Liberty
The God That Failed

Liberty
The God That Failed

Policing the Sacred
and Constructing the Myths
of the Secular State,
from Locke to Obama

by
Christopher A. Ferrara

Foreword by
Patrick McKinley Brennan

First published in the USA
by Angelico Press
© Christopher A. Ferarra 2012
Foreword © Patrick McKinley Brennan 2012

Second Printing

For information, address:
Angelico Press, 4619 Slayden Rd., NE
Tacoma, WA 98422
www.angelicopress.com

Library of Congress Cataloging-in-Publication Data

Ferrara, Christopher A.
Liberty, the god that failed: policing the sacred
and constructing the myths of the secular state, from
Locke to Obama / Christopher A. Ferrara.

p. cm.

Includes bibliographical references and index.
ISBN 978-1-62138-006-1 (pbk: alk. paper)
1. Liberty—History. 2. Liberty—United States—History.
I. Title.
JC585.F495 2012
320.01'1—dc23   2012017001

Cover Image:
The Outbreak of the Rebellion in the United States 1861
Christopher Kimmel, artist; Kimmel & Forster, lithographer
Published by Kimmel & Forster, New York, c.1865
Cover Design: Cristy Deming

CONTENTS

II. THE FIRST AMERICAN REVOLUTION

IV. THE FIRST SECULAR STATE

CHAPTER 18: *The Godless Constitution*

Acknowledgments

A BOOK is not written by the author alone, but rather is a cooperative effort that engages friends and colleagues who put up with the author's obsession and help him along his way. I am indebted to Gary Johannes, Ronald McArthur of Thomas Aquinas College, John Obriski, and John O'Malley for their attentive reading of all or parts of manuscripts of this book, which averted gaffes and pointed to needed improvements in the text. All remaining defects are solely my fault.

Brian McCall of the University of Oklahoma College of Law raised a decisive caveat concerning the problematical term "State," thus prompting a clarification that averted what would have been an inevitable libertarian caricature of the entire work. Jeffrey Langan of Holy Cross College provided a lead to pivotal material concerning the late repentance of John Adams and his end-of-life commiseration with Jefferson. James Bogle, author and barrister of London's Middle Temple, pointed me to the amazing saga of the *San Patricios*. Many others provided suggestions and pointers too numerous to mention.

I owe a special debt to John Rao of Saint John's University, one of the world's great historians, who was an endless source of historical orientation in conversations that guided the direction of my arguments. I am most grateful to him for the privilege of annual participation in the Lake Garda conferences of the Roman Forum, which have provided much of the stimulus for the research and thought that drove this work to completion. I am honored that he and his accomplished wife, Anne, consider me a colleague as well as a friend.

I am also grateful to Miguel Ayuso Torres of the Comillas Pontifical University and Danilo Castellano of the University of Udine for their encouragement and support of my attempt to address "the North American myth." Part of the material on these pages first appeared in a paper I presented in Madrid, which Prof. Ayuso Torres did me the honor of having published in the Spanish journal *Verbo*.

A principal debt is owed to John Riess of Angelico Press, who saw merit in the book and was keen on giving it a public life — not in spite of, but because of, its effort to avoid conventional "conservative" and libertarian narratives of what has gone wrong with the politics of the Western world, especially in America. James Wetmore bestowed, with untiring patience, his typographical artistry in making the text pleasing to the eye. Howard Walsh of Keep the Faith, Inc. was — as he has been for so many years — instrumental in supporting the work that makes a book possible.

Above all, I am indebted, as always, to my heroic wife Wendy, who endured the years of distraction this project entailed. Her accomplishments far exceed anything that could appear on a mere printed page.

i

For a true democrat the best guarantee against
the independence of man is still the freedom of the citizen.
~Augustin Cochin

Foreword

THE CONTEMPORARY enthusiasm for democratic regimes that protect "human rights" should not blind us to the deeper lessons of history. The central Western tradition of reflection on the proper constitution of political regimes has rarely purported to identify a uniquely acceptable form of temporal ruling authority. The naturalness of diverse political forms has been widely acknowledged: democracy, monarchy, and aristocracy, among other possibilities, remain candidates for instantiation as time and place dictate, all other things considered. Until recently, however, among the other things to be considered was the supernatural requirement that the holy Catholic Church's place in the organic unity of political society—whatever its particular form—be given due legal effect. The traditional thesis holds that people were not only allowed, but morally obligated, to institute due political order, most often by accepting and obeying established regimes, and that such order must include legal recognition, first, of the rightful and unique place of the Church and, second, of the obligation of political society—not just of individuals—to offer public worship of the triune God. Such a polity would be a Christian commonwealth.[1]

This ideal was "given the Church's definitive approval in modern times by Leo XIII in his encyclical *Immortale Dei*,"[2] as Henri Cardinal De Lubac has explained. In the words of Pope Leo's restatement of the traditional thesis, "God has divided the human race between two powers. Each of them is supreme in its own field; each is enclosed within the limits perfectly determined and traced out in conformity with its nature and end, and each thus has a sphere in which its own rights and proper activity find exercise."[3] This, Cardinal De Lubac affirmed, "is the perfect blueprint, and it should be the starting point of all practice. . . . This is, of course, no more than the Gospel requires. But insofar as she persists in reminding the world of the fact," Cardinal De Lubac continues, "the Church can never count on peace."[4]

It is of course true that the United States of America was founded on rather different principles and its fundamental law written to give effect to another, very

---

1. For a detailed outline of this ideal of government, see E. Cahill, *The Framework of a Christian State: An Introduction to Social Science* (Dublin: Gill, 1932).

2. Henri De Lubac, *The Splendor of the Church* (San Francisco: Ignatius Press, 1999), 193.

3. Pope Leo XIII, encyclical letter *Immortale Dei* (1885), No. 13.

4. De Lubac, *The Splendor of the Church*, 193–94. This "blueprint" allows, as history attests, a wide range of possible particular organic relationships between the Church and the civil ruling authority, some better than others. See Brad S. Gregory, *The Unintended Reformation: How a Religious Revolution Secularized Society* (Cambridge, MA: The Belknap Press of Harvard Univ. Press, 2012), 129–45; Russell

different blueprint. The Constitution of the United States does not so much as mention God (except pro forma in the dating clause: "in the year of our Lord"), and certainly not the blessed Trinity or the Catholic Church, let alone the polity's obligation to give public worship to the Trinity. The Constitution precludes any hope of a popular transformation of the United States into a Christian common-wealth, moreover, by mandating that "no religious Test shall ever be required as a Qualification to any Office or public Trust under the United States" (Art. VI). The celebrated First Amendment to that Constitution, furthermore, specifically denies the government the authority either to establish "religion" or otherwise to promote its exercise. The U.S. Constitution, then, is both godless and, for reasons that Christopher Ferrara marshals, not indifferent but actively hostile toward the exer-cise of religion, as well as agnostic on the question of the true object of religious worship. And all of this declension and derogation from "the blueprint required by the Gospel" was very much the object and boast of most of those who inspired and led the radical revolution against the English Crown and then went on to frame the Constitution and to arrange its ratification—or so Ferrara argues in *Liberty, the God That Failed.*

This is an uncommon claim, though by no means an unprecedented one, and the reader owes it to himself to judge whether Ferrara has met the relevant burden of proof. Ferrara's mastery of Catholic doctrine, of Enlightenment philosophy and political theory, and of the facts of history, the clarity and rigor of his argument, and his fairness to counter-evidence combine to make this an account to be reckoned with. To praise Ferrara's book is easy, but to predict its reception is another matter. Let it be said emphatically, therefore, that it would be a gross injustice to dismiss this powerful counter-narrative on the presumed ground that Ferrara or those who agree with him are unpatriotic or anti-American. Quite the contrary: *Liberty, the God That Failed* is a reasoned plea to save the United States in the only way Ferrara believes possible—by replacing liberty, the false god that failed the people of the United States, with Jesus Christ, the one God who saves. Nonetheless, especially for his challenging much of the received wisdom of those who are widely (and cor-rectly) admired for advocating a more vigorous Catholic presence in the American public square—characteristically known as Catholic "neo-conservatives"—Ferrara will assuredly arouse an indignant reaction. The neo-conservatives who defend a version of the American proposition of a "separation" of church and state are wed-ded, more specifically, to the implausible thesis, denied by the Popes for millennia, that civil rulers are *per se* incompetent to recognize the truth of the Gospel and its demands for an organic union between Christ's Church and the civil ruling author-ity. Ferrara's respectful insistence upon the demands of the traditional thesis pro-vides an opportunity for productive engagement, but it is no idle concern that some

---

Hittinger, "Introduction to Modern Catholicism," in John Witte Jr. and Frank Alexander (eds.), *The Teachings of Modern Christianity on Law, Politics, and Human Nature* (New York: Columbia University Press, 2006), 3–38; E.A. Goerner, *Peter and Caesar: Political Authority and the Catholic Church* (NY: Herder and Herder, 1965).

Catholics will not recognize the implications of their own tradition when confronted with them. Our contemporary political conceptions are so narrow and relatively uniform that the very act of raising the possibility of an alternative will strike some readers as impious, but Ferrara's tone and learning confirm that this is an alternative that merits the attention of the serious. Ferrara's data and arguments will be welcome tools in the hands of traditionalists, of course, but the book is intended for anyone who is open to re-conceiving political and social life in America. The futility of contemporary political philosophy bounded by "public reason" as stipulated by John Rawls should by now be apparent, and Ferrara has provided us with the true alternative.[5]

Archbishop Charles Chaput, certainly one of the most outspoken, articulate, and insightful members of the U.S. Catholic hierarchy today, recently wrote the following in his book *Render Unto Caesar: Serving the Nation by Living Our Catholic Beliefs in Political Law*: "Virtually all Americans accept the principle of keeping religious and civil authority separate."[6] Chaput's claim is descriptively accurate, and, as already adumbrated, Ferrara's argument offers a direct challenge to the validity of that celebrated "principle." Later in the same book, Chaput also quotes from the opening section of the Second Vatican Council's *Declaration on Religious Liberty, Dignitatis Humanae*: "Religious freedom, in turn, which men demand as necessary to fulfill their duty to worship God, has to do with immunity from coercion in civil society. Therefore *it leaves untouched traditional Catholic doctrine on the moral duty of men and women and societies toward the true religion and toward the one Church of Christ*."[7] That "untouched" traditional Catholic doctrine is the source and spring of Ferrara's argument that Catholic authority must influence civil authority. This includes calling for the state to recognize and worship the Trinity and to enact laws that give effect to the natural and divine laws. What remains to be explained, then, is Chaput's admiring claim that "For the framers, the new federal government had no authority in theological matters."[8] Traditional Catholic doctrine teaches authoritatively that civil rulers are *in principle* theologically competent to recognize the truth of the Catholic Church and of the social kingship of Christ. As Chaput insists in a related context: The Second Vatican Council "did not seek to change [the Church's] basic mission or doctrines."[9] Nor could it. The doctrine that the Church is endowed with the authority and obligation to direct the state in matters touching the supernatural common good is indeed "basic," and is therefore not changeable. This was Jacques Maritain's point when he wrote that that power

5. On the futility of public political philosophy, see Patrick McKinley Brennan, "Political Liberalism's Tertium Quiddity," 43 American Journal of Jurisprudence 239 (1998) (reviewing Michael J. White, *Partisan or Neutral? The Futility of Public Political Theory*).

6. Charles J. Chaput, *Render Unto Caesar: Serving the Nation by Living Our Catholic Beliefs in Political Life* (NY: Doubleday, 2008), 86.

7. Chaput, *Render*, 129 (emphasis supplied by Chaput).

8. Chaput, *Render*, 85.

9. Chaput, *Render*, 107.

"extends as far as the primacy of the spiritual requires; for the Church is not dis-armed, her right is effective and efficient."[10]

The apparent inconsistency just sketched provides some of the context in which even faithful and informed Catholics will receive Ferrara's argument. There is more, however, and it further clarifies the stakes. On the one hand, like many other neo-conservative and some liberal Catholics today, Archbishop Chaput insists that the American constitutional dispensation with respect to religion affords the Church an excellent, indeed a uniquely excellent, guarantee of complete freedom. Referring to the situation in the new government's early years, Chaput writes: "Never before had *any* government conceded to the church full liberty of self-gov-ernment. Thus free of government meddling, Catholics in the United States found an ideal space to thrive. This applied to Catholics as individuals and to the church as a public, believing community."[11] On the other hand, and testing the probity of a roseate account of the place and prospect of the liberty of the Church in the United States, there is the fact that today the Obama Administration is poised to compel the Church to provide many of her workers with contraceptives, steriliza-tion, and abortifacients. This legal subordination of the Church to the judgments of the state, it is popularly said, is necessary to guarantee women's reproductive freedom. Paul Blanshard is today widely regarded to have been a rank anti-Catholic bigot, but the Administration's current policy would seem a fulfillment of Blan-shard's admonition to "admit that the Church in the social sphere is simply one agency within the State."[12]

The U.S. Conference of Catholic Bishops counters the Obama Administration's attempted colonization of the Church with the claim that such governmental action violates "conscience," and this claim is correct as far as it goes. It is not just individual consciences that are being violated, however: the ability of the Church to exercise the freedom that is hers by divine right is also violated. And the result of that injustice, moreover, is that society grows ever less what the Church teaches that society and its members are obligated to become under the command of the divine and natural laws. The Church's reduced ability to fulfill her divine mandate is exactly what the enemy wants. "Without the moderating influence of the spiri-tual sovereignty, [the state] moves as if by instinct toward the most burdensome form of pagan absolutism."[13]

That evil genius of political theory, Thomas Hobbes, knew as much when he dedicated much of his constructive political theorizing, in both *Leviathan* and *De*

---

10. Jacques Maritain, *The Things That Are Not Caesar's* (NY: Sheed and Ward, 1930), 15.

11. Chaput, *Render*, 88.

12. Paul Blanshard, *American Freedom and Catholic Power* (Boston: Beacon Press, 1949), 47. Blan-shard dropped that line from the second edition of his best-selling book, so outrageous was it, but boasted falsely in the later edition that his theses remained "unchanged." See Patrick McKinley Bren-nan, "Are Catholics Unreliable From a Democratic Point of View? Thoughts on the Occasion of the Sixtieth Anniversary of Paul Blanshard's *American Freedom and Catholic Power*," 56 *Villanova Law Review* 199, 206–07 (2011) (the 33rd Annual Donald M. Giannella Lecture).

13. De Lubac, *The Splendor of the Church*, 196.

Cive, to the exigency of eliminating the sacramental life of the Church and her sacred teaching authority in order to make way for a state ruled exclusively by "the mortal god" Leviathan.[14] As Hobbes wrote in *De Cive*, "[O]ur Savior, hath not showed subjects any other laws for government of a city, beside those of nature, that is to say, beside the command to obedience."[15] Hobbes prudently engages in extensive scriptural analysis, "[t]he fundamental point" of which, as Norberto Bobbio has explained, "is that Christ's reign is not of this world. Christ has not come into this world to command. . . . Therefore, there is no reason why there should exist an authority which claims to represent Christ's reign on earth, for this reign is not to be realized." Bobbio concludes: "Facing the problem of the relationship between Church and state, Hobbes thus chooses to unify the two institutions, to the point of fusing them. There are not two powers, but only one: and this is the state. In contrast with the dualistic theses which held throughout this centuries-old controversy, Hobbes's thesis has the merit of being so clear as not to allow for misunderstanding."[16]

The American turn of events described above—the national government's running roughshod over the *libertas ecclesiae* and the demands of true morality, in the name of the liberty of individuals to engage in conduct that violates the moral law as taught by the Church—is shocking, but should come as no surprise, for it has systemic causes. The difficulty is not merely a recent degradation of "religious liberty." The difficulty, rather, is that the American model has never in fact allowed the Church the public mission that is hers by divine right. As Francis Cardinal George recently wrote in a letter to the Catholics of Chicago, the Obama Administration's mandate "reduces the Church to a private club, destroying her public mission in society."[17] But the Church is not a private club, and this is the all-important point on which Catholics must insist. "We must affirm as a truth above all the vicissitudes of time," as Jacques Maritain explained, "the supremacy of the Church over the world and over all terrestrial powers. On pain of radical disorder she must guide the peoples toward the last end of human life, which is also that of States, and, to do that, she must direct, in terms of the spiritual riches entrusted to her, both rulers and nations."[18] When the Church is treated as a private club, lawmakers are free to ignore her teaching and do what they will. "Only the teaching Church is qualified to judge of the *relation* between temporal things and the last supernatural end to which it is her duty to lead us."[19] The American model is, in sum, terminally flawed by failing to allow the Church to guide the temporal powers according to the majestic demands of the divine and natural laws.

14. Thomas Hobbes, *Leviathan*, II.17.

15. Thomas Hobbes, *De Cive*, XVII.11.

16. Norberto Bobbio, *Thomas Hobbes and the Natural Law Tradition* (Chicago: The University Press, 1993), 80–81. Trans. by Daniela Gobetti.

17. Letter dated February 5, 2012.

18. Quoted by Ferrara at 19.

19. Maritain, *The Things That Are Not Caesar's*, 24 (quoting Garrigou-Lagrange).

The American model amounts to a modern invention with a dubious intellectual pedigree. Ferrara's historical narrative follows the development, dissemination, and instantiation in the United States of the novel ideas of Hobbes and, perhaps more, John Locke—"the confused man's Hobbes."[20] Locke would not have been possible without the Protestant revolt, of course, but his admirers and detractors alike agree that John Locke is *the* philosopher of the American founding, and Ferrara's acute reading of Locke establishes—*pace* many revisionist readings—that Locke was out to deliver politics from the influence of the Church, and to accomplish that one must (as Ferrara observes, quoting Pierre Manent), "renounce thinking about human life in terms of its good or end, which would always be vulnerable to the Church's 'trump'" (56). As Ferrara explains, "[t]he *summum bonum*, the supreme good of man, 'which is the primary question raised by the tradition . . . is a perfectly idle question for Locke. . . .' The highest good of man as the possession of God via beatitude—an end even the Greeks perceived, however dimly—now ceases to matter for politics in its new and radically restricted sense" (65, quoting Manent).

What matters for politics in its new and radically restricted sense as understood by Locke is the "liberty" not to be impeded in "the pursuit of happiness." The phrase that Jefferson and the other drafters of the Declaration of Independence seized on appeared first in Locke's *Essay Concerning Human Understanding*, and, as Thomas Pangle explains (in language quoted by Ferrara): "It is, indeed, in the pages of Locke that one finds the most straightforward and lucid statement of hedonistic self-love or 'the pursuit of happiness' as the ground of all duty. . . . [The] new Lockean notion of 'the pursuit of happiness' is explicitly opposed to the classical idea of a '*summum bonum*,' or an *attainment* of happiness" (66). Understood as the right to be virtually unimpeded in the "pursuit of happiness," except by one's own "consent," even if such consent be only "tacit" (a seeming vitiation of the notion of consent—and one that troubles Locke insufficiently), "liberty" becomes the god to be pursued by all, even at gunpoint.

The paradox Ferrara exposes in stunning detail is that the champions of this new sort of liberty are willing, generation after generation, to do the most astonishing things to the people they say are born their equals, including killing them. The "master myth of the liberal meta-narrative" (as Ferrara styles it) is that religion was the cause of endless wars and suffering until the Enlightenment dispelled ignorance and produced peaceful democratic bourgeois living. The truth, though, is that the period in which the Catholic religion has been severed from the state, either completely or in large part, has been the bloodiest in human history. Some 27,000 died effecting liberty from the English Crown, and, as Ferrara demonstrates, we must also face 2 million dead in the French revolutionary wars, the genocide of 300,000 Catholics in the Vendee by the Jacobin regime, 3 million dead following the fall of the Jacobin and Thermidorian regimes, 600,000 dead in the Civil War in America, 16 million dead in World War I (fought to make Europe "safe

---

20. C.B. Macpherson, Introduction to Thomas Hobbes, *Leviathan* (London: Penguin Books, 1985), 25. Quoted by Ferrara at 47.

for democracy"), 7 million dead in the Bolshevik democides, 70 million dead in World War II, 20 million dead in genocides, including 6 million Jews, and so it goes on and on (32–34). Just who imposed all of this suffering? "No, it was not the Vatican," Ferrara observes:

> Nor was it any sort of Christian commonwealth. The wars, persecutions, democides, politicides and genocides that have convulsed Western civilization since the late 18th century have all represented state action by governments that have either persecuted Christianity outrightly and bloodily, or, perhaps even more effectively, quietly and bloodlessly by declaring religion incompetent to "meddle" in politics and consigning it to the realm of socially meaningless private opinion, where "pacifists," "do-gooders," "bleeding hearts," "isolationists," and other unpatriotic sorts have long languished in America. Hence, for example, the seven-point peace plan of Pope Benedict XV [r. 1914–1922], the "peace Pope," to avert World War I was ignored by all the major powers except the still-Catholic Austria-Hungary. (35)

The so-called wars of religion were in fact, as William Cavanaugh has shown, conflicts waged "by state-building elites for the purpose of consolidating their power over the church and other rivals" (quoted by Ferrara 35). Once free of the Church, those unrivaled states show little reluctance to kill, even babies in the womb through state-sponsored abortion. It is worth recalling here that "[i]n a rejection of the Aristotelian teleology repeated ad nauseam . . . , Hobbes held that there is no natural difference between the killing of a man and the killing of an animal."[21]

Most of the world ignored Pope Benedict XV's warning. Pope Benedict XVI (r. 2005–), a man not given to exaggeration, recently issued a new and perhaps wider warning. Referring to the collapse of the Roman Empire, the Pope explained that "the sun was setting over an entire world. Frequent natural disasters further increased this sense of insecurity. There was no power in sight that could put an end to this decline." Today, as well, Benedict XVI continued, "moral consensus is collapsing, consensus without which juridical and political structures cannot function. Consequently, the forces mobilized for the defense of such structures seem doomed to failure. . . . The very future of the world is at stake" (discussed by Ferrara at 636). With this warning, Ferrara observes, the Pope has repudiated any unsubstantiated optimism about "the modern world" and returned to the sober realism of his pre-conciliar predecessors, including this admonition by Pius XII in an encyclical in 1951:

---

21. Annabel S. Brett, *Changes of State: Nature and the Limits of the City in Early Modern Natural Law* (Princeton: Princeton Univ. Press, 2011), 59. "This, then, is the truth: The world under the constant action of Christianity and the sovereignty of Divine law was advancing in civilization and making true progress, until a blight fell upon it. The disorders and anarchies of three hundred years ago came to check and to overthrow the course of its advance. Christianity would have abolished all social evils with greater speed and certainty, if its onward course had not been stayed." Henry Edward Manning, *The Fourfold Sovereignty of God* (1871), 141.

Venerable Brethren, you are well aware that almost the whole human race is today allowing itself to be driven into two opposing camps, for Christ or against Christ. The human race is involved today in a supreme crisis, which will issue in its salvation by Christ, or in its dire destruction. (quoted by Ferrara, 626)

Writing a quarter of a century earlier, Pope Pius XI, whose pontificate proceeded under the motto "The Peace of Christ in the Reign of Christ," did not waver when identifying what is necessary to meet the modern crisis: "The Church alone can introduce into society and maintain therein the prestige of a true, sound spiritualism, the spiritualism of Christianity which both from the point of view of truth and of its practical value is quite superior to any exclusively philosophical theory."[22] Pope Pius XI prescribed the divine law as taught by the Church as the core of the remedy for the world's ills, but his prescription has hardly been heeded, and even today one hears too little of the necessity of it from the Church's authoritative teachers. The Church's traditional teaching remains "untouched," according to the Second Vatican Council, yet it is not preached, not embraced, and sometimes even denied, including by men and women of good will but mistaken judgment. And meanwhile the situation all around sinks further and further from what "the Gospel requires," and the result, alas, is that we live "on the edge of chaos,"[23] in the phrase of Mary Ann Glendon, the President of the Pontifical Council of the Social Sciences, former U.S. Ambassador to the Holy See, and Learned Hand Professor of Law at Harvard Law School.

"[O]n the edge of chaos"—these are the sobering words of judgment of a sage scholar and woman of ardent Catholic faith. Are they a counsel of despair? Certainly not. Christians are people of hope, and Christopher Ferrara's *Liberty, the God That Failed* itself represents reason for hope. It offers both a diagnosis and, still more, a cure: politics of the soul. There is no terrestrial reason to believe that we are capable of such politics at the moment, but all that stands in the way of it is, as Ferrara points out, "a lack of popular will" (635).[24] The increase in such a will must be the object of Christian action and prayer, and of course the greatest prayer of all is the Mass itself. It is not idle to speculate that the deformations of the Mass in recent decades may have contributed to misguided thinking by some Catholics about the form the commonwealth must take. Formlessness is a heresy with legion manifestations.[25] But Christians can counter it with the firm hope that the grace of God is not wanting. Running through the story Ferrara tells is the Enlightenment's relentless effort to drain the world of grace and replace it with what William Blake

---

22. Pope Pius XI, encyclical letter *Ubi arcano* (1922), No. 42.

23. Mary Ann Glendon, *Traditions in Turmoil* (Ann Arbor: Sapientia Press, 2006), xii.

24. On the question of the conditions under which the civil ruling authority's objective obligation to the Catholic Church attaches subjectively, see Francis Connell, "Christ the King of Civil Rulers," 119 *American Ecclesiastical Review*, 244 (1948) and Joseph Fenton, "The Status of a Controversy," 124 *American Ecclesiastical Review* 451, 452 (1951). See also Goerner, *Peter and Caesar*, 153–72.

25. On how denial of form deforms the Mass in particular, see Martin Mosebach, *The Heresy of Formlessness: The Roman Liturgy and Its Enemy* (San Francisco: Ignatius Press, 2006).

called "Newton's Sleep." So it is fitting to recall the words of Cardinal Pie of Poitier, speaking at the grotto at Lourdes: "The supernatural is finished," he quoted nineteenth-century man as boasting, and then continued: "Well, look here, then! The supernatural pours out, overflows, sweats from the sand and from the rock, spurts out from the source, and rolls along the long folds of the living waves of a river of prayers, of chants and of light."[26] The way back from the edge of chaos begins by allowing the supernatural full scope to correct and transform this fallen creation.

PATRICK MCKINLEY BRENNAN

---

26. Quoted in John Rao, *Black Legends and the Light of the World: The War of Words with the Incarnate Word* (The Remnant Press, 2012), 643. Rao's book can be read very profitably in tandem with this one.

To my father, a man of quiet greatness, whose abiding faith, unwavering love, and unshakable fidelity to duty preserved his family from shipwreck in a tempest-ridden world. He is truly the namesake of Saint Joseph.

Introduction

THE RENOWNED Anglican convert to Catholicism, Henry Edward Cardinal Manning, once observed that "All human differences are ultimately religious ones."[1] This is a truth even secular reason is forced to recognize. As the proto-anarchist Pierre-Joseph Proudhon, a professed admirer of Satan, admitted in his *Confessions of a Revolutionary*: "It is surprising to observe how constantly we find that all our political questions involve theological ones." In reply, the renowned Catholic counter-revolutionary of the mid-nineteenth century, Don Juan Donoso Cortés, wrote: "There is nothing in this to cause surprise, except it be the surprise of Proudhon. Theology, being the science of God, is the ocean which contains all the sciences, as God is the ocean in which all things are contained."[2] Recently the Anglican scholar John Milbank has remarked the urgent need to "reassert theology as a master discourse," the only discourse "able to overcome nihilism itself."[3]

The history of Western civilization over the past three centuries is a chronicle of the decline of men and nations in consequence of a theological decision with profound political effects. That decision was the definitive refusal to conduct the art of politics according to the fundamental theological premise that an almighty and eternal God has revealed Himself in the person of Jesus Christ. What confronts us now is the prospect of life in a terminal civilization that has rejected the ancient dictum, in force throughout the West for more than a thousand years, that "Christianity is the law of the land."[4] We are the victims of what Christopher Dawson described as "the reversal of the spiritual revolution which gave birth to Western culture and a return to the psychological situation of the old pagan world. . . ."[5]

The collapsing societies of the West groan under the consequences of what one liberal commentator has characterized as "a fundamental orientation toward politics chosen by early-modern Europeans in order to free themselves from the intellectual and spiritual influence of the Catholic Church. . . ."[6] That is, the condition of contemporary Western civilization reflects the final destruction of the Christocentric social order that endured in one form or another from Imperial Rome under the Emperor Constantine in the 4th century until the fall of the Imperial

---

1. Cited in Wilhelm Röpke, *A Humane Economy* (South Bend: Gateway Editions, 1958), 4, 75.

2. Don Juan Donoso Cortes, *Essay on Catholicism, Authority and Order*, (NY: Joseph F. Wagner, 1925), 1.

3. John Milbank, *Theology and Social Theory* (Oxford: Blackwell, 1993), 6.

4. Christopher Dawson, *Understanding Europe* (NY: Sheed and Ward, 1952), 14.

5. Ibid., 18.

6. Pierre Manent, *An Intellectual History of Liberalism* (Princeton, NJ: Princeton Univ. Press, 1995), viii (preface by Jerrold Siegel).

1

House of Hapsburg under the Emperor Charles I at the dawn of the 20th century. By Christocentric social order is meant civil society with its organs of government, commonly referred to collectively by the modern and misleading term "the State." A brief explanation of our unavoidable use of that term is in order.

A Problematical Term

For purposes of this study, we shall use the term "State"—as opposed to "modern state" or "modern nation-state"—to refer to the *civitas* (political community or civil society) or *res publica* (republic or commonwealth) of Greek and Catholic political philosophy comprising the bimillenial Greco-Catholic tradition of political thought. Although it is of relatively modern derivation (around the 13th century), "State"—a foreshortening of the Latin *status rei publicæ* or "state of the republic"—has supplanted the traditional terminology in all modern translations of the works of Plato, Aristotle and Saint Thomas, as well as vernacular translations of papal encyclicals treating of the *civitas/res publica* and its just constitution. We are thus compelled to adhere to the modern usage "State," but understood strictly as referring to the classical concept so as to avoid libertarian caricatures of what is under discussion.

In its modern sense, the one intended by libertarians and other liberals, "State" means merely the organs of government severed from civil society—a disjunction that serves the libertarian critique of the modern nation-state whose emergence has resulted precisely from the operation of liberal principles, as we shall see. But a severance between government and civil society is quite contrary to the Greco-Catholic conception of the *civitas* as a "body politic" wherein the Church, government and citizenry are organically united in a moral totality while preserving their distinct identities and functions. The classic expression of the body politic metaphor appears in the *Policraticus* of John of Salisbury (c. 1120–1180), the medieval political philosopher whose writings are the most substantial contribution to medieval political thought between Augustine and the Aristotelian synthesis of Saint Thomas Aquinas. According to the metaphor, the Church is the soul of the body politic, the prince its head, ruled by the soul, the judges and governors of the provinces the eyes, ears and tongue, the financiers the stomach, the citizens in their various capacities the limbs, and so forth.[7] This is not to be understood in the crude libertarian sense of "collectivism" but in the Christian sense of the *civitas* as an orderly or "perfect" (meaning only self-sufficient) society of individuals ordered to the eternal destiny of each and the common good of all, including the highest common good, which is beatitude.

In the sense of merely organs of government disjoined from both civil society and the Church, the modern secular nation-state with its central government represents a radical departure from the Catholic view of the rightly ordered *civitas*. In the classical sense we employ here, *the* State is that *civitas* which orders its laws and

---

7. Cf. *Policraticus*, Bk. V, chap. II.

institutions (however imperfectly) to the precepts of Christianity and the final end of man in eternal beatitude or eternal punishment and which respects the Catholic principle of "subsidiarity" (the assignment of political functions to the lowest possible subsidiary levels of authority). We mean, in short, the State as Christian commonwealth in one form or another. This commonwealth may be monarchical, democratic or republican in its political constitution, and we have seen examples of all three forms of government (or mixtures thereof) within the dominant Western mode of social order known as Christendom. No matter what political configuration it displayed, that order was characterized by what the *Policraticus* describes: an organic link between the Church and civil authority in virtue of which the Church was the conscience or "soul" of the body politic. It is that link which has been broken, and the result has aptly been likened to the decomposition of a human body from which the soul has departed. Writing precisely on the subject of true human liberty, Pope Leo XIII expressed the connection thus:

> [A]lthough the civil authority has not the same proximate end as the spiritual, nor proceeds on the same lines, nevertheless in the exercise of their separate powers they must occasionally meet. For their subjects are the same, and not infrequently they deal with the same objects, though in different ways. Whenever this occurs, since a state of conflict is absurd and manifestly repugnant to the most wise ordinance of God, there must necessarily exist some order or mode of procedure to remove the occasions of difference and contention, and to secure harmony in all things. This harmony has been not inaptly compared to that which exists between the body and the soul for the well-being of both one and the other, *the separation of which brings irremediable harm to the body, since it extinguishes its very life.*[8]

The fundamental problem with Liberty to be addressed on these pages is its manifestation as the State without a soul, and thus without a moral compass.

The Subject Defined

One of the great triumphs of the new "fundamental orientation," otherwise known as "classical liberalism," is to have banished from the mind of contemporary Western man the memory that Christendom was the form and pattern of our civilization for nearly all of its history. In place of a civilization ordered to Christ, the forces of liberalism—rather recently in historical terms, and by force of arms at each critical juncture as we shall see—established a new order with a new god whose name is "Liberty."

We ought to call Liberty a god (as many of its early followers literally did)[9] because, like any idol that man sets up for himself, its claims are deemed to surpass

---

8. *Libertas Humana* (1888), n. 18. Emphasis added, here and throughout this book unless otherwise indicated.
9. See Chapter 5.

those of the God who made him and presented Himself to His own creatures as the Word Incarnate. Whereas Christ declared that His apostles were to "make disciples of all nations, baptizing them in the name of the Father and of the Son and of the Holy Ghost" and teaching them "to observe all things whatsoever I have commanded you,"[10] Liberty declared, on the contrary, that the age-old baptism of nations was to be annulled and the Christian commonwealth abolished. Whereas Christ taught that political authority descends to man from God (even in the case of the procurator who unjustly sentenced Him to death), Liberty decreed that political authority ascends from the "sovereign will" of the people, so that even God's law could be subjected to popular repeal. Whereas Christ taught that His truth will make men free, Liberty insisted upon a previously unknown conception of social freedom: the mere absence of restraint on human action, save for that necessary to prevent violence and to protect the ownership, use and enjoyment of private property in the pursuit of whatever each individual deems to constitute happiness. Without the conformity of human law to divine law, the term "violence" inevitably contracted while the terms "property" and "happiness" expanded in proportion to what unrestrained human weakness and popular consensus demanded. Hence today human life *in utero* may, at the option of its "owner," be destroyed and disposed of as waste, or extracted and inventoried at the embryonic stage for sale as a consumer good. And not even the Christian opponents of these crimes against humanity are willing to oppose them on any ground but appeals to the same "sovereign" popular will that put Liberty on its pedestal and maintains it there by the religious devotion of its followers, Christians included.

In sum, Liberty has imposed upon Western civilization what Leo XIII succinctly denounced as "that new conception of law which was not merely previously unknown, but was at variance on many points with not only the Christian, but even the natural law."[11] This new conception of law expressed itself in the revolutionary principles that contemporary man, blissfully ignorant of his own Christian heritage, now unquestioningly accepts as the received wisdom of the ages:

> [T]hat all are equal in the control of their life; that each one is so far his own master as to be in no sense under the rule of any other individual; that each is free to think on every subject just as he may choose, and to do whatever he may like to do; that no man has any right to rule over other men ... that the judgment of each one's conscience is independent of all law; that the most unrestrained opinions may be openly expressed as to the practice or omission of divine worship; and that every one has unbounded license to think whatever he chooses and to publish abroad whatever he thinks. . . .[12]

That these principles would destroy the foundations of our civilization was always self-evident. Only forty years after Leo, Pope Pius XI observed that "With

---

10. Matthew 28:19–20.
11. *Immortale Dei* (1885), n. 23.
12. Ibid., n. 24.

God and Jesus Christ, *excluded from political life*, with authority derived not from God but from man, the very basis of that authority has been taken away, because the chief reason of the distinction between ruler and subject has been eliminated. The result is that human society is tottering to its fall, because it has no longer a secure and solid foundation."[13] But perhaps not even Leo and Pius could have imagined the full extent of the civilizational debacle Liberty has wrought: not only the abortion holocaust, but an epidemic of divorce, the universal practice of contraception, the depopulation of Western nations, the relentless advance of homosexualism, the destruction of the family, the spread of orgiastic consumerism in a morally unbound "free" market, the debasement of art, literature, music, architecture and Western culture as a whole, and finally the emergence of a veritable neopagan social order in which resistant Christians increasingly face persecution for heresies against the orthodoxy of Liberty and not even the stoic virtues of the pagans of Greco-Roman antiquity are evident.

The libertarian acolytes of Liberty argue that it is not Liberty but the State that oppresses us. Rejecting the entire Western tradition, they declare that life in the State—meaning the classic body politic—is not natural to man. The State, they maintain, arises from the unnatural imposition of organs of government upon a naturally free civil society by an age-old conspiracy of nefarious ruling elites, who have somehow managed to persuade generation after generation, in virtually every place on earth, that government is necessary. If only the unnecessary organs of government—kings, parliaments, presidents, congresses, governors, public magistrates, and so forth—could be eliminated, the "monopoly of force" by which the elites have for so long oppressed the world would be ended and civil society would triumph in the freedom and prosperity of the "spontaneous order" that arises from voluntary human cooperation. The State will wither away, just as it does in the dreams of Marxists. It will be the Second Coming of Liberty, whose first coming in 1776 ended with Liberty's crucifixion by the Federalists, who gave the world yet another State (as if there could have been any other outcome).

Democracy, the libertarians concede, is indeed a god that failed, just as communism was a god that failed.[14] Democracy failed not because of Liberty (so the argument goes) but because the State's "monopoly of force" enabled one group to oppress another through taxation, regulation and other violations of the "free-market principle" of untrammeled interpersonal exchange. But the libertarians conveniently overlook the indispensable role of the "free" market itself in fostering democratic tyranny by destroying social adherence to the objective moral order—a role de-ethicized secular governments are only too happy to facilitate with judicial decisions that bar any substantial legal limitation on the market's promotion of vice and corruption. Christians are pressed between what Wilhelm Röpke called

13. *Quas Primas* (1925).

14. Cf. Hans-Hermann Hoppe, *Democracy: The God That Failed* (New Brunswick: Transaction Publishers, 2004), a libertarian critique of the modern nation-state, and *The God that Failed* (NY: Columbia Univ. Press, 1949), a collection of confessional essays by six ex-communists, including Arthur Koestler.

the "bloated colossus of the State" on one side and the "cult of the colossal" in the marketplace on the other. Even the Lutheran liberal Röpke, one of the foremost free-market defenders of the 20th century, was constrained to issue the warning that market competition "must not be allowed to predominate and sway society in all its spheres, or it will poison men's souls [and] destroy civilization...."[15] In Christendom it was not possible for the market to have this effect, for the law of the Gospel, civil law, and the Christian conscience of the individual all worked together for the protection of public morality. In the liberal social order that we know as Liberty, however, that effect was not only inevitable, but legally mandatory.

The libertarians fail to see, or will not acknowledge, that Liberty reigns equally over secular government and free market, constantly maintaining a symbiotic adjustment between these two basic elements of our de-ethicized post-Christian civilization. The de-ethicized government exacts from the de-ethicized market a tribute of taxation and regulation which merely dampens a still immense and growing material prosperity (built on a mountain of credit that can collapse at any time), and in return the market receives from government legal protection against the moral claims of Christianity so that profit may abound from usury and the sale of anything and everything for which entrepreneurs can create a demand, including embryonic human beings. Röpke, who was no advocate of Christendom, observed this symbiosis in his own renowned critique of economic liberalism: "[T]he economic liberalism of the last two centuries has disastrously gone astray in a manner fully paralleling the mistakes of political liberalism and ultimately stemming from the same source."[16]

The dreamers of the libertarian dream are unable or unwilling to recognize that it is not the State as such, which will exist as long as there is human society, but rather a radical change in the *theology* of the State that has led to tyranny. The worst of the "absolute" monarchs of Christendom was a model of limited government compared with the presidents and prime ministers of modern secular regimes who owe no allegiance to Rome. Even a leading libertarian scholar has acknowledged, apparently without recognizing the significance of his admission for libertarianism itself, that "the historic transition from monarchy to democracy represents not progress but civilizational decline."[17]

This study, therefore, presents a counter-narrative of the origin and progress of what contemporary man calls Liberty. It is necessary at the outset to fix the meaning of this notoriously nebulous term whose contours we have just noted. What, *precisely*, do we mean by Liberty for purposes of our discussion? We mean:

First, the supposed emancipation of the body politic from monarchy and from the perennial alliance, in one form or another, between civil and religious authority.

---

15. Röpke, *A Humane Economy*, 128.

16. Wilhelm Röpke, *The Social Crisis of Our Time* (New Brunswick: Transaction Publishers, orig. pub. 1942), 48.

17. Hoppe, *Democracy: The God That Failed*, 69.

Second, the resulting separation of Church and State, and thus of political life from the precepts of revealed religion and ultimately from even the dictates of the natural law, beyond the bare prohibition of bodily or pecuniary injury that interferes with property rights, "public peace" or the "pursuit of happiness."

Third, the corresponding loosening or abandonment of traditional legal injunctions prohibiting adultery, divorce, contraception, abortion, sodomy, obscenity, libel and slander, prostitution, usury, commerce on the Sabbath, public blasphemy and profanity, idolatry, heresy, and other offenses whose traditional legal proscription was rooted in what Western man once recognized as the Law of the Gospel.

Fourth, the "emancipation" of the individual, with his "individual rights," from all but the most minimal legal restraints, leaving him "free" to do, say or claim to be whatever he pleases (even purporting to switch sexes) without regard to the moral, spiritual and social consequences to himself or others—including spouse, children and neighbors—so long as he avoids violence or harm to the property or other purely temporal interests of his fellow citizens and allows them the same "freedom" he demands for himself.

Liberty so defined has given birth to the State in its modern sense: organs of government separated from the Church; government by majority will and the "representatives" of the majority, including a quasi-monarchical "chief executive" who succeeds the Christian king with all the pomp and ceremony of the monarchy, but on a far grander scale than any king could have afforded and with far greater powers at his disposal. We shall see that, paradoxically, the modern state exercises vastly more authority over the individual than any Christian monarch of old—not in spite of, but precisely because of its claim to represent "the will of the people" over and above the authority of any moral code, religion or Church to which a mere king ruling a State in the classical sense was subject, if only out of his own fear of eternal punishment.

The Opposing Narratives

The narrative of Liberty that children imbibe from the pious accounts in public school history books on both sides of the Atlantic goes something like this: In the final decades of the 18th century the oppressed peoples of America and France, yearning to be free, rose up in great popular rebellions, broke the chains of monarchical and ecclesiastical tyranny, stood erect for the first time in centuries, and breathed in the fresh air of the republics they themselves had created in the exercise of their sovereign will. Inspired by these first examples of Liberty, the peoples of the other nations of Europe and Latin America broke their chains in a wave of revolution. Today, Liberty reigns throughout the Western world and Western man enjoys a degree of personal, economic and religious freedom he could scarcely have imagined during the long dark age of oppression under the old order of altar and throne.

The quite different narrative this study will present may be summarized thus: In the final decades of the 18th century radical coteries in America and France, guided by the thought of Hobbes, Locke, and the *philosophes* of the "moderate" Enlightenment, and animated by a burning antipathy toward monarchy and institutional religion, employed propaganda, the exploitation of popular grievances, and political theater to incite a small segment of the populace, almost entirely in key urban centers, to revolt against existing authority. In the resulting power vacuums self-appointed radical leaders seized authority in the name of "the people," declared themselves provisional governments, and crushed all loyalist opposition by intimidation and force. The provisional governments were replaced by permanent "republican governments" the radicals created "in convention" behind closed doors and then presented to the masses as a *fait accompli*, obtaining a token "consent of the governed" or "ratification" by means of hastily arranged plebiscites in which only a tiny percentage of the general population participated. Later attempts to resist or withdraw from these governments, which claimed to represent the "will of the people" in perpetuity, were considered treasonous and were prevented by force, with massive bloodshed whenever necessary. The new governments "conceived in Liberty" in America and France almost immediately imposed far greater burdens on the people than the overthrown kings had ever done, while an unprecedented separation of Church and State was accompanied by growing governmental hostility toward religion and the relentless decline of public morality.

The process in America and France was replicated, more or less, in nearly every Western nation, so that by the turn of the 20th century the whole Western world had been made "safe for democracy," as Woodrow Wilson so famously put it in his address to Congress on April 2, 1917. Today, Western man finds himself under the yoke of ever-expanding "representative" governments which purport to secure "rights" he was supposedly denied under the old order. No longer challenged by any religious body, these governments exercise sole and exclusive authority over secularized market societies which, for all their seeming prosperity, exhibit a degree of moral and spiritual decadence even the most radical of the 18th-century *philosophes* would find appalling. This decadence, though, is only the final outcome of the operation of "moderate" Enlightenment principles.

It is the burden of this book to demonstrate that the revolutionary transformation of the Western world in the name of Liberty was a massive bait-and-switch operation and that Liberty has never delivered what it promised—anywhere, at any time—because Liberty is nothing more than the elevation of a new form of supreme political authority in place of the old one. But this new form of sovereignty, called "government by the people," would respect none of the limits that tradition and custom had placed on the "absolute monarchies" of Christendom. It would, in consequence, lead Western man into an epoch of Church-State separation, the rise of the sacral nation-state (replacing the Church) for which men must die in vast numbers, total wars involving entire national populations, including unprecedented civil and world wars, and central governments with sweeping powers, presiding over individuals whose "individual rights" tend inexorably toward the government-approved destruction of the moral order while providing no real restraint on the growth of government. In short, the epoch in which we live.

In sum, the following pages will present the case for the heretical proposition that Liberty has not made men free, but rather it has relentlessly opposed and driven from the life of the State the very Truth that makes men free. In consequence, as Francis Fukuyama has put it: "The liberal state growing out of the tradition of Hobbes and Locke *engages in a protracted struggle with its own people.*"[18] We are witnessing that very struggle today in the conflict between ever-more-powerful central governments and popular resistance movements, such as the Tea Party movement in America, which are hopelessly handicapped by their acceptance of the very principles that ensure the dominance of the modern nation-state: majority rule and the separation of "secular" politics from contrary "religious" principles.

The Plan of This Book

As should be perfectly obvious already, this book has been written with an unconcealed polemical intent, in recognition of the indispensable preparatory role that the militant polemicists of the so-called Enlightenment played in the radical de-Christianization of Western civilization that afflicts us today. It is a polemic in the full classical Greek sense of the word: *polemos* or war. Just as the advance of Liberty was preceded by a war of words in the treatises and tracts of the Enlightenment (as we shall see on these pages), so must any attempt at a recovery of the vast territory we have lost commence with a polemical counter-attack. These pages are but a modest contribution to a rapidly growing body of recent, more or less traditionalist critiques of the liberal "meta-narrative" of Western history.

Hence this book will treat of philosophy, theology and historical fact not as subjects for "neutral" academic discussion but rather as elements of the arguments it develops. The case presented does not pretend to be (nor could it be) the work of a professional philosopher, theologian or historian, although in building a conceptual and factual framework it relies upon the admissions and analyses of recognized scholars in these disciplines from the respectable academic "mainstream," many of whom would no doubt be entirely adverse to the conclusions to be drawn here.[19] There is no attempt to balance "differing perspectives"—an academic exercise that implies precisely a relativization of the very truths the book presents as indispensable absolutes, the abandonment of which has meant disaster for the West. These pages were written from a perspective on political modernity that is both Christocentric and ecclesiocentric and is defended as simply true. Critics who

---

18. Francis Fukuyama, *The End of History and the Last Man* (NY: Free Press, 1992), 215.

19. Critics need not expend any effort to demonstrate that certain sources cited reject the ultimate conclusions for which they are cited as support. That much can be stipulated here. This work is not intended as a presentation of the thinking of this or that contemporary scholar. Rather, many of the references in question involve what lawyers call "admissions against interest" by an author who may in fact reject the position defended here, which is precisely why the admission is credible and useful as the statement of an adverse party who cannot be dismissed as a partisan of the Catholic perspective from which this study has been written.

would subject this work to the standard of "academic neutrality" would be misplacing their attentions.

The book is divided into four sections that are essentially four short studies linked by central themes. The first is a sketch of the historico-philosophical background necessary to appreciate the falsity of the liberal meta-narrative and in particular its "Whig narrative" thread, according to which the American Revolution was a "moderate" Enlightenment adaptation of classical Western thought that opened the way to essentially conservative regimes of "ordered liberty" and "limited government." The "moderate" Enlightenment is shown to be a radical break with the perennial Greco-Catholic tradition of the Western world as embodied in the Christian commonwealth, which is briefly defended against common prejudices in Chapter 2.

The second section presents a survey of the American Revolution and early history of the Republic, leading up to the Civil War, while the third section examines the Civil War as the second American Revolution. In these two middle sections the historical facts presented are related to the historico-philosophical background of the "moderate" Enlightenment to demonstrate the objectively radical nature of the "American experiment" and the consequences of the new politics it engendered. In the process, numerous golden legends of the *mythos* of Liberty as "conservative" tradition are debunked and its secular saints redimensioned to human proportions. These sections also demonstrate the thesis that beneath the glorious "official" account of the rise of "individual rights," "personal freedom," "government by consent of the governed" and the "illumination" of once-enslaved masses, lies the reality that Liberty is just another name for Power, albeit Power that knows none of the bounds intrinsic to the Christocentric social order relentlessly destroyed in the wave of revolutions of which the American was the first.

The American historical survey is pointedly limited in its focus to the period c.1776 to c. 1877 (with appropriate relation forward) in order to demonstrate that the current state of America is not the result of a 20th-century defection from the "vision of the Founders," nor the wartime tyranny of the Lincoln presidency, as the conservative/libertarian narrative holds. This study vigorously contests the romantic *mythos* of the Jeffersonian Paradise Lost and the closely related Lost Cause of the Confederacy as true heir of Liberty. It will be apparent that we stand today at the end of a sociopolitical trajectory—the trajectory from Locke to Obama—whose inevitable downward path was determined by the "moderate" Enlightenment principles of the Founding, as numerous conservative Protestant critics warned from the very dawn of the republic (cf. Chapters 17 and 22).

The fourth and final section surveys the process by which Christianity was politically subordinated and neutralized as a social force in the new nation, provoking early predictions by concerned Protestants and some of the disillusioned Founders themselves, that a "Christless, godless" America, and with it the whole Western world, would suffer a collapse of the moral order with catastrophic results (cf. Chapter 17). The final section concludes, however, with indications (including recent surprising developments in predominantly Catholic countries) of how we might regain the path from which our civilization was diverted during the age of democratic revolution. Here we explore the real potential of democracy itself for social *metanoia*, thus answering the predictable demagogic criticism that this book is a brief for a quixotic restoration of medieval Catholic monarchy.

As for the anticipated banal objection that what is advocated here is the "impossibility" of a reconversion of the Western world, the final section responds that the time has come to recognize this "impossibility" as the only reasonable course of action to save a dying civilization which, after all, is still composed predominantly of baptized Christians. (We shall see that the currently reigning Pope has intimated as much in an address to which the final pages make reference.) In the midst of a civilizational debacle no one can seriously deny any longer, anyone who calls himself a Christian should at least be willing to make an effort to examine our situation from the frankly Catholic perspective to be presented here. This will require standing outside the framework of liberal premises whose adoption was no less an act of the will than the common faith that sustained Christendom (with the aid of divine grace, of course) for century upon century. As Milbank has observed, the governing assumptions of secular social theory "are bound up with the modification or the rejection of orthodox Christian positions. These fundamental intellectual shifts are . . . no more rationally 'justifiable' than the Christian positions themselves."[20]

This case to be presented, then, will proceed on the ground of reason in the hope that, for the skeptical, faith will follow. Even in the absence of faith, however, reason alone ought to impel the thoughtful reader to confront with eyes wide open the self-evident reality that Liberty is an idol whose reign has oppressed and corrupted us all in one way or another. That conviction was the motive for this work.

---

20. John Milbank, *Theology and Social Theory: Beyond Secular Reason* (Oxford: Blackwell, 1993), 1.

I.

Christendom Deconstructed

1

The Logic of Christendom

TODAY, the principles of the "moderate" Enlightenment are what pass for a conservative inheritance to be opposed to the excesses of liberalism, an inheritance "We the People" were supposed to have "secured to ourselves and our posterity" following the American Revolution. These principles include:

- A hypothetical "social compact" or contract as the foundation of the State.

- The origin of political sovereignty in the "consent" of the governed (invariably presumed to have been given by those who happen to be wielding power).

- "Government by the people" according to the "sovereignty of the people," meaning strict majority rule on all questions, including the most profound moral ones.

- Church-State separation and the non-"interference" of religion in politics.

- The confinement of religion, above all the revealed truths of Christianity, to the realm of "private" opinions and practices one is free to adopt (or to denounce) if it pleases him, but which are to have no controlling effect on law or public policy.

- The unlimited pursuit of gain, including the freedom to buy, sell and advertise anything whatsoever the majority deems permissible by law.

- Total liberty of thought and action, both private and public, within the limits of a merely external "public peace" essentially reduced to the protection of persons and property from invasion by others—in sum, a "free-market society."

- The dissolubility of marriage, and thus the family, as a mere civil contract founded on a revocable consent.

We are witnessing the final outcome of the operation of these "moderate" principles in the life of the individual, the family and the State. That this "conservative" inheritance was actually a radically liberal and inevitably disastrous departure from the millennial Western theologico-political tradition is now considered a proposition bordering on madness even by the most "conservative" opponents of contemporary liberalism. And yet a radical departure it was—a departure that emerged as a full-blown system of thought during the epoch of the "Enlightenment" (roughly 1650–1800), whose first practical triumph, as we shall see, was the American Revolution, "the program of enlightenment in practice"[1] and "the Enlightenment fulfilled."[2] In order to appreciate "the radicalism of the American Revolution," to borrow the title of Gordon Woods's landmark Pulitzer Prize-winning study on the subject, it is necessary first to appreciate what has been dismantled and forgotten in the Age of Liberty whose official inauguration took place in America in 1776. Here the briefest of sketches must suffice.

The Greco-Catholic Synthesis

In his famous Gifford Lectures on the Enlightenment, published under the title *The Heavenly City of the Eighteenth Century Philosophers*, Carl L. Becker observes with the frankness of an honest and accomplished scholar that even before 1776 the *philosophes* of the Enlightenment had overturned in thought the "medieval world pattern, deriving from Greek logic and the Christian story."[3] By this Becker means the synthesis of the two great elements of the Western theologico-political tradition that began in Athens after its fall in the 4th century BC, when Socrates, with "his summons to men to 'care for their souls'... turned the mind of Greece toward a new way of life... a newer and higher ideal of state and society" that "ended with the search for a new God."[4]

The "Greek logic" of the Platonic-Aristotelian system developed for the first time in Western history a philosophical realism, ethics and politics based on the view of man as a creature possessed of a rational and immortal soul who inhabits an orderly universe, a universe in which everything has a fixed and objectively knowable essence determined by nature, which "makes nothing without some end in view, nothing to no purpose."[5] For Plato, these essences were the Forms, residing in a separate realm of perfection of which the sublunary world is but a replication. For Aristotle, with his "hylomorphism," which became the Christian philosophical doctrine of matter and form, every being in the orderly universe is a "substance," a

---

1. Peter Gay, *The Enlightenment: The Science of Freedom* (NY: W. W. Norton & Co., 1996 [1969]), 558.
2. Gordon S. Wood, *The Radicalism of the American Revolution* (NY: Vintage Books, 1991), 191.
3. Carl L. Becker, *The Heavenly City of the Eighteenth-Century Philosophers* (New Haven: Yale Univ. Press [1932], 2003), 5–6. We do not accept Becker's thesis of a veiled continuity between the "heavenly city" as conceived in the tradition of Christendom and the Enlightenment's new notion of a "heavenly" city. As the renowned historian of the Enlightenment Peter Gay has maintained, the thesis is "charming" but simply not true. That the two "cities" perform similar functions does not establish continuity between the old and the new worldviews. Gay calls this the "fallacy of the spurious persistence." Cf. Gay, *The Enlightenment: The Rise of Modern Paganism*, 535. Like Gay, who is not even writing from a Catholic perspective, we insist upon the patent discontinuity between traditional Christianity and the so-called Enlightenment.
4. Werner Jaeger, *Paidea: The Ideals of Greek Culture*, Vol. II (Oxford: Oxford Univ. Press, 1971 [1943]), 8, 46.
5. *Politics*, 1256b20, in *Aristotle: the Politics* (NY: Penguin Books, 1992), 79.

subsisting unity of matter and the form that determines its nature; and the soul, as the Christian tradition would also teach, is the form of man. For Aristotle, as for the Christian philosophical tradition, the forms are to be found in the existing beings themselves which the mind really encounters through the senses in an "adequation" (equalization) of itself to the real world.

In the Greek view of man, assimilated and adapted to the Christian view in light of revelation, the rational soul is ordered by nature to the practice of the virtues of which it alone is capable—above all prudence, fortitude, temperance and justice, the last being the sum of all virtues in social relations. Man's happiness—man being the only creature even capable of rationally seeking and knowingly experiencing happiness—does not consist in mere pleasure or material gain for its own sake, the vice Aristotle called *pleonexia*. It consists, rather, of an activity of the soul in accordance with virtue. And the highest state of virtue is communion with God (Plato) or the contemplation of God for those who are capable of it (Aristotle). This is the *summum bonum* the Greeks sought by unaided reason centuries before the revelation of the New Testament and the concept of the beatific vision.

Why is happiness an activity of the soul in accordance with virtue? Aristotle's answer is teleological: because man *has* a soul, which is clearly of a higher order than the body it rules, and because man is *capable* of exercising virtues, which are clearly of a higher order than the bodily instincts (the need for food, warmth, and so forth) he has in common with the lower animals. Since man is clearly designed for the practice of virtue, his true happiness must consist in virtue, as nature never endows anything without a purpose and "it would be an odd thing if man chose to live someone else's life instead of his own"[6]—that is, the life of a lower animal. With good reason is the bad man called "an animal" in common parlance. Men who live as animals are unhappy and cause unhappiness in others.

Given man's very nature as an ensouled creature whose end is the life of virtue and the encounter with God, both Plato and Aristotle teach that man's perfection requires life in the State, originating in the society of families with its organs of government. The state is "a creation of nature" and "man is by nature a political animal,"[7] as Aristotle so famously observes. Hence for the Greeks, as for the Christian statesmen who will follow them centuries later, the good State is the one whose laws and institutions take care of the soul by promoting and protecting both virtue *and religion* over and above mere security in person and property. For the Greeks of 4th-century Athens, as it would be for the Catholics of Christendom, religion was not merely a private affair but also involved "regular public honoring of the divine."[8]

Accordingly, says Plato, the good citizen—who is the same as the good man—

---

6. *Nicomachean Ethics*, 1178a 4–5.

7. *Politics*, 1253a 3–5.

8. Hans-Georg Gadamer, *The Idea of the Good in Platonic-Aristotelian Philosophy* (New Haven: Yale Univ. Press, 1986), 53.

will "keep himself from all the legislator lists in his count of things base and bad, and exercise himself with all his might in all that is in the contrary table of all things good and lovely" in order to avoid "deformity on the finest thing he has, his soul."[9] The disjunction between "private" and "public" morality that is a dogma of Liberty did not exist for Plato and Aristotle in Athens any more than it would for the Christian in Christendom. "The same things are best for individuals and states,"[10] as Aristotle declares in the *Politics*.

On this point several details of Plato's hypothetical construction of the good State are pertinent, even if others, such as the abolition of the nuclear family and private property, represent pagan wisdom gone astray and are repugnant to the Christian worldview. The first is legislation providing for the religious festivals of the State in keeping with the tight integration of religion and public life in the Greek polity.[11] The religion of the State as a reflection of the religion of the people was, of course, a fundament of political society throughout European history until well into the 19th century. For it is obviously nonsense to say that the individual, but not the collective of individuals making up the State, has duties to God. If there is a true religion, and the great preponderance of people profess it, then the State will naturally and logically profess it as well. Catholic teaching was uncompromising in its defense of this perennial element of Western political organization. Writing more than 2200 years after Plato, Pope Leo XIII declared: "God it is who has made man for society, and has placed him in the company of others like himself, so that what was wanting to his nature, and beyond his attainment if left to his own resources, he might obtain by association with others. Wherefore, civil society must acknowledge God as its Founder and Parent, and must obey and reverence His power and authority. Justice therefore forbids, and *reason itself forbids*, the State to be godless. . . . Since, then, *the profession of one religion is necessary in the State*, that religion must be professed which alone is true. . . ."[12] Leo's successor, Pius X, insisted as recently as 1906 that the members of the State owe God "not only a private cult, but a public and social worship to honor Him."[13] This dictate of practical reason, proceeding from the premise of Christ's divinity and His foundation of a teaching Church, was recognized even by Jacques Maritain, the renowned but inconsistently progressive progressivist and proponent of "integral humanism," when writing in his traditionalist mode:

> We must affirm as a truth above all the vicissitudes of time the supremacy of the Church over the world and over all terrestrial powers. On pain of radical disorder she must guide the peoples towards the last end of human life, which

---

9. *Laws*, 728b in *Plato: the Collected Dialogues*, Bollingen Series LXXI (Princeton, NJ: Princeton Univ. Press, 1989).

10. *Politics*, 1333b37 in *The Complete Works of Aristotle*, ed. Jonathan Barnes, Bollingen Series, LXXI, Vol II (Princeton, NJ: Princeton Univ. Press, 1984).

11. *Laws*, 828b.

12. *Libertas* (1888), n. 21.

13. *Vehementer Nos* (1906), n. 3.

is also that of States, and, to do that, she must direct, in terms of the spiritual riches entrusted to her, *both rulers and nations.*[14]

The radical disorder of which Maritain wrote is the core of the crisis of Western civilization. Also important for our purposes is Plato's advocacy of State censorship of immoral and indecent material in the arts and in literature.[15] Plato defends this basic feature of all traditional Western legal codes with admirable common sense. In Book III of *The Republic*, Socrates prescribes laws forbidding indecent and immoral poetry so that the young elite "may not be bred among the symbols of evil, as if it were in a pasture of poisonous herbs, lest grazing freely and cropping from many such day by day they little by little and all unawares accumulate and build up a huge mass of evil in their own souls."[16] Precisely the same rationale is found in Catholic teaching more than two millennia after Plato: "[L]ying opinions, than which no mental plague is greater, and vices which corrupt the heart and moral life should be diligently repressed by public authority, lest they insidiously work the ruin of the State."[17] The great historian of philosophy, Frederick Copleston, here notes an obvious truth that today is dismissed with howls of liberal outrage: "[T]he principle that animated him [Plato] must be admitted by all who seriously believe in an objective moral law, even if they quarrel with his particular applications of the principle. For, granted the existence of an immortal soul and of an absolute moral code, it is the duty of public authority to prevent the ruin of morality of the members of the State so far as they can...."[18]

According to the same rationale, Plato defends penalties for public offenses against the religion of the State. Public atheists and heretics, or those who set up private temples for false worship, are subject to imprisonment, banishment and even death.[19] Contemporary liberals likewise denounce the idea that public offenses against religion ought to be punished, but this too was a basic feature of traditional Western legal codes, and for perfectly logical reasons. For if religion is the way to eternal happiness, and if the corruption of religious truth leads to eternal misery, the members of the State have a right to protect themselves from the effects of the public dissemination of religious error. Hence Catholic teaching constantly condemned the idea that the best condition of civil society is one in which "no duty is recognized, as attached to the civil power, of restraining by enacted

---

14. Jacques Maritain, *Primauté du spiritual* (Plon, 1927), n. 23, in Michael Davies, *Apologia Pro Marcel Lefebvre*, Vol. II, Chapter 15, accessed at http://www.sspxasia.com/Documents/Archbishop-Lefebvre/Apologia/Vol_tw/Chapter _15.htm.

15. See, e.g., *Republic*, 401b; 377b; 386 ff.; *Laws*, 801b; 817d.

16. *Republic*, 401b.

17. Leo XIII, *Libertas* (1888), n. 23. There are innumerable examples of this teaching in papal encyclicals and even in the recently promulgated *Catechism of the Catholic Church*, which calls for the prohibition and destruction of pornography by the State and the State regulation of mass media to protect public morality. CCC §2354 ("Civil authorities should prevent the production and distribution of pornographic materials").

18. Frederick Copleston, S.J., *A History of Philosophy* (NY: Doubleday, 1985), Vol. I, 227.

19. *Laws*, 907d ff.

penalties, offenders against the Catholic religion...."[20] There is no social truth more obvious than that the spread of religious and moral falsehoods has disastrous temporal as well as eternal consequences. The crisis of our civilization lies in the refusal of political modernity to recognize that the truths of revelation are ineradicably connected both to the integrity of the moral order in society and to human happiness and flourishing in this world and in the next.

The foundational Greek view of the role of the State in the life of the whole man, which would be defended throughout the centuries of Christendom, is summarized in Aristotle's *Politics*:

> But a state exists for the sake of the good life; and not for the sake of life only. . . . It is clear then that the state is not a mere society, having a common place, established for the prevention of mutual crime and for the sake of exchange. These are conditions without which a state cannot exist; but all of them together do not constitute a state, which is a community of families and aggregations of families in well-being for the sake of a perfect and self-suffic-ing life . . . by which we mean a happy and honourable life.... [P]olitical society exists for the sake of noble actions, and not of living together.[21]

Given this function of the State, Plato (like Aristotle) viewed pure democracy as a deadly absurdity, likening its action upon the State to the governance of a sailing ship by a mutinous and drunken crew, who celebrate "the man who is most cun-ning" among them and make him captain, while the true pilot, with his indispens-able knowledge of navigation, is rejected as an impractical stargazer.[22] Of the three basic political constitutions—monarchy, oligarchy and democracy—monarchy is best, provided the monarch is a philosopher-king who governs according to the truth derived from his knowledge of the Forms. In Book V of *The Republic*, however, Plato levels a criticism of kings that applies with equal force to any ruler who fails to govern according to truth and justice: "Unless, said I, either philosophers become kings in our states or those whom we now call our kings and rulers take to the pur-suit of philosophy seriously and adequately . . . there can be no cessation of troubles, dear Glaucon, for our states, nor, I fancy, for the human race either."[23] This admo-nition, *mutatis mutandis*, applied to the Christian ruler whose source of truth included the Gospel revelation expounded by the Church as well as right reason.

The Politics of the Soul

If one phrase could describe the Greek view of Man and State it would be this: the politics of the soul. Indeed, Greek philosophy "led the way into the newfound

---

20. Pius IX, *Quas Primas* (1864). Despite all appearances to the contrary, this Catholic teaching, affirmed by numerous popes, remains intact in principle, even if the practical impossibility of its appli-cation today is conceded.

21. *Politics*, 1280a 30–3; b29; 1281a3 (Bollingen Series).

22. *Republic*, 488 c–d.

23. Ibid., 473d.

land of the soul," producing "a new order of values . . . worked out in the philosophical systems of Plato and Aristotle," which "paved the way for the universal religion, Christianity."[24] As Copleston observes in his monumental history of philosophy: "It would be difficult to exaggerate the importance of Plato in the intellectual *preparatio evangelica* of the pagan world."[25] Likewise, "the natural theology of Aristotle was a preparation for the acceptance of Christianity."[26] Moreover, "the political theory of Plato and Aristotle has indeed formed the foundation for subsequent fruitful speculations on the nature and characteristics of the State."[27] Thus the Catholic Church has never ceased to recognize her debt to the *veterum sapientia* of the Greeks, which "served, surely, to herald the dawn of the Gospel which God's Son, 'the judge and teacher of grace and truth, the light and guide of the human race,' proclaimed on earth."[28]

To the Greek foundations of natural theology, ethics and political philosophy the "Christian story" added its own theological and philosophical superstructure, producing "the synthesis with Hellenism achieved in the early Church,"[29] which reached its fullest and most systematic expression in Thomistic philosophy. The Greco-Catholic synthesis:

• reveals the God for which the Greeks were seeking;

• explains man's tendency to commit evil, and the fact of evil in the world, as consequences of the Fall of man on account of the original sin of our first parents;

• offers fallen man redemption through the grace won by the Redeemer, which repairs the defects of the rational soul clouded by Original Sin;

• completes (in the Aristotelian-Thomistic system of Thomas Aquinas and other medieval scholastics) the Greek picture of philosophical *realism*—a hierarchically ordered universe of divinely created and fixed natures or substances, with man and his rational soul at its visible summit and God as its highest good;

• adds the theological virtues (faith, hope and charity) to the cardinal virtues explored by Plato and Aristotle (prudence, justice, temperance and fortitude), and the concept of punishable transgressions against divine law—sins—to offenses against the natural order, concerning which there had been no explicit divine "ought" or divine prohibition in Greek philosophy.

With the Greco-Catholic synthesis comes an understanding of human freedom as involving, not only the practice of virtue, but liberation of the soul from the effects

24. Jaeger, *Paidea*, 11, 46.
25. Copleston, *A History of Philosophy*, Vol. I, 503.
26. Ibid., 504.
27. Ibid., 242.
28. Pope John XXIII, *Veterum Sapientia* (1962), n. 1.
29. Benedict XVI, "Papal Address at Univ. of Regensburg," 12 September 2006.

of sin. However obscured by sin, the divine ought is written onto our hearts in the form of the natural law, whose first precept is that "Good is to be done and pursued and evil to be avoided."[30] What is good, of course, is specified in the Decalogue— summed up by the love of God and neighbor—revelation as a whole, preeminently the Gospel, and the dictates of right reason, aided by revelation and perfected by grace, which enlightens the darkened soul. In the New Testament "sin" is a translation of the Greek word *hamartia*, which means to "miss the mark." By hitting the mark according to the divine plan, man achieves the end for which the Greeks were seeking in their obscure understanding that *arête*, human fulfillment in the excellence of virtue, and with it the good life in the good State, would seem to require what Plato called *theia moira*—a divine dispensation.[31] That dispensation is sanctifying grace: "Being then freed from sin, we have been made servants of justice."[32]

In the realm of philosophy, the Greco-Catholic synthesis baptized and confirmed the philosophical realism of Aristotle with his simple insistence that the world is just as we see it: an ordered hierarchy of beings with fixed natures and purposes; a vast ensemble of substances composed of matter and the form that makes each of them, above all man, forever one thing and not another. Aristotle, writes G. K. Chesterton, "took things as he found them, just as Aquinas accepted things as God created them." The philosophy of St. Thomas "stands founded on the universal common conviction that eggs are eggs," just as God made them to be. The Thomist, with Aristotle, thus "stands in the broad daylight of the brotherhood of men, in their common consciousness that eggs are not hens or dreams or mere practical assumptions; but things attested by the Authority of the Senses, which is from God."[33] It was Western man's very certitude about the real that the Enlightenment divines, pouring through the opening created by Descartes, Hobbes and Locke, would attack with unrelenting ferocity.

The Christian Commonwealth

Finally, the Christian story solved the dilemma Plato confronted in *The Republic* and *The Laws*: that the good State requires good men, but good men cannot be formed without the assistance of a good State. Taking the road "along which God himself is so plainly guiding us,"[34] to quote Clinias in *The Laws*, the Christian story arrived at a destination neither Plato nor Aristotle could foresee: Christendom. If one phrase could describe the perennial Greco-Catholic synthesis on Man, God and State, it would be this: the politics of the soul in the commonwealths of Christendom.

30. St. Thomas Aquinas, *Summa Theologica* (hereafter *ST*), I–II, 94, 2.

31. Cf. *Republic*, 492e ("And you may be sure that, if anything is saved and turns out well in the present condition of society and government, in saying that the Providence of God preserves it you will not be speaking ill").

32. Romans 6:18.

33. G. K. Chesterton, *Saint Thomas Aquinas* (NY: Random House, 1974), p. 121.

34. *Laws*, 968c.

"Where there is no justice, there is no state," declared Augustine, the first Catholic political philosopher. "But true justice," he argued in *City of God*, "is not to be found save in that commonwealth, if we may so call it, whose Founder and Ruler is Jesus Christ." Hence even in its greatest days the Roman Republic presented "merely a colored painting of justice, as Cicero himself suggests, while meaning to praise it."[35] Justice, Augustine concluded, "cannot be predicated of pagan states, as they do not render justice to God." The just state, therefore, is the Christian state, and an organic relation between the temporal and the spiritual power whose polestar is the Gospel of Christ will insure the justice of its laws.

In all its forms, and with all its human imperfections, the Christian commonwealth perennially exhibited the "Gelasian dyarchy" [36] of two distinct but organically united powers, the temporal subject to the spiritual in matters of morality and justice, where the jurisdictions of the two powers overlap. In all the centuries of its existence the dyarchy never admitted of any divorce between religion and politics, or the secular and the religious. In the universal fellowship of Christendom the Church was the conscience of the State and the soul of the body politic, just as religion (albeit pagan religion) was tightly integrated into the life of the Greek state.

In sum, ancient Greek thought sustains the *logic* of Christendom. Given the acceptance of the theological premise that Christ is God Incarnate, and thus the very *summum bonum* for which the Greeks were seeking, Christendom can be justified not only by an appeal to faith but also to rational principles on the nature of God, Man and State uncovered by the Philosophers in the explorations of unaided reason. Thus, some twenty-two centuries after Plato and Aristotle lived and taught, Pope Leo XIII was able to declare that "the Christian organization of civil society [was] not rashly or fancifully shaped out, but educed from the highest and truest principles, confirmed by natural reason itself."[37]

The Christian commonwealth is the good State for which Plato sought with his utopian method, the State that would be called "Magnesia—or whatever name God will have it called after," which "is not to be equaled in future ages." It is the "dream on which we touched" that would someday "have found its fulfillment in real and working fact...."[38] As the great Harvard classicist Werner Jaeger observes in his monumental work *Paideia*:

> Neither the ancient city-state nor the national ideal of the fourth century, *but the universal fellowship of Christendom laid the foundations for the fulfillment of Plato's hope.* That religious foundation was something far broader than the Greek nation which Plato had addressed. But it was similar to the Platonic

35. Demetrius B. Zema, S.J. and Gerald G. Walsh, S.J., trans., *The Fathers of the Church: Saint Augustine, the City of God*, Books 1–7 and 17–22 (Catholic University of America Press, 1950).

36. From the historic declaration of Pope Gelasius I in his letter to the Emperor Anastasius (494) on the supremacy of the spiritual over the temporal power in cases of conflict: "There are two powers, august Emperor, by which this world is chiefly ruled, namely, the sacred authority of the priests and the royal power. Of these *that of the priests is the more weighty....*"

37. *Immortale Dei*, n.16.

38. *Laws*, 969b.

scheme in this: it was not an abstract universal brotherhood of man; instead it was identical with the concrete Christian ... brotherhood, whose component nations continued to belong to it even in time of war.[39]

In their superficial reading of *The Republic* and *The Laws* contemporary conservatives and libertarians see a "statist" and "totalitarian" conception of social order harboring "the germs of Marxism, National Socialism, Islamicism, and other forms of utopianism."[40] Read with discernment, however, Plato's utopian speculations represent a search for the kind of ecclesiocentric polity that would emerge after the Incarnation, one in which the leavening effect of the Gospel would preclude both totalitarian and majoritarian tyranny. "The perfect design for living given in *The Laws*," writes Jaeger, "is like nothing so much as the year as conceived by the Catholic Church, with its holy rites and liturgies laid down for every day." Plato was seeking no mere State, as the superficial reading would suggest, but rather a great educational system for the formation of souls in which the State would merely play a part. And, notes Jaeger, "if we think of the greatest educational institution of the post-classical world, the Roman Catholic Church, it looks like a prophetic anticipation of many of the essential features of Catholicism." Plato's search thus presupposes precisely what the modern State has denied institutionally: that "[i]n reality only God is worth taking seriously, and what is divine in man," meaning "the logos, the cord by which God moves man.... If humanity is not seen in that divine perspective, it loses its own independent value."[41] And so it has in political modernity.

In the correspondence of Alcuin of York to Charles the Great (Charlemagne) during the Carolingian Renaissance of the late 8th century we find the connection between the hope of Athens and the rise of Christendom being drawn explicitly. Under the influence of the Holy Spirit, wrote Alcuin, "it may be that a new Athens will arise in France.... The old Athens had only the teachings of Plato to instruct it, yet even so it flourished by the seven liberal arts. But our Athens will be enriched by the sevenfold gift of the Holy Spirit[42] and will, therefore, surpass all the dignity of earthly wisdom."[43] This was no pious exultation from a religious zealot blinded by fideism, but the recognition by a great intellect of an historical, intellectual and spiritual reality then unfolding, one that would create the very basis of Western culture: the New Athens that was Christendom.

The "component nations" of Christendom would endure in all or parts of the Western world for some sixteen hundred years—from the edict of Milan in 313 until

39. Jaeger, *Paidea, Vol. II: In Search of the Divine Center* (NY: Oxford Univ. Press, 1986), 258.

40. Mark R. Levin, *Ameritopia* (NY: Simon & Schuster, 2012), Kindle Edition, 440.

41. Jaeger, *Paideia, Vol. III: The Conflict of Cultural Ideas in the Age of Plato* (NY: Oxford Univ. Press, 1986), Kindle Edition, 252–253.

42. The virtues infused by the operation of the Holy Ghost in addition to faith, hope and charity: "wisdom, understanding, counsel, fortitude, knowledge, piety, and fear of the Lord," which "complete and perfect the virtues of those who receive them." *Catechism of the Catholic Church*, §1831.

43. In Christopher Dawson, *Religion and the Rise of Western Culture* (NY: Image Books, 1991 [1950]), 65.

the fall of the House of Habsburg and the Treaty of Versailles in 1918. Their *residua* endure even today in certain predominantly Catholic countries of the Western world, such as Ireland and Malta, although the last remnants of their Christian legal codes and customs are under relentless attack by the European Union, the United Nations and other contemporary agencies of Liberty. It will be the burden of this study to show that the crisis of our civilization lies precisely in its all-but-complete repudiation, in the name of Liberty, of the things that made it Christian.

2

A Brief Defense of Christendom

IF THE Age of Liberty really represents, as we shall demonstrate, a programmatic abandonment of Christian civilization with all the disastrous consequences this has entailed, it is necessary to address at the outset, with the brevity it deserves, the common belief of contemporary man as nurtured from infancy in state schools: that the Age of Liberty has surely delivered men from the long dark age of the tyranny of popes and kings.

Here we make a declaration, once and for all, that should be kept in mind throughout the following chapters: Christendom needs no defense against the charge that it was the enemy of liberty rightly understood. If liberty is defined, not as a mere absence of restraint on human action in the pursuit of whatever one considers happiness, or as the ability to acquire a hitherto unknown abundance of gadgets and other material comforts, but rather as the good life of virtue, the secure possession of truth in individual and social life, and freedom from the bondage of sin for the sake of eternal felicity, then the commonwealths of Christendom were bulwarks of true liberty in comparison with the collapsing secular states of political modernity, which have experienced moral, spiritual and cultural decline from the moment they were established—at the point of a gun in every case, as we shall see.

Indeed, the charge that Christendom smothered true human liberty is refuted merely by pointing to the steady degradation of our post-Christian Western civilization: the ever-deepening cultural depravity of its "free-market" societies and the institutionalized undermining of marriage and family; the prevailing alienation and depression in our "therapeutic age,"[1] as the famed sociologist Philip Rieff has dubbed it, with its endless search for happiness without faith or hope in life eternal; the self-evident disintegration of both public and private morality. Rieff, rightly described as "a Jewish intellectual titan,"[2] provided this withering descrip-

---

1. A reference to Rieff's famed study *The Triumph of the Therapeutic*, which describes how traditional values preserved in communal activity, especially in the Church, have been replaced by "therapeutic values rooted in nothing more than the individual's search for self-fulfillment," assisted, not by priests or confessors, but "professional physicians and therapists, a whole galaxy of mystics, teachers, prophets, gurus, esoteric movements...." Harvey C. Mesesrve, "The Therapeutic Age," Journal of Religion and Health, Vol. 16, No. 2, 77.

2. Benjamin Wachs, "Sociologist Philip Rieff haunts us from the grave," JewishWeekly.com, July 18, 2008, www.jweekly.com/article/full/ 35346/sociologist-philip-rieff-haunts-us-from-the-grave/.

tion of family life in the "transitional civilization" we experience today as the outcome of Liberty in practice (which, as we shall see, brought declining birth rates and liberal divorce laws almost immediately to post-revolutionary America in keeping with Locke's view of marriage as a revocable contract):

> Ecologically, this transitional civilization is becoming one vast suburbia, something like the United States, with divided communities of two, with perhaps two junior members caught in the middle of a private and not always civil war; in relation to these intimate, though divided, communities of two, the public world is constituted as one vast stranger, who appears at inconvenient times and makes demands viewed as purely external and therefore without the power to elicit a genuinely moral response.[3]

Something like the United States, indeed. We shall see as well that the emergence of a neo-pagan America, a "Godless, Christless blank," was predicted by a national movement of alarmed American Protestants in the mid-19th century. This movement in turn pointed to the prophetic warnings of other Protestants, going back to very founding the Republic, about the godlessness of the constitutional regime the enlightened deistic Framers had created.

The "Tyranny" of Christendom

What of the charge that Christendom stands for tyranny by "absolute" monarchs in league with tyrannical popes? The charge is sustainable only upon a complete ignorance of European history and what the modern state system has wrought in terms of death, destruction and governmental impositions on the ordinary citizen. If anything, the monarchies of Christendom were characterized by a radical decentralization of political power in comparison with the massive centralized governments of the modern nation-states. They exhibited what the Catholic Church calls "the principle of subsidiary function" or *subsidiarity*, which assigns governmental functions in an organic manner to the lowest appropriate levels of society.[4]

In his *Democracy: The God That Failed* (whose very title suggested the title of this book), even the radical "anarcho-libertarian" scholar Hans-Hermann Hoppe concedes that the monarchs of former Christendom, bound by a complex web of ancient customary limits on their powers, were far more respectful of legitimate local and personal autonomies than present-day "representative" governments. After referring to the traditional limitations on monarchical power in Catholic Europe and the limited nature of the wars in which monarchs were involved, as opposed to the "total wars" waged in the name of Liberty, Hoppe observes that

---

3. Rieff, *The Triumph of the Therapeutic* (Wilmington, DE: ISI Books, 2005 [1966]), 43.

4. Cf. Pius XI, *Quadragesimo Anno* (1931), n. 79: "Just as it is gravely wrong to take from individuals what they can accomplish by their own initiative and industry and give it to the community, so also it is an injustice and at the same time *a grave evil and disturbance of right order* to assign to a greater and higher association what lesser and subordinate organizations can do. For every social activity ought of its very nature to furnish help to the members of the body social, *and never destroy and absorb them*."

with the rise of universal Western democracy on the ruins of monarchy after World War I, as demanded by Woodrow Wilson, "private government ownership [monarchy] was completely replaced by public government ownership." With that development, "government growth, and an attending process of *decivilization* should have been expected to take off."[5]

In other words, the rise of "government by the people" coincided with the decline of the West. With the fall of monarchy, nothing stood in the way of the process by which the "democratic republicanism" that had replaced kings "produced communism . . . fascism, national socialism and, lastly and most enduringly, social democracy."[6] Curiously enough, it was Wilson himself—hammer of the House of Hapsburg—who exposed the myth of the "tyranny" of Catholic Christendom during a 1909 address republished shortly after his death:

> Did you ever think how the world managed politically to get through the middle ages? It got through them without breakdown because *it had the Roman Catholic Church to draw upon for native gifts*, and by no other means that I can see. If you will look at the politics of the middle ages you will see that *states depended for their guidance upon great ecclesiastics*, and they depended upon them because the community itself was in strata, was in classes, and *the Roman Catholic Church was a great democracy. Any peasant could become a priest, and any priest a chancellor.*[7]

The limited powers of Catholic monarchs in comparison with the modern nation-state reflect precisely the Christian principle ignorantly denounced as a fount of tyranny when it is actually the greatest of all safeguards against it: the revealed truth, as seen in the teaching of Saint Paul, that "there is no power but from God . . . and therefore he that resisteth the power, resisteth the ordinance of God."[8] Or as Christ Himself declared to Pilate: "Thou shouldst not have any power against me, unless it were given thee from above."[9] The ruler is not merely a human authority, but literally a minister of God accountable to Him as such: "The mighty shall be mightily tormented."[10] This truth is not to be confused with the Protestant error of the divine right (direct divine appointment) of kings. From the divine origin of all political authority follows the divine limitation upon its exercise. The ruler, be he a king or a democratically elected official, may not transgress God's law and is rightfully resisted whenever he does: "We ought to obey God rather than men."[11] Hence Saint Augustine's classic formula: *lex iniusta non est lex* (unjust law is not law).

On the other hand, Augustine, in line with the entire political tradition of Chris-

---

5. Hoppe, *Democracy: The God That Failed*, 42.

6. Ibid.

7. Woodrow Wilson, "Robert E. Lee: An Interpretation," *Social Forces*, Vol. II (March 1924) 322–28, accessed at http://leearchive.wlu.edu/reference/essays/wilson/index. html.

8. Romans 13:2.

9. John 19:11.

10. Wisd. 6:7.

11. Acts 5:29.

tendom, defended the Church against the accusation that adherence to the Gospel undermines fidelity to civil authority. Writing to his friend Marcellinus of Carthage, the saint and martyr who served as secretary of state of the Western Roman Empire, Augustine protested: "Let those who say that the doctrine of Christ is incompatible with the State's well-being, give us an army composed of soldiers such as the doctrine of Christ requires them to be; let them give us such subjects, such husbands and wives, such parents and children, such masters and servants, such kings, such judges—in fine, even such taxpayers and tax-gatherers, as the Christian religion has taught that men should be, and then let them dare to say that it is adverse to the State's well-being...."[12]

In *City of God* Augustine developed the theme that the Christian, a citizen of the heavenly City of God sojourning on earth as a citizen of the City of Man, is obliged by his very religion to obey civil authority and to work for the well-being of the State, in whatever form it exists, for "When it is considered how short is the span of life, does it really matter to a man what government he must obey, so long as he is not compelled to act against God or his conscience?"[13] In his commentary on Psalm 124, Augustine observed that the Catholic faithful had even served obediently under Julian, "an emperor unfaithful to God, an apostate, a pervert, an idolator." When Julian commanded them to "honor idols and offer them incense," they refused obedience rather than commit sin, but "when he made them form into ranks and march against a hostile nation, they obeyed instantly. They distinguished the eternal from the temporal master and still in view of the eternal Master they submitted to such a temporal master."[14]

From the standpoint of the unbroken Christian tradition, the Enlightenment novelty of the "right to revolution" and the total overthrow of governments deemed unacceptable by "the people"—meaning the revolutionaries—is contrary to the revealed duty of obedience to civil authority in all things except sin. We shall return to this point in our discussion of Hobbes and Locke in the next chapter, and will touch upon it again in our discussion of the first and second American Revolutions in Sections II and III.

The political tradition of Christendom, then, provides a complete doctrine, rooted in revelation, for both obedience to civil authority and the grounds for licit disobedience to its unjust or immoral commands. Having abandoned the Christian teaching on the divine source and the divinely imposed limits of civil authority, the modern nation-state boasts of its freedom even as it destroys true freedom by an exact inversion of the Gospel: We ought to obey men rather than God, keeping any contrary "private" religious beliefs to ourselves in the exercise of our "religious freedom."

12. *Letter* 138, 2.15.
13. *City of God*, V.17.
14. From *Nicene and Post-Nicene Fathers, First Series, Vol. 8*. Trans, J.E. Tweed; ed. Philip Schaff. (Buffalo, NY: Christian Literature Publishing Co., 1888), accessed at http://www.newadvent.org/fathers/1801125.htm. Psalm 124 is also numbered 125, depending on the numbering system employed. We use the ancient numbering system here.

Economic Freedom

Christendom was no enemy of economic liberty, if this is understood to mean the pursuit of gain within due moral limits—limits long ago transgressed by our "dying capitalist civilization," as Chesterton called it.[15] The Italian city republics or communes of the 12th and 13th centuries, for example, were vibrant centers of commerce with a large middle class. They were no doubt inhabited by innumerable sinners and hypocrites pretending not to be sinners, as is the way of the world since the Fall of Adam. But they were also little "cities of God" in which redemption was everywhere available and near at hand, for social life exhibited the Greco-Catholic integration of religion into all spheres of communal activity, moderating the pursuit of gain with laws against usury and unconscionable bargaining, and animating acts of charity and solidarity with the poor: "At no time were the communes secular in the modern sense. . . . The union of Church and city, which marked the early communes, persisted in new forms, and mutual support between them intensified. . . . Everywhere the cities made the Church's old responsibility for 'miserable persons' their own. . . . Fortified by sacred rites and prayers, the ordered commune extended from citizens on earth to patron saints in heaven, and from there to its wayward souls in purgatory."[16]

Intellectual and Artistic Freedom

If human freedom is viewed under the aspect of the pursuit of truth, goodness and beauty, here too Christendom was a haven of true liberty in comparison with political modernity and its attendant cultural and moral degeneracy. For it was none other than the philosophers, scientists, composers, musicians, and artists of the Christian centuries who gave the Western world deep insights into the nature of man, the university system,[17] innumerable scientific discoveries,[18] and indisputably the greatest works of art, architecture, music and literature the world has ever seen. Who in this Age of Liberty has even remotely approached the philosophical depth of Saint Thomas, or the creative triumph of Michelangelo, Dante, Palestrina, or the mystery-imbued splendor of the architects of Notre-Dame de Chartres?

15. G.K. Chesterton, "On Babies and Birth Control," in *The Well and the Shallows* (San Francisco: Ignatius Press, 2006), 110.

16. Augustine Thompson, O.P., *Cities of God: The Religion of the Italian Communes* (University Park: The Univ. of Pennsylvania Press, 2005), 136, 138, 177.

17. The first universities were successors of the Catholic cathedral schools that had been in existence since the 6th century. The Catholic Church founded literally all of the first universities of Europe, including those at Bologna, Cambridge, Constantinople, Naples, Oxford, Padua, Paris, Salamanca, Salerno, and Toulouse.

18. The scientific achievements of members of the Jesuit order alone are staggering. To provide only two examples: thirty-five lunar craters are named after Jesuit astronomers, and the atomic theory of the Jesuit Roger Boscovich (1711–1787), expounded in his *Theoria philosophia naturalis*, is credited with providing the groundwork for the theories of Faraday, Kelvin and even Einstein. Then, of course, there was Louis Pasteur, the devout Catholic whose discoveries in microbiology established the very basis for all scientific progress in the treatment of communicable diseases.

The punishment of heresy by civil authorities, executing the judgments of ecclesiastical courts, provides indispensable fodder for the catechism of liberal orthodoxy. But as already noted, reason alone informed the Greeks that the religion of the people had to be protected from public attacks for the common good. One of the abounding absurdities of our post-Christian civilization is that contemporary legal codes impose harsh civil and criminal penalties for false advertising that causes the loss of mere money or for political heresy in the form of "hate speech" that offends certain sensibilities, while guaranteeing the absolute "freedom" to spread religious and moral falsehoods that have disastrous temporal and eternal consequences.

As for scientific progress, we need not tarry over the ludicrous schoolboy myth of the persecution and torture of Galileo, seemingly the one and only example of the Church's "opposition" to science. Galileo's friend and patron, Pope Urban VIII, never forbade him to teach his heliocentric hypothesis *as* a hypothesis—as had the monk-scientist Copernicus, seventy years earlier *in a book dedicated to Pope Paul III.* Galileo's "punishment" represented the coddling of a famous intellectual, and even a Protestant biographer mocks the fantasy of torture and harsh imprisonment: "One glance at the truest historical source for the famous trial, would convince anyone that Galileo spent altogether twenty-two days in the buildings of the Holy Office (i.e., the Inquisition), and even then not in a prison cell with barred windows, but in the handsome and commodious apartment of an official of the Inquisition." And Galileo's alleged declaration "E pur si muove" ("Yet it moves"), like Luther's "Here I stand," is a complete fabrication.[19]

"Religious Violence"

Finally, we address here—in the passing manner it merits—the master myth of the liberal meta-narrative: that religion was the cause of endless wars and suffering before the Enlightenment brought an end to religious strife by dispelling ignorance and bigotry and inspiring the revolutions, including the American, that produced peaceful democratic and pluralistic societies. The myth depends upon blindness to the historical reality that the bloodiest wars in Western history, the unprecedented genocides, "democides"[20] and "politicides"[21] that came after 1789, followed by the rise of the worldwide "military-industrial complex"—a perpetual war machine in perpetual preparation for war—were all the work of states opposed in principle to the very idea of Christendom.

To address a facile objection, the difference is not merely one of advances in the technology of killing, but rather a change in the very nature of war. As the distin-

19. Cf. Gerard, J., "Galileo Galilei," *The Catholic Encyclopedia* (1909). Galileo died in the good graces of the Church and was given an elaborate tomb in Santa Croce church in Florence.
20. A term coined by R. J. Rummel to denote the mass killing of unarmed people by governments without any necessary connection to a policy of eliminating a particular race or culture. Rummel, *Death by Government* (New Brunswick, NJ: Transaction Publishers, 2008), 31.
21. "The murder of any person or people by government because of their politics or for political purposes." Ibid.

guished historian R.R. Palmer observes, before the French Revolution—that is, throughout the fourteen centuries of Christendom—wars had been "clashes between governments or ruling families, fought by relatively small armies of professional soldiers. Many people suffered, *but the people as such* was not vitally concerned. When governments became the people's governments, their wars became the people's wars, and their armies the armies of the nation."[22] And so it has been since the Age of Liberty began. The rise of mass democracy introduced the concept of "the nation at war," with men, women and children all playing their roles in "the war effort." Compulsory military conscription, "a kind of blood tax by all modern states, signifies *the loss of freedom* enjoyed by ancient societies," resulting from "the growing power of a state in the process of becoming a leviathan...."[23]

In particular, but without limitation, we note the following immense slaughters involving conscripted national armies that would have been unthinkable during the Christian centuries, beginning with the hitherto unprecedented *levée en masse* (mass conscription) by the Jacobin regime:

• The French revolutionary wars following the 1789 uprising inspired by the American example: 2 million dead.

• The genocide of Catholics in the Vendée by the Jacobin regime: 300,000 dead.

• The Napoleonic wars following the fall of the Jacobin and Thermidorian regimes: 3 million dead.

• The Civil War in America, during which one-half of the nation laid waste to the other half: 600,000 dead.

• World War I, the second bloodiest war in Western history, fought to make Europe "safe for democracy," whose direct consequences were the rise of the madman Hitler in a Germany starved, humiliated, and dismembered at Versailles, World War II, and the rise of Soviet and world communism: 16 million dead.[24]

• The Allied starvation blockade of Germany during and *after* World War I, whose express aim included starving the German population into submitting to the disastrous terms at Versailles: 700,000 dead.

• The genocide of Armenians by the atheist Young Turk regime from 1915–1917—complete with death camps, mass poisoning and gassing—following the "democratic revolution" of 1908: 2 million dead.[25]

22. R.R. Palmer, *Twelve Who Ruled* (Princeton, NJ: Princeton Univ. Press, 1969 [1941]), 60.

23. Romano Amerio, *Iota Unum* (Kansas City, MO: Sarto House, 1996), 445.

24. The famed British politician Lady Astor, when asked during the War: "By the way, where was Hitler born?" is said to have replied immediately: "At Versailles." In Patrick J. Buchanan, *Churchill, Hitler and the Unnecessary War* (NY: Three Rivers Press, 2008), 115.

25. The very word genocide was first coined to describe this slaughter. As R.J. Rummel observes of

• The Russian Civil War (1917–23) between the Red Army and the anti-Bolshevik White Army, assisted by the Allied Forces: 4 million dead, including civilians, from battlefield casualties, disease and starvation.

• The Bolshevik democides perpetrated by Trotsky and Lenin, who had been smuggled from Switzerland into Russia by the German high command during World War I in a successful bid to destabilize the Entente Powers and provoke Russia's withdrawal from World War I: 7 million dead, including the murdered Czar, his wife and five children.[26]

• World War II: the bloodiest war in Western history, causing incalculable losses to Western civilization, including the turnover of eastern Europe to Stalin, presented with a Crusader's sword[27] at Teheran by Winston Churchill in a grotesque parody of the Crusades: 70 million dead.

• The genocides by the Nazi regime: 20 million dead, including 6 million Jews.

• The carpet-bombing of Dresden and Tokyo and the atomic bombing of Hiroshima and Nagasaki, all in 1945: at least 500,000 dead combined.[28]

• The ethnic cleansing of Germans in the eastern provinces of Germany, delivered into the hands of Stalin by moving the Polish border westward at Yalta with the agreement of Churchill and FDR: 2 million dead in an orgy of "mass murder, rape and looting."[29]

• All of the democides, genocides and politicides by Stalin, the monster the

this genocide of Christians, the Young Turks were "practically all atheists," who dreamed the secular dream of "a new Turkey that would unite all enemies into one great nation . . . unweakened by rebellious minorities," and who "only used Islam to incite the Moslem masses against Turkey's Armenians." Rummel, *Death by Government*, 226.

26. The aptly named Alexander Helphand, a/k/a Parvus, who was also an advisor to the genocidal Young Turk regime, assisted the German high command in this endeavor. Cf. Dimitri Kolgonov, *Lenin: A New Biography* (NY: Free Press/Simon and Schuster, 1994), 78 ff.

27. Buchanan, *The Unnecessary War*, 370.

28. The A-bomb dropped on Nagasaki, the home of Japan's largest Catholic population, instantly incinerated Urakami Cathedral: "Fathers Nishida and Tamaya were hearing confessions again after the all-clear. The cathedral was only a third of a mile from where Fat Man detonated and was reduced to rubble in an instant. No one would be sure how many perished inside." Besides the A-bomb's lethal radiation, "there was its intense heat, which reached several million degrees centigrade at the explosion point. The whole mass of the huge bomb was ionized and a fireball created, making the air around it luminous, emitting ultraviolet rays and infrared rays and blistering roof tiles farther than half a mile from the epicenter. Exposed human skin was scorched up to two and a half miles away." In a concrete reinforced hospital a half-mile from ground zero "80 percent of the patients and staff perished." The surviving staff members "were shocked to find many of [the patients] dead, their bodies swollen and their skin peeled off as if they were overripe peaches." Paul Glynn, *A Song for Nagasaki* (San Francisco: Ignatius Press, 1988), 19–20.

29. Serhii Ploky, *Yalta: the Price of Peace* (NY: Viking, 2010), 216.

Allies needed to defeat the monster born at Versailles, and to whom they handed over eastern Europe at Teheran[30] and Yalta in the name of Liberty: at least 56 million dead. [31]

We must also include the genocides perpetrated by regimes that were the direct Asian and Southeast Asian sequelae of the exported Western ideology of Marxism, which began as a radical reaction by Marx, Engels and their adepts against the supposed bourgeois perversion of Liberty by the "moderately" liberal, post-Christian and capitalist social order of Western Europe:

- The Red Chinese regime: 35 million dead.

- The Pol Pot regime: 2 million dead.

- The North Korean regime: 1.6 million dead.

In his landmark study of the history of government-perpetrated genocide, R.J. Rummel compiles statistics for a total of some 150 million victims of "Dekamegamurders" and "Lesser Megamurders" in the 20th century alone.[32] Rummel's study is entitled "Death by Government," but the evidence he marshals of the worst state-sponsored atrocities in history shows that not one of them represents death by *Christian* government, but rather *post*-Christian or atheist regimes.

In response to the massive evidence that the Age of Liberty has been an age of death and devastation on an unprecedented scale, one inevitably receives the tiresome counter-reference to the victims of the Inquisition. But as Erik von Kuehnelt-Leddhin has noted: "all of the victims of the Inquisition burnt at the stake through centuries did not amount to a tiny fraction of those cremated alive one afternoon in Dresden, when among 204,000 killed at least two-thirds perished fully conscious in the fiery flames ... and this without inquest, without the slightest effort to establish real or even a subjectively imputed guilt, [and] at the very end of a war."[33]

The renowned Jewish intellectual Dr. David Berlinski, a self-described agnostic who "cannot pray," provides his own staggering enumeration of statistics on the unparalleled death, misery and devastation of the 20th and early 21st centuries in answer to the ludicrous contention of psychologist Steven Pincker that "something in modernity and its cultural institutions has made us nobler" and that "compre-

---

30. The same Churchill who deplored the smuggling of Lenin into Russia as akin to "a culture of typhoid or of cholera ... poured into the water supply of a great city," would lift his glass to Stalin in the process of preparing to turn over eastern Europe to him at Yalta, declaring, "We regard Marshal Stalin's life as most precious to the hopes and hearts of all of us. . . . I walk the world with greater courage and hope when I find myself in a relation of friendship and intimacy with this great man, whose fame has gone out not only over all Russia, but the world." In Buchanan, *The Unnecessary War*, 376.

31. The Soviet regime's total of 62 million dead from which we have subtracted Lenin's contribution of 6 million. Rummel cites the overall total of 62 million as "the only prudent, most probable tally in a range from a highly unlikely low figure of 28,000,000 ... and an equally unlikely high of 126,900,000. . . ." Rummel, *Death by Government*, 81–82.

32. Cf. *Death by Government*, chaps. 2–3.

33. Erik von Kuehnelt-Leddhin, *Liberty or Equality: The Challenge of Our Time* (Front Royal, VA: Christendom Press, 1993 [1952]), 280.

hensive data again paint a shockingly happy picture."[34] Berlinski offers this droll observation concerning the claim that secular modernity has moved beyond all the human misery provoked by religion:

> Just who has imposed on the suffering human race poison gas, barbed wire, high explosives, experiments in eugenics, the formula for Zyklon B, heavy artillery, pseudo-scientific justifications for mass murder, cluster bombs, attack submarines, napalm, intercontinental ballistic missiles, military space platforms, and nuclear weapons? If memory serves, it was not the Vatican.[35]

No, it was not the Vatican. Nor was it any sort of Christian commonwealth. The wars, persecutions, democides, politicides and genocides that have convulsed Western civilization since the late 18th century have all represented state action by governments that have either persecuted Christianity outrightly and bloodily, or, perhaps even more effectively, quietly and bloodlessly by declaring religion incompetent to "meddle" in politics and consigning it to the realm of socially meaningless private opinion, where "pacifists," "do-gooders," "bleeding hearts," "isolationists," and other unpatriotic sorts have long languished in America. Hence, for example, the seven-point peace plan of Pope Benedict XV, the "peace Pope," to end World War I was ignored by all the major powers except the still-Catholic Austria-Hungary.

Further, we have not even discussed the scores of millions of innocent human beings destroyed *in utero* by state-sponsored abortion, first legalized as a "necessary evil" in Soviet Russia under Lenin's Decree on Women's Health Care (1920),[36] prosecuted as a war crime at Nuremberg,[37] but now defended as the law of the land throughout the Western world (with the exception of the few remaining Catholic countries) even by "conservatives" who profess to deplore this form of genocide while accepting the will of the majority in keeping with the dogmas of Liberty.

What of the "religious wars" that preceded the age of democratic revolution? As William T. Cavanaugh has shown in his magisterial refutation of the "myth of religious violence," the so-called wars of religion in the 16th and 17th centuries were really conflicts waged "by state-building elites for the purpose of consolidating their power *over the church* and other rivals."[38] Hence "these wars were the *birth pangs of the state*, in which the overlapping jurisdictions, allegiances, and customs of the medieval order were flattened and circumscribed into the new creation of the

---

34. David Berlinski, *The Devil's Delusion* (NY: Crown Forum, 2008), 21–25.

35. Ibid., 21.

36. See Laurence H. Tribe, *Abortion: A Clash of Absolutes* (NY: W.W. Norton & Co., 1992), 56 ff, wherein Tribe notes that not even Lenin's wife dared to advocate legalized abortion as a matter of liberty, as the United States Supreme Court would do only 53 years later in *Roe v. Wade.*

37. See e.g., *The United States of America v. Ulrich Greifelt et al.*, Nat'l Archives Collection Of World War II War Crimes Records, Records Of The U.S. Nuremberg War Crimes Trials, Record Group 238, *United States of America v. Ulrich Greifelt et al.* (Oct. 10, 1947–Mar. 10, 1948), Microfilm Publication M894 (38 Reels). Cf. Jeffrey C. Tuomala, "Nuremberg and the Crime of Abortion," (2010). Faculty Publications and Presentations. Paper 26 @ http://digitalcommons.liberty.edu/lusol_fac_pubs/26.

38. William T. Cavanaugh, *The Myth of Religious Violence* (NY: Oxford Univ. Press, 2009), 162.

sovereign state (not always yet nation-state), a centralizing power with a monopoly on violence within a defined territory."[39] Indeed, "the very distinction of politics and religion made possible by the rise of the modern state . . . *was itself at the root of these wars.*"[40] The result, as we shall see in our survey of the American Revolution and its aftermath, was a "transfer of the sacred from Christianity to the nation-state" and "the substitution of the religion of the state for the religion of the church."[41] Citizens would now be expected to lay down their lives in vast numbers, not for Christ or the defense of the Faith, but for the Union or the Republic or the Confederacy.

Thus the "wars of religion" involved complex political alliances having nothing to do with mythical violent quarrels over points of Christian doctrine. Far more than merely religious clashes, they were "military expressions of economic grievances, regional and provincial particularism, competing lusts for power, shifts in class structure, and high rational policy."[42] They were power struggles in which Catholics sometimes allied with Protestants and even Muslims, Catholics fought against Catholics, the Holy Roman Emperor fought against the Pope and the Pope against the Emperor, and Catholic nations fought against Catholic nations.[43] And, with the exception of the Thirty Years War, these conflicts, fought largely by mercenaries or volunteer conscripts, were on a miniscule scale compared to the world wars and genocides of the Age of Liberty that began in 1776. Not even the Thirty Years War, however, was a war over religion *simpliciter*, as opposed to a conflict over territories in which loyalties frequently crossed religious lines, combined with a German civil war—the central conflict—in which the demand of nobles for the right to become Protestant was expediently allied to their drive for political autonomy from the Hapsburg dynasty. The depiction of the War as a pan-European bloodfest between Catholics and Protestants arising from doctrinal differences is a cartoon presented to public school students as part of their indoctrination into the myth of religious violence and the necessity of pluralist democracy to prevent it from ever erupting again.

What Cavanaugh dubs "the creation myth of the wars of religion" was essential to the establishment of the secular liberal state that will tolerate no interference by any

---

39. William T. Cavanaugh, "Beyond Secular Parodies" in *Radical Orthodoxy: A New Theology*, eds John Milbank, Graham Ward, Catherine Pickstock (London: Routledge, 1998), 191.

40. Cavanaugh, *The Myth of Religious Violence*, 118, 162.

41. Ibid., 177.

42. Gay, *The Enlightenment: The Rise of Modern Paganism* (NY: W.W. Norton & Co., 1977), 297.

43. As Cavanaugh summarizes: the Holy Roman Emperor Charles V warred against the Pope (the Schmalkaldic War of 1546–47); Catholic France warred against Charles V in various conflicts over the period from 1521 to 1552, including alliances with Muslim Turks against Charles; Protestant princes were on Charles's side during the emperor's first war against the Schmalkaldic League; Pope Paul IV warred against the Catholic Habsburg monarch, Philip II, in 1552; Protestant and Catholic nobles combined to war upon the commoners of France during the French religious wars (1562–1598), while Protestant and Catholic commoners combined to fight Catholic nobles; and "the latter half of the Thirty Years' War was largely a battle between Catholic France, on the one hand, and the Catholic Habsburgs on the other." Cavanaugh, *The Myth of Religious Violence*, 142–150.

religion or religious body. Cavanaugh's remarkable study provides a startling reminder of what should have been an obvious historical truth: "religion as a distinct category of human activity separable from culture, politics and other areas of life is an invention of the modern West."[44] That invention has been used precisely to justify what John Courtney Murray called the "monism of power" in the secular state.

Then again, as Cavanaugh contends, if nationalism—the worship of the nation-state—is classed as a religion, then it is far and away the most violent religion in human history. The following pages will take note of the role nationalism has played in the "cruel wars, desolations of countries, and oceans of blood" that none other than John Adams, second President of the United States, predicted "*must occur* before rational principles and rational systems of government can prevail and be established"[45]—that is, before Christendom could be eradicated throughout the West and replaced by "the American model." Seen from this perspective, the greatest of all the wars of religion is the one waged for more than a century (from 1789 to 1918) by the forces of Liberty, intent on building their version of the heavenly city on the ruins of every last one of the Catholic states of Europe and Latin America. (We shall survey the vast scope of this project in the second volume of this study.)

Only when the living God who founded a Church and preached His Gospel in the flesh had been banished from political affairs—that is, only when Christendom had been overthrown—was it possible to speak of a secular nation-state; and only then did there emerge the epiphenomenon of nationalism with its demands for total war. But as Milbank has written: "Once there was no secular. Instead there was the single community of Christendom with its dual aspects of sacerdotium and regnum.... The secular as a domain had to be *created or imagined*, both in theory and in practice."[46] The creation or imagination of a secular domain of politics, separated from the precepts of revealed religion, was a primary aim of the Enlightenment and an essential preparation for the American Revolution. We must understand the sheer radicalism of that development before we examine the radicalism of the Revolution itself.

44. Cavanaugh, *Myth of Religious Violence*, 60–85.

45. Adams to Jefferson, September 17, 1823 in *The Works of John Adams, Second President of the United States: with a Life of the Author, Notes and Illustrations, by his Grandson Charles Francis Adams* (Boston: Little, Brown and Co., 1856), Vol. 10; accessed from oll.libertyfund.org/title/2127/193660/310 3830 on 2011-02-08. This author is indebted to Jeffrey Langan for this critical citation in his paper "Revolutionary Guilt."

46. Milbank, *Theology and Social Theory* (Oxford: Blackwell, 1993), 9. Emphasis in original.

3

The Heavenly City Demolished

IN HIS AFOREMENTIONED Gifford Lectures, Carl Becker observed that the 18th-century *philosophes*, following in the path opened up by John Locke, "demolished the Heavenly City of Saint Augustine to rebuild it with more up-to-date materials."[1] What Liberty required for its establishment of the modern state system was, as the brilliant French political philosopher Pierre Manent writes:

> an unprecedented combination that would allow man to erect a "new world" to inhabit, neither "this world" nor "the other world," but a third world or third city *that is neither natural like the city of the Greeks nor supernatural like the city of the Christians*, but simply and purely human: *the city of man*. This third party, which became more and more numerous and ended up subjecting or absorbing the two original camps almost completely, is the party of the Moderns.[2]

To build their city of man the Moderns needed the blueprint for a society that "by its very constitution must prevent the individual from being claimed by either the old city or the old Church."[3] But first they had to erase the inheritance of the Greco-Catholic tradition sketched in Chapter 1, with its orderly universe of created kinds ascending hierarchically to God as the *summum bonum* and terminating, for man, in the beatific vision as his participation and final end in the *summum bonum*. For that vision of man and his place in the universe leads logically and naturally to the social order of Christendom, permeated by religion and the alliance between the temporal and spiritual powers. Manent explains:

> [B]y presenting human life as a hierarchy of goods and ends, Aristotle's teaching was vulnerable to the Christian claim that the good brought by the Church is greater, the end it reveals is higher, than any merely natural good or end. That is why the greatest Aristotelian after Aristotle was a doctor and saint of the Church: Thomas Aquinas. Thomas believed that Aristotle's philosophy contained everything accessible to natural reason. The Christian revelation

---

1. Becker, *The Heavenly City*, 30.
2. Pierre Manent, *The City of Man* (Princeton Univ. Press: Princeton, NJ 1998), 201.
3. Manent, *An Intellectual History of Liberalism*, 36.

added other, higher truths, to these natural ones, but without invalidating them: "Grace perfects nature, it does not destroy it. . . ."

Aristotle's philosophy could thus be used in two conflicting ways: to oppose the Church or to strengthen the Church. The fact that it lent itself to both of these uses sufficed for demonstrating that *it could not be the basis for a new political definition of relationships between the secular city-state and the Church.*[4]

Because the Greco-Catholic synthesis had persisted as part of the intellectual formation of European elites long after Luther had shattered the religious unity of Christendom, so also had the Christian confessional state in Protestant as well as Catholic countries. But it persisted under a configuration in which the spiritual power represented by the Protestant confessions had already been practically subordinated to the temporal power, as in England where the once Catholic King of England became head of the "Church of England" in place of the Pope under the Acts of Supremacy of 1534 and 1559.

But by 1650 philosophy too had begun to undergo its Protestant "reformation" as "everything, no matter how fundamental or deeply rooted, was questioned in the light of philosophical reason and frequently challenged or replaced by startlingly different concepts generated by the New Philosophy and what may still usefully be termed the Scientific Revolution."[5] The rise of the New Philosophy, essentially a kind of philosophical Protestantism run amuck, led inevitably to an attack on the very existence of the Christian confessional state. And this occurred because the erosion of philosophical certitudes, beginning with the very nature of man as an ensouled creature, necessarily undermined those theological certitudes that were still held in common by all Christians, including the need for the soul's redemption by grace. As the renowned liberal historian of the Enlightenment, Jonathan Israel, observes: "once the main thrust of dissent ceased to be theological and became philosophical, there set in an inexorable slackening and loss of coordination in Church-State collaboration in the cultural, educational and intellectual spheres."[6] From 1650 onward the reigning New Philosophy "rapidly overthrew theology's age-old hegemony in the world of study . . . and led a few openly to challenge everything inherited from the past."[7]

An Essential Caveat

Our focus will be on the radical impact of the "moderate" thinkers of the Enlightenment whose triumph we assess in the next chapter. Special consideration will be given to Locke, regarded as the sturdiest of conservatives by the standards of politi-

---

4. Manent, *An Intellectual History of Liberalism*, 11 [paragraph break added].

5. Jonathan I. Israel, *The Radical Enlightenment: Philosophy and the Making of Modernity*, (Oxford: Oxford Univ. Press, 2001), 3–4.

6. Ibid., 8.

7. Ibid., 4.

cal modernity. Hence it is necessary at the outset to dismiss the irrelevant objection that Locke and other such "moderates" did not see themselves as subversives but rather as conservators in good faith of what they considered the fundamentals of the tradition whose revolutionary overthrow followed in their wake.

That these "moderates," including Locke, knew full well they were engaged in intellectual subversion will be clear enough as the argument proceeds. (For one thing, they typically hid behind the cloak of anonymity, fearing the legal consequences of their own writings.) But even assuming the truth of the objection for argument's sake, it has no bearing on what Peter Gay—hardly a Catholic partisan— has rightly called the "discontinuity between Christianity and Enlightenment, a discontinuity *especially radical* when we consider ideas by their function, not their origin."[8] This is a study of the *function* of ideas, not the motives, intentions, character, or professed orthodoxy of the thinkers who stand at their origin.

I. The Cartesian Revolution

The storm of skepticism that became the general climate of the Enlightenment was unleashed in full by *Discourse on the Method* (1637), the work by René Descartes (1596–1650) universally acknowledged as the founding work of "modern philosophy" by the very "Father of Modern Philosophy." Descartes' ultimately nonsensical principle of the certainty of radical uncertainty opened the floodgates to a vast torrent of confusions and absurdities, as we see rather quickly thereafter with such "thinkers" as the Anglican cleric Bishop Berkeley (1685–1753), a "conservative" opponent of Locke who denied the very existence of a physical world in answer to Locke's version of Cartesian skepticism, or the atheist David Hume (1711–1776), who denied the very ability of reason to apprehend cause and effect—including, presumably, his death because of cancer in the very year the American Revolution began. Locke, Berkeley and Hume would come to be known as the great "triumvirate of British empiricists," but Chesterton offers perhaps the most telling comment on such "contributions" to Western thought. Remarking the rise of philosophical modernity alongside political modernity, he wrote: "Since the modern world began ... nobody's system of philosophy has really corresponded to everybody's sense of reality; to what, if left to themselves, common men would call common sense.... A man had to believe something that no normal man would believe...."[9]

Descartes, his contemporary Pierre Gassendi (1592–1655), a Catholic priest, Robert Boyle (1627–1691), and Isaac Newton (1643–1727) were all contributors to the emerging "mechanical philosophy" at the dawn of modern science. According to the mechanical philosophy and its theory of "atomism," the operations of material beings are owing entirely to movements of units of matter (atoms) governed by physical laws rather than to the constitutive forms of the Aristotelian-Thomistic system lying beyond the matter of which things are composed—i.e., the "*meta*

8. Gay, *The Enlightenment: The Rise of Modern Paganism*, 462.
9. Chesterton, *St. Saint Thomas*, 145.

[beyond]-physics" of matter and form of the Greco-Catholic tradition. The "conservative" exponents of the mechanical philosophy, including the Catholics Descartes and Gassendi, insisted that they meant it to apply only to the physical world and not to the realm of the spiritual. This caveat, however, did not prevent a severance in principle of Creation from the eternal divine "ideas" (metaphysical forms) that forever distinguish one being from another. And so it opened wide the door to pantheism (all beings are just modes or aspects of the one and only being, God), evolutionism (nothing has a fixed nature), or sheer materialism (all beings, including man, are merely matter).

These were hardly the outcomes Descartes the Catholic had intended with his "conservative" attempt to counter the threat of atheism in the midst of the religious confusion and growing scientific skepticism of his age. No doubt he persuaded himself that he was defending rather than undermining truth by calling for an epistemological retreat into the mind to discover the "clear and certain ideas" on which all reasonable men could surely agree without having to argue about the dubious data of sensory perception in the world of being on which the Aristotelian-Thomistic system had relied for centuries with such quaint confidence in the authority of the senses. But the Cartesian *cogito* separated man from the world he inhabits and reduced human identity to a thinking substance merely attached to a body in some obscure manner, rather than the unity of body and soul of the Greco-Catholic tradition.

As the great neo-Thomist philosopher Cornelio Fabro concludes: "It was precisely the Cartesian conception of the world, veiled indeed in skillful reticences and continual protests of orthodoxy, which took the crucial step, prior to Hobbes . . . of radically untethering man from transcendence."[10] Thus Descartes' thought is the foremost historical example of how "atheism can eventually stem just as much from a heresy of the Right as from a heresy of the Left."[11] The revolutions that installed Liberty in place of Christendom, beginning with the American, depended entirely on the success of the prior revolution in philosophy that began with Descartes. It was a revolution defined, as the philosopher Edward Feser observes, "more than anything else by its rejection of the fundamental metaphysical and methodological assumptions of the medieval Scholastic tradition."[12] And that revolution received its decisive impetus in England, where both the practice and philosophy of revolution had their birth.

II. The English Genome of Liberty

Thomas Hobbes (1588–1679) and John Locke (1632–1704) were nothing less than the original framers of political modernity. Their major works, published during the period 1650–1695, were written in the historical context of an England convulsed by revolution and civil war. These decades of turmoil were driven largely by

---

10. Fabro, *God in Exile* (NY: Newman Press, 1968), 368.
11. Arthur Gibson, intro. to *God in Exile*, xxxv.
12. Edward Feser, *Locke* (Oxford: One World Publications, 2007), 9.

what would become part of the very genome of Liberty and thus a major element in the American Revolution: fear and loathing of "Popery," meaning a Catholic (or crypto-Catholic) king with allegiance to (or sympathies for) "the Church of Rome"—the very definition of "tyranny" in the Protestant sense of the word. One cannot understand the genesis of Liberty and the sociopolitical order it requires without knowing something about this fulminatingly anti-Catholic epoch of English history.

By the mid-17th century England's Protestant bourgeois elite, including the Puritans within it—Locke himself was born of Puritan parents—had been the beneficiaries of nearly a century-and-a-half of official persecution of the Catholic population by means of legal disabilities, continuing confiscation of property, imprisonment and torture. No one was more honest in describing the history of post-Reformation England than William Cobbett, the renowned Anglican commentator whose *History of the Protestant Reformation in England and Ireland* scathingly depicted "racks and ripping knives" and "scenes of plunder and blood such as the world never beheld before," producing "forty sorts of Protestant religion, instead of the one fold in which our forefathers lived for nine hundred years," with the result that the people of England had been "corrupted and debased" and "barracks, taxing-houses, mad-houses and gaols" had replaced "convents, hospitals, guilds and almshouses...."[13]

The two English Civil Wars of 1642–49 were the proto-revolution against the remnants of the old order of Altar and Throne. The forces of revolution were led by the hyper-Protestant Puritan movement, still within the Church of England, aligned with the Scottish Presbyterians and a nascent capitalist class first empowered by the Henrician theft and redistribution of Catholic Church properties on a vast scale during the previous century. The Civil War period is "one of those historical crossroads, a moment when a whole civilization changes direction.... It was then that modern market institutions and an individualized culture began to emerge as part of a revolt against monarchy and established religion."[14]

The Civil War period features two expedient executions instigated in Parliament to deal with "popery" in the midst of the Catholic Counter-Reformation on the Continent with its threat of a wave of Catholic revival that could sweep over England. In 1645 the Archbishop of Canterbury, William Laud, was executed pursuant to a bill of attainder after his trial for "treason" in 1644 had failed to produce a conviction. Parliament simply ignored a royal pardon by Charles I. Laud's "high church" policy, designed to counter the Puritan attack on the episcopacy and sacramentally oriented Christianity in general, sealed his doom.

Next on the block was Charles himself, taken prisoner in 1647 as the second Civil War wound to its conclusion. Long suspected of "Popery" because of his marriage

    13. William Cobbett, *A History of the Protestant Reformation in England and Ireland* (NY: Benzinger Bros, 1896), Tan Books reprint, 372.
    14. George Shulman, "Hobbes, Puritans and Promethean Politics," *Political Theory*, Vol. 16, No. 3 (1988), 426.

to the Catholic daughter of King Henry IV of France and his opposition to Calvinist rigorism, Charles—by now a prisoner in Windsor Castle—was tried and executed in 1649 by the Puritan proto-revolutionaries whose great leader was Oliver Cromwell. Charles refused to plead to charges of "high crimes" because the "High Court of Justice" created to conduct the trial had simply granted itself authority to try the king in the name of "the people"—a spontaneous self-delegation of authority of the sort that would become common practice in the revolutions of 1776, 1789, 1861 (the American Civil War) and their worldwide sequelae. Charles insisted on the Biblical and Western tradition that authority comes from God, not from people who grant it to themselves in order to be rid of an inconvenient ruler (monarchical or otherwise). After the historical first of a king being tried by his own subjects, Charles was beheaded on January 30, 1649. "I shall go from a corruptible to an incorruptible Crown, where no disturbance can be," he declared just before the blade ended his earthly life.

The execution of Charles never sat well with the common people of England in whose name it had been done by the same sort of self-authorizing cadre of the privileged that would bring revolution to both America and France. The people, in fact, were horrified and shamed by the regicide. Prophetically enough, Katherine Phillips's poetic lamentation predicted untold horrors following the radical loosening of moral restraints the execution signified: "No bounds will hold those who at scepters fly. . . . Oh! to what height of horror are they come/Who dare pull down a crown, tear up a tomb!"[15] "His title was his crime," the poet observed. In his radical libertarian manifesto *The Rights of Man*, Tom Paine would offer precisely that contention regarding Louis XVI, whose "natural moderation" even Paine had to admit, but who had to be deposed simply and only because he was a king.

Cromwell was elevated to the status of Lord Protector of the short-lived Commonwealth of England (1649–60), augmented by his brutal reconquest of Catholic Ireland (1649–53), which decimated the Irish population. Cromwell was a vastly more oppressive ruler than Charles had ever been—a pattern that would be repeated throughout the history of Liberty's overthrow of kings and other governments. Hence during the Restoration reign of Charles II (1660–1685), son of Charles I, it was Cromwell's turn to be executed—symbolically and posthumously by the hanging and decapitation of his rotted corpse in 1661. The Church of England would canonize Charles II's father as a saint-martyr.

The Restoration would provoke a mass departure of the remaining Puritans from the Church of England into various non-conformist sects or to America. The earlier "Great Migration" of Puritans (1620–1640) was already preparing the way for "the revolution of revolutions that was born aboard the *Mayflower* and *Arabella* and matured in the struggles of 1776," the revolution that would come to be viewed as a sacred event in the Puritans' "sacred version of human progress," according to which "[r]evolution . . . functions as a vehicle of providence . . . confirming the

---

15. Katherine Phillips, "Upon the Double Murder of King Charles" (1667).

prophecies of scripture as well as the laws of nature and history." The "patriot ministers" of the Revolution, inspired by the revolutionary theology of the great Puritan divine, Jonathan Edwards, would preach that "Liberty, democracy and American nationhood...were not merely worldly goods; primarily, they were spiritual goods, ordained by God and typed forth in Scripture."[16]

With the Restoration and the reimposition of Anglican supremacy in England, opposition to Church and monarchy would shift from the Puritan movement to a new radical element within the Anglican establishment—an element that included Locke. Following the Popish Plot affair (1678–81), in which allegations of a non-existent Catholic plot to assassinate Charles II incited a new wave of anti-Catholic bigotry, the first Earl of Shaftesbury, Locke's wealthy patron, led a movement to pass the Exclusion Bill, which would have prohibited the Catholic brother of Charles II, James II, from ascending to the throne. Shaftesbury's party came to be known as the Whigs, a term probably derived at least in part from the pejorative "whiggamore," referring to a faction of western Scots who had agitated against Charles II during the Whiggamore Raid insurrection of 1648. "Whig" came to signify an anti-monarchical tendency, bourgeois liberalism and (in its radical form) outright revolutionism in England, later in America, and generally in the revolutionary currents that would sweep the Western world in the 18th century. Ultimately it would produce the "Whig narrative" of history, a "harvest of Puritanism"[17] according to which Western man has inevitably progressed beyond "Popish tyranny" to constitutional monarchy and finally full-blown Liberty in the form of the pluralist and democratic commercial republic. John Milbank refers to this as the "Protestant meta-narrative" that (appropriately secularized) still dominates the mentality of the modern world.

While the Exclusion Bill ultimately failed in the face of Charles's opposition, radical Whig subversion would continue, and Locke himself would surface as a participant. He was implicated in the next Whig move against the Crown: the Rye House Conspiracy (1682–1683). The ultimately aborted plot involved both an armed insurrection against Charles and a separate plan to ambush and assassinate both him and James at the Rye House mansion in order to free England from the "popish tyranny" of the crypto-Catholic king (who finally converted to Catholicism on his death bed) and his Catholic heir apparent. There is no question Locke's patron Shaftesbury was deeply involved, and in a definitive study of the affair historian Richard Ashcraft concludes that there is "not the slightest doubt in my mind that Locke was an active participant...."[18]

---

16. Sacvan Bercovitch, "How the Puritans Won the American Revolution," *The Massachusetts Review*, Vol. 17, No. 4 (1976), 606.

17. Lincoln Konkle, *Thornton Wilder and the Puritan Narrative Tradition* (Columbia, MO: Univ. of Missouri Press, 2006), 30, n. 9; quoting Berkovitch, *American Jeremiad*, 132.

18. Richard Ashcraft, *Revolutionary Politics and Locke's Two Treatises of Government* (Princeton, NJ: Princeton Univ. Press, 1986), 379; cited in Philip Milton, "John Locke and the Rye House Plot," *The Historical Journal*, 43, 3 (2000), 649.

Recent scholarly attempts to absolve Locke of any involvement notwithstanding,[19] he certainly acted like a guilty man: In the late summer of 1683 he fled to Holland, following Shaftesbury, who died there in exile. There Locke hid for five years under an assumed name to avoid extradition and trial. A victim of asthma, he offered the implausible (or perhaps technically truthful) explanation that he had suddenly relocated to the dampness of Holland (along with Shaftesbury!) "for reasons of health."[20] His professed health concerns did not, however, explain his resort to an alias. One Harvard wag observes that Locke "was one of the few major political theorists to go on the lam after being implicated in conspiracy to commit political murder."[21]

Locke's name surfaced again during the Monmouth Rebellion (1685) in reports by two different informants that, while hiding in Utrecht, he had donated £1000 to finance the failed insurrection led by the Duke of Monmouth, which aimed at the overthrow of James II, who had indeed succeeded Charles. Here too scholars have labored to absolve Locke of any involvement, but "Locke's dealings with the revolutionaries were anything but circumstantial."[22]

Then came the end of our seminal period of English turmoil: the "Glorious Revolution" of 1688. The "Glorious Revolution" overthrew James II, who had the effrontery to convert to Catholicism (in 1668), implement toleration of Catholics, and father a male heir to the throne, thus posing the threat of a new Catholic line of succession. James fled for his life as the Protestant William of Orange (James's nephew) and Mary Stuart (James's daughter by Anne Hyde) were brought in by military invasion to "rid the land of popery. . . ."[23] England became a Whig constitutional monarchy when Parliament declared James's abdication and proclaimed William of Orange to be King William III of England to reign jointly with Mary. (James had been captured but was spared execution by William and allowed to escape and live out his life as an exile in France.) In 1689 Locke returned triumphantly from his exile in Holland aboard the royal yacht of the forcibly installed Protestant king. Shortly thereafter Locke's prudently anonymous magnum opus, *Two Treatises of Government*, appeared in print. Its preface hailed William as the king whose title rested in "the Consent of the People" and who had "saved the Nation when it was on the very brink of Slavery and Ruine"—that is, the rule of James II, a Catholic, whose Catholic son would have been the heir apparent to the throne.

In less than forty years (1649 to 1688) England, according to the shifting constituencies of Parliament, went from "a pan-Puritan religious toleration"[24] that excluded

---

19. See Milton, "John Locke and the Rye House Plot."

20. Ibid., 648.

21. "Locke's Life, Times, and Personality," Harvard GOV Theory Review weblog at harvardtheoryreview.blogspot.com/2007/03/lockes-life-times-and-personality.html.

22. Kim Ian Parker, *The Biblical Politics of John Locke* (Waterloo, Ontario: Wilfrid Laurier Univ. Press, 2004), 24.

23. Ibid., 28.

24. Michael de Haven Newsom, "The American Protestant Empire: a Historical Perspective," 40 *Washburn Law Journal* 187, 232 (2001).

Anglicans and Catholics under Cromwell, to varying degrees of legal or *de facto* toleration of non-Anglican Protestants and Catholics under Charles II and James II, to the *non*-toleration of Catholics *and* non-Anglican Protestants after James II was overthrown in the "Glorious" Revolution—or "Reformation the Third" as Cobbett dubbed it in his unreservedly contemptuous history of the "thorough Godly Reformation."[25] In 1701, three years before Locke's death, Parliament adopted the Act of Settlement (which remains in effect three centuries later) precluding any future Catholic monarch in England, thus enshrining in law the one principle on which all the Protestant factions agreed: that Roman Catholics must forever be kept from the seat of sovereign power.

Cobbett, writing in 1825, observed that "Reformation the Third, commonly called the 'Glorious Revolution,' grew directly out of Reformation The Second [the Cromwellian dictatorship]," that "Reformation The Fourth, commonly called 'the American Revolution,' grew directly out of Reformation the Third," and that all of these "reformations" proceeded from "Reformation the First, as naturally as the stem and the branches of the tree proceed from the root."[26] The truth of that observation should be kept in mind as we examine the enduring myth of the "conservative" American Revolution—conservative, that is, by the standards of the same Protestant peoples whose history includes the institutionalized persecution of Catholics and the murder or overthrow of inconvenient Anglican archbishops and kings to preclude even the threat of Catholic influence over the sociopolitical order. That Anglo-Puritan fear and loathing of Catholicism inheres in the very DNA of Liberty down to the present day.

III. The Hobbelockean Worldview

We have thus sketched the historical context in which the co-founders of political liberalism wrote: a great Protestant struggle against the threat of "Popish tyranny" in the course of which the Protestant factions involved did not hesitate to tyrannize each other as well as the Catholics. Indeed, the neutralization of Catholic influence in politics was only part of the religious "problem" that Hobbes and Locke perceived—a problem not attributable to orthodox Christianity as such but to the jockeying for political power by opposing sects arising from the Protestant principle of private judgment. During the era when Hobbes and Locke wrote, English society was threatening to disintegrate under "the corrosive and encroaching pressure of the principle of religious subjectivity proclaimed in opposition to Catholicism."[27] In the midst of this endlessly turbulent epoch—Hobbes in the beginning and middle and Locke near the end—the co-founders of liberalism did what liberals have done ever since then: prescribe a higher dose of liberalism for the ills that liberalism has already provoked.

Between them Hobbes and Locke, but preeminently Locke, introduced the core

25. Cobbett, *A History of the Protestant Reformation*, 325.
26. Ibid., 332.
27. Fabro, *God in Exile*, 225.

concepts of which the entire Enlightenment is but a recapitulation with "moderate" or "radical" variations on a theme. While Locke is known as "the Father of Liberalism," "the Father of Liberty," and "the Father of American Liberty," it was Hobbes who first broached in a blunt and open way what Locke would present a few decades later with guarded ambiguity, all the while bristling at the charge from numerous contemporary critics that he was merely a "Hobbist" in thin disguise. It is right to say, as C. B. Macpherson has said in his introduction to a modern edition of Hobbes's *Leviathan*, that Locke "was the confused man's Hobbes."[28]

It would take a book in itself to explain what scholars such as Macpherson, Strauss, Manent and many others long ago demonstrated: that Hobbes and Locke are two sides of the same coin, with one side, Locke's, being more agreeably "moderate" in appearance. Here, for the limited purpose of background to the American Revolution, it must suffice to outline what they both laid down as foundations of Enlightenment thought in general and the thought of the Founders and Framers of the United States in particular.

In an allusion to the parable of the unclean spirit in the Gospel of Luke,[29] Hobbes's magnum opus *Leviathan* refers to post-Reformation England as the "clean swept house" from which "the Spirit of Rome" had been driven out by the "exorcism" of Henry VIII and was now to be seen "walking by missions through the dry places of China, Japan, and the Indies, that yield him little fruit...." Hobbes declares that preventing the return of that spirit was "all I had the design to say concerning the Doctrine of the Politiques."[30] Referring to the presence of Catholic missionaries in the "dry place" of Japan to which Hobbes had alluded, Locke, in his *Essay Concerning Toleration*, echoed Hobbes's sentiments in observing that the magistrates of that country had no aversion to Christianity as such, "for they tolerate seven or eight sects," but rather it was only "the doctrine of the popish priests that gave them jealousy that religion was but their pretense, but empire their design, and made them fear the subversion of their state."[31] He noted that the "Romish religion" could be extirpated in Japan only "by the death of many thousands ... not only the family that entertained a priest, but also all of both families that were next neighbors on either hand, though they were strangers to the new religion...."[32] Locke proposed far less extreme measures to deal with the

---

28. Thomas Hobbes, *Leviathan* (London: Penguin Books, 1985), 25. All citations to *Leviathan* are to Hobbes's part and chapter and the pages of the Penguin edition.

29. "When the unclean spirit is gone out of a man, he walks through places without water, seeking rest; and not finding, he says: I will return into my house whence I came out. And when he is come, he finds it swept and garnished. Then he goes and takes with him seven other spirits more wicked than himself, and entering in they dwell there. And the last state of that man becomes worse than the first." Luke 11:24–26.

30. *Leviathan*, IV.47.715.

31. *Essay on Toleration*, 158, in *Locke: Political Essays*, ed. Mark Goldie (Cambridge: Cambridge Univ. Press, 1997).

32. A reference to the brutal suppression of the Shimabara Revolt of Japanese Catholics in 1638. These Catholics were the descendants of Japanese who had been converted by the "popish priest" Saint Francis Xavier.

problem of "the papists" and their "dangerous opinions, which are absolutely destructive to all governments but the pope's. . . ."[33] But Hobbes, Locke and the Japanese shoguns were all agreed on one thing: the "spirit of Rome" could never be allowed to dictate the form of political society as it had, and still did, wherever the Catholic faith predominated. Writing in the midst of England's final purgation of its own Catholic past, Hobbes and Locke, like all enlightened thinkers of the early Enlightenment, had "a horror of Roman Catholicism both as a theological monstrosity and a threat to civilized society."[34]

Exorcising the "spirit of Rome" from Western civilization required, of course, a complete rewriting of "the Christian story," to recall Carl Becker's phrase. Commencing the Whig narrative of history, Hobbes and Locke wrote a new story that provided the basic plot for the revolutionary drama of political modernity. The plot elements are laid down in Hobbes's *Leviathan* (1651) and Locke's *Essay on Toleration* (1667), *Two Treatises of Government* (1689), *A Letter Concerning Toleration* (1689), *An Essay Concerning Human Understanding* (1690) and *The Reasonableness of Christianity* (1695). Even contemporary Protestant critics condemned these works as heterodox if not treasonous. Hence, aside from the *Essay Concerning Human Understanding*, Locke (producing much of his *oeuvre* while in exile in Holland) published all his major works anonymously. Both writers—Locke was far more skillful than Hobbes in this regard—observed a semblance of Christian literary convention, including requisite pious references to "Our Lord" and "Our Saviour," but these fig leaves did not conceal a systematic subversion of the entire Greco-Catholic tradition concerning Man, God and State sketched briefly in Chapter 1.

By the time Hobbes and Locke were done, the Christian story had been rewritten and a new story had begun, the story of our Hobbelockean world: the world of secular governments unrestrained by any religion; the absolute rule of the majority; the consequent growth of government beyond all limits hitherto known; the rise of a commercial civilization in which anything can be bought and sold without restraint by Christian morality, and human affairs, including marriage and family, become contractual arrangements; the world in which religion, if one has a religion, is reduced to a purely private affair. In short, the world of Liberty. Let us examine briefly the conceptual foundation of this new world order, of which the American revolutionaries constructed the first new nation.

The Attack on Substance

We have already noted that the new world of Liberty could not be constructed on the old foundation of the orderly hierarchical cosmos of divinely appointed natures or substances strictly ordered to a living and ever-present God at its summit as the *summum bonum* for man. For this worldview logically requires

33. *Essay on Toleration*, 150.
34. Mark Goldie, *Locke: Political Essays*, xv.

something like the Christian commonwealth whose laws and institutions are oriented to man's all-important revealed eternal destiny. Hence, as Manent observes:

> Whether a substance, "substantial form," placed in a hierarchy of substances or forms; or a nature, at once animal and rational, within a hierarchy of natures; or the human soul as the "form" of the human body, it is the teaching of Aristotle, which was essentially adopted by Catholic doctrine, that Descartes, Hobbes [and] Locke will implacably destroy. That man is a *substance* and *one* substance, that is the *Carthago delenda* [Carthage destroyed] of the new philosophy.[35]

In their war on substance Hobbes in *Leviathan* and Locke in the *Essay Concerning Human Understanding* (*ECHU*) conducted nothing short of full-scale assault on man's ability to apprehend the world as it really is through the senses, including human identity itself. They did so in the context of the "mechanical philosophy" earlier noted, seeking to reduce man under his sociopolitical aspect to a material operative governed by law-like tendencies, with spiritual matters shuttled off to the capacious and ever-growing Protestant realm of private judgment. The basic project is a Cartesian division of man into material and spiritual parts, with the spiritual part no longer the subject of politics or political ethics. This strange division of the human self is quite familiar to the modern mind, which uncritically accepts it as received wisdom; but at the time it was a radical innovation which required, first of all, rejection of Aristotelian hylomorphism with its unity of body and soul in the one human person whose indivisible whole had always been the subject of both politics and ethics in the Greco-Catholic tradition.

Hobbes openly attacked the Aristotelian-Thomistic system, and "there is barely a chapter in *Leviathan*...not engaged in guerrilla operations against the neo-Thomism which still formed the backbone of Protestant academic education...."[36] He mocked as one of the "divers absurdities" of Greco-Catholic philosophy the conviction that "there be things universal; that a living creature is Genus or a general thing, &c."[37] All that man can know is the names he gives to the ideas that arise in his mechanical brain upon receiving sensory input from the outside world. Man cannot affirm that any of these ideas corresponds to a fixed and universal reality, not even to what he calls Man. Hence, for Hobbes, "REASON, in this sense, is nothing but Reckoning (that is, Adding and Subtracting) of the consequences of general names agreed upon, for the marking and signifying of our thoughts...."[38]

A frank materialist, Hobbes ridiculed the notion of an immaterial soul and denied the very existence of a spiritual realm, mocking "the Latins" who define God as a "Spirit Incorporeal, and then confess their definition to be unintelligible: or if they give him such a title, it is not dogmatically, with intention to make the

---

35. Manent, *City of Man*, 113.
36. *The Cambridge History of Political Thought* (Cambridge: Cambridge Univ. Press, 1991), 594.
37. *Leviathan*, I.5, 114.
38. *Leviathan*, I.5, 111.

Divine Nature understood; but Piously, to honour him with attributes, of significa-tions, as remote as they can from the grossness of Bodies Visible."[39] Undeterred by the Bible's innumerable references to the realm of spirit, he reduced every reference to a mere metaphor. He even denied that the Holy Spirit is a spirit, reducing Him to "the voice of God in a dream" or divine gifts, "such as are the gifts of sanctity of life, of tongues, and the like."[40]

Locke, in *ECHU*, likewise attacked the existence of universal substances and spiritual realities—not frontally, as Hobbes did, but indirectly by calling their knowability (except for the bare existence of God) into question. Following the Cartesian method (which he had studied), Locke proceeded on the self-contradic-tory premise of the certainty of radical uncertainty—the absurdity on which nearly the whole of subsequent modern philosophy is based. Skeptical of everything but his own skepticism, Locke begins *ECHU* with the declaration that all philosophy before his own had begun "at the wrong end, and in vain sought for satisfaction in a quiet and sure possession of truths that most concerned us, whilst we let loose our thoughts into the vast ocean of Being. . . ."[41]

Not for Locke is "the quiet and sure possession of truths." Instead of beginning with the "vast ocean of Being," as if man could really know things as they are, Locke proposes to question the very process of human understanding: "[I]t came into my thoughts that we took a wrong course; and that before we set ourselves upon inquiries of that nature, it was necessary to examine our own abilities, and see what objects our understandings were, or were not, fitted to deal with."[42] It seems Locke was never troubled by the risible conundrum involved in his insistence that the mind can confirm that what it receives from the senses is not equivalent to the real world and that only primary qualities (shape, extension, number, etc.) but not sec-ondary qualities (color, taste, etc.) really exist. Classical philosophy, on the other hand, "supposes, without examining it, the validity of knowledge,"[43] given the theological premise that a loving God did not create man in His image and likeness only to endow him with senses that deceive him and confine him to a house of mir-rors or a "diving bell," as one commentator has put it.

Locke apparently was unwilling to recognize that to question the authority of the senses is already to undermine belief in the existence of God. But Locke's numerous contemporary critics, including the redoubtable Bishop Stillingfleet, were quite aware that "the seeds of doubt that Locke had sown in the *Essay* . . . may have borne secular fruit in the following centuries . . ." and "that 'his conception of man's capacity to know might readily be (and largely were) to weaken religious

---

39. *Leviathan*, I.12, 171.

40. Ibid., III.34, 438–442.

41. *ECHU*, I.7. All citations to *ECHU* are from *The Works of John Locke: An Essay Concerning Human Understanding*, Kindle Edition (Pearland, Texas: Halcyon Press, Ltd.; 2009), a hypertext repro-duction of the original edition. All references are to book, chapter and section (e.g., II.3.1).

42. *ECHU*, Epistle to Readers.

43. *Catholic Encyclopedia*, Epistemology.

conviction in others.'"[44] By necessary extension, the seeds Locke had planted would undermine the authority of a teaching Church. Thus, as the Locke scholar W.M. Spellman observes (with approval), *ECHU* "shattered the intellectual underpinnings of the confessional state...."[45] Today, such common opinions in matters of religion and morality as "there is no such thing as absolute truth"—a proposition asserted absolutely—or "what is true for you is not necessarily true for others" are faint echoes of the Big Bang represented by Locke's famous application of the Cartesian method, which opened the way to all subsequent epistemological and thus religious skepticism as he was "the first to give a clear statement of epistemological problems"[46] in modern philosophy.

According to Locke, "we know not what it is" that underlies the qualities of objects perceived by our senses, and thus "we have no clear or distinct idea" (the Cartesian method at work) of any substances determining the fixed natures of things and constituting, as it were, the non-material "substratum" of being.[47] Lockean man, his mind a complete *tabula rasa* at birth, can acquire through the senses only *ideas* about the real world, not the real world as such, and thus human knowledge for Locke, as for Hobbes, "hath no other immediate object but its own ideas ... [and] is only conversant about them."[48] For Locke too, man's supposed inability to confirm the existence of distinct substances as instantiated universals, whose natures are ordained by God, extends even to man. In an eerie prefigurement of modern arguments in favor of abortion, Locke opined that one cannot even posit a human nature or substance with certainty, "it having been more than once doubted, *whether the foetus born of a woman were a man* ... which could not be, if the abstract idea or essence to which the name man belonged were of nature's making; and were not the uncertain and various collection of simple ideas, which the understanding put together, and then, abstracting it, affixed a name to it."[49] In all seriousness, he argued that as to an individual he might have identified as a "man" a moment ago "I cannot be certain that the same man exists now, since there is no necessary connection of his existence a minute since, with his existence now ... since I had the Testimony [only] of my Senses for his existence."[50]

Locke further argued that the "self" is not a body-soul unity—that is, not any sort of substance composed of matter and form (the soul)—but simply the continuing consciousness of the individual: "Consciousness alone unites actions into

---

44. Parker, *The Biblical Politics of John Locke*, 33–34, quoting John Dunn, *Locke: 1632–1704* (Oxford: Oxford Univ. Press, 1984), 16–17.

45. W.M. Spellman, *John Locke* (NY: St. Martin's Press, 1997), 52.

46. *Catholic Encyclopedia*, loc. cit.

47. *ECHU*, II.23.3–6.

48. *ECHU*, IV.1.1.

49. *ECHU*, II.3.14. Hobbes likewise provided a rationale for abortion, holding that since "every man by the law of nature, hath right or propriety [property] to his own body, the child ought rather to be the propriety [property] of the mother (of whose body it is part, till the time of separation) than of the father." *De Corpore Politico* (The Elements of Law, Natural and Politic), XXIII.1.

50. *ECHU*, IV.11.9.

the same person.... Self depends on consciousness, *not on substance.*"[51] Hence, Locke concludes: "Persons *not substances* [are] the objects of reward and punishment ... not mattering what becomes of any substance, not joined to, or affected with that consciousness."[52] Even with respect to divine judgment, then, Locke equates "person" with a stream of consciousness, not the soul of orthodox Christianity. Thus what Hobbes attacked openly—the existence of an immaterial soul in man—Locke rather more circumspectly undermined.

The "cautious" Locke was a far more effective philosophical subversive than Hobbes. In the process of declaring substances unknowable he destroyed substance in principle. The *ECHU* seeks "to discredit the notion of substance, to put it out of commission...."[53] This destruction can be further pinpointed in Locke's nominalist hypothesis that God in His omnipotence could endow even inert matter with the capacity for thought: "For I see no contradiction in it, that the first Eternal thinking Being, or Omnipotent Spirit, should, if he pleased, give to certain systems of created senseless matter, put together as he thinks fit, some degrees of sense, perception, and thought...."[54] The consequences of this idea were catastrophic, "for with the collapse of the barrier between matter and thought, it was likewise doomed to fall the distinction between body and soul, with the consequent disappearance of the need of positing in man a spiritual and immortal principal, distinct from the body."[55] Locke's notion of thinking matter made "the operations of things dependent solely on God, on divine decree, so that everything could do anything, because there was no genuine and proper necessary nexus between the reality of a nature and the quality of its actions and operations."[56]

By hypothesizing a divinely superadded capacity for thought in mere matter, Locke, the so-called conservative, was also suggesting, just as his contemporary Anglican critics charged, that "spirit is not an immaterial substance but merely a quality of matter," which in effect is to "deny revelation, miracles, and the survival by the soul of physical death," raising the problem of "what (or what sort of personal identity) is resurrected for Judgment."[57] Locke was seen as "tacitly inviting people to separate (orthodox) faith and (philosophical) reason ... Historically, this was disastrous for the [Anglican] Church, and Locke was unable satisfactorily to reply to the charges."[58]

Worse, in the third letter of his exchange with Bishop Stillingfleet, perhaps his most acute Anglican critic, Locke practically confirmed the charges by arguing that since animals have a certain capacity for perception and thought, "it will follow,

---

51. *ECHU*, II. 27.9,16–17.
52. *ECHU*, II.27.18–20.
53. Manent, *City of Man*, 116.
54. *ECHU*, IV.3.6.
55. Fabro, *God in Exile*, 278.
56. Ibid., 282.
57. R.C. Tennant, "The Anglican Response to Locke's Theory of Personal Identity," *Journal of the History of Ideas*, Vol. 43, N. 1 (Jan.–Mar., 1982), 77.
58. Ibid.

either that God can and doth give to some parcels of matter a power of perception and thinking; or that all animals have immaterial and consequently, according to your lordship, immortal souls, as well as men: and to say that fleas and mites, etc. have immortal souls as well as men will possibly be looked on as going a great way to serve a *hypothesis*."[59] Notice that Locke is implicitly arguing against the mere "hypothesis" of an immaterial soul in man by ridiculing the proposition that an immaterial principle is necessary for consciousness in animals. As the Locke scholar Nicholas Jolley observes:

> [O]n the standard view that the existence of an immaterial soul is a necessary condition of immortality, the thesis that matter thinks in animals is still disturbing, for Locke's philosophy as a whole may well seem to contain the resources *for extending the materialist account to the case of human beings.* . . . Locke may emphasize the difference between animal and human consciousness . . . [b]ut the moral that Locke wishes to draw appears to be that these differences *are differences of degree only, not of kind.* . . . [If] matter can think in animals, then to postulate that the subject of consciousness in us is a wholly different kind of entity—an immaterial soul—may seem an unpardonable metaphysical extravagance of which no one committed to Ockham's razor should be guilty.[60]

Voltaire would seize gleefully upon Locke's destruction of the necessary connection between rational thought, the immaterial soul and immortality, for this ardent devotee of Locke no doubt recognized here the complete overthrow of Scholastic philosophy, the fundamental distinction between matter and spirit, and indeed any understanding at all of a universal structure of being ordained by God to which man is necessarily conformed. The possibilities for revolutionary new realities were endless. As he wrote with evident delight to the Jesuit Tournemine in December, 1735:

> [T]he point is not whether we know if matter can think by itself, a notion rejected by Locke as absurd. The point is not whether we know if our soul is spiritual or not. The point is simply whether we know enough about matter and thought to be bold enough to assert that . . . God cannot communicate thought to the being we call matter. . . .[T]o know what a thing is capable or incapable of doing, we must know that thing most thoroughly. Now we know nothing of matter; rather we know ourselves to have certain sensations, certain ideas . . . but we no more know the substance, the subject, the being in which all this inheres, than we do the make-up of the inhabitants of Saturn.[61]

59. John Locke, *The Works of John Locke in Nine Volumes* (London: Rivington, 1824, 12th ed.), Vol. 3, ¶1200: MR. LOCKE'S REPLY TO THE RIGHT REVEREND THE LORD BISHOP OF WORCESTER'S ANSWER TO HIS SECOND LETTER; accessed from http://oll.libertyfund.org/title/1724/80700/19-22904.

60. Nicholas Jolley, *Locke: His Philosophical Thought* (Oxford: Oxford Univ. Press, 1999), 94.

61. Voltaire, *Lettres Philosophiques*, Lettre XII, Sur Locke, ed. F. A. Taylor, 43; quoted in Fabro, *God in Exile*, 284.

Fabro assesses the outcome of Locke's seemingly innocuous concession to divine omnipotence: "What France was able to give England via the Cartesian *cogito* has now been returned with interest—as we see from Voltaire's heartfelt praise of Locke—via the new materialism catapulting Deism forthwith into materialism and atheism. Locke's hypothesis is based entirely on the existence of God and his omnipotence, it is true; but his followers, gleeful at the long-awaited breaching of the frontier between matter and spirit, convert the hypothesis into a thesis and assert outright the inherent capacity of matter not only to move itself, but also to feel, to understand and to will."[62]

Thus, Locke's confused "conservative" application of the mechanical philosophy, which maintained "verbal assertions of the distinction between the material world and the spiritual," was nonetheless "in fact eliminating any such distinction in the theoretical order and drawing the logical conclusion from his basic principle that certainty consists in the perception of the agreement or disagreement of ideas."[63] As Fabro concludes: "The importance of Locke's influence on the molding of modern materialism and atheism by now are surely quite clear, despite his most outspoken declarations in favor of spiritualism and Christianity. . . . It is no cause for astonishment that the Encyclopaedists, Voltaire and d'Holbach, and later the dialectical materialists, should appeal to Locke and consider him the founder of the new notion of reality."[64]

This "new notion of reality" would become nothing less than the epistemological basis of Liberty. For if "man" is only the name we assign to a collection of perceptible attributes; if "man" is not a substance, a divinely created unity of body and soul with a divinely fixed nature and ends; if even inanimate matter could theoretically be endowed with "man's" capacity for thought; then who is to say that the child *in utero* belongs to the human species, or that a woman may not abort the development of whatever it is within her womb, or even that one "man" may not marry another?

While it can be said that "Locke clung steadfastly, although precariously, to the conviction that there is a divine lawgiver who punishes and rewards,"[65] the emphasis must be on the word precariously, since there is no question that "materialism is the direct consequence of English sense-perceptionism and of Lockean sense-perceptionism in particular."[66] Hobbelockean sense-perceptionism, which openly denies (Hobbes) or negates via Cartesian radical doubt (Locke) any quality of man beyond the sensorily perceivable matter of which his body is composed, was a crucial contribution to the Western world's descent into skepticism about man's very nature and destiny. That development represented a radical break with the Greco-Catholic tradition and thus an essential intellectual preparation for the revolutions that created secular nation-states. Hence "it is in England that the destruction of

---

62. Fabro, *God in Exile*, 284–285.
63. Ibid., 283.
64. Ibid.
65. *Locke: Political Essays*, Intro. by Goldie, xxiii.
66. Fabro, *God in Exile*, 277.

substance is linked most clearly and most closely to the construction of the new body politic, the new world of human liberty."[67]

The State of Nature

Having deconstructed man according to the principle of radical doubt that dismisses the Greco-Catholic metaphysical system, Hobbes and Locke place their deconstructed man into a deconstructed social environment called the "state of nature" from which they purport to derive "the law of nature." The state of nature is imagined to be the natural condition of man, born without any inclination to life in political society. Man in this state lives prior to religion or politics.

The state of nature is, as should be obvious, an imaginary construct that has no basis in either human history or the Christian story. To the lack of any historical record of its existence, Locke can only reply with the contrivance that "it is not at all to be wondered that History gives us but very little account of men that lived the State of Nature" because the "inconveniences of that condition" caused men to leave it so quickly that they created no record of their fleeting "natural" condition, record-keeping being a function of government ("Government is everywhere antecedent to Records....").[68] Locke's attempt to attribute his utter novelty to the "judicious Hooker," a reference to Richard Hooker, an orthodox Anglican political philosopher still very much in the Greco-Catholic tradition, is a sham. His citation to Hooker contains "nothing of the kind," and Hooker "never so much as mentions, let alone embraces, the concept of a state of nature."[69]

The Hobbelockean state of nature conveniently avoids both the happy state of man before Original Sin and his fallen state afterwards, for those two states point, once again, to the role of grace and the Church in the building of political society. As Leo Strauss notes, prior to Hobbes "the state of nature was distinguished especially from the state of grace, and it was subdivided into the state of pure nature [before the Fall] and the state of fallen nature. Hobbes dropped the subdivision and replaced the state of grace by the state of civil society." Hobbes (and Locke) "denied, if not the fact, at any rate the importance of the Fall and accordingly asserted that what is needed for remedying the deficiencies or the 'inconveniences' of the state of nature is, not divine grace, but the right kind of human government."[70]

If the Hobbelockean state of nature was to serve as the vehicle for creating "the new world of human liberty" it could not involve anything like the Greco-Catholic conception of the divine ordination of man to a life of virtue in political society, for

---

67. Manent, *City of Man*, 113.

68. Locke, *Two Treatises of Government*, ed. Peter Laslet (Cambridge: Cambridge Univ. Press, 2005), II.viii.101.

69. Thomas L. Pangle, *The Spirit of Modern Republicanism: The Moral Vision of the American Founders and the Philosophy of Locke* (Chicago: Univ. of Chicago Press, 1988), 132.

70. Leo Strauss, *Natural Right and History* (Chicago: Univ. of Chicago Press, 1965), 184. We refer to Strauss's critiques of Hobbes and Locke for their inherent soundness, without regard to Strauss's own esotericism and indeed atheism.

then the movement from the state of nature into political society would only return us to the Christian commonwealth in some form, and this would thwart the desired final escape from the Church's influence: "In order to escape decisively from the power of the singular religious institution of the Church, one had to renounce thinking about human life in terms of its good or end, which would always be vulnerable to the Church's 'trump.'"[71]

Hence, ironically enough, the Hobbelockean state of nature requires a *denatured* man, the man emerging from the Hobbelockean epistemology we have just noted. No longer viewed as a body-soul substance with fixed ends according to the divine plan by which he is ordained to life in a State that promotes the good of the whole man, this denatured man is ready-made for Liberty. "The idea that man is all that he is prior to any law, political or religious, will be a central element of democratic man's self-consciousness."[72] The state of nature introduces us to "radical man, the individual prior to the citizen and Christian alike."[73] And the Liberal State shall be his dwelling place. This is why, as John Milbank has noted, liberalism in general is "so fantastically peculiar and unlikely," for it presents to us as its first premise "a wholly artificial human being who has never really existed, and then pretend[s] that we are all instances of such a species."[74]

The Ascendancy of Rights Over Law

The fictional Hobbelockean state of nature provides the theoretical justification for a radical shift from the duty-oriented ethic of the Christian story to the rights-oriented ethic of Liberty. For Hobbes the "state of nature"[75] is "the time when men live without a common power to keep them all in awe" and are in consequence engaged in ceaseless "war, as is of every man, against every man."[76] There is no industry, agriculture, navigation of the sea, knowledge of geography, arts, letters or even society. There is only "continual fear, and danger of violent death" and man's life is, as Hobbes so famously puts it, "solitary, poor, nasty, brutish and short."[77]

With Hobbes, for the first time in Western political thought, natural law ceases to be, as it is in the Greco-Catholic tradition, the moral precepts of the Ten Commandments written on the heart, imposing positive duties toward God and fellow man rather than creating "rights" in the solitary individual. For Hobbes, natural law in the state of nature is not God's law written on man's heart, but merely "a precept, or general rule, found out by reason, [Hobbes's notion of reason] by which a man is

71. Manent, *An Intellectual History of Liberalism*, 114.

72. Manent, *City of Man*, 35.

73. Ibid.

74. John Milbank, "The Gift of Ruling: Secularization and Political Authority," *New Blackfriars*, Vol. 85, Issue 996 (March 2004), 212.

75. Hobbes does not use the term "state of nature" in *Leviathan*, but rather in his *Elements of Law and Natural Politic*, where he uses the term repeatedly. Cf. *Elements*, nn. 2, 3, 6, 8–9, 13, 16.

76. *Leviathan*, I.13.185.

77. Ibid., I.13.186.

forbidden to do that which is destructive of his life, or taketh away the means of pre-serving the same, and to omit that by which he thinketh it may be best preserved."[78]

According to Hobbes, while God has decreed the laws of nature, man has no innate understanding of them, as is shown by varying human opinions over what the natural law requires. Hence, man must be guided solely by the decisions of the civil authorities:

> Since therefore such opinions are daily seen to arise, if any man now shall dis-pel those clouds, and by most firm reasons demonstrate *that there are no authentical doctrines concerning right and wrong, good and evil, besides the con-stituted Lawes in each Realme* and government; and that the question whether any future action will prove just or unjust, good or ill, is to be demanded of none, but those to whom the supreme hath committed the interpretation of his Laws.[79]

Hobbes, then, is a legal positivist and a voluntarist: right and wrong are deter-mined solely by the will of the legislator upon emergence from the state of nature, for "Where there is no common power, there is no law; where no law, no injus-tice."[80] The doctrine seems shocking until we realize that it represents the juridical status quo of political modernity: the will of the majority trumps the objective moral order.

For Hobbes, even God is a legal positivist. Hobbes's God is not the loving creator of the universe, who wills for man what is good because it *is* good and implants in him the desire for and recognition of the good as an objective reality. For Hobbes, God's will is law without regard to the merely human categories of good and evil according to reason. Whatever man thinks is good or evil, just or unjust, "is not that by which God Almighty's actions are to be measured and called just. That which he does is made just *by his doing it.* . . ."[81] We must obey God simply because He has "irresistible power"[82] over us, not because love itself commands our obedi-ence in keeping with what J. B. Schneewind calls "the love commandment" enunci-ated by Christ: "Thou shalt love the Lord thy God with thy whole heart, and with thy whole soul, and with all thy strength, and with all thy mind: and thy neighbor as thyself."[83] For Hobbes, God is not love but simply "sovereign power," which means that creation is "emptied of its moral economy. . . ."[84] Hobbes's God "is sov-ereign, but is also a tyrant."[85]

Since the "law of nature" enjoins self-preservation in the perpetual state of war that is the state of nature, natural law reduces to emanations of each man's *right*

---

78. Ibid., I.14.189.
79. *De Cive*, Preface.
80. *Leviathan*, I.13.188.
81. *Works* IV.249.
82. *Leviathan*, II.31.397.
83. Luke 10:27.
84. *The Cambridge History of Political Thought*, 591.
85. Ibid.

to self-preservation by "Peace, as far as he has hope of obtaining it; and when he cannot obtain it, that he may seek, and use, all helps, and advantages of War."[86] Moreover, all's fair in war. Hence when man is in the state of nature "there is nothing he can make use of that may not be a help unto him in preserving his life against his enemies...in such a condition every man has a Right to everything; even to one another's body."[87] As Strauss recognizes: "If, then, natural law must be deduced from the desire for self-preservation, if, in other words, the desire for self-preservation is the sole root of all justice and morality, the fundamental moral fact is not a duty but a right...."[88] With Hobbes we see for the first time in Western thought "The fundamental change from an orientation by natural duties to an orientation by natural rights...." Hobbes, in fact, is "the founder of the specifically modern natural law doctrine."[89] This qualifies Hobbes as the founder of liberalism itself: "If we may call liberalism that political doctrine which regards as the fundamental political fact the rights, as distinguished from the duties, of man and which identifies the function of the state with the protection or the safeguarding of those rights, we must say that the founder of liberalism was Hobbes."[90]

With this change of orientation from natural law to the new doctrine of rights, there came also a new definition of freedom, one that is quite consistent with Hobbes's materialism: "Liberty, or Freedom, signifieth (properly) *the absence of Opposition*; (by Opposition, I mean external Impediments of motion); and may be applied *no less to Irrational, and Inanimate creatures, than to Rational*."[91] According to this definition "A Free-Man, is he, that in things which by his strength and wit he is able to do, is not hindered by what he has a will to."[92] Here we arrive at the first formal definition of Liberty as the mere absence of restraint on human action, rather than man's freedom—and correlative duty—to seek and do good and avoid evil according to the first precept of the natural law (cf. Chapter 1). Already abandoned in principle is the concept of doing good and avoiding evil in order to achieve man's divinely appointed ends, which requires appropriate civil restraints on human action beyond the mere preservation of person and property from harm.

A few decades later the "cautious" and "conservative" Locke, standing in Hobbes's shadow, announces the same new doctrine but with far more prudent language, adding a fundamental development regarding private property. By the end of the 17th century, when his major works appeared, what Macpherson calls the "market men" of English society "had come to terms with the more ambiguous, and more agreeable, doctrine of Locke."[93]

---

86. *Leviathan*, I.14.190.
87. Ibid.
88. Strauss, *Natural Right and History*, 180–1.
89. Ibid., 182.
90. Ibid., 181–2.
91. *Leviathan*, II.21.261.
92. Ibid., 262.
93. C.B. Macpherson, *The Political Theory of Possessive Individualism: From Hobbes to Locke* (Oxford: Oxford Univ. Press, 1962), 106.

Locke's doctrine is essentially the Hobbesian state of nature with an emphasis on private property as the primary means of defending the right to self-preservation. His description of the state of nature pleasingly presents it as one of "Peace, Good Will, Mutual Assistance, and Preservation"[94] with "Men living together according to reason, without a common Superior on Earth, with authority to judge between them," only to concede—literally one page and one section later—that it inevitably devolves into Hobbes's "State of War" on account of the "want of positive Laws and Judges with Authority to appeal to. . . ."[95] Man is born, says Locke, with "a title to perfect Freedom, and an uncontrolled enjoyment of all the Rights and Privileges of the Law of Nature,"[96] but this happy state of perfect equality and freedom is "very uncertain and constantly exposed to the Invasion of others."[97] The inevitable State of War, "once begun, continues, with a *right to the innocent party to destroy the other* whenever he can, until the aggressor offers peace. . . ."[98]

No matter what Locke's apologists in academia labor to find by way of distinctions, Hobbes and Locke are essentially at one in their teaching on a state of nature that is really a state of war, giving rise to a "natural law" that is really a natural right to self-preservation by any means necessary. Like Hobbes, Locke declares that in the state of nature "every man hath a right to punish the Offender, and be Executioner of the Law of Nature," which is none other than the *right* to self-preservation.[99] Locke's statement of this purported natural right is no less harsh than that of Hobbes:

> Man . . . hath by Nature a Power, not only to preserve his Property, that is, his Life, Liberty and Estate, against the Injuries and Attempts of other Men; but to judge of, and punish the breaches of that Law in others, as he is persuaded the Offence deserves, *even with Death itself*, in Crimes where the heinousness of the Fact, *in his Opinion*, requires it.[100]

That is, according to Locke, every man is born with the right to act as judge, jury and executioner concerning all perceived offenses against his person or property in the state of nature. Locke follows this outrageous claim—considered such even by his Protestant critics[101]—with the caveat: "I doubt not but this will seem a very strange Doctrine to some Men."[102] He later repeats the reference to "this strange Doctrine, that in the State of Nature, every one has the executive power of the law

---

94. *Two Treatises* (hereafter "TT"), II.iii.19.280.

95. *TT*, II.iii.20.281.

96. Ibid., II.123.

97. Ibid.

98. Ibid., II.19.

99. Ibid., II.8.

100. *TT*, II.86–87.

101. "The major tenets of natural freedom were condemned by Oxford University, and Locke's fellow revolutionary Algernon Sydney, was executed for holding them." *Cambridge History of Political Thought*, 621.

102. *TT*, II.9.

of nature...."[103] To say the least, Locke's notion of political individualism "is strange: it is one of the major conceptual innovations in early modern political thought."[104] Small wonder Locke, who feared the possible return of the Catholic Stuart monarch James II to the throne, persistently refused to admit to the authorship of *Two Treatises*.[105]

Locke elaborated a natural right to private property as "a corollary of the fundamental right of self-preservation...."[106] As Locke declares: "Men, being once born, have a right to their Preservation, and consequently to Meat and Drink, and such other things as Nature affords for their subsistence." In the state of nature, says Locke, every man "has a property in his own person ... [t]he *Labour* of his Body and the *Work* of his Hands...." What man "removes out of the State that Nature hath provided" and "hath mixed with his Labour" becomes his property. In the state of nature, man is "*absolute lord* of his own person and possessions...."[107]

That man is entitled to use the things of the earth for his subsistence and to the products of his own labor can hardly be disputed. The Greco-Catholic tradition is not to the contrary. But Locke departs from the tradition dramatically in two ways that will become staples of liberal and libertarian thought: First, he declares that man has a property right "in his own person," a novelty quite contrary to the traditional view that man, as a divine creation, has only a custodianship of his body, which he cannot dispose of as he pleases. Secondly, he posits an *absolute* property right, trumping all claims in justice against the owner, according to which man is "absolute lord" of his possessions. Locke "broke with tradition in making [the right to property] a strictly individual right. Certainly, tradition considered it as a natural right, but it emphasized the 'social' aspect of property, its being regulated by law or social duty."[108] Libertarians will seize upon Locke's theory to go even further than Locke did, arguing on Locke's principles for an absolute property right that would render unjust *any* form of taxation or property usage regulation by government.[109]

Locke does allow that in "the first ages of the World" the scope of the absolute lordship of one's property was limited in keeping with the traditional view that God has made the earth for the use of all men. Accordingly, in the "first ages of the World" man was "absolute lord" of only "a very moderate proportion" of the goods of the earth, meaning "such as he might appropriate to himself" while not taking so much that there was not "enough, and as good, left in common" for others.[110]

---

103. Ibid., II.13.

104. *The Cambridge History of Political Thought*, 620.

105. Laslet, intro. to *Locke: Two Treatises*, 66.

106. Strauss, *Natural Right and History*, 235.

107. *TT*, II.25–27.285–287.

108. Manent, *An Intellectual History of Liberalism*, 43.

109. See, e.g., Murray Rothbard, *Ethics of Liberty* (NY: New York Univ. Press, 2002), pp. 100–104, 126, wherein Rothbard expounds on "the law of a free society ... within a framework of absolute property rights," including the right to abortion and the "right to allow a deformed baby to die," which follows from "the larger right to allow any baby, whether deformed or not, to die."

110. *TT*, II.27, 33, 36.

This teaching is famously known as "the Lockean Proviso"—a term coined by the libertarian political philosopher Robert Nozick.

But the Lockean Proviso does not hold for long. It would have operated forever, Locke says, but for "the invention of money, and the tacit Agreement of men to put a value on it" which "introduced (by Consent) larger possessions, *and a Right to them....*"[111] With money comes "the desire of having more than Men needed," and men can indeed have it, since gold, "that little piece of yellow Metal, which would keep without wasting or decay, should be worth a great piece of flesh [meat], or a whole heap of corn...."[112] Owing to the invention of money, man can heap *unlimited* wealth to himself without being guilty of spoilage by taking more from nature than he could use. With money, man can buy all the foodstuffs his gold will buy, vastly more than he himself needs, and then sell them back to others in return for more money. He can buy up all the land in a given region, more land than he could ever occupy or cultivate, and then sell or lease it back for money to those who now have no land. The consent to money makes the right to property both absolute *and* unlimited.

With the advent of money, man moves beyond subsistence and the barter economy into the accumulation of wealth in a market economy—all in the "state of nature"! Locke "specifically puts into the state of nature, money, the consequent inequality of possession of land, and the supersession of the initial spoilage limit on the amount of land a man can rightfully possess. And since ... money leads to this unequal possession of land beyond the spoilage limit by its introducing markets and commerce beyond the level of barter, it must be presumed that Locke is ascribing such commerce also to the state of nature."[113]

So, Locke finds both money and full-blown commercial activity in his state of nature. As Macpherson remarks: "If this at first sight seems incredible, it must be remembered that Locke's state of nature is a curious mixture of historical imagination and logical abstraction from civil society."[114] In fact, as Macpherson has demonstrated, Locke discerns in his state of nature not only money and commerce but also wage-labor for subsistence wages. Since man has a property right to his own labor, he can sell it in order to survive in the world of money and commerce, which has allowed some men to buy up all the available land and means of production. From this it follows that the purchaser of labor becomes the *owner* of it: "the Turfs my servant has cut," says Locke, are part of "the labour that *was mine*, removing them out of the common state they were in...."[115] The idea that in the "state of nature" there is a "natural right" to ownership of the labor of wage-laborers is, as Macpherson observes, "no less intelligible than the ascription of developed commercial economy to the state of nature."[116]

111. *TT*, II.36.
112. *TT*, II.37.
113. Macpherson, *Possessive Individualism*, 209.
114. Ibid., 209.
115. *TT*, II.28.
116. Macpherson, *Possessive Individualism*, 217.

Locke is not saved from the accusation that he is an early proponent of radical laissez-faire capitalism by his allowance that "it would always be a sin, in any man of estate, to let his brother perish for want of affording him relief out of his plenty [so that] charity gives every man a title to so much out of his plenty as will keep him from extreme want, where he has no means to subsist otherwise."[117] In a major innovation, Locke subverts the traditional Christian conception of charity, giving it "a dramatically new and untraditional meaning." He does not "define charity as a duty at all: Lockean charity is a right, a conditional right, of the starving (and only them) to some of the 'surplusage' (and only the surplusage) of the 'rich,' or those who possess 'Plenty' (and only those)...an expression, in desperate circumstances, of the inalienable right and undeniable urge to self-preservation."[118] Hence Locke's conception of social charity is crabbed, to say the least, being essentially that expressed in the English Poor Laws of his time—the Protestant origin of the modern welfare state—that had replaced the vast Catholic system of institutionalized charitable works. In Locke's view, the growth of poverty was the fault of no one but the poor, who had succumbed to "relaxation of discipline and the corruption of manners" and ought to be subjected to a strict regime of "restraint of their debauchery," with appropriate punishments, such as whipping, for the "begging drones" and "idle vagabonds" who "pretend they cannot get work."[119]

All in all, Locke's state of nature bears a suspicious resemblance to England at the time of the "Glorious" Revolution—a society in which the Protestant heirs of Henry VIII's plunder of the Catholic Church were now in the possession of the same land which, in the previous century, had been worked by Catholic tenants with vested interests that were "ripening into a customary freehold estate,"[120] or land which had once been part of the local commons but had been enclosed, often by use of force. Locke's supposedly universal "state of nature," from which all of man's natural rights are to be derived, turns out to be, amusingly enough, the emergent bourgeois market society of post-Reformation England, with its landed Protestant gentry, wealthy Protestant merchants, and large class of dispossessed wage-slaves.

Thus it should not be surprising that Locke's grand new theory of "natural rights" in the "state of nature" posed no impediment to his profitable investments in two slave-trading companies.[121] Nor did Locke's theory affect his work (with

---

117. *TT*, I.42.

118. Pangle, *The Spirit of Modern Republicanism*, 144.

119. *Locke: Political Essays* (Cambridge: Cambridge Univ. Press, 1997), "Essay on the Poor Law," 184–185.

120. Cobbett, *History of the Protestant Reformation*, xv, intro. by Francis Cardinal Racquet.

121. *See* Wayne Glausser, "Three Approaches to Locke and the Slave Trade," *Journal of the History of Ideas*, Vol. 51, No. 2 (April-June 1990), 192–216. Glausser discusses Locke's ownership of shares in both the Royal African Company and the Bahamas Adventurers, his work on the Carolina constitutions and three different scholarly approaches to reconciling Locke's participation in the slave trade with his theory of liberty. Glausser rightly observes, as suggested here, that in his various writings Locke "has built in too many confusions of theory and practice, too many defenses against either being caught in the act or missing the boat." Ibid., 215. That is, Locke's thought involves expedient *ad hoc* adjustments to his own particular circumstances and those of his employers, such as Lord Ashley, who was even more heavily invested in the slave trade than Locke was.

Lord Shaftesbury) in drafting the proposed *Fundamental Constitutions of Carolina* (1669). This strange document provided that the slaves who worked the 48,000 acres comprising an honorary land grant to Locke in America as "Landgrave" (the German title of nobility he thought appropriate for such holdings) were given the right to religious liberty subject to the proviso that "every freeman of Carolina shall have ABSOLUTE POWER AND AUTHORITY OVER HIS NEGRO SLAVES of what opinion or religion whatsoever."[122] (Locke never took possession of his grant, but he did try to sell the title.)

So, while Locke begins his description of the right to private property with "the traditional assumption that the earth and its fruits had originally been given to mankind for their common use," he ends up by "turn[ing] the tables on all who derived from this assumption theories which were restrictive of capitalist appropriation. He has erased the moral disability with which unlimited capitalist appropriation had hitherto been handicapped."[123] Locke's novel teaching on private property "and therewith his whole political philosophy, are revolutionary not only with regard to the biblical tradition but with regard to the philosophic tradition as well."[124] That is, in Locke's thought private property loses both its moral character as a good subject to the claims of non-owners where justice requires and its philosophical character as a natural right subject to a paramount duty under the natural law. With Locke the individual property owner becomes the basic unit of political society and the common good in the traditional sense ceases to exist: "Through the shift of emphasis from natural duties or obligations to natural rights, the individual, the ego, had become the center and origin of the moral world, since man—as distinguished from man's end—had become that center or origin. Locke's doctrine of property is a still more 'advanced' expression of this radical change than was the political philosophy of Hobbes."[125] Locke's doctrine will be a foundation of laissez-faire capitalism and the commercial republics of the modern world.

Regarding this shift from duties to rights, Locke (like Hobbes) denies that the natural law, even in the limited sense he recognizes, is written on man's heart. In *ECHU* he flatly denies that there is any rule of conduct "imprinted on the mind as a duty. . . ."[126] Man has only a Hobbesian desire for happiness and aversion to misery built into his nature, not any understanding of a law that restrains his actions and orders him to the good:

> Nature, I confess, has put into man a desire of happiness and an aversion to misery: these indeed are innate practical principles. . . . [B]ut these are inclinations of the appetite to good, *not impressions of truth on the understanding.*[127]

For Locke, as for Hobbes, men are moved to act by "some uneasiness or trouble

122. *Locke: Political Essays*, Fundamental Constitutions, Arts. [101] [110], 180. Emphasis in original.
123. Macpherson, *Possessive Individualism*, 221.
124. Strauss, *Natural Right and History*, 248.
125. Macpherson, *Possessive Individualism*, 221.
126. *ECHU*, I.2.12.
127. *ECHU*, I.2.3.

or displeasure till it be done, and this is that we call desire, so that desire seems to me to be a pain the mind is in till some good, whether *jucundum* [joy] or *utile* [utility] which it judges possible and seasonable, be obtained."[128] Or, stated otherwise: "The greatest present uneasiness is the spur to action, that is constantly most felt, and for the most part determines the will in its choice of the next action."[129] Removing uneasiness is what Locke means by the "pursuit of happiness":

> Thus, how much soever men are in earnest and constant *in pursuit of happiness*, yet they may have a clear view of good, great and confessed good, without being concerned for it, or moved by it, if they think they can make up their happiness without it. Though as to pain, that they are always concerned for; they can feel no uneasiness without being moved. And therefore, being uneasy in the want of whatever is judged necessary to their happiness, as soon as any good appears to make a part of their portion of happiness, they begin to desire it.[130]

With Hobbes, Locke abandons as a motive for human action any divinely implanted desire to act rightly and refrain from wrongdoing in keeping with natural and supernatural virtues as "the schools" explain them. In *ECHU* Locke, like Hobbes, denies that there is any rule of conduct "imprinted on the mind as a duty...."[131] For Locke, as for Hobbes, the sense of right and wrong is not implanted in man but is developed through his experience of social norms concerning conduct approved or disapproved by men. This is Locke's famous "law of opinion or reputation," enunciated in *ECHU*:

> Virtue and vice are names pretended, and supposed every where to stand for actions in their own nature right or wrong.... But yet, whatever is pretended ... these names, virtue and vice, in the particular instances of their application through the several nations and societies of men in the world, are constantly attributed *only to such actions as, in each country and society, are in reputation or discredit.*[132]

As Nathan Tarcov has demonstrated in his famous study of Locke's *Some Thoughts Concerning Education* (1693), Locke makes reputation or discredit, the esteem of others, the basis for the moral formation of schoolboys, providing "his reconstruction of the model of the liberal gentleman on the basis of the hedonist principles familiar to the readers of the *Essay Concerning Human Understanding.*"[133] That is, virtue is to be learned most effectively, not through the inculcation

---

128. *Locke: Political Essays*, "Pleasure, Pain, the Passions" (1676), 242.
129. *ECHU*, II.21.41.
130. *ECHU*, II.21.44.
131. *ECHU*, I.2.12.
132. *ECHU*, II.28.10. Recall Hobbes's variant of this "law," which he designated the fifth "Law of Nature": "COMPLAISANCE—that is to say, that every man strive to accommodate himself to the rest ... the observers of this law may be called SOCIABLE ... the contrary stubborn, insociable, forward, intractable...." *Leviathan*, I.15.209.
133. Nathan Tarcov, *Locke's Education for Liberty* (Chicago: Univ. of Chicago Press, 1984), 112.

of moral lessons as in traditional Christian curricula, but through the pain of disapprobation and the pleasure that comes with esteem. Unwittingly or not, Locke thus presents the pedagogical foundation for an "education for liberty" in public schools that will be veritable seminaries of conformity to the liberal *Zeitgeist* his own thought will help to engender. Ironically, however, Locke calls for home-schooling in order to achieve his pedagogical vision, as the common schools of his day all provided a standard (albeit Protestant) Christian formation with what he considered ineffectual rote lessons in morality and theology.

The principle that virtue and vice are to be learned by study and reflection upon social conventions will mean in practice the destruction of both public and private morality as those conventions drift ever further from the Biblical precepts to which Locke professed to be a devoted adherent—a drift whose beginning is seen in Locke's own condonation of divorce and even polygamy (discussed below). Despite his pious insistence that reasonable men can discover God's law by consulting social norms, in Locke's ethical system the natural and divine law (beyond pleasure and pain and the instinct for self-preservation) is reduced to a set of precepts handed down from on high. Because in Locke's view God has forged no link between His law and the intrinsic natures of the beings He has created, we see nothing less than what J. B. Schneewind has called "the collapse of modern natural law" in Locke's thought.[134]

Locke, like Hobbes, rejects the *summum bonum* of the Greco-Catholic tradition in favor of a hedonic scale of value: "[T]hat which causes the greater pleasure is the greater good, and that which causes the greater pain, the greater evil."[135] Hence human desire "is not moved by the good it sees or conceives, but by the ill being it feels." Therefore, Locke declares: "[T]he philosophers of old did in vain inquire, whether *summum bonum* consisted in riches, or bodily delights, *or virtue*, or con-templation: and they might have as reasonably disputed, whether the best relish were to be found in apples, plums, or nuts, and have divided themselves into sects upon it."[136] The *summum bonum*, the supreme good of man, "which is the primary question raised by the tradition . . . is a perfectly idle question for Locke. . . ."[137] The highest good of man as the possession of God via beatitude—an end even the Greeks perceived, however dimly—now ceases to matter for politics in its new and radically restricted sense.

For Locke, as for Hobbes, freedom means the absence of restraint on human action: "For *Liberty* is to be free from restraint and violence from others. . . ."[138] If Locke allows that liberty does not mean "for every Man to do what he lists (likes)," this is only because man cannot be free if "every other Man's Humour might domi-neer over him. . . ." Accordingly freedom means that every man may "dispose, and order, *as he lists*, his Person, Actions, Possessions, and his whole Property" as allowed

134. J. B. Schneewind, *The Invention of Autonomy* (Cambridge: Cambridge Univ. Press, 1997), 141.
135. *Locke: Political Essays*, "Of Ethic in General" (c. 1686–8?), 300–301.
136. *ECHU*, II.21.56.
137. Manent, *City of Man*, 130.
138. *TT*, II.57.

by law in such manner as "not to be subject to the arbitrary Will of another, but freely follow his own."[139] That is, the only limit on freedom is that its exercise not subject another to one's arbitrary will. In the *ECHU* Locke declares that no one must be hindered in "the pursuit of happiness"—the very phrase that appears in the Declaration of Independence drafted by that devoted student of Locke's works, Thomas Jefferson. This right to the pursuit of happiness is in keeping with Locke's conception of the natural law as merely a divinely implanted "desire of happiness and an aversion to misery...." All men, says Locke, "must be allowed to pursue their happiness, nay, cannot be hindered...."[140] As Thomas Pangle observes: "It is, indeed, in the pages of Locke that one finds the most straightforward and lucid statement of hedonistic self-love or 'the pursuit of happiness' as the ground of all duty...." The "new Lockean notion of 'the pursuit of happiness' [is] explicitly opposed to the classical idea of a '*summum bonum*,' or an *attainment* of happiness...."[141] Locke sets the stage for Act I in the age-long tragicomedy of a post-Christian civilization in which happiness will come to mean "whatever floats your boat."

To sum up, Hobbes and Locke discard the Christian story of man's origin, his fall from grace, his need for redemption, and his subjection to a natural law inscribed in his nature, while Locke invents a state of nature that corresponds to proto-capitalism and the freedom to amass unlimited wealth without any violation of justice. As even such a decidedly pro-liberal democracy scholar as Walter Berns of Georgetown University is constrained to admit, the "rights discovered by Hobbes and Locke ... presuppose the state of nature, and the idea of the state of nature is *incompatible with Christian doctrine*. According to Christian doctrine, 'the first and great commandment' is to love God, and the second, which is like unto it, is to love one's neighbor as oneself. In the state of nature, however, man is not obliged to love anyone, but merely to preserve himself [and] to preserve the rest of mankind [only] when his own preservation comes not in competition."[142]

The Social Compact

Both Hobbes and Locke employ the fictive state of nature as the origin of their notion of political sovereignty, which will become the foundation of the nation-state's title to authority over its subjects even to the point of life and death: the social compact that takes "naturally free" men out of the state of nature and places them—forever—under subjection to government. The state of nature ends with the "Hobbesian moment" in which men seek to escape the state of nature by forming governments to protect their rights from constant invasion by others.

For Hobbes and Locke, life in the State under a common ruler is not natural to man, as it is in the Greco-Catholic tradition, but purely a *contractual* creation by

139. *TT*, II.57.
140. Locke, *Reasonableness of Christianity* (Stanford, CA: Stanford Univ. Press, 1988), n. 245, 68.
141. Thomas L. Pangle, *Spirit of Modern Republicanism*, 20. Emphasis in original.
142. Walter Berns, "Religion and the Founding Principle," in *The Moral Foundations of the American Republic* (Charlottesville, VA: Univ. of Virginia Press, 1986), 215.

way of an agreement between the parties to surrender to some agreed authority the plenary authority each of the parties has in the state of nature in order to end the state of war. As Hobbes asserts, men decide to enter a contractual commonwealth because, although they "naturally love Liberty and Dominion over others," they realize that their own preservation requires "getting themselves out of that miserable condition of Warre . . . when there is no visible Power to keep them in awe and tie them by fear of punishment to the performance of their Covenants, and observation of [the] Laws of Nature. . . ."[143]

Locke justifies his "Hobbesian moment" by first asking: "If man in the state of nature be so free, as has been said; if he be absolute lord of his own person and possessions, equal to the greatest, and subject to no body, why will he part with his freedom? Why will he give up this empire, and subject himself to the dominion and control of any other power?" The "obvious" answer, says Locke, is that each man's little "empire" of liberty is "constantly exposed to the invasion of others" who are not "strict observers of equity and justice," so that each "empire" is "very unsafe, very unsecure." This constant insecurity of each man's "empire" is what "makes him willing to quit a condition, which, however free, is full of fears and continual dangers" in order to "join in society with others, who are already united, or have a mind to unite, for the mutual preservation of their lives, liberties and estates, which I call by the general name, property."[144]

Given Locke's special emphasis on property, for him the Hobbesian moment is the moment when man realizes that he needs government to protect his property rights: "The great and chief end, therefore, of men's uniting into commonwealths, and putting themselves under government, is the preservation of their property."[145] While Locke sometimes uses the term "property" to include "liberties" in general, for him liberty means the absence of interference with a man's ownership and use of his own person and other possessions: "The commonwealth seems to me to be a society of men constituted *only* for the procuring, preserving, and advancing *their own civil interests.* Civil interests I call life, liberty, health, and indolency of body; and the possession of outward things, such as money, lands, houses, furniture, and the like."[146]

How exactly does man cross the threshold from the state of nature to life under government? In the Hobbelockean view, only the "consent of the governed" to be governed gives rise to political authority. The result is a theory of "mutual subjection" of ruler and subject that, once it has taken root in elite opinion, will lead to revolutions and civil wars not only in America and France but also throughout the Western world in the 18th and 19th centuries.

According to Hobbes, the moment of transition occurs when "a multitude of men do agree, and covenant, every one with every one," that political authority

---

143. *Leviathan*, II.17.
144. *TT*, II.123.
145. *TT*, II.124.
146. *Letter Concerning Toleration* (1689).

over the multitude shall reside with "whatsoever man, or assembly of men, shall be given by *the major part* the right to present the person of them all...."[147] Despite Hobbes's presumption that the sovereign chosen will be a monarch (as opposed to an "assembly of men"), the heart of his view is that "sovereignty, wherever it lay, was simply the aggregate of private wills. It was, therefore, not inappropriate that his critics should reprove him for encouraging the dangers of democracy."[148] This is so even though, for Hobbes, the selection of the sovereign is permanent and the sovereign self-perpetuating: "they that have already instituted a Commonwealth, being thereby bound by Covenant...cannot lawfully make a new covenant...." If the multitude choose a monarch, they "cannot without his leave cast off Monarchy...."[149]

Locke likewise declares that sovereignty is nothing more than a creature of the aggregate of individual consents: "the only way" that man "divests himself of his Natural Liberty, and puts on the bonds of Civil Society is by agreeing with other Men to join and unite into a Community...in a secure Enjoyment of their Properties, and a greater Security against any that are not of it."[150] When "any number of Men have, by the consent of every individual, made a Community, they have thereby made that Community one Body, with a Power to Act as one Body, which is only by the will and determination of the majority."[151] Locke was so intent on establishing personal consent as the basis of political authority that he advanced the ludicrous contention that "a child is born a subject of no Country or Government"[152] because he is not yet capable of giving his "consent" to be governed. Children, he argued, must give their consent "separately in their turns, as each comes to be of Age, and not in a multitude together...."[153] A child, therefore, is merely "under his father's Tuition and Authority, till he come to Age of discretion," at which time he will decide for himself "what Government he will put himself under; what body Politick he will unite himself to."[154]

Locke was forced to this extreme by the obvious objection that if a child is subject to a government without having consented to be so, then political authority must not depend on consent. But then why should a child be subject to even his father's authority if he has not consented to it? Borrowing from the Biblical tradition, Locke would reply that God has placed children under "the Father's empire" and "temporary Government" until such time as the child "leave Father and Mother and cleave to his Wife."[155] Yet the tradition also maintains, and all of history confirms, that God has placed nations as well as children in the charge of

---

147. *Leviathan*, II.xviii.
148. *Cambridge History of Political Thought*, 603.
149. Ibid.
150. *TT*, II.95.
151. *TT*, II.96.
152. *TT*, II.116–118.
153. *TT* II.117.
154. *TT*, II.118.
155. *TT*, II.65, 67.

rulers whose authority does not arise from the consent of those they rule: "By me kings reign . . . by me princes rule, and the mighty decree justice."[156] "Over every nation he hath set a ruler."[157] Here Locke evinces the Protestant's selective deference to the literal meaning of Scripture. Moreover, Locke reduces even the Scripturally enjoined subjection of a child to his parents to an economic *quid pro quo*: "the honour due from a Child places in the parents a perpetual right to respect, reverence, support and compliance too, *more or less*, as the Father's care, cost and kindness in his Education has been more or less."[158]

The Hobbelockean notion that political authority originated in mysterious gatherings of multitudes in the state of nature to bestow their "consent" upon rulers is no less fictional than the state of nature itself. Hobbes makes no real effort to show otherwise, while Locke's apodictic assertion that "Politick Societies *all began* from a voluntary union, and mutual agreement of men, freely acting in the choice of their Govenours and forms of Government"[159] is unsupported by any serious historical argument. He himself admits that "looking back as far as Records give us any account of peopling the world, and the History of Nations, we commonly find Government to be in one hand, yet it destroys not that which I affirm. . . ."[160] And why not? In the mere two pages he devotes to the question in the *Second Treatise*,[161] Locke fails to show that his consent theory is not in fact destroyed by a simple look at the entire history of the human race. For history nowhere shows anything remotely resembling a series of social compacts by men in the state of nature, but it does show everywhere men already living under the rule of kings and emperors to whose authority they have never given any affirmative consent.

And what of the patent historical fact that the predominant mode of governance throughout human history is the hereditary monarchy? This Locke attributes, implausibly enough, to an infantile human attachment to fatherhood, by which the human race became "accustomed to the Rule of One Man." Monarchy, "being simple, and most obvious to men," and even "both easy and safe," was accepted only because "neither experience had instructed in Forms of Government, nor the Ambition or Insolence of Empire had taught to beware of the encroachments of Prerogative, or the inconveniences of power which Monarchy, in Succession, was apt to lay claim to. . . ."[162] That is, we are asked to believe that men submitted to kings because they were unfamiliar with alternative forms of government, and because the successive monarchs of history were not (at least before the English Civil Wars!) sufficiently tyrannical to provoke men to exercise their "natural right" to "self-government"—meaning government by which the majority tells the minority who its

156. Prov. 8:15–16.
157. Ecclus. 7:14.
158. *TT*, II.67.
159. *TT*, II.102.
160. *TT*, II.106.
161. *TT*, II.101–102.
162. *TT*, II.107.

ruler will be, or a rebellious elite overthrows the king and replaces him with another to which "the people" are deemed to have consented.

Here we must note one of the most remarkable facts in the history of Liberty: that nowhere do we find any elaborated "natural law" argument for majority rule. While "Locke and Hobbes were agreed on the necessity of the consent of the majority being taken for the act of the whole," they failed to demonstrate "some law of nature that the major part have the power to rule over the rest of the multitude."[163] On this fundamental point Locke was bested by the long-since-forgotten Robert Filmer, whose work *Patriarcha* (1680) provoked the *Two Treatises*. Locke's "defence of the majority principle against Filmer must be pronounced unsatisfactory," as it rests on nothing more than Locke "simply asserting that it is 'by the Law of Nature and Reason.'"[164] Besides this perfunctory reference to nature and reason, Locke offered the rather Newtonian mechanical argument that the entire multitude must move "that way wither the greater force carries it...."[165] And why is that so? For his part, Hobbes simply assumed the legitimacy of majority rule without even an attempt at a demonstration.

Of course, being unable to demonstrate the existence of any law of nature that requires the entire multitude to follow the decisions of a bare majority of electors constituting a distinct minority of the total population, as opposed to a king, neither Hobbes nor Locke could articulate any "natural" mechanism by which the multitude "consents" to be governed by its ruler. Thus both the social compact and the means of its effectuation are natural law fictions. Yet these fictions are the very foundation of political modernity, including the American Revolution.

Even the Protestant contemporaries of Hobbes and Locke found their new doctrine intolerable, which (along with the Hobbelockean attack on theistic metaphysics) explains why both thinkers had to flee England for their own safety. "Because of the dangers inherent in the contract theory almost all the royalists firmly rejected the notion that civil society is the product of individual wills and pacts.... With Aquinas and Aristotle, the royalists held that civil society and political society were natural, not conventional. Since power does not derive from the people, it does not revert to them...."[166] It did not require a staunch Catholic to recognize that the idea of political authority being created by contract "opened wide the possibility of private judgment of the sovereign's care" by any group of his subjects and implied that a ruler's authority "was hence upheld by nothing more secure than the fact the people habitually obeyed."[167]

Just as Hobbes and Locke both approach epistemology and metaphysics *via* an adaptation of the Cartesian method that is the philosophical analogue of the Protestant principle of private judgment, so also do they apply the principle of private judgment to the very ground of political authority. And while Hobbes is today

163. Laslet, *Two Treatises*, 333 at note, citing Filmer, *Patriarcha*, 82.
164. Ibid.
165. *TT*, II.96.
166. *Cambridge History of Political Thought*, 604.
167. Ibid., 605.

regarded as the "statist" exponent of social contract theory, with Locke being viewed as the "libertarian" exponent, in fact both thinkers equally reduced political authority to a revocable human convention. The Hobbesian sovereign "had feet of clay: 'Hobbes, whilst he pretends on the one hand to bestow gifts upon princes, does with the other treacherously strike a dagger to their hearts.'"[168] For this reason—in what is not at all a paradox—"the liberal minimalist state was discovered in Hobbes at an early stage."[169]

But what *is* paradoxical is that the social contract theory, by severing political authority from its divine source and thus releasing it from the moral check provided by the Church, actually leaves the people defenseless against the very power of the "minimalist" state that supposedly rules only by their consent. After "the Lutheran Reform disarmed religion in the face of temporal power,"[170] Hobbes and Locke secured the final ascendancy of the temporal power over the spiritual by making political authority contractual rather than a participation in God's authority to be exercised according to His justice. In the name of Liberty, Hobbes and Locke together laid out the intellectual groundwork for the most powerful form of government the world has ever known: the modern secular state in all its varieties, from totalitarian to "democratic." There are three basic reasons that this is so.

First, the principle that political authority is founded upon an individual's *consent* to that authority is destructive of authority as such—not only the authority of government, but authority in all areas of human life. The consent principle, first introduced into religion by Luther and then made the foundation of the Hobbelockean theory of sovereignty, is an acid that will burn its way into man's very being, altering the entire order of Western civilization by reducing society more or less to a collection of formally (but not actually) autonomous individuals. Thus did Locke (following John Milton's lead in his tracts on divorce) reduce marriage to a mere compact between the parties, declaring that "the *Conjugal Bonds* [are] more firm and lasting in Man, than the other Species of Animals; yet it would give one reason to enquire, why this *Compact*, where Procreation and Education are secured, and Inheritance taken care for, may not be made determinable, either by consent, or at a certain time, or upon certain Conditions, as will as any other voluntary Compacts...."[171] Locke's endorsement of divorce "was too much for the clerical Elrington, who says: 'To make the conjugal union determinable by consent, is to introduce a promiscuous concubinage.'"[172] But Locke goes even farther by endorsing polygamy: "He that is already married may marry another woman with his left hand....The ties, duration and conditions of the left hand marriage shall be no other than what is expressed in the contract of marriage between the parties."[173]

168. *Cambridge History of Political Thought*, 604, quoting Cumberland (1717), 377.
169. Ibid., 605.
170. Manent, *City of Man*, 27.
171. *TT*, II.81.
172. *TT*, 321, n. 81.
173. *Diary* (1678), 199; cited in Locke, *TT*, 321.

As Manent has observed: "The principle of consent, set in motion by the will of the individual, penetrates and rearranges the relation that appeared up to then invariably inscribed in the eternal order of human nature and above all the relations between parents and children, and man and woman, or in the eternal order of the world, especially those which constitute religion."[174] Even Locke's own friend Tyrell was able to recognize, in response to Filmer's "needling effectiveness," there was "really no stopping ground between the ground he [Tyrell] and Locke occupied and logical individualism [and] final democracy. . . ."[175]

Second, the paradoxical result of logical individualism and final democracy will be subjugation by the collective. Both Hobbes and Locke make it quite clear that the consent to leave the state of nature and enter into a commonwealth results in submission to an absolute authority against which there is no appeal on earth: the supreme sovereign. The supreme sovereign erected by "the will of the people" will finally ascend over monarchy throughout the Western world in the revolutions to come, beginning with those of 1776 and 1789. "From Hobbes to Locke and Rousseau, the idea of the body politic will amount to *absolute sovereignty* variously conceived, founded on and deduced from a state of nature."[176]

As Hobbes puts it, the only way out of the calamitous state of nature is for the warring parties to "confer *all their power and strength* upon one Man, or upon one Assembly of men . . . and therein submit their Wills, everyone to His will . . . and their Judgments to His judgment. . . ." The majority's election of a sovereign creates a unity of the multitude in "one person [which] is called a Common-Wealth. . . . This is the Generation of that great Leviathan, or rather (to speak more reverently) of that Mortal God, to which we owe under the Immortal God, our peace and defense."[177] The "major part" having chosen the sovereign and thus given birth to the mortal god of the State, "he that dissented must now consent with the rest . . . or else be justly *destroyed by the rest*."[178]

It is little different with the verbally more judicious Locke. At the imaginary "consent" meeting of the multitude, everyone in attendance has "quitted" the "natural power" to protect one's own person and property and punish violators of the law of nature, and has "resign'd it up into the hands of the Community. . . . And thus all private judgments of every Member being excluded, the Community comes to be Umpire [and] decides all the differences that may happen between any Members of that Society, concerning any matter of right. . . ."[179] The result is the creation of "one People, one Body Politick under *one Supreme Government*. . . ."[180] Moreover, those who "by actual agreement, and any *express* [Locke's emphasis] declaration" consent to the authority of this supreme government are "*perpetually*

---

174. Manent, *City of Man*, 161.
175. Laslet, intro. *Two Treatises*, 69.
176. Manent, *An Intellectual History of Liberalism*, 37.
177. *Leviathan*, II.17.
178. *Leviathan*, II.18.
179. *TT*, II.87.
180. *TT*, II.89

and indispensably obliged to be and remain unalterably a Subject to it, and can *never again* be in the liberty of the state of Nature. . . ."[181]

The supreme organ of Locke's "supreme government," no matter what form the government takes (democracy, oligarchy, or monarchy) is the legislative branch, to which Locke's executive and "federative" branches are subject (the details of Locke's "division of powers" theory do not concern us here). The legislative is not only "*the supreme power* [Locke's emphasis] of the Commonwealth, but sacred and unalterable in the hands where the Community have once placed it. . . ."[182] While it is the supreme majority of the multitude that elects the legislative body, once elected the legislature is the highest authority on earth: "[A]ll the Obedience, which by which the most solemn Ties any one can be obliged to pay, terminates in this *Supreme Power.* . . ." In a clear reference to the Catholic Church and the papacy, Locke further declares: "nor can any Oaths to any Foreign Power whatsoever, or any domestic subordinate power, discharge any Member of Society from his *Obedience to the Legislative* [Locke's emphasis]. . . ."[183]

Third, and finally, "consent" to the exercise of power by the supreme sovereign will prove to be *pro forma* and entirely trivial, amounting to nothing more than passive acceptance of the status quo. Addressing the objection that, in the real world, most people have not consented to their governments by outward manifestations of a compact with their rulers (such as a loyalty oath or pledge of allegiance), Locke argues that "tacit consent" to the authority of the "supreme power" arises from someone's *mere existence* within a territory:

> The difficulty is . . . how far any one shall be looked on to have consented, and thereby submitted to any government, where he has made no expressions of it at all. And to this I say, that every man, that hath any possessions, or enjoyment, of any part of the dominions of any government, doth thereby give his tacit consent, and is as far forth obliged to obedience to the laws of that government, during such enjoyment, as any one under it; whether this his possession be of land, to him and his heirs for ever, or a lodging only for a week; or whether it be barely travelling freely on the highway; and *in effect, it reaches as far as the very being of any one within the territories of that government.*[184]

If one consents to be governed merely by existing within the territory of a government, the very concept of "government by consent of the governed" is nugatory. Indeed, on Locke's view, one "consents" even to the rule of an "absolute monarch" merely by remaining within his realm without protest. Locke himself exposes "Government by consent of the governed" as the legal fiction it is. In the end, one is simply governed, justly or unjustly, by the powers that be as men always have been throughout history. Even in democracies the act of voting by a relative few

181. *TT*, II.121.
182. *TT*, II.134.
183. Ibid.
184. *TT*, II.119.

merely designates a small number of representatives whose decisions will bind the entire multitude without any formal consent by each subject. This is not to suggest that democracy is a per se invalid mode of political sovereignty but only that its claim to moral superiority over monarchy based on the imaginary "consent" of each subject to all acts of democratic governance is illusory.

With Hobbes and Locke both, therefore, the multitude "consents" to the rule of an absolute sovereign empowered by a majority vote. Aside from the difference that Hobbes's sovereign is consented to in perpetuity while Locke's is consented to at every election, the Hobbesian and Lockean sovereigns are equally powerful. Thus it is fair to speak of a Hobbelockean Leviathan—operative in the modern nation-state—for which Hobbes and Locke together wrote the first charter. Strauss ably sums up the outcome: "In spite of the limitations which Locke demands, the commonwealth remains for him, as it was for Hobbes, 'the mighty leviathan': in entering civil society, 'men give up all their natural power to the society which they enter into.'" Just as Hobbes did, "so Locke admits only one contract: the contract of union which every individual makes with every other individual of the same multitude is identical with the contract of subjection."[185]

The individual who "consents" to be governed by a supreme sovereign in the form of Locke's representative government and its supreme legislature consents to his own subjugation by "representatives" who will turn out to be far more demanding of his life and property than any king. And any subject who purports to revoke his consent and withdraw from the supposedly voluntary social compact will face dire consequences. This will become apparent in our survey of the first century of the American Republic, the first fully working model of "one People, one Body Politick under one Supreme Government," which "shall not perish from the earth" no matter how many members of the irrevocable Lockean compact must die in order to preserve "government of the people, for the people, and by the people."

The Doctrine of Revolution

Hobbelockean subjects are not, however, without an ultimate remedy against abuses, or perceived abuses, by the absolute sovereign they have erected by "consent." Setting the stage for an age of revolution, beginning with the "Glorious" Revolution of 1688, Hobbes and Locke prescribe their remedy: the right to revolution.

It is necessary to remember, first of all, that the political tradition of Christendom recognizes no such right. In his *De Regno*, St. Thomas, adverting to the Gospel injunction to obey civil authority as from God, rejects the notion that some group of subjects may rebel against the ruler at will "in order to set the multitude free." A true tyrant, however, if chosen by the people to rule over them in the first place, may be deposed or his power limited as a matter of self-defense of *a whole people*, provided the deposition does not provoke even greater harm to the common

---

185. Strauss, *Natural Right and History*, 231–2.

good.[186] In the *Summa* St. Thomas goes so far as to condemn revolution as a species of mortal sin—sedition—that is practiced by a few for their personal benefit: "Now Augustine says (*De Civ. Dei* ii, 21) that 'wise men understand the word people to designate *not any crowd of persons*, but the assembly of those who are united together in fellowship recognized by law and for the common good.' Wherefore it is evident that the unity to which sedition is opposed is the unity of law and common good: whence it follows manifestly that sedition is opposed to justice and the common good. Therefore by reason of its genus it is a mortal sin, and *its gravity will be all the greater according as the common good which it assails surpasses the private good* which is assailed by strife."[187]

Hobbes introduces his right to revolution under the guise of a defense of monarchy. One may refuse to obey Leviathan when Leviathan gives a command that would violate the inalienable right of self-preservation. If the sovereign commands a subject to "kill, wound, or maim himself" or to "abstain from the use of food, air, medicine or any other thing without which he cannot live," then that subject "hath the Liberty to disobey." That much, of course, is perfectly consistent with the traditional view on the limits of political authority: that political authority not only may, but must, be resisted in its unjust and immoral commands. Hobbes goes further, however, offering the curious rationale that when a group of men resists the sovereign even *unjustly* "or have committed some capital crime, for which every one of them expected death," they have the right to take up arms to defend themselves against the sovereign's punishment, for "they but defend their lives, which the Guilty man may as well do, as the Innocent."[188] That, of course, is a prescription for revolution. Hobbes also allows that subjects are completely absolved from all further obedience to a sovereign that ceases to protect them, "for the right men have by Nature to protect themselves, when none else can protect them, can by no Covenant be relinquished."[189] The sovereign ceases to protect its subjects not only when it is crippled by a war, but also when it succumbs to a "natural mortality" arising from "intestine discord."[190] This appears to be a veiled justification for the execution of Charles I by the members of the Rump Parliament during the English Civil Wars.

As Jeffrey R. Collins shows in his meticulous examination of Hobbes's political allegiance, both *Leviathan* and the posthumously published *Behemoth* (1682) demonstrate that Hobbes, in his hatred for Catholicism and hierarchical and priestly religion in general, fully accommodated himself, however circumspectly, to the regicide and revolution of the Cromwellian Independents, who had created the "clean swept house" of an England from which the "Spirit of Rome" had been

---

186. St. Thomas Aquinas, *On Kingship* (Ontario, Pontifical Inst. of Medieval Studies, 2000 [1949]), VI.46, 49.

187. *ST*, II–II, Q. 42, Art. 2.

188. *Leviathan*, II.21.

189. Ibid.

190. Ibid.

exorcised.[191] Despite his seemingly royalist defense of the absolute monarchical sovereign in *Leviathan*, Hobbes's treatment of the regicide Cromwell in *Behemoth* "bordered dangerously on open admiration," even if Hobbes, writing during the restored monarchy of Charles II, was careful not to endorse explicitly what the Cromwellians had done to the King's father.[192] Based on his endorsement of the anti-Anglican, anti-episcopal Independents in Chapter 42 of *Leviathan*, Hobbes was widely recognized in his own time as a sympathizer and indeed a theorist of revolution against altar and throne. For this reason, with the ascension of Charles II "the era of public acceptance of his works was over."[193] As Collins concludes: "Hobbes's later critics were vindicated. *Leviathan* was to prove a fitting political theory for Cromwellian revolution."[194]

Here, however, it is Locke who is the less cautious writer for once. In its last two chapters, entitled "Tyranny" and "Dissolution of Government," the *Second Treatise* presents a full-blown doctrine of revolution that justifies overthrow of the sovereign whenever it violates the "trust" placed in it by the people under the social compact. This breach of trust, says Locke, is "a fault that is not proper only to Monarchies; other Forms of Government are liable to it...." When the ruler breaches his trust and declines to heed his subjects on a grievance "of great Consequence," the ruler and subjects return to the state of nature in which there is "no known Superior on Earth" and "the appeal lies no where but to Heaven."[195]

But what constitutes a breach of trust warranting the "appeal to Heaven"? Given that the State has been created by the people for "the Preservation of their Properties," the trust is breached wherever property "is applied to other ends, and made use of to impoverish, harass, or subdue them to the Arbitrary and Irregular Commands of those that have [power]...."[196] Even the members of the "supreme authority"—the legislature—violate the trust and can be overthrown and replaced whenever they "endeavor to grasp themselves, or put into the hands of any other, an Absolute Power over the Lives, Liberties, and Estates of the People; By this breach of trust they *forfeit the power....*"[197]

What does this expansive standard for declaring the forfeiture of political power mean in practice? For Locke the classic example of intolerable "absolute power" is taxation without representation. While "Governments cannot be supported without great Charge, and 'tis fit every one who enjoys his share of the Protection should pay out of his Estate his proportion for the maintenance of it," nevertheless taxes must not be imposed without each individual's consent, "*i.e.*, the Consent of the Majority, giving it either by themselves, or their Representatives chosen by them. For if any one shall claim a *Power to lay* and levy *Taxes* on the People, by his

191. Jeffrey R. Collins, *The Allegiance of Thomas Hobbes* (Oxford: Oxford Univ. Press, 2005), 272.
192. Ibid., 152.
193. Ibid., 270.
194. Ibid., 158.
195. *TT*, II.242.
196. *TT*, II.201.
197. *TT*, II.222.

own Authority, and without such consent of the People, he thereby invades the *Fundamental Law of Property*, and subverts the end of Government."[198]

In other words, Locke declares that no king may impose any tax without the "consent" of fifty-percent-plus-one of his subjects, which means a vote of fifty-percent-plus-one of the "representatives," who in turn were elected by far less than fifty-percent-plus-one of the total population. Any king who taxes without this illusory "consent" of the whole people by a few legislators can not only be resisted in his imposition of the tax but overthrown as a tyrant—a doctrine that will be used to justify the American Revolution despite King George's repeal of the Stamp Act and the Townshend Acts in response to colonial protests. Conversely, of course, no one may resist a tax that has been imposed *with* representation by the "supreme authority" of the "supreme" legislature. Taxation *with* representation, at multiple levels of "government by consent of the governed," will be vastly more burdensome than the exactions of mere monarchs.

Aside from taxing without representation, what does Locke view as sufficient grounds for revolution? According to Locke, the people may revolt "[i]f they see several Experiments made of Arbitrary Power, and that Religion underhand favoured (though publickly proclaimed against) which is readiest to introduce it"[199]—a clear reference to the intolerable Catholicism of James II and the suspected Catholicism of Charles I. The American rebels would likewise cite the suspected "Popery" of George III among the grounds for revolution.

Moreover, for Locke *any* act of a ruler deemed unjust, "even a *single* violation of right,"[200] provides the revolutionary warrant. This is a far cry from St. Thomas's doctrine allowing for the overthrow of a true tyrant *if* he has been chosen by the people in the first place, and *if* what is involved is a threat to the common good as a totality. Departing even further from the political tradition of Christendom, Locke contends that even if "*no* transgression has been committed" revolution is warranted by a perceived "tyrannical *tendency* or design."[201] As Locke argues: "if a long Train of Actings show the Councils all tending that way, how can a Man any more hinder himself from being persuaded in his own Mind, which way things are going; or from casting about how to save himself. . . ."[202] Locke likens this revolutionary state of mind to the passenger on a ship who becomes convinced that the captain is ultimately heading for Algiers (the slave market for Christians captured by Muslims), even if the course is not always in that direction.[203] The American Revolutionaries would develop precisely this sort of Lockean justification for their own rebellion. The Declaration of Independence, which complained that "a long train of abuses and usurpations, pursuing invariably the same Object evinces a design to reduce them under absolute Despotism," is practically a verbatim borrowing from

198. *TT*, II.140.
199. *TT*, II.210.
200. *Cambridge History of Political Thought*, 637.
201. Ibid.
202. *TT*, II.210.
203. Ibid.

the *Second Treatise*: "A long train of Abuses, Prevarications and Artifices, all tending the same way, make the design visible to the people. . . ."[204]

But who determines when an actionable violation of the ruler's trust or a tyrannical "tendency" or "design" warranting his deposition has occurred? "The people shall be judge," says Locke.[205] And how many of the people are sufficient to judge the matter? "The body of the people," says Locke.[206] And how many are sufficient to constitute "the body of the people"? In the end he admits that where the decision to engage in revolution is concerned, "any single man"[207] can judge. Locke asks: "Who shall be Judge whether the Prince or the Legislative act contrary to their Trust?" And Locke answers: "But *every man is Judge* for himself, as in all other cases, so in this. . . ."[208] And "where the body of the people, *or any single man*, is deprived of their right . . . and have no Appeal on Earth, there they have a liberty to appeal to Heaven, whenever they judge the cause of sufficient moment."[209] Accordingly, "the injured party must judge for himself, when he will think fit to make use of that Appeal and put himself upon it."[210] Here we arrive at something even worse than what St. Thomas and the Christian tradition condemn: sedition not only by any "crowd of persons" who deem themselves aggrieved, but even by one grievant.

Thus the Protestant principle of private judgment, which Locke has applied to the validity of human knowledge and the source of sovereignty, is also applied to the justification for rebellion against the sovereign. The individual "appeals to Heaven" and, not surprisingly, does not fail to receive the answer he wishes to hear. It is the same answer the Cromwellians claimed to hear when, for the first time in human history, a group of subjects appointed themselves a tribunal to try their own king for "treason" and sentence him to death; and it is the same answer Locke's fellow travelers heard when they conspired against Charles II and overthrew James II. As Tarcov remarks, on this point Locke slyly subverts the meaning of Scripture, which "restricted the appeal to heaven of the governed to mere prayer" and enjoined upon the Christian "precisely that the subject should *not* take arms against the ruler."[211]

Locke never adequately addressed the patent injustice of his novel doctrine: What if the appellants to heaven arrive at a conclusion not shared by the majority, even the overwhelming majority, of the body politic? What if the majority has no desire at all to overthrow or assassinate the ruler and is in fact willing to put up with the status quo, perceiving no "long train of Abuses, Prevarications and Artifices, all tending the same way" but rather only a sovereign no better or worse than can be expected in a fallen world? Locke's various assurances that revolutions will

204. *TT*, II.225.
205. *TT*, II.240.
206. Ibid.
207. *TT*, II.168.
208. Ibid.
209. Ibid.
210. *TT*, II.242.
211. Tarcov, *Locke's Education for Liberty*, 66.

happen only when "the people are made miserable"[212] merely begs the question: Who are "the people" and by what right do they judge the matter and carry out the deposition of a ruler? The entire Western world will learn, as England had learned from the execution of Charles, the Monmouth Rebellion and "the Glorious Revolution," that "the people" means rump parliaments, revolutionary "committees," "congresses" and "estates" that will seize power by force only to impose a government far more oppressive than the purported tyrant overthrown in the name of Liberty.

It was Locke, then, who first systematically advocated the idea that Liberty depends on a state of "self-governing rebellion" and that "only the actual *practice* of revolution is sufficient to free a people from oppression."[213] The forces of Liberty will follow Locke's teaching (and his own example in the Rye House conspiracy) by freeing the West from "oppression" under the banner of "the will of the people." Locke's doctrine of an "appeal to Heaven" for the revolutionary warrant is a prescription for the age of revolution that will follow, including the American Revolution and the Civil War, depicted by the Southern states as the second American Revolution, whose outcome, as we will see in Chapters 15 to 17, would be an even more powerful central government than that which arose after the first revolution. Lockean revolution will be the trapdoor in the social compact through which the West will fall into the perpetual embrace of an ever more powerful secular nation-state, against which no further rebellion will be possible as the trapdoor swings only downward, and only once.

A further act of intellectual deconstruction was needed, however, to insure that Liberty would remain unchallenged in the "clean swept house" of a post-Christian West. Not only would the "spirit of Rome" have to be exorcised from the new political order, but so also would the very idea of a spiritual authority on earth, for by its nature the Hobbelockean sovereign must have no rival. Like civil society, therefore, religion itself would have to undergo conversion into a contractual association of self-interested individuals subordinated to state power. Hobbes and Locke both set themselves to a task in theory that the American revolutionaries would accomplish in practice.

"Reasonable" Christianity

The process by which liberalism proposes the exclusive cure for the disorders liberalism causes is nowhere more apparent than in the approach of both Hobbes and Locke to the place of religion in the new kind of polity they first imagined and which has since become in practice the modern pluralist and secular state. The Hobbelockean approach to the question was a response to the social chaos Protestant factionalism had provoked in England. In *Leviathan*, published two years after the execution of Charles I, Hobbes declares that his treatise was "occasioned by the

---

212. Cf. *TT*, II.207, 208–209, 223–226.
213. *Cambridge History of Political Thought*, 648.

disorders of the present time...."[214] Some seven years after the restoration of the Stuart monarchy and the posthumous trial and beheading of Cromwell, Locke's *Essay on Toleration* (1667) refers to the problem of "how it comes to pass that Christian religion hath made more factions, wars and disturbances in civil societies than any other...."[215]

It was not, of course, "the Christian religion" that had caused unprecedented faction, war and disturbance in Reformation and post-Reformation England, but rather the internecine political conflicts among Protestant sects. By the 1640s, when Locke was a young lad and Hobbes a middle-aged man, the "godly reformation" of the Henrican rebellion had given way to demands for the "thorough godly reformation" of Cromwell and the Puritan fanatics, who had rebelled against the original rebels. By the 1660s England was in the midst of a long battle for political supremacy among the deposed and then restored Anglican hierarchs, the ascendant and then ousted Presbyterians, and the various sects among those described as Dissenters, Independents and Separatists, especially the Puritans, whose reign under Cromwell was remembered with horror by the common people. [216]

The solution arrived at by both Hobbes and Locke is, quite simply, to subordinate religion to the power of the State and thereby eliminate the political effects of the endless religious disagreements inherent to Protestantism. To reach this result it was necessary for Hobbes and Locke alike to deny the Church-State dualism of the Greco-Catholic tradition discussed in Chapter 1. In the Hobbelockean view there are not two powers on earth, the temporal and the spiritual, each operating within its own sphere but with the former subject to the latter where the jurisdictions of the two powers overlap. For Hobbes and Locke there is no Church with an Ambrose who can excommunicate an emperor Theodosius to punish a brutal abuse of power, thus bringing an errant sovereign to repentance. Hobbes, in fact, declares that "if it were true" that Ambrose excommunicated Theodosius, the excommunication was "a Capitall Crime"[217]—a judgment he conspicuously fails to levy against Cromwell and his collaborators in the outright murder of Charles I.

Hobbes and Locke did not merely seek to separate Church and State, but rather to *subjugate* the Church *to* the State by stripping the Church of any direct or indirect power over politics, reducing churches to the status of private clubs whose authority is strictly limited to enforcing club rules against their respective members. While the two thinkers take differing paths to the negation of the traditional dualism and the complete subordination of the spiritual to the temporal power, they arrive at exactly the same destination—the destination at which Western man resides today.

---

214. *Leviathan*, Conclusion and Review.

215. *Essay on Toleration*, 156–157, 159, in *Locke: Political Essays*.

216. For a comprehensive summary of the complex legal history of the various religious settlements in post-Henrican England leading to the emigration of the Dissenters and the founding of America, see Newsom, *The American Protestant Empire: A Historical Perspective*, 40 Washburn Law Journal (2004), 187 ff.

217. *Leviathan*, III.42.

As Jeffrey Collins has noted, Hobbes was "part of the first generation of English-men raised in an entirely Protestant intellectual environment." Hobbes's youthful formation took place "in a hothouse era for the production of anti-Catholic polemic" in response to such earlier giants of the Catholic Counter-Reformation as Bellarmine and Suarez, who "composed ringing endorsements of transnational papal power that relied on a Thomistic understanding of the Church"[218]—that is, on the millennial Greco-Catholic tradition of the organic relation between Church and State and the duty of the State to profess and defend the true religion.

Hobbes's minimalist Christianity is a reflection of his theory of knowledge, his materialism, and his rejection of the entire Aristotelian-Thomistic system of meta-physics, politics and ethics we have already sketched. He had nothing but contempt for what he regarded as Roman superstitions concerning the realm of the spirit, immaterial substances, doctrines, dogmas and rituals. He rejected the Holy Trinity and replaced it with a Trinity of "personators": Moses, Jesus and the "Spirit" in the sense of an "apostolic succession" of earthly kings.[219] He was "exceptionally reticent on the matter of Christ's divinity and resurrection."[220] His reduction of the Chris-tian religion to the lone article of faith that "Jesus is the Christ"[221]—whatever Hob-bes meant by this—was seen even by Hobbes's Protestant contemporaries for what it was: the pursuit of "an anti-Christian philosophy beneath insincere ('game-some') professions of Christianity."[222] Hobbes's theology, such as it is, is "marked by a rejection of revelation that dramatically alienated him from the Christian theological tradition...."[223] After the restoration of Charles II, Hobbes's Anglican critics "exposed Hobbes's hostility to Christianity with a decisive thoroughness."[224]

In an ironically Catholic way, however, Hobbes at least recognized the necessity of a religious authority of last resort to put an end to the bickering of the sects, and so did his Protestant contemporaries. During the Interregnum between the execu-tion of Charles and the restoration of the monarchy, a group of members of Parlia-ment submitted their *Humble Petition* to Lieutenant-General Cromwell, requesting "His Highness the Lord Protector" declare that "the true Protestant Christian reli-gion, as it is contained in the Holy Scriptures of the Old and New Testament, and no other, be held forth and asserted for the public profession of these nations...." This "true Protestant Christian religion" would be determined by "a Confession of Faith, to be agreed by your Highness and the Parliament . . . and recommended to the people of these nations, that none may be suffered or permitted, by opprobri-ous words or writing . . . to revile or reproach the Confession of Faith to be agreed upon as aforesaid...."[225]

218. Collins, *The Allegiance of Thomas Hobbes*, 21, 23.
219. Ibid., 32, and sections of *Leviathan* cited.
220. Ibid.
221. *Leviathan*, III.43.
222. Collins, op. cit., 256.
223. Ibid., 29.
224. Ibid., 241.
225. *Humble Petition and Advice* (1657), Article 11.

That the people of England had been reduced to petitioning a regicide general to define the articles of Christianity "as agreed" by Parliament did not, of course, suggest to Hobbes that perhaps the Catholics were right about the need for the Petrine office. Quite the contrary, in *Leviathan* Hobbes had already recommended precisely what the *Humble Petition* contemplated: that the political sovereign shall serve as the Protestant equivalent of a Pope. Hobbes's liberal prescription for liberal disorder arises from his belief that, given the fragmentation of religion inherent to Protestantism and the consequent emergence of sects contending for political power, "the only way of saving royal authority, and thus civil peace, was to detach completely the king's power from religion by making the king fully sovereign over it."[226]

As for the role of particular church bodies under the Hobbesian version of the papacy, a church is to be regarded as nothing more than "a Congregation or an assembly of Citizens, called forth to hear the Magistrate [i.e., the 'Pope'] speak unto them." As such, a church is a "company of men professing Christian religion, united in the person of one Sovereign; at whose command they ought to assemble, and without whose Authority they ought not to assemble."[227] The parallel between the unity of particular churches in the universal church under a Pope is unmistakable. Hobbes leaves no doubt of the parallel: "But if Pastors [of churches] not be subordinate to one another, so that there may be *one chief Pastor*, men will be taught contrary doctrines . . . Who that *one chief Pastor* is, according to the law of Nature, hath already been shown: that it is the Civil Sovereign."[228] In just such a way was the King of England made Pope of the Church of England after Henry's rebellion against the Pope of Rome.

As anti-Catholic as they themselves were, even Hobbes's Anglican and Presbyterian contemporaries denounced him for what Leibniz later called "the strange and indefensible claim that 'doctrines touching the divinity depend entirely upon the determination of the sovereign.'"[229] Anglicans and Presbyterians alike defended against "Hobbesism" the sovereignty of the Church as against the State. Implicit in Hobbes's doctrine, with its acceptance of the earlier "Cromwellian captivity" of the Church, was a denial of both supernatural revelation and Christ's divinity itself. Hobbes, like Machiavelli, sought to "instrumentalize" Christianity for service to the State, preserving "the appearance of Christianity" in what was really "an insincere effort to cloak an anti-Christian philosophy."[230]

Having abandoned his earlier adoption of Hobbes's Prince-as-Pope solution, Locke arrived far more circuitously at the goal of state subordination of religion. He had no more use for the doctrines, dogmas and rituals of traditional Christianity than Hobbes did; the two thinkers were in complete agreement on the uselessness of the priesthood, sacraments and catechisms, be they Catholic, Anglican or

---

226. Manent, *An Intellectual History of Liberalism*, 21.
227. *Leviathan*, II.39.
228. Ibid.
229. *Cambridge History of Political Thought*, 613.
230. Collins, *The Allegiance of Thomas Hobbes*, 269, 270.

Presbyterian. As Jonathan Israel points out, Locke, Jean Le Clerc (1585–1633) and Philip van Limborch (1633–1712), whom he met while in exile in Holland, formed a European triumvirate of "reasonable" Christians who "dismissed ecclesiastical authority, as well as tradition and untested dogma, as irrelevant and useless, indeed positively harmful to the Christian cause."[231]

Locke's *Reasonableness of Christianity* (1695) is a veritable charter for the rationalist reduction (and ultimate evaporation) of traditional Christianity that will characterize the entire Enlightenment epoch. For Locke—in an exact reversal of the Greco-Catholic tradition—faith must submit to the judgment of reason based on the private judgment of the reasoner that some proposed article of faith is irrational: "*Reason* must be our last Judge and Guide in every thing," including whether a proposition "be a *Revelation* from God or no [emphasis in original]. . . ."[232] For Locke, Revelation is merely "natural reason enlarged by a new set of discoveries, communicated by God immediately, which reason vouches the truth of, by the testimony and proofs it gives, that they come from God."[233] The proof of revelation is miracles, but miracles are to be judged by reason, which must determine whether a claimed miracle really transcends the laws of nature. Yet, says Locke, "every one being able to judge of those laws only by his own acquaintance with Nature; and notions of its force (which are different in different men) it is unavoidable *that that should be a miracle to one, which is not so to another.*"[234]

Locke thus relativizes his own rational proof of miracles, which in turn are the rational basis on which he would vouch for the truth of any proposed mystery of the Faith. How, then, would he vouch for the miracles performed by Christ and the Apostles? In *Reasonableness* he simply "abandons the project of rationally demonstrating the truly supernatural or miraculous character of the miracles claimed in the New Testament. He excuses himself with the almost shockingly tongue-in-cheek claim to the effect that, since no one ever denied these miracles, they need no further demonstration."[235] Locke thus runs away from the conundrum he himself creates—a conundrum arising from his typically Protestant rejection of the judgment of any ecclesiastical authority commissioned by Christ precisely to verify the authenticity of miracles as well as to resolve disputes of doctrine. Yet he implicitly accepts the judgment of the Church without ever acknowledging it.

Not for Locke were the "Priests [who] everywhere, to secure their Empire, having excluded *Reason* [Locke's emphasis] from having anything to do with religion" produced "a crowd of wrong notions, and invented Rites" so that "the World had almost lost the sight of the One and only true God."[236] With the same supreme confidence in his own powers that led him to declare all philosophy prior to his to

231. Israel, *Radical Enlightenment*, 467.
232. *ECHU*, IV.19.14.
233. *ECHU*, IV.19.4.
234. *A Discourse of Miracles*, in *The Reasonableness of Christianity*, ed. I. T. Ramsey (Stanford, CA: Stanford Univ. Press, 1958), 80.
235. Pangle, *The Spirit of Modern Republicanism*, 201.
236. *Reasonableness* (Stanford Univ. edition), 57.

have begun at "the wrong end," Locke confided to Limborch that "in considering diligently wherein the Christian faith consists, I thought that it ought to be drawn from the very foundations of Holy Writ, the opinions and orthodoxies of sects and systems, whatever they may be, being set aside."[237] Locke's resulting "reasonable Christianity" has no more doctrinal content than the Hobbesian version. He insisted that revelation supported only the one doctrine that he (like Hobbes) deemed necessary to salvation: "that Jesus was the Messiah."[238] But he could not disguise the reality that his notion of the Messiah (like Hobbes's) was radically at odds with the traditional Christian belief in Christ as God Incarnate, the Second Person of the Holy Trinity, whose existence he classified a "speculative opinion."

Locke's Christ does not rescue man from the bondage of Original Sin by an atoning sacrifice without which human redemption and transformation in grace is not possible. For that view of Christ is incompatible with Locke's politics and his epistemological skepticism. Locke's version of the Messiah merely recovers for man the bodily immortality he lost in the Garden of Eden: "Adam being thus turned out of paradise, and all his posterity born out of it, the consequence was that all men should die.... Whereby it appears that the Life, which Jesus Christ restores to all men, is that life which they receive again at the Resurrection."[239] In describing what exactly Christ did that makes Him the Messiah, Locke ignores the Crucifixion and Atonement and specifies nothing beyond a deepening, reaffirmation and universal promulgation of what Moses had already made known to his people: "the profession of one God" as taught by "Moses and the Patriarchs" (with no mention of the Trinity or Christ's divinity), "moral rules," the "encouragement ... to virtuous and pious life," and the "future state" of happiness for those who live rightly.[240] Locke's Messiah also came to mandate Calvinistic liturgical reform by the elimination of "splendor and distinction of habits ... pomp and ceremonies, and all outside performances" from divine worship.[241]

Reasonableness, while filled with pious references to "Our Lord" and "Our Saviour," is a prime example of how throughout his *oeuvre* Locke "leaves one trail for the skeptical and another for the pious, the latter more plainly marked but leading in circles so that eventually the pious will have to follow the skeptics' trail if they wish to get anywhere."[242] But Locke's contemporary Anglican critics were not fooled, and Locke was widely accused of advancing not only latitudinarian but proto-deist, Socinian views. The Socinians were a sect of anti-Trinitarians founded by Faustus Socinius (Sozzini) in post-Reformation Italy. The Socinian creed is best summed up in the so-called Racovian Catechism (1609), named after the city of Rakow in Poland, where Socinius emigrated in the hope of finding greater tolera-

---

237. Locke, *Correspondence*, 4:1901, quoted in Parker, *The Biblical Politics of John Locke*, 31.
238. Locke, *Reasonableness*, 34.
239. Ibid., 28.
240. Ibid., 58, 61, 68, 69.
241. Ibid., 68.
242. Harvey C. Mansfield, "On the Political Character of Property in Locke," quoted in Pangle, *The Spirit of Modern Republicanism*, 164.

tion for his heterodoxy. The Racovian Catechism rejects not only the Trinity, but Original Sin, the eternal punishment of the damned and the Atonement of Christ. Responding to the charge by John Edwards that he was a Racovian—i.e., a follower of the Racovian Catechism and thus a Socinian—Locke, in *A Vindication of the Reasonableness of Christianity* (1695), all but admitted that he denied Christ's divinity and that he placed Him on a par with Adam:

> I expound he [Edwards] says after the antitrinitarian mode, and I make "Christ and Adam to be Sons of God, in the same sense, and by their Birth, as the Racovians generally do." I know not but it may be true, that *the Antitrinitarians and Racovians understand those places as I do*: But 'tis more than I know that they do so. I took not those Texts from those Writers, but from the Scripture it self, giving Light to its own meaning, by one place compared with another: What in this way appears to me its true meaning, I shall not decline, because I am told, that it is so understood by the Racovians, whom I never yet read.[243]

Parker remarks that Locke's claim not to be influenced by Socinian writings "is certainly a prevarication on Locke's part, for by the 1680s his notebooks contain numerous references to Socinian authors and ideas."[244] The myth of Locke the pious and orthodox Christian (like that of the Christian Founders of the United States) has been laid to rest by honest scholarship. Indeed, by the end of his life Locke "probably embraced Unitarianism because he could not find the doctrine of the Trinity in Scripture...."[245] His reductionist Christianity, in keeping with his epistemological skepticism and thinly concealed radical Whig political theory, had already transformed the text of the Bible "into a document of liberation and a license for resistance to all forms of coercive rule in the century after his death."[246]

When all is said and done, Locke's "reasonable Christianity" effectively dispenses with Christian doctrine beyond moral counsel and the lone article of belief that "Christ was the Messiah" as Locke understands the term, the latter being, according to Locke, "the sole doctrine" that Christ and the Apostles "pressed and required to be believed...."[247] Everything else presented to men as Christian teaching arises from "the makers of systems and their followers," who "invent and use what distinctions they please."[248] Locke even declares that the Epistles contain nothing necessary for salvation, although one should receive whatever he is convinced pertains to revelation therein according to his own reasonable interpretation of the text.[249] He thus begins a major work of the Enlightenment army: the instrumentalization of religion via its reduction to a socially useful code of good behavior, a theme that

---

243. In *John Locke: Writings on Religion*, Victor Nuovo contrib. (Oxford: Oxford Univ. Press, 2002), 219.

244. Parker, *The Biblical Politics of John Locke*, 33.

245. Spellman, *John Locke*, 77.

246. Ibid., 78.

247. *Reasonableness*, 43.

248. Ibid.

249. Ibid., 74–75.

will be repeated again and again by Enlightenment divines from Spinoza to Rousseau to Voltaire and to the American Founders, including Franklin, Jefferson and Washington. The net result is Deism.

Commenting on the emergence of Deism as a discrete religious system immediately following the appearance of *Reasonableness*, Fabro describes its function as a libertarian form of religion:

> [I]f man is capable of fashioning for himself or even if he finds within himself a natural religion and ethic, what need is there of revealed religion, especially when this religion [Christianity] stands accused of being full of incomprehensible dogmatic formularies which divide men among themselves? And if the best way to honor God is to practice morality in every day life, of what use are the complicated religious observances and hair-splitting casuistry of positive moral theology. . . . And so the Deist principle, which gave the impression of stretching a rainbow of peace over 17th-century Europe lacerated by the wars of religion, proves in fact to have loosed the hurricane that tore up religion by the roots and prepared the way for the atheism of the 18th-century Enlightenment.[250]

While it cannot be said that Locke himself was a Deist *simpliciter*, his effective reduction of Christ to the status of a most exalted prophet supports Fabro's assessment.[251] One could also call Locke's religion "Christian Deism," according to which Christ came to earth to reveal important information and then departed, never to be seen or heard from again. The Christ of "Christian Deism" founded no Church, revealed no Trinitarian mysteries, established no system of sacraments, has no Vicar who speaks in His name and by His authority, and no longer intervenes in human history. His word can be found only on the pages of a book open to rationalist interpretations, including those of Locke himself. In Locke's religious thought, as well as in that of Hobbes, we can see that "scarcely a century after the Reformation, which had proclaimed the superiority of the Bible over the authoritative Magisterium of the Church in matters of faith, the situation had turned upside down with reason assuming complete ascendancy over faith and philosophy over religion."[252]

As Locke would have it, a faith subordinated to reason would somehow consist of more than what the rationalism of the Deists would allow while drastically less than what was affirmed by Catholics, High Church Anglicans or even Presbyterians.[253] But it was a very short step from Locke's "reasonable" version of Christianity to the "providential Deism" of the Newtonian system, wherein a radically depersonalized God maintains the operation of the universe as a continuing act of will for the good of man. From there it was but another short step to the "non-providential" Deism

---

250. Fabro, *God in Exile*, 235.

251. Ibid., 274.

252. Ibid., 234.

253. Concerning Locke's difficulties in this regard see Samuel C. Pearson, Jr., "The Religion of John Locke," *The Journal of Religion*, Vol. 58, No. 3 (July 1978), 244–262.

that spread throughout Europe in Locke's wake, according to which an impersonal deity set the clockwork of the universe in motion and then withdrew entirely from human affairs. The next step, of course, was frank atheism. Locke's work was recognized early on as the start of this spiritual declivity. Writing in 1753, the American theologian Dr. Samuel Johnson of Kings College lamented "the gradual but deplorable progress of infidelity and apostasy in this age of mighty pretenses and reasoning from the well-meaning but too-conceited Mr. Locke, down to Tindal and thence to Bolingbroke, etc., etc."[254]

In fact, only one year after *Reasonableness* was published (anonymously, of course), John Toland, a self-proclaimed disciple of Locke, sallied into print with his *Christianity Not Mysterious*. In this work Toland carried "reasonable Christianity" to the inevitable next step, arguing that not only the "ridiculous fables of the Church of Rome" ought to be discarded but also miracles and the entire corpus of Trinitarian theology. This would leave intact only what Peter Gay, the great historian of the Enlightenment, calls "the primitive—and largely imaginary—teaching of the man Jesus." As Gay concludes: "[I]n that single amendment the essence of revealed, dogmatic religion evaporated."[255] This evaporation of revealed, dogmatic religion would be nowhere more apparent than in the deism of the Founding Fathers of the American Republic, especially that most devoted student of Locke's thought, Thomas Jefferson, who would allow that Jesus was a great man and moral teacher whose "true" teaching had been obscured by the superstitions of the New Testament, which Jefferson removed from his famous expurgated version of the Bible. Jefferson would confidently predict that the American Revolution, the world's first great experiment in Lockean liberalism, would produce a nation full of enlightened Unitarians.

The "Law" of Toleration

As we have already seen, according to Locke's theory of knowledge, his metaphysics and his politics—which produce outcomes substantially the same as in the Hobbesian system—life in society is a contractualized arrangement between individuals in their autonomous subjectivity, and the role of the State is limited to providing security for life and property. It remained for Locke to fit religion into this scheme, a task he attempted in *Two Tracts on Government* (1660–62), his *Essay on Toleration* (1667) and his *Letter Concerning Toleration* (1689), the latter representing Locke's full-blown doctrine on the place of religion in the State.

Given his system as a whole, for Locke, just as for Hobbes, the specifics of Christian doctrine were a problem to be managed, not a creed to be accepted on faith. "Locke understood that the problem of religion is the *first* problem of political

---

254. Quoted in Theodore Hornberger, "Samuel Johnson of Yale and King's College," *The New England Quarterly*, Vol. 8, No. 3 (Sep., 1935), 386.

255. Gay, *The Enlightenment: The Rise of Modern Paganism*, 327, 377.

theory and practice."[256] Just as Hobbes did, Locke—like Rousseau after him—viewed any church claiming divinely endowed authority as a threat to the good order of society, precisely because such a church poses a challenge to the exclusivity of sovereign power. Thus, after the Catholic Church, Locke saw the Church of England as the greatest threat of all: "The greatest threat to peace according to Locke comes not from the Dissenters but from the Church of England. The monarch must be absolute in order to be free of the national church, which will otherwise use the state to impose uniformity and gain power.... Throughout his writing Locke consistently attacks the Anglican Church as the greatest threat to peace and calls for its disestablishment."[257]

In his *Essay* and subsequent *Letter* concerning toleration, Locke prescribes his liberal cure for the liberal disease of faction: separation of Church and State, a State policy of religious indifferentism, and the mandatory preaching of tolerance by every religion. In the *Essay* Locke enunciates what purports to be a rational argument for religious "neutrality" that, far from being neutral respecting Christianity, "altered the traditional Christian teaching on almost every crucial issue, including the nature of the church, the relationship of grace and nature, the purpose and nature of Christ, the relationship of doctrine and ethics, and the Christian teaching on the freedom of human will and conscience."[258] The *Essay* states that its purpose is nothing less than to explain "the bounds *that God hath set* to the power of the magistrate and the obedience of the subject...."[259] That is, Locke is not merely presenting a case for the prudential toleration of religious error, but rather what he opines is revealed truth on the matter. In the *Letter* Locke will amplify his theological judgments to include his notion of the very nature of the Church and true religion.

Echoing the *Second Treatise*, the *Essay* declares that polities are created by the social contract "only to preserve men in *this world* from the fraud and violence of one another."[260] The duty of the magistrate is limited to "promoting the general welfare, which consists in riches and power" as determined by "the number and industry of your subjects."[261] In Locke's political philosophy the traditional notion of the common good as embracing both the temporal and spiritual welfare of all the subjects of the State is replaced by security for commercial activity and the peaceable possession of property. Hence the magistrate "ought to do or to meddle with nothing but *barely in order to secure the civil peace* and propriety [property] of his subjects."[262] As far as religion is concerned, the magistrate must exercise "an absolute and universal right of toleration,"[263] and there must be "a perfect, uncon-

256. Craycraft, *The American Myth of Religious Freedom* (Dallas: Spence Publishing Co., 1999), 35.
257. *Cambridge History of Political Thought*, 645.
258. Craycraft, op. cit., 37–8.
259. *Essay on Toleration*, 150 (all citations to *Locke: Political Essays*).
260. Ibid., 135.
261. Ibid., 151.
262. Ibid., 136.
263. Ibid.

trollable liberty"[264] as to "speculative opinions and divine worship," including such matters as "the belief of the Trinity," as well as "the place, time and manner of worshipping my God."[265]

In the *Essay* Locke frames his argument for "an absolute and universal right of toleration" and a "perfect, uncontrollable liberty" in matters religious in the same tendentious way that every liberal since has framed it: as an argument against the coercion of religious belief by State power. God, says Locke, would not "have men forced to heaven," nor should "men give the magistrate a power to choose for them their way of salvation."[266] Of course, that is not the issue. Locke cannot have failed to understand that the tradition had never sanctioned the use of the civil power to compel belief in Christianity, but rather to *protect the faith of those who already possess it* by deterring or punishing public attacks on religion and morality that threaten the common good. Hence the same Saint Augustine who declared: "Man cannot believe otherwise than of his own will," also defended the legal punishment of the Donatists on the grounds that "if we were to overlook and forebear these cruel enemies who disturb our peace and quietness . . . we would be rendering evil for evil."[267] Furthermore, as Augustine observed, in many cases the legal penalties for heresy have the effect, not of compelling a mere outward assent that would violate conscience, but rather of provoking true repentance and conversion in those who have "been shaken up in a beneficial way" by their encounter with the law. And if this is not always the case, "Is the art of healing therefore to be abandoned, because the malady of some is incurable?"[268]

Enlightenment polemics for "absolute" religious toleration, including the polemics of the American Founders, all rely upon this Lockean straw man argument. And today, the same liberals who professes horror at any attempt to regulate the public dissemination of religious error—even public calls to worship Satan—will think nothing of fining or imprisoning the false advertisers of condominium timeshares or miracle cures. When it comes to the integrity of mere commercial transactions, the Lockean mind has no trouble discerning both the protective and medicinal aspects of the penal law. But as to religious falsehoods that can have eternal consequences for those who are taken in by them (not to mention drastic temporal consequences where morality is destroyed), Locke and his intellectual descendants illogically insist that the law must offer no protection whatsoever to potential victims, nor any opportunity for the perpetrators to reconsider their conduct under the coercion or deterrence of legal penalties.

This position is defensible only if it is assumed that heresy involves no risk of damnation or even temporal harm, and that indeed is the theological premise on which the liberal argument *must* rest if it is to be taken as anything more than a

264. Ibid., 140.
265. Ibid., 136–137.
266. Ibid., 138.
267. Epistle 93, Ch. 1.
268. Ibid.

mere prejudice against punishment of a certain of type of public offense. Not even a professed uncertainty about damnation would require, as a matter of principle, that no state employ coercion to prevent the diffusion of religious error, any more than uncertainty about the likelihood of war would preclude a state from providing for the common defense. Moreover, if Christ Himself warns "he that believeth not shall be condemned,"[269] and if the worst imaginable form of coercion in matters of belief—the threat of eternal punishment in the fires of hell—is God's own way, on what ground does Locke stand besides an emotional reaction to the abuse of power by his fellow Protestants in turbulent post-Reformation England? In order to make his case, it was necessary for Locke to redefine Christianity itself so as to exclude the very idea of a heresy worthy of punishment—here or in the hereafter.

Locke did not limit his newly conceived right to toleration strictly to matters of religion. In the *Essay* we see in germinal form the modern regime of civil as well as religious liberty: freedom of speech, press and "personal" morality, limited only by the requirement that there be no public breach of the peace. As Locke declares: "*all practical principles, or opinions*" and the "*actions following from them* . . . with all other things indifferent, have a title also to toleration . . . so far as they do not tend to the disturbance of the state or do not cause greater inconveniences than advantages to the community."[270] Among these "indifferent" matters of opinion Locke conveniently includes the opinion "that polygamy and divorce are lawful or unlawful. . . ."[271] The formal collapse of public morality begins with Locke's idea of tolerance.

Locke goes even further toward establishing in theory the laissez-faire social order of the future under the cover of appearing to affirm what he is really denying. Referring to the second table of the Decalogue, Locke allows that the virtues enjoined by the second table are "the vigorous, active part of religion" and that "the countenancing of virtue is so necessary a prop to a state." But having affirmed, as does the tradition, that the maintenance of virtue is necessary to the State, Locke suddenly turns about to declare: "Yet give me leave to say, *however strange it may seem*, that *the lawmaker have nothing to do with moral virtues and vices*, nor ought to enjoin the duties of the second table any otherwise than barely as they are subservient to the good and preservation of mankind under government."[272] What does Locke mean by "the good and preservation of mankind under government"? He means that to the limited extent the magistrate enjoins the practice of virtue— "barely," is Locke's word—it is *not* because the virtues embraced by the second table "oblige the conscience, or are the duties of man to God and the way to his mercy and favour, but because they are the advantages of man with man. . . ."[273] That is, the only basis on which the law can enjoin the practice of virtue is *social utility*, the bare preservation of society, not the defense and inculcation of virtue as

269. Mark 16:16.
270. *Essay on Toleration*, 140.
271. Ibid.
272. Ibid., 144.
273. Ibid.

such. As Locke further declares: "The magistrate *as magistrate* hath *nothing to do with the good of souls* or their concernments in another life, but is ordained and entrusted with his power *only* for the quiet and comfortable living of men in society. . . ."[274]

Locke calls his own contention "strange" because he knows it represents a clean break with tradition, like his "strange Doctrine, that in the State of Nature, every one has the executive power of the law of nature. . . ."[275] As Saint Thomas teaches (referring back to Aristotle), virtue is the very end of human law, whereas the regulation of human behavior under law is oriented toward its end in virtue.[276] Law without virtue as its end is deprived of any objective moral foundation and becomes, as it does for Locke and as it will for Western democracy, a mere means of securing external peace and quiet. Under Locke's view of law, the way is open in principle to the toleration of any and all forms of "private" vice, no matter what their ultimate social effects, including abortion, so long as there is no outward breach of peace. Locke's "strange" idea is now part of the received tradition of liberal and libertarian thought, expressed as the bromide that the State must not "legislate morality"—a claim that is manifestly "both false and absurd."[277]

Locke goes still further, arguing that in certain cases the legislative will to tolerance *legitimately contravenes divine law* and that, moreover, *God accedes* to this contravention. This is so even as to the legislator's decision *not* to tolerate but rather positively to *prohibit* what God's law has ordained! By way of example, Locke cites English public law forbidding the giving of alms to beggars (one of the many "fruits" of early capitalism), enacted despite the divine precept requiring almsgiving, and then makes this astonishing pronouncement:

> God does sometimes (so much does he take care of the preservation of government) make his [sic] law in some degrees *submit and comply with man's law; his law forbids vice, but the law of man often makes the measure of it.* There have been commonwealths that have made *theft lawful* for such as were not caught in the fact. . . . This I only note by the by, to show how much the good of the commonwealth is the standard of all human laws, when it [sic] seems to limit *and alter the obligation of even some of the laws of God, and change the nature of vice and virtue.*[278]

Locke develops his doctrine of toleration far beyond the teaching of the Greco-Catholic tradition that the ruler ought not to prohibit all vices but only those whose practice impacts the common good defined to include both the temporal *and* spiritual welfare of subjects. According to Locke's principle that social utility, meaning the preservation of civil society, is the only basis for law, it is within a

274. Ibid.
275. *TT*, II.13.
276. *ST*, I–II, q. 100, a. 9, obj. 2; see Lawrence Dewan, O.P., "St. Thomas, John Finnis and the Political Good," *The Thomist* 64 (2000), 337–74.
277. John Rist, *Real Ethics* (Cambridge: Cambridge Univ. Press, 2002), 130.
278. *Essay on Toleration*, 145.

magistrate's power to alter the very nature of vice and virtue, even departing from divine law itself if he deems it necessary for "the good of the commonwealth."

Locke is thus ultimately no less a nominalist and positivist than Hobbes, even if, as always, he is more circumspect than the co-founder of "classical liberalism." No matter what he intended, on Locke's principles no less than on Hobbes's, nothing stands in the way of the eventual legalization of not only divorce, but open adultery, public blasphemy and lewdness, the sale of pornography and contraceptive devices, abortion, euthanasia, "gay marriage" and all the other forms of "consensual" and "private" conduct that modern liberals and libertarians alike place beyond the reach of the law because such conduct does not violate property rights or disturb a narrowly defined "public peace."

There are two major exceptions to Locke's regime of universal toleration as expounded in the *Essay*: "papists and fanatics"[279]—in other words, Catholics and Protestant sects which rejected Locke's "latitudinarian Anglicanism"[280] in favor of what he dismissed as "systems." As for the Catholics, the magistrate ought not to tolerate them because "they mix with their religious worship and speculative opinions *other doctrines absolutely destructive to the society wherein they live*, as is evident in the Roman Catholics that are subjects of any prince but the pope."[281] By "destructive" doctrines Locke means those aspects of Catholicism contemporary liberals deride as "triumphalism": the necessity of the Catholic Church for salvation; the universal jurisdiction and indirect temporal power of the papacy; the duty of the State to profess and defend the Catholic religion; the social reign of Christ the King by and through his Church and through social institutions, including governments, made conformable to the law of the Gospel as the teaching Church expounds it. Locke warns that Catholics, "blending such opinions with their religion, reverencing them as fundamental truths, and submitting to them as articles of the faith, ought not to be tolerated by the magistrate in the exercise of their religion, unless he can be secured that he can allow one part without the spreading of the other, and that these opinions will not be imbibed and espoused by all those who communicate with them in religious worship, which, I suppose, is very hard to be done."[282]

As Locke explains in the *Essay*, "papists" cannot be tolerated in this kind of society for the very reason that "where they have power, they think themselves bound to deny it to others . . ."[283] (as if Locke and his fellow proto-republicans would not do the same). Here Locke means that when Catholics are able to do so, they naturally establish a confessional state in keeping with the Greco-Catholic tradition on the nature of political society as a moral totality whose end, *contra* Locke, is not limited to temporalities. Moreover, Catholics are "irreconcilable enemies" of the

279. *Essay on Toleration*, 151.
280. Samuel C. Pearson, Jr., "The Religion of John Locke," *The Journal of Religion*, Vol. 58, No. 3 (July 1978), 245.
281. *Essay on Toleration*, 146.
282. Ibid., 146.
283. Ibid., 152.

Protestant sovereign, because "they owe a blind obedience to [an] infallible pope, who hath the keys of their consciences tied to his girdle, and can, upon occasion, dispense with all their oaths, promises and the obligations they have to their prince ... and arm them to their disturbance of the government...."[284] That is, Catholics will not follow laws and policies that contravene Church teaching. Nor are Catholics to be pitied if the magistrate represses their unacceptable beliefs, "because they receive no other usage than what the cruelty of their principles and practices are known to deserve."[285]

Thus, Catholics in the Lockean state are to be treated in the same manner as public heretics in the Catholic confessional state of millennial standing, and under the same rationale: obviating a threat to the common good (even if Locke defines the common good as mere peace and quiet under a regime of tolerance). That is, the magistrate will, to the extent necessary, suppress opinions that tend to undermine the common faith of the people. Locke preserves this obvious duty of the magistrate even as he radically alters its object. As Craycraft concludes: "Superficially, Locke argues that the state ought to be indifferent to religious opinion. But a closer reading of Locke's theory reveals a rather more sinister teaching; one that has particularly ominous implications for religious orthodoxy. For Locke, the rights of the state are not limited to mere regulation of behavior, *but rather extend to intolerance of certain kinds of opinions as well*, opinions which, not coincidentally, are most closely associated with what he called 'the Papists.' For Locke, the central [and] unifying myth of good, peaceful government is the myth of religious toleration, even if some intolerance has to be exercised to protect the regime of tolerance."[286]

Carrying his dogma of toleration to an astonishing extreme, Locke argues in one of the four manuscript versions of the *Essay* that it is the duty of the magistrate to prevent not only Catholics, *but any religious or social constituency at all*, from becoming so large a faction as to threaten a State happily divided into mutually tolerant and thus harmless groups of citizens. First Locke warns the magistrate to be on the alert whenever men "herd themselves into companies with distinctions from the public, and a stricter confederacy with those of their own denomination and party that other [of] their fellow citizens." But given that "the ties of religion are stronger, and the pretences [of religion] fairer and apter to draw partisans," religious factions that draw what Locke would consider to be too many adherents are "therefore the more suspected and the more heedfully to be watched." Locke recommends that when "any such distinct party is grown or growing so numerous as to appear dangerous to the magistrate and seem visibly to threaten the peace of the state, the magistrate may and ought to use all ways, either of policy or power, that shall be convenient, *to lessen, break and suppress the party*, and so prevent the mischief."[287] When the magistrate so acts, writes Locke, he is not punishing anyone for

---

284. Ibid.
285. *Essay on Toleration*, 152.
286. Craycraft, *The American Myth of Religious Freedom*, 22–3.
287. *Essay on Toleration*, 147.

his beliefs, but rather because "such a number, of any opinion whatsoever, who dissented would be dangerous."[288] While this "danger" is especially clear and present with religious factions—above all the dreaded Roman Catholic faction—Locke insists that it is also present in any faction that sets itself apart from the general public in *any* way, even by "any fashion of clothes," for "a lay cloak may have the same effect with an ecclesiastical cowl or any other religious habit." Indeed, he contends, the magistrate would have to suppress the Quakers simply for being too numerous "were they in no other way distinguished from the rest of his subjects but by the bare keeping on their hats, as much as if they had a set form of religion separate from the state. . . ."

In what appears to be the latest version of the manuscript of the *Essay*, however, Locke prudently deletes this outrageous explicit prescription for State-imposed social conformity and replaces it with a veiled prescription for the same thing, noting that by the very fact of the indifferent toleration of all factions and opinions—except, of course, "papists and fanatics"—the magistrate will be assured of public peace, because when religious sects are indifferently tolerated rather than drawn together by persecution, "they are apt to divide and subdivide into so many little bodies," which act as "a guard upon one another," that "the public can have no apprehension of them so long as they have their equal share of justice and protection."[289] In short, the Lockean strategy for the subjugation of religion by the State is to divide and conquer. But when that fails, outright persecution is always an option, and indeed a duty when it comes to "papists and fanatics." James Madison, "the Father of the Constitution," will make precisely the same divide-and-conquer argument in *The Federalist*, praising the "multiplicity of sects" as a guarantor of social tranquility.

To this day modern pluralist regimes retain in their genetic structure, as it were, the fundamental Lockean theological principle that traditional Roman Catholicism is "the common enemy" of all right-thinking non-Catholic factions, and that, therefore, anti-Catholicism, as the contemporary saying goes, is "the last respectable prejudice."[290] Indeed, anti-Catholicism will be "the deepest bias in the history of the American people," as Arthur Schlesinger observed.[291] Liberty continues to be, as it was from the beginning, a mode of political society that depends for its very existence on keeping the Catholics down; for it is only among the Catholic constituency that there exists, even today, a potentially significant number of people willing to dissent from the Lockean dogma that religion is a matter of personal opinion which must have no bearing on the conduct of politics. Catholicism is the one remaining major constituency still perceived as capable of becoming the sort of faction our Lockean polities cannot tolerate.

Locke's theology of the State is fully developed in the *Letter Concerning Toleration*, which Locke wrote during his exile in Holland, the land of refuge for Conti-

288. Ibid.
289. *Essay on Toleration*, 149.
290. Kenneth L. Woodward, "The Last Respectable Prejudice," *First Things* (October 2002).
291. In Philip Jenkins, *The New Anti-Catholicism* (Oxford: Oxford Univ. Press, 2003), 23.

nental and English radicals of his day. Going beyond the *Essay*, in the *Letter* Locke enunciates a revolutionary theory whose effect, as Craycraft recognizes, "is to establish a particular set of religious opinions as the only acceptable ones in a liberal regime...."[292] Under the guise of an argument for strict governmental neutrality in matters of religion, Locke actually elaborates what will become the common religion of the modern pluralist state, professed by everyone as a set of dogmas standing above the creeds of all particular religions, precisely as Locke hoped it would. As with his other novelties, Locke's anonymous pamphlet incurred the fierce opposition of his more conservative Protestant critics, one of whom characterized it as part of "a plot to bring ruin to church and state" and an exercise in "absurdity and impiety."[293]

In the *Letter* Locke lays down the separation of Church and State, declaring that he will "distinguish exactly the Business of Civil Government from that of Religion, and to settle *the just Bounds that lie between the one and the other*. If this be not done, there can be no end put to the controversies that will be always arising between those that have, or at least pretend to have, on the one side, a concernment for the interest of men's souls, and, on *the other side*, a care of the commonwealth."[294] Locke thus begins with a patently theological premise: that it is possible to draw a bright line between religion and government, with each to stay on its respective side of the line. Here too Locke has radically broken with the Western tradition, which views Church and State as two distinct spheres of influence which nonetheless overlap in many critical areas of social, political and economic life. Locke is in the act of artificially creating the new domain of the purely "secular" in which the dictates of religion will be suspended and such things as abortion on demand will become possible.

As he does in the *Essay* and the *Second Treatise*, Locke argues that political society is formed "*only* for the procuring, preserving, and advancing of their own civil interests ... life, liberty, health, and indolency of body; and the possession of outward things, such as money, lands, houses, furniture, and the like." The "*sole* reason" for entering into political society is "the *Temporal* Good and *outward* Prosperity of the Society...." All civil authority is "bounded and confined to the *only* care of promoting these things." The jurisdiction of the magistrate reaches "*only* to these civil concernments" and is "confined to the care of *the things of this World*, which have *nothing to do* with the world to come."[295] Accordingly, Locke concludes, civil authority is to have no concern whatsoever for the welfare of men's souls. The jurisdiction of the magistrate "neither can nor ought *in any manner* to be extended to the salvation of souls ... [the] care of souls cannot belong to the civil magistrate...." Furthermore, *no man* can be said to have care of the soul of another: "[T]he care of souls is not committed to the civil magistrate, *any more*

292. Craycraft, *The American Myth of Religious Freedom*, 37.

293. John Locke, *A Letter Concerning Toleration* (1689) (Indianapolis, IN: Hackett Publishing, 1983), ed. James H. Tully, introd., 1 (all citations to the *Letter* are to the page numbers of this edition).

294. *Letter*, 26.

295. *Letter*, 26, 28, 48.

than to other men.... The care of each man's soul and of the things of heaven, *which neither does belong to the commonwealth* nor can be subjected to it, *is left entirely to every man's self.*"[296]

With a few sentences Locke dispenses with the entire Greco-Catholic tradition of the cooperation between the two powers where their concerns for human welfare coincide—beginning, of course, with the State's favor, protection and defense of right religion through appropriate legislation. Locke's principles—first applied in America—will negate any possibility of a Christian state wherein political authority, within its sphere of competence, serves the Church's mission of human perfection and salvation. While Locke—ever the prudent one—dutifully utters the pious sentiment that "there is nothing in this world that is of any consideration in comparison with eternity,"[297] nevertheless the "practical upshot of his argument is that there is nothing in 'eternity' worthy of any consideration by government; on close inspection, Locke's elevation of religious affairs to another world may look like a relegation."[298] A relegation—an unprecedented relegation—is exactly what it is.

But what of the perennial role of the Church as the living conscience of the State and the soul of the body politic, which even his fellow Anglicans staunchly defended? In response to the tradition of Christendom, Locke offers only the relativism and skepticism of the latitudinarian Protestant. For Locke, *there is no true Church* to begin with, and thus no infallible guide to the civil authority in matters pertaining to the good of souls. From this theological premise it would follow, of course, that civil authority has no sound basis on which to act in any religious matter. But this premise—and with it Locke's entire argument in favor of an absolute religious tolerance—depends on the further premise that no church was founded by Christ and invested by Him with an infallible teaching authority, but rather that all churches are merely fallible human institutions created by human will alone. And that is precisely how Locke (like Hobbes) defines a church:

> Let us now consider what a church is. A church, then, I take to be a voluntary society of men, joining themselves together of their own accord in order to the public worshipping of God in such manner as they judge acceptable to Him, and effectual to the salvation of their souls.[299]

Locke thus introduces the notion of an ecclesial contract as an analogue to his social contract and his marital and familial contracts, reducing both Church and State to contractual associations in no sense ordained by God according to the ends of human nature. As Locke flatly declares: "*No man by nature* is bound unto any particular church or sect, but everyone joins himself voluntarily to that society in

---

296. *Letter*, 26, 27, 35, 48.
297. *Letter*, 47.
298. Ralph C. Hancock, "Religion and the Limits of Limited Government," *The Review of Politics*, Vol. 50, No. 4 (Autumn, 1988), 684.
299. *Letter*, 28.

which he believes he has found that profession and worship which is truly accept-able to God." In short, for Locke one church is as good as another, if one chooses to join any church at all. All churches are merely instruments to achieve whatever spiritual advantages the isolated individual deems necessary or desirable. As Cray-craft observes, "Like most everything else in Locke's philosophy, religion is reduced to a market commodity."[300]

In sum, under the cover of an argument for State neutrality in matters of reli-gion, Locke has issued a series of sweeping theological pronouncements that would commit Church and State alike to a latitudinarian Protestant view of religion that makes Martin Luther look like a hidebound traditionalist by comparison. Locke has founded his notion of the State on nothing other than his own religious convictions—convictions that are "deep, idiosyncratic, unsentimental, decidedly Protestant, and staunchly anti-Catholic."[301] Those same convictions will lie at the foundations of America's regime of "religious liberty," with its intrinsic hostility to the sociopolitical influence of the Catholic Church.

Only given the full development of his theological premises in the *Letter* is Locke now in a position to declare even more firmly than he did in the *Essay* that the civil authority *must* tolerate all churches and religionists, *and* that all churches and reli-gionists must tolerate each other. Both the function of the State and the function of the Church are to be altered according to the new dictate of Liberty. The policy of toleration Locke had privately recommended to Lord Shaftesbury in the *Essay* is now publicly (but still anonymously) presented in the *Letter* as "*the Law* of Tolera-tion"[302] and "the Duty of Toleration."[303] Locke insists that "*The establishment of this one thing* would take away all ground of complaints and tumults upon account of conscience; and ... there would remain nothing in these assemblies that were not more peaceable and *less apt to produce disturbance of state.* ..."[304] The Law of Toleration is, therefore, as binding on the Church as it is on the State. All churches must be "*obliged* to lay down toleration *as the foundation of their own liberty,* and teach that liberty of conscience is every man's natural right, equally belonging to dissenters as to themselves. ..."[305]

Locke the theologian further pontificates that "the mutual Toleration of Chris-tians in their different professions of Religion" is "the chief Characteristical Mark of *the True Church.*"[306] So there is, after all, a kind of "true church" for Locke: the Church of Toleration. According to Locke, the true Church is to be distin-guished from churches made up of people who "boast of the antiquity of places and names, or of the pomp of their outward worship; others, of the reformation of their discipline; all, of the orthodoxy of their faith—for everyone is orthodox to

300. Craycraft, *The American Myth of Religious Freedom,* 61.
301. Feser, *Locke,* 7.
302. *Letter,* 51.
303. Ibid., 33.
304. Ibid., 51.
305. Ibid.
306. Ibid., 23.

himself—these things, and all others of this nature, are much rather marks of men striving for power and empire over one another than of the Church of Christ."[307]

Where does the Catholic Church fit into a polity governed by the Law of Toleration? In the *Letter* Locke appears to soften his stand toward Catholics, but not really. Rather, his presentation of the intolerability of Roman Catholicism in the well-ordered State is simply more politic and indirect than in the privately circulated *Essay*. While allowing for the toleration of what he calls "speculative opinions" that pose no threat to the regime, such as the Catholic belief in Transubstantiation, he warns that "no opinions contrary to human society, or to those moral rules which are necessary to the preservation of civil society, are to be tolerated by the magistrate."[308] In particular, the magistrate must be ever-vigilant concerning the "secret evil" of certain sects which "arrogate to themselves, and to those of their own sect, some peculiar prerogative covered over with a specious show of deceitful words . . . attribute unto the faithful, religious, and orthodox, that is, in plain terms, unto themselves, any peculiar privilege or power above other mortals, in civil concernments; or who upon pretence of religion do challenge any manner of authority over such as are not associated with them in their ecclesiastical communion. . . ." Such sects intolerably "teach that *Faith is not to be kept with Hereticks*" and that "the privilege of breaking Faith belongs unto themselves: For they declare all that are not of their Communion to be Hereticks." Nor can the magistrate tolerate "those that *will not own and teach the duty of tolerating all men in matters of mere religion.*" Finally, Locke declares: "That Church can have no right to be tolerated by the magistrate [whose members] deliver themselves up to the protection and service of another prince. For by this means the magistrate would give way to the settling of a foreign jurisdiction in his own country. . . ."[309] There was exactly one Church fitting all these descriptions in Locke's England.

While the *Letter* also rejects toleration of atheists (for they cannot be relied upon to honor oaths), it calls not only for pan-Christian but also pan-religious toleration that extends to pagans.[310] Not even the practitioners of outright idolatry are to suffer civil disability on account of their religion, for the question of idolatry is relative, like everything else in Locke's theology except Locke's own opinions: "What power can be given to the magistrate for the suppression of an idolatrous Church, which may not in time and place be made use of to the ruin of an orthodox one?"[311]

As he does in the *Essay*, Locke extends his notion of toleration to essentially any and all opinions that do not actually threaten harm to public peace in the sense of the security of person and property, for "the business of laws is not to provide for the truth of opinions, but for the safety and security of the commonwealth and of every particular man's goods and person."[312] Laying down a dogma of liberalism that would echo throughout the age of democratic revolution, especially in the writings of Jefferson and Madison, Locke declared that "the truth certainly would

307. Ibid.
308. *Letter*, 49.
309. Ibid., 49–50.
310. Ibid., 54.
311. Ibid., 42.
312. Ibid., 46.

do well enough if she were once left to shift for herself. . . . She is not taught by laws, nor has she any need of force to procure her entrance into the minds of men." The idea that truth will prevail against error without the protection of law will be foundational to the coming "free speech" regimes that will inexorably banish religion from political discourse and enforce political correctness against contrary Christian claims on law and public policy.

In fulfillment of Locke's hope, "pulpits everywhere sounded with the doctrine of peace and toleration" following the revolutions whose leading lights were guided largely by Locke's principles. But, as we will see in our survey of the early history of the United States, the operation of the Law of Toleration and the concomitant separation of Church and State have been accompanied by a steady decline in the influence of religion on politics and the rise of governments whose power can no longer be checked by Christian morals. As Jeffrey Collins observes, the "rights-oriented (and thus 'pro-liberal') tradition of Hobbes and Locke" opposed the "Augustinian dualist model of the corporate church and the corporate commonwealth" wherein "the universal morality of Christianity was established outside and above secular standards and the sphere of political action. . . ." Hobbes and Locke, each in his own way, advocated "what might be called a new dualism: the dualism of public power and private religion. Once the church had been co-opted by the state and thus stripped of its capacity to harass the state's masters, religion could be released entirely into a confessional marketplace of free individuals. Politics then surrendered its semi-sacred status and developed more autonomous ideologies of self-justification (including the liberal conceit of the 'morally neutral' state)."[313]

Paradoxically but inevitably, therefore, "[i]ndividualization—the atomizing of society—and state centralization thus worked together."[314] Or, as Peter Gay has suggested in his study of the Enlightenment as "the rise of modern paganism": "political absolutism and religious toleration [are] the improbable twins of the modern state system. . . ."[315] Not so improbable, after all, as we shall see in the following pages. We live in the Hobbelockean world of the massive secular state whose hegemony depends precisely on the political subordination of Christianity via its reduction to a matter of private opinion. But before we arrive at that civilizational turning point, we must first take note of the spread of the new gospel that preceded it.

313. Collins, *The Allegiance of Thomas Hobbes*, 278–280.

314. Ibid., 280.

315. Gay, *The Enlightenment: The Rise of Modern Paganism*, 298–99. Gay contends that this paradox first presents itself in the writings of Jean Bodin, a 16th-century French lawyer and early proponent of religious toleration and an end to "dogmatism" for the sake of civic peace.

4

Triumph of the "Moderate" Enlightenment

DURING THE seventy-two years that elapsed between Locke's death in 1704 and the American Revolution, the deistic European *philosophes* of the Enlightenment developed the Hobbelockean principles that would inspire the deistic American *philosophes* who led the Revolution and penned its key manifestos. Of course, this great intellectual preparation for the American and French Revolutions and the consequent worldwide rise of Liberty did not involve ordinary people, who had no thought of revolution or the abandonment of Trinitarian Christianity in its various Protestant forms. Rather, it involved coteries of "enlightened" intellectuals who dreamed of a new order of the ages that would finally end the perennial alliance between civil and ecclesiastical authority.

I. The Republic of Letters

The *philosophes* on both sides of the Atlantic were engaged in nothing short of a vast project to "change the common way of thinking," as the French Encyclopaedist Denis Diderot put it. The *Encyclopédie* constituted "a *machine de guerre* which served to propagate the ideas of the French Enlightenment."[1] Evoking the same martial theme, Peter Gay describes the entire ensemble of Enlightenment thinkers as "a single army, with a single banner, with a large central corps, a right and left wing, daring scouts, and lame stragglers."[2] Despite their differences, the soldiers in this army fought as one "to free themselves from their Christian heritage, and then, having done with the ancients, turn their face toward a modern world view."[3]

Shaftesbury, Mandeville, Hume, Bentham and Smith in England and Scotland; Toland in Ireland (and then England); Bayle, Montesquieu, Rousseau, Voltaire, Diderot, D'Alembert, D'Holbach, Helvétius and La Mettrie in France; Lessing in Germany; Beccaria in Italy; and, in America, Franklin, Jefferson and Madison—these and other 18th-century *philosophes* would create what J. I. Israel has presented as a "dialogue" between the radical left wing of the Enlightenment army, with its

---

1. *The ARTFL Encyclopédie*, Univ. of Chicago e-text, http://encyclopedie.uchicago.edu/.
2. Gay, *The Enlightenment: The Rise of Modern Paganism*, 8.
3. Ibid.

fulminating enmity toward the Catholic Church, and the "moderate" central core and right wing with its "moderate" disdain for Catholicism and other theological "systems" based on mysteries and sacraments these "moderates," à la Locke, considered "a crowd of wrong notions, and invented Rites."[4] In spite of their differences, together they would build a "republic of letters" decades before republican government in practice was established by revolution in America. For our limited purposes, a look at four key members of this "republic" will suffice to complete our overview of the philosophical context of the American Revolution as a radical event.

Bayle (1647–1706)

Among the Huguenot expatriates in Holland who resided there during Locke's day, Pierre Bayle is indisputably the single most influential figure of the immediate post-Locke period. His *Dictionnaire historique et critique* (1697), appearing in the same year as Toland's *Christianity Not Mysterious* and republished in numerous editions until 1740 and beyond (including an English translation in 1709), established him as "the chief partisan of religious skepticism or of the irremediable opposition between reason and faith in the modern age."[5] Peter Gay assesses Bayle's role most succinctly: "That Bayle is a great teacher of doubt, an instigator of rebellion against Christian belief, is beyond question."[6]

The *Dictionnaire* was Bayle's *magnum opus* of subversion, which accomplished its aim by a new method soon to be imitated by the Encyclopaedists: the reduction of Christianity and its history to a collection of tendentious entries in a bulky encyclopedia filled with intellectual curiosities and rational discussions of everything. By this method the *Dictionnaire* "concealed so much so well that the author virtually disappears behind the elaborate duplicity of the arguments, the sly innuendos of the massive footnotes, and the deft cross references, while the message itself stands forth clearly."[7] And that message is this: the claims of Christianity, particularly Catholicism, are all open to doubt, and thus religious toleration must replace the Catholic confessional state not only in France, but wherever a state religion existed.

Bayle would become "the first citizen of the republic of letters," who had "achieved glory with the easiest possible method, by destroying the views of others." Voltaire even saluted him as "the attorney general of philosophers." The *Dictionnaire* in particular was an instant classic of Liberty on both sides of the Atlantic. It was "one of the most frequently printed and widely used books in the eighteenth century; no self-respecting library was without it." In America, "intellectuals like Thomas Jefferson and Benjamin Franklin read and warmly recommended it," whereas Voltaire praised it as "the first dictionary that had taught men how to

---

4. *Reasonableness*, 57.
5. Fabro, *God in Exile*, 158.
6. Gay, *The Enlightenment: The Rise of Modern Paganism*, 291.
7. Ibid., 293.

think"[8]—that is, to question all Christian doctrine and dogma and the authority of the teaching Church.

Continuing along the line opened up by Locke, Bayle furthered Locke's tentative decoupling of ethics from traditional Christianity and revealed religion in general. One of Bayle's devices was to harp on a comparison between the virtuous atheist and the idolatrous pagans of antiquity who worshipped false gods, the former being more pleasing to God. A seemingly innocuous argument about ancient pagan idolaters versus hypothetical upright atheists soon elides into such declarations about present-day religion as: "The fear and love of the divinity are by no means the only fountainhead of human actions" and "The fear and love of the divinity are not always more active principles than all the others. . . . The love of glory, the fear of infamy, death or torture, the hope of preferment, act with greater force on certain men than do the desire to please God and the fear of transgressing his commandments."[9]

In other words, Christianity is not the only sufficient basis for morality—the fundamental religious theme of the entire Enlightenment, both radical and "moderate." From this it follows that revealed religion in general is not at all necessary to sustain the moral order of society. Hence Bayle, despite his personal profession of what he viewed as orthodox Christianity, "opened a new breach in the dike of deism, through which poured the raging flood of denial of revealed religion on the part of deism and Enlightenment philosophy. . . ." As Fabro concludes: "The importance of Bayle's stand for the emergence and dynamic of modern atheism can, therefore, scarcely be overestimated."[10]

Even from his secular academic perspective, Israel recognizes that there "is much subterfuge in Bayle's plea for freedom of conscience. . . . [H]is real position is not that of a sincere Christian and . . . in reality he was an unbeliever" for whom freedom of conscience "is simply an implement with which to advance secular freedom of thought."[11] Israel absolves Locke of such religious insincerity, even as he admits that Locke's theory no less than Bayle's poses the dilemma that "one cannot in practice, even if one can in theory, separate toleration of other Christian churches and theologies from toleration of irreligion, impiety, atheism and (worst of all in his eyes) Spinozism."[12]

Montesquieu (1689–1755)

Baron de Montesquieu, Charles-Louis de Secondat, is a proto-Liberal Catholic whose magnum opus *On the Spirit of the Laws* (1748) was condemned by the Holy Office (along with the rest of his major works). Mainstream academia views Mon-

---

8. Ibid., 293–295.

9. *Eclairissement*, I, §1, fol., 617; II, fol. 617; quoted in Fabro, *God in Exile*, 166.

10. Fabro, *God in Exile*, 173, 178.

11. J.I. Israel, *Locke, Spinoza and the Philosophical Debate Concerning Toleration in the Early Enlightenment* (Royal Netherlands Academy of Arts and Sciences: 1999), 8.

12. Ibid., 6.

tesquieu as the quintessentially "moderate" Enlightenment thinker whose thought, together with Locke's, typifies the "conservative" inheritance noted in Chapter 1. But he can be characterized as a moderate only if one presumes that the Greco-Catholic tradition embodied in Christendom represents an extreme that can be opposed to the "radical" Enlightenment in order to arrive at the "reasonable" middle ground.

The Montesquieu specialist Paul O. Carrese, for example, observes that "Montesquieu's concept of moderation *demotes moral virtue and internal ethical balance, concepts central to classical and Christian ethics,* so as to comprehend the myriad ideas and actions of human life. His most general formulation of moderation is 'spirit' as a quasi-Newtonian equilibrium between bodies, forces, of ideas."[13] This "quasi-Newtonian equilibrium" will become known as the "separation of powers" and "the consensus of popular opinion" in the coming democratic republics. Like Locke, Montesquieu "coats his controversial medicine with honey," but no less than Locke, Hobbes and the Enlightenment army as a whole, he does away with "a teleology of forms, essences, and natural ends" and advances "Newtonian challenges to the physics and metaphysics of Plato and Aristotle."[14] That is, Montesquieu is a "moderate" only within the mechanical and relativistic framework of Enlightenment thought, which presupposes a radical break with the Christian past.

Despite Montesquieu's profession of Catholicism, Peter Gay, a renowned Jewish scholar who taught at Yale and can hardly be considered an enemy of the Enlightenment, rightly places him in the French deist camp on account of his "sardonic sallies against the clergy, enthusiastic worship of the Architect-Creator, contempt for papist mystifications, disdain for all ritual...."[15] This is particularly apparent in the *Persian Letters* (1721), published anonymously in Holland (where else?), wherein the young Montesquieu launches broadsides against the Church and the *ancien regime* under the guise of an epistolary novel. The *Letters* made Montesquieu famous as his authorship became known.

Montesquieu would have almost as much influence on the American Founders as Locke. Without giving credit to Locke, Montesquieu developed his notion of republican government featuring a "separation of powers." And it was Montesquieu who first enunciated a vision of the rise of a great commercial civilization in which "the spirit of commerce"[16] would be "a cure for the most destructive prejudices; for it is almost a general rule that wherever we find agreeable manners, there commerce flourishes; and that wherever there is commerce, there we meet with agreeable manners."[17] Montesquieu's ethics of "agreeable manners," which included the

---

13. Paul Carrese, "Montesquieu's Complex Natural Right and Moderate Liberalism: The Roots of American Moderation," *Polity*, Vol. 36. No. 2 (2004), 7 (page citations are to the Questia research engine print version of the essay).

14. Ibid., 8, 9.

15. Gay, *The Enlightenment: The Rise of Modern Paganism*, 383.

16. *Spirit of the Laws*, XX.2.

17. *Spirit*, XX.1.

legalization of divorce that would be a *sine qua non* of the "moderate" Enlighten-ment's program,[18] would indeed replace the disagreeable demands of strict Chris-tian ethics, including the traditionally Christian moral limits on "the spirit of commerce" itself.

Carl Becker, writing in the 1930s, captures the objective reality of Montesquieu's supposed "moderation" in an assessment that applies no less to Locke:

> But where could the eighteenth-century reformer, bent on sapping the foun-dations of church and state in the *ancien régime*, find an arsenal better equipped with ammunition for his purpose? Where could he find the cause of constitutional government in France more effectively put forth, more solidly grounded, on 'universal principles'? Where could he find a great variety of facts, analogies, contrasts, indirect refutations, sly left-handed compliments and suave ironical obeisances—all subtly designed to make the practices of the "one true" and "revealed" religion ridiculous. Nowhere, I venture to say.[19]

Voltaire (1694–1778)

François-Marie Arouet, pen name Voltaire, was an avid student of Locke and is (amusingly enough from a Catholic perspective) widely regarded as one of the "moderate dechristianizers" of the Enlightenment. We have already noted that he was particularly enamored of Locke's profoundly subversive suggestion that God could endow matter with the ability to think, an idea that destroys in principle any distinction between matter and spirit. Again and again in his works, Voltaire cloaks himself in Locke's authority as the philosopher "revered as a wise man throughout Europe." The philosophers of France, he declared, "are but the followers of New-ton, Locke and Galileo."[20] In support of his attacks on the entire edifice of the Greco-Catholic tradition, especially its theology and Scholastic philosophy, Vol-taire invokes the "wise Locke," "the wisdom of Locke," "the wise metaphysician Locke," "the judicious Locke," "the *acute* and judicious Locke," "the *sagacious* and

---

18. In Book XVI of *Spirit*, Montesquieu "moderately" advocates divorce. The audacity of this attack on the Church's teaching concerning the indissolubility of marriage can hardly be overstated in the context of 18th-century Catholic France. Here Montesquieu employs his technique of the "scientific" socio-cultural observation. He "observes" the practice of unilateral repudiation of a marriage by the husband in certain non-Catholic countries or in pagan antiquity and pronounces it unjust, but also "observes" that divorce, on the other hand, is "made by mutual consent, arising from a mutual antipathy. . . ." Having none-too-subtly planted the suggestion that divorce is a reasonable practice, he further "observes" that "Divorces are frequently of great political use: but as to the civil utility, they are established only for the advantage of the husband and wife, and are not always favorable to their chil-dren." Montesquieu ends up with the astonishing suggestion that a consensual divorce can be "agree-able" to the natural law, even when only *one* party consents: "A divorce can be agreeable to nature only when it is by consent of the two parties, or *at least of one* of them. . . . In short, the power of divorce can be given only to those who feel the inconveniences of marriage, and who are sensible of the moment when it is for their interest to make them cease."

19. Becker, *The Heavenly City*, 117.

20. *Philosophical Letters*, "On the English Comedy."

judicious Locke," "the respectable and venerable Locke," the "acute and accurate logician" Locke, and "the revered Locke."[21]

In his *Philosophical Letters* (1733–34), a commentary on England based on his exile there from 1726 to 1728 (to escape prosecution for published insults against a member of the nobility), Voltaire sings Locke's praises. He calls Locke "a true philosopher" and declares that "Perhaps no man ever had a more judicious or more methodical genius, or was a more acute logician than Mr. Locke...." In defense of Locke against his orthodox Christian critics, he slyly employs Locke's "modest" hypothesis of thinking matter to drive a wedge between faith and reason, while noting that Locke the "moderate" stood accused of seeking to destroy religion:

> It was in this chapter he presumed to advance, but very modestly, the following words: "We shall, perhaps, never be capable of knowing whether a being, purely material, thinks or not."[22] This sage assertion was, by more divines than one, looked upon as a scandalous declaration that the soul is material and mortal.... It was loudly exclaimed that Mr. Locke intended to destroy religion; nevertheless, religion had nothing to do in the affair, it being a question purely philosophical, *altogether independent of faith and revelation....*
> Exclaim therefore no more against the sage, the modest philosophy of Mr. Locke.... [W]e must not be apprehensive that any philosophical opinion will ever prejudice the religion of a country. *Though our demonstrations clash directly with our mysteries,* that is nothing to the purpose, for the latter are not less revered upon that account by our Christian philosophers, who know very well that the objects of reason and those of faith are of a very different nature.[23]

Voltaire's reference to *"our* mysteries" and *"our* Christian philosophers" was supremely disingenuous. For in declaring that the Christian mysteries are "revered" even when they "clash directly" with the speculations of the new philosophies— thus severing faith from reason with one blow—Voltaire was really saying that the Christian mysteries are nonsense (as he would declare explicitly later in his life, when his fame was such that prudence was no longer necessary). Thus, while paying lip service to the existence of a spiritual soul as purely a matter of revelation, in the *Letters* Voltaire cites Locke for the proposition that reason cannot demonstrate that

---

21. Cf. Voltaire, *The Works of Voltaire: A Contemporary Version,* in 21 vols. [1901]. A searchable e-text of Voltaire's entire corpus is available, appropriately enough, at oll.libertyfund.org in its "Online Library of Liberty."

22. A paraphrase of the passage in Locke's *Essay Concerning Human Understanding,* IV.iii.6, where he declares: "We have the ideas of matter and thinking, *but possibly shall never be able to know whether any mere material being thinks or not*; it being impossible for us, *by the contemplation of our own ideas,* without revelation, to discover whether Omnipotency has not given to some systems of matter, fitly disposed, a power to perceive and think...." Chapter 3 discusses how this "modest" hypothesis supposes man's inability to demonstrate from reason the existence of his own spiritual soul, as Locke's contemporary Anglican critics did not fail to notice.

23. *Philosophical Letters,* Letter XIII, "On Mr. Locke."

the soul is spirit.[24] Like Locke's "moderate" successors in general, Voltaire opens wide the door to the consequences of a merely material life principle in man, a notion that destroys the realm of the spiritual and, with it, all of Catholic and Christian theology, including the teaching on human free will, since the operations of a material soul would be determined completely by the laws of the physical universe.

In the *Letters* Voltaire stakes out the "moderate" Enlightenment's great claim against the spiritual realm: the supremacy of empiricist philosophy over theology, and of "reason" over faith, and the "independence" of secular from religious disciplines—just as Locke had done with far more caution and disguise. And, like Locke, Voltaire advances under the cover of empiricism, along with the rest of the "central corps" of the Enlightenment, to the conclusion that "true" Christianity consists of a few "reasonable" propositions on which, surely, all reasonable men can agree. Hence in his philosophical letter concerning Pascal he declares: "Christianity teaches only humanity, simplicity and charity. To attempt to reduce it to metaphysics is to turn it into a fount of errors."[25] The Jesuit-educated Voltaire knew very well that, as Gay writes, "Christianity taught much more than secular cosmopolitan morality.... But then to preempt the title of 'true Christianity' for deism was a favorite deist trick."[26] We will see James Madison and Thomas Jefferson employing the same trick in their arguments for the "moderate" disestablishment of religion in Virginia and (in Madison's case) the "moderate" religious "neutrality" of the federal government under the First Amendment.

As did all his fellow *philosophes*, Voltaire advocated religious pluralism and toleration as the best means of neutralizing traditional Christianity and its "tyrannical" claims upon the State and the individual conscience. He thus championed the example of England's pluralist constitutional monarchy—the very essence of the "moderate" Anglophile Enlightenment. For Voltaire, England, "if not precisely a deist's paradise, [was] a country in which deism originated and now seems to be professed by the best people. The very pluralism which struck pious Frenchmen as the subversion of social order seemed, at least in Voltaire's account [as it had been in Locke's account], the cause of public felicity."[27] Hence, in the *Letters*, Voltaire was happy that to report that "If one religion only were allowed in England, the Government would very possibly become arbitrary; if there were but two, the people would cut one another's throats; but as there are such a multitude, they all live happy and in peace."[28] We shall see that in *Federalist* No. 51 Madison makes the same argument for the felicity to be had precisely from what he calls "the multiplicity of sects."

Voltaire had to flee Paris following publication of the *Letters*, wandering from place to place until he ended up in the chateau of the Marquise du Châtelet, "an avid collector of lovers"[29] and a would-be *philosophe*. Voltaire and the Marquise

24. Ibid.
25. *Philosophical Letters*, Letter XXV, "On the *Penseés* of Pascal."
26. Gay, *The Enlightenment: The Rise of Modern Paganism*, 390.
27. Ibid., 387.
28. *Philosophical Letters*, Letter VI, "On the Presbyterians."
29. Gay, op. cit., 361.

cohabited and collaborated for the next fifteen years while she was married to the Marquis, with whom she had three children. The arrangement ended when the Marquise, pregnant by yet another lover, died shortly after giving birth to her fourth child at the age of 43. (Voltaire assisted the Marquise in deceiving her husband that the child was of the marriage.) Voltaire's "moderate" deism was a religion conveniently accommodated to his sex life, for the distant deity of deism has no pronouncements to make on the indissolubility of marriage or the evil of divorce, which Voltaire advocated anonymously as an enlightened social reform for Catholic countries. [30]

As for the Catholicism in which he had been reared and educated, Voltaire's *Sermon des cinquante* (1762), which represents his "first frontal attack on Christianity,"[31] sums up the attitude of "moderate" Enlightenment thinkers in both Europe and America:

> May this great God who is listening to me, this God who can surely neither be born of a virgin, nor be eaten in piece of dough, nor have inspired these books filled with contradictions, madness and horror, may this God, creator of all the worlds, have pity on this sect of Christians who blaspheme him.[32]

In 1763 Voltaire published his *Treatise on Tolerance*, a Locke-inspired argument for absolute religious toleration. The pretext for the work was the execution of Jean Calas, a Huguenot merchant of Toulouse condemned to death for the murder of his son, who was found hanging in his room, an apparent suicide. A death sentence was pronounced by the sharply divided judicial *parlement* of Toulouse amidst a public outcry over the rumor that Calas had hanged his own son to prevent his imminent conversion to Roman Catholicism. After Calas went to his death protesting his innocence and forgiving his accusers, Voltaire worked ceaselessly to have the conviction posthumously voided by a royal court in Paris, which finally declared Calas innocent.

In the *Treatise*, Voltaire uses the miscarriage of justice as a launching pad for an attack on the Catholic Church. Proceeding from the premise that "the abuse of the most holy religion has produced a great crime"—as if a death sentence imposed by a civil tribunal for the crime of murder had been a defense of Catholic doctrine— Voltaire declares that it is "to the interest of mankind to examine if religion should be charitable or savage." Having loaded the question in favor of the reader's emotional response, he leaps to an immense *non sequitur* redolent of Locke's arguments in the *Essay* and *Letter* concerning toleration:

---

30. In his *Philosophical Dictionary*, discussed below, Voltaire depicts the plight of a man who leaves his adulterous wife, "needs a woman," but cannot marry another because of the Church's teaching on divorce. "What! a king can abdicate his crown, and without the Pope's permission he cannot abdicate his wife! Is it possible that otherwise enlightened men have wallowed so long in this absurd servitude?" *Philosophical Dictionary*, "Adultery."

31. Peter Gilmour, *Philosophers of the Enlightenment* (Edinburgh Univ. Press, 1990), 147.

32. Quoted in Helmut Georg Koenigsberger, *Politicians and Virtuosi: Essays in Early Modern History* (NY: Continuum International Publishing Group, 1986), 234.

The fewer dogmas, the fewer disputes; the fewer disputes, the fewer misfortunes. . . . Religion is instituted to make us happy in this life and the next. But what is required to make us happy in the life to come? To be just. To be happy in this life, as much as the wretchedness of our nature will permit, what do we need? To be indulgent. It would be the height of madness to pretend to bring all mankind to think exactly in the same manner about metaphysics. We might, with much greater ease, conquer the whole universe by force of arms than subject the minds of all the inhabitants of one single village.[33]

That is, Calas would not have been executed if only Catholicism had confined itself to the teaching that one ought to be just and indulgent, leaving behind useless "metaphysical" disputes that only lead to intolerance and violence. Voltaire, just as Locke did, argues that all religions must be tolerated, no matter what they preach: "It does not require any great art or studied elocution to prove that Christians ought to tolerate one another. I will go even further and say that we ought to look upon all men as our brothers. What! call a Turk, a Jew, and a Siamese, my brother? Yes, of course; for are we not all children of the same father, and the creatures of the same God?"

Voltaire protests that "I am very far from opposing the maxim 'outside the Church there is no salvation'" only to attack it directly by concluding the *Treatise* with a "Prayer to God" that

the trifling differences in the garments that cover our frail bodies, in our insufficient languages, in our ridiculous customs, in our imperfect laws, in our idle opinions, in all our conditions so disproportionate in our eyes, and so equal in yours, that all the little variations that differentiate the atoms called men not be signs of hatred and persecution. . . .[34]

Voltaire was not about to acknowledge that "trifling differences" and "little variations" in Christian doctrine had inevitably produced disastrous changes in morality and social order throughout Christian history—as evidenced by his own behavior, or by that of the Albigensian heretics of France, whose neo-Manichean theological "trifles" had led them to commit suicide in order to avoid sinning after initiation into their sect, or by the later spread of divorce and all its consequences in Protestant countries. In the spirit of the enlightened American Founders, he belittles the early Church's opposition to the Arian heresy, as if it made no difference whether Christ was begotten eternally of the Father or was simply another creature and therefore not divine. Addressing his public, he suggests that the Church's theological pettifoggers are not content that the people "are faithful subjects, dutiful children, tender parents, and good neighbors; that you practice every virtue; that you are friendly, grateful, and worship Jesus Christ in peace. . . ." That

---

33. Voltaire, *Treatise on Toleration and Other Writings* (Cambridge: Cambridge Univ. Press, 2000), 87.

34. Ibid., 92.

Voltaire exhibited none of these qualities himself was perhaps a demonstration of what happens to faith, hope, charity, and finally basic moral integrity in a soul that rejects the authority of revealed truth and the guidance of a teaching Church.

As he aged, Voltaire was ever more vehement in his declarations against the "systems" of Christian theology and the "superstitions" of Catholicism, which he desired to be eliminated from the face of the earth. By the 1760s, Gay notes, he had begun to use the motto *Écrasez l'infâme*—crush the infamy, meaning Christianity. A famous vignette from Voltaire's last years illustrates the supreme contempt with which the "moderate dechristianizers" of the Enlightenment viewed the Catholic religion, including those then agitating for Revolution in America. In 1774, upon hiking to the top of a hill with a friend to admire the view, Voltaire prostrated himself before the rising sun and exclaimed: "I believe, I believe in you. Powerful God, I believe." Rising to his feet, he then remarked: "As for Monsieur, the Son, and Madame, His Mother, that's a different story."[35]

This ridicule of Catholicism was but a rhetorical device, for the ultimate target was, as Gay recognizes, "all revealed religion," which was attacked "indirectly by dwelling on the supposed absurdities of Roman Catholicism."[36] (We will see in due course how the American *philosophes*, especially Jefferson, Adams and Paine, later indulged in the same tactic.) Yet Voltaire continued to profess a belief in the existence of a remote but amorphously personal deity who founded no religion and gave no revelation, but presides over the natural order and will judge malefactors. This is the same God who would have to be invented as a prop for morality even if He did not exist, as Voltaire famously remarked in a letter to Frederick of Prussia in 1770.[37]

It was during his two-year sojourn in Frederick's court, following the death of the Marquise du Châtelet in 1749, that Voltaire conceived the *Dictionnaire philosophique* (1764), his landmark but prudently anonymous contribution to the "moderate" Enlightenment's assault on revealed religion. In the *Dictionnaire* Voltaire adopts the Enlightenment stratagem of undermining Christianity through the persona of a perplexed Christian expressing seemingly insuperable (but ultimately sophistical) grounds for doubt. He "poses—transparently, for transparency is of the essence of the ironic game—as a good Christian bewildered by the unending controversies of theologians . . . as an intelligent ignoramus who cannot bring himself to believe that important matters like the soul (which geniuses like Locke and Newton considered to be impenetrable mysteries) can be clear to mere priests, as a wide-eyed traveler in space and time who is surprised to discover the rationality of

---

35. Quoted in Gliozzo, "The Philosophes and Religion: Intellectual Origins of the Dechristianization Movement in the French Revolution," *Church History*, Vol. 40, No. 3 (Sep. 1971), 274.

36. Gay, *The Enlightenment: The Rise of Modern Paganism*, 377.

37. Quoting himself, Voltaire wrote: "If God did not exist, He would have to be invented. But all nature cries aloud that he does exist: that there is a supreme intelligence, an immense power, an admirable order, and everything teaches us our own dependence on it." In *Voltaire's Correspondence*, ed. T. Besterman, Vol. 77 (Geneva: 1962), 119–120.

the Chinese and the humanity of the Roman Stoics and thus by implication the irrationality and inhumanity of modern Christians."[38]

The *Dictionnaire* was an immense success even as Voltaire "frantically denied any part in the devilish work."[39] Devilish indeed. Draping himself in Locke's mantle at every opportunity, Voltaire mounts a full-scale frontal attack on Christianity and Catholic dogma in particular. Successive entries—and these are only a smattering—deny or undermine belief in Original Sin, the spiritual soul, the bodily Resurrection, the existence of Hell and Purgatory, the Trinity, the divinity of Christ, transubstantiation, the divine founding of the Catholic Church, the authenticity of the Gospels, the apostolic succession, and the priesthood. Other entries defend Locke's philosophy, his "reasonable Christianity," and his barely disguised denial of Christ's divinity, with Voltaire citing Locke as an adherent (with Newton) of latter-day Arianism.[40] Basing himself on Locke's nominalist epistemology, Voltaire, under the curious entry "Monsters," argues that it is very difficult indeed to distinguish a monster from a normal specimen of animal since the very existence of fixed species is dubious. Following his master in laying down an early foundational argument for one of Liberty's final extremities—legalized abortion— he even adopts the "judicious" Locke's argument calling into question (as Hobbes had also done) the humanity and ensoulment of the fetus:

> We have already asked, with the judicious Locke, *what is the boundary of distinction between the human and merely animal figure*; what is the point of monstrosity at which it would be proper to take your stand against baptizing an infant, against admitting it as a member of the human species, against according to it the possession of a soul? *We have seen that this boundary is as difficult to be settled as it is difficult to ascertain what a soul is*; for there certainly are none who know what it is but theologians.

For obvious reasons, practically all of Voltaire's *oeuvre* was placed on the Index of Forbidden Books along with Montesquieu's *Persian Letters* and *The Spirit of the Laws*. No less than Locke, but with great and powerful literary flourishes of which his philosophical mentor was incapable, Voltaire subverted the very foundations of the Greco-Catholic tradition. He was "a man of rare genius and unequalled skill when it came to the work of destruction. To demolish ancient things was the task in which he excelled and which he delighted to perform."[41] But Voltaire, like his "moderate" confreres, left nothing to replace the resulting rubble. Nothing, that is, save Liberty. Which is to say, nothing but the power of the State, which would bring Liberty to the masses and maintain it at the point of a gun.

---

38. Gay, *The Enlightenment: The Rise of Modern Paganism*, 395.

39. Ibid., 393.

40. "The great Newton and Locke embraced it. Samuel Clarke, the celebrated rector of St. James, and author of an excellent book on the existence of God, openly declared himself an Arian, and his disciples are very numerous." *Philosophical Dictionary*–"Arianism."

41. Frederic R. Coudert, *The Spirit of the Laws* (London: Colonial Press, 1900), introd., iii.

Rousseau (1712–1778)

Born in Geneva eight years after the death of Locke, Jean-Jacques Rousseau is to France what Locke is to England: the great liberal visionary who provides the blueprint for the final overthrow of altar and throne in the nation known as "the eldest daughter of the Church." With Rousseau, however, we encounter not an extreme radical but rather a "moderate" one whose thought J. I. Israel rightly describes as a "Janus-headed mixing of elements from both the radical and the mainstream Enlightenment," and in particular "Spinoza with Locke," as an outcome of the "moderate" Enlightenment's "dialogue with the *Spinosistes....*"[42] Consequently, "no other Enlightenment thinker had anything like as many professed disciples as Rousseau."[43]

Rousseau was a great admirer of Voltaire, to whom he deferred as an elder and predecessor on the path of enlightenment. Voltaire, however, despised Rousseau, ridiculing (rightly enough) his conception of man as naturally innocent, free and happy until society corrupts him, and his elevation of moral sentiment above what Voltaire considered an ethical rationality. But the disciples of both Voltaire and Rousseau would ultimately be reconciled by the greatest and most revered of the American *philosophes*, Benjamin Franklin, during his sojourn in Paris as America's minister to France (1776–1785) in the very midst of the Revolutionary War. It was through the medium of Freemasonry that Franklin, revered in Parisian society as the semi-divine "electrical ambassador," would accomplish the reconciliation of these two opposing camps among the French disciples of Liberty upon Voltaire's triumphant return to Paris in 1778, the year of his and Rousseau's death. Fittingly enough, the two divines would be deified with tombs in the Panthéon, the Parisian Temple of Liberty (and former Catholic church) to which their remains were transferred with great pomp and ceremony during the French Revolution neither man would live to see.

Rousseau abandoned Catholicism after his early conversion to it from Calvinism—a decision in keeping with his lifelong predilection for mistresses and affairs with other men's wives. One of Rousseau's mistresses, a chambermaid by the name of Thérèse Levasseur (whom he would invalidly marry in 1768), bore him five children out of wedlock. Each he promptly deposited in succession in a Paris orphanage between 1746 and 1752. Rousseau's religious defection, adultery, criminal neglect of his own children, and utter disregard of the sacrament of matrimony did not deter him from writing *Emile: Or On Education* (1762). In what he considered his most important work, he presents to the world, through the fictional child Emile, Emile's tutor, and his bride-to-be, Sophie, a complete program for the rearing and education of the enlightened, "reasonably" religious and upright citizen. Giving the "Moses" of the Enlightenment his due, *Emile* contains repeated references to "the wise Locke" and his thoughts on child rearing. Like Locke, who had no children,

---

42. Israel, *Radical Enlightenment*, 269, 719, 720.
43. Ibid., 717.

Rousseau wrote with great confidence on a subject concerning which he was a manifest incompetent.

Much as Locke did, Rousseau loudly professed his personal adherence to the Gospel even as he advanced the Enlightenment's indispensable attack on Catholicism and the reduction of Christianity to a few "reasonable" precepts sufficient to secure good behavior, toleration and a belief in God amounting to a vague providential deism. In Book IV of *Emile*, the doubt-ridden Savoyard Vicar serves as a mouthpiece for Rousseau's condemnation of "a church which decides everything and permits no doubts" and imposes "absurd decisions" on its members. The Vicar declares that he is done with "general and abstract ideas; the jargon of metaphysics" which has "never led to the discovery of any single truth, and it has filled philosophy with absurdities." The Vicar knows this, of course, because his infallible private judgment—"the inner voice of feeling" informed by the "senses through which I receive impressions"—tells him so. The Church may err, but the Vicar is infallible as he looks inward and ponders the "simple" truth, which is that "the visible order of the universe proclaims a supreme intelligence" and "the world is governed by a wise and powerful will." This deity, says the Vicar, "is what I call God." Thus freed from the claims of metaphysics and the sects, the Vicar is finally able to offer his "first homage to the beneficent Godhead. I worship his Almighty power and my heart acknowledges his mercies." Is the soul immortal? "I know not," says the Vicar. As for the eternal punishment of the wicked, "I cannot tell, and I have no empty curiosity for the investigation of useless problems." Nevertheless, the Vicar finds it "hard to believe that they will be condemned to everlasting torments. If the supreme justice calls for vengeance it claims it in this life."

Concerning the morality to which one is to be held under this "beneficent Godhead," Rousseau, just as Locke did, denies that the natural law is inscribed in the soul as precepts to reason. But, unlike Locke, he declares through the Savoyard Vicar that conscience is man's "divine instinct" and thus "what I *feel* to be right *is right*, what I *feel* to be wrong is wrong; conscience is the best casuist. . . . [H]e who obeys his conscience is following nature and he need not fear that he will go astray. . . . The morality of our actions consists *entirely in the judgments we ourselves form with regard to them*."

For Rousseau, as for the "moderate" Enlightenment generally, the role of religion is simply to foster man's good behavior as supported by appropriately "decorous worship"[44] of the beneficent Godhead; and all sincerely professed religions are equally good and useful for that purpose. Hence, further on in Book IV, Rousseau's voice of Reason recites the "moderate" Enlightenment's *credo*:

> I serve God in the simplicity of my heart; *I only seek to know what affects my conduct.* As to those dogmas which have no effect upon *action or morality*, dogmas about which so many men torment themselves, I give no heed to them. *I regard all individual religions as so many wholesome institutions. . . . I*

44. Schneewind, *The Invention of Autonomy*, 481.

think them all good alike, when God is served in a fitting manner. True worship is of the heart. God rejects no homage, however offered, provided it is sincere. Called to the service of the Church in my own religion, I fulfill as scrupulously as I can all the duties prescribed to me, and my conscience would reproach me if I were knowingly wanting with regard to any point.

As Schneewind wryly observes: "No wonder that the Catholic French establishment had the book burned."[45] And not only the Catholic establishment. The book was also burned in Calvinist Geneva,[46] for even the Protestant sect from which Rousseau had emerged recognized that *Emile* undermined traditional Christianity in any form, promoted utter religious indifferentism, and deprived morality of any basis in revelation, including the threat of hell. Rousseau's way of thinking would reduce morals to a convention among men based on "feeling" and "instinct," a convention whose inefficacy was manifest in Rousseau's own life, a major public scandal throughout Europe. Faced with imprisonment, Rousseau fled France to Berne, and from there to the court of Frederick II, where Voltaire had sojourned some twelve years earlier.

Rousseau's *The Social Contract* (1762) is his sociopolitical *magnum opus* wherein he presents variations on the by-now indispensable Hobbelockean themes: the state of nature, the social contract, and submission to the authority of government only by "consent" of the governed. Rousseau's "radical man" in the mythical state of nature is an innocent brute; a speechless, pre-cultural creature who knows nothing of good or evil but has a natural sentiment of pity, and thus may be said to be essentially good even if he lives like an animal. Man in the state of nature simply follows his animal instincts and exercises his Hobbelockean "natural liberty and an unlimited right to everything he tries to get and succeeds in getting...."[47] As Rousseau famously declares at the beginning of *The Social Contract*: "Man is born free, and everywhere he is in chains"[48]—a ludicrous assertion that Emile Faguet demolished with a single witticism: "It would make just as much sense to say that cows are born carnivores, yet everywhere they eat grass."[49]

As with Hobbes and Locke, the need for self-preservation compels Rousseau's innocent brutes to leave the state of nature and enter into civil society. While Rousseau rejects the absolute monarchy of the Hobbesian Leviathan, he advocates a different form of political absolutism: the "general will," to which the parties to the social contract surrender all their rights upon leaving the state of nature. Putting aside the ultimately rhetorical distinction between Locke's "supreme authority" governing by the will of the majority and Rousseau's absolute "general will" as

---

45. Ibid.

46. Haig A. Bosmajian, *Burning Books* (Jefferson, NC: McFarland & Co., Inc., 2006), 10.

47. Jean Jacques Rousseau, *Social Contract*, I.8., e-text at constitution.org.

48. *Social Contract*, I.1, e-text at constitution.org; *The Social Contract and Other Political Writings*, ed. Victor Gourevitch (Cambridge: Cambridge Univ. Press, 2007).

49. "Dire: les moutons sont nés carnivores, et partout mangent de l'herbe: serait aussi juste." In *Joseph DeMaistre: Considerations on France* (Cambridge: Cambridge Univ. Press, 1994), trans. and ed. Richard Lebrun, xxii.

expressed by the majority, Rousseau's version of the social contract is quite in line with the Hobbelockean system. His theory

> includes the standard contractarian argument, to be found in Hobbes and Locke and others, that a necessary condition of political sovereignty is the surrender by each contractor of the right of private judgment that he possessed in the state of nature. Leviathan [Hobbes], or the community [Locke], or the general will [Rousseau] substitutes for the multiplicity of private judgments on the good of a binding public judgment. *Rousseau endorses the absolute sovereignty of this public reason in common with Hobbes, and in effect Locke, malgré lui* [in spite of himself] precisely because he accepts the view that the maintenance of an authoritative public judgment is incompatible with the retention of the individual of the right to judge the justice of the laws. . . . The theory of absolute sovereignty holds that political association is possible only on condition that the "state" decides these matters for all.[50]

As Rousseau himself declares in one of his most famous formulations: "[I]n order . . . that the social compact may not be an empty formula, it tacitly includes the undertaking, which alone can give force to the rest, that whoever refuses to obey the general will shall be compelled to do so by the whole body. This means nothing less than that *he will be forced to be free.* . . ."[51] The Western world has ever since been plagued by what Simon Schama calls "the impossibly paradoxical nature of this bargain. . . ."[52] The impossibility of the paradox would become bloodily apparent during the Civil War in America.

Rousseau attempts to resolve the impossible paradox by addressing the rhetorical question "how a man can be both free and forced to conform to wills which are not his own. How are the opponents [of the majority] subject to laws to which they have not consented?"[53] Rousseau answers his own question with a legal fiction redolent of both Hobbes and Locke. Speaking in the first person, he argues that every citizen has already "consented" to every law adopted by the majority because "the tally of the votes yields the declaration of the general will," and the general will is "what I had willed," so that if he were to oppose the will of the majority he would have "done something other than what I had willed, and it is then that I would not be free."[54] On the basis of such nonsense did the Enlightenment stake its entire claim that each individual's "consent" to be governed by elected "representatives" confers a title to political authority superior to that of hereditary monarchs and a "freedom" that is not possible under monarchical rule. (Again, we are not suggesting that majority rule—democracy—is a *per se* invalid form of government; we

---

50. John Charvet, "Rousseau, the Problem of Sovereignty and the Limits of Political Obligation," in *Critical Essays on the Social Contract Theorists: Hobbes, Locke and Rousseau,* ed. Christopher W. Morris (Lanham, MD: Rowman & Little, 1999), 205–206.

51. *Social Contract,* I.7.

52. Simon Schama, *Citizens* (NY: Alfred A. Knopf, 1989), 161.

53. *Social Contract,* IV.2.7.

54. Ibid. IV.2.8.

merely refuse its claim to moral superiority over monarchy based on a pro forma "consent of the governed" to political decisions that the governed, as often as not, would reject if given the option of rejection.)

The term "civil religion" as such was first employed by Rousseau in Book VI, Chapter 8 of *The Social Contract*, entitled "Of Civil Religion." Rousseau prescribed for his ideal state "a purely civil profession of faith, the articles of which it is up to the Sovereign to fix, not precisely as dogmas of Religion but as sentiments of sociability, without which it is impossible to be either a good Citizen or a loyal subject."[55] This civil religion would replace "the cult we have rejected"[56]—namely, traditional Christianity—as the religion of the State. Christianity would remain a tolerable "private" preference so long as its adherents observed the primary "negative dogma"[57] of the civil religion: intolerance of those who will not tolerate the beliefs (or unbelief) of others. That negative dogma would become the super-dogma of the civil religion that would surpass Christianity in almost every nation of the post-Christian West.

The "Moderates" Prevail

According to the modern liberal perspective, the "radical" Enlightenment is represented by such atheistic and materialistic "Hobbists" and "Spinozists" as La Mettrie and Diderot, who advocated "non-providential" Deism, pantheism, or outright atheism, the overthrow of "absolute" monarchy in favor of direct democracy, the absolute equality of citizenry, the abolition of all hereditary privileges of nobility, and the leveling of society. The "moderate" Enlightenment, on the other hand, is presented as an alarmed "conservative" reaction to the excesses of the radicals by thinkers more in line with Locke.

Israel, who questions the extent of Locke's influence on the early Enlightenment before 1730, is nonetheless constrained to admit that by the 1730s, less than thirty years after Locke's death, there was "[i]ncontrovertibly . . . an international 'cult' of Newton and Locke," and that Voltaire's "intellectual, as distinct from rhetorical and literary, contribution to the Enlightenment, consists of little more than introducing Newton and Locke to the continent . . . or mere propaganda for English philosophy."[58] Further, the Encyclopaedists, including d'Alembert, praised Locke (while stealthily promoting the ultra-radical Spinoza) because by then Locke was considered "intellectually safe . . . innovative, perhaps, but entirely supportive of revealed religion, Providence, and the political social order."[59] Hence by the 1740s "much of the European mainstream . . . firmly espoused the ideas of Locke and Newton which indeed seemed uniquely attuned and suited to the moderate Enlightenment purpose."[60]

55. Cf. *The Social Contract*, IV.8.32.
56. *The Social Contract*, IV.8.33.
57. Ibid.
58. Israel, *Radical Enlightenment*, 515 (internal citation and quotation omitted).
59. Ibid., 516.
60. Ibid., 11.

Thus did the "dialogue" with the benighted Spinozists produce a Lockean "middle ground" involving propositions that Locke's contemporary critics, only a few decades earlier, had condemned as radically subversive of traditional Christianity and society. And this triumph of Lockean (and Montesquieian) "moderation" occurred even as post-Locke philosophers of the Enlightenment's radical wing were revealing what Israel admits are "certain potentially radical implications"[61] in Locke's thought, to put it mildly. Already, then, the Western world had begun to witness the process by which the terms "conservative" and "liberal" would undergo an utter relativization, becoming nothing more than expressions for drifting opinion with no mooring in the abandoned Greco-Catholic tradition.

The "moderate" Enlightenment is said to have produced a "viable synthesis of old and new"[62] that can be summarized thus: a minimalist "reasonable" Christianity (admitting a "core" of "reasonable" doctrines), "Christian deism" or a "providential deism" to replace traditional Christian theology; government in the form of a liberal constitutional monarchy or republic instead of a hereditary "absolute" monarchy; a rights-oriented political theory founded on private property and laissez-faire capitalism; and religious toleration or pluralism ("papist" Catholicism excepted) replacing or derogating from the Christian confessional state. But what Israel calls the "struggle for the middle ground" between the radical and the "mainstream" Enlightenment ended with the predominance of a "moderate" version of the New Philosophy that was radical by any objective historical standard of Western civilization up to that time.

II. Manuscripts and Masons

Despite their disdain for the "systems" of traditional Christianity, the "moderate" Enlightenment illuminati of both Europe and America were not without a religious confession of their own. They sought "not only to destroy an old faith, but to supply a new faith, which would be in conformity with the new age" in order to "give supreme significance to the rise of science [and] the growth of the state. . . ."[63] As Bernard Fay observes, the deistic *philosophes* who detested Christian doctrine nevertheless had a "mystic preoccupation [that] always haunted their minds. They all had the souls of prophets."[64]

Becker's great contribution to our understanding of the Enlightenment as an objectively radical break with "the Christian story" is his recognition that the "prophets" of the "moderate" Enlightenment sought to build a "heavenly city" that was "shifted to earthly foundations," a city in which "the business of justification [was] transferred from divine to human hands" and God was "differently conceived and more indifferently felt." In short, they replaced Christ—even Locke's reductionist Christ—with an "Author of the Universe" who does not actively intervene in

---

61. Israel, *Radical Enlightenment*, 517.

62. Ibid., 11.

63. Charles A. Gliozzo, "The Philosophes and Religion," loc. cit., 282.

64. Bernard Fay, *Revolution and Freemasonry* (NY: Little, Brown and Company, 1935), 64.

human affairs. Once this Author had "performed his essential function of creation, it was proper for him to withdraw from the affairs of men into the shadowy places where absolute being dwells."[65] The Author of the Universe, who is the "Nature's God" of the Declaration of Independence, is the conveniently remote and inaccessible deity of Deism, the religion *par excellence* of the Enlightenment.

With a vague Deism as their theological foundation, the "prophets" of the Enlightenment turned to a man-made institution dedicated to a new God for the New Order of the Ages, an institution that would help spread the gospel of Liberty throughout the Western world. What united many *philosophes* and other "enlightened" men of substance in 18th-century England, Holland, France, the Continent at large and America, despite the differences among them, was a kind of substitute for a church universal: Freemasonry.

In contemporary academia, especially in America, it is fashionable to dismiss attention to Freemasonry as the stuff of paranoid conspiracy theories. But attempting to understand the rise of Liberty without reference to Freemasonry would be like attempting to understand the development of Christendom without reference to the Catholic Church. No scholar has examined Freemasonry and its relation to the Enlightenment more closely than Margaret Jacob of U.C.L.A., whose classic works on the subject, *The Radical Enlightenment* (1981) and *Living the Enlightenment* (1991), made the serious study of Freemasonry respectable in the American academy. It is Jacob who observes that in the Masonic lodges one finds "nascent political modernity"[66] developing during the first half of the 18th century. Freemasonry, she concludes, "transmitted and textured the Enlightenment,"[67] becoming nothing less than "the cult of the Enlightenment, presenting a set of distinctive values by which men and some women might now organize their lives."[68] And it was the Enlightenment that "provided the rudiments of a new Western identity," helping to create the "secular men"[69] (formal Masons or not) who ever since have wielded the levers of power in political modernity.

The standard accounts of the origin of Freemasonry assign the date of June 24, 1717, "during the height of the Enlightenment period."[70] On that date a group of four lodges in London held an "ever-memorable meeting" at which they united to form Europe's first Freemasonic "Grand Lodge," the Premier Grand Lodge of England. This event marked the transition from the "operative" Freemasonry of the medieval stonemason guilds comprised of various craftsmen, which had all but disappeared by 1717 (there being no more cathedrals to build in post-Reformation Europe), to the "speculative" Freemasonry of cosmopolitan gentlemen steeped in

65. Becker, *Heavenly City*, 31, 49.
66. Ibid., 224.
67. Margaret Jacob, *Living the Enlightenment* (NY: Oxford Univ., 1991), 224.
68. Ibid., 35.
69. Ibid., 21.
70. John Salza, *Freemasonry Unmasked* (Our Sunday Visitor Publishing Division: 2006), 22. The author is a former member of the Craft who renounced his membership when he realized its incompatibility with his own Catholicism.

the thought of the Enlightenment, including its deistic natural religion and its Lockean-Newtonian-Baconian empiricism. Jacob, based on groundbreaking research, argues for an earlier date for the transition: 1710 or before, when Toland (the disciple of Locke we encountered in the previous chapter) joined with radical Huguenot expatriates in Holland to establish the Knights of Jubilation in the Hague, a secret society with a Grand Master and constitutions of the same genre that would be standard for Freemasonry throughout the world.

The precise date of its origins aside, the "father" of modern speculative Freemasonry is John Theophilius Desgauliers (1683–1744), another of the French converts to radical Whiggism residing in England in the years immediately after the death of Locke. The son of a Huguenot clergyman who fled to England following revocation of the Edict of Nantes, he graduated Oxford with distinction, becoming the close friend and assistant of Newton (godfather to his child) and a fellow of the Royal Society. Desgauliers was made the third grand master of England in 1719, and "through his influence many men of learning and position flocked to the Fraternity,"[71] including many members of the prestigious scientific fellowship of the Royal Society to which he and Newton belonged.

Desgauliers "received vital assistance in the creation of speculative Masonry" from the Rev. James Anderson, a latitudinarian Presbyterian minister with whom he (and others) drafted the first Masonic constitutions, published under Anderson's name in a volume entitled *Anderson's Constitutions of* 1723.[72] The work of Desgauliers and Anderson reflects what would become basic Freemasonic themes that are also the "moderate" Enlightenment's mainstays of Liberty: "a strongly latitudinarian religious vision" and "a willingness to allow the state to control the church and thereby to maintain religious peace. . . ."[73]

Desgauliers was instrumental in devising the theology of the surrogate religion that was Masonry's substitute for traditional Christianity. He was "not interested in an apology for Christianity as revealed religion," because he was "a Newtonian Christian" whose God was not the Holy Trinity or even the God of Abraham but an entirely new deity: the "Great Architect and Organizer of the World,"[74] to which Masons refer by the initials G.A.O.T.U. (Great Architect of the Universe). That English Freemasonry included not only Desgauliers but many other members of the Royal Society accounts for its ritual fixation on geometric and architectural expressions of the divine "logic" of the universe. In fact, as Jacob summarizes:

> It was *only* in the Masonic lodges, of all the new forms of sociability, that the deity of enlightened culture, the Grand Architect of the Universe, was ceremonially invoked. These pious invocations, first articulated within a British

---

71. William R. Denslow and Harry S. Truman, *10,000 Famous Freemasons* (Missouri Lodge of Research: 1957), Part I, 309. Former President Truman, a proud 32nd degree Mason, wrote the preface to this reference work.

72. Jacob, *The Radical Enlightenment* (Lafayette, LA: Cornerstone Books, 2006 [1981]), 94–95.

73. Ibid., 95.

74. *Living the Enlightenment*, 105.

context, seemed to equate the Grand Architect with the deity of the new science, the guarantor of order and harmony originally proclaimed by Descartes, but codified most especially by Newton. . . . Yet, as clerical critics were quick to point out, the Masonic deity was at best suspect, or at worst the God of the deists.[75]

GAOTU *was* the God of the deists; the God that Locke, Toland, Collins, Shaftesbury, Voltaire and all the others had progressively "revealed" to the world as a replacement for the divisive God of Christianity, who had audaciously declared in the flesh such things as: "I came not to send peace, but the sword" and "if he will not hear the church, let him be to thee as the heathen and publican."[76] *Anderson's Constitutions* imposed upon the members of "the Craft" precisely that minimalist and instrumentalized religion that was the *credo* of the "moderate dechristianizers" of the Enlightenment, although the Brothers could retain adherence to orthodox Christianity as a matter of personal preference to be left outside the Lodge door:

> A Mason is oblig'd by his Tenure, to obey the moral law; and if he rightly understands the Art, he will never be a stupid Atheist nor an irreligious Libertine. But though in ancient Times Masons were charg'd in every Country to be of the Religion of that Country or Nation, whatever it was, yet 'tis now thought more expedient *only to oblige them to that Religion in which all Men agree, leaving their particular Opinions to themselves*; that is, to be good Men and true, or Men of Honour and Honesty, by whatever Denominations or Persuasions they may be distinguish'd; whereby *Masonry becomes the Center of Union*, and the Means of conciliating true Friendship among Persons that must have remain'd at a perpetual Distance.[77]

Anderson's Constitutions are a prime example of the "moderate" Enlightenment's actual radicalism. Atheism and libertinism are resoundingly rejected in opposition to the evil "Hobbists" and "Spinozists," but so is orthodox Christianity. The "moderate" replacement of Christianity with "that Religion in which all Men agree, leaving their particular Opinions to themselves" was a radical break with the "Gothic" Constitutions regulating the old stonemason's lodges (a reference to the Gothic cathedrals on which the "operative" masons of Christendom had labored). For example: "The first charge is this that you be true to God and Holy Church and use no error or heresy."[78] Like the "moderate" Enlightenment as a whole, Freemasonry rejects the "details" of revealed religion.

Not surprisingly, the works of Locke "have been held to belong among the classics of Masonic writing. . . ."[79] Jean Rousset de Missy, a co-founder of the proto-Masonic Knights of Jubilation, was instrumental in bringing about a definitive

75. Jacob, *Living the Enlightenment*, 31.

76. Matt. 10:34; 18:17.

77. *Anderson's Constitutions of 1723*, Article I. "God and Religion."

78. Hermann Gruber, "Masonry (Freemasonry)," *The Catholic Encyclopedia*, Vol. 9 (NY: Robert Appleton Company, 1910).

79. Fabro, *God in Exile*, 270.

French translation of the *Two Treatises* that was distributed throughout the Continent. Rousset aimed to use Locke's thought to justify the Dutch Revolution of 1747, "just as it would be used, decades later, to justify the American Revolution."[80] Also standard Masonic fare was Montesquieu's *Spirit of the Laws*, published twenty-two years after Montesquieu himself was inducted into the Grand Lodge of London during a visit to that city in 1730.[81]

It hardly needs to be demonstrated that Freemasonry's invention of a secretly practiced "religion in which all men agree" was, as Jacob observes, "radically out of step with the prevailing mores of British, indeed of *every European society*."[82] Freemasonry "exported onto the Continent . . . the legacy of liberal Protestantism with its emphasis on natural religion. It had been forged by nearly a half century of revolution under the impact of the new science."[83]

At one in their worship of GAOTU, the "Craftsmen" would, with astonishing rapidity, come to comprise nothing less than a worldwide "mystical body" of Liberty with its own dogma, levels of spiritual initiation, temples, liturgy, sacraments and sacramentals, and even catechisms, such as *A Catechism of the Mystery of Freemasons*, published in 1726. The Freemasonic surrogate religion includes an entire "system of morality veiled in allegory and illustrated by symbols."[84] The Freemasonic creed, being a creature of Enlightenment thought, naturally excludes the tenets of traditional Christianity, including the Trinity, the Fall, the redemption, and sanctifying grace, thereby reflecting "the new spirit of naturalism, rationalism, and deism expressed by men such as Thomas Hobbes and John Locke."[85] Just as *Anderson's Constitutions* had purged operative Freemasonry of its Catholic elements as part of "the paradigm shift from revelation to reason," so did the dogmas, rituals and "degrees" also promulgated by the Grand Lodge of London, the veritable Vatican of Freemasonry, "reflect the influence of Enlightenment philosophy . . . eliminat[ing] Christian prayer and any references to the Catholic religion."[86] With the religion of Freemasonry, writes Jacob, "the Enlightenment is brought full circle: Having disdained traditional religion, it is being enlisted in the service of a *new religiosity*," according to which the Mason "is not only virtuous, he is at the same time a *philosophe*, a word borrowed during the 1740s to mean an adherent of the secular and the freethinking."[87]

In less than a lifetime after its emergence in London in 1717, Freemasonry had built consecrated temples in virtually every city of every nation in the Western world. The first Masonic lodges were established in France around 1725, and by the eve of the French Revolution there were seven hundred lodges in Paris alone.

80. Jacob, *The Radical Enlightenment*, 56.
81. Bernard Fay, *Revolution and Freemasonry* (Boston: Little, Brown and Company, 1935), 177.
82. Jacob, *Living the Enlightenment*, 71.
83. Ibid., 72.
84. Waite, *Encyclopedia of Freemasonry*, 50, 163.
85. Salza, *Freemasonry Unmasked*, 23.
86. Ibid., 24.
87. Jacob, *Living the Enlightenment*, 146 (internal quotation omitted).

William Doyle, a renowned historian of the Revolution, observes that Frenchmen who sought the "newer, truer wisdom believed themselves most likely to find it in the 'royal art' of Freemasonry." Consequently, "[f]ew towns of any consequence were without one or more lodges by the 1780s ... despite several papal condemnations of a deistic cult that had originated in Protestant England, the élite of society flocked to join."[88] Francois Furet, generally considered the foremost living historian of the Revolution until his death in 1997, describes the Masonic lodges of France as part of an "enlightened community" of opinion-makers "whose kings were the writers"—first and foremost those whose thought we have just surveyed. The French lodges, he writes, were part of an elite that was "capable of criticizing everything" and was "presiding over a tremendous reshaping of ideas and values." Indeed, observes Simon Schama, the French Masonic lodges belonged to a veritable "empire of words" that included the literary and scientific academies, societies of thought and museums.[89] In France—and everywhere else it took root—Freemasonry was "a potent agency in propagating the new ideas. It was from Freemasonry that Republican France borrowed its slogan, 'Liberty, Equality, Fraternity.'"[90]

Masonic lodges were established in the American colonies by the 1730s through the work of Benjamin Franklin, with a sudden expansion of membership in the 1750s. By 1760, writes Fay, "there was no town, big or small, where Masonry had not spun its web. Everywhere it was preaching fraternity and unity."[91] On the eve of the American Revolution "there were dozens of lodges up and down the continent."[92] Not only Washington, but Franklin—a veritable Masonic demigod, as we shall see—Madison, Hamilton, Samuel Adams, James Otis and a host of other American revolutionaries belonged to the Craft, including some of the most radical Whigs in colonial America and numerous signers of the Declaration of Independence, perhaps as many as fifty-two out of fifty-six.[93] Franklin was appointed Provincial Grand Master of Pennsylvania in 1749.[94] Washington was initiated into "the Craft" at the Fredericksburg Lodge on November 4, 1752, and was elevated to the status of Master Mason on August 4, 1753, remaining a faithful Mason until his death.[95]

As it established itself throughout Europe and the American colonies in the 18th century, exulting that it was "spread over the surface of the earth,"[96] Freemasonry

88. Doyle, *Oxford History of the French Revolution*, 64–65.

89. Schama, *Citizens*, 181.

90. Cornwell B. Rogers, *The Spirit of Revolution in 1789* (Princeton, NJ: Princeton Univ. Press, 1949), 56, n.9.

91. Ibid., 231–232.

92. Wood, *Radicalism of the American Revolution*, 223.

93. Philip Davidson, *Propaganda and the American Revolution* (Chapel Hill: Univ. of North Carolina Press, 1941), 101. Davidson asserts that fifty-two of the fifty-six signers were Masons. A review of Denslow and Truman's reference work reveals that at least twenty-four of the signers were Masons, while the reputed Masonic affiliation of others cannot be confirmed by documentation from the lodges or official Masonic histories.

94. Waite, *New Encyclopedia of Freemasonry*, Vol. II, 59.

95. Denslow and Truman, Part 2, 300.

96. Jacob, *Living the Enlightenment*, 149.

aimed to offer "all that the Church of old had offered, for the Church of the Middle Ages was at the same time a center where the people met, the guardian of dogmas and essential truths, the protectress of morality, the dispenser of spiritual and material help, and the stage manager of social life."[97] A Mason, wrote one American member of the Craft in 1750, belonged "not to one particular place only, but to places without number, and in almost every corner of the globe; to whom, by a kind of universal language, he can make himself known—and from whom, we can, if in distress, be sure to receive relief and protection."[98] The French lodges and other "circuits of enlightened opinion," writes Furet, were "engaged in more deliberate and concerted action towards the incipient revolution than history has recorded."[99] Jacob agrees: "almost predictably, wherever we find revolutionaries on the European scene, so too we find our Freemasons. What labyrinths of political intrigue have yet to be uncovered can only be speculated."[100]

For our purposes there is no need to speculate. It suffices to understand from the indications given here that the international Freemasonic fraternity would help convert the entire Western world to religious latitudinarianism and secular republicanism in the same way that the Catholic Church had converted it to Christendom: by serving as a leaven of social order, by becoming the religion of movers and shakers, by preparing the way for a revolutionary change in civilization. To illustrate this fact of history, Fay proposes an apt analogy between a Masonic lodge and a Roman Catholic parish. In both places politics are not discussed, nor will one find records of political plots. A Masonic lodge is "devoted strictly to Masonic work, just as a church is devoted to strictly Christian activities." As with the Catholic Church, the political aims of Masonry are accomplished not by the organization proper but by associated groups and charismatic leaders who have its backing. Thus, Fay concludes, while each organization abstains from direct political action, Freemasonry and the Catholic Church "have never ceased being opposed to each other"[101] on the field of politics in the classical sense. This is a truth we will revisit in the second volume of this work when we survey the Catholic counter-Enlightenment and its opposition to the empire of Liberty.

In the late 18th century, observes R. R. Palmer, "[t]he fact that Washington and other American leaders were Masons made European Masons feel akin to them...."[102] The transatlantic Masonic network, "with its mysterious rituals and its select membership ... created an international and interclass sense of fellowship among men fired by ideas of liberty, progress and reform."[103] As it spread from London to France and the rest of the Continent, and across the sea to America,

97. Fay, *Revolution and Freemasonry*, 116.
98. Wood, *Radicalism of the American Revolution*, 224.
99. François Furet, *Revolutionary France: 1770–1880* (Oxford: Blackwell, 1988), 14, 60.
100. Jacob, *The Radical Enlightenment*, 225–226.
101. Fay, *Revolution and Freemasonry*, 224–225.
102. Palmer, *The Age of the Democratic Revolution*, Vol. I, 245.
103. Ibid.

Freemasonry "wove enlightened ideas into a tapestry of rituals and oaths" creating a social organism of "all-pervasive religiosity" wherein Masons found "that 'heavenly city' offered by the new secular philosophies of the eighteenth century...."[104] The Pulitzer Prize-winning historian of the American Revolution, Gordon Wood, could not be more emphatic on the role of this international, quasi-religious brotherhood in the American Revolution:

> It would be difficult to exaggerate the importance of Masonry for the American Revolution.... For thousands of Americans, it was a major means by which they participated directly in the Enlightenment.... *Freemasonry was a surrogate religion for an Enlightenment suspicious of traditional Christianity.* It offered ritual, mystery and congregativeness without the enthusiasm and sectarian bigotry of organized religion....[105]

§

This brief look at Freemasonry completes our survey of the intellectual landscape at the dawning of the Age of Democratic Revolution, whose beginning coincided with the height of the late Enlightenment. While in its most virulent phase the Enlightenment was a furious and unrelenting attack "against Christianity itself, against Christian dogma in all its forms, Christian institutions, Christian ethics, and the Christian view of man,"[106] that phase does not concern the first volume of this study. Here we chronicle how the "moderate" Enlightenment will press the same attack in a far more subtle way, thus prevailing as the vehicle for advancing the strategy of the Enlightenment army as a whole throughout the Western world.

We have arrived, then, at the threshold of the first of the Enlightenment-bred revolutions that would turn the Western world definitively away from its Christian past and resolutely toward its post-Christian future. What we have seen thus far ought to be sufficient to demonstrate that even at its most "moderate," the intellectual climate that gave birth to Liberty—epistemologically skeptical, materialistic, and ethically relativized; latitudinarian, deistic and hostile to established religion; republican, favorable to revolution, and Masonic—was inimical to any form of Christocentric social order.

Moving now from the realm of philosophy to the realm of historical events emerging from the function of ideas in human action, we will see how the rise of Liberty under the banner of the "moderate" Enlightenment would require precisely the end of Christian civilization through the revolutionary creation of that vast and never-before-seen Hobbelockean realm known as the secular. Writing in 1764, Voltaire exulted: "Everything I see scatters *the seeds of revolution which will definitely come,* though I won't have the pleasure of being its witness.... Enlightenment has gradually spread so widely that it will burst into full light at the first right

104. Jacob, *The Radical Enlightenment*, 22.
105. Wood, *The Radicalism of the American Revolution*, 223.
106. Gay, *The Enlightenment: The Rise of Modern Paganism*, 59.

opportunity. . . . The young people are lucky; they will see some great things."[107] In the process of intellectual preparation for the coming of these "great things," Locke, "who repudiated the self-denying ordinances of Christian ethics" and "called for liberation from the shackles of antique and medieval rules of thought," had been nothing less than "a Moses, writing the law, showing the way, dominating the scene, exacting gratitude, but stopping short of the promised land."[108] The *philosophes* who, like Voltaire, had been faithful to Locke's testament in the midst of what they regarded as the desert of Christendom would finally see the land of milk and honey in a place called America.

107. To Chauvelin, April 2, 1764, *Letters*, Vol. IV, 231; quoted in Gay, *The Enlightenment: The Science of Freedom*, 103.

108. Gay, *The Enlightenment: The Rise of Modern Paganism*, 321.

II.

The First American Revolution

5

The House That Locke Built

BY THE 1770s, North America's Catholic moment had passed. In a foreshadowing of the American Revolution, the royal government of the Catholic colony in Maryland, chartered by Charles I and governed by the successive Lords Baltimore, the Calverts of Ireland, was overthrown in the Puritan rebellion of 1650–52 following the execution of Charles by the Cromwellians. The new Protestant governor of Maryland, installed by Cromwell, repealed Maryland's Act Concerning Religion (1649) which guaranteed religious freedom to all Trinitarian Christians, both Catholic and Protestant. Protestantism was established as the official religion of Maryland and Catholics were subjected to a regime of legal restrictions, including disqualification from public office and prohibitions on public worship. While the Calverts regained control of Maryland during the Stuart Restoration in England and reinstated the Act Concerning Religion, the Puritans finally triumphed after the "Glorious Revolution" of 1688, and Maryland became a Protestant colony with all the attendant legal persecution of Catholics. The great "Catholic experiment" in Maryland had ended.

The long age of Catholic exploration of the New World by the Spanish, French and Portuguese that began in 1492 and could have led to a Catholic North America, had ended with the Treaty of Paris (1763), concluding the Seven Years' War (1754–63) of which the French and Indian War was but the North American campaign. Under the Treaty, Britain gained control of French Canada, Florida (wrested from Spain) and the entire eastern half of North America. France (to Voltaire's regret) ceded the Catholic territories of Louisiana to Spain as compensation for the loss of Florida to Britain. (Louisiana would ultimately be reacquired by Napoleon and sold to the United States.) King George III's Royal Proclamation of 1763 imposed British rule on former French Canada and led to the disqualification of Canadian Catholics from public office and other legal disabilities for Catholics. (George's repeal of that penal regime via the Quebec Act of 1774 would be a major pretext for the Revolution.) In the first of many broken promises to the Indians, the Proclamation reserved to them the territories west of a line running through the Appalachian Mountains. Without the support of the French, however, the Indians would be unable to resist the relentless Western expansion of Anglo settlers, who promptly disregarded the Proclamation and every subsequent government promise to the native tribes.

Hence by the 1770s North America was a predominantly British possession. The thirteen colonies were separated by a continent from the Spanish mission territory of Upper California in New Spain, which was being evangelized by Blessed Juniper Serra (1713–1784). In the colonies the Catholic population just before the American Revolution was a tiny and threatened minority of around 25,000 souls, subject to varying degrees of legal discrimination. In this Protestant social order, an ocean away from the King and Parliament, the English genome of Liberty already expressed in the Puritan mini-revolution in Maryland would express itself throughout the continent with world-changing consequences.

Moses and the Promised Land

If Locke was the Moses of the Enlightenment, laying down the law for its progress and showing the way to the Promised Land, then the American Revolution was indeed "the program of enlightenment in practice"[1] and "the Enlightenment fulfilled."[2] We have seen how Locke created on paper the blueprint for nothing less than "the new world of human liberty." As Kenneth Craycraft notes, however, "it took another hundred years for a practical experiment in Lockean liberalism to be attempted."[3] The experiment commenced in 1776.

To the American revolutionaries, "[w]ith the Lockean premises they had about how knowledge was acquired, everything suddenly seemed possible."[4] They believed themselves capable of "creating their own world,"[5] a conviction fostered by the commonly shared "liberal premises of Lockean sensationalism: that all men are born equal and that only the environment working on their senses made them different."[6] Change the environment, they believed, and it is possible to remake political man into something other than the "slave" of the "absolute monarchs" who had reigned in Christendom for so many centuries.

Thomas Jefferson, the philosophical leading light of the Revolution and principal author of the "Lockean inspired Declaration of Independence,"[7] was a diligent student of Locke's writings. As we have seen, Locke's very words—"the pursuit of happiness," "long train of abuses"—appear in the Declaration. The Declaration, as the historian Donald D'Elia remarks, is a veritable "transcript of Locke's partisan 17th-century Whig political theory."[8] Jefferson's papers include an annotated copy of Locke's *A Letter Concerning Toleration*, which we have already examined as the very model of the modern pluralist state, while Jefferson's Virginia Statute for Religious

---

1. Peter Gay, *The Enlightenment: The Science of Freedom*, 558.
2. Wood, *Radicalism of the American Revolution*, 191.
3. Craycraft, *The American Myth of Religious Freedom*, 69.
4. Wood, *Radicalism*, 191.
5. Ibid.
6. Ibid., 236.
7. Murray Rothbard, *For a New Liberty* (Von Mises Institute: 2002), online edition, 4.
8. Donald D'Elia, *The Spirits of '76* (Front Royal, VA: Christendom Publications, 1983), 12.

Freedom bears a direct verbal correspondence to the *Letter*.[9] Joining the European *philosophes* of the Enlightenment, Jefferson worshipped Locke, Bacon and Newton as the *"three greatest men that have ever lived, without any exception"* because they "laid the foundation of those superstructures which have been raised in the Physical & Moral sciences."[10] Steeped in the deism of the Enlightenment and the science of Bacon and Newton, Jefferson, like the rest of the Founders, "had a deep aversion to speculative philosophy" and was "scornful of metaphysicians of the stature of Plato and Aristotle," although, like Locke (who wrote during an Epicurean revival), he was "quite partial to Epicurus" and thus to a Lockean ethics of pain, pleasure and utility.[11] "Utility to man" declared Jefferson, is "the standard and test of virtue."[12]

Ben Franklin's writings contain "explicit and repeated indications of the debt he owed to Locke and to Bacon."[13] John Adams, Sam Adams, Madison and Hamilton were all Locke-influenced writers and thinkers. Madison's landmark document *Memorial and Remonstrance Against Religious Assessments*, which inveighed against public support for religious instruction and the establishment of Christianity in general, is wholly Lockean in its rejection of any role for the State in matters religious. Thus it has been argued that if Madison "was specially indebted to a single source, that source was Locke."[14] *The Federalist Papers*, written by Madison, Hamilton and Jay under the pseudonym "Publius," are not only a defense of the "American experiment" in Lockean liberalism but also a "classic work of the Enlightenment" whose pages are "made of Hobbes and Harrington, Locke and Montesquieu, Hume and the *Encyclopedie*."[15] The *Federalist* reflects the entire socio-political program of the Enlightenment as first laid down by its Moses, including "the dialectical movement away from Christianity to modernity" and "the pessimistic though wholly secular appraisal of human nature coupled with optimistic confidence in human arrangements"[16]—a confidence that would be shattered during the Founders' own lifetimes.

It is apparent, in short, that as Fukuyama concludes: "Despite the efforts of some recent scholars to see the roots of the American regime in classical republicanism, the American founding was thoroughly if not wholly imbued with the ideas of

9. S. Gerald Sandler, "Lockean Ideas in Jefferson's Bill for Establishing Religious Freedom," *Journal of the History of Ideas* 21 (1960): 110–116 in Craycraft, *The American Myth of Religious Freedom*, 35.

10. Jefferson to John Trumbull, February 15, 1789, *Jefferson Writings*, ed. Merrill D. Peterson (New York: Library of America, 1984), 939–940 (e-text).

11. Joseph F. Costanzo, S.J., *Political and Legal Studies* (West Hanover, MA: The Christopher Publishing House, 1982), 102–105.

12. Jefferson to Thomas Law, June 13, 1814, in *The Jeffersonian Cyclopedia* (Funk & Wagnall: 1900), §5518.

13. Pangle, *The Spirit of Modern Republicanism*, 19.

14. Lance Banning, "Madison, the Statute and Republican Convictions," in *The Virginia Statute for Religious Freedom: Its Evolution and Consequences in American History*, eds Merrill D. Peterson and Robert C. Vaughan (NY: Cambridge Univ. Press, 1988), 118; in Craycraft, *The American Myth of Religious Freedom*, 70.

15. Gay, *The Enlightenment: The Science of Freedom*, 563.

16. Ibid.

John Locke."[17] Locke is, quite simply, "America's philosopher."[18] This is true of "both Locke's epistemology of experience and theory of toleration," which have had great significance for "the shape and direction of American thought and experience"[19] and thus for the shape and direction of Western thought in general. The American Revolution was—as libertarians are happy to declare—"grounded in a radically revolutionary development of Lockean theory...."[20]

Of course Locke was not the only or strictly predominant influence on the thinking of the Founders, as if he were a posthumous mastermind guiding the entire revolutionary process and the subsequent course of Western and even world history. But to admit this is not to mitigate the radicalism of the Founders' philosophy with respect to the nearly bimillenial tradition that had preceded it, for their other sources of inspiration (and their own education) hardly steered them in the direction of the tradition. Bayle, Shaftesbury, Voltaire, Montesquieu, Rousseau, Bolingbroke, Hume and the other Enlightenment divines were uniformly "religious nonconformists who sought to disassociate the legitimacy for government from religious authority."[21] The Founders followed and indeed wrote the most important chapter in the "Whig narrative" of history, and there is no denying the "commanding influence of Locke and other Enlightenment and Whig thinkers on the founding generation."[22]

Thus, Gordon Wood does not in the least exaggerate when he observes (with admiration) that the Revolution produced "a change of society, not just of government.... America, at a stroke it seemed, had overturned two millennia of Western history."[23] What is commonly hailed as "the genius of the Founders" represents a radical implementation of Locke's concept of "one Body Politick under *one Supreme Government* . . . ,"[24] his Law of Opinion and his Law of Toleration, all of which were noted in Chapter 3. In the following pages we will survey how Locke's principles, which became those of the "moderate" Enlightenment generally, were employed to design and build the first "temple of Liberty" in America.

Mythical Justifications

At the outset, however, we must dispense with the first of the many golden legends that comprise the Whig narrative of America as the beginning of the *Novus Ordo Seclorum*—the New Order of the Ages. The prime legend is that the American Revolution was a "conservative" movement of judicious Christian statesmen who

17. F. Fukuyama, *The End of the History and the Last Man* (NY: Free Press, 2006), 159.

18. Craycraft, *American Myth of Religious Freedom*, 35.

19. David A. J. Richards, *Toleration and Constitution* (NY: Oxford Univ. Press, 1986), 107–108.

20. Murray Rothbard, *The Ethics of Liberty* (NY: New York Univ. Press, 2002), 23.

21. Steven K. Green, "Understanding the 'Christian Nation' Myth," 245 *Cardozo Law Review* 245, 250 (2010).

22. Ibid.

23. Wood, *Radicalism*, 169, 339.

24. *TT*, II.vii.89.

soberly guided the masses toward the safe harbor of God-given "individual rights" to life, liberty and the pursuit of happiness. The legend is refuted, first of all, by the very inadmissibility of a "right to revolution" in the Christian political tradition, given that all political authority rests ultimately on divine authority. Recall here the discussion in Chapters 2 and 3 on the crucial distinction in the Christian teaching between resistance to particular unjust or immoral measures of a ruler and the total overthrow of existing authority, which Saint Thomas called the mortal sin of sedition by some "crowd of persons" (Saint Augustine) who deem themselves to be "the people." Recall as well Augustine's observation that Christians obeyed even Julian the Apostate in all things except sin, serving faithfully in his armies.

In fomenting a revolution against George III, whom none other than Colonel George Washington had called "the best of kings"[25] in a missive to the monarch during the French and Indian War, the Founders themselves were well aware "of their political modernism—their sense of participation in radical innovation, both theoretical and practical."[26] Nowhere is this awareness more evident than in No. 14 of *The Federalist Papers* wherein Madison, writing as *Publius*, hails "the glory of the people of America"—meaning Madison and the revolutionary cadres—who had "accomplished a revolution which has no parallel in the annals of human society. They reared the fabrics of governments [state and federal] which have no model on the face of the globe."

Mainstream historians of the first rank long ago exposed the golden legend for what it is. For example, in his Pulitzer Prize-winning study of the American Revolution, Gordon Wood observes that:

> We Americans like to think of our revolution as not being radical; indeed, most of the time we consider it downright conservative.... But if we measure radicalism by the amount of social change that actually took place ... then the American Revolution *was not conservative at all*; on the contrary, it was as radical and as revolutionary as any in history.... In fact, it was one of the greatest revolutions the world has known, *a momentous upheaval that not only fundamentally altered the character of American society but decisively affected the course of subsequent history*.... [I]n destroying monarchy and establishing republics they [the American revolutionaries] were changing their society as well as their governments, and they knew it.[27]

The late Murray Rothbard, now an icon of the contemporary "Austro-libertarian" movement, happily trashes the golden legend in his multi-volume paean to the Revolution. After noting the obvious—that "all mass revolutions ... by bringing the masses into violent action, are therefore per se highly radical events"—

---

25. "We, the officers of the Virginia regiment ... can not help testifying our grateful acknowledgments, for your 'high sense' of what we *shall always esteem a duty* to our country and the best of kings. Signed for the whole corps, GEORGE WASHINGTON." In Jared Sparks, *The Life of George Washington*, Vol. II (NY: Harper & Bros., 1847), 466.

26. Pangle, *The Spirit of Modern Republicanism*, 8.

27. Wood, *Radicalism*, 1, 5.

Rothbard observes that "the deep seated radicalism of the Revolution . . . was inex-tricably linked both to the radical revolutions before and to the ones, particularly the French, that came after. From the researches of Caroline Robbins and Bernard Bailyn we have come to see the indispensable linkage of radical ideology in a straight line from the English Republican revolutionaries of the seventeenth cen-tury through the commonwealthmen of the late seventeenth and eighteenth centu-ries, to the French and American revolutionaries."[28] Among other radical elements, Rothbard points out that the Revolution introduced guerilla warfare, overthrew not only British rule but all other existing forms of government in the colonies, and resulted in the forcible confiscation and redistribution of Tory real estate and personal property on a vast scale—a "statist" abuse of power he somehow finds just and appropriate despite his otherwise dogmatic defense of "anarcho-capitalism" and an "absolute right" to private property.[29]

Rothbard further remarks with satisfaction that although many of the new state constitutions were "conservative reactions against initial revolutionary condi-tions"—in other words, governments that were, in the end, no "freer" than the one thrown off—"the very act of making them was radical and revolutionary: men did not have to submit blindly to habit, to custom, to irrational 'prescription.' After *violently throwing off* their prescribed government, they could sit down and con-sciously make over their polity by the use of reason." Rothbard fails to explain how "reason" justifies the violent overthrow of habit, custom and previous prescrip-tions for government—as if the established order were not itself the product of reason—or why, on his view, "reasonable" men should not continuously be engaged in revolution to prevent the formation of new "unreasonable" habits, cus-toms and prescribed forms of government. Nevertheless, as Rothbard concludes approvingly: "For all these reasons, for its *mass violence* and for its libertarian goals, the American Revolution was ineluctably radical."[30] Indeed it was, as even a casual student of the Revolution will learn.

Let us also dispense at the outset with another golden legend: The Revolution was not, as public school history texts solemnly declare, a justified rebellion against "taxation without representation." The Tory counter-propagandists demonstrated quite handily that "every Englishman is taxed, and not one in twenty is repre-sented."[31] Where taxation is concerned, what matters, of course, is whether the tax is just or unjust in amount and application, not whether it is "authorized" by some putative "representative" elected by a bare majority of a plurality of the population. Today, taxation *with* representation has led to confiscatory levies an "absolute mon-arch" like King George would have considered madness, but which are impregnably defended as *ipso facto* just precisely because "representatives" approved them.

28. Murray S. Rothbard, *Conceived in Liberty* (Auburn, AL: Von Mises Institute, 1999), Vol. IV, 442.

29. Ibid., 426–427 ("every state carried out confiscation of Tory property . . . the result of this dis-tribution was a significantly more democratic and less concentrated ownership of land. . . .").

30. Ibid., 442, 444, 446.

31. Philip Davidson, *Propaganda and the American Revolution*, 271; quoting Soame Jenyns in *Mas-sachusetts Gazette*.

The very idea that the justice of a tax depends on "representation" is one of those "self-evident" truths and "natural rights" for which neither Locke (who first enunciated the idea) nor the revolutionary leaders could find any support in history or in the tradition of political thought.[32] Rather, as Tench Coxe, a Federalist delegate to the Continental Congress admitted, "self-evident as the truth appears, we find no friend of liberty in ancient Greece or Rome asserting that taxation and representation were inseparable." Nevertheless, "no taxation without representation" was "a novel truth [that] henceforth the people of the earth will consider . . . the only rock on which they can found the temple of Liberty."[33] That taxes in the "temple of Liberty" would be vastly greater than they were under the "tyrannical" King George is perhaps the primary example of the illusory nature of Lockean "government by consent of the governed."[34]

Neither was the Revolution a righteous uprising against King George's "tyranny" in general. As Wood concludes: "There should no longer be any doubt about it; the white American colonists were not an oppressed people; they had no crushing imperial chains to throw off."[35] The Revolution was no spontaneous rising up of great masses of common men against political and economic oppression by a despot across the sea—the "best of kings," as Washington had called him. Quite the contrary, "the colonists knew they were *freer*, more equal, more prosperous, and less burdened with cumbersome feudal and monarchical restraints [so-called] than any other part of mankind in the eighteenth century."[36] Even the great libertarian sage Rothbard "makes clear that . . . Americans were willing to fight against British coercion, but many, if not most, saw themselves as British subjects fighting unjust laws; remove the laws, as before, and they would become peaceful subjects once more."[37]

32. Previous claims of a right to consent to taxation were always founded on recognition of the sovereign's inherent power to levy taxes for the support of a commonwealth, and did not involve the idea that a tax was per se unjust unless enacted by "representatives."

33. *Pamphlets on the Constitution of the United States Published During Its Discussion by the People,* Paul Leicester Ford, ed. 1888, 148; cited in Pangle, *The Spirit of Modern Republicanism,* 36.

34. Despite the grossly exaggerated claims for the authority of *Magna Carta* (1215) during the time of William Blackstone and other 18th-century Protestant legal commentators, the Charter certainly provides no historical foundation for any natural right not to be taxed without "representation." The original *Magna Carta* was "won from [King] John at sword's point" by a group of rebellious barons following the Battle of Runnymede. The Charter as originally written thus constitutes an extorted peace treaty between the king and barons who considered themselves overtaxed, rather than freely willed royal legislation reflecting objective principles of natural justice bearing on the point. Upon appeal to the Pope from King John, Innocent III annulled the Charter on August 2, 1215, only two months after John had been induced to approve it, and the rebellious barons were excommunicated. The Charter as reissued in 1225 by John's successor, Henry III, pointedly omits chapters xii and xiv, requiring that no scutage (payment in lieu of military service) or other "aid" be imposed except upon agreement of a Great Council of the kingdom. With the omission of these two chapters the king's "right of taxation" was restored. See "Magna Carta," *Catholic Encyclopedia,* Vol. IX (1910).

35. Wood, *Radicalism,* 4.

36. Ibid.

37. Robert Klassen, "Conceived in Liberty: A Review," www.lewrockwell.com/klassen/klassen-26.html.

The Allure of "Liberty"

The myths aside, at its ideological core the Revolution was not driven by claims of specific injustices, which after all could be and were remedied by the colonials' demands for repeal, but rather by its radical leaders' unappeasable demand for "Liberty." And what is Liberty? Historian Philip Davidson provides this amusing description of the confused understanding of the new idol among rank and file colonials:

> What did liberty mean? Who can tell? To one it may have meant simply free-dom from English restrictions, perhaps nothing more than freedom from the Stamp Act; to another it may have meant complete freedom from England; to still a third it may have meant internal freedom from local oppressors. It may have meant political, economic, religious freedom—free government, free land, free trade, free religion, free liquor, free anything the people want. It meant just as much or as little as 'Liberty, Fraternity, Equality' in another revolution.... The power of the word was its vagueness. Who would not choose Liberty to Slavery? Some there might have been who would not fight for the merchants, or for the political bosses, some there might even be who would not fight for the preachers, but it was a craven spirit who would not fight for Liberty.[38]

At the level of the average colonial, the Revolution demonstrates, in short, what Davidson calls "the compulsive appeal of a vague concept...."[39] But however imperfectly Liberty was understood by the common man in pre-revolutionary America, in the minds of those who wielded it as a philosophical concept its mean-ing was crystal clear and quite in accord with the Lockean thinking we have already examined: freedom from any external authority not subject to the "consent" and "sovereign will" of "the people"; freedom, above all, from the "tyranny" of kings, popes and the Catholic Church.

As this book will argue thematically, when all is said and done the ultimate meaning of Liberty has always been emancipation from the claims of the Catholic Church on men and societies. And this requires "the Church's complete subordina-tion to the body politic."[40] David Hume, who died in the very year the American Revolution began, summed up the 18th-century "spirit of Liberty" as precisely a rejection of the age-old alliance between ecclesiastical and political authority according to which the latter was subject to the former when necessary for the defense of faith and morals. As discussed in Chapter 3, this is the very "problem" addressed by Hobbes and Locke in their respective approaches to the instrumental-ization and subjugation of the spiritual by the temporal power. As Hume declared:

---

38. Davidson, *Propaganda*, 137–138.
39. Ibid., 136–137.
40. Manent, *An Intellectual History of Liberalism*, 8.

In all ages of the world priests have been enemies to liberty. . . . Liberty of thinking, and of expressing our thoughts, is always fatal to priestly power, and to those pious frauds, on which it is commonly founded; and, by an infallible connexion, which prevails among all kinds of liberty, this privilege can never be enjoyed, at least has never yet been enjoyed, but in a free government. . . . All princes that have aimed at despotic power have known of what importance it was to gain the established clergy. . . .[41]

By "free government" Hume meant—as did Hobbes and Locke—a state free from the influence and control of any religious body. America would become the first such state in the history of the Western world, not because of any "conservative" response to given injustices but because of the inevitable progression, especially in the northern colonies, of the Lockean principles derived from the Protestant principle of private judgment: that "individual consent [is] the only proper basis for all man's organizations, civil and ecclesiastical,"[42] and that this consent may be revoked and the established order overthrown on the ground of individually perceived wrongs. The Protestant radicals in America were only following their private judgment, based on their Lockean "appeal to heaven" for the warrant to revolt. As Edmund Burke declared in his address to Parliament in 1775 concerning attempts to conciliate the American radicals:

All Protestantism, even the most cold and passive, is a sort of dissent. But the religion most prevalent in our northern colonies is a refinement on the principle of resistance; it is the dissidence of dissent, and the Protestantism of the Protestant religion. . . .[43]

Especially in the northern colonies, therefore, Whig radicals, "speaking the language of Locke," agitated in favor of his "consent or compact theory of government, the right of free man in society to determine the character of the government which in the last analysis he creates."[44] What the radicals sought and what they achieved— with resort to demagogic propaganda, political theater, censorship, violence, intimidation, and dictatorial rule, as we shall see—was no conservative reform. Rather, it was "a radical change in the conception of state power. Almost at a stroke the Revolution destroyed all the earlier talk of paternal or maternal government, filial allegiance, and *mutual* contractual obligations between rulers and ruled."[45]

But the radical leaders of the American Revolution sought far more than a change of government. They were a movement motivated by "a utopian hope for a

41. David Hume, "On the Parties of Great Britain," *Essays Moral, Political and Literary*, I.IX.3.

42. Sidney Mead, *The Lively Experiment: The Shaping of Christianity in America* (NY: Harper and Row, 1963), 61; cited in Catharine L. Albanese, *Sons of the Fathers: The Civil Religion of the American Revolution* (Philadelphia: Temple Univ. Press, 1976), 127.

43. Edmund Burke, *Speech on Conciliation with the Colonies, The Founders' Constitution*, Volume 1, Chapter 1, Document 2, @ http://press-pubs.uchicago.edu/founders/documents/v1ch1s2.html.

44. Davidson, *Propaganda*, 46.

45. Wood, *Radicalism*, 187.

new moral and social order. . . ."[46] and "new way of life, a new attitude toward all the interests of man in society."[47] The colonies would be swept up in the radicals' "soaring dreams" which were followed by the same radicals' "eventual disappointments"[48] when (as we shall discuss in due course) they realized their "experiment" had not produced the anticipated utopia of enlightened men exercising enlightened "self-government."

And an experiment it was. The radicals knew they were attempting something never before attempted: the creation of a non-monarchical representative democracy that would profess no religion and be tied to no Church. They knew that they had proceeded by means of "a revolution which has no parallel in the annals of human society," as James Madison put it in Federalist No. 14. It was revolution that, as Madison boasted, had established a form of government for which "an exact model did not present itself" anywhere "on the face of globe" or in human history, but which, thanks to the courage and vision of the Founders (including himself), had spared America from the fate of "laboring under the weight of some of those forms which have crushed the liberties of the rest of mankind." But, "Happily for America, happily, we trust, for the whole human race," the Founders had "pursued a new and more noble course."[49]

The Revolutionary Minority

This "new and more noble course" for "the whole human race" required, just as Locke's principles did, the final overthrow of the Catholic social order of altar and throne, the corrupted remnants of which were manifest in the reign of George III. But how would the radicals rid themselves of a troublesome monarch who had the disconcerting tendency to address the very injustices of which the radicals were complaining so loudly? How would they transform a sufficient number of rank and file colonists from opponents of particular unjust laws into opponents of monarchy per se, willing to take up arms in a rebellion against their own King?

Philip Davidson observes that while there were in the colonies in the 1760s "conditions tending toward a separation of England and America," including "gradual divergence of institutions, customs, language and interest," nevertheless the continuing benefits of union with England, the persistent loyalty or indifference of a majority of the colonists, and the interminable dissensions among "a million or so straggling settlers, but loosely united in their disparate, quarrelsome governments," all meant that "the Revolution was at best but the work of an aggressive minority."[50] With "Locke as the source of the rallying cry of the Revolution,"[51] however, the radical minority relied on what would become the tools of the Lockean practice

46. Wood, Radicalism, 189–90.
47. Davidson, Propaganda, 46.
48. Wood, Radicalism, 190.
49. The Federalist Papers (New Rochelle, NY: Arlington House), 104.
50. Davidson, Propaganda and the American Revolution, xv–xvi.
51. Pangle, The Spirit of Modern Republican Republicanism, 36.

of revolution over the next century: agitation and propaganda, mob violence and intimidation, the creation of revolutionary cadres and committees to expose, censor, harass and crush all "enemies of the Revolution" and "enemies of the People," and, finally, bloodshed whenever and wherever necessary. The same pattern would be followed in every subsequent revolution in the name of Liberty. In short, to build "the temple of Liberty" the "apostles of Liberty" would trample on the liberties of their opponents. Let us examine in brief how they proceeded to clear the ground for the creation of their brave new world.

6

Imposing the
Revolutionary Will

IT WAS ULTIMATELY the very existence of a monarchy allied to the Anglican Church—a government not "consented" to and a Church not "consented" to—that was held to justify revolution in the minds of its radical Whig leaders. And it was so even if the monarch whose authority was thrown off turned out to be quite mild, indeed positively benign, compared with what was to follow. The grease on the wheels of the revolutionary juggernaut was that deeply ingrained, Enlightenment-bred fear and loathing of any sort of union between civil and ecclesiastical power, which is to say fear of the Beast whose head was to be found in Rome.

Stoking the Fear of "Popery"

In his Pulitzer Prize-winning study of the Revolution, Bernard Bailyn observes that for the American radicals it was ultimately not a question of particular tax measures of the Crown such as the Stamp Act but rather "that the ultimate design behind the Stamp Act was an effort to forge the fatal link between ecclesiastical and civil despotism" incessantly derided as "Popery" by revolutionary propagandists and demagogues. Popery meant nothing other than "the conjunction of the Church of Rome with aggressive civil authority...." This the revolutionaries saw "as the greatest threat, the classic threat" to what they called Liberty.[1] As John Adams argued with the usual late-Enlightenment fustian, America was meant "for the illumination of the ignorant, and the emancipation of the slavish part of mankind all over the earth," including Catholic Europe, but "Unless the colonists united against the Stamp Act ... there would be established in that land the same civil and ecclesiastical tyranny from which men had freed themselves by the Protestant Reformation."[2] In fact, "Colonists everywhere had a traditional dislike, distrust and even fear of Roman Catholicism" which was easily exploited by raising the threat of a quasi-Catholic established Anglican Church in America, even if "there was no real danger of the establishment...."[3]

---

1. Bernard Bailyn, *The Ideological Origins of the American Revolution* (Cambridge, MA: Belknap Press of Harvard Univ. Press, 1992 [1967]), 98, n.3, 99.
2. Davidson, *Propaganda*, 123, quoting and explaining the arguments of Adams.
3. Ibid., 122.

A typical example is a sermon by one Reverend Holly in defense of resistance to British taxation and other violations of "Liberty." If the colonists were to submit to British "tyranny," Holly warned, it would only be a matter of time before their consciences would be

> bound by Popish chains, which, when thoroughly fastened upon us, away must go our Bibles, and in lieu thereof we must have imposed upon us, the superstitions and damnable heresies and idolatries of the church of Rome. Then we must pray to the Virgin Mary, worship images, believe their doctrine of purgatory, and the Pope's infallibility, and such like. And last of all, the deepest plot of hell and Rome, the holy inquisition, must guard the Catholic faith of the church of Rome, and bind us thereto with all its terrors and cruelty.[4]

Given the colonials' congenital fear and loathing of Catholicism, inherent in the English genome of Liberty, the Quebec Act was a far greater pretext for the Revolution than any tax measure. It was enumerated among the "Intolerable Acts" precisely because it had granted legal status to the Catholic Church and extended "the boundaries of a 'papist' province,"[5] thereby "threatening the colonists with a horde of 'Popish slaves' in the North and the West...."[6] Sam Adams, the consummate revolutionary propagandist, warned that on account of the Act "arbitrary power, and its great engine, the Popish religion, are, to all intents and purposes established in that province" with the terrifying result that the king would "have no other subjects in this part of his domain than Roman Catholics."[7] The Quebec Act gave revolutionary propagandists "their real opportunity to play upon the colonial hatred of Rome" by stoking suspicions of "the popish designs of the British government."

The idea that "King and Parliament did intend to establish Popery on all the Continent of North America" was "assiduously propagated" by revolutionary propagandists and "did much to prepare people for the Declaration of Independence, for the hatred of Roman Catholicism was real...."[8] King George was depicted as suspect of Catholicism, and rumors of his secret conversion were circulated throughout the colonies. In his epic poem *McFinigal*, the Revolutionary era painter and poet John Trumbull launched a typical accusation. The King, he declared, had

> Assumed all rights divine, as grown
> The churches head, like good Pope Joan;
> Swore all the world should bow and skip
> To her almighty Goodyship....

4. Davidson, *Propaganda*, 204.
5. Bailyn, *Ideological Origins*, 119.
6. John C. Miller, *Sam Adams: Pioneer in Propaganda* (Stanford, CA: Stanford Univ. Press, 1964), 323.
7. Cited in Davidson, *Propaganda*, 13.
8. Ibid., 127–128.

> Struck bargains with the Romish churches
> Infallibility to purchase;
> Set wide for Popery the door,
> Made friends with Babel's scarlet whore.[9]

The historian Daniel Barber notes that the hatred of "Popery" constantly cultivated by the radicals' propaganda "remained so strong through the early part of the Revolution that the President of Princeton University [John Witherspoon] believed the common hatred of Popery, caused by the Quebec Act, *the only thing* that cemented the divergent religious groups in the colonies together sufficiently to allow them to make war, an opinion which was shared by British observers."[10] Here we see in action Locke's idea, expressed in his *Essay Concerning Toleration*, that in opposing the rise of Catholicism in political society "the differing parties will sooner unite in common friendship with us, when they find we really separate and set ourselves against *the common enemy*, both to our church and all Protestant professions. . . ." But in this instance the Anglican Church itself had been identified with the "common enemy" by the Protestant dissenters and Masonic deists who were driving the revolutionary propaganda machine. Moreover, it was argued, by allowing the establishment of Catholicism in Quebec, King George the crypto-Catholic "had absolved the allegiance of the colonists to him, for he had broken his coronation oath"[11]—a rationale that reflects perfectly the Lockean idea that a ruler may be overthrown and replaced whenever he is perceived to have violated his amorphously conceived "trust."

The Attack on Monarchy

The problem of propaganda the radicals faced, however, was that despite the specter of "Popery," King George was really not much of a tyrant. The colonies, in fact, enjoyed *de facto* independence, as demonstrated by their success in beating back by 1770 every unwanted revenue measure except the tea tax. Hence, as Rothbard admits in his paean to the Revolution: "the old and obsolete Whig ideal of virtual independence under a figurehead king of both Britain and America could only be shattered if the king were to be attacked personally."[12]

Enter the great radical rabble-rouser Thomas Paine, the transplanted Englishman, ex-Methodist preacher, and twice-fired tax collector who came to America in 1774 to become nothing less than an aide to George Washington and the fast friend of Thomas Jefferson. It was Paine, writes Rothbard, who became "the voice of the American Revolution and the greatest single force in propelling it to completion and independence."[13] Sidney Hook, another devotee of the Revolution, likewise

9. John Trumbull, *McFinigal: An Epic Poem* (NY: American Book Exchange, 1881), 26–27.
10. In Erik von Kuehnelt-Leddihn, *Leftism Revisited* (Washington, DC: Regnery Gateway, 1990), 50.
11. Davidson, *Propaganda*, 128.
12. Rothbard, *Conceived in Liberty*, Vol. IV, 135.
13. Ibid., 137.

lauds Paine as the man responsible for "inspir[ing] two of the greatest revolutions in human history"—both the American and the French.[14] Bernard Bailyn, citing Harold Laski, writes that Paine "was with the exception of Marx the most influential pamphleteer of all time...."[15] It was Paine's propaganda that overcame what Rothbard dismisses as mere "personal loyalty to the British crown . . . a political taboo of almost mystical force against attacking the head of state" and "long-standing habits" of respect for established authority that supposedly "impeded a rational analysis of the deeds of King George III."[16] It was Paine, Rothbard enthuses, who was able "to rupture this taboo, smash the icon, and so liberate America from its thrall...."[17]

In *Common Sense* Paine argued for the American Revolution as necessary to remove "The remains of monarchical tyranny in the person of the king."[18] That is, he advanced the novel contention, first suggested by the "cautious" and "conservative" Locke, that hereditary monarchy *in itself* is tyranny and must *by the very fact of its existence* be overthrown. Hence it simply did not matter whether King George was a tyrant in fact. Likewise, in *The Rights of Man*, Paine later justified the French Revolution despite "the natural moderation" of Louis XVI as a monarch "so little disposed to the exercise of that species of power." As Paine wrote, in terms applicable to both France and America: "It was not against Louis XVI, but against the despotic principles of the government, that the Nation revolted.... The Monarch and the Monarchy were distinct and separate things; and it was against the established despotism of the latter, and not against the person or the principles of the former, that the revolt commenced, and the Revolution has been carried."[19] Such arguments won Paine honorary French citizenship and a seat on the National Convention (although he narrowly escaped execution for voting against the regicide of Louis XVI).

Rothbard is brimming with libertarian admiration for Paine's attack on monarchy *per se*: "Not stopping at indicting George III, Paine pressed on to a comprehensive attack on the very principle of monarchy." "How indeed," Rothbard wonders, "had the natural equality of men before the law become transposed into subjection to a monarch?"[20] Rothbard hails Paine for concluding his "magnificent pamphlet" with these "stirring lines":

O ye that love mankind! Ye that dare oppose, not only the tyranny, but the tyrant, stand forth! Every spot of the old world is overrun with oppression. Freedom hath been hunted round the globe. Asia, and Africa, have long expelled her. Europe regards her like a stranger, and England hath given her

---

14. *Common Sense, the Rights of Man and Other Essential Writings of Thomas Paine* (NY: Meridian Books, 1984), Introduction, ix.

15. Bailyn, *Ideological Origins*, p. 286.

16. Rothbard, loc. cit., 135.

17. Ibid.

18. *Common Sense*, 27.

19. Ibid.; *The Rights of Man*, 133.

20. Rothbard, *Conceived in Liberty*, IV, 137.

warning to depart. O! receive the fugitive, and prepare in time an asylum for mankind.[21]

It seems not to have occurred to Rothbard that Paine's "stirring lines" might actually have been perceived by a reasonable reader of the time as windy demagoguery unsupported by any serious historical or philosophical argument.[22] *Common Sense* was certainly viewed that way by the Loyalists, whose counter-pamphlets warned quite prophetically that should Paine and his fellow radicals succeed in establishing their new "government by consent of the governed," they would only "turn loose upon the colonists a rabble of cheap politicians far worse than England's most incompetent officials. . . ."[23] No less than John Adams, who would live to become bitterly disillusioned by the results of the Revolution, called Paine "a star of disaster" whose radical call for mass democracy in America arose from "honest ignorance or foolish superstition on the one hand or from willful sophistry and knavish hypocrisy on the other." Adams fretted about the effect "so popular a pamphlet might have among the people."[24]

Rothbard also hails Paine for drawing—contrary to all tradition—a "sharp and quasi-anarchist distinction between 'society' and 'government'", according to which society is natural but government a mere "necessary evil" to which men must resort in their mythical Lockean "state of natural liberty."[25] But Paine and his fellow Lockean radicals failed to address in their propaganda the entirely predictable outcome of the Revolution: not anything like a return to a happy libertarian "state of nature" that has never existed but rather the replacement of an "absolute monarch" in England with a "Supream Government" (to recall Locke's phrase) at home. Here again the Tories were prophetic, warning that the colonists were already "slaves to [the Continental] Congress [and] that submission to it would entail far greater burdens to them than ever subjection to Great Britain would."[26]

Indeed, the radicals were not at all averse to appointing *themselves* an interim "Supream Government" without the "consent" of anyone but themselves and a rump composed of their vocal supporters. As the Tory counter-propagandists were only too happy to note, the "Sons of Liberty," the committees of correspondence

---

21. *Common Sense*, 50; Rothbard, *Conceived in Liberty*, IV, 139.

22. Rothbard, ibid., 137, cites Paine's reliance on the "the great English tradition of Milton and Sidney" *contra* monarchy. Aside from his poetry, John Milton (1608–1674) defended the regicide of Charles I, advocated divorce and rejected the divinity of Christ and the immortality of the soul. Algernon Sidney (1623–1683) was put to death for his role in the Rye House plot to assassinate Charles II. These two contemporary polemicists, considered beyond the pale even by conservative Protestants of their own time, hardly constitute "a great English tradition." Quite the contrary, the entire English tradition—not to mention the entire history of the Western world—supported monarchical government. Rothbard explains the history of monarchy in the West as the result of a perennial duping of the masses by priests and other intellectuals in the service of power-hungry rulers. See, e.g., Rothbard, "Anatomy of the State," http://www.lewrockwell.com/rothbard/rothbard62.html.

23. Davidson, *Propaganda*, 167–68.

24. In Bailyn, *Ideological Origins*, 288.

25. Rothbard, *Conceived in Liberty*, Vol. IV, 138; *Common Sense*, 24, 25.

26. Davidson, *Propaganda*, 316.

and safety, and the Continental Congress had not been elected by the people at large to represent them but rather had been self-appointed or chosen at town meetings attended by "not one fourth of the freeholders" or county meetings at which "not a hundredth of the people had consented to the choice."[27] Yet, in violation of the radicals' own fundamental principle of "Liberty," these *ad hoc* bodies (and others they created) routinely made decisions and enforced policies without any "consent of the governed." As one Tory pamphlet summed up with appropriate irony: "as there can be no TAXATION without representation, so there can be no REPRESENTATION without an ELECTION."[28] But, as Rothbard notes approvingly, "the Tories and the conservatives found that their attacks on independence were in vain" because "there is a fascination belonging to the word *Liberty* that beguiles the minds of the vulgar. . . ."[29] Here one can only agree with Rothbard.

Political Theater

Given the material comfort and natural human disinclination to upheaval among rank and file colonists, the Revolution was not, of course, set in motion entirely on the strength of anti-Catholic and anti-monarchical propaganda, no matter how "stirring." The radical apostles of Liberty also relied on another tool in the revolutionary toolbox they were helping to design for the future: staged provocations to generate public outrage.

The indisputable maestro of these provocations was Sam Adams, a second cousin of John Adams. One of the innumerable Freemasons on the revolutionary stage,[30] Adams "owned no superior as a propagandist. No one in the colonies realized more fully than he the primary necessity of arousing public opinion, no one set about it more assiduously."[31] At Harvard Adams gained a "profitable acquaintance with Locke and the liberal writers of the eighteenth century."[32] At age forty-two, writes an admiring biographer, Adams had "failed at one job after another . . . quit his legal studies, performed poorly as a clerk in Mr. Cushing's countinghouse, lost the thousand pounds his father had given him to enter business, botched his work as a tax collector, and run his family's brewery to the ground."[33] Yet he found his true calling as a politician and rabble-rousing leader of the movement for Revolution.[34] Adams's revolutionary activities proved to be a handy diversion from accusations that he had embezzled (but more likely simply failed to collect) thousands of

---

27. Ibid., 273.

28. "To the Worthy Freeholders and Others, Inhabitants of the Province of Georgia," July 27, 1774, in Davidson, *Propaganda*, 273.

29. Rothbard, *Conceived in Liberty*, Vol. IV, 140.

30. Reputedly a member of the Saint John's Lodge in Boston, although no written record of his membership survives. Cf. Denslow and Truman, Part One, 5–6.

31. Davidson, *Propaganda*, 2.

32. Ibid.

33. Dennis B. Fradin, *Sam Adams: the Father of American Independence* (NY: Clarion Books, 1998), 23.

34. Ibid.

pounds from the public treasury during his service as tax collector of Boston and Suffolk counties—a shortfall Adams attempted to cover up by shifting revenue from one year to another on the books.[35] Apparently, for Adams the dictum "no taxation without representation" was no bar either to his employment as a tax collector or the suit he was finally forced (by public pressure) to file against tax delinquents, including "two carpenters, two shoemakers, and 'Jack a free Negro.'"[36]

It was Adams's Sons of Liberty who led opposition to the Stamp Act in 1765, which included the highly successful use of mobs to "compel repeal of the Stamp Act by putting those who were to administer and enforce it in fear of their lives."[37] Adams organized and united the mobs, whose amusements at the time included ransacking and destroying the homes of Crown officials such as Lieutenant Governor Thomas Hutchinson (whom Adams's propaganda had falsely accused of initiating the Act) and pitched battles in the street over the mutilation of opposing effigies of the Pope on the annual "Pope Day," during which the combatants were sometimes "carted dying off the field of battle."[38]

Adams's mobs employed the device of Boston's famous Liberty Tree in their terror campaign against the Stamp Act. After Andrew Oliver, the stamp collector, and other officials were hung in effigy from the Tree, Oliver was summoned there to solemnly declare his resignation under threat of force—a threat backed up by the destruction of the stamp office and the ransacking of Oliver's home.[39] Thereafter, in Boston and the other colonies, the Liberty Tree became the site of the "Tree Ordeal" by which various royal officials and other perceived enemies of Liberty would be coerced into resignations or oaths of loyalty to "the people." Oliver, in fact, was later summoned before Liberty Tree to take a second solemn oath before a mob of two thousand, after the Sons of Liberty feared that he was "reconsidering his enforced resignation."[40]

The repeal of the Stamp Act in 1766 did not lessen Adams's appetite for agitation. Through his newspaper the *Independent Advertiser*, he "was familiarizing New Englanders with colonial rights and John Locke's political theory...."[41] Meanwhile, on the ground Adams was busily helping to orchestrate two more events that would be cited in support of a Lockean "appeal to heaven" for the warrant to rebel against George. The Boston "Massacre" (1770) and the Boston Tea Party (1773), both occurring in the city that served as the "Revolutionary cockpit,"[42] illustrate

35. Miller, *Sam Adams*, 58–60.

36. John K. Alexander, *Sam Adams, Revolutionary Politician* (Oxford: Roman & Littlefield, 2004), 27.

37. Hiller B. Zobel, *The Boston Massacre* (NY: W.W. Norton & Co., 1970), 28.

38. John C. Miller, *Sam Adams: Pioneer in Propaganda* (Stanford: Stanford Univ. Press, 1960), 68.

39. Arthur M. Schlesinger, "Liberty Tree: A Genealogy," *The New England Quarterly*, Vol. 25, No. 4 (Dec. 1952), 438.

40. Ibid., 438–39.

41. Davidson, *Propaganda*, 22.

42. Richard Maxwell Brown, "Violence and The American Revolution," from *Essays on the American Revolution*, eds Stephen G. Kurtz and James H. Hutson (Chapel Hill: Univ. of North Carolina Press and NY: W. W. Norton & C., Inc., 1973), 83.

how the advance of Liberty required a great deal of stagecraft as opposed to a spontaneous upwelling of popular demands for freedom from "tyranny." The work of such scholars as John C. Miller, Samuel Eliot Morison, and Hiller Zobel long ago demonstrated beyond serious dispute that both productions were early examples of revolutionary political theater.

As for the "massacre," the historical record is now clear: it was provoked by a mob of Adams's "Sons of Liberty" after years of Adams-organized mob violence in the city, including the razing of Lieutenant Governor Hutchinson's house, which Adams had the temerity to deplore in public. The mob involved in the "massacre," numbering in the hundreds, cornered a British guard of twenty, taunting and stoning the soldiers and daring them to fire, which several finally did (without orders) after one of them was knocked to the ground by a flying club. Even with a rather diffident defense by John Adams (whose selection as defense counsel was orchestrated by Sam), evidence of the colonials' aggression against Captain Preston and his men was so plain that the colonial jury promptly acquitted Preston of all charges. (It must be said that Adams rose to the occasion in his historic summation, which included the famous phrase "facts are stubborn things.") In a separate trial only two of the seven defendants were found guilty of even manslaughter, for which the penalty imposed was branding of the thumb. In yet another trial the jury did not even have to leave the courtroom to declare an acquittal of the customs official (Mainwaring), fancifully accused of firing on the colonials from the window of the Custom House. In fact, though, all the customs officials were indisputably miles from the scene at the time. The prosecution's star witness, "the little French boy," was a demonstrable liar whose perjury had been suborned by "divers high Whigs."[43]

An infuriated Sam Adams tried to convict Preston and the others in the press, blaming the jury rather than the evidence for the outcome. The trial evidence had included testimony regarding the deathbed statement of Patrick Carr, a fatally wounded member of the mob that had advanced on the soldiers, who confessed in his last moments that "the townspeople had been the aggressors and that the soldiers had fired in self-defense." Adams discredited Carr by the surefire method of describing him as "an Irish papist" who had "in all probability died in the faith of a roman catholick."[44] In a colony where men killed each other over the annual privilege of ripping apart an effigy of the Pope, what more did Adams need to say? Despite the loss at trial, Adams "squeezed every ounce of propaganda out of the 'Boston Massacre,'"[45] using it "not only to embitter Americans toward Great Britain but to prove the necessity of fighting British troops before they had opportunity to gain a foothold in the country."[46] Paul Revere provided Adams with a helpful engraving, now part of American folklore, which quite fictitiously depicted

43. Miller, *Sam Adams*, 188.

44. Zobel, *The Boston Massacre*, 286–287; Miller, *Sam Adams*, 189.

45. Samuel Eliot Morison, *The Oxford History of the American People* (NY: Oxford Univ. Press, 1965), 200 (hereafter *HAP*).

46. Miller, *Sam Adams*, 190.

"the soldiers in line of battle firing a point blank volley at twenty respectable citizens."[47] At the sight of the engraving "the continent rang with outraged screams."[48]

Nevertheless, owing to Parliament's repeal of the Townshend Act import duties, as requested by Lord North on March 5, 1770, the very day of the "massacre," the non-importation agreements organized by the radicals fell apart and "a general wave of prosperity set in."[49] As Arthur Schlesinger observes: "In the circumstances, patriotic ardor tended everywhere to cool during the next few years.... [E]ven Sam Adams, the 'Grand Incendiary of the Province,' could find little fuel for a blaze."[50] Morison makes the same point in his monumental history of the American people: "It proved difficult to whip up resentment against Britain when the colonies were enjoying the greatest prosperity within memory." Things were so good for the colonists that even John Hancock "told the royal governor that he was through with agitating," while Adams fretted that "the people will be so accustomed to bondage as to forget they were ever free."[51] That the colonists were not, in fact, in bondage was unthinkable for Adams and his fellow radicals, given that for them the very existence of a monarchy constituted "slavery."[52] Adams was convinced that behind the repeal of the Townshend Acts was a plot to increase the power of the Crown by using the revenue generated by the remaining duty on tea to put Crown appointees on the payroll, including Hutchinson, who had been elevated from Lieutenant Governor to Governor. But, as Morison notes, "this issue was rather arid; rural taxpayers were apt to say it was all right with them if the king paid the governor! Adams needed a spectacular emotional issue."[53]

Three years later Adams found his issue. The Boston Tea Party was "a far greater triumph" for Adams than the "Boston Massacre." By "precipitating the American Revolution [it] deserves to rank as the masterpiece of Sam Adams's effort to create an unbridgeable gap between Great Britain and her American provinces" and to paint himself and his fellow radicals as "patient, peace-loving men driven to rebellion by intolerable British tyranny...."[54] In this case the "intolerable tyranny" was the duty on prime British bohea tea, which, even with the duty, the colonies were able to import through the East India Tea Company at half the price paid in London—a bargain Parliament saw as the way to undercut and put out of business smugglers of the inferior Dutch product. From the average colonist's perspective, the British move resulted simply in a bargain price for a fine cup of tea. Yet, as Morison writes, while "It was difficult to find a constitutional issue in this device to

47. Morison, *HAP*, 201.
48. Ibid., 200.
49. Ibid.
50. Schlesinger, "Liberty Tree: A Genealogy," 448.
51. Morison, *HAP*, 201.
52. As Jefferson wrote to Adams in 1800: "You [Adams] have proven that it was monarchy, and not merely British monarchy, you opposed ... 'where annual election ends, tyranny begins' [Jefferson quoting himself]." Jefferson to Adams, February 26, 1800, in *The Writings of Thomas Jefferson* (Washington: Thomas Jefferson Memorial Association, 1904), 153.
53. Morison, *HAP*, 202.
54. Miller, *Sam Adams: Pioneer in Propaganda*, 276.

undercut the tea-runners . . . the radicals were equal to it. They had all summer to think it over, to write articles against the 'illegal monopoly' given the great chartered company, and to write poems about the 'pestilential herb' and the 'cup infused with bane by North's insidious hand.'"[55]

Miller wryly remarks that while the Stamp Act had been repealed, along with all of the Townshend Act duties except the one on tea, now the colonists would be "tempted to drink themselves out of their liberties with cheap tea." Adams and other "patriot propagandists vainly attempted to wean the people from tea" by declaring that it was "infected with plague which destroyed colonial liberties," would "induce tremors and spasmodic affections" and even "turn strong men into 'weak, effeminate and creeping valetudinarians.'" Yet, as fellow radical James Otis lamented, it seemed Bostonians would "part with all their liberties, and religion too, rather than renounce it." Worse, no less than John Hancock and other Whig merchants "joined with the rankest Tories in importing British tea and paying the tax."[56] The British bohea was apparently so good that it topped the allure of Liberty. Or perhaps the citizens of Boston simply did not see a threat to Liberty in the payment of a modest import duty for their favorite tea.

Unable to persuade Bostonians that Liberty was at stake in this tempest in a teacup, Adams and his Liberty Boys attempted to terrorize the royal tea merchants into resigning and refusing to handle the tea; but rather than consent to their own financial ruin, the merchants agreed only that they would store the merchandise pending further instructions from England. Out of options, Adams staged his Tea Party. A mob of his self-appointed Sons of Liberty donned their Mohican Indian costumes and tossed hundreds of chests "of the finest tea that ever tempted New Englanders' palates" into Boston Harbor. New Englanders, as Miller writes, were "charmed, as was John Adams, by the 'sublimity' of the tea party," and it now became "a patriotic duty to follow Boston's leadership."[57]

Adams's provocation started "a headlong plunge toward revolt . . . that led to war between the mother country and the colonies."[58] England could not let the act go unpunished without forfeiting all authority over the rebels; there would have to be retribution, which came, among other measures, in the form of the so-called Intolerable Acts (1774). As Morison concludes: "That is why this comic stage-Indian business of the Boston Tea Party was so important. It goaded [England] into a showdown, which was exactly what Sam Adams and the other radical leaders wanted."[59] Yet, as we shall see, it would be the same Sam Adams, ensconced as a member of the new post-Revolutionary government of Massachusetts, who would call for the hanging of anyone who resisted state taxation with the same tactics he himself had employed against the Crown's rather piddling tea tax only a few years earlier.

55. Morison, *HAP*, 203.
56. Miller, *Sam Adams*, 286.
57. Ibid., 294.
58. Ibid., 296.
59. Morison, *HAP*, 204.

The Deification of Liberty

Even before the first shots were fired at Lexington and Concord, it was apparent that Liberty was to be depicted as something far loftier than the new form of political power that it really was. The radicals' successful propaganda campaign to the masses involved what Conor Cruise O'Brien has aptly described as the Jeffersonian vision of "an absolute and deified Liberty, incarnate in the American and French Revolutions."[60] From the Whig radical leaders down to the rabble engaging in organized violence against the "enemies of American liberty," there was at work the invocation of a mystical entity perceived as struggling to be enfleshed in a new form of polity that would change the whole world with its saving Word.

In his massive study of the revolutionary movements of the 18th, 19th, and early 20th centuries, historian James H. Billington traces the development of what he calls "the revolutionary faith." By this he means the belief that "a perfect secular order will emerge from the forcible overthrow of traditional authority," a "rational order" that would replace "the rule of kings with the rule of law" and free humanity at last "from the arbitrary authority of the past in favor of rational perfectibility in the future. . . ."[61] The revolutionary faith is a "flame" that began its journey around the world when, as Billington writes, "some European aristocrats transferred their lighted candles from Christian altars to the Masonic lodges."[62] This "flame" is the revolutionary analogue to the action of the Holy Ghost, who "renew[s] the face of earth" and produces "a new man."[63] As Thomas Paine, the rabble-rousing evangelist of the gospel of Liberty, declares in *Common Sense*: "We have it in our power to begin the world over again. A situation, similar to the present, hath not happened since the days of Noah until now. The birthday of a new world is at hand. . . ."[64] Defending the French Revolution based on "the principles of freedom" established in America, Paine further declares in *The Rights of Man* that "the name of a Revolution is diminutive of its character, and it rises to a REGENERATION OF MAN."[65] This regeneration is to be effected by the "flame" first ignited in America; the flame that, like the Holy Ghost, transforms but does not consume its recipient: "From a small spark, kindled in America, a flame has arisen not to be extinguished. Without consuming . . . it winds its progress from nation to nation, and conquers by a silent operation. Man finds himself changed, he scarcely perceives how."[66]

In her groundbreaking study *Sons of the Fathers*, Catherine L. Albanese provides the historical evidence that the American Revolution "was *in itself* a religious experience, a hierophany [revelation of the sacred] collectively manifested and received,

60. Conor Cruise O'Brien, *The Long Affair: Thomas Jefferson and the French Revolution* (Chicago: Univ. of Chicago Press, 1996), 271–272.

61. James H. Billington, *Fire in the Minds of Men* (NY: Basic Books, Inc., 1980), 4.

62. Ibid., 6.

63. Psalm 130:30, Ephesians 4:24.

64. *Common Sense*, 63.

65. *The Rights of Man*, 120, 153, 189 (in part quoting Lafayette's farewell to Congress).

66. Ibid., 265.

which provided the fundamental basis for American civil religion as we know it."[67] For after all, America was the place where Liberty finally replaced what the Christian religion had once wrought in social order: the alliance of altar and throne. But, as we have seen, by its very nature the State—and most certainly the Lockean state—must profess some form of religion. And every religion must have its god.

It was in America, during the years preceding the Revolution, that Liberty first "revealed" itself as a god and began its public ministry to the world. Albanese provides an overview of the historical evidence of both the reification and deification of Liberty in the immediate pre-Revolutionary period. In her historical survey we first see a reified Liberty taking form as "the Genius of Liberty" or "the Spirit of Patriotism."[68] But after the "Boston Massacre," Liberty reified became Liberty deified. If, as Jefferson envisioned, the Capitol Building was to be "the first temple dedicated to the sovereignty of the people, embellishing with Athenian taste the course of a nation looking far beyond Athenian destinies,"[69] then the latter-day Greek deity occupying that latter-day Athenian temple would have to be the sovereignty of the people incarnate: the Goddess Liberty.

In fact, the goddess *Libertas* is of Roman provenance, "a female personification of liberty and personal freedom" to which a temple was built on the Aventine Hill circa 238 BC by order of Tiberius Gracchus before the Second Punic War. In 46 BC the Roman Senate voted to build "a temple to Libertas in honour of Julius Caesari, but it was not built. A statue of Libertas was set up in the Forum." The goddess "is usually portrayed as a matron with a laurel wreath or a pileus (a conical felt cap given to freed slaves, hence the symbol of liberty)."[70] The Liberty cap would figure prominently among the paraphernalia of the Age of Democratic Revolution, and the Roman denarius of 42 BC depicts the head of the goddess in a manner almost identical to what is seen in the Statue of Liberty.[71]

Albanese's study of the orations commemorating the "massacre" shows that the colonial orators were "particularly assiduous in bringing the goddess to the fore" and that "appeals to the Goddess Liberty [were] far more frequent than invocations to the Judaeo-Christian God."[72] In these orations, and in innumerable others that would follow, Liberty is identified precisely as a goddess occupying a temple. Among other examples, Albanese cites the Boston Massacre oration of radical leader James Lovell, a member of the revolutionary Committee of Secret Correspondence and a signer of the Articles of the Confederation, who acquainted his listeners with "the dimensions of the new religion":

67. Catherine L. Albanese, *Sons of the Fathers*, 6.

68. Ibid., 72–77.

69. Jefferson to Latrobe, July 12, 1812, *The Writings of Thomas Jefferson*, ed. H.A. Washington (NY: Derby & Jackson, 1859), 75.

70. "Libertas," Encyclopædia Britannica, online edition, accessed at <http://www.britannica.com/E Bchecked/topic/1389461/Libertas>.

71. Cf. image in *Sear Roman Coins and Their Values* (RCV 2000 edition) number 1447, available at http://wildwinds.com/coins/sears5/s1447.html.

72. Albanese, *Sons of the Fathers*, 73.

Watchful, hawk-eyed jealousy, ever guards the portal of the temple of the Goddess Liberty. This is known to those who frequent *her altars*. Our whole conduct, therefore, I am sure, will meet with the utmost candor of her Votaries, but I am wishing we may be able to convert even her basest Apostates.[73]

After 1770, writes Albanese, "songs began to appear which celebrated the Goddess" and "preachers took up the cause of the Goddess in their turn." For example, Jacob Duché, the Chaplain to the Continental Congress who delivered its opening prayer, gave a sermon explaining how Liberty "true to her divine source, is of heavenly abstraction" and that both Liberty and the "divine virtue" which is her "illustrious parent" come to dwell "in the hearts of all intelligent beings" where "they ought jointly *to be worshipped*."[74] The revolutionary troops of North Carolina were bucked up with a sermon reminding them that at one time "the heavenly goddess seemed to have fixed her temple" in Britain, where Liberty had "her saints and her confessors, and a whole army of martyrs," but now that "the gates of hell have prevailed against her" in the mother country, it fell to the colonials to bank her "sacred fires." Indeed, warned another preacher, Simeon Howard, unless Liberty were defended in America the "heaven-born virgin, seeing her votaries slain, her altars overthrown and her temples demolished" would have "no refuge on earth" and "would be obliged, like the great patron of liberty, the First-born Son of God, to ascend to her God and our God . . . till *with him she shall again descend to reign in triumph on earth*."[75] Thus, when it came to Liberty, even the most Protestant of orators was willing to contemplate something like the Assumption of the Blessed Virgin Mary.

Equally telling is the testimony of apostates from the cult of Liberty. One such was the Anglican prelate Jonathan Boucher, who confessed in one of his discourses that during the Stamp Act controversy he had been "Contented to swim with the stream . . . and, with but little reflection, had embraced those doctrines which are most flattering to human pride. . . . *I too bowed at the altar of Liberty*, and *sacrificed to this idol* of our groves, upon the high mountains, and upon the hills, and under every green tree."[76]

The sign and sacrament of this veritable cult of the Goddess Liberty was the Liberty Tree in Boston—the same tree from which Andrew Oliver and other royal officials were hung in effigy and before which he and other "enemies of American liberty" were haled to offer their coerced resignations and oaths of loyalty to the revolutionary cause. As Oliver's brother wrote, Liberty Tree had been "consecrated

73. James Lovell, "Boston Massacre Oration," April 2, 1771; in Albanese, *Sons of the Fathers*, 77–78.

74. Jacob Duché, "The Duty of Standing Fast in Our Spiritual and Temporal Liberties" (July 7, 1775), in *Patriot Preachers*, ed. Moore, 80; cited in Albanese, 78.

75. Simeon Howard, Election Sermon (1780), in Albanese, 78.

76. Boucher's Discourses, in *The History of the Church of England in the Colonies* (London: F. & J. Rivington, 1844–1848), 322.

as an idol for the mob to worship" and was the place for imposing the discipline of the "Tree Ordeal [on those] whom the Rioters pitched upon as State delinquents."[77] In addition to being both a totem and locus of the power of Liberty, Liberty Tree was a place of worship where revolutionary liturgies were enacted. In Providence, Rhode Island a Liberty Tree was dedicated during a ceremony in which the participants laid their hands on the sacred object as a local minister invoked the worldwide unity of a kind of mystical body of Liberty:

> We do, in the name and on behalf of the true sons of Liberty, in America, Great Britain, Ireland, Corsica, or wherever they may be dispersed throughout the world, dedicate and solemnize . . . this tree to be a Tree of Liberty. May all our councils and deliberations under its venerable branches be guided by wisdom . . . and may the sons of Liberty often repair hither, to confirm and strengthen each other. When they look towards *their sacred Elm*, may they, like the House of David, grow stronger and stronger, while their enemies, like the House of Saul, grow weaker and weaker. Amen.[78]

Another such liturgy, at the Boston Liberty Tree, featured an oil paper obelisk constructed by Paul Revere which contained "some verse to the Goddess of Liberty, including the cry: 'Goddess! we cannot part, thou must not fly . . .'" and "a sketch of America as an Indian chief lying under a pine tree while the angel of Liberty hovered above."[79]

The "sacred elm," writes Albanese, became "a kind of transcendent cosmo-historical tree around which the other Liberty Trees and liberty signs of the colonies took root . . . Like the sacrament it was, Liberty Tree was the reality which oriented the patriots, yet it pointed beyond itself to another source of power"[80]—the power invoked by Paine with his talk of remaking the world and regenerating man in a disquieting analogy to the working of divine grace. In fact, as Arthur Schlesinger pointed out long ago, it was none other than Paine who elaborated Liberty Tree's provenance as a divine gift. Upon seeing Liberty Tree after his arrival in America, the "congenital rebel . . . at once grasped its significance" and "conjured up a fit origin for the Tree. . . . [H]e explained that the Goddess Liberty had transplanted the 'fair budding branch' from 'the gardens above' to this 'peaceable shore,' where the 'fame of its fruit' drew men from many nations."[81] In Paine's widely published ode to Liberty Tree, set to the tune "The Gods of the Greeks," the former tax collector— the "Matthew" of the new gospel—praised the "freemen" of America who "with one spirit endued . . . one friendship pursued/And their temple was *Liberty Tree*. . . ."[82]

77. Peter Oliver, "The Origin and Progress of the American Rebellion to the Year 1776"; in Schlesinger, "Liberty Tree: A Genealogy," 438.

78. Silas Downer, "A Discourse Delivered in Providence . . . at the Dedication of the Tree of Liberty" (Providence, RI: John Waterman, 1768), 15–16, in Albanese, *Sons of the Fathers*, 60.

79. Ibid., 61.

80. Ibid., 17.

81. Schlesinger, "Liberty Tree: A Genealogy," 435–436.

82. "Liberty Tree. A New Song," by "Atlanticus," *Pennsylvania Ledger*, August 12, 1775, in Schlesinger, op. cit., 436.

Liberty Tree begat Liberty Pole, which either replaced a Liberty Tree felled by the British authorities or was erected as an alternative totem. One Tory pamphleteer observed with contempt that the Liberty Pole "had come to mean the '*Happiness of Assembling in the open Air,* and performing *idolatrous and vociferous* Acts of Worship to a stick of wood'. . . ."[83] As with Liberty Tree, Liberty Pole was a place where enemies of the revolution were brought to express their coerced repentance or loyalty to the revolution. For example, in 1775 two Tories in New York City "were 'used in a most cruel manner by a mob of two hundred men' for refusing on bended knee to curse King George at the Liberty Pole."[84] And woe unto him who committed the sacrilege of harming the sacred stick. In Sandwich, Massachusetts, for example, "[t]hree miscreants . . . who destroyed the Liberty Pole one night were forced publicly to confess that they had behaved 'most Wickedly, Maliciously and Injuriously (being instigated by the Devil and our own evil Hearts). . . .'"[85]

Liberty Tree emerged as the sacramental sign and symbol of the French Revolution as well, very probably under the influence of Paine, the honorary French citizen who nearly fell victim to the wrath of the Goddess when he was in Paris "stepping up French resistance."[86] In France, Liberty Tree was, as Billington writes, "a symbol of regeneration rooted in the earth but reaching up to heaven . . . a living totem: an acceptable new form of verticality amidst the leveling impulses of the revolutionary era."[87] But in France "the tree of Liberty was now said to be fertilized by the blood of kings" as opposed to "the blood of patriots and tyrants" to which Jefferson alluded. In the annual commemoration of the execution of Louis XVI, "the planting of a tree of Liberty was the central, obligatory ritual."[88]

We have focused on these "liturgical" details of the deification of Liberty by the colonial radicals because they rather dramatically demonstrate the falsity of the golden legend of a "conservative" and even "Christian" American Revolution. Both the radical Whig leaders at the top and the rabble dancing around Liberty Trees and Liberty Poles at the bottom saw themselves as participants in a mystical and sacred cause that embraced all of humanity: the cause of Liberty. The identification of Liberty as a Goddess was thus far more than the sort of classical trope common to 18th-century rhetoric. As florid as they were, 18th-century rhetoricians were hardly in the habit of deifying the objects of their esteem. Liberty alone received this honorific in the patriots' speeches, sermons, songs and poems. This does not, of course, mean that the American revolutionaries *literally* worshipped Liberty as a divinity. Rather, the deification of Liberty and the rituals surrounding Liberty Tree and Liberty Pole were a spontaneous expression of Liberty's status as an idol. In this sense, Liberty was something to which one is so slavishly attached—be it money, fame or some other earthly *desideratum*—that it competes with the true

---

83. "The Dougliad," *New-York Gazette and Weekly Mercury,* April 23, 1770; in Schlesinger, op. cit., 445.
84. *New York Gazetteer,* March 9, 1775; cited in Schlesinger, op. cit., 451.
85. Schlesinger, op. cit., 449.
86. Ibid., 453 & n. 68.
87. Billington, *Fire in the Minds of Men,* 46.
88. Ibid.

God as the object of one's devotion. The patriots, Albanese concludes, "seemed held as securely captive by the power of Liberty as their fathers had been by the sovereignty of God. 'Free' patriots were literally unfree as they walked in the service of the Goddess, yet enslavement to her virtues . . . created for them another form of freedom or at least the illusion of it."[89]

Another aspect of the idolatry at work here is a rather febrile and half-understood theology of Liberty, according to which the Goddess, while not God the Father Himself, is in some way related to Him, even espoused to Him, as suggested by the "heaven-born virgin" of Simeon Howard's sermon. Hence Albanese writes of a *hieros gamos* between "the Goddess and their God"[90]—that is, a mythic coupling between divinity and a lesser being by virtue of which the latter acquires divine attributes. The *hieros gamos* between God and Liberty—with the "wife" proclaiming man's Lockean independence from any authority not "consented" to on the basis of persuasive arguments—even causes the divine Husband himself to change His ways. As Gordon Wood observes, in the American intellectual climate created by the Locke-inspired attack on the doctrine of the natural law of patriarchal authority, "Even the authority of the supreme father of all, God himself, was not immune to challenge. . . . God, like any parent, had to earn the respect of his children, and he had to earn it through love and affection, not fear."[91]

Finally, the deification of Liberty must be seen under another aspect: the neo-paganism that characterizes the Enlightenment as a whole. In his magisterial study of Enlightenment thought, Peter Gay, who calls the American Revolution "the program of enlightenment in practice,"[92] defines the Enlightenment as "a mixture of classicism, impiety and science, and the *philosophes* as modern pagans. . . ." The Enlightenment was, quite simply, "the rise of modern paganism."[93] Already far removed from the theology and perennial philosophy of the Catholic Church, the great majority of American colonials practiced forms of non-conformist Christianity which (the widely detested High Church Anglicanism of the colonial minority aside) were practically devoid of sacrament, ritual, and mystical theology. And yet the human need for some form of ritual tribute to the divine cannot be eradicated from a soul made by and for a mysterious God. Hence the need for Liberty Tree as "an acceptable new form of verticality amidst the leveling impulses of the revolutionary era," to recall Billington's words.

Given this historical context one can appreciate why grown men who considered themselves Christians, and who lived more than seventeen centuries after the advent of Christ, were reduced to offering hosannas to trees and poles as totems of a deified Liberty. The participants in this puerile nonsense were nominal Christians who exhibited an almost neo-pagan regression to an elemental faith in a powerful but distant God, a God who could indeed be thought of as acting through a

---

89. Albanese, *Sons of the Fathers*, 79.
90. Ibid., 80.
91. Wood, *Radicalism*, 158.
92. Peter Gay, *The Enlightenment: The Science of Freedom*, 558.
93. Cf. ibid., 125.

demiurge in the sacred but embraceable person of Liberty. The evangelical Great Awakenings of the Christian sects notwithstanding, it was this sort of God—the neo-pagan Nature's God of the Declaration of Independence—that the Whig radicals of pre-Revolutionary America invoked and which would become the inoffensive generic deity of the national civic religion, a subject to which we shall return in the fourth and final section.

The Interim Dictatorship of Liberty

Despite the religious devotion of its most ardent followers, "Liberty" has never been established anywhere without trampling on the rights of its unbelieving opponents, whose unpardonable sin is their refusal to see in Liberty's advance anything but another form of sovereign power likely to prove far less agreeable than the "tyrannical" status quo. Given the natural reluctance of people to overthrow everything that stands in favor of a promised utopia, the leaders of the American Revolution could not rely on propaganda, political theater and quasi-religious fervor alone to overcome local resistance to the revolutionary tide they were trying to create. Whenever necessary, the colonial radicals, like all the apostles of Liberty before and after them, did not hesitate to employ other means. These included violence, coercion, the confiscation and destruction of property, the seizure of political power by cliques proclaiming themselves "the body of the people," and a purge of all "enemies of the Revolution."

Sam Adams, as we have seen, was "something of a specialist in group violence."[94] While the violence characteristic of the revolutionary movement as a whole was part of a long history of mob violence in the colonies, upon Adams's first successes with the Boston mobs "[f]orce had been introduced into the Revolutionary movement in a form long familiar, but now newly empowered by widely shared principles and beliefs. *It would never thereafter be absent*."[95] Zobel remarks that it is no defense to argue that the mobs of the Revolution "did not cause wholesale or even retail slaughter, and that compared to the Paris rabble in 1789 the Bostonians acted decently and decorously," for the purpose of the mobs in both revolutions was the same: to impose the desired political result by sending the message, "Do what the mob asks, or the mob will destroy your property and perhaps destroy you."[96]

In a seminal essay on violence in the American Revolution, historian Richard Maxwell Brown observes that the Revolution "made a contribution to the demonic side of our national history, for its origin was violent and the concept of popular sovereignty lent itself frequently to majoritarian tyranny."[97] Historian G. B. Warren essays how the mobs justified their actions with reference to the "curious, amorphous entity called the 'Body of the People,'" or simply the "Body," which came to

---

94. Richard Maxwell Brown, "Violence and The American Revolution," 90.
95. Bailyn, *Pamphlets of the American Revolution*, 585; in Zobel, *Boston Massacre*, 28.
96. Zobel, *Boston Massacre*, 28.
97. Brown, *Violence*, 82.

mean any gathering of radicals, "both mobs as well as formal legal assemblies." Thus, a town meeting protesting the Tea Act in 1773 became in the minds of the attendees "a mass meeting of the 'Body' supposedly representing all the people of the province."[98]

Tarring and feathering was a principal means by which the "Body" imposed "popular punishment for modern delinquents" deemed enemies of the revolutionary movement.[99] The "Body" employed tarring and feathering "without respite from 1773 through 1775 in such cities as Boston and Charleston" as well as the countryside of New England and the middle colonies.[100] This form of torture was wielded not only against crown officials but also against loyalists and merchants "who violated the patriotic policy of the nonimportation of British goods." Even those who merely defended the Crown were liable to be tarred and feathered. By way of example, Brown recounts the "fate of Dr. Abner Beebe of East Haddam Connecticut, who had spoken 'very freely' in favor of the crown . . . 'for which he was assaulted by the Mob, stripped naked, and hot pitch was poured on him, which blistered his Skin. He was then carried to the Hog Sty and rubbed over with Hogs Dung. They threw Hogs Dung in his face and rammed some of it down his throat'. . . ." after which Beebe's home was vandalized.[101]

Wood demonstrates that "at the height of the patriot frenzy in 1774–76 many of the revolutionaries wanted nothing less than a reconstruction of American society." He provides a compelling summary of how radical mobs aimed for this goal by means of "elaborate procedures and rituals for dealing with individuals who held royal commissions or whose allegiance to the revolutionary cause was in doubt." In addition to the usual tarring and feathering, the radicals effected armed arrests of men of wealth and position (such as James Allen of the Allen family of Pennsylvania) or even insignificant traders with the Crown (such as a Maine lumberman) for actions or even attitudes "contrary to the known sentiments of the people." Whig committees and mobs were always intent on getting their political opponents to "recant their former ties to the crown" so that they could be "reintegrate[d] back into the community." In an early form of political reeducation, the radicals "singled out suspected loyalists, subjected them to elaborate interrogations, and urged them to sign confessions of guilt and repentance."

Wood cites the classic example of one Isaac Hunt, who was "escorted around the city in a cart, while he publicly recanted his questioning of a revolutionary committee's authority." In the case of backsliding, such as "having drunk British tea or having denounced the Continental Congress," the radicals "went to great lengths to get these individuals to swear new oaths of fidelity as 'marks of friendship' to the people."[102] As Wood observes: "All revolutionaries in the eighteenth century were fascinated with oath-taking. . . . The American revolutionaries, like the French a few

98. G. B. Warden, *Boston: 1689–1766* (Boston: 1970), 218–219; in Brown, *Violence*, 110.
99. *Boston Evening Post*, November 6, 1769; in Brown, *Violence*, 104.
100. Brown, *Violence*, 104.
101. Ibid.
102. Wood, *Radicalism*, 215.

years later, could not administer enough oaths. . . . Whig committees sought . . . to make the oaths a 'touchstone of public virtue, and a trial of faith, and woe unto those who are found faithless.'"[103] With these oaths, extracted under threat of force, the radicals were destroying the old hierarchical society and "creating new social bonds by making individuals swear a new 'attachment to the body of the people' (the terms most commonly used in these mob rituals)."[104]

Until the radicals effectively silenced it, the colonial opposition press did not hesitate to protest "Whig tyranny." For example, the *New York Gazetteer* protested that the First Continental Congress and its committees "arraign [assume] the highest authority on earth, insolently trample on the liberties of their fellow subjects; and without the shadow of a trial, take from them their property, grant it to others, and not content with this, hold them up to contempt and expose them to the vilest injuries."[105] An article in the *Massachusetts Gazette* charged that the Congress, ostensibly summoned to address the "Intolerable Acts," had assumed a life of its own, ignoring the expiration of its own stated purpose: "[C]an there be any strong instance of tyranny and usurpation, than for a number of men under the cloak of an obsolete and expired authority, to continue themselves in office, and decide upon the property of their fellow citizens? . . . *I have no notion that freedom can be established by opposing arbitrary principles in one instance, and tamely submitting to them in another.*"[106] Or, as another dissenter declared in the *Virginia Gazette*: "Is there no Danger to Liberty when every Merchant is liable to have his House, Property and even Life invaded or threatened by a mob, who may be assembled at any time by the call of unknown Leaders, by the Ringing of the Bells . . . and hanging out a Flag?"[107]

As Davidson demonstrates in his definitive study of Revolutionary War propaganda, the Whig propagandists and their "muscle" would not tolerate anti-Whig propaganda and "were determined to control the press." The Sons of Liberty "began the intimidation of the printers" and "Tory preachers, writers and printers were all the objects of actual violence and coercion." For example, the Anglican cleric Samuel Seabury's "capable pamphlets" attacking the Continental Congress were "tarred and feathered by some committees, burned by others and condemned by all." Seabury's pamphlets were so effective, however, that "mere answers were insufficient," and a band of radicals "invaded his house while he was away and finally captured him." During the Townshend Act controversy the *Boston Chronicle* was "boycotted and actually attacked"; it eventually shut down completely. When all other efforts at censorship failed, the printing press of James Rivington, "the most capable of the Tory printers," was destroyed. The editor of the *New Hampshire Gazette* was "under the close supervision of the committees" and was "warned never again to print anything reflecting upon the Continental Congress or the

---

103. Wood, *Radicalism*, 215, quoting *The Patriots* by Robert Munford.
104. Ibid.
105. Davidson, *Propaganda*, 275.
106. *Mass. Gazette and Boston Weekly News-Letter*, July 7, 1774; in Davidson, *Propaganda*, 275
107. *Va. Gazette* (Purdie), January 20, 1774; in Davidson, *Propaganda*, 285.

cause of American independence." The *New York Mercury* was forbidden to publish the British version of the Battle of Lexington after "Hancock and Adams came to town . . . determined still to suppress every account but their own." The *New York Gazetteer* was forced to close for two years when a mob invaded its offices and destroyed the type, after which the editor fled to England. When Charles Inglis "felt impelled" to answer Paine's *Common Sense* in a pamphlet entitled "The Deceiver unmasked. . . . In answer to a pamphlet falsely called Common Sense," a mob assembled and consigned the entire edition of the pamphlet to the flames. *Common Sense* went unanswered by opposing pamphlets because "The Tory pamphleteers were gone. Seabury and Galloway were under close watch, and Cooper, Chandler, Leonard and Sewall had left America."[108] The examples could be multiplied but the point is made: the Whig apparatus practically drove the opposition press out of existence.

But the Whigs were not content with merely silencing their opponents in the press. They sought to suppress Tory activities in general. Whig mobs, committees and councils "broke up their meetings, persecuted their speakers, and drove their preachers from the pulpits."[109] And "Whig tyranny" was no local *ad hoc* affair but rather a continental policy coordinated from the top by an unelected revolutionary government whose "recommendations" set the pace for revolutionary despotism: the Continental Congress. To insure that it would be able to keep actual and potential opposition under its thumb, the First Continental Congress (1774)—again, with no real authority to do so—had declared that cessation of trade with Britain under the Continental Association would be enforced by committees to be chosen "in every county, city and town . . . to observe the conduct of all persons touching this association" and to identify (by majority vote) and publish in the newspaper the names of all those violators who were to be "universally contemned as *the enemies of American liberty. . . .*"[110] The creation of these local surveillance committees was part of a process by which the Whig radicals ultimately erected a veritable pan-colonial police state to crush all opposition to the Revolution. By the time of the calling of the Second Continental Congress in May of 1775, weeks after the Battles of Lexington and Concord, the revolutionaries in every colony, as even Rothbard admits, had institutionalized a virtually totalitarian oppression of the political opposition:

> Everywhere Tories were deprived of civil rights and freedom of speech and press; they were especially taxed and arrested for the duration of the war on mere suspicion and without benefit of habeas corpus. They were herded together and shipped into prison camps far from British lines, in which they were sometimes forced to work for the Revolution; they were tarred and feathered, banished, and their lands and properties were confiscated by the

108. Davidson, *Propaganda*, 170–172; 251–254; 307.
109. Ibid., 298.
110. S.E. Morison, ed., *Sources and Documents Illustrating the American Revolution, 1764–1788* (Oxford, 1929), 124; in Brown, *Violence*, 111.

State. Sometimes they were even executed. They were forced to take test oaths, they were disenfranchised and barred from public office, and they were generally forbidden to practice as professional men. In many cases, family punishment was imposed, and relatives of absent Tories were jailed for the behavior of their errant kinsmen and held hostages. Local vigilante action kept watch on suspected Tories and imposed harsh penalties on them. Banishment from the country—with little money allowed to be taken out—was a favorite punishment for Tories and suspected Tories.[111]

Nor did the radicals' police state confine its oppression to known or suspected Tories. For all his admiration of the Revolution, it is Rothbard himself who admits that the Second Continental Congress "urged the imprisonment of *anyone* who might, in the opinion of the provincial committees of safety, 'endanger the safety of the colony or the liberties of America'. . . ."[112] And this from a self-constituted body that had "not a foot of land on which they had the right to execute their decisions . . . not one civil officer to carry out their commands, nor the power to appoint one," and which had been "elected" by "tumultuary assemblies which had no recognized legal existence. . . ."[113] Here the revolutionaries relied heavily (even if unknowingly) on Locke's doctrine of "tacit consent" and Rousseau's "general will," not to be confused with the actual will of an actual majority of "the people." (See Chapter 3.)

Rothbard further admits that the "concept of 'enemy of American liberty' was quickly extended from violators of the continental boycott to *anyone critical of the Revolution.*" The historian John C. Miller, in his most ironically entitled *Triumph of Freedom*, fleshes out this aspect of the revolutionary police state:

> Loyalists who scoffed at the Congress and swore that they would do as they pleased were summoned before the committees to answer for their opinions and conduct; and if the committees failed to persuade, the mob took over. *Thus was created a police system, secret, efficient, and all-powerful.*
>
> Letters were seized in the post office, those addressed to England receiving special attention from the committeemen; and spies kept watch upon the movements of suspected persons.
>
> In October 1775, the Continental Congress directed the committees to take into custody every person "who, going at large, might in their opinion endanger the safety of the colony or liberties of America." Zealously the committees fell to this work; suspects were rounded up, oaths of fidelity were imposed, and in stubborn cases imprisonment and disfranchisement were inflicted.
>
> "It is as much as a person's life is worth to speak disrespectfully of the Congress," declared a Loyalist in 1775. "The people . . . are all *liberty mad.*"[114]

---

111. Rothbard, *Conceived in Liberty,* Vol. IV, 423–34.

112. Ibid., 424.

113. George Bancroft, *History Of The United States of America, from the Discovery of the American Continent* (Boston: Little, Brown and Company, 1875), 353–54.

114. John C. Miller, *Triumph of Freedom, 1775–1783* (Boston: Little, Brown, 1948), 40.

Liberty mad indeed. Suspects were subject to appearances before the "commit-tees of safety" for such "offenses" as "criticizing the Continental Congress, belittling the Massachusetts Army, criticizing Presbyterian prominence in the Revolution, and a host of other 'errors of opinion.'"[115] The very definition of "Tory" was an expansive thing, eventually equating with anyone who would not swear an oath to the Revolution because he felt bound in conscience to remain loyal to the King. A Loyalist who "was true to his convictions, creed and king was detested, reviled and if prominent, ruined in business, tarred and feathered, mobbed, ostracized or imprisoned; and all this at the will of a committee, *self constituted and responsible to no one.*"[116]

The Tyrannical Apostle of Liberty

On July 4, 1776, the Second Continental Congress—purporting to speak as the "representatives" of several million colonials who had never elected them—declared that the colonies were independent from England and that they now con-stituted a union of independent states:

> We, therefore, the Representatives of the united [sic] States of America, in General Congress, Assembled ... do, in the Name, and by Authority of the good People of these Colonies solemnly publish and declare, That these united Colonies are, and of Right ought to be Free and Independent States, that *they are Absolved from all Allegiance to the British Crown*, and that all political connection between them and the State of Great Britain, is and ought to be totally dissolved.

As Professor Peter Onuf of the University of Virginia explains, the Declaration of Independence was part of a hidden "clockwork" that had been set up, not by "the Body of the people," but rather by self-appointed patriot leaders who had to main-tain "the myth of spontaneous resistance" as a "crucial prop to congressional legiti-macy." The Second Continental Congress, "[e]xploiting an early burst of popular enthusiasm for the war effort, quickly and successfully assumed *a quasi-monarchi-cal authority....* In other words, *Congress sought to take the king's place.* But this pretension would be seen as legitimate only if it made no claims on its own behalf"[117]—that is, only if the Congress claimed to act for "the people."

After the Congress arrogated to itself the authority to declare the colonies inde-pendent of England, the radical leaders in the newly minted independent States of the United States of America imposed strict conformity, in both word and deed, to the revolutionary cause, crushing all opposition to the Revolution. Here it is appropriate to focus on the preeminent role of the very author of the Declaration:

115. Rothbard, *Conceived in Liberty*, Vol. IV, 66.
116. Alexander C. Flick, *Loyalism in New York During the American Revolution* (NY: Columbia Univ., 1901), 47–48; in Rothbard, *Conceived in Liberty*, ibid.
117. Peter S. Onuf, "Jefferson, Federalist," in *Essays in History* (Charlottesville, VA: Univ. of Virginia Press, 1993), Vol. 35, 26, 27.

Thomas Jefferson, the idol of contemporary libertarians. As the constitutional historian Leonard Levy observes: "Jefferson and Washington agreed that only those who swore loyalty to American Independence should enjoy the rights of citizenship, and that all others were 'secret enemies.'"[118] In keeping with what Washington and Jefferson had decided for the rest of America, by 1778 all states "had adopted loyalty or test oaths, 'weapons of savage coercion,' that failed to distinguish between loyalty itself and the ritual of swearing it."[119]

The loyalty oath statute Jefferson drafted for the Virginia legislature is typical of these totalitarian measures. The purpose of the loyalty or test oath was, of course, to flush out suspected Tories whose hidden thoughts were threats to the revolutionary cause. Jefferson's definition of a Tory, written in defense of the loyalty oath, is supremely illustrative of the manner in which he and his fellow radicals imposed what they called Liberty on those who would dissent even inwardly from their program:

> A Tory has been properly defined to be *a traitor in thought,* but not in deed. The only description, by which the laws have endeavored to come at them, was that of non-jurors, or persons refusing to take *the oath of fidelity to the state.*[120]

Jefferson's loyalty oath, whose provisions were paralleled in the other newly created states, compelled all free males above age sixteen to "swear or affirm that I renounce and refuse all allegiance to George the third [sic], king of Great Britain, his heirs and successours [sic]," to profess absolute allegiance to Virginia "as a free and independent state," and to turn over to the authorities anyone known to be involved in "treasons or traitorous conspiracies which I now or hereafter shall know to be formed against this or any of the United States of America."[121] Whoever refused to take the oath was disarmed, stripped of his voting rights, and barred from holding public office, serving on juries, suing for money or acquiring property. Jefferson also participated in drafting a statute that subjected non-jurors to triple taxation.[122] Ironically enough, today the Thomas Jefferson Center for the Protection of Free Expression cites loyalty oaths as one of the great threats to freedom of speech, providing just one example of how the "Jefferson legend" and the actual historical figure fail to correspond.[123]

Jefferson was not content with a loyalty oath producing mere verbal conformity to the Revolution. He actively supported and probably helped to draft a Virginia statute prohibiting "crimes injurious to the independence of Virginia, but less than treason." As Levy describes it, this act "was in part a loosely drawn interdict against

118. Leonard Levy, *Jefferson and Civil Liberties: the Darker Side* (NY: Quadrangle/New York Times Book Company, 1963), 28.

119. Ibid.

120. Jefferson, *Notes on the State of Virginia*, ed. David Waldstreicher (NY: Macmillan, 2002), Query XVI, Proceedings as to Tories, 189.

121. Laws of Virginia, May 1777, Ch. III, in Hening's Statutes at Large, Vol. IX, 281.

122. Levy, *Jefferson and Civil Liberties*, 30–31.

123. See "Pall of Orthodoxy: The Insidious Persistence of Loyalty Oaths," fepproject.org/commentaries/loyalty.html.

freedom of political expression."[124] Under penalty of a fine of up to twenty thousand pounds and a prison term of up to five years, the act criminalized "any word, open deed, or act" in defense of "the authority, jurisdiction, or power, of the king or parliament of Great Britain," or even an attempt to "persuade [others] to return to a dependence upon the crown of Great Britain. . . ."[125]

An expanded version of the act, *signed by Governor Jefferson* in 1780, defined "new verbal crimes"[126] deemed "injurious to the Independence of America, but less than treason," including writing, preaching or other statements expressing the view that "the United States of America, or any or either of them ought to be dependant [sic] on the crown of Great Britain, or on the British parliament," any statement acknowledging "the king of Great Britain to be the lawful sovereign of the United States of America," any attempt to induce another "to promise any obedience or allegiance to the king or parliament of Great Britain," and any attempt to "dissuade or discourage any person" (outside of one's immediate family) from joining the revolutionary army "when called upon by due authority. . . ."[127] The law Jefferson signed included a preposterous ban on "directly by writing, printing, or open speaking, wish[ing] health, prosperity, or success to the king of Great Britain. . . ."[128]

Jefferson's major contributions to "Whig tyranny" even extended to his support for what Levy calls "the Age of Enlightenment's rudimentary precursor of modern internment camps for political suspects."[129] In 1777 (two years before Jefferson became Governor), the Governor's council, citing an imminent threat of British naval invasion, ordered the removal from military zones and internment of "all persons who refused to take an oath of loyalty to the American cause," said prisoners to be released only if they took the oath. The council later conveniently immunized itself and the governor from all suits arising from such internments, so that "Jefferson thus participated in retroactively constitutionalizing the executive act by which political suspects and non-jurors were interned because they *might* commit a crime at some future time."[130] The Virginia legislature later invested Governor Jefferson with the power to imprison, or to remove and intern in "places of security," anyone as to whom "there may be just cause to *suspect* . . . disaffection to the independence of the United States, and of attachment to their enemies. . . ."[131] While Jefferson did not personally order any internments, he did "exercise his power to imprison the disaffected or politically suspect, and many languished in jail without a hearing or even a court martial."[132]

124. Levy, *Jefferson and Civil Liberties*, 28.
125. Laws of Virginia, October 1776, Ch. V, in Hening's Statutes, Vol. 9, 170.
126. Levy, *Jefferson and Civil Liberties*, 29.
127. Laws of Virginia, May 1780, Ch. XIV, in Hening's Statutes, 268–270.
128. Ibid.
129. Levy, *Jefferson and Civil Liberties*, 31.
130. Ibid., 32. Emphasis in original.
131. Hening, Statutes of Virginia, May 1780, Vol. X, 309–315, cited in Levy, *Jefferson and Civil Liberties*, 32.
132. Levy, *Jefferson and Civil Liberties*, 33.

But Jefferson went still further in trampling on the rights of the "enemies of American liberty." Rothbard notes that it was Jefferson who pushed through the Virginia legislature a bill of attainder against Tory counter-revolutionary Josiah Philips, a common laborer-turned-brigand and citizen of Virginia who took up arms against the Revolution. By this draconian measure, *drafted by Jefferson himself*,[133] the Virginia legislature pronounced Philips guilty of high treason and various other crimes, including murder and arson, ordered him to stand trial within a month, and declared that upon his failure to appear for trial—after having already been declared guilty!—"it shall be lawful for any person, with or without orders, to pursue and slay the said Josiah Philips, *and any others who have been of his associates or confederates. . . .*"[134]

Jefferson's bill, writes Levy, declared "an open hunting season on the unnamed men whose guilt for treason and murder was legislatively assumed. . . . [A] man might be shot on the mere supposition that he was an 'associate' of Philips."[135] Philips and several of his men were ultimately captured and put on trial, thus mooting the bill of attainder. They were not tried for treason, murder or arson, however, but for the theft of some felt hats and a ball of twine worth about two pounds in total, for which petty theft they were promptly convicted and executed. Virginia Attorney General Randolph had not pursued treason, murder or arson charges because the evidence was lacking. And it was also necessary to avoid the defense that Philips was a prisoner of war fighting against the American revolutionaries on a military commission from Lord Dunmore, the royal governor of Virginia, which in fact he was, as Randolph himself later admitted.[136]

As even Rothbard concedes, Jefferson the libertarian icon "was willing to use a hated and despotic outlawry procedure rarely used in the American colonies and *dying out even then in comparatively statist England*."[137] But Rothbard has it backwards: England was comparatively *libertarian* alongside Jefferson's "free and independent" Virginia. Indeed, Jefferson's bill of attainder was based on the old English model but *without* the "elaborate common law procedure [that] insured some standard of fairness" when outlawry had been employed in England.[138] Josiah Philips, moreover, was "attainted" in direct violation of Section 8 of the Virginia Declaration of Rights, adopted by the Virginia legislature only two years earlier.[139]

Long after the Revolutionary War was over, Jefferson defended his bill of attain-

133. Cf. *The Writings of Thomas Jefferson* (NY: G.P. Putnam's Sons, 1898), ed. Paul Leicester Ford, Vol. II, 149 ff; Rothbard, *Conceived in Liberty*, Vol. IV, 424.

134. Laws of Virginia, May 1778, Ch. 12, in Hening's Statutes, Vol. IX, 463–64.

135. Levy, op. cit., 35.

136. As Randolph stated, Philips "had a commission in his pocket at that time. He was, therefore, only a prisoner of war." In Levy, *Jefferson and Civil Liberties*, 37.

137. Rothbard, *Conceived in Liberty*, Vol. IV, p. 423–34.

138. Levy, op. cit., 34.

139. Ibid., 36. Section 8 provided that "in all capital or criminal prosecutions a man hath a right to demand the cause and nature of his accusation, to be confronted with the accusers and witnesses, to call for evidence in his favor, and to a speedy trial by an impartial jury of twelve men of his vicinage,

der, the loyalty oath, and the other deprivations of civil liberties he had either supported or drafted during the war.[140] Concerning the bill of attainder, he wrote in 1815, six years after the end of his second term as President, that "society had a right to *erase from the roll of its members* anyone who rendered his own existence inconsistent with theirs; to withdraw him from the protection of their laws, and to remove him from among them by exile, or even by death if necessary. . . . I was thoroughly convinced of the correctness of the proceeding [against Philips], and *am more and more convinced by reflection.*"[141] This was but one of many examples of how, as Levy puts it, "Something in his [Jefferson's] make-up, more than likely a stupendous ego, inhibited second thoughts."[142] But then the leaders of the American Revolution in general could hardly be described as a humble lot.

Jefferson's involvement in such brutally compulsory "statist" measures, including what he himself approvingly described as an oath of "fidelity to the state," is only one of many embarrassments to contemporary libertarians in their effort to sustain the fiction that Jefferson was a courageous champion of libertarian principles and "limited government" whose liberating vision was subverted by conniving Federalists. We shall further expose the "Jefferson legend" as this discussion proceeds, including his positively autocratic second term as President and the illusory "Revolution of 1800" during his first term. Suffice it to note for now that Jefferson saw nothing wrong with fining, imprisoning, interning or even executing on sight opponents of the Revolution; and in this he was no different from his fellow "apostles of Liberty."

The Southern Secession Prefigured

A slave-owner who wrote of having one of his dozens of escaped slaves "severely flogged in the presence of his old companions,"[143] Jefferson was the same radical who declared in the Declaration that all men are created equal and endowed by their Creator with the right to "Life, Liberty and the pursuit of Happiness." The same lover of Liberty who issued impassioned denunciations of slavery and calls for abolition of the slave trade also believed that Negroes were racially inferior,[144]

---

without whose unanimous consent he cannot be found guilty; nor can he be compelled to give evidence against himself; that no man be deprived of his liberty, except by the law of the land or the judgment of his peers."

140. Ibid., 36–41.

141. Jefferson to Girardin, March 12, 1815, in Levy, *Jefferson and Civil Liberties*, 40, and Jefferson to William Wirt, May 12, 1815, Liberty Fund e-text, oll.libertyfund.org/?option=com_staticxt&staticfile=show.php%3Ftitle=807&chapter=88129&layout=html&Itemid=27.

142. Levy, *Jefferson and Civil Liberties*, 172.

143. Jefferson to Reuben Perry, April 16, 182, cited in William Cohen, "Thomas Jefferson and the Problem of Slavery," *The Journal of American History*, Vol. 56, No. 3 (Dec. 1969), 516.

144. "Comparing them by their faculties of memory, reason and imagination, it appears to me that in memory they are equal to the whites; in reason much inferior, as I think one could scarcely be found capable of tracing and comprehending the investigations of Euclid; and that in imagination they are dull, tasteless and anomalous. . . . [N]ever yet could I find that a black had uttered a thought above the level of plain narration; never seen even an elementary trait of painting or sculpture." From Winthrop

wrote of breeding his slaves as if they were a capital asset,[145] and never ceased utilizing his (conveniently enough) already acquired 180–200 human chattels and their offspring to provide the forced labor that was the source of his wealth and privilege as a Virginia plantation owner. Jefferson's duplicity is aptly summarized by the historian William Cohen:

> He was a sincere and dedicated foe of the slave trade who bought and sold men whenever he personally found it necessary. He believed that all men were entitled to life and liberty . . . yet he tracked down those slaves who had the courage to take their rights by running away. He believed that slavery was morally and politically wrong, but he still wrote a slave code for his state and opposed a national attempt in 1819 to limit the further expansion of the institution. He believed that one hour of slavery was worse than ages of British oppression, yet he was able to discuss the matter of slave breeding in much the same terms that one would use when speaking of the propagation of dogs and horses.[146]

Jefferson, Washington and Madison, a veritable "holy trinity" of the Founding, were easily the most prominent examples of "the incongruity of these slaveholding patriots who trembled at the peril of becoming 'British slaves.'"[147] No one said it more succinctly than Samuel Johnson in his immortal reply to the Continental Congress on the alleged "tyranny" of "taxation without representation": "We are told that the subjection of Americans may tend to the diminution of our own liberties. . . . If slavery be thus fatally contagious, how is it that we hear the loudest yelps for liberty among the drivers of negroes?"[148]

The same "drivers of negroes" had for some time been fretting over the prospect that royalist jurists and governors would free the slaves in order to enlist them against the colonial radicals. In 1772 a slave taken to England by his master had sued successfully for his freedom, winning a decision by Lord Chief Justice William Mansfield that as Parliament had never authorized slavery in the colonies "no court could compel a slave to obey an order depriving him of his liberty."[149] Mansfield's explosive decision in what is known as Somersett's Case prompted a flurry of peti-

---

Jordan, *White over Black: American Attitudes Toward the Negro, 1550–1812*, Chap. 12, in O'Brien, *The Long Affair*, 261–62.

145. "I know no error more consuming to [an estate] than that of stocking farms with men almost exclusively. I consider a woman who brings [a child] every two years as more profitable than the best man on the farm. *What she produces is an addition to capital*, while his labor disappears in mere consumption." Jefferson to John Wayles Eppes, June 30, 1820, in University of Virginia Electronic Text Center collection at 1820, n. 391.

146. William Cohen, "Thomas Jefferson and the Problem of Slavery," *The Journal of American History*, Vol. 56, No. 3 (Dec., 1969), 525.

147. Albanese, *Sons of the Fathers*, 25.

148. Samuel Johnson, "Taxation No Tyranny," in *The Works of Samuel Johnson*, ed. Arthur Murphy (NY: Alexander V. Blake, 1837), 437.

149. Paul S. Boyer, Clifford E. Clark, Sandra Hawley, Joseph F. Kett, Andrew Rieser, *An Enduring Vision: A History of the American People* (Florence, KY: Wadsworth Publishing, 2009), 110.

tions by slaves in Massachusetts seeking application of the decision to the whole colony. Among these were three petitions by slaves in Boston and one to the General Court and the military governor and commander-in-chief, Thomas Gage, wherein the slaves identified themselves as "a Grate number of Blackes of the Province" and protested as follows:

[W]e have in common with all other men a naturel right to our freedoms without Being depriv'd of them by our fellow men as we are a freeborn Pepel and have never forfeited this Blessing by aney compact or agreement whatever. But we were unjustly dragged by the cruel hand of power from our dearest friends and sum of us stolen from the bosoms of our tender Parents and from a Populous Pleasant and plentiful country and Brought hither to be made slaves for Life in a Christian land. Thus we are deprived of every thing that hath a tendency to make life even tolerable, the endearing ties of husband and wife we are strangers to. . . . Our children are also taken from us by force and sent maney miles from us. . . . Thus our Lives are imbittered. . . .[150]

Abigail Adams wrote to John Adams to express her fears over the "conspiracy of negroes" who had "draw[n] up a petition to the governor, telling him that they would fight for him provided he would arm them, and engage to liberate them if he conquered."[151]

The demand for emancipation spread to other colonies. In Virginia, for example, governor Lord Dunmore was forced to take refuge in a British ship off Yorktown after his proclamation in the fall of 1773 had (expediently enough) promised the slaves freedom in return for their defense of the Crown. The Virginia House of Burgesses (soon to become the revolutionary Virginia House of Delegates) denounced Dunmore's "Scheme, the most diabolical . . . to offer Freedom to our Slaves, and turn them against their Masters."[152] In December 1776, slave-owner George Washington wrote to the Massachusetts legislature concerning "a Crisis like the present, when our Enemies are prosecuting a War with unexampled severity; when they have call'd upon foreign Mercenaries and have excited Slaves and Savages to Arms against us. . . ."[153]

The slave population in the colonies "began to anticipate the arrival of British troops as their path to liberation," and "both blacks and whites began to seek a clear link between British forces and slave liberation."[154] In fact, following Dunmore's proclamation in Virginia, black privates in the British regiments participated in a skirmish in which the colonials were routed and two of their colonels

150. Sidney Kaplan, *The Black Presence in the Era of the American Revolution* (Amherst MA: Univ. of Massachusetts Press, 1989), 13.

151. Charles F. Adams, ed., *Letters of Mrs. Adams, the Wife of John Adams* (Boston, 1841), Vol. II, 24; in Sidney Kaplan, "The 'Domestic Insurrections' of the Declaration of Independence," *The Journal of Negro History*, Vol. 61, No. 3 (July 1976), 249.

152. In Kaplan, "The 'Domestic Insurrections' of the Declaration of Independence", 250.

153. John C. Fitzpatrick, ed., *The Writings of George Washington*, Vol. V, 261, University of Virginia archive, etext.virginia.edu/washington/fitzpatrick/.

154. Kaplan, "Domestic Insurrections," 250.

captured.[155] With that kind of outcome in view, slave-owner Madison had earlier confided as follows to William Bradford:

> If [sic] america and Britain should come to an hostile rupture, I am afraid an Insurrection among the slaves may and will be promoted. . . . [L]ately a few of those unhappy wretches met together and chose a leader, who was to conduct them when the English Troops should arrive—which they foolishly thought would be very soon and that by revolting to them they would be rewarded with their freedom. Their intentions were soon discovered and proper precautions taken to prevent the Infection. . . . *It is prudent that such attempts should be concealed as well as suppressed.*[156]

The Spirit of 1776 could hardly abide the prospect of slaves fighting for their freedom on the side of the Crown. And this, of course, included the slaves who were tending to Jefferson's every need while maintaining his 5000-acre plantation, and who had built (and would rebuild repeatedly) his mansion at Monticello, which he had managed to acquire while bound in the chains of King George's intolerable tyranny. Indeed, the Declaration of Independence itself charges George with having "excited domestic insurrections amongst us"—meaning the revolt of slaves. Sidney Kaplan put it mildly when he remarked that the Declaration is "perhaps doubly flawed as an indictment of the monarch for stirring up an enslaved and oppressed people to seek their freedom from freedom-seeking revolutionaries. . . ."[157] But the Spirit of 1776 was quite in keeping with the spirit of Locke's *Fundamental Constitutions of Carolina*, which (as we saw in Chapter 3) provided that the English slaveholder in America "shall have *absolute power and authority over his negro slaves* of what opinion or religion whatsoever."

Eighty-five years after the Declaration was issued, Senator Jefferson Davis of Mississippi, soon to be President of the Confederate States of America, would bid farewell to the United States Senate by reminding his fellow senators that the Founders themselves had excluded their slaves from "the great principles" of the Declaration, which "have no reference to the slave; else, how is it that among the items of arraignment against George III was that he endeavored to do *just what the North has been endeavoring of late to do, to stir up insurrection among our slaves?* Had the Declaration announced that the negroes [sic] were free and equal, how was the prince to be arraigned for raising up insurrection among them? And how was this to be enumerated among *the high crimes which caused the colonies to sever their connection* with the mother-country?"[158] As we will see in Chapter 11, the Southern secession, portrayed by the Confederate leadership as the second American Revolution, would be justified by the same fear of slave insurrection and emancipation.

155. Kaplan, "Domestic Insurrections," 252.
156. Madison to Bradford, November 26, 1774; in Kaplan, op. cit, 254.
157. Ibid., 253.
158. Farewell Address, Senate Chamber, U.S. Capitol, January 21, 1861, in Jefferson Davis, *The Rise and Fall of the Confederate Government* (NY: D. Appleton and Company, 1881), Vol. I, 224.

The mythology of the American Revolution requires that the hypocrisy of the slave-owning "apostles of Liberty"—a hypocrisy clearly recognized by their own contemporaries—be excluded from the Liberty narrative, just as Madison counseled concealing the suppression of revolts by slaves hoping to be freed by the British. Hence, for example, the outright deception involved in the use of Jefferson's lapidary remarks inscribed on the Jefferson Memorial, which conclude with the ringing declaration from his autobiography that "Nothing is more certainly written in the book of fate that these people [the slaves] are to be free." In service of the myth, the builders of the Memorial deliberately cropped the words immediately following:

> Nor is it less certain than that the two races, equally free, *cannot live in the same government*. Native habit, opinion, *has drawn indelible lines between them*. It is still in our power to direct the process of emancipation *and deportation* peaceably and in such slow degree as that the evil will wear off insensibly, and their place be *pari passu* filled up by free white laborers. . . .[159]

Auguries of France

Given the convenient inconsistency with which the "apostles of Liberty" have always and everywhere followed their gospel since it was first "revealed" by Locke, it should not be surprising that although the Declaration of Independence "had been made in the name of liberty . . . the very first acts under it were to deprive a large portion of the colonies not only of liberty of action, but of liberty of thought and opinion."[160] Along with these, they were also deprived of their property and even their very lives whenever it was deemed expedient.

The quantity of bloodshed aside, the imposition of the revolutionary will was no less radical in America than it would be in France a few years later. R. R. Palmer, whom Rothbard cites as an "eminent historian," provides what Rothbard calls "a critically important comparison of the degree of radicalism in the American and French Revolutions."[161] Palmer shows that Whig tyranny in the colonies and new states actually produced more refugees per thousand of population than did the Jacobins during the Terror: 24 per thousand in America versus 5 per thousand in France.[162] Rothbard goes Palmer one better and proposes a "corrected rate" of 50 Americans per thousand, yielding "fully *tenfold* the exile rate of the supposedly more radical French Revolution."[163] Palmer observes that this purge of the Tory and Royalist opposition, whose members never returned, deprived the fledgling United States of "an important nucleus of conservatism," whereas in France the

---

159. Thomas Jefferson, *Autobiography*, Yale University e-text @ yale.edu/lawweb/avalon/jeffauto-.htm.

160. North Callahan, *Royal Raiders* (Indianapolis: Bobbs Merrill, 1963), 8; in Rothbard, *Conceived in Liberty*, Vol. IV, 423.

161. Ibid., 425.

162. Palmer, *Age of Democratic Revolution*, 188.

163. Rothbard, *Conceived in Liberty*, Vol. IV, 425.

return of the émigrés had an obvious moderating effect, including, of course, the restoration of the monarchy from 1814–1848.[164] Rothbard relies on Palmer's analysis in support of his contention, with which one must agree, that "A myth has been promulgated by neoconservative historians that the American Revolution was a uniquely mild revolution, so mild as not to be a revolution at all."[165]

In view of the massive evidence we have barely sketched here, Palmer draws the obvious parallel between the French and the American Revolutions:

> Revolutionary government as a step toward constitutional government, committees of public safety, representatives on a mission to carry revolution to the local authorities . . . oaths, detention, confiscation, aversion to 'moderatism,' and Jacobins who wind up sober guardians of the law—how much it all suggests what was to happen in France a few years later! With allowance for differences in scale and intensity, there was foreshadowed in the America of 1776 something of the *gouvernement révolutionaire* and even the Terror of France in 1793—except for the death sentences and the horrors that went with them, and except for the fact that the victims of these arbitrary proceedings never returned to political life as an organized force. . . .[166]

As Palmer concludes: "The Revolution could be carried out, against British and loyal American opposition, *only by the use of force.* Its success 'was impossible* without a revolutionary government which could enforce its will.'"[167] Even Rothbard, whose praise for the Revolution is unbounded, is constrained to recognize that "Liberty" was imposed by means contrary to the very principles professed by its self-appointed vanguard: "Thus, a Revolution and revolutionaries dedicated to the cause of liberty moved to suppress crucial liberties of their opposition—an ironic but not unsurprising illustration of the inherent contradiction between Liberty and Power, a conflict that can all too readily come into play even when Power is employed on behalf of Liberty."[168]

Rothbard's suggestion that an amorphous "Power" is to blame for abuses committed in the name of an equally amorphous "Liberty" inadvertently exposes a fundamental truth that the very conduct of the American radicals, before and after the Revolution, should have made obvious to him—a truth that is thematic here: that Liberty *is* Power. Liberty is Power directed to the destruction of the old order so that the new order, and the new man who would be subject to it, could emerge from the ruins. Liberty is Power seeking to dominate society in a way never before seen in the history of the West, or indeed in the history of civilization as a whole. Liberty is Power in the form of the modern state that the Founders, following their Lockean blueprint, created by the imposition of their collective will on the mass of ordinary people.

164. Palmer, *Age of Democratic Revolution*, 189–90; Rothbard, *Conceived in Liberty*, loc. cit., 425–426.
165. Rothbard, 423.
166. Palmer, 199.
167. Ibid., 198.
168. Rothbard, *Conceived in Liberty*, Vol. IV, 67.

Today, confronted with the increasingly oppressive demands of that same state, which they never cease to denounce, Rothbard's libertarian disciples insist that what we need is Liberty without Power, society without government, or at least "limited government" according to the supposedly betrayed "Jeffersonian vision" that, with poetic irony, Rothbard's own libertarian paean to the Revolution exposes as a sham. (Further on we shall see how the same Jefferson, though elevated to the status of an icon by contemporary libertarians, was in reality just another "statist.")

As the tradition that Locke and his progeny rejected teaches, and as all human experience, including the outcome of the American Revolution itself confirms, the very Creator invoked by the Founders has ordered human affairs so that men shall live in societies under the authority of rulers of one sort or another. And those who rule, no matter how they characterize themselves or their intentions, will always exercise power over their subjects according to a given theologico-political system. The Founders themselves would live to learn that Liberty is just another name for Power. But they would learn something else: that Liberty is Power unrestrained by moral or theological limits, not even the purely "rational" ones the Founders had in mind, because a deified Liberty, the new Word made flesh, would become a law unto itself.

7

New Yokes For Old

OF THE LAW that He had given, Christ declared: "my yoke is easy, and my burden is light."[1] The Founders of the American Republic promised a similar liberation through adherence to law—"a government of laws, not of men," John Adams called it.[2] But immediately after the Revolution it was apparent that the colonies had thrown off the yoke of constitutional monarchy only to take on their shoulders the far heavier double yoke of "representative" government by the newly constituted States and the central government in Washington. As Thomas Paine predicted in 1777 in his *Crisis Papers*, the "United States of America" (the name he had coined for the new nation aborning) "will sound as pompously in the world or in history, as 'the kingdom of Great Britain'. . . ."[3] What Paine did not predict, however, was that behind the pomposity of the name would be a new kind of sovereign whose authority and might, exercised always in the name of Liberty, would make "absolute monarchy" look puny by comparison.

The Yoke of "Republican" State Government

Ironically enough, the post-Revolutionary movement for a strong national government was justified largely by a revolt against taxation *with* representation in Massachusetts and other New England states. Burdened by heavy taxes and unpayable debts arising from the new government's "sound money" policy favoring creditors by requiring specie for payment, farmers in Massachusetts attempted to replicate the tactics of the Revolution. They organized committees of correspondence and county conventions to circumvent existing authority, used mobs to shut down the courts in order to prevent the issuance of judgments and warrants of execution for taxes and other debts, and ultimately formed a militia to storm the courthouse and federal arsenal in Springfield in February 1787.

The latter event is called the Shays Rebellion after its leader, Daniel Shays, a veteran of the Revolutionary War. Shays' service was so distinguished that he received a ceremonial sword from no less than General Lafayette, who would bear the holy fire of revolution to France. Shays' reward for loyal service to the "sacred cause of

---

1. Matthew 11:30.
2. *Massachusetts Constitution*, Part The First, Art. XXX (1780); see John Adams, *Works*, IV, 230.
3. Thomas Paine to Lord Howe, January 13, 1777, *The Crisis*, No. II.

Liberty" was a judgment against him for back taxes and the impending loss of his farm. He had also witnessed others lose everything they had to the "republican government" of Massachusetts, including a woman whose very bed was taken from her by the tax collectors of Liberty.[4] The Massachusetts state militia crushed the rebellion, and Shays fled to Vermont.

The Shays Rebellion was, as Morison observes, a "grim joke on the leaders of the American Revolution who were now running the state government." Chief among these was none other than Sam Adams, "now a respectable member of the state council," who indignantly proposed to "hang anyone who used the methods he had employed in 1774."[5] Adams exemplified perfectly how under the banner of Liberty the revolutionary leaders had merely replaced one sovereign with another whose demands were already more onerous than those of the Crown. Adams, writes Miller, "denounced the Shaysites just as Luther hurled anathemas against the peasants during the Peasants' Revolt" (which Luther himself had instigated). Now that the Revolution was over, so far as Adams and his fellow politicians were concerned, "no people could be more free than those who lived under a constitution they themselves had established."[6] And who were "they"? As the participants in the rebellion learned, "they" meant the former revolutionary leaders, who would brook no opposition to *their* authority. Miller puts it most succinctly: "Like other revolutionists, Sam Adams disapproved of revolutions when they were begun by other people."

So there was Sam Adams, the former paladin of Liberty, ramming a bill through the Massachusetts Senate to suspend the writ of habeas corpus so that the Shaysites could be imprisoned without trial. And even after the rebels had been crushed, Adams demanded blood. "Once the rebellion was crushed," writes historian John K. Alexander, "most politicians, sensing that the public wanted mercy, endorsed clemency for the rebels," but "Adams refused to pander to the popular mood. He wanted the ringleaders hanged because, as he reportedly said: 'in monarchies, the crime of treason and rebellion may admit of being pardoned or lightly punished; but the man who dares to rebel against the law of a republic ought to suffer death.'"[7] What could be more ironic than the former leader of opposition to monarchical "tyranny" in Boston declaring that monarchs can afford to be more lenient with disobedient subjects than he could? It would be hard to find a better proof text for the proposition that Liberty is just another name for Power. But Adams was hardly alone in demonstrating this truth: Governor Bowdoin himself had demanded, with high royal dudgeon, "the most vigorous measures, effectively to vindicate the insulted dignity of government."[8]

Accordingly, fourteen of the Shaysites received a death sentence. But the new

---

4. Cf. Howard Zinn, *A People's History of the United States* (NY: Harper Collins, 2005), 93–94.

5. Morison, *HAP*, 303.

6. Miller, *Sam Adams*, 372–373.

7. Alexander, *Revolutionary Politician*, 202–203.

8. David P. Szatmary, *Shays Rebellion: The Making of an Agrarian Insurrection* (Amherst, MA: Univ. of Mass. Press, 1980), 81.

sovereign erected by "the people" was merciful, despite Adams's braying for blood: only several hangings actually took place, while other death sentences were commuted at the last minute to short prison terms or expunged by pardons, including the pardon extended to Shays himself, who died in penniless obscurity.[9] By comparison, King George and the royal authorities had sentenced neither Adams nor any of his fellow Sons of Liberty to death or even a minimal prison term despite year after year of violent uprisings against the Crown. Indeed, as Miller remarks, had Thomas Hutchinson, the royal governor of Massachusetts "heard Sam Adams inveighing against the Shaysites in 1786 he would scarcely have believed it was the one-time incendiary of the colonies speaking."[10]

But Adams was only defending the Lockean "supreme legislature" for which he and his fellow radicals had cleared the ground with their revolution. While a strong opponent of any sort of monarchical chief executive, Adams "had been firmly attached to Locke's theory of the supremacy of the legislature; no principle of government was more fundamental to him than that 'in a constituted commonwealth . . . there can be but one supreme power, which is the legislature, to which all the rest are and must be subordinate.'"[11] And it was the supreme legislature of the supreme republican government of Massachusetts that the Shaysites had dared to defy.

The impoverished Massachusetts radicals of the rural regions learned another bitter lesson: that the Revolution had resulted in the ascendancy of a new privileged class that viewed "republican government" as the means by which its newly acquired Revolutionary spoils were to be secured against any further radicalism. Thus, for example, a petition by a group of farmers to the Massachusetts General Court protested in vain that President Washington's Secretary of War, Henry Knox, had been granted a vast tract of land "superior in extent to any Lord of Europe" even though Knox had done no more for his country "than hundreds of us, no verily."[12]

The situation was not much different in the other states, where former rebels had likewise become iron rulers now that they held power. Even that great lover of the American Revolution, Murray Rothbard, is constrained to note that "many of the state constitutions, under the influence of conservative theorists, turned out to be conservative reactions against revolutionary conditions. . . ."[13] Rothbard fails to explain how these mysterious "conservative theorists" managed to gain control of a political process supposedly unleashed by a widespread yearning for radical Liberty. Perhaps Rothbard is not comfortable admitting that the same revolutionaries who had decried the petty "tyranny" of a distant king had no compunctions about imposing far greater burdens on their own neighbors once they had ascended to positions of authority. In this, of course, they were no different from all the

9. Zinn, op. cit., 295.

10. Miller, *Sam Adams*, 373.

11. Ibid., 375.

12. In Nathan O. Hatch, *The Democratization of American Christianity* (New Haven: Yale Univ. Press, 1989), 31.

13. Rothbard, *Conceived in Liberty*, Vol. IV, 446.

revolutionaries who would follow their example in the coming "age of democratic revolution."

Gordon Wood provides a more frank assessment of the ironic but entirely predictable rise of big government *after* the Revolution and *because* of it:

> Almost at a stroke the Revolution destroyed all the earlier talk of paternal or maternal government, filial allegiance and mutual contractual obligations between rulers and ruled.... [T]he state in America emerged as something very different from what it had been....
>
> *As sovereign expressions of the popular will, these new republican governments acquired an autonomous public power their monarchical predecessors never possessed or even claimed....*
>
> The republican state governments sought to assert their *newly enhanced public power* in direct and *unprecedented* ways—doing for themselves what they had earlier commissioned private persons to do. They carved out exclusively public spheres of action and responsibility *where none had existed before.* They now drew up plans for improving everything from trade and commerce to roads and waterworks and helped to create a science of political economy for Americans. And they formed their own public organizations *with paid professional staffs supported by tax money,* not private labor....
>
> *The power of the state to take private property was now viewed as virtually unlimited*—as long as the property was taken for exclusively public purposes.[14]

What Wood describes is the rise of the ever-busy and ever-more-intrusive modern bureaucratic state governments, whose expanding power, funded by taxes far higher than the relative pittances England had attempted to levy from afar on the colonies, was justified on a ground no mere monarch could invoke: that "the people" had "consented" to them through their representatives. It was on this very ground that Sam Adams had stood to declare that kings could be more forgiving of rebellion than the republican rulers of Massachusetts. Wood explains how the new "republican governments" of America used the ideas of "representation," "consent" and "the will of the people" to restrict the same personal rights monarchs were bound by tradition to respect:

> The people under monarchy, of course, had possessed long-standing rights and privileges *immune from tampering* by the prerogative powers and privileges of the king. *But under republicanism could such popular rights continue to be set against the government?* In the new republics, where there were no more crown power and no more prerogative rights, *it was questionable whether the people's personal rights could exist apart from the people's sovereign power*—the general will expressed in their assemblies.... To be sure, as the Pennsylvania constitution together with other revolutionary constitutions declared, "no man's property can justly be taken from him, or applied to public uses, with-

14. Wood, *Radicalism*, 188 (paragraph breaks added).

out his own consent," but this consent, in 1776 at least, meant "that of his legal representatives."[15]

Lockean "virtual representation" was the great fiction by which the sovereignty of the monarch, freed from the restraints of tradition, was transferred to the governors and legislatures of the new state governments. Peter S. Onuf, a preeminent scholar of the American Revolution, describes the process thus:

> As "sovereignty" was transferred from king to people, it travelled a circuitous route. Deposing the king created *a vacuum of legitimate authority that representatives of the people quickly filled.* The most significant consequence of this upheaval ... was the invention of *the American idea of state sovereignty* ... [which] marked the final stage in the rise of the assemblies. Facing an increasingly uncertain future in the last years of imperial rule, *the representatives gained expansive new powers* under the first new state constitutions.[16]

It was no different after the Revolution. As Wood admits, albeit from an approving perspective, "limiting popular government and protecting private property and minority rights without at the same time denying the sovereign public power of the people ... remains the great dilemma of America's constitutional democracy."[17] But this "dilemma" never existed before the Revolution first subjected an entire people to the virtually illimitable power of Lockean "representative" governments unbound by the customs and traditions that had limited monarchical rule and to which the American revolutionaries themselves had rather cynically appealed in decrying the "tyranny" of George III.

In another supremely ironic twist, it was the growing power of the state governments that became an argument in favor of a strong federal government as a counterweight. In his famous memorandum "Vices of the Political System of the United States" (1787), written on the eve of the Philadelphia Convention, none other than James Madison, the very "Father of the Constitution," would cite the endless proliferation of conflicting state laws and regulations and the tyranny of the majority in "republican" state governments as grounds for adopting a federal constitution that would bring to the new nation legal uniformity and control over state deprivations of Liberty.[18] Madison noticed—a bit late in the game for the "liberated" colonies— that majoritarian tyranny in the States, imposing "the selfish interests of a dominant faction," seemed to arise "from the very nature of republicanism."[19] He posed to himself this question: "Whenever therefore an apparent interest or common passion unites a majority what is to restrain them from unjust violations of the

15. Wood, 188–189.

16. Onuf, "Jefferson, Federalist," in *Essays in History*, Vol. 35, 27.

17. Wood, *Radicalism*, 188–189.

18. James Madison, "Vices of the Political System of the United States," Univ. of Chicago e-text, press-pubs.uchicago.edu/founders/documents/v1ch5s16.html (Univ. of Chicago Press).

19. Charles F. Hobson, "The Negative on State Laws: James Madison, the Constitution and the Crisis of Republican Government," *The William and Mary Quarterly*, Third Series, Vol. 36, No. 2 (Apr. 1979), 222.

rights and interests of the minority, or of individuals?" His astonishing answer was an *extended* republic—a national government—that would "temper" the small republics in the States: "As a limited Monarchy tempers the evils of an absolute one; so an extensive Republic meliorates the administration of a small Republic."[20]

During the Convention Madison would argue unsuccessfully for an outright Congressional negative over state laws that would create a relationship between the national and the state governments "analogous to that between the state and county governments," the theory being that a national majority, unlike state majorities, would "embrace a multitude of diverse interests so that it would have a built-in protection against domination by a single party"[21]—a view whose naiveté was apparent even at the time. After the Convention, in *The Federalist* No. 62, Madison argued for a federal constitution that would counter the "mischievous effects of mutable government" in the States, which "poisons the blessings of liberty itself" by producing "laws . . . so voluminous that they cannot be read, or so incoherent that they cannot be understood," with "[e]very new regulation concerning commerce or revenue, or in any manner affecting the value of different species of property" producing a "a new harvest to those who watch the change," so that "it may be said with some truth that laws are made for the *few*, not for the *many*."[22]

Madison's arguments are another demonstration of how Liberty has always advanced its drive for Power. Just as the Founders had cited the abuses of the King and Parliament to justify revolution and the creation of "republican governments" in the States, so did Madison and his fellow Framers cite the even greater abuses of the new state governments to justify a new federal government under a new constitution. Pointing, as always, to the ills of one sovereign in order to usher in a new and greater one as the cure, Liberty was now saying again: Come to me, and I will free you. And so "the people"—that is, Madison and his fifty-four collaborators—went to Philadelphia to prescribe another cure that would turn out to be far worse than the disease. Only seventy-four years later, the Civil War would snuff out more than 600,000 lives and lay waste to half a nation in order to preserve what the Framers "conceived in Liberty."

The Philadelphia Convention

Upon learning of the Shays Rebellion while serving in France as the United States Minister Plenipotentiary (from 1785 to 1789), Jefferson wrote to Madison to confide that "a little rebellion now and then is a good thing, and as necessary in the political world as storms in the physical."[23] But the rebellion "had alarmed all American leaders except Jefferson,"[24] and "added strength to the demand for a revision of the

20. Madison, "Vices of the Political System of the United States," 12.2.
21. Hobson, op. cit., 232.
22. *The Federalist*, No. 62, eds Kendall and Carey, 280–281.
23. Jefferson to Madison, January 30, 1787.
24. Morison, *HAP*, 304.

Articles of Confederation."[25] As John Alexander shows, the resistance in one state to the tax collectors of Liberty was "skillfully exploited" by "American politicians who wanted to revamp the Union's government," and "exaggerated reports of rebellion brewing throughout New England" helped convince George Washington to attend the upcoming convention in Philadelphia which promptly "disregarded its instructions and drafted a totally new Constitution" instead of simply amending the Articles of Confederation.[26]

Here we encounter the next of the golden legends in the history of Liberty: that the Founding Fathers, acting as wise and selfless Framers of the Constitution, assembled in Philadelphia in order to devise and bequeath to America and the whole world an inspired model of freedom and "limited government" whose results were so beneficent as to suggest divine guidance for their project. The reality is quite other. There is no denying that the Constitution is a masterpiece of legal draftsmanship. But there is also no denying that what the delegates to the Constitutional Convention created was a central government with sweeping powers they had been given no warrant to create when the state legislatures appointed them and sent them to Philadelphia. A brief examination of some basic historical facts is necessary to demonstrate how the first "temple of Liberty" was planned by a few men behind closed doors and then erected over the nation without even the semblance of a mandate from the mass of the people.

Under the Articles of Confederation, the Continental Congress was little more than an *ad hoc* alliance of thirteen independent states; it had no chief executive, no judiciary, and no power to impose direct taxes, coin or borrow money, pay debts, or regulate interstate commerce. Moreover, the Congress had no power to change the Articles themselves except by proposing a formal amendment that would have to be submitted to the state legislatures for their unanimous ratification.

Faced with these impassable roadblocks to their will, Madison and his collaborators in the plan to create a new national government engineered a "spontaneous" resolution of the impasse: The Virginia legislature would hold a convention of state delegates in Annapolis, Maryland to be entitled "Meeting of Commissioners to Remedy Defects of the Federal Government." Although no one but Madison's cronies in Virginia had called for any such "meeting of commissioners" to decide a national question, five states sent a total of twelve delegates, including Madison. But, as the eminent early 20th-century historian John W. Burgess put it, "a coup d'état attempt by so small a body could not but fail."[27] The Annapolis Convention adjourned without accomplishing anything except a recommendation for another convention of state delegates "to devise such further provisions as shall appear to them necessary to render the constitution of the federal government adequate to the exigencies of the Union."

25. Miller, *Sam Adams*, 374.
26. Alexander, *Revolutionary Politician*, 203.
27. John W. Burgess, *Political Science and Comparative Constitutional Law*, Vol. I, *Sovereignty and Liberty* (Boston: Ginn & Co., 1893), 103.

Thus, on February 21, 1787 the Continental Congress, authorized by no one except itself, "invited" the States to assemble at Philadelphia "for *the sole* and express purpose of revising the Articles of Confederation" so as to "render the federal constitution adequate to the exigencies of government, and the preservation of the Union." The stage had been set for the creation of a new government whose powers would soon dwarf those of the overthrown king. By the time the delegates to the Philadelphia convention were done with their work in secret session, they had completely scrapped the Articles, which they had been commissioned only to "revise," and had created in their place a new federal government that would have all of the powers the Continental Congress lacked and would reign supreme over the several states. A simple reading of the key provisions of Article I and Article VI, clause 2 of the proposed Constitution, establishing the powers and supremacy of Congress, suffices to demonstrate this:

Article I—The Legislative Branch . . . .

SECTION 8—POWERS OF CONGRESS

The Congress shall have Power *To lay and collect Taxes*, Duties, Imposts and Excises, *to pay the Debts* and provide for the common Defence and *general Welfare* of the United States. . . .

To *borrow money* on the credit of the United States;

To *regulate Commerce* with foreign Nations, and among the several States. . . .

To *coin Money, regulate the Value thereof*, and of foreign Coin. . . .

To *constitute Tribunals* inferior to the Supreme Court;

To *define and punish Piracies and Felonies* committed on the high Seas, and Offenses against the Law of Nations;

To *declare War.* . . .

To *raise and support Armies.* . . .

To provide and maintain *a Navy.* . . .

To provide for calling forth the Militia to execute the Laws of the Union, *suppress Insurrections* and repel Invasions. . . .

To make *all Laws which shall be necessary and proper for carrying into Execution the foregoing Powers*, and *all other Powers vested by this Constitution* in the Government of the United States, or in any Department or Officer thereof.

Article VI—Debts, *Supremacy*, Oaths

[Clause 2] This Constitution and the laws of the United States which shall be made in pursuance thereof, and all treaties made, or which shall be made, under the authority of the United States, *shall be the supreme law of the land*, and the judges in every State shall be bound thereby, *any thing in the constitution or laws of any State to the contrary notwithstanding.*

Add to these sweeping powers the Constitution's correlative limitations on the powers of the States in Article I, §10:

SECTION 10—POWERS PROHIBITED OF STATES

No State shall enter into any Treaty, Alliance, or Confederation ... coin Money; emit Bills of Credit; make any Thing but gold and silver Coin a Tender in Payment of Debts ... or Law impairing the Obligation of Contracts, or grant any Title of Nobility.

No State shall, without the Consent of the Congress, lay any Imposts or Duties on Imports or Exports, except what may be absolutely necessary for executing it's [sic] inspection Laws: and the net Produce of all Duties and Imposts, laid by any State on Imports or Exports, *shall be for the Use of the Treasury of the United States.* ...

No State shall, without the Consent of Congress, lay any duty of Tonnage, keep Troops, or Ships of War in time of Peace, *enter into any Agreement or Compact with another State,* or with a foreign Power, or engage in War. ...

Finally, under the proposed Constitution the new national government would assume the power to tax the importation of slaves, while guaranteeing both the continuation of the transatlantic slave trade at least until 1808 (twenty years hence) and *the return of all escaped slaves* (a provision that remained in force until the adoption of the Thirteenth Amendment in 1865):

Article I, §9:

The Migration or Importation of such Persons as any of the States now existing shall think proper to admit, shall not be prohibited by the Congress prior to the Year one thousand eight hundred and eight, but a tax or duty may be imposed on such Importation, not exceeding ten dollars for each Person.

Article IV, §2, Clause 2:

No person held to service or labor in one state, under the laws thereof, *escaping into another,* shall, in consequence of any law or regulation therein, be discharged from such service or labor, *but shall be delivered up on claim of the party* to whom such service or labor may be due.

As a further protection of the property rights of slaveholders, Article 1, Section 2, Paragraph 3 provided (until modified by the Fourteenth Amendment in 1868) that "Representatives and direct Taxes shall be apportioned among the several States which may be included within this Union, according to their respective Numbers, which shall be determined by adding to the whole Number of free Persons ... three fifths of all other Persons." In other words, under the Constitution's infamous "Three-Fifths Compromise" a slave was to be counted as 3/5 of a white man.

Deeply embarrassed by this provision, contemporary libertarian defenders of the "wisdom of the Framers" try to explain it away as merely a census measure for political purposes and not the expression of a belief that a black man is only three-fifths of a human being—as if anyone, even then, had seriously argued such a thing. Refuting a straw man, libertarians evade the real point of the three-fifths compromise: that in the "temple of Liberty" slaves, whose essential humanity was not denied, were nevertheless not considered citizens of the United States but rather a form of property that, as such, possessed no civil rights whatever, so that *northern opponents of ratification, agreeing with the constitutional non-person legal status of the slaves, objected to counting them at all* as members of the population.[28] That is, in the "temple of Liberty" racism was universal, but the political benefit of owning slaves was not. It would be none other than the three-fifths rule that would make it possible for Thomas Jefferson to squeak out an electoral vote victory in the presidential election of 1800. And, so, it was literally the case that he "rode into the Temple of Liberty on the shoulders of slaves"[29]—including those he himself owned and had flogged for attempting to escape.

To sum up, the Framers at Philadelphia, the majority of whom (30 out 55 delegates) were lawyers, had devised a central government with the power to tax the entire nation, borrow and spend, pay debts, mint money, regulate all interstate and foreign commerce, protect the institution of slavery, raise an army and navy, declare and wage war, conduct foreign relations, enter into nationally binding treaties with any and all foreign powers, impress state militias to put down insurrections against itself by force, establish a federal judiciary, and "promote the general welfare"—John Locke's very phrase, as we noted in Chapter 3 in our discussion of his view of the function of the State as "promoting the general welfare, which consists in riches and power."[30] And, in case the Framers had missed something, Congress was further authorized to pass *any laws* deemed "necessary and proper" to execute the powers granted by the Constitution, with all of this legislation constituting "the supreme law of the land" overriding contrary state statutes, judicial decisions and constitutions.

At the same time, the independent sovereignty of the States was expressly negated by the prohibitions on minting money, conducting foreign relations, entering treaties, regulating interstate or foreign commerce, taxing imports or exports without Congressional consent (with any net revenue turned over to the federal government), entering into treaties, declaring or engaging in war, or even maintaining troops unless Congress so authorized. Madison had not gotten the outright federal negative over state laws he had argued for, but "the supremacy clause, the judiciary article, and the restrictions on the States constituted the judicial substitute for the legislative negative on state laws."[31]

In short, the Framers' secret deliberations in Philadelphia had produced the very model of Locke's "supreme government" with its "supreme legislature"—and this without even considering the potentially vast power of the newly devised Presi-

---

28. John C. Miller, *The Wolf by the Ears* (Charlottesville, VA: Univ. of Virginia Press, 1991), 222.
29. Ibid.
30. *Essay on Toleration*, 151.
31. Hobson, "The Negative on State Laws," 229.

dency and federal judiciary, whose authority has not ceased to expand since the Constitution was ratified. In the name of Liberty the delegates at the Constitutional Convention had created the acorn that would grow inexorably into the federal oak tree whose limbs, branches and twigs would extend to every corner of the nation. Given the plain language of the Constitution, not to mention our long and bitter experience with its implementation and interpretation by the federal judiciary the Constitution itself created, the claim that the Framers created a "limited government" of "checks and balances" borders on the ridiculous.

The Motives At Work

What were the motives of the fifty-five delegates who went to Philadelphia, including the sixteen who either walked out of the Convention in protest or refused to sign the final document? Responsible scholarship long ago dispensed with the golden legend of selfless statesmen acting under an inspiration to bring Liberty to America and the world. The end of the hagiography of the Founders and the Framers is widely identified with the publication in 1913 of *An Economic Interpretation of the Constitution of the United States* by the renowned historian Charles A. Beard. The political scientist Alan Gibson rightly describes Beard's study as "the most important work ever written on the American founding, because it liberated scholars to critically study the Founders rather than merely celebrate them."[32] Despite a fusillade of critical reviews of Beard's work since its publication, his basic thesis—with important modifications—remains intact: the Constitution served economic interests either possessed or represented by delegates. The delegates were, in fact, hardly representative of the common man but rather were drawn from "the uppermost layer of the Revolutionary leadership" and were "disproportionately lawyers and professional politicians." And while American society at the time "was made up mostly of modest farmers, only two delegates could be so classified." In fact, "virtually all of the delegates to the Convention were from coastal regions and cities." They were, in short, "economic elites" from the Eastern seaboard whose makeup was "disproportionately wealthy, urban and commercial."[33]

Historians, above all Forrest McDonald, have refuted the Beard thesis to the extent that it posited what McDonald called "a consolidated economic group" controlling the Convention, but in the process they have only succeeded in refining Beard's oversimplified demonstration of the economic interests at play in the Convention's give-and-take.[34] Among the delegates were not only the holders of Continental securities that would be worthless unless the new government redeemed

---

32. Alan Gibson, "Whatever Happened to the Economic Interpretation: Beard's Thesis and the Legacy of Empirical Analysis," paper delivered at annual meeting of Midwest Political Science Association, April 15, 2004, 1. See also, Gibson, *Understanding the Founding: the Crucial Questions* (Lawrence, KS: Univ. of Kansas Press, 2007), 15–38.

33. Ibid., 92–93, 114.

34. Forrest McDonald, *We the People: the Economic Origins of the Constitution* (New Brunswick, NJ: Transaction Publishers-Rutgers University, 1991 [1958]), 349.

them at par value, but the holders of private debt instruments whose value was threatened by the paper currency many states were printing, merchants whose livelihood depended on interstate commerce, and slave-owners. As even a cursory review of the Constitutional provisions set forth above will reveal, the Framers protected every one of these economic interests: the Constitution authorized federal redemption of the securities of the Continental Congress at par value; it forbade the States to issue paper currency while requiring them to allow only specie (gold and silver coins) as payment for debts; it prohibited the States from impairing contracts for private debt or commercial exchanges; it preempted state regulation of interstate and foreign commerce; and it required the interstate rendition of escaped slaves while guaranteeing the continuation of the international slave trade for at least another twenty years.

As for the protection of the interests of slave owners, it was the Constitution that provided the basis for the Fugitive Slave Act of 1793 and the Fugitive Slave Law of 1850, both of which mandated the return of escaped slaves, the latter requiring federal marshals to effect the rendition. In his First Inaugural Address, as we shall see, Lincoln defended the Fugitive Slave Law as warranted by the "plainly written" provision of Article IV of the Constitution, which he was bound to follow, declaring: "I have no purpose, directly or indirectly, to interfere with the institution of slavery where it exists."

Whatever the status of Beard's specific thesis today, post-Beard scholarship, and indeed the plain language of the Constitution itself, demonstrates that "the Constitution can be thought of as an economic document, at least in the sense that it was meant to abolish the 'currency' system of finance that had been adopted by many of the States during the mid-1780s and also in the sense that it was meant to promote and protect commercial interests."[35] For Madison especially, the Constitution was a document whose principal aim was to insure central regulation of economic interests in a Lockean polity set up as "an arena for competitive power, where the private bargaining of free men, groups and interests would take place...."[36] For Hamilton and the other "strong" Federalists, however, there was a more grandiose motive at work: the building of a great nation-state governed by men of virtue, whose construction would confer upon its Founders "everlasting fame" and would, as Hamilton put it in *The Federalist* No. 11, "baffle all the combinations of European jealousy to restrain our growth," allowing America to become "mistress of the world."[37] And so she did.

Under either Madison's or Hamilton's view the Constitution was indubitably "a grant of power to a centralized nation state,"[38] and it was successfully defended as such by both men in *The Federalist*. The idea that Madison, Hamilton and the

---

35. Gibson, "Whatever happened...?", 114.

36. Isaac Kramnick, "The Great National Discussion: The Discourse of Politics in 1787," *William and Mary Quarterly*, 3d. Ser., Vol. 45, No. 1 (Jan. 1988), 30.

37. Ibid., 28.

38. Ibid., 23.

other elite and wealthy delegates to the Philadelphia Convention were motivated by love of an abstract Liberty for the common man is nothing but a pious fable. Their business was to arrange for the exercise of power over millions of people by a newly created central government—power that would arise, to be sure, in the name of Liberty, but which had never existed before and would soon dwarf the power that had been overthrown by the Revolution.

"The Tyranny of Philadelphia"

The delegates at Philadelphia knew that what they had crafted behind closed doors would be a "tough sell" when it came to ratification by the States. Indeed, sixteen of the delegates had refused to sign the resolutions comprising the proposed Constitution for various reasons, and the New York delegates (except Hamilton) had "withdrawn in disgust."[39] (Gouverneur Morris, however, created the illusion of unanimity by appending to the resolutions the statement: "Done in Convention by the unanimous consent of the States present. . . ."—without revealing the walkouts and dissents.) The delegates also knew that the Constitution would never receive approval from the same state legislatures that had sent them to Philadelphia. As Beard observes: "One of the first objects of the Constitution was to restrict the authority of state legislatures, and it could hardly be expected that they would voluntarily commit suicide."[40]

To avoid these difficulties, the delegates, exceeding their authority once again, devised the strategy of *avoiding the state legislatures altogether* by "inviting" them to submit the proposed Constitution for approval by ratification "conventions" composed of delegates popularly elected in each state. Obviously, a small group of delegates would be far easier to lobby than a body of state legislators adamantly opposed to any limitation of the authority they now exercised as leaders of "republican governments." Sam Adams, for example, while asserting the authority of the Massachusetts state government to tax farmers, repossess their land and personal property for non-payment, suspend the writ of habeas corpus, and hang tax resistors, would oppose the federal constitution on grounds that it was a threat to Liberty, although he was ultimately persuaded to drop his opposition by the wealthy elites of Boston, who were all in favor of it.[41]

The delegates further proposed that approval by conventions in only nine of the thirteen states be sufficient to ratify the Constitution as to those states. This of course virtually compelled all thirteen states to fall into line once conventions in nine states had ratified, as ratification by nine would effectively abolish the Confederation, leaving four states on the outside looking in. Faced with this cleverly contrived piece of

---

39. Morison, *HAP*, 311.

40. Charles A. Beard, *An Economic Interpretation of the Constitution of the United States* (NY: Dover Publications, 2004 [1913]), 221.

41. In disgust, Adams was finally heard to declare: "Well, if they must have it, they must have it." Quoted in Miller, *Sam Adams*, 379.

demagogy, the state legislatures acceded to the plan to submit the proposed Constitution, as it famously commences, to "We the People" for ratification.

When he rose to oppose ratification in his oration before the Virginia ratifying convention, Patrick Henry would open by focusing precisely on this substitution of "We the People" for the States that were supposed to have been the ratifiers. Speaking of the delegates at Philadelphia, he declared: "Sir, give me leave to demand, what right had they to say, We the People. . . . [W]ho authorised them to speak the language of, We the People, instead of We, the States?. . . *The people gave them no power to use their name.* That they exceeded their power is perfectly clear." It was indeed perfectly clear, but then the Revolution itself had been one example after another of elite cadres taking actions "We the People" had never actually authorized. Henry predicted that "that poor little thing—the expression, We the People, instead of the States" would prove to be no little thing at all, for it implied that the people at large were to be the direct subjects of the new federal government and that this government would thus be "a national government," a republican government that would be "consolidated, not confederated."[42] Thus, he warned, "The tyranny of Philadelphia may be like the tyranny of George III."[43] Not even Henry could have foreseen that this would turn out to be a vast understatement.

Moreover, the "We" in "We the People" would mean the tiniest of minorities. Given that in nearly every state only propertied white males could vote, and further given the widespread indifference or lack of knowledge concerning the legal import of the Constitution's detailed text, no more than about five percent of the total American population at the time, or about 160,000 white male voters, actually cast votes for delegates to the ratifying conventions. Of these 160,000 voters about 60,000 were probably opposed to ratification.[44] Thus, contrary to popular belief, it was not the States as such that ratified the Constitution but only a few hundred *ad hoc* delegates at ratifying conventions whose votes represented the will of about 100,000 propertied electors in a nation of some 3.5 million people, not including the slave population. As for the slaves, they had no vote on what the Framers decided with respect to them: that if they escaped, they would be returned to their owners as recovered chattels.

The legal scholar Wythe Holt shows that had all the delegates to the ratification conventions been able to attend in all the States, the Constitution would have failed to pass. "[T]he proponents of the Constitution," he writes "were forced to scramble, scheme, organize, and pray for a victory that almost eluded them." When all the delegate votes were tallied, the Constitution was "ratified" by a mere "twenty-one

---

42. Opening Speech to Virginia Ratifying Convention, June 4, 1788.

43. In *The Life of John Marshall* (Boston: Houghton Mifflin Company, 1916), Vol. I, 428.

44. Beard, op. cit., 250–251. While Beard's version of an economic interpretation of the Constitution has been severely criticized, there is no dispute over his analysis of how few Americans actually voted on the subject of ratification. As Alan Gibson observes, "approximately 160,000 voted for delegates to attend state ratifying conventions to approve or reject the proposed constitution. There was *no* national referendum on the Constitution. . . ."

votes out of the 355 votes cast."[45] Those twenty-one votes by "We the People" would dramatically affect the history of the entire world.

Professor Burgess, who was no less than dean of the political science faculty of Columbia University, was perhaps the first major scholar to write honestly about how the delegates at Philadelphia usurped power by creating an entirely new national government on paper and then bypassing the state legislatures in order to effectuate their plan: "It certainly was not understood by the Confederate Congress, or by the legislatures of the commonwealths, *or by the public generally*, that they [the delegates] were to undertake any such problem. It was generally supposed that they were there for the purpose simply of improving the machinery of the Confederate government and increasing somewhat its powers." But what the Convention did, "stripped of all fiction and verbiage, was *to assume constituent powers,* ordain a constitution of government and of liberty, and demand the plebiscite thereon, *over the heads of all existing legally organized powers.* Had Julius or Napoleon committed these acts they would have been pronounced a coup d'état."[46]

Burgess goes on to note that "Of course the mass of the people were not at all able to analyze the real character of this procedure. It is probable that many of the members of the convention itself did not fully comprehend just what they were doing. . . . Really, however, *it deprived the* [Continental] *Congress and the legislatures of all freedom of action by invoking the plebiscite.* It thus placed those bodies under the necessity of affronting the source of their own existence unless they yielded unconditionally to the demands of the convention."[47] Professor Beard provides a helpful analogy: If Congress today were to call for a national convention to revise the Constitution, and the delegates to that convention junked the Constitution entirely, disregarding its own provisions for amendment and calling for votes by ratifying commissions on an entirely new form of government, we would be able to appreciate the magnitude of what the delegates in Philadelphia did.[48] Thus Beard rightly describes the whole procedure as "a revolutionary programme."[49] That is, the delegates to the Convention in Philadelphia conducted a veritable revolution against the Confederation.

Far more recently than Burgess and Beard, no less an authority than R. R. Palmer observed as a matter of simple historical fact that "the Philadelphia convention proceeded, not to amend the Articles [of Confederation], but to discard them. It *repudiated the union which the thirteen states had made.* . . . The men at Philadelphia did circumvent the state governments, and in a sense *they betrayed those who sent them.* They did so *by adopting the revolutionary principle of the American Revolution,* which had already become . . . an accepted routine"—that is, an appeal to

45. Wythe Holt, "To Establish Justice: Politics, the Judiciary Act of 1789, and the Invention of the Federal Courts," 1989 *Duke L.J.* 1421, 1475–76 (1989).
46. John W. Burgess, *Political Science and Comparative Constitutional Law,* 104–105.
47. Ibid., 105–6.
48. Beard, *Economic Interpretation,* 63, 217–218.
49. Ibid., 63.

"the people."[50] But, as Palmer further observes, voting for the ratifying conventions was light because "most people lost interest, or never had any, in abstract debates concerning governmental structure at the distant federal level."[51] In other words, "the people of the United States" in their millions did not realize what would be visited upon them in their name and cannot be said to have "consented" to it in any meaningful way. That is why it is no exaggeration to speak of what happened at Philadelphia as a coup d'état, one of the innumerable usurpations by which Liberty has advanced in every Western nation.

If this claim still seems extravagant, consider the response of the very "Father of the Constitution" to the charge that he and his fellow delegates had violated their limited commission to revise the Articles and had arrogated to themselves authority no one ever gave them. In *The Federalist* No. 40, Madison, writing as "Publius," provides a justification for the Convention's revolutionary activities that could have been written by John Locke himself. After some lawyerly quibbling about what it meant to "revise" the Articles, Madison gets to the heart of the matter: what the delegates had done in Philadelphia was no different from what the leaders of "the people" had been doing ever since the time of colonial resistance to England. Since the whole process of establishing independence had been moved along by a few "representatives" assuming authority on their own initiative, why should anyone complain if the members of the Convention, seeing all the irregularities that had preceded them, should continue in the same path? As Madison writes:

> It could not be unknown to them [the Convention] that the hopes and expectations of the great body of citizens, throughout this great empire, were turned with the keenest anxiety to the event of their deliberations. . . . They had seen the LIBERTY ASSUMED by a VERY FEW deputies from a VERY FEW States, convened at Annapolis, of recommending a great and critical object [a new constitution], wholly foreign to their commission. . . . They had seen, in a variety of instances, assumptions by [the Continental] Congress, not only of recommendatory, but of operative, powers. . . . They must have reflected, that in all great changes of established governments, forms ought to give way to substance; that a rigid adherence in such cases to the former, would render nominal and nugatory *the transcendent and precious right of the people to "abolish or alter their governments as to them shall seem most likely to effect their safety and happiness"*. . . .[52]

In other words, the leaders of "the people" had been cutting corners and assuming authority not given all along, so why stop now! This way of acting was, after all, only an exercise of Locke's newly discovered "transcendent and precious right of the people" to "abolish or alter their government" whenever "they"—in this case, Madison and his thirty-eight co-signers—deemed it expedient. Thus, just as Beard,

---

50. Palmer, *Age of Democratic Revolution*, Vol. I, 230.
51. Ibid., 231.
52. Federalist No. 40, in *The Federalist Papers*, Arlington House ed., 252.

Burgess and Palmer contend, Madison himself admitted *a revolutionary change of government* existing under the Articles of Confederation. All that was necessary was that "the people" (here about 100,000 voters out of more than three million citizens) later be induced to accept what had been done in their name. This *modus operandi* was necessary, Madison argued, because

> it is impossible for the people spontaneously and universally to move in concert towards their object; and it is therefore essential that such changes be instituted by some INFORMAL AND UNAUTHORIZED PROPOSITIONS [emphasis in original], made by some patriotic and respectable citizen or number of citizens.[53]

Like all his fellow revolutionaries, Madison presumed to know the object of "the people" and that he was entitled to lead them toward "their" object by "informal and unauthorized" steps. This was the Lockean practice of revolution in its essence: that any group of citizens, or even a single "respectable citizen," may throw off established authority, abandon the rules of the game, and take any action deemed necessary for the sake of Liberty, bringing "the people"—or at least some token assemblage thereof—along after the fact. (In Chapters 11 to 13 we will see how the self-authorizing leaders of the Confederate States of America would follow the same *modus operandi* in staging their own revolution via secession from the government created by their own "revolutionary fathers," as Jefferson Davis would call them.)

Madison also advanced an argument that only a lawyer (albeit a non-practicing one in this case) could propose without blushing: Since the States and the Continental Congress had usurped power in calling the Constitutional Convention to begin with, no one ought to complain that the delegates had followed suit by usurping power from the usurpers:

> [I]f there be a man whose propensity to condemn is susceptible of no control, let me then ask what sentence he has in reserve for the twelve States who USURPED THE POWER of sending deputies to the convention, a body *utterly unknown to their constitutions*; [and] for Congress, who recommended the appointment of this body, *equally unknown to the Confederation....*

In what lawyers call a "fall-back" argument, Madison concluded by allowing that even if "it shall be granted for a moment that the convention were neither authorized by their commission, nor justified by circumstances in proposing a Constitution for their country: does it follow that the Constitution ought, for that reason alone, to be rejected? If, according to the noble precept, it be lawful to accept good advice even from an enemy, shall we set the ignoble example of refusing such advice even when it is offered by our friends?"

In other words, all's well that ends well. The Convention had given "good advice" even if it had no authority or justification to give it. But whether the proposed

---

53. *Federalist Papers*, 253.

Constitution was "good advice" could hardly be left to the determination of Madison and the others who had usurped power in the first place. Nor could the votes of 100,000 people, most of whom had probably not even read the document but had merely relied on the representations of the delegates for whom they voted, establish that the Constitution was "good advice" for the millions who had no involvement in the process. Yet those same millions awoke one day to find themselves subjects of a new federal government they had never requested from their "representatives," only to be told that "We the People" had received the blessing of "government by consent of the governed."

The old Virginia radical Richard Henry Lee remarked that it was "really astonishing that the same people, who have just emerged from a long and cruel war in defense of liberty, should now agree to fix an elective despotism upon themselves and their posterity."[54] As an official U.S. government historical source admits, however, "it is probable that a majority of people in the entire country opposed it [the Constitution]."[55] In truth, neither "We the People" nor even the States as such adopted the Constitution—except, of course, to acquiesce in the whole scheme once it had been imposed upon them by the few who had created it and the few who "ratified" it in their name. But, as we saw in our examination of Locke's political theory, mere acquiescence suffices for Lockean "government by consent of the governed." For, as Locke taught, merely to inhabit a polity created by means of the newly invented "social compact" is to consent tacitly to its "supreme authority." And where that consent is by explicit agreement, there are even more drastic Lockean consequences, as we shall see in our discussion of the Civil War.

The Rout of the Anti-Federalist Prophets

What, then, of the great battle between the Federalists and the anti-Federalists before, during and after ratification of the Constitution? According to another golden legend, the anti-Federalists, led by such as Patrick Henry, were the true believers in the ideals of the Revolution, whereas the Federalists, led by Madison, Hamilton and Jay (the pseudonymous authors of *The Federalist Papers*), were the evil subverters of the Revolution, who "stole" it from the people and imposed a "statist" outcome on what should have been a monumental triumph for Liberty. That we are dealing with a legend should be apparent, first of all, from what happened with the state governments, whose quondam revolutionary leaders could hardly wait to exercise their own newfound powers, as we saw with Sam Adams and his demand for the hanging of the tax resisters who dared to disobey the "republican government" of Massachusetts. Beyond this, however, a brief examination of

54. Lee to John Lamb, June 27, 1788, in Ballagh, ed., *Letters of R. H. Lee*, II, 475, cited in Kramnick, "The Great National Discussion: The Discourse of Politics in 1787," *William and Mary Quarterly*, 3d. Ser., Vol. 45, No. 1 (Jan. 1988), 23–24.

55. Bruns, op. cit., at National Archives federal website.

some key historical facts will suffice to demonstrate that, all the heated rhetoric of the time aside, in the end the conflict between the Federalists and the anti-Federalists was no different in substance from the illusory conflict today between liberals and "conservatives" over just *how* big and powerful the federal government should be.

It has to be said, first of all, that the rhetoric of the anti-Federalists, however unavailing, was positively prophetic. Chief among the prophets was Patrick Henry, whose protest against "the tyranny of Philadelphia" we have already noted. As Henry argued elsewhere, the "tyranny of Philadelphia" might be *worse* than that of King George. In another of his fiery orations before the Virginia ratification convention, Henry ridiculed the "checks and balances" of the proposed government as an ideal construction on paper and the "division of powers" as nothing more than the walls of the buildings of different agencies in what would be a monolithic government. Drawing a supremely ironic comparison, Henry argued that unlike an English monarch, who was motivated by his narrow self-interest to preserve the prosperity of the nation to be handed on to his successor, "The President and Senators have nothing to lose. They have not that interest in the preservation of the Government, that the King and Lords have in England. They will therefore be regardless of the interests of the people."[56] Focusing on the "necessary and proper clause" of Article I, §8 of the proposed Constitution, Henry warned that the implied powers conveyed by this clause were potentially unlimited: "Implication is dangerous, because it is unbounded; if it be admitted at all, and no limits be prescribed, it admits of the utmost extension. . . ." At the climax of his two-day oration Henry thundered: "Must I give my soul, my lungs, to Congress? Congress must have our souls, the state must have our souls. This is dishonorable and disgraceful."[57]

No less prophetic, and considerably more amusing, was the pseudonymous "Brutus," generally believed to have been Robert Yates, a New York jurist and delegate to the Philadelphia Convention who was among the sixteen delegates refusing to sign the Philadelphia resolutions comprising the proposed Constitution. Like Patrick Henry, "Brutus" (a pseudonym evidently intended to evoke the assassination of Caesar in order to prevent the overthrow of the Roman Republic) also focused on the mischief of the "necessary and proper clause," as well as the "supremacy clause," warning that "the government will have complete judicial and executive authority to carry all their laws into effect, which will be paramount to the judicial and executive authority of the individual states: in vain therefore will be all interference of the legislatures, courts, or magistrates of any of the States on the subject; *for they will be subordinate to the general government*, and engaged by oath to support it, and will be constitutionally bound to submit to their decisions."[58]

---

56. Address to the Virginia Ratifying Convention, June 9, 1788, Univ. of Chicago e-text, press-pub s.uchicago.edu/founders/documents/v1ch11s13.html.

57. In *Patrick Henry: Life, Correspondence and Speeches*, ed. William Hirt Henry (NY: Charles Scribner's Sons, 1891), Vol. III, 471.

58. *The Anti-Federalist Papers*, "Brutus," No. 6; Constitution Society e-text @ http://www.constitution.org/afp/brutus06.htm. The title "Anti-Federalist Papers" loosely designates an indeterminate

Furthermore, wrote "Brutus," the taxing power would make the federal government into a colossus the people would find themselves powerless to resist:

> The general legislature [Congress] will be empowered to lay any tax they chuse [sic], to annex any penalties they please to the breach of their revenue laws; *and to appoint as many officers as they may think proper to collect the taxes.* . . . And the courts of law, which they will be authorized to institute, will have cognizance of every case arising under the revenue laws, the conduct of all the officers employed in collecting them; and the officers of these courts will execute their judgments. There is no way, therefore, of avoiding the destruction of the state governments . . . unless the people rise up, and, with a strong hand, resist and prevent the execution of constitutional laws. The fear of this, will, it is presumed, restrain the general government, for some time, within proper bounds; *but it will not be many years before they will have a revenue, and force, at their command, which will place them above any apprehensions on that score.*[59]

The result of the power to tax, the "necessary and proper" clause, and the "supremacy" clause would, "Brutus" predicted, be a national government that

> will enter the house of every gentleman, watch over his cellar, wait upon his cook in the kitchen, follow the servants into the parlour, preside over the table, and note down all he eats or drinks; it will attend him to his bed chamber, and watch him while he sleeps; it will take cognizance of the professional man in his office or study; it will watch the merchant in his counting house or his store; it will follow the mechanic to his shop and in his work, and will haunt him in his family and in his bed; it will be the constant companion of the farmer in all his industrious labor . . . ; it will penetrate into the most obscure cottage; and finally, *it will light upon the head of every person in the United States.* To all these different classes of people and in all the circumstances in which it will attend them, the language in which it will address them will be, GIVE! GIVE![60]

Professor Bailyn pokes fun at these predictions as a "florid peroration that conjures up the horrors of totalitarian states."[61] But Bailyn overlooks the fundamental point "Brutus" used hyperbole to convey: that the new government would be a voracious center of power, fed by taxes that would never be enough to satisfy it, and that it would not be long before its supreme authority became unchallengeable. If the Civil War, taking place within a single lifetime of Brutus's prophecy, did not demonstrate this, it is hard to see how Bailyn, writing in 1967, could have

---

collection of writings against *The Federalist Papers*, whose most definitive collection is that edited by Herbert Storing, entitled *The Complete Anti-Federalist.*

59. Herbert J. Storing, *The Complete Anti-Federalist* (Univ. of Chicago Press: 1981), 396–97.

60. Ibid.

61. Bailyn, *Ideological Origins*, 336.

overlooked that the federal government had at least by then become precisely the irresistible colossus predicted.

"Brutus" had relied for his prophecies on a source that commanded respect among the American *philosophes* of the post-Revolutionary America: *The Spirit of the Laws* by Montesquieu, whose stature approached even that of Locke among learned Americans. Montesquieu had observed that "It is natural for a republic to have only a small territory," such as the republic of Athens, but that in "an extensive republic" a man of wealth "soon begins to think that he may be happy and glorious, by oppressing his fellow-citizens; and that he may raise himself to grandeur on the ruins of his country." Moreover, "In an extensive republic the public good is sacrificed to a thousand private views...."[62] And, in fact, never in human history had a republic the size of the continental United States existed. Bailyn notes that "Cato," also citing *The Spirit of the Laws*, warned that "factionalism in an extended republic would lead inevitably to a standing army" and that the same factionalism "would produce *the threat of secession* [and] the 'creation of a permanent force, to be kept on foot,' in order to preserve the state, a necessity created also by the difficulty of executing revenue laws, always the source of opposition to a government...."[63] Cato, of course, was deadly accurate in his prediction.

Madison, replying to these objections, offered the spectacularly false counter-prediction that the sheer size of the American Republic would be a protection against demagoguery and the abuse of power. The larger multitude, he argued, would produce "a greater probability of a fit choice" for representatives of the people in Congress. And since each representative would be chosen "by a greater number of citizens... than in a small republic, it will be more difficult for unworthy candidates to practice with success the vicious arts by which elections are too often carried...." Moreover, he continued, "the suffrages of the people being more free, will be more likely to center on men who possess the most attractive merit...." Finally, he contended, unlike in a pure democracy, in an extended republic governed by representatives "the greater number of citizens and extent of territory" would render "factious combinations less to be dreaded...." because, given the sheer number of people and factions involved, it would be "less probable that a majority of the whole will have a common motive to invade the rights of other citizens...."[64]

Precisely the opposite has proved to be true on all counts. Madison failed (or refused) to see the fatal defect in the untried "American experiment": that, as Erik von Kuehnelt-Leddihn observes, "Constitutionally very little can be done to prevent the degeneration of a republic into a democracy...."[65] And a *mass* democracy, embracing ever more millions of people, could not fail to produce an ineluctable concentration of power in its central government, no matter what "checks and

---

62. Montesquieu, *The Spirit of the Laws*, VIII.16.
63. Bailyn, op. cit., 348.
64. *Federalist* No. 10, Yale Law School e-text yale.edu/lawweb/Avalon/federal/fed10.htm.
65. Von Kuehnelt-Leddihn, *Liberty or Equality*, 115.

balances" Madison and the other Framers believed they had created. Gordon Wood merely remarks an undeniable fact of history when he concludes: "The American Revolution created this democracy, and we are living with its consequences still."[66]

This is not the place to conduct an extended comparative analysis of Federalist and anti-Federalist arguments. What matters for this part of our discussion is that, at least until the Civil War, the anti-Federalists offered little more than rhetorical resistance to the course of events their own beloved Revolution—which, after all, they had conducted shoulder-to-shoulder with the men who were now Federalists—had made inevitable. After the Shays Rebellion, the drive for a "strong" national government became unstoppable. No less than George Washington, "the Father of his Nation," had cloaked the entire Federalist cause in the mantle of his quasi-mystical leadership. It was Washington himself who had presided over the Philadelphia Convention where, as one official source approvingly observes, "the delegates . . . spent four months, from May to September, behind closed doors, hammering out the framework of a new, more powerful national government."[67] And, as Morison observes: "Washington and almost all military leaders of the war, and many civilians as well, had long felt that the Confederation could never become a respectable government *without the power to tax.*"[68] Hence a leading anti-Federalist and delegate to the Constitutional Convention, Luther Martin of Philadelphia, wrote vehemently of a veritable conspiracy against Liberty by the other delegates, whom he denounced as "harpies of power" who "shield their secret intentions with 'the virtues of a Washington.'"[69] Martin refused to sign the Convention's resolutions.

Further, no less than Thomas Jefferson, "the Father of Liberty" and the very author of the Declaration of Independence, lent his support (however lukewarm) to ratification of the proposed Constitution after receiving the famous explanatory letter of 1787 from Madison, his good friend and fellow Virginian and the Constitution's "Father." Jefferson supported ratification even though Madison's letter had argued for "a Government which instead of operating, on the States, should operate *without their intervention on the individuals composing them,*" and for a nationwide "*controlling power*" over the States by which "*the general authority may be defended against encroachments of the subordinate authorities. . . .*" That is, Madison proposed precisely the opposite of the Catholic principle of subsidiarity (distribution of authority to the lowest appropriate level) discussed in the Introduction and Chapter 2. With ultimate irony, Madison's letter even defended the aforementioned (but never obtained) "constitutional negative on the laws of the States" by analogy to "the royal negative" over the English parliament, without which "the unity of the system would be destroyed. . . ." He argued to Jefferson that such a negative was needed to address the "mutability of the laws of the States" which are "found to be

66. Wood, *Radicalism*, 369.

67. National Constitution Center (Philadelphia), "Delegates to the Constitutional Convention: Who Were These Men?," @ http://www.constitutioncenter.org.

68. Morison, *HAP*, 304.

69. In Bailyn, *Ideological Origins*, 333.

a serious evil" and an "injustice . . . so frequent and so flagrant as to alarm the most steadfast friends of Republicans."[70]

Contrary to the mythology of Liberty, Jefferson was a federalist from the very beginning of his revolutionary career, even if his Democratic-Republican brand of federalism (the Republican Party we know today would not emerge until 1854, during the controversy over the Kansas-Nebraska Act) varied in style from that of Madison and Hamilton. Indeed, his most famous document, the Declaration of Independence, rested upon the Continental Congress's quintessentially *federalist* arrogation of central authority to act as a *de facto* federal union of the colonies in order to declare independence from England. The Declaration purported to be in the name of "the people" even though the Congress "had no such legitimating pedigree" and "its pretensions were most revolutionary. . . ."[71] It should be no surprise, then, that Jefferson called *The Federalist Papers*, an extended argument for ratification of the Constitution, the "best commentary on the principles of government ever written."[72]

With the support of, respectively, the Father of His Nation, the Father of the Constitution and the Father of Liberty, the anti-Federalists never had a chance. As Roger Bruns writes: "Against this kind of Federalist leadership and determination, the opposition in most states was disorganized and generally inert. The leading spokesmen were largely state-centered men with regional and local interests and loyalties. Madison wrote of the Massachusetts anti-Federalists, 'There was not a single character capable of uniting their wills or directing their measures. . . . They had no plan whatever.'"[73] Further, not even as charismatic a figure as Patrick Henry had argued that there must be no federal constitution or federal government at all but only that ratification should be conditioned on limitations of federal power in a Bill of Rights like Virginia's. Even the most passionate and radical advocates of another constitutional convention to undo "the tyranny of Philadelphia" were ultimately reduced to silence by Madison's promise of just such a Bill of Rights, ratified two years after the Constitution. In fact, given that the majority of the general population was probably against the Constitution, "*Only* the promise of amendments had ensured a Federalist victory."[74]

The Illusory Tenth Amendment

Contemporary "conservative" and libertarian proponents of Liberty argue that the Bill of Rights would have allowed "Jeffersonian limited government" to prevail if only the federal courts had not abandoned a "strict construction" of the Constitution. The focus of this argument is generally the last provision of the Bill, the Tenth

---

70. Madison to Jefferson, October 24, 1787, Univ. of Chicago e-text, http://press-pubs.uchicago.-edu/founders/documents/v1ch17s22.html, *The Founders' Constitution*, Chapter 17, Document 22.

71. Onuf, "Jefferson, Federalist," 27.

72. Quoted in "A More Perfect Union: The Creation of the U.S. Constitution," U.S. National Archives and Records Administration, extracted from intro. to Roger A. Bruns, *A More Perfect Union: The Creation of the United States Constitution* (Washington, DC: National Archives Trust Fund Board: 1986); e-text @ www.archives.gov.

73. Bruns, "A More Perfect Union," loc. cit.

74. Bruns, op. cit., National Archives website.

Amendment, which provides: "The powers not delegated to the United States by the Constitution, nor prohibited by it to the States, are reserved to the States respectively, or to the people."

Libertarians revere Jefferson as a veritable progenitor of constitutional "limited government" even though he played no part whatever in the Philadelphia Convention because he was still serving as Minister Plenipotentiary in Paris. While the Constitution was in the process of being ratified by the States, Jefferson was abandoning even the pretense of diplomatic neutrality in Paris by cheering on the Third Estate's dictatorial usurpation of power from Louis XVI upon declaring itself the National Assembly. In July of 1789, only weeks from the end of his mission, the supposed apostle of "limited government" delightedly informed his fellow meddler in French affairs, Tom Paine, that the National Assembly had "set fire to the four corners of the kingdom," would "perish with it themselves rather than relinquish an iota of their plan for a total change of government," and "are now in complete and undisputed possession of the sovereignty.... They have prostrated the old government and are now beginning to build one from the foundation."[75] Jefferson had the supreme audacity to conspire with and render positive assistance to the revolutionaries by assisting General Lafayette in drafting the Declaration of the Rights of Man (inspired by his own Declaration of Independence), adopted by the National Assembly on August 26, 1789 pursuant to "authority" which, like the Continental Congress, it had bestowed upon itself.

By the time Jefferson had returned to America in late 1789, eleven states had already ratified the Constitution's unamended text and the Bill of Rights had been drafted and proposed for ratification. Yet today libertarian commentators cite Jefferson's interpretation of both documents as if they were part of the organic law of the United States. As one libertarian commentator writes, with a remarkable degree of naiveté for such an otherwise skeptical scholar: "Jefferson believed that the keystone of the entire document [the Constitution] was the Tenth Amendment. After delegating a few [!] express powers to the central government, the citizens of the States reserved all others to themselves, and to the States respectively. The Tenth Amendment announced, essentially, that the citizens of the free and independent states were sovereign. They were the masters, not the servants, of the federal government which they had created by ratifying the Constitution in state political conventions."[76]

Putting aside the patent historical fact that it was not the States as such that had ratified the constitution in the first place but rather ratifying conventions *in* the States elected by "We the People"—meaning about 100,000 voters out of 3.5 million inhabitants—it hardly required a legal sage to recognize that the federal government's promise not to eclipse the powers "reserved to the States ... or the people" would not amount to much over time. For that same federal government had been given authority under the Constitution itself to pass all laws "necessary and proper"

---

75. *Jeffersonian Cyclopedia*, §7529.
76. Thomas DiLorenzo, "The Jefferson of Our Time," www.lewrockwell.com/dilorenzo/dilorenzo-137.html.

to the exercise of its own sweeping powers, including the power to "promote the general welfare," and "We the People" had already agreed that federal law, as construed by the Article III federal judiciary, including the *Supreme* Court, would constitute "the supreme law of the land." To cite the Tenth Amendment against an expansion of federal power is, therefore, to beg the question: what *is* the scope of federal power and thus the corresponding limit on the power of the States? Hence the Supreme Court, as the very creature of the Framers' creation of a federal supremacy,[77] observed long ago that the Tenth Amendment "states but a truism that all is retained which has not been surrendered."[78] Much more recently, even a "conservative" majority of the Court reiterated what should have been apparent from the start, and indeed was apparent to the anti-Federalists: that the Tenth Amendment is "essentially a tautology" with no meaning apart from an analysis of the scope of federal authority as established by the broad powers enumerated in Article I, the "necessary and proper clause," the "general welfare clause" and the "commerce clause," all of which created a "framework" of federal power that it has been

> sufficiently flexible over the past two centuries to allow for enormous changes in the nature of government. The Federal Government undertakes activities today that would have been unimaginable to the Framers.... *Yet the powers conferred upon the Federal Government by the Constitution were phrased in language broad enough to allow for the expansion of the Federal Government's role.*[79]

Present-day "conservative" and libertarian defenders of the myth of the "stolen" Revolution and the Federalist betrayal of "the Jeffersonian vision" of Liberty thus find themselves bemoaning the inevitable outcome of the Constitution being what it is: the framework for a supreme federal government to which "We the People," in an exercise of Lockean compact theory, had "consented" to submit themselves. As Morison observes with admiration: "[T]he genius of the Convention of 1787, its greatest contribution to political science, was to get away from this horizontal separation between the state governments and federal government, and give the latter *a direct line to each individual citizen.*"[80]

Anything like a complete survey of the early history of the federal government is impossible here. But landmark examples of the early exercise and expansion of federal power during the administrations of the first five Presidents—Washington, Adams, Jefferson, Madison and Monroe—will suffice to dispel the myth that the Founders' inspired plan for Liberty was subverted by evil Federalists and will also demonstrate why even President Jefferson would call himself a federalist in the very name of Liberty. The federal government's inexorable tightening of its "direct line to each individual citizen" is the subject to which we now turn.

---

77. Article III, §3 of the Constitution provides: "The judicial Power of the United States, shall be vested in one supreme Court, and in such inferior Courts as the Congress may from time to time ordain and establish."

78. *United States v. Darby*, 312 U.S. 100, 124 (1941).

79. *New York v. U.S.* 505 U.S. 144 (1992).

80. Morison, *HAP*, 311.

8

The Acorn Becomes an Oak

THE FEDERAL GOVERNMENT'S "direct line" to each citizen was made evident almost immediately by its first President, the unanimous choice of the Electoral College. Even as the defeated anti-Federalists "continued to scream for a new Federal Convention and sneered at the Bill of Rights,"[1] George Washington began a roughly ten-year period of Federalist ascendancy with such acts as instituting the inaugural address, creating the first Cabinet, signing into law the first federal tax (a customs duty), grudgingly accepting the then stupendous presidential salary of $25,000 per year, and putting the federal judiciary into operation, appointing John Jay as the first Chief Justice of the same Supreme Court that would, predictably enough, find that federal power in general was supreme over the States in every case of conflict, precisely as the Supremacy Clause dictated.

Meanwhile, Washington's Secretary of the Treasury, Alexander Hamilton, was presiding over the Treasury Department, a creation of Congress nowhere explicitly mentioned in the text of the Constitution but certainly authorized by the "necessary and proper" clause, which empowered Congress to enact "all Laws which shall be necessary and proper for carrying into Execution the foregoing Powers . . . vested by this Constitution in the Government of the United States, *or in any Department* or Officer thereof." The anti-Federalists could hardly complain that a federal government authorized to create departments had created the Department of the Treasury to finance its operations.

The Treasury Department staff immediately ballooned to over 800 officials, as the Federalists began to build new "hierarchies of patronage and dependence" that "ran from the federal executive through Congress down to the various localities."[2] This patronage and dependence included redemption at par value of state debt securities through payment by the newly created Bank of the United States. As Morison remarks favorably, Hamilton, with Washington's approval, had "turned dead paper into marketable securities, and provided for their redemption by taxes that the nation was well able to bear."[3] Patrick Henry protested in vain that he could find "no clause in the Constitution authorizing Congress to assume the debts of the States."[4]

---

1. Morison, *HAP*, 319.
2. Wood, *Radicalism*, 263.
3. Morison, *HAP*, 326.
4. Virginia Remonstrance Against the Assumption of State Debts, December 16, 1790.

As for Washington's Secretary of State, Thomas Jefferson (recently returned from Paris, where he and Tom Paine had been aiding and abetting the French Revolution), he was doing all he could privately to advance the Jacobin cause. This was the same Jefferson who had written from France, concerning the Shays Rebellion, that "the tree of liberty must be refreshed from time to time with the blood of patriots and tyrants." In 1793, while serving as Secretary of State, Jefferson penned his infamous "Adam and Eve" letter defending the September Massacres of 1792 in Paris during the early stages of the Revolution, only a few months before the execution of Louis XVI:

> The liberty of the whole earth was depending on the issue of the contest, and was there ever a prize won with so little innocent blood? . . . My own affections have been deeply wounded by some of the martyrs of this cause, *but rather that it should have failed, I would have seen half the earth devastated.* Were there but an Adam and an Eve left in every country, and left free, it would be better than as it now is.[5]

Thus did Jefferson (along with his fellow radicals) blithely justify the mass murder of thousands of Parisian prisoners in the name of freeing mankind from the "tyranny" of monarchy. According to the same consequentialist ethical calculus, Vladimir Lenin would declare in an eerie parallel: "It does not matter if three-quarters of mankind is destroyed; all that counts is that ultimately the last quarter should become Communists."[6]

The Whiskey Rebellion

The federal government's "direct line" to the people was deployed with dramatic effect on August 7, 1794, when President Washington, pursuant to the federal Militia Act of 1792, called up 13,000 state militiamen from New Jersey, Maryland, eastern Pennsylvania and Virginia to crush the Whiskey Rebellion (1791–94). The rebellion had arisen in parts of Pennsylvania, Maryland, Virginia, North and South Carolina and Georgia over Congress's next revenue measure: an excise tax on domestically distilled spirits based on the gallon capacity of stills. The tax was imposed to finance Hamilton's plan for the federal assumption of state war debts, a federal bailout that redounded to the benefit of speculators who had bought up

5. Jefferson to William Short, January 3, 1793. The entire letter is set forth in Conor Cruise O'Brien, *The Long Affair: Thomas Jefferson and the French Revolution* (Chicago: Univ. of Chicago Press, 1996), 145–147. O'Brien refutes the desperate attempts of leftist and libertarian scholars to explain away the "Adam and Eve" letter. For example, O'Brien notes, the claim that Jefferson was not "fully aware of the violent turn the revolution had taken" when he wrote to Short is refuted by the fact that in November 1792, two months before he wrote the letter, the American papers had "carried news of the September massacres in Paris," while Jefferson's own *National Gazette* in Philadelphia had "scolded" the Federalist newspapers for calling the French revolutionaries "barbarous and inhuman when *justly incensed they had made examples of two or three thousand scoundrels.*" Ibid., 150.

6. Cited in René Fuelop-Miller, *Fyodor Dostoevsky: Insight, Faith and Prophecy* (NY: Charles Scribner's Sons, 1950), 105.

debt certificates issued by both the States and the Continental Congress. The original owners of the certificates were soldiers who had received them as pay during the Revolution and were forced to sell them "at a few cents on the dollar to feed themselves. . . ." Now the same speculators who had bought the certificates were foreclosing on the former soldiers' farms "because they had no money to pay their debts, all the while voting in state legislatures to tax them heavily so as to enrich the speculators even more by paying off the war debt certificates—their *own* certificates, as they saw it."[7]

In his account of the Whiskey Rebellion, the lawyer, jurist and Pennsylvania Congressman H.M. Brackenbridge records with evident disdain the sentiment of the common people of western Pennsylvania that "since the introduction of the excise law . . . it were better for them to be under the British; and at this time such language began to be common," although he had never heard "any person of *note* breathe the idea." There was even talk "that arms and ammunition could be obtained from the British" to aid in resisting the tax.[8] Like all the revolutions in the name of Liberty that would follow, beginning with the French, the American Revolution was benefitting wealthy elites while imposing new burdens on the simple poor and the working classes, "who had much less stake in the American government than its elite defenders. . . . Probably, having little, they were zealous to protect it all, and deeply resented the power of some distant government to force itself into their very hearthsides to search for untaxed whiskey."[9]

The whiskey tax was only one of several grievances in the regions of the rebellion that related to the feathering of elite nests in the Revolution's aftermath. Another major grievance providing context to the rebellion in trans-Appalachia was the ruthlessness of land speculators who, as absentee owners, were snapping up huge swaths of choice western land and ejecting small farmers and other longstanding occupants. None was more ruthless than the high-handed George Washington himself, who systematically amassed "63,000 acres of trans-Appalachia, becoming one of the largest absentee landlords the western country knew during his day."[10] During a meeting aimed at ousting Scottish squatters from lands he had acquired in a western Pennsylvania county, and knowing that the eastern courts in which the actions for ejectment would be litigated would never defy the great man, Washington regally withdrew a silk handkerchief from his pocket and declared: "I will have this land as surely as I now have this handkerchief." But his legal victory against the "Miller's Run Scots" would "exacerbate the local image of Washington as a rapacious speculator and grasping landlord."[11]

Washington, along with his fellow absentee landlords, "monopolized much of

7. Wythe Holt, "The Whiskey Rebellion of 1794: A Democratic Working-Class Insurrection," Paper presented at The Georgia Workshop in Early American History and Culture (2004), 8.

8. H.M. Brackenridge, *History of the Western Insurrection* (Pittsburgh: W.S. Haven, 1859), 139. This reference is owed to Holt's paper.

9. Holt, 38.

10. Thomas P. Slaughter, *The Whiskey Rebellion* (NY: Oxford Univ. Press, 1986), 82.

11. Ibid., 85.

the area's best land while local farmers labored to scratch a living from what remained. He owned thousands of acres and did not even live or farm on them, although he tried to hide these facts by having his agent build dummy dwellings on the tracts."[12] He had acquired his vast holdings "in the manner usual to most speculators: in making and holding his purchases he lied, he knowingly and repeatedly broke the laws of Great Britain, Pennsylvania, and Virginia, he cheated the soldiers in his command who trusted him, taking the best lands for himself when he distributed land allocated to his command, he browbeat, he sued (exhibiting disgust for the lack of respect squatters had for the law!), and he threatened."[13] Hence by the time of the Whiskey Rebellion, Washington and the other land speculators had become "the most despised men in the western country."[14]

The historical context, then, was ripe for a rebellion against an excise tax imposed by the administration of President Washington and his federalist cronies, who had reaped generously the spoils of a war against the King that the common soldier had fought with the expectation of a new and radical freedom from government. And because the excise taxed whiskey to fund federal redemption of the state debt certificates, it was perceived as a scheme to extract from working class whiskey producers and consumers the money to pay the claims of a few wealthy creditors who had provided no benefit to the taxpayers. On the contrary, the speculators were reaping huge profits on debt instruments that originally belonged to taxpayers themselves; and many thought the certificates should be redeemed in favor of the original holders, who had borne the brunt of the hardships of the war. Further, the tax favored large distilleries, which could afford to opt out of the per-gallon tax by paying a single annual fee of $54—far beyond the reach of a small producer— and then pass the cost along to their customers.[15] Still worse, all legal proceedings pertaining to the tax, including criminal prosecutions for evading it, had to be litigated in the new federal courts. In western Pennsylvania, the center of the rebellion, that meant a journey of hundreds of miles east, at great expense, to the federal courthouse in Philadelphia.

For all these reasons, Wythe Holt has called the rebellion "a democratic working-class insurrection."[16] Opposition to the tax quickly became widespread and often violent. Tax resisters, aping the American revolutionaries only a few years earlier, put up Liberty Poles, held protest "congresses" with "delegates," and engaged in a campaign of disobedience and confrontation of officials involved in collecting the federal duty, including the old reliable tarring and feathering. At a congress in Pittsburgh, a group calling itself the Mingo Creek Association, some of whose members had been revolutionaries against King George, issued what are known as the Mingo Creek Resolutions, which declared, among other things ironic, that the common people of western Pennsylvania were suffering "treatment . . . worse than

12. Slaughter, *The Whiskey Rebellion*, 85.
13. Holt, 36; Slaughter, 82.
14. Ibid., 36; Ibid., 82.
15. Slaughter, 30.
16. Ibid.

the colonies met with from the King of Britain, as it appears in the first Petition to Congress in 1774 and the Declaration [of Independence] of the representatives of the united colonies in 1775."[17] The opposition reached its peak with the march of an army of 7000 on Pittsburgh and a mock attack on Fort Pitt and the federal arsenal, involving thousands who were not even directly affected by the whiskey tax.[18] It seems the rebels were animated by the naïve impression that they were entitled to "the popular autonomy and prosperity the revolutionary experience had promised them,"[19] instead of the installation of wealthy elites in the District of Columbia (created the year before the rebellion began) who were already exercising more power over them than the overthrown King in distant England.

President Washington's imperious Proclamation on the Whiskey Rebellion (1794) may rank as the single greatest piece of irony in the irony-laden and hypocrisy-filled history of Liberty we shall be exploring in this study. Focusing on the uprising in western Pennsylvania, particularly Pittsburgh, Washington condemned "combinations to defeat the execution of the laws laying duties upon spirits distilled within the United States," and recited as "treasonable acts" in a series of "Whereas" clauses a litany of *the very things the Revolutionary leaders and their mobs had done* to resist the revenue measures of the Crown and to intimidate Crown officials charged with imposing and collecting duties in Boston and elsewhere:

> the influence of certain irregular meetings whose proceedings have tended to encourage and uphold the spirit of opposition by misrepresentations of the laws calculated to render them odious. . . .
>
> endeavors to deter those who might be so disposed from accepting offices under them through fear of public resentment and of injury to person and property. . . .
>
> [endeavors] to compel those who had accepted such offices by actual violence to surrender or forbear the execution of them. . . .
>
> circulation [of] vindictive menaces against all those who should otherwise, directly or indirectly, aid in the execution of the said laws. . . .
>
> . . . . injuring and destroying the property of persons who were understood to have so complied. . . .
>
> inflicting cruel and humiliating punishments upon private citizens for no other cause than that of appearing to be the friends of the laws. . . .
>
> intercepting the public officers on the highways, abusing, assaulting, and otherwise ill treating them. . . .
>
> going into their houses in the night, gaining admittance by force, taking away their papers, and committing other outrages. . . ."[20]

17. In Holt, 53, citing Rawle papers of Society of Hamiltons District, May 5, 1794.

18. Slaughter, 4.

19. Ibid.

20. See Yale Law School e-text of the Proclamation at yale.edu/lawweb/avalon/presiden/proclamations/gwproc03.htm.

Raising the irony to the level of the exquisite, Washington cited in defense of the federal government precisely what the American revolutionaries had deemed insufficient in defense of the Crown—i.e., that the duties had been reduced in response to protests, and that the government had been willing to conciliate:

> ... the endeavors of the legislature to obviate objections to the said laws *by lowering the duties* and by other alterations conducive to the convenience of those whom they immediately affect ... and the endeavors of the executive officers *to conciliate a compliance with the laws by explanations, by forbearance, and even by particular accommodations.* ...

But, Washington lamented, the traitorous tax resisters, especially those in the western part of the new State of Pennsylvania, had not been interested in a redress of grievances, which was sufficient for the loyal population at large. Rather, the rebels—exactly like the "Sons of Liberty," whose example Washington had conveniently forgotten—had only been interested in provoking insurrection against duly constituted authority. Hence the federal government's efforts at conciliation had been

> disappointed of their effect by *the machinations of persons whose industry to excite resistance has increased with every appearance of a disposition among the people to relax in their opposition and to acquiesce in the laws,* insomuch that many persons in the said western parts of Pennsylvania have at length been hardy enough to perpetrate acts, which I am advised amount to treason. ...

Some of the tax rebels, notes Holt, "were amazed that the Washington administration wanted to hang them for the same sorts of actions which had been praiseworthy and heroic a short time before, while Hamilton and Washington never seemed to notice this deadly irony."[21] And so, in the late summer of 1794, President Washington assembled his federalized army of 13,000—as large as any he had commanded during the American Revolution[22]—to crush the rebellion in western Pennsylvania as a test case for the exercise of federal authority. Having done so, he declared: "I, George Washington, President of the United States, command all persons, being insurgents ... to disperse and retire peaceably to their respective abodes. And I do moreover warn all persons whomsoever against aiding, abetting, or comforting the perpetrators of the aforesaid *treasonable acts.* ..." Commander-in-Chief Washington and Hamilton personally accompanied the federally marshaled army in its "stiff hike over the Alleghenies"[23] into western Pennsylvania—a military operation of rather mammoth proportions.[24]

Two delegates from a meeting of local citizens at Parkinson's Ferry, in southwestern Pennsylvania, went to meet with Washington in Bedford County to persuade him that order was being restored and that he need not send his avenging army. He

21. Holt, 53.
22. Holt, 1.
23. Morison, *HAP,* 341.
24. Cf. Slaughter, 212 ff.

replied sternly that "the army, unless opposed, did not mean to act as execution-ers," but that he "considered the support of the laws an object of the first magni-tude" and that he required "unequivocal proofs of *absolute submission*" to the federal government, which had not been forthcoming. "I believe they are scared," said Washington with satisfaction as the two rushed back to warn their fellow ben-eficiaries of Liberty that Washington's mighty hosts were coming.[25]

In our irony-filled history of Liberty's first century in America we must note that Washington, now quite convinced there would be no significant resistance, put the entire federal army under the authority of his trusted cavalry commander, who was also Governor of Virginia, General Henry "Light-Horse Harry" Lee, the future father of Robert E. Lee (b. 1807). To heap irony upon irony, when son Rob-ert was still a toddler, Henry would serve a year in debtor's prison after having led an army to vindicate the federal debt collectors of Liberty. To heap the ironies still higher, sixty-six years after a federal army invasion of Pennsylvania led by his own father to suppress a local tax revolt, Col. Robert E. Lee would resign his commis-sion in the United States Army on the grounds that he could not participate in a federal army invasion of Virginia, which had just *entirely seceded* from the Union. Evidently, invading one's *own* state to impose the requirements of Liberty was a different matter.

The whiskey rebels fled in panic before the advancing army, whose members—most of whom had to be drafted—were enraged at being derided as "the Water-melon Army" and were itching for a fight to prove their mettle.[26] Two of the rebel leaders were convicted of treason, a capital offense, of which the Father of His Coun-try generously pardoned them. Holt notes the "harsh irony" that the federal district attorney in charge of prosecuting the rebels, who had been a Loyalist supporter of King George during the Revolution, sought to prosecute twenty-four of them for the non-existent crime of "liberty pole raising" and for "speeches just like those his Washington administration colleagues had made two decades previously."[27]

In his Thanksgiving Day Proclamation the following January, Washington hailed the "internal tranquility we have enjoyed," and "the recent confirmation of that tranquility by the suppression of an insurrection which so wantonly threatened it," and thanked "the Great Ruler of Nations" for the "seasonable control which has been given to a spirit of disorder in the suppression of the late insurrection."[28] King George might well have expressed similarly regal sentiments had he succeeded in suppressing the "late insurrection" in Boston over his comparatively trivial tea tax.

The suppression of the Whiskey Rebellion was, Morison writes admiringly, "a severe but successful test of the new government in its domestic relations."[29] The supreme irony of the affair, in which Liberty Poles had been raised by tax rebels in

　25. Slaughter, 216.

　26. Ibid., 205–206.

　27. Holt, 53.

　28. Proclamation of January 1, 1795; cf. Yale Law School e-text, yale.edu/lawweb/Avalon/presiden/proclamations/gwproc11.htm.

　29. Morison, *HAP*, loc. cit.

opposition to none other than George Washington and his new government "conceived in Liberty," was apparently lost on Morison as well. But then the prevailing *mythos* of Liberty obscures what should be obvious indications of "the duplicity and the self-serving vision which motivated the famous gentlemen in the Washington administration."[30]

The Jay Treaty and Washington's Farewell Warning

During Washington's second term, the Jay Treaty (ratified in 1795) evoked outraged opposition from the anti-Federalist forces, leading to the emergence of Jefferson and the Democratic-Republicans as a formal political party. Under the Treaty, Great Britain was given most favored nation trade status and a promise of United States neutrality in Britain's ongoing war with post-revolutionary France. In return Great Britain would relinquish outposts in the Northwest Territory and pay reparations to American ship owners whose vessels had been captured by the British navy during Anglo-French hostilities. Jay and the Washington administration had the benefit of the argument, expressed by Jay, that the Revolutionary War alliance with France under Louis XVI could hardly continue with "the republic that had decapitated the king."[31]

At this point Jefferson was still involved in his love affair with the French Revolution, as reflected in his "Adam and Eve" letter of 1793. He joined with Madison in depicting the Jay Treaty as a betrayal of France, whose aid to the colonies had made possible the American victory over England, and as a sign of dangerous monarchical tendencies in the new federal government. But the Federalists, supported again by Washington's overwhelming prestige, secured Senate ratification, and Washington signed the Jay Treaty into law. The federal government "conceived in Liberty" had just done a deal with the very locus of "Popish tyranny," heralding the beginning of America's global foreign policy designs. Then again, one could hardly blame the Federalists for taking sides against the French when the Paris regime was in the midst of waging the French Revolutionary Wars (1792–1802) that would convulse all of Europe and claim millions of lives in the drive to remake all of Europe in the image of Liberty.

In his Farewell Address (1796), the outgoing President Washington established the theme that every subsequent President, including Jefferson, would follow unswervingly: the Age of Revolution was over, and now had come the Age of Obedience. As Washington admonished:

> This government, the offspring of our own choice . . . has a just claim to your confidence and your support. *Respect for its authority, compliance with its laws, acquiescence in its measures, are duties enjoined by the fundamental maxims of true liberty.* . . . The very idea of the power and the right of the people to

---

30. Holt, 53.

31. Bernard Fay, *The Revolutionary Spirit in France and America* (NY: Cooper Square Publishers, 1966), 353.

establish government presupposes the duty of every individual *to obey the established government.*

The message could not have been starker: Liberty means obedience to the federal government. And obedience to the federal government means preservation of the federal Union, which must endure forever: "These considerations speak a persuasive language to every reflecting and virtuous mind, and exhibit *the continuance of the Union as a primary object of patriotic desire.*" Sixty-five years before the Civil War began, George Washington enunciated the political dogma that made the War inevitable: to be an American is to be devoted to the Union even unto death. Why this should be so has always been one of the mysteries in the catechism of Liberty. But then this was the bed that North and South had made together in their joint rebellion against "absolute monarchy."

The Alien and Sedition Acts, the Quasi War, and "Nullification"

Thanks to the Jay Treaty, during the Presidency of John Adams (1797–1801) America found herself in hostilities with the French Directory, successor to the revolutionary government under Robespierre, who had been executed two years earlier (in July 1794) following the Terror. In keeping with the spirit of Jefferson's "Adam and Eve" letter, the Republicans, who would still neither see nor hear any evil in the French Revolution, were secretly encouraging the French to seize American ships, "stoutly defend[ing] the spoliations as a natural answer to Jay's treaty."[32]

By this time Jefferson, returned from France and serving as Vice President under Adams, "had come to see Washington as an apostate to the cause of Liberty."[33] As he had earlier confided privately to his friend and fellow "apostle of Liberty," Philip Mazzei, who was roaming Europe promoting the creed of republicanism: "It would give you a fever were I to name to you the apostates who have gone over to these heresies, men who were Sampsons in the field & Solomons in the Council, but who have had their heads shorn by the harlot England."[34] America, Jefferson lamented, had been given over to "an Anglican, monarchical and aristocratical party" in place of "that noble love of liberty & republican government which carried us triumphantly thro' the war...."[35] Soon enough, however, President Jefferson would be governing with a hand far heavier than Washington's, defending federal supremacy just as his predecessor had done.

---

32. Morison, *HAP*, 348.

33. O'Brien, *The Long Affair*, 204.

34. Jefferson to Mazzei, April 24, 1796, in Howard R. Marraro, "The Four Versions of Jefferson's Letter to Mazzei," *William and Mary College Quarterly Historical Magazine*, 2d Ser., Vol. 22, No. 1 (January, 1942), 24. The authenticity of the version quoted, Jefferson's English original, is not disputed. The letter caused Jefferson no end of embarrassment when it found its way into the French and then the American Federalist press.

35. Ibid.

When President Adams sent a diplomatic commission to France to negotiate a settlement of the situation, three representatives of Talleyrand, the apostate Catholic bishop who had become French Minister of Foreign affairs, approached the commissioners and demanded, among other things, a massive bribe before France would even begin to negotiate. The dispatches evidencing the blackmail were published by order of President Adams, with "X," "Y," and "Z" designating the redacted names of the blackmailers—hence, the infamous XYZ Affair.

The XYZ Affair provoked the next expansion of federal power. Riding a wave of popular outrage against France, which had hitherto been the darling of public opinion, the Federalist-dominated Congress passed a flurry of legislation to levy new taxes, raise an army, and establish a Department of the Navy. The newly beefed-up Navy proceeded to engage French ships that were interfering with American commerce. The resulting undeclared Quasi-War with France (1798–1800) delighted the British, who now hastened to assist America in a complete and supremely ironic reversal of the alliance in effect during the Revolution. The burgeoning U.S. Navy was now protecting both U.S. and British shipping from the French in the Caribbean, while the British navy was protecting American shipping from French interference in transatlantic commerce.

In 1798, amidst the now-reigning Francophobia, Adams signed into law the four bills known collectively as the Alien and Sedition Acts. The Alien Friends Act and the Alien Enemies Act authorized the President to arrest, imprison or deport aliens considered dangerous to the republic or whose home countries were at war with America. The Naturalization Act increased the residency period required for citizenship from five to fourteen years. Section 1 of the Sedition Act, punishing criminal conspiracies against the federal government, had the support of even some Republicans in Congress. Section 2, however, made it a federal offense to write, print, or publish, or to assist in writing, printing or publishing, any "false, scandalous and malicious writing or writings against the government of the United States, or either house of the Congress of the United States, or the President of the United States, with intent to defame the said government."[36] That is, federal law now forbade Americans to speak against the President or Congress in the same manner the Whig radicals had spoken for years, with complete impunity, against the King and Parliament. Quite conspicuously, however, the Sedition Act exempted the Vice President (i.e., Jefferson) from its prohibitions.

The passage of the Alien and Sedition Acts brought into stark relief the reality that, just as the anti-Federalists had warned, the Constitution on its face created a government of potentially vast powers whose limits were anything but clearly fixed by the fundamentally ambiguous Tenth Amendment. The question was whether the document the Framers had written provided any explicit means to oppose the Acts beyond repeal by Congress or judicial review by the Article III judiciary, a process that had yet to develop with the Marshall court.

---

36. 5th Congress, 2nd Session, Chapter 74, July 14, 1798: An Act for the Punishment of Certain Crimes against the United States ("Sedition Act"), § 2.

In response to the crisis, Jefferson would invoke—nay, invent—a constitutional remedy: neither repeal nor judicial review of allegedly unconstitutional federal laws but "nullification" of them by the state legislatures, even the legislature of a lone state defying the consensus of its co-states. But this mechanism of state legislative nullification of federal law is found nowhere in the text of the Constitution. Quite the contrary, the Supremacy Clause implies *federal* nullification of *state* laws by Congress: "the Laws of the United States . . . shall be the supreme Law of the Land; and the Judges in every State shall be bound thereby, *any Thing in the Constitution or Laws of any State to the Contrary notwithstanding.*"

Three years away from his own inauguration as President, Jefferson joined Madison in opposing the Alien and Sedition Acts by way of the Kentucky and Virginia Resolutions of 1798—an amazingly audacious move for Jefferson, given that he was a sitting Vice-President whose actions undermined the Adams administration and were arguably a violation of Section 1 of the Sedition Act. Jefferson anonymously authored the "resolves" that were adopted, *mutatis mutandis*, by the Kentucky General Assembly, although they were apparently intended for North Carolina. His draft of October 1798 declared that "the several States composing, the United States of America, are not united on the principle of unlimited submission to their general government. . . ." When the federal government acts in a manner deemed to violate what Jefferson viewed as the "compact" according to which the federal government is "not a party, but merely the creature," then, the Resolutions declare, "every State has a natural right in cases not within the compact . . . to nullify . . . all assumptions of power by others within their limits. . . ." Further, he opined, every state "has an equal right to judge for itself, as well of infractions as of the mode of measure of redress."[37]

How ironic it was that only eleven years after the Constitutional Convention, Jefferson's resolutions were already complaining of "unlimited submission," not to the distant monarch who had been overthrown twenty-two years earlier, but to the very government the Framers had created to replace that monarchy according to the "sovereign will of the people." Contrary to libertarian legend, however, Jefferson opposed the Sedition Act not because it violated any inherent right to freedom of expression but rather because it exceeded the powers granted to the federal government as supposedly limited by the Tenth Amendment. Jefferson had no problem with *the States* criminalizing seditious speech or conspiracies, as his draft resolutions made clear: "[T]he power to create, define, and punish such other crimes is reserved, and, of right, appertains solely and exclusively *to the respective States*, each within its own territory." The states, Jefferson argued, had "*retain[ed] to themselves* the right of judging how far the licentiousness of speech and of the press may be abridged. . . ."[38] As we shall see in due course, President Jefferson found *state* prosecutions for seditious libel quite useful to his purposes, and during

---

37. *Kentucky Resolutions* (1798), nn. 1 and 9.
38. In Levy, *Jefferson and Civil Liberties*, 56.

his second term he quite forgot the limited view of federal power he had advocated in his draft resolutions.

Not willing to go as far as Jefferson would, the General Assembly's formal Resolutions of 1798 deleted Jefferson's draft reference to a "nullification" remedy supposedly found within the constitutional "compact." Rather, Kentucky merely called upon the other States for "an expression of their sentiments on the acts . . . plainly declaring whether these acts are or are not authorized by the federal compact." The Assembly further expressed the hope that the co-States "will concur with this commonwealth in considering the said acts as palpably against the Constitution" and that, "recurring to their natural right in cases not made federal, will concur in declaring these acts void, and of no force, and will each take measures of its own for providing that neither these acts, nor any others of the General Government not plainly and intentionally authorized by the Constitution, shalt be exercised within their respective territories."

In its Resolutions of the following year, the Kentucky General Assembly clarified that while "a nullification, by those sovereignties, of all unauthorized acts done under colour of that instrument [the Constitution], is the rightful remedy"—meaning nullification by *all* the States together as "sovereignties," not by Kentucky alone—nevertheless Kentucky "will *bow to the laws of the Union*, yet . . . does at the same time declare, that it will not now, nor ever hereafter, cease to oppose *in a constitutional manner*, every attempt from what quarter soever offered, to violate that compact." That is, contrary to what contemporary libertarians misleadingly suggest, Kentucky implicitly conceded that opposition "in a constitutional manner" to federal laws deemed unconstitutional by the States did not involve *single*-state "nullification" of such laws while the co-states obeyed them, as this would obviously lead to absurd results. Hence Kentucky bowed to the will of the other states in obeying "the laws of the union."

This was Madison's position as well. In his later *Notes on Nullification* (1835), the "Father of the Constitution" pronounced an "absurdity," as well as "naked and suicidal," the concept of "a *constitutional* [his emphasis] right in a single state to nullify a law of the U.S." The bizarre outcome of such a principle would be that:

> In some of the States, the carriage-tax would have been collected, in others unpaid. In some, the tariff on imports would be collected; in others, openly resisted. In some, lighthouses w[ould] be established; in others denounced. In some States there might be war with a foreign power; in others, peace and commerce. Finally, the appellate authority of the Supreme Court of the U. S. would give effect to the Federal laws in some States, whilst in others they would be rendered nullities by the State Judiciaries. In a word, the nullifying claims if reduced to practice, instead of being the conservative principle of the Constitution, would necessarily, and it may be said obviously, be a deadly poison.

The notion of nullification, wrote Madison, ignored "the essential distinction between a *constitutional* right and the *natural* and universal right of resisting intolerable oppression"—i.e., civil disobedience to particular unjust laws, with all its consequences. Thus Madison's resolutions, as adopted by the Virginia Senate, made no call for "nullification," but merely a "solemn appeal to the like dispositions of the other states, in confidence that they will concur with this commonwealth in declaring, as it does hereby declare, that the acts aforesaid, are unconstitutional; and that the necessary and proper measures will be taken by each, for co-operating with this state, in maintaining the Authorities, Rights, and Liberties, referred to the States respectively, or to the people." Those "necessary and proper measures" were, as the Resolutions declared, to "transmit a copy of the foregoing Resolutions to the executive authority of each of the other states, with a request that the same may be communicated to the Legislature thereof; and that a copy be furnished to each of the Senators and Representatives representing this state in the Congress of the United States." That is, the Madisonian remedy for the Alien and Sedition Acts was a protest and petition to Congress, Locke's "supreme authority," for repeal.

At no time, in fact, did Madison ever advocate the "nullification" doctrine attributed to Jefferson. Quite to the contrary, he rejected it entirely; and (as we shall see) he later devoted considerable energy to the argument, intended to defend the memory and legacy of his friend, that *Jefferson himself* had never advocated it! The historian Robert M.S. McDonald remarks "Madison's clear aversion to Jefferson's constitutional brinkmanship" and his rejection of Jefferson's suggestion that "Madison's resolutions be amended to declare 'that the said acts are . . . null, void and of no force, or effect.'" Madison pointed out to Jefferson that there was no warrant in the text of the Constitution for State legislatures to "nullify" federal laws in the first place, since "it was not the [state] assembly, after all, that had ratified the Constitution: *it was a special convention of citizens*. Thus the legislature did not have the power to nullify. Were it to claim that prerogative it would expose itself to 'the charge of Usurpation in the very act of protesting ag[ain]st the usurpations of Congress.'"[39] That it was "We the People," not "We the State legislatures" that had ratified the Constitution would figure prominently in Justice Marshall's early defense of the independent sovereign power of the federal entity the Framers, led by Madison himself, had—like it or not—patently endowed with direct authority over the individual citizens of the United States.

As McDonald observes: "It is not surprising that Madison resisted Jefferson's somewhat impetuous tinkering with the Constitutional process, a project that could lead, no less certainly than the Adams administration's constitutional improvisation, to the dissolution of his cherished union of states."[40] The subjection of the individual citizen to that "cherished union" led ultimately to the Civil War, an event the anti-Federalists had likewise predicted with prophetic accuracy. For the Lockean sovereign the Framers created could hardly countenance great masses of its subjects simply walking away from its authority.

39. Robert M.S. McDonald, "The Madisonian Legacy: A Jeffersonian Perspective," in *Madison and the Future of Limited* Government, ed. John Samples (Washington, DC: Cato Institute, 2002), 65.
40. Ibid.

Jefferson's "nullification" theory was contrary to the reigning Lockean notion of political sovereignty, despite Jefferson's own devotion to the Moses of the Enlightenment. The American historian Abbot E. Smith observes that nullification "was an entirely new doctrine, based upon conceptions of the nature of sovereignty and of the meaning of the word 'compact' which were strange to the men of 1798."[41] For Jefferson—at least before he himself ascended to the Presidency—the federal union was a mere league that had no existence apart from its members. But for Madison and the other Framers—a view not disputed by the vast majority of state legislatures during the Nullification Crisis—"[t]he purpose of ratifying the compact *not by the state legislatures but by the people of the States* was to make it not a treaty, or league, but a constitution, creating a government with sovereign powers."[42] The prevailing understanding of the federal compact was that of "*Lockeian political philosophy*, and signified the basis upon which all government rested, according to that philosophy."[43] That is, it was a social compact that had erected a sovereign power to which the parties (barring revolution) were irrevocably subject, the "one Body Politick under one supreme Government"[44] of the Second Treatise, discussed in Chapter 3.

To the objection by Jefferson and "the nullifiers" (including present-day libertarians) that the "sovereignty of the people" could not be divided between state and federal governments, Madison replied with "the empirical statement that in the government of the United States sovereignty *had been divided*."[45] If the "sovereign people" of the United States had been deemed to "consent" to the Constitution by means of the ratifying conventions, why could they not also "consent" to make themselves subject to successive levels of political authority? Jefferson's notion of "indivisible" sovereignty, as if the supposedly "sovereign people" were ontologically incapable of creating a *hierarchy* of power, was a convenient contrivance to avoid the implications of Lockean compact theory at the federal level.

Given the prevailing Lockean view of what the federal government was—not a league but a sovereign in its own right, created by "We the People"—Virginia and Kentucky had no success in rallying the other states to declare the Alien and Sedition Acts void for unconstitutionality. Quite the contrary, Kentucky and Virginia had only succeeded in provoking counter-resolutions from all the Northern states, which declared the Kentucky and Virginia Resolutions "a very unjustifiable interference with the general government and constituted authorities of the United States" (Delaware), "evil and fatal" (Rhode Island), "inflammatory and pernicious sentiments and doctrines" (New York), and "unconstitutional in their nature, and dangerous in their tendency" (Vermont). Massachusetts, remarking the salient fact that

---

41. Abbot Emerson Smith, *James Madison: Builder—A New Estimate of a Memorable Career* (NY: Wilson Erickson, 1937), 231.

42. Ibid., 229.

43. Ibid.

44. *TT*, II.89.

45. Smith, *James Madison: Builder*, 230. Emphasis in original.

the state legislatures had not ratified the Constitution in the first place, but rather "We the People," maintained (just as Madison did) that "the people . . . have not constituted the state legislatures the judges of the acts or measures of the Federal Government" and that the text of the Constitution had confided to the state legislatures only "the power of proposing such amendments of the Constitution, as shall appear to them necessary to the interests, or conformable to the wishes of *the people whom they represent*."[46]

On the other hand, the Northern states would later deem it expedient to speak of nullification when it came to the federal Fugitive Slave Acts of 1793 and 1850, mandating the interstate rendition of escaped slaves pursuant to the Constitution's own slave rendition clause. Thus was demonstrated the highly expedient character of the "states' rights" doctrine in general and "nullification" in particular, which comprised not so much a coherent doctrine as a political threat by the losing side of a legislative debate in Congress. As Professor Morison writes: "Almost every man in public life between 1798 and 1860 spurned it ['states' rights'] when his section was in the saddle, and embraced it when his constituents deemed themselves oppressed. Almost every state in turn declared its absolute sovereignty, only to denounce as treasonable similar declarations by other states."[47] Such was the confusion and inconsistency provoked by the very idea of a "sovereign people" creating the very authorities to which it was supposed to be subject.

In any event, the dominant movement during these endless debates over federal sovereignty vis-à-vis the States was a steady expansion of federal power. And this occurred according to the very terms of the document by which "We the People" had created the federal government of which, according to Locke's insoluble paradox—the paradox of Liberty itself—they were both creators and subjects unto death.

The Fries Rebellion

In 1799, reprising President Washington's crushing of the Whiskey Rebellion in 1794, President Adams crushed the Fries Rebellion, named after its leader, John Fries of Pennsylvania. Fries was another Revolutionary War hero who, like Daniel Shays, would find that his reward for service to the cause was persecution by the federal tax collectors of Liberty. Perhaps there was poetic justice in this, as Captain Fries had been a company commander in the army of militia that marched with Washington to crush the Whiskey Rebellion, during which, as one sternly approving historian notes, Fries "served his country faithfully."[48]

Fries and his fellow rebels, most of whom were Federalists, engaged in nonviolent resistance to federal agents conducting assessments for the first direct federal

46. *See* "COUNTER-RESOLUTIONS OF OTHER STATES IN RESPONSE TO THOSE OF VIRGINIA, &c.," www.constitution.org/rf/vr_04.htm.

47. Morison, *HAP*, 394–395.

48. W.W.H. Davis, A.M., *The Fries Rebellion, 1798–99* (Doylestown, PA: Doylestown Publishing, 1899), 10.

tax: an excise on land, houses, and slaves—the so-called House Tax, imposed for the ostensible purpose of paying for the expense of the Quasi War with France. The rebellion also involved the farcical "Hot Water War," in which an angry housewife poured buckets of hot water on a revenue officer from the window of her now-taxable home. After Fries and his men marched on a local jail and freed some of the tax rebels imprisoned there, Adams called out the militia to apprehend the ringleaders. Fries and others were handed up by pro-government citizens. Fries at first eluded capture, only to be caught when his hiding place was betrayed by his barking dog, whose name, most ironically, was "Whiskey."[49]

After being indicted for "war, insurrection, and rebellion against the United States," Fries and two others were convicted of treason and sedition in federal district court and sentenced to be hanged. Fries, whose lawyer assured him this could never happen for such a minor offense, "fainted away."[50] But Fries and the other defendants were granted new trials when it was learned that one of the jurors had declared publicly before trial that the defendants should hang. They fared no better at their retrials.[51]

Two days before the execution, however, Adams pardoned the condemned men. In language reminiscent of Washington's proclamation on the Whiskey Rebellion, Adams's proclamation spared the "traitors" because "the late wicked and treasonable insurrection against the just authority of the United States of sundry persons [has] . . . been speedily suppressed without any of the calamities usually attending rebellion. . . ."[52] King George could not have said it any more regally. But there was no need for a hanging, as the American people had gotten the message conveyed so dramatically by Washington in his march across the Alleghenies to put down the Whiskey Rebels: obey or die.

The Apotheosis of Washington

In the midst of the criminal prosecution of Fries, the death of President Washington on December 14, 1799 marked the beginning of the process of his virtual apotheosis as "the Father of His Nation." As Washington was a faithful Freemason, who had sworn his oath of office on a Masonic bible, "[h]is Masonic lodge was permitted to prepare arrangements for the funeral procession." He was given "the traditional Masonic funeral rites" by "the Reverend James Muir, minister of the Alexandria Presbyterian Church, and Dr. Elisha Dick, both members of Washington's Lodge. . . ."[53] As his biographer Joseph J. Ellis recounts, while Washington lay dying and fully aware that he was in his last hours, "there were no ministers in the

49. Jane Shaffer Elsmere, "The Trials of John Fries," *The Pennsylvania Magazine of History and Biography*, Vol. 103, No. 4 (October 1979), 432–445 at 435.

50. Ibid., 438.

51. Ibid., 438–442.

52. John Adams, Proclamation of May 21, 1800.

53. "The Papers of George Washington: The Funeral," University of Virginia Library, accessed at http://gwpapers.virginia.edu/project/exhibit/mourning/funeral.html.

room, no prayers uttered, no Christian rituals offering the solace of everlasting life. . . . He died as a Roman Stoic rather than as a Christian saint."[54]

Six years before his death, Washington had consecrated the Capitol Building according to a Masonic ritual. The world-renowned historian Simon Schama, of Oxford, Harvard and Columbia, notes that the Masonic apron Washington wore when he "baptized" that edifice in a "supremely Masonic act" was embroidered by Adrienne Lafayette, the wife of General Lafayette, Washington's Masonic brother-in-arms, who joined the Lodge of Saint-Jean de Candeur in 1775.[55] Steven Bullock describes the bizarre ritual in his classic study of Freemasonry in the early Republic:

> If, as Thomas Jefferson argued, the Capitol represented "the first temple dedicated to the sovereignty of the people," then the [Masonic] brothers of the 1793 ceremony served as its first high priests. Clothed in ritual vestments, Washington and his brothers consecrated the building by the literal baptism of corn, oil and wine—symbols of nourishment, refreshment and joy, or, as some versions interpreted them, Masonry, science and virtue, and universal benevolence.[56]

Credulous acceptance of the "conservative" thread of the Liberty narrative, with its golden legend of the Christian Founding (cf. Chapter 18), requires that Americans find nothing amiss with this sort of thing.

Congress chose Washington's fellow Freemason, "Light-Horse Harry" Lee,[57] to deliver the funeral oration.[58] As Washington's close associate and most brilliant cavalryman during the Revolutionary War, Henry Lee uttered the immortal words: "First in war, first in peace and first in the hearts of his countrymen," to which he added such measured encomia as "vice shuddered in his presence and virtue always felt his fostering hand." Two weeks later, the Yale-educated historian and Protestant preacher Benjamin Trumbull delivered a funeral discourse in Connecticut with the cautionary title "The Majesty and Mortality of created Gods." He reminded his audience of the divine admonition in Psalm 82 that the rulers of this world, no matter how great, "shall die like men, and fall like one of the princes," and that it behooves them to contemplate frequently "their mortality . . . [and] their responsibility to a tribunal higher than their own. . . ."[59]

Sixty-five years after Washington's death, the interior of the dome in the rotunda

---

54. Joseph J. Ellis, *His Excellency George Washington* (NY: Alfred A. Knopf, 2004), 269, quoted in Brooke Allen, *Moral Minority*, 34–35.

55. Schama, *Citizens*, 29.

56. Steven C. Bullock, *Revolutionary Brotherhood* (Chapel Hill: Univ. of North Carolina Press, 1996), 137.

57. A member of Hiram Lodge No. 59, Westmoreland County, VA. Cf. Denslow and Truman, 68.

58. "The Papers of George Washington: Immediate Response," University of Virginia Library, accessed at http://gwpapers.virginia.edu/project/exhibit/mourning/response.html.

59. Benjamin Trumbull, *The Majesty and Mortality of created Gods Illustrated and Improved. A Funeral Discourse, Delivered at North-Haven, December 29, 1799. On the Death of George Washington; who died December 14, 1799.* (New Haven: Read & Morse, 1800).

of the Capitol Building that Washington had baptized according to Masonic ritual would be adorned by a fresco literally entitled "The Apotheosis of Washington." It depicts the sainted Revolutionary Father "rising to the heavens in glory, flanked by female figures representing Liberty and Victory/Fame...."[60] The fresco would become a major icon in the American civil religion (cf. Chapter 21). And Washington would become, not a "created God" in the sense of Trumbull's discourse—the earthly ruler who, as God's creation, acts as God's minister, accountable to Him—but a purely human semi-divinity in a nation whose Constitution and laws make no reference to divine authority. One of the first things that would be forgotten during the "progress" of Liberty is the direct accountability of civil authorities to God and their duty to obey His law.

The "Revolution" of 1800

The Fries Rebellion and the Alien and Sedition Acts, including the conviction of a member of Congress and several Republican editorialists for "seditious libel," provided much of the political fodder by which Jefferson, tied with Burr in the Electoral College, squeaked through to victory in the election of 1800 after 35 tie-breaker ballots in the House. The Republicans had conducted a campaign whose theme was the Federalist "reign of Terror."[61] But already an American dynamic had been established according to which the foes of Big Government run for election against the evil perpetrators of Big Government, only to perpetuate Big Government themselves once they occupy the seats of power.

Which brings us to the next of the golden legends in the history of Liberty: Jefferson's so-called "Revolution of 1800." According to this legend, President Jefferson, coming to power on a rising tide of discontent with Federalist power-building and disregard for Liberty, slayed the federal dragon and restored the true principles of Liberty by rolling back federalist encroachments on the sovereignty of "the people" and the several states. It does not take much examination, however, to see that "the Revolution of 1800," much like the "Reagan Revolution" of the 1980s, was more apparent than real. What began as a seeming reduction in federal power ended with a dramatic net expansion—a pattern all too familiar in our American experience with Liberty.

To begin with, in his First Inaugural Address in 1801, Jefferson stunned his own fellow Republicans when he famously declared: "We are all Republicans, we are all Federalists. If there be any among us who would wish to dissolve this Union or to change its republican form, let them stand undisturbed as monuments of the safety with which error of opinion may be tolerated where reason is left free to combat it." Now that he was President, Jefferson wanted it known that "the essential principles of our Government" included "preservation of the General Government *in its whole constitutional vigor*" and "*absolute acquiescence* in the decisions of the major-

---

60. "The Apotheosis of Washington," www.aoc.gov/cc/art/rotunda/apotheosis/Overview.cfm.
61. Morison, *HAP*, 355.

ity, the vital principle of republics. . . ." That only three years before his own inauguration Jefferson had anonymously advocated state "nullification" of federal law under the "compact theory" of the Kentucky Resolutions only demonstrated that the most consistent thing about this "apostle of Liberty," who recaptured and flogged his own slaves, was his inconsistency. As Professor Onuf writes: "Jefferson's celebration of the Union in his Inaugural—a union he was prepared to destroy in 1798 through state 'nullification' of federal authority—thus seems disingenuous, if not downright hypocritical. . . . Jefferson has never lacked defenders, of course, least of all in these precincts [the University of Virginia]. . . . [But] Jefferson's friends have been complicit in an interpretation of the Inaugural and of his political career generally that systematically discounts and misrepresents his principled commitment to the American experiment in *federal* republican government. . . . [W]hen Jefferson called himself a 'federalist,' he meant what he was saying."[62]

Jefferson, in fact, sought nothing less than to make the United States of America the center of a veritable "empire of Liberty." As he had written twenty years before he assumed the Presidency: ". . . .[W]e shall form to *the American union* a barrier against the dangerous extension of the British Province of Canada and add to the Empire of liberty an extensive and fertile Country thereby converting dangerous Enemies into valuable friends."[63] He sounded the same theme in a letter to his successor as President, James Madison, but adding the element of a conquest of Canada, following the acquisition of Florida and Cuba:

> We should then have only to include the north [Canada] in our Confederacy, which would be of course *in the first war*, and we should have such an empire for liberty as she has never surveyed since the creation; and I am persuaded no Constitution was ever before so well calculated as ours for *extensive empire* and self-government.[64]

Having begun his presidency by declaring "We are all republicans, we are all federalists," Jefferson, no less than Washington, invoked the necessity of obedience to federal power and the preservation of "the Union," further declaring in his inaugural address:

> I know, indeed, that some honest men fear that a republican government can not be strong, that this Government is not strong enough. . . . I believe this, on the contrary, *the strongest Government on earth*. Let us, then, with courage and confidence pursue our own *Federal and Republican principles*, our *attachment to union* and representative government.

The one-time anonymous proponent of the "nullification" of federal law had ascended to the highest office in the land as a Republican Federalist—a prototype of the modern "Big Government conservative," who pledged to reduce bureaucracy

62. Onuf, "Jefferson, Federalist," 22–23.
63. Jefferson to George Rogers Clark, December 25, 1780, in Boyd, Julian P., ed. *Papers of Thomas Jefferson*, Vol. 4 (Princeton, NJ: Princeton Univ. Press, 1951), 237–238.
64. *Writings*, ed. H. A. Washington, Vol. 5, 444.

and taxes even as he touted "the strongest government on earth" and presided over what was ultimately an expansion of federal power.

Jefferson was true to his self-contradictory program, which involved—here we see already the perennial theme of American national politics—"seeking common ground on which to build his new government."[65] Thus, during his first term, the same President Jefferson who insisted upon abolishing internal excise taxes (while retaining import duties), reducing the national debt and cutting back on the size of the army and navy, also left intact the entire nascent federal bureaucracy, including Hamilton's Treasury Department and the Bank of the United States, which Jefferson had opposed when he was Secretary of State.

"Wholesome Prosecutions"

While Jefferson pardoned convicts under the Sedition Act or abandoned pending prosecutions—all the beneficiaries of this leniency being fellow Republicans—he had no qualms about state-level prosecution for "seditious libels" uttered against the national government. In fact, in the middle of his first term he explicitly endorsed "selected" state law libel prosecutions of Federalists, confiding to Governor McKean of Pennsylvania in early 1803 that "the federalists having failed in destroying the freedom of the press by their gag-law [the Sedition Act, which expired in 1801], seem to have attacked it in an opposite direction . . . by pushing its licentiousness and its lying to such a degree of prostitution as to deprive it of all credit." This "dangerous state of things," he continued, could be addressed "by the laws of the States. . . . And I have, therefore, long thought that *a few prosecutions of the most prominent offenders* would have a wholesome effect in restoring the integrity of the presses. *Not a general prosecution, for that would look like persecution; but a selected one.*"[66]

Jefferson's "confidential" letter to McKean gave the nod to McKean's request for his authority to prosecute one of these "prominent offenders": the Federalist editor of the Philadelphia *Port-Folio*, Joseph Dennie, who had given extensive publicity to the famous allegation (recently confirmed by DNA testing[67]) that Jefferson had fathered a child by his slave, Sally Hemings. Dennie, however, was prosecuted "not for libeling Jefferson but for a tirade against democracy," having committed

65. Dawson, *Partisanship and the Birth of America's Second Party*, 192.
66. Jefferson to Thomas McKean, February 1803, in *Jeffersonian Cyclopedia*, §5967.
67. In a monumental embarrassment for the keepers of the Jefferson legend, in 2000 a research committee of the Thomas Jefferson Foundation reported its finding that a DNA study in 1998, published in the prestigious scientific journal *Nature*, "combined with multiple strands of currently available documentary and statistical evidence, indicates a high probability that Thomas Jefferson fathered Eston Hemings, and that he most likely was the father *of all six of Sally Hemings's children appearing in Jefferson's records.*" (Cf. "Report of the Research Committee on Thomas Jefferson and Sally Hemings," Thomas Jefferson Foundation, January 2000, Conclusions, monticello.org/site/plantation-and-slavery/vi-conclusions.) Unable to refute the DNA analysis, which found in the Hemings line a genetic marker that could only have come from a male in the Jefferson line, the keepers of the legend offer the desperate

the grave offense of publishing ballads that "openly glorified monarchy."[68] He was promptly acquitted.

The Louisiana Purchase

The same Jefferson who had harped on a strict construction of the Constitution when he was out of power conveniently ignored his own counsel in proceeding with the Louisiana Purchase (1803) from Napoleon with federal funds, thereby doubling the size of the United States and subjecting the Territory's inhabitants to a veritable conquest by the federal government. As Jefferson freely admitted to his Attorney General, John Breckinridge: "The Constitution has made no provision for our holding foreign territory, still less for incorporating foreign nations into our Union. The Executive [i.e., Jefferson] in seizing the fugitive occurrence which so much advances the good of their country, *have done an act beyond the Constitution. . . .*"[69]

Writing to John Dickinson, "Penman of the Revolution" and author of "the Liberty Song," Jefferson cynically admitted that what he saw as the incapacity of the federal government to acquire new territory "presents a handle to the malcontents among us, though they have not yet discovered it." What the malcontents had not yet figured out was that the federal government "has no powers but such as the constitution has given it; and it has not given it a power of holding foreign territory, and still less of incorporating it into the Union." Nevertheless, Jefferson proposed to hide this difficulty from the "malcontents" by "ratify[ing] & pay[ing] our money . . . for *a thing beyond the constitution*, and rely on the nation to sanction an act done for its great good, *without its previous authority.*"[70] In other words, Jefferson would act without authority from "the people" and then count on their passive acceptance of a *fait accompli*—the very *modus operandi* of Liberty since 1776, as we have seen in the preceding survey. Jefferson agreed to pay $15 million even though Congress had authorized only $2 million (for New Orleans alone).

This is not to suggest that under the broad powers granted to the federal government in the Constitution, including the power to provide for the common defense and to promote the general welfare, the federal government actually was incompetent to acquire new territory. The point, rather, is that Jefferson was willing to ignore his own professed commitment to "strict construction" whenever it was

---

suggestion that his younger brother Randolph was the father, even though Randolph never resided at Monticello and rarely visited. Even more desperately, they suggest that one of Randolph's sons was the father, though they would have been too young to father any of Hemings's children. (Cf. Jeanette K.B. Daniels, AG, CGRS, Marietta Glauser, Diana Harvey, and Carol Hubbell Ouellette, "Thomas Jefferson and Sally Hemings: A Look at Some Original Documents," *Heritage Quest Magazine*, May/June 2003).

68. Fawn McKay Brodie, *Thomas Jefferson: An Intimate Portrait* (NY: W.W. Norton & Company, 1974), 548, n. 42.

69. Jefferson to John Breckinridge, August 12, 1803, in ed. Jerry Holmes, *Thomas Jefferson: A Chronology of His Thoughts* (Lanham, MD: Rowman & Littlefield Publishers, Inc., 2002), 189.

70. Jefferson to John Dickinson, August 9, 1803, in Everett Somerville Brown, *The Constitutional History of the Louisiana Purchase, 1803–1812* (Berkeley: Univ. of California Press, 1920), 23.

expedient to do so. In this he would prove to be no different from the Federalists, and indeed arguably far worse than they during his second term.

Irony of ironies, it was the *Federalists* of New England who objected to the Louisiana Purchase as an unwarranted expansion of federal power that had "violated the original agreement among the parties to the Constitution" and, even more important, "threatened to radically reshape the face of the nation" and "upset the political and social balance" between North and South by opening up a vast new territory for slavery, which in fact it did.[71] The Purchase led Senators Timothy Pickering and William Plumer, Congressman Roger Griswold and other New England Federalists to undertake nothing less than a plan for "a *new confederacy,* exempt from the corrupt and corrupting influence of the *aristocratic democrats* of the South."[72] This Northern Confederacy would secede "from the Jefferson-tainted Union to form a separate and commercially powerful confederacy, where it was assumed that the Federalist vision of society and polity would dominate."[73]

This is not to suggest that this failed movement for Northern secession sought a stronger central government than the one over which Jefferson was already presiding. Quite the contrary, the New England Federalists viewed Jefferson as a traitor to the republican principles he espoused, a dangerous political opportunist prone to tyranny (as his second term would demonstrate), a man who "would stoop to any means to obtain political power." Pickering and his colleagues denounced Jefferson and his fellow Southern slaveholders as hypocrites who "are looked upon by the giddy headed, and ill informed sovereign majority, to be the guardians of the Rights of Man."[74] And, when Congress passed the Breckinridge Bill, which gave Jefferson the power to appoint all the officials in Louisiana's provisional government, Plumer, the Federalist Senator from New Hampshire, protested (quite rightly) that "Had such a bill been passed by federalists, it would have been denounced as *monarchal.*"[75]

Another motive for a Northern Confederacy was the federalist John Pickering's impeachment from the federal bench, following a Senate trial at which he was not allowed to appear in person to defend himself. The charges against him were based on his alcoholism and consequent episodes of bizarre behavior, but a "Jeffersonian strict construction" of the Constitution could not support the claim that Pickering's drinking problem constituted the requisite "Treason, Bribery, or other high Crimes and Misdemeanors" required for impeachment of a federal official under Article II, §4. Confronted with this problem, "the Republican-controlled House of Representatives, *with the approval of Thomas Jefferson,* simply redefined 'misdemeanor' to

---

71. Kevin M. Gannon, "Escaping 'Mr. Jefferson's Plan of Destruction': New England Federalists and the Idea of a Northern Confederacy, 1803–1804," *Journal of the Early Republic,* Vol. 21, no. 3 (Autumn 2001), 423.

72. Pickering to George Cabot, January 29, 1804; quoted in Gannon, op. cit., 414. Emphasis in original (per Gannon).

73. Gannon, op. cit., 414.

74. Ibid., 421.

75. Ibid., 424.

include aspects of Judge Pickering's drunken behavior...."[76] Senator Plumer offered the sarcastic remark that "This business of *amending* the constitution is found to be a tedious process—the good work of *reform* cannot be delayed."[77] Pickering was expediently replaced by "a New Hampshire Jeffersonian who had also been one of the chief prosecution witnesses against Pickering in the Senate trial." John Quincy Adams protested that "If proceedings like ours were had in a court of law . . . it would be considered a *Mere Mock Trial*." The impeachment of Pickering demonstrated "the lengths to which the Jeffersonians were willing to go to secure their objectives."[78]

The Louisiana Purchase represented a great advance for the institution of slavery under the same President who had professed his belief that the slaves must be freed (in order that they might be deported forthwith). When Jefferson took power in 1801, America, the self-proclaimed "temple of Liberty," was the largest slave-holding country in the world, followed by the British Empire. Between America (900,000 slaves) and Britain (800,000 slaves), some 1,700,000 blacks were subjected to involuntary servitude by the same ruling classes that considered themselves "the most truly free and enlightened people on earth."[79] Jefferson himself continued to buy and sell slaves while President, using third parties to conceal his involvement in the transactions.[80] He observed a politic silence over the serious worsening of the lot of the slaves in the Louisiana Territory once it became an American possession. Under Napoleon the territorial legal code had recognized the right of slaves to receive religious instruction, to observe the Sabbath day of rest, to cultivate plots of land for their own sustenance, and to be buried in consecrated ground, while also forbidding the sale of a child away from his mother before the age of fourteen or the separate sale of husbands and wives.[81] Under the Americans, however, the Black Code passed by the federally established territorial legislature abolished these rights, and slaves were classified as real estate.[82]

Miller asks: "Would the 'Empire of Liberty' prove to be an 'Empire of Slavery'? . . . By not making the exclusion of slavery from that region an administration measure, Jefferson seemed to have opened a new world for the plantation system and slavery, the 'malign twins,' to conquer."[83] Indeed he did. While Jefferson oversaw the Congressional ban on the importation of slaves into the United States in 1808—a ban that was largely evaded by running slaves under the American flag and claiming "freedom of the seas"—he would (notes Miller) ultimately become "an

---

76. Ibid., 428.

77. William Plumer, entry of Jan. 7, 1804, in E.S. Brown, ed. *William Plumer's Memorandum*, cited in Gannon, op. cit., 429. Emphasis in original.

78. Gannon, op. cit., 429.

79. Miller, *Wolf by the Ears*, 130.

80. Ibid., 107. Miller notes that Jefferson sold about fifty slaves while President in order to raise cash to pay creditors, and that not even in his last will and testament did Jefferson free his slaves.

81. Ibid., 144.

82. Ibid.

83. Ibid., 145.

ardent exponent of the establishment of slavery in the entire Louisiana Purchase"
on grounds that the federal government had no power to interfere in the property
rights of slaveholders but ample power to *protect* that right.

Jefferson's Second Term

By the time of his second term (1805–1809), Jefferson was already under the accusation that he had "deserted his own principles with the acquisition of Louisiana;
as he certainly did when, in his Second Inaugural Address, he recommended
spending federal money on roads and other internal improvements."[84] In the same
address he defended the Louisiana Purchase on the positively Madisonian grounds
that the bigger the Union the better, as its sheer size would (so the theory goes)
mitigate the influence of factions:

> I know that the acquisition of Louisiana has been disapproved by some, from
> a candid apprehension that the enlargement of our territory would endanger
> its union. *But who can limit the extent to which the federative principle may
> operate effectively?* The larger our association, the less will it be shaken by local
> passions. . . .

Jefferson took the occasion of his second inauguration to intimate, in the most
dramatic setting possible, the potential for further state law libel prosecutions of
Federalists as "wholesome punishments" for their abuse of freedom of speech:

> During this course of administration, and in order to disturb it, the artillery
> of the press has been leveled against us, charged with whatsoever its licen-
> tiousness could devise or dare. These abuses . . . might, indeed, have been
> corrected by the wholesome punishments reserved to and provided by the
> laws of the several States against falsehood and defamation, but public duties
> more urgently press on the time of public servants. . . .

This less-than-subtle threat was in line with a Presidency that, during its second
term, veered toward nothing short of autocratic rule. Let us examine briefly the key
events of this era of Jeffersonian "Republican Federalism."

The Burr Case

In 1807 the same Jefferson who only a few years earlier had argued (in the Kentucky
Resolutions) for the "compact theory" of federal union, sought the death penalty for
Aaron Burr, his own former Vice President, on account of Burr's plot to have the
Louisiana Territory secede from the Union and, incorporating parts of Mexico, con-
stitute itself a separate nation. Burr was to have the assistance of no less than James
Wilkinson, the federal governor of northern Louisiana and the commanding gen-
eral of the United States Army. Wilkinson's prominence in the national government

---

84. Morison, *HAP,* 371.

was remarkable, given that he himself was a veteran of secession schemes, having failed in his bid (during the 1780s) for Kentucky and Tennessee to secede from the Union in an alliance with Spain, to whose king he had pledged allegiance as part of the plot. Very much in Jefferson's own "Spirit of 1776," Burr's grandiose scheme to create a new republic in the Southwest involved the cooperation of the Creoles, who, not surprisingly, objected to being made subjects of President Jefferson and the federal government without their consent. Despite its grandiosity, the Burr Conspiracy "was the most formidable secession conspiracy prior to 1860, one which probably would have succeeded had not Wilkinson ratted on Burr."[85]

After the conspiracy fell apart, Jefferson ordered that Burr be arrested and tried for treason, a capital offense. Even before Burr was apprehended, however, Jefferson had publicly declared his guilt in a "Special Message on the Burr Conspiracy" delivered to Congress. Burr, said Jefferson, had plotted the treasonable "severance of the Union of these States," only to discover that "that the attachment of the western country to the present Union was not to be shaken." He revealed that he had issued orders "for the employment of such force either of the regulars or of the militia, and of such proceedings also of the civil authorities, as might enable them to seize on all the boats and stores provided for the enterprise, to arrest the persons concerned, and to suppress effectually the further progress of the enterprise." He lamented that "In Kentucky, a premature attempt to bring Burr to justice, without sufficient evidence for his conviction, had produced a popular impression in his favor, and a general disbelief of his guilt." But he assured the now Republican-controlled Congress that Burr and his fellow conspirators "will be delivered to the custody of the law, and left to such course of trial, both as to place and process, as its functionaries may direct," including a trial in Washington, which would be "equally desirable *for the criminals* as for the public. . . ."[86]

This amazing public presidential pronouncement of Burr's guilt before his trial was, as Leonard Levy writes, part of a plan whose "object was not to secure justice—or innocence—fairly determined, but to secure a conviction, no matter how, on the charge of high treason."[87] In attempting to execute that plan, Jefferson "did not turn the case over to the United States Attorney, but acted himself as prosecutor, superintending the gathering of evidence, locating witnesses, taking depositions, directing trial tactics, and shaping public opinion as if judge and juror for the nation."[88]

Eager to please their President, the Republican-controlled Senate, without debate, passed by acclamation a bill suspending the writ of habeas corpus for three months and authorizing the President or his designate to arrest anyone charged in the Burr affair. But this was precisely as authorized by the Constitution, Article I,

---

85. Ibid., 369–370.

86. Thomas Jefferson, "Special Message on the Burr Conspiracy," January 22, 1807, Yale Law School e-text, yale.edu/lawweb/avalon/jeffburr.htm.

87. Levy, *Jefferson and Civil Liberties*, 71.

88. Ibid.

§9: "The privilege of the Writ of Habeas Corpus shall not be suspended, *unless when in Cases of Rebellion* or Invasion the public Safety may require it." The House, however, refused to go along, although it would be much more cooperative with Jefferson's coming dictatorial moves.

The Military Dictatorship in Louisiana

At the same time Jefferson was seeking to apprehend Burr he was also, as Levy recounts, providing "undeviating support to Wilkinson's despotic rule in New Orleans," where Wilkinson, having "ratted" on Burr, was acting as a military dictator on the pretext that an invasion by Burr's men was imminent. Wilkinson suspended the writ of habeas corpus, declared martial law, and generally "unleashed a saturnalia of lawlessness." Certain of Burr's co-conspirators were arrested by the military without warrants, only to be released on writs of habeas corpus or for lack of evidence. A defense attorney was subjected to a warrantless arrest merely because he had obtained a habeas writ for one of the suspects, as was a judge who protested Wilkinson's conduct and thus incurred the charge of being "actively engaged in these nefarious projects." Also tossed into jail on Wilkinson's orders was the editor of the *Orleans Gazette*. Summing up Jefferson's view of Wilkinson's program, Levy writes: "Jefferson's reaction to his general's conduct was to applaud a job well done."[89] In a letter to the Governor of New Orleans, Jefferson mocked Federalist protests against the infringement of civil liberties he had sanctioned:

> On great occasions, every good officer must be ready to risk himself in going beyond the strict line of law, when the public preservation requires it. . . . The Feds, and the little band of Quids, in opposition, will try to make something out of the infringement of liberty by the military arrest and deportation of citizens, but if it does not go beyond such offenders as Swartout, Bollman, Burr, Blennerhasset, Tyler, & c., they will be supported by the public approbation.[90]

Writing to Wilkinson on the same day, Jefferson assured his man in the field that "your conduct, as now known, has placed you on a ground extremely favorable with the public."[91] In other words, violations of the liberty of a few people were acceptable so long as the public could be brought along—the same rationale Jefferson had used to justify what he himself viewed as the unconstitutional acquisition of Louisiana. The following year Jefferson assured his correspondent, Dr. James Brown, that "There are extreme cases where the laws become inadequate even to their own preservation, and where the universal resource is a dictator, or martial law."[92]

89. Levy, *Jefferson and Civil Liberties*, 82–83.
90. Jefferson to Claiborne, February 3, 1807, in ed. Paul Leicester Ford, *The Writings of Thomas Jefferson* (NY: G. P. Putnam's Sons, 1898), 14.
91. Jefferson to Wilkinson, February 3, 1807, in Lipscomb, XI, 150.
92. *Writings*, ed. H. A. Washington, Vol. IV, 379.

In view of all of this, Levy reminds us of Jefferson's rather significant earlier contention in a document entitled the Declaration of Independence: that "among King George's III's serious crimes were those making the 'Military independent of and superior to the Civil Power' and 'transporting us beyond the Seas to be tried.'"[93]

Burr's Acquittal and Jefferson's Rant Against the Independent Judiciary

As he defended a military dictatorship in the Louisiana Territory, which he had conquered by buying it for cash from its previous conqueror, Jefferson's plan to railroad Burr to the gallows failed completely and spectacularly. In a bit of exquisite irony, the trial judge, Supreme Court Chief Justice John Marshall, *strictly construed* Article II, §3 of the Constitution, which defines "treason" as consisting "only in levying War against [the United States], or in adhering to their Enemies, giving them Aid and Comfort" and requires "the Testimony of two Witnesses to the same overt Act. . . ." As Marshall concluded, a mere plan to secede from the Union that did not ripen into acts of war against the United States could not constitute treason. Hence Marshall refused to hold Burr over on the charge of treason but only on the high misdemeanor of attempting to levy war on Mexico. Levy here remarks the ironical fact that, contrary to Justice Marshall, "Jefferson's lax concept of treason smelled of the English doctrines of the seventeenth century that he himself had repudiated during the Revolution."[94]

The jury, composed almost entirely of Republicans,[95] found Burr not guilty.[96] Jefferson's rage was unbounded. He now declaimed against the very idea of an independent judiciary, complaining of the "error in our Constitution, which makes any branch independent of the nation" and "proclaims impunity to that class of offenders which endeavors to overturn the Constitution, and are themselves protected in it by the Constitution itself. . . ."[97] He called for a constitutional amendment that would allow the President to remove any federal judge from office upon the issuance of a joint address to Congress. The amendment, which died in committee, was in direct opposition to the position Jefferson had taken in 1789, when he argued for an independent judiciary "as a means of enforcing civil liberties against the government. . . ."[98] But this was hardly the only *volte-face* of which the icon of libertarianism would be guilty, now that power was his to wield.

---

93. Levy, *Jefferson and Civil Liberties*, 85.

94. Ibid., 79.

95. "[A] polling of the jury found that fourteen of the Grand Jurors were Republicans (Jefferson's party) and two were Federalists (supporters of Marshall's point of view)." See "History and Legacy: The Aaron Burr Trial," apva.org/marshall/justice/aaron_burr_trial.php.

96. The former Vice President, however, died in disgrace in 1836, although he did manage to establish a law practice in New York after avoiding a trial for murder on account of the duel with Hamilton in 1804.

97. Jefferson to William Giles, the Senator from Virginia, April 1807, in *Jeffersonian Cyclopedia*, § 1220.

98. Levy, *Jefferson and Civil Liberties*, 81.

Jefferson's Naval Expansion and
Plan for Compulsory Military Service

Jefferson's next expansions of federal power came during the conflict between Britain and France during the Napoleonic Wars (1803–1815) following the French Revolution. As of 1806, in desperate need of personnel, the British had taken to impressing British-born seamen on American vessels, many of them deserters from the British navy whose claims of American citizenship were not recognized by England. After the *H.M.S. Leopard* broadsided the *U.S.S. Chesapeake* in the process of impressing a British-born deserter, Jefferson, in the midst of public outcry, asked Congress for the money to build 188 more gunboats—thus beginning the restoration of the same navy he had boasted of reducing during his first term. (The gunboat program was an early federal boondoggle, however, as these tiny ships were no match for British frigates.)

At the same time, Jefferson was expressing his support for universal compulsory military service in aid of his "empire of Liberty." In May 1808, for example, he wrote to Gen. John Armstrong praising a bill for a vast conscripted militia that had almost passed Congress:

> Against great land armies we cannot attempt defense but by equal armies. For these we must depend on a classified militia, which will give us the service of the class from twenty to twenty-six, *in the nature of conscripts*, comprising a body of about 250,000, to be specially trained. This measure, attempted at a former session, was pressed at the last, and might, I think, have been carried by a small majority. But considering that great innovations should not be forced on a slender majority, and seeing that the general opinion is sensibly rallying to it, it was thought better to let it lie over to the next session, when, I trust, it will be passed.[99]

The Embargo Acts

With the Embargo Act, a series of laws demanded by Jefferson and enacted by Congress from 1806 to 1808, Jefferson became, as Levy writes, a "presidential autocrat," who "disdained all criticism, brooked no opposition, and imperiously employed the most odious means to achieve his ends."[100] The Embargo regime, so Jefferson and the Republicans argued, would avoid war with England and France by withdrawing American shipping from the seas, where it had been subject to attack during the Napoleonic Wars. The real target, however, was Britain, whose dependence on trade with America would supposedly bring her to her knees.

The embargo policy benefitted Napoleon while punishing England as the object of Napoleon's "Continental System"—a blockade of all trade with Britain during the Napoleonic Wars. Lawrence Kaplan's scholarship on this subject demonstrates

---

99. Jefferson to Armstrong, May 1808, in *Jeffersonian Cyclopedia*, §5179.
100. Levy, *Jefferson and Civil Liberties*, 95, 125.

that Jefferson's policy, while ostensibly applicable neutrally to both Britain and France, actually "brought the United States into the service of Bonaparte's Continental System," and that "[i]t cannot be denied that Jefferson was fully aware that the embargo constituted a service to Napoleon." In a letter to General Turreau, the genocidist of the "twelve infernal columns" who laid waste to the Vendée and whose reward was to be made Napoleon's minister to the United States, Jefferson admitted that "The embargo which appears to hit France and Britain equally is for a fact more prejudicial to the latter than the other by reason of a greater number of colonies which England possesses and their inferiority in local resources."[101]

The embargo policy was a political and economic disaster that turned the nation against Jefferson and led directly to the War of 1812. For some fifteen months Jefferson exerted a personal stranglehold on America's entire maritime economy, obtaining from Congress a series of embargo measures that he either drafted himself or had drafted by his Secretary of the Treasury, Albert Gallatin.[102] In an escalating series of federal controls and penalties, the acts prohibited any American vessel from heading to a foreign port, deputed the U.S. navy to intercept and seize offending vessels, imposed onerous bonds to be forfeited in the event of embargo violations, required Jefferson's *personal permission* for the departure of any ship from an American port adjacent to foreign territory, directed federal customs agents to detain ships pending Jefferson's approval, and authorized warrantless searches of ships and the seizure of cargoes suspected of being forbidden exports. The Embargo, "begun as a means of coercing and starving England and France into respect for American rights, rapidly became an instrument of coercion against American citizens."[103]

Widespread civil disobedience to the embargo "simply enraged the president, whose executive temper remained at the flash point. He even considered starving out American communities to break their spirit. . . . To resist him, even to say anything countenancing a spirit of disobedience, was the mark of an enemy to be overcome by naked power."[104] For example, acting pursuant to the same federal statute that Washington had invoked to crush the Whiskey Rebellion, Jefferson issued "a proclamation of insurrection" and called out the militia to prevent exports from the Lake Champlain region into Canada.

But Jefferson went even further to punish disobedience to his will—further than any Federalist president had dared to go. In 1807 the Republican-dominated Congress authorized the President to use the regular army and navy to put down "insurrections" in lieu of the militia, with the decision to deploy being left to the President's discretion under the statute, subject to a presidential finding and public proclamation of "insurrection." This move was accompanied by Jefferson's demand, expressed in a speech to Congress by his son-in-law, John Eppes, and in

101. Lawrence S. Kaplan, *Jefferson and France: An Essay on Politics and Political Ideas* (New Haven: Yale Univ. Press, 1967), 112, 125.
102. The entire policy is recounted by Levy, op. cit., chaps. 5–6, which are relied upon here.
103. Ibid., 105.
104. Ibid., 106–107.

his own presidential address, for an expansion of the standing army to 9,000, after Jefferson had reduced it during his first term from 5,000 to 3,000. Thus the libertarian icon who had loudly deplored the evil of the Federalist standing army before he was President now proposed to *triple* its size. Levy wryly observes that "The congressional Republicans, although caught unaware by this stunning blow to their cherished doctrines against standing armies, recovered with great agility [and] quickly convinced themselves that considerations of national security justified their abrupt reversal of position."[105] The Republicans gave Jefferson an overwhelming majority in the House with the Senate vote being unrecorded.[106]

The only strong opposition to Jefferson's military expansion came from *Federalists* in the House, who warned that Jefferson would use the additional troops to enforce his embargo.[107] They were right. By the late summer of 1808

> the regular army, the previously dreaded "standing army in time of peace," was regularly employed in the enforcement of the embargo laws in the Northeastern United States. By the same time, naval gunboats and revenue cutters patrolled the inland waterways and coasts of the nation. On a prolonged, widespread and systematic basis . . . the armed forces harried and beleaguered the citizenry . . . as if it were normal for American soldiers to enforce against American citizens their own laws. . . . Substantial segments of the people genuinely believed their own government was at war with them.[108]

Worse, in deploying the regular armed forces against American citizens, Jefferson dispensed with the necessity of the presidential finding and proclamation of "insurrection" required by the congressional authorization of 1807.[109]

The Federalists had a field day when two of Jefferson's own judicial appointments issued decisions in 1808 upholding the rights of citizens against his dictatorial embargo. In the first case, Supreme Court Justice William Johnson[110] struck down Jefferson's attempt to have a customs collector in Charleston, South Carolina detain a ship based on nothing more than Jefferson's instructions through Gallatin without any statutory authorization. Undeterred, Jefferson had his Attorney General, Caesar Rodney, issue an opinion that attacked Johnson's decision and purported to overrule it, prompting the press to denounce Jefferson's "contempt for constitutional government."[111]

In the second case, Jefferson directed that a group of embargo violators in the Lake Champlain region, who had recaptured a raft of lumber from federally summoned militia, be indicted and tried for the capital offense of treason. But Justice

105. Ibid., 111.

106. Ibid., 112 & n. 45.

107. Donald R. Hickey, "Federalist Defense Policy in the Age of Jefferson," *Military Affairs*, Vol. 45, No. 2 (April 1981), 67.

108. Levy, *Jefferson and Civil Liberties*, 119–120.

109. Ibid., 125.

110. At that time Supreme Court justices served as trial judges for the federal circuit courts.

111. Levy, 129.

Brockholst Livingston, a *Jefferson* appointee to the Supreme Court, followed the same strict construction of the offense of treason by Justice Marshall that had led to the acquittal of Burr, holding that the defendants had not levied war against the United States but rather had engaged in private conduct aimed at recovering their own property. Livingston's instructions to the jury, admonishing it that treason "is almost universally punished with death," could not have been more contemptuous of Jefferson's design to hang the defendants for taking back their own lumber. Particularly stinging was Livingston's observation that the notion of treason underlying the indictment would not be countenanced *even in England*: "Can it be seriously thought that an American jury . . . can be brought by engrafting construction on construction, to leave far behind them, English judges and English juries, in their exposition of the crime of treason?"[112] Having received a virtual directed verdict for the defense, the jury acquitted the "insurrectionists" after only a few minutes of deliberations.[113]

Levy notes the supremely ironic development that Jefferson's only judicial victory concerning the embargo was the decision by a *Federalist* judicial appointment, Judge John Davis, who "sustained the constitutionality of the embargo laws in an opinion of sweeping nationalism" based on "a broad reading of the commerce power and the inherent sovereignty of the United States—a construction of the Constitution that Jefferson, before becoming President, had condemned as irreconcilable with civil liberty."[114]

This decision was followed by Jefferson's demand for his fifth and final Embargo Act, providing forfeiture penalties amounting to "many times the combined value of ship and cargo," stripping vessel owners of affirmative defenses under admiralty law, thus guaranteeing conviction, and authorizing use of the armed forces to seize, without warrants, suspected illegal exports not only in ports adjacent to foreign territory but anywhere in the United States at the discretion of the President or his delegate. The Fifth Embargo, passed by the Republican-dominated Congress over fierce *Federalist* opposition in January 1809, a few weeks before Jefferson's second term ended, was, writes Levy, "the most repressive and unconstitutional legislation ever enacted by Congress in time of peace."[115] An historian as sober as Morison remarks that "George III and Lord North had been tender by comparison."[116]

Jefferson, in short, had succeeded in making the Federalists look like libertarian Republicans. Morison sums up the debacle: "The embargo was intended to be the crowning glory of Jefferson's second administration. . . . It proved to be his greatest mistake. It altered the policy of Britain and Napoleon not by one hair, it failed to protect the American merchant marine, and it convinced a good many people that the Virginia Dynasty was bound to be Napoleonic."[117]

112. *U.S. v. Hoxie*, 26 F. Cas. 397, 399 (C.C. Vt. 1808).
113. Levy, *Jefferson and Civil Liberties*, 130–131.
114. Ibid.
115. Ibid., 140.
116. Morison, *HAP*, 375.
117. Ibid.

Now it was the Federalists' turn to complain of a federal "reign of terror," as the Federalist-dominated state legislatures of New England reminded Jefferson of his own position in the Kentucky Resolutions and even considered calling a convention to declare state nullification of the embargo. Meanwhile, Jefferson's own fellow Republicans in New England turned against him, and "Jefferson was shaken by a battery of resolutions from New England town meetings, some threatening secession." Under sustained attack, and with Congressional Republicans defecting in droves, Jefferson finally signed a bill repealing the embargo three days before his term ended and he retired to Monticello.[118] But the Embargo Act was immediately superseded by the Non-Intercourse Act of 1809, which, while permitting American shipping to other foreign destinations, kept in place the federal embargo on all shipping to British and French ports.

Jefferson the Federalist

The embargo laws were but the crowning application of Jefferson's dictum, first uttered during the Burr affair, that in "extreme cases . . . the universal resource is a dictator, or martial law." Libertarian legends notwithstanding, Jefferson and "the new Republicans" were, in the end, facilitators of a relentless advance of federal power in the name of Liberty—indeed, in the name of Jefferson's "*empire* of Liberty." As Jefferson had proudly declared during his first term: "We feel ourselves strong, and daily growing stronger. The day is within my time as well as yours, when we may say by what laws other nations shall treat us on the sea. And we *will* say it."[119]

For Jefferson, as it was for all his fellow "apostles of liberty," what mattered was *who* wielded power in Liberty's name: he and his fellow Republicans or the evil Federalists. In the "right" hands—that is, in Republican hands—the peremptory authority of the federal government over the States was a good thing. Thus it was that Jefferson, in imposing the Embargo on the nation, "had stretched the powers of that government *far beyond anything advocated by Hamilton. . . .*"[120] Since the Federalists had been routed in 1800, "The precautions [Jefferson] had recommended that the American people adopt against Hamilton and the federalist party—eternal vigilance against the corruptive effects of power and unremitting opposition to the encroachments of the federal government . . . could now safely be dispensed with."[121]

No one denounced Jefferson's hypocrisy more scathingly than John Randolph, the Republican Senator from Virginia, who had served as foreman of the grand jury in the Burr Trial. It was Randolph who famously declared that Jefferson had spelled Federalism backwards for four years, only to spell it forwards again in his second term. The Pulitzer Prize-winning historiographer William Cabell Bruce

---

118. Ibid.

119. Jefferson to William Short, Oct. 3, 1801, in ed. Kees de Mooy, *The Wisdom of Thomas Jefferson* (NY: Citadel Press, 2003), 44.

120. Miller, *Wolf by the Ears*, 203.

121. Ibid.

describes the sentiments of Randolph and other Republican critics of Jefferson's turnabout:

> The Republican creed, it has been happily said, was the Federalist creed spelled backwards, and, after spelling it backwards to a certain extent, as in the repeal of the Internal Taxes, the reduction of the Army and Navy, and the like, Jefferson and the new Republicans under the influence of the love of power begotten by power, and the over-riding necessities which render governmental responsibility and minority opposition two such very dissimilar things, began to spell the Federalist creed forward again, and did not cease until they had done almost everything that Jefferson and his original Republican adherents had condemned the Federalists for doing-not indeed until Randolph could wrathfully say that Jefferson had not differed more from his predecessor than he had from himself.[122]

While Jefferson's rhetoric envisioned an empire arising from the free cooperation of republican citizens and the republican governments of their respective states, this was only part of what Peter Onuf has called a "penchant for ideological posturing and empty abstractions. . . ." and "bromides about harmonious, voluntary and affectionate union among republicans."[123] Like all politicians, however, Jefferson said one thing and did another. In the end, should coercion be necessary to preserve the "empire of Liberty," Jefferson was ready to exercise it. As he wrote from Monticello in 1812:

> What does this English faction with yon [in New England] mean? Their newspapers say rebellion, and that they will not remain united with us unless we will permit them to govern the majority. If this be their purpose, their antirepublican spirit, it ought to be met at once. But a government like ours should be slow in believing this, *should put forth its whole might, when necessary, to suppress it*, and promptly return to the paths of reconciliation.[124]

Two years later Jefferson wrote: "I see our safety in the extent of our confederacy, and in the probability that in the proportion of that the sound parts will always be sufficient to *crush out local poison*."[125] Despite his own advocacy of the "compact theory" in the Kentucky Resolutions some twenty-six years earlier, there is not the least suggestion here that individual states were free to leave the union with impunity.

In sum, Jefferson and his fellow Republicans had "forged an account of the nation's history that justified violation of the very liberties they celebrated."[126] For Jefferson the Republican, as for Washington the Federalist, "liberty and union were inextricable: the destruction of one necessarily entailed destruction of the other. It was only by sustaining the federal republic that the essential distinction between

122. William Cabell Bruce, *John Randolph of Roanoke*, Vol. 1 (NY: G. P. Putnam, 1922), 280.
123. Peter S. Onuf, *Jefferson's Empire* (Charlottesville, VA: Univ. of Virginia Press, 2000), 55, 126.
124. Jefferson to Elbridge Gerry, June 11, 1812, in *Jeffersonian Cyclopedia*, §794.
125. Jefferson to Horatio Spafford, March 17, 1814, in *Jeffersonian Cyclopedia*, §802.
126. Onuf, *Jefferson's Empire*, 108.

Europe and America could be sustained."[127] Fifty years later, Abraham Lincoln would be motivated by precisely the same sentiment of Liberty.

The War of 1812

By 1812–14 America, now under President Madison, had declared war on Britain and attempted the very conquest of Canada Jefferson had earlier suggested—no doubt to "promote the general welfare" and "provide for the common defense." Writing in 1812, Jefferson in retirement opined that conquering Canada for the "empire of Liberty" would be an easy affair: "The acquisition of Canada this year, as far as the neighborhood of Quebec, will be a mere matter of marching, and will give us experience for the attack of Halifax the next, and the final expulsion of England from the American continent."[128]

Jefferson was once again spectacularly wrong. The disastrous War of 1812 culminated in the utter humiliation of the British sack of Washington and the burning of the original White House and numerous other government buildings during the Battle of Bladensburg in August 1814. The War ended with neither side gaining or losing any territory, yet it provided a rich vein of patriotic folklore (the Battle of New Orleans, the penning of the National Anthem after the bombardment of Fort McHenry, etc.) and is hailed in history books as "the second War of Independence" from England. Moreover, along with a staggering national debt from the war, America acquired that thing called "a sense of nationalism," which provided ample support in Congress for a still bigger and better military. This meant, of course, more federal spending and thus more taxes, according to what was now the *Republican* plan for an expanding federal government, to which the *Federalists* (especially in the New England states) were opposed.

As Morison writes of the "Republican conversion" during the period 1815–1823: "President Madison and his party adopted to the nationalism of Washington and Hamilton as if they had been born to it."[129] After his retirement to Monticello, Jefferson's own nationalism was expressed in his continued advocacy of compulsory universal military service. The burning of Washington, he argued, demonstrated that the federal government had been "too indulgent" in relying upon volunteer militia for the national defense and that the time had come to compel all qualified males to serve a tour of military duty, as he had wished while serving as President, for the citizens had been "indolent" with respect to their duties to the federal government:

> In the beginning of our government we were willing to introduce the least coercion possible on the will of the citizen. Hence a system of military duty was established *too indulgent to his indolence*. This [the War of 1812] is the first opportunity we have had of trying it, and it has completely failed; an issue

---

127. Ibid., 114.
128. Jefferson to William Duane, August 1812, in *Jeffersonian Cyclopedia*, §1093.
129. Morison, *HAP*, 400.

foreseen by many, and for which remedies have been proposed. That of class-ing the militia according to age, and allotting each age to the particular kind of service to which it was competent, was proposed to Congress in 1805, and subsequently; and, on the last trial, was lost, I believe, by a single vote. Had it prevailed, what has now happened would not have happened. Instead of burning our Capitol, *we should have possessed theirs in Montreal and Quebec. We must now adopt it, and all will be safe....* With this force properly classed, organized, trained, armed and *subject to tours of a year of military duty,* we have no more to fear for the defence of our country than those who have the resources of despotism and pauperism.[130]

Universal military service was for Jefferson the means by which not only the con-quest of Canada, but also the defense of the entire "empire of Liberty," could be accomplished without a vast standing army. But since the people were too content with their lot to serve in the military, they must be compelled to do so. As he wrote to John Eppes in 1814: "I think the truth must now be obvious that our people are too happy at home to enter into regular service, and that *we cannot be defended but by making every citizen a soldier,* as the Greeks and Romans who had no standing armies; and that in doing this *all be marshaled, classed by their ages,* and every ser-vice ascribed to its competent class."[131] Jefferson's supremely "statist" idea presents yet another major embarrassment to the libertarian presentation of Jefferson as the staunch defender of "limited government." The real Jefferson envisioned a kind of neo-Roman republic, protected by a vast Praetorian guard of ordinary citizens per-forming military service for the State in order to protect, not any mere emperor, but Liberty itself in the form of "the Union."

The Hartford Convention

To add to a growing heap of historical ironies in the Age of Jefferson, during the War of 1812 it was the *Federalists* of the New England states who gathered at the Hartford Convention (1814–15) to consider possible secession from the Union as an expression of their opposition to Washington's war policy. The aim was to enter a separate peace with England and constitute the New England states as a separate and distinct republic, much as the New England Federalists had proposed in oppo-sition to the Louisiana Purchase some twelve years earlier.

Jefferson, writes Onuf, "welcomed a war with the New England Federalists that he knew the loyal Republican states would win."[132] We have already noted how Jef-ferson argued that the government "should put forth its whole might, when neces-sary, to suppress" such secessionist tendencies, so that the wayward states would "promptly return to the paths of reconciliation."[133] Here, as elsewhere, Jefferson

130. Jefferson to Dr. Thomas Cooper, September 10, 1814, in *Jefferson: Political Writings,* eds Joyce Oldham Appleby and Terence Ball (Cambridge Univ. Press: 1999), 139–140.

131. Jefferson to John W. Eppes, 1814, *Jeffersonian Cyclopedia,* §551.

132. Onuf, *Jefferson's Empire,* 123.

133. Jefferson to Elbridge Gerry, 1812, *Jeffersonian Cyclopedia,* §794.

exhibited the convenient inconsistency that, to the end, would characterize his political thought (as well as that of most of the revolutionary leaders who ascended to power in the new government). Thus did Jefferson advocate precisely what Lincoln would do: wage war against seceding states.

The Monroe Doctrine and the Republican "Conversion"

The Republican conversion to Federalism was fully confirmed during the administration of James Monroe (1817–1825), the fifth President and the last Revolutionary War hero to serve in that office. The Monroe Doctrine, promulgated with Jefferson's advice, declared: "The American continents . . . are henceforth not to be considered as subjects for future colonization by any European powers."[134] The effect of the doctrine, soon to be backed by America's growing economic and military might, was to create "two separate spheres of influence: the Americas and Europe. The independent lands of the Western Hemisphere would be solely the United States' domain."[135] The potential growth of the "empire of Liberty," versus the "despotism" of Europe, was thus assured in keeping with Jefferson's advice to Monroe:

> Our first and fundamental maxim should be, never to entangle ourselves in the broils of Europe. Our second, never to suffer Europe to intermeddle with cis-Atlantic [sic] affairs. America, North and South, has a set of interests distinct from those of Europe, and peculiarly her own. She should therefore have a system of her own, separate and apart from that of Europe. While the last is laboring to become the domicile of despotism, our endeavor should surely be, *to make our hemisphere that of freedom.*[136]

Jefferson's libertarian defenders invariably point to his advice to avoid entanglements in Europe as evidence of his commitment to "limited government." They ignore, of course, not only his authoritarian second term as President and his advocacy of federal enforcement of slave ownership but also his seminal advice to make the United States the policeman of Liberty throughout the Americas. Jefferson prescribed a role for the federal government that would lead inevitably to aggressive southwestern expansion ("Manifest Destiny"), the acquisition of veritable colonies (Cuba, Puerto Rico, Guam and the Philippines) and unilateral intervention in Latin American affairs (the so-called "Roosevelt Corollary" to the Monroe Doctrine). His assertion that the United States had some sort of inherent right to prohibit European control over any part of Latin America is one of those mysterious self-authenticating dictates by which those who rule in Liberty's name have justified a relentless acquisition of additional power and territory—beginning, of course, with Jefferson's own acquisition of Louisiana and the subjection of its inhabitants, including slaves, to a government they had never chosen.

134. James Monroe, Seventh Annual Message to Congress, December 2, 1823.

135. "The Monroe Doctrine," U.S. Department of State historical note @ http://www.state.gov/r/pa/ho/time/jd/16321.htm.

136. Jefferson to Monroe, October 24, 1823, in *The Monroe Doctrine: Also, Jefferson's Letter to Monroe* (Veterans of the Foreign Wars of the U.S., 1920), 4.

The Marshall Court

The Republican "conversion" to Federalism was accompanied by a series of early Supreme Court decisions in which Chief Justice John Marshall, during a tenure that spanned thirty-five years and six presidencies (1801–35), began the process of drawing out the plain implications of the Constitution's "supremacy clause" and its grant of broad powers to the federal government. Unlike Jefferson, Marshall was a *bona fide* Revolutionary War hero, an officer in the Continental Army who fought at Brandywine, Germantown, Monmouth, Stony Point and Paulus Hook and was with General George Washington at Valley Forge. He had also sat on Virginia's ratification convention, and he was one of the leaders of the movement for ratification. No Republican, not even Jefferson, could cite against Marshall superior credentials in the matter of Liberty and what it meant under the Constitution.

What Liberty meant according to the Marshall Court—and what it has meant to every bench of the Supreme Court since—is simply this: a federal government whose supremacy over the States and whose direct action upon individual citizens would dwarf the authority of King George and Parliament over pre-Revolutionary America.

In *McCulloch v. State of Maryland* (1819), the Marshall Court held that it was well within Congress' power to establish the Bank of the United States under the "necessary and proper clause," and it declared—as even Jefferson had made obvious already with his embargo acts and other measures—that the federal government "is supreme within its sphere of action." This "sphere of action" included what the Court found to be the federal government's "implied" powers, meaning those necessary to effect its specifically enumerated powers. Since Congress had been given the enumerated powers to tax and collect revenue and to issue and regulate currency, it also had the implied power to create a bank if Congress decided that such means would be "necessary and proper" to execution of the enumerated powers.

Dispensing with the "tautology" of the Tenth Amendment less than thirty years after its adoption, the Court observed that, unlike the Articles of Confederation, which expressly *excluded* any incidental or implied powers, the Constitution expressly *includes* them in the "necessary and proper" clause. But, the Court continued:

> Even without the aid of the general clause . . . empowering congress to pass all necessary and proper laws for carrying its powers into execution, the grant of powers itself necessarily implies the grant of all usual and suitable means for the execution of the powers granted. . . . *Even the* 10th amendment, *which was framed for the purpose of quieting the excessive jealousies which had been excited, omits the word 'expressly,' and declares only, that the powers 'not delegated to the United States, nor prohibited to the States, are reserved to the States or to the people;'* thus leaving the question, whether the particular power which may become the subject of contest, has been delegated to the one government, or prohibited to the other, to depend on a fair construction of the whole instrument.[137]

---

137. 17 U.S. at 406.

The Tenth Amendment, in other words, begs the question of where Federal powers end and State powers begin, leaving that question precisely to the *federal* courts to decide in their supreme authority to interpret the Constitution under the supremacy clause.

What, then, of "states' rights"? Just as Patrick Henry had predicted, the Marshall Court pointed out the obvious implications of the manner in which the Constitution had been ratified—not by the "We the States," which the Framers had skillfully bypassed, but rather by "We the People" (again, about 100,000 propertied white males), who had voted directly for delegates to the ratifying conventions that were devised precisely to remove the state legislatures from the ratification process:

> But the constitution acts directly on the people, by means of powers communicated *directly from the people. No state, in its corporate capacity, ratified it; but it was proposed for adoption to popular conventions.* It springs from the people, precisely as the state constitution springs from the people, and acts on them in a similar manner. It was adopted by them in the geographical sections into which the country is divided. *The federal powers are just as sovereign as those of the States.* The state sovereignties *are not the authors of the constitution* of the United States.[138]

Libertarians cavil that Marshall's reference to "geographical sections" is a reference to the States, and therefore it was the States that ratified the Constitution. But they fail to demonstrate how popularly elected conventions that happened to take place within the borders of each state constituted a corporate ratification by each state government, when no state legislature had ratified the Constitution. Libertarian commentators also conveniently overlook the Preamble's invocation of "the People," not "the States," as the ones who "ordain and establish this Constitution. . . ." If anything, the Preamble indicates that "We the People" *subjected the state governments*, along with themselves, to the federal government. That, in fact, was the very idea behind bypassing the state legislatures in the first place.

The libertarian argument that the substitution of "We the People" for "We the States" was a mere stylistic interpolation by the Committee on Style at the Philadelphia Convention[139] is exposed as ludicrous by history itself. With good reason had Patrick Henry denounced this "stylistic" change by the delegates as a usurpation of power, protesting that "[t]he people gave them no power to use their name. That they exceeded their power is perfectly clear."

And so it began. The Supreme Court had adopted precisely that conception of federal sovereignty advocated by "the Father of the Constitution" himself. Additional Supreme Court decisions during this early period upheld the Court's own

---

138. 17 U.S. at 377–78.

139. See, e.g., Thomas E. Woods, Jr., "Some Guy: Ron Paul Doesn't Know the Constitution," lewrockwell.com/woods/woods170.html. Libertarian polemicists of this sort, intent on preserving the myth of the "Jeffersonian vision of limited government," ridicule as constitutional ignoramuses those who (with Patrick Henry) simply remark the obvious about what the Constitutional text actually says and how it was actually ratified.

power to nullify state court decisions contravening federal laws or treaties[140]—Jefferson's "nullification" in reverse, under the Supremacy Clause—the President's power to compel the States to provide militia whenever he deems it necessary in his sole discretion,[141] and Congressional power to regulate interstate commerce by such measures as breaking up state-sanctioned transportation monopolies.[142] In the latter case, *Gibbons vs. Ogden*, the Court again brushed aside the Tenth Amendment, holding that the federal government's power over interstate commerce and navigation was not only supreme but *exclusive*:

> But it has been urged with great earnestness, that, although the power of Congress to regulate commerce with foreign nations, and among the several States, be co-extensive with the subject itself ... yet the States may severally exercise the same power, within their respective jurisdictions. In support of this argument, it is said that they possessed it as an inseparable attribute of sovereignty before the formation of the constitution, *and still retain it* ... [and] that this principle ... *is secured by the tenth amendment.* .... We do not find, in the history of the formation and adoption of the constitution, that any man speaks of a general concurrent power, in the regulation of foreign and domestic trade, as still residing in the States. The very object intended, more than any other, *was to take away such power.*[143]

Indeed, the Tenth Amendment expressly provides that only the powers "*not* delegated to the United States by the Constitution ... are reserved to the States respectively. ...." Since the Constitution delegates power over interstate commerce to the federal government, *ipso facto* the States retain no such power.

And so it would be with any other claim of a "retained" state power deemed to trench upon a federal power or upon measures deemed "necessary and proper" to the exercise of a federal power. Such was the consequence of granting broadly worded enumerated powers to the federal government along with the power to pass any and all "supreme" laws deemed "necessary and proper" thereto. Within a few years of the creation of the Republic, the promise of the Tenth Amendment had already been exposed as largely, if not entirely, illusory.

The Death of "Jeffersonian Liberalism"

The preservation of "the Union" was so important to Jefferson in retirement that he opposed the Missouri Compromise of 1820, by which Missouri would be admitted to the United States as a slave state provided there would be no further extension of slavery above the parallel marked by Missouri's southern border (except for Missouri itself). Jefferson viewed the drawing of a geographical line restricting slavery as the death knell of his beloved Union, for it would "reduce the Southern states to

---

140. *Martins v. Hunter's Lessee* (1817), *Cohens v. Virginia* (1821).
141. *Martin v. Mott* (1827).
142. *Gibbons v. Ogden* (1824).
143. *Gibbons*, 22 U.S. at 7.

a subordinate, minority status under a 'consolidated' federal regime ..."[144]—the same regime, of course, that he himself had helped to consolidate. He bizarrely compared the Federalist proponents of slavery restriction to the counterrevolutionary and anti-Republican Holy Alliance of European Christian monarchs created in 1815, for the "Holy Alliance" in America was threatening the integrity of the sacred Republican union of the States. Yet, as Onuf points out, it was Jefferson himself who had proposed to ban slavery in the new western states in his draft of the Government Ordinance of 1784.[145]

In defense of the property right in slaves, Jefferson "took up the shield of states' rights which he had laid aside during the embargo and the War of 1812."[146] The same man who, as President, "had exercised powers of such scope and force as were undreamed of by John Marshall or John Quincy Adams," had "plunged from the presidency to carping criticism of the federal government in a single degeneration."[147] Yet, at the same time, Jefferson supported the Fugitive Slave Act of 1793 by which the federal government was empowered to assist in the rendition of both fugitives from justice and escaped slaves, the latter precisely as warranted by Article IV, §2, Clause 2 of the Constitution. The Act made it a federal offense to aid or abet the escape of a slave, and it provided for rendition of escaped slaves without trial based on nothing more than the oral testimony or affidavit of the slave-owner. White fugitives from justice, however, were entitled to due process of law.

So, according to Jefferson, the federal government had no authority to *restrict* the ownership of slaves, but ample authority to punish those who interfered with the property right in slaves, and further authority to mandate the recovery of slaves as lost chattels that could be seized by law enforcement officials without due process and shipped back to the "owners" as human cargo. Jefferson, as Professor Miller observes, "jettisoned his earlier notion that property must be legitimately acquired in order to merit the protection of the laws."[148] He was willing "to accord Congress power only to *protect* slavery in the territories, and he converted the doctrine of states' rights into a protective shield for slavery by a hostile federal government." Having trampled on the property rights of countless Americans in the North when he enforced the Embargo as President, Jefferson in retirement now insisted that slaves in the South were private property with which the federal government had no right to interfere but only a duty to protect. Jefferson thereby demonstrated that "his constitutional theories were convertible and that, depending upon the exigencies of the occasion, they were as serviceable to the advocates of slavery as to the advocates of freedom."[149]

But that was not the end of Jefferson's duplicity on this score. In the context of discussing his scheme for the emancipation and immediate deportation of slaves

144. Onuf, *Jefferson's Empire*, 117.
145. Ibid., 112.
146. Miller, *Wolf by the Ears*, 228.
147. Levy, *Jefferson and Civil Liberties*, 148.
148. Miller, *Wolf by the Ears*, 230.
149. Ibid., 229, 231.

to Haiti, Sierra Leone or some other suitable location outside the United States—a program he advocated to his dying day—Jefferson estimated the value of the property involved:

> There are in the United States a million and a half people of color in slavery. To send off the whole of these at once, nobody conceives to be practicable for us, or expedient for them. Let us take twenty-five years for its accomplishment, within which time they will be doubled. *Their estimated value as property*, in the first place (*for actual property has been vested in that form, and who can lawfully take it from the possessor?*) at an average of two hundred dollars each, young and old, would amount to six hundred millions of dollars, which must be paid or lost by somebody.[150]

Who would compensate slave-owners for such staggering losses, and who would pay for the cost of deportation? At first Jefferson proposed that the state governments impose new taxes to fund a staged deportation of emancipated slaves from Virginia to Haiti, but his proposed bill before the Virginia legislature never reached the floor. Jefferson soon realized, however, that given the exploding black population, which then stood at one-and-a-half million, the amount of compensation that would have to be paid to the owners would approach a billion dollars, the value of "a prime field hand" being four hundred dollars "at a time when free labor was paid at the rate of one dollar a day and a good house cost six hundred dollars."[151] The state governments could not possibly raise the necessary funds.

Thus in 1824 Jefferson, conveniently abandoning his "limited government" philosophy, began to advocate a massive federally-funded plan to emancipate and deport slaves, using the revenue generated from the federal sale of public lands. The execution of this plan, Professor Miller concludes, "required the expansion of the powers of the federal government and its intervention into the private affairs of American citizens far beyond anything dreamed of in the philosophy of Alexander Hamilton."[152] As with his dictatorial embargo, here Jefferson revealed that "his aversion to 'energetic' government could be conveniently suspended when great social and economic problems were involved. . . ."[153]

But at this time in American history the entire national debt was only in the millions of dollars, and Jefferson knew the American people would never stand for a federal expenditure of the enormous sum required for his plan. And so he settled upon the idea of simply deporting *slave children* from the United States, thereby cutting off future population growth: "Jefferson calculated that if sixty thousand black children were born annually, fifty vessels could carry off the annual increase, leaving the parents and grandparents to die off in the course of nature." He further recommended that, in effectuation of this plan, "black slave children be taken from

---

150. Jefferson to Jared Sparks, February 4, 1824, in *The Political Writings of Thomas Jefferson*, ed. Merrill D. Peterson (Chapel Hill: Univ. of North Carolina Press, 1993), 205, Questia Library ed.

151. Miller, *Wolf by the Ears*, 269.

152. Ibid., 269–70.

153. Ibid., 270.

their parents at the age of five years, raised as wards of the States, and prepared for their pending expatriation by instruction in skills that would prove useful to them in their new homeland." Meanwhile, by their forced labor, the children could earn part of the cost of compensation to their owners and transportation to Haiti or Sierra Leone.[154]

Writing to Jared Sparks, a renowned historian, educator and Unitarian minister who later became President of Harvard, Jefferson defended his monstrous idea with a comment worthy of Stalin, Mao or Pol Pot: "The separation of infants from their mothers . . . would produce some scruples of humanity. But this would be straining at a gnat, and swallowing a camel."[155] In the same correspondence he writes that the scheme of "emancipating the afterborn, leaving them, on due compensation, with their mothers, until their services are worth their maintenance, and then putting them to industrious occupations, until a proper age for deportation," was "the result of my reflections on the subject five and forty years ago [in *Notes on the State of Virginia*] and I have never yet been able to conceive any other practicable plan."[156]

Yet even as he advocated the forcible deportation of black slave children to "solve" the social problem of slavery by allowing the adult slave population to die off, Jefferson vigorously supported extension of the institution of slavery into the new territories. Concerning Jefferson's opposition to the Missouri Compromise, Professor Miller writes that it "seemed to mark the strange death of Jeffersonian liberalism."[157] But as Jefferson own words and deeds over a lifetime had demonstrated, Jeffersonian liberalism was a collection of lofty platitudes that imposed no real impediment to the expansion of federal power under the banner of Liberty but, on the contrary, only concealed it. By 1817, Miller writes, "the Jeffersonian Republicans had 'out-Federalized Federalism' by adopting the entire Federalist program. . . .The dismaying fact was that the Jeffersonian Republicans conquered federalism by stooping to embrace its policies."[158]

Inconsistent to the end, however, Jefferson in retirement conveniently "reverted to his earlier view that the States constituted the only effective barrier to the onrushing Leviathan State, which, he lamented, many of his own former followers seemed eager to mount and ride to power."[159] But it was Jefferson himself who had mounted and ridden the Leviathan with voluptuous abandon when citizens of the several states made bold to defy his authority as President. And it was Jefferson who, even in retirement, exalted the Union and its growing power as the mainstay of the "empire of Liberty."

154. Ibid., 269–71.
155. Jefferson to Jared Sparks, February 24, 1824, in Lipscomb and Bergh, *The Writings of Thomas Jefferson*, Vol. 16, 13.
156. Ibid., 10.
157. Miller, *Wolf by the Ears*, 231–32.
158. Ibid., 210.
159. Ibid., 216.

Interring the Jefferson Legend

With his death approaching, Jefferson knew full well that "the vagaries of life had left a vulnerable legacy," as even a Library of Congress biography admits.[160] To fund the lavish life a retinue of slaves had helped make possible, Jefferson accumulated massive debts that were satisfied in part by the post-mortem sale of his already heavily mortgaged human chattels. "Fear for his reputation and public legacy led him to beg his closest friend, James Madison, to 'take care of me when dead.'"[161]

Today, libertarians are engaged in the same mission in defense of Jefferson. For without him, to whom can they point as an example of Liberty fulfilling its promises? What becomes of their defense of Liberty if even Jefferson, the very Apostle of Liberty, revealed that Liberty in practice means Power in disguise? Led by such dearly departed gurus as Murray Rothbard, libertarians of the so-called Austrian School hold fast to the idea, unsupported by any real evidence of comparative human happiness, that true freedom was won for America and the world with the overthrow of King George and the creation of "republican government." Firmly convinced that Liberty delivered what it promised in 1776 (when? where? how?), libertarian historians draw a bright line at the beginning of the Lincoln era, depicting his actions as a betrayal of the principles of "Jeffersonian democracy" expressed in the Declaration of Independence and the Kentucky Resolutions, especially "states' rights." The following is a typical example of this "libertarian narrative"[162] of Liberty:

> Jefferson was the apostle of states' rights, enunciated in his famous Kentucky Resolve of 1798; Lincoln waged the bloodiest war in American history to destroy the Jeffersonian states' rights doctrine. Jefferson authored America's Declaration of Secession from the British empire, known as the Declaration of Independence. Lincoln's overriding purpose in his war was to destroy the secessionist and states' rights principles of the Declaration (while using slick rhetoric designed to pretend that he revered the document).[163]

Missing from this historical cartoon are all the inconvenient details of Jefferson's career examined on the preceding pages, including these:

• His drafting of legislation imposing a compulsory oath of loyalty to the Revolution and the State of Virginia and renouncing loyalty to the King, providing severe legal penalties for refusal to take the oath, and punishing even "verbal crimes" against the Revolution.

• His call for the outlawry and shooting on sight of Tory counter-revolutionaries who should have been treated as prisoners of war, pursuant to a bill of attainder he himself drafted and pushed through the Virginia legislature.

---

160. "Thomas Jefferson: Legacy," http://www.loc.gov/exhibits/jefferson/jeffleg. html.
161. Ibid.
162. Onuf, *Jefferson's Empire*, 85.
163. Thomas Di Lorenzo, "The Latest Defamation of Jefferson," www.lewrockwell.com/dilorenzo/dilorenzo100.html.

• His imprisonment of political criminals in virtual concentration camps while revolutionary governor of Virginia.

• His meddling in French affairs while Minister to France, including outright conspiracy with Lafayette and the National Assembly in the overthrow of Louis XVI.

• His support for the early Jacobin massacres as expressed in the "Adam and Eve" letter.

• His lifelong ownership of slaves, some of whom he had flogged for attempting to escape, and his continued slave trading while President.

• His endorsement of state law prosecutions for "seditious libel" against the President and Congress.

• His endorsement of the draconian Fugitive Slave Law of 1793.

• His "we are all Federalists" Inaugural Address.

• His expansionist acquisition of the Louisiana Territory and the subjection of its inhabitants to the federal government without their consent, even though he himself believed this to be unconstitutional.

• His supine acceptance of the drastic worsening of the lot of the slaves in Louisiana under federal law.

• His approval of an expedient and quite illegal "amendment" of the Constitution by the Republican-controlled House to expand the definition of "high crimes and misdemeanors" in order to facilitate the impeachment of his Federalist opponent, Judge Pickering, for drunkenness.

• His attempt to stage-manage the conviction and execution of Aaron Burr merely for allegedly planning to sever Louisiana from the Union, a prosecution based on an expansive interpretation of the definition of "treason" rejected by the Supreme Court.

• His failed effort, following Burr's acquittal, to eliminate the independent, life-tenured federal judiciary from the Constitution—which he had earlier supported as essential to civil liberties—on the grounds that no branch of government should be "independent of the nation."

• His support for General Wilkinson's military dictatorship in the Louisiana Territory in response to Burr's illusory "threat" to the Union.

• His declaration that "where the laws become inadequate even to their own preservation . . . the universal resource is a dictator, or martial law."

• His dictatorial embargo of American shipping, including the federal seizure of ships and cargos without due process.

• His instigation of "treason" trials and his demand for the death penalty for American citizens who had merely attempted to recover their own property from federal agents.

• His retention of the entire fledgling federal bureaucracy, his expansion of the U.S. military, and his budgetary expenditures for federal projects during his terms as President.

• His support for the federal military conquest of Canada and a federally prosecuted war against Great Britain as necessary to America's final emancipation from "tyranny."

• His fervent advocacy of compulsory universal military service, which almost passed Congress during his presidency.

• His call for war on the secessionists of the Hartford Convention should they secede from the Union.

• His opposition to any restriction on the extension of slavery into the territories because it would divide the Union and impair property rights guaranteed by the Constitution.

• His scheme for the government-subsidized forcible separation of slave children from their parents and their deportation to Haiti or Sierra Leone.

• His support for the Monroe Doctrine, which made America the hemispheric policeman of Liberty.

• His entire grandiose vision of an "empire of Liberty" whose center and summit would be a militarily mighty United States with armed forces raised through the compulsory military service he advocated.

Not even Rothbard, who otherwise sings the praises of Jefferson and the "libertarian creed" of the Founders, could ignore completely the truth about Jefferson's career. Wrote Rothbard:

> The Jeffersonian drive toward virtually no government foundered after Jefferson took office, first, with concessions to the Federalists . . . and then with the *unconstitutional* purchase of the Louisiana Territory. But most particularly it foundered with the *imperialist drive toward war* with Britain in Jefferson's second term, a drive which led to war and to a one-party system which established *virtually the entire statist Federalist program*: high military expenditures, a central bank, a protective tariff, direct federal taxes, public works.[164]

But where can one find any sign of the "Jeffersonian drive toward virtually no government" if that very drive "foundered" precisely when Jefferson took office, both as governor of Virginia and as President of the United States? It is easy enough for Rothbard (who fails to mention the tyrannical Embargo) to say that *after* Jefferson left office he was "horrified at the results" and "brooded at Monticello. . . ." But these psychological touches do not alter the basic picture: When he actually wielded power, the Apostle of Liberty was no less vigorous than the Federalists and

---

164. Murray Rothbard, "The Libertarian Heritage: The American Revolution and Classical Liberalism," in *For a New Liberty*, e-text excerpt lewrockwell.com/rothbard/rothbard121.html.

in fact far outdid them. Rothbard perpetuates the myth of "Jeffersonian democracy" even as he admits the historical facts that explode it.

Also missing from the libertarian cartoon is their icon's central role in creating the conditions that made the conflict over which Lincoln presided well nigh inevitable. By the time Jefferson died in 1826, the state governments, the first five presidents (including Jefferson), Congress and the Supreme Court had already demonstrated what Liberty in its first incarnation required of "the people" who had supposedly clamored for it: obedient subjection to the government in Washington under pain of death. Seeing the way things were going during his retirement, the same Jefferson who had ruled autocratically as President and sought the death penalty for Aaron Burr on grounds of a plot to sever Louisiana from the sacred Union, began grumbling privately that perhaps the peaceable agrarian South should secede from the bellicose industrial North:

> I would rather the States should withdraw which are for unlimited commerce and war and confederate with those which are for peace and agriculture. I know that every nation in Europe would join in sincere amity with the latter, and hold the former at arm's length. . . .[165]

Contrary to Jefferson's prediction, not a single European nation would support the secessionist South. He spent his last days lamenting what he saw as the "ideological apostasy of many Jeffersonian Republicans to the worship of strange Federalist gods."[166] The "true Republicans," according to him, were now to be found only in the South, which was "rapidly becoming a minority section." But it was Jefferson himself who had apostatized as President, leading his fellow Republicans down the road to Federalism "in everything but name"[167] when it suited his purposes. And it was President Jefferson who, with the conquest of Louisiana, made slavery an issue that would provoke the attempted Southern secession from a federal government whose supreme authority he himself had imposed upon the nation during the Embargo in a manner still without precedent in American history. There is no question that, as Professor Miller concludes, "the overall effect of his actions as President was manifestly to foster the spread of slavery and thereby enhance the political power of the South" and that the Louisiana Purchase in particular had "opened up a new world for slavery to conquer."[168] Jefferson's own self-contradictory words and deeds helped set the stage for the Civil War.

---

165. Jefferson to William H. Crawford, June 20, 1816, in ed. Randolph, *Memoirs, Correspondence, and Miscellanies*, Vol. III, 284.

166. Miller, *Wolf by the Ears*, 210.

167. Ibid.

168. Ibid., 234.

9

The Founders' Season of Regret

JEFFERSON'S LAST YEARS marked the end of a long season of regret for him and other Founders of the first rank. Perhaps the single most telling piece of evidence in the overwhelming case against the myth of a "conservative" American Revolution is the recognition by many of the Founders themselves that their radical experiment in republican government was already exhibiting alarming signs of degeneration. In responding to the anticipated objection that this critique of Liberty in its first incarnation is mere *post hoc* special pleading from a Catholic perspective, it will be helpful to consider what Gordon Wood observed in his Pulitzer Prize-winning study of the Revolution's radicalism:

> This democratic society was not the society the revolutionary leaders had wanted or expected. No wonder, then, that those of them who lived on into the early decades of the nineteenth century expressed anxiety over what they had wrought. Although they tried to put as good a face as they could on what had happened, they were bewildered, uneasy, and in many cases deeply disillusioned. Indeed, a pervasive pessimism, a fear that their revolutionary experiment in republicanism was not working out, runs through the later writings of the founding fathers. *All the major revolutionary leaders died less than happy with the results of the Revolution.*[1]

Wood shows that the Founders' reasons for disillusionment over their own creation varied greatly: alarm at the rise of a government that already threatened to become all powerful; disgust at the emergence of a mass democracy ruled by cheap politicians; revulsion over the crass commercialism and lust for lucre that had consumed the entire nation only a few decades after the Revolution; among those few Founders (almost all of the second rank) who were orthodox professing Christians, horror at the degeneration of Christian faith and morals; and, among the Revolutionary illuminati, especially Jefferson, disdain for the proliferation of Christian sects whose various bizarre and ineffectual enthusiasms were a far cry from the cool and rational Unitarianism Jefferson had so confidently predicted would become America's national religion within a generation. (In Chapter 19 we will examine how the "sect plague" of the Second Great Awakening contributed to the subordination of Christianity by the power of the secular state the Founders created.)

---

1. Wood, *Radicalism of the American Revolution*, 365.

Things Fall Apart

In general, the Founders who survived into the early decades of the 1800s "were unsettled and fearful not because the American Revolution had failed but because it had succeeded, and succeeded only too well." For they had succeeded in overthrowing an existing "tyrant" only to see him replaced in short order by a tyrannical majority goaded by pandering politicians rather than the noble and disinterested rulers the Founders had envisioned in their utopian boasting that Liberty would be something more than what it was and what they themselves had revealed it to be in their own exercise of public office: just another name for Power. As the prophecies of Patrick Henry and other anti-Federalists began to come true before their eyes, many of the Founders were aghast at a "radically new understanding of political patronage and office holding, one that virtually repudiated all that the revolutionaries of 1776 had sought." With the Presidency of Andrew Jackson, the still-surviving Founders were confronted with the greatest irony of all: that Jacksonianism was "infusing into American democracy more elements of monarchy than even the Federalists had dared to try." Moreover, through the "spoils system" the Jacksonian Revolution would centralize and consolidate Presidential power even as the Jacksonians pandered to the masses with "the most enthusiastic democratic rhetoric that any modern country had ever experienced."[2] The rise of the professional politician, who could be any Tom, Dick or Harry that talked a good line, spelled early doom for the Founders' gauzy vision of a neo-Roman republic of virtuous solons, animated only by a desire to serve the public good.

Many of the Founders were appalled by the rapid moral deterioration of their creation. Wood summarizes what they saw in the decades following the Revolution: "Everything seemed to be coming apart, and murder, suicide, theft and mobbing became increasingly common responses to the burdens that *liberty* and the expectation of gain were placing on people." Almost overnight, Wood notes, America had become a nation of heavy drinkers: "nearly all Americans drank—men, women, children, and sometimes even babies—everywhere and anywhere, all day long." Washington, who ran his own distillery in Mount Vernon, nevertheless complained that "distilled spirits 'were the ruin of half the workmen in this Country,'" while John Adams "was mortified that his countrymen were more intemperate than *any other people in the world*."[3]

And whereas before the Revolution "only New Englanders had recognized the absolute right to divorce . . . after the Revolution all the States except South Carolina developed new liberal laws on divorce."[4] This development was accompanied by a diminution in family size. Beginning in 1800, the fertility rate in America steadily declined even as material prosperity rose, dropping by some 25% between 1800 and 1860. The 19th-century phenomenon of the gradually diminishing family

---

2. Wood, *Radicalism*, 368, 300, 302.
3. Ibid., 306.
4. Ibid., 184.

was seen as well in post-revolutionary France and, much earlier, in England, where Liberty had its first violent stirrings in the 17th century.[5]

As early as 1806, a mere seventeen years after ratification of the Constitution, Adams viewed with horror the mass democracy the federal government had already revealed itself to be, despite his dream that he had been engaged in "the illumination of the ignorant, and the emancipation of the slavish part of mankind all over the earth." The co-drafter of the Declaration of Independence and the second President of the United States, who had regally spared the Fries Rebellion tax resisters from the death penalty, penned this lament: "I once thought our Constitution was a quasi or mixed government, but they have made it, to all intents and purposes, in virtue, spirit and effect, a democracy. We are left without resources but in our prayers and tears, and we have nothing that we can do or say but *the Lord have mercy upon us....*"[6]

No one was more eloquent in expressing disgust and disillusionment over the results of the Revolution than Adams's dear friend and faithful correspondent, Benjamin Rush, a signer of the Declaration of Independence, a member of the Continental Congress, the most eminent American physician of his day, credited with healing the rift between Adams and Jefferson over the federalist question and Adams's humiliating loss in the presidential election of 1800, which had marked the end of his political career. Commiserating with Adams in 1812, Rush lamented: "We are indeed a bebanked, a bewhiskeyed, and a bedollared nation."[7] The "American experiment," Rush admitted, "*will certainly fail. It has already disappointed the expectations of its most sanguine and ardent friends.*"[8]

Rush further complained to Adams that the political order the Revolution created already featured such things as Jefferson expressing theological objections to Christianity on the floor of Congress while ridiculing a motion for a national day of fasting. Sounding the very theme of the NRA movement some fifty years later, he wrote of "the *national sins* of our country that have provoked the wrath of Heaven to afflict us with war [the War of 1812]." Flirting with heresy against the American civil religion, Rush identified as one of these national sins the "idolatrous worship paid to the name of George Washington by all classes and nearly all parties of our citizens, manifested in the impious application of names and epithets to him which are ascribed in Scripture only to God and Jesus Christ." With sardonic but only slight exaggeration, he enumerated the litany: "'our Saviour,' 'our Redeemer,' 'our cloud by day and our pillar of fire by night,' 'our star in the east,' 'to us a Son is born,' and 'our guide on earth, our advocate in heaven.'"[9]

5. Cf. Herbert S. Klein, *A Population History of the United States* (Cambridge: Cambridge Univ. Press, 2002), 76–82.

6. Adams to Benjamin Rush, September 19, 1806, in *The Spur of Fame: Dialogues of John Adams and Benjamin Rush*, eds Schutz and Adair (Indianapolis: Liberty Fund, 1966), 72.

7. Rush to John Adams, June 27, 1812, in *The Spur of Fame*, 247.

8. Wood, *Radicalism*, 366.

9. Rush to Adams, June 27 and July 8, 1812, in *The Spur of Fame*, 247, 250.

Many of the Founders of the second rank, including Rush himself, John Jay, Elias Boudinot, Noah Webster, and John Randolph, "ended by abandoning the Enlightenment and becoming a Christian enthusiast."[10] A deeply disheartened Rush wrote to Adams to express the conviction that had been the very foundation of the perennial social order rejected by the Framers of the Constitution: "nothing but the Gospel of Jesus Christ will effect the mighty work of making nations happy."[11] In a letter to Noah Webster, Rush provided a startling contemporaneous confirmation of the thesis advanced here, predicting as early as 1798 nothing short of disastrous worldwide consequences from the deistic Founders' Enlightenment-bred utopian effort to build a political society on the insights of unaided reason without reliance on the Gospel:

But Alas! my friend, I fear all *our attempts* to produce political happiness by the solitary influence of human reason, will be as fruitless at [as] the search for the philosopher's stone. It seems to be reserved to Christianity alone to produce universal, moral, political and physical happiness. Reason produces it is true, great and popular truths, but it affords motives too feeble to induce mankind to act agreeably to them. Christianity unfolds the same truths and accompanies them with motives, agreeable, powerful & irresistible. I anticipate nothing but suffering to the human race while the present systems of paganism, deism and atheism prevail in the world.[12]

Adams—the same American *philosophe* who had boasted of his role in the illumination of the world, who had mocked the Christian dogma of the Trinity[13] and ridiculed the Catholic Mass[14]—would come to the same conclusion as Rush, attributing America's already evident decline to precisely the Enlightenment philosophy he himself had embodied and helped to put into practice. Writing in 1806, after the fall of the Jacobins, the collapse of the Thermidorian regime and the rise of the Emperor Napoleon in revolutionary France, Adams made this remarkable admission in reply to Rush's concern about the fate of America: "If the philosophers had not undermined the Christian religion and the morals of the people *as much in America as they have in Europe*, I should think civilization would take its

10. Wood, *Radicalism*, 366.

11. Ibid.

12. Rush to Webster, July 20, 1798, in K. Alan Snyder, *Defining Noah Webster* (Fairfax, VA: Allegiance Press, 2002), 136.

13. "Had you and I been forty days with Moses on Mount Sinai to behold the divine Shekinah, and there told that one was three and three, one: We might not have the courage to deny it, but We would not have believed it." Adams to Jefferson, September 14, 1813, in *The Works of John Adams*, 67–68.

14. "This afternoon's entertainment was to me most awful and affecting; the poor wretches fingering their beads, chanting Latin not a word of which they understood; their pater nosters [sic] and ave [sic] Marias; their holy water; their crossing themselves perpetually; their bowing to the name of Jesus, whenever they hear it; their bowings and kneelings and genuflections before the altar...." John Adams to Abigail Adams, October 9, 1774, in *Familiar Letters of John Adams and His Wife Abigail Adams during the Revolution* (NY: Hurd and Houghton, 1876), 46–47.

flight over the Atlantic. But as it is, I see nothing but that we must, or rather that we shall, follow the fate of Europe."[15]

Yet Adams himself was one of the "philosophers" he professed to deplore; and it was his philosophy—a progeny of Locke's as the great Moses of the Enlightenment—that had already provoked in America what Wood calls an "epistemological crisis." It was a crisis arising from the eminently Lockean notion, now appallingly adopted by the common man as well as the enlightened elites, that people have "the ability to determine all by themselves the truth or validity of any idea or thing presented to them," which left the great mass of Americans "prey for all the hoaxers, confidence men and tricksters . . . who soon popped up everywhere."[16]

America was already experiencing the result in practice of Jefferson's lofty pronouncement of the "moderate" Enlightenment principle that "truth is great and will prevail if left to herself . . . and has nothing to fear from the conflict . . . errors ceasing to be dangerous when it is permitted freely to contradict them."[17] The notion that truth and error must be allowed to engage endlessly in a public contest for the minds of men met with the ridicule of a contemporary Pope, Gregory XVI: "Some are so carried away that they contentiously assert that the flock of errors . . . is sufficiently compensated by the publication of some book which defends religion and truth. . . . Is there any sane man who would say poison ought to be distributed, sold publicly, stored, and even drunk because some antidote is available and those who use it may be snatched from death again and again?"[18] The Pope described the final outcome of the Enlightenment-bred, unbridled "freedom of thought" over which Adams, a man of the Enlightenment, was now wringing his hands: "When all restraints are removed by which men are kept on the narrow path of truth, their nature, which is already inclined to evil, propels them to ruin."[19]

"Rivers of Blood Must Yet Flow"

Adams did recognize that he and his collaborators in revolution might have had something to do with the seemingly worldwide spectacle of men propelling themselves to ruin. He viewed the French Revolution and its pan-European aftermath with pangs of conscience for what he and the other Founders had wrought. Quite simply, "Adams believed that the American Revolution set off unrest around the world."[20] In 1806 he anticipated the coming revolutions in South America, "an abyss into which I dare not look."[21] Five years later, writing at the height of the Napoleonic Empire, the now aged Founder unburdened to Rush his sense of guilt:

15. Adams to Rush, March 26, 1806, in *Spur of Fame*, 55.
16. Wood, *Radicalism*, 362.
17. The Virginia Act For Establishing Religious Freedom (1786).
18. Gregory XVI, *Mirari Vos* (1832), n. 15.
19. Ibid., n. 14.
20. Douglas Adair, in *Spur of Fame*, 60, n. 16.
21. Adams to Rush, June 22, 1806, in *Spur of Fame*, 60.

Have I not been employed in mischief all my days? *Did not the American Revolution produce the French Revolution? And did not the French Revolution produce all the calamities and desolation to the human race and the whole globe ever since?* I meant well, however ... and awful, dreadful, and deplorable as the consequences have been, I cannot but hope that the ultimate good of the world, of the human race, and our beloved country is intended and will be accomplished by it. . . .[22]

A stunning confession, coming as it did from the same mordantly anti-Catholic American *philosophe* who had once condemned the Catholic social order of Europe thus: "the most refined, sublime, extensive, and astonishing constitution of policy ... framed by the Romish clergy for the aggrandizement of their own order ... to spread and rivet among the people ... a state of sordid ignorance and staring timidity ... Thus was human nature chained fast for ages in a cruel, shameful, and deplorable servitude to him [the Pope], and his subordinate tyrants. . . ."[23]

As the historian Jeffrey Langan has shown, however, some six years later, during the Adams-Jefferson correspondence of 1812–1826, Jefferson, the old crypto-Jacobin, played the role of "spiritual advisor" to Adams, the "hand-wringing liberal" and "guilt-filled revolutionary," attempting to buck up the sagging revolutionary faith of his old nemesis.[24] In September of 1826, writing to Adams about the calamitous events in France and the Bourbon Restoration that seemed to have brought the French Revolution to an end, Jefferson waxed to the theme of his infamous "Adam and Eve" letter: that no amount of bloodshed and devastation was too great for the prize of Liberty, which sooner or later would come to France:

A first attempt to recover the right of self-government may fail, so may a second, a third, etc. But as a younger and more instructed race comes on, the sentiment becomes more and more intuitive, and a fourth, a fifth, or some subsequent one of the ever renewed attempts will ultimately succeed.

In France, the first effort was defeated by Robespierre, the second by Bonaparte, the third by Louis XVIII and his holy allies; another is yet to come, and all Europe, Russia excepted, has caught the spirit; and all will attain representative government, more or less perfect. . . .

To attain all this, however, *rivers of blood must yet flow, and years of desolation pass over*; yet the object *is worth rivers of blood, and years of desolation*. For what inheritance so valuable, can man leave to his posterity? You and I shall look down from another world on these *glorious achievements to man*, which will add to the joys even of heaven.[25]

In reply, Adams told Jefferson of his pleasure at hearing read to him "the sure

---

22. *The Spur of Fame*, 207.

23. John Adams, *A Dissertation on the Canon and Feudal Law* (1765).

24. Jeffrey Langan, "Revolutionary Guilt," paper delivered at the Trialogos Conference, Tallinn, Estonia (2007), 3.

25. *Jeffersonian Cyclopedia*, §7771 (paragraph breaks added).

words of prophecy in your letter of September 4," but added: "It is melancholy to contemplate the cruel wars, desolations of countries, and oceans of blood, which *must occur* before rational principles and rational systems of government can prevail and be established."[26]

What is one to make of this exchange between two supremely prideful figures, neither of whom had suffered a scratch during the Revolution, pondering the fate of millions of ordinary mortals who "must"—but of course—drown in oceans of blood in order to establish the "rational principles" they had both helped loose upon the world? One is reminded of Nietzsche's lines on how "Homer makes his gods look down upon the fates of men" and "every evil is justified in the sight of which a god finds edification...."[27] Adams, at least, had enough of a conscience to express "melancholy" over the oceans of blood required for the "glorious achievements" of those poor, struggling worldlings Jefferson evidently expected to be surveying with a contented smile from his empyrean perch in Unitarian heaven.

John Adams and Thomas Jefferson both died on July 4, 1826, the very anniversary of the founding of a republic whose rapid descent into a vulgar democracy headed by an elected quasi-monarch they had lived long enough to regret, even though it was "only an extension of all that the revolutionary leaders had advocated."[28] It appears that neither had foreseen, however, that during the generation that would immediately follow them, the oceans and rivers of blood they deemed necessary to establish their notion of government throughout the world would drench the very soil of the nation they had helped to invent.

26. Adams to Jefferson, September 17, 1823, in *The Works of John Adams, Second President of the United States: with a Life of the Author, Notes and Illustrations, by his Grandson Charles Francis Adams* (Boston: Little, Brown and Co., 1856), Vol. 10; accessed from oll.libertyfund.org/title/2127/193660/3103 830 on 2011-02-08. This author is indebted to Jeffrey Langan for this critical citation in his paper "Revolutionary Guilt."

27. Friedrich Nietzsche, *The Genealogy of Morals* (Mineola, NY: Dover Publications, 2003), 44.

28. Wood, *Radicalism*, 368.

10

Slouching Toward Sumter

THE DEFEAT OF incumbent President John Quincy Adams by Andrew Jackson of Tennessee in the election of 1828 marked the end of the era of the charismatic Founders and Framers and the beginning of the era in which the unprecedented central government they had created in the name of Liberty would reveal its might fully and with terrifying power. It was the era in which those who invoked the "Spirit of 1776" would wage their final losing battle with the illimitable sovereign that very spirit had set in motion without restraint by an established Church, a Christian moral code, or any other authority higher than itself as the avatar of "We the People." It was the era in which Locke's "one supreme government" in operation would impose with unprecedented political vengeance Rousseau's "general will" and all those who refused to obey would be "forced to be free."[1]

The Nullification Crisis

Only six years after Jefferson's death, America witnessed the Nullification Crisis (1832–33), which arose over the federal tariffs of 1828 and 1832. President Jackson, a Freemason[2] who owned upwards of a hundred-fifty slaves and had run for office as an advocate of states' rights, was confronted by South Carolina's attempt to nullify the tariffs in accordance with its Ordinance of Nullification (1832). The Ordinance had been drafted with the support of South Carolina's own John C. Calhoun, the two-time Vice President who had resigned from that office during the Jackson administration in order to advance the Southern cause in the Senate. A War Hawk during the War of 1812 who served as Secretary of War under President Monroe, Calhoun had been a staunch proponent of a strong federal government and even a supporter of the Missouri Compromise as a means of settling the slavery controversy: "Let us not be disturbers of this Union,"[3] he had declared when recommending extension of the Compromise line to the Pacific. But like so many of the politicians of Liberty, first and foremost Jefferson, Calhoun's positions were as

---

1. Cf. Chapter 4 and *Social Contract*, I.7.

2. Jackson was a Royal Arch Freemason who served as Grand Master of the Grand Lodge of Tennessee, a post to which he was elected on October 7, 1822. Denslow and Truman, Part One, 284.

3. In Margaret L. Coit, *John C. Calhoun: An American Portrait* (Columbia, SC: Univ. of South Carolina Press, 1991 [1950]), 450.

consistent as the direction of the wind. "Calhoun never admitted that he himself had changed his views on state rights, the tariff, or any other subject. He . . . always claimed to be entirely governed by deduction from first principles rather than any consideration of practicality or political advantage."[4]

The Ordinance of Nullification declared the tariffs to be in excess of Congressional authority under the "true meaning and intent" of the Constitution and thus null and void, and that South Carolina "will not submit to the application of force on the part of the federal government, to reduce this State to obedience. . . ." Evoking Locke's doctrine of revolution, the Ordinance warned that if force were applied or authorized by Congress "the people of this State will henceforth hold themselves absolved from all further obligation to maintain or preserve their political connection with the people of the other States; and will forthwith proceed to organize a separate government, and do all other acts and things which sovereign and independent States may of right do."[5] The Ordinance concluded by noting that it had been adopted "in the fifty-seventh year of the Declaration of the Independence of the United States of America."

In other words, South Carolina was prepared to do just what the American revolutionaries, including Madison, the still-living "Father of the Constitution," had done only fifty-seven years earlier: exercise the Lockean warrant for revolution and declare its independence from a government deemed to have breached the Lockean trust. But, as we have seen, the holders of power in Washington, beginning with George Washington himself, had long since made it clear that the age of revolution had ended with the overthrow of King George and that the age of obedience— obedience to them—had begun. The Framers had made their bed of the "sovereignty of the people," and "We the People" would now be expected to lie therein tranquilly in perpetuity, without further tossing and turning. Thus, in response to the Ordinance, President Jackson issued a Proclamation Regarding Nullification (1832) along Madisonian lines as enunciated by the Marshall Court:

> The Constitution of the United States then forms a government, not a league. . . . It is a government in which all the people are represented, *which operates directly on the people individually, not upon the States.* . . . [E]ach State having expressly parted with so many powers as to constitute, jointly with the other States, a single nation, *cannot, from that period, possess any right to secede,* because such secession does not break a league, but destroys the unity of a nation; and any injury to that unity is not only a breach which would result from the contravention of a compact, but it is *an offense against the whole Union.*[6]

4. Daniel Walker Howe, *What Hath God Wrought* [*Oxford History of the United States*] (Oxford Univ. Press: 2007), Kindle Edition, 400.

5. *South Carolina Ordinance of Nullification*, November 24, 1832, Yale Law School e-text, yale.edu/lawweb/avalon/states/sc/ordnull.htm.

6. *Proclamation Regarding Nullification*, December 10, 1832, Yale Law School e-text, yale.edu/lawweb/avalon/presiden/proclamations/jack01.htm.

Jackson's words foreshadowed Lincoln's own rationale for preventing southern secession by force of arms. In his later message to Congress in 1833 Jackson declared that, as President and head of the executive branch, he was bound to "take care that the laws be faithfully executed," while Congress had "the power not merely to lay and collect taxes, duties, imposts, and excises, to pay the debts and provide for the common defense and general welfare, but 'to make all laws which shall be necessary and proper for carrying into effect the foregoing powers and all other powers vested by the Constitution in the Government of the United States or in any department or officer thereof. . . .'" Such "necessary and proper" laws obviously included the tariffs at issue, he maintained.[7]

South Carolina's actions were, Jackson continued, "subversive of the supremacy of the laws and of the integrity of the Union," because they amounted to *de facto* secession: "a State in which, by an usurpation of power, the constitutional authority of the Federal Government is openly defied and set aside, wants only the form to be independent of the Union."[8] By ratifying the Constitution, the people of South Carolina, like those in the other states, had entered into a compact with the federal government, and "[t]o this compact, in whatever mode it may have been done, the people of South Carolina have freely and voluntarily given their assent, and to the whole and every part of it they are, upon every principle of good faith, *inviolably bound.*"

All of this was fully in accord with Locke's notion (discussed in Chapter 3) that once a party has expressly consented to be subject to a sovereign pursuant to the social compact, that party is *"perpetually and indispensably* obliged to be and remain unalterably a Subject to it, and can *never again* be in the liberty of the state of Nature"[9]—unless, of course, there is a revolution, which in this case the President of the federal sovereign was not about to countenance. Echoing Locke and the Declaration of Independence, but wielding them both *against* South Carolina's claim to the revolutionary warrant, Jackson declared that while "a State or any other great portion of the people, suffering under long and intolerable oppression and having tried all constitutional remedies without the hope of redress, may have a natural right . . . to absolve themselves from their obligations to the Government and appeal to the last resort"—this was pure Locke—nevertheless the tariffs were not grounds for revolution. Moreover, South Carolina had not even attempted to exhaust its legal remedies under the Constitution.

Finally, Jackson concluded, the Founding Fathers had bequeathed a "rich inheritance" and "the sacred obligation of preserving it by the same virtues which conducted them through the eventful scenes of the Revolution and ultimately crowned their struggle with the noblest model of civil institutions." The federal government and the Union were "founded upon the great principle of popular representation"

7. *Message to the Senate and House Regarding South Carolina's Nullification Ordinance,* January 16, 1833, Yale Law School e-text @ http://avalon.law.yale.edu/19th_century/ajack001.asp.

8. Ibid.

9. *TT,* II.119.

and were "the objects of the hopes of the friends of civil liberty throughout the world. . . ." Therefore, for the sake of mankind, the Union had to be defended against South Carolina's usurpation.[10]

The still-living "Father of the Constitution" was of like mind. Madison harshly rejected the very idea that one State "may arrest the operation of a law of the United States, and institute a process which is to terminate in the ascendancy of a minority over a large majority, in a Republican System, the characteristic rule of which is that the major will is the ruling will."[11] In his *Notes on Nullification* (1835), written precisely to address South Carolina's contentions, Madison claimed that not even Jefferson had advocated a *constitutional* right on the part of individual states to declare federal laws null and void but rather only "the natural right, which all admit to be a remedy against insupportable oppression"—another reference to Locke's doctrine of revolution. But, Madison continued, "It cannot be supposed for a moment that Mr. Jefferson would not revolt at the doctrine of South Carolina, that a single state could constitutionally resist a law of the Union while remaining within it, and that with the accession of a small minority of the others, overrule the will of a great majority of the whole, & constitutionally annul the law everywhere." For it was none other than Jefferson, "the apostle of republicanism . . . whose own words [in his inaugural address] declare that 'acquiescence in the decision of the majority is the vital principle of it.'"

Opinions may differ on whether Madison succeeded in absolving Jefferson of complicity in the nullification crisis, but one may not reasonably deny Madison's own rejection of the doctrine attributed to his friend. He vigorously denied that his own Virginia Resolutions of 1798 had advocated nullification, referencing his own Report to the Virginia House of Delegates in 1799, wherein, on the contrary, he had advised the delegates that state declarations of the unconstitutionality of federal laws are mere "*expressions of opinion*, unaccompanied with *any* other effect than what they may produce on opinion by exciting reflection." On the other hand, judicial review of allegedly unconstitutional laws, presumably by the Article III judiciary, could be "carried into immediate effect by force" and would be the means by which "the latter [the judiciary] enforces the general will"—a startling reference to Rousseau's doctrine of coerced Liberty.[12]

Scorning nullification as a "newfangled theory," Madison contended that the only nullification of federal law possible was that attendant upon outright dissolution of the federal compact, bottomed on the Lockean justification (recited in the Declaration of Independence) of "abuses or usurpations, releasing the parties to it from their obligation" and warranting the overthrow of the government.

10. *Message to the Senate and House Regarding South Carolina's Nullification Ordinance,* January 16, 1833. Yale Law School e-text @ http://avalon.law.yale.edu/19th_century/ajack001.asp.
11. *Notes on Nullification* (1835–36), *Writings* (Hunt) IX, 588–89, in Koch, *Madison and Jefferson,* 287.
12. James Madison, *Report of 1799 to the Virginia House of Delegates,* e-text @ http://www.constitution.org/rf/vr_1799.htm.

No "nullification" remedy was to be found in the text of the Constitution as such; the only way out of the Union was to *break* it in a revolutionary act or, at the very least, to engage in civil disobedience of an unjust law and suffer the legal consequences.

Madison put the alternative just that starkly in the *Notes*. While the contention that a single state could declare a federal law null and void "as one of the parties to the Constitution" while "not ceasing to avow its adherence to the Constitution" was a "contradiction in terms" and an "inlet to anarchy," nevertheless "there is nothing which excludes a natural right in the States individually . . . suffering under palpable and insupportable wrongs, from seeking relief by *resistance and revolution*." Madison made clear the point of the Lockean doctrine: the Lockean compact once having been formed, revolution is the only escape hatch. Twenty-seven years before it began, Madison had sketched the rationale for secession and the Civil War.

Exposing the infirmity of the principle of private judgment advanced by South Carolina, Madison ridiculed the "sophism" involved in the claim that "an unconstitutional law is no law" when the very question of unconstitutionality could hardly be South Carolina's alone to determine. The doctrine that every state had an equal right to assert its reading of the Constitution as "the infallible one, and . . . act upon it ag[ainst] the construction of all others" would, he argued, "be subversive of all constitutions, all laws, and all compacts." Of course, Madison had a point. But he failed to perceive that the Protestant principle of the "infallible" private judgment of individuals was the very basis of the "American experiment" and Enlightenment political theory in the first place. The only difference was that, for such as Madison, private judgment becomes infallible only when it is shared by fifty-percent-plus-one of a governing electorate or legislature, or when a lone dissenter invokes (as even Madison would allow) the Lockean revolutionary warrant based on the "appeal to heaven," citing supposedly "intolerable" abuses.

Following the principle of private judgment as applied to politics, Madison insisted that "We the People" were bound by the final authority they themselves had erected in the Constitution, much as the members of Protestant churches agree to be bound by the decisions of their elders—but only until they decide to break away and found their own churches in protest. It was "We the People" who had determined that federal law was to be supreme in the Republic they had created, failing which there would be no final authority to resolve disputes among the members of the federal compact. "A political system which does not contain an effective provision for a peaceable decision of all controversies arising within itself, would be a Govt. in name only," he wrote. A government "cannot be either peaceable or effective by making every part an authoritative umpire," but rather "[t]he final appeal in such cases must be to the authority of the whole, not to that of the parts separately and independently." It was this exigency, said Madison, that had "dictated the clause declaring that the Constitution & laws of the U. S. should be the supreme law of the Land, anything in the constn [sic] or laws of any of the States to the contrary notwithstanding."[13] Indeed, on its face the Supremacy Clause in Article VI made the "nullification" doctrine untenable:

> This Constitution and the laws of the United States which shall be made in pursuance thereof ... shall be *the supreme Law of the Land* ... any Thing in the Constitution or Laws *of any State* to the Contrary *notwithstanding.*

The federal Constitution and statutes could hardly be supreme over state constitutions and statutes if any state were free to "nullify" any federal enactment it deemed *ultra vires.* Nor would it do to argue that federal law is supreme only within the "sphere" of federal authority, for the Constitution is quite clear that the very extent of that "sphere" is determined, not by each state as it sees fit, but by the final arbiter the Constitution itself designates: the Article III federal judiciary, including the *Supreme* Court, whose decisions are, as the very name implies, likewise "the supreme Law of the Land."

What of the contention advanced by today's libertarian exponents of nullification, who cite Jefferson's draft of the Kentucky Resolutions: that it would be absurd to allow the federal government created by the "sovereign people" to be the final arbiter of the extent of its own powers over them? But why is this absurd if, under the Founders' own principles, it was the "sovereign people" in the first place who had "consented" to give the federal government precisely such final authority via the Supremacy Clause? Observing the obvious, Madison asked: "But is not the Const[itution] itself necessarily the offspring of a sov[ereig]n aut[horit]y?" And under the Founders' principles the American people have continuously "consented" to the role of the Article III judiciary "We the People" themselves established as final arbiter of disputes over the scope of federal authority.

What is absurd, rather, is that each and every party to the constitutional compact would be equally entitled to interpret it as against all the others, and against the interpretations of the President, the Congress and the federal judiciary. The result would be a virtual infinitude of "final authorities" on the limits of federal power: the three branches of the federal government, each individual state, and the people residing in each state to the extent they rejected Jefferson's idea that state legislatures should have the final say on which federal laws are valid. But, again, that absurdity is implicit in the political theory whose logical outcome Madison and his collaborators thought they could contain with documentary provisions for a final authority at the federal level.

One staunch contemporary libertarian defender of the myth of Jeffersonian "limited government" under the regime of state "nullification" of federal laws argues that since the Supremacy Clause provides that "only the Constitution and *laws which shall be made in pursuance thereof* shall be the supreme law of the land ... [c]iting the Supremacy Clause merely begs the question," because "[a] nullifying state maintains that a given law is not 'in pursuance thereof' and therefore that the Supremacy Clause does not apply in the first place."[14] But where does the

---

13. From James Madison, "Notes on Nullification," *Writings* 9:606–7, Univ. of Chicago e-text, press--ubs.uchicago.edu/founders/documents/a6_2s43.html.

14. Thomas E. Woods, Jr., "Nullification: Answering the Objections," http://www.tomwoods.com/nullification-answering-the-objections. Emphasis in original.

Constitution confer upon the States the right of each to decide for itself which laws are "in pursuance" of the Constitution and which are not, especially when it was not the States but "We the People" who are said to have ratified the Constitution?

The same commentator belittles as a "foolish, ill-informed argument" the objection that "nullification" of federal law by any state as it sees fit makes nonsense of the Supremacy Clause and indeed the entire federal government the Framers created. He dismisses this statement of the obvious as "the reply we often hear from law school graduates and professors" and scoffs that one must "never . . . confuse legal training with an education." But it is precisely our naïve commentator's *lack* of legal training that blinds him to what any minimally trained lawyer can discern in the Constitution's lawyer-drafted provisions: that the broad grants of federal power and the corresponding limitations on state power in Article I, the "necessary and proper" clause in Article VI, the "general welfare" clause, the Supremacy Clause, the Tenth Amendment's silence on just what powers the States are supposed to have retained, and the role of the Article III judiciary in construing the constitutional text—including the court rather tellingly denominated Supreme—all present gigantic loopholes that could only mean a relentless expansion of federal power over time, just as the anti-Federalists predicted.

It is, therefore, libertarian polemicists who indulge in "foolish, ill-informed argument" when they invoke the anonymously published "nullification" theory of Thomas Jefferson—who did not even attend the Constitutional Convention—as if it were part of the organic law of the United States. Jefferson's opinions provide no magical incantation that will draw the federal genie back into the bottle or turn the federal oak back into an acorn. But not all libertarians are thus deluded. The libertarian gadfly Kirkpatrick Sale, for example, has protested thus: "Let's wake up these 'real Constitution' die-hards and the ardent 'Tenthers' and tell them that it's a waste of time to try to resurrect that document in order to save the nation—because *the growth of government and the centralization of power is inherent in its original provisions* [a]s the anti-Federalists were trying to say all along from the very beginning of the ratification process. . . . [W]e have a big overgrown government because *that's what the Founding Fathers founded. . . ."*[15]

Here it is necessary to insert a caveat to ward off an anticipated demagogic attack on this element of our discussion. The intent here is not at all to suggest that "nullification" would *per se* be a morally wrongful usurpation of federal authority, or that federal authority is anything other than what it has become: oppressive. Quite the contrary, under the higher law that governs all human positive law one is morally obliged to declare null and void an unjust and immoral federal law, including laws purportedly made "in pursuance" of the Constitution. An unjust law is no law at all, as Saint Augustine and the whole Greco-Catholic tradition affirm. Moreover, under the principle of subsidiarity enunciated in Catholic social teaching (cf. Chapter 1), a moral argument can be made for disregarding federal laws that unjustly trench

---

15. Kirkpatrick Sale, "Getting Back to the Real Constitution?", at http://www.counterpunch.org/20 10/10/28/getting-back-to-the-real-constitution/.

upon political functions rightly belonging to lower orders of authority. This too is a matter of natural law and natural justice, as the Church teaches.

The point, rather, is that "nullification" *is not to be found in the text of the Constitution and Bill of Rights viewed as a human compact.* And it is intellectually dishonest to maintain that the Framers built state "nullification" of federal acts and even secession-at-will into the organic law of the United States, especially when the Constitution provides, if anything, for *federal* nullification of *state* law deemed contrary to "the supreme law of the land." Aside from the judicial review or legislative repeal the Constitution does provide as remedies, the only ground of nullification available to the States is the higher law, which means civil disobedience. Contemporary libertarians ought to admit what the anti-Federalists saw from the beginning: that the Framers created a powerful central government whose enactments would be supreme, trumping all state laws in cases of conflict, because "We the People" *were deemed to have consented to this arrangement* as both authors and subjects of the constitutional compact. It is that simple.

The Nullification Crisis revealed the impossible paradox of Locke's theory of sovereignty, according to which the subjects of the "one supreme government" consent to be ruled by it. Just who had "consented" to be ruled by whom after the Revolution, and who had reserved the right to terminate that consent in cases of conflict? The Civil War would present the bloody answer to these questions: the party that succeeds in crushing the opposition by force determines who is the ruler, who is the subject, and who may withdraw from the ruler-subject relation. *The mythical limitless power of "absolute monarchy" actually existed in the form of the Union*, but without the traditional limits imposed on the Christian sovereign, including his recognition that God, not "We the People," is the ultimate Author of all sovereignty to which all earthly sovereigns must bend the knee.

At any rate, the contemporary libertarian advocacy of a "nullification" remedy in the Tenth Amendment encounters a major embarrassment in the historical fact that not a single state legislature, *not even in the South*, supported South Carolina's Ordinance of Nullification. Virginia "regarded nullification as a caricature of her resolves of 1798, Georgia 'abhorred the doctrine'"[16] and Alabama denounced it as "unsound in theory, dangerous in practice, and essentially revolutionary."[17] Quite simply, "South Carolina stood alone."[18] Accordingly, in March of 1833 Congress passed not only a compromise tariff proposed by Calhoun himself (reducing the tariff by fifty percent) but also the Force Act, which essentially gave President Jackson the power to use military force as he saw fit to detain ships (à la Jefferson during the Embargo), collect the tariff from South Carolina, and suppress any opposition to federal authority by local militia, with federal marshals being empowered to set up jails for any resulting prisoners.

16. Morison, *HAP*, 437.
17. *Cyclopedia of American Government*, eds Andrew McLaughlin and Albert Bushnell Hart (NY: D. Appleton & Co., 1914), Vol. II, 566.
18. Ibid.

The compromise tariff, writes historian Daniel Walker Howe, "passed with handsome majorities from both sections in the House and won in the Senate the votes of most Northerners and exactly half the Southerners. The northern business community had come to recognize that their enlightened self-interest lay in tariff rates that could endure rather than ones that inflamed southern agitation. Most Southerners saw the measure as a significant amelioration of their grievance and were now content to back Jackson for reelection rather than pursue any more drastic remedy such as the one South Carolina was touting."[19] The Force Act passed the Senate 32–1 after Calhoun and other Southern opponents left the chamber to avoid having to vote on the bill. South Carolina retreated, accepted the compromise tariff, and repealed its Nullification Ordinance as Jackson, following the examples of Washington, Adams, and Jefferson, was preparing for military action. Only seven years after Jefferson's death, secession from the Union had been declared forever out of bounds in the name of Liberty.

The Nullification Crisis, then, was resolved in accordance with the views of the Constitution's "father." In vain do present-day libertarians complain about Madison's alleged inconsistency on the question of nullification. As we have seen, he was quite consistent, having called originally (at the Constitutional Convention in 1787) for an outright federal veto over all state legislation, but having settled for the Supremacy Clause as a middle ground approach to achieve "a due *subordination of the States* and to establish some measure of central control over their internal affairs."[20] Here again, those aggrieved by Liberty as incarnated in the Constitution are reduced to complaining about the results of the document saying what it says.

But South Carolina was not done. And neither was Calhoun. As Jackson accurately predicted: "The tariff was only the pretext, and disunion and a Southern Confederacy the real object. The next pretext will be the negro or slavery question."[21] In 1837, rising to object to petitions for the abolition of slavery addressed to the Senate, Calhoun declared that slavery was "[t]he peculiar institution of the South . . . on the maintenance of which the very existence of the slaveholding States depends. . . ." and that if the slaves were emancipated "we would soon find the present condition of the two races reversed. They and their northern allies would be the masters, and we the slaves. . . ."[22] That is, the perpetual enslavement of the black man was only the respectable status quo, whereas even the spectre of white enslavement or loss of liberty—including the liberty to own human chattels—was intolerable. This was the Southern position in its essence.

In a Senate committee report he authored to express support for the President's message calling for measures to prevent "the circulation of incendiary abolition petitions," the paladin of nullification and secession made it clear that the issue was

---

19. Howe, *What God Hath Wrought*, 401–02.

20. Hobson, "The Negative on State Laws," 228.

21. In ed. Frank Moore, *The Rebellion Record* (NY: G. P. Putnam, 1862), Vol. III, 44.

22. *Speech on the Reception of Abolition Petitions*, February 6, 1837, http://oll.libertyfund.org/index.php?option=com_staticxt&staticfile=show.php%3Ftitle=683&layout=html#chapter_107122.

not one of high moral principles but rather the property right in slaves and the Southern prosperity it insured. Referring to "the vast amount of property involved, equal to at least $950,000,000"—meaning nearly a billion dollars worth of enslaved human beings—Calhoun declared that "[t]o destroy the existing relations" between masters and slaves "would be to destroy this prosperity, and to place the two races in a state of conflict, which must end in the expulsion or extirpation of one or the other."[23]

Employing the Southern euphemism for slavery—"our institutions"—Calhoun promised a bloodbath upon any attempt to interfere with slavery, which was intrinsic to the South as a people and the very basis of Southern liberty:

> We of the South cannot, will not surrender our institutions. To maintain the existing relations between the two races inhabiting that section of the Union is indispensable to the peace and happiness of both. *It cannot be subverted without drenching the country in blood.* . . . Be it good or bad, it has grown up among our society and institutions, it is so interwoven among them that *to destroy it is to destroy us as a people.*[24]
>
> . . . .
>
> It [slavery] is to us a vital question. It involves not only our liberty, but, what is greater (if to freemen anything can be) *existence itself.* The relation which now exists between the two races in the slave-holding States has existed for two centuries. It has grown with our growth, and strengthened with our strength. *It has entered into and modified all our institutions, civil and political.* None other can be substituted. We will not, cannot, permit it to be destroyed. . . . [I]f, instead of denying all jurisdiction, and all interference in this question, the doors of Congress are to be thrown open; and we are to be exposed here, in the heart of the Union, to an endless attack on our rights, our character, and our institutions . . . if this is to be our fixed and permanent condition as members of this confederacy, we will then be compelled to turn our eyes on ourselves. Come what will, should it cost *every drop of blood, and every cent of property*, we must defend ourselves. . . . It is not we, but the Union which is in danger.[25]

It should not be surprising that Calhoun's speeches are archived today by the "Liberty Fund" as classic texts of Liberty, including his declaration in 1847 that "the relation now existing in the slaveholding States between the two [races], is, instead of an evil, a good—a positive good."[26] Calhoun had framed the *sine qua non* of the coming Civil War: preservation of the "peculiar institution" against even the threat

23. In *Speeches of John C. Calhoun* (NY: Harper and Brothers, 1843), 195.

24. Ibid., 224.

25. Ibid., 209–210.

26. John C. Calhoun, *Union and Liberty: The Political Philosophy of John C. Calhoun*, ed. Ross M. Lence (Indianapolis: Liberty Fund, 1992); Chapter: REVISED REPORT; accessed from http://oll.libertyfund.org/title/683/107124/1935247.

of abolition or any attempt to exclude its extension into the territories. And he would be instrumental in the annexation of Texas as a new slave state, a major step toward the war.

The Indian Removal Policy

The Jackson era provides an object lesson in how "republican government" at *both* the state and federal level tramples on the hapless people who get in its way. The problem was what to do with the Indians as the Temple of Liberty relentlessly expanded westward. Regarding the left bank of the Mississippi in the Louisiana Territory, for example, President Jefferson had thought that while "sheer obstinacy might cause the Indians to refuse land cessions to a benevolent government, their primitive honesty would incline them to pay their debts."[27] Thus he devised the scheme of encouraging the Creeks, Chickasaws, and Choctaws to make purchases of goods in federal stores at cost—the government thus driving out private merchant competition—so that when the Indians' debts for necessaries "get beyond what the individuals can pay, they become willing to lop them off by a cession of lands" to their sole creditor: the federal government.[28] Jefferson's cynical resort to federal monopoly power is but another example of how the facts of his career demolish the myth of his apostleship of "limited government."

The Indian problem would ultimately be "solved" in the 1860s and 1870s by herding the tribes from the wilderness areas of the far West, into which they had already been driven, onto discrete reservations. This development was in keeping with "the powerful sense of national destiny" and the "processes of conquest and nation building [which] seemed to alter the essential nature of the [West]; through a sort of patriotic transubstantiation, a number of western landscapes quickly became American Canterburys" that could no longer simply be left to the Indian tribes.[29] In the 1830s, however, the Western wilderness became the dumping ground for Indians in the path of Liberty's progress.

President Jackson proposed to deal with the Indians according to the distinctly Jeffersonian plan of deporting undesirables in order to eliminate the social problem caused by their inconvenient presence among the beneficiaries of the Revolution. In December 1829 he requested that Congress appropriate funds for the forcible removal of all the southeast Indians beyond the Mississippi River to western reservations. This would complete implementation of "the benevolent policy of the Government, steadily pursued for nearly thirty years," which was only part of the long process by which "[t]he tribes which occupied the countries now constituting the Eastern States were annihilated to make room for the whites."[30] After all, Jackson declared: "What good man would prefer the country to be covered with

---

27. R. S. Cotterill, *The Southern Indians: The Story of the Civilized Tribes before Removal* (Norman, OK: Univ. of Oklahoma Press, 1954), 139.

28. Jefferson to William Henry Harrison, in *Jeffersonian Cyclopedia*, §3927.

29. Mark David Spence, *Dispossessing the Wilderness: Indian Removal and the Making of the National Parks* (Oxford: Oxford Univ. Press, 2000), 4–5.

30. *First Annual Message to Congress*, December 8, 1829.

forests and ranged by few thousand savages to our extensive Republic . . . occupied by more than 12,000,000 happy people, and filled with all the blessings of liberty, civilization and religion?"

The Georgia legislature, emboldened by Jackson's election in 1828, had already led the way in this ethnic cleansing. Although the independence of the Cherokee nation in Georgia was supposedly secured by a federal treaty in 1791, "the State of Georgia had been chopping away at their lands for more than thirty years, and regarded the treaty as obsolete"[31]—a position that undoubtedly had something to do with the happy discovery of gold on Cherokee land. In the year of Jackson's election, Georgia simply declared by fiat that it now owned all Indian lands in the northwestern counties of the state, prohibited gold mining by Indians, nullified all laws of the Cherokee nation, and disqualified Indians from testifying against whites in judicial proceedings, thereby neatly precluding any claims for judicial relief.[32] The last provision paralleled the Southern state slave codes applicable to blacks.

Jackson did nothing about this, ignoring a storm of protest directed to the White House. On the contrary, conveniently invoking the same "states' rights" doctrine he had rejected during the Nullification Crisis, he declared a federal hands-off policy regarding state legislation against the tribes: "For the justice of the laws passed by the States within the scope of their reserved powers they are not responsible to this Government."[33] Jackson's path toward accommodation of Georgia's removal of the Cherokee had been prepared nearly thirty years earlier by Jefferson, in yet another example of the mythic character of "Jeffersonian limited government." In 1802, President Jefferson had entered into a compact with Georgia under which, in return for Georgia's surrender to the federal government of its *pro forma* claim to a western boundary at the Mississippi (which other former colonies had been granted as well), the federal government would insure the extinguishment of any Indian titles to land within Georgia's borders. The Georgia Compact was "[t]he real seed of the movement that resulted in the wholesale removal of the Southeastern tribes. . . ."[34]—and not just in Georgia.

Despite nationwide but ultimately futile opposition to Indian removal from religious organizations and churches, the Indian Removal Act of 1830 passed the House and Senate in April-May of that year, thanks in part to an increase in Southern representation in the House on account of the always helpful three-fifths rule. Ignoring a Supreme Court decision declaring that the State of Georgia had no jurisdiction over the Cherokee nation—just as Jefferson had ignored the decision of Justice Johnson during the Embargo—President Jackson "remained determined to coerce Indian removal, and he responded defiantly by withdrawing federal

31. Morison, *HAP*, 450.

32. Mary Hershberger, "Anticipating Abolition: the Struggle Against Indian Removal in the 1830s," *The Journal of American History*, Vol. 86, No. 1 (June 1999), 21.

33. *First Annual Message to Congress*, (1829).

34. In Frederick E. Hoxie, "What Was Taney Thinking? American Indian Citizenship in the Era of Dred Scott," 82 Chi.-Kent L. Rev. 329, 335 (2007), quoting Tim Alan Garrison, "The Legal Ideology of Removal: The Southern Judiciary and the Sovereignty of Native American Nations," 20 (2002).

troops from Georgia, leaving no buffer between the Cherokee and the state, which moved immediately to force the Indians out."[35]

The "republican government" of Georgia then enacted legislation requiring all white men residing in Cherokee zones—that is, white missionaries—to obtain a license and swear to uphold the laws of Georgia or face fines and prison. A Georgia jury convicted eleven missionaries of failing to comply with the law and sentenced them to expulsion or four years' hard labor. Two of the missionaries chose prison over expulsion, whereupon they were "marched in chains to the state penitentiary in Milledgeville." When the Supreme Court reversed their convictions on the previously enunciated grounds of Georgia's lack of jurisdiction over the Cherokee, "Georgia threatened violent resistance if blocked" and refused to release the prisoners, who were finally expelled after Jackson was reelected.[36] This was another example of the morally standardless doctrine of "nullification" at work.

In 1835 Senator Henry Clay condemned the conduct of the Georgia government on the floor of the Senate, noting that it marked the beginning of a series of state-sponsored violations of Indian rights:

> Georgia was the first that made these encroachments; she originated the plan of invading the Indian rights, and she had carried it far beyond all others. . . . By the first act Georgia abolished the Government of the Cherokee nation. No nation (said Mr. C.) can exist without a Government of some kind. These people had formed and established a Government in imitation of our own. But it was wholly immaterial what the humble form of that Government might be. Georgia had abolished it. She next proceeded to divide their territories into counties, and distribute them by lotteries among their citizens, every head of a family being entitled to the land drawn against his number. She did indeed reserve a small pittance of a few acres for those Indians who wished to remain within her limits, but under circumstances that rendered them worthless. She gave them no rights, no franchise, no single privilege. They were denied the power of testifying in courts of justice. No Indian could be a witness in favor of his fellows.[37]

The federally mandated removal of the Indians culminated with the infamous "Trail of Tears" in 1838, when federal troops under General Winfield Scott, serving under President Van Buren, rousted the Cherokee and led them on a forced march from Georgia to the West, during which a fourth of them died. Similar depredations occurred in Florida, where federal troops forcibly removed the Osceola Indians and marched them West after years of warfare in the Everglades. Clay's speech to the Senate in 1835 recited the long list of broken treaties with the Cherokee and the brutal injustices perpetrated upon them by the "republican government" of Georgia. But, to quote the always sober Professor Morison, while Clay's oration

---

35. Hershberger, op. cit., 30–31.

36. Ibid., 32.

37. *Congressional Globe*, February 4, 1835; quoted in *United States v. State of Mich.*, 471 F. Supp. 192, 202–03 (W.D. Mich. 1979).

"drew tears from the eyes of senators, they did nothing for the Cherokee except to expedite their removal."[38]

One prominent abolitionist, James Birney, noted that the removal of the Indians was reminiscent of Jefferson's approach to the deportation of the slaves. Birney scored as erroneous and inhumane Jefferson's advice in 1811 that while "It may perhaps be doubted whether many of these people would voluntarily consent to such an exchange of situation. . . . This should not, however, discourage the experiment, nor the early trial of it. . . ."[39] As Hershberger demonstrates, the widespread (but ineffectual) public opposition to *state* and federal tyranny over the Indians of the Southeast was a major factor in the emergence of the movement to abolish slavery, so that the Indian Removal crisis was another milestone on the road to the Civil War.[40]

The Texas Revolution

By the 1830s neighboring Mexico had been radically destabilized by the influence of the American Revolution, the French Revolution, the activities of Freemasonry, and the forcible installation of Napoleon's brother Joseph as King of Spain in 1808 during the Napoleonic Wars. In 1821 (after the fall of Napoleon and during the Bourbon Restoration in France), the Mexican War of Independence ended in a repudiated treaty to establish a constitutional monarchy independent of Spain, followed by the fleeting reign of the revolutionary general Iturbide as Emperor of Mexico in 1822, the overthrow of Iturbide, and the creation of a Mexican republic under Antonio Lopez de Santa Anna in 1823. Like the American revolutionaries who had risen to power in the name of Liberty, Santa Anna would rule with a far heavier hand than the distant king of the mother country or the overthrown Catholic emperor Iturbide (who was executed by firing squad upon his ill-fated return to Mexico from exile).

In Mexico the link between revolution and international Freemasonry could not have been more apparent. Santa Anna himself was a Mason (albeit ultimately a repentant one)[41] and none other than the United States Minister to Mexico during the John Quincy Adams administration, Joel R. Poinsett (for whom the Poinsettia plant he imported to South Carolina from Mexico is named), was instrumental in spreading the Masonic Spirit of 1776 south of the border. Elected "as grand high priest of the Grand Chapter of South Carolina" and Deputy Grand Master of the Grand Lodge of South Carolina in 1821, Poinsett massively breached diplomatic protocol by introducing York Rite Freemasonry to Mexico in competition with the already established Scottish Rite, assisting in the establishment of a Mexican Grand

38. Morison, *HAP*, 451.

39. Jefferson to John Lynch, January 21, 1811, in Lipscomb and Berg, *The Writings of Thomas Jefferson*, XIII, 12; Hershberger, op. cit., 38.

40. Hershberger, *Anticipating Abolition*, loc. cit.

41. At first a member of Mexico's Scottish Rite, he later "appeared to become a Yorkist." Denlsow and Truman, Part 2, 96–97. His Masonic affiliation saved his life after his capture by fellow Mason Sam Houston.

Lodge. Professor Morison describes the result of Poinsett's Masonic meddling: "All Mexico became divided into *Escoceses* and *Yorkinos*; civil war broke out, and Poinsett's name became the rallying point for one party and the target for the other. The Scots won, and Poinsett was recalled under a cloud."[42] Poinsett's activities prompted protests from Rome and the Mexican hierarchy that he was interfering in Mexican affairs and fomenting revolution. Despite his carefully worded denial of any intention of "extending *our order* and *our principles* into a neighboring country" for "political influence" as opposed to "pure and philanthropic purposes,"[43] Poinsett "has gone down in history as an interloper except to a minority such as his biographer, J. Fred Rippy, who defended his subject's interference in Mexican domestic affairs...."[44] Even an admiring Masonic biographer concedes that Poinsett (like Jefferson in France) "deviated from his role" as an ambassador, and lauds him on that account as a "revolutionary diplomat."[45]

While the Indians were being removed from Georgia and other places where they posed an obstacle to expansion of the United States, American settlers were bringing their slaves into the Mexican province of Texas (*Tejas*) under the cover of land grants to Anglophone immigrants willing to establish colonies there. The Santa Anna government, attempting to mitigate its own instability, had encouraged the colonization project as a buffer against anticipated United States aggression. It thus had a preference for Irish immigrants who, "among all European peoples, were identified as the most desirable settlers" because "they were loyal Catholics, having suffered cruel persecutions in defense of their faith... were regarded as having outstanding moral virtues [and] were not friendly to England or the United States, so that in the case of war, Mexico could rely on brave [Irish] soldiers... to defend its borders."[46] (And, indeed, it would be Irish immigrant soldiers who would defect from the U.S. Army and defend Mexico's borders during the coming Mexican-American War.)

The Mexican Constitution of 1824 prohibited slavery and established Catholicism as the sole and exclusive religion of the Mexican state. Accordingly, the land grants did not permit any importation of slaves and required that all settlers be (or at least become) Catholics in that Catholic country. Both legal strictures were evaded in the amazingly rapid advance of the Spirit of 1776 once it gained a foothold in Anglo-American colonies of only a few thousand settlers. One such colony was headed by Virginia-born and Missouri-bred Stephen F. Austin, for whom Austin, Texas would be named. A Mexican lieutenant made this prescient comment on

42. Morison, *HAP*, 419.

43. In Denslow and Truman, Part 2, 352.

44. Paul Rich and Lic. Guillermo De Los Reyes, "Towards A Revisionist View Of Poinsett: Problems In The Historiography Of Mexican Freemasonry," published paper, www.h-net.org/~latam/essays mason2. html. The co-authors are professors at the University of the Americas.

45. Leon Zeldis, "Poinsett: A Revolutionary Diplomat," in Pietre-Stones Review of Freemasonry @ http://www.freemasons-freemasonry.com/zeldis16.html.

46. Graham Davis, *Land!: Irish Pioneers in Mexican and Revolutionary Texas* (Texas A&M Univ. Press, 2003), 32.

Austin's outpost of slavery on Mexican soil: "The Americans in general are, in my opinion, lazy people of vicious character. Some of them cultivate their small farms, but this task they usually entrust to their Negro slaves, whom they treat with considerable harshness. In my judgment, the spark that will start the conflagration that will deprive us of Texas will start from this colony."[47]

With the influx of 25,000 Protestant Americans and their slaves in the early 1830s, the Anglo-American population outnumbered the native *Tejanos* by ten to one and the Irish Catholic settlers were a small minority. Among the wave of Protestant settlers were numerous folk heroes of Liberty, including the Southerners Sam Houston (of Tennessee by way of Virginia), Davey Crockett (from Tennessee), and Jim Bowie (of Kentucky and Louisiana) along with innumerable shady characters looking for a quick killing.

In 1835, with Mexico being racked by one civil war and revolution after another since winning its independence from Spain, Santa Anna dissolved the republican constitution and moved to consolidate the power of Mexico's central government. In response, the Anglo-Texans repeated a familiar process: they created Committees of Correspondence and Safety, held a Convention, issued a Declaration of Independence, formed a provisional government, and declared the independence of all of Texas from Mexico under their authority. The Texas Declaration of Independence, signed by fifty-two self-appointed "Plenipotentiaries" claiming to represent a new "Republic of Texas," included the requisite Protestant denunciations of the "army and the priesthood, both the eternal enemies of civil liberty" and the "despotism of the sword and the priesthood," as well as Mexico's intolerable "support of a national religion" (Catholicism) and its unpardonable failure to "to establish any public system of education, although possessed of almost boundless resources."[48] Of course, the revolutionaries could have left Texas and returned to the "land of the free and the home of the brave," as Francis Scott Key had called it some twenty years earlier. But instead they arrived at a more elegant solution: simply declare that Texas was another land of the free and home of the brave, thereby purporting to take possession of an entire Mexican province without benefit of such niceties as an actual legal title, while asserting political authority over all the inhabitants.

Thus, Mexico's naïve policy of encouraging American immigration in order to create a buffer zone against the United States had had precisely the opposite result: the creation of an American buffer zone against Mexico, soon to become an American possession. Daniel Cloud, a young lawyer arrived in Texas from Kentucky, could not have drawn more clearly the link between the Anglo-revolutionary heritage of rebellion, the Spirit of 1776, and the Texas Revolution:

> Inheriting the old Saxon spirit of 1640 in England, 1776 in America, the inhabitants of Texas throw off the chains of Santa Anna, assert their independence,

47. Lieutenant Jose Maria Sanchez, in *The West*, documentary, Episode 2, *Empire Upon the Trails*.
48. See *Texas Declaration of Independence*, November 7, 1835, http://www.tsl.state.tx.us/treasures/republic/declare-01.html.

assume a national sovereignty, and send a corps of diplomatic agents to the parent state of Washington [DC].[49]

After the siege of the Alamo and the slaughter of its defenders by Santa Anna, during which Davey Crockett and Jim Bowie were killed, came the culmination of this miniature replica of the American Revolution: the Battle of San Jacinto (1836). To cries of "Remember the Alamo," General Sam Houston charged to victory over Santa Anna, routing his army and securing the wounded captive general's signature on the treaties that ended the Texas War of Independence and wrested Texas from Mexico's control. The inscription on the monument to the battle which stands in Houston today proudly declares: "The slaughter was appalling, victory complete, and Texas free! . . . San Jacinto was one of the decisive battles of the world. The freedom of Texas from Mexico won here led to annexation and to the Mexican-American War, resulting in the acquisition by the United States of the States of Texas, New Mexico, Arizona, Nevada, California, Utah and parts of Colorado, Wyoming, Kansas and Oklahoma. Almost one-third of the present area of the American Nation, nearly a million square miles of territory, changed sovereignty." Changes of sovereignty at gunpoint are the very essence of Liberty in its march through the nations.

Although his adherence to Freemasonry was fickle, Santa Anna saved his own life by giving a "Masonic distress sign to . . . Sam Houston,"[50] his fellow Mason, who founded the Grand Lodge of Texas in 1837.[51] In appreciation for the treatment he had received from Houston and his subordinate John Stiles during his captivity, Santa Anna "presented his Masonic apron to Stiles," which was "displayed at a meeting of Friendship Lodge No. 16, Clarksville, Texas."[52] As for the Irish colonists, they had been faced with the "terrible dilemma of which side to support," given that they were loyal Catholics and friendly with the Mexican settlers, with whom they "cooperated in sharing town government, worshipped at the same Catholic church, and were bonded together by sharing the hardships of pioneer life."[53] But, caught in the revolutionary crossfire, many of the Irish were driven into the Anglo-Texan camp by Santa Anna's brutal attempt to crush the revolution, only to be forced to defend their holdings after the war against "American freebooters challenging the original claims."[54]

Thus, in a scant fifteen years the American presence in Mexico had grown from tiny colonies that were supposed to consist only of non-slaveholding Catholics to the overwhelmingly Protestant and slave-holding Republic of Texas under President Sam Houston, complete with an American-style constitution legalizing chattel slavery. The pertinent provision is almost amusingly emphatic in its protection of

49. Letter to his brother, December 26, 1835; quoted in Davis, *Land: Irish Pioneers*, 109.
50. Denslow and Truman, Part 2, 96.
51. Houston "presided over the meeting which established the Grand Lodge of Texas" and was "undoubtedly a Royal Arch Mason." Denslow and Truman, Vol. I, 256.
52. Denslow and Truman, Part 2, 97.
53. Davis, *Land: Irish Pioneers*, 114.
54. Ibid., 239.

the property right in human beings who happened to have dark skin: "All persons of color who were slaves for life previous to their emigration to Texas, and who are now held in bondage, shall remain in the like state of servitude, provided the said slave shall be the bona fide property of the person so holding said slave as aforesaid." In the Republic of Texas slaves could not even be emancipated by their owners without consent of the Congress of Texas, unless the emancipated slave was exiled from the Republic. Citizenship in the Republic did not extend to "Africans, the descendants of Africans, and Indians."[55] And, of course, the Catholic *ethos* of former *Tejas* was explicitly declared abolished: "No preference shall be given by law to any religious denomination or mode of worship over another, but every person shall be permitted to worship God according to the dictates of his own conscience."[56] It might be more accurate to call this new incarnation of Liberty the Protestant *Masonic* Republic of Texas, for the very assembly that formed the Grand Lodge of Texas took place in the Senate Chamber of the State Capital,[57] President Houston presiding,[58] and every president of the short-lived Texas Republic was a Mason.[59]

In 1837 the Republic of Texas received diplomatic recognition by the United States under President Jackson, Houston's fellow Southerner and fellow Mason, a member of the same Masonic lodge.[60] Houston sent commissioners to Washington to explore the possibility of the annexation of Texas, an idea warmly approved by Houston's other fellow Southerner and Mason, former ambassador Poinsett,[61] now serving as Secretary of War and supervising the Indian removal operation. By 1842 the new President of Texas, the aptly named Mirabeau Buonaparte Lamar, yet another fellow Mason,[62] was attempting to seize vast northern swatches of Mexico

---

55. *The Constitution of the Republic of Texas* (1836), General Provisions, §§ 9–10, University of Texas Law School e-text, http://tarlton.law.utexas.ed/constitutions/ text/ccRights.html.

56. Ibid., Declaration of Rights, Article 3.

57. See http://www.grandlodgeoftexas.org/node/1238.

58. To this day Masonic degrees are conferred in the Senate Chamber. ("On August 21st [2010] starting at about 9 AM a Master Mason's Degree will be conferred in the Senate Chamber of the State Capital by Canyon Lake Lodge No. 1425. All Master Masons are invited. You will need to bring a current dues card, a picture ID (if a Texas Mason) and an apron.") See, www.grandlodgeoftexas.org/node/2507.

59. "The second president of the Republic of Texas, Mirabeau B. Lamar, was a Mason, as were *all* of the Presidents of the Republic of Texas." In "A History of Free Masonry and Public Schools in Texas," http://www.eastforklodge.org. (emphasis in original). "To separate the Grand Lodge of the Republic of Texas from the Republic of Texas is not easily accomplished." In "The Grand Lodge of the Republic of Texas," duckcreek1419.org/Masonic%20History/m-dec.htm.

60. Cumberland Lodge No. 8 in Nashville, TN. Cf. medlibrary.org/medwiki/Grand_ Lodge_of_Tex s#Grand_Lodge_of_the_Republic_of_Texas. Jackson's record of Masonic membership begins in 1801, at Greenville Lodge No. 3. He served as Grand Master of the Grand Lodge of Tennessee, to which he introduced no less than General Lafayette. He assisted in laying the Masonic cornerstone of Jackson City (across the Potomac from Washington) in 1836. Denslow and Truman, Vol. I, 283–84.

61. James Haley, *Sam Houston* (Norman, OK: Univ. of Oklahoma Press, 2004), 196. (Houston's commissioner, Peter Grayson, wrote to Houston from Washington to advise that Poinsett's "warmth on the subject seems equal to our own. . . .").

62. Lamar was apprenticed as a Mason in Columbus, Ohio, reaching the degree of Fellowcraft in Harmony Lodge of Galveston on July 21, 1840 while President of Texas. Cf. Denslow and Truman, Part II, 49.

to create an even bigger republic. He was to be succeeded by Houston in his second term as President of Texas after the venture failed.

Facing the prospect of a British-mediated recognition of the Texas Republic by Mexico on condition that slavery be abolished within its borders, the Southern states, conveniently forgetting Jeffersonian "strict construction" of the Constitution—just as Jefferson had done whenever it suited his purposes—maneuvered in Congress to obtain annexation. The leader of the Southern faction was President John Tyler of Virginia, a substantial slave-owner himself who had ascended to the Presidency from the office of Vice President upon the death of President Harrison in 1841. The Constitution made no provision for annexing a foreign country. Moreover, the Southern states were unable to obtain the constitutionally required 2/3 vote of the Senate ratifying a treaty with Texas, including a version proposed by Senator John C. Calhoun of "nullification" fame. The Southern bid for annexation was hardly helped by Calhoun's infamous letter to the British minister in Washington, Richard Pakenham. In this bizarre missive, Calhoun protested British intervention in Mexico and argued against the abolition of slavery in Texas on grounds that included the contention that the proportion of "deaf and dumb, blind, idiots and insane of negroes" was seven times higher in "the States that have changed the ancient relation between the races [than in] the States adhering to it."[63] Undeterred by the strict constitutional limits he had trumpeted during the Nullification Crisis, Calhoun joined Tyler in the move to obtain a wholly irregular Congressional "resolution" for annexation adopted by a bare majority of both Houses, which passed only days before the end of Tyler's term. Texas accepted the invitation to annexation and was incorporated into the Union on December 29, 1845. The Lone Star Republic became the Lone Star State—and a new stronghold of slavery. In keeping with the Anglo-Protestant-Masonic revolutionary dynamic of Liberty, however, the same sorts of cadres that had declared secession from Mexico and then clamored for annexation by the United States would declare the secession of Texas from the United States a mere sixteen years later.

Thus was completed the first step in a program of Southern expansionism led by Southern Presidents and the Southern contingent in Congress. The annexation of Texas supported allegations of a conspiracy by "Slave Power" to establish a Southern slave empire that would extend into Mexico and embroil America in a foreign war. In a most ironic analogue to later Southern arguments, opponents of the annexation protested that it constituted a breach of the constitutional compact that would justify secession by the *Northern* states. The prominent jurist William Jay, son of John Jay, elaborated the argument that "[t]he compact between the States embodied in the Constitution was destroyed by the South...when Texas was admitted by a simple majority of both Houses rather than by a two-thirds vote of the Senate, as required for transactions with a foreign power." The annexation, said Jay, signaled an "indefinite extension of the southern boundary" and a "perpetual

63. Calhoun to Pakenham, April 18, 1844, in ed. Richard K. Crallé, *The Works of John C. Calhoun* (NY: D. Appleton and Company, 1855), Vol. V, 337.

slave-holding control of the federal government," so that "'continuance of the union' would 'enslave the North rather than free the South.'"[64] The policies of incoming President Polk could not have been better designed to lend support to this theory of a Slave Power conspiracy.

The Conquest of Mexico, Nativism, and Southern Imperialism

The annexation of Texas prompted Mexico to sever diplomatic ties with the United States, now under President James K. Polk. Polk was another Southern gentleman—from Tennessee by way of North Carolina—who owned numerous slaves by inheritance and continued to own and operate a large cotton plantation in Mississippi until his death in 1849, shortly after the end of his one term as President. A member of the Royal Arch order that Joel Poinsett had introduced into Mexico with calamitous results, Polk was among the Freemasons of the South (including Poinsett and Andrew Jackson) who played leading roles in the advance of Liberty for slaveholders through territorial conquest.[65]

Polk had run for office on a pro-slavery platform amidst Southern cries of "54-40 or Fight," meaning 54 degrees, 40 minutes latitude, an extension of the northern boundary of the United States in the Oregon Territory into British-held Canada all the way up to Alaska. Southern agitation for annexation of Oregon (ultimately achieved peacefully by treaty with England) was meant to render more palatable to Northern politicians Polk's plan for a southwestern expansion of slavery. Elected at the peak of the anti-Catholic Nativist movement in America (roughly 1835–1855), Polk's jingoism was in keeping with the belief of the "anti-Catholic, anti-immigrant forces . . . that native-born Americans held the God-given right to conquer the continent from the Atlantic to the Pacific and to 'cleanse the dominions of Romish and foreign blight.'"[66]

Looking to the southwest, Polk very much wanted to acquire California as the next advance toward America's "manifest destiny" under the Monroe Doctrine. Unable to induce Mexico to sell California, however, he simply contrived a war with her. The pretext was debts Mexico owed United States citizens on indemnities for damage suffered to American properties during the revolutions and civil wars that had been convulsing Mexico since her break with Spain. Mexico refused even to discuss the terms Polk proposed: the ceding of New Mexico and Upper California and acceptance of the Rio Grande as the southern border of the United States, in return for America's assuming Mexico's debts (a mere $3 million) and paying an additional negotiated price for the same territory she had already adamantly

---

64. In Robert William Fogel, *Without Contract or Consent: the Rise and Fall of American Slavery* (NY: W. W. Norton & Co., 1989), 325.

65. Initiated into the three degrees of Royal Arch Freemasonry on April 5, 22 and 24, 1825, in the Lafayette Chapter of his home town of Columbia, TN. His remains were reinterred on the grounds of the State Capitol in Nashville with Masonic ceremonies. Denslow and Truman, Part 2, 353–54.

66. Peter F. Stevens, *The Rogue's March: John Riley and the St. Patrick's Battalion, 1846–48* (Washington, DC: Potomac Books, Inc., 2005 [1999]), 28.

refused to sell. When President Herrera declined to receive the American ambassador, John Slidell, Polk ordered General Zachary Taylor to cross the Nueces River
(then the southernmost border of Texas) and occupy the eastern bank of the Rio
Grande. A resulting skirmish with Mexican cavalry, producing American casualties, was all Polk needed for a Congressional declaration of war on May 13, 1846.
Only John Quincy Adams and "13 other congressmen, viewing the conflict as the
work of expansionist slave-owners, voted against it."[67]

Future Civil War generals Taylor and the Freemason Winfield Scott,[68] both Virginians, were among the U.S. generals participating in the Mexican conquest by an
invasionary force in which Southern generals and Southern volunteers (especially
from Tennessee) predominated. Also participating in the officer ranks with distinction were Lieutenant Ulysses Grant, under Taylor, Captain Robert E. Lee, under
Scott, and Thomas ("Stonewall") Jackson. Lee, whose notorious father Henry
"Light-Horse Harry" had served with distinction as a general under Washington
during the Revolutionary War, was promoted to colonel on account of his service
to Scott. Scott declared that "his success in Mexico was largely due to the skill, valor
and undaunted energy of Robert E. Lee" and would later hail Lee as "the greatest
military genius in America."[69] Lee's greatest laurel was the American victory at the
Battle of Chapultepec Castle (1847), for his role in that victory helped make possible the capture of the forts that protected Mexico City, the occupation of the Mexican capital, and the defeat of Mexico.

For his participation in the Battle of Chapultepec and the siege of Mexico City,
the future Confederate hero "Stonewall" Jackson earned several promotions. At
Mexico City, he unquestioningly obeyed an order to mow down a crowd of panicked civilians in the main thoroughfare with artillery fire when the city was not
evacuated by the deadline General Scott had established. Though he "abhorred
such action," Jackson "felt no reason to question a directive from his superiors. 'My
duty is to obey orders' he said then and always."[70] Yet he had earlier refused a direct
order by General Worth to retire his forces from the battlefield during the fighting
at Chapultepec.[71] Also distinguishing himself in the war was Jefferson Davis, who
would become Secretary of War during the administration of President Franklin
Pierce (1853–57). As Colonel Davis, the future President of the Confederate States
led the Mississippi Rifles, suffering a foot wound during the Battle of Buena Vista
after having participated in the Siege of Monterey.

One of the bloodiest battles of the war took place at the monastery of Churubusco near Mexico City on August 20, 1847. Among the defenders of the monastery
were a brigade of several hundred defectors from the American army known as the

67. Stevens, Rogue's March, 127.

68. Dinwiddie Union Lodge, No. 23, inducted 1805. Denslow and Truman, Part 2, 115.

69. In eds Armistead Lindsay Long and Marcus Joseph Wright, Memoirs of Robert E. Lee (NY: J. M.
Stoddart and Company, 1887), 61.

70. James I. Robertson, Jr., Stonewall Jackson: the Man, the Soldier, the Legend (NY: MacMillan Publishing USA, 1997), 69.

71. Ibid., 67.

San Patricios or Saint Patrick's Brigade, so named because it was composed mostly of Irish Catholic immigrants. The *San Patricios* were led by the Irishman John Riley, who had served as an artillery sergeant in the British army. In a Catholic version of the last stand at the Alamo, sixty percent of the *San Patricios* were wiped out during the battle. The *San Patricios* are viewed by Mexicans as martyr-heroes of Mexican history, with "medals, memorial plaques, annual ceremonies, and public schools honoring them. . . ."[72] During the battle General Scott had suffered the loss of more than 1,000 men or twelve percent of his 9,000-man army, the worst losses for the American forces during the entire Mexican War. General Santa Anna (returned from exile) declared that "if he had commanded a few hundred more men like them, he would have won the battle."[73] While a hundred of the *San Patricios* escaped, Riley and numerous others were captured and would face the death penalty.

The *San Patricios* are dismissed as craven deserters in the American narrative of the glorious Mexican conquest. But it was no ordinary group of deserters that not only left the American ranks but fought for Mexico as the single most formidable brigade in the Mexican army, marching under a green silk banner bearing the Mexican coat of arms, the legend *Erin go Brag* ("Ireland forever") and an image of Saint Patrick. A brief digression concerning the *San Patricios* is worthwhile for what it reveals about a theme of this study: Liberty's intrinsic hostility toward Catholicism or anything resembling a Catholic and "papist" social order.

Because the regular United States Army lacked the manpower to conquer Mexico, the Polk administration had to resort to recruiting among the immigrant population. Thus nearly half of the American Army of Occupation (at first called the "Army of Observation") was composed of European immigrants without citizenship. Most of these were Irishmen who had fled Protestant-ruled Ireland during the potato famine or "Great Hunger" of 1845–1847. From the time of the Forgotten Famine of 1817, when John Riley was a boy, the Catholics of Ireland, dispossessed of their tenancies by Protestant landowners and living on the edge of starvation, "lay virtually prostrate beneath their Anglo-Irish Protestant lords." Gustave De Beaumont, the French man of letters who accompanied Alexis de Tocqueville on his celebrated journey to America during the 1830s, once observed that almost two centuries after Cromwell's conquest of the Emerald Isle—during the English birth pangs of Liberty we examined in Chapter 3—Ireland was "still full of Catholics' terror of his name." Tocqueville himself wrote in 1821 that in Ireland "All of the rich Protestants whom I see speak of Catholics with extraordinary hatred and scorn. The latter, they say, are savages and fanatics, led into all sorts of disorders by their priests."[74]

Recruited from the slums of America's industrial cities, Riley and his desperately poor fellow Irish immigrants were promised good pay, a wholesome diet, honor and promotions, and an opportunity to avenge past wrongs by fighting the English in the Oregon Territory. Instead they would receive the same abiding Protestant

72. Robert Ryal Miller, *Shamrock and Sword* (Norman, OK: Univ. of Oklahoma Press, 1989), 183.
73. Ibid., 90.
74. Stevens, *The Rogue's March*, 13.

hatred of Catholics they had endured in Ireland. But then they had come to a nation founded by Protestants who had rebelled against the authority of other Protestants; and America in the 1840s, "imbued with the historical and cultural traits of its pilgrim, puritan, and Anglican founders, was still England's child."[75] While the government desperately needed Irish bodies, the Mexican War was being waged at the height of the Nativist (anti-immigrant) movement and the cusp of the Know-Nothing movement that was its political arm (so named because those who attended its secret meetings professed to know nothing about them).

It was not long before Irish recruits realized they had "been sold a proverbial bill of goods by the U.S. Army, its own pledge a Nativist fraud."[76] Irish immigrant soldiers were brutally mistreated by an entirely Protestant officer corps that systematically subjected them to a double standard of military justice and punishment: comparative leniency for native-born soldiers and the harshest possible penalties for the Irish and other immigrants, even for trivial or non-existent offenses. Southern officers in particular treated all the regulars, especially the Irish immigrants, like the slaves that some had brought along with them. In addition to this abuse, the living conditions were horrible even for the military; the promised wholesome food turned out to be rancid beef and maggot-filled hardtack, and many succumbed to dysentery from contaminated drinking water.[77]

"Nativist prejudice, combined with contempt for Roman Catholicism, was widespread in the American Army," notes historian Robert Ryal Miller. And such incidents of anti-Catholic mob violence as the burning of the Ursuline Convent in Charlestown, Massachusetts in 1834 and the burning of St. Augustine's Church and other church properties during the anti-Catholic riots in Philadelphia in 1844 were still recent memories. The Irish recruits were taunted as "micks" and "potato heads" by both the officers and non-Catholic regulars, who "disparaged the Catholic Church [in Mexico], calling its rituals 'absurd' and 'flummery.'"[78] For the Irish in the Army of Occupation, "Nativist epithets and unrelenting brutal discipline furnished little proof that America had 'adopted them.'"[79] Worse, having been deprived of Catholic chaplains, Irish soldiers were forced by many officers to attend Protestant services, and they were punished for refusing to do so. The objection of one Dennis O'Tool, who was urged (but not required) by his lieutenant to attend a Protestant service, typified the feelings of the Irish recruits: "Sure, Lieutenant, the Blessed Virgin knows I'm bad enough already without sinning my soul any more by going to hear a swaddling preacher mocking the holy religion."[80]

Finally, Irish immigrant recruits had to contend with the knowledge that instead of fighting the English, as the recruiters had falsely suggested, they were going to be

---

75. Stevens, *The Rogue's March*, 21.

76. Ibid., 94.

77. Ibid., 40–57, 142.

78. Miller, op. cit., 157–162.

79. Stevens, op. cit., 64.

80. George Ballentine, *Autobiography of an English Soldier in the United States Army* (NY: Stringer & Townsend, 1853), 41.

fighting Mexicans—members of their own religion. The administration had "failed to comprehend the inherent problems of sending immigrant Catholic troops into battle against Catholic Mexico at the behest of a Protestant nation."[81] The historian Peter F. Stevens paints a vivid picture of the scene on the east bank of the Rio Grande just before the declaration of war: "the crosses crowning graceful bell towers" of the Catholic churches of Matamoras were plainly visible only a few hundred yards away, and the Irishmen could hear the ringing of the church bells and see the priests in white vestments sprinkling holy water on the cannons defending the city. In that moment they knew that, as Catholics who had "fled a Catholic land conquered by another army trumpeting Anglo-Saxon superiority and reviling papists," they had been "sent to provoke a war" against their fellow Catholics in a Catholic land just across the river. The conviction that they were on the wrong side of a foreign war was nurtured by English-language leaflets appealing to Catholic guilt. Their consciences were also pricked by a widely publicized 1843 open letter from the famed Irish barrister and crusader for Catholic emancipation, Daniel O'Connell, who "had blasted America's proposed annexation of Texas, slavery, and Northerners and Southerners alike for anti-Catholic bigotry." O'Connell "exhorted Irishmen never to volunteer in an American campaign for annexation on behalf of slave-owners. 'It was not in Ireland you this learned this cruelty. Your mothers were gentle, kind, and humane. . . . How can your souls have become tainted with such a darkness?'"[82]

With the Army of Occupation encamped alongside the Rio Grande, Irish soldiers and other immigrants who had been mocked, physically abused and humiliated for months by Protestant superiors and regulars, jumped one after the other into the river and swam to the other side. So many were defecting that Gen. Taylor, in "a blatant violation of the Articles of War," issued a "shoot-to-kill" order amounting to summary execution for "desertion" when war had not yet been declared. Scores of soldiers defied the order and defected anyway.[83] To stem the tide of desertions, after war had been declared Taylor urgently requested that the administration provide Catholic chaplains. Polk sent two Jesuit priests on a "secret" mission to serve unofficially in that capacity, it being of course quite impossible for the United States of America to have official Catholic chaplains. At least de facto, however, the two *sub rosa* Jesuits were the first Catholic chaplains in the history of the U.S. Army.[84]

While some of the *San Patricios* were no doubt induced to join the Mexican army by offers of land and money or by the senselessly brutal discipline of the officer corps, there is no denying the fundamental role of Catholic loyalty in the defections. As John Riley would put it, writing after the war: "listening only to the advice of my conscience for the liberty of a people which had had war brought

81. Stevens, *The Rogue's March*, 58.

82. Cf. "Letter of Daniel O'Connell on American Slavery" (1843), Johns Hopkins digital archive, http://www.archive.org/details/letterofdanielocooocon; Stevens, op. cit., 63.

83. Stevens, op. cit., 76, 81–87.

84. Ibid., 134–35.

them by the most unjust aggression, I separated myself from the North American forces...."[85] Nor was this merely Riley's after-the-fact justification of his own actions. The notable autobiography of George Ballentine, an English artilleryman in the Army of Occupation, reveals that "[a]s the majority of these deserters were Irish, the cause commonly assigned by the officers for their desertion, was, that, as they were Catholics, they imagined that they were fighting against their religion in fighting the Mexicans."[86] Although in Ballentine's view the "barbarous modes of punishment" were a greater factor than religion in driving immigrant soldiers to desert, this would not explain why the Catholics among them not only deserted but took up arms and fought valiantly for the Mexican side under Riley. As Catholics whose roots in an endemically hostile Protestant America were tenuous at best, they could be expected to respond to appeals to the Catholic conscience during what was essentially a Protestant invasion of a Catholic country. And it was an invasion in which thousands of their fellow Catholics, including civilian bystanders, were being killed by Protestant soldiers, churches and chapels damaged by bombardments or desecrated and robbed by out-of-control volunteer regiments, and religious processions disrupted. As a pamphlet authored by Santa Anna himself declared:

> Irishmen, listen to the words of your brothers, hear the accents of a Catholic people.... Is religion no longer the strongest of human bonds? ... Can you fight by the side of those who put fire to your temples in Boston and Philadelphia? ... If you are Catholic, the same as we, if you follow the doctrines of our Saviour, why are you seen sword in hand murdering your brethren? ... Are Catholic Irishmen to be the destroyers of Catholic temples [and] the murderers of Catholic priests ... in this pious nation?[87]

The *San Patricios* captured during the Battle of Churubusco, including Riley, were tried by a *pro forma* court-martial on the outskirts of Mexico City. Riley and several others were spared the death penalty by General Scott, who overruled the judgments of the drumhead court-martial because under the Articles of War a death sentence could not be imposed on those who had deserted before the Congressional declaration of war. (That conclusion was an implicit recognition that General Taylor's earlier shoot-to-kill order was both illegal and immoral.) To his great credit, Scott resisted all pressure to put at least Riley to death, vowing that "Sooner that the life of Riley should be taken, he would rather with his whole army be put to the sword" during the coming final assault on Mexico City.[88] After a few pardons and reductions of sentence by Scott, the *San Patricio* prisoners were either hung or flogged and branded on the cheek with the letter D (for deserter) in a mass display of public retribution, despite the pleas of the Archbishop of Mexico and even American citizens residing in Mexico City, who petitioned Scott for "a pardon

85. Miller, op. cit., 161–163, 142.
86. Ballentine, op. cit., 281–82.
87. Miller, 162–63.
88. Stevens, op. cit., 264.

to Captain John O'Reilly [sic] of the Legion of Saint Patrick, and generally speaking for all deserters to the American service."[89]

At San Angel, Riley and six other *San Patricios* received fifty lashes and branding, their flayed backs "hav[ing] the appearance of a pounded piece of raw beef, the blood oozing from every stripe." Since the letter D had been branded upside down on Riley's right cheek, he was branded a second time on the left cheek. The flogging and branding were followed by the simultaneous mass hanging of sixteen other *San Patricios*, attended by "five Catholic priests in canonicals, with a crucifix in one hand"[90] while Riley and the other prisoners were forced to watch. The sixteen were hung from the backs of mule-drawn carts driven out from under them. Their bodies were carted off to a nearby cemetery or buried on the spot by Riley and the others, who were required to dig the graves. Then, for good measure, the prisoners were forced to kneel while their heads were shaved with straight razors, "leaving each scalp a bloody latticework." One Captain Davis wrote that had he not been ordered to attend the barbaric spectacle "nothing on earth could have influenced my witnessing what I did."[91] The infliction of these punishments was supervised by Gen. David E. Twiggs of Georgia, another Southern leader of the Mexican conquest, who was wounded in battle and served as military governor of Veracruz, receiving a ceremonial sword from Congress. When counting off the fifty lashes for Riley, Twiggs dragged out the count in an effort to maximize blood loss and then pretended to lose count, adding nine more lashes in the hope of achieving the death penalty Scott had refused to impose.[92]

Thirty more *San Patricios* were hanged *en masse* near Mixcoac under the supervision of Colonel William Selby Harney of Tennessee, still another slave-owning Southern hero of the Mexican War. Harney's long history of brutality included raping and hanging Indian girls during the Seminole Wars in Florida and the fatal bludgeoning of one of his own female slaves because she lost his keys, resulting in an indictment for murder and his temporary flight from St. Louis. Despite the admitted fatal beating, Harney was acquitted because "people in Harney's day felt little anguish for slave and servant victims of such violence." As one of his friends had assured him when urging him to return to St. Louis for trial: "Accidents such as yours have happened to others here of which no notice was taken either by the people or any of the courts."[93] The War Department's own files reflect multiple courts martial and Harney's notorious "profanity, brutality, incompetency, peculation, recklessness, insubordination, tyranny and mendacity."[94]

With a dramatic flourish, Harney timed the simultaneous hanging of the thirty to coincide with the raising of the Stars and Stripes over the captured Chapultepec

89. Ibid., 261.
90. Ibid., 104–105.
91. Stephens, 269.
92. Miller, 103; Stephens, 267.
93. George Rollie Adams, *General William S. Harney: Prince of Dragoons* (Lincoln, NE: Univ. of Nebraska Press, 2001), 47–48.
94. Miller, 106–107.

Castle, visible two miles distant from the gallows. When only twenty-nine *San Patricios* were presented for hanging, Harney demanded that the thirtieth, one Francis O'Conner, who had lost both his legs at Churubusco and was dying, "be transported from the medical tent to the gallows where he was propped up alongside his companions."[95] When told of the condemned man's condition, Harney shouted: "Bring the damned son of a bitch out! My order was to hang 30 and by God I'll do it!" When asked if the hanged men could be taken down from the gallows, Harney replied: "No, I was ordered to have them hanged, and I have no orders to *unhang* them."[96] Harney was promoted to brigadier general.

Despite the mass executions, the *San Patricio* brigade continued to gain Irish recruits—and not only deserters. The Irish desertions from America's invading army would coincide with the "growing realization that the United States was not fighting a war of liberty, but that it was fighting a war of conquest, and it was fighting against the people who were fellow Catholics...."[97] Which brings us to the point of this digression concerning the *San Patricios*: that a Protestant war of conquest led by anti-Catholic Nativists against a neighboring Catholic nation *was* a war of Liberty in the sense we have been examining on these pages.

From the Mexican perspective, of course, the conflict was an unjust war of aggression by an imperialist power intent on territorial expansion, which it indubitably was. From the American perspective, at least according to ephemeral popular sentiment whipped up by the press, the war had "offered reassurances that the beliefs undergirding American romanticism still had meaning." Americans were regaled by tales of victory against all odds in "the halls of Montezuma," and the war "was even compared with the American Revolution, its heroes with those of 1776."[98] As Walt Whitman enthused in one of his pro-war newspaper columns: "There is hardly a more admirable impulse in the human soul than patriotism."[99] As the war dragged on, however, a "spectrum of opposition" developed in Congress that included both conservative and radical Whigs, "anti-administration Democrats... [and] a radical clutch of abolitionists, pacifists, and reformers."[100] By war's end, writes Miller, "war guilt haunted many Americans. Some citizens regarded it as unjustified aggression against a weak neighbor; others envisioned a plot of slaveholders to extend their territory...."[101] Congressional opposition to the war as unjust and unconstitutional included, ironically enough, men who would be on opposite sides of the Civil War: Congressman Abraham Lincoln from Illinois, and Congressman Alexander H. Stephens (future Confederate Vice President) and Senator Robert Toombs (future Confederate Secretary of State), both from Georgia.

95. Ibid., 107–08.

96. Stevens, op. cit., 271, 276.

97. Ibid., 143.

98. K. Jack Bauer, *The Mexican War, 1846–48* (Lincoln, NE: Univ. of Nebraska Press, 1992 [1974]), intro. by Robert Johannsen, xviii.

99. Ibid.

100. Ibid., 358.

101. Miller, op. cit., 167.

Under the Treaty of Guadalupe Hidalgo (1848), Mexico formally ceded fifty-five percent of its territory to the United States. In addition to Texas, to which Mexico relinquished any claim, the Mexican Cession comprised what are now the States of California, Nevada, Utah, Arizona and New Mexico. In return, the United States paid a paltry $15 million plus assumption of the preexisting $3 million debt to American citizens. Now stretching "from sea to shining sea," the United States had opened up a huge new arena for the expansion of slavery and the conflict over it that would lead to civil war. The Mexican War, the first American war on foreign soil and the first involving occupation of a foreign capital, was "an adventure in imperialism of the South, in partnership with the restless inhabitants of the West. It was provoked by a Southern president and fought largely by Southern generals and by Southern volunteers. It furnished the training school of practical experience for most of the Confederate and Union officers who participated in the Civil War."[102]

This is not to suggest that there was no imperialist impulse from the North at work in the war. William J. Worth, a Freemason[103] from Albany who served as a brigadier general during the war and personally tore down the Mexican flag from the National Palace in Mexico City, expressed the Northern attitude this way: "Why [does] Mexico matter? Have not our Anglo-Saxon race been land stealers from time immemorial and why shouldn't they? When their gaze is fixed upon other lands, the best way is to make out the deeds."[104] But Worth was a Northern imperialist who served Southern aims. Shortly after the war ended he engaged in a plot to overthrow Spanish colonial rule in Cuba and annex Cuba to the United States. The Havana Club, a group of Cuban Freemasons and slaveowners, proposed the idea to Worth through its representative, the Freemason and revolutionist Ambrosio José Gonzales, who (after an exchange of Masonic signals to confirm their brotherhood) offered Worth $3 million to lead an armed invasion by an American expeditionary force employing Mexican War veterans. Worth accepted. The plan, which had the endorsement of John C. Calhoun and involved Robert E. Lee and other Southern military leaders, became an extension of Southern imperialist designs. But the expedition was prohibited by executive order of newly-elected President Zachary Taylor, who wished to preserve United States neutrality, and the expeditionary ships were seized by the government.[105] Gonzales, however, would find an outlet for his revolutionary passions by serving as a colonel in the Confederate Army.

102. Eaton, *A History of the Old South*, 365.
103. He received a Masonic burial; a memorial was dedicated to him at the Grand Lodge of New York. Denslow and Truman, Part 2, 351.
104. In Stevens, op. cit., 68.
105. The details and participants in the scheme, including their Masonic affiliation and the evidence of Lee's involvement are discussed in Antonio Rafael de la Cova, *Cuban Confederate Colonel: The Life of Ambrosio José Gonzales* (Columbia, SC: Univ. of South Carolina Press, 2003), 2–27. The author notes Lee's otherwise inexplicable presence in New York City on three separate occasions just before the planned but aborted departure of the mission.

Between battlefield deaths and disease, the Mexican War had cost America 25,000 lives. Mexico had suffered a like number of casualties in addition to the economic devastation of a conquered nation that now had to cope with "tens of thousands of orphans, widows, and cripples."[106] In his memoirs, written with frantic energy as he was dying of throat cancer some forty years later, none other than General Grant condemned both the annexation of Texas, which he had "bitterly opposed," and the resulting Mexican War, which he described as "one of the most unjust ever waged by a stronger against a weaker nation."[107] As he confessed elsewhere: "I know the struggle I had with my conscience during the Mexican War. I have never altogether forgiven myself for going into that. I had very strong opinions on the subject. I don't think there was ever a more wicked war than that waged by the United States upon Mexico. I thought so at the time, when I was a youngster, only I had not moral courage enough to resign."[108] In defense of John Riley and his fellow Catholic *San Patricios*, who never really were Americans, it is at least arguable that they had more than the courage merely to resign; they had the courage to leave the army of an unjust aggressor and defend the victims of its unjust aggression.

One of the supreme ironies of the history of Liberty is that only fourteen years after his prominent role in this naked conquest of America's neighbor to the south, Colonel Robert E. Lee would tender his resignation to General Scott—a fellow Virginian who would *not* secede—and assume command of one of the Confederate armies opposing an invasion of the *American* South by a Northern army whose head would be Grant. Jefferson Davis, who had also distinguished himself during the conquest of Mexico, would see his fledgling Confederate States of America conquered in much the same manner. Lee's and Davis's Mexican exploits had helped bring on the very war that would pit them against their former comrades-in-arms. And just as the Mexicans had hated the *gringos* who conquered their agrarian nation, so would Confederates come to hate the "damn Yankees" who would conquer the agrarian South.

That the Mexican War was a morally indefensible prequel to disaster for the South was intimated by none other than Calhoun, who predicted that the conquest of Mexico would be seen as proof positive of the Slave Power conspiracy, provoke a massive anti-slavery backlash, and destroy the Southern-leaning balance of power in Congress.[109] Rising to protest the war in the Senate, he had spoken of a "mysterious connection between the fate of this country and that of Mexico" and warned that "Mexico was to us forbidden fruit; and that, if we should consume that fruit, it would be almost tantamount to the political death of our own institutions."[110] In the same vein, but from a Northern perspective, Grant confessed in his memoirs:

---

106. Miller, 169.

107. In *Personal Memoirs of Ulysses S. Grant* (NY: Cosimo, Inc., 2007), 16.

108. In Geoffrey Perret, *Ulysses S. Grant: Soldier & President* (Modern Library Paperbacks: 2009), Kindle Edition, 52.

109. Fogel, *Without Consent or Contract*, 301.

110. *Abridgement of the Debates of Congress from 1789 to 1856* (NY: D. Appleton & Co., 1861), Vol. XVI, 58.

"The southern rebellion was largely the outgrowth of the Mexican war. Nations, like individuals, are punished for their transgressions. We got our punishment in the most sanguinary and expensive war of modern times."[111] In the next section we will see that an extraordinary movement of prominent conservative Protestants would make much the same confession during and after the Civil War, petitioning Congress to show national repentance by amending the "godless Constitution" to acknowledge the authority of Christ and the Gospel over the United States—the very thing the entire American experiment, following the thought of the "moderate Enlightenment," had been designed to negate. Congress would reject the petition in the name of the Founding Fathers.

In the aftermath of the Mexican conquest, the lot of Catholics in what remained of Mexico deteriorated steadily as the Mexican forces of Liberty, led by Freemasons, relentlessly dismantled the country's ancient Catholic social order. Restored to power after his exile, Santa Anna became a dictator once again, this time under the title "Most Serene Highness," only to be forced into exile for the last time in 1855, ending up in Staten Island, of all places, before finally being allowed to return to Mexico and die in 1867—an impoverished and discredited former dictator whose memoirs declared that he had "defended the Apostolic Roman Catholic religion (the only one in which I believe and in which I must die)."[112] By 1857 Mexico's new Federal Constitution of the United Mexican States—condemned by Pope Pius IX—would declare the separation of Church and State and the "sovereignty of the people," the sale of Church property and the abolition of ecclesiastical civil privileges, while a series of laws would impose state secularity, including civil divorce and marriage, along with outright legal persecution of Catholic clergy and faithful. By the end of the 19th century the seesaw battle between Catholic conservatives and Masonic liberals for the fate of Mexico had ended in favor of the liberals, and Mexico settled permanently into that paradoxical condition typical of the advance of Liberty in Catholic countries, beginning with France in 1789. As the Catholic historian Ambrose Coleman described it:

> [T]he people are, for the most part, devoutly Catholic, while the politicians are Masonic. As a consequence the Church has been despoiled of her property and visited with persecution. The trouble with the people of these countries [South America] is that they allow themselves to be ruled by politicians. *The same may be said of the United States,* with a difference, however: there, politicians are allowed to misappropriate funds and plunder tax-payers; in Mexico and South America the Catholics, somehow or other, permit themselves to be persecuted by Masonic politicians.[113]

111. *Personal Memoirs of U.S. Grant* (1885), Vol. I, Chapter 3, Gutenberg Project e-text, gutenberg.org/files/4367/4367-h/p1.htm#ch3.
112. Denslow and Truman, Part Two, 96.
113. Ambrose Coleman, *The Friars in the Philippines* (Boston: Marlier, Callanan & Co., 1899), 137.

The Compromise of 1850

The next milestone on the road to the Civil War was the Compromise of 1850. Quite in keeping with the Constitution's protection of slaves as property and the federal government's obligation to protect that property, Congress enacted the Compromise to balance the rights of free states and slave states with respect to the extension of slavery in the new territories of California, Texas and New Mexico. The Compromise included the Fugitive Slave Act of 1850, an amazingly draconian piece of legislation designed to correct lax enforcement of the Fugitive Slave Act of 1793 (which, again, Jefferson had supported). The 1850 Act provided for $1,000 fines (the price of an average house) on any federal official who failed to secure the apprehension of an escaped slave, imposed a duty on every law enforcement officer in the United States to effect the immediate rendition of escaped slaves without trial based on the *ex parte* affidavit of a slave-catcher, and even mandated that rank and file citizens, under penalty of fines and imprisonment, assist in the recapture of escaped slaves.

The Act became Exhibit A in the case against the Slave Power conspiracy, and with good reason. For not only had federal marshals been enlisted in the work of returning escaped human chattels, the Act "'also required every freeborn American to become a manhunter.' A new and wider circle of voices from the press, pulpit, and rostrum now joined in the denunciation of this evil. . . ."[114] Passage of the Act inspired Harriet Beecher Stowe's *Uncle Tom's Cabin*, a runaway best-seller that more than any other polemic turned Northern public opinion against the South. As University of Virginia historian Michael F. Holt observes, however, contrary to the legend of a vast underground railroad for fugitive slaves "in most instances the new law was peacefully enforced. However much Northerners might revile the law, the vast majority of them believed that it must be obeyed as long as it was the law of the land."[115] Precisely the same attitude obtains today with respect to legalized abortion or any other moral outrage made law in the name of Liberty; for Liberty, as George Washington had insisted in his Farewell Address, means respect for the authority of the federal government, "compliance with its laws, acquiescence in its measures. . . ." Rather than alleged federal tyranny, the South would cite precisely the Northern states' failure to abide by federal law—the Fugitive Slave Act—as grounds for secession. That the Act *did* constitute federal tyranny over people with black skin was of no moment to the members of Congress, Northern and Southern, who had voted for its passage.

The Kansas-Nebraska Act

Acting in accordance with the Constitution's protection for the institution of slavery, in 1854 Congress passed the Kansas-Nebraska Act, principally authored by

114. Fogel, *Without Consent or Contract*, 342.
115. Michael F. Holt, *The Fate of Their Country: Politicians, Slavery Extension, and the Coming of the Civil War* (NY: Hill and Wang, 2004), 86–87.

Illinois Senator Stephen A. Douglas and signed into law by President Franklin Pierce, a "doughface" Democrat who favored the South's position. The Act repealed the Missouri Compromise, with its ban on slavery extension above the compromise line, and authorized the inhabitants of the new Kansas and Nebraska Territories to decide for themselves whether to allow slavery as a matter of "popular sovereignty." As the Act declares, the people are "free to form and regulate their domestic institutions their own way, subject only to the Constitution of the United States." [116] While the Constitution protected slavery from federal interference, it did not prevent any *state* from banning slavery within its borders (while remaining obligated under federal law to return slaves escaped from slave-holding states). As with life in the womb today, the fate of the slaves in Kansas and Nebraska, or for that matter anywhere else in the United States, depended upon the will of the majority.

Holt observes that the Kansas-Nebraska Act "is arguably the most consequential piece of legislation ever passed by Congress."[117] As yet another example of Southern power in Congress, it stoked the fires of Northern outrage, ending the existence of the Whig party and giving birth to the modern-day Republican Party as a now avowedly anti-slavery faction, which would grow to include former members of the defunct Free Soil Party formed to oppose slavery extension into the territories during the elections of 1848 and 1852. But it cannot be maintained that the outrage that made the issue of slavery extension a cause of the Civil War was motivated solely by Christian moral revulsion, although it certainly existed. Nor did the same Northern states that had generally (at least until that time) enforced the Fugitive Slave Act agitate against slavery simply because slaves had been excluded from "the Temple of Liberty." Rather, the contest over slavery was, as Holt and others have demonstrated, largely a political struggle revolving around the growing power of the supposedly "limited" federal government and an economic struggle over the ramifications of the expansion of a slave-based economy into the new states and territories. The struggle was political because expansion of slavery into new territory, with slave populations counted as three-fifths of the white population, would mean a continuing increase of Southern power in Congress and in the Electoral College based upon the census. The struggle was economic because, without denying the existence of widespread moral opposition to slavery in the North, "far more Northerners opposed slavery's extension because they believed that their own social and economic system based on free labor required fresh Western lands [and] northern farmers, artisans and wageworkers could not compete fairly with slaveholders whose workforce went unpaid...."[118]

For these very reasons, however, neither could the South claim it was defending any great moral principle in the political and economic struggle over an institutionalized chattel slavery that now represented, as even many Southern leaders

116. Kansas-Nebraska Act, §14.

117. Holt, "The Slavery Issue," in *The American Congress: the Building of Democracy* (NY: Houghton Mifflin, 2004), 198.

118. Holt, *The Fate of Their Country*, 26–27.

admitted, an anomaly in the Western world and a moral embarrassment to the South. This is not to deny, on the other hand, that the North—the same North that in general was cooperating with the shipment of slaves back to their Southern owners like stray cattle—was likewise "a pervasively racist society" that "wanted to keep slaves out of the West in order to keep blacks out. . . . [S]ome Midwestern states, indeed, legally banned the entry of blacks within their borders."[119] In fact, the never-enacted Wilmot Proviso (1846), which would have barred slavery in any of the territory acquired by the conquest of Mexico, was, as David Wilmot himself declared, "the White Man's Proviso."[120]

Looking ahead to the Civil War, we can consult Professor Morison for his usual balanced view of the American historical landscape: "The attitude of *both* the Union and the Confederacy toward the Negroes was ambiguous, inconsistent, and even hypocritical. . . ."[121] We must bear this in mind as we later examine the romantic narratives woven by both sides in what Pope Pius IX would see for what it was: a "deplorable intestine war."

"Bleeding Kansas" and a Bleeding Senator

Three more key developments turned the Northern tide against slavery. After passage of the Kansas-Nebraska Act, the Kansas Territory inevitably became a battleground over slavery extension. In the Spirit of 1776, competing factions of pro- and anti-slavery immigrants in the Territory set up rival provisional territorial governments during the spring of 1856, and the Territory "was soon awash with secret societies and informal militias . . . capable of deadly mischief on both sides."[122] Since the pro-slavery provisional government had been established first—quite illegally, in keeping with the *modus operandi* of Liberty—a local federal grand jury indicted members of the equally irregular anti-slavery government for "high treason." After a federal marshal effected the peaceable arrest of the indictees at Lawrence on May 21, 1856, a local pro-slavery sheriff, who had been wounded by an unidentified gunman, led a mob in razing the headquarters of the anti-slavery Emigrant Aid Society, destroying the presses of two anti-slavery newspapers, and pillaging the shops and houses of Northern settlers.[123] The Emigrant Aid Company then issued the famous Sharp rifles to free-state militia and the shooting began in earnest: Northern "Jayhawks" versus Southern "Kickapoo Rangers" and assorted "border ruffians" from Missouri.

As Professor Morison observes with appropriately amused contempt: "These were merry times in Kansas for men who enjoyed fighting."[124] And the fighting was

119. Holt, 27.
120. Ibid.
121. Morison, *HAP*, 574.
122. Ross Drake, "The Law that Ripped America in Two," *Smithsonian Magazine*, May 2004, 2.
123. Fogel, *Without Consent or Contract*, 379.
124. Morison, *HAP*, 591.

over slavery, an issue the pro-slavery faction was now determined to keep from the direct popular vote recommended by Senator Douglas, precisely as provided by the Kansas-Nebraska Act, because it knew the anti-slavery faction would win by a landslide. Thus the same Southerners "who had supported Douglas' notion of popular sovereignty when it suited their purposes now abandoned both it and Douglas," and the territorial legislature passed laws making opposition to slavery a felony and aiding a fugitive slave a capital offense.[125] "Bleeding Kansas" represented nothing less than a western preliminary to the Civil War.

The nation was further propelled toward civil war by the Southern reaction to a tirade against the pro-slavery Kansas faction, entitled "The Crime Against Kansas," delivered May 19, 1856 on the Senate floor by the radical Republican Senator Charles Sumner of Massachusetts. When Sumner indulged in crass and defamatory invective against Senator Butler of South Carolina, one of the sponsors of the Kansas-Nebraska Act, Butler's relative Preston Brooks, a representative from South Carolina, decided that Southern "chivalry" and "honor" required him to administer a beating to Sumner in keeping with the Southern custom of "punishing an inferior for an insult [by] a thrashing with a cane or whip." Brooks happened to have a selection of canes, as he walked with a limp on account of a wound suffered in a duel to vindicate his "honor" in some other dispute. Brooks waited three days before walking up to the defenseless Sumner in the nearly empty Senate chamber and savagely beating him about the head with his weapon of choice, "a gutta-percha cane with a gold head," leaving his victim "unconscious and bleeding profusely." He continued beating the unconscious Sumner until the cane broke. Another representative from South Carolina, Laurence Keitt, assisted Brooks by wielding his own cane to fend off the elderly Senator John Crittenden of Kentucky, who was rushing to Sumner's aid: "Let them alone, God damn you!" shouted Keitt. The Southern press hailed the "chivalrous" deed and Brooks's admirers presented him with inscribed memorial sticks. Sumner was injured so badly that he required years of medical treatment and could not regularly attend the Senate. Brooks had made Sumner—an otherwise eminently unlikable man—into a martyr for the anti-slavery cause. To the public mind the attack, in the context of the violence in Lawrence, Kansas, "showed that not even a U.S. Senator was safe from Southern aggression."[126]

Two days after the caning of Sumner, the fanatical John Brown and a band of abolitionists killed five pro-slavery settlers in retaliation for the "sack of Lawrence," as the anti-slavery press was calling it. The Pottawatomie Massacre, as it came be known (for the river Brown and his men had crossed), would be followed three years later by Brown's raid at Harper's Ferry.

125. Drake, 5.
126. Michael S. Green, *Politics and America in Crisis: the Coming of the Civil War* (Santa Barbara, CA: ABC-CLIO, LLC, 2010) 94; Fogel, 379–80; Morison, 592.

Know-Nothingism and the Election of 1856

The events in Kansas and the nearly fatal assault on Senator Sumner—both intrinsically connected to slavery—"traumatized the nation"[127] and caused a significant loss of Northern support for the Democratic Party. The ascendancy of the Republican Party and the election of Lincoln were heralded by the results of the presidential election of 1856. A key development in that election was the division of the anti-Catholic Know-Nothing movement into Northern and Southern factions.

As Holt has observed, Know-Nothingism "sprouted like kudzu across the South during the hot summer of 1854. . . . Know-Nothingism originally grew in the South for the same reasons it spread in the North—nativism, anti-Catholicism, and animosity toward unresponsive politicos—not because of conservative Unionism." The embarrassed former Governor of Tennessee, William B. Campbell, put it this way in 1855: "I have been astonished at the widespread feeling in favor of their principles—to wit, Native Americanism and anti-Catholicism—it takes everywhere."[128] In the same year the future President Lincoln echoed Campbell concerning the nation as a whole:

> Our progress in degeneracy appears to me to be pretty rapid. As a nation, we began by declaring that "all men are created equal." We now practically read it "all men are created equal, except Negroes." When the Know-Nothings get control, it will read "all men are created equal, except Negroes and foreigners and Catholics." When it comes to this I should prefer emigrating to some country where they make no pretence of loving liberty—to Russia, for instance, where despotism can be taken pure, and without the base alloy of hypocrisy.[129]

That Lincoln's own prosecution of the dictates of Liberty would exhibit the "base alloy of hypocrisy" does not alter the truth of his observation concerning Know-Nothingism, both North and South. Typical of anti-Catholic bigotry in the antebellum South was the renowned Presbyterian minister James Henry Thornwell of South Carolina, President of South Carolina College (precursor to the University of South Carolina). Thornwell "view[ed] with no little favor the general attitudes of the 'Know-Nothing' party [and] . . . [h]is close friendship with R. J. Breckinridge brought him into intimate contact with one of this country's more virile opponents of Catholicism."[130] His writings are illustrative of how "from 1839 to the Civil War the prophetic zeal for righteousness which, in the North, was expended upon American slavery received expression in the South by repeated and vitriolic attacks

---

127. Fogel, 379.

128. Michael F. Holt, *The Rise and Fall of the American Whig Party: Jacksonian Politics and the Onset of the Civil War* (NY: Oxford Univ. Press, 1999), 856.

129. Lincoln to Joshua Speed, August 24, 1855, in *The Yale Book of Quotations*, ed. Fred R. Shapiro (New Haven: Yale Univ. Press, 2006), 460.

130. Paul Leslie Garber, *James Henley Thornwell: Presbyterian Defender of the Old South* (1939), doctoral thesis, Duke University, reprinted from *Union Seminary Review*, February 1943, 20, http://www.-archive.org/details/jameshenleythornoogarb.

upon Catholicism."[131] A masterful pro-slavery polemicist known as "the Calhoun of the Church,"[132] Thornwell issued this dire warning about the Catholic threat in 1845:

> The slaves of the Papacy are taught to conceal their weapons until they are ready to strike—to disguise their hemlock and nightshade until they can prepare the deadly potation with the certain prospect of success. But when once they become master of the scepter and the sword, they are to strike for Rome, sell the liberties of the country to their spiritual lord, raise the banner of inhuman persecution, and purge the land from the damning stain of heretical pravity with the blood of its noblest sons. LaFayette is reported to have said that if ever the liberties of this country should be destroyed, it would be by the machinations of Romish priests.[133]

The Know-Nothing movement had achieved major successes in the 1854 elections and by 1856 was formally organized as the American Party. But the party self-destructed at its 1856 convention in Philadelphia when the Southern wing gained control, adopted pro-slavery resolutions, and nominated as its presidential candidate the pro-slavery, ex-Whig Millard Fillmore, the former Vice President who had served as President after the sudden death of President Zachary Taylor. (Andrew Jackson's nephew, Andrew Jackson Donelson, was nominated for Vice President.) The result was a massive defection of Northern Know-Nothings from the American Party.

Without Know-Nothing votes from the North, many of which went to the 1856 Republican candidate John Frémont, Fillmore lost disastrously, carrying only Maryland. While the Democrat James Buchanan won the election, Know-Nothings in the Northern states would overwhelmingly cast their votes for Lincoln in 1860, as their attention was shifted from "the key Know-Nothing issue (the papal conspiracy to subvert American institutions) to the key Republican issue (the Slave Power conspiracy to subvert northern liberties and economic welfare)—from a foreign menace to a southern menace." The Republican Party was able to attract the support of Know-Nothing laborers whose enmity toward factory owners was accompanied by fear of losing their jobs to slave labor. The Republicans appealed to the working man to join their "crusade against the conspiracy by the 'great capitalists' of the North and the planters of the South 'to exclude white laborers from the territories and hand them over to the sole occupancy of slaves and slave-breeders.'"[134] Thus did pro-slavery Know-Nothings in the South drive large numbers of Know-Nothings in the North into the arms of Lincoln.

---

131. Garber, 19.

132. Eugene D. Genovese, *Slaveholders' Dilemma: Freedom and Progress in Southern Conservative Thought* (Columbia, SC: Univ. of South Carolina Press, 1994), 36.

133. James Henley Thornwell, Letter VIII, "Infallibility and Civil Government," in *The Collected Writings of James Henley Thornwell*, eds John B. Adger and John L. Girardeau (NY: Robert Carter & Bros., 1873), Vol. III, 550.

134. Fogel, 380.

The Dred Scott *Decision*

The 7-to-2 decision in *Dred Scott v. Sandford* (1856)[135] seemed to confirm Southern dominance over the levers of federal power and thus was instrumental in the gathering anti-slavery coalition that would put Lincoln in the White House. Dred Scott's decade-long journey through the American legal system had begun in a Missouri state court, where he sued for his freedom after being taken by his master, Dr. John Emerson, an Army surgeon, from the slave State of Missouri to Fort Snelling in the free State of Illinois, and then to the free Territory of Wisconsin (Minnesota today). While in the Territory, Scott had married another slave, Harriet, with his master's "consent" (the requirement of which violates natural law, as Catholic teaching recognizes; cf. Chapter 12). The civil marriage ceremony was performed by Harriet's master, a justice of the peace, who then conveyed Harriet to Dr. Emerson. The Scotts ultimately had four children. Upon Dr. Emerson's death, his wife, Irene, inherited the entire Scott family as chattels and "the Scotts worked as hired slaves with the rent going to Irene Emerson." Scott sued after the widow Emerson "refused to sell Scott to himself" and thereby emancipate him and his family.[136]

Given these facts, under numerous Missouri Supreme Court precedents Scott and his family had indubitably been emancipated. At that time Missouri followed the common law rule that "a master who takes his slave to reside in a State or territory where slavery is prohibited, thereby emancipates his slave."[137] That rule, recognized by a number of other Southern jurisdictions, reflected the English common law as enunciated in Somersett's Case, the previously mentioned decision by Lord Chief Justice Mansfield in 1772, which had excited such furor among the slave-owning colonial radicals, including Washington and Adams (cf. Chapter 6). In keeping with the rule, the Supreme Court of Illinois had likewise held that emancipation occurs upon the residence of a slave within its borders.[138]

Instructed in then prevailing Missouri law, a jury found that Scott and his family had indeed become free. But, in a blatantly political decision, the Missouri Supreme Court, abandoning its own precedents, reversed the jury's verdict because "[t]imes are not now as they were when the former decisions on this subject were made. Since then not only individuals but States have been possessed with a dark and fell spirit in relation to slavery. . . ."[139] That is, the court openly admitted it was abolishing the established legal rule merely because the political tide had turned against slavery. "Times may have changed, public feeling may have changed, but principles have not and do not change," the dissenting justice protested in vain.[140]

---

135. The decision was actually handed down on March 6, 1857. "Sandford" is a misspelling; the defendant's name was "Sanford."

136. Paul Finkelman, "Scott v. Sandford: The Court's Most Dreadful Case and How It Changed History," 82 Chi.-Kent L. Rev. 3 19–20 (2007).

137. *Scott v. Emerson*, 15 Mo. 576, 590 (1852) (Gamble, J., dissenting, and citing numerous Missouri precedents).

138. *Id.* at 589.

139. *Id.* at 585 (majority opinion).

140. *Id.* at 591–92 (Gamble, J., dissenting).

To dispense with the complex procedural history that followed, Scott's subsequent federal suit ended up in the United States Supreme Court, where the parallel with the contemporary abortion controversy as an example of Lockean legal positivism and result-oriented jurisprudence could not have been clearer. The opinion by Chief Justice Roger B. Taney was accompanied by separate opinions from the other six justices in the majority, although Taney's opinion effectively became the "majority opinion" of the Court.[141] While he died in near-poverty, Taney was a former slave-owner from a wealthy Maryland family that "had made its fortune in landholding, slaves, and tobacco planting," and the majority, including Taney, consisted of "[s]even Democrats—five pro-slavery Southerners and two Northern doughfaces [pro-slavery Northerners]," who "dominated the Court."[142]

Despite the undisputed facts militating in favor of the Scott family's emancipation, Taney held that "[t]he facts upon which the plaintiff relies, did not give him his freedom...."[143] First of all, he reasoned, the federal court had no jurisdiction over Scott's case and should have dismissed it because Scott, being a slave of African descent, could not be a "citizen" of Missouri in "the sense in which that word is used in the Constitution of the United States." He thus had no right to bring a suit against Sanford, a citizen of New York State, under Article III's provision for federal suits by a "citizen" of one state against a "citizen" of another—so-called "diversity jurisdiction."[144] This conclusion, said Taney, was dictated by the will of the Framers, as shown by the fact that "a negro of the African race was regarded ... as an article of property, and held, and bought and sold as such, in every one of the thirteen colonies which united in the Declaration of Independence, and afterwards formed the Constitution of the United States."[145] According to Taney, it did not matter for purposes of diversity jurisdiction that black freedmen in several states had enjoyed the privileges of state citizenship at the time of the Founding, including the right to vote in state elections. Absent a constitutional amendment, "a negro of the African race," even if emancipated, was not, and never could be, "a 'citizen' within the meaning of the Constitution of the United States."[146]

What of the Declaration of Independence to which Taney himself had alluded, with its proclamation that "*all* men are created equal" and are "endowed by their Creator with certain *unalienable* rights," including the rights to "life, *liberty*, and the pursuit of happiness"? Taney allowed that the words of the Declaration "would seem to embrace the whole human family, and if they were used in a similar instru-

---

141. We avoid entirely the endless debates among legal historians about whether, according to their "box scores," a majority of five justices had actually agreed on Taney's opinion where it concerned Negro citizenship or federal jurisdiction. What matters is that a majority of the justices agreed that Scott was still a slave. And, for better or worse, Taney's opinion became "the opinion of the court." See, e.g., Don E. Fehrenbacher, *Slavery, Law and Politics: the Dred Scott Case in Historical Perspective* (NY: Oxford Univ. Press, 1981), abridged ed., Chapter 6, 168–172.

142. Finkelman, 82 Chi.-Kent L. Rev. at 40.

143. *Dred Scott v. Sandford*, 60 U.S. 393, 395, 15 L. Ed. 691 (1856).

144. *Id.* at 400.

145. *Dred Scott*, 60 U.S. at 408.

146. *Id.* at 393, 404–405.

ment *at this day* would be so understood. . . ." But as far as the Founders were concerned, it was "too clear for dispute, that the enslaved African race were not
intended to be included, and formed no part of the people who framed and
adopted this declaration; for if the language, as understood in *that* day, would
embrace them, the conduct of the distinguished men who framed the Declaration
of Independence would have been utterly and flagrantly inconsistent with the principles they asserted. . . ."[147]

Taney ignored the obvious: the principles those "distinguished men" had
asserted were that God, not the Founders, had created *all* men in a state of essential
equality and that God, not the Founders, had endowed *all* men with certain
unalienable rights. That being so, it ought not to matter whether the Declaration
was construed "this day" or "that day." Hence only two honest conclusions were
possible for Taney: Either the authors of the Declaration meant to assert that members of "the African race" were not men, or they were indeed "flagrantly inconsistent
with the principles they asserted"—just as their Loyalist and English critics had suggested, including Dr. Johnson with his famous jibe about colonial "drivers of
negroes" yelping for Liberty. Taney attempted to evade the problem by resorting to
the logical fallacy of vouching: such distinguished men as the authors of the Declaration could not possibly have been hypocrites. But that left only the conclusion
that the authors did not believe that members of the African race were men—at
least not men in the full sense—but rather an inferior caste divinely ordered to servitude and subjugation. That, as we shall see, was precisely the position of the future
President and Vice President of the Confederate States of America, who insisted that
the members of the African race be viewed forever just as the Founders had viewed
them.

This explains how Taney justified his conclusion that even blacks who had managed to become emancipated were nonetheless still disqualified from citizenship. It
was membership in the African race *as such*, not slave status, that had disqualified
the slaves and all their descendants, free or not, from membership in the American
political community. At the time of the Founding, members of the African race
were regarded as "a subordinate and inferior class of beings, who had been subjugated by the dominant race, and, *whether emancipated or not*, yet remained subject
to their authority, and had no rights or privileges but such as those who held the
power and the Government might choose to grant them."[148] Taney had taken the
same position nearly thirty years earlier when serving as President Andrew Jackson's Attorney General, arguing "that blacks in the United States had no political or
legal rights, except those they 'enjoy' at the 'sufferance' and 'mercy' of whites," and
that "blacks 'even when free' were a 'degraded class' whose 'privileges' were
'accorded to them as a matter of kindness and benevolence rather than right.'"[149]

Taney did not explain how his position could be reconciled with what the "dis-

147. *Dred Scott*, 60 U.S. at 410.
148. *Id.* at 404–405.
149. Finkelman, 82 Chi.-Kent L. Rev. at 32.

tinguished men" had declared concerning the equality and unalienable rights of all men; he merely adverted to the Constitution's treatment of slaves as property:

> There are two clauses in the Constitution which point directly and specifically to the *negro race* as a separate class of persons, and show clearly that they were not regarded as a portion of the people or citizens of the Government then formed.
>
> One of these clauses reserves to each of the thirteen States the right to import slaves until the year 1808.... And by the other provision the States pledge themselves to each other to maintain the right of property of the master, by delivering up to him any slave who may have escaped from his service . . . pledg[ing] themselves to maintain and uphold the right of the master in the manner specified, *as long as the Government they then formed should endure. . . .*
>
> And these two provisions show, conclusively, that neither the description of persons therein referred to, *nor their descendants*, were embraced in any of the other provisions of the Constitution; for certainly these two clauses were not intended to confer on them *or their posterity* the blessings of liberty, or any of the personal rights so carefully provided for the citizen.[150]

Taney's blatant non-sequitur would have disastrous consequences for the nation: Slaves are treated as property in the Constitution. Therefore, members of the "negro race" descended from slaves, *even if emancipated*, have none of the rights of citizens. But the Constitution says nothing about the "negro race," much less that the "negro race" *as such* is an "inferior class of beings" whose members, "whether emancipated or not," have "no rights or privileges" except those granted by "the dominant race." The constitutional text refers only to "free persons" versus "three fifths of all other Persons," "a person held to service of labor" and "migration or importation of . . . persons [i.e., slaves]."[151] As a matter of strict construction, which Taney purported to be doing, the legal inferiority of slaves attached to their slave status, *not to their race.*

Here Taney ventured his infamous distinction between Indians and Africans, which he seriously proposed as intrinsic to the Constitution's guarantee of rights and privileges only to "citizens." The Indians, according to him, were capable of being citizens in the constitutional sense because they had been "a free and independent people, associated together in nations or tribes, and governed by their own laws,"[152] whereas the members of the African race had always been "a subordinate and inferior class of beings"—and so they must remain. As the legal scholar Frederick Hoxie has noted, however, Taney conveniently omitted mention of the reference to Indians in the Declaration of Independence as "merciless Indian savages, whose known rule of warfare is an undistinguished destruction of all ages,

---

150. *Dred Scott*, 60 U.S. at 411.
151. *U.S. Constitution*, Art. 1, § 2, Clause 3; § 9, Clause 1; Art. 4, § 2, Clause 3.
152. *Dred Scott*, 60 U.S. at 403, 405.

sexes and conditions." Nor had he mentioned the Supreme Court's own prior declaration in *Johnson v. McIntosh*, an opinion by Justice Marshall, that the Indians
were "fierce savages" who could *not* be "blended with the conquerors or safely governed as a distinct people."[153] Yet, according to Taney, absent a constitutional
amendment—impossible to obtain over Southern opposition—America was to be
governed for all time by the posited idiosyncratic differentiation of red-skinned
people from black-skinned people.

But Taney did not stop with his purely racial disqualification of Scott as a federal
plaintiff, which would have sufficed to end his bid for freedom in the federal courts.
Under the guise of construing the Constitution, Taney wished to pronounce on the
merits of Scott's claim despite his own finding of a lack of jurisdiction. Nor was he
content merely to affirm Scott's loss in the federal district court, which had applied
the expedient change of Missouri state law already noted. In what has to be seen as
a gratuitous exercise of judicial power for political ends—mirroring the politics of
the Missouri high court—Taney opined that Congress had no authority to enact
those provisions of the Missouri Compromise banning slavery north of the compromise line (where Scott had been), or otherwise to ban slavery in the federal territories, despite the Constitution's express provision that "Congress shall have
Power to dispose of and make *all needful Rules and Regulations respecting the Territory* or other Property belonging to the United States. . . ."[154]

In an argument one commentator rightly calls "absurd and silly,"[155] and
another, just as rightly, "bizarre,"[156] Taney reasoned that Congress's power to make
"*all* needful rules and regulations" in the territories did not include a rule or regulation barring importation of property in the form of slaves, because a federal territory is "acquired to become a State, and not to be held as a colony and governed
by Congress with absolute authority. . . ."[157] The argument is absurd, silly and
bizarre because it means that while a state could ban slavery within its territory by
a simple vote of *state* representatives (remaining liable to return escaped slaves
from slave states), Congress could not do so in a federal territory by a vote of *federal* representatives. The Constitution made no such distinction; it said nothing at
all on the subject.

Further, under the Kansas-Nebraska Act the people residing in a territory could
vote directly on whether to ban or establish slavery therein—a result the Southern
states had hailed until it became apparent that the votes would not go their way.
Taney's opinion, however, implicitly held that even a direct popular vote to ban slavery in a territory would be unconstitutional: "And if Congress itself cannot do
this—if it is beyond the powers conferred on the Federal Government—it will be
admitted, we presume, that it could not authorize a Territorial Government to

---

153. Frederick E. Hoxie, "What Was Taney Thinking? American Indian Citizenship in the Era of
Dred Scott," 82 Chi.-Kent L. Rev. 329, 331 (2007).

154. *U.S. Constitution*, Art. 4, §3.

155. Finkelman, 40.

156. Fehrenbacher, *Slavery, Law and Politics*, 195.

157. *Dred Scott*, 60 U.S. at 447.

exercise them. It could confer no power on any local Government, established by its authority, to violate the provisions of the Constitution."[158] The absurd result was that a referendum abolishing slavery in a territory on Monday would be unconstitutional, but not on Wednesday if the territory had become a state on Tuesday. By that reasoning, a vote to *establish* slavery in a federal territory would be equally unconstitutional, although this was apparently of no concern to Taney. But "[t]he weakness of his argument on the Territories Clause did not stop Taney, who was determined, as few Justices have been, to reach a specific result. Weak arguments or faulty logic would not stand in his way. His goal was to prohibit congressional regulation of slavery in the territories, and any argument, it seems, would do the trick."[159]

Taney held further that the Fifth Amendment's protection against deprivation of life, liberty, or property without due process of law prohibited any ban on slavery in the territories because the text of the Constitution expressly "guaranties to the slaveholder the title to his property, and gives him the right to its reclamation throughout the entire extent of the nation. . . . [N]o other right of property is placed by the Constitution upon the same high ground, nor shielded by a similar guaranty."[160] Thus, he concluded, "an act of Congress which deprives a citizen of the United States of his liberty or property [i.e., slaves], merely because he came himself or brought his property into a particular Territory of the United States, and who had committed no offence against the laws, could hardly be dignified with the name of due process of law."[161]

But Scott was not an *escaped* slave liable to "reclamation" under the Constitution's slave rendition clause and the Fugitive Slave Act. Rather, he was a slave whose master had knowingly and willingly taken his "property" to reside for years in jurisdictions where slavery was illegal, allowing Scott to marry and produce children therein under a prevailing common law rule that required emancipation in precisely such circumstances. And what of the deprivation of *Scott's* liberty interest under the Fifth Amendment? If, according to Taney, "it was a violation of 'due process' to take property from people who merely entered a federal jurisdiction. . . . [by] applying that logic to the slaves themselves, abolitionists might have argued that it was a denial of 'liberty' to allow someone to be enslaved in a federal territory." And they did so argue.[162] Even in strict terms of the property right in slaves, Congress, for example, "which had full lawmaking power for the District of Columbia, allowed local officials there to ban abolitionist publications *just as the Southern states did*."[163] If the States and Congress alike could ban abolitionist property within their respective jurisdictions, why not slave-owner "property"?

From Taney's tortured reasoning it followed that Scott and his entire family had

158. *Dred Scott*, 60 U.S. at 451–52.
159. Finkelman, 40.
160. *Dred Scott*, 60 U.S. at 490.
161. *Id.* at 450.
162. Finkelman, 43 & n. 128 (citing sources).
163. Ibid., 42.

never ceased to be Dr. Emerson's chattels, that the Scott family had passed by operation of law to Irene Emerson, and that her brother, John Sanford, acting as executor of the Emerson estate, had committed no wrong by *imprisoning Scott, his wife, and the children* to prevent the escape of Irene Emerson's property.[164] It was of no moment that such treatment of human beings was now recognized as evil by many Americans, as it had been for centuries in Catholic Europe (cf. Chapter 12). The Constitution said what it said, and only a duly adopted amendment could alter the otherwise perpetual lot of the African race in America—"land of the free and the home of the brave," in the words of Francis Scott Key, who was none other than Taney's brother-in-law and former law partner.[165] Wrote Taney:

> It is not the province of the court to decide upon the justice or injustice, the policy or impolicy, of these laws. . . . No one, we presume, supposes that any change in public opinion or feeling, in relation to *this unfortunate race*, in the civilized nations of Europe or in this country, should induce the court to give to the words of the Constitution a more liberal construction in their favor than they were intended to bear when the instrument was framed and adopted. . . . If any of its provisions are deemed unjust, there is a mode prescribed in the instrument itself by which it may be amended; but while it remains unaltered, *it must be construed now as it was understood at the time of its adoption*.[166]

There is something of the tragicomical about Taney's foray into what is now known as "original meaning" jurisprudence. According to this school of constitutional interpretation, championed today by Justice Antonin Scalia, neither morality nor justice must enter into the search for the meaning of constitutional terms freighted precisely with concerns of morality and justice. Even the definition of "citizen," and with it the very status of human beings in civil society, is to be determined solely by the purported understanding of an original cohort of 18th-century, slave-owning Protestant revolutionaries and their contemporaries. This approach is supposed to avoid the "arbitrary" results of a "living constitution," but as we shall see in the concluding chapter, it results in the morally vacuous document contemporary judicial "conservatives" offer as the only opposition to the moralizing of judicial liberals construing the same text.

Yet Taney's conclusion was clearly driven by politics as much as by an "original meaning" that was suspiciously conformable to the desired result. He and the majority could just as plausibly have reasoned that as the Constitution was silent on whether the federal government's power over federal territories extended to a ban

164. *Dred Scott*, 60 U.S. at 398–399. There is controversy over whether Irene Sanford ever really vested control of the Scott family in her brother. But as no one disputed that John Sanford was the one claiming authority over the family as slaves, it is his name that appears on the caption of the case. See Finkelman, op. cit., 25.

165. See, e.g., Abraham Resnick, *They Too Influenced a Nation's History* (Lincoln, NE: iUniverse, Inc., 2003), 74.

166. *Dred Scott*, 60 U.S. at 426.

on slavery within them, the Court should defer to the judgment of Congress and the "democratic process" in the same way deference would be shown to the *abolition* of slavery within a state. Furthermore, since he had insisted on reaching the merits, Taney could readily have found that Scott attained his freedom under Illinois law, even if Missouri's high court had shamelessly abandoned its own precedents to achieve the result it desired. Why, dissenting Justice McLean asked, had Taney deferred to the Supreme Court of Missouri, rather than the Supreme Court of Illinois?[167] Why indeed, especially given Taney's own dictum that a court must never act, as Missouri's high court had done, based on "change in public opinion or feeling"? McLean cited the common law rule of the locality of slavery as a creature of positive law operating only within a given territory. "By virtue of what law is it," he queried, "that a master may take his slave into free territory and extract from him the duties of a slave?"[168]

Even more persuasively, dissenting Justice Curtis opined that Scott's master Emerson, being a military officer, had certainly emancipated his slaves by residing for two years at Fort Snelling with full knowledge of the illegality of slavery in the Wisconsin Territory. And what of Scott's marriage to Harriet, to which Emerson and Harriet's master had "consented"? "In my judgment," Curtis opined, "there can be no more effectual abandonment of legal rights of a master over his slave, than by the consent of the master that the slave should enter into a contract of marriage, in a free state, attended by all the civil rights and obligations which belong to that condition."[169] Curtis would resign from the Supreme Court in protest over Taney's decision, although he cited other reasons.

The dissents in *Dred Scott* reveal ample room for a just result in favor of the Scott family's freedom, and arguably reveal Taney's creative constitutional "construction" as a rather monstrous positivistic injustice—to the South's delight. More than a century-and-a-quarter later, none other than the "originalist" Justice Scalia, dissenting in part from the Supreme Court's refusal to overturn *Roe v. Wade*, would write that "Justice Curtis's warning [in *Dred Scott*] is as timely today as it was 135 years ago: '[W]hen a strict interpretation of the Constitution, according to the fixed rules which govern the interpretation of laws, is abandoned, and the theoretical opinions of individuals are allowed to control its meaning, we have no longer a Constitution; we are under the government of individual men, who for the time being have power to declare what the Constitution is, according to their own views of what it ought to mean.'"[170]

Yet it must be said that the Constitution Taney had construed in favor of the white citizen's perpetual domination of black-skinned human beings was quite consistent with Locke's own constitutional draftsmanship for Carolina, which we encountered in Chapter 3: "every freeman of Carolina shall have absolute power

167. *Dred Scott*, 60 U.S. at 559–560.

168. *Id.* at 534–535, 548, 559–560 (McLean, J., dissenting).

169. *Id.* at 598–600 (Curtis, J., dissenting).

170. *Planned Parenthood of Se. Pennsylvania v. Casey*, 505 U.S. 833, 984 (1992) (Scalia, J., dissenting). I am indebted to Finkelman, op. cit., for this telling connection.

and authority over his negro slaves of what opinion or religion whatsoever."[171] The *Dred Scott* decision was a major milestone in Locke's Progress toward civil war. It was an attempt to navigate the Lockean conceptual jumble of antebellum America, a man-made nation-state whose rulers sought "to balance ambitions of equality with the racial privileges chiseled into governmental institutions . . . a nation that was at once decentralized, expanding, and united."[172]

Justice Taney was an otherwise outstanding jurist and a man of impeccable character. He was also a Catholic—the first Catholic ever to serve on the Supreme Court. But he was a Catholic bobbing in a rising Lockean tempest he had attempted to suppress with a quasi-legislative judicial decision that had only heightened the storm. His iron enforcement of the "law of the land" prefigured that of the modern Catholic jurist who, when confronted with such outrages as the mass extermination of unborn children in the womb—as Justice Scalia himself would be—adheres rigorously to Locke's dogmatic disjunction between "public" and "private" morality and the body versus the soul as the only object of politics. (Cf. Chapters 3 and 20.) It was a testament to the *ethos* that surrounded Taney that all six of his surviving children became Protestants.[173]

As for Dred Scott, the outraged sons of Scott's original master, Peter Blow, who had financed Scott's freedom litigation, were finally able to wrest control of Scott and his family from "the intractable Irene Emerson" after she remarried a prominent abolitionist, Calvin C. Chaffee. Chaffee was humiliated to learn that his wife owned "the most famous slave in the nation," and he prevailed upon her to turn Scott and family over to the Blow sons, who promptly freed them.[174] Scott died of tuberculosis in 1858.

Taking notice of the patent parallel between *Dred Scott v. Sandford* and *Roe v. Wade*, Justice Scalia's dissent in *Casey* scores the Court's disastrous attempts in both cases to resolve "an issue involving life and death, freedom and subjugation" by a purported "common mandate rooted in the Constitution." This study prescinds, for obvious reasons, from Scalia's alternative approach of simply punting such issues into the Colosseum of mass democracy (which admittedly would have been preferable to Taney's opinion) (cf. Chapter 23). The Court, rather, should have had the courage to declare the correct answer to the moral question concerning human freedom that *Dred Scott* inescapably presented under the Fifth Amendment, just as the Court should have done in *Roe* regarding the humanity of the unborn child and its right to life under the Fifth and Fourteenth Amendments. But we can agree with Scalia's assessment of *Dred Scott* as a disastrous judicial failure, whose "apparent consequences for the Court and its soon-to-be-played-out

171. *Locke: Political Essays,* Fundamental Constitutions, Arts. [101] [110], 180.

172. Hoxie, 82 Chi.-Kent L. Rev. at 329.

173. Cf. Steve O'Brien, "The Justice: Roger B. Taney," *The Latin Mass: The Journal of Catholic Culture and Tradition,* Vol. 20 (Winter 2011), 54.

174. Alan Axelrod, *Profiles in Folly: History's Worst Decisions and Why They Went Wrong* (NY: Sterling Publishing Co., 2008), 191–192.

consequences for the Nation" may well have been reflected, as he suggests, in the "expression of profound sadness and disillusionment" to be seen in the famous portrait of Taney at Harvard Law School.[175]

Lincoln's Election and Buchanan's Warning

Owing in part to Northern outrage over the decision in *Dred Scott*, on November 6, 1860, Abraham Lincoln was elected the sixteenth President of the United States. As Fogel shows in a meticulous analysis of election statistics, the election of Lincoln was made possible by a Republican coalition that included ex-Whigs and northern Know-Nothings who "deserted the Fillmore [Southern] Know-Nothings because they wanted to fight *both* the pope *and* Slave Power."[176]

But Lincoln could not have won without the help of the Southern pro-slavery faction itself. The seven Deep South "Cotton States" had walked out of the Democratic convention in Charleston when the party voted down a plank calling upon the federal government to guarantee slavery extension in the territories—yet another example of how the tail of slavery extension was wagging the dog of American politics. A reconvened Democratic convention in Baltimore had nominated Stephen Douglas, while the dissident Southern Democrats had subdivided into two spinoff parties: the pro-secession Southern Democrat Party, which nominated John Breckinridge, and the anti-secession Constitutional Union Party, which nominated John Bell and had only one plank in its platform: preservation of the Union.

The division of the Democrats insured a Republican victory in both the popular vote and the Electoral College. In the popular tally Lincoln received 1,855,993 votes, Douglas 1,381,944 votes, Breckinridge 851,844 votes, and Bell 590,946 votes. In the Electoral College Lincoln won 180 electoral votes, Bell 39, Breckinridge 72 and Douglas 12. The overwhelming majority of Democrat voters declined to cast their ballots for Breckinridge, the secession candidate. Had the Democrats been united—and their division related entirely to slavery—Lincoln could have been defeated by Douglas or a "fusion" candidate. The hopeless Breckinridge candidacy could not have been better designed to insure Lincoln's victory and marginalize the South.[177]

By the time of Lincoln's election, the Cotton States were already on the verge of secession from the Union over the slavery issue. A month earlier John Brown's aborted lunatic attempt to start a war of slave liberation at Harper's Ferry, Virginia (where he was captured by Captain Robert E. Lee) had provoked outrage in the deep South bordering on mass hysteria. Rising Northern opposition to slavery (for whatever motive) had led to state attempts to nullify the Fugitive Slave Act. Despite the Supreme Court's 1859 decision in *Ableman v. Booth*, another authored by Justice Taney, holding that state courts had no power to interfere with federal court

175. *Casey,* 505 U.S. at 1001–02.
176. Fogel, *Without Consent or* Contract, 381; and see 382–85.
177. See, e.g., Jeffrey A. Jenkins and Irwin L. Morris, "Running to Lose?: John C. Breckinridge and the Presidential Election of 1860," *Electoral Studies,* Vol. 25, Issue 2, June 2006, 306–328.

enforcement of the Act, civil disobedience of its provisions had become widespread in the context of the growing Northern abolition movement, fed by such polemics as *Uncle Tom's Cabin* and the galvanizing oratory and eloquently written personal account of the escaped slave Frederick Douglass, a protégé of the leading abolitionist William Lloyd Garrison. In fact, there was talk of secession in the *Northern* states over the Act.

The anti-slavery coalition, which succeeded in electing Lincoln owing to the fractures in the Southern constituency, had overturned the longstanding Southern dominance of the federal government centering around the Virginia dynasty in the Presidency. The South had controlled the Presidency for 40 out of 52 years, and the Speaker of the House had been a Southerner for 28 of the preceding 35 years. Before Lincoln's election, every Senate president *pro tem* had been a Southerner from the time the Constitution was ratified, and the majority of both the Cabinet and the Supreme Court had been Southerners. Based on the census, which included millions of slaves under the three-fifths clause, until the off-year elections of 1858 the South had enjoyed a 25-vote majority in the House, posing a formidable obstacle to passage of any bill contrary to Southern interests.[178]

Having lost control of the House and the Presidency by 1860, the South was no longer in control of the federal political process. Before 1860, pro-slavery interests had obtained from Washington the annexation of Texas, the conquest of Mexico, the enactment of a federal statute compelling the return of escaped slaves without due process of law, the major Supreme Court victories in *Dred Scott* and *Ableman*, the repeal of the Missouri Compromise, and the right to extend slavery by popular approval under the Kansas-Nebraska Act. But now those same interests were moving the Southern states toward revolution—the outcome Liberty required whenever the political process did not produce the result demanded by radical elites.

Hoping to head off secession and probable civil war, on December 3, 1860 the outgoing President James Buchanan, a Northerner with Southern sympathies, used his Fourth Annual Message to Congress to deliver a lecture on the by now canonical Lockean concept of political sovereignty as a "compact" (which we examined in Chapter 3), but with a strange twist. Lamenting "the long-continued and intemperate interference of the Northern people with the question of slavery in the Southern states," which "has at length produced its natural effects," Buchanan observed that "[t]he different sections of the Union are now arrayed against each other, and the time has arrived, so much dreaded by the Father of his Country, when hostile geographical parties have been formed."[179] But the South, Buchanan opined, was not on the verge of secession because of "the claim on the part of Congress or the Territorial legislatures to exclude slavery from the Territories," for these "evils might have been endured by the South without danger to the Union (as others have been)

---

178. Fogel, 339. Fogel provides this summary of Southern political dominance over the federal government.

179. Fourth Annual Message to Congress, December 3, 1860, www.presidencyucsb.edu/ws/index.-p hp?pid=29501#axzz1VIc39k00.

in the hope that time and reflection might apply the remedy." In other words, *the problem was not the political process as such.* Rather, Buchanan saw the immediate cause as "the incessant and violent agitation of the slavery question throughout the North for the last quarter of a century [which] has at length produced its malign influence on the slaves and inspired them with vague notions of freedom." Because propaganda had incited vague notions of freedom in the breasts of slaves, in the South "a sense of security no longer exists around the family altar" and "[t]his feeling of peace at home has given place to apprehensions of servile insurrections." Recall that the Declaration of Independence cited the same apprehensions of servile insurrections among the slaves as one of the grounds for revolution.

Nevertheless, Buchanan continued, the election of Lincoln "does not of itself afford just cause for dissolving the Union," for "[i]n order to justify a resort to revolutionary resistance, the Federal Government must be guilty of 'a deliberate, palpable, and dangerous exercise' of powers not granted by the Constitution," and nothing of the sort had happened yet. Further, argued Buchanan, while territorial legislatures had purported to ban slavery in the Territories, Congress had not done so, and the Supreme Court (in *Ableman* and *Dred Scott*) had "solemnly decided that slaves are property, and, like all other property, their owners have a right to take them into the common Territories and hold them there under the protection of the Constitution...." Hence in *Ableman* the Supreme Court struck down Wisconsin's attempt to defy the Fugitive Slave Act, whose validity had been established "over and over again by the Supreme Court ... with perfect unanimity" based on the slave rendition clause in the Constitution itself.

Buchanan allowed that a future failure on the part of the Northern states to rectify their refusal to treat slaves as property under the Constitution and the Fugitive Slave Act would mean—again under Locke's prevailing doctrine of revolution—that "the Constitution, to which all the States are parties, will have been willfully violated by one portion of them" and that "the injured States, after having first used all peaceful and constitutional means to obtain redress, would be justified in revolutionary resistance to the Government of the Union...." Seizing on Lockean-Madisonian doctrine, however, Buchanan declared that it was *only* by "revolutionary resistance" that the South could leave the Union, because in no way was the Union "a mere voluntary association of States, to be dissolved at pleasure by any one of the contracting parties," which would make of the Union "a rope of sand, to be penetrated and dissolved by the first adverse wave of public opinion in any of the States."

Buchanan's admonitory address went on to note that the idea of "nullification" and a Union revocable at will by any one state had not been floated "until many years after the origin of the Federal Government" only to be rejected by the Southerner Andrew Jackson (and all the States but South Carolina) during the Nullification Crisis. He sounded the fundamental Lockean theme that the social compact, once expressly consented to, is *irrevocable*: the Constitution "was formed by the States; that is, by the people in each of the States acting in their highest sovereign capacity," and was "intended to be perpetual, and not to be annulled at the pleasure of any one of the contracting parties." We will reserve for discussion in the next chapter what we have already noted in Chapter 3: the lack of any traditional moral or philosophical basis for the theory of a perpetually indissoluble Union as asserted by Lincoln in view of Locke or, for that matter, Locke's doctrine of the right to revolution invoked by the South. We note here Buchanan's invocation of the "perpetual union" theory only to provide additional historical context for the war that the practical application of Locke's theories in America had made inevitable.

But Buchanan had his own peculiar twist on Lockean social compact theory as applied to the Union created by the Constitution. While the South could escape the Union only by revolutionary resistance, in his view neither the President nor Congress had any power under the Constitution to use force to oppose this revolution, for "the power to make war against a State is at variance with the whole spirit and intent of the Constitution. . . . If [the Union] can not live in the affections of the people, it must one day perish. Congress possesses many means of preserving it by conciliation, but the sword was not placed in their hand to preserve it by force."

Buchanan's argument, a desperate bid to avoid civil war, verged on the nonsensical, given the Lockean premise of a perpetual social compact arising from express consent from which *revolution* was the only escape, as Buchanan himself had just asserted. Secession from the perpetual compact could hardly constitute revolution if the compact—the Constitution—conferred no power on the government it had created to put down a rebellion against its own authority. But, like it or not, Section 8 of the Constitution enumerated among Congressional powers precisely the power "To provide for calling forth the Militia to . . . *suppress Insurrections. . . .*" As Buchanan would have it, "revolutionary resistance" by way of secession would be a quiet exit from the Union through a massive loophole in the compact. This was a loophole Locke himself surely would not have recognized, however, for it would mean that his "one body politic under one supreme government" could be destroyed at will by any group of dissenting subjects; it would mean, in fact, that governmental authority does not exist at all, but rather only interludes of non-resistance. Then again, having denied the ultimate divine source of all civil authority (as we saw in Chapter 3), on what ground besides sheer force could even Locke stand to demand obedience to authority?

If the Constitution had expressly provided for a right of secession by the States, there could be no moral objection to the Southern states' secession nor any criticism of it from the perspective of this study of the follies of political modernity. But Buchanan's conclusion that the seceding states could not be subjected to force, however desirable that conclusion might have been for the avoidance of bloodshed, did not follow from his own premise that secession constituted revolutionary resistance to the federal government. His argument was deficient in logic but noble in intent, for he had hoped "to gain time for reflection . . . that thus the good sense of the people would assert itself."[180] The problem, however, was that his reading of the Constitution was only an opinion regarding a "penumbral" or implicit right of secession to be found in the "spirit" of the document. Disagreement over that

180. Clement Eaton, *A History of the Old South*, (Long Grove, IL: Waveland Press, 1975), 3rd ed., 491.

opinion by the contending parties could only mean a resort to violence—that is, civil war. And that war would have to be morally justified by both sides.

Indeed, Buchanan himself admitted that his view of the Constitutional compact was far from uncontested and that the secession issue would have to be decided by Congress: "The course of events is so rapidly hastening forward that the emergency may soon arise when *you* may be called upon to decide the momentous question whether you possess the power by force of arms to compel a State to remain in the Union. I should feel myself recreant to my duty were I not to express an *opinion* on this important subject." That is, Buchanan knew his opinion was only that. Lincoln, of course, would have a different opinion, as would the Congressional majority that would bow to his wishes. Thus Locke's internally contradictory theory of sovereignty, as put into practice by Madison and the Framers, had set in motion an inexorable dynamic of civil war in the name of Liberty: a deadly duel of opposing sovereigns, each demanding the allegiance of the very subjects who were supposed to be their authors.

§

The survey in this and the preceding chapters of signal events in the early history of the Republic should suffice to demonstrate that the coming Civil War would reflect Liberty's own self-contradictory imperatives: the call to rebellion against established authority in order to build a "temple of Liberty" wherein no further rebellion would ever be permitted; the cry for an end to "tyranny" by the same radicals who insisted on their own right to buy, sell and forcibly repossess their fellow human beings as chattels; the demand that the federal government protect institutionalized slavery in the States, followed by the demand that the federal government keep its hands off the States entirely.

At first, Liberty had meant freedom from King George; but after the Revolution it meant dutiful submission to former revolutionary leaders at all levels of government. And now, as civil war loomed, Liberty meant the freedom of the States to exit the Union and return to the way things were before the Constitution was ratified. Under Lincoln, however, Liberty would mean what his predecessors had all required: obedience to the national government "We the People" had vested with authority over themselves—"a new birth of freedom," as he would call it during his address on a "great battlefield" of the war. And it should come as no surprise that both sides in that unbelievably bloody and destructive conflict over the shape-shifting idol called Liberty would invoke the names of Washington and Jefferson.

III.

The Second
American Revolution

11

The South Rises

WE HAVE ALREADY NOTED that the libertarian disciples of Liberty blame Lincoln above all for the supposed demise of what one libertarian commentator (typical of the rest) hails as the "classical vision of the American republic" and "the republic the framers established."[1] But it was the very "republic the framers established" on Locke's principles that had made the Civil War inevitable, as the Tory propagandists had predicted back when the Continental Congress was already exceeding its purported authority by acting as a federal union. To quote one prophetic Tory broadside by Thomas Bradbury Chandler:

> Even a final victory [over England] would effectually ruin us; as it would merely introduce *civil wars* among ourselves. . . . *And till one part of this country shall have subdued the other,* and conquered a considerable part of the world besides, this peaceful region must become, and continue to be, a theater of inconceivable misery and horror.[2]

As the previous discussion should make clear, Lincoln would do on a vast scale what his predecessors had already done on a smaller scale, and according to the same principles as they: that Liberty demands subjection to the new federal republic; that the essence of the new republic is "the Union" of the several States; that, as Jefferson himself declared, "in extreme cases" the President of the republic is entitled to exercise dictatorial powers, including the use of armed forces against American citizens—powers that, as we have seen, were either granted or ratified by Congress according to its own sweeping authority under the Constitution. Lincoln would merely wield the hammer first forged in the furnace of the American Revolution. The oppression of Loyalists and other dissenters by the Continental Congress and the revolutionary governments and committees of safety that comprised a virtual police state was no different in principle from the oppression of secessionists by the Lincoln administration. In both cases, the opponents of sheer power wielded in the name of Liberty were ruthlessly and systematically bludgeoned into submission.

---

1. Thomas E. Woods, Jr., "Theodore Roosevelt and the Modern Presidency," www.lewrockwell.com/woods/woods79.html.

2. Thomas Bradbury Chandler, "What Think Ye of Congress Now (1775)," in Davidson, *Propaganda and the American Revolution*, 289.

The Avoidance of Romance

But the assertion of raw power in Liberty's name would not be confined to the Northern side of the conflict. The "theater of inconceivable misery and horror" that was the Civil War was, at its essence, the result of an attempt by the eleven seceding states of the South, declaring themselves a new nation, to assert against the federal government—however selectively, as we shall see—the very principles by which that government had been created to replace the overthrown king and parliament. In the process, both sides of the conflict would reveal to its victims that Liberty means Power, that Liberty had always meant Power, and that once incarnated in the United States of America, or for that matter the Confederate States of America, Liberty could permit no further operation of the principles by which the Word revealed by Locke had been made flesh to dwell among men.

In order to understand this, it is necessary to prescind from either the Northern or the Southern romantic narrative of the Civil War. In his magnum opus *Patriotic Gore*, Edmund Wilson—no partisan of the Northern narrative—explicates through the literature and rhetoric of the wartime period the pretensions of modern "patriotic" wars in general, with their "songs about glory and God, the speeches about national ideals, the demonstrations of logical ideologies."[3] Wilson's masterful survey of the writings of thirty leading wartime Americans, of the North and the South, exposes what we have already developed thematically respecting the American Revolution: that "when once the dominant power has been routed and dispossessed" there remains the problem of "defending the society set up by the revolution against the return of the former regime," and that "once the insurgent party has succeeded in imposing its own authority, if it feels itself strong enough to go further, it will devour as much as it can, and its slogans will lose all meaning."[4] This was a process the Union would complete with its final subjugation of the South, even as the Confederacy imploded under the strain of attempting to be the Union's successor and opponent on the field of battle, which required that it demand submission to its own central authority despite the doctrine of "states' rights" that the Southern romantic narrative places at the heart of the "Southern cause."

Wilson, like this study, is unaccepting of both Northern and Southern claims to righteousness. While the North proclaimed "its Armageddon-like vision, derived from its traditional theology, of the holy crusade which was to liberate the slaves and to punish their unrighteous masters," the South proclaimed "with equal fanaticism" its own holy crusade of "rescuing a hallowed idea of gallantry, aristocratic living, fine manners, and luxurious living from the materialism and vulgarity of the Northern society."[5] Some have even amplified the Southern myth into nothing

---

3. Edmund Wilson, *Patriotic Gore* (NY: Farrar, Strauss and Giroux, 1962), Norton paperback ed. (1994), xii.

4. Ibid.

5. Ibid., 438.

less than a battle for the remnants of Christendom in America. Yet it was the very nerve center of the Confederacy, Virginia, that led the way to the total disestablishment of Christianity by the governments of all the States (a subject treated in the next section), doing so under the influence of that holy icon of the Southern cause: Thomas Jefferson, a nominal Anglican deist who ridiculed Trinitarian Christianity and proclaimed the equality of all men while living a life of luxury made possible only by a large retinue of heavily mortgaged slaves.

That both the North and the South would appeal to Jefferson's legacy during the Civil War is a telling indication of the ideological confusion his own life exhibited: an apostle of Liberty who owned slaves and had them flogged for attempting to escape; an advocate of emancipating the slaves who declined to emancipate his own slaves, even after death; a proponent of states' rights who ignored them completely when he was President; an advocate of limited government who vastly expanded federal power; a defender of free speech who crushed it when he was Governor of Virginia and called for sedition prosecutions by the States while he was President. Jefferson was a veritable incarnation of the internal contradictions that would tear asunder the first Temple of Liberty from 1861 to 1865.

The Secession of the "Cotton States"

By late 1860, driven by the press and the incendiary rhetoric of the pro-secession politicians known as "fire-eaters," the movement for Southern secession was past the point of no return. On December 14, with secession seemingly imminent and only six days before South Carolina actually seceded, Robert E. Lee wrote to his wife, Mary Custis Lee, who was no less than the daughter of George Washington Parke Custis, the adopted son of George Washington. Lee confided to her his disapproval of the posture of the "Cotton States" and what it would mean for the fate of border states like Virginia:

> I am not pleased with the course of the 'Cotton States,' as they term themselves. In addition to their *selfish, dictatorial bearing*, the threats they throw out against the 'Border States,' as they call them, if they will not join them, argues little for the benefit or peace of Virginia, should she determine to coalesce with them. While I wish to do what is right, I am unwilling to do what is wrong at the bidding *of the South or of the North.*[6]

A few months later, Mrs. Lee herself would condemn the conduct of the Cotton States in a letter to her friend Elizabeth Stiles in Georgia, asking if she "could approve of all these riotous proceedings" and "has all love & pride in their Country died at the South?" The Cotton States, she wrote, seemed "willing to tear her [the country] in pieces & some even to exult to see her glorious flag trailing in the dust. It should rather have drawn tears from their eyes. We have lived & fought & prospered under this flag for so many years & tho the South has suffered much from

6. In Michael Fellman, *The Making of Robert E. Lee* (NY: Random House, 2000), 81.

the meddling of Northern fanatics, yet do they expect to fare better now; are there no rights & privileges but those of negro slavery?"[7]

On January 21, 1861, while he was still in Texas on assignment with the Army, Lee wrote the famous letter to his son "Rooney." Agreeing with President Buchanan's final message to Congress, Lee declared to his son that although the South had been aggrieved "by acts of the North.... I can anticipate no greater calamity for the country than a dissolution of the Union. It would be an accumulation of all the evils we complain of, & I am willing to sacrifice every thing but honour for its preservation. I hope therefore that all Constitutional means will be exhausted, before there is a resort to force. *Secession is nothing but revolution.*" The Framers, he opined, would have failed in their work if the Union could "be broken by every member of the confederacy at will.... Anarchy would have been established & not a government...."[8]

On January 23 Lee wrote again to Mary Custis from Texas. By this time five states had seceded—South Carolina, Florida, Mississippi, Alabama and Georgia—although it seems only news of the first four secessions had reached Lee. Lee declared: "As far as I can judge from the papers, we are between a state of anarchy and civil war. May God avert both of these evils from us.... I see that four States have declared themselves out of the Union; four more apparently will follow their example. Then, if the Border States are dragged into *the gulf of revolution*, one half of the country will be arrayed against the other."[9] As the Southern leadership itself would proclaim, the Civil War was indeed a revolution—nothing less than the second American Revolution, launched on the basis of the same principles that had inspired the first: that breach of the compact between "the sovereign people" and their government justifies dissolution of the government and the formation of a new one by the same "sovereign people."

Yet, in keeping with the Spirit of 1776, whose mythical "conservatism" we examined in Chapter 5, present-day Southern partisans of a traditionalist bent defend the Southern secession as a "conservative" act. The proponents of this view, quite remarkably, offer in defense of American Revolution II the same myth that persists regarding American Revolution I: that it was no revolution at all, but really a conservative affair. In defense of this line, the Catholic historian Harry W. Crocker III writes: "The new nation [the Confederate States of America] was created out of motives of preservation, not destruction, of conservatism rather than revolution. For inspiration, the South looked to its past; one Georgia delegate wanted the new nation to be named 'The Republic of Washington.' Instead, George Washington

---

7. Mary Custis Lee to Elizabeth Stiles, February 9, 1861, in *Women's Letters: America from the Revolutionary War to the Present*, eds Lisa Grunwald and Stephen J. Adler (NY: Random House, 2008). The letter is part of the Lee papers of the Colonial Dames Collection of the Georgia Historical Society.

8. Washington and Lee University digital archive, http://leearchive.wlu.edu/reference/essays/rach al/index.html.

9. In Henry Alexander White, *Robert E. Lee and the Southern Confederacy: 1807–1870* (G. P. Putnam's Sons, 1900), 98.

ended up on the Great Seal of the Confederacy."[10] For reasons that should be perfectly obvious at this point in our survey of the history of Liberty, a reprise of the American Revolution could no more be considered a conservative act than any other revolution against an existing government based on Locke's novel theories.

Some proponents of the "conservative" Southern revolution thesis recite, as if it were the essence of "true conservatism," the radically liberal dictum of the great libertarian divine Ludwig von Mises: "No people and no *part* of a people shall be held against its will in a political association that it does not want."[11] The dictum reduces to the nonsensical proposition, representing Liberty in its active revolutionary phase, that no government has any authority over any group of people that deems its authority at an end. From this it follows—just as Lee confided to his son—that there is neither government nor law but only anarchy punctuated by periods of relative calm maintained by force and social conformity, or Liberty in its resting phase. Mises's dictum is but a restatement of Locke's doctrine of the right to revolution, part of the "moderate" Enlightenment inheritance we surveyed in Chapter 3 and thus part of what passes for a "conservative" tradition in a radically liberal, post-Christian West.

Lee would abandon his opposition to secession once Virginia had seceded, but the pre-secession Lee was surely right. As distinguished from licit resistance to particular unjust or immoral state actions, a total secession from the authority of a duly constituted government (at least absent a prior peaceable agreement with that government) is patently a rebellion and thus a revolution against it. Indeed, the Confederates would proudly call themselves Rebels, complete with a "rebel yell," and their leaders would invoke the first American Revolution as their warrant for the second. Recall once again the discussion in Chapters 2 and 3 of the Christian tradition, elaborated by St. Paul, St. Augustine and St. Thomas, on obedience to civil authority, even pagan emperors, as rooted in divine authority and the concomitant duty to refrain from insurrections.

By 1860, the federal government had indubitably acquired legitimacy as a constituted civil power despite its originally contested revolutionary origins, for revolutions have to stop somewhere.[12] For that very reason, less than thirty years after the Civil War began, Pope Leo XIII would call upon the Catholics of France to submit to the authority of the Third Republic despite its remote origins in the French

10. H.W. Crocker, III, *The Politically Incorrect Guide to the Civil War* (Washington, DC: Regnery Publishing, Inc., 2008), Kindle Edition, 202.

11. See, e.g., Thomas E. Woods, Jr., "The Left is Pro-Empire," www.lewrockwell.com/woods/woods55.html, quoting Ludwig von Mises, *Nation, State and Economy* (Indianapolis: Liberty Fund, Inc. 2006 [1919]); cf. online PDF edition, 37. Purporting to express sober conservative opposition to Leftist hysteria, Woods quotes the Misesian dictum and then declares: "Leftists can talk a dramatic game about bringing the empire down, but they seek to do so while at the same insisting on its absolute supremacy over all other institutions and power centers, such that the very invocation of states' rights —or, heaven forbid, secession—is enough to render them apoplectic."

12. As a practical matter, even a government established by revolution must be held to have acquired legitimacy at least "by prescription" once it becomes clear that "the rightful ruler cannot be restored." Catholic writers on the subject have suggested that this transition to legitimacy occurs within

Revolution, which had been inspired precisely by the American example. The very fact that an illicit rebellion had overthrown the King of France in 1789, producing anarchy, had given rise, wrote Leo, to the "social need [that] justifies the creation and the existence of new governments. . . ."[13] France could not remain forever in a state of anarchy, and a peaceful restoration of the *ancien régime* was no longer conceivable more than sixty years after the Revolution of 1830 had ended the Bourbon Restoration.

Citing St. Paul and St. Augustine and the example of Christian obedience to Julian the Apostate, Leo reminded the French faithful of the revealed truth— binding even on the infuriated Protestant slave-owners of the antebellum South— that men have a duty to respect existing civil authority despite particular grievances against it. In the light of revelation, "the Church, the guardian of the truest and highest idea of political sovereignty, since *she has derived it from God*, has always condemned men who rebelled against legitimate authority and disapproved their doctrines." While the Third Republic had enacted anti-Catholic laws, the faithful were obliged to recognize "the very considerable distinction between constituted power and legislation. . . ." An unjust and immoral law may be opposed and even resisted, but the government that enacted it may not be overthrown on that account. Quoting the Epistle to the Romans, the Pope observed that "in all hypotheses, civil power, considered as such, is from God, *always* from God: 'For there is no power *but* from God.'" Hence, despite the injustices the French people were enduring, they were obliged not to rebel against what was now, however unfortunately, a "constituted power." The divinely imposed obligation to refrain from rebellions against the established government was "all the more imperative because an insurrection stirs up hatred among citizens, *provokes civil war*, and may throw a nation into *chaos and anarchy*, and this great duty of respect and dependence will endure as long as the exigencies of the common good shall demand it, since this good is, after God, the first and last law in society."[14] While Leo's policy of *Ralliement* (reunification) was controversial to the extent it appeared to counsel a prudential accommodation to the new order on the part of French monarchists, his teaching against the evils of insurrection as such was not in question.

But the "Rebels" of the South were not acting in the bimillenial tradition defended by Catholic saints and the detested Popes of Rome. They were following the new doctrines of Hobbes, Locke and the American revolutionaries. Those doctrines provided the warrant for the Southern secession, which the pre-secession Lee had rightly called "nothing but revolution"—that is, the Second American Revolution. The Southern fire-eaters would not be deterred by the ancient wisdom reflected in Pope Leo's admonition that revolutions stir up hatred and civil war, leading to chaos and anarchy—all of which would follow the secession with

---

"two or three generations." Ryan and Boland, *Catholic Principles of Politics* (NY: The MacMillan Company, 1950), 93. At any rate, a line must be drawn somewhere respecting the duty to obey constituted governments in order to avoid the absurdity of endless revolution and counter-revolution.

13. *Au Milieu des Solicitudes* (1892), n. 18.

14. Ibid., nn. 16, 17, 19.

predictable immediacy. Yet Lee himself had uttered the same admonition, albeit privately.

With the secession of South Carolina on December 20, 1860—that is, a "convention" in Charleston purporting to speak for the people of that state—American Revolution II was underway. "The tea has been thrown overboard. The Revolution of 1860 has been initiated," declared the *Charleston Mercury*.[15] The early 20th-century historian James Ford Rhodes, known for his meticulous examination of contemporaneous publications in order to determine the motives behind political decisions, observed that "The comparison of events in Charleston to the Boston 'tea party' occurs more than once in the agitation that immediately preceded the act of secession. It was a welcome assertion to the people that they were animated by the spirit of 1776."[16]

Following South Carolina's lead, each of the seceding states would issue an "ordinance" or other decree of secession purporting to withdraw all the people within the borders of that state from the United States, whether they liked it or not; and many did not like it at all. As the renowned historian Clement Eaton, a North Carolinian, observes in his classic history of the Old South, "the Southern people as a whole left the Union reluctantly." And to be quite sure that they left it "the secession conventions, except in Texas and Virginia (after it already had seceded), *refused to submit the secession ordinances to a vote of the people*, suggesting that they feared the people might reject them."[17] But what else is new? The cadres of Liberty in the secession conventions were only following Madison's view in Federalist No. 40 that since "it is impossible for the people spontaneously and universally to move in concert towards *their* object ... some patriotic and respectable citizen or number of citizens" must do it for them. For who knows the people's object better than a group of patriotic and respectable citizens?

Eaton summarizes evidence that the second American Revolution, like the first, probably did not have the support of an actual majority of the people of the South. Aside from the refusal of secession conventions in nine States to submit their decisions to a popular vote, Easton cites: (1) the overwhelming opposition to secession in the Southern press before Lincoln's election, (2) the failure of a majority of Southern voters to cast their ballots for the secessionist candidate Breckinridge in the election of 1860, (3) the very strong pro-Union sentiment in Georgia, Alabama, and Louisiana (which would later undermine the Confederacy), rendering debatable "what the real sentiment of the people was," (4) the opposition to secession by both Jefferson Davis and Alexander Stephens, future President and Vice President of the Confederacy, and (5) the resistance of the States of the Upper South to secession "almost until the last moment"—especially Virginia, as discussed below. As Eaton also remarks: "Illusions upon illusions, notably a belief that secession would

15. James F. Rhodes, *History of the United States from the Compromise of 1850 to the McKinley-Bryan Campaign of 1896* (NY: Cosimo, Inc. 2009 [1895]), Vol. III, 4.
16. Ibid.
17. Eaton, *A History of the Old South*, 510.

not be followed by war, and that the *élan* of the Southern people would prevail against technology and numbers, played a decisive role in the disastrous decision."[18] But, again, this was a decision by a few "patriotic and respectable citizens" who did not bother to seek the popular approval that might have averted disaster.

What were the grounds for secession? We can dispense immediately with the argument that tariffs were a ground because the duties on imported goods compelled the South to purchase its goods from the North. As we have seen, the tariff issue was resolved by the compromise Tariff of 1830, proposed by Calhoun, the very voice of nullification, supported by Andrew Jackson, a slave-owning Southern President, and ultimately accepted by every Southern state *including* South Carolina, the very *situs* of the crisis. Thereafter it was the Southern states, allied with Massachusetts, Connecticut, Maine, and the majority of the New York delegation to Congress that enacted the Tariff of 1857, "the lowest tariff enacted by Congress since 1816." As the historian Richard Hofstadter has shown, the major tariff conflict was not between "manufacturers and cotton," that is, between the North and the South, but rather between wool growers and wool manufacturers over the extent to which foreign wool would be taxed to protect domestic growers. The Tariff of 1857 obviated the conflict by exempting from duties certain grades of wool that did not compete with domestic production. Hence at the time of secession "there was no open hostility on [the tariff] issue . . . between these manufacturers and the South that might have been exploited for a partisan purpose."[19]

The *sine qua non* of the Southern secession came down to one issue: slavery. In keeping with Locke's theory and the Declaration of Independence, the Southern states alleged a breach of the constitutional "compact" between the States that gave rise to the federal government. But no matter how they framed their arguments for secession, they could not articulate any breach besides a perceived threat to the property right in slaves as guaranteed by the Constitution and the Fugitive Slave Act of 1850. The Declaration of Secession by Calhoun's home state of South Carolina, the leader of the band, is preeminently illustrative of the historical reality versus the romantic myth. The document sounds entirely in breach of compact, and the alleged breach concerns only the constitutionally protected property right in slaves. A close reading of the Declaration reveals the Lockean principles of Liberty at work in an argument for "nothing but revolution," as Lee had put it.

First, the Declaration appealed to the supposedly sacred principles discovered by the Founders and the Framers, which South Carolina now vainly expected "the republic the framers established" to observe. Citing the "struggle for the right of self-government" against England and the Declaration of Independence, it asserted "the two great principles asserted by the Colonies: the right of a State to govern itself; and the right of a people to abolish a Government when it becomes destructive of the ends for which it was instituted." The national government, it claimed,

18. Eaton, 510.

19. Richard Hofstadter, "The Tariff Issue on the Eve of the Civil War," *The American Historical Review*, Vol. 44, No. 1 (October 1938), 51–53.

was "subject to the two great principles asserted in the Declaration of Independence." The Declaration added to these principles an argument based on Lockean social compact theory:

> We maintain that in every compact between two or more parties, the obligation is mutual; that the failure of one of the contracting parties to perform a material part of the agreement, entirely releases the obligation of the other; and that *where no arbiter is provided, each party is remitted to his own judgment* to determine the fact of failure, with all its consequences.

This was yet another American invocation of Locke's by-now-canonical "breach of trust" justification for the overthrow of established government, with the breach of trust to be determined by the private judgment of each individual party to the social compact. Having recited this quintessentially Lockean rationale, the Declaration argued that under the Articles of Confederation "each State retain[ed] its sovereignty, freedom and independence, and every power, jurisdiction and right which is not, by this Confederation, expressly delegated to the United States in Congress assembled." The same was true under the Constitution, the Declaration observed optimistically, but "to remove all doubt" the Tenth Amendment was added, "which declared that the powers not delegated to the United States by the Constitution, nor prohibited by it to the States, are reserved to the States, respectively, or to the people." But what *were* the retained, non-delegated powers that, according to the Declaration, trumped the Supremacy Clause of the Constitution? The Declaration offered no details, whereas the Supreme Court had long ago revealed the Tenth Amendment to be a truism amounting to the pious hope that the federal government would be submissive to the will of the States in cases of conflict over the extent of its powers.

Finally arriving at the actual grounds for secession, the Declaration pointed out that the very text of the Constitution, in Article IV, provides that escaped slaves "shall be delivered up, on claim of the party to whom such service or labor may be due," that "the General Government," acting pursuant to that provision, had passed both the Fugitive Slave Act of 1793 and the Fugitive Slave Act of 1850, and that "[f]or many years these laws were executed." But now, thanks to the abolition movement, Maine, New Hampshire, Vermont, Massachusetts, Connecticut, Rhode Island, New York, Pennsylvania, Illinois, Indiana, Michigan, Wisconsin and Iowa "have enacted laws which either *nullify the Acts of Congress* or render useless any attempt to execute them. In many of these States the fugitive is discharged from service or labor claimed, and in none of them has the State Government complied with the stipulation made in the Constitution." At the same time, however, slaveowners in some of the Northern states continued to enjoy the ownership of their *non-*fugitive slaves.

Thus South Carolina, the original champion of State "nullification" of federal law during the tariff crisis of 1832–33, was now declaring that *state nullification was a breach of the constitutional compact*. In addition to these alleged breaches of the compact, the Northern states, said South Carolina, had combined to "inaugurate a

new policy, hostile to the South, and destructive of its beliefs and safety," by granting citizenship to fugitive slaves in some states (thereby affecting the balance of
political power in the national government) and by electing Lincoln, "whose opinions and purposes are hostile to slavery" and who was about to take office as President. Hence, South Carolina concluded, "the guaranties of the Constitution will
then no longer exist; the equal rights of the States will be lost. The slaveholding
states will no longer have the power of self-government, or self-protection, and the
Federal Government will have become their enemy." Accordingly, "appealing to the
Supreme Judge of the world for the rectitude of our intentions"—a direct reference
to Locke's *Second Treatise*—South Carolina declared that "the Union heretofore
existing between this State and the other States of North America, is dissolved, and
that the State of South Carolina has resumed her position among the nations of the
world, as a separate and independent State."

According to the gravamen of its Declaration of Secession, then, South Carolina
was not seceding because of "tyranny" as such, or "taxation without representation," or indeed any other alleged abuse of federal power, but rather because the
federal government had *failed* to exercise its power to protect Southern property
rights in slaves as provided by federal law. "Thus," South Carolina declared, "the
constituted compact has been deliberately broken and disregarded by the non-
slaveholding States, and the consequence follows that South Carolina is released
from her obligation." The argument could not be clearer: the slave-holding states
were seceding from the non-slaveholding states over the economic issue of slavery.
That the "Southern cause" would *become* a defense of the homeland against invasion cannot alter the historical reality that the secession that led to the war was justified on the basis of one, and only one, breach of the compact between the States:
the refusal of some states to respect the property right in slaves and the failure of
the federal government to remedy that disrespect.

This was the Lockean "breach of trust" doctrine in its essence: a government
deemed ineffective in addressing any particular issue can be deemed no longer to
exist. But notice the incoherence of the argument: South Carolina, entering the
Union as a sovereign state like all the others, had the right to secede from the
Union because the federal government had *failed to override the sovereignty of the
Northern states* by compelling them to abide by the Fugitive Slave Act, which
(according to South Carolina) the Northern states had no right to nullify with their
contrary laws. South Carolina thus wanted it both ways: absolute sovereignty for
itself, including the right to "nullify" federal legislation it deemed unconstitutional
(as it had attempted to do with the tariffs of 1828 and 1832), but subjection to the
federal government on the part of the Northern states when it came to federal legislation on slavery.

To be perfectly fair, one could construct a narrow and thus coherent argument
for South Carolina's secession: Since the Constitution by its very terms required the
interstate rendition of escaped slaves, the Fugitive Slave Act was patently within
federal authority. And so the Northern states' attempt to nullify it was a breach of
the constitutional compact by both the Northern states and the federal govern-

ment, which had breached its constitutional duty to enforce the Act. But the argument thus constructed means precisely what we are suggesting here: that failure to protect the property right in slaves was the *only* grounds for secession based on breach of compact. And, in fact, South Carolina made *no* argument in favor of a general right to secede from the Union at will; it knew it had to allege at least a colorable breach of the constitutional compact in its attempt to justify secession.

Only three secession conventions besides South Carolina's—those in Georgia, Texas, and Mississippi—even bothered to issue detailed declarations of the purported grounds for secession in support of their "ordinances" of secession. Like South Carolina's convention, the others failed to present any argument for the right of a state to secede from the United States at will. Rather, they all contrived to present the same "breaches" of the constitutional compact: *failure* to exercise federal authority over the Northern states in order to protect the property right in slaves; the Northern states' failure to obey federal law; and the allegedly unconstitutional restriction of slavery extension in the territories.[20]

Georgia's declaration of secession, issued January 29, 1861, complained that the non-slave-holding states had "refused to comply with their constitutional obligations to us with respect to that property," even though at the time the constitution was ratified "the political and social inequality of the African race was fully conceded by all...." The declaration further complained of the exclusion of slavery from the territories and ended with a peroration protesting that Congress had "outlawed $3,000,000,000 of *our property* [i.e., slaves] in the common territories of the Union...." Just how central the property right in slaves was to Georgia's secession is seen in an address by Benjamin Harvey Hill to members of the secession convention before it met to vote on secession. While arguing passionately against secession until all constitutional remedies had been exhausted, even the pro-Union Hill—the only delegate to the Convention who was not a Democrat—thundered to his audience: "If the Union and the peace of slavery cannot exist together, then the Union must go; *for slavery can never go, the necessities of man and the laws of Heaven will never let it go*, and it must have peace."[21]

The Texas declaration boldly invoked nothing less than natural law and divine revelation on the subjugation of the black man as grounds for secession, citing the Northern states' "unnatural feeling of hostility to these Southern States and their beneficent and patriarchal system of African slavery, proclaiming *the debasing doctrine of equality of all men*, irrespective of race or color—a doctrine at war with *nature*, in opposition to the experience of mankind, and in violation of the plainest *revelations* of Divine Law."[22]

The Declaration of Secession by Jefferson Davis's home State of Mississippi,

20. These declarations are archived online by Yale Law School. Cf. avalon.law.yale.edu/subject_menus/csapage.asp.

21. In *Senator Benjamin H. Hill of Georgia: His Life, Speeches and Writings* (Atlanta: H.C. Hudgins & Co., 1891), 244.

22. Cf. "A Declaration of the Causes which Impel the State of Texas to Secede from the Federal Union," Yale Law School e-text, www. avalon.law.yale.edu/19th_century/csa_ texsec.asp.

which seriously asserted the necessity of black slave labor because "none but the black race can bear exposure to the tropical sun," could not have been more emphatic about violation of the property right in slaves as grounds for secession:

> *Our position is thoroughly identified with the institution of slavery—the greatest material interest of the world.* Its labor supplies the product which constitutes by far the largest and most important portions of commerce of the earth. . . . *[A] blow at slavery is a blow at commerce and civilization.* That blow has been long aimed at the institution, and was at the point of reaching its consummation. There was no choice left us but submission to the mandates of abolition, or a dissolution of the Union, whose principles had been subverted to work out our ruin.[23]

Here it must be noted that in his Farewell Address to the United States Senate on January 21, 1861, given twelve days after Mississippi's secession, then Senator Davis declared that he had "for many years advocated, as an essential attribute of State sovereignty, the right of a State to secede from the Union," so that even if Mississippi "was acting without sufficient provocation, or without an existing necessity, I should still, under *my* theory of Government, because of my allegiance to the State of which I am a citizen, have been bound by her action. I, however, may be permitted to say that I do think she has justifiable cause, and I approve of her act."[24] In other words, Davis was not defending Mississippi's secession on the basis of his personal theory of a *per se* right of the States to secede from the Union with or without cause. Rather, Mississippi had "justifiable cause" for secession: that the federal compact had allegedly been breached by the federal government's failure to defend Mississippians' property rights in slaves, "the greatest material interest of the world."

As Davis would later concede in his post-Civil War apologia, the seceding states had a moral obligation "not to break up the partnership *without good and sufficient cause.* . . ."[25] What, then, was the "good and sufficient cause" for secession? It was simply and only a threat to the institution of slavery. Davis's explanation of Mississippi's rationale before the Senate is devastating to the myth of Southern secession as a noble crusade, coming as it did from the future President of the Confederacy himself. Mississippi, he protested, has "heard proclaimed the theory that all men are created free and equal, and this made the basis of an attack upon her social institutions; and the sacred Declaration of Independence is invoked to maintain the equality of the races." It was true that no less than Thomas Jefferson had proclaimed that in the communities that were declaring their independence "no man was born . . . booted and spurred, to ride over the rest of mankind; that men were created equal . . . that there was no divine right to rule; that no man inherited the

23. *Mississippi Declaration of Secession* (1861), University of Mississippi e-text, www.olemiss.edu.

24. In ed. William J. Cooper, *Jefferson Davis: the Essential Writings* (NY: Random House, 2004), 190–191.

25. Jefferson Davis, *A Short History of the Confederate States of America* (NY: Belford Company, Publishers, 1890), 52.

right to govern; that there were no classes by which power and place descended to families; but that all stations were equally within the grasp of each member of the body politic." But these principles, Davis insisted—evoking Justice Taney's argument in *Dred Scott*—"have *no reference to the slave*," but only to "the men of the political community." By the will of the Founders themselves, Davis continued, the slaves "were not put upon the footing of equality with white men—*not even upon that of paupers and convicts; but . . .* were discriminated against as *a lower caste*, only to be represented in the numerical proportion of three fifths."[26] As already noted in Chapter 6, Davis reminded his fellow Senators that the Founders never meant to embrace the slaves—least of all their own!—within the Declaration. That is precisely why the Declaration had "arraigned" King George for "stirring up insurrection among them." And that, Davis concluded, was "just what the North has been endeavoring of late to do—stir up insurrection among our slaves. . . ."

Writing sixteen years after the war's end, the former President of the Confederacy could still do no better than an elaborate restatement of the same claim of breach of compact the Southern states had enunciated twenty years earlier: violation of the property right in slaves. "It was not," he argued, "the passage of the 'personal liberty laws' [protecting escaped slaves from *ex parte* seizure without a jury trial], it was not the circulation of incendiary documents, it was not the raid of John Brown, it was not the operation of unjust and unequal tariff laws, nor all combined, that constituted the intolerable grievance, but it was the systematic and persistent struggle to deprive the Southern states of equality in the Union—generally to discriminate in legislation against the interests of their people; culminating in their exclusion from the Territories, the common property of the States, as well as by the infraction of their compact to promote domestic tranquility."[27]

But *how* was the South discriminated against and excluded from the territories with regard to any matter *except* slavery? Davis identified no other discrimination constituting "infraction of [the] compact to promote domestic tranquility." Attempting to draw a distinction between slavery as "an *occasion*, [rather than] the *cause* of the conflict,"[28] Davis revealed this to be a distinction without a difference. His entire post-war argument for secession reduced to nothing more than the pre-war argument: that the Northern states had failed to respect the property right in slaves as applied to the territories and had thus breached the federal compact. Here Davis discussed in particular, not any allegation of federal tyranny, but rather the failure of the States of the North to *obey the federal government* respecting the *Dred Scott* decision, which Davis defended as—irony of ironies—the supreme law of the land:

> In 1854 a case (the well-known "Dred Scott case") came before the Supreme Court of the United States, involving the whole question of *the status of the*

---

26. Davis, *The Rise and Fall of the Confederate Government* (NY: D. Appleton and Company, 1881), Vol. I, 224.

27. Ibid., Vol. 1, 83.

28. Ibid., 78. Emphasis in original.

African race and the rights of citizens of the Southern states to migrate to the Territories, temporarily or permanently, *with their slave property*, on a footing of equality with the citizens of other States with their property of any sort.

Having identified the question presented in *Dred Scott*, Davis recited the elements of the decision on which his breach of compact argument rested:

The salient points established by this decision were:

1. That persons of the African race were not, and could not be, acknowledged as "part of the people," or citizens, under the Constitution of the United States;

2. That Congress had no right to exclude citizens of the South from taking *their negro servants, as any other property*, into any part of the common territory, and that they were entitled to claim its protection therein;

3. And, finally, as a consequence of the principle just above stated, that the Missouri Compromise of 1820, in so far as it prohibited the existence of African servitude north of a designated line, was unconstitutional and void....[29]

But, Davis continued, "[i]nstead of accepting the decision of this then august tribunal—*the ultimate authority* in the interpretation of constitutional questions— as conclusive of a controversy that had so long disturbed the peace and was threatening the *perpetuity* of the Union, it was flouted, denounced, and utterly disregarded by the Northern agitators, and served only to stimulate the intensity of their sectional hostility." Note that, long after the war, Davis referred to flouting and denunciation of *Dred Scott* by "agitators" and to an increased "intensity of . . . sectional hostility" rather than to any specific state or federal action constituting a Southern grievance warranting secession. For, again, the complaint of the South was a *lack* of governance concerning one matter: the property right in slaves—a pocketbook issue, and only that.

With the flouting and denunciation of *Dred Scott*, Davis concluded: "What resource for justice—what assurance of tranquility—what guarantee of safety— now remained for the South?" Aside from the non-cooperation of Northerners in the return of escaped slaves, however, Davis presented no evidence that property in slaves had been impaired *within* any of the slave-holding States—because, in fact, it had not been. Rather, Davis repeated his pre-war argument that the election of Lincoln entitled the Southern states to engage in a preemptive secession for fear of what Lincoln *might* do with their slaves: "Still forbearing, still hoping, still striving for peace and union, we waited until a sectional President, nominated by a sectional convention, elected by a sectional vote—and that the vote of a minority of the people—was about to be inducted into office, under the warning of his own distinct announcement that the Union could not permanently endure 'half slave and half free'. . . .'" But, as we will see, Lincoln would repeatedly insist that he had

29. Davis, *Rise and Fall*, 84.

no intention nor any power under the Constitution to abolish slavery where it already existed, and he would affix his approving (and quite unnecessary) signature to a proposed constitutional amendment that would perpetuate the institution in the slave-holding States.

Alluding vaguely to how "the temper of the triumphant party had been tested in Congress and found adverse to any terms of reconciliation consistent with the honor and safety of all parties"—meaning the prompt return of escaped slaves and a guarantee that slaves could be transported into the territories like any other form of property—Davis's post-war apologia concludes just as the original state declarations of secession had done: "No alternative remained except to seek the security out of the Union which they had vainly tried to obtain within it. *The hope of our people may be stated in a sentence.* It was to escape from injury and strife in the Union, to find prosperity and peace out of it." That is, the hope of the South was that secession would secure a peace and prosperity that depended upon a slave-based economy. As of 1881 the very head of the extinct Confederacy was unable to articulate any other concrete rationale for the secession that—prescinding for the moment from the morality of President Lincoln's conduct during the conflict—had predictably plunged the nation into a war Davis himself had warned would be "a long and desperate struggle."[30]

The "Cornerstone" Address

Not only the President, but the Vice-President of the Confederacy declared that the grounds for secession were a perceived threat to the "institution" of chattel slavery. On March 21, 1861, a month after his installation as provisional Vice-President and days before the firing on Fort Sumter, the eloquent and erudite Alexander H. Stephens, who had represented Georgia in the U. S. House of Representatives from 1831 to 1859, delivered his infamous "Cornerstone Address." Having previously opposed secession, Stephens now made the case for it in a way that no Christian, then or now, could view as anything other than an appalling brew of blind racism and pseudo-scientific justifications for the permanent subjugation of "the negro." Yet not one word of it was delivered with malice toward the black man (Stephens was apparently well liked by his own slaves), but rather in the measured tones of one who was quite certain he was defending eternal verities. He had expressed precisely the same racial views in a speech in Georgia on his retirement from Congress two years earlier, declaring that "African slavery with us rests upon principles that can never be successfully assailed by reason and argument. . . ."[31] Stephens would now relate these unassailable principles to his case for secession.

30. Davis, *A Short History of the Confederate States*, 59.

31. "Farewell Speech of Hon. A.H. Stephens," July 2, 1859, in Henry Cleveland, *Alexander H. Stephens in Public and Private, with Letters and Speeches* (Philadelphia: National Publishing Company, 1866), 647.

Admitting in public what Lee had admitted in private, that secession was revolution, Stephens declared: "we are passing through *one of the greatest revolutions in the annals of the world*—seven States [soon to be eleven] have, within the last three months, thrown off an old Government and formed a new." This revolution, said Stephens, "amply secures all our ancient rights, franchises, and privileges." In particular, the new Confederate Constitution (to which we shall turn shortly), had "put at rest forever all the agitating questions relating to our peculiar institution— African slavery as it exists among us—*the proper status of the negro in our form of civilization. This was the immediate cause of the late rupture and present revolution.*"

Stephens acknowledged that at the time of the framing of the United States Constitution, "the prevailing ideas . . . were, that the enslavement of the African was in violation of the laws of nature; that it was wrong in principle, socially, morally and politically" and that "the general opinion of the men of that day was, that, somehow or other, in the order of Providence, the institution would be evanescent and pass away." But these ideas, Stephens declared to applause, "were fundamentally wrong. *They rested upon the assumption of the equality of races. This was an error.* It was a sandy foundation, and the idea of a Government built upon it—when the 'storm came and the wind blew, it fell.'" The invocation of the Gospel of Matthew in defense of white supremacy is stunning. But even more stunning is the following declaration:

> Our new Government is founded upon exactly the opposite ideas; its foundations are laid, *its cornerstone rests,* upon the great truth that *the negro is not equal to the white man; that slavery, subordination to the superior race, is his natural and moral condition.* [Applause.] This, our new Government, is *the first, in the history of the world, based upon this great physical, philosophical, and moral truth.*[32]

Expounding upon this "great physical, philosophical, and moral truth," the new Vice-President of the Confederacy called upon the authority of science, for scientific progress had upheld the truth of the Southern position against the moral fanaticism of the North:

> This truth has been slow in the process of its development, like all other truths in the various departments of science. It is so even amongst us. Many who hear me, perhaps, can recollect well that this truth was not generally admitted, even within their day. *The errors of the past generation still clung to many as late as twenty years ago.* Those at the North who still cling to these errors with a zeal above knowledge, we justly denominate fanatics. All fanaticism springs from an aberration of the mind; from a defect in reasoning. It is a species of insanity. One of the most striking characteristics of insanity, in many instances, is, forming correct conclusions from fancied or erroneous premises; so with the anti-slavery fanatics: their conclusions are right if their

---

32. *Southern Pamphlets on Secession*, ed. John L. Wakelyn (Chapel Hill, NC: Univ. of North Carolina Press, 1996), Appendix B, 401–411.

premises are. *They assume that the negro is equal, and hence conclude that he is entitled to equal privileges and rights, with the white man. . . .*

In their "insane" opposition to slavery, said Stephens, the abolitionists had ignored the findings of science and thus "were warring against a principle. They were attempting to make things equal which *the Creator had made unequal.*" But Stephens was confident that the principle on which "our social fabric is firmly planted" would eventually receive "full recognition . . . throughout the civilized and enlightened world." Scientific progress would insure this outcome and prove to the world that the basis of Southern society was scientifically as well as morally sound, and indeed ordained by God Himself:

> It was so with the principles announced by Galileo—it was so with Adam Smith and his principles of political economy. It was so with Harvey, and his theory of the circulation of the blood. It is stated that not a single one of the medical profession, living at the time of the announcement of the truths made by him, admitted them. Now, they are universally acknowledged. May we not therefore look with confidence to the ultimate universal acknowledgment of *the truths upon which our system rests? It is the first Government ever instituted upon principles in strict conformity to nature, and the ordination of Providence in furnishing the materials of human society.*

The "scientific racism" Stephens espoused was no conservative idea, but rather represented an element of the post-Enlightenment liberalism of his day opposed even by the conservative Protestant divines of the South, who nonetheless defended the "peculiar institution" as Biblically sanctioned.[33] Stephens concluded his oration with the expected references to the Bible, privately interpreted in the same Protestant manner by which Locke—himself an investor in slaves, as we saw in Chapter 3—had redefined the Gospel to suit his new vision of the State as an agency for the protection of proto-capitalist property rights. The Confederacy, Stephens argued, was founded on the *right* kind of slavery—not white slavery, which of course was immoral, but Negro slavery, ordained by God for the foundation of Southern civilization:

> Many Governments have been founded upon the principles of certain classes; but the classes thus enslaved, were *of the same race, and in violation of the laws of nature.* Our system commits no such violation of nature's laws. *The negro by nature, or by the curse against Canaan, is fitted for that condition which he occupies in our system.* The architect, in the construction of buildings, lays the foundation with the proper material—the granite—then comes the brick or the marble.
>
> *The substratum of our society is made of the material fitted by nature for it,* and by experience we know that it is the best, *not only for the superior but for*

---

33. Eugene D. Genovese, *A Consuming Fire: The Fall of the Confederacy in the Mind of the White Christian South* (Athens, GA: Univ. of Georgia Press, 1998), 82.

the inferior race, that it should be so. It is, indeed, in conformity with the Creator. . . . The great objects of humanity are best attained, when conformed to his laws and degrees [sic], in the formation of Governments as well as in all things else. Our Confederacy is founded upon principles in strict conformity with these laws. This stone which was rejected by the first builders "is become the chief stone of the corner" in our new edifice.

As Edmund Wilson concludes, with no little respect for Stephens as an intellectually consistent polemicist of Liberty: "From the moment this man of principles has established a principle that makes slavery obligatory, every step of the course of the South follows from his previous postulates."[34] And, as the renowned historian of the antebellum South, Eugene D. Genovese, points out: " . . . Stephens could not have been clearer in his 'Cornerstone Speech,' *and no Southerner of any importance contradicted him.*"[35]

The immense embarrassment the Cornerstone Address poses to the Southern romantic narrative was not the least mitigated by its author's attempt to "clarify" it in the diary he kept during his brief imprisonment at Fort Warren after the war. Alluding to the "extemporaneous" nature of his remarks, but retracting nothing of substance, Stephens simply dug the same hole deeper, repeating all the basic points of the address and the earlier retirement speech:

> . . . *Slavery was without doubt the occasion of secession*; out of it rose the *breach of compact*, for instance, on the part of several northern States in refusing to comply with Constitutional obligations as to rendition of fugitives from service, a course betraying total disregard for all constitutional barriers and guarantees. . . .
>
> I admitted that the fathers, both North and South, who framed the old Constitution, while recognizing existing slavery and guaranteeing its continuance under the Constitution so long as the States should severally see fit to tolerate it in their respective limits, were perhaps all opposed to the principle . . . . But, on the subject of slavery—so called—(which was with us, or should be, nothing but *the proper subordination of the inferior African race to the superior white*) great and radical changes had taken place in the realm of thought; many eminent latter-day statesmen, philosophers, and philanthropists held different views from the fathers. . . .
>
> The relation of the black to the white race, or *the proper status of the colored population among us*, was a question now of vastly more importance than when the old Constitution was formed. *The order of subordination was nature's great law*; philosophy taught that order as *the normal condition of the African amongst European races. Upon this recognized principle of a proper subordination, let it be called slavery or what not, our State institutions were formed and rested.* The new Confederation was entered into with this distinct under-

34. Wilson, *Patriotic Gore*, 411.
35. Genovese, *A Consuming Fire*, 111.

standing. *This principle of the subordination of the inferior to the superior was the "corner-stone" on which it was formed. . . .*[36]

Davis was not outdone by Stephens in defending the divinely ordained perpetual subjugation of the black man for the benefit of antebellum slave-owners: "My own convictions, as to negro slavery, are strong. . . . [W]e recognize the negro as God and God's book and *God's Laws*, in nature tell us to recognize him—*our inferior, fitted expressly for servitude* . . . the *innate stamp of inferiority is beyond the reach of change*. . . . You cannot transform the negro into anything one-tenth as useful or as good as what slavery enables him to be."[37] In his repetitious and disjointed two-volume apologia for the Confederacy, *The Rise and Fall of the Confederate Government* (1881), Davis sounded the familiar slave-owner refrain: slavery was really the best thing for the slaves. The slaves, he wrote, had been

sold by heathen masters, [and] were transferred to shores enlightened by the rays of Christianity. There, put to servitude, they were trained in the gentle arts of peace and order and civilization; they increased from a few unprofitable savages to millions of efficient Christian laborers. Their *servile instincts rendered them contented with their lot*, and their patient toil blessed the land of their abode with unmeasured riches. . . . Never was there a happier dependence of labor and capital on each other. The tempter came, like the serpent in Eden, and decoyed them with the magic word "freedom."[38]

This was the gravamen of the South's legal argument for secession and revolution under the banner of Liberty: the preservation of the slaves in their "contented lot," so that they could go on producing "unmeasured riches" for their masters in accordance with their "servile instincts," unperturbed by devilish temptations to freedom. Freedom was for the white race, as was the practice of revolution to defend it. So it was in 1861, no less than in 1776.

§

In the Cornerstone Address, Vice President Stephens voiced the Southern politicians' dream of a new Southern empire in which the Negro would forever have his proper place: "We are now the nucleus of a growing power which, if we are true to ourselves, our destiny, and high mission, *will become the controlling power on this continent*. . . . We have all the essential elements of a high national career." Eighty-five years after the overthrow of King George, the spirit of Liberty was in search of new Power.

36. In *Recollections of Alexander H. Stephens: His Diary Kept When a Prisoner at Fort Warren, Boston Harbour, 1865; Giving Incidents and Reflections Of His Prison Life and Some Letters and Reminiscences* (NY: Doubleday, Page & Company, 1910), 172–174 (parentheses around first paragraph omitted).
37. William C. Davis, *Jefferson Davis: the Man and His Hour* (LSU Press/Harper Collins, 1991), 319.
38. Davis, *Rise and Fall*, Vol. II, 192.

12

The "Peculiar Institution"

AS THE PRIOR DISCUSSION suggests, the "Southern cause" should not be seen as a "conservative" opposition to the progress of Liberty but rather as a conflict over the direction Liberty would take in a dispute over power, territory and property—that is, slaves. In order to appreciate this fully it is necessary to have clearly in view the moral and legal contours of the institution the South seceded and fought a war to defend.

Southern slavery, as Clement Eaton observes, "was an immensely complex thing that was remote from the stereotype of general cruelty presented by the abolitionists as well as the romantic legend of the happy slaves."[1] In keeping with our commitment to avoid both the Northern and the Southern romantic narratives, our primary focus must be the incontestable status of slaves as property under the antebellum legal system (as well as the Constitution). We make no pretense to settle the endless academic disputes among specialists over the quality of the food, shelter, medical care, and general treatment the slaves might have received in a given region or under a given master as compared with conditions in free-labor or peasant economies. That some slaves had it better than others is not the issue. The issue is slavery as such: the bondage of blacks for more than two centuries for no other reason than their race, and the legal and social standing of the black race during the antebellum period, when Southern slavery was a Western anomaly.

The Southern Anomaly

"Our *peculiar* institution" is the euphemism Southern leaders habitually employed to identify what Stephens described in the Cornerstone Address as "African slavery as it exists amongst us—the *proper status of the negro* in our form of civilization." The word peculiar was well chosen, for antebellum slavery in the American South was an anomaly in the Western world of the mid-19th century. The antebellum South was a slave-based socioeconomic order in which slaves constituted an amazing forty percent of the general population, and cotton and sugar harvested and processed by slave labor were the king and queen, respectively, of the economy.

Why the "peculiar institution" was called peculiar even by its defenders is evi-

---

1. Eaton, *A History of the Old South*, 249.

dent from its grand historical context. As Hilaire Belloc observed, the slave-owning state is not the capitalist state of concentrated ownership of capital and property-less wage-dependent "free" laborers; nor is it—Southern romanticism not-withstanding—the distributist state of widely dispersed ownership of the means of production as seen in pre-capitalist Christendom. The slave-owning state is the "Servile State . . . which was found among our forefathers everywhere. It is the Ser-vile State in which we Europeans all lived when we were pagan two thousand years ago."[2] In the same vein the famed American convert to Catholicism, Orestes Brownson, observed in 1857 that slavery "belongs to a past age, to a heathen rather than a Christian republic. . . ."[3] In pagan Rome and pagan Greece alike, where the origins of our civilization are found, wrote Belloc, "most of the people you would have seen working at anything were slaves, and above the slaves were the owners: the free men. . . ." For all its past achievements and advantages in terms of security and stability, "[t]he great disadvantage of the slave-owning state is clearly apparent: in it the mass of men are degraded: they are not citizens: they cannot exercise their own wills. . . . Slavery is a most unhappy condition in so far as it wounds human honour and offends human dignity; *and that is why the Christian religion gradually dissolved slavery* in the process of many centuries: slavery is not sufficiently consis-tent with the idea of man's being made in the image of God."[4]

There can be no denying that the Catholic Church accepted the reality of slavery as a tolerable evil from the first days of her existence under Roman persecution. Hence Saint Paul's admonition to slaves to obey their masters rather than rebel.[5] But as Saint Augustine famously observes in *City of God*, slavery is a consequence of Original Sin and the Fall, before which "no man was a slave either to man or to sin." According to the divine plan, "God wanted rational man, made to his image, to have no dominion over man, but only man over beast." Thus slavery is "penal in character" and represents bondage for both master and slave—the bondage of sin. As such, slavery is a condition to be overcome by divine grace and Christian love, not by insurrection and rebellion where "there is no chance of manumission."[6] The Catholic view of slavery as an evil to be tolerated until it can be eliminated under the influence of the Christian religion is a far cry from Calhoun's previously men-tioned attempt to portray it as "a positive good," which the South had the right to extend into the territories even at the cost of war and massive bloodshed. More-over, the Church *had never tolerated slavery on the racial grounds advanced by the South*: i.e., that enslavement is the "natural condition" of the black race alone but immoral as to whites, as Stephens, Davis and other Confederate leaders maintained in a convenient theological modification suited to Southern requirements.

The "enlightening rays of Christianity" to which Davis appealed had peacefully

2. Hilaire Belloc, *Economics for Helen* (IHS Press, 2010), Kindle Edition, 1687–1697.

3. In Kenneth J. Zanca, *American Catholics and Slavery 1789–1866, An Anthology of Primary Docu-ments* (Lanham, MD: University Press of America, 1994), 132.

4. Belloc, *Economics for Helen*, loc. cit.

5. Ephesians 6:5, 7.

6. *City of God*, Bk. 19, Ch. 15.

abolished slavery from Europe centuries before the Civil War. Owing to the preaching of Church Fathers such as Gregory of Nyssa, in whose sermons we find a "most energetic and absolute reprobation of slavery," and the constant influence of the Church over increasingly liberal civil legislation down through the centuries of Catholic Christendom (a process of Christian reform interrupted by the barbarian invasions), by the Middle Ages "slavery, properly so called, no longer existed in Christian countries; it had been replaced by serfdom, an intermediate condition in which a man enjoyed all his personal rights except the right to leave the land he cultivated and the right to freely dispose of his property." But even serfdom "soon disappeared in Catholic countries, to last longer only where the Protestant Reformation prevailed."[7]

In the New World outside of America, slavery, long in decline, was rapidly disappearing everywhere during the 1700s and 1800s. In the whole Western world outside of the antebellum South, only Brazil could still be fairly characterized as a slave society in the decades before the Civil War. But as Frank Tannenbaum at Columbia University and Stanley Elkins at Smith College demonstrated with their groundbreaking studies,[8] the influence of Catholicism in Latin America had greatly ameliorated the abuses of slavery as compared with the American South, particularly in Brazil. Thus, for example, in Brazil slave marriages were recognized as legally binding, manumission was quite freely practiced and could be effected by any means, formal or informal, and there were no laws compelling manumitted slaves to emigrate. As a result, the ratio of slaves to freedmen was 3:1 in Brazil as compared with 16:1 in the Cotton States and 8:1 in the United States as a whole.[9] Further, upon manumission the former slave acquired all the rights of citizens, not merely a release from bondage—a development that would not happen in America, North or South, until after the Civil War.[10]

Throughout Spain's Catholic colonies in the New World, the Spanish Church was "the 'prime arbiter' of the social and intellectual life" of the colonies and "insisted upon its right to determine 'the moral religious and even social conditions' under which [slave] labor was conducted. It was the aim of the Spanish Church to preserve as much of the legal personality of the slave as possible," including the right of slaves "to personal security, to private property, and to purchase their freedom." Slaves could marry even against the wishes of their masters, and decrees of the Spanish

---

7. P. Allard, "Slavery and Christianity," *The Catholic Encyclopedia* (NY: Robert Appleton Company, 1912).

8. Cf. Frank Tannenbaum, *Slave and Citizen: the Negro in the Americas* (NY: Vintage Books/Random House, 1946) and Stanley Elkins, *Slavery: A Problem in American Institutional and Intellectual Life* (Chicago: Univ. of Chicago Press, 3d ed., 1976).

9. Carl N. Degler, "Slavery in Brazil and the United States: An Essay in Comparative History," *The American Historical Review*, Vol. 75, No. 4 (Apr. 1970), 1011, 1012. The author, clearly intent on convicting the Church of the sins of the South, contrives to dispute the validity of slave marriages in Brazil by speculating that while the Church mandated their validity, "it is not likely" that Brazilian slave-owners were any more respectful of the marriage bond than their American counterparts. Ibid., 1008. No evidence is cited to refute Tannenbaum and Elkins on this score.

10. Tannenbaum, *Slave and Citizen*, 63–64.

Crown, under pressure from the Church, "severely restricted the rise of large-scale, gang-system plantations—of capitalist plantations that produced primarily for a world market," like those of cotton- and sugar-producing states in America. In both the Spanish and French colonies, "the Catholic Church, as the guardian of souls of the Christian slaves, proclaimed that it had the authority to review the practices of masters, and so it established ecclesiastical courts in which a number of countries recognized that slaves had certain civil rights." Masters were tried for brutality and other violations of the rights of slaves in secular and religious courts, often on petitions not only by slaves themselves but "sympathetic free persons."[11]

The Church not only condemned the slave trade in Catholic countries, but also insisted "that slave and master were equal in the sight of God" and that "masters bring their slaves to church to learn the doctrine and participate in the communion."[12] As Tannenbaum notes, slaves in Brazil formed religious fraternities among themselves and "adopted the Lady of the Rosary as their own special patroness, sometimes painting her black."[13] Tannenbaum, a Jewish Austrian immigrant, can hardly be accused of Catholic partisanship in summarizing the standing of the slave in Catholic Latin America as compared with Protestant North America:

> the element of human personality was not lost in the transition to slavery from Africa to the Spanish or Portuguese dominions. He [the slave] remained a person even while he was a slave. . . . He was never considered a mere chattel, never defined as unanimated property, and never under the law treated as such. . . . This legal tradition and juridical framework were strengthened by the Catholic religion and were part of its doctrine. It made him a member of the Christian community. It imposed upon both the slave and the master obligations to respect and protect the moral personality of the other. . . .[14]

In short, while "the Latin-American environment was favorable to freedom, the British and American were hostile. Legal obstacles were placed in the way of manumission, and it was discouraged in every other manner."[15] In England, however, the decades-long campaign by the evangelical Anglican convert and conservative social reformer, William Wilberforce, had succeeded in abolishing the slave trade by 1807, and slavery itself by 1833, wherever it still remained in the British Empire. (Wilberforce died three days after learning that the Slavery Abolition Act of 1833 had passed overwhelmingly in the House of Commons and would certainly pass in the House of Lords—a stunning reversal of two centuries of state-sanctioned slavery in the Empire.)[16]

---

11. Robert William Fogel, *Without Consent or Contract* (NY: W.W. Norton & Company, 1989), 37–39, 397.

12. Tannenbaum, 63.

13. Ibid., 63–64.

14. Ibid., 97–98. Emphasis in original.

15. Ibid., 65.

16. Wilberforce was also an advocate of Catholic emancipation in England, speaking in favor of it as a member of the House of Commons in 1813.

But as of 1861 the "enlightening rays of Christianity" had yet to shine on the strict property rights of the slave-owners of the antebellum South, where slavery was the "cornerstone" of Southern civilization.

The antebellum slave class provided the laboring foundation of what passed for a hierarchical society in a nation whose Founders—led by Washington, Madison, and Jefferson, all slave-owning Southerners—had proudly abolished all titles of nobility as a matter of constitutional law.[17] The Confederate Constitution did likewise.[18] The Constitutions of both rival powers, in the same spirit of the Enlightenment from which the first had issued, leveled the field for the emergence of a Montesqueian commercial civilization based on "absolute" Lockean property rights. At the top of the Southern pseudo-hierarchy was the politically dominant slaveholder or master class, at the very vertex of which were the major planters. The influence of the master class, especially the planters, would drive the Cotton States into secession and then the whole South into a sectional war with the North over the Southern "way of life."

The "way of life" Southern partisans laud in their romantic narrative was made possible only by a vast slave labor force of some four million blacks that allowed the master class to reap the benefits of an agrarian capitalism while remaining above the stark and undignified competition of the industrial North, with its free-labor force, or the drudgery of the yeoman farmer of the Southern lower class. As the famed antebellum physician William Henry Holcombe of Mississippi put it: "The Northeast loves to make money, the Southerner to spend it."[19] The Southern Agrarian novelist and essayist Stark Young, a Mississippian writing in defense of the Old South in the celebrated anthology *I'll Take My Stand*, was quite frank about the foundations of this bygone "way of life" or what Stephens called "our peculiar institution." As Stark wrote in 1930: "[W]e must make it clear that in talking of Southern characteristics we are talking largely of a certain life in the Old South a life founded on land and *the ownership of slaves*. Of the other people of the South who lived in that epoch we know less, the people who worked their own farms with their own hands, respectable and sturdy, a fine yeomanry partly, and partly the so-called 'poor whites' . . . [I]*t is not they* who gave this civilization its peculiar stamp."[20] Polemicists of the Southern romantic narrative have never been able to extract a Southern civilizational "essence" that would explain the Civil War apart

17. *U.S. Const.* Art I., §9, Clause 8: "No Title of Nobility shall be granted by the United States: And no Person holding any Office of Profit or Trust under them, shall, without the Consent of the Congress, accept of any present, Emolument, Office, or Title, of any kind whatever, from any King, Prince or foreign State."

18. Art. I, §9, ¶11: "No title of nobility shall be granted by the Confederate States; and no person holding any office of profit or trust under them, shall, without the consent of the Congress, accept of any present, emolument, office, or title of any kind whatever, from any king, prince, or foreign state."

19. Genovese, *The Political Economy of Slavery* (Middletown, CT: Wesleyan Univ. Press, 2d ed., 1989), 30.

20. Stark Young, "Not in Memoriam, But in Defense," in *I'll Take My Stand* (Baton Rouge: Louisiana State Univ. Press, 1994 [1930]), 336–37.

from slavery, or more precisely the ownership of slaves by the Southern upper class and the life of wealth and privilege it made possible.

The Southern Slave as Chattel

The fundamental legal characteristic of the "peculiar institution" was, of course, chattel slavery. Since colonial times and continuing during the antebellum period (1820–1860), slaves were not merely involuntary servants but chattels—movable personal property—for all relevant legal purposes, despite the noble theological or "scientific" outer garment in which the institution's defenders attempted to cloak it. Slaves were inventoried like "plantation tools, silverware, furniture, linen, and livestock. . . ."[21] Like any other chattel, they were subject to being bartered, traded, sold to the highest bidder, pledged, mortgaged, attached by creditors, bequeathed in wills, and even given as gifts to children, relatives or friends—all with no more respect for ties of marriage and family than a particular owner, purchaser, creditor or beneficiary might wish to accord without any legal compulsion to do so.[22] Not even manumission of a slave by a generous master was permitted where it would prejudice the rights of a creditor with a lien on the human chattel; and slaves freed by will could still be sold into bondage to a new owner to satisfy the decedent's unpaid debts or a disinherited widow's "elective share" of the estate in a challenge to her disinheritance.[23] Perhaps the most famous example of this legal reality is the sale of 130 of Thomas Jefferson's already mortgaged slaves in 1827 to pay off the massive debts he had left behind, the slaves being his *only saleable asset.*[24]

No matter how much evidence one amasses concerning the benevolence of certain slave-owners, which can hardly negate the cruelty of others, there can be no denying what the fugitive slave James W. C. Pennington wrote of the "peculiar institution": that "'the being of slavery' lay in 'the chattel principle,'" so that "even slaves who seemed for the moment to live good lives would inevitably be drawn into the worst abuses of the system by the price that was on their heads and the trade it represented." And, as we shall see, "[s]ale from 'the mildest form of slavery' to 'the worst of which the system is possible' and from 'the comparatively favorable circumstances' of slavery in the Upper South to the desperate abuses of slavery in the Lower South was . . . 'the legitimate working of the great chattel principle.'"[25]

Owing to an agrarian revolution that paralleled the Industrial Revolution in England, launched by the invention of the cotton gin and new methods for refining sugar, between 1790 and 1860 slaves were in demand as human capital on a new and

21. Daina Ramey Berry, "'We'm fus' rate bargain': Value, Labor and Price in a Georgia Slave Community," in ed. Walter Johnson, *The Chattel Principle: Internal Slave Trades in the Americas* (New Haven: Yale Univ. Press, 2002, Kindle Edition), 55.

22. Cf. Gutman, *Slavery and the Numbers Game*, 133–135; Genovese, *A Consuming Fire*, 109–110.

23. Tannenbaum, *Slave and Citizen*, 67–71.

24. Herbert E. Sloan, *Principle and Interest: Thomas Jefferson and the Problem of Debt* (Charlottesville, VA: Univ. of Virginia Press, 2001 [1995]), 11.

25. In *The Chattel Principle*, Walter Johnson, introd., 1–2.

vaster scale. The "peculiar institution" underwent a rapid revival even as the last remnants of slavery were fading in the industrial North. The demand for good quality slaves reached unprecedented heights during the "Negro fever" and "Cotton fever" of the 1850s (following the depression years of the 1840s), during which the rising international demand for Southern cotton placed the Cotton States in the position of a near-monopoly that could be exploited only by a dramatic intensification and diversion of the use of slave labor to the cash crops.

The one million slaves in the South when the transatlantic slave trade ceased in 1808 were four million by 1860. To Northern outrage, that number was augmented by a clandestine resumption of the transatlantic trade to meet demand from 1858 to 1860, during which "thousands of Negroes were brought from Africa and smuggled in through the Southern ports." While these illegal slave-traders were indicted in federal courts, "no jury in the South would convict them" even though their illegal activity was "denounced by certain prominent Southerners on the ground that it would lead to secession, and that the Union must not be sacrificed."[26]

To protect this vast pool of human capital at the height of the demand for it—especially after Nat Turner's slave rebellion in 1831, which claimed the lives of scores of whites in Virginia—longstanding colonial era "slave codes" were enforced with new vigor and amended to add additional protections for owners. This was particularly the case in the slave states admitted after 1800—Alabama, Arkansas, Florida, Kentucky, Louisiana, Mississippi, Missouri, Tennessee and Texas—to which slaves were moved during the agrarian revolution in a mass migration to the west and deep South known as the Second Middle Passage, the first being the original passage from Africa.

The slave codes tightly restricted the mobility of slaves, typically requiring written passes for their movement outside the plantation; severely punished their attempts to escape, including the death penalty; forbade their employment for wages and criminally penalized anyone who hired them; subjected them to search and seizure at will; sharply circumscribed their freedom of association for worship and other purposes; and barred their testimony against whites in civil or criminal proceedings. Slaves were legally disqualified from owning, transferring or inheriting property. The penalty for slave rebellion, or plotting to rebel, was death, with the state reimbursing the owner for the loss of his executed slave. Slaves were denied freedom of assembly and their preachers could not preach without the presence of a white auditor. They were not entitled to trial by jury and were generally tried informally by justices of the peace.[27]

Slave code provisions even prohibited teaching a slave to read or write, evidently a specific juridical response to the prospect of rebellions like the one led by Turner, a highly intelligent slave who had taught himself to read, reinventing himself as a spellbinding religious visionary and Biblical "prophet." A typical example is an 1830

26. Wilson, *Patriotic Gore*, 361.
27. Eaton, *History of the Old South*, 260–61.

North Carolina statute declaring that "whereas the teaching of slaves to read and write has a tendency to excite dissatisfaction to their minds and to produce insurrection and rebellion to the manifest injury of the citizens of this state," any whites providing such instruction were subject to fines and any free black doing so was subject to a whipping of nine to twenty lashes.[28]

The slave codes were enforced by slave patrols, which "kept general order within county districts and towns [and] were appointed and paid by local authorities, generally committees made up of the local justices of the peace." These "white paterollers" had authority to "enforce curfews and whip offenders for minor violations" and were responsible for ascertaining that slaves off the plantation had the requisite passes.[29] In both the original slave states and the newly admitted ones, the slave codes assured slave-owners "that their claim to property-in-persons would be protected, that their rights to discipline their slaves would be unchallenged, and that slaveholders and non-slaveholders alike would cooperate in the return of fugitives and the suppression of slave rebels. Behind the master class stood the power of the state in the form of militia, police, juries, and patrols."[30]

To be sure, less draconian remnants of slave codes, holdovers from colonial times, still existed in Northern states. For example, northern slave codes placed tight restrictions and financial requirements or even prohibitions on residency by emancipated slaves. We must not forget that the Temple of Liberty was pervasively racist. Moreover, the rigor of enforcement in the antebellum South varied according to circumstances. Nevertheless, as Genovese summarizes: "At the end of the antebellum period the laws remained Draconian and the enormous power of the masters had received only modest qualification. The best that might be said is that the list of capital crimes had shrunk considerably, in accordance with the movement toward general sensibility, and that the ruthless enforcement of the eighteenth century had given way to greater flexibility during the nineteenth."[31]

Since slaves were property before they were human in the antebellum legal system, it followed that crimes *against* slaves by whites were diminished in culpability. A typical common law outcome, as explained in an 1829 decision by Thomas Ruffin of the Supreme Court of North Carolina, was that "the master is not liable to an indictment for a battery committed upon a slave. . . . The power of the master must be absolute to render submission of the slave perfect." Hence, while the law generally punished the *wanton* killing of a slave, even with the death penalty in some jurisdictions, "[a]ny mitigating struggle or circumstance (and there always appeared to be one) could negate the crime entirely."[32] Thus, the law typically

---

28. Clayton E. Jewett and John O. Allen, *Slavery in the South: A State-by-State History* (Westport, CT: Greenwood Press, 2004), 193.

29. Ibid., 197.

30. Berlin, *Generations of Captivity* (Cambridge, MA: Belknap Press of Harvard Univ. Press, 2004), Kindle Edition, 1830–34.

31. Eugene D. Genovese, *Roll, Jordan, Roll: The World the Slaves Made* (Vintage Books: Kindle Edition, 2011 [1976]), 845–851.

32. Jewett, op. cit., 194.

provided that a master or overseer who killed a slave "during the administration of moderate correction" could not be punished for homicide.[33] And, given the bar of slave testimony against whites in criminal or civil proceedings, the barrier to conviction was often impossibly high.

Another fundamental aspect of the law of antebellum slavery untouched by Davis's "enlightening rays of Christianity" was the Southern legal system's refusal to recognize the validity of slave marriages and the resulting family bonds. Even in her toleration of slavery as an evil arising from Original Sin to be eliminated by Christian means, the Catholic Church had never ceased to condemn the reduction of slaves to chattels over whom the master's command is so complete that it extends to the very requisites of a slave's nature as a fellow human being essentially equal to the master in the sight of God. As St. Thomas observes, a master simply has no authority over the marriage or procreation of a slave, nor the slave any duty to obey a master's command forbidding marriage or procreation:

> [A] slave is bound to obey his master in those things which his master can command lawfully; and just as his master cannot lawfully command him not to eat or sleep, so neither can he lawfully command him to refrain from marrying.... [C]onsequently if the master command his slave not to marry, the slave is not bound to obey his master.
>
> [S]ince by nature all men are equal, [a subject] is not bound to obey another man in matters touching the nature of the body, for instance in those relating to the support of his body *or the begetting of his children.* Wherefore servants are not bound to obey their masters ... in the question of contracting marriage or of remaining in the state of virginity or the like.[34]

In the antebellum South, however, even *with* a master's illicitly required consent slave marriages were still considered legally void. Slaves were property, and "property could not enter into a legal contract," for "[t]he master-slave relationship superseded relationships between slaves, which differed from those between free men and women joined in lawful wedlock...."[35] Slaves could hardly be permitted to enter into relationships that would legally impair their owners' property rights. With their owners' "permission"—or in secret without permission—slaves did commonly marry in legally non-binding ceremonies of various kinds, ranging from traditional religious nuptials to *ad hoc* affairs, including "jumping the broom" after a Bible reading in the master's "Big House." And some owners, going beyond the law, not only permitted traditional religious ceremonies but respected the resulting marriage bond as indissoluble. Depending on the circumstances, an owner might well have an incentive to encourage indissoluble slave marriages, if only to foster the stability and future growth of his labor supply. But, unlike Latin

---

33. Eaton, *A History of the Old South*, 251.

34. *ST*, III (Supplement), Q. 52, Art. 2 and II–II, Q. 104, Art. 5.

35. Cf. Paul Finkelman, John F. A. Sanford, *Dred Scott: A Brief History with Documents* (Boston: St. Martin's Press, 1997), 16 ff.

America, where Catholic sacramental marriages had the force of law, none of these "concessions" to human nature by Southern slave-owners were reflected in antebellum legal codes. In the slave states the marriage of a slave "even with the master's consent, produced no civil effect."[36] Thus, as one typical judicial decision put it, any purported slave marriage could be "dissolved at the pleasure of either party, or by the sale of one or both, depending on the caprice or necessity of the owners.'"[37] For that reason the civil marriage of Dred Scott to his fellow slave Harriet Robinson was considered legally null and void and thus no impediment to his legal status as a recoverable chattel under the Fugitive Slave Law.[38]

Abolitionist fables of slave "stud farms" in the South aside, there is no denying that slave couples and families, marriages notwithstanding, were commonly broken up for sale and resale. Like Thomas Jefferson before them, plantation owners throughout the antebellum South routinely sold or mortgaged slaves to finance their "way of life" and pay debts. Above all other events, however, the Second Middle Passage wreaked havoc on the family life of slaves. During America's agrarian analogue of the Industrial Revolution, the lure of huge profits from cotton and sugar crops, harvested and processed according to the new methods, led to transshipment of vast numbers of slaves from the States of the Atlantic seaboard and Upper South, especially Virginia and Maryland, to fertile deep South and interior plantations in Georgia, Kentucky, Tennessee, South Carolina, Mississippi, Texas, Arkansas, Louisiana and Alabama.

Uprooting and destroying slave families, the Second Middle Passage "was the central event in the lives of African-American people between the American Revolution and slavery's final demise in December 1865."[39] Between 1790 and 1860 approximately 1.1 million slaves, "the majority of them between the ages of 15 and 30," were relocated to cotton or sugar plantations by their migrating owners, by kidnappers and smugglers, and, in the majority of cases, by traders called "Georgia men" who packed their human inventory into wagons, boxcars and ships,[40] with the men manacled together in "coffles."[41] In Virginia alone between 1850 and 1860 some sixty-eight thousand slaves were shipped out of state in trade.[42] Almost a quarter million slaves were sent to the Southern interior during the 1850s, and more

36. William Goodell, *The American Slave Code* (NY, 1853), 107; in Tannenbaum, *Slave and Citizen*, 75.

37. Ibid., quoting *Howard v. Howard*, December 1853, in *Judicial Cases Concerning American Slavery and the Negro*, ed. Helen T. Cotterall, Vol. 2 (Washington, D.C., 1929).

38. Cf. Paul Finkelman, John F. A. Sanford, *Dred Scott: A Brief History with Documents* (Boston: St. Martin's Press, 1997), 16 ff.

39. Berlin, *Generations of Captivity* (Kindle), 1782–1783.

40. Calvin Schermerhorn, "The Everyday Life of Enslaved People in the Antebellum South," *OAH Magazine of History*, April, 2009, 31.

41. Eaton, *A History of the Old South*, 236.

42. See, e.g., Richard Sutch, "The Breeding of Slaves for Sale and the Western Expansion of Slavery: 1850–1860," in Engerman and Genovese, eds *Race and Slavery in the Western Hemisphere: Quantitative Studies* (Princeton, NJ: Princeton Univ. Press, 1975), Appendix, Table 4, 207.

than half of those went west of the Mississippi.[43] The Second Middle Passage clearly "counts as one of the great forced migrations in world history. . . ."[44]

By its very nature the interregional slave trade provided a powerful economic incentive for breaking up families, as the whole point of the trading was to buy and sell the most valuable human commodities: "young slaves of eight or ten years of age to mid-teens, mothers with offspring, young females in early womanhood, and prime adult males. These categories quickly translated themselves into a traffic in fragmented families."[45] Traded like cattle on the open market, slave children suffered separation from their parents in about half of these sales, and at least a quarter of the sales broke up marriages.[46] John W. Blassingame, analyzing records of the post-Civil War Freedman's Bureau, estimated that in the antebellum South overall "approximately a third of slave marriages were broken up by the masters"[47] through local and interregional sales. But not only the sales by "Georgia men" caused family and marital dissolution. Given that slave marriages and families often involved slaves who lived on different plantations, even the migration of owners with their own slaves broke up both marriage and family; or the owner might sell off some family members before migrating with a "stock" that was "leaner," fitter, and less costly to maintain.[48] Two typical advertisements from the 1830s depict the grim reality of the destruction of marriage and family among the slaves:

NEGROES FOR SALE.—A negro woman, 24 years of age, and her two children [where was the husband/father?], one eight and the other three years old. Said negroes will be sold SEPARATELY or together, *as desired.* The woman is a good seamstress. She will be sold low for cash, or EXCHANGED FOR GROCERIES.

. . . .

ONE HUNDRED AND TWENTY NEGROES FOR SALE.—. . . one hundred and twenty *likely young negroes* of both sexes and every description. . . . [Where were their parents, grandparents and other relations?] The lot now on hand consists of plough-boys [parents? grandparents? other relations?] . . . well-qualified house servants of both sexes [where are their parents, spouses, children, other relations?], *several women with children* [where were the

43. Berlin, *Generations of Captivity,* 1868.

44. Herbert G. Gutman, *Slavery and the Numbers Game: A Critique of Time on the Cross* (Chicago: Univ. of Illinois Press, 2003 [1975]), 103.

45. Michael Tadman, *Speculators and Slaves: Masters, Traders and Slaves in the Old South* (Madison, WI: Univ. of Wisconsin Press, 1996), 136.

46. Schermerhorn, op.cit., 31. Tadman notes that statistical analysis of marriage certificates obtained by freed slaves in Mississippi, for example, shows that twenty-three percent of recorded previous marriages were "forcibly broken by masters during slavery" when the sample includes slaves over fifty. Tadman, op. cit., 135.

47. John W. Blassingame, *The Slave Community: Plantation Life in the Antebellum South* (NY, 1972), 90; in Eaton, *A History of the Old South,* 250.

48. Gutman, *Slavery and the Numbers Game,* 106–7.

fathers, husbands, parents, other relations?], *small girls* suitable for nurses [mothers? fathers? grandparents? other relations?], and SEVERAL SMALL BOYS WITHOUT THEIR MOTHERS [or their fathers, grandparents and other relations].... [T]he subscriber ... is enabled to sell as cheap or cheaper than *any other person in the trade*.[49]

The disastrous impact of both the local and interregional slave trade on slave marriages and families cannot be effaced by the dubious "cliometric" statistical analyses of revisionist historians. Chief among these is *Time on the Cross*, the famed study in which Robert Fogel and Stanley Engerman attempted to estimate from sale records in New Orleans the percentage of slave marriages broken by sale (while ignoring the question of family impact).[50] The records they used gave no indication of marital status and the entire exercise was guesswork, despite the impressive mathematical formulae into which unproven variables were inserted. *Time on the Cross* was just as famously torn to shreds by Herbert G. Gutman in his *Slavery and the Numbers Game*, wherein he notes, among many other glaring flaws in analysis, the patently unreasonable assumption that the entirety of a large statistical cohort of slave women around age 25 who were sold separately in New Orleans had never been married or had a child, the failure to consider the impact of non-sale migrations on marriages and families, the failure to consider the breakup of mother-child relationships among *unmarried* slave women (as suggested by the advertisements cited here), and the risible contention that sales of children away from their parents occurred "at an age when it would have been normal for them to have left the family."[51] The last suggestion, as Gutman rightly observes, "not only senselessly cheapens the process by which slave families were involuntarily broken, but reveals an ideological bias that has no place in the writing of history, even 'cliometric history'.... There is no possible way to compare the decision of a white teenage youth to quit his Maryland or Virginia home for Georgia or Alabama to the sale of a black teenage youth from his Virginia or Maryland slave family."[52]

Another factor Fogel and Engerman failed to consider was the breakup of slave marriages and families via estate sales. Since slaves were chattels in the antebellum legal system, it was quite common for wealthy slave-owners to parcel out their human chattels to different beneficiaries under the terms of their wills. We have already noted the famous post-mortem auction of Jefferson's slaves. Gutman cites the classic example of the will of William Fitzhugh, the eminent Virginia statesman and planter of the colonial era, whose will parceled out his fifty-one slaves in aliquot shares among his wife and four children. Another typical will, from 1841, required the executor in North Carolina to sell, either separately or together if

---

49. In Tannenbaum, *Slave and Citizen*, 77–78. Emphasis in original.

50. Cf. *Time on the Cross: the Economics of American Negro Slavery* (NY: Little, Brown & Co., 1974), Vol. I, 126 ff.

51. Gutman, *Slavery and the Numbers Game*, 138.

52. Cf. *Slavery and the Numbers Game*, 101–08, 115–23, 125–30.

possible—although estate law mandated separate sales—"5 of 11 children" of the still-living slave Hanna, "the other six having been sold."[53]

In his later work *Without Consent or Contract* (1989), Fogel retreated from the devastated edifice of his and Engerman's "cliometric" attempt to minimize the damage Southern chattel slavery wrought to the marriages and families of slaves. Fogel conceded that there was large-scale interference in slave marriages and families by plantation owners, including prohibitions on marrying anyone off the plantation, and that "by far the most common form of interference, besides limiting marriages to partners available on the plantation, was the destruction of marriages through the internal slave trade." Citing traditional historical sources instead of dubious data extrapolations, Fogel now concluded that "ex-slave narratives reveal that in a third of the slave households headed by a single parent the marriage was destroyed because the mother or father was either *sold or given away*."[54] But these traditional sources should have made it apparent from the start that whether by sale, hiring, or inheritance, "[f]ragmentation of slave families was in fact inevitable...."[55] No amount of "cliometric" numbers-gaming based on isolated data sets could obscure the living historical reality conveyed by traditional research into such sources as the Charleston City Council's matter-of-fact description of the slave trade in 1856. Expressing the sentiment of its meeting to address the subject, the Council deplored a spectacle it did nothing to prohibit:

> It was thought a common spectacle to see troops of slaves, of all ages and both sexes, uniformly dressed, paraded for air, exercise and exhibition, through the streets and thoroughfares. This spectacle of a large number of negroes, for the most part single, brought together from all quarters, *without regard to family ties*, for purposes purely of speculation and cupidity, entailed on this community by strangers, citizens of other states, was repugnant to the moral tone and sense of our people.[56]

Having duly noted its sense of personal repugnance, the Council exhibited the legal nominalism and moral schizophrenia inherent to political modernity—from legalized chattel slavery to legalized abortion. The Council members were at pains to note that what they deplored personally was, of course, perfectly legal and just:

> [T]his community entertains no morbid or fanatical sentiment on the subject of slavery. The discussions over the last twenty years have led it to clear and decided opinions as to *its complete consistency with moral principle and with the highest order of civilization*. It regards the removal of slaves from place to place, and *their transfer from master to master, by gift, purchase or otherwise*, as incidents necessarily connected with the institution.

53. Gutman, 134, 138–39.
54. Fogel *Without Contract or Consent*, 152.
55. Edwin W. Phifer, "Slavery in Microcosm: Burke County, North Carolina," *Journal of Southern History*, XXVIII (May 1962), 137, in Gutman, op. cit., 135.
56. Tadman, "The Interregional Slave Trade in the History and Myth-Making of the U.S. South," in *The Chattel Principle*, 135.

Even at the lowest estimates, the slave trade wrenched hundreds of thousands of slaves from the spouses, families, webs of kinship, and local cultures they had established in the Upper South; it made them strangers in strange lands, forced to rebuild family, kinship, and culture anew. Every compilation of slave testimonies during this period contains innumerable stories like that of Madison Jefferson of Virginia, saddled with the names of the two slave-owning icons of Virginia history. He recounted living in a condition where "we don't know how long master may keep us, nor into whose hands we may fall." Like so many other slaves, he knew of frequent sales of men "in one direction, and their wives in another; their social affections and sympathies forming no part in the cold and mercenary calculations of the slave-owner; indeed, these separations, by a refinement of cruelty, are frequently made for punishment."[57]

In fact, no form of slave discipline was more effective than the threat of being sold away from loved ones, and "reliance on punitive sales had long been a tactic used by masters to rid themselves of non-compliant slaves. . . . This most-feared possibility was made real in innumerable ways. Not only did planters threaten to sell slaves who persistently refused to comply, but they saw to it that insubordinate slaves, as well as other bond people, constantly witnessed auctions and the endless processions of human chattels driven by diverse whites to distant destinies in captivity."[58] The breakup of slave families was forbidden by the Catholic Emperor Constantine as early as AD 334,[59] but in the antebellum South, more than fifteen centuries later, it was still common practice according to the law of the land.

The local and interregional slave trade was enormously profitable both for the original owners who sold their assets and the new owners who used them to plant, harvest and process cotton and sugar during the agrarian revolution. The slave trade "became the largest enterprise in the South outside of the plantation itself, and probably the most advanced in its employment of modern transportation, finance, and publicity. It developed its own language: prime hands, bucks, breeding wenches, and fancy girls. . . . [T]he slave trade, with its hubs and regional centers, its spurs and circuits, reached into every cranny of southern society. Few Southerners, white or black, were untouched."[60] Nor were slave traders a band of social outcasts shunned by polite Southern society, as the romantic narrative portrays them in an effort to hide the embarrassment of Southern chattel slavery. Even in South Carolina, notes Michael Tadman, "traders were among the wealthiest and most influential in their communities; indeed, in terms of wealth they were part of a tiny group at the top of American society. They also served in city, state, and national politics. . . . In the antebellum period, then, traders were no outcasts from southern society."[61]

---

57. In *Slave Testimony*, ed. John W. Blassingame (Louisiana State Univ. Press, 2003 [1977]), 218–19.

58. *Society and Culture in the Slave South*, ed. William Harris (NY: Routledge, 1992), 164, 168.

59. Cf. Orlando Paterson, *Slavery and Social Death: A Comparative Study* (Cambridge, MA: Harvard Univ. Press, 1985), 189.

60. Berlin, *Generations of Captivity*, 1858–1862.

61. Tadman, op. cit., 137.

A vivid example of the well-respected antebellum Southern entrepreneur who became rich selling men, women and children is Nathan Bedford Forrest, who would later become the Confederate Army's most celebrated cavalryman and, after the war, Grand Wizard of the first Ku Klux Klan. A modern definitive biography traces his career from slave trader to member of the elite planter class. The biographer recounts how Forrest and his partners made their killing at the height of the "Negro fever" of the 1850s, when demand for slaves was at its peak and prices had been driven to all-time highs: at least $1500 for a male hand and $1300 for a female—the equivalent of the price of a new car in today's dollars.[62] Forrest's company built up a large inventory of human beings with such advertisements as "FIVE HUNDRED NEGROES WANTED—WE will pay the highest cash price for all good negroes offered. . . ." Another advertisement represented that Forrest and company had "constantly on hand the best selected assortment of Field Hands, House Servants & Mechanics at their Negro Mart," invited prospective buyers to "examine their stock before purchasing elsewhere," and promised "the highest market price always paid for good stock."[63]

Like all slave traders, Forrest allowed his customers to inspect the merchandise by "prob[ing] teeth and limbs, particularly looking for signs of sickness or violence. Whipmarks were indications of ill temper, laziness, or insolence."[64] Potential investors in slaves "assessed each purchase with as much shrewdness and concern for value as any western horse trader or northern manufacturer. . . . [P]rices were systematically affected by such characteristics of slaves as their age, gender, health, skills, and reliability. . . . Masters put a price on each skill and defect of a slave. . . . Masters even put a price on 'virtues' and 'vices.' Slaves labeled as runaways, lazy, thieves, drunks, suicidal, or having 'heredity vices' sold for average discounts of up to 65 per cent as compared with slaves of the same age who were 'fully guaranteed.'"[65] All of this was part of an agrarian capitalist "free market" in which Southerners "fell into the vicious practice of investing in slaves to produce more cotton to buy more slaves and land."[66]

There was, finally, an aspect of chattel slavery that did not involve bargain and sale. At the hands of masters, the female slave was too often a sexual as well as a marketable chattel. Mary Boykin Chesnut, author of the famous Civil War chronicle *A Diary from Dixie*, recounts having been repelled by the sight of a mulatto girl for sale on the auction block in Charleston, which made her feel "faint—seasick." She later records her disgust at the profusion of mulatto children born to planter fathers whose identity was known to all but never admitted openly. "We are surrounded by prostitutes," she wrote of the slaves with whom their masters coupled.

62. *The Chattel Principle: Internal Slave Trades in the Americas*, ix.

63. Brian Steel Wills, *The Confederacy's Greatest Cavalryman: Nathan Bedford Forrest* (Lawrence, KS: Univ. Press of Kansas, 1992), 30.

64. Ibid.

65. William Fogel, "Slavery: A Highly Developed, Flexible Form of Capitalism," in Harris, *Society and Culture in the Slave South*, 81–82.

66. Eaton, op. cit., 244.

"Like the patriarchs of old our men live all in one house with their wives and their concubines, and the mulattoes one sees in every family exactly resemble the white children...." While "every lady tells you who is the father of all the mulatto children in everybody's household ... those in her own she seems to think drop from the clouds, or pretends so to think." In a mordant allusion to the Book of Genesis, she derides the master to whom "wife Leah does not suffice. Rachel must be *added*, if not *married*." Yet these same adulterers "seem to think themselves patterns—models of husbands and fathers." Expressing her "heretical" abolitionist sentiments, she writes: "I wonder if it be a sin to think slavery a curse to any land.... God forgive us, but ours is a *monstrous* system and wrong and iniquity." Referring to Senator Sumner, whose nearly fatal beating by Representative Brooks of South Carolina we have already noted, she concludes: "Sumner said not one word of this hated institution which is not true."[67]

But then the South was full of people who professed to loathe slavery in the midst of the war the South was waging because it had seceded to defend the "hated institution." And many of these people, including Mary Chesnut herself, had no hesitancy accepting the benefits that flowed to them from the labor of slaves. In this connection, however, Chesnut records for history the essence of what we are aiming for here, which C. Vann Woodward describes as "the hypocrisy of the stern puritanical code these libertarian patriarchs imposed on their womenfolk and children."[68] The Southern romantic narrative conceals precisely this *libertarian* patriarch: shamelessly breeding children with female slaves, just as the infidel Jefferson did with Sally Heming, but seeing himself as a staunchly conservative defender of the Protestant notion of Christendom against the forces of an apostate (but no less Protestant) North. Only within the overall framework of Protestantism and its privatized revelation could there be such an illusory "clash of civilizations."

The Labor and the Lash

How hard were Davis's "efficient Christian laborers" required to labor? Slave labor conditions varied greatly depending upon location and the needs and temperament of the master. Just as there were many "souths," so were there many "slaveries." The gang system, the task system, small farm labor, and domestic service all employed slaves in the antebellum South's slave-based economic order. Working conditions ranged from a relatively moderate amount of work in such task-oriented enterprises as the tobacco plantations of Virginia, to the "first light to full dark," six- and even seven-day work week of the slave gangs that worked plantations in the Deep South and western interior, especially the "dreaded sugar plantations,"[69] where life

67. In ed. C. Vann Woodward, *Mary Chesnut's Civil War* (New Haven: Yale Univ. Press, 1981), 15, 29–31. Emphasis in original. This edition contains all of the diary manuscripts Chesnut produced, including material suppressed in the later *Diary from Dixie.*

68. Ibid., li.

69. Tadman, "The Interregional Slave Trade," loc. cit., 126.

was even worse than it was for the wage-slaves of England's "dark satanic mills" or the farmhands of the American North, who also worked from dawn to dark.

In an embarrassed afterword to the 1989 edition of *Time on the Cross*, Fogel and Engerman refined their earlier contention that free northern farmers, who specialized in livestock and dairying, worked on average ten percent more hours than southern slaves. They conceded the obvious point that southern slaves in the plantation gangs worked more intensely per hour under masters, overseers, and Negro slave drivers than did a cattle or dairy farmer, and that "the greater the intensity of work per hour, rather than more hours per day, or days per year, was the principal form of the exploitation of slave labor. The gang-system played a role comparable to the factory system, or, at the later date, the assembly line, in regulating the pace of labor."[70]

The "regulation" of slave labor in general depended heavily on physical punishment. Beatings with whips, "sticks, pistols, knives, fists, feet, shovels and tongs"[71] hardly comported with Davis's "gentle arts of peace and order." Nor did such punishments as staking to the ground, ducking in cold water, deprivation of food, and confinement in the private jails built by plantation owners, however infrequently these "negative incentives" were employed in comparison with the old reliable whipping. The famous photograph in *Harper's Weekly* of the escaped slave Gordon, his back crisscrossed with scar tissue from repeated whippings, did not reflect some unusual mode of punishment (except as to severity) but rather the common practice for disciplining laggardly, disobedient, escaped or simply insufficiently productive slaves, even if the prudent master, like any good capitalist, would avoid abusing his most important capital assets to the point of impairing their utility.

Regarding the standard practice of whipping, Fogel's and Engerman's "cliometric" analysis in *Time on the Cross*, based on the record of punishments in the diary of a single cotton planter from Louisiana, Bennet H. Barrow (the primary existing documentary evidence) has been demolished by Gutman. Gutman shows that the very data on which Fogel and Engerman relied, taken together with numerous telling diary entries they conspicuously ignored, demonstrate that Barrow, a typically "paternal" slave-owner, routinely collectively whipped all his adult field hands, both male and female, that he whipped at least half of his slave children during one annual period, that he whipped even his house slaves, and that (as shown in a dissertation Gutman cites) he "employed practically every known form of chastisement slaveholders use," including "chains . . . humiliation, such as making a man wear woman's clothing and parade around the quarters, 'staking out'; 'hand sawing' [beating with a handsaw blade]; and dousing or ducking in water which occurred in October or November."[72]

Consider these entries reflecting life on the Barrow plantation for his slaves: "had

70. Fogel and Engerman, *Time on the Cross*, 267–68.
71. Schermerhorn, op. cit., 34.
72. Gutman, *Slavery and the Numbers Game*, 18–28 & 25.

a general whipping frollick ... broke my sword cane over one of their skulls. ... Whipped about half today. ... Whipped every hand in the field this evening. ... Gave my negroes about my lot the worst Whipping they ever had. ... Gave every cotton picker a Whipping last night. ... Gave my driver [i.e., a black slave driver] a few licks this evening, not knowing who had done bad work ... had a general Whipping among the house ones. ... More hands attempting to shirk ... gave a number of them a good flogging. ... Whipped all my grown cotton pickers today. ..."[73] Yet Barrow's diary entries provided the entire statistical basis for the supposedly groundbreaking "finding" in *Time on the Cross* that the punishment of slaves had been greatly exaggerated in prior historiography.

Even Fogel and Engerman are constrained to admit, however, that "*whipping was an integral part of the system* of punishment and rewards. ..." According to them—a conclusion widely and justly ridiculed—whipping was merely part of the process by which "[p]lanters sought to imbue their slaves with a 'Protestant' work ethic and to transform that ethic from a state of mind into a high level of production."[74] But it is self-evident that, as Gutman observes acidly, "[m]ost of Barrow's slaves were whipped for *not* conforming to the Protestant work ethic."[75] With unintentional humor, Fogel and Engerman explain why the antebellum slave-owner did not whip his slaves with malice (as if that were the issue) but rather for sound economic reasons. While some masters "excluded it [whipping] altogether ... [m]ost accepted it, but recognized that to be effective, whipping had to be used with restraint and in a coolly calculated manner." This cool and calculated whipping was preferable to withholding food or incarcerating the slave in a private jail "because the cost of substituting hunger and incarceration for the lash was greater for the slave-owner than for the northern employer of free labor." Hence the "decline of whipping as an instrument of labor discipline outside of the South" could be laid to "economic considerations" rather than moral disapproval of the practice in the North. Uncooperative free laborers "could be fired—left to starve beyond the eyesight and expense of the employer," whereas "[u]nder slavery, the master desired forms of punishment which, while they imposed costs on the slave, did so with minimum impairment to the human capital which the master owned. Whipping generally fulfilled these conditions."[76]

There is no denying that what Davis called the "patient toil" of millions of slaves had indeed created "unmeasured riches" for their owners. But as Fogel and Engerman themselves demonstrate with their "cliometric" attempt to revise the history of slavery to depict something resembling a market process, the slaves' "patient toil" was commonly extracted or optimized by brute physical coercion or the threat of it (not to mention the ever-present threat of sale away from loved ones) rather than a mythical acquired Calvinist zeal for hard work, even if "positive incentives"

73. Gutman, 21–24.
74. Fogel and Engerman, *Time on the Cross*, Vol. I, 147.
75. Gutman, *Slavery and the Numbers Game*, 27.
76. Fogel and Engerman, *Time on the Cross*, 147.

(a suit of clothes, an extra portion of meat, some whiskey, cash gifts, etc.) were not wanting for some slaves.

"Cliometric" analysis aside, a decision of the Alabama Supreme Court in 1861 is profoundly illustrative of the central role of physical coercion in maintaining the "peculiar institution." The case involved an appeal by a slave-owner from a jury verdict against him on a claim for "trespass" he had brought against the hirer of one his slaves, who had allegedly trespassed against the slave owner's chattel by whipping him too severely. In upholding the verdict, Alabama's high court, only a few weeks before the Civil War began, observed the fundamental antebellum legal principle that "Absolute obedience, and subordination to the lawful authority of the master, are the duty of the slave; and the master or hirer may employ so much force as may be reasonably necessary to secure that obedience." Since, the court concluded, "[t]he law cannot enter into a strict scrutiny of the precise force employed, with the view of ascertaining that the chastisement had or had not been unreasonable," the jury's verdict that the whipping had not been so excessive as to constitute trespass by damage to the slave must stand. The court did note, however, "that the master, hirer, or overseer, should ever bear in mind, that the main purpose of correction is to reduce an offending and refractory slave to *a proper state of submission*, respect and obedience to legitimate authority."[77]

The Slave-Owner's Burden

The pro-slavery arguments of Davis and Stephens examined in the preceding chapter were but part of a vast antebellum Southern polemic designed to demonstrate that the "peculiar institution" was no mere tolerable evil but rather a "positive good," as Calhoun had called it in the Senate speech he spent the rest of his career trying to explain away. Going even further, however, the same polemic seriously depicted the institution as a sacrificial burden heroically shouldered by the master class. More than a century and a half after Cotton Mather enunciated it, the pro-slavery spokesmen of the antebellum South were still preaching his discredited gospel of the divine ordination of slavery and the natural subjugation of the Negro. According to this thread in the Puritan narrative of salvation history, the slave-owner was no less than God's vice-regent, even an *alter Christus*, charged with the duty of saving his Negro slaves as the "miserable children of Adam and Noah,"[78] still under the curse of Ham. The "peculiar institution" was, after all, a *Christian* institution.

This apologetic was in keeping with a trend according to which, "with the exception of the Society of Friends, every denomination in the South had compromised with slavery until by midway in the nineteenth century religious leaders were either silent or offered divine justification for the traffic in human chattels."[79] As one Confederate partisan enthuses, apparently without recognizing the implications of

77. *Tillman v. Chadwick*, 37 Ala. 317, 319 (1861).
78. Cf. Cotton Mather, *Rules for the Society of Negroes* (1693).
79. *Society and Culture in the Slave South*, 164.

his observation for the sincerity of this typically Protestant theological adjustment: "Before Nat Turner's Rebellion [in 1831], there were at least three times more anti-slavery societies in the South than in the North."[80] The evil—Lee's own word—of chattel slavery was somehow transformed into a Christian duty the slave-owner was nobly discharging in accordance with God's plan, caring for his slaves in sickness or in health, never punishing them too severely, and shining upon them the "enlightening rays of Christianity" to which Davis referred. That the ownership of slaves was accompanied by a splendid estate, fine possessions, "unmeasured riches," as Davis put it, and a life of leisure for the master class did not make it any easier for them to bear their heavy burden under God.[81]

In his Bancroft Prize-winning study of antebellum slavery, *Roll, Jordan, Roll*, Eugene Genovese shows how the members of the Southern master class, responding to the rising abolition movement, developed the original Puritan narrative into an entire counter-theology of self-justification for the ownership of fellow human beings whose involuntary servitude had made them rich or quite well-to-do. Genovese cites the rather amusing example of James Chesnut of South Carolina, the wealthy politician-planter husband of Mary Chesnut. During the war Captain James Chesnut would assist in delivering the ultimatum to Major Anderson to abandon Fort Sumter or be fired upon. Mrs. Chesnut records that her husband once complained bitterly that his many slaves "steal all of my hogs, and I have to buy meat for them, and they will not make cotton." Asked if any had ever run away he replied: "Never. It's pretty hard work to keep me from running away from them!"[82] Of course, Chesnut was not about to run away from the wealth his slaves produced, despite their excessive demands for food; and when his slaves did run away during the war "he would have an opportunity to calculate his economic relationship to them more realistically,"[83] Genovese remarks with nice irony.

Davis's "enlightening rays of Christianity" did extend to baptism and a rough Protestant Christianity for many (but far from all) slaves. This the slaves combined with elements of their own folk religion, producing "a mélange [that] selectively appropriated those ideas that best fit their own sacred universe and secular world. With little standing in the church of the master, these men and women fostered a new faith . . . a theological amalgam that white clerics found unrecognizable. . . ."[84] That faith included a Biblical exegesis quite contrary to that of their masters: a reading of Scripture that foretold their divinely ordained emancipation from captivity in the here and now.

Dinesh D'Souza discusses how in the process of studying antebellum slavery Genovese, who returned to the Catholic Church in 1996, expected to find that Christianity had reconciled slaves to their condition according to the convenient

80. Crocker, *Politically Incorrect Guide to the Civil War*, 439–40.

81. Cf. Eugene D. Genovese, *Roll, Jordan, Roll: The World the Slaves Made* (Vintage Books: Kindle Edition, 2011), 1754–2006.

82. Ibid., 1904–1905.

83. Ibid., 1909.

84. Berlin, *Generations of Captivity*, 2181–2182.

theology of their masters. He was amazed to find instead what historians now universally acknowledge: that the slaves read the Bible to teach that "the hope of salvation in the next world was inextricably connected to the demand for freedom in this world." Hence the lines from the Negro spiritual that is part of American folklore and sums up the entire slave theology of liberation: "Go down Moses, way down to Egypt land, and tell Pharaoh, let my people go." The Puritan theology of African slaves as bearers of the curse of Ham—a rationale most Southern divines abandoned in embarrassment—was, as D'Souza writes, "complete nonsense. Nowhere does the Bible even imply that Ham was black." By the eve of the Civil War, the slaves who read the Bible had certainly deduced this on their own, drawing from the Book of Exodus "an analogy between their own condition and that of the Israelites under Egyptian captivity." Moses became a prophet and sign of hope to the antebellum slaves of the South—so much so that many of them named their children after him.[85]

A Morality and Theology of Convenience

None of this is to suggest that all slave-owners were conscious hypocrites or brutal slave-drivers à la Harriet Beecher Stowe's Simon Legree. The focus here is on the objective merit of the defense of chattel slavery as the ground of Southern secession and consequent war, not the subjective disposition or culpability of individual slave-owners. There is no doubt that the brutality of the institution is exaggerated in abolitionist and neo-abolitionist sources. And it must also be said that even in the midst of their subjugation, acting within the interstices of a legal system that treated them as property and deprived them of the most basic rights, slaves were able to extract important concessions from their owners, develop a primitive, extra-legal slave economy that supplemented what the masters provided by way of sustenance, and build (or rebuild when destroyed) families and kinship networks, along with an entire black American culture. Further, in innumerable creative ways slaves were able to avoid, evade, postpone, shirk, or passively resist the demands of their masters, who after all were totally dependent upon them for their wealth—a dependency even slaves could exploit within limits. Thus a kind of reciprocal bargaining process—radically stunted, of course, by the fact of legally imposed and physically coerced involuntary servitude—to some extent asserted itself in given circumstances. All of this has been shown in magisterial studies by Genovese, Ira Berlin, and other leading historians of American slavery.

But neither can one accept Davis's ridiculous depiction of the slave-owning class as benevolent Christian patrons of beloved charges whose "servile instincts" left them all "contented with their lot." The *ethos* of slave culture is steeped in an ancestral longing for freedom from bondage, no matter how lenient the master. And while many slave-owners forged close bonds with at least some of their slaves, even a familial affection, wherever this occurred it did not alter a legal and social relation

---

85. Dinesh D'Souza, *Life After Death* (Washington: Regnery Publishing, Inc., 2009), 197–98.

that was never to be disregarded. A telling indication of the dark moral underside of even the "happiest" master-slave relation is an observation by Mary Chesnut in her diary. Chesnut recounts the last days of her wealthy father-in-law, owner of five square miles of plantations now devoid of slaves. His beloved slave Scipio "has never deserted old Chesnut: six feet two, a black Hercules and gentle as a dove in all his dealings with the blind old master. . . . Partly patriarch, partly *grand seigneur,* this old man is of a species we will see no more; the last of the lordly planters who ruled this Southern world. His manners are unequalled still, but beneath this smooth exterior *lies the grip of a tyrant whose will has never been crossed.*"[86] Even at its most benign, the master-slave relation in the antebellum South was at bottom a benevolent tyranny, and both parties to the relation never forgot it. Old man Chesnut, wrote his daughter-in-law, "came of a race that would brook no interference with their own sweet will by man, woman, or devil."[87]

What Chesnut provides with this anecdote of an iconic antebellum planter is what Genovese has so brilliantly dissected in his historical analysis of antebellum slavery. The reciprocity that developed in master-slave relationships could never be allowed to destroy the fundamental legal reality, so that what arose—when it did arise, which was far from always—was not Christian fraternity but something analogous to the relation between a master and his dog. Noting the English novelist Anthony Trollope's observation (quite untrue) "that slaves love their masters in the same way that dogs do," Genovese addresses the quaintly naïve arguments of Mrs. Henry Rowe Schoolcraft, the rather schoolmarmish planter class aristocrat from South Carolina who wrote a pro-slavery novel in answer to *Uncle Tom's Cabin.* Schoolcraft agreed with Trollope's supremely condescending assessment of the emotional and intellectual capacity of the black slave, but professed to see nothing wrong with such a degenerate form of human relations. She thought it quite fitting for the slaves she simply assumed were not divinely fitted for anything higher and were thus suitably pampered by their owners, just as faithful dogs would be: "The slave can never be treated with the hardness of heart that poor white operators are, because the fact of his being dependent makes his master love to patronize him. . . . How thankful I am to God that the slave, who seems given up to the will of his master, should have the very strongest passion of that master's heart enlisted to protect him and provide for his every want." This romantic fantasy of the pampered slave, content in his dog-like devotion, loving his master with an unconditional love born of total submission of mind and will, was just as God had mandated from all eternity: "South Carolinians are 'old fogies,' and consequently they do not believe with the Abolitionists that God is a progressive being," and "[t]here scarcely ever was a time in the history of the world, when one man did not enslave his fellow-man."[88]

Thus was the chattel slavery of the antebellum South smugly dressed up as perennial Christian conservatism. As Genovese observes, with an ideology of this

86. In Wilson, *Patriotic Gore*, 298–99.
87. Mary Boykin Chesnut, *A Diary From Dixie* (D. Appleton and Company, Kindle Edition), 397.
88. Genovese, *Roll, Jordan, Roll*, 2008–2011.

sort, the members of the master class who cared about being Christians—and they certainly did care—could reconcile their "demand for absolute obedience while repudiating its theoretical foundation" and thus live with themselves as "morally responsible beings who were doing their duty."[89] Such was the self-justification of even the most benevolent slave-owner. Eaton cites the example of Charles Colcock Jones of Georgia, who "undoubtedly was an exceptional planter." Jones never whipped his slaves, fed them well, bought from them the produce he allowed them to raise, and even built them a chapel and provided Sunday schooling. Like any good Protestant, Jones "searched the Scriptures for justification of the institution, and, of course, found what he was seeking."[90]

But, as Genovese notes—making the crucial distinction—what the antebellum master class would never admit to itself was that the "historical ubiquity of slavery *had nothing to do with race....*"[91] Their "peculiar" system of chattel slavery was foreign to the Old Testament, being based upon the supposedly "natural subjugation" of only one race among men. Had not Alexander Stephens condemned any form of white-on-white slavery as a "violation of the laws of nature" in his Cornerstone Address? Further, as the Southern Protestant divine George F. Simmons had preached—at the risk of lynching—the Mosaic form of slavery the Southern planters pretended to emulate "contained no permission for the sale of slaves.... 'They cannot be part of our property; nor can they be treated as such.'"[92]

Beneath the soft garb of the South's "Christian" chattel slavery lay the hard political economy of the works of Adam Smith (cited by Stephens in the Cornerstone Address), David Ricardo, Thomas Malthus, and Jean-Baptiste Say, from which educated planters familiar with these works drew their own conclusions on the relative utility of slave versus free labor, including the "law" that "all races required some form of servitude in order to progress."[93] Thus the "conservative" critique of capitalism by the antebellum master class was entirely within the framework of post-Enlightenment economic liberalism, which is to say within the framework of Liberty. That is precisely why the very icon of Liberty, Thomas Jefferson, was able to prosper from the forced labor of several hundred of his fellow human beings while professing to deplore the very "cornerstone" of the supposedly high civilization of the South. Nor is it presentism to highlight this hypocrisy, which was well understood and prominently exposed at the time to the great irritation of the antebellum South's indignant intelligentsia. Recall Samuel Johnson's ridicule a century earlier of the Continental Congress, where one could hear "the loudest yelps for liberty among the drivers of negroes."

In the end, it was only a utilitarian and consequentialist ethic, the same ethic behind the "dark satanic mills" of England, that could be cited in defense of an

---

89. Ibid., 2071–2074.
90. Eaton, *A History of the Old South*, 252.
91. Genovese, *The Southern Tradition*, 33.
92. Genovese, *Consuming Fire*, 114.
93. Genovese, *The Southern Tradition*, 33.

institution in which one man not only owned another but the other's offspring to the *nth* generation: The slaves, so the argument goes, were "better off" as slaves, just as the industrial workers in the dark satanic mills were better off in the mills according to their English capitalist overlords. In fact, the Southern argument was precisely that slaves on the Southern plantations had an easier life than industrial wage-slaves in the Northern cities. Assuming this to be true solely for argument's sake—while ignoring chattel slavery's frequent destruction of marriage and family bonds—the argument is essentially that the exploitation of human beings by slave-owners was morally justified by reference to an even worse alternative form of exploitation by others. That is, the end ("Christianizing" or "uplifting" the Negro) justifies the means (slavery), which is utilitarianism. Or, stated otherwise, slavery can be pronounced good because its overall consequences (better food, clothing, housing, religion) are superior to the *status quo ante* (life in Africa or in an industrial city), which is consequentialism.

These are not the arguments of a Christian but rather of an entrepreneur who professes Christianity, perhaps in all sincerity, yet also wishes to justify the source of his wealth without an overly scrupulous application of the Gospel. That is exactly what a 19th-century laissez-faire capitalist was, be he a Southern agrarian capitalist turning up his nose at the dog-eat-dog free-labor industrialism of the North, or a Northern factory owner intent on paying his human capital as little as possible for as much labor as possible. Four years before the Civil War, Robert E. Lee (who at that time still owned slaves by inheritance from his father-in-law) voiced the prevailing utilitarian/consequentialist moral judgment of the Southern master class on its own behavior: "There are few, I believe, in this enlightened age, who will not acknowledge that slavery as an institution is a moral and political evil in any country." And yet, he hastened to add, "[t]he blacks are immeasurably better off here than in Africa, morally, physically, and socially."[94]

Whoever would multiply such anti-slavery testimonies among the Southern leadership—and many such testimonies there were—would only succeed in diminishing the grounds for secession over the slavery question. For the slave-owning critics of slavery, like Jefferson decades earlier, were articulating a liberal morality of convenience. "In the abstract, Lee and the others had it both ways: they had been able to lament slavery as an evil, but cling to it as an institution, leaving its fate in the hands of God or some other long-range force."[95]

In fact, Lee did not free all of the 196 slaves Mary Custis had inherited from her father, George Washington Parke Custis, until January 1, 1863—the very date of the Emancipation Proclamation, and the last date for compliance with a court order compelling Lee to honor the terms of the Custis will mandating their freedom, which Lee had tried to delay. In his effort to generate income for the Custis estate, Lee rented out most of the slaves, thereby "ruptur[ing] the Washington and Custis tradition of respecting slave families. By 1860 he had broken up every family but

---

94. Charles Bracelen Flood, *Lee: The Last Years* (NY: Houghton Mifflin, 1998), 50.
95. Alan T. Nolan, *Lee Considered* (Chapel Hill: Univ. of North Carolina Press, 1991), 20.

one on the estate, some of whom had been together since Mount Vernon days."[96] Lee's own account books show that he routinely hired constables to arrest fugitive slaves and return them to Arlington, despite the testamentary direction that they be freed.[97]

It was all well and good for Lee to tell Mary in 1856 that God, "with whom a thousand years are but a single day," would somehow abolish slavery through His "work by slow things."[98] But what of the slaves—including Lee's—to whom a day might seem like a thousand years and who had long prayed to the same God for an end to their captivity, even if their purely material conditions in a given case might be significantly better than those of peasants or industrial workers in Europe? Peasants and wage-slaves at least had legally recognized marriages and families. Was that not infinitely more important to a human being than quantity of food or quality of habitation? As for religion, a black man hardly required enslavement in the antebellum South in order to find Christ. The "peculiar institution" was not a church.

Here Lee echoed the theologically expedient preaching of the South's Protestant divines, who at one and the same time decried the abuses of antebellum chattel slavery—especially its disregard of the bonds of marriage and family—professed to favor gradual emancipation, yet deplored the Northern regime of free-labor and held up Southern slavery as a morally superior relation between labor and capital. Citing the sermons of Thornwell and Benjamin Palmer as examples, Genovese neatly summarizes their utter incoherence: "Now, how could Thornwell and Palmer, honest and clear-thinking men, have simultaneously praised slavery as a superior labor system, damned the free-labor system as morally monstrous and politically insupportable, and looked kindly on the prospects for emancipation?"[99]

A Famous Escapee from Republican Slavery

While the abolitionist cartoon of every slave-owner a monster à la Simon Legree is not antebellum slavery as it really was, we have dispensed as well with the opposing cartoon of plantations filled with "happy darkies," singing their happy songs and laboring dutifully in grateful devotion to their benevolent Christian owners. That there were no slaves yearning for freedom, or at most just a few troublemakers among the happy and contented slave masses depicted by Davis and Stephens, was the great delusion of the Southern master class. The proud owners of their fellow human beings would be stunned to see how, at the approach of the Union armies, "'faithful' house servants as well as field hands deserted in droves. The 'moment of

96. Elizabeth Brown Pryor, *Reading the Man: A Portrait of Robert E. Lee Through His Private Letters* (Penguin Group: Kindle Edition, 2007), 5608–5611.

97. Ibid., 5746–5756.

98. Lee to Mary Custis, December 27, 1856, in Fitzhugh Lee, *General Lee* (NY: The University Society, 1905), 63–64.

99. Genovese, *A Consuming Fire*, 10, 57, 67–68.

truth' had arrived for the masters, but they reacted by accusing the slaves of ingratitude."[100] They could not believe that their "'loyal' and 'pampered' servants ... chose to leave at the first chance of freedom."[101] They seemed blissfully unaware that many slaves had affected an attitude of happy subservience, thus deftly exploiting the masters' belief in their slaves' tranquil stupidity: "We wear the mask that grins and lies," wrote the black poet Paul Laurence Dunbar of the life of his ex-slave parents.[102]

Few among the leaders of the antebellum South could see any rectitude in the eloquent speeches and writings of Frederick Douglass, one of the many slaves born of an illicit union between his slave mother and her master. For all his radicalism and proto-feminism, it was Douglass who issued an immortal indictment of the racist Temple of Liberty from North to South. In his *My Bondage and My Freedom* Douglass recounts how he fled America entirely in 1845 "to seek a refuge from republican slavery in monarchical England," for even in the North he was subject to racist segregation and to capture and return to his owner like a runaway horse. Douglass spent only a single night in England before making his way to Catholic Ireland, where he was astonished by what he found in Dublin:

> I breathe, and lo! the chattel becomes a man. I gaze around in vain for one who will question my equal humanity, claim me as his slave, or offer me an insult. I employ a cab—I am seated beside white people—I reach the hotel—I enter the same door—I am shown into the same parlour—I dine at the same table—and no one is offended. No delicate nose grows deformed in my presence. I find no difficulty here in obtaining admission into any place of worship, instruction, or amusement, on equal terms with people as white as any I ever saw in the United States. I meet nothing to remind me of my complexion. I find myself regarded and treated at every turn with the kindness and deference paid to white people. When I go to church, I am met by no upturned nose and scornful lip to tell me, "*We don't allow niggers in here!*"[103]

As he recounted in his *Narrative of the Life of Frederick Douglass, An American Slave*, Douglass had long been affected by his encounter with two Irishmen working the docks in the Baltimore shipyard where he had worked for his master as a slave: "Are ye a slave for life?" one of them asked. "When Douglass replied that he was, the 'good Irishman seemed [...] deeply affected' by his response and said 'it was a pity [...].'" Their advice that he seek his freedom "caused him to resolve 'from that time to run away'...."[104] Among the Catholics of Ireland, he confided in a letter to William Lloyd Garrison, "I find myself not treated as a color, but as a

100. Eaton, *A History of the Old South*, 253.

101. Pryor, *Reading the Man*, 5686–5689.

102. Ibid.

103. Frederick Douglass, *My Bondage and My Freedom* (NY: Miller, Orton and Mulligan, 1855), 365, 371. Emphasis in original.

104. In Patricia J. Ferreira, "Frederick Douglass in Ireland: the Dublin Edition of His Narrative," *New Hibernia Review*, Vol. 5, No. 1, Earrach/Spring 2001, 53.

man—not as a thing, but as a child of the common Father of us all."[105] Of his six months among the Irish, Douglass wrote to Garrison: "I have spent some of the happiest moments of my life since landing in this country, I seem to have undergone a transformation, I live a new life."[106]

While in Ireland, Douglass met and became fast friends with Daniel O'Connell, author of the aforementioned letter condemning the annexation of Texas and calling upon Irish American immigrants to renounce any participation in building a Southern slave empire. O'Connell was, like Douglass, a spellbinding orator who had led another sort of emancipation movement against oppression by a Protestant master class: the movement for Catholic emancipation that had culminated in the passage of the Emancipation Act in 1829, removing the disqualification of Catholics from public office and the requirement of the Oath of Supremacy, which O'Connell had refused to take because it was contrary to the Catholic faith. A successful trial lawyer and a member of Parliament following the Emancipation Act (being one of the few Irishmen wealthy enough to qualify for the franchise), O'Connell "was no revolutionary: he believed in the rule of law, rejected violence and had a deep-seated wariness of the Pandora's box of societal forces unleashed by revolutions." But he also "passionately opposed slavery. Upon meeting an American, before shaking hands, he routinely asked whether the visitor was a slaveholder. If the answer was yes—no handshake."[107]

Unlike O'Connell and the generality of Catholic Ireland, the Protestant master class of the antebellum South could not or would not see that Douglass's withering critique of the institution to which he had been subjected his whole life extended beyond utilitarian considerations of the quality of a slave's food, lodging, clothing and general treatment, as compared with that of other unfortunate souls in other unfortunate circumstances. The critique went directly to the fundamental "moral and political evil," as Lee had called it: the black slave's perpetual legal reduction to a human chattel simply and only because of the color of his skin, with all that this entailed for his social, political, intellectual, marital, familial, and spiritual life. On this ground, writes Fogel, the indictment of slavery would stand "even if slaves were treated as well as the favorite Arabian steed of a very rich man, because people are not horses."[108] As the Irish Catholic journalist William Howell Russell observed during his journey to America in 1861—and this from a perspective sympathetic to the South:

> The constant appeals to the physical comforts of the slaves, and their supposed contentment, have little or no effect on a person who acts up to a higher standard of human happiness than that which is applied to swine or the beast

---

105. In Frederick May Holland, *Frederick Douglass, The Colored Orator* (NY: Haskell House Publishers, Ltd., 1969 [1891]), 116.

106. Douglass, *My Bondage and My Freedom*, 370.

107. Tom Chaffin, "Frederick Douglass's Irish Liberty," *New York Times*, February 25, 2011, opinionator.blogs.ny-times.com/2011/02/25/frederick-douglasss-irish-liberty/.

108. Fogel, *Without Consent or Contract*, 392.

of the fields, "See how happy my pigs are." Slavery is a curse, with its time of accomplishment not quite at hand—it is a cancer, the ravages of which are covered by fair outward show, and by the apparent health of the sufferer.[109]

In public testimony on why he abandoned Marxism and returned to the Catholic Church, Eugene Genovese revealed the part played by the stunning discovery during his work on *Roll, Jordan Roll* of the centrality of the "religious dimension" in the life of antebellum slaves: "the extraordinary struggle of those black slaves to keep the faith against all odds," despite the "humiliation felt by people who, through no fault of their own, have to watch their children suffer at the hands of those who presume to run their lives." Recalling the humiliation his own father had suffered on account of reversals of fortune during the Great Depression, leaving him a bitter man until the day he died, Genovese observed:

> What must black slaves, who suffered immeasurably worse, have felt? And yet they repelled the sense of humiliation and impotence. They forged a vibrant culture of hope based upon unshakable faith in the Lord's deliverance. Studying their creative resistance to the degradation their masters were trying to impose upon them, I began to appreciate the meaning of the Crucifixion and the Atonement. For while Jesus suffered bodily torments, they were hardly the worst anyone had or has suffered. But His humiliation, abasement and momentary sense of being forsaken did encapsulate the worst a man might suffer. And the slaves, I believe, grasped the depth of the sacrifice more deeply than all others.[110]

As we saw in Chapter 3, the Crucifixion and the Atonement are precisely what Locke the slave-owner excised from his "reasonable Christianity." And it was a "reasonable Christianity" that lay beneath both the radically Lockean property rights philosophy of the Industrial Revolution in England and the northern United States, as well as the agrarian revolution of the antebellum South, the personal piety of the individual entrepreneur notwithstanding. Both variants of Locke's "absolute" property right in operation were dependent on human capital in the form of chattel slaves or wage-slaves made available by state action.

It is important to recall here (also from Chapter 3) Locke's provision in the *Fundamental Constitutions of Carolina*, which he wrote some two hundred years earlier to protect his own "absolute" property right in human chattels: "every freeman of Carolina shall have *absolute power and authority over his negro slaves....*"[111] Just as in the antebellum South, Locke's slaves were allowed to profess a religion, provided that "no slave shall hereby be exempted from that civil dominion his master hath over him, but be in all things in the same state and condition he was in before."[112]

---

109. In Zanca, *American Catholics and Slavery*, 120.

110. "Eugene Genovese: From Marxism to Christianity," Calvin College, January Series Lecture, Part 5, 1–20–98 at 6:00, www.youtube.com/watch?v=xYYTSEodYy4&NR=1.

111. *Locke: Political Essays*, Fundamental Constitutions, Arts. [101] [110], 180.

112. Ibid., Art. 107.

Locke was aware that the influence of Christianity posed a threat to the absolute property right in slaves, hence the former had to be subordinated to the latter by an appropriately Puritan and Lockean theological adjustment. The American master class had the same awareness. Hence, for example, colonial Maryland and colonial Virginia both enacted statutes providing that baptism effected no change in slave status.[113]

The Southern Jeremiahs and the Popes

The facile objection that our critical view of antebellum chattel slavery indulges in the moral hindsight of "presentism" is negated by the many contemporary warnings of the more conscientious Southern Protestant divines, who were not blind to the evils their Northern counterparts condemned. Quite the contrary, while doggedly defending black (but not white) slavery as Biblically sanctioned, they publicly reprobated their fellow Southerners for failing to reform the abuses of the "peculiar institution," warning of divine chastisement if reforms were not introduced. In his Lamar Lectures, Genovese collects testimony after testimony by "Southern Jeremiahs" that "Southern slavery, as legally constituted and daily practiced, fell well short of Biblical standards," that "God had a quarrel with [the masters] for treating their slaves as brutes," that "the South could defend slavery only if it met its Christian responsibility to the slaves," and that "a sweeping revision of the slave codes" was urgently needed if the South wished to avoid divine disfavor of its "holy" cause.[114]

Above all, these godly defenders of the peculiar institution had pleaded—quite in vain—for "recognition of slave families at law," and they had "long cringed before the widespread criticism of the South's unwillingness to recognize slave marriages and prevent the separation of slave families."[115] Some twenty years before South Carolina's secession, for example, the Reverend Robert L. Dabney, typical of the rest of these Jeremiahs, had "excoriated 'unprincipled' masters who inflicted starvation, oppression, and cruel punishments on their slaves...." He "urged protection of the family relation," and warned that "[i]f Southerners did not correct these abuses, they would be turning away from Jesus." Southerners, he declared, "can only stand on the Bible if they acknowledge that they have no right to separate a man and a wife or in any other way violate Christian teaching."[116] John Leadley Dagg, the renowned evangelical Baptist, President of Mercer University in Georgia, and author of Manual of Theology, the veritable hornbook of the Southern Baptist creed, warned in 1857 that "The failure of our laws to protect marriage among slaves ... is only a part of the general evil. We have not labored, in every possible way, to promote the welfare, for time and eternity, of our slave population, as of dependent and helpless immortals whom God has placed in our

---

113. Zanca, American Catholics and Slavery, 113.
114. Genovese, A Consuming Fire, 5, 9, 11–12, 14, 15, 17, 67–68.
115. Ibid., 17.
116. Ibid., 11–12.

power and at our mercy."[117] Summing up the warnings of the Southern Jeremiahs, a pro-slavery, white supremacist educator from Tennessee declared in 1861: "Our divine Master has most emphatically ordained family relations as sacred: The Legislatures of all the Southern States have with equal emphasis repudiated these relationships as to four million of their people. The Legislatures of each of these States has thus absolutely *nullified* the law of Christ."[118]

A small but telling example of this morally degraded state of affairs is found in the correspondence of the prominent planter aristocrat and U.S. Congressman and Senator Robert Woodward Barnwell of Charleston. Writing to his cousin Robert Barnwell Rhett some seventeen years before South Carolina's secession, Barnwell expresses disdain for slave-owners outside of South Carolina, who lack the élan to uphold slavery "as a political institution essential to the preservation of our civilization ... to be maintained and defended in the same high strain *as liberty itself.*" Rather, "the greater part of the slaveholders in the other states are mere negro-drivers believing themselves wrong and only holding on to their negroes as something to make money out of. And we [South Carolinians] have retrograded and must soon fall into the same category." Only three months later, however, Barnwell himself is scheming with Rhett to avoid a creditor by "sell[ing] the negroes under mortgage to me" before the creditor can seize Rhett's human chattels "through the power of the Court." Yet, in the same letter, Barnwell laments that "the infamous conduct of our Southern Senators combined with the folly and apathy of those whom they represent, seem to me to indicate that our institutions are doomed & that the Southern civilization must go out in blood." Barnwell was at that time unwilling to go out with them: "Nor do I feel as I once did, that I am bound to abide ... the fate of my country. It seems to me that when a country degrades itself, its citizens may abjure the country with the disgrace it has drawn upon them."[119] But Barnwell would serve in the Confederate Congress throughout the coming war, watching his own prophesy come true.

The Southern Jeremiahs' warnings about the cracks in the "cornerstone" of Southern civilization were quite in line with contemporaneous Catholic teaching on the evils of Negro slavery. Even Bishop Verot of Savannah, a Confederate partisan, delivered a sermon in which, while arguing that the Church had not condemned slavery as *intrinsically* evil, he "insisted that slaves had the right to marry and that 'the laws of marriage must be observed among them exactly as among the whites'" and "made it clear that a master did not have the same rights over a slave that he had over an animal."[120] In that sermon, published under the title *A Tract for the Times* (1861) within weeks after South Carolina's secession, Verot joined the Protestant Jeremiahs of the South in posing the question "whether God can bless a

117. Genovese, *A Consuming Fire*, 67–68.

118. Ibid., 22. Emphasis in original.

119. Barnwell to Rhett, November 1, 1844 and February 19, 1845; in John Barnwell, "Hamlet to Hotspur: Letters of Robert Woodward Barnwell to Robert Barnwell Rhett," *The South Carolina Historical Magazine*, Vol. 77, No. 4 (October 1976), 252, 255–56.

120. Rev. Benjamin J. Blied, Ph.D., *Catholics and the Civil War* (Milwaukee: 1945), 63.

country and a state of things in which there is a woeful disregard of the holy laws of marriage." Echoing the natural law teaching of Thomas Aquinas already noted, he declared that while slave-owners can claim titles "only to labor and service, they cannot change the nature of men" and "deprive them of the faculty of marrying," which would lead to "the shocking, hideous and abominable conclusion ... that they must live in concubinage and adultery." Further, he admonished, "It is unreasonable, unchristian, and immoral to separate a husband from his wife and children, and to sell the husband North, and the wife South, and the children East and West." The Confederacy, he warned, "must rest on morality and justice, and it could never be entitled to a special protection from above unless it professes to surround Slavery with the guarantees that will secure its morality and virtue"—none of which had been forthcoming. Writing of "the wrongs which the South ought to acknowledge and confess," he cautioned that "if these wrongs be persevered in, this may be the reason that the Almighty, in his justice and wise severity, may sweep Slavery out of the land. . . ."[121] This was a prophesy soon to be fulfilled.

Rising above the politics and sectionalism by which the American hierarchy, both North and South, would be affected, Pope Gregory XVI's encyclical *In Supremo Apostolatus* (1839) condemned "the inhuman slave trade in Negroes and all other men" and warned the Catholic faithful that "no one in the future dare to vex anyone, despoil him of his possessions, reduce to servitude, or lend aid and favour to those who give themselves up to these practices, or exercise that inhuman traffic by which the Blacks, as if they were not men but rather animals, having been brought into servitude, in no matter what way, are, without any distinction, in contempt of the rights of justice and humanity, bought, sold, and devoted sometimes to the hardest labour." There can be no question that the papal condemnation would apply to the foreign slave trade practiced in America and protected explicitly by Article 1, § 9 of the Constitution until 1808, the domestic slave trade that continued thereafter, with its frequent destruction of marriages and families, and the generalized "contempt of the rights of justice and humanity" evident in the status of American slaves under the slave codes.

The predictable efforts of Southern partisans to limit the Church's condemnation strictly to the slave trade rather than the institution of chattel slavery as such could hardly be squared with Pope Leo XIII's encyclical *In Plurimis* (1888), promulgated on the occasion of the freeing of slaves in Brazil by Dom Pedro II in honor of Leo's golden jubilee as a priest. Leo made explicit reference to *In Supremo Apostolatus*, noting that fifty years earlier "Gregory XVI also severely censured those neglecting the duties of humanity and the laws, and restored the decrees and statutory penalties of the apostolic see, and left no means untried that *foreign nations, also, following the kindliness of the Europeans*, should cease from and abhor the disgrace and brutality of slavery." While counseling against violent or precipitate

---

121. Bishop Augustine Verot, *A Tract for the Times* (New Orleans: Catholic Propagator Office, 1861), 15, 18–19. Accessed at Duke Univerity Library Ebook and Texts Archive, http://www.archive.org/details/tractfortimesslao1vero.

means to achieve emancipation, the Pope declared that the "*condition* of slavery, in which a considerable part of the great human family has been sunk in squalor and affliction now for many centuries, *is deeply to be deplored*; for the system is one which is wholly opposed to that which was originally ordained by God and by nature."[122] Here the Church echoed the teaching of Saint Augustine in *City of God* more than fourteen centuries earlier.

Belatedly recognizing the religious dimension of the question, the authors of *Time on the Cross*, in their 1989 afterword, issued a public apology for their cold-bloodedly secular, neo-liberal and econometric view of Southern slavery as not so bad, after all. The authors confessed a lack of familiarity with the historical and religious sources, admitting that "We had to overcome . . . our 'obtuse secularism' and understand the role of religious inspiration in the shaping of the antislavery ethic."[123] Oddly enough, the same obtuse secularism is evident in the polemic of contemporary Southern partisans, who portray the Lost Cause of the South as a "Christian crusade" for high ideals of civilization (a polemic further addressed in Chapter 16, where we assess the "Southern cause" *post mortem*), yet at the same time find themselves uttering unchristian, neo-liberal and utilitarian arguments in defense of "Christian" chattel slavery—the same arguments advanced by the ante-bellum master class itself.

"Southern-fried" Liberty

All in all, it is quite remarkable that partisans of the "Southern cause" as a "conservative" libertarian movement fail to recognize that the cause centered around a resolute defense of the perpetual state-imposed subjugation of an entire class of human beings via legal codes, legal disabilities, and penal and physical coercion whenever necessary. And the whole system was justified by a self-serving Protestant Biblical exegesis and theodicy that saw the "finger of God" in chattel slavery in the same way the industrialists saw it in their unrestrained "free market." The allure of the Southern romantic narrative is such that many of its proponents are willing to ignore the patent moral rot at the center of the "Southern-fried" version of Liberty.

Like the revolution of 1776, the revolution of 1861 was led by slave-owning libertarians who (just as Jefferson did) professed to deplore slavery while luxuriating in its benefits. Contemporary devotees of the Confederate romance do not see "the paradox of the slaveholding South's devotion to 'liberty'" and its "daily betrayal of its liberal self. . . ."[124] Southern-fried Liberty demanded a revolution for the preservation of its own hypocrisy—an hypocrisy matched by the equally racist North when Lincoln expediently adopted emancipation as a great crusade, but only after the Civil War was well underway and Northern public support was waning. Neither

122. *In Plurimis* (1888), nn. 3, 17.

123. Ibid., 274–75.

124. Richard E. Beringer, Herman Hattway, Archer Jones, and William N. Still, Jr., *Why the South Lost the Civil War* (Athens, GA: Univ. of Georgia Press, 1986), 358 (internal quotation omitted).

side in a fratricidal civil war between Protestant regional factions would exhibit the simple Christian acceptance of the black man as fully human that Douglass had experienced in the Catholic *ethos* of Ireland.

But not all modern Southern partisans have been afflicted by this blindness. Allen Tate, a poet and essayist of the Southern Agrarian school sounded basic themes which "informed their critique of slavery as well as the capitalist exploitation of man and nature."[125] Writing in 1968, Tate observed with regret that what was good about the Old South—its genteel manners, its disdain of dog-eat-dog capitalism, its appreciation of the value of leisure—was bound up with an evil that could no longer endure. Even the "Southern myth" advanced by William Faulkner tried to assimilate this reality:

> The South, afflicted with the curse of slavery—a curse like that of Original Sin, for which no single person is responsible—had to be destroyed, the good along with the evil. The old order had a great deal of good, one of the "goods" being the result of evil; for slavery itself entailed a certain responsibility which the capitalist did not need to exercise if it was not his will to do so. . . .
>
> The evil of slavery was two-fold, for the "peculiar institution" not only used human beings for a purpose for which God had not intended them; it made it possible for the white man to misuse and exploit nature itself for his own power and glory.[126]

This is not to imply that the North had any moral right to invade and destroy the South on account of slavery. Not even Lincoln was willing to assert such a right until long after the Civil War had commenced. Rather, it was the status of chattel slavery as the "cornerstone" of Southern civilization that made the South vulnerable to destruction in a war that would not have happened but for the Southern secession triggered by the slavery issue.

Whither the Cause for Secession?

Given the legal and moral contours of antebellum chattel slavery, what is one to make, finally, of the South's case for secession? Certainly the Southern states had a colorable, if dry, contractual argument for "breach of compact" regarding the constitutionally protected property right in slaves—for whatever Locke's compact theory is worth as a ground of political sovereignty and the supposed right to revolution. The point demonstrated by the foregoing discussion, however, is that *the only argument they had* was a property-based breach of compact: interference with a morally indefensible institutionalized chattel slavery; or, even more narrowly, its extension into the territories, as there was no credible threat to the institution where it already existed in the Southern states.

125. Eugene Genovese, *The Southern Tradition* (Cambridge, MA: Harvard Univ. Press, 1994), 13.
126. Tate, "Faulkner's *Sanctuary* and the Southern Myth," *The Virginia Quarterly Review*, Summer 1968, 418–427; accessed at http://www.vqronline.org/articles/1968/summer/tate-faulkners-sanctuary/.

Narrower still, the issue reduced to slavery extension in the territories *before they became states*. For once admitted to the Union as a new state, a former territory was free *qua* state to ban slavery within its borders as a matter of "states' rights," even if the constitutional duty to return escaped slaves to slave states remained. Jefferson Davis himself had admitted this much in his 1849 address during the Congressional debates on the admission of the Oregon Territory to the Union: " . . . I will render the admission that but for the Constitution, the right to property in slaves could not have been extended beyond the States which possessed them. . . . The question, then, *is reduced to this*: 'Has the Federal Government, under the grants of the Constitution, the power to prohibit "slavery" in the *Territories* of the United States?'"[127] Hence Southern leaders had vehemently opposed President Zachary Taylor's recommendation of immediate statehood for Texas, California, and New Mexico, seeing that it might well lead to abolition within those states. Threatened with secession over the issue during a meeting with Southern leaders in February 1850, even Taylor—the Southern imperialist and hero of the Mexican conquest—had had enough. If the Southern states seceded, he warned, "I'll take command of the army myself, and if you are taken in rebellion against the Union I will hang you with less reluctance than I hanged deserters and spies in Mexico."[128]

When all was said and done, then, the secessionists could not appeal to high principles of morality or justice but only to Southern-fried Liberty. They advocated a Lockean revolution based on allegedly intolerable grievances relating to property in slaves as opposed to a tax on tea—in other words, American Revolution II. But this will hardly do for those who insist upon a noble and high-minded Southern cause that was not merely the Southern half of a violent North-South struggle over property rights. Southern partisans have long labored to distill a kind of romantic essence of the secession. This is typically expressed as a vaguely delineated irreconcilable clash between the cold, ignoble, and inhuman industrial civilization of the North and the warm, noble, and humane agrarian civilization of the South—as if it were somehow impossible for a nation to contain distinct regions with differing economies, local manners, customs, and rhythms of life. (Also overlooked here are the vast rural areas of the North with their own slower-paced, agrarian *ethos*.)

The claim that the North and the South in 1861 were two "different civilizations" is, as the historian Grady McWhiney, a Louisianan, concludes, "one of the great myths of American history"[129]—that is, one of the great myths of Liberty, or rather Southern-fried Liberty with its romantic "War of Southern Independence." The myth was seen and exposed as such contemporaneously by Hinton Rowan Helper, son of a yeoman farmer from North Carolina, in his classic work *The Impending Crisis of the South*, published four years before the Civil War began. In his relentless empirical attack on the "peculiar institution" as the seed of the South's own economic self-destruction, Helper mockingly observed the lack of a respectable

127. In Varina Davis, *Jefferson Davis* (NY: Belford Company, 1890), Vol. I, 388, 392.
128. In John S.D. Eisenhower, *Zachary Taylor* (NY: Times Books, 2008), 110.
129. Beringer, et al., *Why the South Lost the Civil War*, 75.

Southern literature and independent intellectual culture, noting that Southerners had the very books in which they defended chattel slavery "printed on Northern paper, with Northern types, by Northern artisans, stitched, bound and made ready for the market by Northern industry; and yet fail to see, in all this, as a true philo-sophical mind *must* see, an overwhelming refutation of their miserable sophisms in behalf of a system against which humanity in all its impulses and aspirations, and civilization in all its activities and triumphs [including Catholic Christendom, as we have seen], utter their perpetual protest."[130]

Only post-war romanticism obscures the reality that "slavery made 'the South' and by contrast 'the North' and the sectional division. From colonization through nationhood and territorial expansion, the South's peculiar labor system—more than climate, ethnic, or political variations—delineated the regions. It was the major disparity between countrymen who, from a global perspective, shared more than they differed."[131] In a nation filled with Protestants belonging to the same basic denominations, the distinctiveness of the two regions never approached a fundamental civilizational difference *apart from slavery*. Rather, North and South "were complimentary elements in a society that was everywhere primarily rural, capitalistic, materialistic, and socially stratified, racially, ethnically, and religiously heterogeneous, and stridently chauvinistic and expansionist"—as we saw in our look at the leading Southern role in the Mexican War. Further, "[r]acism was not much stronger in the South than it was in the North—its expression merely took different forms."[132]

Thus when one searches the literature for hard evidence of how—apart from slavery—the posited civilizational conflict translated into a *political* rupture at spe-cific points, one encounters little more than romantic rhetoric. For example, Harry Crocker, in his *Politically Incorrect Guide to the Civil War*, recites the usual romantic sentiment that "the goal of Southern life was leisure and what Bagehot called 'the conservatism of enjoyment. . . .'"[133] But the fact remains that this "conservative" life of leisure and enjoyment depended entirely upon a class of slaves owned by a class of slave-owners, and that this socioeconomic order is what the South had seceded to "conserve" as its "peculiar institution." Indeed, posing the question: "Was the war really all about slavery?" Crocker provides this answer: "In the sense that *the South was defined by slavery*, yes."[134] Hence Crocker himself lends support to the conclusion of another study: that aside from regional distinctions short of civilizational distinctions, "[o]nly slavery gave the South its own identity, despite the efforts of some southern writers before the Civil War to pretend otherwise."[135]

Crocker quotes approvingly (however drolly) this description of the "spirit of the

130. In Wilson, *Patriotic Gore*, 369. Emphasis in original.
131. Jason Phillips, *Diehard Rebels: The Confederate Culture of Invincibility* (Athens, GA: Univ. of Georgia Press, 2007), 42.
132. Beringer, et al., *Why the South Lost the Civil War*, 75.
133. Crocker, *The Politically Incorrect Guide to the Civil War*, 385.
134. Ibid., 231.
135. Beringer, et al., *Why the South Lost the Civil War*, 66.

South," as if it constituted a persuasive existential argument in favor of secession: "The girls were always beautiful. The men wore varnished boots, raced horses and played cards. And drank mint-juleps till the time came round for fighting duels with their second cousins or tar-and-feathering some God-damn Yankee. . . ." Elsewhere he quotes a description of the "spirit of antebellum Virginia" as something evoked by "a mint-julep stirred with a sword-blade."[136] But what does this sort of thing have to do with the hard historical reality that there would have been no secession, no "conservative" revolution, and therefore no war, death and devastation, in the absence of antebellum chattel slavery?

And why would a Catholic historian view with such affection a degenerate Protestant milieu in which dueling was still an acceptable way of defending one's honor? Here it is worth noting James Henley Thornwell's contempt for the decree of the twenty-fifth session of the Council of Trent (1545–63) by which, three centuries earlier, the Catholic Church had declared dueling a mortal sin punishable by the excommunication of the participants, facilitators, and spectators. This, said one of the South's most prominent Protestant ministers, was typical of the Church's "arbitrary claims to secular authority" which "merge the State in the Church" and allowed "the Pope [to] set his feet upon the neck of kings. . . ."[137] No doubt Thornwell, like Southern Protestants generally, would also have viewed the Catholic Church's condemnations of chattel slavery as further intolerable meddling in temporal affairs.

A more prominent historical example of this search for a romantic essence of the South's revolutionary break with the North is Frank Lawrence Owsley's 1930 essay "The Irrepressible Conflict." A member, with Tate, of the Southern Agrarian literary school associated with Vanderbilt University in the 1930s, Owsley wrote of how "the North was commercial and industrial, and the South was agrarian," how "[t]he life of the South was leisurely and unhurried for the planter, the yeoman or the landless tenant," and how among Southern amusements were such things as "fine balls and house parties of the planter or the three-day breakdown dances which David Crockett loved, or horse races, foot races, cock and dog fights, boxing, wrestling, shooting, fighting, log-rolling, house raising or corn-shucking." Yes, but what of it? From these romantic reminiscences of the Southern way of life Owsley leaps to the immense *non sequitur*, really only a tautology, that "the irrepressible conflict" lay in the "eternal struggle between the agrarian South and the commercial and industrial North to control the government. . . ." He refers passingly to the Northern states' demand for "internal improvements—roads, railroads, canals—at national expense to furnish transportation for its goods to Southern and Western markets," to which expenditures "the South objected . . . because it had less need of transportation than the North. . . ."[138] But how could such jejune political questions have risen to

136. Crocker, 382–83.

137. James Henley Thornwell, Letter VIII, "Infallibility and Civil Government," in *The Collected Writings*, Vol. III, 548.

138. In *I'll Take My Stand* (Baton Rouge: Louisiana State Univ. Press, 1994 [1930]), 71, 72, 73.

the level of the posited romantic clash of civilizations that could only end in a fight to the death? As we have seen, before 1858 these disputes were hashed out in the halls and back rooms of a Congress effectively controlled by the South, most of the time under a President from Virginia or another Southern state.

Determined to deny that slavery had anything to do with the secession, Owsley, following the Southern partisan line, declares without the least attempt at a demonstration that slavery was "no essential part of the agrarian civilization of the South—though Southerners under attack assumed it was."[139] They did indeed "assume" it was, and neither Owsley nor any other Southern partisan polemicist has ever demonstrated that that assumption was some sort of defensive delusion induced by mounting abolitionist propaganda and political pressure in the late-1850s. Recall Calhoun's declaration before the Senate as early as 1837 that slavery "cannot be subverted without drenching the country in blood. . . . It is to us a vital question. It involves not only our liberty, but, what is greater (if to freemen anything can be) *existence itself.* . . ."

The high romance of the Civil War as a noble Southern defense of a morally superior way of life cannot survive an objective reading of the speeches and manifestos of Calhoun, Davis, Stephens, Hill and a host of other Southern leaders. On this score, Genovese simply remarks the obvious: "Virtually all Southern spokesmen, clerical and lay, readily acknowledged that the South was fighting to uphold slavery."[140] What the slave states sought to "conserve" from the American Revolution in particular was the only thing their own declarations of secession had deemed under imminent threat from the Union: not chivalry, Christian morals, the "conservatism of enjoyment" or agrarian life as such, but the original constitutional protection of the institution of Negro chattel slavery. If there was any "clash of civilizations" between North and South it arose precisely and only from that institution, absent which the historical record is devoid of any coherent rationale for secession. "And nobody who has read the letters, state papers, newspapers and other surviving literature of the generation before 1861 can honestly deny that the one main, fundamental reason for secession of the original states which formed the Southern Confederacy was to protect, expand and perpetuate the slavery of the Negro race."[141]

Catholics who would defend the secession and subsequent war as a noble and even "conservative" Southern undertaking should be embarrassed by the intellectual honesty of the Jewish scholar Frank Tannenbaum. In Catholic Latin America, he observed, "the abolition of slavery was achieved in every case without bloodshed, without violence, and without civil war" because in those Catholic countries of the New World where slavery still existed "slavery and freedom were, socially and morally speaking, very close to each other. . . . The passage from slavery to freedom was always possible for the individual, and in practice frequent." Moreover, once

---

139. Ibid., 76.
140. Genovese, *A Consuming Fire*, 3.
141. Morison, *HAP*, 608.

freed the Latin American slave became simply a citizen like any other, because "there was for legal and practical purposes no separate class of freedman. The freedman was a freeman." But in the Protestant *ethos* of the antebellum South "the Negro was considered a slave *by nature*" and "the Southern slave-holding community had by law and custom, by practice and belief, developed a static institutional ideal, which it proceeded to endow with a highly ethical basis," thus converting what was at best a tolerable evil to be obviated as soon as possible into the moral bulwark of Southern civilization with a conveniently discovered Biblical foundation. "Revolution was the result because change as a principle had been denied."[142]

To repeat a point that critics might be tempted to overlook: There is no suggestion here that the federal government would have been morally justified in initiating a war against the South to stamp out slavery. Again, this was a *casus belli* Lincoln himself at first flatly rejected, as Southern partisans themselves insist in attempting to prove that slavery had nothing to do with the Civil War (thereby extinguishing their own argument for secession). As Pope Leo XIII cautioned in his aforementioned encyclical: "the Church has deprecated any precipitate action in securing the manumission and liberation of the slaves, because that would have entailed tumults and wrought injury, as well to the slaves themselves as to the commonwealth. . . ."[143] That is, the system of slavery is indeed an evil to be abolished, but only by peaceful means. It is crucial to note, however, that by "precipitate action" the Pope did not mean some outcome of the political process declared "tyrannical" by the loser and cited as grounds for revolution à la Locke, but rather "recourse to *violence and sedition*" as opposed to "the remedy of patience. . . ."[144] The difference is between the Missouri Compromise, on the one hand, and John Brown's easily suppressed insurrection on the other. The South might have had a colorable constitutional argument against the Compromise, as Justice Taney had opined in the disastrous *Dred Scott* decision, and as Congress had recognized in repealing the Compromise via the Kansas-Nebraska Act. But the real question is whether a turning of the political tide against the South on the matter of slavery justified secession and the war it would provoke when there was no serious threat of violent action to abolish the institution where it was already long established.

Further, from the proposition that slavery must not be abolished by violence follows the converse proposition that neither could defense of the institution be justified by means that, to quote Leo again, "would have entailed tumults and wrought injury, as well to the slaves themselves as to the commonwealth." That is precisely the argument against precipitate *secession* made by a leading figure of the South, the aforementioned Benjamin Hill, in his impassioned plea for patience and prudence before members of the Georgia secession convention in Milledgeville, Georgia in November 1860. Echoing President Buchanan, Hill stressed that "the mere election of Mr. Lincoln" was no grounds for secession, as Lincoln had not yet done

---

142. Tannenbaum, *Slave and Citizen*, 105, 106–7, 108.
143. *In Plurimis* (1888), n. 9.
144. Ibid., n. 9.

anything to interfere with the institution of slavery. The Southern states, he argued, had a duty to exhaust all constitutional remedies before the drastic remedy of secession could be applied.

Hill warned with prophetic accuracy that destruction of the Union through secession would paradoxically serve abolitionist aims by destroying the Constitutional framework under which slavery was then protected: "the inexorable logic of this [abolitionist] party . . . must array them against the whole Constitution of the United States; because that instrument, in its very framework, is a recognition of property in slaves." To prove his point, Hill quoted Henry Ward Beecher, who had stated the matter with stark simplicity: "The dissolution of the Union is the abolition of slavery."[145] Mary Chesnut's father-in-law, a patrician lord of the planter class, saw likewise: "Without the aid and countenance of the whole United States, we could not have kept slavery." Old man Chesnut knew that "for all the noise of the abolitionists, the Union was the great protector of slavery, just as many abolitionists had charged."[146] Secession would not only fail to serve, but would positively disserve, its stated end.

In sum, the case for the Southern secession must stand or fall on the argument presented for the purported breach of compact respecting property in slaves. But to defend that argument is to defend in turn the Lockean doctrines of sovereignty and the right to revolution on which it rested. As we have seen, however (cf. Chapter 3), there is no support in the pre-"Enlightenment" Western tradition for the overthrow of a government and the creation of a new one by some group of subjects who, following Locke, deem the existing government to have breached its trust in some particular matter of law or public policy. Only true and proper tyranny would justify the subjects deposing an elected tyrant in self-defense or (the morally preferable course) limiting his power. Such could hardly have been the case with a sectional disagreement over the territorial extension of chattel slavery in America—a moral and political evil in any country, as even the South's leading general admitted. Therefore, he who would defend American Revolution II, arising from the slavery question, must logically defend American Revolution I, arising from King George's supposedly "intolerable" acts. And he who would defend both revolutions is left with no ground on which to stand in opposing "the right to revolution" as such, and thus the mainspring of the movement by which the forces of Liberty destroyed the whole of Christendom.

---

145. In *Benjamin Hill: His Life, Speeches and Writings*, 239–40.
146. In Beringer, et al., *Why the South Lost the Civil War*, 71.

13

Loosing the Dogs of Civil War

BY THE TIME Lincoln took the oath of office on March 4, 1861, seven of the eleven states of the Confederacy had already seceded from the Union: South Carolina, Mississippi, Florida, Alabama, Georgia, Louisiana, and Texas. Exactly one month before Lincoln's inauguration, following faithfully the example of their revolutionary forebears, delegates from all of those states except Texas convened in Montgomery, Alabama. Guided by a "Committee of Twelve" the delegates at large, purporting to be "Deputies of the Sovereign and Independent States," adopted the provisional Constitution of the Confederate States of America (CSA) on February 8 and created its provisional government, electing Davis as President and Stephens as Vice President, who were provisionally inaugurated on February 9. At the Convention the "process of national imagining began in earnest...." In search of a founding mythology the delegates "had one ready-made in the form of the American Revolution and they returned again and again to that deep well of symbolism."[1] Thomas R. R. Cobb, a delegate from Georgia, even proposed that the new nation be dubbed "The Republic of Washington."[2]

The Confederate Constitution

Typically for the history of Liberty, the Montgomery Convention was not composed of common people demanding a new government but rather of wealthy elites who purported to determine who would govern the masses during the coming war: thirty-three planters, all major slave-owners, and forty-three lawyers, all but one of whom owned slaves.[3] Putting the lie to the Southern partisan claim that the secessionists generally (unlike Davis and Lee) had no expectation of war on account of the exercise of their "clear right" to secede, while the Convention was meeting "the same states were raising troops in preparation for war."[4] In fact, Stephens was rejected as provisional President when he told the Convention "that he would be unwilling to strike the first blow if it came to war."[5] Further, like Davis,

---

1. Anne Sarah Rubin, *A Shattered Nation: the Rise and Fall of the Confederacy, 1861–1868* (Chapel Hill, NC: Univ. of North Carolina Press, 2005), 14.
2. Ibid.
3. Eaton, *A History of the Old South*, 505.
4. Nolan, *Lee Considered*, 36.
5. Davis, *Jefferson Davis: the Man and His Hour*, 303.

Stephens "had been too reluctant to embrace secession" and "[o]thers in his own delegation, like Thomas Cobb, loathed him for his presumed Unionism."[6] Davis, however, would be quite willing to strike the blow the Convention expected.

The hurriedly drafted provisional Confederate Constitution was in force only from February 8 to March 11, 1861, when it was replaced by a permanent Constitution adopted by the delegates at Montgomery, which now included a delegation from Texas.[7] Like the provisional document, the permanent one was based on its U.S. counterpart. And, as with the U.S. counterpart, the framing of the Confederate Constitution was driven by the economic interests of the delegates who framed it. In this case, the overriding economic interest was slavery—or more precisely, *Negro* slavery. Unlike the U.S. Constitution construed in *Dred Scott*, the permanent Confederate Constitution expressly mentioned skin color, providing that the Confederate Congress could pass no law "impairing the right of property in *negro* slaves."[8] The Confederate Constitution required the interstate rendition of escaped slaves in language identical to that of the U.S. Constitution, but the delegates at Montgomery went further, providing constitutional protection for slavery in any territories the Confederacy might acquire:

> The Confederate States may acquire new territory. . . . In all such territory *the institution of negro slavery, as it now exists in the Confederate States, shall be recognized and protected by Congress and by the Territorial government*; and the inhabitants of the several Confederate States and Territories shall have the right to take to such Territory any slaves lawfully held by them in any of the States or Territories of the Confederate States.[9]

Hence the largest substantive difference between the United States and Confederate Constitutions was the latter's absolute and perpetual protection of the institution of negro slavery—the enslavement of one race, and one race only—in both the Confederate States and territories.[10] Art. I, §9,¶1 provides, however, that "importation of negroes of the African race from any foreign country other than the slaveholding States or Territories of the United States of America, is hereby forbidden; and Congress is required to pass such laws as shall effectually prevent the same." This ban on foreign (but not domestic) slave trade was designed to attract European support for the Confederacy. The bid would fail.

Otherwise, apart from some other technical differences (such as one six-year term for the President, a presidential line-item veto, and a ⅔ vote of Congress for certain federal expenditures), the newest documentary expression of Liberty tracked

---

6. Davis, *Jefferson Davis*, 303.

7. By a vote on March 2, the Confederate Congress had authorized the Texas delegation to sign the Provisional Constitution already adopted by the other six states.

8. Art. I, §9 (4).

9. Art. I, §3(1); Art. IV, §2(3).

10. The Confederate Constitution did, however, attempt to tighten the Congressional purse strings by requiring a two-thirds vote of both houses of Congress for any appropriation of revenue, "unless it be asked and estimated for by some one of the heads of departments and submitted to Congress by the President; or for the purpose of paying its own expenses and contingencies." Article I, §8.

the United States Constitution and Bill of Rights word-for-word, with the Bill of Rights being incorporated into the body of the document. It provided for a strong Congress with the power to "lay and collect taxes, duties, imposts, and excises," mint and borrow money, regulate interstate and foreign commerce, raise an army and navy, wage war, conduct foreign policy, enter into treaties, and so forth (Article I); a strong President (Article II), and a judiciary that included a Supreme Court (never actually put into operation) with overarching judicial power (Article III).[11] The Confederate Congress was further granted the express power "to dispose of and make all needful rules and regulations concerning the property of the Confederate States, including the lands thereof."[12] The "general welfare" language of the U.S. counterpart was omitted, however.

The Confederate Constitution even contained both a "necessary and proper clause" and—amazingly enough—a *supremacy* clause providing precisely as the United States Constitution had done: "This Constitution, and the laws of the Confederate States made in pursuance thereof, and all treaties made, or which shall be made, under the authority of the Confederate States, shall be the supreme law of the land; and the judges in every State shall be bound thereby, anything in the constitution or laws of any State to the contrary notwithstanding."[13] The supremacy of federal law over the Confederate States would be pivotal to the central government's defense of its mass conscription program and suspensions of the writ of habeas corpus during the war. Counterpoised to this sweeping grant of federal power was merely the Confederate Constitution's version of the Tenth Amendment, taken verbatim from the United States Constitution's demonstrably unavailing provision: "The powers not delegated to the Confederate States by the Constitution, nor prohibited by it to the States, are reserved to the States, respectively, or to the people thereof."[14]

Thus the national government of the Confederacy was a veritable clone of the government from which it had seceded, granted every bit as much power over its purported subjects as the government in Washington. And, most tellingly, while its Preamble declares that each of the Confederate states is "acting in its sovereign and independent character," the Confederate Constitution contains no clause providing for at-will secession from the Confederacy. That this supposed "inherent right of the sovereign States" was not specified, even after the raging debates over its existence that had preceded secession from the Union, could only be interpreted as an implicit recognition that secession from the Confederacy, like secession from the Union, would require a demonstrable "breach of compact."

Jefferson Davis's later message to the Confederate Congress upon ratification of the Confederate Constitution only further confirms the centrality of the property right in human chattels to the secession and formation of the Confederate States of

11. See *Constitution of the Confederate States of America*, Art. I, §8, Yale Law School e-text, www.yale.edu/lawweb/avalon/csa/csa.htm.

12. Art. IV, §3 (2).

13. Art. VI, §3.

14. Art. VI, §6.

America. After some preliminary complaints about long-settled tariff disputes and the North's perversion of the federal government "into a machine for their control in their domestic affairs"—in other words, the South had lost control of Congress and the Presidency due to population shifts and changes in public opinion—Davis inevitably focused on the heart of the matter: "interests of such *transcendent magnitude* as at all times to create the apprehension in the minds of many devoted lovers of the Union that its permanence was impossible."

By this, of course, Davis meant "African slaves imported into the colonies by the mother country," as to which the United States Constitution had provided "no . . . delegation of power to the Congress authorizing it in any manner to legislate to the prejudice, detriment, or discouragement [of] owners of that *species of property*, or excluding it from the protection of the Government." The slaves of the South, Davis continued, had been "elevated from brutal savages into docile, intelligent, and civilized agricultural laborers," and "[u]nder the supervision of *a superior race* their labor had been so directed as not only to allow a gradual and marked amelioration of their own condition, but to convert hundreds of thousands of square miles of the wilderness into cultivated lands covered with a prosperous people. . . ."[15] For this prosperous people of the superior race, "the labor of African slaves was and is *indispensable*," and "[w]ith interests of such *overwhelming magnitude* imperiled, the people of the Southern States were driven by the conduct of the North to the adoption of some course of action to avert the danger with which they were openly menaced"—the danger being loss of a prosperity built upon slave labor. For this reason the slave states had formed a new *federal* government whose constitution mimicked that of the federal government from which they had just seceded.

The outcome of the Montgomery Convention extinguishes the claim that the South seceded from the Union for the noble purpose of vindicating the autonomy of each individual State according to the Jeffersonian ideal of a purely voluntary league—the appealing legal fiction Jefferson himself had ignored when he was President. If the elites who met in private and then announced to the masses what their Confederate government would be had envisioned a merely voluntary league, the Southern states would have seceded strictly as individual states and there would have been no Montgomery Convention to produce a Southern replica of the federal government. At most there would have been a loose confederation among the seceding states along the lines of the Articles of Confederation. But that loose confederation was the very thing the delegates in Philadelphia had destroyed behind closed doors seventy-four years earlier in order to create the very document the Montgomery Convention had just adopted almost verbatim. There was, however, this difference: much greater protection was provided for the one interest of "transcendent magnitude" that had brought them all together in the act of secession: "the right of property in negro slaves."

A year after the Convention, following their unopposed election, Jefferson Davis

---

15. Message to Congress April 29, 1861 (Ratification of the Constitution), http://avalon.law.yale.edu/19th_century/csa_m042961.asp.

and Alexander Stephens would be formally inaugurated as President and Vice President of the permanent government of the Confederate States of America on Washington's Birthday (February 22), "which seemed a fitting date for the formal launching of the permanent government established by the Second American Revolution."[16] While Davis would later deny that he had ever been a revolutionary—"Sovereigns never rebel," he declared to a crowd in 1886[17]—it was he who invoked "the principles of our revolutionary fathers" and "the experiment instituted by our revolutionary fathers" in his Second Inaugural Address, delivered in front of a statue of Washington, with Davis hailing "the memory of the man most identified with the establishment of American independence. . . ."[18]

To show their supposed continuity with the first Revolution, the Confederate States adopted a Great Seal whose center depicts Washington on his horse, pointing ahead to the field of battle against the King's men. "Since from immemorial times a formal seal or signet has been the accepted evidence of sovereignty, the architects of the Southern Confederacy in keeping with this tradition at once turned their attention to providing the needed device."[19] While the Seal would never actually come into use, as the Confederacy did not last long enough, its adoption represented the spirit of the war on both sides. The George Washington of the South would ride against the George Washington of the North. The two powers, each invoking the Founding Fathers and the Spirit of 1776, having separated their respective mass of subjects one from the other in mutual enmity, would collide in an annihilating explosion—the matter and anti-matter of Liberty. The Northern mass would not only survive the collision but grow immensely more powerful from the titanic energies it would unleash.

Hostilities Commence

During a meeting of the Cabinet of the provisional Confederate government on April 9, 1861, a leading fire-eater from Georgia, Robert Toombs, former United States Senator and briefly tenured as the Confederate Secretary of State, pleaded with the still provisional President Davis not to authorize the bombardment of Fort Sumter. This was an act the war hawks were demanding on the ground that Lincoln had signaled bellicose intentions by authorizing a reprovisioning of the fort's small garrison. (During an earlier reprovisioning by outgoing President Buchanan in January, cadets at the Citadel in Charleston had fired on the supply ship *Star of the West*—the literal, if not historical, first shots of the war.) Toombs, who fell one vote short of being chosen President of the Confederacy at the Montgomery Convention, made this entirely accurate prophesy:

16. Shelby Foote, *The Civil War: A Narrative* (NY: Vintage Books, 1986 [1958]), Vol. I, 132.

17. Ibid., Vol. III, 1056.

18. Second Inaugural Address, February 22, 1862, *Papers of Jefferson Davis* at Rice University Library, accessed at http://jeffersondavis.rice.edu/Content.aspx?id=107.

19. George H. Shirk, "The Great Seal of the Confederacy," digital.library.okstate.edu/Chronicles/vo30/v030p309.pdf.

The firing on the fort *will inaugurate a civil war greater than any the world has yet seen.* ... Mr. President, at this time it is *suicide, murder,* and you will lose us every friend at the North. You will wantonly strike a hornet's nest which extends from the mountains to the ocean, and legions now quiet will swarm out and sting us to death. It is unnecessary; *it puts us in the wrong;* it is *fatal.*[20]

By this time, however, the hawks on both sides were itching for war: the Northern hawks because they viewed possible loss of Southern markets to the English as economically devastating; the Southern hawks because they demanded a demonstration that the Confederacy could assert its sovereignty in a convincing way and thus survive. As the *Charleston Mercury* had put it, beating the drums for war *now*: "Border states will never join us until we have indicated our power to free ourselves—until we have proven that a garrison of seventy men cannot hold the portal of our commerce. Let us be ready for war. ..."[21]

For his part, as the late Shelby Foote observes, a newly inaugurated President Lincoln was awaiting "an act of aggression by the South, asserting in the interim just enough pressure to provoke such an action, without exerting enough to *justify* it."[22] If Lincoln was hoping for an unjustified action, he got his wish when the Southern war hawks prevailed. "Strike a blow," demanded the Virginian fire-eater Roger Pryor from a balcony in Charleston, hoping that the firing on Sumter would finally move his state to join the first seven seceders.[23] Offered the honor of launching the first artillery shell, however, Pryor quailed: "I could not fire the first gun of the war." Another Virginian is widely believed to have done the honors: Edmund Ruffin, a slaveholding "farm-paper editor and old-line secessionist, sixty-seven years of age."[24] At 4:30 AM on April 12, 1861, the "first" shot of the Civil War arced its way across Charleston Harbor and slammed into the fort, launched by an old fire-eater who would never see a day of combat. But after the South had lost the war, Ruffin, "still hating," would die from another shot: the one he fired into his own head.[25]

Southern partisans have contrived elaborate preemptive action rationales to justify firing on the fort. They generally point to Secretary of State Seward's "well-meant misrepresentation"[26]—he had spoken too soon—that Lincoln would accept the fort's evacuation and not attempt to have the fort's garrison of a few dozen men reprovisioned. The matter has been debated endlessly, although "[m]odern scholarship has doubted that President Lincoln cleverly manipulated the situation in Machiavellian fashion so that the South would fire the first shot. ..."[27] Not debatable, however, are the following facts: Jefferson Davis ordered General P. G. T. Beau-

---

20. In Foote, *The Civil War,* Vol. I, 47.
21. In Paul Calore, *Naval Campaigns of the Civil War* (Jefferson, NC: McFarland & Co. 2001), 28.
22. Foote, *The Civil War,* Vol. I, 44.
23. Ibid., 44.
24. Ibid., 49.
25. Foote, *The Civil War,* Vol. III, 971.
26. Ibid., 47.
27. Eaton, *A History of the Old South,* 506.

regard to "reduce" Fort Sumter if its commander would not order its evacuation. Beauregard sent a delegation to demand the fort's surrender from Major Robert Anderson, a pro-slavery, former slave-owning Kentuckian and Southern sympathizer. Despite his Southern sympathies, Anderson replied that his sense of honor and duty to his government would not allow him to abandon the fort. Beauregard, in the first step on his path to Civil War glory, ordered artillery batteries in Charleston Harbor to bombard the fort. Lincoln ordered the bombardment of nothing. Even assuming Lincoln positively hoped the South would fire first, only one conclusion is possible, as expressed by the historian James Randall: "To say that Lincoln meant that the first shot would be fired by the other side *if a first shot was fired*, is not to say that he maneuvered to have the first shot fired."[28] That is, the decision to fire the first shot and commence the next chapter in Liberty's sanguinary history was the South's alone.

Add to those facts the South's acts of war before and just after Fort Sumter, without the North having fired a shot: the seizure of Forts Morgan and Gaines in Alabama (January 4–5), the Federal Arsenal at Apalachicola and Fort Marion in Florida (January 6–7); the firing on the *Star of the West* (January 9); the seizure of Forts Jackson and Philip in Louisiana (January 10); the seizure of various forts and other federal property in Mississippi (January 10); the seizure of Fort Pickens in Florida (January 14), Fort Massachusetts in Mississippi (January 19), the Federal Arsenal at Augusta, Georgia (January 24), the US Mint at New Orleans (January 31), and the US munitions depot in Napoleon, Arkansas (February 12); the Confederate takeover of the already captured mint in New Orleans (March 31); the seizure of Fort Quitman in Texas, the US Mint at Dahlonega, Georgia (April 8), Fort Macon in North Carolina (April 14), the Federal Arsenal at Harper's Ferry (April 18), and the Norfolk Naval Yard (April 20). Add to these all the federal courthouses and post offices in the seceding states.

Consider as well the attempt by a secret secessionist society in Baltimore to take over the city by force of arms on April 19, when rioters attacked the Sixth Regiment of Massachusetts volunteers, killing four and wounding thirty of them. When the conspirators requested support from Richmond, the Governor of Virginia sent two thousand muskets and promised twenty heavy guns, while Davis called up thirteen regiments to reinforce the insurrection after telegraphing the Governor: "Sustain Baltimore, if practicable. We reinforce you."[29] Davis had thought to end the war quickly by encircling Washington, but the dogs he had unleashed were not so easily controlled.

Given these undisputed first acts of aggression, the claim that the South was "provoked" into firing on Fort Sumter to begin a war it never wanted or expected, and that Lincoln had no cause to call up 75,000 volunteers on April 15 in response, moves from dubious to ridiculous. Yet few there were in the South who were willing

---

28. Richard N. Current, *Lincoln and the First Shot* (Prospect Heights, IL: Waveland Press, Inc., 1990 [1963], reprint Harper & Row edition), 194. Emphasis in original.

29. Rhodes, *A History of the United States*, Vol. III, 380.

to state openly what the *Daily Lynchburg Virginian* proclaimed almost a year to the day after Sumter: "We dared a revolution, and provoked a war."[30] Objectively speaking—and quite apart from the immoral acts in which the North would engage in violation of just war doctrine—Lincoln could not possibly have been expected passively to accept the proposition that numerous federal facilities that had been United States property by agreement of all the States only days before now suddenly belonged to something called the Confederate States of America and could be confiscated by deadly force if necessary. Nor could he be expected to accept the sudden creation of a rival nation across the Potomac with control of the Mississippi River.

The mission by Confederate commissioners to Washington in the days before the firing on the fort to propose a peace treaty and the purchase of all property seized by the Confederacy—an implicit admission that the United States was its rightful owner in the first place—must have seemed preposterous to Lincoln, who refused to see the commissioners. Even Davis's sympathetic biographer admits that "Davis could not see, of course, Lincoln's point of view, nor could he see that he himself, in Lincoln's place, would never have agreed to negotiate in the face of ultimatums and naked threats of violence."[31] But a challenge to existing authority by a demand that it accept a *fait accompli* is basic to the revolutionary operations of Liberty, as the creation of the United States itself had demonstrated eighty-five years earlier. This time, however, the brazen tactic would backfire with immense consequences, for the forces of Liberty in the South were not acting against a distant king of mild disposition but rather against the opposing forces of Liberty on their very doorstep, possessed of vastly more human and material resources than the South would ever be able to muster.

The "Border States" Secede

On April 17, five days after the firing on Fort Sumter, Virginia seceded based on the vote of an ongoing "secession convention" meeting in secret, which, like the other secession conventions, had acted without prior popular approval, protracting the proceedings long enough for the expected precipitating event. Before Sumter, however, the significantly pro-Union convention could have gone either way, and at one point its votes were 2-to-1 against secession. Secessionists "had tried to exploit the emotional aftershock of Lincoln's election, but in these early months they were overridden by those who thought the Union still offered the best guarantee of liberty and prosperity."[32] But Lincoln's reaction to the bombardment of Sumter and the seizure of federal facilities had turned the tide in the convention.

Following Virginia's example, conventions in the remaining States of the Confederacy—Arkansas, Tennessee and North Carolina—would secede in May, all

30. *Daily Lynchburg Virginian*, April 4, 1862, in Richard E. Beringer, *The Elements of Confederate Defeat* (Athens, GA: University of Georgia Press, 1988), 121.

31. Davis, *Davis: the Man and His Hour*, 322.

32. Pryor, *Reading the Man*, 6094–6097.

acting without prior popular approval. Lincoln's call for the 75,000 volunteers was what the Southern war hawks had been waiting for: a galvanizing event that would trigger war fever throughout the South. What loyal son of the South would not be galvanized by the prospect of an invasion of his home state by federal troops? Never mind that the entire scenario was avoidable, as Lee had thought. This was war! There would follow a thousand gala balls at which the cream of Southern youth would lift a glass to the honor of the new Confederacy before signing up and marching off to die in a war the South was ill-equipped to wage, much less to win.

Lee's virtual hagiographer, Douglas Southall Freeman, recounts how Lee had been telling himself "that secession could not become an accomplished fact until the voters of Virginia had passed on the ordinance of secession." A meaningless ratification of the *fait accompli* by a miniscule percentage of Virginia's population would come more than a month after the war had begun. "The people" would hardly have reversed Virginia's involvement in the war after her militiamen had already seized the federal arsenal at Harper's Ferry, which Lee himself had defended against John Brown. Lee had been naïve in hoping that Virginia would not follow the Cotton States based on the agitation of a secessionist minority. Secession was entirely predictable given the history of Liberty with its "INFORMAL AND UNAU-THORIZED PROPOSITIONS," as Madison had called them in defending the junking of the Articles of Confederation during another closed-door session: the one that had produced the Constitution now at the heart of a civil war. After all, Lee, then still in Texas on assignment with the Army, had already "with his own eyes, seen how the Texas committee of safety had committed an act of war by seizing United States property [Fort Quitman] without waiting for the people to confirm or disavow the ordinance of the convention. . . ."[33]

But now, "like Washington, his great model [who] had embraced the revolutionary cause," Lee would resign his commission as a colonel, reject Lincoln's offer to command the entire U.S. Army, and take up the cause of defending Virginia from the Northern invasion he had feared. For as Lee saw it, "her action controlled his; he could not wait for the uncertain vote of the people when war was upon him."[34] The demands of Liberty in Virginia could hardly wait for an "uncertain vote of the people," for had not the secession convention already informed the people of what their will was in the matter? So Lee felt bound to follow "Virginia"—or at least what the convention purported to decide on behalf of Virginia.

As Alan T. Nolan shows in his provocative study of Lee, a mere twenty-two days had elapsed from Lee's acceptance of a commission as a colonel in the United States Army to his "joining the forces preparing for war against the federal government!"[35] Yet, only weeks before, he had confided to his wife's cousin that "I wish for no other flag than 'the Star spangled banner' & no other air than 'Hail Columbia'. . . ."[36] He

33. Freeman, *R. E. Lee: A Biography*, Vol. I., 439–40, Univ. of Chicago e-text, http://penelope.uchi-cago.edu/Thayer/E/Gazetteer/People/Robert_E_Lee/FREREL/home.html.

34. Ibid., 440.

35. Nolan, *Lee Considered*, 41–42.

36. Lee to Martha Custis Williams, January 22, 1861, in Nolan, *Lee Considered*, 33.

368 LIBERTY, THE GOD THAT FAILED

had "explod[ed] with rage when secessionists tried prematurely to force his resigna-tion," and when he learned of the secession of Texas he had broken down. A friend recounted that "I shall never forget his look of astonishment . . . his lips trembling and his eyes full of tears. . . ." When asked "do you intend to go South or remain North?" Lee had replied: "I shall never bear arms against the United States,—but it may be necessary for me to carry a musket in defence of my native State, Virginia, in which case I shall not prove recreant to my duty."[37]

The historian Elizabeth Brown Pryor's discussion of Lee's fateful decision fairly remarks that "The way Lee envisioned his own role in the conflict was particularly convoluted. Here his pronouncements often appear at odds not only with them-selves but with realistic expectation. He could not raise his sword against the United States—but if called on to carry a musket for Virginia, he would not shirk. . . . One of the more intricate steps in this psychic Virginia reel is the word 'defence.' It appears Lee thought that if he stayed in the old army, he might be able to maintain a position that resisted offensive operations; and that if Virginia seceded, he could restrict himself to actions that checked aggression."[38] Of course, Lee did neither, but rather ended up the foremost military leader of a Confederacy engaged in an all-out war with the government he had served for thirty years.

There is no denying the immense sacrifice Lee made at the end of his tortured deliberations about where his loyalty lay. But, as Pryor rightly notes, "[t]here was no linear path to rectitude in Lee's case, and every avenue was strewn with irrecon-cilable principles." Lee thought it dishonorable to participate in military action against his home state, yet "in military circles it was 'dishonorable' to resign because of unwelcome orders. Lee acted on this definition of honor at the very time he was 'dishonoring' vows of thirty years."[39] Recall here that sixty-seven years earlier Lee's own father, "Light-Horse Harry," had led a federal army's march into western Penn-sylvania during the Whiskey Rebellion under the command of no less than George Washington, the greatest Virginian of all. On the basis of what coherent moral stan-dard was it honorable for Lee's father to lead a federal army that included Virgin-ians in a march on Pennsylvania in 1794, but dishonorable for Lee to lead an army that would include Pennsylvanians in a march on Virginia in 1861? Was only the soil of one's home state so sacred that it must not be trod by federal boots?

Moreover, Lee's was not the only "honorable" course for a Virginian in the U.S. Army to take. Pryor points out that "there were numerous options available to him, options that others in his situation did choose." Some two-fifths of the officers from Virginia remained in the U. S. Army, suffering opprobrium and shunning by their fellow Virginians. "Others opted not to fight on any side. West Point's Dennis Hart Mahan, another proud Virginian, chose not to uphold a cause he believed unworthy and sat out the war."[40] Members of Lee's own family sided with the

---

37. Pryor, *Reading the Man*, 6033–6035, 6040–6042.
38. Ibid., 6060–6066.
39. Ibid., 6208–6211.
40. Ibid., 6168–6179.

Union, including his cousin Samuel Phillips Lee, a naval officer who would be instrumental in the Union naval blockade. In answer to the question whether he would go North or South he replied: "When I find the word Virginia in my commission I will join the Confederacy."[41] Lee's own sister Anne "was also not in agreement with Robert, and her son, Louis Marshall, fought with General John Pope against his uncle. No one in that family ever spoke to Lee again."[42] Had all these men acted contrary to honor, while Lee and those who went his way were the only honorable Virginians?

The point here is not to judge Lee in hindsight, even if it is eminently arguable that, objectively speaking, he made the wrong decision in view of its disastrous consequences, including 75,000 casualties from his two failed attempts to carry a "defensive" war North. Again, his personal sacrifice was immense: he could have had the command of the entire United States Army. The point, rather, is one that serves our overall critique of the "progress" of Liberty: Lee was a living embodiment of the fatally conflicted framework of competing Lockean authorities the Framers had erected—the States versus the Federal Government. Both claimed the allegiance of their subjects, and both were supposedly authored by the "sovereign will of the people," who were somehow rulers and subjects of both governments at one and the same time. (In Chapter 16 we will consider the problematicity of conflicting claims of loyalty to these synthetic jurisdictions, which did not even exist before 1789 and were essentially cartographic conventions, not organic traditional societies.)

And just who *were* these sovereign people? Were they *United* States citizens first, state citizens first, or both equally at once? Attempting to reason his way out of this classic conundrum of Liberty, which had torn Lee, Jefferson Davis would later offer the contention that when he was serving as the United States Senator from Mississippi his status was merely that "of an ambassador from the State he represented to the Federal Government, as well as being, in some sense, a member of the Government."[43] That one could simultaneously be both ambassador to and member of the same government—in "some sense"—is among the many strange propositions emerging from the Framers' application of Lockean political theory to their unprecedented creation.

Explaining the astonishing legerdemain by which conventions of a few men had suddenly announced that the people of Virginia and the other seceding states were no longer part of the United States and were now citizens of the Confederate States, whether they liked it or not, Davis offered a curious rationale. According to him, "the primary and paramount allegiance of the citizen is due to the sovereign only. . . ." But *which* sovereign? The primary and paramount sovereign the citizen must obey, Davis opined, is "the people of the State to which he belongs." But the citizens of the several states were also citizens of the *United* States. On what ground

---

41. A. A. Hoehling, *Thunder at Hampton Roads* (NY: Da Capo Press, 1993), 6.

42. Pryor, 6189–6890.

43. Davis, *A Short History of the Confederate States of America*, 59.

did Davis make the larger "sovereign people" subject to the smaller "sovereign people," especially when many among the smaller sovereign objected to being removed from the territory of the larger and losing their citizenship therein? Davis did not try to evade the patent conflict of loyalties by proposing the fiction that there really is no such thing as United States citizenship—the bizarre contention Stephens advanced in his own two-volume apologia.[44] He simply declared that the sovereign people *qua* state are superior to the sovereign people *qua* United States and that everyone in a given state must abide by what the smaller sovereign had purportedly decided.

On this premise, Davis concluded that at the moment the "sovereign people" of a state—meaning, again, a few men meeting in convention—"withdraws from its association with its confederates in the Union," then "the allegiance of the citizen requires him to follow the sovereign. Any other course is rebellion or treason. . . ." So, based on a vote in secret by a few delegates, it was now rebellion or treason not to follow out of the Union those who were being accused of rebellion and treason for leaving it! These "plain and irrefutable truths," wrote Davis, negated the charge that the secession was a rebellion. Here we see what Davis's biographer remarks concerning his method of argument: "the logic of his arguments was the same as it had always been, which is to say almost none at all other than the automatic assumption that his opinion, whatever it might be, was the right one. Stating his position as fact, he thereafter built his arguments according to their 'proof' by using such 'facts' as givens, not mere opinions."[45]

Many in the seceding states begged to differ with such a vertiginous Lockean excursus on the duty of every man to follow the bouncing sovereign. Hence the declaration of anti-secessionist Virginians at the Second Wheeling Convention, who walked out of the secession convention at Richmond in protest of its actions, which they denounced as "a usurpation . . . to the manifest injury of the people, which, if permitted, will inevitably subject them to a military despotism." The Richmond Convention, declared the delegates of the Wheeling Convention, had "required the people of Virginia to separate from and wage war against the government of the United States" and had "attempted to transfer the allegiance of the people to an illegal confederacy of rebellious States, and required their submission to its pretended edicts and decrees. . . ." Indeed, on what ground besides their own will in the matter did the Richmond Convention assert that its edicts and decrees were not "pretended"? In fine Lockean fashion, the dissenting Virginians then seceded from the secession, forming their own provisional government on June 20, 1861, which would ultimately seek and obtain admission to the Union as the State of West Virginia on June 20, 1863.

Southern partisans have cultivated the popular belief that the members of the Virginia secession convention, faced with an impending invasion from the North, had no choice but to vote for secession, however reluctantly, as a matter of

---

44. Cf. Stephens, *A Constitutional View of the Late War Between the States*, Vol. I, 34.
45. Davis, *Davis: the Man and His Hour*, 676.

self-defense. But the thesis of unavoidable self-defense founders on the facts of what the western counties did: refusing to go along with the secession, creating a separate state, achieving incorporation into the Union, and thereby avoiding the brunt of the war precisely because they did not see any need to "defend" Virginia, which would end up back in the Union anyway, but in a devastated condition. What is more, West Virginia actually did what many Virginians (including Lee) piously professed to desire: she adopted a plan of gradual emancipation of the slaves within her borders which provided for the automatic emancipation of slave children born after a certain date and otherwise at age 21 or 25.[46]

Who, then, were the "traitors" in Virginia: those who refused to follow the Richmond Convention into the Confederacy with Robert E. Lee, or those who refused to follow the Second Wheeling Convention and remain in the Union, *as Lee's own fellow Virginian and superior officer*, General Winfield Scott, had done? Given the dramatic split in Virginia, who were the real "sovereign people" of Virginia in April 1861? Here we see the farcicality of the aforementioned dictum of Ludwig von Mises, cited by contemporary libertarians in defense of secession as a "conservative" remedy for political grievances: that "No people and no *part* of a people shall be held against its will in a political association that it does not want." How many secessions are justified on the basis of this notion before one arrives at the true and legitimate "government of the people"? If Virginia had the right to secede from the United States because a group of people within the state no longer wished to be subject to the federal government, and if West Virginia had the right to secede from Virginia because a group of people in the western part of the state *did* wish to be subject to the federal government, then why not further subdivisions of Virginia via secession down to the smallest town or even a group of citizens within a town? What besides sheer force prevents an infinite regression of secession movements once the first secession occurs?

And what of Missouri, where a pro-Confederate faction of the General Assembly adopted an Ordinance of Secession, but another convention declared the Assembly dissolved? What of Kentucky, where Confederate troops invaded and a group of pro-Confederates declared itself the new state government over and against the pro-Union General Assembly, while other Kentuckians called for the intervention of Union troops, who drove out the Confederate forces? The Confederacy claimed both Kentucky and Missouri and seated claimants to authority from both states in the Confederate Congress, while other claimants to authority from the same states sat in the United States Congress.

Locke's application of the Protestant principle of private judgment to political sovereignty was wreaking havoc in America, just as it had in 1776. And all of this jockeying for power by political cadres who did not bother consulting the masses demonstrates why "consent as a basis for Southern loyalty to Confederate institutions proved problematic. The notion that individual citizens had consented to

46. Cf. An Act for the Admission of West Virginia into the Union, in Virgil Anson Lewis, *History of West Virginia* (Philadelphia: Hubbard Brothers, 1889), 385–387.

Confederate rule began on shaky ground, as both the government and its leaders were chosen by the South's elite, with no popular ratification by its citizens."[47] But then the same had been true of the Continental Congress; and it was true of the Philadelphia Convention that effectively overthrew the Articles of Confederation the Continental Congress had adopted in favor of a Constitution whose protection for the institution of slavery was now the flashpoint for secession and civil war.

Whither the Casus Belli?

Again, what the Southern cause *became* once the Civil War began—a defense of the homeland in each Confederate state against invasion from the North—must be distinguished carefully from the secession and initial acts of Southern aggression in firing on a federal supply ship, seizing federal forts, arsenals, mints and post offices, bombarding Fort Sumter, and abruptly asserting a new Southern federal jurisdiction over the lower half of the United States, beginning just across the Potomac within sight of the White House. Any or all of these acts allowed Lincoln to claim justification for an invasion of the South to recover federal property and restore "the Union." What *exactly* had the North done to justify these *initial* acts of war by the South? An examination of Confederate polemics fails to reveal any clearly demonstrable *casus belli*.

Vice President Stephens, for example, was as blind as Davis concerning an objective assessment of the Southern position. Without seeming to notice the devastating implicit admission in his argument, he justified war with the North on the grounds that Lincoln and the Republicans had adopted a "policy to wage war for *the recapture of former possessions*, looking to the ultimate coercion and subjugation of the people of the Confederate States to their power and domain. . . . With such an object on their part persevered in, no power on earth can arrest or prevent a most bloody conflict."[48] When one nation—and the Confederacy claimed to be a nation—seizes the possessions of another by force, who is responsible for starting the ensuing war if not the nation guilty of the seizure? A nation whose possessions have been seized by another has a fairly strong argument for invading the nation that seized them in order to *recapture*—Stephens's own word—what was *captured* by a hostile power. The Confederate leadership could hardly have expected that Lincoln would meekly accept their attempt at a massive *fait accompli*.

Here the Southern position exhibited yet another of the self-serving inconsistencies that riddle arguments on both sides of any conflict over the direction of the supposed progress of Liberty. If the seceding states, acting in the name of Liberty, had formed a unified *nation*, as the South maintained, then what was underway was a war between two nations—the United States of America versus the Confederate States of America. That being the case, the *entire territory* of each nation was

---

47. Mark A. Weitz, *More Damning than Slaughter: Desertion in the Confederate Army* (Lincoln, NE: Univ. of Nebraska Press, 2005), 31.

48. Current, *Lincoln and the First Shot*, 169.

subject to invasion by the other without regard to the political subdivisions of either. If there was to be a war at all between the United States and the Confederate States over property, territory and jurisdiction, then the "Yankee invasion" of the "sovereign State of Virginia" at Manassas, for example, would have to be on the same moral plane as the "Rebel invasion" of the "sovereign State of Pennsylvania" at Gettysburg. Southern romanticism aside, the internal state lines of the Confederacy were no more "sacred" than those of the Union, which is to say not sacred at all, but rather mere cartographic conventions arrived at by agreement after the territory in question had been seized from the Crown or acquired by purchase or conquest in the rather recent past. The entity called the "State of Texas," for one, did not even exist until sixteen years before the Civil War began.

There is indeed something suspiciously artificial and shifty about the territorial claims of both sides in the war: the indignant rhetoric about "states' rights" versus "preservation of the Union," when neither the States nor the Union had existed 85 years earlier; or a "war of independence" between a Confederate "nation" invented in 1861 against an American "nation" invented in 1776 after an earlier war of independence; or polemics concerning a "Yankee race" versus a "Southern race," both of which were composed of white Anglo-Saxon Protestants who had fought as one against England. The dubious territoriality at the heart of the Civil War is itself a function of liberalism, a point we shall develop more fully in assessing the war's aftermath in Chapter 16.

In any case, the justification of self-defense by each Southern state could not be imported backwards in time to justify the acts that provoked the war in the first place and without which there would have been no need for self-defense. Nor can the prior secession find justification in a romantic narrative of the subsequent defensive war, including the undeniable bravery, valor, and nobility of countless men on both sides who were called upon to lay down their lives because of what the politicians had decided in their name. That *Lincoln* did not wage the Civil War on account of slavery but rather solely to "save the Union," as we will see, is beside the precise point under consideration here: that the South seceded on account of the slavery question and then seized federal properties, bombarding one of them with intent to kill, and that absent these events there would have been no war—at least not the one that began in 1861 and ended in 1865.

No one had doubted the grounds for war more than the South's greatest general. Lee's most admiring biographer recounts that for Lee secession "meant the wreck of the nation, 'the beginning of sorrows,' the opening of a war *that was certain to be long and full of horrors*."[49] We have noted that in the same letter in which Lee counseled his son that "secession is nothing but revolution," the future head of the Army of Northern Virginia wrote that while "[t]he South, in my opinion, has been aggrieved by the acts of the North, as you say. . . . I can anticipate no greater calamity for the country than a dissolution of the Union. It would be an accumulation of all the evils we complain of. . . ." A day later (January 22, 1861) Lee confided to his

---

49. Douglas Southall Freeman, *R. E. Lee: A Biography* (NY: Scribner & Sons, 1914), 439–40.

wife's cousin that notwithstanding the South's legitimate grievances, "I see *no cause of disunion, strife and civil war* & pray it may be avoided."[50] On February 16, 1861, days before the firing on Fort Sumter and while still a colonel in the United States Army, Lee confided to Charles Anderson, the very brother of the commander of the fort, that "I do not believe in secession as a constitutional right, *nor is there a sufficient cause for revolution. . . .*"[51] On the very day he sent his resignation from the United States Army to his fellow Virginian, General Winfield Scott (April 20, 1861), Lee wrote to his sister to declare: "We are now in a state of war *which will yield nothing*. The whole South is in a state of *revolution*, into which Virginia, after a long struggle, has been drawn. . . . *I recognize no necessity for this state of things. . . .*"[52]

No less than Jefferson Davis likewise undermined the Southern *casus belli* by stressing that he, unlike others, knew that the war would not be a brief and relatively bloodless affair. In his *Short History of the Confederate States of America*, looking back on the meteoric rise and fall of the government over which he had presided so disastrously, Davis was at pains to make it clear for the historical record that while in the antebellum South "[t]he opinion generally prevailed that secession would be peacefully accomplished," this was "an opinion from which I *publicly dissented*, with the result that. . . . I was regarded as 'too slow,' and being behind the public sentiment of my own State." Davis wanted history to record that he had warned that secession would mean "a long and desperate struggle" and that "few realized how totally deficient we were in all that was necessary to the active operations of an army."[53] In his massive two-volume work, *The Rise and Fall of the Confederate Government* (1881), Davis went even further, seeking to establish for the record nothing less than his own pre-secession prophecy of doom for the South. He quoted from an account of a conference of the Mississippi delegation to the United States Congress in Jackson in the fall of 1860, during which he had declared that "he was opposed to secession as long as the hope of a peaceable remedy remained. He did not believe we ought to precipitate the issue, as he felt certain from his knowledge of the people, North and South, that once there was a clash of arms, *the contest would be the most sanguinary the world had ever witnessed*."[54]

Explaining after the war why the South had lost it, Davis wrote that the Confederacy simply did not have the means to wage the war he knew secession would trigger, for "[t]he foundries and armories were in the Northern states, and there were stored all the new and improved weapons of war," whereas "[i]n the arsenals of the Southern states were to be found only arms of the old and rejected models." Further, the South "had no manufactories of powder, no navy to protect our har-

50. Nolan, *Lee Considered*, 33.

51. *The Nation*, Vol. XLIV (NY: Evening Post Publishing Company, 1887), No. 1137, 322; see also Nolan, *Lee Considered*, 36.

52. Lee to Anne Marshall, April 20, 1861, in George Cary Eggleston, *The History of the Confederate War: Its Causes and Its Conduct* (London: William Heineman, 1910), 208.

53. Jefferson Davis, *A Short History of the Confederate States*, 54, 59, 75.

54. Jefferson Davis, *The Rise and Fall of the Confederate Government* (NY: D. Appleton and Company, 1881), Vol. 1, 59.

bors, no merchant ships for foreign commerce." Thus, Davis concluded: "It was evident to me . . . that if we should be involved in war, the odds against us would be far greater than what was due merely to our inferiority in population. Believing that *secession would be the precursor of war between the States*, I was consequently slower and more reluctant than others, who entertained a different opinion, to resort to that remedy."[55]

Davis was not a Catholic and perhaps was unfamiliar with the traditional Catholic teaching on the ethical criteria for a just war. But these criteria—a matter of natural morality and justice rather than theology—were well known outside the Catholic world through the widely published works of Saint Augustine, generally acknowledged as the originator of the just war doctrine, and Saint Thomas Aquinas. Their works in turn were foundational to those of the more modern political and legal thinkers on the subject, both Catholic and non-Catholic, including Francisco de Vitoria (1486–1546), Francisco Suarez (1548–1617), Hugo Grotius (1583–1645), Samuel Pufendorf (1632–1704), Christian Wolff (1679–1754), and Emerich de Vattel (1714–1767). Vattel's legal commentaries in particular would have been familiar to any American intellectual of the 19th century. In fact, both Davis and Stephens—President and Vice President of the Confederate States—cite Vattel repeatedly in their respective apologia.[56]

By his own words Davis demonstrated that an armed conflict with the North over secession and his own decision to bombard Fort Sumter objectively violated every traditional criterion for a just war, classically formulated as follows: "that the damage inflicted by the aggressor on the nation or community of nations must be lasting, grave, and certain; that all other means of putting an end to it must have been shown to be impractical or ineffective; that there must be *serious prospects of success*; that *the use of arms must not produce evils and disorders graver than the evil to be eliminated.*"[57] For one thing, before the firing on Fort Sumter and the seizure of practically every federal fort, arsenal, mint and post office in the seceding states, the North had never aggressed militarily against the South and the only arguable "damage inflicted by the aggressor" was by way of the political process, not armed aggression. It was, rather, *the South* that had confiscated and inflicted damage on federal possessions, fired on federal military personnel with intent to kill, and then proposed to purchase from the federal government the very possessions it had just taken at the point of a gun. And it was the South that had purported to withdraw subjects of the United States from its authority in order to make them subjects of the Confederate States—against the will of many of them, who would resist the Confederacy throughout the war, call for federal assistance, and even send regiments to the North. The Civil War was bilateral folly, but as between Davis and Lincoln, can it seriously be maintained that Davis had the better argument for

55. Davis, *Rise and Fall*, 57–58.
56. Davis, *Rise and Fall*, Vol. I, 145, 706; Alexander H. Stephens, *A Constitutional View of the Late War Between the States* (Philadelphia: National Publishing Co., 1867), Vol. I, 4, 48, 83, 116, 170, 204, 392, 492, 656.
57. Cf. *Catechism of the Catholic Church*, §2309.

use of force to remedy "damage inflicted by the aggressor"? The question should answer itself.

Further, Davis, like Lee, knew that "serious prospects of success" were gravely in doubt; and, like Lee, he suspected that the war would produce "evils and disorders graver than the evil to be eliminated"—assuming that a perceived political threat to the institution of slavery could even be considered an "evil" to be eliminated in the first place. Yet Davis gave the order to fire on Fort Sumter knowing full well that that act would launch the very war he himself had publicly predicted would be the bloodiest the Western world had yet seen.

In defense of Davis, however, it must be said that in the concrete circumstances in which he found himself, with emotions all around him at a fever pitch, none of the caveats he issued could have counteracted the rhetoric of the fire-eaters nor halted the political tide that led to secession and the creation of the Confederate States of America. And without the border states in the Confederacy, the seven Cotton States had little chance of survival as a nation. "Strike a blow!" Pryor of Virginia had demanded with precisely that reality in view. Only acts of war provoking the threat of a Northern invasion could rally a Confederacy of sufficient size to pose a serious challenge to the Union. Thus, given the familiar dynamic of Liberty as precipitate action by a self-appointed cadre of radicals who will have their way no matter what, "Davis could only move ahead: he could not back up. He had too many panting soldiers to think of, too many blood-minded enthusiasts to take into account. If he should retreat, *the Confederacy would have no chance to grow or even to live*. His own position of leadership would be imperiled. The hot-headed Carolinians might take the initiative from him. They might begin the firing at any moment, regardless of the instructions from Montgomery."[58] In other words, no war meant no viable Confederacy, and so the war hawks of the South would not be denied their war whether or not Davis gave the order to fire.

Joining many voices of moderation the Southern war hawks refused to heed were the South's industrialists, an economic minority whose wealth did not depend upon the ownership of slaves. Among the industrialists was a well-founded "widespread fear of defeat and ruin for the South generally and themselves in particular." They, "much more than the planters or swaggering politicians, appreciated the census statistics on the material strength of the contending parties and scoffed at the illusions pervading the dominant class." One of them, Rufus L. Patterson of North Carolina, signed North Carolina's Ordinance of Secession, but "with deep misgivings, for he saw as inevitable defeat at the hands of a stronger foe, and what was worse, the specter of 'civil war at home.'"[59] Both fears would be fully realized.

On Christmas Eve of 1860, a prominent prophet of the North predicted disaster for the South. William Tecumseh Sherman, whose middle name honored the great Indian chief, was a lover of the South, a West Point graduate like Lee who was then

58. Current, *Lincoln and the First Shot*, 150.
59. Genovese, *Political Economy of Slavery*, 202.

superintendent of the Louisiana State Military Academy. Four years before the Civil War had converted this painter of water colors and connoisseur of Shakespeare into a lover of war whose criminal "March to the Sea" would eviscerate a Confederacy already driven to its knees, Sherman wept over news of South Carolina's secession four days earlier, which would force his resignation from the Academy.[60] He warned a professor of Latin and Greek at the Academy that secession would mean the entire nation would be "drenched in blood"—an echo of Calhoun's warning to the Senate in 1837. He sketched with uncanny accuracy the future course of events:

> It is all folly, madness, a crime against civilization! You people speak so lightly of war; you don't know what you are talking about. War is a terrible thing. Where are your men, and your appliances of war? The North can make a steam engine, locomotive or railway car; hardly a yard of cloth or a pair of shoes can you make. You are rushing into war with one of the most powerful, ingeniously mechanical and determined people on earth—right at your doorstep! You are bound to fail. Only in your spirit and determination are you prepared for war. In all else you are totally unprepared, with a bad cause to start with. *At first you will make headway, but as your limited resources begin to fail, shut out from the markets of Europe as you will be, your cause will begin to wane.* If your people will but stop and think, they must see that in the end you will surely fail.[61]

Sherman's prophecy was not much more than a statement of the obvious, however. In terms of population alone, the South with its nine million people, nearly four million of whom were slaves, was no match for the North with its twenty million. Worse, because the slaves were legal non-persons disqualified from military service, the manpower disparity between the North and the South was almost four-to-one in the North's favor.[62] And that was only the beginning of the North's list of massive advantages. Yet, ignoring these facts, "[e]ven men who should have known better ... went willingly to war or urged others to do so, giving scant mind to the staying power of their own people and caring little about the absence of proper preparation."[63]

The hard historical evidence precludes any claim that the Southern *casus belli* appears inadequate only in historical hindsight. Quite apart from which side fired the first shot, it is hardly presentism to say that it ought to have been clear to any cool-headed Southerner (as it was to Lee and Davis) that defense of the "peculiar institution"—meaning essentially its extension into the territories—was no grounds for a war that was likely unwinnable and would be devastating both to the very institution to be defended and to the South as a whole. Writing from a Confederate

60. Wilson, *Patriotic Gore*, 180.
61. Foote, *The Civil War*, Vol. I, 58.
62. Foote, 60.
63. Beringer, et al., *Why the South Lost the War*, 82.

partisan perspective, even a libertarian scholar opines: "It is doubtful that the abolitionists of the North or the fire-eaters of the South, both small groups who were unrepresentative of their respective regions, appreciated the risks to liberty by the war they both so emotionally demanded."[64] But from the dominant emotional perspective of the Southern political leadership and the wealthy elites who had installed it, who indeed were *not* representative of the masses of yeoman farmers and other common people who had not voted on secession, this was a war that Liberty required. Ignoring the warnings of their more rational fellow Southerners, the fire-eating politicians and planters of the South would get what they asked for. Yet almost none of them would later be found on the battlefield.

Early Portents of Doom

By the date of Jefferson Davis's inauguration in 1862, then Brig. Gen. Ulysses S. Grant had already won the Battle of Fort Henry (February 6) and the Battle of Fort Donelson (February 16) for the Union, thus opening up the Tennessee and Cumberland Rivers as arteries of invasion leading to the heart of the Confederacy. The bumbling Union Army had recovered from its defeat at the First Battle of Bull Run (First Manassas) the previous July. In an early harbinger of doom for the Confederacy, during the immense bloodbath at Shiloh (April 6–7), ultimately a Union victory, the intrepid General Albert Sidney Johnston (no relation to General Joseph Johnston) was fatally wounded by friendly fire—one of three Confederate generals, including "Stonewall" Jackson, inadvertently killed by their own men.[65]

On April 28, 1862 Union forces under Maj. Gen. Benjamin Butler occupied New Orleans. Despite Butler's brutal and corruption-ridden regime of martial law, a Confederate counteroffensive would fail in part for lack of support among the general population; for Butler had seen to it that "the huge illiterate majority" of the city was fed and clothed, his sanitation policies had "cleansed the city of disease," and "for many years after the war the poor continued to praise him...."[66] Further, since colonial times New Orleans, under Catholic influence, had been an urban center of black freedmen and increasingly independent urban slaves, and "the Catholic Church—unlike the established Protestant denominations—welcomed them."[67] By the early 19th century "slaves and free people of color, especially women...comprised at least half of the Catholic population of the city."[68] By the immediate antebellum period thousands of free blacks in New Orleans constituted a veritable black "middle caste," attaining "an unprecedented prosperity

64. In John V. Denson, *A Century of War: Lincoln, Wilson and Roosevelt* (Auburn, AL: Von Mises Institute, 2006), 88.

65. Donald Cartmell, *The Civil War Book of Lists* (Franklin Lakes, NJ: New Pages Books, 2001), 82.

66. Chester G. Hearn, *When the Devil Came Down to Dixie: Ben Butler in New Orleans* (Baton Rouge: Louisiana State Univ. Press, 2000), 4.

67. Berlin, *Generations of Captivity*, 1020–1021 (Kindle location).

68. Stephen Jay Ochs, *A Black Patriot and a White Priest* (Baton Rouge: Louisiana State Univ. Press, 2000), 165.

and creating their own churches, schools, literary associations, and fraternal organizations. . . ."[69]

New Orleans presented another early harbinger of Confederate doom. Less than two months before the city fell, the Confederate Army command disbanded the 1st Louisiana Native Guard, a black local militia formed for public relations purposes and headed by the freedman André Cailloux, a Catholic. As one Catholic commentator writes, if blacks had been given "any encouragement at all to enlist in the Confederate Army, especially with a promise of eventual emancipation for all blacks, [it] might have helped alter the outcome of the War." But then "if the Confederate leaders had been willing to entertain such ideas at the beginning of the War, neither secession nor the War would have occurred."[70] What the Confederacy spurned, General Butler prudently exploited. He reconstituted the Guard with Cailloux at its head, making him Captain of Company E. "The black population of New Orleans responded enthusiastically to Butler's initiative, and the Native Guard soon grew to three regiments."[71] We will see how the Confederacy's doom was sealed by the planter-dominated Confederate Congress's adamant refusal, despite the urging of Davis and Lee, to emancipate even a single slave to fight for the South because to do so would have negated the very grounds for secession and war.

With the loss of Forts Henry and Donelson, the slaughter at Shiloh, and the fall of New Orleans, Davis had already seen the fulfillment of his prediction that secession would lead to a "long and desperate struggle." Soon he would see fulfilled his further prediction that "the contest would be the most sanguinary the world had ever witnessed." Faced with the prospect of a long and bloody war, Davis turned to God. At best a diffident believer in the vaguely providential deity of "moderate" post-Enlightenment liberalism before the war, he had never joined any church "and could not even recall whether he had ever been baptized." But in the midst of the trials of war he "began to think about God and religion in more personal terms than ever before." On May 1, 1862—three days after New Orleans was lost—Davis was baptized in the Confederate White House; and later that day, at the age of 52, he received Confirmation at Saint Paul's Episcopal Church in Richmond.[72]

As the war progressed, Davis "sometimes blamed Confederate failures on divine displeasure with the South."[73] The thesis of divine displeasure was not unreasonable given the death and devastation the South would suffer on account of the decisions of its politicians—a disaster on which the bold motto of the Great Seal of the Confederacy provided an unintentionally ironic commentary: *Deo Vindice* (God will vindicate). Like the revolutionaries of the first American Revolution, the revolutionaries of the Confederacy proclaimed that God had willed the creation of their new nation. As a Confederate Army pamphlet declared: "The only proper view of

69. Berlin, *Generations of Captivity*, 2048–49.

70. Donald R. McClarey, "The Hero and the Priest," the-american-catholic.com/2011/01/17/the-hero-and-the-priest/.

71. Ibid.

72. William J. Cooper, Jr., *Jefferson Davis, American* (NY: Vintage Books, 2000), 417.

73. Davis, *Jefferson Davis: The Man and His Hour*, 602.

this *revolution* is that which regards it as the child of providence."[74] But this was only in keeping with the "millennialism of American Civil religion" generally, which combined the Puritan idea "that pilgrims founded a new Israel with the republican ideology that the young nation represented humanity's greatest experiment in government."[75] For the South, that view would prove impossible to reconcile with the war's outcome, unless a Confederate were willing to concede that Providence had ordained the chastisement of the Southern people, just as the Southern Jeremiahs had feared.

74. Phillips, *Diehard Rebels*, 15.
75. Ibid., 14.

14

The North Rises

WE HAVE SEEN enough to dispel the Southern romantic *mythos* of a noble "conservative" crusade for the highest ideals of civilization, launched by leaders who were forced into secession and a war they had never asked for and which the North started. Let us turn now to the romantic *mythos* of the North, whose central character is the sixteenth President of the United States.

A Holocaust for Liberty

With the Union capture of New Orleans, an immense new holocaust for Liberty was well underway. Thanks to the tactical brilliance of Robert E. Lee, the outmanned and outgunned Confederate forces, especially Lee's valiant Army of Northern Virginia, would hold out defensively for years, although Lee's major northern offensives at Antietam and Gettysburg would both end in disaster. The South would inevitably be subjected to an unprecedented practical application of the Rousseauian dictum tied to the Lockean social compact: "whoever refuses to obey the general will shall be compelled to do so by the whole body. This means nothing less than that *he will be forced to be free....*"[1] And since it was only at the point of a gun that the "whole body" could force the seceding part to be "free," the North too would pay a terrible price in blood and treasure, albeit one it could sustain while continuing even to prosper in the midst of hostilities.

Holocausts for Liberty do not come cheap, however. In order to fund the massive armies that would be needed to force the South to be free, the tax collectors of Liberty—more demanding from the start than old King George had ever been—immediately introduced the first federal income tax in United States history, albeit as a temporary wartime measure. The Revenue Act of 1861 provided that "upon the annual income of every person residing in the United States, whether such income is derived from any kind of property, or from any profession, trade, employment or vocation carried on in the United States" there would be a tax of 3% on the excess over $800 (about $18,000 in current U. S. dollars). With the Revenue Act of 1862 that flat tax was replaced by a graduated tax of 3% on incomes above $600 (about $13,000 in current dollars) and 5% on incomes above $10,000 (equivalent to

---

1. *Social Contract*, I.7.

around $200,000 today).[2] As for the seceding States, the income tax bill, with interest, would become due once what was left of them had been dragged back into the Temple of Liberty.[3] The Revenue Act of 1861 had been signed into law by Abraham Lincoln, the first Republican President.

The Lincoln Legend

Like the Founding Fathers both the South and the North invoked, Lincoln came to be depicted as nothing less than a secular martyr-saint who gave his life for "the sacred cause of Liberty," just as Christ purchased the Church with His own blood, as Saint Paul had put it. With each decade following his assassination, "Lincoln became more and more the object of adulation; a full-blown 'Lincoln legend' appeared."[4] Observing this phenomenon in the 1920s, H. L. Mencken wrote:

> The growth of the Lincoln legend is truly amazing. He becomes the American solar myth, the chief butt of American credulity and sentimentality. Washington, of late years, has been perceptibly humanized; every schoolboy now knows that he used to swear a good deal, and was a sharp trader, and had a quick eye for a pretty ankle. But meanwhile the varnishers and veneerers have been busily converting Abe into a plaster saint. . . . Worse, there is an obvious effort to pump all his human weaknesses out of him, and so leave him a mere moral apparition, a sort of amalgam of John Wesley and the Holy Ghost. What could be more absurd?[5]

The related fable of Lincoln the devout Christian is sufficiently debunked in the biography by his close friend, confidant and former law partner, Colonel Ward H. Lamon, wherein we read: "His extremely general expressions of religious faith called forth by the grave exigencies of his public life, or indulged in on occasions of private condolence, have too often been distorted out of relation to their real significance or meaning to suit the opinions or tickle the fancies of individuals or parties. . . . Mr. Lincoln was never a member of any Church, nor did he believe in the divinity of Christ, or the inspiration of the Scriptures in the sense understood by evangelical Christians. . . . When a boy, he showed no sign of that piety which his many biographers ascribe to his manhood. When he went to church at all, he went to mock, and came away to mimic. . . . It was not until after his death that his alleged orthodoxy became the principal topic of his eulogists. . . ."[6]

According to the "Lincoln legend," the sainted and probably crypto-Christian President fought a great war to "free the slaves," bringing unity and equality to all of America. But as Mencken observes, "his handling of the slavery question was that

2. Compare Revenue Act of 1861, § 49 and Revenue Act of 1862, § 90.
3. See Revenue Act of 1861, § 53.
4. "Abraham Lincoln," *The Columbia Encyclopedia*, Sixth Edition (2001–2007).
5. H. L. Mencken, *Prejudices: Third Series* (NY: Alfred A. Knopf, 1922), 173–174.
6. Ward Hill Lamon, *The Life of Lincoln: From His Birth to His Inauguration as President* (Boston: James R. Osgood & Company, 1872), 486–487.

of a politician, not that of a fanatic. Nothing alarmed him more than the suspicion that he was an Abolitionist. Barton tells of an occasion when he actually fled town to avoid meeting the issue squarely."[7] The truth is that, the loudly professed fears of the South notwithstanding, Lincoln, like Jefferson, had no intention of abolishing slavery where it already existed, but on the contrary had every intention of preserving it precisely as the text of the Constitution required.

Moreover, Lincoln, like Jefferson—like the majority of Americans at the time, both North and South—viewed the black man as innately inferior to the white man, even if human. Lincoln declared in the course of the Lincoln-Douglas polemics that "There is a natural disgust in the minds of nearly all white people at the idea of an indiscriminate amalgamation of the white and black races. . . ." While, contrary to the opinion of President Davis, President Lincoln held that the Declaration of Independence "includes all men, black as well as white," this did not mean that "because I do not want a black woman for a slave I must necessarily want her for a wife. I need not have her for either. I can just leave her alone. In some respects she certainly is not my equal; but in her natural right to eat the bread she earns with her own hands without asking leave of anyone else, she is my equal and the equal of all others."[8] That is, the black man was equal to the white man, but only in the most essential Lockean sense of having the right to self-preservation.

Thus, like Jefferson, Lincoln called for the mass deportation of former slaves should they be emancipated, as this was the only policy that could address the impossibility of the coexistence of the two races in America:

> But Judge Douglas is especially horrified at the thought of the mixing of blood by the white and black races. Agreed for once—a thousand times agreed. . . . *I have said that the separation of the races is the only perfect preventive of amalgamation.* . . . Such separation, if ever effected at all, *must be effected by colonization.* . . . Let us be brought to believe it is morally right, and at the same time favorable to, or at least not against, our interest *to transfer the African to his native clime, and we shall find a way to do it, however great the task may be.*[9]

In other words, Lincoln, like Jefferson, believed that "freedom" for the slaves meant their removal from America and thus the elimination of the problem their existence posed for white society.

Lincoln's First Inaugural Address, standing alone, suffices to dispel the myth that he waged the Civil War to free the slaves. Assuring the South that it had nothing to fear from him concerning the issue of slavery where it already existed, he noted that the mandatory slave rendition clause in Article IV "is as plainly written in the Constitution as any other of its provisions," and that "[i]t is scarcely questioned that this provision was intended by those who made it, for the reclaiming of what we call

---

7. Mencken, *Prejudices*, 174.

8. Abraham Lincoln, "The Sacredness of Judicial Decisions," Speech of June 12, 1857, in Marion Mills Miller, ed., *Great Debates in American History* (NY: Current Literature Publishing Company, 1913), Vol. IV, 395–396, 398–399.

9. Ibid.

fugitive slaves; and *the intention of the law giver is the law.*" Consequently, he declared, "All members of Congress swear their support to the whole Constitution— *to this provision as much as to any other.*" In other words, the President and Congress had a *duty* under the Constitution to preserve the institution of slavery. Hence, quoting one of his campaign speeches, Lincoln promised the Southern states that:

> I *have no purpose, directly or indirectly, to interfere with the institution of slavery* in the States where it exists. I believe *I have no lawful right to do so*, and I have no inclination to do so. Those who nominated and elected me did so with full knowledge that I had made this, and many similar declarations, *and had never recanted them.*

Moreover, Lincoln reaffirmed, the Republican Party platform had promised "the maintenance inviolate of the rights of the States, and especially the right of each State to order and control its own domestic institutions according to its own judgment exclusively"—slavery being, after all, a matter of "states' rights." Therefore, Lincoln, *on his very oath to uphold the Constitution*, was prepared to give the Southern states the benefit of what they viewed as the constitutional "compact," precisely as they had demanded, the only issue being the spread of slavery beyond where it already existed into the territories:

> One section of our country believes slavery is right, and ought to be extended, while the other believes it is wrong, and ought not to be extended. *This is the only substantial dispute.* The fugitive slave clause of the Constitution, and the law for the suppression of the foreign slave trade, are each as well enforced, perhaps, as any law can ever be in a community where the moral sense of the people imperfectly supports the law itself. *The great body of the people abide by the dry legal obligation in both cases. . . .*

That is, there was room in the Union for both those who defended slave ownership as an inviolable property right, and those who denounced it as intolerable evil, with the Constitution providing the means for both parties to get along by protecting the rights of slave owners as a "dry legal obligation." The same rationale supports the alleged constitutional right to treat children in the womb as disposable chattels owned by the mother.

Leaving no doubt of his commitment to the slavery status quo, Lincoln went even further in giving assurances to the South. Two days before his inaugural address the Senate, on March 2, 1861, had passed a proposed constitutional amendment that had passed the House several days before. The proposed amendment (never ratified by the States) provided: "No amendment shall be made to the Constitution which will authorize or give to Congress the power to abolish or interfere, within any State, with the domestic institutions thereof, *including that of persons held to labor or service by the laws of said State.*"[10] Referring to this amendment in his address, Lincoln said: "[H]olding such a provision to now be implied constitutional

---

10. House of Representatives electronic archive, www.house.gov/house/Amendnotrat.shtml.

law, I have no objection to its being made express and irrevocable." That is, Lincoln had no objection *to the perpetual existence of the institution of slavery* wherever it had already been established in the United States. Neither had the Founders and Framers any objection, which is why the Constitution had guaranteed the rendition of escaped slaves in the first place. In an extraordinary gesture, Lincoln later signed the text of the proposed amendment to indicate his approval, even though a Presidential signature is not required to commence the ratification process. As a House of Representatives archival note points out, this was "the only proposed (and not ratified) amendment to the Constitution to have been signed by the President."[11]

So much, then, for the legend of Lincoln the Abolitionist. No wonder the abolitionist rhetorician Wendell Phillips, referring to the dogs used to hunt down escaped slaves, denounced him as "the slave-hound of Illinois," declaring in an editorial in *The Liberator* that "We gibbet a northern hound today, side by side with the infamous Mason of Virginia."[12] Then again, Southern partisans who insist that Lincoln had no intention of warring over slavery fail to see that they have extinguished their own position. The South could hardly justify secession and war over the election of a President denounced as a pragmatic "slave-hound" by Northern abolitionists and who at worst viewed the question narrowly as one of the extension of slavery into the territories.

Till Death Do Us Part

What animated Lincoln as he took office after the first wave of secessions was not the abolition of slavery but preservation of "the Union" *with or without slaves.* Confronted with the Southern secession, Lincoln could have argued for its suppression based on the Christian political tradition, proceeding from divine revelation, on the duty to obey constituted government and refrain from rebellions, given the divine source of all civil authority (cf. Chapters 2, 3, and 11). But, of course, that tradition had been abandoned in America in favor of the new principles undergirding Liberty: the social compact, the "sovereign will of the people" as the source of civil authority, and the right to revolution. The first American Revolution had enshrined these Lockean doctrines as the "conservative" American inheritance of both the North and the South.

Thus Lincoln's argument for preservation of the Union in his First Inaugural Address proceeded within the same Lockean framework the Framers had erected and to which the South itself was now appealing. The Address presents a kind of mystical excursus on Locke's compact theory, for Locke's theory is indeed shrouded in mystical confusion. Instead of simply asserting that the Southern states had a duty under God to respect the authority of the government they themselves had helped to constitute more than seventy years earlier, Lincoln developed

11. Ibid.
12. *The Liberator*, XXX, 99 (June 22, 1860), in Frank Luther Mott, *A History of American Magazines: 1850–1865*, Vol. II (Cambridge: Belknap Press of Harvard Univ. Press, 1938), 292.

the theme of a Union that was somehow intrinsically both indestructible and irrefrangible without reference to divine authority.

Beginning mystically enough, Lincoln, echoing all his predecessors in office, declared that "the Union" must endure forever: "I hold, that in contemplation of universal law, and of the Constitution, the Union of these States is *perpetual*. Perpetuity is implied, if not expressed, in the fundamental law of all national governments." By operation of this mysterious "universal" and "fundamental law of all national governments" the Union could never end. This was also true, according to Lincoln, because of the history of the Union before the Constitution:

> [T]he proposition that, in legal contemplation, the Union is perpetual, [is] confirmed by the history of the Union itself. *The Union is much older than the Constitution.* It was formed in fact, by the Articles of Association [sic] in 1774. It was matured and continued by the Declaration of Independence in 1776. It was further matured and *the faith of all the then thirteen States expressly plighted and engaged that it should be perpetual,* by the Articles of Confederation in 1778. And finally, in 1787, one of the declared objects for ordaining and establishing the Constitution was "to form a more perfect Union." But if [the] destruction of the Union, by one, or by a part only, of the States, be lawfully possible, the Union is less perfect than before the Constitution, having lost the vital element of perpetuity.

While the word "perpetual" appears nowhere in the Constitution, it does appear in the superseded Articles of Confederation, which had declared, with no authority whatsoever from the people at large, that "the Articles of this Confederation shall be inviolably observed by every State, and *the Union shall be perpetual. . . .*"[13] Lincoln did not explain how the perpetuity clause of the junked Articles could have any relevance seventy-two years after ratification of the Constitution. Nor did he explain why the alleged perpetuity of the Union did not permit some states to leave it while allowing others to perpetuate it if they so chose.

But such legal fine points did not matter for Lincoln's argument. Rather, the Address evoked a pseudo-mystical rationale for forcing the South to remain in the Union: that *"the faith"* of the original thirteen states had "plighted and engaged" that the Union be endowed with a living quality akin to the indefectibility claimed for the Catholic Church, the "vital element of perpetuity." In support of this vital element of perpetuity Lincoln appealed to "the mystic chords of memory, stretching from every battle-field, and patriot grave, to every living heart and hearthstone," which mystic chords he hoped "will yet swell the chorus of the Union, when again touched, as surely they will be, by the better angels of our nature." Adherence to the Union, then, was a *spiritual* imperative, a sacred ancestral duty imposed from beyond the grave, to be heeded under an influence no less than angelic.

Then again, the idea of a perpetual Union was not foreign to the Southern polemic. Far from it. In the "secession is nothing but revolution" letter to his son,

---

13. *The Articles of Confederation* (1778), Art. XIII.

no less than Lee had observed: "The framers of our Constitution never exhausted so much labor, wisdom, and forbearance in its formation, and surrounded it with so many guards and securities, if it was intended to be broken by every member of the Confederacy at will. *It was intended for 'perpetual union'. . . .*" Departing from Lee's view, however, the Southern secessionist fire-eaters had argued that while "perpetual," the Union was not *inescapable* by those states that wished to depart from it without prejudice to its perpetuity among the remaining states. Not according to Lincoln, however—or the pre-war Lee, for that matter. Lincoln opined that none of the States, not even one, could ever be allowed to leave the Union's quasi-marital embrace. Quite fantastically, in a remark that must have been considered scandalous at the time, he declared: "A husband and wife may be divorced, and go out of the presence, and beyond the reach of each other; but the different parts of our country cannot do this. They cannot but remain face to face; and intercourse, either amicable or hostile, must continue between them." Till death do they part. The Union was forever, even if matrimony of the Protestant variety was not.

But why should the Union, unlike Protestant matrimony, be considered indissoluble merely because the parties happened to be geographically contiguous? Were not states all over the world contiguous with, yet legally independent of, their neighbors—America and Canada, for example? Given that there was no question of any appeal here to the divine source of all civil authority, according to what traditional legal or moral principle was, say, the supposedly sovereign Commonwealth of Massachusetts bound forever to the supposedly sovereign State of South Carolina? The answer is that Lincoln was not presenting a traditional legal or moral argument. As a Lockean liberal of the North, he was pitting Locke's confused and self-contradictory theory of sovereignty against the Lockean liberals of the South. For the South had forgotten one of Locke's axioms, the truth of which the Moses of the Enlightenment had never bothered to demonstrate. As we saw in Chapter 3, it was none other than Locke who, while viewing marriage as a mere revocable contract, taught in his *Second Treatise* that "he, that has once, by actual agreement, and any express declaration, given his consent to be of any commonwealth, *is perpetually and indispensably obliged to be, and remain unalterably a subject to it. . . .*"[14] This sort of perpetual union was indeed what the authors of the Articles of Confederation had implied, without bothering to consult the millions of parties to the "marriage" ceremony they had performed.

Since the States had (supposedly) ratified the Constitution, thereby giving their express consent to belong to the commonwealth of the United States, under Locke's theory they were bound to remain within it forever according to the same Lockean principle of "government by consent of the governed" reflected in the Declaration of Independence and the Articles of Confederation. Indeed, by the very act of invoking "states' rights" under the Constitution *before* they had seceded, the Southern states had implicitly ratified their prior express and thus (per Locke) irrevocable consent, *qua* states, to be part of that Union. Lincoln freely conceded the

14. *TT,* II.121.

Lockean corollary that "Whenever they [the people of the United States] shall grow weary of the existing Government, they can exercise their *constitutional* right of amending it, or their *revolutionary* right to dismember or overthrow it."[15] But while the "right to revolution" that is Locke's escape hatch from the perpetual compact was the option the South had exercised—there being no right of at-will secession from a perpetual Union expressly consented to—the Union had a correlative right to oppose that revolution by putting it down.

The Southern states had, of course, raised the Lockean counter-argument that the Union was automatically dissolved on account of "breach of compact." But Lincoln was not admitting that any such breach had occurred; and it was Lincoln, not the South, who held the powers of chief executive of the supreme sovereign "We the People" had created with the supposed consent of the Southern states themselves. Yet, for his part, Lincoln had conveniently overlooked the historical reality that, as Justice Marshall observed in the *McCulloch* decision, it was not the state legislatures but rather "We the People," acting through ratifying conventions, that had ratified the Constitution. Thus it was only "We the People," not the States *qua* States, who could be said to have expressly "consented" to the federal compact. Then again, Lincoln would reply, given the supposed "consent" of "We the People" to the direct authority of the federal government over them, by what right did any state secession convention purport to withdraw the people residing within its borders from the United States, thereby depriving them of their national citizenship? The Second Wheeling Convention in western Virginia had rejected and refused to obey precisely that purported act of withdrawal, calling it a "pretended decree."

The deadly North-South debate over secession is perhaps history's most dramatic demonstration of the treacherous nature of Locke's murky, self-negating, and nonsensical "consent" theory of sovereignty. To recur to the questions already posed: Who were the rulers and who were the subjects at the state and federal level? Just who had consented to what, just who had represented whom, in the creation of the United States of America and the several states that composed it? What cause sufficed for a revocation of "consent to be governed" by means of secession, and who had authority to declare for others that a sufficient cause existed and act accordingly? Under the old order of Christendom, on the other hand, when political grievances arose it was not a question of determining "consent" to be governed or grounds for revocation of consent. Rather, the question was whether the ruler's subjects could resist particular injustices without denying or overthrowing the ruler's authority as such by means of revolution.

Having laid out his Lockean argument for the indissolubility of the Union, Lincoln stated the inevitable Lockean conclusion: "It follows from these views [!] that no State, upon its own mere motion, can lawfully get out of the Union. . . ." And then he uttered the threat that has always been the mainstay of Liberty—the use of force against those who dissent from its dictates as issued by those who govern in the name of "the people":

15. *First Inaugural Address.* Emphasis in original.

I shall take care, as the Constitution itself expressly enjoins upon me, that the laws of the Union be faithfully executed in all the States. . . . In doing this there needs to be no bloodshed or violence; and there shall be none, *unless it be forced upon the national authority.* . . . In *your* hands, my dissatisfied fellow country-men, and not in mine, is the momentous issue of civil war. The government will not assail you. You can have no conflict without being yourselves the aggressors. You have no oath registered in Heaven to destroy the government, while I shall have the most solemn one to "preserve, protect, and defend it."

Since Lincoln had given himself a warrant from Heaven to preserve the Union—without, of course, suggesting that his authority as President ultimately derived from and was limited by divine authority—he had rhetorically prepared the public for an all-out war to "save" the Union. At the same time, of course, the Southern leadership—being self-appointed, as the Confederacy was still a revolutionary government—was preparing its public for an all-out war to dissolve the Union and defend the Confederacy it had just created.

Long after commencement of the war for which agitators on both sides had clamored and the South had obligingly launched by firing on Fort Sumter, Lincoln continued to insist that his aim was not the abolition of Southern chattel slavery, but only restoration of the Union. He was so clear on this point that Horace Greeley wrote an editorial in the *New York Tribune* of August 1862 condemning Lincoln's failure to make slavery the paramount issue in the war. Lincoln replied:

My paramount object in this struggle is to save the Union, and *it is not either to save or destroy slavery. If I could save the Union without freeing any slave, I would do it*; and if I could save it by freeing some and leaving others alone I would also do that. *What I do about slavery, and the colored race, I do because I believe it helps to save the Union.* . . . I have here stated my purpose according to my view of official duty, and I intend no modification of my oft-expressed *personal* wish that all men everywhere could be free.[16]

So, even as men were dying to "save the Union," Lincoln remained "pro-choice" concerning slavery, precisely in the manner of modern politicians concerning abortion. The South could have its slaves and the war would end so long as the South submitted to the federal government. And Congress agreed. In July 1861 the House and Senate passed a joint resolution declaring:

[T]his war is not waged upon our part in any spirit of oppression, or for any purpose of conquest or subjugation [!], or purpose of overthrowing or inter-fering with *the rights or established institutions of those States*, but to defend and maintain the supremacy of the Constitution and to preserve the Union with all the dignity, equality, and rights of the several States unimpaired; and that as soon as these objects are accomplished the war ought to cease.

The resolution, which passed by a vote of 119-to-2 in the House and (with slight

---

16. In Harry Hansen, *The Civil War: A History* (NY: Signet, 2002), 274–275.

changes of wording) in the Senate by a vote of 30-to-5,[17] demonstrated that it was the sense of Congress, as well as the mind of the President, that in the Temple of Liberty slavery was fully acceptable, whereas refusal to submit to the power of the President and Congress was intolerable.

But the Civil War would morph into something quite other than the dispute with which it began. For the South, the war would become a crusade for the defense of homesteads against the Northern aggression the South itself had provoked with the first acts of war. But for the North, weary of the conflict as an assertion of federal supremacy to "save the Union," a mere jurisdictional space, a new and higher moral cause would be needed to sustain flagging popular support. As the conflict entered its third year and the South—not yet at the end of its limited resources—was proving more difficult to conquer than had been anticipated, Lincoln would find his cause: the "Armageddon-like vision" of the "holy crusade ... to liberate the slaves," to recall Edmund Wilson's phrase.

Northern Tyranny in the Name of Liberty

To vindicate Liberty in its sacred incarnation in the Union, Lincoln exercised to the fullest the framework of power that prior Presidents, especially Jefferson, had already deployed. Indeed, he bent that framework to preserve it, becoming a naked dictator, just as Jefferson had done during his enforcement of the Embargo of 1808–09. Tellingly, during his campaign for the presidency Lincoln had cloaked himself in the memory of his precursor in authoritarian rule: "All honour to Jefferson," he wrote in a famous letter published in the *Cincinnati Daily Gazette*. For it was Jefferson who, "in the concrete pressure of a struggle for national independence ... had the coolness, forecast, and capacity to introduce into a merely revolutionary document, an abstract truth, and so to embalm it there, that today, and in all coming days, it shall be a rebuke and a stumbling block to the very harbingers of re-appearing tyranny and oppression."[18]

There would be no further declaration of independence for the South, however. The "struggle for national independence" in the face of "tyranny and oppression" had ended with the Union to which the South must belong forever. Yet the ultimate absurdity involved in Liberty's incarnation in the Union was that only "tyranny and oppression" could maintain its perpetual existence. An historian as respectful of the Northern position as Professor Morison is forced to admit that "Lincoln wielded a greater power throughout the war than any other President of the United States prior to Franklin D. Roosevelt; a wider authority than *any British ruler between Cromwell and Churchill.* Contemporary accusations against him of tyranny and despotism read strangely to those who know his character, but not to students of

---

17. In Edward McPherson, *The Political History of the United States of America during the Great Rebellion* (NY: Philp & Solomons, 1864), 286. This is a compendium of legislative proceedings and other material prepared by the Clerk of the House of Representatives pursuant to an act of Congress.

18. Lincoln to Henry L. Pierce, et al., April 6, 1859.

his administration. Lincoln came near to being the ideal tyrant of whom Plato dreamed, yet nonetheless *he was a dictator* from the standpoint of American constitutional law."[19]

In defense of Plato, however, it must be said that Lincoln was precisely the sort of tyrant Plato would have condemned in the name of his master Socrates, who was the victim of a morally standardless democracy ruled by sophists. The State that condemned Socrates to death bears no little resemblance to the State that, under Lincoln, killed hundreds of thousands of its own members in the name of "We the People." In Plato's *Gorgias* "it is not Socrates but the State that is on trial," for the degenerate democracy that had taken Socrates' life needed to "be brought into harmony with Socrates' teaching" so as to become the "new spiritual society" for which Plato was seeking—that is, Christendom, as Werner Jaeger and so many other scholars of Greek thought have recognized.[20] Lincoln, then, was no Platonic philosopher king but rather the ruler of what was already a post-Christian nation-state, as even conservative American Protestants were lamenting in the very midst of the Civil War (a development to be taken up in the next section). Lincoln followed to the bitter end none other than Jefferson's dictum that "where the laws become inadequate even to their own preservation . . . the universal resource is a dictator. . . ."

The list of Lincoln's tyrannical acts is seemingly endless. We enumerate here only the keynotes of Lincolnian tyranny: increasing the size of the Army and Navy without a Congressional authorization; the commandeering of the public purse to make military purchases without Congressional appropriations; the suspensions of the writ of habeas corpus even in defiance of Supreme Court decisions to the contrary; the mass arrest and incarceration of suspected enemies of the Union without due process, including the jailing of political opponents without trial; the raids on all the telegraph offices in the Union and the seizure of all telegrams; the censorship and shutting down of the opposition press and the arrest of critics of the administration; the declarations of martial law; the naval blockade of the South, the cutting of railway lines, and the interception of traffic on rivers and canals. All of this was in conjunction with the merciless prosecution of total war against the Confederacy by a massive army of more than 2 million, including 210,000 black soldiers, half freedmen from the North and half escaped slaves from the South. Sheridan's Shenandoah campaign and Sherman's all-but-unopposed "March to the Sea," the completion of his own prophecy of how the war would go, were intended to punish and demoralize entire populations by wrecking the infrastructure of Southern society. By that phase of the war, the dwindling Confederate forces could offer only scattered and purely defensive resistance, as with the trench warfare at Chancellorsville and Fredericksburg.

When even more bodies were needed for hurling into the conflagration, Lincoln demanded and got from Congress precisely what Jefferson had advocated: compulsory conscription. The federal draft in 1863 and 1864, however, produced precious

19. Morison, *HAP*, 658.
20. Jaeger, *Paidea*, 155, 159.

little beyond the huge mass of volunteers already serving. The draft became a mockery as the permitted practice of buying out of it for $300 or hiring a substitute resulted in less than 10% of those selected in the lottery actually serving. The New York draft riots from July 13–16, 1863 were the worst civil disturbance in American history, with burning, looting, and lynching of blacks by Irish immigrants and other rioters who refused to fight in a "nigger war" down South from which the rich had been exempted. (Similar outcomes would follow from the Confederacy's earlier attempt to impose conscription on unwilling masses who saw the war as unwinnable and a threat to the very home and hearth it was supposed to be defending.)

Through it all, however, Lincoln deftly preserved his son Robert from the slaughter, arranging a cushy adjutancy for him with General Grant after his graduation from Harvard, although Robert wanted to see combat. Mrs. Lincoln was "sick with fear" over what might happen to poor Robert. Yet Lincoln knew that in "the shot-torn ranks of the nation's armies" there were "hundreds of thousands of other sons whose mothers loved and feared for them as much as Mary Lincoln did for hers."[21] As we will see in our look at the Confederate approach to conscription, however, the children of the fearless politicians of Liberty on both sides would regularly be spared from its calamities on the battlefield, as were the fearless politicians themselves at every level of government. Dying for Liberty—the Northern or the Southern version—was overwhelmingly the burden of the common soldiers who were supposedly its primary beneficiaries.

The Emancipation Proclamation

On January 1, 1863, Lincoln issued the Emancipation Proclamation, thus purporting to govern America by presidential decree without an act of Congress. It is no longer controversial to observe that Lincoln's aim was not to "free the slaves," but rather to dangle them as bait before the rebel states in the hope of enticing them back into the Union without further hostilities. Thus the Proclamation "emancipated" *only* slaves in the States deemed to be in rebellion, while allowing slavery to continue in the non-rebel states, including Delaware, Maryland, Missouri, West Virginia (newly seceded from Virginia) and Kentucky. The Proclamation's purely strategic aim is evident also from its allowance of the continuation of slavery in Southern areas *already occupied by Northern forces* and thus supposedly "liberated." Why allow slavery to continue in Northern-occupied "free" New Orleans or "free" Norfolk? Because, quite clearly, ending slavery was *still* not really the issue. The issue was still the assertion of federal power, now cloaked in the cause of emancipation. And, conveniently enough, those two port cities were nexuses of the still-ongoing domestic slave trade, with New Orleans being the largest slave market in the country at the time. Slaves were also needed to load and unload non-human cargoes in the Northern-occupied ports, and many were working for the war effort

21. Foote, *The Civil War*, Vol. III, 816.

in Northern factories (at the same time slaves toiled at the manufacture of Southern implements of war at the Tredegar Iron Works in Richmond).

Even more cynically, the Proclamation offered the rebel states a hundred-day window for keeping their slaves without federal interference, so long as within that time they elected representatives to Congress at elections in which a majority of the qualified voters had participated. This show of submission to the federal government would be deemed "conclusive evidence that such state, and the people thereof, are not then in rebellion against the United States." Absent such submission, however, the Proclamation implicitly invited slaves in the rebel states to conduct uprisings now that they had been "emancipated," advising them to "abstain from all violence, *unless in necessary self defense*," and promising that "the Executive government of the United States, including the military and naval authorities thereof, will recognize the freedom of said persons" and receive them "into the armed service of the United States" to fight against the Confederacy.

Professor Morison states the obvious: "This proclamation . . . *freed not one slave*, since it applied only to rebel states where it could not be enforced. The *loyal slave states*—Delaware, Maryland, West Virginia—occupied New Orleans, and occupied parts of Virginia were excepted. The South, indignant at what she considered an invitation to the slaves to cut their masters' throats, was nerved to greater effort; for it meant that only a Southern victory would prevent unconditional surrender."[22] James Webb, a renowned historiographer and former Secretary of the Navy, remarks the preposterous result of this bogus "emancipation":

> [T]he Confederate soldier knew that slave-owners in Delaware, Maryland, Missouri and Kentucky, the slaveholding states that remained in the Union, were allowed to keep their slaves when the war began. This was also true of West Virginia when it broke off from Virginia in 1862 and became a separate state. The consequence of this reality was that in virtually every major battle of the Civil War, *Confederate soldiers who did not own slaves were fighting against a proportion of Union Army soldiers who had not been asked to give theirs up.*[23]

That being the case, what was all the fighting about? Triggered by the slavery issue, it was a war for political and territorial supremacy between the United States of America and the Confederate States of America. But, quite apart from the evil of slavery, no one can deny what the Southern cause became once the invasion by the North began: a defense of home and hearth. The young soldiers, averaging less than twenty-one years of age, who fought so bravely on the side of the Confederacy, laying down their lives by the tens of thousands, could hardly have been motivated solely or even substantially by the issue in which the Southern leadership had found its breach of compact and warrant for secession. As Webb writes: "It is impossible to believe that such men would have continued to fight against unnatural odds—

---

22. Morison, *HAP*, 654.

23. James Webb, *Born Fighting: How the Scots-Irish Shaped America* (NY: Broadway Books, 2004), 223–4.

and take casualties beyond the level of virtually any modern army—simply so that 5 percent of their population who owned slaves could keep them or because they held to a form of racism so virulent that they would rather die than allow the slaves to leave the plantations. Something deeper was motivating them, something that appealed to their self-interest as well."[24] That something deeper was a defense of the homeland against a brutal assertion of power by a government that, indeed, the South had once embraced as a great blessing of Liberty only to find—as Liberty's subjects invariably do—that Liberty was just Power by another name.

Shelby Foote recounts an oft-cited incident in which his Union captors asked a captured Virginia private: "What are you fighting for, anyhow?" The prisoner replied: "I'm fighting because you're down here."[25] In keeping with our commitment to steer between the romantic narratives of both sides, however, we must ask: Yes, but *why* was the North "down there" in the first place? There was only one reason: the secession and first acts of war by the South under the leadership of Southern politicians and the wealthy elites behind them, whose notion of Liberty required a defense of the property right in slaves. Yet this was a property right Lincoln had repeatedly promised to recognize as required by the Constitution itself; and even the Emancipation Proclamation cynically exempted slave states that returned to the Union.

As we will see, the Confederate cause would collapse as the common people of the South realized in growing numbers that the Confederacy could not protect home and hearth, that the continued prosecution of the war was actually a threat to both, and that they were being asked by an increasingly oppressive central government in Richmond to offer the ultimate sacrifice for the sake of a seemingly endless, bloody conflict in which, not being the owners of any slaves, they had no real stake. Then too, many members of the slave-owning class would become disillusioned with the war and withdraw their support.

§

We have examined the Southern and Northern romantic narratives sufficiently to see that they both disguise a war that was essentially yet another struggle over power, property, and territory in the name of Liberty, driven by elites and politicians rather than the mass of common people. It now remains for us to return to the Confederate side of the conflict, where we will see on a smaller scale precisely the tyranny of Lincoln, denounced precisely as such by the Southern opposition— first and foremost Confederate Vice President Alexander H. Stephens. We will see how the Confederacy undermined its own claim to be the true heir of Liberty, how it imploded under the strain of the internal contradictions of its cause, and how the leaders on both sides of the Civil War heaped a vast mountain of bodies on the altar of the Temple to which each side asserted paramount title.

24. Ibid., 223.
25. Foote, *The Civil War*, Vol. I, 65.

15

The South Falls

IN HIS MONUMENTAL three-volume narrative of the Civil War, Shelby Foote, a refined Southern gentlemen from Mississippi who could hardly be accused of Northern sympathies, calmly debunks the myth of the Confederacy as a citadel of "states' rights," "limited government" and assiduous respect for civil liberties. In recounting a speech by Jefferson Davis before the Confederate Congress in 1861, during which the President of the Confederacy denounced the tyranny of the President of the Union, Foote observes the historical reality excluded from the Southern romantic narrative: "Yet even as he spoke, thus stigmatizing his opponent across the Potomac, Davis was faced with the necessity for emulating his 'tyrannous' example."[1]

Southern Tyranny in the Name of Liberty

Edmund Wilson, openly contemptuous of the North's "Armageddon-like" cause, nonetheless observes that "if the Confederacy was really to stand up to the Federal Government, it would have to have recourse to Lincoln's methods, to organize an efficient machine and accept a wartime discipline."[2] That is, in order to defeat what it was fighting, the Confederacy would have to *become* what it was fighting. Writing in the early 20th century, Albert Burton Moore, a Southerner descended from Confederate military officers, remarked the same truth in his landmark study of the colossal problems with compulsory military conscription in the Confederacy:

> The people must, if necessary, submit to the paradoxical logic of establishing the principle of States' rights or decentralization by a process of centralization. . . . The hazy convictions, soon to be clarified and deepened, which gave rise to these acts explain the tame submission of the masses of a proud, brave and high-spirited people to many acts of the Confederate Government that were *scarcely less than despotic.*[3]

---

1. Foote, *The Civil War*, Vol. I, 132.
2. Wilson, *Patriotic Gore*, 425.
3. Albert Burton Moore, *Conscription and Conflict in the Confederacy* (Univ. of South Carolina Press: 1996 [1924]), 4.

Under the banner of Liberty, President Davis and the Confederate Congress exercised extraordinary wartime authority no less severe in principle than Lincoln's, often in disregard of the letter of the Confederate Constitution, approving such measures as military conscription, *ad valorem* taxes on all property, including land and slaves, martial law, impressment of crops and other property for use by the Confederate Army, suspensions of the writ of *habeas corpus*, the banishment of male citizens within Confederate territory who would not declare allegiance to the Confederacy pursuant to the Confederacy's Alien Enemies Act of 1861,[4] summary executions, and mass arrests and imprisonment in Tennessee and elsewhere in order to "save the Confederacy."[5] In short, "the Confederate government enforced the draft, suppressed dissent, and suspended civil liberties and democratic rights at least as thoroughly as did the Union government." Further, "the Confederate army suppressed Unionists with more ruthlessness, especially in east Tennessee and western North Carolina, than Union forces wielded against Copperheads in the North or Confederate sympathizers in the border states."[6] The rationale—wartime necessity—was the same as Lincoln's; the only difference was geographical.

The Pulitzer Prize-winning historian Mark E. Neely, Jr. shows that, unlike in the North, "freedom to travel within the Confederate states was severely limited by a domestic passport system," which is one of the reasons Neely concludes: "The Confederate citizen was not any freer than the Union citizen—and perhaps no less likely to be arrested by military authorities. In fact, the Confederate citizen may have been in some ways less free than his Northern counterpart."[7] Moore's study notes that Governor Joseph E. Brown of Georgia, who became a nemesis of the Davis regime in his defense of "State's rights" against conscription, vehemently protested that there would be no need for a draft if Davis would abolish the internal passport system and end the deployment of provost officers to round up draft dodgers, reassigning to combat duty "the almost countless swarm of young, able-

---

4. See "Proclamation of Banishment," August 14, 1861, issued by President Jefferson Davis to implement the Alien Enemies Act: "I, Jefferson Davis, President of the Confederate States of America, do issue this my proclamation: . . . do hereby warn and require, every male citizen of the United States, of the age of fourteen years and upwards, now within the Confederate States, and adhering to the Government of the United States, and acknowledging the authority of the same, and not being a citizen of the Confederate States, to depart from the Confederate States within forty days. . . . [A]ll persons above described, who shall remain within the Confederate States after the expiration of said period of forty days . . . will be treated as alien enemies. Provided, however, that this proclamation shall not be considered as applicable, during the existing war, to citizens of the United States residing within the Confederate States with intent to become citizens thereof, and who shall make declaration of such intention in due form, acknowledging the authority of this Government. . . ." In Frank Moore, ed., *The Rebellion Record* (NY: G. P. Putnam, 1862), Vol. II, 526.

5. For a discussion of these governmental acts as unwarranted or dubiously warranted by the Confederate Constitution, see David P. Currie, "Through the Looking Glass: The Confederate Constitution in Congress, 1861–1865," *Virginia Law Review*, 90:1257 (2004).

6. James M. McPherson, Gary W. Gallagher, Reid Mitchell, Joseph T. Glatthaar, *Why the Confederacy Lost* (NY: Oxford Univ. Press, 1992), 24–25, Questia Library ed.

7. Mark E. Neely, Jr., *Confederate Bastille: Jefferson Davis and Civil Liberties*, Questia Library ed. (Milwaukee: Marquette Univ. Press, 1993), 16.

bodied officers, who are to be seen in all our railroad stations, and in all our hotels. . . ."[8]

The mythology of the Confederacy as libertarian citadel fails to mention that almost from the war's beginning President Davis was condemned as an enemy of Liberty by his critics in the South no less vehemently than Lincoln by his Liberty-loving critics in the North. Numerous Confederate leaders "repeatedly denounced President Davis as a military despot because of such measures as conscription, impressment, and the suspension of habeas corpus."[9] Among these determined Confederate opponents of the Davis administration were Governor Brown, Confederate Senator William Lowndes Yancey of Alabama, the famed fire-eating "Orator of Secession," Tennessee Representative Henry Foote (former U.S. Senator from Mississippi), Robert Toombs, and no less than Vice-President Stephens himself, who had been a U.S. Representative from Georgia. But then, denunciations of existing authority in the name of Liberty, only to be followed by denunciations of the successor authority in the name of Liberty, should be a familiar pattern at this point in our discussion.

Two of the "statist" aspects of Richmond's war policy ranked foremost among the causes of dissension within the Confederacy. The first was impressment of private property for use by the Confederate army, which provoked early popular outrage against the Davis administration. Small farmers in particular were severely impacted by systematic confiscation of their food crops to feed troops. Newspaper accounts record popular complaints about how "the country is plum full of [Confederate] cavalry. . . . stealing all the time" and how "[t]he Yankees cannot do us any more harm than our own soldiers have done."[10] Meanwhile, wealthy and politically influential planters raising cotton with slave labor escaped economic harm from Richmond, generally failing to keep their promise to divert cotton fields to food production and continuing the "monotonous round of growing more cotton to buy Negroes to raise more cotton."[11] To protect their property during the war, planters would move some 150,000 slaves into the far western reaches of the Confederacy.

The refusal of the planters voluntarily to offer the services of their slaves to the war effort, once it became apparent that the war would not be ending quickly, led the government in Richmond to attempt to impress them as property. The Confederate Congressman from Georgia, Warren Akin, summed up the situation in an oft-quoted remark: "Have you ever noticed the strange conduct of our people during this war? They give up their sons, husbands, brothers & friends, and often without murmuring, to the army; but let one of their negroes be taken, and what a houl [sic] you will hear." Wrote another legislator: "The patriotic planters would willingly put their own flesh and blood into the army, but when you asked them for a

---

8. Moore, *Conscription and Conflict*, 306.

9. Currie, "Through the Looking Glass: The Confederate Constitution in Congress," 90 *Virginia Law Review*, 1257, 1273 (2004).

10. David Williams, *Rich Man's War: Class, Caste and Confederate Defeat in the Chattahoochee Valley* (Athens, GA: Univ. of Georgia Press, 1998), 4

11. Weitz, *More Damning than Slaughter*, 115.

negro, the matter approached the point of drawing an eye-tooth."[12] In June of 1862, scarcely a year after the war began, Mary Chesnut's diary records that "every man is [sic] in Virginia and the eastern part of South Carolina is in revolt because old men and boys are ordered out as reserve corps—and worst of all, sacred property, that is, negroes, seized and sent to work on fortifications."[13]

The planters' reluctance to part with their human property even temporarily was no doubt motivated by the likelihood that it would be returned to them in far worse condition, for impressed slaves "were invariably overworked, underfed, poorly clothed, brutally treated, exposed to enemy gunfire, and given inadequate medical attention," and the period of their impressment often "rendered them almost useless—if not downright dangerous—upon their return to the plantation."[14] Hence Richmond's attempts to impress slaves were met by legal challenges and outright refusals to comply with Richmond's requisitions. "The outrage that such selfishness provoked among Confederate army officers grew exponentially toward the war's end," writes historian Bruce Levine, prompting one Confederate general to call for "Some very severe example such as trial by c[ourt]. m[artial]. and shooting if necessary." General Lee himself would complain that in response to Richmond's requisition of 20,000 slaves for non-combat military details, "not one has yet been received for laboring purposes, and to any inquiries on the subject I get no satisfactory reply."[15]

Confederate Conscription

Even more divisive than government impressment of private property was military conscription. In the heady weeks following the fall of Fort Sumter, Vice President Stephens had boasted that "Lincoln may bring out his 75,000 troops against us," but "We fight for our homes, our fathers, our mothers, our wives, our brothers, sisters, sons, and daughters. . . . We can call out a million of peoples if need be, and if they are cut down we can call another, and still another, until the last man in the South finds a bloody grave."[16] For his part, President Davis uttered what had become a familiar refrain since the colonies threw off King George: the armies of the South, he declared, were "the last hope of liberty."[17] By the spring of 1862, however, only a year after the fall of Fort Sumter, the war had lost its romance, and it was now apparent that it was becoming precisely what the future President Davis had predicted in 1860: "the most sanguinary the world had ever witnessed." In an agrarian society whose *ethos* was rugged individualism and "States' rights," many,

---

12. Leon F. Litwack, *Been in the Storm So Long: The Aftermath of Slavery* (Vintage: 2010, Kindle Edition), 1069–70.

13. Chesnut, *Mary Chesnut's Civil War*, 373.

14. Litwack, *Been in the Storm So Long*, 1071 (Kindle Edition).

15. Bruce Levine, *Confederate Emancipation: Southern Plans to Free and Arm Slaves during the Civil War* (Oxford Univ. Press, USA: 2005, Kindle Edition), 135–37.

16. In *The Rebellion Record*, ed. Frank Moore (NY: G. P. Putnam, 1861), 176.

17. Foote, *The Civil War*, Vol. I, 55.

especially in the border and mountain regions, were already questioning whether the "last hope of liberty" really required that they be slaughtered by the tens of thousands and placed in bloody graves for the sake of a war they had never asked for and which the politicians had promised would be over in a few weeks.

In April of 1862, with the one-year enlistments of the first wave of volunteers about to end, the Confederacy was forced to resort to a draft, passing the First Conscription Act. Since it preceded the equivalent Union measures of 1863, the Conscription Act had the dubious distinction of being the first nationwide military draft in American history—another bitter irony in the trail of ironies that marks the war-filled history of Liberty. The primary object of the Act was a military stop-loss: the one-year voluntary enlistments were converted into mandatory three-year terms, thus providing the basic forces that would sustain the Confederate war effort until it collapsed. All other white men between the ages of 18 and 35 would be subject to the draft for service of three years if President Davis called upon them. Davis was given the power to use state officials to enroll draftees, with the consent of the state governors, and where state officials were not available, the power to use Confederate officers to enforce the draft directly. "In spite of the theory of the independence and sovereignty of the States," writes Moore, the Act "dispensed with the instrumentality of the States in the recruitment of armies . . . it substituted the direct call for the call through the States. . . . [I]t did not harmonize with the individualistic instincts of Southerners and with their conception of genuine manhood."[18]

The conscription scheme would prove largely unenforceable in the face of state and popular resistance, as the Confederate government simply did not have the administrative resources for nationwide enforcement of the draft. Conscription would open a great fault line in the Confederacy, contributing mightily to the divisions that accelerated its disintegration under relentless pressure from the North, with its vastly larger pool of able-bodied men. Conscription altered the spirit of the Confederate war effort: a noble and popular defense of the homeland in the form of the States and localities had become a government-imposed duty to die for a central government in Richmond. A volunteer army of state citizens was effectively converted into a drafted federal army, held to three years of service after its members had honored their one-year commitments and many had already sacrificed their lives.

The Conscription Act marked the beginning of a process of declining morale, class division, resentment over exemptions from the draft, desertion and straggling that steadily eroded the Confederate forces, despite the valiant service of those who stayed and fought to the end. The Union of course had its own problem with desertion on the part of those who saw no compelling reason to engage in a "nigger war" down South. But the North's situation was critically different in one respect: its vastly larger male population allowed the Union Army to absorb the losses from desertion, whereas the Confederate Army simply did not have the men to spare.

---

18. Moore, *Conscription and Conflict*, 13, 16.

One of those who did fight valiantly to the end was Sam R. Watkins of Tennessee, a state sharply divided over secession and the "Southern cause." Watkins survived the battles of Shiloh, Corinth, Perryville, Murfreesboro, Shelbyville, Chattanooga, Chickamauga, Missionary Ridge, Resaca, Adairsville, Kennesaw Mountain, New Hope Church, Zion Church, Kingston, Cassville, Atlanta, Jonesboro, Franklin, and Nashville. Of his company of 120 men, Company H, Watkins was one of only seven survivors by war's end. His memoir *Company Aytch* (for "H" with a Southern drawl) is considered an essential primary source of Civil War history. By the end of 1861, wrote Watkins, he and his fellow soldiers of the First Tennessee Regiment had "found out that the glory of war was at home among the ladies and not upon the field of blood and carnage and death, where our comrades were mutilated and torn by shot and shell." Upon learning that their one-year commitment had been extended to three years, the men of the regiment felt betrayed:

> They had done their duty faithfully and well. They wanted to see their families; in fact, wanted to go home anyhow. . . . War had become a reality; they were tired of it. . . . From this time till the end of the war, the soldier was simply a machine, a conscript. It was mighty tough on the rebels. We cursed the war, we cursed [General] Bragg, cursed the Southern Confederacy. All our pride and valor had gone, and we were sick of the war and the Southern Confederacy.[19]

An early sign of trouble for Confederate conscription was Louisiana's outright refusal to comply with the conversion of one-year volunteers into three-year draftees. Governor Moore released all one-year men from service, declaring: "the law is the law. We kept them 15 months, three months beyond their enlistment."[20] Without any federal-level administrative mechanism to enforce the draft, the Confederacy would find its forces depleted at critical junctures by draft resistance on the part of both individuals and state governments, desertion, straggling, and furloughs from which soldiers never returned. Conscription in the Confederacy "was so unpopular that the government needed lawyers to fend off the suits of those who wished to escape the Confederate ranks."[21]

In yet another of the innumerable ironies of the history of Liberty, the lower courts of the Confederate States consistently granted exemptions from conscription, often on the basis of habeas writs, prompting the Confederate Congress more than once to suspend habeas corpus. But the highest courts of each State consistently ruled in favor of Richmond. Many of the judges on the state high courts had served in the United States district court system (the Confederacy's federal Supreme Court never got off the ground and its federal district courts did little). As former U.S. federal judges, they had little difficulty arriving at perhaps the greatest irony of all: decisions solemnly quoting Justice Marshall and the United States

19. Sam R. Watkins, *Company Aytch* (NY: Touchstone, 2003[1881]), 31.
20. Weitz, *More Damning than Slaughter*, 78.
21. Neely, *Southern Rights*, 57.

Supreme Court and affirming the supremacy of federal law over state law and the direct authority of the Confederate government over the individual citizens of the Confederacy.

Moore cites a telling example: a decision by the Supreme Court of Alabama holding that in the matter of conscription "the claim and call of the Confederate States must prevail over the claim and call of the State government, on the ground that the Confederate Constitution, and laws made in pursuance thereof, *are the supreme laws of the land.*" In like manner, the Mississippi high court declared flatly: "When the Constitution grants Congress and the States power over the same object or person . . . the power of the State is *subordinate to that of the federal government.*"[22] Was federal supremacy over the States the principle for which the South had seceded and for which so many were dying? And given that even *state* courts were defending that principle, what did it portend for the future of the Confederacy were it to survive long enough for its Article III *federal* judiciary to become established as the final arbiter of federal power under a supremacy clause that was a mirror image of that in the United States Constitution?

Confederate conscription was morally compromised and fatally crippled from the start by exemptions which, like those built into the later Northern draft, were designed to favor the wealthy and privileged, including the entire political class presiding over the war effort from Richmond and state and local government offices. The Act, writes Moore, "exempted most of the civil service retinue of the Confederate and State governments and a large number of professional and industrial classes."[23] And, as in the North, a draftee could buy his way out of combat by hiring a substitute, a provision that led to massive fraud as substitutes bid up the prices for their services to obscene levels, only to desert and sign on again as someone else's substitute. By the time it was finally abolished in 1863—far too late to undo the damage—the system of substitution had "produced moral turpitude, popular discontent, and class animosity; it was greatly reducing the fighting strength of the army."[24]

One exemption in particular provoked widespread outrage: that for planters, statutorily defined as the overseers of twenty or more slaves, which led to the measure being ridiculed as the "20-Nigger Law." In his study of the Davis administration's failed attempt to overcome planter resistance to the conscription of slaves, historian Bruce Levine notes that "[e]xempting planters and overseers from conscription antagonized many who had initially rallied to the Confederate cause but who increasingly resented being forced to make what they saw as disproportionate sacrifices on its behalf."[25] This is not the biased assessment of an anti-Confederate liberal scholar but rather a reality widely acknowledged by contemporaneous Southern critics of the government in Richmond. These included not only General

22. Moore, *Conscription and Conflict*, 171–72.
23. Ibid., 16.
24. Ibid., 32–33.
25. Levine, *Confederate Emancipation*, 23.

Lee, but his aide-de-camp, Col. Charles Marshall, whose memoirs yield irrefutable historical evidence of the role that the defense of slavery had played not only in secession and the war but also in skewing the entire framework of law in favor of slaveholders. Slavery, wrote Marshall, "claimed important modifications of the common law governing social relations in favour of slavery, regarding the institution not only as conferring a benefit upon the owner but as something the whole people were bound to support...." For example, he noted, "Slaves were represented in the State legislatures in all the States, being treated as persons for this purpose, while for other purposes, when the interest of the owner required it, they were regarded simply as chattels." As chattels, however, slaves "were not taxed as other property, but an arbitrary value was set upon them, without reference to their actual value," whereas "[a]ll other kinds of property were taxed according to value."[26]

The institutional favoritism toward slaveholders in general and the planter exemption in particular reflected the political reality that had led to secession in the first place: the dominance of the planter elites in the Southern political class. The political clout of slave-owners, writes Levine, "comes through even in the most basic statistical analysis. Simply put, masters dominated government."[27] In *The Impending Crisis*, Hinton Helper observed four years before the Civil War that although non-slaveholding whites comprised seven-tenths of the South's population "[t]he magistrates in the villages, the constables in the districts, the commissioners of the towns, the mayors of the cities, the sheriffs of the counties, the judges of the various courts, the members of the legislatures, the governors of the States, the representatives and senators in Congress—are all slaveholders." Further, "[t]he lords of the lash are not only absolute masters of the blacks, who are bought and sold, and driven about like so many cattle, but they are also the oracles and arbiters of non-slaveholding whites, whose freedom is merely nominal...."[28] That is, Southern-fried Liberty was a rich man's possession and a poor man's burden.

Even allowing for Helper's evident bias and class resentment, what he resented was a sociopolitical fact that fatally undermined the Southern cause. More than ninety percent of Confederate congressmen were slave-owners, and forty percent were large slaveholders as defined by the statutory exemption, even though only five percent of the Southern population owned twenty or more slaves.[29] Colonel Marshall's memoirs located the political origin of the "20-Nigger Law" in precisely the political dominance of the planter class. He admitted that the planter exemption was subject to "the charge of being partial in its operation and conferring a special privilege upon a favoured class..."; and he deplored the injustice that under the exemption even the owners of fifteen slaves were allowed to purchase their way out of combat with a substitute, whereas "persons of smaller means, whose circumstances rendered it very onerous for them to leave their families or their affairs,

26. Charles Marshall, *Lee's Aide-De-Camp*, ed. Frederick Maurice (Lincoln, NE: Univ. of Nebraska Press, 2000), 41–42.
27. Levine, *Confederate Emancipation*, 132–33.
28. In Wilson, *Patriotic Gore*, 371.
29. Levine, loc. cit.

could only avoid being conscripted by purchasing the services of a substitute at a price which they were much less able to pay than the owner of fifteen slaves...." Marshall posed to himself the question: "Why was this peculiar privilege conferred upon this particular class?" and then provided the telling answer:

> In no aspect is the measure defensible on the grounds of expediency. Its explanation is to be sought, I think, in the controlling influence that circumstances had given to the owners of slaves in the management of affairs in the Southern States. They represented a very large proportion of the wealth of the country, were generally better educated, and had more leisure to devote to public affairs than the non-slaveholders, as a class.[30]

Marshall recorded for posterity the effect of the planter exemption on both the army and the people at large:

> The effect of the measure upon the army and upon the people was however very injurious. The Federal Government sedulously endeavoured to inculcate the idea that the war was a slaveholders' war, in which the non-slaveholding people of the South had no interest, *while it was generally agreed by the people of the South that the object of the war was to defend slavery.* It may well be imagined that, in these circumstances, they viewed with surprise, not to say indignation, the exemption of a part of the class of slaveholders from the common burden of the country. This provision of the law was severely commented upon in the army. I heard the remark made that the slaveholders would have to be taught that they owned naught but their slaves, and that *they could not stay at home and send their countrymen to fight their battles.*[31]

In *Company Aytch*, Sam Watkins famously recounts the common, non-slaveholding soldier's contempt for the privileged planter class whose interests they were dying to defend: "A law was made by the Confederate States Congress about this time allowing every person who owned twenty negroes to go home. It gave us the blues; we wanted twenty negroes. Negro property suddenly became very valuable, and there was raised the howl of 'rich man's war, poor man's fight.'"[32] Long-simmering, widespread resentment was also reflected in a complaint received by President Davis in early 1864: "a protest written by 'many soldiers' in 'the ditches' of Georgia who were 'ask[ing] ourselves what we are fighting for.' They, too, were 'tired of fighting for this negro aristockracy [sic],' tired of fighting 'for them that wont fight for themselves.' 'This war and the hardships and dangers must fall on all classes alike or we are determined it shall cease as far as we are concerned....'"[33] This attitude was typical of the deserters who, unlike the stalwart Watkins, would abandon the Confederate cause and return to home and hearth or hide out in the swamps and hills.

30. Marshall, *Lee's Aide-De-Camp*, 40–41.
31. Ibid., 42.
32. Watkins, *Company Aytch*, 31–32.
33. Levine, *Confederate Emancipation*, 24.

Reviewing the sad history of America's military drafts, one commentator observes that the Confederacy's conscription law was "an even greater fiasco" than the Union's, with exemptions for newspapermen, railroad employees, lawyers, school teachers, and druggists, with the result that "schools were established without pupils, and newspapers without readers, while drugstores sprang up everywhere."[34] Nor can this commentator be accused of liberal bias against the Southern cause, for in his definitive work on the subject, Moore, a classic Southern gentlemen and scholar, sketches with evident contempt the ludicrous outcome of the exemption scheme:

> The evidence is irrefutable that there was much fraud connected with exemption, and that many persons secured exemption who had no legal or moral right to it. Men bestirred their wits to engraft themselves onto some of the exempted classes, even at the expense of their accustomed vocations. They turned to teaching, preaching, selling drugs, mining, manufacturing, milling, blacksmithing, wagonmaking, tanning, shoemaking, harnessmaking, salt prospecting, charcoal burning, railroading, carpentering, cattle driving, etc. Amorphous drug stores, county schools, mills, salt pits, impromptu shops and backyard tanneries simultaneously sprang into being. The South only a short while before was lacking in skilled labor, now it was overstocked with mechanical adepts.[35]

And it is Moore who expresses the contempt of a Southern gentleman, not a Union sympathizer, in remarking the righteous hypocrisy of the wealthy and privileged war hawks who avoided a war in which so many of the poor were required to make the ultimate sacrifice on their behalf for the sake of Liberty's "Southern-fried" variant—the "glorious" and "sacred" cause of Southern independence:

> Those who could stay out of the army under color of law were likely to be advocates of a more numerous and powerful army, and were most eloquent expounders of the principle that the war must not cease until the "atrocious foe" had been driven from the sacred soil of the South and a grand and glorious independence had been established. Not so with many of those who were not favored with position and wealth. They grudgingly took up their arms, and condemned the law which had snatched them from their homes, as dear as life itself to them, and forced them to incur the dangerous and onerous burdens of the soldier's life, while their neighbors whose lives and families were not dearer to them were left at home. *The only difference was the circumstance of position and wealth. . . .*[36]

Moore cites a famous letter from one Norman Harrold, a conscript from North

34. Myra McPherson, *Long Time Passing: Viet Nam and the Haunted Generation* (Bloomington: Indiana Univ. Press, 2001), 91.

35. Moore, *Conscription and Conflict*, 111.

36. Ibid., 18–19.

Carolina, which would become a hotbed of resistance to the Confederate White House in Richmond. Never sent, the letter nonetheless sums up the attitude of many conscripts in the upland counties who owned no slaves and did not see what stake they had in the fight with the North. Dripping with bitter sarcasm regarding the Southern narrative of the war as a holy crusade for the highest principles, the letter salutes President Davis as "Czar of all chivalry and Kahn of Cotton Tartery [sic]," announces Harrold's intent to go North, and declares that he "gazes for the last time upon our holy flag—that symbol and sign of an adored trinity, cotton, niggers and chivalry." Harrold concludes with a reference to Davis as "the bastard president of a political abortion."[37]

The prominent anti-Confederate agitator, William "Parson" Brownlow of Tennessee (who would become that state's Reconstruction-era governor), spoke for many when he declared in his newspaper: "The honest yeomanry of these border States, whose families live by their hard licks, four-fifths of whom own no negroes and never expect to own any, are to be drafted—forced to leave their wives and children to toil and suffer, while they fight for the purse-proud aristocrats of the Cotton States, whose pecuniary abilities will enable them to hire substitutes."[38]

Abandoning the Sacred Cause

In short, the Conscription Act, the product of a "wealth-sponsored government,"[39] "removed any doubt that the rich would expect the poor to fight."[40] In the South as well as the North, the Civil War, like all armed conflicts launched in the name of Liberty, was indeed "a rich man's war and a poor man's fight."[41] And by late 1862, the scheme of substitutions and exemptions that made a mockery of Confederate conscription, combined with the slaughters of Confederate soldiers at Shiloh (11,000), Fair Oaks and Seven Pines (6,000), the Seven Days' Battle (20,000), Second Manassas (8,300), South Mountain (2,600) and Lee's astonishingly bloody failed incursion into the North at Antietam (10,000), had not only depleted the Confederate forces but had provoked a rising tide of desertions.

During a debate over the declining condition of the Confederate Army in the Confederate Senate during the late summer and fall of 1862, the subjects under review were General Lee's requests for an expansion of the First Conscription Act "to include all able-bodied men between the ages of eighteen and forty-five" and the appointment of a permanent court martial "with authority to inflict the death penalty in an attempt to reduce straggling and desertion. . . ."[42] During the debates Senator Yancey rose from his seat to protest the Davis administration's policies,

37. Moore, *Conscription and Conflict*, 20–21.
38. Brownlow, "Rise, Progress and Decline of Secession," in Neely, *Southern Rights*, 111.
39. Moore, 50.
40. Weitz, *More Damning than Slaughter*, 78.
41. Neely, *Southern Rights*, 75.
42. Foote, *The Civil War*, Vol. I, 780.

"shouting that if he had to have a dictator, he wanted it to be Lincoln, 'not a Confederate.'" Governor Brown agreed, "declaring that the people had 'much more to fear from military despotism than from subjection by the enemy.'"[43]

The Confederate command in general was encountering what the historian Mark A. Weitz calls "the American practice," which had "existed since the earliest days of organized colonial armies." Composed largely of farmers whose primary allegiance was to land and family—the very things the Confederacy was supposed to be defending from Northern aggression—the "revolutionary armies" of both the first and the second American revolutions were plagued by desertions as many of their members simply went home when it became apparent that the fighting was endangering what mattered most to them. To address the "American practice" General Washington had "insisted on putting deserters to death, claiming that without severe punishment he could not stop the practice." Unable to stem desertions even in his own fiercely loyal Army of Northern Virginia, Lee and the men in his command likewise "had come to realize that shooting deserters held the key to stopping the practice of desertion." As Lee explained to Confederate Secretary of War James Seddon, "he had shot some men in 1862, and then stopped, whereupon desertion immediately increased."[44]

But the Confederacy "over the course of the war . . . wavered between full pardons and executions"[45] for deserters. This intermittent leniency contributed to the failure of conscription. Beyond the initial success at converting the one-year men to three-year men, providing a Confederate army steadily reduced by horrendous casualties, conscription was provoking more desertions and legal escapes from service than it was yielding in new soldiers. "There were able-bodied men at home to replenish the wasted armies," notes Moore, "and the demand for them had become so importunate by the summer of 1863 that thoughtful patriots tried to discover how they had escaped through the meshes of the law." The answer at which the public arrived is that "most of those who were skulking behind were men of wealth for the security of whose rights and interests the war was begun. Those who had a philosophical slant of mind tried to discern what manner of men these were, who could with equanimity of mind and peace of soul enjoy the good things of life while their fellow country-men were enduring the worst tortures for the common defense."[46] General Bragg and seventeen other Confederate Generals issued a joint complaint to President Davis, through the War Office, that the conscription laws had " . . . 'allowed more than 150,000 soldiers to employ substitutes. . . .' And they expressed the honest conviction that not one in a hundred of these substitutes was then in the service."[47]

The problem of desertion combined with the doctrine of state's rights to produce a perfect storm of disunity within the Confederacy. By the end of 1862, writes

43. Ibid.
44. Weitz, *More Damning than Slaughter*, 156–157.
45. Ibid., 6–7, 281.
46. Moore, *Conscription and Conflict*, 38.
47. Ibid., 39–40.

Weitz, "virtually every state saw strong resistance to the draft, and even South Carolina, the birthplace of secession, experienced violent resistance to conscription. The Confederacy was slowly collapsing under the weight of its own conceptual framework."[48] The deteriorating state of affairs, notes Edmund Wilson, is contemporaneously recorded in Mary Chesnut's diary, which chronicles "the fatal incapacity of the Southerners for agreeing or working together" and how "the recalcitrance of the Southerners against any sort of central control, which has led them to secede from Union, is also . . . obstructing their success with the war."[49] Thus did things stand when the end began for the Confederacy at Gettysburg and Vicksburg.

The Beginning of the End

Desertion, euphemistically described as "absenteeism," and straggling, desertion by hanging back in the hope of arriving too late for the next slaughter, had "depleted Lee's army before each of his major invasions into the North." By mid-1863 a veritable "desertion epidemic" had left Lee with "no alternative but to execute deserters without hesitation."[50] By the time of the Battle of Gettysburg on July 1–3, 1863, the Confederate Army had been hobbled by rising desertion and staggering casualties in the battles already mentioned, as well as those at Perryville (3,300), Fredericksburg (5,300), Stones River (11,739), Chancellorsville (13,000), and Champion Hill (4,000). Desertion had been "running rampant in [Lee's] army before and after Gettysburg" and it was Lee "who wanted to shoot these men and cautioned Seddon about being lenient."[51]

At the same time, the Confederate war effort and Southern morale as a whole had been drastically undermined by the devastating loss of Lee's right-hand man, the brilliantly successful and already legendary corps commander Stonewall Jackson, who died of pneumonia after being gravely wounded by friendly fire less than two months before Gettysburg during the Battle of Chancellorsville. That battle is called Lee's "masterpiece" by Civil War enthusiasts who view senseless slaughters as if they were fascinating chess games in which the pieces just happened to be human beings. "One more year of Stonewall would have saved us," wrote Mary Chesnut optimistically.[52] But Jackson simply "could not be replaced, and without this brilliant corps commander Lee was never again able to execute the strategy that had heretofore characterized his operations."[53]

Jackson, however, had (like Lee) depended heavily on the tactic of hurling outmanned regiments at numerically superior forces in "daring" raids, bleeding his army white. Quoting General Lawton, Chesnut brings the deified Stonewall down to earth: "He had shown small sympathy with human infirmity. He was a one-idea-ed

48. Weitz, *More Damning than Slaughter*, 115.
49. Wilson, *Patriotic Gore*, 285.
50. Weitz, op. cit., 150, 160.
51. Ibid., 181.
52. Chesnut, *A Diary from Dixie*, 269.
53. Mark Mayo Boatner, III, *The Civil War Dictionary* (NY: David McKay Company, Inc., 1959), 138.

man. He looked upon broken-down men and stragglers as the same thing. He classed all who were weak and weary, who fainted by the wayside, as men wanting in patriotism. If a man's face was as white as cotton and his pulse so low you scarce could feel it, he looked upon him merely as an inefficient soldier and rode off impatiently. Like the successful warriors of the world, he did not value human life where he had an object to accomplish. He could order men to their death as a matter of course."[54] Lincoln needed such "successful warriors" as much as Davis did, which is why he had removed the comparatively timid General McClellan from his command as general-in-chief of the Union Army and then from the Army of the Potomac. McClellan simply lacked the stomach for the slaughter. As he had confided to his wife after the Battle of Seven Pines: "I am tired of the sickening sight of the battlefield, with its mangled corpses and poor suffering wounded. Victory has no charms for me when purchased at such cost."[55]

Lee too was one of those "successful warriors" who could order men to their death without pause. And he did so at Gettysburg. The enormous casualties there—Lee's second failed attempt to carry the war North—were, objectively speaking, a mortal blow to the Confederate cause, even if Confederate stalwarts did not see it that way at the time. The crowning debacle of that defeat was, of course, Pickett's famous charge on July 3. Despite the "vehement objection" of his lieutenant general, James Longstreet, Lee "was determined to attack again the third day" of the battle.[56] Against Longstreet's advice, he ordered the inexperienced Maj. Gen. George Pickett and two other commanders under Longstreet to lead an advance of some 12,500 men across three-quarters of a mile of open field against an elevated Union position behind a rock wall on the aptly named Cemetery Ridge. The result was a slaughter, with casualties of fifty percent overlapping with 5,000 captured Confederates. "It seemed madness to order a column in the middle of a hot July day to undertake an advance of three fourths of a mile over open ground against the center of that line," wrote Col. E.P. Alexander. And no one knew this better than Lee: "'It's all my fault, I thought my men were invincible,' he told Longstreet the next day, making specific admission that he had been wrong in overruling his chief lieutenant's objection that the charge was about to fail."[57]

What happened to Lee men's at Cemetery Ridge had an eerie equivalence to what had happened to the Union forces at Marye's Heights the previous December during the Battle of Fredericksburg. Some 8,000 Union soldiers were mowed down by cannon and rifle fire as they advanced futilely, one brigade after another, up a slope toward the Confederate position behind a rock wall. In fact, cries of "Give them Fredericksburg! Fredericksburg!" had resounded from the Union ranks as they mowed down the *Confederate* ranks in Pickett's charge. One Sgt. Hirst shouted:

54. Chesnut, 261–62.
55. In David J. Eicher, *The Longest Night: A Military History of the Civil War* (NY: Simon & Schuster, 2001), 279.
56. Boatner, *The Civil War Dictionary*, 337.
57. Foote, *The Civil War*, Vol. II, 569.

"Now we've got you. Sock it to the blasted rebels. Fredericksburg on the other leg!"[58]

Lee now came under attack by the same press that had been beating the drums for secession and war. The *Charleston Mercury* declared that "It is impossible for an invasion to have been more foolish and disastrous." But, as Foote remarks, Lee's men "had been mishandled and they knew it." Even the Chief of the Bureau of War, R.G.H. Kean, lamented that "Gettysburg has shaken my faith in Lee as a general. To fight an enemy superior in numbers at such terrible disadvantage of position in the heart of his [the enemy's] own territory, when the freedom of movement gave him the advantage of selecting his own time and place for accepting battle, seems to have been a great military blunder. . . . God help this unhappy country."[59]

In total, the Battle of Gettysburg had resulted in an astounding 50,000 casualties for both sides combined, with some 28,000 for the Confederacy. "No one," writes Shelby Foote,

> felt the responsibility harder than Lee, though, *far from inaugurating, he had opposed the war at the outset*, when some who were now loudest in their lamentations had called for secession or coercion [preventing secession by force] whatever the consequences, and had allowed themselves to be persuaded that all the blood that would be shed could be mopped up with a congressman's pocket handkerchief; whereas it now turned out that, at the modest rate of a gallon for every dead man and a pint for each of the wounded, perhaps not all the handkerchiefs in the nation, or both nations, could soak up the blood that had been spilled at Gettysburg alone.[60]

Lee's Northern offensive was ended forever. But now even the grand defensive strategy, which had depended on Northern war-weariness to win eventual Southern independence, was failing catastrophically. Two days after Gettysburg, an inadequately defended Vicksburg, Mississippi, under siege since May, fell to Grant's army and 30,000 Confederate P.O.W.s were placed in Union custody.

The defeats at Gettysburg and Vicksburg signaled the objective incapacity of the Confederacy to win the war. The war was by no means over. There would be further Confederate victories, including those at the battles of Cold Harbor and the Crater (a total debacle for the Union), and the outcome for the Union was doubtful until the Battle of Atlanta a year later. But after the summer of 1863, the overall course of the Southern cause was relentlessly downward as the Confederacy's thinning human and material resources began to be exhausted, even if the Confederate command and many in the ranks continued to persuade themselves that God would soon vindicate their holy cause. General Longstreet, however, faced reality early on. After the predictable failure of Pickett's charge he knew "that the army would not recover from this day. . . . He knew that as a good doctor knows it, bending down

58. George C. Rable, *Fredericksburg! Fredericksburg!* (Chapel Hill: Univ. of North Carolina Press, 2002), Prologue, 1.

59. Foote, Vol. II, 642.

60. Ibid., 579.

perhaps for the last time over a doomed beloved patient. 'All that was left now was more dying. It was final defeat.'"[61]

While Vicksburg was under siege by Grant, the Confederate position at Port Hudson on the other side of the Mississippi, near Baton Rouge, was under siege by General Banks. The Union victory there, a week after the fall of Vicksburg, would elevate to martyr status the black soldiers of the 1st Louisiana Native Guards led by André Cailloux. Captain Cailloux, now fighting for the Union side, would die while leading his men during a hopeless assault on the Confederate position. In her account of Cailloux's death, historian Drew Gilpin Faust notes that "[d]espite a truce called to permit the removal of the dead and wounded, rebel sharpshooters prevented Union troops from retrieving the bodies of black soldiers. Cailloux lay on the field until July 8, when Port Hudson surrendered. After forty-one days exposed to the elements, his body could be identified only because of a ring he still wore."[62]

Just how much of a public relations blunder the Confederacy had made in disbanding New Orleans's colored regiment more than a year earlier was shown by Cailloux's funeral: "'immense crowds of colored people' made the streets 'almost impassable'.... Benevolent societies lined Esplanade Street for more than a mile. A parade of fellow soldiers and civic society members accompanied the coffin, draped in an American flag and borne by a hearse pulled by a team of fine horses, to St. Louis Cemetery."[63] The funeral Mass, attended by thousands, was offered by the controversial Father Claude Paschal Maistre, a liberal maverick of abolitionist sentiments who was constantly at loggerheads with the Archbishop of New Orleans, Jean-Marie Odin, a Confederate partisan (but no supporter of slavery). (Odin suspended Maistre, who briefly established an independent congregation; but he was reconciled with Odin's successor, Archbishop Napoleon Perche, who restored him to a parish.[64])

Cailloux had become a martyr-saint in Lincoln's belatedly adopted cause of emancipation. Yet General Butler's successor, Nathaniel Banks, evincing the racism of the North, purged black officers from the Louisiana regiments in keeping with his "aim of winning the support of more white New Orleanians in the wake of Butler's tumultuous tenure."[65] As for Lincoln, it is a testament to the racism and white supremacy of Protestant America as a whole that he penned this hush-hush private response to the Governor of Louisiana to a petition for the right to suffrage for the free blacks of New Orleans, given their "emancipation" by Lincoln himself and the courageous service of blacks during the siege of Port Hudson: "I *barely* suggest for

61. Michael Shaara, *The Killer Angels* (NY: Random House, 1974), 356, 358; in Phillips, *Diehard Rebels*, 91. Shaara's Pulitzer Prize-winning novel draws from Longstreet's memoirs.

62. Drew Gilpin Faust, *This Republic of Suffering* (Vintage: Kindle Edition, 2008), 943–947.

63. Ibid. at 950–53.

64. Stephen J. Ochs, *A Black Patriot and a White Priest* (Baton Rouge: Louisiana State Univ. Press, 2000), 254.

65. Ibid., 156.

your *private* consideration whether *some* of the colored people may not be let in [to the suffrage]—as, for instance, the very intelligent, and especially those who have fought gallantly in our ranks."[66]

With the fall of Vicksburg and Port Hudson, the Union regained total control of the Mississippi River, breaking the geographical backbone of the Confederacy and splitting it in two. Longstreet admitted that the disaster at Gettysburg and the fall of Vicksburg meant for him "that our last hope was gone, and that it was now only a question of time with us." Chief of Ordnance Josiah Gorgas lamented: "Yesterday we rode on the pinnacle of success; today, absolute ruin seems to be our portion. The Confederacy totters to its own destruction." Even President Davis admitted: "We are now in the darkest hour of our political existence."[67] Robert Garlick Hill Kean, the fire-eater from Alabama who was head of the War Bureau, reported that "steadfastness is yielding to a sense of hopelessness of the leaders."[68] "We are without doubt gone up; no help can be had," wrote the staunch Confederate Congressman Dargan from Alabama. "The failure of the Government to reinforce Vicksburg, but allowing the strength and flower of the Army to go north, where there could be but one fate attending them, has so broken down the hopes of our people that even the little strength yet remaining can only be exerted in despair."[69] One prominent planter lamented: "Vicksburg is gone and as a consequence Mississippi is gone, and in the opinion of allmost [sic] every one here the Confederacy is gone." Gen. E. Kirby Smith, commander of the trans-Mississippi Confederate forces reported that "The people, particularly in Arkansas and Louisiana, [were] lukewarm, dispirited, and demoralized [and] to a great extent prepared for returning to their allegiance" to the Union.[70]

While there is no denying the fierce loyalty of many Southerners to the cause of Southern independence that the war became after it had been launched by the conflict over slavery, especially the men in Lee's army, there is also no denying "the admittedly impressive evidence of disaffection and disillusionment from the summer of 1863 forward . . . indicat[ing] a complex mood of deepening gloom punctuated by desperate bursts of hope" and over all a "loss of will" to continue the fight.[71] Gettysburg and the related fall of Vicksburg had been the equivalent of Napoleon's Russian campaign: the fatal misstep in Lee's brilliant career, the turning point in a war that Lee had never wanted and had rightly predicted would ultimately "yield nothing" for the South. Exhausted and debilitated by what he did not

---

66. Ibid., 189–90.

67. Foote, Vol II, 641–642.

68. In Bruce Levine, *Confederate Emancipation: Southern Plans to Free and Arm Slaves during the Civil War* (Oxford Univ. Press, USA, Kindle Edition), 21.

69. Foote, *The Civil War*, Vol. II, 652.

70. Gary W. Gallagher, *The Confederate War: How Popular Will, Nationalism, and Military Strategy Could Not Stave Off Defeat* (Cambridge, MA: Harvard Univ. Press, 1997), 44, and James M. McPherson, "American Victory, American Defeat," in *Why the Confederacy Lost*, ed. Gabor S. Boritt (NY: Oxford Univ. Press, 1992), 15–42; both cited in Levine, *Confederate Emancipation*, 178.

71. Levine, *Confederate Emancipation*, 178.

yet know were the sequelae of a heart attack, Lee offered to resign in favor of a younger man, but Davis rejected the offer.

Nonsense at Gettysburg

On November 19, 1863, Lincoln traveled to Gettysburg to deliver his immortal address. Uttering not one word about the abolition of slavery as a *casus belli*, Lincoln enunciated the real reason so many had to die:

> Four score and seven years ago our fathers brought forth on this continent, a new nation, *conceived in Liberty,* and dedicated to the proposition that all men are created equal. Now we are engaged in a great civil war, testing whether that nation, or any nation so conceived and so dedicated, can long endure. . . . [W]e here highly resolve that these dead shall not have died in vain—that this nation, under God, shall have a new birth of freedom—and that government of the people, by the people, for the people, shall not perish from the earth.

The Civil War was waged for *Liberty,* in which the nation had been "conceived." Liberty required preservation of the nation that was the fruit of its womb, and preservation of "the nation" meant that no state could be allowed to defy the Lockean "supreme authority" of the national government, no matter how many had to die, no matter how much devastation had to be inflicted. What the Tory pamphleteer Thomas Chandler had predicted back in 1775 was precisely what was happening in 1863: "till one part of this country shall have subdued the other . . . this peaceful region must become, and continue to be, a theater of inconceivable misery and horror."

Commenting on the Gettysburg Address at the very height of the "Lincoln legend," the irrepressible Mencken did not hesitate to remark the absurdity of what Lincoln had done in the name of Liberty:

> But let us not forget that it is oratory, not logic; beauty, not sense. Think of the argument in it! Put it into the cold words of everyday! The doctrine is simply this: that the Union soldiers who died at Gettysburg sacrificed their lives to the cause of self-determination—"that government of the people, by the people, for the people," should not perish from the earth. It is difficult to imagine anything more untrue. The Union soldiers in that battle actually fought against self-determination; it was the Confederates who fought for the right of their people to govern themselves. . . . *Am I the first American to note the fundamental nonsensicality of the Gettysburg address?* If so, I plead my æsthetic joy in it in amelioration of the sacrilege.[72]

Putting aside Mencken's acceptance of the illusory Lockean notions of "self-determination" and the "right of people to govern themselves," his point is well taken. The Gettysburg Address does indeed mask nonsense: "freedom" delivered at

---

72. Mencken, *Prejudices,* 175.

the point of a gun. But it should be exceedingly obvious at this point in our long discussion that Liberty itself is nonsense: the call for the violent overthrow of all established authority as "tyrannical," followed by the claim that Liberty demands perpetuation of the newly established authority by force, or its overthrow by force as yet another "tyranny." The same nonsense had been preached by politicians and propagandists on both the Northern and Southern sides of the conflict, with the common man paying the price in blood, as always.

In a speech a year after the Gettysburg Address, Lincoln could not have been more explicit on the point. The war, he admitted, "has deranged business... destroyed property and ruined homes; it has produced a national debt and taxation unprecedented, at least in this country; it has carried mourning to almost every home, until it can almost be said that the 'heavens are hung in black.'" But the past three years of death and devastation would not change either Lincoln's or Davis's course, for as Lincoln put it in words that Davis could have uttered: "We accepted this war for an object, a worthy object, and the war will end when that object is attained." For Lincoln, the object was "restoring the national authority over the whole national domain, and for the American people, as far as my knowledge enables me to speak, I say we are going through on this line if it takes three years more."[73] For Davis the object was establishing the authority of a *new* domain, the Confederate States of America as an independent sovereign: "we are fighting for INDEPENDENCE, and that, or extermination, we *will* have.... The war came, and now it must go on until the last man of this generation falls in his tracks, and his children seize the musket and fight in our battle."[74] But as of the date of the Gettysburg Address, the domain over which Davis presided was already falling to pieces.

Seceding from the Secession

Even before the Gettysburg Address, Davis had written to Lee in late July of 1863 to confide that "this war can only be successfully prosecuted when we have the cordial support of the people," but that "[I]n various quarters there are mutterings of discontent, and threats of alienation are said to exist, with preparation for organized opposition." Robert Toombs, the one-time Confederate Secretary of State who had warned Davis more than two years earlier that the firing on Fort Sumter "will inaugurate a civil war greater than any the world has yet seen... it is suicide, murder," was now reported to be "ready for another revolution, and curses everything Confederate from the President down to the horse boy."[75]

Vice President Stephens was also "'ready for another revolution' whose cause would be the same as the First and Second, staged respectively in 1776 and 1861:

73. "Speech at a Sanitary Fair in Philadelphia," June 16, 1864, in *Abraham Lincoln: His Speeches and Writings*, ed. Roy P. Basler (Cleveland, OH: World Publishing, 1946), 752.

74. Rhodes, *History of the United States*, Vol. IV, 515.

75. Foote, Vol. II, 647–49.

both of which, as Stephens saw it, had been betrayed." For Stephens the primary foe was now exactly what the Confederacy was supposed to have escaped: "the Demon of Centralism, Absolutism, Despotism. Away with the idea of getting our independence first, looking after liberty afterward. Our liberties, once lost, may be lost forever."[76] Of like mind was Congressman John P. Murray of Tennessee: "This is the people's revolution, and they will tolerate no subversion of their ancient liberties. . . . [I have] never understood that political doctrine that teaches that in order to get liberty you must first lose it. . . ."[77] Murray apparently did not grasp the essence of the history of Liberty. Concerning the Conscription Act, Governor Brown protested: "No act of the government of the United States prior to the secession of Georgia struck a blow at constitutional liberty so fell as has been stricken by the conscription act."[78] South Carolina Senator William Boyce wrote to Davis to protest: "Is not our Federal Government in the exercise of every possible power a national central military despotism? . . . Indeed, if you were appointed Military Dictator, what greater powers could you exercise than you now do? . . ."[79] Boyce went on to offer an assessment of Richmond's policies that called into question the entire basis for secession and war:

> The truth is, that the Government at Washington *has not dared to exercise power on the grand scale that our Government has.* The Lincoln Government has not ventured to resort to an effective conscription; it has not resorted to taxation as we have; it has no tax in kind; it does not prohibit imports; it does not monopolize the exports; it does not rely on impressments. It plays the tyrant, but it hesitates to seize the sceptre.[80]

The opinions of these leaders, writes Foote, "made waverers of many among their listeners who had been steadfast up to then, and defeatists of those who were wavering already."[81] The people were "[p]rofoundly shaken by the double defeat of Gettysburg and Vicksburg, and [they] looked to their leaders for reassurance. From some they got it, while from others all they got was 'I told you so'—as indeed they had, with a stridency that increased with every setback."[82] During the elections of 1863, disillusioned voters swept large numbers of secessionist politicians from office, replacing them with Unionist Whigs who, while still committed to the war effort, had argued against secession in 1861 and were now perceived as wiser heads, better entrusted with the fate of the Confederacy than reckless fire-eaters. The people "turn[ed] instinctively to those old leaders, who foretold their present situation, for counsel and instruction."[83] An editorial in the *Milledgeville Confederate Union* of

76. In Wilson, *Patriotic Gore*, 426.
77. In Beringer, *Elements of Confederate Defeat*, 132.
78. Moore, *Conscription and Conflict*, 256, 279.
79. Beringer, et al., *Why the South Lost the Civil War*, 289–90.
80. Boyce to Davis, September 29, 1864, reprinted in *The New York Times*, October 24, 1864.
81. Foote, *The Civil War*, Vol. II, 648–49.
82. Ibid., 652.
83. Beringer, *The Elements of Confederate Defeat*, 13 (internal quotation omitted).

Georgia summed up this voter sentiment: "We are learning by bitter experience that hotspurs and demagogues are unfit to govern a country. Such men brought us into trouble, and seem to be incapable of taking us out. They were suffered to lead the country in 1861, and none of the blessings they predicted have been realized, while most of the evils apprehended by more considerate men have to come to pass."[84]

The secessionist politicians who were overwhelmingly representatives of the planter class had assured the people that secession was essential to the defense of Southern liberty, but the subjects of the Confederacy were discovering anew that Liberty is just another name for Power. And now the Protestant dynamic of Liberty—rebellion, followed by dissension from the leaders of the rebellion, followed by more rebellion—was tearing apart the Confederate States of America. Invoking the memory of the first of the great Protestant rebels, Mary Chesnut wrote in her diary that "Martin Luther had a right to protest and free himself from the thralldom of the Roman Catholic Church, but [then] everybody began to protest against Luther—as it seemed good to them—freely exercising their right of private interpretation—!... Seceding can go on indefinitely with the dissatisfied seceders."[85] And how could it be otherwise within a political framework arising from a Lockean application of the Protestant "right of private interpretation" to the question of sovereignty back in 1776?

Chesnut's "dissatisfied seceders"—the Calvins, Zwinglis, Bucers and Melancthons of the Confederacy—were multiplying daily. The "increasingly forthright opposition to the central government by regional States Rights leaders" was accompanied by "the formation and expansion of societies dedicated to sabotage of the entire confederate effort...."[86] In the "Appalachian chain of discontent," where "masses of ordinary folk [had] opposed the Confederacy from the very beginning,"[87] secret societies such as the Heroes of America and the Sons of America began to mount organized para-military resistance to the government in Richmond. Far more than a few cowards running from the field of battle, their members, writes Foote, were predominantly

> natives of a mountainous peninsula more than a hundred miles in width and six hundred miles in length, extending from the Pennsylvania border, southwest through western Virginia and eastern Tennessee, down into Northern Georgia and Alabama. Owning no or few slaves, and indeed not much of anything else in the way of worldly goods, a good portion of these people wanted no part of "a rich man's war and a poor man's fight."[88]

Eastern Tennessee provided the most prominent example of how common people simply refused to acknowledge that a Confederate government created out of thin air by wealthy elites in Richmond had the authority to remove them from the

84. *Milledgeville Confederate Union*, August 25, 1863, in *Why the South Lost*, 277.
85. Chesnut, *Mary Chesnut's Civil War*, 121.
86. Foote, *The Civil War*, Vol. II, 652.
87. Beringer, et al. *Why the South Lost the Civil War*, 74.
88. Foote, *The Civil War*, Vol. II, 651.

Union, rule over them, and draft their sons for military service. The Unionists of East Tennessee conducted an underground resistance "comparable to that demonstrated in Nazi-occupied Europe or French-occupied Algeria," burning bridges, cutting telegraph lines, and training a veritable "army of liberation" in Kentucky. As early as the fall of 1861, Richmond was forced to commit an occupying army of 11,000 men to the eastern counties of Tennessee in order to keep them in the Confederacy, but "[t]he most strenuous Confederate efforts at pacification failed to suppress these dedicated Unionists, and East Tennessee remained a cancer in the vitals of the Confederacy."[89] In the Confederacy, too, Liberty had to be imposed at the point of a gun on those to whom its benefits were far from apparent.

As the war wore on throughout 1863, events "validated Lee's prediction to [Secretary of War] Seddon that executing deserters might not be enough, that more drastic action would be required." General Pillow told Seddon that the number of deserters "had become so great that they could not shoot them all."[90] According to the assistant secretary of war, "fifty to a hundred thousand southern soldiers were absent without leave after the fall of Vicksburg and the Gettysburg defeat. 'The Confederacy wants more men,' wrote Captain Samuel T. Foster, of the 24th Texas Cavalry, of Patrick Cleburne's division. 'Lee wants men. Bragg wants men. They are wanted everywhere; but where are they to come from?'"[91] The situation was made immeasurably worse by Bragg's humiliating defeat after winning the Battle of Chickamauga in September of 1863. Having routed General Rosecrans's army and laid siege to Chattanooga, in November he was routed in return during the Battle of Missionary Ridge by 75,000 Union reinforcements that overwhelmed his army and drove it into a panicked retreat from what should have been a commanding position on the ridge. "The humiliation plunged the Army of Tennessee's morale to new depths and forced Bragg to resign his command."[92]

The Cleburne Memorial

On January 2, 1864, Maj. Gen. Patrick Cleburne provided a devastatingly frank assessment of the Confederacy's position in a famous memorandum to General Johnston, commander of the Army of Tennessee. Cleburne was no defeatist, but a bona fide hero of the Confederate Army. An Irish immigrant to America who had left Ohio to join the Confederate cause, he had been wounded in the face at the Battle of Richmond and would be killed at the Battle of Franklin in November. He had led his division brilliantly against the Union forces at the Battle of Stones River, earning promotion to major general in December of 1863. Cleburne had become known as the "Stonewall of the West," and Lee called him "a meteor shining from a

89. Kenneth M. Stampp, *The Southern Road to Appomattox* (El Paso, TX: Univ. of Texas Press, 1969), 19.

90. Weitz, *More Damning than Slaughter*, 160.

91. In Levine, *Confederate Emancipation*, 24.

92. Levine, *Confederate Emancipation*, 27.

clouded sky."[93] But Cleburne's "Memorial" (memorandum) painted a dire future for the Confederacy and ended his own chances for promotion:

> We have now been fighting for nearly three years [and] have spilled much of our best blood, and lost, consumed, or thrown to the flames an amount of property equal in value to the specie currency of the world. . . . [But] the fruits of our struggles and sacrifices have invariably slipped away from us and left us nothing but long lists of dead and mangled. Instead of standing defiantly on the borders of our territory or harassing those of the enemy, we are hemmed in today into less than two-thirds of it, and still the enemy menacingly confronts us at every point with superior forces. . . .
>
> Our soldiers can see no end to this state of affairs except in our own exhaustion; hence, instead of rising to the occasion, *they are sinking into a fatal apathy*, growing weary of hardships and *slaughters which promise no results*. In this state of things it is easy to understand why there is a growing belief that some black catastrophe is not far ahead of us, and that unless some extraordinary change is soon made in our condition we must overtake it.
>
> The consequences of this condition are showing themselves more plainly every day; restlessness of morals spreading everywhere, manifesting itself in the army in a growing disregard for private rights; *desertion spreading to a class of soldiers it never dared to tamper with before*; military commissions sinking in the estimation of the soldier; our supplies failing; our firesides in ruins.[94]

Equally devastating was Cleburne's recognition that the happy and contented slaves of the Confederate romance advanced by Davis and Stephens were in fact defecting to the Union in large numbers and betraying the Confederate Army. With the approach of the Union forces, the masters were finding "every household surrounded by spies" who were providing the Union with intelligence concerning "our valuable men . . . our positions, purposes and resources. . . ." The male slaves had become "recruits awaiting the enemy with open arms. . . ." Cleburne warned that if the slaves were not emancipated in return for fighting on the side of the Confederacy, then slavery would continue to be, not the Confederacy's supposed strength, but "one of our chief sources of weakness." The Confederate Congress, dominated by wealthy planters, would reject Cleburne's idea when it was finally presented to them as proposed legislation, resisting to the bitter end the emancipation of their human property and belying the Southern narrative of a war for Southern liberty having nothing to do with the preservation of chattel slavery.

93. Craig L. Symonds, *Stonewall of the West: Patrick Cleburne and the Civil War* (Lawrence, KS: Univ. of Kansas Press, 1997), 158.

94. In *The War of the Rebellion, A Compilation of the Official Records of the Union and Confederate Armies*, Series I, Vol. 52, Pt. 2, 586–592; Cornell University archival text at http://ebooks.library.cornell.e du/m/moawar/text/waroo110.txt. Hereafter "Official Records."

A Civil War Within A Civil War

After the Cleburne Memorial reached President Davis and his Cabinet, the order was issued to General Johnston "to suppress 'not only the memorial itself, but likewise . . . all discussion and controversy respecting or growing out of it.'"[95] While the document could be suppressed, the decomposition of the Confederate cause could not. By the end of 1863, "deserters had established themselves in all eleven Confederate states as quasi-military forces to be reckoned with" and had "literally become the third army in the American Civil War, turning the conflict into a two-front war for the Confederacy." Roving deserter bands "staked out large areas of the Confederacy from Virginia to Texas" and by 1863—still a year before Sherman's criminal March to the Sea—"the rhetoric of the 'Union invader' ravaging civilians in the South paled in comparison with the reality of Confederate deserters, unable to reach home or with no home to return to, preying on civilians."[96]

There were little secessions-from-the-secession in state after state, as deserter bands established primitive functioning governments in Alabama, Virginia, North Carolina, South Carolina, Texas, and Mississippi. Some deserter organizations were "literally negotiating with the government for terms to keep them from killing Southerners" in the midst of what had become "a civil war within a civil war."[97] Much of Georgia had always been pro-Union, and northern Georgia had actually sent companies to join the Union army; now its mountain region was becoming a deserter haven. In Florida, deserters even won elections for justice of the peace and the county commissioner's court in the fall of 1863, prompting Florida's governor to observe that the situation in his state amounted to "reconstruction of the United States government." The same thing happened in southwestern Virginia, where a deserter organization ran winning candidates for sheriff and justice of the peace. The whole of Southern Mississippi was under the control of deserters.[98]

In February 1864 Lincoln called up 500,000 more men, then in March 200,000 more. In response, all the Confederacy could do was lower and raise the draft age to 17 years and 50 years, "robbing thus the cradle and the grave, as some complained, or as Davis put it, regarding the half-grown boys about to be drafted and thrown into the line, 'grinding the seed corn of the nation.'"[99] Tens of thousands had left the Confederate army via desertion or medical and family furloughs from which they never returned. Another exit strategy was a return to allegiance to the Union under the North's offer of full amnesty with no obligation of military service in the Union army in return for the taking of an oath to the United States and a laying down of arms—in essence, early surrender on an individual basis. Even if the official Confederate figure of 104,000 desertions for the total army during the war is accepted at face value—and the number was undoubtedly far higher—it represents

---

95. Levine, *Confederate Emancipation*, 28.
96. Weitz, *More Damning than Slaughter*, 183, 188, 208.
97. Ibid., 194, 200, 206, 207, 210.
98. Ibid., 163, 200, 208, 213.
99. Foote, *The Civil War*, Vol II., 124–125.

a desertion rate "higher than for any previous American war" or for any American war thereafter.[100] And this rising tide of desertion embraced far more than the simple cowards who had mostly turned tail early. As the war dragged on, especially by late 1864, what prompted desertion was more often simply that, even in Lee's exemplary and fiercely loyal army, desertion "was an easy decision to make, a choice between a wretched existence in the army for no compelling reason and an uncertain future that at least represented a better chance for survival."[101]

Stephens versus *Davis*

With Atlanta having fallen in September and Sherman marching virtually unopposed toward Savannah and the sea, the Confederacy was coming apart under the pull of home and family combined with an unsustainable tension between the spirit that had led to secession—the Spirit of 1776—and the demands of the central government in Richmond. And no one had been more prominent in exposing that tension than the very Vice President of the Confederacy. Alexander Stephens was, to the bitter end, a man of principles. Edmund Wilson observes that with Stephens the "case against Lincoln as the founder of a centralized state" was no "mere piece of partisan rationalizing," for "[h]e had resisted the 'despotism' of Jefferson Davis as uncompromisingly as he had that of Lincoln." And Wilson wonders whether Stephens was right; for Southerners "had fought against the British Crown; they had fought against the dictatorship of Lincoln; why should they not repudiate their own President when he sought to become a dictator too?"[102] What Wilson does not seem to notice, however, is the very point of this study. This continuing fight against tyranny had led inexorably to the very outcome those who fought it professed to decry from the time they overthrew King George: more government than ever before, proclaimed nonetheless as a great advance for Liberty.

As Stephens explained in his post-war apologia, he had vehemently opposed Richmond's impressment of private property, the suspensions of the writ of habeas corpus, and, above all, conscription as "not only radically wrong in principle, but as violative of the [Confederate] Constitution, and as exceedingly injurious to our Cause in their effects upon the people." Ignoring the fact that the First Conscription Act had converted one-year volunteers into mandatory three-year enlisted men who were effectively draftees, Stephens insisted that "Richmond was not saved by conscription . . ." but rather that Lee had won his early brilliant victories with an army "composed chiefly, and almost entirely, of volunteers already enlisted. . . ."[103] In short, Stephens rejected the reality that, as Wilson writes, "if the Confederacy was really to stand up to the Federal Government, it would have to have recourse to

---

100. Weitz, 14.

101. J. Tracy Power, *Lee's Miserables: Life in the Army of Northern Virginia from the Wilderness to Appomattox* (Chapel Hill: Univ. of North Carolina Press, 1998), 307.

102. Wilson, *Patriotic Gore*, 425.

103. Stephens, *A Constitutional View*, Vol. II, 570–71.

Lincoln's methods. . . ." That is, the Confederacy would have to become the South-ern-fried equivalent of the Union. But the argument that the rights of the individ-ual Confederate States could be defended only by their submission to centralized authority, particularly in the matter of conscription, was no longer sufficiently per-suasive to sustain the war effort, if it ever was. Typical of the disillusionment of state officials is the declaration by Louisiana's chief of ordnance: "The government can no longer protect the citizenry and they should at least be left in the best possi-ble condition to take care of themselves."[104]

Throughout 1864, Davis's popularity was plummeting, and by early 1865 some of the States in the Confederacy considered calling conventions to depose Davis, while the *Richmond Examiner,* flagship of the opposition press, openly called for a military dictatorship under General Lee, who rejected both plans.[105] Stephens, who had returned to Richmond from his self-imposed absence to preside over the Confederate Senate, formed a triumvirate of opposition to the Davis administra-tion with his friend and ally Governor Brown and Governor Zebulon Vance of North Carolina. Confederate historian Moore, being after all a Southern partisan, derides Stephens as one who "could see the ghost of despotism stalking abroad." Governor Vance is depicted as "the most dangerous man with whom Davis had to deal" because of his "masterly leadership of untutored, provincialistic, and suspi-cious peasant farmers of North Carolina. . . ." Moore meant yeoman farmers, who owned no slaves but had wives and children they preferred not to leave behind in order to lend their bodies to an increasingly pointless slaughter mandated by Rich-mond in the South's losing analogue of the North's winning crusade for Liberty. Both Brown and Vance, according to Moore, were the "twin Nemeses" of Davis, "unbending States' rightists in principle [who] were admirably equipped to tor-ment the souls of the military strategists at Richmond." The two were "like divinely ordained sentinels upon the isolated peak of particularistic patriotism . . . preach-ing with equal skill two sermons for State protection: one against the devastating swords of the Federal troops; the other against the compressing tentacles of the 'insatiable political octopus' at Richmond."[106]

But what of the "divinely ordained sentinels" of Liberty in a Confederate Con-gress controlled by planters, who, as Lee so famously complained, "do not seem to be able to do anything except to eat peanuts and chew tobacco, while my army is starving"? What of the "divinely appointed sentinels" of Liberty among the press, the politicians, and the state conventions whose members had voted for secession to protect the property right in slaves, launching a war for which the South was woefully unprepared on behalf of a wealthy planter class that had exempted itself and its property from the conflict? Vance and Brown and the other governors who resisted conscription were "guilty" of placing the survival of their states before the survival of a Confederate government that had not even existed before 1861. But

104. Weitz, *More Damning than Slaughter,* 272.
105. Moore, *Conscription and Conflict,* 337.
106. Ibid., 270, 295–96.

was not "my sovereign state first" the very principle for which the Confederacy had supposedly been fighting?

Furthermore, in a Confederacy that had arisen from an alleged breach of the Lockean compact regarding the eminently Lockean property right in slaves owned by a few, what about the compact between the Confederacy and its citizens to defend the common man's far more elemental property right to home and hearth? Was it morally wrong for those Moore disparages as "provincialistic and suspicious peasant farmers" in North Carolina to conclude, after years of "slaughters which promise no results," to recall Cleburne's phrase, that it was time for the bloodletting to stop because "killing or wounding Union soldiers was not putting food on their tables at home or clothing their families"?[107] It was not so much an ephemeral Confederate nationalism that failed, although it did fail. Rather, as Weitz concludes, "it was the government and the rich."[108] Nowhere was this truth more apparent than in the Confederacy's last-gasp attempt to provide for the conscription of slaves.

Thinking the Unthinkable

As the war dragged on throughout 1864, the South was bled dry of its willing white male populace. The conscription of slaves had been floated throughout the war, but as Levine notes in his important study of this question: "[t]he masters' domination of southern politics helps explain why the War Department had spurned suggestions about arming slaves throughout the first three and a half years of the conflict. . . ."[109] That and the deeply ingrained Southern belief in the "natural subjugation" of the black race as a "cornerstone" of Southern civilization, to recall Stephens's infamous and never-retracted but rather adamantly defended Cornerstone Address. Accordingly, President Davis had "resisted the notion throughout the war, thinking it at first unnecessary and later impractical, not to mention that it tended to undermine the institution of slavery itself, *the very foundation of their cause*. . . ." It was for this reason that Davis had "tried to prevent widespread knowledge of the petition from Cleburne. . . ."[110]

By the fall of 1864, however, Davis had already seen that there was no choice but to propose Cleburne's unthinkable idea to the Confederate Congress. Atlanta had fallen, Lee's army was under siege by Grant's in Petersburg-Richmond, Sherman was plundering his way toward Savannah, and Lincoln's reelection had crushed hopes for a new war policy in Washington. The War Bureau was reporting that "a vast number of deserters were at large and were so bold that they did not go to the trouble to hide themselves."[111] The attempt to draft men between the ages of seventeen and fifty pursuant to the Conscription Act of February 16, 1864 had failed dismally. There were simply no more white men to be drafted, and those that had

---

107. Weitz, *More Damning than Slaughter*, 125.
108. Weitz, 293.
109. Levine, *Confederate Emancipation*, 133.
110. William C. Davis, *Jefferson Davis: the Man and His Hour*, 597.
111. Moore, *Conscription and Conflict*, 338.

deserted could not be rounded up. Even among those remaining in service, the utter futility of the war was so apparent that many spoke openly of leaving the ranks to go home, as if no one could doubt the reasonableness of their decision. Three such unfortunates interrupted Nathan Bedford Forrest's breakfast with the advice that they had decided to return to their homes and families. He had them executed on the spot.[112]

Hence in an address to the Confederate Congress on November 7, Davis now argued for "a radical modification in the theory of the law." By this he meant the government's outright purchase of slaves from their owners for service as non-combatants, or even as combatants in extreme necessity, followed by emancipation of the slave conscripts in return for "faithful service" in the war.[113] The address, which had only intimated the idea of enlisting slaves as full-fledged soldiers, provoked a storm of outrage "throughout the South from both slave-owners and non-slave-owners."[114] Collating many examples of the opposition, Levine shows that it was

> not only powerful but also broadly based, attracting support from across the Confederacy's political spectrum. Vociferous opponents included founders of the Confederacy, prominent army officers, state governors, members and former members of the president's cabinet, and leaders of both the Senate and House of Representatives. It embraced former Whigs, such as Charles C. Langdon, the ex-mayor of Mobile, and congressmen Thomas S. Gholson of Virginia, James T. Leach of North Carolina, and William G. Swan of Tennessee. It also boasted a great many long-time Democrats, including Mississippi congressman Henry C. Chambers and Georgia's Howell Cobb, who at one time or another served as governor, speaker of the U.S. House of Representatives, U.S. secretary of the treasury, chairman of the February 1861 convention that founded the Confederate government, and general in the Confederate army. The opposition included both prewar secessionist firebrands and people who had resisted secession until the last minute.[115]

Among the sources Levine cites are the *Macon Telegraph and Confederate*, which reminded Congress of why the South seceded and went to war: "Was it not to prevent the destruction of slavery and its manifold economic, political, and social consequences that the South had opted first for secession and then for war?" *The Memphis Appeal* argued that the war was "occasioned ... more by the institution of negro slavery [than] by any other subject of quarrel. For it [slavery] and its perpetuation we commenced and have kept at war." It was, noted the *Charleston Mercury*, "the mere agitation in the Northern States to effect the emancipation of our slaves that largely contributed to our separation from them." The *North Carolina Standard* protested that this "proposition surrenders *the great point upon which the two*

112. Phillips, *Diehard Rebels*, 152.
113. Davis, *Rise and Fall*, Vol. I, 515.
114. Levine, *Confederate Emancipation*, 34.
115. Ibid., 41.

sections went to war." The *Lynchburg Republican* declared that if the slaves were to be emancipated, "then the Confederacy will have proven 'not worth one drop of the precious blood which has been shed in its behalf.'" [116]

Yet only days before, the *Richmond Enquirer* had supported the desperate measure in an editorial arguing that "The conscription of negroes should be accompanied with freedom . . . this is no part of abolitionism; it is the exercise by the master of the unquestionable right of manumission; it is remunerating those who defend our cause with the privilege of freedom." Nor should anyone think that this would mean "putting the negro on an equality with our friends, brothers, and fathers," for after all "[m]any of the soldiers in their childhood were fondled and nursed by faithful negro nurses, and yet no question of equality was ever raised. Many a man has manumitted slaves without ever being subjected to the suspicion of being an abolitionist." Issuing a direct challenge to the master class, the *Enquirer* declared: "The issues involved in this war are too exalted in their importance and character for us to permit them to be compromised by being degraded to a question of property. We bear in our midst a half million of fighting material which is property— shall we use that property for the common cause?" The editorial noted that the Confederate government had impressed "horses, cattle, wheat, and every other property except slaves" and that "[t]his very exception is an imputation that *this war is for slavery and not for freedom.* By conscripting the negroes we show to the world the earnestness that is in our people; . . . and we explode the false accusation that we are fighting for slavery, or a slaveholders' Confederacy."[117] In reply, the *New York Times* reprinted the editorial in full under the headlines: "DESPERATION OF THE SOUTH; ARMING OF THE NEGROES. Freedom to All Who Fight for Slavery. The Most Significant Sign of Weakness. CONSCRIPTING THE SLAVES."[118]

The Cleburne Memorial had voiced a similar challenge to the slaveholders who controlled Congress. It warned that Lincoln "has already in training an army of 100,000 negroes as good as any troops," and that "every fresh raid he makes and new slice of territory he wrests from us will add to this force." Even if all the substitutions and exemptions from service were abolished, all those "improperly absent" and now "without the Confederate lines" could somehow be rounded up, and all those below age eighteen and above age forty-five could be conscripted, this would "exhaust the white race" and leave "no reserve to meet unexpected disaster or to supply a protracted struggle." Surely, Cleburne had argued, "[a]s between the loss of independence and the loss of slavery, we assume that every patriot will freely give up the latter—give up the negro slave rather than be a slave himself."

If the masters would commit their slaves to combat and emancipate them as a reward, Cleburne had written, "[i]t will leave the enemy's negro army no motive to

116. Ibid., 55–57.
117. "Using the Slaves," *The Richmond Enquirer*, October 18, 1864, reprinted in *New York Times*, October 24, 1864, Internet Archive, www.nytimes.com/1864/10/21/news/desperation-south-arming-negroes-freedom-all-who-fight-for-slavery-most.html.
118. Ibid.

fight for, . . . will exhaust the source from which it has been recruited" and "remove forever all selfish taint from our cause and place independence above every question of property." The masters must not delude themselves any longer about happy slaves willing to fight for the perpetuation of their own bondage, for on account of Northern agitation "the negro has been dreaming of freedom, and his vivid imagination has surrounded that condition with so many gratifications that it has become the paradise of his hopes." At this point, "[t]he hope of freedom is perhaps the only moral incentive that can be applied to him in his present condition. It would be preposterous then to expect him to fight against it with any degree of enthusiasm. . . ." Moreover, "It is a first principle with mankind that he who offers his life in defense of the State should receive from her in return his freedom and his happiness, and we believe in acknowledgment of this principle." Was this not the very promise kept as to the galley slaves who had contributed to the great victory in the "sea fight of Lepanto where the Christians checked forever the spread of Mohammedanism over Europe"?

Thus, Cleburne had concluded, it was imperative for the salvation of the Confederate cause that Richmond enlist the slaves and their families by offering them the only incentive that would work—ending their status as chattels, unable to marry legally and subject to separation and sale:

> give the negro not only his own freedom, but that of his wife and child, and . . . secure it to him in his old home. To do this, *we must immediately make his marriage and parental relations sacred in the eyes of the law and forbid their sale. . . .*
>
> If, then, we touch the institution at all, we would do best to make the most of it, and *by emancipating the whole race upon reasonable terms*, and within such reasonable time as will prepare both races for the change, secure to ourselves all the advantages, and to our enemies all the disadvantages that can arise, both at home and abroad, from such a sacrifice.
>
> Satisfy the negro that if he faithfully adheres to our standard during the war *he shall receive his freedom and that of his race*. Give him as an earnest of our intentions such immediate immunities as will impress him with our sincerity and be in keeping with his new condition, enroll a portion of his class as soldiers of the Confederacy, and we change the race from *a dreaded weakness to a position of strength.*[119]

Cleburne's petition, of which Davis had earlier "tried to prevent widespread knowledge,"[120] passionately summed up every argument the planter-dominated Confederate Congress would adamantly reject even as the Confederacy was tottering to its fall. The same elites who had driven secession, demanded the firing on Fort Sumter, and then thwarted Richmond's attempt to impress their slaves for

---

119. Cleburne Memorial (paragraph breaks added).
120. William C. Davis, *Jefferson Davis*, 597.

service in labor details during the ensuing war, would now refuse to emancipate their slaves in return for enlistment in the Confederate Army.

On February 3, 1865 Vice President Stephens and two other Confederate representatives met with President Lincoln and Secretary of State Seward aboard a steamboat anchored at Newport News, in Hampton Roads, Virginia. Stephens asked Lincoln: "Mr. President, is there no way of putting an end to the present trouble?" He made a vague reference to the risible proposal of Francis P. Blair that the two belligerents put aside their differences and unite to invade Mexico—just like the days of the Mexican War, less than twenty years earlier, when North and South together had advanced the Monroe Doctrine, named after the slave-owning President from Virginia. It was exquisitely ironic, however, that both Davis and Lincoln had opposed the conquest of Mexico when they served together in Congress. Foote recounts that Lincoln brushed aside the idea, stating simply that "restoration of the Union is a *sine qua non* with me" and that "he could never agree to bargain with men in arms against the government in his care." When one of the Confederate commissioners present (Senator Hunter) suggested that Charles I had dealt with rebels in arms against his government, Lincoln replied that he knew little of such historical details, but that "My only distinct recollection of the matter is that Charles lost his head."[121] Lincoln, that is, would not emulate the weakness of the king whose beheading marked the very beginning of our journey through the annals of Liberty (cf. Chapter 3). But we have seen enough by now to appreciate the radical difference between monarchs and presidents in dealing with uprisings against their authority.

The outcome of the Hampton Roads peace conference was clear, and (as Foote notes) it suited Davis: surrender not being an option, the Confederacy must fight to the bitter end. But with what troops? The only remaining pool of manpower from which to draw was the slaves. Hence on February 7, four days after Hampton Roads, Mississippi Senator Albert Gallatin introduced a bill that would have authorized President Davis to enlist up to 200,000 slaves as volunteers or by impressment, followed by emancipation after the war. The bill had the support of both Davis and Lee. Lee's famous earlier letter to Robert M.T. Hunter, the Confederate Senator from Virginia, is primary evidence of how, even at the very end of the Confederacy's existence, the clearly dying institution of slavery still had to be acknowledged as central to the Southern cause. Answering Hunter's objections to the conscription and emancipation of the slaves, Lee wrote that "the relation of master and slave, controlled by humane laws and influenced by Christianity and an enlightened public sentiment [is] the best that can exist between white and black races . . . in this country." Nevertheless, he continued—echoing Cleburne's warning—"we must decide whether slavery shall be extinguished by our enemies and the slaves be used against us, or use them ourselves at the risk of the effects upon *our* social institutions." And then the unthinkable, whose acceptance Cleburne had also urged: "My own opinion is that we should employ them without delay . . . [and] the best means

121. Foote, *The Civil War*, Vol. III, 776.

of insuring the efficiency and fidelity of this auxiliary force would be to accompany the measure with a well-digested plan of gradual and general emancipation."[122]

Despite Lee's intervention, the measure was immediately voted down over-whelmingly by the planter-controlled Congress. This Congressional obstruction-ism elicited condemnation in the Richmond press. Charles Button of the *Lynch-burg Virginian* denounced "some prominent gentlemen from Virginia ... whose more secret opinions have been made known to us confidentially" and who "have opposed with the most vehemence and bitterness the conscription of slaves" because "they want to fall back into the arms of Lincoln, hoping to save their property."[123] The *Richmond Enquirer* condemned "certain members of Congress, representing large slaveholding constituencies" for reasoning that "As *the object of the war was the safety of slave title*, we must seek that object by another course. We shall throw ourselves upon the protection of the enemy. They will grant us, at least, the temporary use of our own slaves.'"[124]

The final outcome of the legislative process was a ludicrous compromise autho-rizing Davis to "*ask* for and accept from the owners of slaves, the services of such number of able-bodied negro men as he may deem expedient," provided that "nothing in this act shall be construed to authorize a change in the relation which the said slaves shall bear toward their owners, except by consent of the owners and of the States in which they may reside. . . ." The act specified a recruitment quota of 300,000 still-enslaved blacks, but with no enforcement mechanism in the event of the owners' refusal to provide them beyond a "call on each State" to obtain black recruits "as the proper authorities thereof may determine." But the bill was limited to "not more than twenty-five per cent. of the male slaves between the ages of eigh-teen and forty-five, in any State. . . ."[125]

Even this toothless measure, essentially an elaborate invitation to the masters to consider lending *some* of their slaves—*as* slaves—to the Confederate cause, barely passed the House on February 20 by a vote of 40-to-37. On March 8, after further procedural wrangling, the bill passed the Senate by the barest of margins, 9-to-8, but only after the Virginia legislature had instructed Virginia's two Senators, Hunter and Allen T. Caperton, to vote in favor. The measure finally became Con-federate law on March 13, 1865. Yet Hunter, while "obliged, by instructions of the Legislature of Virginia" to vote in favor, "spoke at length in opposition ... on the ground of the principle involved and expediency. *It gave up the principle on which we went to war*, and would add no strength to our armies."[126] This former Speaker of the U.S. House of Representatives, a former Confederate Secretary of State, and now president *pro tem* of the Confederate Senate, exposed the damning implicit admission at the heart of the bill: "If we are right in passing this measure, *we were*

122. Lee to Hunter, January 11, 1865, in *Official Records*, Series IV, Vol. III, 1012–1013.
123. In Levine, *Confederate Emancipation*, 138.
124. Levine, *Confederate Emancipation*, 138.
125. Cf. *Official Records*, Series IV, Vol. III, 1161–62.
126. *The Daily Dispatch*, March 8, 1865, Tufts University archival text at www.perseus.tufts.edu/hop per/text?doc=Perseus%3Atext%3A2006.05.1317%3Aarticle%3Dpos%3D16.

wrong in denying the old government the right to interfere with the institution of sla-
very and to emancipate slaves."[127]

Indeed, was not the Confederate Congress now authorizing precisely what the Union had done—effectively emancipating slaves by making them soldiers—and this contrary to the letter of the Confederate Constitution with its special protection for the institution of slavery? As Hunter further declared on the Senate floor: "The Government had no power under the Constitution to arm and emancipate the slaves, and the Constitution granted no such great powers by implication."[128] In the same vein was Governor Brown of Georgia. In an address to the Georgia legislature just before House approval of the bill, Brown made the obvious point that "If we admit the right of the Government to impress and pay for slaves to free them we concede its power to abolish slavery." But under the Confederate Constitution, "No slave can ever be liberated by the Confederate Government without the consent of the States."[129]

Passage of the bill unleashed a storm of condemnation from both slave-holding and non-slaveholding leaders, both civilian and military. Their rhetoric exposed for what it was the myth of a noble secession from the Union for high ideals of patriotism, defense of the *patria,* and Liberty. They expressed not only the bare economic motives behind the original secession but also the doctrine of white supremacy enunciated in Vice President Stephens's Cornerstone Address—a doctrine, it must be remembered, that Americans both North and South, including Lincoln, more or less accepted. Senator Hunter summed up the entire property-based argument for secession and war with a single sentence: "What did we go to war for, if not to protect our property?" Likewise, the Confederate Congressman from Tennessee, Henry S. Foote, posed the question: "If this government is to destroy slavery, why fight for it?"[130] Brig. Gen. Howell Cobb, the former Governor of Georgia who had been no less than Secretary of Treasury under President Buchanan, bitterly protested: "The day you make soldiers of them [Negroes] is *the beginning and the end of the revolution. If the slaves will make good soldiers our whole theory of slavery is wrong."*[131]

Foote notes that the very head of the Confederate War Bureau denounced the measure as "passed in a panic . . . a colossal blunder, a dislocation of *the foundations of society* from which no practical results will be reaped by us." The same Robert Toombs who had warned that the bombardment of Fort Sumter would be "suicide, murder," likewise condemned the measure. Having joined most of his

127. In *The American Annual Cyclopedia and Register of Important Events,* Vol. IV, "Congress, Confederate" (NY: D. Appleton & Co., 1865), 218.

128. Ibid.

129. In Robert F. Durden, *The Gray and the Black: the Confederate Debate on Emancipation* (Baton Rouge: Louisiana State Univ. Press, 1972), 252.

130. Frank E. Vandiver, "Proceedings of the Second Confederate Congress," *Southern Historical Society Papers,* 51, p. 276, in Levine, *Confederate Emancipation,* 5.

131. In James I. Robertson, Jr., *Soldiers Blue and Gray* (Columbia, SC: Univ. of South Carolina Press, 1998), 30.

fellow plantation owners in ignoring Richmond's demand that he divert his land from cotton production to food production to feed the Confederate Army, Toombs now issued a protest from his plantation, dated March 24, 1865 and printed in full in the *New York Times* weeks later. The one-time Confederate Secretary of State's jeremiad provides a window into the mentality of the wealthy planters who drove the secession yet now lamented the war and the wreck of the South:

> I have the most painful apprehensions for the future and they arise solely from my entire conviction of the total incapacity of Mr. DAVIS, and consequently the utter failure of all his petty schemes. We have given him all the men who would volunteer, allowed him all the men he could catch at first from eighteen to thirty-five, then up to forty-five, then all from seventeen to fifty; and the army is smaller to-day and less efficient than on the day the first Conscript Bill was passed. Now Congress has given him all the negroes, and the result will still be the same, superadded to the most fatal consequences which have ever darkened our prospects. . . .
>
> *If two-thirds of the white freemen (as Mr. DAVIS says) have ingloriously abandoned their flag, and ran away from a standard in which all the hopes of a true man are centered* . . . do we expect that the negro slaves will stand by it? . . .
>
> In my opinion, the worst calamity that could befall us would be to gain our independence by the valor of our slaves, instead of our own. . . . *The day that the Army of Virginia allows a negro regiment to enter their lines as soldiers they [the Army] will be degraded, ruined and disgraced.* . . .
>
> [I]f you put our negroes and white men into the army together, you must and will put them on an equality; they must be under the same code, the same pay, allowance and clothing. There must be promotions for valor, or there will be no morale among them. *Therefore, it is a surrender of the entire slavery question.*[132]

In an effort to salvage the debacle of the slave conscription bill, President Davis bypassed Congress and the Confederate Constitution by promulgating an administrative decree promising emancipation to any slave who enlisted in the army. Irony of ironies, *Davis had thereby issued his own desperate equivalent of Lincoln's Emancipation Proclamation.* But the plan to conscript the slaves was a total failure. The masters' recalcitrance and the slaves' calculation that the advancing Union armies were the quickest road to freedom resulted in two hundred or fewer black recruits as opposed to the 200,000 the plan's proponents imagined would rush into the Confederate ranks. Levine succinctly sums up the outcome:

132. "Toombs, of Georgia.; WHAT HE THOUGHT OF THINGS IN MARCH, 1865 HIS OPINION OF JEFF. DAVIS," *The New York Times*, June 4, 1865, Internet archival text www.nytimes.com/1865/06/04/news/toombs-georgia-what-he-thought-things-march–1865-his-opinion-jeff-davis.html. Paragraph breaks added.

Far from rescuing the Confederacy from defeat, they [the slaves] ultimately became indispensable instruments of its destruction. Slaves resisted their masters' commands, escaped from their masters' control, aided and entered the ranks of advancing Union armies.... By the time that a handful of black Southerners donned gray uniforms in Richmond in the spring of 1865, nearly 200,000 were already wearing Union blue and helping to force the Confederacy to its knees.[133]

Levine's conclusion cannot be dismissed as the biased revisionism of a contemporary liberal historian indulging in presentism, for it only states what Maj. Gen. Patrick Cleburne, one of the Confederate Army's finest, had warned in January 1864: "All along the lines slavery is comparatively valueless to us for labor, but of great and increasing worth to the enemy for information. It is an *omnipresent spy system*, pointing out our valuable men to the enemy, revealing our positions, purposes, and resources, and yet acting so safely and secretly that there is no means to guard against it. Even in the heart of our country, where our hold upon this secret espionage is firmest, *it waits but the opening fire of the enemy's battle line to wake it*, like a torpid serpent, into venomous activity." Davis had ordered Cleburne's Memorial suppressed only to end up following his recommendations, but far too late for them to be effective. For as Cleburne had also warned presciently: "there is danger that this concession to common sense may come too late."

Unlike their comrades, many Confederate military leaders were filled with disgust by the politicians' refusal to allow interference with the masters' property rights even at the Confederacy's eleventh hour. Typical of these expressions is a letter from Maj. Thomas P. Turner complaining of the Virginia slave-owners that while "wives and daughters and the negroes are the only elements left us to recruit from, it does seem that our people would rather send the former even to face death and danger than give up the latter."[134] In the same vein was the Confederate captain Francis Dawson, who wrote that the majority of slave-owners "would I am convinced rather have placed in the army two sons than one negro."[135] Mary Chesnut's diary records that while "General Lee and Mr. Davis want the negroes put into the army ... the men who went into the war to save their negroes are abjectly wretched. Neither side now cares a fig for these beloved negroes, and would send them all to heaven in a hand-basket, as Custis Lee says, to win in the fight."[136]

But no one could have been more disgusted than Lee about what his headquarters reported was "the unwillingness of owners to permit their slaves to enter the service."[137] On March 24, 1865, only days before his surrender at Appomattox, the Confederate general-in-chief, commanding the remnants of the Confederate Army

133. Levine, *Confederate Emancipation*, 150–51.
134. In *The Library of Congress Civil War Desk Reference*, eds Margaret E. Wagner, Gary W. Gallagher, James M. McPherson (NY: Simon and Schuster, 2002), 157.
135. In Gaines M. Foster, *Ghosts of the Confederacy: Defeat, the Lost Cause and the Emergence of the New South, 1860 to 1913* (NY: Oxford Univ. Press, 1987), 23.
136. *A Diary From Dixie*, 224 (Kindle Edition).
137. Levine, *Confederate Emancipation*, 139.

in northern Virginia and fighting desperately to survive Grant's massive assault on Petersburg-Richmond, wrote to Davis to suggest with amazing understatement that he lean on the Governor of Virginia to compel the slave-owners to produce their slaves or else the war was over: "I have the honor to ask that you will call upon the governor of the State of Virginia for the whole number of negroes, slave and free, between the ages of eighteen and forty-five. . . . The services of these men are now necessary to enable us to oppose the enemy."[138]

In any event, the plan was far too late and far too ridiculous to succeed. William C. Oates, the intrepid Confederate colonel who literally gave his right arm to the Confederate cause and would become the post-war Governor of Alabama, later observed: "No sensible Negro would have volunteered under that law, if honestly explained to him, unless it was for the purpose of availing himself of the opportunity it would have given him to desert to the other side, where he could, beyond doubt, have obtained his freedom."[139] Mary Chesnut had likewise wondered in 1863: "but would they fight on our side or desert to the enemy?"[140] A year later the question was no longer relevant, as the slaves had calculated that their freedom was in the offing. "If we had *only* freed the slaves at first and put them in the army—that would have trumped their trick," Alcott Green tells her. Years before, says Green, old man Chesnut's head slaves "were keen to go in the army—free, and bounty after the war. Now they say coolly they don't want freedom if they have to fight for it. That means they are pretty sure of having it anyway."[141] In perfect agreement with this Southern view was Frederick Douglass, who wrote that the Confederacy's eleventh-hour embrace of emancipation was on "the verge of madness," for it "called upon the negro for help to fight . . . against Lincoln the Emancipator for Davis the enslaver." But then "desperation discards logic as well as law, and the South was desperate."[142]

The abysmal failure of the black conscription plan exposed the delusion of a happy and contented slave population eager to assist their masters in defending the *status quo antebellum*. A typical confession in this regard is a letter from Augustin L. Taveau, a South Carolina planter, published in the *New York Tribune* only days after Lee's army had surrendered at Appomattox:

> [T]he conduct of the Negro in the late crisis of our affairs has convinced me that we were all laboring under a delusion. . . . I believed that these people were content, happy, and attached to their masters. But events and reflection have caused me to change these positions. . . . If they were content, happy, and

---

138. In *Official Records*, Series 1, Vol. 46, Part 3 (the Appomattox Campaign), 1339, Ohio State electronic archive, ehistory.osu.edu/osu/sources/recordView.cfm?Content=097/1339.

139. In Mark Perry, *Conceived in Liberty: Joshua Chamberlain, William Oates, and the American Civil War* (NY: Penguin Books, 1997), 321.

140. *A Diary from Dixie*, 224.

141. Chesnut, *Mary Chesnut's Civil War*, 679. Emphasis in original.

142. Frederick Douglass, *The Life and Times of Frederick Douglass* (Mineola, NY: Dover Publications, 2003 [1892]), 262.

attached to their masters, why did they desert him in the moment of his need and flock to an enemy, whom they did not know; and thus left their perhaps really good masters, whom they did know from infancy?[143]

None other than Edmund Ruffin, the slave-owning fire-eater who had fired the first shot (or one of the first shots) on Fort Sumter, would record in his diary his bitter disillusionment over the realization that the loyalty of the slave population to their benevolent masters had been largely illusory. While he had "before believed in the general prevalence of much attachment & affection of negro slaves for the families of their masters," events had revealed only "some few cases of great attachment & fidelity [but] many more of signal ingratitude & treachery of slaves to the most considerate & kind of masters," and still more cases of "entire disregard of all such supposed ties of attachment & loyalty."[144] A few months later, Ruffin would commit suicide by using a forked stick to fire a rifle into his mouth. His last diary entry declared his "unmitigated hatred to Yankee rule . . . & to the perfidious, malignant & vile Yankee race."[145]

This is not to suggest that there had been any general uprising of slaves before it became apparent that the end was near for the institution. For where was a slave to go and how would he survive in the midst of the Confederacy once he had rebelled against his master, the penalty for which was death? The process was rather one of a steady stream of escapees to the North during the war, followed by a massive abandonment of the plantations wherever the Union armies approached. The *Richmond Sentinel* described a typical scene: "'Proceeding up our rivers, on the banks of which the slaves are most numerous,' northern vessels 'had little more to do than display their colors'. . . . 'The negroes at once threw down their hoes, axes and spades, and quitted their plows, and flocked to the Yankee steamers and other craft by *tens of thousands.*'"[146] Mary Chesnut's diary likewise records a report that as Yankee gunboats are proceeding up the Santee River, shelling and burning as they go, "the negroes rush down to them."[147]

But perhaps the most telling evidence that the happiness, contentment, and loyalty of the slaves had been a delusion was the Confederate government's own belated recognition that only the promise of freedom could induce them to fight for the South. For if the institution of antebellum chattel slavery had been so benign and of such benefit to the slaves, why were they not willing and eager to fight to preserve it just as it was? Why instead, as Cleburne had warned, were the slaves "spies surrounding every household" and the young men among them "recruits awaiting the enemy with open arms"? The failure of the Southern leadership to recognize this reality until it was far too late had, William Oates was convinced, contributed to

143. In Zinn, *A People's History of the United States*, 194.

144. William Kauffman Scarborough, ed., *The Diary of Edmund Ruffin* (Baton Rouge: Louisiana State Univ. Press, 1972–1989), Vol. 3, p. 692; in Levine, *Confederate Emancipation*, 84.

145. Eric H. Walther, *The Fire-Eaters* (Baton Rouge: Louisiana State Univ. Press, 1993), 229–230.

146. Levine, *Confederate Emancipation*, 83–84.

147. Chesnut, *Mary Chesnut's Civil War*, 402.

the South's defeat: "After slavery was practically dead, the Confederacy had clung to its putrid body and expired with it."[148]

Governor Brown's Indictment of Richmond

A vehement opponent of black conscription during the last days of the war, Governor Brown issued a wide-ranging indictment of the Davis administration in his address to the Georgia Senate and House of Representatives on February 18, 1865: "Our constitution has been violated and trampled under foot; and the rights and sovereignty of the States, which had been disregarded by the Government of the United States, *which formed with slavery the very foundation of the movement that brought into being the Confederate Government,* have been prostrated and almost destroyed by Confederate Congressional encroachment and executive usurpation." Richmond's conscription laws had caused the common soldier to conclude that what was supposed to have been "the people's war"—like all the wars of Liberty—was "the Government's war, and that he was no longer a freeman, but the slave of absolute power."

Brown recited a litany of unconstitutional acts emanating from Richmond over the past four years that not only dwarfed Southern complaints about the federal government prior to secession, but also inadvertently rendered trivial by comparison the litany of King George's "intolerable acts" in the Declaration of Independence:

Direct taxes of enormous burden have been levied by Congress, without the census or enumeration imperatively required by the Constitution. . . .

Impressments of private property for public use . . . have been carried to an extent which is tyrannical and oppressive in the extreme. . . .

By a pretended conscription, not authorized by the Constitution, the Government has placed our agriculturists under heavy bonds to sell to it at the impressment prices fixed by its agents, and denies to them the privilege to sell the fruits of their labor in open market, or to exchange them for other commodities which are necessary to the support of themselves and their families. . . .

The Government disregards that provision of the Constitution which prohibits Congress from making any appropriation of money for a longer term than two years for the support of the armies of the Confederacy, and as a means of perpetuating the war beyond the period of the existence of the present Congress, without the assent of the people at the next elections, it proposes to pledge the tithe of the more valuable annual productions of the agricultural class of our people for years to come . . . and to continue the pledge of the incomes of this particular class after the termination of the war for the payment of the Treasury notes issued for the support of its armies. . . .

Citizens who belong neither to the land nor naval forces of the Government, or to the militia in actual service, are arrested by Provost guards and

---

148. In Perry, *Conceived in Liberty,* 321.

Government detectives, under charges of treason or other indictable offences, or disloyalty, without warrant or other process from the courts and imprisoned at the pleasure of the Government. . . .

Good and loyal citizens, who travel on railroads or steamboats, or through towns or cities, upon lawful business, are arrested if they fail to carry passes, while Federal spies procure or forge passes, and travel over our thoroughfares at their pleasure. . . .

While the old men and boys of this State . . . have been obliged to take up arms to resist the enemy, thousands of young able-bodied men of this and other States . . . are protected by Confederate authority, on account of their wealth or other influence, from service in the field, and under pretext of some nominal employment for the Government, are allowed to remain out of the reach of danger, and devote most of their time to their speculations or other individual pursuits. . . .

By its efforts to grasp absolute power, the Confederate administration has greatly weakened our arms, and results have shown its utter inability, with all the power placed in its hands, to recruit and fill them up to a number sufficient to meet the emergency.

So fatal have been the results of our wretched conscription policy . . . well adapted to control European serfs . . . that it has driven our men in despair to delinquency and desertion, till the President has informed the country, in his Macon speech, *that two thirds of those who compose our armies are absent, most of them without leave.*[149]

Brown queried what was the point of a war for Southern independence—the cause for which Davis now said the Confederacy was fighting—if "the courts must be closed, and State lines obliterated to accomplish this object." Rights and liberties, he declared, "are not secondary to our independence, but our independence is only necessary to protect our rights and our liberties. . . . If this is the sort of independence for which we are fighting, our great sacrifices have been made to but little purpose." He professed that he had not despaired of the Confederate cause, that it was just a matter of immediate and urgent reform and—irony of ironies—a return to respect for the Confederate Constitution. But he declared that, like the Lincoln administration, "Our government is now a military despotism. . . ." Once again Liberty had revealed itself as sheer Power. Further, the "Lincoln dynasty informs us distinctly that reconstruction and subjugation are the only alternatives to be presented to us. . . ." Barring a radical change of policy in Richmond, Brown predicted, "[t]he present policy, if persisted in, must terminate in reconstruction either with or without subjugation." And so it did.

149. Confederate Records of the State of Georgia, 2:837–844, 847, 853–854; *New York Times*, March 8, 1865, archival reprint, www.nytimes.com/1865/03/08/news/gov-brown-s-message-he-defends-georgia-against-char-ge-cowardice-scathing-expose.html. Paragraph breaks added.

Lee's Surrender

There were thirty-three black regiments in Grant's Army when Richmond fell to it on April 2, less than two months after Brown's indictment of Richmond. As the remnants of Lee's proud Army of Northern Virginia were forced to abandon the city, Confederate demolition squads set fire to tobacco and munitions warehouses rather than have them fall into Union hands. The munitions exploded, giving the appearance of an enemy bombardment, and the fires spread out of control, destroying much of Richmond. Like Davis, "[t]he old war-scarred city seemed to prefer annihilation to conquest."[150] Foote recounts how the *Richmond Whig* denounced Davis for the burning of Richmond, declaring: "If there lingered in the hearts of our people one spark of affection for the Davis dynasty, this ruthless, wanton handing over to the flames [of] their fair city, their homes and altars, has extinguished it forever."[151]

One week later, without prior notice to Davis, Lee surrendered the starving and ever-loyal remnant of his army to Grant at Appomattox. It was Palm Sunday. In what had to be among the most generous terms ever offered a defeated separatist army, Grant proposed, and Lee accepted, a surrender that would allow his men to keep their horses and sidearms and simply go home on parole. Grant then disbursed 25,000 rations to feed Lee's men. For the rest of his life, Lee "never allowed an unkind word about Grant to be spoken in his presence."[152]

The moment of surrender was replete with irony: two generals who had fought as young officers in the same army that had conquered Mexico twenty years earlier—over the strong opposition of a young Congressman Lincoln, who had protested that the Mexican war was unconstitutional and premised on a Southern President's lies—now shook hands on the first terms of Lincoln's ruthless conquest of another power to the South. On April 12, Lee's men marched toward a line of Federal troops waiting to receive them in surrender. Instead of launching humiliating taunts, however, the Union soldiers were "lifting their muskets to the position of Carry Arms in a salute to the Confederate States Army." Lee's biographer cites this tribute to Lee's beaten men by General Joshua Chamberlain of Maine:

> Before us in proud humiliation stood the embodiment of manhood, men whom neither toils and sufferings, nor the fact of death, nor disaster, nor hopelessness could end from their resolve; standing before us now, thin, worn, and famished, but erect, and with eyes looking level into ours, waking memories that bound us together as no other bond....[153]

Davis, however, hung on long past the bitter end, weeks after the remnants of his government began making plans behind his back to seek terms for a definitive peace. With Lee's army surrendered, the war was effectively over, but Davis refused to accept reality when General Johnston declared: "It would be the greatest of

150. Foote, *The Civil War*, Vol. III, 889.
151. Ibid.
152. Flood, *Lee*, 11.
153. Ibid., 27.

human crimes for us to attempt to continue the war." His highest remaining field officers and his entire cabinet, except Secretary of State Benjamin, were now arrayed against him, and soon it would all end forever with his capture.[154]

Expressing contempt for his fellow Confederates who would not part with their slaves for the sake of a Southern cause that had been rooted in slavery but had become a war for Liberty—at least in the minds of some—Davis had said: "If the Confederacy falls, there should be written on its tombstone: Died of a theory."[155] And so it was written.

A Revolution of the Politicians

Lee's admiring biographer observes that "Slavery had been the principal issue that led to this war, but nine out of ten of these foot soldiers and artillerymen had never owned a slave. They were fighting because the Union Army had invaded the South."[156] But, absent slavery, there would have been no secession, no war, no invasion. To deny that the Confederate States of America were born in a defense of slavery is to deny history. As William Davis rightly observes in his definitive biography of Jefferson Davis: "Slavery and slavery alone is what brought the Confederate States together, however much they might try to argue more elevated arguments about states' rights. *No other substantive issues bound them in* 1861, and since then it was only the war, the Yankee enemy at the gates, and Jefferson Davis that held them together."[157]

Yet it is also true, as his biographer observes, that by late 1864 Davis and other diehard Confederate leaders "had come to see a higher goal," that of a "Confederate nationalism" transcending loyalty to the individual states of the confederacy. We have already noted that so far as Davis was concerned, "we are fighting for INDE-PENDENCE, and that, or extermination, we *will* have. . . ." But while his biographer views Davis's fanatical determination as "admirable," he notes "that others in Richmond . . . regarded him as deluded and his cause as lost, and began working quietly on their own to halt the war short of extermination," which they did.[158]

The common people of the devastated South were not interested in the extermination Davis saw as preferable to defeat in the "Liberty or death" tradition of 1776. They were no longer willing, if they ever were, to sacrifice life and property for a political entity that was, in the end, no more appealing than the Union from which the South had seceded based on the decisions of politicians—including Davis himself—who had refused to submit their decisions to prior popular approval. In fact, "the people had never sanctioned the course of the politicians, but 'when the ball of revolution had received such momentum, it could not be stopped.' *No one had consulted the popular will*, and the people had become 'the dupes of dema-gogues and partizan [sic] tricksters who have carved out for them and forced them

154. William C. Davis, *Davis,* 616.
155. Davis, *Rise and Fall,* Vol. I, 518.
156. Flood, *Lee,* 5.
157. Davis, *Davis,* 598.
158. Ibid., 600.

to execute.'"[159] And what had the people gotten in return? They were promised Liberty—the Southern-fried version—and had gotten instead the usual outcome: more government than ever before. With "magnificent understatement" one politician admitted at war's end that "'[s]ecession seems not to have produced the results predicted by its sanguine friends. There was to be no war, no taxes worth prating about, but an increase of happiness, boundless prosperity, and entire freedom from all Yankee annoyance.' But instead the war brought conscription, destruction, and infringement of civil liberties."[160]

Following the fall of Atlanta in September 1864, Governor Vance had already admitted what was long obvious: "[T]he great popular heart is not now, and never has been in this war. *It was a revolution of the Politicians, not the People*; and was fought at first by the natural enthusiasm of our young men, and has been kept going by State and sectional pride, assisted by that bitterness of feeling produced by the cruelties and brutalities of the enemy."[161] But hatred of the "perfidious, malignant & vile Yankee race," as Ruffin had called them, was no basis for an enduring nation, especially when the suffering masses could see that a war supposedly waged for Liberty was stripping from them the very foundations of their earthly happiness: loved ones, tranquil possession of home and hearth, and the pursuit of a livelihood undisturbed by the incessant demands of government. In the course of the war many Southerners, especially those who had opposed secession from the beginning, deeply resented the immense burdens they had had to endure for the sake of the planters who had dragged the South into secession and bloody conflict. Edmund Wilson recounts how on the eve of Lee's surrender, Mary Chesnut, now a refugee in North Carolina, learned from Colonel Chesnut that "many of their own fellow Southerners are rejoicing over the ruin of the planter class. 'They will have no Negroes now to lord it over!' he says he heard one of them say. 'They can swell and peacock about and tyrannize now only over a small parcel of women and children, those who are their very own family.'"[162]

Drastically disadvantaged from the start by the overwhelming numerical superiority of the Union Army and the technological and industrial advantages possessed by the North, the Southern cause finally collapsed when people simply ceased believing in the latest promises of Liberty, issuing this time from Richmond instead of Washington. As the Bancroft Prize-winning historian Charles Royster observes:

> The authorities grew increasingly dictatorial, yet the populace more frequently defied them with impunity.... With broad coercive powers, with unprecedented success in military mobilization, with war-making industrial

159. In Beringer, et al., *Why the South Lost the Civil War*, 291; quoting *Raleigh Daily Conservative*, January 2, April 5, 1865.

160. In Beringer, *Elements of Confederate Defeat*, 130.

161. In Mark L. Bradley, *This Astounding Close: the Road to Bennett Place* (Chapel Hill: Univ. of North Carolina Press, 2000), 75; see also Cornelia Philips Spencer, *The Last Ninety Days of the War in North Carolina* (NY: Watchman Publishing Co, 1866), 27–28.

162. In Wilson, *Patriotic Gore*, 298.

resourcefulness hardly conceivable a few years earlier, with the loyalty of most officials at all levels, the Confederate government spun its gears and pulleys vigorously as it slowed down and fell apart. It suffered a government's most ignominious fate: issuing demands and orders to citizens who no longer believed in its power to protect, reward, or punish them. A nation relying on appeals was doomed when it could no longer convince. A nation relying on coercion was doomed when it could no longer coerce.[163]

Many indeed wondered what had been the point of a war to defend a government no less oppressive than the one that had sent invading armies to march through the South. Edward A. Pollard, one of the pro-secessionist (but anti-Davis) editors of the *Richmond Examiner*, offered this devastating post-mortem in 1868:

> A strong characteristic running through the whole government of the Southern Confederacy, and pervading all its legislation, was a feeble but persistent echo to Washington. History will remark this as one of the most curious circumstances of the war. A Government in the position of a seceder, if not of a rebel, was so utterly destitute of statesmanship, so devoid of intellectual force and originality, as to follow with halting and apish imitations upon the Government it had forsaken and denounced. . . . *Richmond was a Chinese copy of Washington*, with all its patches of departments and bureaus, with all its stripes of "fed tape," with all its traditions of official circumlocution, with all its ancient stenches of the lobby and back-stairs.[164]

The Treasurer of North Carolina, Jonathan Worth, observed that "many men having large influence over public opinion do not take pains to conceal the conviction that the establishment of our Independence would be no permanent blessing to us."[165] That is, many men could see that the Southern states would only end up where they had left off after the first American Revolution: under the thumb of a federal government "conceived in Liberty" but dominated by demagogues. "We were not fit for Independence or we would have had it," wrote William Preston Johnston, Jefferson Davis's aide-de-camp in July of 1865. "Many of our wisest & truest men, thought, after seeing the results in the war, that we would with our doctrine of Secession & State Rights, be at the mercy of such pestiferous demagogues as Joe Brown & such agitators & destructives as Toombs and Wigfall." As one of Alexander Stephens's friends had put it in a letter to Stephens after Atlanta fell to Sherman: "I am not one of those who desire to see the last dollar spent, and the last man killed in setting up the Independence of the Southern states, that I have no assurance will last as many years as we will spend in obtaining it."[166]

John Bigelow, United States minister to France during the reign of Napoleon III,

163. Charles Royster, *The Destructive War: William Tecumseh Sherman, Stonewall Jackson, and the Americans* (Vintage: Kindle Edition, 2011; Knopf ed. 1991), 3965.

164. Edward A. Pollard, *The Lost Cause Regained* (NY: G. W. Carleton & Company, Publishers, 1868), 27.

165. Royster, *The Destructive War*, Kindle Edition, 3965–3968.

166. Ibid., 3971–3974, 3979–3981.

took an appropriately measured view of the conflict, albeit from a Northern perspective. Bigelow distinguished between the field of battle, where men rose to the heights of bravery and honor, and the field of politics, where some men goaded and compelled masses of others to lay down their lives for the aims of a relative few. He praised the "admirable military qualities of the Confederate army" as a source of "not only regional but national pride," allowing that "it might have been difficult to organize an army of better soldiers or more competent officers in the whole United States than those who fought under the flag of the Confederacy. . . ." Nevertheless, "[t]he best judgment, talent and virtue of the South were not responsible for the rebellion, *were never fairly represented in its prosecution,* and but for the ascendancy which a group of desperate demagogues had acquired in the politics of the South by causing it to be believed that they only could be trusted to protect the people from the confiscation of their slave property, the South would never have permitted its solicitude about slavery to ripen into rebellion."[167]

Lee himself would echo that assessment, even if he applied it to demagogues on both sides. He had "never cared for politicians, including Confederate congressmen,"[168] and he made that clear when testifying before a U.S. Senate subcommittee:

> I may have said and I may have believed that the position of the two sections which they held to each other was brought about by *the politicians of the country*; that *the great mass of the people, if they had understood the real question, would have avoided it.* . . . I did believe at the time that it was an unnecessary state of affairs and might have been avoided, if forbearance and wisdom had been practiced *on both sides.*[169]

As Lee explained to his men in his General Order No. 9: "I determined to avoid the useless sacrifice of those whose past services have endeared them to their countrymen." Lee, at least, had not been willing to suffer extermination rather than defeat.

The End of Lincoln

In four years of war and devastation, two rival federal governments, each invoking the memory of the Founders, had sacrificed a million lives in a struggle to vindicate their competing visions of the progress of Liberty. As always in the history of Liberty, the common man had marched and paid with his life and the survivors would find themselves less free than they had been before the shooting began. And now the leaders on both sides would ask the survivors to live together peaceably once again, rebuilding the Temple built in common by the sainted revolutionary fathers of the North and the South.

But Lincoln would not be presiding over the process of reconstruction. Two days

---

167. John Bigelow, "The Southern Confederacy and the Pope," loc. cit., 473–74.
168. Flood, *Lee: the Last Years*, 124.
169. Ibid.

after Lee's men had laid down their arms to a Union salute while Davis and the remnants of his government were on the run, the reign of Abraham Lincoln, "savior of the Union," would come to an end on April 14, 1865, Good Friday. Lincoln met his fate on the famous balcony at Ford's theater, where he was taking in a light comedy—a fitting Good Friday diversion for a Deist (at best) who had no belief in the divinity or atonement of Christ.

John Wilkes Booth was no obscure fanatic but a rich and famous celebrity widely considered the greatest American stage actor of his day. Wilkes and his fellow conspirators had plotted to assassinate not only Lincoln but also Vice President Johnson (whose assassin could not go through with the deed) and Secretary of State Seward (whose assassin succeeded only in wounding his target with a knife). Playing his greatest role, Booth leapt from the balcony to the stage after having dispatched the President, shouting: "*Sic semper tyrannis*"—"thus always to tyrants." The same Latin motto appears on the reverse side of the Seal of Virginia, created in 1776. In leaping to the stage Booth literally fulfilled the traditional show business idiom for good luck: he broke his leg.

The plan had been to kill off the line of Presidential succession in the hope of destabilizing the Union and resuscitating the Confederate war effort. (The last skirmish of the war, at Palmito Ranch, Texas, was still a month away.) Like the Confederate war effort itself, this was very much in the Spirit of 1776 as reflected on the Virginia seal. It was also very much in the spirit of the events which gave rise to the genome of Liberty we examined in Chapter 3: the overthrow of James II by force in 1688, the Rye House Plot to assassinate Charles II and James II in 1683 (in which John Locke, the "Father of American Liberty," was involved), and the execution of Charles I in 1649 by the original Puritan rebels, whose fellow Puritans colonized America and prepared the way for the Revolution without which Lincoln would never have been sitting on the balcony of Ford's theater that Good Friday evening in the aftermath of his relentless devastation of the South in the name of Liberty.

Then again, Lincoln's waging of the Civil War was no less in the Spirit of 1776 than the war against Mexico, the Texas Revolution, and President Jefferson's Lincoln-like tyranny during the Embargo, when he deployed American troops against the American people. The same spirit was at work in John Adams's crushing of the Fries Rebellion and George Washington's march along with an army of fifteen thousand to put down the Whiskey Rebellion because a few Americans had dared to resist the federal tax collectors of Liberty. So was that spirit behind the American revolutionary leadership's oppression of its royalist opposition. Indeed, one and the same Spirit had animated all the landmark acts of force and violence since the head of King Charles fell into the basket in 1649, prompting the poet to utter the prophesy we recall here: "Oh! to what height of horror are they come. . . ." Like the Ouroboros—the snake that consumes itself tail-first to recreate itself in an eternal cycle—Liberty has always sought self-perpetuation by devouring its own in revolutions, wars, and plots. One is not surprised to learn that the serpent symbol of the Ouroboros appears on Masonic emblems in the temples of a surrogate religion dedicated to the foundation of the New World Order called Liberty, whose "first temple dedicated to the sovereignty of the people,"[170] as Jefferson described the Capitol Building, was consecrated by Washington according to a Masonic ritual.[171]

At Mary Lincoln's insistence, Lincoln was buried in his hometown of Springfield, Illinois at the Oak Ridge Cemetery. His tomb, devoid of any sign of a Christian death or burial, for he was no Christian, befits a secular saint in the pantheon of Liberty. "Now he belongs to the ages," declares the lapidary motto above the sarcophagus. Referring to the tomb, a Presbyterian minister in Washington delivered the famous funeral sermon in which he declared: "The friends of Liberty and of the Union will repair to it in years and ages to come, to pronounce the memory of its occupant blessed...." Similar veneration would be accorded the "Recumbent Statue" of Robert E. Lee in the Lee Chapel at Washington and Lee University, a National Historical Landmark. And Jefferson Davis would be immortalized by a 351-foot-tall obelisk—third tallest in the world—in a blatant imitation of the Washington Monument, the world's second tallest obelisk at 555 feet. The world's tallest obelisk, the 567-foot-tall San Jacinto Monument, commemorates the Americans who fought in the Battle of San Jacinto and wrested control of Texas from "papist" Mexico during the Texas Revolution. Thus the world's three tallest obelisks, all national landmarks, are monuments to heroes of American insurrections in the Spirit of 1776.

§

Eight days before Lincoln was interred on May 4, General Johnston surrendered his Army of Tennessee without consulting an enraged Davis. Six days before that surrender, on April 20, Lee wrote to Davis, "sensing that he was dealing with a desperate leader who might be considering a guerilla war if all else failed." In terse language, he told Davis to face reality: "To save useless effusion of blood, I would recommend that measures be taken for the suspension of hostilities and the restoration of peace."[172] But there were many in the South who had viewed the entire war as a useless effusion of blood, and none more famously than that battle-scarred veteran of Johnston's army, Sam Watkins:

> Our cause was lost from the beginning. Our greatest victories—Chickamauga and Franklin—were our greatest defeats. *Our people were divided upon the question of Union and secession.* Our generals were scrambling for "Who ranked." *The private soldier fought and starved and died for naught....* Amid the waving of flags and handkerchiefs and the smiles of the ladies, while the fife and drum were playing Dixie and the Bonnie Blue Flag, we bid farewell to home and friends. The bones of our brave Southern boys lie scattered over our loved South. They fought for their "*country*" [emphasis in original] and gave their lives freely for that country's cause: and now they who survive sit, like Marius amid the wreck of Carthage, sublime even in ruins....[173]

170. Jefferson to Latrobe, July 12, 1812, *Jeffersonian Cyclopedia*, § 461.
171. See, Chapter 8, note 56.
172. Flood, *Lee*, 45.
173. Watkins, *Company Aytch*, 230.

16

Post Bellum, Post Mortem

THE RUIN OF THE SOUTH in an ultimately pointless war was the eminently predictable outcome of the principles of Lockean liberty operating in their first fully functional laboratory: an unprecedented extended republic founded on the Protestant principle of private judgment applied to politics, in a nation populated overwhelmingly by Protestants for whom private judgment was the air they breathed. Before we can draw out the lessons on Liberty the Civil War teaches us, it is necessary to assess the war's aftermath, beginning with an autopsy of the Confederacy.

Knights of Liberty

On the Southern pages of Civil War romance, we must consider a claim appealing to traditionalist sensibilities: that the "Lost Cause" of the South was a desperate, losing struggle to preserve the last remnants of European tradition and Christian social order in America. This chapter of the Southern romantic narrative relies heavily on the work of a group of post-war Southern historians centered around Virginia, preeminently the Confederate general Jubal A. Early. They labored to transform a failed revolution in the Spirit of 1776, ignited by a sectional dispute over slavery extension, into the purified memory of a veritable Christian crusade to defend the holy people of a holy land against apostate Northern hordes.

   Southern exceptionalism replaces American exceptionalism in the Liberty myth of the Confederacy. Like the United States of 1776, the Confederate States of 1861 is depicted as unique among nations, chosen by God for a special purpose. The Southern people are depicted as a superior race—superior of course to the black man who had provided the human substratum of the Southern "way of life," but superior as well to the white man of the North in every department: breeding, education, refinement, and even courage. Southern exceptionalism fueled the "fatal hubris of invincibility," the delusion that "grimy Yankees were crumbling before the stalwart knights of the sunny South."[1] But no less than their Northern counterparts, they were knights in service of a human government, not the reign of

---

1. Phillips, *Diehard Rebels*, 46.

Christ—a government whose very constitution, like that of the United States, rejected true knighthood, nobility, and monarchy and made no mention of Christ. That is, they were knights of political modernity, riding into battle for the same essential cause as the knaves of the North they considered inferior beings: the cause of Liberty; but Liberty with slaves, just as the Framers had so wisely provided. It was this crusade, not a crusade for the Word Incarnate, that Confederate religion served—in opposition to the Northern crusade for Liberty without slaves.

The Anglican Bishop of Savannah, Stephen Elliot, illustrated the point with a fiery funeral oration that had denounced "ye Christians of the North" and called them "to that bar in the name of sacred Liberty which you have trampled under foot; in the name of the glorious Constitution which you have destroyed" and "our slaves whom you have seduced."[2] Likewise, the Rev. James Warley Miles of Charleston wrote: "It would be impiety to doubt our triumph, because we are working out a great thought of God—namely, the higher development of Humanity in its capacity for Constitutional Liberty."[3] In a patriotic tract circulated by the Confederate Army, Frances Blake Brockenbrough had urged her son to war because "We are contending for the great principle of the American Revolution; that all authority is derived from the consent of the governed"—but not the consent of their slaves. Her son must be a Christian soldier, she wrote, like such "humble Christians" as "Cromwell, Gardiner, and Havelock, thunderbolts of war... devout as they were heroic."[4] In the great Anglo-Protestant tradition of Liberty, Brockenbrough's selection of model Christian soldiers, published for the inspiration of Confederate troops, included the "humble" regicide general who overthrew the Stuart monarchy and began Liberty's long march of conquest through Christendom (Cromwell), and the fallen Protestant hero of a battle to prevent the Catholic Prince Charles Edward Stuart, the grandson of James II residing under papal protection in Rome, from regaining the throne of England for the Stuarts during the Jacobite Uprising of 1745 (Gardiner).

In a remarkable demonstration of just how tightly the Southern cause had been bound to "Christian" chattel slavery, the exponents of the Confederacy as Christian crusade developed the argument that it was precisely slavery that had kept the South so staunchly Christian and saved it from the fate of both the North and revolutionary Europe. The South, it was argued, was really the world's only remaining bastion of Christendom (as the Protestant mind understood that term), an oasis of stability where false notions of freedom had not corrupted social order. And slavery indeed was the *sine qua non* of this happy state of affairs! The *Richmond Examiner* could not have stated the Southern claim more clearly: "we are the *only* religious and conservative people in Christendom.... It is nothing but our social institutions and *our domestic slavery* that distinguishes us from the rest of the nations of

2. Ibid., 37.

3. In Genovese, *A Consuming Fire*, 37.

4. *A New Tract for Soldiers*, No. 18, "A Mother's Parting Words to Her Soldier Boy," 1, 5. Duke University Ebook and Texts Archive, http://archive.org/details/motherspartingwo00broc.

Europe." Thanks to slavery, the South had avoided the terrible situation in which "all men are equals, [and] all must be competitors."[5]

With the skill of a consummate polemicist, James Henley Thornwell wove his defense of slavery into a depiction of the South as a fortress against the radicalism and revolutionism threatening the whole world: "The parties in this conflict are not merely abolitionists and slaveholders—they are atheists, socialists, communists, red republicans, jacobins, on the one side, and the friends of order and regulated freedom on the other. In one word, the world is the battle ground—Christianity and Atheism the combatants. . . ." At the same time Southern Protestant apologists for slavery were denouncing Northern Protestant abolitionism as a Trojan horse for all manner of anti-Christian radical forces, they were deploying their notion of Christendom as a Trojan horse filled with human chattels. That the Catholic countries of pre-revolutionary Europe had been strongholds of Christianity for centuries after slavery disappeared seems to have escaped Thornwell's notice, probably because he and his fellow evangelical Presbyterians did not regard Catholicism as Christian.[6]

Yet in the South, as in the North and revolutionary Europe, all men *were* declared equal in precisely the modern egalitarian sense the antebellum Southern polemicists professed to deplore. To this objection would come the reply that in the South only *white* men were considered equal under the Declaration of Independence, whereas in Europe and the North—including its still-Catholic nations, which of course did not qualify as part of what the Protestant mind considered Christendom—there was no distinction among men based on race. It was precisely this racial distinction (so the argument goes) that was the genius of the Southern system with its "order and regulated freedom." Had not President Jefferson Davis insisted for this reason on the limited application of the Declaration to whites only? Had not Vice President Stephens cited the weight of scientific authority as well as the Bible and divine law in support of "the proper status of the negro in our form of civilization"?

According to the argument, then, it was the legally mandated slavery of the Negro race—and the Negro race alone, for white slavery was indeed immoral, as Stephens and Southerners in general recognized—which insured that this European and Northern business of equality would not go too far in the South. The slaves were a kind of anchor against the mania for equality; a human placeholder for the hierarchical society the Union and the Confederacy alike had legally abolished in their practically identical Constitutions.

But what of the objection that blacks were not equal to whites in the North either, so that the North ought to have been a bastion of Christendom according to the Southern rationale? The proponents of the Southern Christendom theory

---

5. *Examiner,* July 17, 1861, in *Religion and the American Civil War,* eds Randall M. Miller, Harry S. Stout (New York: Oxford University Press, 1998), 340.

6. Cf. Thornwell, "The Validity of the Baptism of the Church of Rome," *Collected Writings,* Vol. III, 283 ff, wherein he develops the standard evangelical arguments for the invalidity of Catholic baptisms on account of numerous Roman "heresies."

would reply that as blacks of the North were not *slaves*, the North, with its dog-eat-dog regime of free labor, lacked the missing ingredient for the preservation of Christendom in a world gone mad for equality and unbridled competition. *Slavery* insured the "order and regulated freedom" of the Republic the Founders and Framers had established with the protection of slavery in view; the peculiar institution represented the genuine Christian inheritance of the Founding.

As Eugene Genovese demonstrated in his Averitt Lecture on the subject, the conservative, pro-slavery Protestant divines of the South were quite prepared to concede to the conservative, anti-slavery Protestants of the North that "*you northern conservatives share our revulsion against growing infidelity and secularism . . .* the rapid extension of the heresies of liberal theology . . . the social and political abominations of egalitarianism and popular democracy . . . the mounting assault upon family and upon the very principle of authority. *You share our alarm* at the growing popularity of the perverse doctrines of Enlightenment radicalism and the French Revolution. . . ." But, the polemic continued, "you fail to identify the root of this massive theological, ecclesiastical, social and political offensive against Christianity and the social order: *the system of free labor.* . . . You fail to see that *only the restoration of some form of personal servitude* can arrest the moral decay of society. . . . In truth, the South stands virtually alone in the transatlantic world as a bastion of Christian social order because it rests upon a Christian social system."[7]

That is, the South had stood alone because the South alone still defended a "Christian" system of slave labor. Southern Christians had "marched to war behind their Lord of Hosts, convinced that he blessed their struggle to uphold a biblically sanctioned slavery."[8] But this remarkably refined theological sophistry could not alter the reality that the South, no less than the North, was heir to the American Revolution and its radical abandonment of the very essence of the true Christendom: an organic relation between Church and State under the old order of Altar and Throne. Hence what Genovese calls the "slaveholders' dilemma" of attempting to reconcile their revolutionary inheritance with their Protestant brand of Christian conservatism.

Just as Lincoln had done on the Northern side of the conflict, the revolutionary and military leaders of the Confederacy instrumentalized religion for purely secular and material ends. The Protestant preachers of the South routinely denounced the godless and barbarian North from their pulpits, to which Northern preachers responded with their own charges of Southern brutality and infidelity to the Gospel. For the Confederacy, the religion of the holy Christian war for "sacred Liberty," which the North had "trampled under foot," kept the cause alive long after it had become objectively untenable. Phillips shows how a combination of "grim justice and joyful religion worked together to rejuvenate the army" despite the mortal blows at Gettysburg and Vicksburg. He cites by way of example the testimony of the Alabamian Sam Pickens, who witnessed ten executions of deserters on September

7. Genovese, *Slaveholders' Dilemma*, 37–38.
8. Genovese, *A Consuming Fire*, 3.

5, 1863—one of whom had to be shot sixteen times—followed by sixteen Protestant-style total immersion baptisms of Confederate soldiers on September 6.[9]

But the ironic motto of the Confederacy's Great Seal—God Will Vindicate—reflected a religiosity in service of war that, unlike the North's Armageddon-like mission, could only undermine the Southern cause. As Phillips observes, the Confederate diehard had to confront the simple question: "If the Confederacy enjoyed divine favor, why was it losing the war?"[10] In the end, "The South's religious views served as a trap for Confederate will. When victories decreased and casualty lists lengthened, doubts about God's favor (never very far beneath the surface) began to arise and Southern will weakened accordingly."[11]

Here we must recall the "Southern Jeremiahs" we encountered in Chapter 12, including John Leadley Dagg, who had warned that the moral infirmities of the "peculiar institution" were a violation of Christian duty and grounds for God's wrath. "The Southern Jeremiahs," writes Genovese, "lived to say, 'I told you so.' They had, after all, long warned against a misreading of the signs of the times." One after the other, they declared (with Dagg) that "God had inflicted defeat . . . upon the Confederacy because its people had failed in their duty to their black dependents. . . ." Genovese cites the prominent examples of George Flournoy, the former Texas attorney general, who "concluded that God had cursed slavery in the wake of the Southerners' failure to improve the moral and material condition of the slaves," and Henry William Ravenel, the renowned botanist and Episcopalian of South Carolina, who "admitted that the slaveholders had erred in failing to reform the slave codes in time [and] . . . especially regretted the failure to protect slave marriages and families."[12] After the Confederacy was destroyed, these Protestant divines "ruefully allowed that God had punished the South for failing to do justice to its slaves," yet "they reiterated their conviction that they had not sinned in upholding slavery per se" and they mourned "the destruction of their cherished 'Christian' slave society."[13]

Slavery aside, at the level of laws, institutions and public policy the Confederate cause was no more a Christian crusade or even an explicitly religious one than the North's. "There is neither Christianity nor religion of any kind in this war," declared the *Richmond Examiner* in August of 1863. "We prosecute it in self-defense, for the preservation of our liberty, our homes and our Negroes."[14] Nor did the Southern legal system overall exhibit a more Christian cast than the Northern. In keeping with the American Revolution—and the logic of Protestantism in general—by the eve of the Civil War all the Southern states except South Carolina had joined the Northern states in legalizing divorce; all had abandoned official establishments of Christianity; and all but Maryland (which did not secede) had abandoned religious tests for office. New York and North Carolina alike "abolished any remnants

9. Phillips, *Diehard Rebels* 28.
10. Phillips, *Diehard Rebels*, 32.
11. Beringer, *Why the South Lost the Civil War*, 98.
12. Genovese, *A Consuming Fire*, 67–68.
13. Ibid., 71, 101.
14. Stout and Grasso, op. cit., in *American Religion and Civil War*, 338.

of religious establishments"[15] immediately after the Revolution, with Maryland, Georgia, South Carolina, and Virginia soon following.

Virginia's abolition of all state support of Christianity back in 1786 was in accordance with the latitudinarian thinking of the Southern Founder and Framer, James Madison, and his fellow nominal Anglican and deist, Thomas Jefferson, the Founder who was the South's most sacred icon of Liberty—venerated equally in the North, of course, in keeping with the spirit of Liberty animating both sides of the Civil War. The persistence of the myth of a Confederate Christendom seems not to have been affected by the historical reality that it was two deistic, slave-owning plantation owners from Virginia, the capital state of the Confederacy, who led the way to federal Church-State separation in the first officially secular nation-state in world history, under a Constitution of which Madison is called the father—a development Section IV will examine in detail. Nor has the myth been affected even by the Confederate Constitution's own prohibition of the establishment of Christianity (or any other religion) in religion clauses identical to those in the First Amendment to the U.S. Constitution, whose provenance was both Jeffersonian and Madisonian, as we shall see.

While Jefferson Davis called publicly for fasting ten times during the war, even the unchurched Lincoln did so three times. And, as in the North, "in the southern pulpit the doctrine of the church's 'spirituality'—the strict separation of church and state—reigned. . . ."[16] It reigned as well in Richmond. Confederate army regulations "never mentioned the role, duties, or even presence of chaplains in the ranks. Demonstrating their own indifference to religion—despite presidential appeals for fast days—Jefferson Davis and others in high places thought paid chaplaincies a misallocation of scarce resources. *Separation of church and state was carried to an extreme that could not have helped army esprit de corps in the long run. . . .* No wonder clerical morale during the war was not much better than that of the civilian population as a whole."[17] By comparison, the far more numerous Union chaplains had the rank, pay and allowances of a captain in the cavalry. And the denominational breakdown by percentage was virtually the same for chaplains of the South and the North.[18]

To the extent Confederate politicians like Davis had preached a civic religion in which the Southern cause was God's cause, "[m]uch of that rhetoric, after all, originated in the North"[19] with the Puritan narrative of a Protestant New World as part of God's plan from all eternity. There was a "Confederate jeremiad"[20] no less than a

15. Steven Green, *The Second Disestablishment: Church and State in Nineteenth-Century America* (NY: Oxford Univ. Press, 2010, Kindle Edition), 421.

16. Stout and Grasso, 320.

17. Bertram Wyatt-Brown, "Church, Honor and Secession," in *American Religion and the Civil War,* Kindle Edition, 104.

18. Cf. website of National Civil War Chaplains Museum, www.chaplainsmuseum.org/i/?page_id =21.

19. Stout and Grasso, 325.

20. Ibid., 326.

Northern one, as Lincoln had cynically acknowledged when he noted toward the war's end that both sides "read the same Bible and pray to the same God, and each invokes his aid against the other." Nor was Lincoln to be outdone by Davis when it came to exalted religious rhetoric. In his Proclamation Appointing a National Fast Day on March 30, 1863 he declared: "But we have forgotten God.... Intoxicated with unbroken success, we have become too self-sufficient to feel the necessity of redeeming and preserving grace, too proud to pray to the God that made us! It behooves us then, to humble ourselves before the offended Power, to confess our national sins, and to pray for clemency and forgiveness." And it was Lincoln who, in his Proclamation for Thanksgiving on July 15, 1863, following the Union victory at Gettysburg, called upon the citizenry to "render homage due to the Divine Majesty, for the wonderful things He has done in the Nation's behalf, and invoke the influence of his Holy Spirit."[21] Just as the War of Independence had "incorporated and reaffirmed" the Puritan tradition of God's chosen Protestant people as the heralds of human progress, so had the South "wanted to believe it was divinely chosen." The Southern days of prayer and fasting, like those of the North, were a "symbolic claim both to God's special favor and to an important component of the American heritage"[22]—the heritage of a divinely sanctioned holy war for Liberty.

Apart from the division over slavery, Protestant religious thought in the North and the South "displayed striking similarities; for each saw its own region as the legitimate 'new Israel.' Each side operated from the same beliefs, seeing victory as a sign of God's favor, defeat as a sign that the people had strayed from Him and thus lost favor...."[23] And as we saw in Chapter 12, even the theological differences between the two sections over slavery were the result of convenient theological modifications by Southern Protestant ministers in the mid-1800s. As of 1844 some 14.5 million Americans out of a national population of 17.5 million were members, or under the influence, of an evangelical church.[24] Given the universal disestablishment of religion, North and South, during the antebellum years all of America was an "'antebellum spiritual hothouse'... [and] [i]n response to the growing religious pluralism and the absence of a spiritual order *created by disestablishment*, orthodox and evangelical leaders called for voluntary societies and associations to achieve the realization of a Christian America."[25] The antebellum South could not even claim a greater presence of the Christian clergy among the populace than in the North. Quite the contrary, "there were over twice as many clergymen in New York than in all thirteen slave states put together, and the same number as preached in all the South served the single state of Pennsylvania. To put it another way, in the North, out of 187 inhabitants one was a minister, and in the South, the ratio

21. In eds John G. Nicolay and John Hay, *Abraham Lincoln: Complete Works* (NY: The Century Co., 1920), Vol. II, 370.

22. Drew Gilpin Faust, *The Creation of Confederate Nationalism: Identity and Ideology in the Civil War South* (Baton Rouge: Louisiana State Univ. Press, 1988), 26.

23. Beringer, et al., *Why the South Lost the Civil War*, 274.

24. Green, *The Second Disestablishment*, 1186 (Kindle location).

25. Ibid., 1208.

was one to 329." And the North's Unitarian moment had long since passed with the Second Great Awakening.

And while "Confederates took great pride in the invocation of God in their own constitution, as opposed to the 'Godless instrument' still in effect in the North,"[26] the most conservative Protestants of the South recognized that what the Confederate Constitution and the Confederacy itself lacked was precisely a specifically Christian character. Thus, for example, in 1861 James Thornwell—the same anti-Catholic bigot who so skillfully developed the conservative Protestant theology of slavery just cited—presented the General Assembly of the Presbyterian Church of the Confederate States of America a paper in which he called upon the Confederate Congress to amend the Confederate Constitution to recognize explicitly the authority of Christ over the Confederate nation. His proposed amendment would have read: "We, the people of these Confederate States, distinctly acknowledge our responsibility to God, and the supremacy of His Son, Jesus Christ, as King of kings and Lord of lords; and hereby ordain that no law shall be passed by the Congress of these Confederate States inconsistent with the will of God, as revealed in the Holy Scriptures."[27] Unwittingly, Thornwell was advocating Confederate recognition of what Catholics call the Social Kingship of Christ, a doctrine they commemorate and reaffirm on the Feast of Christ the King.[28]

As Thornwell observed in his paper, despite a generic invocation of God the Confederate Constitution "still labours under one capital defect. *It is not distinctively Christian*" and thus did not "express the precise relations which the Government of these States ought to sustain to the religion of Jesus Christ."[29] The Confederate Congress had "to some extent, rectified the error of the old Constitution, but not so distinctly and clearly as the Christian people of these States desire to see done." Thornwell argued that "it is not enough for a State which enjoys the light of Divine revelation to acknowledge in general terms the supremacy of God; *it must also acknowledge the supremacy of His Son*, whom He hath appointed heir of all things, by whom also He made the worlds. To Jesus Christ all power in heaven and earth is committed. To Him every knee shall bow, and every tongue confess. *He is the Ruler of the nations, the King of kings, and Lord of lords*."[30]

As the Southern cause collapsed, Jefferson Davis himself wondered whether the "Confederate constitution should not have stopped at recognizing God but should have gone on to express its belief in 'the Saviour of mankind' and perhaps even . . . specifically have countenanced Christianity. Might this, he wondered, have saved his dying nation?"[31] But the Confederate States were no more likely than the United States to depart from the Lockean framework within which both sides were operating, wherein a Christian commonwealth was excluded as a matter

26. Faust, *Confederate Nationalism*, 31.
27. Thornwell, 549–50.
28. Cf. Pius XI, *Quas Primas*.
29. Thornwell, 549–50.
30. Ibid., 551.
31. Davis, *Jefferson Davis: the Man and His Hour*, 602.

of principle in keeping with what Thornwell called "the fatal delusion that our government is a mere expression of human will...."[32] The failed movement for a Christian constitution for the Confederacy paralleled a far more vigorous Northern movement for a "Christian Amendment" to the U.S. Constitution, the National Reform Association, which continued well beyond the end of the Civil War as we will see in Chapter 18. Thornwell, in fact, was little more than a lone voice crying out in the wilderness of the Confederacy. "When he died [in 1862] his principles and his proposal seem to have died with him."[33]

Quite telling in this regard (as Chapter 18 will show) is the longstanding Northern movement for a Christian commonwealth in America. From the time of the Second Great Awakening through the antebellum period and during the Civil War itself, it was conservative evangelicals of the North, led by such luminaries as Timothy Dwight, the President of Yale, who publicly agitated for a national submission to the reign of Christ and condemned the "godlessness" of the Constitution. In fact, as we will see, it was Dwight and John M. Mason, the evangelical Presbyterian minister of renown from New York, who led public opposition to the presidential candidacy of Jefferson, the iconic Southern agrarian, on the ground that America would be punished for electing an "infidel"—which, by any objective standard of Christianity, Jefferson certainly was.

As these indications make clear, the more historical facts one considers, the more the depiction of the South as the defeated land of the godly and the North as the victorious land of apostates is revealed as a cartoonish oversimplification. Before, during and after the Civil War, America as a whole exhibited the religious enthusiasms and divisions of any predominantly Protestant nation—a nation founded, after all, in a Protestant rebellion against the last remnants of Catholic social order represented by the "popery" of George III. There was plenty of Protestant piety of various flavors—and plenty of apostasy—in both the northern and southern wings of the Temple of Liberty. A more accurate picture is that the far more populous and urban northern wing exhibited both piety and apostasy on a much larger scale.

But even if one allows that in the South a generically more "conservative" strain of Protestantism prevailed than in the North—an ultimately trifling distinction given the intrinsic liberalism of the Protestant religion—how does this validate the myth of the Lost Cause, given that the Southern states fully retained their "Bible belt conservatism" after the war? In fact, they still retain it today relative to the Northern states, in the sense of a theological "conservatism" that drifts inexorably toward moral dissolution in Protestant social order regardless of the geographical latitude at which it exists. As Orestes Brownson would observe only six years after the war: "democracy may be a good form of government; but combined with

---

32. Thornwell, "Relation of the State to Christ," 551.

33. "Relation of the State to Christ," *Christian Nation*, February 9, 1902, Vol. 36, 4. This Northern publication reprinted Thornwell's paper with praise, noting that he had withdrawn it from the consideration by the Assembly when it was clear that it would not receive full and fair discussion.

Protestantism . . . its inevitable tendency is to lower the standard of morality, to enfeeble intellect, to abase character, and to retard civilization, as even our short American experience amply proves."[34]

A Catholic Crusade?

Citing Jefferson Davis's initiation into the Anglican Church at age 52 during the war, some Southern partisan romantics—apparently sensing a need to obviate the sheer Calvinism innate in the Southern cause—propose that the South was really engaged in an "Anglo-Catholic" crusade. This fanciful notion is advanced regardless of the official disestablishment of the Anglican Church in Virginia immediately after the American Revolution, the lack of any established Anglican Church anywhere in the Confederacy, and the status of Anglicans as a tiny minority in the evangelical-dominated South. According to this story, Davis (who was sent to a Catholic school by his father) converted to Catholicism on his deathbed. There is no evidence for the claim, which apparently represents a Southern partisan analogue of the fairy-tale deathbed conversion of George Washington.

Varina Davis's loving biography of her late husband makes no mention of any conversion to Catholicism, on his deathbed or otherwise. And, tellingly, there is not a single reference to the Catholic faith in Davis's *Short History of the Confederate States of America* or his two-volume *Rise and Fall of the Confederate Government*, spanning some two thousand pages of oppressively detailed memoirs. Quite the contrary, Davis explained clearly why he was an Anglican and not a Catholic—despite his attendance at a Catholic school as a boy, his decided Catholic sympathies, and his affection for the Sisters of Charity who had cared for his family at Savannah during the war. "[S]pirituality," he once wrote, is "supreme over matter," which is why "the simple singing of an excited congregation of 'Methodists,' has stirred in my heart a deeper feeling than the noble ceremonial of the High Mass. . . . *All modes of Christian worship are in themselves good*, they are the different kind of roads suited to the great variety of travellers, and why not to the different mood of the same traveller, if by such diversion he may the more certainly reach the end of his journey. . . ." Not for him was the notion that "none but the Papists can be saved" or, on the other hand, that "all the Papists must be condemned." For Davis, who pronounced Luther "a benefactor of mankind," the Christian religion was happily composed of "flocks scattered on a thousand hills . . . all cared for by the one great Shepherd, who will seek every sheep that is lost without inquiring from which flock it is astray." Like the Protestant and partisan of Liberty he was, he declared that the flock that suited his taste was the one created by Henry VIII to accommodate his divorce: "The catholicity of St. Paul [Episcopal Church] suits me well."[35] There is no

---

34. Orestes Brownson, "Introduction to Last Series," *Brownson's Quarterly Review* (January 1873), in *The Works of Orestes A. Brownson* (Detroit: H. F. Brownson, 1887), Vol. XX, 285.

35. In Felicity Allen, *Jefferson Davis: Unconquerable Heart* (Columbia, MO: Univ. of Missouri Press, 1999), 440.

indication in Davis's writings that he recognized the salvific necessity of any church, much less the Catholic Church.

Proponents of the myth of a Confederate "Anglo-Catholic crusade" argue that American Catholics naturally aligned themselves with the Confederacy in preference to the Union. But that claim founders on the basis of one undeniable fact: the preponderant alignment of American Catholics was with the Union. By 1860, thanks to waves of Irish immigration, Catholicism had become the single largest religious denomination in the North, whereas "Southern Catholics were a minority in a culture dominated by evangelical orthodoxy." Although the Irish Catholics of the Northern states "were known for their commitment to the Democratic Party and enmity toward blacks, they were frequently deeply loyal to the Union."[36] All told, some 140,000 Irish Catholic immigrants fought in the Union army, most serving in the Irish Brigade with its Irish regiments. The Irish Sixty-Ninth Regiment, for example, carried into battle both the green flag of Ireland and the Stars and Stripes. The same regiment was also found alongside the heavily Irish New York City police force in putting down the largely Irish draft riots of 1863.[37]

On the Southern side, the destruction and incompleteness of records has always made it impossible to determine precisely the overall strength of the Confederate army as a whole, much less its ethnic breakdown, although Irish Catholics certainly fought valiantly for the Confederacy. The historian Philip Thomas Tucker estimates that some 30,000 Irish-born Catholics fought for the South in various regiments, while noting also that *Irish Catholic brothers fought against each other* in the war.[38] For example, Brigadier General James McIntosh served the Confederacy, while Second Lieutenant John B. McIntosh fought for the Union. And both sides saw Catholic clerics assisting the cause. In the North, for example, Father William Corby, who later became president of the University of Notre Dame, ministered to dying Northern troops of the Irish Brigade during the Battle of Gettysburg. In doing so, he placed himself under Confederate fire, and a statue in his memory was erected on the battleground. On the Southern side, Father Abram Joseph Ryan achieved fame and fond memory by ministering to dying Catholics in the Confederate ranks.

The Catholic Church as an institution never expressed support for either side of the conflict, although individual members of the upper hierarchy, such as Archbishop John Hughes in New York and Archbishop John Mary Odin in New Orleans, called for allegiance to civil authority along regional lines. Individual prelates on both sides, however, were open partisans for the existing government.[39] In the vexed State of Virginia, closely divided over the issue of secession, Bishop McGill of the Diocese of Richmond produced two books, in one of which he

---

36. Eds David S. and Jeanne T. Heidler, *Encyclopedia of the American Civil War* (NY: W. W. Norton & Co., 2000), 374.

37. Iver Berstein, *The New York City Draft Riots: Their Significance for American Society and Politics in the Age of the Civil War* (Oxford: Oxford Univ. Press, 1990), 113.

38. Philip Thomas Tucker, *Irish Confederates: The Civil War's Forgotten Soldiers* (Abilene, TX: McWhitney Foundation Press, 2006), 17.

39. Cf. Blied, *Catholics and the Civil War*, 36–39.

"deplored the fact that the Christian rulers of this country did not permit the marriage of slaves and permitted owners to separate husband from wife and children
from parents." Commenting on the war he wrote: "It is not certain that the present
dreaded calamities, which afflict the country, are not the scourge of God, chiefly
for this sin, among the many that provoke his anger. . . ."[40] After the Confederacy
fell, even the Confederate partisan Bishop Verot of Savannah "bluntly attributed
the defeat to the slaveholders' failure to treat their slaves in accordance with scriptural injunction."[41]

The American hierarchy at large declined to embrace either Northern abolitionism on the one hand or the South's "slavery is the Christian thing to do" polemic
on the other. This was in keeping with American Catholic quietism in general. In
order "to prove that Catholics were 'good Americans', the American hierarchy practiced a studied non-involvement in politics and political issues, especially the most
political issue of the day, slavery."[42] Hence the only synodal declaration on the war
appears to have been that of the Third Provincial Council of Cincinnati, issued sixteen days after the surrender of Fort Sumter. The assembled bishops spoke only of
deplorable strife in which the Church—unlike the Protestant sects—had no stake:

> It is not for us to enquire into the causes which have led to the present
> unhappy condition of affairs. . . . The spirit of the Catholic Church is emi-
> nently conservative, and while her ministers rightfully feel a deep and abiding
> interest in all that concerns the welfare of the country, they do not think it
> their province to enter into the political arena. They leave to *the ministers of
> the human sects* to discuss from their pulpits and in their ecclesiastical assem-
> blies the exciting questions which lie at the basis of most of our present and
> prospective difficulties. Thus, while many of the sects have divided into hos-
> tile parties on an exciting political issue, the Catholic Church has carefully
> preserved her unity of spirit in the bond of peace, literally *knowing no North,
> no South, no East, no West.*
>
> Had this wise and considerate line of conduct been generally followed
> throughout the country, we are convinced that much of the embittered feel-
> ing which now unfortunately exists, would have been obviated, and that
> brotherly love, the genuine offspring of true Christianity, instead of *the fratri-
> cidal hatred which is opposed to its essential genius and spirit,* would now bless
> our country, and bind together all our fellow-citizens in one harmonious
> brotherhood. . . .[43]

Then again, Archbishop Purcell of Cincinnati penned a Thanksgiving reflection
in 1864 which declared that the North "did not commence this war" and asked
"[w]here in the north was the draft, the conscription, enforced as ruthlessly and as

40. Ibid., 62–63.
41. Genovese, *A Consuming Fire*, 67.
42. Zanca, *American Catholics and Slavery*, 34.
43. John Francis Maguire, *The Irish in America* (Charleston, SC: Forgotten Books, 2010), 461.

indiscriminately as in the south? Where was the citizens' property confiscated, without compensation, for the alleged uses of government, as it was in the south?" He referred to "Irish Catholic refugees from Georgia, from Arkansas, from Alabama, and other southern states" who had told him of how they "were stripped of their money and their clothes and cast into prison, when they refused to go into the ranks of the confederate army." And Archbishop Hughes of New York advised Bishop Lynch of Charleston that in his view "the constitution having been formed by the common consent of all the parties engaged in the ... approval thereof, I maintain that no state has a right to secede, except in the manner provided in the document itself."[44]

A *"Deplorable Intestine War"*

Looking abroad, some Southern partisans have suggested that no less than Pope Pius IX (reigning from 1846 to 1878) lent the weight of his office to the Lost Cause as "Anglo-Catholic crusade." The only documentary evidence in support of the claim is a letter from Pius to Jefferson Davis, dated December 3, 1863. The Pope wrote in response to a letter from Davis purporting to reply to the Pope's prior missive to the leading American prelates of the North and the South—Hughes of New York and Odin of New Orleans—calling upon them to use their good offices to bring an end to the conflict. The Pope's letter to Davis, addressed to the "Illustrious and Honorable Mr. Jefferson Davis, President of the Confederate States," was provided to A. Dudley Mann, the Confederate emissary who went to Rome in a failed attempt to attain diplomatic recognition of the Confederacy.

Mann portrayed the salutation as an implicit diplomatic recognition of the Confederate States, but it was nothing of the kind, as the Confederacy's Jewish Secretary of State, Judah Benjamin, recognized. On the other hand, Rome had continuing diplomatic relations with the United States at the consular and mission level before and during the war even if there was no formal ambassadorship. Benjamin dismissed the papal salutation as a "formula of politeness to his correspondent, not a political recognition of the fact. *None* of our political journals treat the letter as a recognition in the sense you attach to it, and ... the Nuncio at Paris ... had received no instructions to put his official visa on our passports...."[45] In his biography of Jefferson Davis, William Davis (no relation) notes that "through the whole course of diplomatic efforts, the only glimmer of recognition—and that meaningless" was the papal letter, and that while "the foolish old Dudley Mann, who engineered the correspondence, called it 'a positive recognition of our government'.... Davis and Benjamin were not fooled."[46] Rome itself "considered the letter merely a polite acknowledgment of Davis's letter. Apparently papal offi-

---

44. Blied, *Catholics and the Civil War*, 41–43.

45. Benjamin to Mann, February 1, 1864, in John Bigelow, "The Southern Confederacy and the Pope," *The North American Review*, Vol. 159 (1893), 469.

46. Davis, *Jefferson Davis: the Man and His Hour*, 545.

cials attached no significance to the epistolary form 'President of the Confederate States of America.'"[47]

Furthermore, Southern partisans overlook Pius IX's diplomatic correspondence with the Union side of the conflict, which can just as readily be construed as support for the Union's position. For example, in June 1862 Alexander W. Randall, then United States minister to Rome, sent a letter to the Pope presenting his credentials along with Randall's contention that the war involved the South's "treason, and rebellion, on the one hand, and law, order, and constitutional Government, on the other." The North, he wrote, was defending "Government and institutions against an armed rebellion seeking to overthrow them." In reply the Pope wrote: "We have listened with satisfaction to the sentiments *Your Excellency* has well expressed as to the duty of supporting government, of contributing to its stability, and of observing just laws. *And it has ever been the maxim of the Church to support constituted authority* and just laws." The Pope went on to observe that "we feel justly proud" that the United States had chosen Archbishop Hughes with the "most important mission" of representing the United States in Rome.[48]

If anything, the Pope's letter to Randall (for whatever such diplomatic missives are worth) can be read more readily as positive support than the letter to Davis. The latter, transmitted via an emissary who presented no diplomatic credentials and had none, contained no expressions of approval whatsoever for the South's position. Rather, Pius IX deplored the entire conflict and stated his wish that it be ended amicably:

> We have lately received with all kindness, as was meet, the gentlemen sent by your Excellency to present to us your letter dated on the 23d of last September. We have received certainly no small pleasure in learning both from these gentlemen and from your letter the feelings of gratification and very warm appreciation with which you, Illustrious and Honorable Sir, were moved when you first had knowledge of our letters written in October of the preceding year to the Venerable Brethren, John, Archbishop of New York, and John, Archbishop of New Orleans, in which we again and again urged and exhorted those Venerable Brethren that because of their exemplary piety and episcopal zeal they should employ the most earnest efforts, in our name also, in order that *the fatal civil war* which had arisen in the States should end, and that the people of America might again enjoy *mutual peace and concord, and love each other with mutual charity.* And it has been very gratifying to us to recognize, Illustrious Sir, that you and your people are animated by the same desire for peace and tranquility.... Oh, that the other people also of the States and their rulers, considering seriously *how cruel and how deplorable is this intestine war,* would receive and embrace the counsels of peace and tranquility![49]

47. In David J. Alvarez, "The Papacy in the Diplomacy of the American Civil War," *The Catholic Historical Review,* Vol. 69, No. 2 (Apr. 1983), 243.

48. In *United States Ministers to the Papal States* (Washington, DC: Catholic Univ. Press, 1933), 351–52.

49. In Bigelow, *The Southern Confederacy and the Pope,* 469.

Unlike the wildly optimistic Mann, Secretary of State Benjamin—who had an estranged French Catholic wife he married in a Catholic ceremony—was astute enough to see that the Pope's reference to a "fatal *civil* war" and a "cruel and deplorable *intestine* war" was an implicit rejection of the Confederacy's fundamental claim: that it was a sovereign nation at war with an invading foreign power. "[T]he war now waged by them [the North] is foreign, *not an intestine or civil war, as it is termed by the Pope*," he replied testily to Mann.[50]

Nevertheless, Benjamin exploited the letter's propaganda value, causing it to be published in the Southern and European press to the consternation of Washington. In response to an inquiry by Rufus King, the United States minister to Rome, the Pope's Secretary of State, Cardinal Giacomo Antonielli, assured King that Secretary of State Seward's interpretation of the letter "was correct since the missive possessed no political significance. He added that Pius would have replied in the same spirit to a communication from Abraham Lincoln." Deep into the war, both Antonielli and the Pope personally expressed to King "renewed support for the Union," and the Holy Father personally informed King during an audience that "as much as he deprecated the War and desired that it might cease, he could never, as a Christian and the head of the Catholic Church, lend any sanction or countenance, to the system of African slavery."[51]

Still worse for this piece of the Southern romantic narrative, Cardinal Antonielli, known to be doctrinally inimical to insurrections of any sort in keeping with Catholic teaching, told King that "he had carefully studied the American question; that he had read our Constitution and could plainly perceive that the so-called Confederate States had sought an unconstitutional remedy for their alleged wrongs, and were endeavoring to dissolve by force a Union consecrated by law."[52] Antonielli repeated this advice to Bishop Patrick Neeson Lynch of South Carolina when he journeyed to Rome as a Confederate representative in a second attempt to obtain diplomatic recognition.[53] (By then Archbishop Hughes had already made his own diplomatic mission to the Holy See as "an agent of the North," defending Union policy and providing reports of the Union's early successes in battle.)[54] Lynch's mission failed. The Pope received him only in private audience, "not as a Confederate representative," and Cardinal Antonielli "assured [King] that Lynch was received only as a bishop making his *ad limina* visit." In further conversations with both Pius and Antonielli, Lynch "made no progress toward recognition."[55] On the contrary, Antonielli advised the United States minister that Lynch "had never been received, or recognized, in any way, as an accredited representative of Jefferson Davis; and that, like every other good Catholic, resident in the U.S., it was his bounden duty to

50. Ibid., 470.
51. King to Seward, October 25, 1864, in *United States Ministers to the Papal States*, 321.
52. King to Seward, August 22, 1864, in *United States Ministers*, 315–16.
53. Blied, *Catholics and the Civil War*, 68.
54. Alvarez, "The Papacy in the Diplomacy of the American Civil War," 231–33.
55. David G. R. Heiser, "Bishop Lynch's Civil War Pamphlet on Slavery," *The Catholic Historical Review*, Vol. 84, No. 4 (October 1998), 682–83.

honor, respect, and obey the constituted authorities of the Government, under whose protection he lived."[56] For his trouble, Bishop Lynch was reduced to taking a loyalty oath to the United States and seeking a presidential pardon before he could be readmitted to the country and his episcopal see in Charleston.

Most ironically, it was the Protestant ex-minister to France under Lincoln, John Bigelow, writing after the war, who would defend Pius IX and the Church against the suggestion that Rome had aligned itself with a government whose constitution expressly declared that it was formed for the perpetuation of institutionalized chattel slavery and whose member States had cited its preservation as the grounds for secession:

> Could anything accentuate the infatuation of these men in their attempt to equip from the old world a republican fortress for the protection and propagation of slavery in the new, it had to be sought in this effort to enlist the Pope and his church in their support. It is not so very surprising that neither Davis nor Benjamin nor any of their agents abroad was aware of the hostile attitude which the Church of Rome had always occupied towards chattel slavery, and that wherever it has prevailed in Catholic countries it has prevailed by permission or encouragement from the civil, not from the ecclesiastical, power.
>
> The studies of these statesmen may be presumed not to have ranged very widely in the domain of Ecclesiastical history. But how a bishop could have indulged the expectation for one moment, if Bishop Lynch did indulge it, that Pius IX, with a half dozen bulls of his predecessors, against holding our fellow-creature in bondage, staring him in the face, could have taken the first step towards countenancing this pro-slavery crusade in the United States, is quite incomprehensible.[57]

In fairness, however, it must be said that Pope Pius was undoubtedly personally sympathetic to the South in its wartime plight and that he is reported to have confided privately to a British diplomat that—quite apart from the question of slavery and its abolition—he hoped the South would succeed.[58] And when Davis was briefly imprisoned in Fortress Monroe following the fall of the Confederacy, the Pope would send him condolences in the form of a likeness of himself inscribed in Latin with the words of the Gospel: "Come unto me all ye who are weary and heavy laden, and I will give you rest."[59] It would have been natural for Pius to sympathize with the Confederacy given his own experience with the forces of Liberty. In 1848,

---

56. King to William Hunter, June 2, 1865, in *United States Ministers*, 341.

57. Bigelow, "The Southern Confederacy and the Pope," 474 (paragraph breaks added).

58. O. Russell to J. Russell, July 30, 1864; in Alvarez, op. cit., 246.

59. Varina Davis, *Jefferson Davis*, Vol. II, 448. Whether the Pope also sent a crown of thorns woven by his own hands remains a subject of controversy. Varina Davis makes no mention of it in her biography of her late husband, although she does mention the papal portrait. That the crown exists and adorns the portrait is certain; but whether it was woven by the Pope or by Varina Davis cannot be ascertained. In correspondence with this author, historian Michael Shumaker advised that an Italian member of the Sons of Confederate Veterans "consulted someone at the Vatican Secret Archives and found that Pope Pius IX definitely sent the crown. . . . However, there was no annotation as to whether

during the European revolutions of that year, the Pope had been forced to flee Rome for his life after Masonic "liberators" shot and killed his Minister of the Interior. During the 1850s Garibaldi's Masonic armies battled for control of the Papal States, and by March of 1861 Victor Emmanuel II had been declared King of Italy. By this time Pius had long abandoned his own earlier liberalism and become a staunch foe of political modernity—that is, a foe of Liberty. And, as the historian James Hennessey has suggested, the Pope's pro-Confederate sympathies would have been fueled by his resentment over the United States' recognition of the new Kingdom of Italy and his belief that "a reunited United States would be too powerful a nation."[60]

What spoils this element of the Southern romantic narrative, however, is the reality that the Protestant slave-owners of the American South would have been the first to applaud the overthrow of the papal monarchy in Italy in the name of Liberty and under the same Lockean principles that had been cited to justify revolution and the overthrow of the "papist" George III some ninety years earlier. Liberty was coming to Europe in the same way it had arrived in America with the assistance of the southern colonies: at the point of a gun. Further, the South, which had seceded and deliberately fired the first shot in a war to preserve its "peculiar institution," was hardly in the same position as the Pope, who was under persecution simply and only because he was a Catholic monarch despised by "liberators" who were following the very principles that had united North and South in 1776.

Even if, as the romantic narrative holds, "the pope preferred the South" because it was "a rural, hierarchical, more traditionally religious society than the North" and the Church "deprecated nationalism—the centralizing, aggressive power of the state,"[61] the Pope had to have been disabused of that sentiment if he was kept abreast of the developments in the Confederacy we have surveyed here, which paralleled developments in *Il Mezzogiorno*, the agrarian southern region and society of the revolutionary Kingdom of Italy. As the historian Enrico del Lago has shown, citing other major studies, in both the Confederacy and the *Mezzogiorno* the adoption of centralizing measures by the revolutionary leadership was seen as "the betrayal of the promise to respect regional autonomy not long after the formation of the national government," so that "almost from the beginning of their turbulent history both the Confederacy and the Italian kingdom faced a crisis of legitimacy, a crisis that led to the end of the former and to the near collapse of the latter during the crucial period between 1861 and 1866." Confederate centralization under Jefferson

His Holiness wove it." No documentation is available to confirm this double-hearsay account. To the contrary is the fawning biography of Davis by Felicity Allen, who writes: "They [Jeff and Varina Davis] hung a circlet of real thorns over this [papal] portrait on the wall of Jeff's study. Varina used the same symbol to assuage her children's grief over their father's suffering in Fortress Monroe: she told them it was 'a crown of thorns, and glory.'" Allen notes that Strode's account "mistakenly says (*Tragic Hero*, 302; *Letters*, 472) pope wove crown and sent it to JD (poss. because it hung in Conf. Mus. on pope's pic. with no ident., author's inquiry at Vatican fruitless)." Allen, *Jefferson Davis: Unconquerable Heart*, 442 & n. 25.

60. James J. Hennessey, *American Catholics: A History of the Roman Catholic Community in the United States* (NY: Oxford Univ. Press, 1981), Kindle Edition, 3328–3329.

61. Crocker, *The Politically Incorrect Guide to the Civil War*, 947–50.

Davis "dealt a particularly harsh blow to the belief in the Confederacy as a guardian institution of states' rights with the implementation of wartime measures such as conscription, suspension of the writ of habeas corpus, and military impressment of both commodities and slaves." Just as the elite southern agrarians of the Kingdom of Italy became disillusioned with the central government's failed program, so did the planter elites of the Confederacy reach the point of "disaffection . . . if not out-right revolt, against the very nation that they had created." In fact, the last desperate attempt to conscript the slaves "signaled the complete failure of the Confederate government to protect the very basis of power of the slaveholding elite that formed the economic and social backbone of the new nation."[62]

At any rate, private papal expressions of sympathy for the Confederacy were hardly positive papal support for the cause of secession in order to preserve institu-tionalized chattel slavery, leading to what the Pope called a "deplorable intestine war"—not a "war of Northern aggression" as the Southern romantic narrative would have it. The Pope's official policy toward the Confederacy was always dictated by "the prudence of cultivating relations with Washington." Although Pius would express grave humanitarian concerns over the "cost of preserving the Union by mil-itary operations and the consequent carnage," once "the fortunes of war turned irre-versibly against the South, the Vatican found it expedient to repair its relations with Washington. In the end the papacy recognized the primacy of political objectives."[63]

And, in the end, North and South would be more united by their shared Protes-tantism and their acceptance of the principles of political modernity than they had been divided over the question of slavery. Citing Allen Tate, a Catholic partisan of the Lost Cause admits:

Unfortunately . . . the South did not adopt an agricultural and hierarchical religion to support its civilization. Even the "High Church" Episcopalianism exemplified by Bishop Polk and embraced by President Davis was not very widely practiced by ordinary Southerners. Instead, too much of the South adopted, as Tate puts it, "the *Teutonic Puritanism of the New England textile manufacturers.*"

The result was tragic. Without the right religion to support and sustain its civilization, the South, it can be said, lost the War Between the States even before the first shots were fired. . . .[64]

And what could have been more Teutonically Puritan than the depredations of the Second Middle Passage, the sale of slaves like cattle, and the "plodding justifica-tions"[65] of chattel slavery by Southern ministers and both the President and Vice President of the Confederacy? In his *Without Consent or Contract*, a chastened Rob-

62. Enrico Del Lago, *Agrarian Elites: American Slaveholders and Southern Italian Landowners, 1815–1861* (Baton Rouge: Louisiana State Univ. Press, 2005), 342–45.
63. Alvarez, "The Papacy in the Diplomacy of the American Civil War," 248.
64. Gary Potter, "Catholicism and the Old South: Part 2," http://catholicdiscussion.wordpress.com /2008/04/10/catholicism-and-the-old-south-by-gary-potter-pt-2/.
65. Wyatt-Brown, "Church, Honor and Secession," loc. cit at 1532.

ert Fogel, having absorbed more traditional historical sources, observed that the masters of the antebellum plantations, like their northern counterparts in the textile industry, were intent on "the creation of a new kind of worker, well suited to serve as a cog in the large-scale systems of production (the agribusinesses) that they were building.... In this respect the masters were similar to the men who developed the factory system; manufacturers also sought to transform the individualistic culture of rural laborers into a new culture of collective discipline."[66]

Tate provides a religious diagnosis of the South's failure quite in keeping with our theme of Liberty as precisely the abandonment of Christendom, or anything like it, in favor of rationalist political arrangements born of the Enlightenment, separating faith from reason and Church from State. Southerners, he writes, "had a religious life, but it was not enough organized with a right mythology. In fact, their rational life was not powerfully united to the religious experience, *as it was in mediæval society....* Lacking a rational system for the defense of their religious attitude and its base in feudal society, they elaborated no rational system whatever, no full-grown philosophy.... The South would not have been defeated had it possessed a sufficient faith in its own kind of God."[67] The female rebel firebrand of Tennessee, Ellen Renshaw House, put it far more succinctly in her Civil War diary: "We have depended too much on Gen. Lee too little on God...."[68]

As Tate observes, because "the South never created a fitting religion" that really distinguished it religiously from the North, its conflict with the North was never religious but rather economic and political. The South, in short, was "a feudal society without a feudal religion." For that matter, because the South lacked a feudal religion its serfs were not really serfs at all, for the serf of Catholic Christendom was never treated as a legal chattel. Without a supernatural vision that would allow it to rise above Enlightenment-bred political philosophy, the Southern cause failed because the South "continued to defend itself on the political terms of the North." Having the same religion as the North, the South "tried to encompass its destiny within the terms of Protestantism, in origin, *a non-agrarian and trading religion; hardly a religion at all, but a result of secular ambition.*" The Southern polemicists "could merely quote Scripture to defend slavery ... while they defended their society as a whole with the catchwords of eighteenth century politics." Hence "the modern Southerner inherits the Jeffersonian formula ... that the ends of man may be established by political means."[69]

The *post bellum* creators of the myth of the Lost Cause could never admit that, in keeping with the very nature of Protestantism, the South no less than the North had been in a state of spiritual and cultural decline before the war, although the Southern Jeremiahs had warned of precisely that development—and with it the risk of divine disfavor. The myth required belief in the proposition that "the Southern

66. Fogel, *Without Consent or Contract*, 398.
67. Tate, "Remarks on the Southern Religion," in *I'll Take My Stand*, 166, 168, 173–174.
68. Ellen Renshaw House, *A Very Violent Rebel: The Civil War Diary of Ellen Renshaw House*, ed. Daniel E. Sutherland (Knoxville: Univ. of Tennessee Press, 1996), 161–62.
69. Tate, "Remarks on the Southern Religion," 168, 174.

culture did not decline . . . ; it was destroyed by outsiders in a Trojan war. The 'older' culture of Troy-South was wiped out by the 'upstart' culture of Greece-North. *Sunt laminae rerum*; and the Yankees were therefore to blame for everything. . . ."[70]

A Conflict of Two Leviathans

The Civil War had claimed the lives of 620,000 soldiers and left another 500,000 wounded. There were some 700,000 fatalities all told, including civilian deaths. The battlefield death toll from wounds and disease equaled that of the Revolutionary War, the War of 1812, the Mexican War, the Spanish American War, World War I, World War II, and the Korean War, combined. But the rate of death, notes Drew Gilpin Faust, was "six times that of World War II. A similar rate, about two percent, in the United States today would mean six million fatalities." And Confederate soldiers "died at a rate three times that of their Yankee counterparts; one in five white southern men of military age did not survive the Civil War."[71] The war produced a nation filled with widows and shattered families in both the North and the South, the total destruction of the Southern economy, and "physical devastation, almost all of it in the South," including "burned or plundered homes, pillaged countryside, untold losses in crops and farm animals, ruined buildings and bridges, devastated college campuses, and neglected roads," all of which "left the South in ruins."[72]

The devastated South had learned the same lesson President Washington had first inculcated in the national psyche when he marched with his men to crush the Whiskey Rebellion: There is no escape but death or exile from a government "conceived in Liberty." The only difference—the fatal difference—between the two presidential teachers of this lesson was that the first did not encounter violent resistance. The tax rebels of Pennsylvania had scattered at the news of Washington and his men marching over the Alleghenies. But the rebels at Bull Run, and for years thereafter, stood their ground against Lincoln and "the Federals." And so they had to die. Yet they would have died just as surely had Washington, not Lincoln, been President in 1861, for if "the father of his country" was willing to use military force to put down a localized tax revolt, there can be no question he would have employed force to prevent eleven states from seceding outright from the Union.

Those who invite armed conflict, however, cannot credibly claim to be its innocent victims when the conflict spirals wildly out of control. It takes two belligerents to make a war. The apocalypse of the Civil War would not have happened without the Southern secession, which Lee, who saw "no cause for disunion, strife and *civil war*," had called "nothing but revolution" before he took off the Union blue and put on the Confederate gray. And the consequence of that revolutionary act, leading ineluctably to the South's first acts of military aggression, was what Davis himself predicted would be a "clash of arms . . . the most sanguinary the world had ever

70. Tate, "Faulkner's *Sanctuary* and the Southern Myth," loc. cit.

71. Drew Gilpin Faust, *This Republic of Suffering* (NY: Vintage Books, 2008), xi.

72. *Historical Times Illustrated Encyclopedia of the Civil War*, ed. Patricia L. Faust (NY: Harper Perennial, 1986), 187.

witnessed." The South's course could have been justified—if at all—only by a *casus belli*. And that was clearly lacking in the South's attempt to contrive a breach of Locke's social compact based on the institution of chattel slavery, whose post-war abolition even the South's greatest general professed to welcome with joy.

The South's defeat, claimed Benjamin Hill, was not the fault of its two great leaders, Lee and Davis, but rather the people themselves, who were unwilling to lay down their lives in even larger numbers for the sacred cause because they had come to doubt it: "The truth is, we failed because too many of our people were not determined to win. Malcontents at home took more men from Lee's army than did Grant's guns.... [W]e failed to win independence because our sacrifices ceased, our purpose faltered, and our strength was divided."[73] But how many more Southerners should have died in order to achieve independence from Lincoln only to be required to submit to the authority of Davis? Of what benefit was the glorious "war of Southern independence" to the vast majority of the common people of the South: the yeoman farmers; the blacksmiths, wheelwrights, carpenters and other tradesmen; the peddlers, small merchants and innkeepers; the people of the mountains and swamps; the poor whites; the women who lost husbands and the children who lost fathers? Of what benefit was the war to the four million slaves, whose humanity was of no account in the Confederate saga? In 1861 as in 1776, it seems, armed rebellion in the name of Liberty was permissible only for white people, whereas the slaves had no Lockean remedy for centuries of "natural subjugation" by their lordly masters.

Would the yoke of the Confederate States really have been any lighter for these multitudes, slave or free, than the yoke of the United States? Had not both of these new yokes, forged in the fires of revolution and laid upon the masses with promises of new freedom, proven far heavier in terms of the daily intrusions of government than that long-forgotten yoke of the "papist" monarchy of King George, who had never conscripted his colonial subjects to die in wars, nor impressed their property, nor even maintained his unpopular taxes against their protests? Was it not obvious that the Southern rebellion had only made the already heavy yoke of the federal government immensely heavier, for both North and South, than it was when the Southern states still were a major force in Congress? Had not the Southern people suffered the predictable penalty for kicking against the goad of Liberty their revolutionary forefathers had first applied to their ancestors with the warning that it must not be resisted?

In sum, the Civil War—the Second American Revolution—was no more a stark conflict between tyranny and freedom than the first. A more accurate picture is that of an all-out war between *two* federal leviathans: one powerful and well-provided, the other a fledgling upstart with more pride than capacity to impose its will. Both leviathans, with their substantially identical Constitutions, had Presidents and Congresses that exercised authority and demanded sacrifices from the ordinary citizenry vastly in excess of the comparatively minimal governmental

---

73. Hill, "Address to Historical Society," *Speeches and Writings*, 406.

intrusions that had supposedly justified the first revolution against a king and parliament of distant memory.

At the beginning of the war the federal government had a standing army of 17,000; by war's end, it had almost two million men in arms. The rebellion of the Southern states against the very government they had joined with the North to create in the originating act of rebellion led to a hopeless war against that government; it was that war which produced a geometric acceleration of what had been a slow but inevitable process of centralization that could at least have been retarded by political compromise. Instead, the war provided the Big Bang of the cosmion that is the modern nation-state. The Civil War *made* the one federal leviathan that towers over us today. Thus did the George Washington of the North, first President of the United States, who demanded "[r]espect for its authority, compliance with its laws, acquiescence in its measures," finally prevail over the George Washington of the South, the general on horseback depicted on the Great Seal of the Confederacy, who had led the rebellion against a namesake king only to preside over a new form of government that would crush the South with a merciless might King George had never possessed.

The Jeffersonian Mirage

For reasons that by now should require no demonstration, the outcome of the Civil War cannot be seen as a betrayal of the fabled founding ideal of "Jeffersonian limited government," which Jefferson's own presidency revealed to be a mirage. In light of the details missing from the libertarians' historical cartoon, surveyed throughout the first section, it is inconceivable that even President Jefferson, "the apostle of republicanism" as Madison called him, would have sat still for the secession of eleven states from the very Union he considered his sacred legacy to mankind and the hope of the world. It was, after all, precisely in order to address what he himself had decried before Congress as an attempted "severance of the Union of these States" that he had called for the execution of Burr as a traitor and supported a military dictatorship in the Louisiana territory—a dictatorship with all the features of the one that Lincoln imposed on the rebel states of the South. Yet while Jefferson's own Republican contemporaries (such as John Randolph) did not fail to oppose and condemn his hypocrisy and duplicity, especially during his second term and the tyrannical Embargo, contemporary libertarians seem determined to replace the "Lincoln legend" with a "Jefferson legend," raising Saint Thomas to the altar of Liberty and invoking his name against Lincoln and the Leviathan whose power Jefferson himself did not hesitate to exercise, perpetuate and even expand.

In acting to prevent Southern secession, however, Lincoln was enforcing the Lockean principles of political authority the Founders and Framers, including Jefferson, had built into the American republic and had acted to enforce themselves. While Lincoln waged a devastating war whose horrendous outcome was not warranted by the professed aim of "saving the Union," it is still the case that the South was brought into submission by the same Lockean "supreme sovereign" the South itself had helped to create as a replacement for the king the South itself had helped to overthrow. This is the reality "conservatives" and libertarians alike less-than-candidly fail to acknowledge.

The Claremont Institute, a "conservative" think tank, astutely remarks libertarian inconsistency on this point: "Given the affinity of libertarians for Lockean liberalism, their favorable disposition towards Southern secession, an act based on Calhoun's rejection of the principles of the American Founding, is hard to fathom."[74] But it is really not hard to fathom, for it is entirely understandable that libertarians (or anyone else) would sympathize with the plight of the devastated, underdog South, whose legions of young men died, not for any property right in the slaves that they (unlike their leaders) did not own, but for the defense of their homeland against what they thought was foreign aggression—aggression, to be sure, that had been brought down on their heads by the South's reckless politicians and planter elites. The South's catastrophic blunder was that it failed to recognize the idol it had helped to erect—Liberty—for what it really was in disguise: illimitable power arising from "the will of the people" as executed by elected officials under a hitherto unprecedented compact amounting to a vow of "till death do us part." And that vow unto death had been required of the common man no less by the Confederacy than by the Union it had purported to replace.

Sympathy for Underdogs

While our judgment of both parties to the Civil War is rationally negative, emotionally we arrive, finally, at something like the sentiment expressed by Shelby Foote, whose Southern gentleman credentials were impeccable: "If pride in the resistance my forebears made against the odds has leaned me to any degree in their direction, it ought to amount to no more, in the end, than the average American's normal sympathy for the underdog in a fight."[75] But from our perspective, the underdogs were legion on both sides of the conflict: they were the ordinary citizens and valiant soldiers who were called upon to shoulder its impossible burdens, loaded onto their backs by the high and mighty rulers of the North and the South. Outrage and contempt are the natural reaction to both Northern and Southern claims of righteousness when one considers the horrible fate the pontificating politicians all managed to escape: the vast battlefields strewn with tens of thousands of corpses, the young faces frozen in death-agony, the skeletons in shallow graves exposed by rain, the shattered bodies and severed arms and legs and heads, the screaming and dying wounded, the multitudes of amputees, the wives without husbands, the children without fathers, and the ruinous consequences of it all, ramifying endlessly down the generations.

The question must be answered: For what? At the end, we are left with nothing more than what James Swanson rightly describes as "two myths—the legend of America's emancipating, secular saint, and the legend of the Lost Cause."[76] Neither

74. "The Case Against Secession," http://www.claremont.org/publications/pubid.171/pub_detail.asp.
75. Foote, *The Civil War*, Vol. I, 816.
76. James L. Swanson, *Bloody Crimes* (NY: Harper Collins, Inc., 2010), Kindle Edition, 5612.

was worth the loss of even a single life. And what is so exquisitely tragic about the South's downfall was that no war had ever been necessary to preserve the things that made her so attractive, and make her attractive even today: the manners of her people, Southern hospitality, the leisurely pace of life, the agreeable climate, the elegant cities, the enchanting natural beauty of her almost mystical low country and the mountain regions, and her relative social conservatism. In one of his unguarded moments, recorded in a fragmentary note he left behind, even Lee admitted that the war seemed to have been pointless: "Looking at the late war from this point of view, it is difficult to find results which justify the conflict.... Political quarrels were the motive of the war, but what difficulties in the way of the development of the country have been removed by it?"[77]

The Civil War was a fight in which an objective viewer of the bloody follies of Liberty ought not to have a dog. Like Foote, we ought to view the senseless carnage as the outcome of hubris played out on killing fields with the lives of common people: "We think that we are a wholly superior people. If we'd been anything like as superior as we think we are, we would not have fought that war. But since we did fight it, we have to make it the greatest war of all time."[78] But if the Civil War was the result of false principles in operation—the fictive social compact, the "sovereignty of the people," the "absolute" right to property, the absolute will of self-constituted political bodies calling themselves representatives of "the people," the right to revolution—then it is wrong to look for glory in it. Rather, we should find in its annals only a book of terrible lessons learned about this thing called Liberty.

The Lessons Learned

One of the primary lessons the Civil War ought to teach us is a major theme of this study: the perpetual failure of Liberty to deliver the promised glorious and unprecedented perfection of human freedom, lying always just ahead on an ever-receding horizon. What "blessings of liberty" had the political creation called "the Union" bestowed upon its subjects that entitled it to slay them in large numbers for attempting to escape its authority? Was not the Union itself founded in a rebellion that was supposed to have established "government by consent of the governed"? On the other hand, what claim did the fleeting Confederate States have on its purported subjects that justified *its* demand for the ultimate sacrifice from vast numbers of them? By what right under God had a hastily formed "wealth-sponsored" government in Richmond required yeoman farmers and other ordinary people with wives and children to leave behind everything that mattered to them in this world in order to die in an unwinnable war in which they had no real stake, beyond an abstract "independence" from one central government only to be subjected immediately to another at the cost of their lives?

Another lesson learned is that when sovereignty is said to rest on nothing more

---

77. "War," essay fragment in Lee's handwriting [c. 1868], in Pryor, *Reading the Man*, 9322–9325.
78. In Ken Burns, *The Civil War*, PBS Documentary, Episode 9 at 1:01:45.

than an illusory "consent of the governed," rather than God and fear of His justice on the part of both ruler and subject, the ultimate support for government devolves into raw power—the essence of Liberty under its political aspect, as both the Union and the Confederacy had revealed to the hapless masses who were subjected to their authority. The only difference between the two belligerents was that the South had far less power to wield in the name of Liberty, and had wielded it far less efficiently.

Less obvious, but no less important, is the lesson that in two rival nations that were already post-Christian in principle—as their most conservative Protestant divines recognized (cf. Ch. 18)—Christianity had been instrumentalized for war, but was otherwise of no account in the outcome. Both the Union and the Confederacy had their Bible-quoting ideologues, their days of prayer and fasting, their lofty public religious rhetoric, their battlefield chaplains ministering to the dead, the dying, and the soon-to-be-dead, their pious invocations of divine providence. But neither side had any intention of fighting for anything remotely resembling what had been overturned once and for all in 1776: the politics of the soul in the commonwealths of Christendom.

The Civil War also provides a lesson on the point first raised in Chapter 13: the artificiality and shiftiness of the territorial claims of those who wield force in the name of Liberty. Behind the claims at work in the Civil War one sees yet another liberal inconsistency: a self-serving oscillation between the organic-unitive and territorial-exclusive notions of political society according to the rhetorical needs of the moment. Hence in 1776, during the rebellion against King George, it was "the American people" or "the American nation," not Northern and Southern "races," to which the adepts of Liberty in both the Northern and Southern colonies had appealed in declaring the independence of the "*United* States of America." But during the secession of the Southern states in 1861, the Southern revolutionaries adverted to "states' rights" possessed by strict political subdivisions drawn on maps. On the other hand, when it suited their purposes, the appeal was to a "Southern civilization" without state borders whose organicity apart from the formerly organic "American people" of 1776 was a convenient fiction that concealed political, economic and religious differences revolving around slavery. Southern Protestants were as hetero-populous in the socioeconomic sense as Northern Protestants: blueblood and *nouveau riche* slave-owners in the Deep South; highly educated Virginia aristocrats with their slaves, oriented to the Washington society just across the Potomac; barely literate yeoman farmers, illiterate poor whites in the southern reaches of the Appalachian mountain chain, and positively primitive denizens of the Florida and Louisiana swamps; Southwestern pioneers, many of whom were from Northern states; and some four million descendants of the slaves originally kidnapped from Africa by the Protestant ancestors of both Northern and Southern wealthy elites. Yet what emerged from all the bilateral conceptual juggling leading up to the war was a strictly demarcated "Confederate States" versus a just-as-strictly demarcated "United States," giving rise to hostilities between vast armies that would not have been mowing each other down on battlefields if not for the drawing of the jurisdictional lines.

The groundbreaking work of the legal scholar Richard T. Ford of Stanford Law School confirms our view of an expedient shifting of sociopolitical concepts to cloak the creation of territorial constructs for power-wielding by the political vanguards of Liberty that drove both sides of the conflict:

> The opposed representations of territorial jurisdiction—"organic" [the "American people"] and "synthetic" [the contractual "compact" between the States]—are employed by various actors as arguments for or against a given controversial action. For instance, a jurisdiction may be described as synthetic by someone who wishes to change the jurisdiction against the wishes of affected parties [the Southern "breach of compact" argument], while the same jurisdiction may be described as "organic" by those who wish to assert "rights" to the jurisdiction [Lincoln's "preservation of the Union" argument].[79]

As Ford notes, "the famous historical shift from status [the subject of a king] to contract ['self-rule' by compact with the ruler] was accompanied by an equally significant shift from status to locus." That is, as sovereignty became a mere human compact, its extension likewise became a human convention within an agreed upon space literally delimited by parallel lines on a mapped grid. American jurisdictional development "was marked by synthetic sub-national jurisdictions," including the entities called "states," which are not identified by name in the Constitution because they are "generic in status" and new ones can be created by fiat.[80]

Ford offers one of those brilliantly obvious insights that eludes superficial thinking: this arrangement of territorial jurisdiction in America "was only possible through the intersection of *modern cartography and political liberalism. . . . Territorial jurisdiction is a foundational technology of political liberalism.*"[81] He argues that we ought to "see liberalism as a certain way of drawing the map of the social and political world." What he calls the "old, preliberal map"—the map of Christendom, not yet separated into the discrete nation-states of emerging political modernity— "showed a largely undifferentiated land mass, with no borders. Society was conceived as an organic and integrated whole."[82] Political sovereignty was not territorial, but rather "in pre-modern Europe, what appear to modern eyes to be territorial communities were in fact simply groups united by kinship, common interests and customs." That is, a Christian sovereign ruled over a people who happened to occupy a certain general region, but not a precisely bounded territorial space in the modern sense. There were no strictly delineated national or local borders, and property boundary descriptions before modern cartography were narratives imprecisely referenced to landmarks. Ford quotes Sir Henry Maine for the observation that "the double proposition that 'sovereignty is territorial,' i.e., that it is always associated with the proprietorship of a limited portion of the earth's surface . . . is altogether

79. Richard T. Ford, "Law's Territory (A History of Jurisdiction)," 97 *Mich. L. Rev.* 843 (1999), 861–62.
80. *Id.* at 890.
81. *Id.* at 890, 897 (author's ellipses omitted).
82. *Id.* at 897.

untenable so far as regards a large part of modern history. . . . It is . . . not true that the territorial character of sovereignty was always recognised. . . ."[83]

In this pre-modern world without borders, writes Ford, "*liberal theorists, drew lines*, marked off different realms, and created the sociopolitical map with which we are still familiar." His rather stunning conclusion—and this from a frankly liberal academic—lends support to our counter-narrative: "Liberalism is a *world of walls*, and each one *creates a new liberty*."[84] Seen in this light, the Civil War was essentially a practical function of Liberty: armed conflict between territorial spaces created by sheer acts of will rather than by the organic existence of peoples over centuries; the erection of new walls to "create a new liberty" as needed. Thus the liberals of the Montgomery Convention had hastily erected a conceptual wall of territorial jurisdiction snapped to a grid at the nothernmost borders of "the Confederate States of America," while Lincoln and his fellow liberals in Washington had resolved to tear down that wall and "restore" the previously agreed upon jurisdictional space—"the Union"—even at the cost of devastating its southern half.

Without "the intersection of modern cartography and political liberalism," there would have been no synthetic "states" to assert "states' rights" and secede from the "United States"—a vast synthetic jurisdiction—based on a "breach" of the "compact" that is Locke's synthetic origin of territorial sovereignty. Nor would there have been a synthetic "Union" with defined borders and neatly detachable state sub-units whose reassembly could have been the object of Lincoln's war effort. In short, had antebellum America, like the Europe of medieval Christendom, been "a largely undifferentiated land mass, with no borders," it is difficult to see how the Civil War could have happened. On a "pre-liberal map" there would have been only an indeterminate number of disgruntled elites and radicals, leading localized insurrections without any means of instantly asserting jurisdiction over vast, predefined territorial spaces, immediately drawing all their inhabitants into a war under pain of "treason" against "the sovereign."

Here we encounter the political reality hidden beneath the vaunted "division of power" in the state-federal hybrid emerging from the deliberations of the 55 men that Jefferson, still in France, had called "an assembly of demi-gods."[85] The reality is that the creation of the synthetic political subdivisions called "the States" had corralled the American population into large jurisdictional spaces that actually facilitated central control by the federal governments of both the United and the Confederate States of America. What were supposed to be buffers against the central government were actually funnels that focused its authority upon vast stretches of territory via the centralized authorities of the States themselves, which did the central government's bidding in directing populations to war, although the process broke down significantly as the Confederacy's cause was increasingly seen as lost.

---

83. Ford, "Law's Territory," 97 *Mich L. Rev.* at 872–73.

84. *Id.* at 897.

85. In John R. Vile, *The Constitutional Convention of 1787: A Comprehensive Encyclopedia of America's Founding* (Santa Barbara, CA: AVC-CLIO, 2005), 214.

The appeal to "states' rights" had only provoked the division of one synthetic nation into two, with the States continuing to serve as funnels of federal power in each of the opposing "nations." Occasional threats to "nullify" this or that federal law notwithstanding, today the States are permanently locked into their function of funneling federal power (while adding ever-increasing demands of their own). The "divided" power portrayed by the Framers was really a monolithic construction of jurisdictional blocks put in place by the monolith itself, and the claims of the States to be co-equal "sovereigns" of whom the federal government was a mere servant to be dismissed at will were never more than metaphorical. For all its moving parts, the Founders' creation was, from the beginning, Locke's "one Body Politick under one Supreme Government. . . ."[86]

Finally, we encounter a lesson summarized by none other than Thomas Paine in his pamphlet *Agrarian Justice*: "An army of principles will penetrate where an army of soldiers cannot. . . . It will march on the horizon of the world, and it will conquer."[87] An army of principles—Paine's principles—had conquered both sides in the Civil War long before the war began. A people united in principle will be united in practice once a great practical difference between them has been removed—in this case the servitude of the African race that had been the common legacy of North and South, but had evolved over time into the South's peculiar institution. The principles that had conquered both North and South in the American Revolution would irresistibly unite them again, once the artificial lines of the appropriate jurisdictional spaces had been restored to their pre-war coordinates.

§

We have noted how Sam Watkins penned the lament that in a war spawned by the demands of planters and politicians, "the private soldier fought and starved and died for naught. . . ." But even he had to find a way to make sense of the "long and unholy war" he had somehow survived. Wrote Watkins:

> But when we pass away, the impartial historian will render a true verdict, and a history will then be written in justification and vindication of those brave and noble boys who gave their all in fighting the battles of their homes, their country, and their God.
>
> "The United States has no North, no South, no East, no West." "*We are one and undivided.*"[88]

The Confederacy having failed, Watkins—writing twenty years after the fact—sounded the theme its own former leaders had already sounded, and Lee above all: the theme of Reconstruction and Reconciliation. According to the master narrative of Liberty, the one and undivided nation was the nation that men on both sides of the Civil War had really died for. Thus began the era of the Great Never Mind.

86. *TT*, II.89.
87. *Agrarian Justice* (1797), in *Paine: Collected Writings* (NY: Penguin Books, 1955), 411.
88. Watkins, *Company Aytch*, 247. Emphasis in original.

17

Purifying the Temple: Confederates and Indians

"I, ROBERT E. LEE, at Lexington, Virginia, do solemnly swear, in the presence of almighty God, that I will henceforth faithfully support, protect and defend the Constitution of the United States, and the Union of the States thereunder, and that I will, in like manner, abide by and faithfully support all laws and proclamations which have been made during *the existing rebellion* with reference to the emancipation of slaves, so help me God."[1] With these words, in an oath subscribed before Charles A. Davidson on October 2, 1865, Lee swore allegiance once again to the government against which he had fought for four years. Lee submitted the oath in connection with his prior application for a pardon from President Johnson, "the most controversial act of his life."[2]

To the diehards of the Confederacy, including Jefferson Davis, imprisoned in Fortress Monroe following his capture on May 10, "this was a betrayal of men scarcely cold in their graves. . . . Lee was kneeling before the enemy and was admitting that everything—secession, creation of the Confederacy, fighting the Northern armies that had marched into the South—had been wrong." But Lee the realist saw it as "the only way for a Confederate to secure his civil rights and to pave the way for Southerners once again to elect their own leaders."[3] In one of those amazing accidents of history, however, the pardon application was lost when Secretary of State Seward, thinking it was only a copy of the original received by the President, filed it away. It was not until 1970 that the application was uncovered in the National Archives. On August 5th, 1975, by a joint resolution of Congress signed by President Gerald Ford, Robert E. Lee was posthumously granted full rights of citizenship.[4]

---

1. "From Washington: General Lee Takes the Amnesty Oath. . . ." *New York Times*, October 16, 1865, electronic archival copy, www.nytimes.com/1865/10/17/news/washington-gen-lee-takes-amnesty-oath-veteran-reserve-corps-post-office.html. See also Emory M. Thomas, *Robert E. Lee: A Biography* (NY: W.W. Norton & Co., 1995), 280 (reproducing amnesty oath).

2. Flood, *Lee*, 64.

3. Ibid.

4. Cf. "President Gerald R. Ford's Remarks Upon Signing a Bill Restoring Rights of Citizenship to General Robert E. Lee," www.fordlibrarymuseum.gov/library/speeches/750473.htm.

Reconstruction and the Great Never Mind

So great was Lee's stature after the war that his example overcame any objection to seeking pardon from the hated Yankees. Although President Johnson had issued a parole (not a pardon) of all the military leaders and soldiers of the Confederacy, Lee advised innumerable former members of the Confederate Army to take the oath in order to receive a Presidential pardon and full restoration of civil rights. One such was Captain George Wise, whose conversation with his father, Henry A. Wise, former Governor of Virginia and Confederate brigadier general, is often cited in Civil War histories: "[T]he ex-governor said: 'You have disgraced the family!' 'General Lee advised me to do it.' 'Oh, that alters the case. Whatever General Lee says is all right, I don't care what it is.'"[5]

How did Lee explain his own military leadership of the "existing rebellion"—his own words under oath—followed by his request for a pardon after the rebellion had failed? In a letter that "was to be quoted for generations," he cited George Washington as an example of a "true patriotism" seemingly unbound by any objective moral standard for the actions it demands:

> I need not tell you that true patriotism sometimes requires of men *to act exactly contrary, at one period, to that which it does at another*, and the motive which impels them—the desire to do right—is precisely the same. The circumstances that govern their actions, change, and *their conduct must conform to the new order of things*. . . . Washington himself is an example of this. At one time he fought in the service of the King of Great Britain; at another he fought with the French at Yorktown, on the orders of the Continental Congress, against him. He has not been branded by the world with reproach for this, but his course has been applauded.[6]

But why must the conduct of a "true patriot" always "conform to the new order of things"? What if the new order of things was morally questionable? What if, just as Lee himself had observed before hostilities began, secession was "nothing but revolution" and would lead to "a war that was certain to be long and full of horrors" and "yield nothing" for the South? By what authority did a "patriotic" secession convention, opposed by many Virginians, decree a "patriotic" revolution against the existing government? What authority to demand war was possessed by the planters and lawyers who made up the Montgomery Convention and announced the formation of a provisional government that the masses who would die on the battlefield had no role in creating and no real stake in defending? Why would "true patriotism" not have counseled Lee to abstain entirely from the conflict rather than be involved in massive bloodshed for which both sides were offering morally dubious rationales, as Lee himself had admitted privately concerning the Cotton States' "selfish, dictatorial bearing" and "threats" to the border states in the days before the war?

---

5. In Myrta Lockett Avery, *Dixie After the War* (NY: Doubleday, Page & Co., 1906), 71.
6. In Flood, *Lee: the Last Years*, 102.

Further, Lee had outdone Washington by performing not one, but two about-faces in the name of "true patriotism": It was "true patriotism" that had led him to resign from the United States Army to take up the cause of Virginia, fighting against the very government he had been serving as a "true patriot" only days before. Then it was "true patriotism" that had led him to seek pardon from that same government and urge all his fellow Southerners to do the same. How did the mere invocation of patriotism justify such changes of position without further moral inquiry? What was the *moral* ground for submitting once again to the authority of the Federal Government after hundreds of thousands of young men, proudly calling themselves Rebels, had bravely sacrificed life or limb to oppose its authority under Lee's own leadership? Was it simply that in the end Lee and the South had been unable to muster sufficient opposing force? Was it simply, therefore, that "might makes right"?

It seems that "might makes right" is precisely the dictum Lee followed. On November 4, 1866, Lee sent an oft-quoted letter to the future Lord Acton, a liberal Catholic disciple of the excommunicated theologian Johann Joseph Ignaz von Döllinger.[7] Acton had barely escaped excommunication himself for, among other things, traveling to Rome and "organizing a party of resistance to the proposed definition of papal infallibility" by Pope Pius IX—the same Pope that Southern partisans depict as a tacit supporter of Southern secession and the "Southern cause" in general.[8] A great proponent of the Whig narrative of Liberty, Acton had written to Lee (in another oft-quoted letter) to tell him that "I saw in States Rights the only availing check on the absolutism of sovereign will, and secession filled me with hope, not as the destruction, but as the redemption of Democracy; and I mourn for the stake which was lost at Richmond. . . ." In Acton's view, Lee was "fighting the battles of *our* liberty, *our* progress, *our* civilization"[9]—showing precisely that the "Southern cause" was quite in line with Liberty's march through the nations. Lee, who had written before the war that "secession is nothing but revolution," replied to Acton that on the question of secession "the judgment of reason has been displaced by the *arbitrament of war*, waged for the purpose as avowed of maintaining the union of the States." Referring to the "*fratricidal* war which has taken place," Lee advised Acton that the South "now accepts in good faith its constitutional results. . . ."[10]

Those "constitutional results" included the Thirteenth Amendment, abolishing slavery, which had been ratified by the requisite number of states as of December 1865, including all the former Confederate States except Mississippi (which did

---

7. Paul Maria Baumgarten, "Johann Joseph Ignaz von Döllinger," *The Catholic Encyclopedia*, Vol. 5 (NY: Robert Appleton Company, 1909), <http://www.newadvent.org/cathen/05094a.htm>.

8. Herbert Thurston, "John Emerich Edward Dahlberg Acton, Baron Acton," *The Catholic Encyclopedia*, Vol. 1 (NY: Robert Appleton Company, 1907), <http://www.newadvent.org/cathen/01114a.htm>.

9. In Denson, *A Century of War*, 88.

10. Ibid., 88–89.

not ratify until March 16, 1995!) and Texas (which ratified on February 18, 1870). Concerning the Thirteenth Amendment, Lee told Acton that "the South . . . receives without reserve the amendment which has already been made to the Constitution for the extinction of slavery," which Lee claimed was "an event that has long been sought, though in a different way, and by none has it [the abolition of slavery] been more earnestly desired than by citizens of Virginia." Thus did Lee undermine the entire cause for secession and war.

In his postwar statements Lee repeatedly expressed the view that the South's claims regarding secession and slavery had been decided against the South by the outcome of the war. The most prominent example is the "Rosecrans Letter" or White Sulphur Letter of 1868, solicited from Lee by the Union general William Rosecrans, a Democrat, for use in support of the presidential candidacy of Horatio Seymour, the Democrat candidate opposing Grant in the presidential election of that year. Drafted by the Virginia lawyer Alexander Stuart, the White Sulphur Letter was personally reviewed and edited by Lee and signed by him and other former Confederate leaders. The letter declares: "Whatever *opinions* may have prevailed in the past with regard to African slavery or the right of a State to secede from the Union, we believe we express the almost unanimous judgment of the Southern people when we declare that *they consider these questions were decided by the war,* and it is their intention in good faith to abide by that decision."[11]

So, in Lee's view the Civil War had been an immensely bloody and destructive arbitration of a political dispute. And he was right. Within the Lockean framework in which the North and South had operated, the North's interpretation of the Constitution had prevailed simply because, as Genovese observes, "the North won a test of physical strength. . . . [I]t would be hard to imagine a clearer example of the doctrine that might makes right—a doctrine supposedly anathema to liberals."[12] But has the doctrine ever really been anathema to liberals? That hardly seems to be the case with the liberals of the North. And it certainly was not anathema to Southern "conservatives" such as Lee, who by any objective historical standard of conservatism—the standard of the Christian centuries under the order of altar and throne—were merely the "moderate" products of post-Enlightenment liberalism, "conservative" Lockean liberals who, as Genovese himself notes (citing the thought of Calhoun), were "not monarchists or supporters of aristocracy" in the sense of the nobility abolished by the constitutions of both the North and the South. "They accepted the principle of the sovereignty of the people and associated themselves with the democratic insistence that any regime, to claim legitimacy, must rest on popular support."[13] But those who cite the "sovereignty of the people" and loss of popular support as the ground for revolutionary resistance to existing authority must accept the outcome when the "sovereign people" is beaten in a test of force

11. In Nolan, *Lee Considered,* 142–143.

12. Eugene D. Genovese, *The Southern Tradition: the Achievement and Limitations of an American Conservatism* (Cambridge, MA: Harvard Univ. Press, 1994), 28.

13. Ibid.

and the popular will no longer supports the effort to annul Locke's irrevocable social compact. And that is precisely what Lee counseled.

The question thus presents itself: Where, in the end, was the moral justification for "arbitration" by war instead of the political process? There is no denying that even if the South had lost in the political process its losses would have been infinitely less than those it sustained in a war that Lee himself admitted "will yield nothing" just before the war began and that Jefferson Davis knew would be "the most sanguinary the world had ever witnessed." And what of the enormous irreparable harm to countless innocent bystanders, the common people who had no stake in Lee's "arbitrament of war"—"a revolution of the Politicians, not the People," as Governor Vance had called it? That harm would not end with the end of the war, for the South still had the radical Reconstruction to endure.

In the years between Lincoln's assassination and Grant's election, the dominant radical Republican faction in Congress, capitalizing on the public's outrage over the assassination, treated the former Confederate States as if they were conquered foreign provinces. President Johnson, a pro-Union slave-owner from Tennessee whom Lincoln selected to balance the Republican ticket, had at first pursued a lenient reconstruction policy along the same lines as Lincoln's. But here too the politicians and wealthy elites of the South helped bring Northern repression down on the heads of the common people. As Morison writes, the Lincoln-Johnson reconstruction policy was "wrecked by a combination of Southern folly and Radical malevolence."[14]

In 1865–66, many heroes and partisans of the Confederate cause were elected or appointed to positions in state governments without prior legal prohibition by Congress. The South was theirs to rule again. Slavery having been abolished by the Thirteenth Amendment—which Lee professed to welcome—the blacks of the South were now freedmen; but they were still without the rights of white citizens, including the right to vote. Abandoning all prudence, the newly elected former Confederate leaders exploited that legal lacuna by adopting in 1865–66 various state statutes and local ordinances known collectively as the Black Codes. Piously invoking their "Christian duty" to regulate the lives of freedmen for their own good, Southern legislators, with amazing audacity, attempted to preserve as much of the institution of agricultural chattel slavery as possible given the bare fact of emancipation.

While the statutory language and specific provisions varied from state to state, the Black Codes generally established the same basic restrictions on the rights of former slaves: denial of the right to vote, hold public office or sit on juries; the barring of testimony by blacks in civil or criminal proceedings involving whites; mandatory contracts of employment for specific terms; authorization for the arrest of "fugitives from labor" and their forcible return to employment; jailing or fining for "vagrancy," defined as roaming at large without suitable employment;

14. Morison, *HAP*, 707.

and prohibitions on employment outside agriculture without a special license, "in order to discourage those who aspired to be artisans, mechanics, or shopkeepers, or who already held such positions. . . ."[15]

Mississippi's code, for example, defined as "vagrants" those "unable or unwilling to pay a new tax to support Negro indigents," while the Alabama code "included as vagrants 'any runaway, stubborn servant or child' and any laborer 'who loiters away his time' or fails to comply with the terms of his employment." Ostensibly applicable to whites as well as blacks, the vagrancy laws were designed precisely as black population control measures. There were even prescriptions for "the hours of labor (from sunrise to sunset), the duties, and the behavior expected of black agricultural workers." The codes also typically provided that blacks who could not pay fines incurred for various violations could be hired out against their will in order to work off the fines. "By adopting harsh vagrancy laws and restricting non-agricultural employment, the white South clearly intended to stem the much-feared drift of freedmen toward the cities and to underscore their status as landless agricultural laborers."[16]

In addition to state codes, a regime of local ordinances made life in many Southern towns and cities all but impossible for blacks. Leon Litwack's major study summarizes these local codes:

> To enter the town, a black person needed his employer's permission, stipulating the object of the visit and the time necessary to accomplish it; any freedman found on the streets after ten o'clock at night without a written pass or permit from his employer would be subject to arrest and imprisonment. No freedman could rent or keep a house within the town limits "under any circumstances," or reside within the town unless employed by a white person who assumed responsibility for his conduct. To hold any public meetings or to assemble in large numbers for any reason, blacks needed the mayor's permission, as they also did to "preach, exhort or otherwise declaim" to black congregations. Nor could they possess weapons or sell, barter, or exchange any kind of merchandise without special permits. A freedman found violating these ordinances could be punished by imprisonment, fines, and forced labor on the city streets.[17]

Litwack records the admission by one Mississippi planter that the adoption of the Black Codes had only provoked Congressional retaliation: "We showed our hand too soon. We ought to have waited till the troops were withdrawn, and our representatives admitted to Congress; then we could have had everything our own way."[18] And the retaliation came: Federal officials in the Freedmen's Bureau and the courts suspended the operation of the Black Codes. On April 9, 1866 Congress, overriding President Johnson's veto—the first successful override in the Senate's

15. Litwack, *Been in the Storm So Long,* 367.
16. Ibid., 368.
17. Ibid.
18. Ibid.

history—enacted the Civil Rights Act of 1866. The Act provides in pertinent part that

> all persons born in the United States . . . are hereby declared to be citizens of the United States; and such citizens, of every race and color, without regard to any previous condition of slavery or involuntary servitude . . . shall have the same right, in every State and Territory in the United States, to make and enforce contracts, to sue, be parties, and give evidence, to inherit, purchase, lease, sell, hold, and convey real and personal property, and to full and equal benefit of all laws and proceedings for the security of person and property, as is enjoyed by white citizens, and shall be subject to like punishment, pains, and penalties. . . .

On June 13, 1866, Congress introduced the Fourteenth Amendment, ratification of which was now made a condition of each state's readmission into the Union. This raised the interesting but ultimately pointless legal objection that states deemed "out" of the Union had no legal standing to ratify the Amendment. Libertarian arguments that the Amendment was never properly ratified, or that its ratification in several states was "irregular," have proved to be as unavailing as objections to the manner in which the Constitution itself was ratified by "popular" conventions that bypassed the very state legislatures that had sent delegates to Philadelphia for the limited purpose of modifying the Articles of Confederation. To recall once again what Madison himself explained in Federalist No. 40, the forces of Liberty have never caviled at shortcuts to imposing what they deem to be the true object of the popular will. Why should ratification of the Fourteenth Amendment have been an exception?

The Amendment's five sections provide, among other things, that all persons residing in the States, including the former slaves, are deemed citizens of the United States—thus extinguishing the *Dred Scott* decision—and that the States are forbidden to "make or enforce any law which shall abridge the privileges or immunities of citizens of the United States; nor shall any State deprive any person of life, liberty, or property, without due process of law; nor deny to any person within its jurisdiction the equal protection of the laws." That is, by ratifying the Fourteenth Amendment the Southern states agreed that the provisions of the federal constitution were directly binding upon them, including (as we shall see in the next section) the First Amendment's separation of Church and State. The "states' rights" doctrine, on life support from the beginning, was now definitively pronounced dead, along with the Black Codes.

To remove many members of the former Confederate leadership from power at both the state and federal level, the Amendment disqualified them from holding office if they had sworn an oath to the Confederacy: "No one shall be a Senator or Representative in Congress, or elector of President and Vice President, or hold any office, civil or military, under the United States, *or under any State*, who, having previously taken an oath, as a member of Congress, or as an officer of the United States, or as a member of any State legislature, or as an executive or judicial officer of any State, to support the Constitution of the United States, shall have engaged in insurrection or rebellion against the same, or given aid or comfort to the enemies thereof. . . ." This provision helped insure the neutralization of a former Confederate faction in Congress.

The crowning blow came with the Reconstruction Acts of 1867. Under the Acts, Congress imposed military rule on the ten former Confederate states not yet readmitted to the Union (all but Tennessee), dividing them into five military districts ruled by military governors. The electorates of the ten states were not only reconstituted to include the newly emancipated slave populations, but all former Confederate leaders were disqualified from holding office. Newly enfranchised black voters, who constituted a majority in South Carolina, Alabama, Florida, Mississippi and Louisiana, led the way to the election of constitutional conventions in each of the ten states, which adopted new state constitutions. These state constitutional conventions turned Liberty against the former master class, imposing the new pattern of enfranchisement and disenfranchisement, the political equality of emancipated slaves, and the liberalization of voting requirements tending toward universal suffrage. The Black Codes were formally abolished.

As draconian as the Reconstruction Acts were, Morison makes the astute observation that their imposition had proceeded from the very premise on which the South itself had insisted: If secession was constitutionally permitted, then the South could hardly argue consistently that it had not become a separate nation which the North had conquered, wherein the former Southern states of the United States no longer existed. On the other hand, the North could hardly argue consistently that the South was a conquered foreign nation if secession was illegal and the Southern states had never ceased to be part of the United States. Both sides could appeal to the other's premise. Here yet again we see the ambiguity and self-contradiction inherent to Locke's doctrines of the social compact and the right to revolution.

Such, in summary, was the Congressional response to the South's attempt to recreate antebellum slavery by means of statutes and ordinances. Whereas under Lincoln and previous Presidents, especially Jefferson, it was the Chief Executive who boldly exercised federal authority, now it was Congress's turn to wield the powerful levers of Liberty. After Congress passed the Tenure of Office Act (1867), which made it illegal for a President to fire any of his appointed officials without Senate approval, President Johnson tested the constitutionality of the Act by dismissing Secretary of War Stanton, who promptly "barricaded himself in his office and refused to permit access to War Department records."[19] The radical Republicans' attempt to impeach Johnson in May 1868 failed by only a single vote. But by this time there "was no longer any effective opposition to the Radicals within party ranks, and the reconstructed states gave them plenty of docile delegates," which would lead to the election of General Grant as President in 1868.[20]

19. William F. Swindler, "The Politics of 'Advice and Consent,'" 56 *American Bar Association Journal* (1979), 540.

20. Morison, *HAP*, 720–21.

Despite the draconian measures of Radical Reconstruction, the Southern states submitted tamely, one by one, to the superior sovereign, merging with it once again. Morison observes that "a Europe accustomed to the persistence of Irish, Polish, and other national grievances" was astonished "by Southern acceptance of the result. . . . Lee, Johnston and almost every Southern leader except Davis advised their people to accept the verdict of battle and endeavor to be good citizens in a reunited country. The great majority did so . . . retaining only a nostalgic loyalty to the Stars and Blues."[21] In the great spirit of reconciliation that now filled the Temple of Liberty, it was a famous New York lawyer, Charles O'Conor, who had led Davis's defense team and obtained his release from Fortress Monroe on a writ of habeas corpus. In December 1868 the indictments of Lee, Davis, and some thirty other Confederate leaders for treason were all dismissed, and on Christmas Day the outgoing President Johnson issued an unconditional and universal amnesty to all former Confederates, which "left only 300 persons unpardoned and ineligible to vote in the entire South."[22]

One of Johnson's earlier exercises of executive clemency for former Confederates merits particular mention: On August 30, 1865 Johnson granted amnesty to his fellow Scottish Rite Freemason, Albert Pike, the eccentric genius who wrote a major pamphlet defending secession and had served as a brigadier general in the Confederate Army and Confederate commissioner to the Indian Territory. In 1871 Pike, "Sovereign Grand Commander" of the Scottish Rite in America, published *Morals and Dogma of the Ancient and Accepted Scottish Rite of Freemasonry*, the famous Masonic manual for the Southern Jurisdiction of the Rite. As Sovereign Grand Commander, Pike was literally President Johnson's Masonic superior. Johnson's "close association with Freemasonry was one of the factors that led to his impeachment trial," as the leading anti-Mason Thaddeus Stevens "was a ringleader against Johnson in 1868."[23] Pike is the only Confederate general to be honored with an outdoor statue in Washington, DC, and Pike's remains were interred in "The House of the Temple" in Washington, headquarters of the Scottish Rite's Southern Jurisdiction, U.S.A. and a national landmark. The worldwide Masonic fraternity of Liberty knew no North or South, East or West.

The spirit of reconciliation was prevailing and the Temple of Liberty was being exorcised of its evil spirit of dissension. And among the exorcists were former Confederate leaders, including Stephens, who was elected to the United States Congress as a representative from Georgia in 1873 and was reelected repeatedly until his retirement in 1882. The fiery preacher of the Confederacy's right to secede in order to defend the "natural subjugation" of the Negro as the "cornerstone" of Southern civilization, who had declared in 1862 that the Confederacy would fight on until "the last man in the South finds a bloody grave," now readily accommodated himself to a South that was indeed full of bloody graves but was entirely without slavery.

21. Morison, *HAP*, 706–707.
22. Ibid., 718.
23. Denslow and Truman, Part One, 299.

Like so many wily politicians in the annals of Liberty, Stephens had landed firmly on his feet, unscathed by the massive bloodshed he had helped to instigate.

Yet as of 1867, Lee still found "person after person railing against the Reconstruction Acts, against the Republican Party, against Washington, against the damn Yankees." His advice to one such woman was: "Madam, do not train up your children in hostility to the government of the United States. *Remember we are all one country now.* Dismiss from your mind all sectional feeling, and bring them up to be Americans."[24] In 1870, the year of his death, Lee would say: ". . . . I am rejoiced that slavery is abolished. I believe it will be greatly for the interests of the South. . . . I would cheerfully have lost all I have lost by the war, and have suffered all I have suffered, to have this object attained."[25] So Lee would gladly have lost the war in order to achieve the very thing the South had fought the war to prevent! But why the rejoicing if slavery had been such a boon to the slaves compared with the alternatives, and the black man would be lost and fall into ruin if emancipated, as Lee and the Confederate polemic had so long maintained?

Charles Bracelen Flood recounts an incident after Lee's application for a pardon that is offered to illustrate Lee's nobility. As reported by a Union colonel from West Virginia, during a Sunday service at St. Paul's Episcopal Church in Richmond attended by Lee "a negro in the church arose and advanced to the communion table" to the "great surprise and shock" of the congregation. "This," writes Flood, "was the South's worst nightmare," for instead of waiting in the black section until all the whites had received their Anglican communion wafers "this black man had come to the front of the church as if he were a social equal." Only months before, a Negro who had dared to do this "would have been hustled from the church, jailed for disturbing the peace, and quite possibly flogged." With Richmond under federal occupation, however, the congregation could do nothing "while the minister stood dumbfounded." But Lee, the colonel reported, "ignoring the action and presence of the negro, arose in his usual dignified and self-possessed manner, walked up the aisle to the chancel rail, and reverently knelt down to partake of the communion, and not far from the negro," whereupon the other congregants proceeded to the altar.[26] The question arises: If Lee is to be lauded for this noble gesture of racial harmony, where was the nobility in a Southern cause dedicated to maintaining the antebellum status quo under which the same black man would have been arrested and possibly flogged?

In the White Sulphur Letter Lee had represented that the former Confederate leaders excluded from office and the franchise sought only "a restoration of their rights under the Constitution" and the "re-establishment, in the Southern states, of that which has justly been regarded as the birth-right of every American, the right of self-government. Establish these on a firm basis, and we can safely promise, on behalf of the Southern people, that *we will faithfully obey the Constitution and laws*

24. Flood, *Lee*, 152.
25. Statement by Lee to Rev. John Leyburn, May 1, 1870, in Freeman, *R. E. Lee*, Vol. IV, 401.
26. Flood, *Lee: the Last Years*, 65–66.

*of the United States, treat the negro populations with kindness and humanity and ful-
fill every duty incumbent on peaceful citizens,* loyal to the Constitution of *their country.*"[27] That being the case, what was the point of the Southern secession, the Civil
War, and the loss of upwards of a million lives, including civilians?

Even the unrepentant Davis, who refused until his end to seek a pardon, would
eventually issue an astonishing call for *perpetual union with the North* and final
abandonment of the cause of Southern secession. It appears in the concluding lines
of his monumentally obstinate apologia for that very secession, published in 1881:

> In asserting the right of secession, it has not been my wish to incite its exer-
> cise. I recognize the fact that the war showed it to be *impracticable*; but this
> did not prove it to be wrong; and *now that it may not again be attempted*, and
> that the Union may promote the general welfare, it is needful that the truth,
> the whole truth, be known, so that crimination and recrimination forever
> cease; and then, on the basis of fraternity and faithful regard for the rights of
> the States, there may be written on the arch of the Union, *Esto perpetua.*[28]

Davis's description of the Southern secession as "impracticable" is a strong candidate for the greatest understatement in Western political history. But his call for
permanent union was no fickle sentiment of the moment. Seven years later,
addressing a gathering of former Confederates in Mississippi—his last public
address—Davis declared the death of his ideas and a glorious future for Liberty in
the Union:

> I feel no regret that I stand before you this afternoon a man without a coun-
> try, for my ambition lies buried in the grave of the Confederacy. There lies
> consigned not only my ambition, but the dogmas on which the Confederate
> government was based. . . . The past is dead; let it bury its dead, its hopes, its
> aspirations; before you lies the future—a future full of hope and golden
> promise; a future of expanding national glory, before which all the world shall
> stand amazed. Let me beseech you to lay aside all rancor, all bitter sectional
> feeling, and take your place in the ranks of those who will bring about a con-
> summation devoutly to be wished—a reunited country.[29]

Lee died in 1870 while serving as President of Washington College. Like any good
post-Enlightenment liberal, he had accepted the position only after he had
"received private assurances that Washington College would favor no particular
Christian denomination . . . "—another nail in the coffin of the mythical "Southern
cause" as "Anglo-Catholic" crusade.[30] Davis survived Lee by nineteen years; and
while Lee immediately ascended to the pantheon of Liberty, it would take several

27. In Freeman, *R. E. Lee*, Vol. IV, Chap. XXI, 376–77.

28. Davis, *Rise and Fall*, Vol. II, 764; and see Foote, *The Civil War*, Vol. III, 1054 (on Davis's dictation
to Varina).

29. In ed. William Cooper, *Jefferson Davis: The Essential Writings* (NY: Random House, 2003; 2004
paperback edition), 437.

30. Flood, *Lee*, 84.

years for Davis to be forgiven sufficiently to join him in its Southern wing, to the cheers of vast crowds even while he was still alive.

In examining the statements of both regarding permanent reconciliation in the Union, however, one cannot help but ask: What were Lee and Davis saying in the end if not a very elaborate "never mind"? For all their talk of Southern honor, given their own counsel to forget the past, forget the Confederacy, and be glad of reunion, just whose "honor" had really been at stake in the war over secession if not their own personal honor—purchased at the cost of a vast number of other peoples' lives? Was it "honor" at all that was really at stake, in the sense of a vindication of high moral principles, or was it rather, as Elizabeth Pryor suggests, "'pride,' that second cousin of honor"? Could not the same be said of all the leading generals in this senseless war, both North and South? Sam Watkins said it best, with appropriately mordant sarcasm (and this for all his admiration of Lee): "[T]he generals did all the fighting, and that is today why generals, and colonels, and captains are great men. They fought the battles of our country. The privates did not. The generals risked their reputation, the private soldier his life."[31]

Lee once expressed the sentiment that "The warmest instincts of every man's soul declare the glory of a soldier's death. It is more appropriate to the Christian than the Greek to sing: 'Glorious his fate, and envied his lot, who for his country fights and for it dies.'"[32] But for which country had all those young men died their enviable, glorious deaths? Was it the Confederate States of America, which had suddenly vanished without a trace and whose existence Lee had implicitly consigned to oblivion with his request for a pardon from Washington and his call for reunification with the North? Or did Lee mean the individual "sovereign states" or the homes and farms from which these legions of the fallen had come? Yet the States, homes and farms of the South would never have had to be defended in the first place if not for the creation of a short-lived Confederate "country"—to recall Sam Watkins's contemptuous quotation marks—by a group of wealthy and privileged elites who had met to decide the fates of millions of others in Montgomery back in 1861. How many of those planters and lawyers, if any, had joined the 258,000 men who died Lee's glorious death of a soldier for a Southern cause Lee afterwards pragmatically reduced to an arbitration of political disputes whose outcome must be accepted because "We are all one country now"? If, according to Lee, it was not only possible but morally incumbent on the South to resume being one country with the North, why did the South secede in the first place? Where was the moral justification for the "arbitrament" of a war that had—with complete predictability—claimed so many lives, destroyed so many families, and left the South in ruins?

In a groundbreaking essay published more than forty years ago, Kenneth Stampp, of Berkeley and Oxford and winner of Gettysburg College's Lincoln Prize for his achievements as a Civil War historian, did for the Southern romantic narra-

31. Watkins, *Company Aytch*, 51.
32. Nolan, *Lee Considered*, 127.

tive what other scholars had done concerning the Whig narrative of the "conservative" American Revolution: he led the way in exposing its *mythos* with hard historical facts. "It is instructive," he wrote, "to contrast the myth of a special southern national identity with the reality of, say, Polish nationalism, which survived more than a century of occupation, partition, and repression. After Appomattox the myth of southern nationalism died remarkably soon."[33] And it was none other than Lee and Davis, the defunct Confederacy's foremost leaders, who lowered it into its grave. In the aftermath of the romantic "clash of civilizations" that never really was, "[t]he values the South shared with the North proved to be bonds, not wedges, and they were bonds that neither could escape."[34] Hence Alexander Stephens had been at pains to note in 1861 that in the Confederate Constitution "all the essentials of the old Constitution, which have endeared it to the hearts of *the American people*, have been preserved and perpetuated." Southerners "could no longer escape this heritage, and rather than seeking to escape it they claimed it as their own. But in doing so they confessed rather pathetically the speciousness of southern nationalism."[35] Once slavery was removed from the picture, the cause of division in the Temple of Liberty would be removed along with it, as Lee and other Southern leaders now insisted. In the end, Southern nationalism proved to be "that most flimsy and ephemeral of dreams. . . ."[36] This is why, as we have argued here, the "Southern cause" was not a "conservative" departure from the "progress" of Liberty, but rather a struggle over the path that progress would take in the same general direction: Liberty plus slaves versus Liberty without slaves, but Liberty in either case.

The Great Never Mind, then, was part of the process by which the Civil War was assimilated by the one undivided nation into the one undivided Liberty narrative, whose "conservative" and liberal threads were quickly merged into a garment acceptable to all Americans. Rather than admitting that "the war was a tragic failure and trying to understand it or even condemn it, Americans, North and South, chose to view it as a glorious time to be celebrated. . . ."[37] The post-war partisans of North and South were unwilling to recognize, as the *North Carolina Christian Advocate* did in 1863, that God will not favor either side in a war when "in the origin and progress of the war, each party to the conflict is equally guilty."[38] Instead, both sides "celebrated the war's triumphant nationalism and martial glory."[39]

Speaking in 1963, Allen Tate, long since disabused of his own Confederate partisanship of thirty years earlier, recorded his disgust at "seeing 'men dressed up in Gray and Blue playing out like children an episode of the great tragedy of American

33. Stampp, *The Southern Road to Appomattox*, 15.

34. Beringer, et al., *Why the South Lost the Civil War*, 75.

35. Stampp, *The Southern Road to Appomattox*, 13–14.

36. Ibid., 13.

37. Nolan, *Lee Considered*, 170–171, in part quoting Beringer, et al., *Why the South Lost the Civil War*, 416–17.

38. In Beringer, et al., 270.

39. Nolan, *Lee Considered*, 170–171, in part quoting Beringer, loc cit.

history.' A man who had once passionately admired the Confederacy now rejected the romanticism of the Lost Cause, symbolized by the reenactors' glorification of war."[40] Five years later, a thoroughly chastened Tate would describe the writings of the Lost Cause revisionists as

> not a literature of introspection, but a literature of romantic illusion; and its mode was what I have called elsewhere the Rhetorical Mode. I like Yeats' epigram about rhetoric—it is the way we quarrel with others, not ourselves—and rhetoric in the Reconstruction South was a good way of quarreling with the Yankees, who were to blame for everything. The quarrel raged with some cunning and versatility, for it elicited a good deal of fiction in which the Southern gentleman was the Chevalier Bayard redivivus, the Poor White a picturesque buffoon who spoke a quaint dialect, and the Negro Rousseau's Natural Man spoiled by having been deprived of the benefits of slavery.[41]

Even in losing the war Southerners could claim "[t]heir cause had been just and their failure only the result of overwhelming numbers." Yet, at the same time, "the death of chattel slavery, along with the surrender of dreams of separate nationhood, allowed the South to claim victory in partnership with the North...."[42] That is precisely what Lee did in making the stupefying pronouncement that he would gladly have lost the war to *end* slavery. And the myth-makers of the North, cultivating their own romantic *mythos* of the Emancipation Crusade, were only too happy to give the defeated South its due by "romanticizing Lee and his men, painting them as underdogs or epic warriors."[43] Thus did both parties to a gigantic and bizarre catastrophe contribute their respective grandiose pages to the Liberty narrative.

Southern Statues for the National Pantheon

This study has declined to recognize any of the plaster saints ensconced in Liberty's pantheon, be it the Northern or the Southern wing. Just as ridiculous as the apotheosis of Washington and Lincoln is the apotheosis of the leaders of the Confederacy, especially its generals, who even during the war were already being raised to the status of divinely anointed saviors. Typical of such adoration is an ode in the Atlanta journal *Southern Confederacy* to General Beauregard, who oversaw the bombardment of Fort Sumter, was the victor at First Bull Run, and fought off a Union invasion of Petersburg until Lee's army arrived:

40. In Wallace Hettle, *Inventing Stonewall Jackson: A Civil War Hero in History and Memory* (Baton Rouge: Louisiana State Univ. Press, 2001, Kindle Edition), 120, quoting Allen Tate, "The Battle of Gettysburg: Why It Was Fought," lecture at Lothrop Memorial Auditorium, Univ. of Minnesota, 4 February 1963, in *Allen Tate Papers*, Princeton Univ. (PU).

41. Tate, "Faulkner's *Sanctuary* and the Southern Myth," loc. cit.

42. Beringer, et al., 416.

43. Pryor, *Reading the Man*, 9572–9575.

> Our trust is now in thee,
> Beauregard,
> In thy hand the God of Hosts
> Hath placed thy sword
> And the glory of thy fame
> Hath set the land aflame
> Hearts kindle at thy name,
> Beauregard![44]

But nothing matches the adoration that would surround the memory of Lee and Jackson, above all Lee. Thanks to the tireless work of post-war Confederate historians of the Lost Cause, Lee would become nothing less than another George Washington—the George Washington of the Second American Revolution. As Emily Mason's *Popular Life of Robert Edward Lee* would observe concerning's Lee's acceptance of the presidency of Washington College: "It is remarkable that the institution which enjoyed the munificence and inherited the name of the hero of the first American Revolution, should have opened its arms to receive . . . the foremost man of the second."[45]

The Lee Memorial Association, emerging on top in the struggle to appropriate Lee's memory, saw to it that a marble "Recumbent Statue" of Lee would dominate the sanctuary of the Lee Chapel of the renamed Washington and Lee University. In this Protestant place of worship devoted to a man, the central alcove in the sanctuary containing the statue is flanked by portraits of Lee on the right and Washington on the left—a veritable "holy of holies" for the Southern cult of Liberty. Beneath the alcove is the burial crypt of the entire "holy family" of the Lees, including the transferred remains of "Light-Horse Harry." There is even a separate burial plot at the entrance to the chapel museum for the remains of Lee's horse, Traveller, the sacred stallion that bore the holy Knight of the South.[46] Later plans to demolish Lee Chapel and build a new one in its place were scuttled by a wave of outraged opposition, including this editorial blast: "Lay not a hand upon it—change it not either in interior or exterior appearance—for it is a holy thing!"[47]

Only four years after Lee's death, Benjamin Hill heaped nearly hysterical praise on the already apotheosized Confederate general. Lee, said Hill, had combined all the virtues of all the great military leaders in Western history—Caesar, Frederick, Napoleon, Washington—while having no faults to speak of. Lee was "as gentle as a

44. In Thomas Lawrence Connelly, *The Marble Man: Robert E. Lee and His Image in American Society* (Baton Rouge: Louisiana State Univ. Press, 1977), 21–22.

45. Ibid., 97.

46. Cf. Lee Chapel history, http://chapelapps.wlu.edu/secondary.asp?ID=7&NavOrder= 20.

47. In Ollinger Crenshaw, *General Lee's College: the Rise and Growth of Washington and Lee University* (NY: Random House, 1969), 303.

woman in life; modest and pure as a virgin in thought; watchful as a Roman vestal in duty; submissive to law as Socrates, and grand in battle as Achilles." He was "obedient to authority as a servant, and royal in authority as a true king." In private life he was a "citizen without wrong; a neighbor without reproach; a Christian without hypocrisy; a man without guile."[48] There is no denying that Lee was an impressive, dignified, accomplished, and highly intelligent man, and it is right to view him sympathetically as a supremely tragic figure who had nothing to gain and everything to lose from the decision that put him on the path to the catastrophic rise and fall of the Confederacy. But he was only a man—a man, moreover, who by his own admission had committed grave blunders that may well have lost the war for the South. Yet if Hill had declared that Lee was the greatest man who ever walked the face of the earth save Jesus himself, he would not have been saying much more than he said in this dithyramb, which sounded all the themes of a Lee Legend to match those of Washington and Lincoln.

Later, "Freeman and other Lee writers—like Carl Sandburg in his Lincoln biography and Parson Weems's writing about Washington—relate every anecdote, including second- and third-hand accounts originating long after the fact, that portray their subject as superhuman...."[49] Nolan's study of Lee collects examples of such excesses in Lee biographies: Freeman's panegyric-laden four volumes devote no less than four columns to Lee's virtues alone, from his abstemiousness to his wisdom, and present him as a Christ-like figure to whom a woman brings her baby for a blessing. Fishwick's biography lauds the "Apollo on horseback... fighting bravely as did the knights of old," and likens Lee to both "Saint George, slaying Yankee dragons" and Saint Francis of Assisi because "literally everything and everybody loved him." Typifying the nonsense that permeates the Liberty narrative in general, Gamaliel Bradford admits the obvious truth that "after all, in fighting for the Confederacy Lee was fighting for slavery, and he must have known perfectly well that if the South triumphed... slavery would flourish for another generation, if not for another century," and that Lee, "fighting, as he believed, for freedom, for independence, for democracy, was fighting also to rivet the shackles more firmly on millions of his fellow men." Yet Bradford somehow reaches this conclusion: "In Lee, no pride, but virtue all; not liberty for himself alone, but for others, *for everyone*."[50]

Elizabeth Brown Pryor ably sums up the development of the Lee cult that began immediately after his death, "as if an open season of adoration had been declared." She writes:

> [T]he words became ever more superlative, the images more sublime. Admirers spoke of a mystical aurora that had appeared at his death. His office was kept untouched as a sacred memorial, and some began to refer to Lexington, with its twin graves of Jackson and Lee, as "Mecca.".... Lee was compared to

---

48. "Address Delivered before the Southern Historical Society," February 18, 1874, in *Benjamin Hill: His Life, Speeches and Writings*, 406.
49. Nolan, *Lee Considered*, 172.
50. Ibid., 173.

Washington, to Napoleon, to Caesar, even to Ulysses S. Grant. Some came perilously close to blasphemy, adorning Lee with the vision of prophets, the qualities of Christ, the power of a "divine example." It all survived well until the late twentieth century, when a popular painting placed Lee at the right hand of Christ, in a triptych whose other secular saint was Elvis Presley.[51]

The life of Frederick Douglass has become the property of liberals, but there is much in his writings that resonates with the Christocentric worldview in its confrontation with the vainglory of political modernity. In a famous protest that Lee's more reasonable admirers admit was warranted, Douglass wrote of the growing idolatry of Lee: "We can scarcely take up a newspaper that is not filled with nauseating flatteries of the late Robert E. Lee. . . . It would seem from this that the soldier who kills the most men in battle, even in a bad cause, is the greatest Christian."[52] And why should a Christian not be at least dubious concerning claims of epic greatness for men who, however admirable, surely would have disappeared from historical memory if not for their central roles in massive battlefield carnage—the Northern as well as the Southern "great men" of a conflict Pope Pius IX rightly called "a deplorable intestine war."

Over the years Lee would become "the closest thing to a saint in the Protestant South . . . canonized not only as the South's military hero but also as its supreme religious symbol."[53] The height of this cultic *dulia* had to be the comment in one contemporaneous newspaper clipping, found among the Lee family papers, that "in Lee's 'composition original sin seemed omitted.'"[54] But even this was not enough. Lee would be elevated to the status of a Christ-figure, whose sufferings compared with those of the Man of Sorrows Himself. Concerning Lee's decision to resign his commission and turn down command of the U.S. Army, the principal orator at the sacred unveiling of the "Recumbent Statue" at Lee Chapel in 1883 seriously proposed the borderline blasphemy that "[s]ince the Son of Man stood on the Mount" to be tempted by the devil with all the kingdoms of the world, "to the Cross of Calvary and beyond, no follower of the meek and lowly Saviour can have undergone a more trying ordeal."[55]

For Southerners, Lee's Birthday would serve as the equivalent of Washington's Birthday. The celebrations included prescribed public school rituals for honoring the memory of a man who would become no less a "virtual demigod"[56] than Washington, and perhaps even more so. Thomas Lawrence Connelly's study of Lee recounts how in the early 1900s, for example, the commissioners of public

---

51. Pryor, *Reading the Man*, 9524–9525.

52. Ibid., 9572–9575. Douglass's protest was quoted favorably by a Lee aficionado who was to deliver an address on Lee at the Lee Chapel in Lexington. Cf. Kevin Levin, "The Historical Legacy of Robert E. Lee," http://cwmemory.com/2007/10/08/the-historical-legacy-of-robert-e-lee/.

53. Connelly, *The Marble Man*, 95.

54. Pryor, *Reading the Man*, 9523.

55. Connelly, 97.

56. Ibid., 91.

education in Georgia and Alabama issued instruction booklets for the correct observance of the holy day. Georgia's booklet, entitled *Selections for the Observance... of the Birth of Robert E. Lee in the Schools of Georgia*, included the poem "The Sword of Robert E. Lee" by Father Abram Ryan, the famed battlefield chaplain and "poet-priest of the South." Ryan's patriotic doggerel hailed Lee's glorious sword, held "high in the air/Beneath Virginia's sky," which inspired those who saw it "To follow—and to die!" According to one set of rubrics for the solemn reading of the poem, at the words "Flashed the sword of Lee!" the student reader was expected to "Sway weight of body forward to R. foot as right arm swings out to R. oblique at shoulder level, then swing straight above head; head tilted back; face up. Pleased expression."[57]

Also read solemnly in Southern public schools was Ryan's "Conquered Banner." Written in mourning on a discarded shoe box after Lee's surrender at Appomattox, the rediscovered poem, "read or sung in every Southern household" as well as in the schools, became "the apotheosis of the 'Lost Cause.'"[58] The poem winds to its lugubrious conclusion with the exhortation: "Furl that banner, softly, slowly!/Treat it gently—it is holy,/For it droops above the dead/Let it droop there, furled forever,—/For its people's hopes are dead." What precisely were the "people's hopes" represented by the drooping banner finds no explanation in the poem. We are told, however, that "Once ten thousands hailed it gladly./And ten thousands *wildly, madly,*/ Swore it should forever wave."

The defeated South erected a pantheon of revolutionary heroes akin to the one erected after 1776, with Lee at its center. The post-war task was to link the two pantheons as wings of the one national Temple of Liberty. Led by a determined nucleus of Virginian activists and writers of the Lost Cause movement, the drive to elevate Lee and Stonewall Jackson to national status began early and was not to be resisted. And the effort would succeed. For after all, both men were exemplary of the Anglo-Puritan revolutionary dynamism that had given birth to a nation then still only a lifetime old. Lee's own father had been instrumental in General Washington's triumph over King George and had served as a member of the Continental Congress. And Lee, Jackson, Washington, "Light-Horse Harry," Jefferson and Madison were all sons of Virginia, the proud heart of American Liberty.

The future Lord Acton, arch-liberal opponent of Pius IX and supporter of the Southern secession, whose correspondence with Lee we have already mentioned, was pleased to observe as early as 1862 that "in Northern cities 'Stonewall Jackson is the national hero.'" Immediately after Jackson's death, in the very midst of the Civil War, the *Washington Daily Morning Chronicle*, while hailing the Confederacy's loss of a key general, praised "his heroism, his bravery, his sublime devotion, his purity of character.... He is not the first instance of a good man devoting himself to a

57. Connely, *Marble Man*, 114.
58. H. Taylor, "Father Abram J. Ryan," *The Catholic Encyclopedia* (NY: Robert Appleton Company, 1912), accessed at: http://www.newadvent.org/cathen/13282b.htm.

bad cause." No less than Abraham Lincoln himself thanked the newspaper for its "excellent and manly article . . . on Stonewall Jackson."[59]

Within thirty years of Lee's death in 1870, writes Connelly, "[a] mania for Lee swept through the country, as if America could not praise him enough, or read enough of his army's exploits." *Harper's* would hail him as "the pride of the whole country," while the *Chautauquan* would declare nothing less than that—of course—Lee belonged to America's "'first triumvirate of greatness' with Abraham Lincoln and George Washington." After 1900, "the entire nation accepted the Lee imagery and enshrined the General as an American hero of the same status as George Washington and Abraham Lincoln."[60] A bust of Lee would be included in New York University's Hall of Fame.

The "nationalization" of Lee would be accompanied by an expedient adjustment of the Lost Cause narrative. In what Connelly calls "the Virginia argument," Lost Cause polemicists began to distance Virginia, home of the sainted Lee, from the rest of the Confederacy. Secession was now to be blamed entirely on the radical hot-heads of the Cotton States, whose "selfish, dictatorial bearing," "threats" and "riotous proceedings" both Robert and Mary Custis Lee had condemned in their private pre-war correspondence, as we saw in Chapter 12. In his "A Rebel's Recollections," serialized in *The Atlantic Monthly* in 1874, the Southern novelist George Cary Eggleston depicts the politicians of the Cotton States—rightly enough—as "types of a class" who had "brought upon the South odium with 'their bragging, their intolerance, their contempt for the North, their arrogance,'" whereas noble Virginia had felt that "secession was unwise, and was indignant toward those Southerners who were 'endangering the peace of the land.'" Forced into a posture of self-defense by the foolhardy Cotton States, Virginians had no choice but to defend themselves when Lincoln "called for troops to put down the rebellion," and "they freely offered themselves upon the altar of an abstract principle of right . . . which they knew must work hopeless ruin to themselves."[61] The "Virginia argument" conveniently ignored the path taken by the western Virginia counties (noted in Chapter 13), which saw no need of self-defense, rejected secession, and became the State of West Virginia, thereby escaping the devastation of an utterly pointless war.

According to this retelling of history, Lee would be reinvented as the great healer of the nation with his call for reconciliation in the Union. Both Theodore Roosevelt and Woodrow Wilson would hail him as "a great nationalist who helped to save the Union by his resignation to defeat after the war."[62] We have seen that both Lee and Davis did indeed speak a nationalist vocabulary after their Confederacy's downfall, with Davis even proclaiming America's glorious future as a *perpetually* reunited

59. Gary W. Gallagher, "Shaping Public Memory of the Civil War: Robert E. Lee, Jubal A. Early and Douglas Southall Freeman," in Alice Fahs and Joan Waugh, eds *The Memory of the Civil War in American Culture* (Chapel Hill: Univ. of North Carolina Press, 2004), 55–56.

60. Connelly, 12–13, 98.

61. Connelly, 106–107.

62. Ibid., 4.

nation. Unfortunately for all the Southern soldiers who lost their lives or limbs, the nationalism of Lee and Davis did not manifest itself before secession and the attack on Fort Sumter that Davis had authorized to commence a war he knew—and said—would be the bloodiest the Western world had yet seen, and which Lee knew would "yield nothing" even before it began.

The national veneration of Lee was an important part of the process by which memory would be "purified" and the Temple of Liberty finally purged of the evil spirit of dissension. Veneration of Lee would become *de fide* with the posthumous republication of Woodrow Wilson's 1909 tribute to Lee, his fellow Virginian, in 1924. Recalling the "delightful memory of standing, when a lad, for a moment by General Lee's side and looking up into his face," Wilson declared that Lee "does not need the eulogy of any man. His fame is not enhanced, his memory is not lifted to any new place of distinction by any man's words of praise, for he is secure of his place ... [and] is recognized now as a national hero." Lee, that is, was too marvelous for words. He embodied, said Wilson—who had made the world safe for democracy—"the consummate fire of a democratic nation."[63] And so he had.

But what of the President of the Confederate States? Jefferson Davis would never achieve the status of universal American icon, although he became a beloved figure in the South. According to Benjamin Hill, he "was as great in the cabinet as Lee was in the field." There were some, Hill said, who "affect to praise Lee, and condemn Davis," but "[h]and in hand, they moved in front of the dire struggle of their people for independence—a pair of noble brothers. . . ." And surely "as heart in heart, and wing to wing, they fly though the courts of Heaven, admiring angels will say, What a noble pair of brothers!" Kneeling rhetorically in the midst of this effusion, Hill pledged his undying devotion to the pair: "I would be ashamed of my own unworthiness if I did not venerate Lee. I would scorn my own nature if I did not love Davis."[64] And this from a "reconstructed" politician, a member of the Georgia secession convention who went on to win seats in the U.S. House and Senate after the war.

Even an entirely admiring biographer of Lee's final years looks askance at this Southern hagiography, noting that Lee was in reality "a central figure in a stupendous failure," but that after his death "the national memory would simplify Lee" and that he and his horse Traveller "were instantly transformed into a stone statue, his name revered in the South and his campaigns studied in the world's military academies."[65] That both Lee and Davis had failed stupendously at the cost of hundreds of thousands of lives did not matter to Hill, nor would it matter to the long train of Lost Cause hagiographers who would follow him. On the contrary, the sheer number of deaths that Lee and Davis (along with the rest of the Confederate leadership) left in their wake was only a testament to their "heroic determination"

63. Wilson, "Robert E. Lee: An Interpretation," *Social Forces*, Vol. II (March 1924) 322–28, accessed at http://leearchive.wlu.edu/reference/essays/wilson/index. html.
64. In *Hill: His Life, Speeches, and Writings*, 410.
65. Flood, *Lee*, 32.

and "sense of honor"—as was Lincoln's own massive contribution to the mountain of dead for the hagiographers of the Emancipation Crusade.

Just as surely as the Founders and Lincoln were finally redimensioned to human size, so were Lee, Jackson, and Davis in modern studies.[66] We have followed suit here in order to remove from the field of inquiry such distractions as honor and glory on battlefields, the romance of lost causes, and the admirable qualities of particular leaders. The subject under examination is Liberty, whose revolutionary principles—followed by North and South alike—have in practice produced death and devastation on an unprecedented scale since the age of "democratic revolution" commenced with the first one in 1776. The Civil War is arguably the single greatest folly in Liberty's march through the nations. No one has captured the bilateral insanity of the conflict better than Edmund Wilson:

> [A]s soon as a war gets started, few people do any more thinking about anything except demolishing the enemy.... [A] Southerner like Lee who had opposed secession and did not approve of slavery, was ready to fight to the death for both, and ... a Northerner like Sherman who knew the South, who had always got on well with Southerners and who did not much object to slavery, became more and more ferocious to devour the South.... We have seen, in our most recent wars, how a divided and arguing public opinion may be converted overnight into a national near-unanimity, *an obedient flood of energy which will carry the young to destruction and overpower any effort to stem it.*[67]

The heroes in this long and bloody tale are not the great generals who led legions of the young to their deaths under the Stars and Stripes or the Stars and Bars—competing standards of Liberty so similar that they caused confusion on the battlefield. The heroes, rather, were the valiant victims in the ranks who marched bravely to their slaughter on both sides of the war, in service of what they had been led to believe was a higher cause rather than the mere power struggle it actually was. The prophets in this tale are the unheeded and unremembered opponents of the violent upheaval that began this era of Liberty's endless saga of glory—at the end of which, as with the chapter that began in 1776, there was less true freedom than before. And after the Civil War was over, even the "emancipated" slaves found themselves among the latest victims of Liberty's empty promises.

---

66. See, e.g., Nolan's *Lee Considered*, and Davis's *Jefferson Davis*, a balanced presentation of the life of a man who simply could not admit he was wrong. See also Connelly's *The Marble Man*, which argues simply for the reduction of Lee to the level a human being instead of an icon, and Pryor's *Reading the Man*, which employs the Lee correspondence in an attempt to excavate the real Lee from the marble slab in which his hagiographers have entombed him. Jackson is brought down to earth in Wallace Hettle's *Inventing Stonewall Jackson* and Peter Cozzens's *Stonewall Jackson's Valley Campaign: Shenandoah 1862*.

67. Wilson, *Patriotic Gore*, xxxii.

The Jim Crow Era and the Klan

By the time Reconstruction had ended, the blacks of the South had no illusions that Washington would ever deliver "forty acres and a mule"—yet another promise Liberty had failed to keep. Over the course of the Grant administration (1869–77), "Jim Crow"[68] Democrats, including re-enfranchised former Confederate leaders such as Stephens, recaptured state legislatures throughout the South and won seats in Congress, bringing an end to the radical Republican ascendancy. With antebellum slavery abolished, along with any attempt to reinstate it via the Black Codes, what remained in the South was what had always lain beneath the surface of the institution: the doctrines of white supremacy and the inferiority of the black race. (Of course this was still very much in evidence in the North as well, for the Temple of Liberty had always been as racist as it was anti-Catholic.) Continuing Southern attempts to defeat black voting rights through state laws and constitutional amendments were met with another federal Constitutional amendment, the Fifteenth, adopted in 1870, which provides in pertinent part that "The right of citizens of the United States to vote shall not be denied or abridged by the United States or by any State on account of race, color, or previous condition of servitude."

Yet Southern opponents of Liberty for the black man still had life-tenured friends on the Supreme Court. Contrary to Lee's promise in the White Sulphur Letter that Southern blacks would be treated with "kindness and humanity" if only white civil rights were fully restored, the abandoned Black Codes were replaced by a panoply of "Jim Crow" laws that would more or less remain in effect from 1876 to 1965. These included elaborate black voter disqualification schemes, prohibitions on the sale of real estate to blacks in white neighborhoods, and the "separate but equal" public accommodations approved by the Supreme Court in its landmark decision in *Plessy v. Ferguson* (1896). In *Plessy*, the same Court that had upheld the continued bondage of Dred Scott and struck down the Civil Rights Act of 1875 in *Wabash, St. Louis, and Pacific Railroad Company v. Illinois* (1886), upheld by a 7-to-1 majority the criminal conviction of Homer Plessy, a black man who had engaged in civil disobedience by refusing to leave his seat in a "whites only" railroad car. The Court found nothing discriminatory in the state policy of providing separate public accommodations for blacks, so long as they were of equal quality (which they were not).

Later statutes and Supreme Court decisions would chip away at the Jim Crow regime of "whites only" drinking fountains, bathrooms, swimming pools, and lunch counters, the "blacks in the back of the bus" rule challenged by Rosa Parks, and of course the segregated public schools addressed in *Brown v. Bd. of Education* (1954), overruling *Plessy* 9-to-0 and issuing the famous dictum: "separate educational facilities are inherently unequal." During the so-called Second Reconstruction, passage of the federal Civil Rights Act of 1964 and the Voting Rights Act of 1965

---

68. The phrase "Jim Crow" appears to have been derived from the popular vaudeville caricature of blacks by the comedian and song-and-dance artist Thomas Rice, who performed in blackface under the title "Jump Jim Crow."

finally dismantled the last remnants of state-sponsored racial discrimination and segregation in the South—a full century after the end of the Civil War. It must be stressed that neither the prudence nor the effectiveness of these federal laws and judicial decisions is at all implied here, much less a defense of the public schools, seminaries of state-imposed conformity that are a *sine qua non* of Liberty (cf. Chapter 22). Rather, these federal actions are cited merely for the state of affairs they reflected.

While the vast majority of Southerners, led by the vast majority of former Confederate leaders, had come to terms with the outcome of the war as determinative of the questions of slavery and secession, a hard core of Confederate diehards refused to admit defeat—including even those who (following Lee) had taken oaths of allegiance to the United States. For them, divine favor was still with "the Southern cause" and "the death of the Confederacy somehow confirmed God's love for the South and fit within his higher plan for the region. . . . [T]hey looked forward to resurrection and redemption." Hence the slogan of the Lost Cause: "the South will rise again," an "intended . . . analogy to Christ's resurrection."[69] The most militant members of this constituency built what came to be known as an "Invisible Empire" divided into "Realms," "Dominions," "Provinces" and "Dens"—namely, the Ku Klux Klan. Before and during the Jim Crow era (roughly 1865 to 1965), successive iterations of the Klan and spin-off organizations would develop and practice an ideology of white supremacy, anti-Catholicism, nativism and anti-Semitism, combined with lynchings, shootings, house burnings and other acts of terror against blacks and "nigger-loving" whites.

The first Klan was formed in 1865 by Confederate War veterans in Pulaski, Tennessee as a para-Masonic "fraternity." While he would later dissemble by denying membership, it is beyond dispute that General Forrest, of Civil War cavalry fame, was a key member.[70] We have seen that before he was General Forrest, Nathan Bedford Forrest reaped profit from trading slaves like cattle, but he was wiped out financially during the war. He was initiated into the Klan by Captain John W. Morton, "Grand Cyclops" of the Nashville Klan "Den" and Forrest's former chief of artillery. This was admitted by Morton himself in his laudatory biography of Forrest, which presented as historically accurate various third party accounts of the first Klan's brief history. Morton also revealed that Forrest became "Grand Wizard" of the Klan, demolishing the contrary claims of Southern partisans who present Forrest as a model of Southern nobility, courage and honor.[71] In fact, as noted by the definitive modern biography of Forrest, "[u]nder Forrest's control, the Ku Klux

---

69. Phillips, *Confederate Diehards*, 182, 183.

70. Denslow and Truman, Part 2, 63. Forrest apprenticed at Angerona Lodge No. 168 on October 29, 1877.

71. John Watson Morton, *The Artillery of Nathan Bedford Forrest's Calvary: the 'Wizard of the Saddle'* (Nashville, TN: Publishing House of the M.E. Church, South, 1909), 345; see also John C. Lester, Daniel L. Wilson, *Ku Klux Klan: Its Origin Growth and Disbandment* (NY: Neal Publishing Company, 1905), 27.

Klan became a major counterrevolutionary force in Tennessee and the rest of the South."[72]

Other prominent members of the first Klan included none other than the Masonic divine Albert Pike, who had been granted amnesty by his fellow Mason, President Andrew Johnson. Pike served as the Klan's chief judicial officer while also reigning as "Sovereign Grand Commander" of Scottish Rite Freemasonry.[73] The Klan's "Prescript" was written by former Confederate general John B. Gordon. The Prescript prescribed certain questions for applicants, including: "Are you opposed to Negro equality both social and political?", "Are you in favor of a white man's government in this country?," and the exquisitely ironic: "Are you in favor of constitutional liberty, and a government of equitable laws instead of a government of violence and oppression?"[74]

The Klan's "creed," as Morton called it, acknowledged "our relation to the United States Government, the supremacy of the Constitution, the constitutional laws thereof, and the union of the States thereunder"[75]—another indication of the ephemeral quality of "Southern nationalism" as a pretext for secession and war. In fact, it would be the American flag, not the Confederate flag, that the Klan would display at its rallies and marches from the beginning of its existence. One libertarian commentator, a Southern partisan and follower of Murray Rothbard, bristling at the suggestion that the Klan could be associated with the noble Confederate ideal of libertarianism, denied that "the Confederate flag [is] 'the proud symbol of the Ku Klux Klan.' In fact, the KKK—a nationalist, nativist outfit if there ever was one— used the US flag *exclusively*. . . ."[76] But so did the former states of the Confederacy, and on the advice of no less than Robert E. Lee.

Like ex-Confederate Army revanchists in general, Morton depicted the Klan as a noble movement of "Chivalry, Humanity, Mercy and Patriotism." The Klan, he contended, was merely a defensive organization formed to protect whites against the abuses of the carpetbagger state governments and the black freedmen militia during Radical Reconstruction. Even Morton conceded, however, that in the neighborhoods where Klan "dens" were operating, "no negro could be induced to budge beyond his doorsill after nightfall." He attributed this fear to "leading features of the negro character," including a "vivid imagination" and a "superstitious nature." The Klan members roaming the countryside, making nocturnal visits to the homes of terrified blacks, lining the roads in their ghostly white robes and

72. Wills, *The Confederacy's Greatest Cavalryman*, 337.

73. Lester and Wilson, *Ku Klux Klan*, 27.

74. Cf. Lester and Wilson, op. cit, Appendix II, 171–72, and State Univ. of New York at Albany electronic archive, www.albany.edu/faculty/gz580/his101/kkk.html.

75. Morton, *The Artillery of Nathan Bedford Forrest's Calvary*, 337–38 (election as Grand Cyclops), 343–44 (induction of Forrest) and, generally, 337–45.

76. Llewellyn H. Rockwell, Jr., "Bristling Dixie," http://www.lewrockwell.com/Rockwell/klanflag.h tml; citing David M. Chalmers, *Hooded Americanism: The First Century of the Ku Klux Klan, 1865–1965* (Garden City, NY: Doubleday & Co., 1965)("the definitive treatment at the time. It features many pictures of the Klan in operation. *Not one shows a Confederate flag. Many feature the US flag*").

hoods in order to deter blacks from congregating or holding meetings, were regarded as "the 'hants' of dead Confederate soldiers" and the "incarnation of the powers of darkness," which some Klan members deliberately pretended to be.[77]

Morton's romantic depiction aside, the Klan represented that constituency of white Southerners who "hoped to persuade black Southerners to return to the status quo antebellum, in which they would perform labor much as they had when they were slaves." And when "such attempts at persuasion demonstrably failed, the Klan turned to more violent means to control the new voters.... By spring 1868, the Klan was fully launched throughout Tennessee as a vigilante army."[78] Quoting from the account of the prominent Texas lawyer Thomas W. Gregory, who would serve as Attorney General of the United States during the Wilson administration, even Morton damned the Klan in the process of attempting to defend it. Gregory observed that while "ninety percent of the work of the Klan involved no act of personal violence," but rather shows of intimidation designed to cow the superstitious Negro, there were indeed Klan actions of "a much more drastic nature." The "sheeted horsemen did not merely warn and intimidate.... In many instances negroes and carpetbaggers were whipped, and in very rare instances shot or hanged." In addition to these "rare" instances of shooting and lynching, the Klan routinely issued "[n]otice to leave the country" which was "rarely declined; and if declined, the results were likely to be serious." And those who "advocated and practiced social equality of the races, and incited the hostility of the blacks against the whites, were given a single notice to depart in haste, and they rarely took the time to reply."[79]

Morton seriously published as a defense of the Klan Gregory's discussion of how the Klan imposed its extra-judicial punishments, including execution. The Klan would conduct "a full and ample investigation, *ex parte* 'tis true, but all the facts were first found out and thoughtfully weighed, for and against him, and the sentence carefully considered"—all without participation of the "defendant," of course.[80] Morton cites as if it were a high moral accolade the testimony of the Reconstruction judge and famed novelist Albion Tourgée, who represented Homer Plessy in the *Plessy* case. Tourgée, who escaped a Klan death sentence by "the narrowest of margins," gained lasting literary fame with his fact-based historical novel *A Fool's Errand* wherein he described the Klan and its "Invisible Empire" as "a daring conception for a conquered people" that "[o]nly a race of warlike instincts and regal pride could have conceived or executed...."[81] The Klan purported to be a revolutionary white supremacist army and secretive shadow government—in short, a bid for American Revolution III and the restoration of Southern-fried Liberty.

77. Morton, 338–339.

78. Wills, *The Confederacy's Greatest Cavalryman*, 338, quoting Wyn Craig Wade, *The Fiery Cross: the Ku Klux Klan in America* (NY: Simon & Schuster, 1987), 46.

79. Morton, 341.

80. Ibid.

81. Albion W. Tourgée, *A Fool's Errand: A Novel of the South During Reconstruction* (NY: Cosimo Classics, 2005 [1879]), Kindle Edition, 323.

Writing as the Fool in the novel's title, the character who recognizes the folly of the North's plan to subdue this toweringly prideful people, Tourgée expresses the admiration for the Invisible Empire he had acquired in the process of attempting to deal with it while protecting himself and his family. But his admiration is akin to that of a pathologist for the hardiness and adaptability of a peculiar pathogen:

> The Fool saw them resisting bravely every step leading to the adoption of this plan, protesting with indignation, denouncing with rage, and finally submitting almost with tears. No conquered foe ever passed under the yoke which they conceived to mean servitude and infamy to them, with more unwilling step, or with more deeply muttered curses. He saw men and women afflicted with the keenest sense of personal humiliation because of their enforced submission to the power of a people they had always deemed their inferiors,—the traditional foe of the South, the "groveling and greedy Yankee,"—and then still further degraded by being placed on a level, in legal and political power and privilege, with a race despised beyond the power of language to express, whom they had always accounted too low and mean even for contempt,—mere ethnological ciphers, who had no power, except when acting in conjunction with some significant figure in the notation of human races.[82]

Even in defeat, the continued subjugation of the Negro was deemed essential to a restoration of Southern "pride" and "honor." And now the Southern biblical polemic shifted from an attempt to justify chattel slavery to "an intellectually feeble and arguably blasphemous attempt to provide religious sanction for white hegemony and segregation."[83] After the war, just as before it, the "clash of civilizations"—such as it was—revolved around the perpetual servile status of the black race in Southern society. As the Fool observes:

> The Fool deemed it likely that actual violence was not at first intended. It was probably believed that mere intimidation, the appeal to superstitious fears and the threat of corporeal punishment, would have the effect thoroughly to demoralize and disintegrate the colored vote, and leave the white [pro-black] minority powerless. When, from the unexpected manhood of the recent slaves and the long-suffering "Unioners" [Union sympathizers in the South], it was found that this result would not follow a mere display of force and the assumption of ghostly habiliments, some degree of violence followed as an almost necessary consequence. The pride of a haughty people, the resentment of one that deemed itself bitterly wronged, and the ambition of those greedy for power, were all staked on the issue of the struggle.[84]

And it is the Fool on his fool's errand who recounts via the medium of a novel the "blackmail, bullying, flogging, rape of women, castration of men, contemptuous violence to children, burning of Negro houses, stabbings, drownings and

---

82. Tourgée, *A Fool's Errand*, 322.
83. Genovese, *A Consuming Fire*, 75.
84. Tourgée, *A Fool's Errand*, 324.

hangings of anyone who offered serious resistance. Thousands, both black and white—though less, of course, the latter—were slaughtered by the Ku Klux Klan. Tourgée and his family had been through all of this."[85]

In testimony before a Congressional Committee investigating the Klan on June 27, 1871, Forrest, in keeping with the Klan's nature as a para-Masonic secret society, skirted with perjury. He "maneuvered, dodged and evaded the barrage of questions, with surprising deftness. There is no doubt he knew far more than he was saying." At one point, questioned about his role in organizing the Klan, Forrest "took the Fifth" even before the Supreme Court had elucidated the Fifth Amendment privilege against self-incrimination: "I do not think I am compelled to answer any question that would implicate me in anything. I believe the law does not require that I should do anything of the sort."[86] In one of many clear signs that "Forrest was deceiving the committee," he portrayed as a vaguely recalled "man named Saunders" the leader of a company of scouts under Forrest's direct command during the war. He was referring to Benjamin F. Saunders, a former slaveholder and the Klan organizer for North Carolina.[87]

Forrest did reveal that as of the date of his testimony the Klan of which he professed to know so little had 40,000 members in Tennessee and 550,000 throughout the South.[88] By then, Klan members were being federally prosecuted pursuant to the Force Acts of 1870–71, which made it a federal offense to use force or intimidation to prevent blacks from voting. Congress had compiled thirteen volumes of testimony documenting "hundreds of examples of the Klan's violence and terror tactics, from whippings and beatings to shootings and killings."[89] Tennessee itself, which gained readmission to the Union in 1866—the first former Confederate state readmitted—enacted legislation in 1868 that imposed criminal penalties for Klan membership, and Governor "Parson" Brownlow met force with force during his strong-arm tenure as Governor, using the militia to continue what amounted to an offshoot of the Civil War in that state. The Klan was crushed in Tennessee.

The Force Act prosecutions and the Tennessee law had snuffed out the first Klan by 1872, but Forrest claimed to have supported its earlier official disbandment. It was Forrest himself, acting as "Grand Wizard," who issued a so-called disbandment order in 1869, as revealed by Morton in his fawning biography.[90] Forrest knew, however, that his order only directed the abandonment of "masks and costumes" and professed to deplore acts of "private revenge" while the Klan continued to operate at the local level. He also knew that the order "merely dissociated Imperial Headquarters from responsibility from the behavior of rank-and-file Klansmen, which was probably all that Forrest hoped it would do."[91] As Forrest's biographer

85. Wilson, *Patriotic Gore*, 535.
86. Wills, *The Confederacy's Greatest Cavalryman*, 364.
87. Ibid.
88. Lester and Wilson, op. cit., 28–30.
89. Wills, op. cit., 365.
90. Morton, *The Artillery of Nathan Bedford Forrest's Calvary*, 345.
91. Wade, op. cit, 59; in Wills, 358.

observes, Forrest took this action as Grand Wizard "less because the Ku Klux Klan had become a monster than because it was a monster he no longer believed he could restrain or regulate as he saw fit."[92] But even Morton concedes that after the first Klan finally dissolved in 1872, former members continued the Invisible Empire through such organizations as "the Palefaces," "White League," "White Brotherhood," and "Knights of the White Camelia."[93] Later iterations of the original Klan have continued its "mission" to the present day.

The South's Moral Victory

In the decades following the Civil War, black Americans had to be among the most disillusioned "beneficiaries" of Liberty, no matter which half of the country they inhabited. Enslaved for more than two hundred years by a Protestant master class that portrayed itself as a divinely ordained host of noble saviors, treated as inferior beings in both the North and the South since their arrival in the holds of slave ships in the 17th century, unwelcome in the hardly less racist Northern states where chattel slavery had been abolished, the former slaves and their children found themselves consigned to a "separate but equal" apartheid even by the post-Civil War Supreme Court. Shelby Foote, a Mississippian, rightly observed in his classic narrative of the Civil War that despite the war's outcome the black man, "locked in a caste system of 'race etiquette' as rigid as any he had known in bondage," could "repeat with equal validity what an Alabama slave had said in 1864 when asked what he thought of the Great Emancipator whose proclamation went into effect in that year. 'I don't know nothing bout Abraham Lincoln, cep they say he sot us free, and I don't know nothin' about that neither.'"[94]

The period between the first Reconstruction and the second Reconstruction of the 1960s supported a postwar rationale for the South's contribution to the glorious Liberty narrative. For although the South had lost the war and its peculiar institution, it had maintained white supremacy and the doctrine of states' rights related to that regime, even in the face of early Supreme Court challenges. The South had thus preserved its "honor" as the proponents of the Lost Cause then understood it. "In this way, the South could claim 'a moral if not a military, victory,' conspiring with historians 'to prove that no one—no white man at least—had lost the Civil War.'"[95] And today the South's greatest general, who sent more Northerners to their graves than any other, is a national hero almost on the level of George Washington himself. In the inscrutable designs of Liberty, all things are assimilated to its relentless progress.

92. Wills, 359.

93. Morton, *Artillery*, 343.

94. Foote, *The Civil War*, Vol. II, 1045.

95. Beringer, et al., *Why the South Lost the Civil War*, 417, quoting Shy, *People Numerous and Armed*, 245.

Indian "Pacification"

Even after the Confederacy was dead and buried—with the blessing of its two most prominent leaders!—there remained another separatist nation-within-a-nation to be dissolved, and another benighted race to be subdued, before the Temple of Liberty could be purged of all dissension. During the Grant administration, the federal government completed the process of Indian removal in which North and South had happily cooperated before the war under Andrew Jackson, the Southern proponent of states' rights. That process had continued with the Gold Rush of the 1850s in California, Oregon and Washington, the Idaho Gold Rush in the 1860s, and relentless white expansion into the Western frontier during the Civil War and Reconstruction periods. Now it was time to finish the job.

Forced from their ancestral territories, the Indian tribes had been driven onto Western reservations, then from the reservations into outright wastelands when white settlers or gold prospectors occupied the land. Even Indians consigned to barren Western regions "were destined not to enjoy for very long their restricted domains, for valuable mines discovered on what was thought to be waste land attracted hordes of fortune-seekers to the country."[96] The same sequence of events was repeated over and over again: "The Indians resisted the invaders and exchanged shots. Then the Federal troops intervened, new treaties were imposed on the tribe, and again they were forced to retire to a new reservation, often far distant, and destined in turn to become the ground of similar disputes."[97] The Creeks, for example, were forced to relocate a dozen times until "the whole tribe was finally wiped out by General Jackson, afterward President of the United States."[98]

According to the schoolbook narrative of Liberty, however, the Indians who resisted white expansion were mindless savages who wantonly murdered innocent Americans engaged in a courageous mission to settle the Western frontier and expand Liberty's great domain of freedom and opportunity for all. Any other perspective on the conflict is dismissed as bleeding heart liberalism. The myth is demolished, however, by the Grant administration's own official assessment of the history of relations between the Indians and the federal government. In 1869 Grant appointed a commission (pursuant to an Act of Congress) composed of "nine men, representing the influence and philanthropy of six leading States, to visit the different Indian reservations, and to 'examine all matters appertaining to Indian affairs.'"[99] The Commission's report included these devastating admissions concerning the treatment of Indians in the Temple of Liberty:

> While it cannot be denied that the government of the United States, in the general terms and temper of its legislation, has evinced a desire to deal gener-

96. Fr. E. Laveille, S. J., *The Apostle of the Rocky Mountains: The Life of Father De Smet, S.J.* (NY: P. J. Kennedy & Sons, 1915), Tan Books ed. (2000), 322.

97. Ibid.

98. Marshall, *Christian Missions*, Vol. II, 240, quoted in Laveille, *Life of De Smet*, 322.

99. Helen Hunt Jackson, *A Century of Dishonor*, in *The American Reader: The Words that Moved a Nation* (NY: HarperCollins, 2000), 292.

ously with the Indians, it must be admitted that *the actual treatment they have received has been unjust and iniquitous beyond the power of words to express.*

The history of the government connections with the Indians is a shameful record of broken treaties and unfulfilled promises. The history of the border white man's connection with the Indians is *a sickening record of murder, outrage, robbery, and wrongs committed by the former as the rule,* and occasional savage outbreaks and unspeakably barbarous deeds of retaliation by the latter as the exception....

The testimony of some of the highest military officers of the United States is on record to the effect that, *in our Indian wars, almost without exception, the first aggressions have been made by the white man,* and the assertion is supported by every civilian of reputation who has studied the subject.

In addition to the class of *robbers and outlaws who find impunity in their nefarious pursuits upon the frontiers,* there is a large class of professedly reputable men *who use every means in their power to bring on Indian wars, for the sake of the profit to be realized from the presence of troops and the expenditure of government funds in their midst.* They proclaim death to the Indians at all times, in words and publications, making no distinction between the innocent and the guilty. *They incite the lowest class of men to the perpetration of the darkest deeds against their victims, and, as judges and jurymen, shield them from the justice due to their crimes....*

The murders, robberies, drunken riots, and outrages perpetrated by Indians in time of peace taking into consideration the relative population of the races on the frontier *do not amount to a tithe of the number of like crimes committed by white men in the border settlements and towns....*

It is hardly to be wondered at that inexperienced officers, ambitious for distinction, when surrounded by such influences, have been incited to attack Indian bands without adequate cause, *and involve the nation in an unjust war....*[100]

In its efforts to "pacify" the Indians so as to avoid the time and expense involved in exterminating them, the Grant administration called upon the services of a remarkable Catholic priest, the Belgian-born Father Pierre-Jean De Smet, S.J. (1801–1873). His astonishing missionary and diplomatic voyages to the Rocky Mountain and Great Plains tribes over a period of thirty years (1838–1868), together with his fellow "Black Robes," produced innumerable conversions to Catholicism among the Potawatomi, the Flatheads, the Coeur d'Alènes, the Crows, the Kalispells, the Flatbows, the Kootenais, the Blackfeet, the Yanktons, the Mandons, the Aricaras, the Grosventres, and even the bellicose Sioux.

Revered and beloved as a great spiritual figure by the chiefs and people of the tribes who knew him as "Black Robe" and "the white man whose tongue does not lie," Father De Smet had earlier been asked by the Superintendent of Indian Affairs

---

100. Report of Commission of Citizens (November 23, 1869), in *Report of Commission of Indian Affairs*, 47–48 (1869); cited in *United States v. State of Mich.*, 471 F. Supp. 192, 202 (W.D. Mich. 1979).

to preside over the Fort Laramie Council (1851) at which peace was negotiated with various prairie and mountain tribes. In typical fashion, however, the government violated the Fort Laramie accords when the Senate unilaterally "amended" the treaty by reducing from a period of fifty years to a mere fifteen years the already paltry annuity of $50,000 to the signatory tribes in recompense for damages and ceded lands, despite the admission of the Indian Affairs commissioner that "The treaty . . . should have been sent back to the Indians for the purpose of obtaining their sanction to the modification. . . ."[101]

Nevertheless, during the Buchanan administration, Father De Smet had been tasked by the Secretary of War to broker a peace with the Indians of Oregon, brutalized during the "White conquest" of that territory by "thousands of adventurers" seeking gold, including "deserters, thieves, murderers, the scum of the United States," who seized the Indians' cultivated land and villages.[102] While Father De Smet had succeeded in negotiating a peace accord, the government had rejected his plan to provide the Indians a reserve with plentiful game and arable soil under the authority of the "Black Robes." Washington paid no heed to an admiring General Haney's advice that "The history of the Indian race on our continent shows that the *missionaries succeeded when military and civil authorities failed. . . .* [I]t would be wisdom to profit by the lessons of experience, and adopt Father De Smet's plan."[103] But the Temple of Liberty could hardly allow part of its precincts to be administered by papist priests.

In 1862 a disillusioned Father De Smet, surveying the history of Washington's dealings with the Indians, wrote to his brother: "Heaven will mete out justice to a country that permits such atrocities." Joining other prophets of national chastisement, he confided to the Mother Superior of the Sisters of Mary that "The civil war is in my opinion a punishment, and alas, little is being done to propitiate heaven."[104] Yet he continued to lend his good name to the government's "pacification" efforts in the hope of a just result, failing to broker peace with the Sioux in 1864 (while baptizing eight hundred of them), but securing a peace agreement with fifteen thousand Indians in Colorado, having been summoned to the task by the Commissioner of Indian Affairs, who wrote: "Your relations with the Indians and your marvelous influence over them are well known facts."[105]

In 1868, the last year of the Johnson administration, the same military authorities "who had just brought the civil war to a close, now asked the aid of a missionary to induce a few thousand Indians to lay down their arms."[106] The Black Robe went alone to the Yellowstone region to meet with chiefs Four Horns, Black Moon, No Neck, and Sitting Bull at a successful peace council that took place beneath a banner

101. Helen Jackson, *A Century of Dishonor* (Boston: Little Brown, 1885), 75–76, DSI reproduction.

102. *Life of De Smet*, 273.

103. Ibid., 280.

104. Fr. De Smet to Francis De Smet, April 16, 1862; De Smet to Mother Superior of Sisters of Mary, March 1, 1862, quoted in *Life of De Smet*, 323.

105. Colonel Bogey to Father De Smet, February 13, 1867, quoted in *Life of De Smet*, 273.

106. Ibid., 348.

of the Blessed Virgin Mary, followed by a council of thousands of Indians that produced a historic peace with the warring Sioux. As General Stanley observed: "Father De Smet *alone of the entire white race* could penetrate to these cruel savages and return safe and sound." The Sioux "savages" received him "with extraordinary enthusiasm" and "[h]is counsels were at once agreed to, and representatives sent to meet the Peace Commission"—a result that has been "looked on as the most remarkable event in the history of the Indian wars."[107] As Stanley later declared: "we can never forget, nor shall we ever cease to admire the disinterested devotion of the Rev. Father De Smet . . . to arrest the shedding of blood. . . ."[108] All three generals involved in the peace negotiations declared that "but for the influence over even the most hostile of tribes which your years of labor among them have given you, the results we have reached here could not have been accomplished."[109]

During the Grant administration, however, Father De Smet's service to the Temple of Liberty ended with a bitter resignation following the government's final betrayal of the Indians. Grant's "Indian Peace Policy" deprived vast numbers of converted Indians of their Black Robes, Catholic churches and schools by reassigning the Indian agencies supervising the reservations to assorted Protestant denominations even though, by numbers, Catholic missionaries were entitled to the vast majority of the agencies (receiving only eight instead of the forty their numbers warranted). Not even the missions founded by Father De Smet himself were spared. "If it be true," wrote one journalist, "that the Indians are condemned to annihilation, should they not be allowed to choose the faith in which they wish to die? Baptized and instructed as Catholics, the Indians have been divided between the various denominations, and the missionaries, who collected money in Europe for evangelizing these poor savages, *are now expelled from the missions they founded.*"[110]

Despite his selfless service at risk of life to a government "conceived in liberty and dedicated to the proposition that all men are created equal," Father De Smet's repeated pleas to the Grant administration were rudely ignored, for the priest had outlived his usefulness in bringing about Indian pacification. Among the missives that received no reply from Washington was this plea to the Secretary of the Interior: "All that the Catholic bishops and missionaries aim at, in this country of religious liberty, is to be allowed their rights, in accordance with their call from above, to evangelize the Indians who have received them with joy, and not to be turned out of the missions where they have labored for years with zeal and fervor for the salvation of the Indians. . . ." Snubbed by Washington, and unable to resign himself to seeing "his neophytes become Methodists and free-thinkers," Father De Smet resigned his federal commission.[111]

107. William Fanning, "Pierre-Jean De Smet," *The Catholic Encyclopedia* (NY: Robert Appleton Company, 1908), Vol. IV (New Advent online edition).

108. Stanley to Bishop Purcell, July 12, 1868, quoted in *Life of De Smet*, 358.

109. Gens. Harney, Sanborn and Terry, Address of July 3, 1868, quoted in Laveille, *Life of De Smet*, 358.

110. Ibid., 364.

111. Ibid., 366.

As for the Indians, they "sent frequent messages to the Great Father in Washington [i.e., Grant], entreating him to give them back their Catholic agents, their priests and their Catholic schools." Like Father De Smet's entreaties, theirs fell on deaf ears. In 1871 the Coeur d'Alène tribe wrote to Pope Pius IX in tribute to the Black Robe, "who came and lived with us and awakened us, directing us in the path that leads to heaven." Pius IX, himself a captive in Rome surrounded by the forces of Liberty who had been "unifying" Italy at gunpoint, replied by conveying his apostolic blessing in a papal brief addressed to the head of the Coeur d'Alènes—the first such papal communiqué to an Indian chief.[112]

The history of the next six years of the Grant administration records the uprising by Sitting Bull, the Battle of Little Bighorn with "Custer's Last Stand," the federal seizure of the Black Hills from the Sioux (yet another treaty violation), the surrender of Crazy Horse, the end of the Great Sioux Wars, and the final subjugation of the Indian populations by the federal government. But it did not have to end that way. Father De Smet's biographer cites a government agent's report of what the Black Robe and his fellow missionaries had done for the Indian tribes who loved and revered them:

> Thanks to the untiring labors of the missionaries, the Indians have made great progress in agriculture. They are being instructed in the Christian religion; they have abandoned polygamy, are pure in morals, and edifying in conduct. The work of these Fathers is truly marvelous.[113]

Another agent marveled at what he found among the mountain tribes administered by the Catholic missions: "I could hardly believe my eyes. Am I among the Indians—among people the world calls savages?"[114] Such testimony from "Protestant pens," notes the De Smet biography, "permits us to realize, faintly, what the Indians might have become if the United States had left to Catholics the task of civilizing them, instead of following a policy of extermination."[115] For that matter, what would America as a whole have become had Catholicism informed its culture, laws and institutions from the beginning, as it might have done had England not gained hegemony on the North American continent following the French and Indian War? For one thing, in a Catholic *ethos* the Civil War would have been inconceivable.

As Father De Smet predicted: "The curtain will soon fall upon the unhappy remnants of the Indian tribes, and they will henceforth exist only in history. The whites are spreading like torrents. . . . Today the very names are hardly known of hundreds of tribes that have entirely disappeared."[116] He confided that he would have "consecrated the remainder of my days to their [the Indians'] spiritual and

---

112. *Life of De Smet*, 367–370.
113. Ibid., 271, quoting "Explorations from the Mississippi River to the Pacific Ocean," Vol. I, 308.
114. Ibid., quoting "Reports of Governor Stevens to the President," *Selected Letters*, 2d Series, 206–217.
115. Ibid., 271.
116. In *Life, Travels and Letters of Pierre-Jean De Smet*, eds Hiram Martin Crittenden and Alfred Talbott Richardson (NY: Francis P. Harper, 1905), Vol. IV, 1219–1220.

temporal welfare,"[117] but he died in Saint Louis on May 23, 1873, at the beginning of Grant's second term.

Paradise Never Found

By the end of the Grant administration in 1877, the defiled Temple of Liberty had been fully purged. The price was the better part of a million lives and incalculable devastation in what had been the bloodiest civil war in all of Western history, and the final betrayal and subjugation of the Indian tribes. A central government with powers that, even before the war, had been greater than any exercised by King George over the distant colonies was now irremovably entrenched on the Potomac, its all-seeing eye unblinkingly surveying the vast territory it now ruled without challenge. Thus did things stand only a hundred years from the date of the Declaration of Independence.

In only seventy years following ratification of the Constitution in 1789—a single lifetime—the reign of Liberty in America had meant the rise of state governments far more demanding of the people than England had ever been; the forcible suppression of "insurrections" by government troops; treason trials and death sentences for tax resisters and other opponents of government power; the punishment of even plans for secession as treasonable; higher taxes and more regulations, even at the state level, than England had ever imposed; steadily expanding federal powers defended by the Supreme Court; a growing federal bureaucracy and military establishment, and acts of Presidential autocracy (including those of Jefferson) no Christian sovereign would dare to have ventured. And all of this *before* the Civil War itself, which was only a demonstration on a vaster scale of Jefferson's dictum that in "extreme cases . . . the universal resource is a dictator, or martial law."

As Lee had said of the Civil War in his testimony before the U.S. Senate in 1866: "[T]he great mass of the people, if they had understood the real question, would have avoided it. . . ." But then the great mass of the people had never asked for the American Revolution or the formation of the Continental Congress to act as the first "perpetual" federal union. Neither had they voted to issue the Declaration of Independence, convert the colonies into the United States of America, or wage war on Great Britain. The great mass of the people had likewise never voted to subject themselves to the Articles of Confederation, much less to a Constitution written behind closed doors in Philadelphia by a few men they had no voice in choosing. Nor had the great mass of the people voted to become subjects of the federal government under that same Constitution, whose ambiguous provisions the average American at the time—as now—would have been unable to appreciate in their vast implications. And, finally, the great mass of the people in the South had not clamored for secession from the Union, war with the North, or the creation of the Confederate States of America as a rival federal government, with the power to tax them, draft them, send them onto battlefields to be slaughtered, impress their property, or exile them from their homelands as suspected "alien enemies."

---

117. *Life of De Smet*, 220.

In fact, the great mass of the people had never asked for Liberty at all—with or without slaves. Back in 1776, the generality of colonists were content to go about their workaday lives and drink the Bohea tea imported by the British East India Company, even if they had to pay King George's tax. We have seen that at every step of the way since the Boston Tea Party, Liberty had to be imposed on the masses, both North and South, by an enlightened few who knew better. But after a turbulent four score and seven years of Liberty, no doubt there were many thoughtful Americans who wondered whether King George's trifling tea tax and his quartering of a modest number of troops in riot-torn Boston had been such terrible injustices after all. By the end of the Civil War could anyone really say that the American people had ever been freer—less burdened by the demands of government—under the state and national "republican governments" of either the Union or the Confederacy than they had been when America was a loose network of prosperous and de facto independent colonies separated by an ocean from the Crown and Parliament? Even a libertarian commentator has observed that King George was a benevolent ruler by comparison with the President and Congress, apparently without realizing that his astounding admission undermines the entire libertarian case in defense of Liberty:

> Granted, the British . . . sent regiments to Boston, closed the port, and quartered soldiers in colonists' homes. But only after repeated attempts to conciliate the colonies had gotten them nowhere and had prompted only more defiance. There is no comparison, absolutely none, between the final British crackdown and what's happening in "free" America. The Bostonians asked for what they got. We didn't. . . .
>
> No, Old England's taxes weren't popular over here. But when America complained, London listened. The 1765 Stamp Act was repealed by Parliament the very next year after the colonists protested. Parliament tried again in 1767 with the Townshend Acts, taxing imported glass, paper, lead, and tea. The colonies roared again, and the British backed down again, *repealing everything but the tea tax in 1770.* . . .
>
> *Tyrants?! I just wish to God that our Congresses and Presidents were so responsive to the American people's wishes.* . . . If you plan to spend the Fourth celebrating the liberty you haven't got, by all means go ahead. Me? I'm going to drink a loyal toast *to one of the most benevolent rulers this suffering country ever had, a small-government man and a pillar of constitutional rectitude* compared to despotic megalomaniacs and reckless warmongers like Woodrow Wilson, Franklin Roosevelt, LBJ, Clinton, and George W. Bush. His Majesty, God bless him![118]

The same commentator overlooks the comparative despotism of earlier Presidents, including Jefferson, as well as the burdens imposed on the people by the

---

118. John Attarian, "Hurrah for King George!" http://www.lewrockwell.com/attarian/attarian-9.html.

governors and legislatures of the new "republican" state governments, but the point is made.

Yet libertarians such as this one appear not to have not learned history's lessons. They praise the "libertarian principles" of the American Revolution while rejecting the position of its own Founders, including their idol Jefferson, that submission to the national government the Founders created was essential to what the Founders called Liberty. Despite the undeniable expansion of state power immediately following the Revolution, and in consequence of it, they wish to pretend, as Murray Rothbard does, that "after achieving impressive partial victories against statism, the classical liberals began to lose their radicalism, their dogged insistence on carrying the battle against conservative statism to the point of final victory."[119] But it was the very radicalism of the American Revolution that gave birth to the ever-expanding modern state system in the first place. Concerning the Constitution, a masterfully Lockean document, libertarians ignore the reality that "the growth of government and the centralization of power is inherent in its original provisions [as] the anti-Federalists were trying to say all along from the very beginning of the ratification process."[120] In short, they wish to have their Lockean cake and eat it too by advertising to a Jeffersonian Paradise Lost that never existed *even when Jefferson was President of the United States.*

The rise of the first fully operational Hobbelockian Leviathan in America merely followed the pattern that Liberty would make familiar throughout the Western world. As the constitutional scholar Isaac Kramnick of Cornell University rightly observes: "Like most revolutions, the American began as a repudiation of the state, of power, and of authority in the name of liberty. Like most revolutions, it ended with *a stronger state*, the revival of authority, and the taming of liberty's excesses."[121] What Kramnick calls "the taming of liberty's excesses," however, was a form of government that would show King George to have been a timid pushover by comparison. What Christian sovereign ever presided over the slaughter of more than 600,000 of his own subjects and deemed it "a new birth of freedom," as Lincoln had, or declared, as Davis had, that "Independence . . . or extermination, we *will* have" and that a civil war launched in the name of Liberty for slave states "must go on until the last man of this generation falls in his tracks, and his children seize the musket and fight in our battle"? There is bloodshed of course in the annals of Christendom, but nothing approaching this sort of madness, or the greater madness still that would follow in the 20th century.

No one has equaled Alasdair MacIntyre's mordant description of the sheer deadliness of the new configuration of state power that first emerged in America:

> The modern nation state, *in whatever guise*, is a dangerous and unmanageable institution, presenting itself on the one hand as a bureaucratic supplier of goods and services, which is always about to, but never actually does, give its

119. Rothbard, *For a New Liberty* (Von Mises Institute, 2002), online edition, 17.
120. Sale, "Getting Back to the Real Constitution?" www.counterpunch.org/sale10282010.html.
121. Kramnick, "The Great National Discussion: The Discourse of Politics in 1787," loc. cit., 31.

clients value for money, and on the other as a repository of sacred values, which from time to time invites one to lay down one's life on its behalf. . . . [I]t is like being asked to die for the telephone company.[122]

Whither Christianity?

And where was Christianity during the first century of the history of the first modern nation-state? How had a nation filled with an assortment of Christian denominations, the same denominations that had contended so vigorously over the question of slavery, found itself saddled with a federal Leviathan in Washington whose drive for supremacy had snuffed out hundreds of thousands of lives under a President who professed no discernible religion? Why had the Christian churches been unable to counter the power of a government that had protected the institution of chattel slavery as a matter of constitutional law only to wage war with the very states in which it had been protected? How could the supposed Christian "conservatism" of the Southern appeal to Liberty be reconciled with the revolutionary act of secession from the federal government in order to defend, via the creation of a new and substantially identical federal government, the permanent subjugation of the black race? How could chattel slavery be defended or condemned by members of the same Protestant denominations, invoking the same Bible, depending on which side of a geographical line the members resided?

Here too the Founders and Framers had built well according to their Lockean master plan. For as the power of the state and federal governments was on the rise, the influence of Protestant Christianity, with its ever-multiplying sects, was on the decline. This was precisely as the Moses of the Enlightenment had envisioned in the works he had written "to distinguish exactly the Business of Civil Government from that of Religion, and to settle the just Bounds that lie between the one and the other."[123] Having examined the political outcome of the "moderate" Enlightenment principles canonized by Locke and built into the first Temple of Liberty, we will now examine the religious outcome. To do so, we must survey the foundations of the Republic under a different aspect.

---

122. Alasdair MacIntyre, *After MacIntyre: Critical Perspectives on the Work of Alasdair MacIntyre,* ed. John Horton and Susan Mendus (Notre Dame, IN: Notre Dame Univ. Press, 1994), 303.

123. Locke, *Letter Concerning Toleration,* 26.

IV.

The First Secular State

18

The Godless Constitution

WE HAVE ALREADY NOTED how the trials of the Civil War drove Jefferson Davis to seek a more orthodox Christian faith and how he wondered during the final days of the war whether an explicit constitutional recognition of Christ might have averted disaster for the Confederate nation. During the Civil War there emerged in the North a national movement of conservative evangelical Protestant ministers, theologians, academics, lawyers and jurists, mostly Presbyterians, that posed precisely that question, but to America as a whole. Called the National Reform Association (NRA), the roll of its elected officers included no less than William Strong, a retired Justice of the Supreme Court.

The National Reform Association

The records of the NRA conventions during and after the war are an historical treasure trove of admissions by prominent American Protestants that the war had been the outcome of a grave defect in the Republic—the same defect James Henley Thornwell had seen in the political organization of the Confederacy, despite its Constitution's generic invocation of divinity. It was a defect, argued the NRA, that must be laid at the feet of the sainted Founders themselves in their attachment to the political philosophy and rationalism of the Enlightenment: the failure to recognize divine authority over the nations and the primacy of God's law over human law. Typical of these admissions is the following from the proceedings of the NRA's 1874 Convention in Pittsburgh, quoting a sermon by Rev. Horace Bushnell in July of 1861, three months after the War began. Bushnell took aim precisely at the Constitution as a godless Lockean social compact, whose ambiguities allowed it to be cited for secession by the South (for breach of the compact) and for the crushing of the secessionists by the North (for attempting to revoke the compact once it had become irrevocable by express consent):

> It is a remarkable, but very serious fact... *that our grand Revolutionary fathers left us the legacy of this war in the ambiguities of thought and principle which they suffered in respect of the foundations of government itself....* [T]hey organized a government, such as we, at least, have understood to be *without moral or religious ideas; in one view merely a man-made compact....*

Proximately our whole difficulty is an issue forced by slavery; but if we go back to the deepest root of the trouble, we shall find that it comes by *trying to maintain a government without moral ideas, and concentrate a loyal feeling around institutions that, as many reason, are only human compacts.* . . . [1]

Lamenting the Godless Constitution, NRA's proceedings record such historical events as the reported encounter between Alexander Hamilton and Dr. John Rodgers, the "eminent chaplain of the Revolution," following adjournment of the Constitutional Convention: "Mr. Hamilton, we are greatly grieved that the Constitution has no recognition of God or the Christian religion," protested the theologian, whereupon Hamilton is said to have replied: "I declare, we forgot it!"[2] Also noted was that Benjamin Franklin, the consummate Deist, thought it politic to make a historical record of the Convention's amazing rejection of his motion (no doubt a provocation designed to break the logjam during the debates) that the members engage in some sort of prayer to some sort of deity at the opening of each session: "The convention, except three or four persons, thought prayers unnecessary!"[3]

A historical fact the NRA proceedings mention repeatedly was the rather infamous and *unanimous* declaration of the fledgling United States Senate in Article XI of the Treaty of Tripoli, approved by President John Adams on June 10, 1797:

As the Government of the United States of America *is not, in any sense, founded on the Christian religion*; as it has in itself no character of enmity against the laws, religion, or tranquility of Mussulmen . . . it is declared by the parties, that no pretext arising from religious opinions, shall ever produce an interruption of the harmony existing between the two countries.[4]

1. *Proceedings of the National Reform Convention to Aid in Maintaining the Christian Features of the American Government and Securing a Religious Amendment to the Constitution of the United States* (Philadelphia: Christian Statesman Association, 1874), 53 (hereafter "*Proceedings* [1874]").

2. *Proceedings* (1874), 41; see also, Benjamin Franklin Morris, *Christian Life and Character of the Civil Institutions of the United States* (Philadelphia: George W. Childs, 1864), 248.

3. Sparks, *Works of Benjamin Franklin*, Vol. 5, 155, in Phillip Schaff, *Church and State in the United States* (NY: Charles Scribner's Sons, 1888), 124. Resolutely apologetical historians have proposed desperate excuses for the Framers' embarrassing failure to consult God during their drafting of the Constitution, including the excuses that Franklin's motion was "untimely"—prayers to God being no less subject to parliamentary deadlines than other agenda items, after all—and that the Convention lacked the funds for a preacher. See, e.g., Schaff, ibid. (referring to Hamilton's argument on the "untimeliness" of the motion), and *Religion and the Founding of the American Republic*, §VI, Pt. 2: "Religion and the Federal Government," Library of Congress e-text www.loc.gov/exhibits/religion/rel06.html (noting that "Franklin's motion failed, ostensibly because the Convention had no funds to pay local clergymen to act as chaplains").

4. Yale Law School's Avalon Project maintains a digital text of the Treaty. Cf. yale.edu/lawweb/avalon/diplomacy/barbary/bar1796t.htm. The superseding 1805 version of the Treaty, in Article XIV, removes the explicit rejection of Christian principles but retains the declaration that "As the Government of the United States of America, has in itself *no character of enmity* against the Laws, *Religion* or Tranquility of Mussulmen. . . . It is declared by the contracting parties that no pretext arising from Religious Opinions, shall ever produce an interruption of the Harmony existing between the two Nations." This alteration does not diminish the historical significance of both the Senate's and the President's express disavowal of any Christian foundation of the United States government.

The Treaty, which temporarily resolved America's problem with the Barbary pirates in the Mediterranean before the First Barbary War, was clearly drafted to assure the Muslim captors of American seamen that they had no reason to fear any sort of Christian crusade from the non-Christian, religiously "neutral," Islam-friendly government in Washington.[5] As one humanist commentator is only too happy to note, the entire text of the Treaty was read aloud to the Senate before the ratification vote, and not one senator objected to Article XI's bold public disavowal of any Christian foundation for the United States government.[6] Ratification of the Treaty was only the third unanimous vote in the Senate's history, out of 339 votes taken up to that point.[7] Moreover, the text of the Treaty was published in major newspapers, including the *Philadelphia Gazette*, without any official protest.[8]

The NRA cited the Treaty of Tripoli, along with President Jefferson's refusal to proclaim a day of fasting and prayer as the factual basis for one of its resolutions in support of submission to Congress of its proposed "Christian Amendment" to the Constitution (discussed below):

> Resolved, That ... it is a striking and solemn fact that our present National Constitution is *so devoid of any distinctive Christian feature,* that one of our Chief Magistrates [Jefferson] once refused to appoint a day of fasting and prayer in an hour of public calamity, because the nation, *in its Constitution, recognized no God*; and another [John Adams], in contracting a treaty with a Mohammedan power, hesitated not to declare that "the Government of the United States *is not, in any sense, founded on the Christian religion.* It has in itself no character of enmity against the laws and religion of Mussulmans."[9]

Moreover, the NRA declared, the Treaty of Tripoli only confirmed that the Constitution was so devoid of Christian content as to be suitable for a Muslim nation without the least amendment:

> The people of the United States are awakening to the fact that the National Constitution *is destitute of any explicit acknowledgment of God or the Christian religion.* Although it is the fundamental law of a great Christian people, its want of a distinct Christian character has led even such men as Dr. Woolsey, ex-President of Yale College, to state that *it would need no change to adapt it to a Mohammedan nation.*[10]

5. Some scholars argue that U.S. Consul General Joel Barlow unilaterally inserted Article XI into the Treaty, and that it does not appear in the Arabic original. But that does not alter the fact that the Treaty was ratified as presented by Barlow, and that what Barlow presented to the Senate is the only official Treaty of Tripoli.

6. Edward Buckner, "Does the 1796–97 Treaty with Tripoli Matter to Church/State Separation?" stephenjaygould.org/ctrl/buckner_tripoli.html.

7. Brooke Allen, *Moral Minority*, 142.

8. *Proceedings* (1874), 11.

9. *Proceedings of the National Convention to Secure the Religious Amendment of the Constitution of the United States* (Philadelphia: Jas. B. Rodgers Co., 1872), xiii (hereafter "*Proceedings* [1872]").

10. *Proceedings* (1874), 21.

The Deism of the Founders

As the unanimous Senate vote on the Treaty of Tripoli made embarrassingly clear, the organic law of the Republic was not merely Godless, but *Christless*—also the gravamen of Thornwell's complaint to the Confederate Congress. The 1874 NRA proceedings quote a sermon by Rev. Thomas Robbins nearly sixty years earlier: "The great evil of our country, in my view, is that we have attempted to strike out a new path to national prosperity regardless of the dictates of experience and the testimony of the word of God. *We have not been a religious but a political people....* [I]n our collective national capacity we do not worship the God of heaven, *we do not acknowledge his Son, we do not receive His Holy Word.*"[11] The proceedings also cite a sermon in 1820 by James R. Wilson, chaplain to the New York State legislature, who did not spare even the quasi-divinized Washington from this assessment:

There is not only in the theory of our government no recognition of God's laws and sovereignty, but its practical operation, its administration, has been conformable to its theory. *Those who have been called to administer the government have not been men making any public profession of Christianity....* Washington was a man of valor and wisdom. He was esteemed by the whole world as a great and good man; *but he was not a professing Christian.*[12]

The NRA candidly exposed the truth, now readily acknowledged today in revisionist studies, that "our grand revolutionary fathers" were not the pious Christian statesmen of legend and therefore did not bequeath to America a Christian commonwealth. They were deists. It is not possible to assess the religious foundations of the American Republic objectively without recognizing what R.R. Palmer observes in his landmark study *The Age of the Democratic Revolution*: "As for leaders of the American Revolution, it should be unnecessary to demonstrate that most of them were deists.... Like Jefferson in the Declaration of Independence, they appealed to the laws of Nature's God. They seem not to have felt, however ... that these laws placed serious limits on their freedom of political action."[13] Neither did Locke, philosophical father of the Revolution, a participant in the Rye House plot against Charles II, and the first respectable theologian of a "reasonable Christianity" that would not disturb the good order of the State.

In Chapter 3 we examined how in Locke's reductionist version of the Christian religion, good behavior is the essence of religious practice, Christ is a Messiah in the sense of a divinely appointed moral advisor, the Trinity is relegated to the category of "speculative opinions" reason cannot verify, "Romanist" dogmas such as transubstantiation are denied outright, and the divinity of Christ, the divine inspiration of Scripture, and belief in the immateriality and immortality of the soul

---

11. Ibid., 45.

12. Boller, *George Washington & Religion*, 14–15. The sermon has arguably been wrongly attributed to Rev. Bird Wilson, son of the lesser-known Founder James Wilson (no relation to Rev. James R. Wilson).

13. Palmer, *Age of Democratic Revolution*, 194.

are undermined. We saw as well that Locke's Christianity was a gateway to the full-blown Deism that followed his teaching almost immediately in Toland's *Christianity not Mysterious*. As David Holmes explains in his study *The Faiths of the Founding Fathers*, Deism is "what is left of Christianity after casting off everything that is peculiar to it. The Deist is one who denies the Divinity, the Incarnation, and the Atonement of Christ, and the work of the Holy Ghost; who denies the God of Israel, and believes in the God of Nature."[14]

To the extent that it can be called a religion, Deism is the religion of Liberty because it removes the living God and His claims on men and nations from the field of politics, shuttling all revealed truths at odds with "the will of the people" into the realm of private opinion. What remains is the distant and amorphous deity of the Masonic temple, which we encountered at the end of Chapter 3: "First Cause," "Author," "Creator," "Almighty Being," "Divine Artist," "Divine Author of All Good," "Grand Architect," "God of Nature," "Nature's God," or, to use a phrase of the arch-Mason Benjamin Franklin's devising, "Author and Owner of our System."[15] While Deism is not strictly atheism, "it is equally impossible to call the movement 'Christian'. Deists repeatedly called into question any teaching or belief of Christianity that they could not reconcile with human reason. . . . Thus Deism *inevitably undermined the personal religion of the Judeo-Christian tradition.*"[16]

In America, Deism became identified with Unitarianism, which arose as a form of opposition to the Second Great Awakening and culminated with the election of the Unitarian Henry Ware as Hollis Professor of Divinity at Harvard in 1805. Peter Gay's monumental survey of Enlightenment thought notes that "By the early 1730's most of the leading deists had already done their work," and that by the 1770's the "natural religion" of the Deists "was a serious competitor to Christianity, at least among intellectuals. . . ."[17] The *philosophes* of America were no exception to this trend. As Holmes observes: "Among educated eighteenth-century Americans . . . the idea of reason as a liberator from the shackles of repressive religion and tyrannical government won widespread acclaim. . . . Thus it would be surprising if Deism—which was viewed as cutting-edge thought—had not influenced the founding fathers, for most were young men when the movement began to spread. . . ." In fact, "*Four of the five first presidents* began their studies during the formative years of Deism" at institutions where "Enlightenment rationalism unseated Christian orthodoxy" in the final decades of the 1700s.[18] Holmes points out that the very center of Deism in Virginia was the College of William and Mary, the alma mater of both Monroe and Jefferson, whose chancellor was none other than George Washington from 1788 until his death in 1799. Washington, who never

14. David L. Holmes, *The Faiths of the Founding Fathers* (Oxford: Oxford Univ. Press, 2006), 39–40; quoting L.W. Gibson, "Deism," in *The Church Cyclopedia* (NY: M.H. Mallory, 1883), ed. A.A. Benson, 224.

15. Ibid., 47.

16. Ibid., 46, 47.

17. Gay, *The Enlightenment: The Rise of Modern Paganism*, 372, 382.

18. Holmes, *Faiths of the Founding Fathers*, 49–50.

attended college, held the post even while he served as the first President of the United States.[19] (Here again the myth of a Southern Christendom is undermined by historical fact.)

Deism, "reaching its climax" as an alternative to Christianity at the time of the Founding, "affected the religious thought or behavior of practically every educated man in the Atlantic civilization of which the United States was a part."[20] Thus, as Holmes concludes, "Deism influenced, in one way or another, most of the political leaders who designed the new American government. . . . [I]f census takers trained in Christian theology had set up broad categories in 1790 labeled 'Atheism,' 'Deism and Unitarianism,' 'Orthodox Protestantism,' 'Orthodox Roman Catholicism' and 'Other,' and if they had interviewed Franklin, Washington, Adams, Jefferson, Madison and Monroe, they would undoubtedly have placed *every one of these six founding fathers* in some way under the category of 'Deism and Unitarianism.'"[21] With his election thirty years after the death of Monroe, Lincoln continued the line of deist Presidents—assuming generously that he was even a deist.

In short, the American Republic, of which the North and the South alike claimed to be the true heirs, was inarguably the brainchild of late-Enlightenment Deists, not traditional Christians—that is, of men who had no intention of establishing a Christian commonwealth. Thus the conservative Protestants in both the Confederacy and the Union who militated for a Christian constitution during the Civil War were advocating a radical departure from the path laid down at the Founding, from which the Congress of neither the Confederacy nor the Union was willing to depart. Here it suffices to focus on the three Founders in the line of presidential succession most often invoked by both North and South: the Father of His Country, the Father of the Constitution, and the Father of Liberty—that is, Washington, Madison, and Jefferson, Liberty's "holy trinity" of Virginia slaveholders.

George Washington: Masonic Stoic

We have seen that the "Father of his Country" was featured prominently on the Great Seal of the Confederacy and that it was even proposed to name the Confederate States the Republic of Washington. But as the NRA proceedings candidly observed, Washington was no professing Christian. That he was a Deist is the *most* one could say of his practice and profession of religion. Washington was a nominal Episcopalian who was never confirmed, refused to receive Holy Communion, insisted on standing while everyone knelt in prayer at the Anglican services he irregularly attended,[22] and never used the words "Savior," "Redeemer," or "Son of

---

19. See "Washington,"alumni.wm.edu/notable_alumni/george_washington. shtml.

20. Adair and Harvey, op. cit., 312.

21. Holmes, *Faiths of the Founding Fathers*, 50–51.

22. Ibid., 62. Holmes calls Washington's refusal to kneel a "puzzling idiosyncrasy" instead of the scandal it clearly was and a sign of immense pride. Concerning Washington's pride, there is a revealing anecdote in Morison's history: During the Constitutional Convention, Alexander Hamilton bet Gouverneur Morris a dinner if he would slap Washington on the back and say: "How are you today, my dear

God."[23] In the thousands of letters Washington wrote, "the name of Jesus Christ never appears."[24] The Anglican pastor of Washington's own parish, the Reverend James Abercrombie, when asked about Washington's religion, answered simply: "Sir, Washington was a deist."[25]

In true Deistic and Masonic fashion, Washington's First Inaugural Address invokes "the Almighty Being who rules over the universe," "the Great Author of every public and private good," "the invisible Hand which conducts the affairs of men. . . ." and "the benign Parent of the Human Race."[26] In his Farewell Address, which we have already considered under another aspect, Washington bid farewell with a single reference to "the Almighty," while recommending "religion and morality" strictly on utilitarian grounds: as "indispensable supports" to "political prosperity" and "private and public felicity," and as "security for property, for repu-tation, for life," which would be in danger "if the sense of religious obligation desert the oaths which are the instruments of investigation in courts of justice. . . ."[27] Further, Washington declared, "reason and experience both forbid us to expect that national morality can prevail in exclusion of religious principle." Apparently, any religion would supply "the religious principle" so long as it pro-vided support for good behavior.

Here we see the Enlightenment's instrumentalization of religion, reducing its role to what Locke in the *Essay Concerning Toleration* called "the countenancing of virtue" as a "necessary prop to a state." Religion is good and useful because it serves social ends, not because man, much less the State, has a divinely imposed duty to profess any particular religion, to reverence God in holy obedience to His law, or to recognize Christ as Redeemer, without whom there is no salvation. Washington himself endorsed what Brooke Allen rightly calls "the Lockean proposition" that, to quote Washington, "While men perform their social duties faithfully, they do all that society with propriety can demand or expect; and remain responsible to their Maker for the religion, or modes of faith, which they may prefer or profess."[28]

Nothing but this sort of religiously indifferent Deism would explain why the "Father" of a supposedly Christian country would studiously avoid references to Christ and Christianity in key addresses to an overwhelmingly Christian audience that would undoubtedly have warmed to such references, referring instead to a faceless and nameless Being, Author, Hand and Parent. With Washington, more-over, there is another fact demonstrating his Deism: He was a Freemason who, as

---

General?" Morris took the bet, only to report afterwards that "after the look Washington gave him, he wouldn't do it again for a thousand dinners." Morison, *HAP*, 308.

23. Holmes, op. cit., 65.

24. A. W. Greeley, "Washington's Domestic and Religious Life," *Ladies Home Journal*, April 1896, quoted in Brooke Allen, *Moral Minority* (Chicago: Ivan R. Dee, 2006), 34–35.

25. Paul F. Boller, *George Washington & Religion*. (Dallas: Methodist Univ. Press, 1963), 16.

26. See yale.edu/lawweb/avalon/presiden/inaug/wash1.htm.

27. See yale.edu/lawweb/avalon/washing.htm.

28. George Washington, "Letter to Annual Meeting of the Quakers," September 28, 1789, cited in Brooke Adams, *Moral Minority*, 40.

Walter Berns remarks, "sounds more like the Freemason he was than a pious Christian in an orthodox sense."[29]

In Chapter 3, we examined the strange and ubiquitous sect of Freemasonry and its crucial role as "surrogate religion" in the advance of Liberty. In Chapter 8, we saw that Washington, a faithful member of the Craft, swore his presidential oath on a Masonic bible, consecrated the Capitol Building according to a Masonic ritual, and received a Masonic funeral. Bullock's study documents Freemasonry's "exalted position" during the period encompassed by the first five presidential terms (1790–1826), when Masonry "formed a part of the post-Revolutionary infrastructure of power and authority" and was to be found "in almost every place where power is of importance."[30]

Twenty-seven years after Washington's death, however, the kidnapping and murder of William Morgan in 1826 for having revealed Masonic "secrets" provoked a decline in the pervasive influence of this Enlightenment-bred, quasi-religious order over American life. As the perpetrators suspiciously evaded criminal prosecution, there was a national reaction against Freemasonry, led by the Protestant churches (not to mention the long series of condemnations of Masonry by the Popes in Rome over the preceding century). An Anti-Masonic third party ran a candidate opposing Andrew Jackson, a Freemason,[31] in the presidential election of 1828; and in 1834, ex-President John Quincy Adams (ousted by Jackson) would run a losing campaign for the governorship of Massachusetts on the Anti-Masonic ticket. But Albert Pike, author of the Masonic canon *Morals and Dogma*, whose career as a secessionist pamphleteer and Confederate military officer we have already noted, was "the key figure in mid-nineteenth-century revival of the Scottish Rite." By 1884, writes historian Steven Bullock, "Masonry had experienced extraordinary growth. Its membership rolls far exceeded their 1826 peak," although (as Pike lamented), "Victorian America no longer accorded Masonry its older role as the cornerstone of the Republic."[32] In the next volume of this study, we will see how Masonry, having done its work in America, helped spread the "sacred flame of Liberty" throughout the Western world.

But the Masonic religion to which Washington adhered was only a reflection of the overwhelming consensus of the Enlightenment *philosophes*, both in Europe and America, which we noted in Chapter 3: that revealed religion was a contemptible fiction that had resulted in the "enslavement" of the individual and political society by the practitioners of priestcraft—above all the priestcraft of Roman Catholicism. While Freemasonry was indeed "the cult of the Enlightenment," to recall Margaret Jacob's phrase, the religion of the Enlightenment, Deism, extended far beyond the members of the Craft.

---

29. Berns, "Religion and the Founding Principle," in *The Moral Foundations of the American Republic*, ed. Robert H. Horowitz (Charlottesville, VA: The Univ. of Virginia Press, 1986), 212–13.

30. Bullock, *Revolutionary Brotherhood*, 220–221, 310.

31. Elected Grandmaster of the Grand Lodge of Tennessee on October 7, 1828 and made an honorary member of Federal Lodge No. 1, Washington, D.C. during his first term as President. Cf. Denslow and Truman, Part 1, 283–84.

32. Bullock, *Revolutionary Brotherhood*, 316.

It may well be, however, that Washington was not even a believing Deist. Not only did he avoid even those references to Jesus as a great moral figure which we see in the writings of the arch-deists Jefferson and Paine, he also "eschewed the loaded word 'God' whenever possible, opting instead for some nondenominational moniker like Superintending Power, Great Ruler of Events, Higher Cause, Grand Architect of the Universe—all of which terms he used interchangeably with Providence, a force hardly distinguishable from the pagan idea of 'Fortuna.'"[33]

Washington's last act on earth was "to take his own pulse, the consummate Enlightenment gesture...."[34] The account of Washington's last hours by Tobias Lear, his personal secretary, demolishes *post hoc* legends of a deathbed conversion to orthodox Christianity or (even more fantastically) Catholicism. The historian Peter Henriques, a member of the editorial board for the George Washington Papers and of the Mount Vernon committee of George Washington Scholars, summarizes what Lear recorded: "In Washington's final hours, as faithfully recounted by Lear, there is no reference to any religious words or prayers, no request for forgiveness, no fear of divine judgment, no call for a minister (although ample time existed to summon one if desired), no deathbed farewell, no promise or hope of meeting again in Heaven."[35] Washington's view of the afterlife, to the extent he entertained the idea, was "not a bright one, and certainly not a Christian one," but rather was indicated by his references to "the shades of darkness," "the shades below," the "tomb of my ancestors," "the dreary mansions of my Fathers," and "that country from which no Traveller returns."[36]

Throughout his life Washington deftly avoided answering any questions about his religious beliefs or lack thereof. For example, Jefferson records in his diary Benjamin Rush's account of how, upon Washington's departure from government, certain Protestant clergymen contrived to submit to him an address that would include a point designed to "force him at length to declare whether he was a Christian or not...." But, writes Jefferson, "the old fox was too cunning for them. He answered every article of their address particularly *except that*, which he passed over without notice."[37] Washington, as John Adams wrote of him, had "the gift of silence."[38]

In her own historical study of the religion of the Founders, Brooke Allen remarks the problem that a deistic—or worse, neo-pagan—Washington poses for the Christian Founding: "In a Christian country, then, how could the greatest American not be a great Christian too? ... The Greatest American could not be allowed to rest in peace as what he had been, an undogmatic and perhaps skeptical

---

33. Brooke Allen, *Moral Minority*, 36.

34. Ibid., 33. Tobias Lear, Washington's faithful secretary, recorded that moments before he died Washington "withdrew his hand from mine, and felt his own pulse." Peter R. Henriques, "The Final Struggle between George Washington and the Grim King: Washington's Attitude toward Death and an Afterlife," *The Virginia Magazine of History and Biography*, Vol. 107, No. 1 (Winter 1999), 84.

35. Henriques, op. cit., 91, 93.

36. Ibid., 96.

37. *Memoirs, Correspondence*, Vol. IV, 512.

38. In David McCullough, *John Adams* (NY: Simon and Schuster, 2001), 593.

Enlightenment gentleman.... So began the creation of the priggish George Washington ('I cannot tell a lie') we all learned about as children. It is a false and cartoonish portrait."[39] Only after Washington's death did there emerge the pious fables with which we are all familiar: the tale of the cherry tree; Washington's kneeling in the snow to pray at Valley Forge; Washington's retreating into the woods during lulls in Revolutionary War combat to pray in solitude, and so forth. There are even ridiculous tales, spun by certain Catholics, that Washington was favored with personal apparitions of the Virgin Mary. In his sober debunkation of "the ingenuity of the pietistic folklorists" who created the legend of Washington the Pious Christian, the historian Paul Boller writes: "the popular legends about Washington—the Valley Forge and the Morristown stories and the innumerable tales of Washington at prayer—must be dismissed as totally lacking in any kind of evidence that would hold up in a court of law."[40] Many of these tales were first published by the Anglican parson Mason Locke Weems, whose very name qualifies him as a writer of the mythology of Liberty. It was Weems who seriously depicted Washington's death as follows:

> Swift on angels' wings the brightening saint ascended; while voices more than human were warbling through the happy regions, and hymning the great procession towards the gates of heaven. His glorious coming was seen afar off; and myriads of mighty angels hastened forth, with golden harps, to welcome the honoured stranger. High in front of the shouting hosts, were seen the beauteous forms of Franklin, Warren, Mercer, Scammel, and of him who fell at Quebec, with all the virtuous patriots, who, on the side of Columbia, toiled or bled for liberty and truth.... O Columbia! such the brother band of thy martyred saints, that now poured forth from heaven's wide opening gates, to meet thy Washington; to meet their beloved chief, who, in the days of his mortality had led their embattled squadrons to the war. At sight of him, even these blessed spirits seem to feel new raptures, and to look more dazzlingly bright. In joyous throngs they pour around him—they devour him with their eyes of love—they embrace him in transports of tenderness unutterable; while from their roseate cheeks, tears of joy, such as angels weep, roll down.[41]

Returning to earth and the realms of serious history and bearable prose, Boller pronounces "conclusive" the direct testimony of Rev. Abercrombie, Bishop White and others as to Washington's complete abstention from Communion in the Anglican Church and his failure to give any indication of a belief in the divinity of Christ or the authority of Scripture. Boller further finds that Washington (contrary to the fables) never knelt in the snow to pray at Valley Forge, did not say grace over all his meals, and did not study the Bible except possibly "for purposes of whimsy." After

---

39. Brooke Allen, *Moral Minority*, 28.

40. Paul F. Boller, *George Washington & Religion* (Dallas: Methodist Univ. Press, 1963), 22.

41. Mason Locke Weems, *A History of the Life and Death, Virtues and Exploits of General George Washington* (Philadelphia: J. P. Lipincott Co., 1918), Chapter 12; see Univ. of Virginia e-text, xroads.virginia.edu/~cap /gw/weems.html.

an exhaustive review of Washington's writings, wherein there is a "massive silence regarding Christ," and the recorded testimony of those who had direct knowledge of Washington's religious practices, Boller concludes:

> [I]f to believe in the divinity and resurrection of Christ and his atonement for the sins of man and to participate in the sacrament of the Lord's Supper are requisites for the Christian faith, then Washington, on the evidence which we have examined, can hardly be considered a Christian, except in the most nominal sense.... He was ... more of a "Unitarian" than anything else in his apparent lack of doctrinal convictions.[42]

Thomas Jefferson: Enlightened Infidel

Equally contemptuous of orthodox Christianity, of course, was the very "Father of Liberty," the third President. Jefferson, like Lincoln, spent much of his political career dodging the accusation that he was an infidel. On this score, the NRA proceedings in 1874 cite John M. Mason, one of the great "pulpit orators" of the Revolution, who declared in 1800, in opposition to the presidential candidacy of Jefferson, that if Americans were to elect "such an infidel as Mr. Jefferson" to the Presidency, he warned, "you will declare, by *a solemn national act* that there is no more religion in your collective character, than in your written Constitution; you will put a *national* indignity upon the God of your mercies; and provoke him, it may be, to send over your land that deluge of judgments which his forbearance has hitherto suspended."[43]

A blatant non-Christian under any orthodox meaning of the term, Jefferson, like Washington and Madison, was a nominal Anglican. Yet he refused to serve as godfather for children of his Anglican friends because "godfathers had to profess a belief in what he viewed as the unreasonable doctrine of the Trinity."[44] Like nearly all Enlightenment thinkers who worshipped the trinity of Bacon, Newton and Locke, Jefferson had no use for the triune God, whose second Person became flesh and dwelt among us. For Jefferson, God was best described as an "ethereal gas."[45] He confidently predicted that on account of the American Revolution "there is not a young man now living in the United States who will not die a Unitarian."[46] The Unitarian deity Jefferson invoked in his inaugural addresses was a suitably innocuous "Infinite Power which rules the destinies of the universe" and a "Being in whose hands we are."[47]

42. Boller, *George Washington & Religion*, 90–91.

43. John M. Mason, "The Voice of Warning," in *The Complete Works of John M. Mason* (NY: Charles Scribner, 1854), Vol. IV, 570–71. Emphasis in original.

44. Holmes, *Faiths of the Founding Fathers*, 87.

45. *The Writings of Thomas Jefferson*, ed. Bergh and Lipscombe (1904), 274–275; in Costanzo, *Political and Legal Studies*, 102.

46. Jefferson to John Adams, Aug. 22, 1813, quoted in Pangle, *The Spirit of Modern Republicanism*, 83.

47. See Yale Law School Avalon Project e-text at www.yale.edu/lawweb/Avalon/presiden/inaug/.htm.

Throughout his inept and silly theologizing, Jefferson was guided by Locke: "Jefferson's debt to Locke in theological matters was so great that in some instances he accepted Locke's interpretation of the gospels over what he believed to be the doctrines of Jesus himself."[48] Much in the spirit of his mentor Locke, who relegated the Trinity to the category of "speculative opinions," Jefferson rejected the foundational Christian dogma as "The hocus-pocus phantasm of a God like another Cerberus, with one body and three heads,"[49] "the confection of Platonizing priests,"[50] and the "abracadabra of the mountebanks calling themselves the priests of Jesus."[51] While Locke had never openly rejected the divinity of Christ (even as he presented arguments that tended to negate it), Jefferson openly denied that Christ, whom he admired as a great moralist, had "ever claimed divinity though 'ascribing to himself every *human* [Jefferson's emphasis] excellence.'"[52] The atonement of Christ was for Jefferson "a compound of 'follies, falsehoods, and charlatanisms,'" whereas "predestination and original sin were 'heresies of bigotry and fanaticism.'"[53]

In keeping with his view of Christ as a sublime humanist and moralist, Jefferson literally rewrote the New Testament by excising from it anything of the supernatural, leaving only "the morals of Jesus." The so-called Jefferson Bible was, as Jefferson wrote, produced by "cutting verse from verse out of the printed book and arranging the matter which is evidently his [Christ's]."[54] Jefferson thought that what he considered the true teaching of Jesus, the excellent man, could be extracted like "diamonds in a dunghill"[55] from the Gospel, which he viewed as nothing but "the history of a person called Jesus" as distinguished from the "pretensions . . . of those who say he was begotten by God, born of a virgin, suspended and reversed the laws of nature at will, and ascended bodily into heaven. . . ."[56] Of Christ's teaching in the Gospel Jefferson wrote: "It is not to be understood that I am with him (sic) in all his doctrines. I am a Materialist; he takes the side of Spiritualism; he preaches the efficacy of repentance towards forgiveness of sin; I require a counterpoise of good works to redeem it."[57]

Jefferson had no hesitancy advising his own nephew that he should prefer to be an atheist rather than avoid a rational critique of Christian dogma: "Do not be frightened from this inquiry by any fear of its consequences. If it ends in a belief that

48. Sanford Kessler, "Locke's Influence on Jefferson's 'Bill for Establishing Religious Freedom,'" *Journal of Church and State* 231 (1983), 247–248, in Craycraft, *American Myth of Religious Freedom*, 69.

49. Jefferson to Rev. James Smith, December 8, 1822; from *Jefferson's Works*, ed. H. A. Washington, Vol. 7, 269–70.

50. Costanzo, *Political and Legal Studies*, 107.

51. Quoted in James Hutson, "James Madison and The Social Utility of Religion: Risks and Rewards," Library of Congress monograph at www.loc.gov/loc/madison/hutson-paper.html.

52. Ibid., citing Jefferson to Rush, April 21, 1803, in Padover, *The Complete Jefferson* (1943), 955.

53. Hutson, op. cit.

54. Jefferson to John Adams, October 13, 1813, *The Writings of Thomas Jefferson*, Lipscomb and Bergh, Vol. 13, 389–90.

55. Ibid.

56. Jefferson to Carr, August 10, 1787, in Pangle, *The Spirit of Modern Republicanism*, 84–85.

57. Padover, op. cit., 184–185; cited in Costanzo, op. cit., 107.

there is no god, you will find incitements to virtue in the comfort & pleasantness you feel in its exercise. . . ."[58] Jefferson "strictly" concurred with Richard Price, the Welsh non-conformist minister and political philosopher, that atheism would be preferable to what Price had called the "demonism" of "popery."[59]

James Madison: A Religious Void

As for "the Father of Our Constitution," the inaugural address of the fourth President contains the by now obligatory deistic reference to "that Almighty Being whose power regulates the destiny of nations." Like Washington, Madison cultivated "the gift of silence" concerning religion. James Hutson, one of America's leading historians, a past member of the faculties of Yale and William and Mary, and currently head of the Manuscript Division of the Library of Congress, observes that "one peers into a void when trying to discern evidence of personal religious belief" in the life of Madison.[60] The religious void that is Madison's recorded life does not bespeak any sort of devout Christianity, which tends, after all, to manifest itself in praise (or at least some mention) of Christ. It is clear enough that Madison, yet another nominal Anglican who was never confirmed, practiced an "essentially Deistic form of Anglicanism."[61]

Like Washington, the proud Madison could not bring himself to kneel in prayer with his fellow Anglicans. According to William Meade, the Protestant Episcopal Bishop of Madison's home state of Virginia, on those occasions when Madison invited ministers to his house to conduct family prayers, "he did not kneel himself at prayers."[62] And although Madison attended church services, he did so at a time when "No office holder in the republic wanted to be branded an infidel, as Jefferson had been, and Madison surely would not have wanted to offend the sensitivities of his political base in Orange County, composed largely of evangelical Baptists."[63] Nevertheless, Madison, as we will learn, was a relentless foe of any ties between government and religion. And he and his friend Jefferson would lead the movement for the disestablishment of Anglicanism and the separation of religion from the State not only in Virginia but in the national government—setting the first example for the entire Western world.

58. Jefferson to Peter Carr, August 10, 1787, in *Jefferson: Political Writings*, eds Joyce Appleby and Terence Ball (Cambridge: Cambridge Univ. Press, 1999), 255.

59. Jefferson to Richard Price, Jan. 8, 1789, Library of Congress e-text, www.loc.gov/exhibits/jefferson/60.html.

60. Huston, "James Madison and the Social Utility of Religion: Risks vs. Rewards," loc. cit.

61. Holmes, *Faiths of the Founding Fathers*, 97.

62. William Meade, *Old Churches, Ministers and Families of Virginia*, Vol. II (Philadelphia: J. P. Lippincott & Co., 1899), 99.

63. Hutson, op. cit.

The NRA's Christian Amendment

The banishment of Christ from the organic law of the Republic by the deistic Founders and Framers was no accident of history, but a practical necessity. As the political scientist Ralph C. Hancock has put it: "the politics of liberation depend upon the glory of an unintelligible God, whether such a being is named or not."[64] The remote and unintelligible deity of the Founding presented no obstacle to "the emancipation of the slavish part of mankind all over the earth," as John Adams (another Deist) had boasted, whereas "one does not debate with the son of God."[65] It was this spiritual legacy that the NRA movement frankly confronted after the Civil War, identifying it as a source of the late conflict.

Hence in 1874 the NRA presented to Congress a Memorial and Petition to address what it considered the "capital defect" in the Constitution: its conspicuous failure to acknowledge not only God, but Christ as God Incarnate, even though virtually the entire population of rank and file Americans professed one form or another of the Christian religion. As the legal historian John Witte, Jr. of Emory University notes: "A reference to 'the Year of our Lord' sneaks into the dating of the instrument. But nothing more. The 'Godless Constitution' has been both celebrated and lamented ever since."[66] The NRA was foremost in the camp of lamentation. Referring to "our national sins, which have provoked the Divine displeasure"—that is, the Civil War and the War of 1812—and the need "of imploring forgiveness through Jesus Christ," NRA's petition proposed that the Constitution's Preamble be amended to read as follows:

> We the People of the United States, [*humbly acknowledging Almighty God as the source of all authority and power in civil government, the Lord Jesus Christ as the Ruler among the nations, his revealed will as the supreme law of the land, in order to constitute a Christian government,*] and in order to form a more perfect union. . . .[67]

The proposed amendment was quite similar to Thornwell's proposed amendment to the Confederate constitution. To recall Thornwell's wording: "[W]e, the people of these Confederate States, distinctly acknowledge our responsibility to God, and the supremacy of His Son, Jesus Christ, as King of kings and Lord of lords; and hereby ordain that no law shall be passed by the Congress of these Confederate States inconsistent with the will of God, as revealed in the Holy Scriptures."

Remarkably, the NRA's "Christian amendment," like Thornwell's, contained in a nutshell the same theologico-political doctrine with which we began this entire study: what the Catholic Church calls the "Social Kingship" of Christ, the great Christian corollary of Greek wisdom concerning the State as a moral totality

---

64. Hancock, "Religion and the Limits of Limited Government," 696.

65. Peter Gay, *The Enlightenment: The Rise of Modern Paganism*, 171.

66. John Witte, Jr., *Religion and the American Constitutional Experiment: Essential Rights and Liberties* (Boulder, CO: Westview Press, 2000), 61.

67. *Proceedings* (1872), vii.

oriented to the eternal destiny of man as an ensouled being. For if Christ is God, then the Gospel logically must undergird the laws and institutions of political society, as it is irrational to hold that only individuals but not societies are subject to divine authority. Now, in the aftermath of the Civil War, a group of conservative Protestants—most of whom, ironically, were more or less afflicted by America's endemic anti-Catholic bigotry—was calling for the recovery of that quintessentially Catholic doctrine, the very thing Locke regarded as "destructive of society" in his call for the non-toleration of Catholics in England.

A most striking example of this Protestant recognition of a signal Catholic teaching is found in a sermon by an NRA vice-president, Dr. J. R. W. Sloane, published in *The New York Times* of May 1, 1863, nine years before the NRA's 1872 convention. Sloane, a nationally prominent Presbyterian minister and theologian, condemned the Constitution's explicit protection of the institution of slavery and protested: "We have disobeyed and dishonored God. . . . We have no recognition of His name or authority in the Constitution of the United States." If the Constitution were lost and dug up by an archaeologist thousands of years hence, "no mortal would be able to tell whether it was the Constitution of a Christian or a pagan land, from any word or sentence found in it." Moreover, he declared, the Bible is not merely "for the individual," but rather "a large portion of this inspired volume is taken up in prescribing the duties and obligations *of nations. His law binds man in every relation in life.*"[68] And the biblical prescriptions for nations include their recognition of Christ and His kingship: "We have refused to recognize the Lord Jesus Christ as King *of Nations. . . . The claims of the Messiah have been entirely ignored.*" A more forthright declaration of the Social Kingship could hardly be found in papal encyclicals on the subject.

Thus, Protestants who had imbibed a loathing of the Catholic Church with their mothers' milk had nonetheless understood and accepted implicitly a Catholic teaching reviled by the men of the Enlightenment, including the leading Founders and Framers, and had found the Republic gravely wanting according to the standard of that teaching. Here we encounter another of the many surprises hidden by the Whig/libertarian narrative of American history, which depicts a nation living in happy concord under the new regime of pluralism and "religious freedom" won for them and the whole world by the Revolution.

As we shall see, the NRA's approach to application of the Social Kingship doctrine to America was doomed to incoherence because of the Protestant principle of private judgment in matters of faith and morals and the movement's acceptance of the principle of majority rule even in matters of morality. Yet the doctrine was accepted in principle and advanced quite courageously by the participants in NRA's conventions, who were denounced as "fanatics" by the liberal press of their day for so much as suggesting that a nation composed almost entirely of professing

68. "Sermon of Rev. J. R. W. Sloane," *The New York Times*, May 1, 1863, available in online archive @ nytimes.com/1863/05/01/news/sermon-of-rev-jrw-sloane.html.

Christians should have laws and institutions reflective of their religion—as had every nation in human history before 1776.

The "Original Sin" of the Nation

The NRA, whose third president was Justice Strong, had come into being based on the shared conviction of the delegates to its national conventions that the Republic had offended God in formulating its organic law without the least reference to Him or His authority. At the opening of its convention in 1874, the NRA's General Secretary declared that by "neglect of God and his law, by omitting all acknowledgment of them in our Constitution," the Framers had committed "the crowning, *the original sin of the nation....*"[69]

On that score the NRA proceedings of 1874 present evidence that the Constitution's godlessness had preoccupied the most conservative Protestants from the very dawn of the Republic.[70] Referring to "the friends of the Christian institutions of our government" over the century since the Founding, the proceedings declare that "[m]ultitudes of them ... were painfully aware that our written Constitution contained no acknowledgment of God, or the Christian religion. The chain of testimony to its religious defect ... indicates how widely and deeply this defect was deplored." The following examples taken from the proceedings are illustrative:

1788: Luther Martin, the delegate from Maryland to the Constitutional Convention, wrote with bitter sarcasm of the Constitution's failure to prescribe even bare belief in God as a qualification for national office: "There were some members so unfashionable as to think that a belief in the existence of a Deity ... would be some security for the good conduct of our rulers, and that, in a Christian country, it would be at least decent to hold out some distinction between the professors of Christianity and downright infidelity or paganism."

1793: Only four years after the Constitution was ratified, John M. Mason, one of the great "pulpit orators" of the Revolution, gave a sermon entitled "Divine Judgments" in which he lamented that "that very Constitution which the singular goodness of God enabled us to establish does not even recognize His being," a shameful truth that "should crimson our faces...." In another sermon, entitled "Voice of Warning," Mason declared: "The Federal Constitution makes no acknowledgment of that God who gave us our national existence.... *This neglect has excited in many of its best friends more alarm than all other difficulties.*"

It was Mason who declared in 1800, in opposition to the presidential candidacy of Jefferson, that "the Federal Constitution makes no acknowledgment of the God that gave us our national existence and saved us from internal anarchy and war." The Founders, he added, had "forgotten our Christianity," and the only way to make amends for that "reproach of religion and to avert the descending vengeance"

---

69. *Proceedings* (1874), 4; quoting John Alexander, Esq.
70. Ibid., 41–58. The following quotations are from these pages of the 1874 *Proceedings*.

was by "national acts" which would "prove that the Constitution has not, in this instance, done justice to the public sentiment." But if Americans were to appoint "such an infidel as Mr. Jefferson" to the Presidency, he warned, "you will declare, by *a solemn national act* that there is no more religion in your collective character, than in your written Constitution; you will put a *national* indignity upon the God of your mercies; and provoke him, it may be, to send over your land that deluge of judgments which his forbearance has hitherto suspended."[71] For believing Christians, including those of the NRA movement, the War of 1812 and the Civil War were more than arguably fulfillments of that prophecy.

1811: Continuing in this admonitory vein, Samuel Austin, President of the University of Vermont, warned his congregation in a published sermon that the Constitution "has one capital defect *which will issue inevitably in its destruction.* It is entirely disconnected from Christianity."

1812: Hon. Samuel Taggart, a former U.S. Congressman and Presbyterian minister, sounded the warning that America had broken with all historical precedent in forming a nation without any acknowledgment of God: "Perhaps there is no one feature in the Constitution of the United States which has been the subject of more numerous encomiums, or more unqualified praise, upon both sides of the Atlantic, than this, 'that it takes no notice of, and is not at all connected with religion.' In this instance, the United States are exhibiting *a new and singular spectacle to the world* ... a phenomenon which the world *has never witnessed before.* It is a bold experiment, and one which, I fear, *can only issue in national apostasy and national ruin.*"

1812–1813: Not long before the burning of Washington during the War of 1812, no less than the President of Yale, Timothy Dwight, likewise linked the prospect of America's ruin to the Framers' neglect of God. Decrying "the sinful character of our nation," Dwight's famous discourse in the chapel of Yale College indicted the Constitution as the locus of that sin:

> We formed our Constitution *without any acknowledgement of God*; without any recognition of His mercies to us, as a people, of His government, or even of His existence. The Convention, by which it was formed, *never asked even once, His direction, or His blessing, upon their labours.* Thus we commenced our national existence under the present system, *without God.*[72]

In later published remarks the President of Yale declared that "it is highly discreditable to us that we do not acknowledge God in our constitution," when even "the grossest nations and individuals, in their public acts ... always recognize the superintendency of a Supreme Being. *Even Napoleon does it.* We, however, have neglected to do it." The result, Dwight continued, was "the corruption which is now rapidly extending in this country [which] gives reasonable apprehension that

---

71. John M. Mason, "The Voice of Warning," in *The Complete Works of John M. Mason* (NY: Charles Scribner, 1854), Vol. IV, 570–71. Emphasis in original.

72. *Proceedings* (1874), 44. This address is also cited as historical evidence in Isaac Kramnick and R. Laurence Moore, *The Godless Constitution: the Case Against Religious Correctness* (NY: W. W. Norton & Co., 1997), 105–106.

we are soon to suffer the punishment to which we have exposed ourselves." Less than a year later, the Capitol was sacked.

1815*:* In the aftermath of the War of 1812, the Reformed theologian Alexander McLeod decried *"the public immoralities of the Constitution* of our Federal government" in which "God is not at all acknowledged, and holding men in slavery is authorized. *No association of men for moral purposes can be justified in an entire neglect of the Sovereign of the world."*

1820: James R. Wilson, chaplain to the New York State legislature, declared in a widely published sermon that "In the United States the refusal to acknowledge God has probably been *more explicit that it ever was in any other nation"* and that the American people had "rejected the government of God, and with *a degree of ingratitude, perhaps without a parallel,* formed a Constitution in which there is not the slightest homage to the God of heaven."

1833*:* Justice Story's famous *Commentaries* on the Constitution noted a grave problem with the unprecedented American form of government: "It yet remains to be solved in human affairs, whether any free government can be permanent where the public worship of God and the support of religion constitute *no part of public policy or the duty of the State in any assignable shape.* The future experience of Christendom, and chiefly of the American States, must settle this problem, as yet *new in the history of the world. . . ."*

1845: The theologian D. X. Junkin, noting that the aridly secular oath of the President prescribed by the Constitution "could as well be taken by a Pagan or a Mohammedan, as by the Chief Magistrate of a Christian people," objected that the Constitution appeared to have been drafted according to "the prejudices of the infidel few" rather than "the consciences of the Christian millions" and that "[i]n these things the minority . . . has hitherto managed to govern the majority"—an outcome typical for the advance of Liberty by its enlightened *avant garde*, as we have already seen.

1859: The political scientist J. H. McIlvaine of the College of New Jersey, noting that "the Constitution of the United States has rigorously abstained from all recognition of or allusion to Christianity, or the being of a God," ridiculed the claim by certain commentators that this omission manifested "a cordial zeal for the purity of religion by keeping it separate from government"—the Madisonian rationale to be examined in the next chapter. "[U]nfortunately," he continued, "they do not inform us what is to preserve the purity of government after it has been sequestered from religion—has thus solemnly excommunicated itself."

1861: Writing shortly after the Battle of Bull Run, Horace Bushnell, a Yale graduate and prominent Congregational clergyman and theologian, fixed the blame for the Civil War squarely on the Godless Constitution in the sermon we have already noted, warning that while the American people at large might be "closer to God than our political doctrines . . . *we have been gradually wearing our nature down to the level of our doctrines. . . .* Our merely terranean, almost subterranean, *always godless fabric*, becomes more and more exactly what we have taken it to be in our philosophy." Here again we see the recognition that the builders of the Republic were not representative of the religion of the overwhelming majority of the American people, who awoke one day to find themselves the subjects unto death of that same Republic. (In the second volume of this study we shall examine the parallel development in France, a perennially Catholic nation that somehow came under the domination of a cadre of deists and atheists ruling from Paris and citing the American Revolution as their warrant and inspiration.)

1863: Professor Pomeroy of New York University voiced the essence of the Catholic teaching in rejecting the Lockean "theory of our National Constitution . . . that the State, as an organic body, has nothing whatever to do with religion, except to protect the individuals in whatever belief or worship they may adopt; that religion is entirely a matter between each man and his God," noting that, on the contrary, "there is a growing opinion among thoughtful men all over the country, that this thing should be abandoned, and that as a State we should acknowledge the claims of God upon us, and own Him to be the Supreme Ruler of nations, as well as of the single individuals who make up the nation."

Perhaps the most decisive testimony cited was a lengthy editorial in the *New York Independent* of September 26, 1861, before that respected journal veered leftward following the Civil War. Summing up the sense of Christians who decried the Godless Constitution, the editor leveled these astonishing accusations against the document and the government it had created:

> To sum up the iniquity of this nation in one comprehensive charge, it is GODLESSNESS: not atheism in the philosophical sense of denying the existence of God, but that *practical atheism which ignores the law and authority of God and the requirements of religion in both public and private affairs.* . . .
>
> [W]e have shown our godlessness as a nation *by ignoring the name and authority of God in the framework of our political institutions* [emphasis in original]. Neither the name of God, nor any reference to His law, His government, or His providence, can be found in the Constitution of the United States. . . . [T]he Constitution has nothing to do with religion *except as a barrier between it and the State.* . . .

The editorial went on to provide an assessment demonstrating that the "wall of separation" between Church and State was no mere artifact of evil Supreme Court decisions not yet handed down, which supposedly "perverted the will of the Founders" and misconstrued Jefferson's famous letter to the Danbury Baptists (to which we will return in the next chapter). Rather, the political status quo already reflected what the Founders had set in motion with their new conception of sovereignty:

> [W]e have set up ourselves, our concrete nationality, "We the People," as the original source of all authority and power, and *have worshipped the work of our own hands.* From this *atheistic error in our prime conceptions of government* has arisen the atheistic habit of *separating politics from religion*; the voter must not carry his religious scruples to the political caucus . . . the minister must not bring politics into the pulpit, though the legislature should license

dramshops and brothels, though Sodom should be replaced by the Salt Lake of Utah, though man made in the image of God should be sold like a brute under the eaves of the national capitol.

The piece concluded with a ringing indictment of the sheer legal positivism that was even then becoming dominant under a federal charter that made no reference to any authority higher than "We the People":

> Nay, in the very Senate chamber, when Senators are warned that a measure is unjust and against the law of God, it is sneeringly, scornfully answered that *there is no higher law than the Constitution.* "We the People" made that, and "We the People" can make and unmake laws as we please. This godless habit of thought and action *has taken possession of the public mind in all political institutions and affairs.*[73]

Stung by these words from the *Independent's* own editorial past, the current editor, employing rhetoric familiar to today's victims of political correctness, described participants in the NRA's 1874 convention, including retired Supreme Court Justice Strong, as "fanatics."[74]

The proceedings of NRA's 1872 convention also abound with such testimonies. For example, the aforementioned Dr. John M. Mason, one of the most influential American Presbyterian theologians and preachers of the late 18th and early 19th century, made the rather devastating point that in commencing an undertaking as momentous as the founding of a nation, even Muslims or pagans would have paid more attention to God than the Framers had:

> While many, on various pretenses, have criminated the Federal Constitution one objection has urged itself forcibly on the pious mind. That no notice whatever should be taken of that God who planteth a nation and plucketh it up at His pleasure, is an omission *which no pretext whatever can palliate.* Had such a momentous business been transacted by Mohammedans, they would have begun, "In the name of God." *Even the savages whom we despise, setting a better example, would have paid some homage to the Great Spirit.* But from the Constitution of the United States, it is impossible to ascertain what God we worship, or whether we own a God at all.[75]

Also cited was another sermon by James R. Wilson of Albany in which he decried the godlessness of the Constitution in 1831, while the "Father of the Constitution" was still alive:

> When the [Revolutionary] war was over and the victory over our enemies won, and the blessings and happiness of liberty and peace were secured, the Constitution was framed and God was neglected. *He was not merely forgotten. He was absolutely voted out of the Constitution.* The proceedings, as published

---

73. Ibid.
74. See NRA *Proceedings* (1874), 55 (footnote).
75. *Proceedings* (1874), 42.

by Thompson, the secretary, and the history of the day, show that the question was gravely debated whether God should be in the Constitution or not, and after a solemn debate *he was deliberately voted out of it. . . .*

"A Most Unnatural, Impossible Monster"

Several interventions at NRA conventions protested against the very concept of a "religiously neutral" republic. For example, at the 1872 convention Prof. Tayler Lewis, an eminent Greek scholar whose father was an officer in the Revolutionary War, adverted to the Greco-Catholic political tradition in denouncing as unnatural state "neutrality" respecting religion:

> If there is any truth that may be said to be practically as well as theoretically, then it is certain that what we call politics *must be religious or anti-religious, Christian or anti-Christian. . . . The State cannot be neutral*; it must be religious or irreligious. So it was held by the most eminent legislators before the birth of Christ. An irreligious community, one that did not acknowledge the gods, or something divine as the ground of civil obligations, *was a most unnatural, as well as impossible monster.*[76]

Lewis went on to utter a conclusion that was already anathema in America, even though (as we saw in Chapters 1–3) it was rooted in the entire history of the Christian West before the American Revolution: "Every modern state must be Christian or anti-Christian. Neutrality is impossible." Neutrality is impossible, said Lewis, for the very reasons Christ Himself had pronounced in the Gospel: "He that is not for me is against me, he that gathereth not with me, scattereth abroad. . . . Every plant which my Father in Heaven hath not planted shall be rooted up." Here NRA exposed the fiction of the "religiously neutral" state whose very "neutrality" necessarily involves an official rejection of the claims of Christianity on both men and nations, and thus an "anti-theology of the state" we shall examine in the following chapters.

Likewise, at the 1874 convention the President of Wesleyan University, Dr. Joseph Cummings, answered the charge that the NRA was composed of fanatical innovators by observing that all of human history attested to the necessity of a religious foundation for the State:

> From the earliest religion has been regarded as the foundation of national prosperity. In Egypt, Palestine and the Oriental nations, religion has been the main object of government. . . . Plutarch, speaking of the legislators of Greece and Rome, says that religion is the cement of civil union and the essential support of government. "A city might as well be built on the air without any earth to stand on, as a Commonwealth or kingdom be constituted or founded without religion." *Our principles are not novel or fanatical. They are sanctioned by the experience of ages.*[77]

76. *Proceedings* (1872), 42–43.
77. *Proceedings* (1874), 36.

The NRA's dramatic accusation, even then the very height of political incorrect-ness, was that the Framers had created precisely that "most unnatural [and] impos-sible monster" Lewis had described: the first nation in Western history whose organic law had excluded any reference to religious foundations.

"No nation has ever existed without a religion, and the religion of our nation is Christianity," declared the president of the 1874 convention, Felix R. Brunot, whose grandfather was none other than the foster-brother of General Lafayette, serving under him as a physician during the Revolutionary War.[78] Brunot's address pro-vided a supremely ironic twist: an unfavorable spiritual and moral comparison between the American government and the *British* government and the govern-ments of a still largely Christocentric Europe (including even post-Jacobin France, only four years after the fall of its professedly Catholic Emperor, Napoleon III):

> In Great Britain the Bible is the law which stands behind all other laws. Chitty[79] says, in notes to Vattel,[80] "In cases of doubt it is now an admitted rule among *all European nations*, that our common religion, Christianity, pointing out the principles of natural justice, should be equally appealed to by all as an unfailing rule of construction." *It is not so here. In the United States there is no ultimate appeal but the Constitution.* The laws must agree with the Constitu-tion, and being contested, they have not binding authority in the courts, unless they so agree. Our Christian laws, institutions and usages have *no legal basis in the fundamental law of the land.*[81]

The Social Compact Rejected

The NRA's critique of the godlessness of the federal regime was not confined to the four corners of the Constitution. The NRA proceedings are rife with historically notable objections by renowned preachers, jurists and academics to the Locke-inspired political theory of America's Enlightenment-bred founding elites, which limited the role of the State to the protection of material interests and located the source of sovereignty, not in God and His law, but in a social compact arising from "the will of the people." Recall in this context Thornwell's parallel warning to the Confederate Congress concerning "the fatal delusion that our government is a mere expression of human will. . . ."

At the NRA Convention of 1872, the eminent jurist M. B. Hagans gave an address in which he declared "All nations and each nation is of God. . . . It does not accord with the logic of history or the philosophy of our being, or the facts of experience, to say that the State is *a social or economic compact, or that it is founded on the will of*

---

78. Cf. *A Genealogical and Biographical History of Allegheny County*, Pennsylvania, ed. Dr. Thomas Cushing (Baltimore: Genealogical Publishing Co., 1975), 210.

79. Joseph Chitty, Esq., an English barrister and renowned legal commentator of the late 19th cen-tury.

80. I.e., Chitty's annotations to Emmerich de Vattel's *The Law of Nations* (1758) (Philadelphia: T. and J. W. Johnson, 1844, Sixth American Edit.), iv.

81. *Proceedings* (1874), 33.

the people, and therefore has no relation to God." Flatly rejecting the foundation of Hobbelockean politics, Hagans concluded that the State "*is not, therefore, a compact, nor does it exist by the will of the people*," but rather must be "the acceptable minister of God in history" which "strives for a growth into the perfect humanity of its members" and has "a distinct rational and moral end, because God constituted men rational and moral beings." This was a concise recapitulation—by a Protestant jurist—of the Greco-Catholic tradition on the nature of the State, which we examined in Chapter 1.

On the same theme, Hagans observed that in America "the State has no relations to God, *for the Constitution we have made omits even the mention of any supremer sovereignty than itself*, and we can see none." The result was that "the State, recognizing no other or higher sovereignty than itself in its fundamental law, falls short ... of one of its greatest purposes—the education of the citizens in the formation and growth of moral character."[82] Still another address along these lines declared: "As government is an ordinance of God, and is not an invention or institution of man, the fruit of some *imaginary social compact* ... a devout people, worshippers of the living God, should be allowed, in setting up their government, to signify that they do it *in his name*."[83]

NRA's publication *Christian Statesman* gave this rationale for calling a National Convention to secure the "religious amendment" to the Constitution:

The Constitution makes no acknowledgment of Almighty God, the author of national existence; nor of Jesus Christ, who is the Ruler of Nations.... It does not reflect the views of the great majority of the people upon these matters. *It dishonors God....* It has introduced, or furthered, views and measures which are now struggling for baneful ascendancy in State and national politics: such as, *That civil government is only a social compact; That it exists only for secular and material, not moral, ends*; that Sabbath Laws are unconstitutional, and that the Bible must be excluded from our public schools.

The National Association which has been formed for the securing of such an amendment to the National Constitution as will remedy this great defect, indicate that this is a Christian nation, and place all Christian Laws, Institutions and Usages in our government as an undeniable legal basis in the fundamental law of the nation....[84]

The NRA proceedings for 1874 take note of a sermon to the Massachusetts legislature by the Protestant Episcopal bishop of Western Massachusetts, Alexander H. Vinton, wherein he lamented that "our own nation, like France, has chosen the social compact theory of government," which "seemed to alienate religion, and to stand alone, in perfect human sufficiency." While the Framers had supposed they could contain the worst excesses of social compact theory with "conservative

82. *Proceedings*, (1872), 12.
83. Ibid., 68.
84. Ibid., xv.

checks," Vinton observed, "the great question is are these checks sufficient? Is there not the same capacity for mischief in our modified system, as in its simpler forms?"[85]

Taking aim at the Constitution's proclamation that "We the People" were the origin of the Republic's sovereign power, Dr. Sloane, a professor of history at Princeton as well as a Protestant minister, observed that a sovereignty based on popular will provided no ultimate basis for legal authority:

Each day I pass the frowning walls of a gloomy prison in which some hundreds of human beings are confined, some of them for the term of their natural life, on behalf of the safety of society . . . yet we are told that the power which thus isolates those persons, cuts them off from all that makes life desirable . . . and consigns them to separation and solitude . . . derives its power from the people, is accountable only to them, *has no soul, no moral character, and is responsible to no higher tribunal than the majority of citizens!* If the theory thus claimed to be embodied in the present preamble of the Constitution in the words "We the People of the United States of America do ordain this Constitution" is true, then society has no right to put the murderer to death, no right to punish as such, and, indeed, is ultimately *without right to protect itself against ignorance, intemperance, or any other evil which threatens its destruction.*[86]

Of like mind with the NRA was none other than Pope Leo XIII, writing seven years after the NRA's 1874 convention in order to affirm the constant teaching of the very Church that, most ironically, the preponderance of the NRA delegates no doubt viewed as a citadel of antique tyranny:

[V]ery many men of more recent times, walking in the footsteps of those who in a former age assumed to themselves the name of philosophers, say that all power comes from the people. . . . But from these, Catholics dissent, who affirm that *the right to rule is from God*, as from a natural and necessary principle.[87]

Like the NRA, Leo too made short work of Locke's nonsensical social compact, according to which the subjects are the rulers but the rulers are the subjects, leaving no ultimate ground of authority besides sheer force, as the Civil War had demonstrated:

It is plain, moreover, that the pact which they allege is openly a falsehood and a fiction, and that it has no authority to confer on political power such great force, dignity, and firmness as the safety of the State and the common good of the citizens require. Then only will the government have all those ornaments

85. *Proceedings* (1874), 49.
86. *Proceedings* (1872), 29.
87. Leo XIII, *Diuturnum* (1881), n. 5.

and guarantees, when it is understood to emanate from God as its august and most sacred source.[88]

The correspondence between the NRA's view of sovereignty and the teaching of the Catholic Church might seem astonishing at first blush, until one considers that the NRA's position, like the Church's, was rooted in the logical necessity of divine authority as the ground of human authority without which there is really no authority at all, but only contractual arrangements for breach of which the only ultimate sanction is force—with the stronger force prevailing in the inevitable clash of wills, as in the case of the Civil War.

Prophesies Fulfilled

Speakers at the NRA conventions issued a series of prophecies about the effect the Godless Constitution and its underlying political philosophy would have on public morality and the remnants of the Christian legal tradition in the States. "Step by step," Dr. Sloane declared, "the enemy gains, and the Christian sentiment is overbalanced by a contemptible minority of the people, because, in an unfortunate hour, *they accepted a Constitution which has no clause recognizing the great moral power which has made and preserves the nation.*"[89]

Almost exactly a hundred years before the Supreme Court, citing the Fourteenth Amendment, legalized abortion in all fifty states, the aforementioned intervention by Tayler Lewis warned that America's *"perilous experiment of ignoring a divine ruler has been tried and its failure is rapidly developing itself.* God will allow no such silence, much less any profession of indifference. . . . The word of Christ shall show itself to be true: 'He that is not for me is against me, he that gathereth not with me scattereth abroad.'"[90] The NRA's General Secretary quite accurately predicted the emergence of the judicial landscape we now inhabit:

> [T]he written Constitution must be amended to conform to the facts as they have actually been evolved. If this be not done, *the Constitution will in time conform everything to itself.* The facts, the usages, the legislative and judicial actions, everything, in a word, that is out of harmony with the written instrument, *will give way before its moulding and controlling influence, and disappear.*[91]

Even more explicitly prophetic was the President of Wheaton College, Prof. Charles Blanchard, whose address to the 1874 convention, entitled "The Conflict of Law," predicted that, failing adoption of the proposed Christian Amendment, no state law favorable to Christianity "can stand a suit in the Supreme Court of the United States. . . . This conflict of law is inevitable and irrepressible. *Our laws will*

---

88. Ibid., n. 12.
89. *Proceedings* (1872), 31.
90. Ibid., 43.
91. Ibid., 6.

be heathenized or our Constitution Christianized, and Americans must soon decide which they will have done."[92] In like manner, Felix Brunot's address warned that while "Our nation is Christian . . . the Constitution is unchristian. . . . Can this anomaly continue? Impossible. One by one your Christian laws . . . and all the Christian features of State Constitutions, must come to the test of the Constitution of the United States; *and they must fall before it.*" Already, warned the Presbyterian minister T. P. Stevenson, "our divorce legislation, in many States, is a reproach to the Christian name." Under state divorce laws one could "have as many wives as he likes . . . provided he takes one at a time." In St. Louis and other places, he noted, "the Bible has already been excluded from the schools. The legality of the resolution of the Cincinnati School Board, prohibiting prayer and the reading of the Scriptures, has been affirmed by the Supreme Court of the State. They are succeeding everywhere. . . ."[93]

Such predictions were all the more remarkable given the Supreme Court's refusal at that time to apply the Bill of Rights (and thus the First Amendment's requirement of "religious neutrality") to the States. In *Barron v. Baltimore* (1833), handed down before the adoption and ratification of the Fourteenth Amendment, the Court—under Chief Justice Marshall, no less—declined to apply to the States the Fifth Amendment's guarantee against deprivation of property without due process of law. Marshall, writing for the unanimous Court, held simply that the first Ten Amendments "contain no expression indicating an intention to apply them to the State governments. This court cannot so apply them."[94] Even in the year following the NRA convention of 1874, by which time the Fourteenth Amendment was part of the Constitution, the Court held in *United States v. Cruikshank* (1875) that the First Amendment, "like the other amendments proposed and adopted at the same time, was not intended to limit the powers of the State governments in respect to their own citizens, but to operate upon the National government alone," and that the Second Amendment likewise "has no other effect than to restrict the powers of the national government. . . ."[95]

Despite these holdings, however, the NRA movement had rightly discerned the irresistible gravitational force the Constitution was exerting on the States long before the 1925 *Gitlow* decision formalized that effect via the "incorporation" doctrine under the Fourteenth Amendment. Addressing the 1872 convention, T. P. Stevenson provided a sketch of the process:

A German secularist lands on our shores. . . . The American Constitution is held out to him as the fundamental bond of our political union. He finds in it no recognition of the God in whom he does not believe, or of a law whose authority he denies. He assents to it and becomes a citizen. A school tax is levied on his property. He pays it and demands that the reading of the Bible cease

92. *Proceedings* (1874), 71.
93. Ibid., 64, 74 & *Proceedings* (1872), 63.
94. *Barron*, 32 U.S. at 250.
95. *Cruikshank*, 92 U.S. at 552, 553.

in the schools. "It was," he says, "no part of the compact by which I became a citizen that I should be taxed to maintain public instruction in the Christian Scriptures."

It may be said that in becoming a citizen he accepted the Constitution of Ohio ... and thus did become the party to an acknowledgment of the Christian religion ... as the religion of the State. But acknowledgments of God have not always been found in our State Constitutions. If it is good for the National Constitution to be devoid of religious character, why is it not good for the Constitution of a State, *of all States*? *And must not the National Constitution exert a powerful and constant influence to draw the State Constitutions to its own likeness in this respect*?[96]

Again and again, NRA participants warned that, unless amended in the manner proposed, the Constitution itself would be the club by which the defenders of the Christian legal tradition in America would be beaten into submission by a liberal minority. "The appeal of the enemy is to the Constitution," declared Stevenson. The increasingly immoral ruling class of Chicago, warned the attorney R.G. McNiece, "quotes the United States Constitution as authority for such rebellion against the Almighty." The Rev. D. McAllister, General Secretary of the NRA, remarked that "[t]he potent weapon with which they strive to smite down the religious observances and institutions of the country, is the United States Constitution"[97] and that "the enemies of our Christian institutions of government glory in the fact that the Constitution of the United States contains no acknowledgement of God or the Christian religion."[98] O.N. Stoddard of Wooster University lamented that "[t]he opposers of our Christian laws and customs point triumphantly to the Constitution, and lo, it is dumb." Under the influence of the Godless Constitution as wielded by anti-Christian forces, predicted Tayler Lewis, it would not be long before "our whole political page becomes *a pure, unbelieving, irreligious, Christless, Godless blank.*"[99]

The proceedings of 1874 warned of the final consequences of the Constitution's incongruity with the religion of the people of the several states:

[I]t is a serious matter if [the] Constitution should be found wanting in any principle or any matter of fact. The deficiency will in due time work mischief. Error in the Constitution will work as powerfully as truth, *and what is left out may one day be formally declared un-American.* And one such serious matter there is; one most unnecessary and unfortunate omission. *God and Christianity are not once alluded to;* although the Constitution is itself the product of a Christian civilization, and although it purports to represent the mind of a

---

96. *Proceedings* (1872), 59. Paragraph break added.
97. Ibid., 6.
98. *Proceedings* (1874), 38, 40.
99. *Proceedings* (1872), 54, 59.

Christian people, who in all the State Constitutions made explicit reference to both God and religion.[100]

The key phrase here is *"purports* to represent the mind of a Christian people." As the NRA recognized, the Constitution did not in fact represent the mind of the people identified in "We the People," but rather the mind of the drafters, who were by and large deists of the late Enlightenment and saw themselves (to recall Adams's rather fustian boasting) as the vanguard of Kant's dictum that "Enlightenment is man's emergence from his self-incurred immaturity." Given its provenance, the Constitution was admirably suited to the purposes of the NRA's contemporary liberal opposition, as the NRA understood quite well, even if contemporary neo-conservatives cling to the myth of a "conservative" American Revolution. The 1874 proceedings even present a catalogue of the "Demands of Liberalism" in light of the Constitution, including two demands that must have seemed fantastic to many at the time but that have been more than fulfilled under the Constitutional regime:

> We demand that all laws looking to the enforcement of "Christian" morality shall be abrogated, and that all laws shall be conformed to the requirements of natural morality, equal rights, and impartial liberty.
>
> We demand that not only in the Constitution of the United States and in the several States, but also in the practical administration of the same, no privilege or advantage shall be conceded to Christianity or any other special religion; *that our entire political system shall be founded and administered on a purely secular basis. . . .*

In view of these liberal demands, which were even then gaining ground almost daily, the NRA's resolutions at its 1872 convention included the proposition that "the continued ignoring of God and religion exposes us to the guilt of *formal national Atheism.*"[101] And formal national atheism is precisely what has eventuated.

Ultimate Incoherence

The NRA's accurate diagnosis of Liberty's genetic infirmities was not, however, accompanied by an adequate prescription for a cure. Having proposed a Christian amendment to the Constitution, the NRA had no vehicle for securing the Christian commonwealth the amendment implied. In the end, the NRA movement succumbed to the same fatal deficiency that characterizes Protestantism in all its varieties: the lack of an authoritative teaching Church with final authority to resolve disputes over faith and morals and unite Christians as a force standing in opposition to abuses of state power.

The "spirit of Rome," to recall Hobbes's phrase, had well and truly been exorcised from the Constitution just as it had been from the Protestant nation-states emerging from the Reformation. And this was just as the NRA participants themselves

---

100. *Proceedings* (1874), 14.
101. *Proceedings* (1874), 15, citing resolutions of 1872.

approved; for in no way, they stressed, were they seeking "the union of Church and State," but only the "relation of religion and the state."[102] Thornwell's proposed amendment to the Confederate constitution likewise accepted in principle the Founders' "attempt to realize the notion of popular freedom, without the checks of aristocracy and a throne, and without the alliance of a national Church." "The conception was a noble one," wrote Thornwell, although the Founders had erred by "accept[ing] a partial for a complete statement of the truth"[103] in that, while rightly separating Church from State, they did not make the Republic subject to Christ and His law by an express constitutional provision.

But how is a state to be Christian, as both the NRA and Thornwell envisioned, unless its relation to the Law of the Gospel is mediated by a universal authority to define and maintain the integrity of faith and morals? The NRA, at war with itself, could appeal only to the very thing it had rejected as the ground of political sovereignty: "the will of the people." Answering the charge that a Christian Constitution would mean discrimination against non-Christians, the NRA quietly extinguished its own position in self-contradiction, arguing that if America's charter recognized the nation's duty "to conform to the law of religious or Christian morality," nevertheless

> the people of the United States . . . will protect the rights of every citizen, and persecute no man for his religion until that religion drives him to disobey the law *which expresses the will of the majority* concerning the moral duty of the citizen; and that will is *always open to revision by constitutional means.*[104]

Unable to point to any earthly spiritual authority higher than human consensus—for there is none in Protestantism—the NRA was reduced to advocating a Christian moral order determined by an unstable majority will—the same will whose already alarming drift from Christian morals the NRA itself was lamenting. And what other outcome could there be in the absence of the Church-State union we examined in Chapter 1, according to which the Church is the conscience of the State and the "soul" of the body politic as it had been during all the centuries of Christendom?

The NRA's insuperable problem was earlier identified by the renowned Protestant convert to Catholicism, Orestes Brownson, who addressed it with ruthless logic in an essay entitled "Catholicity Necessary to Sustain Popular Liberty" (1845), written only a year after his conversion.[105] Just as the NRA would observe some thirty years later, Brownson observed that "the Constitution is a dead letter . . . it has been becoming in practice, and is now, substantially, a pure democracy, with no effective constitution but the will of the majority. . . ." Only religion could save

---

102. *Proceedings* (1874), 1.

103. Thornwell, *Collected Writings*, Vol. IV, 550.

104. *Proceedings* (1872), 37.

105. *Brownson's Quarterly Review,* October 1845, e-text available @orestesbrownson.com/catholicitynecessarytosustainpopularliberty.html.

America from the majoritarian tyranny. Here too, Brownson anticipated the NRA's program. Yet, he argued, the *Protestant* religion could not save America because Protestantism, "like democracy itself, is subject to the control of the people, and must command and teach what they say. . . ." Hence, he continued:

> The holding of slaves is compatible with Christian character south of a geographical line, and incompatible north; and Christian morals change according to the prejudices, interests, or habits of the people—as evidenced by the recent divisions in our own country among the Baptists and Methodists. The Unitarians of Savannah refuse to hear a preacher accredited by Unitarians of Boston. . . . The Protestant sect governs its religion, instead of being governed by it. If one sect pursues, by the influence of its chiefs, a policy in opposition to the passions and interests of its members, or any portion of them, the disaffected, if a majority, change its policy; if too few or too weak to do that, they leave it and join some other sect, or form a new sect.

Answering the charge that he would place religion in America under the dominion of the Pope, Brownson turned that very charge into the proof of his argument: "this is good proof of our position, that Protestantism cannot govern the people—for *they* govern *it*—and therefore that Protestantism is not the religion wanted; for it is precisely a religion that can and will govern the people and be their master, that we need." Of course, only one Church fits that description; only one is headed by a figure whose authority—spiritual, not political, Brownson stressed—is accepted as final and binding by the faith of its members. "The Roman Catholic religion, then," he concluded, "is necessary to sustain popular liberty, because popular liberty can be sustained only by a religion free from popular control, above the people, speaking from above and able to command them—and such a religion is the Roman Catholic."

But it was precisely union with the Catholic Church and its monarchical head that the NRA's Protestant members, their Southern counterparts, the Republic's Protestant and deist progenitors, Hobbes, Locke and the Enlightenment divines had all rejected as one. The NRA movement, like any Protestant movement, had no ground on which to stand save the majority will of a Protestant people that was already squandering what was left of its moral inheritance from the dreaded Church of Rome. And in the name of constitutional liberty the same Protestant majority would acquiescence in the extinction of even that residuum of Christian moral order.

The Framers, Brownson noted, had thought they could restrain the tyranny of the majority "by a written Constitution. But they intrusted the preservation of the Constitution to the care of the people, which was as wise as to lock up your culprit in prison and intrust him with the key." Writing only three years before his death, in the very year of the NRA's 1873 convention, Brownson—now a bitterly disillusioned former Americanist—echoed the NRA in its dire predictions about America's future. Unlike the NRA, however, he linked the coming catastrophic moral decline precisely to the tendencies of Protestant Christianity:

Where the people are Catholic and submissive to the law of God, as declared and applied by the vicar of Christ and supreme pastor of the church, democracy may be a good form of government; *but combined with Protestantism or infidelity in the people, its inevitable tendency is to lower the standard of morality, to enfeeble intellect, to abase character, and to retard civilization, as even our short American experience amply proves.* Our republic may have had a material expansion and growth; but every observing and reflecting American, whose memory goes back, as mine does, over fifty years, sees that *in all else it is tending downward, and is on the declivity to utter barbarism.*[106]

Nevertheless, while the NRA's prescription for what ailed America was only a different strain of the same disease, its diagnosis could well have been written by the Popes themselves in their own critique of political modernity. Recall the diagnosis by Pope Leo XIII quoted in the Introduction, concerning "that new conception of law which was not merely previously unknown, but was at variance on many points with not only the Christian, but even the natural law."[107] Recall as well from the Introduction the later diagnosis by Pius XI, which could have been adopted as an NRA resolution: "With God and Jesus Christ excluded from political life, with authority derived not from God but from man, the very basis of that authority has been taken away, because the chief reason of the distinction between ruler and subject has been eliminated. The result is that human society is tottering to its fall, because it has no longer a secure and solid foundation."[108]

It is crucial to note that the NRA's damning diagnosis of the Republic addressed, not some perversion of the "true Constitution" by evil Federalists or Supreme Court decisions that betrayed the "vision of the Framers," as the "conservative" libertarian narrative insists, but rather precisely what the Framers had wrought. The NRA boldly proclaimed in public, to cries of "fanaticism" in the press, the self-evident truth that the Constitution created by the men Marty E. Marty calls "the Deist founders and proto-Unitarians of the late 18th century"[109] was so far removed from a Christian project that not even the Lockean "Nature's God" of the Declaration of Independence had found a place in its text.

"Whether Christian or Pagan"

The 43rd Congress of the United States recognized as much when it rejected the NRA's "Christian Amendment" out of hand. A House Judiciary Committee report, published in the Congressional Record on February 18, 1874, declared that

106. Orestes Brownson, "Introduction to Last Series," *Brownson's Quarterly Review* (January 1873), in *The Works of Orestes A. Brownson* (Detroit: H. F. Brownson, 1887), Vol. XX, 285.

107. *Immortale Dei* (1885), n. 23.

108. *Quas Primas* (1925).

109. Martin E. Marty, "Sidney E. Mead: Historian of Religion in America 1904–1999," harvardsquarelibrary.org/unitarians/mead.htm.

an examination of the record of the debates at the Constitutional Convention had revealed that:

> the fathers of the Republic in the convention which framed the Constitution ... decided that this country, the foundation of whose government they were laying, was to be the home of the oppressed of all nations of the earth, *whether Christian or Pagan*, and in full realization of the dangers which the union between church and state had imposed upon so many nations of the Old World, [decided] with great unanimity that it was inexpedient to put *anything into the Constitution or frame of government* which might be construed to be a reference to *any religious creed or doctrine.*[110]

The Report concluded: "it is inexpedient to legislate upon the subject of the above memorial" and asked that the members of the Committee "be discharged from the further consideration thereof, and that this report, together with the petition, be laid upon the table." That is, the Committee would not even allow the proposed constitutional amendment to reach the floor of the House for a vote so that the constitutional amendment process could begin *as the Constitution itself provides.* For to do so would be contrary to the sacred will of the Founders and Framers in creating a Republic that would neither profess nor even favor the Christian religion, or indeed any religion at all. Thus was the Godless Constitution preserved intact against the NRA's Christian insurrection. The NRA eventually abandoned its campaign for the amendment (it failed in committee three times in all, including an attempt in 1896), although the organization continued to hold conventions and later existed in vestigial form as recently as 2004.[111]

$$\S$$

We have focused so intently on the proceedings of the National Reform Association because they provide little known but all but dispositive historical evidence against the myth of the Constitution as the charter for a Christian republic. The very existence of the NRA movement also provides a decisive rebuttal to the charge of special pleading from a Catholic historical perspective. Indeed, even contemporary liberals have been honest enough to recognize what conservative Protestants had recognized literally from the day the Framers' ink was applied to parchment: that a Godless Constitution is exactly what the Framers had in mind. Furthermore, the record evidence in the NRA proceedings negates the neo-conservative and libertarian contention that the liberals are indulging in historical revisionism in order to defend judicial activism by the Supreme Court.

Brooke Allen, whose book *Moral Minority* is part of a body of recent literature debunking the Legend of the Christian Founding, aptly sums up the reality versus

---

110. "House Reports," Vol I., 43d Congress, 1st Session, Report No. 143.

111. See Anthony Cowley, "From Whence We Came: A Background of the National Reform Association," www.natreformassn.org/ecp/chap1.html. The website is no longer functional and now exists only as an archival page.

the myth: "Our nation was founded not on Christian principles but on Enlightenment ones. God only entered the picture as a very minor player, and Jesus Christ was conspicuously absent."[112] Walter Berns, also remarking the obvious, writes: "If the Founders had intended to establish a Christian commonwealth (and, under the circumstances, it could not have been any other variety of religious commonwealth), it was remiss of them—indeed, sinful of them—not to have said so and to have acted accordingly."[113] But the Founders had no intention of establishing a Christian commonwealth because nearly all the leading lights among them were simply not Christians. As the NRA had discerned, the builders of the Temple of Liberty were Enlightenment-bred deists determined to prevent religion from having any control over the government they had created behind closed doors in Philadelphia. Yet, trapped within the framework of Protestant Christianity and its principle of private judgment, the NRA could offer no means to prevent the moral and spiritual catastrophe its proceedings so accurately predicted, and which all of former Christendom endures today.

112. Brooke Allen, "Our Godless Constitution," *The Nation*, February 21, 2005.
113. Berns, "Religion and the Founding Principle," 211.

19

A House Divided

THE NRA MOVEMENT was unable to recognize that the ascendancy of the State over Christianity in America was not solely the result of fatal omissions in the Constitution or the errors of Enlightenment political philosophy. These were necessary, but not in themselves entirely *sufficient*, conditions for that outcome. Other essential conditions were a uniquely American exacerbation of the fragmentation of Protestant Christianity inherent to the English genome of Liberty, which we examined in Chapter 3, and the beginning of a breakup of the institution of the family viewed, like the Protestant churches, as a contractarian association.

Divided Sects

As Locke foresaw, the unchallenged monism of state power that is at the essence of Liberty would be insured by a multiplicity of Christian sects. In Chapter 3 we saw how, in the *Essay Concerning Toleration*, Locke advised that when any sect is "grown, or growing so numerous as to appear dangerous to the magistrate" the magistrate "may and ought to use all ways, either of policy or power, that shall be convenient, *to lessen, break and suppress the party*, and so prevent the mischief"[1]—the "mischief" being the mere existence of a dominant religious faction capable of posing a challenge to the State. Both Jefferson and Madison, following Locke, expressly recognized the division of Christianity into sects as a primary safeguard of Liberty. In his *Notes on the State of Virginia*, Jefferson observes that the "several sects perform the office of a Censor morum over each other," preventing any one sect from installing the "Procrustean bed" of "uniformity" via government.[2] Likewise, in Federalist No. 51, written to persuade the holdout states to ratify the Constitution, Madison declares, with the supreme religious indifference of the Deist he was, that:

> In a free government the security for civil rights must be the same as that for religious rights. *It consists in the one case in the multiplicity of interests, and in the other in the multiplicity of sects.* The degree of security in both cases will depend on *the number of interests and sects*; and this may be presumed to depend on the extent of country and number of people comprehended under the same government.... In the extended republic of the United States, and

1. *Essay on Toleration*, III.I.2, in Cambridge Edition, 148.
2. *Notes on the State of Virginia*, 193 (Waldstreicher ed.).

among the great variety of interests, parties, and sects which it embraces, a coalition of a majority of the whole society could seldom take place on any other principles than those of justice and the general good. . . . [3]

Like Locke, Madison viewed the very multiplicity of sects as necessary to secure "justice and the general good," by which he means what Locke means: "to preserve men in *this world* from the fraud and violence of one another"[4] and "promoting the general welfare, which consists in riches and power" as determined by "the number and industry of your subjects."[5] Christianity divided poses no threat to the power of the State as the guarantor of a "social peace" limited to the absence of aggression against property rights, including the right to own slaves (as Madison, Jefferson and Washington did) or, as contemporary libertarians contend, the right to abortion as incident to Lockean "self-ownership." (It was precisely this limited role of the State that Calhoun had insisted upon in the face of "interference" with "our institutions" by the Christian "fanatics" of the abolition movement who had petitioned the Senate for legislation emancipating the slaves.) Lockean polities require for their equilibrium and survival a divide and conquer strategy toward Christianity as their only serious rival. This is why, to recall Peter Gay's startling observation, "political absolutism and religious toleration [are] the improbable twins of the modern state system."

In America, the constitutional subordination of revealed religion the NRA attempted to oppose was mightily assisted by the post-Revolutionary disintegration of what was left of traditional Christianity's power and authority as a socially constitutive force. The result, writes Sidney Mead, is that in America the "struggle between Church and State is actually between the one coherent institutionalized civil authority, and about three hundred collectively incoherent religious institutions whose claims tend to cancel each other out."[6] Just as a Locke-inspired Declaration of Independence from the authority of the king launched the American Revolution, so did the Second Great Awakening (c. 1800–1850) launch what Alexander Campbell, the British-born leader of the Restoration Movement in America, called a "declaration of independence of the kingdom of Jesus."[7] From roughly 1780 to 1840, the example of the Revolution and the resulting republic inspired Campbell and a host of other Protestant revivalist leaders such as Lorenzo Dow, Elias Smith, Barton Stone, Francis Asbury, Joseph Smith and John Leland, to mount an assault on ecclesiastical authority and the Christian creeds, replacing traditional Christianity with a seemingly infinite variety of "fresh religious ideologies around which new religious movements coalesced."[8] In his landmark study of the democratization of Christianity in America, Nathan Hatch observes that the new American republic "became a city on a hill, not because it kept faith with Puritan tradition, but because

---

3. *The Federalist Papers*, 324, 325.

4. *Essay on Toleration*, 135, in *Locke: Political Essays*.

5. Ibid., 151.

6. Sidney E. Mead, "The Nation with the Soul of a Church," *Church History*, Vol. 36, No. 3 (Sept., 1967), 277.

7. Alexander Campbell, Fourth of July Oration, *The Millennial Harbinger*, Vol. I, No. VII (1830).

8. Hatch, *The Democratization of American Christianity*, 57.

it sounded the death knell for corporate and hierarchic conceptions of social order. In sum, a government so enlightened as to tell the churches to go their own way *must also have the prophetic power to tell them which way to go.*"[9]

And so it did. The American Revolution, as Hatch observes, taught people "a powerful new vocabulary, a rhetoric of liberty, that would not have occurred to them were it not for the Revolution." Applying that vocabulary to ecclesiastical as well as political authority, newly arisen religious demagogues, whose appeals to the masses paralleled those of the new political demagogues, provoked a mass departure from the established denominations, represented in the failed NRA movement, into the "freedom" of a "personal relationship" with the American Jesus who founded no Church and taught no elaborate doctrine or dogma.

"The democratic revolution of the early republic," writes Hatch, "sent external religious authority into headlong retreat and elicited from below visions of faith that seemed more authentic and self-evident. . . . These new expressions of faith . . . did not merely diverge from received authority; increasingly, they failed to take into account the standard theological categories that served as guides for religious experience and formed the common denominator of theological discussion between disputants. . . . In the wake of the Revolution, dissenters confounded the establishment with an approach to theological matters that was nothing short of guerrilla warfare."[10] In consequence, as Gordon Wood observes, nowhere in Christendom "had religion become so fragmented and so separated from society" as in post-Revolutionary America.[11] All of former Christendom, lamented Harrison Gray Otis in the early 1800s, "has been decomposed, broken in pieces . . . [in the] fiery furnace of democracy."[12] "Every congregation has power to originate a new Christianity for its own use," observed the German Reform theologian John Nevin in the mid-1800s.[13]

The leaders of the dissenters involved in this process appealed, as did their political counterparts, to Locke's theory that all authority, including religious authority, originates in the consent of the people to a compact. We have already seen how, for Locke, a church is nothing more than a "voluntary society of men, joining themselves together of their own accord in order to the public worshipping of God in such manner as they judge acceptable to Him. . . ."[14] But the application of the fiction of "government by consent of the governed" to the formation of new Christian sects produced the same result in religion it had already produced in politics: the replacement of one "absolute sovereign" with numerous others. In an ironic commentary on what they called the "sect plague," Nevin and his fellow Reform German theologian Philip Schaff warned that the rebellion against religious authority would mean the enslavement of Protestant Christians by self-

9. Hatch, 186.
10. Ibid., 34.
11. Wood, *Radicalism*, 333.
12. Ibid., 332.
13. Hatch, 167.
14. *Letter Concerning Toleration*, 28.

appointed "popes" whose reign was more of a danger than that of the Pope of Rome: "The most dangerous foe with which we are called to contend is again not the Church of Rome but the sect plague in our own midst; not the single of the seven hills, but the numberless popes—German, English and American—who would fain enslave Protestants once more to human authority, not as embodied in the church indeed, but as holding in the form of mere private judgment and private will."[15]

From the "Free Will Baptists" to the Church of Jesus Christ of the Latter Day Saints; from the camp meetings of Lorenzo Dow and other itinerant preachers, replete with dancing, jerking, barking and "holy laughter," to the relative sobriety of James O'Kelly's Republican Methodists; from the Churches of Christ, the Disciples of Christ and the new evangelical Baptists and Methodists on the evangelical "right," to the Universalists on the Jeffersonian "left"—in all of this profusion of "free" and personalized religiosity, America became a "religion-mad country."[16] After the Revolution, Protestant Americans declared their independence from existing ecclesiastical authority *en masse*, following little "popes" into a mind-boggling assortment of new religious sects and movements.

Nowhere is this religious revolution more evident than in the history of the "Church of Jesus Christ of Latter Day Saints," invented in 1823 by one Joseph Smith, who claimed to have received the Mormon canon in the form of golden plates buried on a hill in Manchester, NY whose location was revealed to him by an angel named Moroni. Smith ended up being shot to death during a gun battle with rival Mormons at a jail in Carthage, Illinois where he had been imprisoned after surrendering on charges of riot. (Acting as mayor of nearby Nauvoo, Illinois, Smith had ordered the destruction of a rival Mormon faction's printing press.) But Smith's new religion survived. His successor, Brigham Young, acting as President of the Quorum of Twelve Apostles, led the cult into the salt flats of the Utah desert because not even Protestant America could tolerate their preposterous heresies. There the cult flourished against all odds—the quintessential American religion, conceived in Liberty. Today, having expediently jettisoned its polygamy based on "continuing revelation," the cult is now an acceptable dish in the American smorgasbord of religions, even for a Presidential candidate.

The Second Great Awakening and its aftermath were an explosive new fragmentation of an already divided American Christianity, thus further insuring its impotence before a political authority whose unity and power were growing with each passing year. In 1841 Schaff observed with disgust that in America "Every theological vagabond and peddler may drive...his bungling trade, without passport of license, and sell his false ware at pleasure. What is to come of such confusion is not now to be seen."[17] In fact, what was to come of the confusion was already evident:

---

15. In Hatch, *Democratization of American Christianity*, 165.

16. Harold Bloom, *The American Religion: The Emergence of a Post-Christian Nation* (NY: Simon & Schuster, 1993), 37.

17. Philip Schaff, *The Principle of Protestantism as Related to the Present State of the Church* (Chambersburg, PA: Publication Office of the German Reformed Church, 1845), 116.

the same collapse of morality the NRA deplored, beginning with the liberalization of divorce and property law, leaving the divided Christian house impotent before the monism of power emanating from Washington.

Divided Families

We have already noted (cf. Chapter 9) that after the American Revolution all the States except South Carolina enacted liberalized divorce laws, thereby all but universally enacting the Lockean (and latitudinarian Protestant) view of marriage as a mere contract born of mutual consent. Even before the Revolution, however, Jefferson was already agitating for legalized divorce. In 1772, following his master Locke, he crafted a case for a bill of divorce in the Virginia legislature on behalf of his client Dr. James Blair—the only way a divorce was then attainable under Virginia law. His notes for the case reflect the argument that it is "[c]ruel to continue by violence an union made at first by mutual love, but now dissolved by hatred ... [t]o chain a man to misery till death. Liberty of divorce prevents and cures domestic quarrels. . . . Preserves liberty of affection (which is natural right)." Citing Locke, the notes propose that marriage "may be made at the time of contracting dissoluble by consent ... as other compacts."[18] Jefferson lived to see the beginning of the "liberty of divorce" he envisioned. The moral havoc wreaked by liberalized divorce laws, which provided legal sanction for the dissolution of marriages and families as mere civil compacts, is so obvious as not to require a demonstration; one need only consult the self-evident results of America's divorce culture. Allied to the emergence of legalized divorce as an attack on the family was the steady decrease in its size beginning in 1800, already noted in Chapter 9.

Far less obvious in their moral implications, however, are the radical changes in property law that followed the Revolution. Gordon Wood observes that "the Revolution's assault on patriarchy inevitably affected relationships within the family" and resulted in early claims for "women's and daughters' rights that conservatives later regarded as 'tending to loosen the bonds of society.'"[19] Nowhere was this assault more direct than in the area of estate law. Animated by a Lockean philosophical antipathy toward the traditional Christian conception of patriarchy—which Locke undermined in the *First Treatise, Some Thoughts Concerning Education,* and the *Essay Concerning Human Understanding*—the legislatures of the new states "struck out the power of family and hereditary privilege" by "abolish[ing] the legal devices of primogeniture and entail where they existed, either by statute or by writing the abolition into their constitutions."[20] That is, the States abolished the perennial legal protection of the unity of family estates, thus indirectly attacking family unity itself, by prohibiting restrictions on inheritance in cases of intestacy to male lineal descendants (entail) and the eldest surviving son in the lineage (primogeniture).

18. In Frank L. Dewey, "Thomas Jefferson's Notes on Divorce," *The William and Mary Quarterly,* Third Series, Vol. 39, No. 1, The Family in Early American History and Culture (Jan. 1982), 216–217.
19. Wood, *Radicalism,* 183–184.
20. Ibid., 183.

The law now mandated "an equality of property which is of the spirit and principle of a genuine republic."[21] Over time, this radical change of laws as old as Christendom would have its effect even where wills were drawn to avoid inheritance by operation of law. Traditionally, a testator would prefer the eldest son or divide the estate equally between male heirs, with provisions for unmarried daughters being common. Traditional inheritance patterns assumed, however, that female children would marry men of means who were perpetuating family lines and estates of their own. The idea that women were left destitute by traditional inheritance patterns is a liberal romantic myth, but one that was essential to conversion of the family as well as the state into a democratic compact.

In *Democracy in America*, Tocqueville noted that the American abolition of entail and primogeniture was part of the process by which newly awakened "democratic instincts," the mania for equality, and the demand for "every kind of independence" profoundly affected family life. He was "astonished that ancient and modern political writers have not attributed to estate laws a greater influence on the course of human affairs," for such laws "have an incredible influence on the social state of peoples. . . . Man is armed by them with almost a divine power. . . . The legislator regulates the estates of citizens once and rests for centuries. . . ." By subjecting hereditary landed estates to a legally mandated "equal inheritance," the state legislatures had brought about what Tocqueville called a "revolution in property" through which estates "are constantly fragmented into smaller portions." The law of equal partition thus "acts on the very souls of property owners" because the "family spirit is in a way materialized in the land. The family represents the land, the land represents the family."

As of the 1830s, when Tocqueville wrote, estate law's "work of destruction is nearly ended. . . . The least trace of ranks and hereditary distinction is destroyed; estate law has done its leveling everywhere."[22] Yet, Tocqueville observed, the equal partition of the estate of a landed patriarch upon his death "destroys the intimate connection between the spirit of the family and the preservation of the land" as the heirs divide and sell off the family estate and the family members go their separate ways. In this way, he concluded, estate law "succeeds in profoundly attacking landed property and in making *families as well as fortunes disappear with rapidity.*" Here, as elsewhere, Liberty delivered precisely the opposite of what it had promised.

Tellingly, Jefferson proudly linked the legal abolition of traditional inheritance patterns to the disestablishment of Christianity and the creation of a system of general public education as parts of his legislative program in Virginia, "by which every fibre would be eradicated of antient or future aristocracy; and a foundation laid for a government truly republican." As he explained:

21. Stanley N. Katz, "Republicanism and the Law of Inheritance in the American Revolutionary Era," 76 *Michigan Law Rev.* (1977) 1, 7; cited in Wood, *Radicalism*, 183.

22. *Democracy in America*, ed. Mansfield and Winthrop (Chicago: Univ. of Chicago Press, 2000), I.I.3, 47–48, 50. All subsequent references to this work are to the Mansfield and Winthrop edition, citing volume, part, chapter and page.

The repeal of the laws of entail would prevent the accumulation and perpetuation of wealth in select families.... The abolition of primogeniture, and
equal partition of inheritances removed the feudal and unnatural distinctions
which made one member of every family rich, and all the rest poor.... The
restoration of the rights of conscience relieved the people from taxation for
the support of a religion not theirs; for the establishment was truly of the religion of the rich, the dissenting sects being entirely composed of the less
wealthy people; and these, by the bill for a general education, would be qualified to understand their rights, to maintain them, and to exercise with intelligence their parts in self-government....[23]

The claim that traditional patriarchal inheritance patterns "made one member
of every family rich, and all the rest poor" was sheer demagoguery. As already
noted, testators routinely made provisions for all their male heirs and for unmarried female heirs as well. Nor were family members cast into the street in cases of
intestacy.

Just as the overthrow of the patriarchal Pope had resulted in the disintegration
of Christianity into innumerable sects, and the overthrow of the patriarchal monarch the disintegration of political society into mass democracy, so would the overthrow of patriarchal primacy within the family bring on its disintegration into a
group of individuals, each with his own rights, living under the same roof until
divorce or the death of the father effected the dissolution of a domestic society
viewed as no less contractual than any other arrangement in Lockean social order.

§

The fragmentation of American religion and the liberalization of divorce and estate
law were inevitable operations of the consent principle in the relentless dissolution
of the remnants of Christian civilization in America. The tradition established by
Hobbes and Locke, writes historian Jeffrey Collins, was directed against "an Augustinian, dualist model, of the corporate church and corporate commonwealth—in
which the universal morality of Christianity was established outside and above secular standards and the sphere of political action...." The opposing Hobbelockean
model, first made operative in a religiously fragmented America, is one in which a
"monolithic state presided over a polity of atomized individuals."[24] Speaking of the
Union, Lincoln had famously declared in 1858 that "a house divided against itself
cannot stand," audaciously quoting Christ Himself concerning the unity of the
Kingdom of God on earth. A divided Christian house, both ecclesial and familial,
was no match for the undivided house Lincoln had reconstructed by brute force—
the Western world's first secular state, resting on the foundation of a godless Constitution the NRA had been powerless to alter.

23. *Memoirs, Correspondence*, Vol. I, 42.
24. Collins, *The Allegiance of Thomas Hobbes*, 279.

20

The Constitutional Subjugation of Religion

HAVING ESTABLISHED that the Godless Constitution is not a figment of liberal historical revisionism or Catholic special pleading but rather a reality deplored by the most conservative Protestants since the dawn of the Republic, we are now in a position to examine more closely how the Framers' handiwork produced precisely the outcome the NRA (and Catholics like Brownson) predicted.

The Constitution was written into polished form by the head of the Constitutional Convention's committee on detail, Gouverneur Morris of Pennsylvania. If anyone can be called "the" literal drafter of the document, Morris can. Like other key Founders, Morris prudently hid his deism behind the façade of a nominal Episcopalianism. In his *Anas*, Jefferson, after discussing the failed attempt to get the "old fox" Washington to declare whether he was a Christian, writes of Morris: "I know that Gouverneur Morris, who pretended to be in his [Washington's] secrets and believed himself to be so, has often told me that General Washington believed no more of the system [Christianity] *than he did*."[1]

It was Morris who uttered the famous declaration to the delegates of the Constitutional Convention that he had come not only as "a representative of America" but also "in some degree as a Representative of the whole human race; for the whole human race will be affected by the proceedings of this Convention."[2] And so it was. Jefferson, writing in 1826, predicted that the radically new form of government "which we have substituted" would "be to the world, what I believe it will be (to some parts sooner, to others later, *but finally to all*), the Signal of arousing men to burst the chains, under which monkish ignorance and superstition had persuaded them to bind themselves...."[3] The faithful followers of the myth of the "conservative" American Revolution close their eyes to such pronouncements.

---

1. Thomas Jefferson, *The Anas* from *The Writings of Thomas Jefferson*, Univ. of Virginia e-text, 434, etext.lib.virginia.edu/etcbin/toccer-new2?id=JefBv012.sgm&images=imagesmodeng&data=/texts/english/modeng/parsed&tag=public&part=all.

2. Quoted in Morison, *HAP*, 308.

3. Jefferson to Roger Weightman, June 24, 1826, Library of Congress e-text @ http://www.loc.gov/exhibits/jefferson/214.html.

This business of freeing the world from its monkish ignorance and superstition was the culminating practical project of the Enlightenment, designed precisely to preclude the intrusion of divine claims into politics—above all the claims of Christ on men and nations so handily excised from the "Jefferson Bible." John Adams explained in perfect Enlightenment style why the Framers had rejected any divine intrusion into their work: "It was the general opinion of ancient nations that the Divinity alone was adequate to the important office of giving laws to men," he wrote, but the new state and federal governments of America "have exhibited, perhaps, *the first example* of governments erected on the simple principles of nature"— principles that had somehow eluded man's understanding until 1787. Further, Adams declared, it must not be pretended that those involved in devising these new governments "had interviews with the gods, or were in any degree under the influence of Heaven, more than those at work upon ships or houses, or laboring in merchandise or agriculture...." Rather, Adams predicted: "[I]t will forever be acknowledged that these governments were contrived *merely by the use of reason and the senses*."[4] Nor would Locke have had it any other way.

Christianity Subordinated

Given our discussion of the Lockean political foundations of the American Republic in Chapter 3, it should be obvious that, as the legal historian John Witte observes, a century after Locke proposed his paradigm of the modern, religiously "neutral" and pluralist state, "American Enlightenment writers pressed Locke's theses into more concrete legal and political forms."[5] With Locke's principles in mind, the "enlightened" and deistic Founders knew that what they called Liberty could not be established so long as government remained in any way subject to the dictates of revealed religion. Quite simply, religion had to be subordinated to politics, but especially the Christian religion with its claims on both men and nations.

"The origin of free government in the modern sense," writes Walter Berns, "coincides with and can *only* coincide with, the solution of the religious problem, and the solution of the religious problem consists in *the subordination of religion*."[6] As Berns concludes approvingly elsewhere: "The Constitution was ordained and established to secure liberty and its blessings, not to promote faith in God. Officially, religion was *subordinate to liberty*...."[7] Or, as George Will has put it: "A central purpose of America's political arrangements is the *subordination* of religion to the political order, meaning the primacy of democracy.... It is the intent of the Founders."[8] More specifically, as Hancock recognizes, "America is based upon *a*

4. *The Works of John Adams* (Boston: Little, Brown & Co., 1865), 291–292.
5. Witte, *Religion and the American Constitutional Experiment*, 32.
6. Walter Berns, *The First Amendment and the Future of American Democracy* (NY: Basic Books, 1976), 26.
7. Berns, "Religion and the Founding Principle," 214.
8. George Will, "Conduct, Coercion and Belief," *Washington Post*, April 22, 1990, in Craycraft, *American Myth of Religious Freedom*, 20.

Lockean subordination of Christianity to secular ends."[9] Locke's political theory, says Thomas Pangle, is aimed at "moderating religion and *subordinating* it to the needs of a society designed according to rational principles."[10]

The Founders followed Locke's aim unswervingly, and they achieved it with spectacular success. The foundation of their plan was, of course, the Constitution itself, which enacts the Lockean paradigm into law by forbidding any religious test for federal office and denying government any power to "establish" religion—i.e., to profess, defend, promote, lend official support to, or be guided by Christianity. As those clauses read:

> Article III, clause 6:
> *No* religious Test shall *ever* be required as a Qualification to *any* Office or public Trust under the United States.

> Amendment I:
> Congress shall make *no* law respecting an *establishment of religion*, or prohibiting the free exercise thereof. . . .

The NRA's protests had focused on what the Constitution fails to state: any recognition of Christ and His authority over both men and nations or even the authority of God and religion in general. But the NRA all but ignored the problems posed by what the Constitution *does* say; it even positively approved the Church-State separation mandated by the Establishment Clause of the First Amendment. Golden legends aside, the intendment of the Constitution's religion clauses is perfectly clear: not merely to preclude an established church in America but also to insulate the federal government from the influence of any religion. Contrary to the romantic myth of a Confederate Christendom, the same is true of the identically worded clauses in the Confederacy's virtual carbon copy of the U.S. Constitution.

Article III, Clause 6 in and of itself makes an American Christian commonwealth a legal impossibility, for on its face it forbids the national government to require a profession of belief in Christ by office holders or even a belief in the remote and amorphous deity of the "moderate" Enlightenment. In the very midst of the Constitutional Convention, Luther Martin, whose testimony we noted in Chapter 18, condemned precisely "[t]he part of the system [Constitution] which provides, that no religious test shall ever be required as a qualification to any office or public trust under the United States. . . ." which eliminated any "distinction between the professors of Christianity and downright infidelity or paganism."[11] But neither the NRA movement nor its Southern analogue in the movement led by James Thornwell had objected to the elimination of any religious test for office. Thornwell, in fact, defended this provision in the Confederate Constitution.

9. Hancock, "Religion and the Limits of Limited Government," 686.

10. Pangle, *The Spirit of Modern Republicanism*, 214.

11. Luther Martin, "The Genuine Information (1787)," in Farrand, ed., *Records of the Federal Convention*, 3:227.

The Conceit of Religious Neutrality

As for the First Amendment, the defenders of Liberty have always argued that its religion clauses merely insure the federal government's "neutrality" toward religion, thereby safeguarding the "religious freedom" of all. But without even discussing the endlessly debated "meaning" of the Amendment (which we shall consider in due course), it must be said first of all that, just as the NRA observed, when a government declares itself "neutral" respecting the revealed truths of Christianity, it has *ipso facto* constituted itself an anti-Christian confessional state that has adjudged the Gospel to be a mere collection of debatable private opinions that can have no influence on law or public policy. The disastrous consequences for the sociopolitical order are inescapable, as the NRA protested far too late to reverse the process.

In his withering examination of the self-contradictions in Lockean and Jeffersonian liberalism, Thomas Pangle states the obvious: "Government cannot be neutral as regards religion. By manifesting indifference to theological controversy, government necessarily promotes indifference among citizenry."[12] Jefferson himself was quite pleased to note this fact: "our sister states of Pennsylvania and New York . . . have made the happy discovery that the way to silence religious disputes, is to take no notice of them. . . ."[13] As the NRA protested, however, the founder of the Christian religion had warned His subjects that "He who is not with me is against me, and he that gathers not with me scatters."[14] The glib reply that Christ also taught that one must render unto Caesar what is Caesar's and to God what is God's, overlooks *Caesar's* duty to render unto God what is His—that is, obedience to His law and reverence for His majesty. Caesar's duty to God is the very reason for the "Gelasian dyarchy," discussed in Chapter 1, which was the foundation of Western civilization for more than a thousand years: i.e., the submission of the temporal power to the spiritual power when the two powers come into conflict in matters pertaining to law or public policy.

Scholars from all points on the political spectrum—including, among innumerable others, Levy and Berns on the left, Manent and Fish in the gadfly left-of-center, Mead in the staunchly Americanist and Unitarian middle, Milbank and Pickstock on the Anglican right-of-center, and MacIntyre, Schindler, Rowland and Craycraft on the Catholic right—have converged on the fundamental insight that the claim of "religious neutrality" by the so-called "procedural state" is a mere conceit that hides a contrary reality. Legally mandated state "neutrality" toward religion—seen for the first time in the Constitution of the United States, as the NRA protested—is *ipso facto* the subordination of religion to secular purposes. The Constitution that makes no mention of God or Christ, and whose religion clauses preclude by their very terms anything like a Christian state (as the Treaty of Tripoli expressly affirmed), is the result of a judgment that the national government shall neither be with Christ

---

12. Pangle, *The Spirit of Modern Republicanism*, 83.
13. Jefferson, *Notes on the State of Virginia* (Boston: Lilly and Wait, 1832), 168; Pangle, op. cit., 83.
14. Matthew 12:30.

nor gather with Him. The Constitution's religion clauses are, in fact, the Founders' new and revolutionary answer to the theologico-political question that has confronted Western man since the fall of Athens four hundred years before the Incarnation. And why should anyone be surprised by the Founders' answer, given that the leading lights among them were plainly not orthodox Christians but rather deistic American *philosophes*?

The Novelty of the Secular State

We have already noted John Milbank's observation that "Once there was no secular. Instead there was the single community of Christendom with its dual aspects of *sacerdotium* and *regnum*. . . . The secular as a domain had to be *created or imagined* (Milbank's emphasis), both in theory and in practice."[15] We have seen that it was Locke who first invented the idea of a "secular" realm in society, reserved to the instrumental acts of government in defense of property rights and bodily security, wherein the truths of revealed religion would be deemed politically inoperable according to what can be called the "politics of the body." It was the Framers who built the first working model of what is now commonly known as the "secular state."

What is lost on Americans today, although it was quite apparent to the NRA movement not so very long ago, is that the government the Founders created was an utter novelty that departed from the entire Western tradition on the relation between religion and the State as maintained, after a fashion, even in the colonies and new state governments. No one understood this better than the Constitution's very "father." In his posthumously published *Detached Memoranda* (c. 1817),[16] written after his retirement from the Presidency to record his thoughts on "religious liberty," Madison boasts that it was indeed the United States that had "the noble merit of *first* unshackling the conscience from persecuting laws, and of establishing among religious sects a legal equality." Until the "American experiment" began, the Western world had labored under the yoke of "the erroneous idea of a national religion," which had been remedied by the "separation between Religion & Govt in the Constitution of the United States."[17] America, Madison later wrote, was the first nation to reject "the prevailing opinion in Europe, England not excepted, . . . that Religion could not be preserved without the support of Government, nor Government be supported with[out] an established Religion, that there must be at least an alliance of some sort between them." Some three years before his death, the Father of the Constitution looked with satisfaction on the results of the religion clauses in operation: "the lapse of time, now more than fifty years, since *the legal support of Religion was withdrawn*, sufficiently prove[s], that it does not need the support of

15. Milbank, *Theology and Social Theory*, 9.

16. The *Detached Memoranda* were first published in 1946 in the *William and Mary Quarterly* after being found among Madison's papers by a biographer conducting research. They are unquestionably authentic, despite the desperate attempts of "conservative" commentators to suggest (without proof) that perhaps they were not written by Madison.

17. James Madison, *Detached Memoranda*, in "The Founders' Constitution," Vol. 5, Amendment I (Religion), Document 64, Univ. of Chicago e-text.

Government. And it will scarcely be contended that government has suffered by *the exemption of Religion from its cognizance, or its pecuniary aid.*"[18]

Most rank and file Americans of Madison's time (and certainly the NRA movement some forty years later) would have disagreed with Madison's suave assurance that the divorce of religion and government was a great boon to both. What is more, Madison knew this. In the *Detached Memoranda*, written twenty-five years after ratification of the First Amendment, he complained that the idea of an alliance between religion and government still had a hold on the American people: "The idea just as it related to the Jewish nation under a theocracy, having been improperly adopted by so many nations which have embraced Xnity [sic], is too apt to lurk even in the bosoms of Americans," for "a union of all to form one nation under one Govt in acts of devotion to God is an imposing idea."[19] Writing about this "imposing idea" five years later, Madison fretted that despite the shining example of Liberty found in the Constitution, some of the States had retained "a strong bias towards the old error, that without some sort of alliance or coalition between Govt & Religion neither can be duly supported...."[20] It was precisely this "bias towards the old error" the NRA movement attempted to recover (by then the state establishments of religion had already disappeared) while incoherently lauding the separation of Church and State.

What Madison and the other Framers wrought was radically different even from the remnants of the traditional pattern of Church-State relations that had existed in the colonies and persisted for some time in the new states. In his definitive study of the First Amendment's "Establishment Clause," Leonard Levy notes that as of the date of the First Amendment's ratification (1791), seven of the fourteen states (Vermont being the fourteenth) continued to maintain establishments of Protestantism or Christianity by way of earmarked tax support for the denomination of the taxpayer's choice. Before then (and up to about 1790), nine of the thirteen colonies had formal establishments of religion of one type or another: either the Anglican Church as the sole established Church of the colony (Maryland, Virginia, North Carolina, South Carolina and Georgia), the "general" establishment of Christianity, or the "multiple" establishment of the tax-supported denominations of each taxpayers' choice (New York, Massachusetts, Connecticut, and New Hampshire). Only four of the colonies (Rhode Island, Pennsylvania, Delaware and New Jersey) never had any form of established religion.[21]

Moreover, even in states without any sort of religious establishment, other legal measures supported Christianity in its various colonial forms. Hence *all but two* of the new States had precisely what the Constitution rejects: religious tests for public

---

18. Letter to Rev. Adams (1833), in Daniel L. Dreisbach, *Religion and Politics in the Early Republic: Jasper Adams and the Church-State Debate* (Lexington, KY: The Univ. Press of Kentucky, 1996), 117–121, at 120.

19. *Detached Memoranda*, loc. cit.

20. Madison to Edward Livingston, July 10, 1822, in *Writings*, Vol. IX, accessed from http://oll.libertyfund.org/title/1940/119268.

21. Levy, *The Establishment Clause*, 77.

office that disqualified atheists, agnostics and other non-Christians. Some states denied the franchise to non-Christians, prohibited court testimony by anyone "refusing to swear or affirm the existence of God," and barred atheists from holding or conveying property in trust. In general, "anyone who rejected the doctrine of the Trinity suffered civil disabilities." Profanity and blasphemy were punishable as criminal offenses *in every state*, and the observance of the Christian Sabbath was legally enforced. In short, "Christianity was regarded by state jurists as part and parcel of the law of the land."[22] And so it had been throughout the history of the Christian West.

The basic scheme predominating in the colonies, and to a great extent in most of the States even after ratification of the Constitution and the First Amendment, reflected the logical and historically unbroken recognition that revealed religion must be the lodestar of the State. And, as such, it must be protected and defended by law and made part of the juridical basis of public morality for the common good. As Levy remarks, until the Constitution's religion clauses were imposed upon the States by way of the Fourteenth Amendment and implementing Supreme Court decisions (which we will discuss further on), "the States were free . . . to erect and maintain exclusive establishments of religion,"[23] although the States, following the new order at the federal level, had abolished religious establishments by the time the NRA movement arose. That the States were *not* free to sponsor established churches once the federal judiciary imposed the pattern of the national government upon them is a well nigh conclusive demonstration that the new regime the Founders created was anything but "neutral" toward Christianity. And, as we saw in the preceding chapter, under the "gravitational" pull of the Constitution, the emergence of official hostility to Christianity at the state level was well underway before Supreme Court intervention via the Fourteenth Amendment, as the NRA's proceedings document contemporaneously.

"Articles of Peace" or Declaration of War?

What of the argument that the religion clauses are merely pragmatic "articles of peace" between the various Christian sects, made necessary by the potential for civil strife and even bloodshed were any sect to gain political power at the national level? One of the leading exponents of this position was John Courtney Murray, S.J., the liberal Catholic theologian whose work supposedly influenced the Fathers of Vatican II to endorse the "American model"—a claim that does not survive close scrutiny.[24] According to Murray, who ignored the bold declarations of the Framers already noted, the drafters of the Constitution "were not radical theorists intent on constructing society in accord with the a priori demands of a doctrinaire blueprint" but rather practical lawyers, for the most part, who were concerned only

---

22. Levy, *The Establishment Clause*, 77.
23. Ibid., 94–106.
24. The Council's document on religious liberty, *Dignitatis Humanae*, begins by insisting that the Council "leaves untouched *traditional Catholic doctrine* on the moral duty of men *and societies* toward

with crafting a legal framework "for the preservation of the public peace, under a given set of conditions." The First Amendment, said Murray, is therefore "not true dogma, but only good law,"[25] so that Catholics ought not to see any malign religious intention behind the First Amendment.

The "peace treaty" argument fails, first of all, because—as the Protestants of the NRA protested so vociferously—it does not account for the Constitution's failure to mention God or Christ even in the most generic way, or its rejection of any religious test for office, even the barest belief in God, much less in Christ or the Trinity. There would hardly have been a civil war if the Constitution, following the more or less traditional pattern in the colonies and states—who were only following the perennial pattern of Christian civilization—had invoked Christ and required that office holders at least profess a belief in His divinity. There was no armed conflict in the States that retained these remnants of Christendom for a time even after the Constitution and Bill of Rights became law. And it is worth noting, in anticipation of later discussion, that it would have been quite impossible to find in the Constitution a right to abortion or a right to "privacy" that embraces sodomy[26] had the Preamble read as suggested by the NRA movement: "We the people of the United States, humbly acknowledging Almighty God as the source of all authority and power in civil government, the Lord Jesus Christ as the Ruler among the nations, his revealed will as the supreme law of the land, in order to constitute a Christian government. . . ."

Further, the "peace treaty" argument ignores the reality that the Constitution is not merely a pragmatic religious truce hammered out in Philadelphia by devout Christian statesmen, but rather it is the embodiment of an entirely new conception of government based on the Lockean notion of sovereignty and the subordination of Christianity to secular concerns: the politics of the body under a social compact replacing the politics of the soul in a state whose existence is ordained by God and rests upon His ultimate authority. It is remarkable that the NRA, a movement of Protestants in the 19th century, recognized and deplored this fact, while Murray, a mid-20th century liberal Catholic, paid it no mind (at least in this context, although he would inconsistently recognize it elsewhere, as we shall see).

At any rate, the point is placed beyond dispute by the two "patron saints" of "religious liberty" in America, Madison and Jefferson, whose efforts were indubitably a preparation for the drafting and ratification of the First Amendment and "the

---

the true religion and toward the one Church of Christ"—that is, their duty to profess the Catholic religion once they come to know it. *Dignitatis Humanae*, Art. 1. The remainder of the document is a bewildering attempt to recognize "religious liberty" without repudiating the traditional Catholic doctrine, leaving the document plagued by what Craycraft calls an "undeniable ambiguity" that "makes it difficult to give a definitive and final understanding of the Council's intention." Craycraft, *The American Myth of Religious Freedom*, 122 (disagreeing with Murray).

25. John Courtney Murray, S.J., *We Hold These Truths*, (Kansas City: Sheed and Ward, 1960), 56–57.

26. *Lawrence v. Texas*, 539 U.S. 558 (2003) (holding that "the intimate, adult consensual conduct at issue here was part of the liberty protected by the substantive component of the Fourteenth Amendment's due process protections").

godless constitution" which it amends. While Madison protested that the Constitution is not "the off-spring of a single brain," namely his, but rather "the work of many heads and many hands" (including Morris and Hamilton),[27] there is no doubt that the thought of Locke, Madison's "master,"[28] guided the genesis of the First Amendment, which is based on Madison's initial draft.[29] And there can be no denying that Madison is "the single most significant Founder, at least in terms of his writings. . . ."[30]

Perhaps the most important of those writings is the *Memorial and Remonstrance* (1785), which Madison wrote in support of his joint campaign with Jefferson to disestablish Christianity in Virginia. In this document "the Father of the Constitution" follows Locke in advancing the idea that religion "must be left to the conviction and conscience of every man; and it is the right of every man to exercise it as these may dictate. This right is in its nature an unalienable right. It is unalienable, because the opinions of men, *depending only on the evidence contemplated by their own minds* cannot follow the dictates of other men. . . ."[31] To modern ears, Madison's talk of an "unalienable" right to profess whatever religion one finds acceptable sounds like the received wisdom of the ages. But the claim that there is a natural right to profess any religion of choice, no matter what it teaches and no matter how its spread might affect the Christian beliefs and morality of other people, was a radical break even from the Protestant conception of Christendom as seen in the colonies.

In *Memorial and Remonstrance*, Madison defends one of the newly discovered Lockean "natural rights" proclaimed by the Founders: "the sacred principle of religious liberty," as he calls it in the *Detached Memoranda*. This right joins Locke's other natural rights novelties: the right to government by "consent" of the governed, the right to government by majority rule instead of hereditary monarchy, the right not to be taxed without "representation," and the right to engage in revolution against any government that violates the vaguely defined "trust" placed in it by "the people." The Madisonian right to "religious liberty" reduces religion, just as Locke did, to a rational sifting of persuasive evidence by autonomous individuals—"the evidence contemplated by their own minds," as the *Memorial* states. Religion so defined is not the product of the influence of divine grace upon the human will and the consequent assent of faith to a proposition based on the authority of the One revealing it, but rather it is an exercise in self-persuasion by the supremely

27. Madison to William Cogswell, March 10, 1834, in Max Farrand, ed., *The Records of the Federal Convention of 1787* (RFC) (New Haven, Conn., 1937), 3:533.

28. Leonard Levy, *The Establishment Clause*, 129.

29. Ibid., 96. That draft read as follows: "The civil rights of none shall be abridged on account of religious belief or worship, nor shall any national religion be established, nor shall the full and equal rights of conscience be in any manner, or on any pretext, infringed." 1 *Annals of Congress* 452.

30. Paul J. Weber, "James Madison and Religious Equality: The Perfect Separation," *The Review of Politics*, Vol. 44, No. 2 (April 1982), 163. This author attempts to demonstrate that by "perfect separation" between government and religion Madison meant something other than "absolute" separation, but the argument reduces to semantic quibbling over what "absolute" means.

31. Madison, *Memorial and Remonstrance on the Religious Rights of Man* (Univ. of Chicago: e-text), 1.

authoritative individual conscience in the exercise of reason alone. Hence Madisonian religion, like Lockean religion, cannot be subject to the authority of any man or indeed *any Church*.[32] Madison, just as Locke did—and this, after all, is the Protestant principle—makes every man a pope and every church a mere voluntary association of popes each of whom reserves the right literally to found his own religion should it please him to do so. This is the essence of "religious liberty" in the Lockean-Madisonian sense, and it is thus the *theological* basis for all of Madison's work regarding the First Amendment.

Likewise, Jefferson, in his *Notes on the State of Virginia* and in the text of his Virginia Statute for Religious Freedom, protesting the religious test for office and other elements of established religion in Virginia, declared that the right to "religious liberty" precludes any action by civil authority to defend religious truth or to restrain the spread of religious error: "[T]o suffer the civil magistrate to intrude his powers into the field of opinion and to restrain the profession or propagation of principles, on the supposition of their ill tendency, is a dangerous fallacy, which at once destroys all religious liberty, because he being of course judge of that tendency, will make his opinions the rule of judgment. . . ." Hence, Jefferson concluded: "our rulers can have no authority over such natural rights, only as we have submitted to them.—The rights of conscience we never submitted, we could not submit. . . ."[33]

Thus, for Jefferson and Madison, as for Locke, there is a natural right to religious liberty, i.e., a right whose object is the private and public profession of any religion whatsoever. And this right exists *because* religion is merely a matter of opinion, with the magistrate's opinion being no more trustworthy than anyone else's. This is so even if the magistrate is guided by the teaching of the established church, because the teaching of any church is equally a matter of opinion. To recall Locke's argument in the *Letter Concerning Toleration*: "Yet, nevertheless, you bid me be of good courage and tell me that all is now safe and secure, because the magistrate does not now enjoin the observance of his own decrees in matters of religion, but only the decrees of the Church. *Of what Church, I beseech you?* Of that, certainly, which likes him best. . . ." That is, the right to "religious liberty" in the Madisonian and Jeffersonian sense depends upon a Lockean relativization of the truth claims of Christianity.

Locke's *Letter Concerning Toleration* was published anonymously because Locke knew the outrage his argument for indifferent toleration of all religions (except Catholicism, of course) would provoke. But a hundred years later, with Locke's notion still unrealized in any existing polity, Madison and Jefferson had no hesitancy in proclaiming the new "sacred principle of religious liberty." The "sacred principle" of the supposed right to profess and spread abroad any religion depends upon Madison's and Jefferson's theological conclusion, inherited from Locke, that there is neither one true religion to inform the life of the State nor one true Church

---

32. Cf. Craycraft, *American Myth of Religious Liberty*, 73–78 for an excellent treatment of this aspect of Madison's thought, to which this author is indebted.

33. *Virginia Statute for Religious Freedom*; *Notes on the State of Virginia*, 192 (Waldstreicher ed.).

with which the State should ally itself for the protection and promotion of religious truth. For if there *were* such a religion and such a church, neither Madison nor Jefferson could logically justify the indifferent toleration of religious error. Locke himself recognized in the *Letter* that if there were many ways to salvation, "there would not be so much as a pretence left for compulsion" regarding the spread of religious error, since there would not be any such thing as a heresy with eternal consequences.

Madison and Jefferson, following Locke, eliminate the "pretence" for compulsion by declaring that no religion or church can claim to hold the key to eternal salvation, or even temporal well being, so that the State has no obligation to heed and defend the teaching of any particular religion or church for the common good. In the Madisonian-Jeffersonian view of religion, which is the Lockean view, heresy is not "injurious" to anyone but merely harmless opinion belonging to the Lockean category of "things indifferent," as we saw in both the *Essay* and *Letter* on toleration. As Jefferson famously declared: "But it does me no injury for my neighbor to say there are twenty gods or no God. It neither picks my pocket nor breaks my leg."[34] Hence, he opines: "The legitimate powers of government extend to such acts only as are injurious to others,"[35] meaning only physical or other purely material injury. This "non-aggression principle" is the foundation of contemporary libertarianism, which demands a rigorous application of the principle to permit literally any conduct that does not involve the physical invasion of another's person or property. Like Locke before them, Madison and Jefferson alike reject the principle that the State has any duty to assist the Church in protecting souls against the consequences of the spread of religious error. As practitioners of the new Lockean politics of the body, for them (as for Locke), *there is no such thing* as religious error—or rather, no such thing as *harmful* religious error, as they both certainly considered orthodox Christianity, especially Catholicism, to be replete with errors against reason.

Therefore, for Madison and Jefferson (as for Locke) any attempt by civil authority to promote and protect religious orthodoxy is, as Jefferson said apropos the then prevailing law of Virginia, "religious slavery."[36] Pilate's mocking question to Christ—"What is truth?"—thus becomes the foundation of an entirely new conception of religious freedom, which is no longer the freedom of the true religion to propagate itself and be reflected in the laws and institutions of the people who profess it. As the NRA saw quite clearly, under the "religiously neutral" regime the Framers erected, "We the People" would no longer have the religious freedom to constitute themselves a Christian commonwealth. The result is that in return for its "liberty," religion, being nothing more than a matter of fallible opinion, must relinquish any right to influence the political process, just as required by Locke's Law of Toleration. Moreover, every religion must preach and teach the dogma of toleration if it wishes to be tolerated by government. To recall Locke's prescription, all

---

34. Ibid.
35. Ibid.
36. Ibid.

churches are "obliged to lay down toleration as the foundation of their own liberty, and teach that liberty of conscience is every man's natural right, equally belonging to dissenters as to themselves. . . ."[37] In this way, as Locke confidently predicted, "there would remain nothing in these assemblies that were not more peaceable and less apt to produce disturbance of state. . . ."[38]

In sum, "religious liberty" means the neutralization of religion in the public square and thus the impotence of religion before the power of the State. Precisely as the NRA protested, under the First Amendment regime, which is the Law of Toleration in practice, religion is to be separated strictly from the State according to the "sacred principle" Madison and Jefferson have discovered. As Madison puts it: "A perfect separation between ecclesiastical and civil matters" is the best course, for "religion and Government will both exist in greater purity, the less they are mixed together."[39] For Madison (as for Locke) the "purity" of religion depends upon the refusal of civil authority to defend any particular religious truth by means of legal sanctions, whereas the "purity" of government requires its divorce from religion. To recall the testimony of NRA leader J. H. McIlvaine, however, the proponents of Madison's view "do not inform us what is to preserve the purity of government after it has been sequestered from religion. . . ." The answer, as history demonstrates, is that nothing will.

With these considerations in view, it is clear that Madison and Jefferson, under the guise of religious neutrality, were arguing for the imposition of a new *theology* of the State in preference to the old one involving some form of Church-State alliance. Further, this new theology of the state required the divorce of government not only from any established church, which was radical enough, but from *any form of religion*. Hence in the *Memorial and Remonstrance* Madison opposed as "a dangerous abuse of power" a proposed bill in the Virginia legislature, sponsored by Patrick Henry, to "make provision for teachers of the Christian religion" and to provide a general assessment for the support of the Christian denomination of each taxpayer's choice. Madison vigorously opposed the measure even though, as Levy points out, it declared "that all Christian sects and denominations were equal before the law, none preferred over others" and recited a purely secular motive of "the furtherance of public peace and morality rather than Christ's kingdom on earth or the encouragement of religion."[40] Madison's position is patently irreconcilable with Murray's argument that the First Amendment involves nothing more than pragmatic "articles of peace" between Christian denominations, *for that is exactly what Henry's proposal was.* Madison, rather, was issuing a veiled declaration of war on religion in its traditional alliance with the State. To do this, he needed to advance theologically founded arguments about the nature of religion and its proper place in political society.

37. *Letter*, 51 (Tully edition).
38. Ibid.
39. Madison to Edward Livingston, July 10, 1822, in *The Writings of James Madison*, ed. G. Hunt (NY: G. P. Putnam's Sons, 1900–1910), 9:98–103, at 102.
40. Levy, *The Establishment Clause*, 62.

Woven into Madison's appeal to freedom of conscience and his prudent Lockean nod to religion as "the duty which we owe to our Creator" is the real message of the *Memorial*: that the establishment of Christianity in any way, shape or form as the religion of the State is tyranny *per se*, and that Western man must finally end this age-old tyranny:

> [E]xperience witnesseth that ecclesiastical establishments, instead of maintaining the purity and efficacy of religion, have had a contrary operation. *During almost fifteen centuries has the legal establishment of Christianity been on trial.* What have been its fruits? More or less, in all places, pride and indolence in the clergy; ignorance and servility in the laity; in both, *superstition, bigotry, and persecution....*
>
> What influences, in fact, have ecclesiastical establishments had on civil society? In some instances they have been seen to erect a spiritual tyranny on the ruins of civil authority; in many instances they have been seen upholding the thrones of political tyranny; *in no instance have they been seen the guardians of the liberties of the People.*[41]

Like any respectable deist of the American Enlightenment, Madison saw nothing but slavery and superstition in the ecclesiocentric social order of Christendom, instead of the great hierarchy of values "the *philosophes* could not understand ... and refused to make any attempt to understand...."[42] Having glibly equated any sort of established Christianity with tyranny, Madison, with a magisterial wave of his pen, dismisses the fifteen centuries of Christendom as *contrary* to Christianity:

> [T]he establishment proposed by the Bill is not requisite for the support of the Christian Religion. To say that it is, *is a contradiction to the Christian Religion itself,* for every page of it disavows a dependence on the powers of this world: *it is a contradiction to fact; for it is known that this Religion both existed and flourished, not only without the support of human laws,* but in spite of every opposition from them, and not only during the period of miraculous aid, but long after it had been left to its own evidence and the ordinary care of Providence. *Nay, it is a contradiction in terms; for a Religion not invented by human policy, must have pre-existed and been supported, before it was established by human policy....*[43]

The argument that the State contradicts Christianity by legally supporting it is nothing short of sophistry, wherein Madison resorts to a blatant *non sequitur* in drawing the conclusion that merely because Christianity has at times been "without the support of human laws" it ought never to enjoy such support. What is really at work here, however, is not a logical argument but an *a priori* theological judgment about the nature of religion. Just as Locke does, Madison the theologian purports to instruct mankind on what Christianity requires of Church-State relations, even as he argues that the State must take no position in matters religious.

41. *Memorial and Remonstrance*, nn. 7–8.
42. Peter Gay, *The Enlightenment: The Rise of Modern Paganism*, 236.
43. *Memorial and Remonstrance*, n. 6.

Based on the theological premise that state support of Christianity is "a contradiction to the Christian Religion itself," Madison arrives at his theologically premised conclusion: "We maintain therefore that in matters of Religion, no man's right is abridged by the institution of Civil Society and that Religion is wholly exempt from its cognizance." But on what ground does Madison stand to overrule the contrary belief of Christians such as Patrick Henry (not to mention Catholics throughout the history of the West), who hold that civil society *must* take cognizance of religion by professing, defending and protecting it for the common good? (As we saw in the previous chapter, this was the very program of the Protestant-led NRA movement less than thirty years after Madison's death.) The ground on which Madison stands is *Madison's religion.* Like Locke, Madison advocates a kind of confessional state that pretends to be religiously neutral even as it imposes a particular reading of Christianity on the body politic. Craycraft suggests that Madison's argument, like Locke's, involves something subtler than a mere self-contradiction. Since Madison was no fool, Craycraft surmises that Madison must have been employing irony by appealing to Christianity to justify a political regime that divorces itself from Christianity. Perhaps irony would explain why a man of superior intellect would seriously argue that Christianity forbids the State to be Christian. Or perhaps Craycraft is being too kind to Madison. Perhaps Madison, the slave-owner who complained of religious "slavery," was simply a sophist.

On the question of "religious liberty," Thomas Jefferson was no less the dogmatic theologian than Madison. His Virginia Statute, whose enactment in 1786 finally disestablished the Christian religion in Virginia, is another theologically premised foundational document in the historical movement to divorce government from religion, and is even more important than Madison's *Memorial.* Jefferson proposed his statute in opposition to a General Assessment bill which, among other things, declared that Christianity was the "established religion" of Virginia and provided for a tax assessment under which taxpayers could designate the Christian church of their choice to receive the tax assessed. The General Assessment was followed by Patrick Henry's more secularized bill along the same lines.

In the Virginia Statute, Jefferson issues this dogmatic definition as a veritable pontiff of Liberty: "Almighty God hath created the mind free; that all attempts to influence it by temporal punishment, or burthens, or by civil incapacitations, tend only to beget habits of hypocrisy and meanness, and are a departure from *the plan of the Holy Author of our religion.*"[44] Thus Jefferson, no less than Madison—and both of them no less than Locke—claimed to know the will of God on the proper relation between religion and the State. And by adopting Jefferson's statute, the Virginia legislature, paving the way for ratification of the First Amendment, likewise declared that it was God's will to disestablish the Christian religion—by means of the very law that declares that the State must not impose "civil incapacitations" on

---

44. *The Virginia Statute for Religious Freedom* (1786), Univ. of Virginia e-text, www.lva.lib.va.us/whatwedo/k12/bor/vsrftext.htm.

Christianity! The Virginia Statute's "principles and language have inspired support-ers of religious freedom around the world,"[45] including Madison, who clearly had something more in mind for the First Amendment than legalistic "articles of peace" with no doctrinal import.

Like Madison, Jefferson was animated by a dogmatic certitude concerning what constitutes acceptable religion. Thus the Virginia Statute denounces "the impious presumption of legislators and rulers, civil as well as ecclesiastical, who being them-selves but fallible and uninspired men ... hath established and maintained *false reli-gions* over the greatest part of the world, and through all time."[46] By "false religions" Jefferson meant Roman Catholicism and other variants of Trinitarian Christianity, which he regarded as "a counter-religion made up of the deliria of crazy imagina-tions" that teaches there are "three gods" and has corrupted "the simple doctrines of Jesus...."[47] Not for Jefferson the theologian were the "metaphysical insanities of Athanasius, of Loyola, and of Calvin," which he regarded as "mere lapses into poly-theism, differing from paganism only by being more unintelligible."[48] Jesus, accord-ing to him, had taught only a "benevolent morality" which had been corrupted by "artificial systems, invented by ultra-Christian sects (the immaculate conception of Jesus [sic], his deification, the creation of the world by him, his miraculous powers, his resurrection and visible ascension, his corporeal presence in the Eucharist, the Trinity; original sin, atonement, regeneration, election, orders of the Hierarchy, etc.)...."[49] The day will come, he confided to John Adams, "when the mystical gen-eration of Jesus, by the Supreme Being as his father, in the womb of a virgin, will be classed with the fable of the generation of Minerva in the brain of Jupiter."[50]

In short, Jefferson was a foe of revealed religion as such, who envisioned a polit-ical regime the very structure of which would tend toward the extirpation of what he considered religious superstitions from the body politic. University of Virginia historian William L. Miller notes that Jefferson, the very man "who shaped the phrases and formed the ideas that gave the nation its soul, looked upon the old religions of mysteries, creeds, and emotion-charged symbols, the 'shackles' on the human mind of 'revealed' religion, as an impediment—perhaps the most impor-tant impediment—to the truths on which rested his new nation with all its hope for the world."[51] But Jefferson rejoiced "that in this blessed country of free inquiry and belief, which has surrendered its creed and conscience to neither kings nor priests, the genuine doctrine of one only God is reviving, and I trust that there is

45. "Religious Freedom Day," https://www.rutherford.org/publications_resources/legal_features/Religious_Freedom_Day.

46. *Virginia Statute,* loc. cit.

47. Jefferson to Dr. Benjamin Waterhouse, Monticello, June 26, 1822, in *Memoirs, Correspondence and Miscellanies from the Papers of Thomas Jefferson,* ed. Thomas Jefferson Randolph (Charlottesville, VA: F. Carr and Co., 1829), Vol. III, 349.

48. Jefferson to Jared Sparks, November 4, 1820.

49. Jefferson to W. Short, October 31, 1819.

50. Jefferson to Adams, April 11, 1823.

51. William Lee Miller, *The First Liberty: Religion and the American Republic* (NY: Knopf, 1987), in Craycraft, *American Myth of Religious Freedom,* 88.

not a young man now living in the United States who will not die an Unitarian." Jefferson, then, saw himself as an evangelist of true religion, and his Virginia Statute as part of the process by which, to recall his earlier quoted words, newly enlightened men would "burst the chains, under which monkish ignorance and superstition had persuaded them to bind themselves. . . ."[52]

The *Memorial and Remonstrance* and the Virginia Statute are, as the constitutional scholar Leo Pfeffer concludes, "a historic basis for the adoption, five years later, of an amendment to the Constitution that opens with the words 'Congress shall make no law respecting an establishment of religion or prohibiting the free exercise thereof.'"[53] Here, however, one cannot overlook the Virginia Declaration of Rights (1776), drafted by George Mason, who is considered to be another of the fathers of the First Amendment. The Virginia Declaration, which later became part of the Virginia Constitution, influenced the political theology of both Madison and Jefferson. With clear echoes of Locke's Law of Toleration, the Virginia Declaration delivers the stern homiletic advice, which appears in the Virginia Constitution to this day, "that it is the mutual duty of all to practice Christian forbearance, love, and charity towards each other," from which it follows that "all men are equally entitled to the free exercise of religion."[54] And what of those who, standing with the Western tradition on the right and duty of the State to defend revealed truth, do *not* believe that all men are *equally* entitled to the free exercise of religion, but rather that true charity itself requires that religions that teach heresy or promote immoral conduct not be allowed to spread their errors to the temporal and eternal detriment of orthodox Christian believers? Mason, like Jefferson and Madison, prejudged the theological question by declaring Locke's Law of Toleration to be a divinely imposed duty without exception.

Madison's *Memorial and Remonstrance*, Jefferson's Virginia Statute, and Mason's Virginia Declaration are rife with theological judgments foundational to the adoption of the First Amendment. It is thus impossible to maintain convincingly, as Murray and the other proponents of his position attempt to do, that the First Amendment does not involve "true dogma, but only good law."[55] Like the documents that were its precursors, the First Amendment (combined with Article III, clause 6) rests upon the Lockean dogmatic teaching that no religion has the right to be the religion of the State or the State's moral preceptor, no matter how preponderant that religion may be among "We the People," no matter what authority or mission God may have given it, no matter what the truth and glory of its teaching, no matter how important that teaching may be for public morality, justice, and the temporal and eternal welfare of humanity.

52. Jefferson to Waterhouse, June 26, 1822, in *The Writings of Thomas Jefferson* (Jefferson Memorial Association), 384–385; Jefferson to Roger Weightman, June 24, 1826, in Library of Congress digital collection, www.loc.gov/exhibits/jefferson/214.html.

53. Leo Pfeffer, "Madison's 'Detached Memoranda': Then and Now," *The Virginia Statute for Religious Freedom*, 285; in Craycraft, *American Myth of Religious Freedom*, 73.

54. *The Virginia Declaration of Rights*, Art. 16; Constitution of Virginia, Art. I, §16.

55. Murray, *We Hold These Truths*, 56–57.

The Constitution's religion clauses are not, therefore, mere "articles of peace" among Christians, but they are rather a definitive legal embodiment of the Lockean theological premises we examined in Chapter 3. Hence even if by some miracle America awoke to find that every one of its citizens had become Catholic overnight, the Constitution would forbid any special recognition or support of the Catholic Church by the federal government, even as part of a general or "multiple" establishment of Christianity along the lines of state law prior to the Fourteenth Amendment. This legal reality is precisely what the NRA attempted unsuccessfully to alter with its proposed Christian Amendment to the Constitution, without which not only the national government but also the state governments and all local governments, indeed the entire juridical structure of America, would become, as Tayler Lewis warned, "a pure, unbelieving, irreligious, Christless, Godless blank."

The time has come to recognize what was patently evident to the NRA movement, to recall its citation to the editorial in the New York *Independent*: that "the Constitution has nothing to do with religion except as a barrier between it and the State." Craycraft stands on the evidence of history and a mountain of respectable scholarship when he concludes that in the thought of Jefferson and Madison we see that the intent behind the First Amendment "was not the expansion of religious liberty, *but the protection of the state from religious influence*."[56] That much ought to be obvious even without the aid of scholarly analysis, since Madison and Jefferson could not have been clearer in their intent, and their role in the creation of the American regime of "religious liberty" was indubitably decisive.

The "Non-Preferentialism" Fiction

Contrary to the evidence we have just reviewed, however, certain "conservative" defenders of Liberty have maintained that the words "*no* religious test" and "Congress shall make *no* law respecting an establishment of religion" can at least be read "narrowly" to permit "non-preferential" government support of "religion in general." First of all, not even the staunchest "conservative" defenders of the Founders' Lockean novelty today would argue that the First Amendment permits "non-preferential" support of *Christianity* in general to the exclusion of non-Christian religions. And they would view with horror the demand of the NRA movement for a Christian Amendment to the Constitution. Thus, even if the "non-preferentialist" reading were correct, it fails to support the golden legend of the Christian foundations of the American republic, which the NRA movement and other perceptive Christians (including Orestes Brownson) could see were non-existent.

That problem aside, the "non-preferentialist" interpretation is nonsensical because the Bill of Rights, including the First Amendment, is supposed to be a *limitation* on federal power, not a grant of additional legislative authority to Congress to prefer religion. As Levy states: "To argue . . . that the amendment permits congressional aid and support to religion in general or to all denominations without

56. Craycraft, *American Myth of Religious Freedom*, 18.

discrimination leads to the impossible conclusion that the First Amendment added to Congress's power. Nothing supports such a conclusion. Every bit of evidence goes to prove that the First Amendment, like the others, was intended *to restrict Congress to its enumerated powers.*"[57] Levy's point is not logically disputable by the same "conservatives" who insist on the limitation of federal power to what is enumerated in the Constitution's unamended text, which confers no power on Congress to aid religion in any way and fails even to mention God. If *"no religious test"* for office, *"no law respecting an establishment of religion,"* and no mention of God or His law anywhere in the Constitution do not mean that Congress has no power to prefer, aid or defend religion in general—non-preferentially or otherwise—then words have lost their meaning.

Not to the contrary are such customary historic practices as war-related presidential calls for fasting and thanksgiving (a custom long since abandoned), the early use of government buildings for Protestant services attended by certain Congressmen (another abandoned custom), congressional chaplains, military chaplains, the invocation "God save the United States and this honorable Court" at the beginning of Supreme Court sessions, oaths on the Bible, and (much more recently) the motto "In God We Trust" on currency, none of which, in any event, even remotely establish Christianity as the religion of the Republic. Historical customs of this kind are not *authorized* by the First Amendment but rather were viewed even by Madison and Jefferson as (barely) tolerable *de minimis* transgressions of the principle of Church-State separation according to "the sacred principle of religious liberty," Madison himself having grudgingly proclaimed days of fast and thanksgiving as President during the War of 1812. In the *Detached Memoranda*, however, Madison maintains that "in strictness" neither the presidential proclamations nor the congressional chaplains could be justified under the amendment as written, since "they seem to imply and nourish the erroneous idea of a national religion."[58] Moreover, when viewed under the aspect of the churchless, non-sectarian civil religion that has indeed developed in America since the Revolution (to be discussed in Chapter 21), these apparent breaches of Church-State separation are actually quite consistent with the First Amendment's ban on any form of "established" Christianity.

The presidency of Thomas Jefferson provides a telling historical example of why reliance on such customs to support a "non-preferentialist" reading of the Establishment Clause is unavailing—putting aside, once again, the fact that these customs do nothing to create the Christian polity of legend. As the NRA noted, Jefferson notoriously refused to proclaim national days of fasting and thanksgiving (a strictly non-sectarian custom George Washington had followed) precisely because he saw them as barred by the First Amendment. Yet, on January 3, 1802, Jefferson, clearly in order to rebut Federalist charges that he was an atheist, conspicuously attended a church service conducted in the Hall of the House of Representa-

57. Levy, *The Establishment Clause*, 105.
58. *Detached Memoranda*, loc. cit.

tives by the Baptist preacher John Leland as part of festivities that included Leland's presentation to the President of a 1000-lb. "Mammoth Cheese" stamped with the motto: "Rebellion to Tyrants is Obedience to God."[59] Jefferson's participation in the service was "contrary to all former practice," as one Federalist critic noted, but the resulting publicity "offset the negative impressions created by his [Jefferson's] refusal to issue religious proclamations. . . ."[60]

Jefferson's behavior, like that of his Federalist critics, only demonstrates that then, even more so than today, it behooved a politician to make a show of "my faith" for the sake of public opinion while nonetheless insisting upon the strictest possible separation of Church and State. Moreover, the very minister whose service Jefferson attended was a fulminating advocate of Church-State separation. Leland, whose stump preaching had influenced Madison,[61] rejected the very idea that America is a Christian nation and condemned the various State establishments of Christianity as artifacts of the Antichrist, calling them "Anti-Christocracies."[62] He had nothing but praise, however, for the Constitution, "which certainly had the advantage of any of the state constitutions," because it "forbids Congress ever to establish *any* kind of religion, or require *any* religious test to qualify *any* officer in *any* department of federal government. Let a man be Pagan, Turk, Jew or Christian, he is eligible to any post in that government." [63] This state of affairs is precisely what had given rise to the NRA movement and its prophecies of the moral collapse of America on account of the national government's practical atheism.

Despite his token appearance at Leland's service, it was none other than Jefferson who, only two days before, had sent off his famous Letter to the Danbury Baptists, commiserating with them about the need for Church-State separation in Connecticut and praising the Constitution for effecting a "wall of separation" in the national government:

> Believing with you that religion is a matter which lies solely between Man & his God, that he owes account to none other for his faith or his worship, that the legitimate powers of government reach actions only, & not opinions, I contemplate with sovereign reverence that act of the whole American people which declared that their legislature should "make no law respecting an establishment of religion, or prohibiting the free exercise thereof," thus building *a wall of separation between Church & State.*[64]

59. Hatch, *The Democratization of American Christianity*, 96.

60. James H. Hutson, "Thomas Jefferson's Letter to the Danbury Baptists: A Controversy Rejoined," *The William and Mary Quarterly* 3d, Vol. 56, No. 4 (October 1999), 785.

61. See Levy, *The Establishment Clause*, 136.

62. Ibid.

63. *The Writings of the Elder John Leland*, ed. L. F. Greene (NY: G. W. Wood, 1845), 191.

64. Jefferson to Nehemiah Dodge, Ephraim Robbins, & Stephen S. Nelson, a committee of the Danbury Baptist association in the State of Connecticut, January 1, 1802, Library of Congress e-text, loc.gov/loc/lcib/9806/danpre.html.

The proponents of "non-preferentialism" have labored without success to demonstrate that the "wall of separation" letter has been misunderstood, but it says what it says.[65] And Jefferson's letter, along with Madison's *Memorial and Remonstrance*, found its way into the Supreme Court's 1878 decision in *Reynolds v. United States*, handed down only four years after the NRA's 1874 convention. Citing the "wall of separation" metaphor "almost as an authoritative declaration of the scope and effect of the [First] amendment," given that it came from Jefferson, the Court upheld the federal statute prohibiting Mormon polygamy in the territories not on religious grounds, *which the Court noted would be forbidden by the Constitution*, but rather strictly on the grounds that the criminal law may reach conduct "in violation of social duties or subversive of good order."[66]

Early on, then, the Supreme Court took the Madisonian-Jeffersonian view of the First Amendment, and that view ultimately determined a long line of Supreme Court decisions applying the Establishment Clause to the States via the Fourteenth Amendment. The line began with *Cantwell v. Connecticut,* wherein the Court observed matter-of-factly: "The First Amendment declares that Congress shall make no law respecting an establishment of religion or prohibiting the free exercise thereof. The Fourteenth Amendment has rendered the legislatures of the States *as incompetent as Congress* to enact such laws."[67] That is precisely the outcome predicted by the NRA, even before the "incorporation doctrine" later enunciated in *Gitlow v. New York* (1925).

Seven years after *Cantwell,* in *Everson v. Board of Education,* the Court made its passing remark in *Cantwell* the foundation of its Establishment Clause jurisprudence. In *Everson,* the Court upheld—just barely, by a vote of 5-to-4—the use of tax dollars by a New Jersey township to reimburse the transportation costs of parents who sent their children to private schools, but only because the measure benefited private schools in general and religious schools only incidentally. The Court's rationale was drawn directly from the thought of Madison and Jefferson as seen in the *Memorial* and the Virginia Statute. The Court cited both documents as foundational to the American movement, centered in Virginia, to enshrine the legal principle that "individual religious liberty could be achieved best under a government which *was stripped of all power* to tax, to *support*, or *otherwise to assist* any or all religions. . . ."[68] The Court then observed that "the provisions of the First Amendment, in the drafting and adoption of which Madison and Jefferson played such

---

65. Jefferson's metaphor appears to have originated with Roger Williams, the radically non-conformist Protestant theologian whose notion of "soul-liberty" is also considered foundational to the Constitution's religion clauses: "When they [the Church] have opened a gap in the hedge or wall of separation between the garden of the church and the wilderness of the world, God hath ever broke down the wall itself, removed the Candlestick, etc., and made His Garden a wilderness as it is this day. . . ." Roger Williams, "Mr. Cotton's Letter Lately Printed, Examined and Answered," *The Complete Writings of Roger Williams*, Vol. 1, 108 (1644).

66. *Reynolds v. United States*, 98 U.S. 145, 164 (1878).

67. *Cantwell v. Connecticut*, 310 U.S. 296, 303 (1940).

68. *Everson v. Board of Education*, 330 U.S. 1, 11 (1947).

leading roles, had *the same objective* and were intended to provide *the same protection* against governmental intrusion on religious liberty as the Virginia statute."[69]

The Court further noted that while, "[p]rior to the adoption of the Fourteenth Amendment, the First Amendment did not apply as a restraint against the States," nevertheless most states "did soon provide similar constitutional protections for religious liberty." That is, the States—again, even without the *Gitlow* incorporation doctrine—had conformed themselves to the Constitution as the national charter, just as the NRA had warned they were doing. Yet, just as Madison had lamented in the *Detached Memoranda*, the *Everson* court noted that "some states persisted for about half a century in imposing restraints upon the free exercise of religion and in discriminating against particular religious groups." That is, "some states" were persisting in what Madison called the "old error" of "some sort of alliance or coalition between Govt & Religion." Having noted the happy passing of this deplorable situation, however, the *Everson* Court enunciated a reading of the Establishment Clause that made Jefferson's "wall of separation" the law of the land:

> The "establishment of religion" clause of the First Amendment means at least this: Neither a state nor the Federal Government can set up a church. Neither can pass laws which *aid one religion, aid all religions, or prefer one religion over another. . . .* No person can be punished for entertaining or professing religious beliefs or disbeliefs, for church attendance or non-attendance. No tax in any amount, large or small, can be levied to support *any religious activities or institutions, whatever they may be called, or whatever form they may adopt to teach or practice religion.* Neither a state nor the Federal Government can, openly or secretly, *participate in the affairs of any religious organizations or groups and vice versa.* In the words of Jefferson, the clause against establishment of religion by law was intended to erect "*a wall of separation between Church and State.*"[70]

In case after case the Supreme Court has construed the "wall of separation" as requiring it to strike down even the most minimal intrusion, or imagined intrusion, of religion into the functions of state governments no less than the federal government, including state laws requiring profession of a belief in God for the holders of public office (the last remnant of the state establishments of Christianity),[71] the reading of the Bible[72] and the posting of the Ten Commandments in public school classrooms[73] or in courthouses,[74] state reimbursement to parents for the cost of educating their children in secular subjects at Catholic schools,[75] the

---

69. Recall that Jefferson was in Paris during the Constitutional Convention. The Court's reference to Jefferson's leading role in the drafting of the Amendment pertains primarily to the influence of the Virginia Statute.

70. *Everson*, 330 U.S. at 16.

71. *Torcaso v. Watkins*, 367 U.S. 488 (1961).

72. *Abington Township School District v. Schemp*, 374 U.S. 203 (1963).

73. *Stone v. Graham*, 449 U.S. 39 (1980).

74. *McCreary County, Ky. v. American Civil Liberties Union of Ky.*, 545 U.S. 844 (2005).

75. *Lemon v. Kurtzman*, 403 U.S. 602 (1971).

assignment of public school teachers to provide "special education" services to parochial school students,[76] a state statute requiring the balanced teaching of evolution and creation science in the public schools,[77] partial tuition reimbursements for parents with students in parochial schools,[78] a non-denominational invocation at a public school commencement exercise,[79] and even a moment of silence in public school classrooms as required by the laws of twenty-five states, merely because such laws "could effectively favor the child who prays over the child who does not."[80]

What of the customs already mentioned—executive calls for days of thanksgiving, military chaplains, legislative chaplains, and so forth? As Levy observes, the Supreme Court has had "enough cunning to avoid rendering judgments in such cases" and has exercised a "prudent abstention" from challenges to any of these customs, except for that of legislative chaplains.[81] As to the chaplains, the Court upheld the practice only because it is "deeply embedded in the history and tradition of this country," "has coexisted with the principles of disestablishment and religious freedom," involves generic invocations of the deity which, as the Founders believed, "harmonize[d] with the tenets of some or all religions," and therefore is "a tolerable acknowledgment of beliefs widely held among the people of this country."[82] That is, since the practice does not lead to any *particular* religious truth determining law or public policy, much less the dreaded Christianity, a ceremonial chaplain does not threaten any material breach of the Jeffersonian "wall of separation."

Those who argue that these holdover religious customs of the early Republic evince the "meaning" of the First Amendment engage in a form of constitutional analysis relying on "bad history," which assumes that "the Founders thought in constitutional terms in all of their actions" and "allows for no inconsistencies between politically popular policies and overarching constitutional principles."[83] As the NRA movement had recognized, the text of the First Amendment had an objective signification that would, if only by its "gravitational" pull on the States, put an end to holdover customs at all levels of government. Indeed, Noah Webster happily predicted as early as 1787 that "The time will come (and may the day be near!) when all test laws, oaths of allegiance, abjuration, and partial exclusions from civil office, will be proscribed in this land of freedom."[84] The Jeffersonian "wall of separation" was laid down in principle in 1789, and it was only a matter of time before practice caught up with principle.

76. *Grand Rapids School District v. Ball*, 473 U.S. 373 (1985); *Aguilar v. Felton*, 473 U.S. 402 (1985).
77. *Edwards v. Aguillard*, 482 U.S. 578 (1987).
78. *Committee for Public Education and Religious Liberty v. Regan*, 413 U.S. 756 (1973).
79. *Lee v. Weisman*, 505 U.S. 577 (1992).
80. *Wallace v. Jaffree*, 472 U.S. 38, 73 (1985).
81. Levy, *Establishment Clause*, 154.
82. *Marsh v. Chambers*, 463 U.S. 783, 786, 792 (1983).
83. Green, "Understanding the 'Christian Nation' Myth," 245 *Cardozo Law Review* at 255.
84. Noah Webster, "On Test Laws, Oaths of Allegiance, Abjuration, and Partial Exclusions from Office" (Mar. 1787), in 4 *The Founders' Constitution* 636 (Philip B. Kurland & Ralph Lerner, eds 1987), cited in Green, op. cit.

In *Wallace v. Jaffree,* the decision that banned even a moment of silence in public school classrooms, the late Justice Rehnquist, dissenting, complained that the Supreme Court's Establishment Clause jurisprudence has "been expressly freighted with Jefferson's misleading metaphor for nearly 40 years." But Rehnquist failed to demonstrate that Jefferson did not mean what he said about the wall of separation between Church and State in the letter that Rehnquist dismissed, quite in vain, as a "short note of courtesy...." Rehnquist was forced to admit that President Jefferson, abiding by the wall of separation, refused even to indulge in the meaningless ceremonial proclamations of a national day of thanksgiving and prayer addressed to what Washington, in one of his own such proclamations, reduced to "a great and glorious Being" with no connection to any particular religion.[85]

Rehnquist also argued in vain that when Madison advocated for the First Amendment on the floor of the House of Representatives, it is "totally incorrect" to suppose that he was intending to advance the same divorce of religion from government he had advocated in *Memorial and Remonstrance* and during the fight to pass the Virginia Statute abolishing all government aid to Christianity in Virginia.[86] As already shown, the *Detached Memoranda* (which Rehnquist failed to mention) demonstrate that that was exactly Madison's intent. Some thirty years after the First Amendment's ratification, the *Memoranda* express his satisfaction with the "*separation* between Religion & Govt in the Constitution of the United States" and his belief that "in strictness" not even presidential proclamations of thanksgiving to a non-denominational "Being" or congressional chaplains could be justified under the Amendment, since such practices "seem to imply and nourish the erroneous idea of a national religion." Here we see the expedient selectivity of the search for the "intent of the Framers" by those who deny their intent to frame a secular republic.

The *Wallace* decision merely completed the process so clearly foreseen by the NRA movement, according to which "our whole political page becomes a pure, unbelieving, irreligious, Christless, Godless blank."[87] With or without the incorporation doctrine and the later Supreme Court decisions on application of the First Amendment's religion clauses to the States, that process would inevitably have unfolded under the gravitational pull of the national charter. The NRA's prediction in this regard was a prophecy fulfilled.

Originalists versus *Non-Originalists: A Non-Debate*

Today we are witness to endless academic and judicial debates between "originalists" and "non-originalists" over the meaning of the First Amendment and the rest of the Constitution. The originalists, the party of the "conservatives," insist that the Constitution, being merely a legal document, ought to be construed as of the time

---

85. *Wallace,* 472 U.S. at 92, 102.
86. *Id.* at 99.
87. *Proceedings* (1872), 59.

of its ratification, while the non-originalists, the party of the liberals, argue that the Constitution, being a "living" document, should be construed in keeping with changing circumstances affecting its application. Within the originalist camp is a division between "textualists" and "intentionalists." The former, among which Justice Scalia is the most prominent, hold that the Constitutional text on its face, given its "original meaning" at ratification, should control, while the latter hold that the drafters' "original intention," as demonstrated by historical materials, should control.

Justice Scalia's "textualist" originalism seeks to discern the meaning of a given Constitutional provision, including the First Amendment, as it was "originally understood"[88]—literally the "18th-century meaning"[89] or "original public meaning"[90] of the text. This peculiar hermeneutic is as dubious as it is arbitrary. In the first place, since the Constitution itself provides no rule governing its interpretation in doubtful cases, the "originalists" have no authority for declaring that the rule ought to be an elusive "public understanding" of people in the 18th century, and more precisely the 18th century during the period when the unamended text of the Constitution and the ten amendments of the Bill of Rights were ratified (1789–1791). Moreover, what about the 19th-century Fourteenth Amendment, which reorients the entire constitutional framework to the status of a charter not only for the national government but for every state and political subdivision in America? This tectonic shift accelerated the very outcome the NRA was already lamenting long before *Gitlow*: the arid secularity of political life and a conception of rights that is nothing but social libertinism, including the inevitable legalization of abortion.

Scalia himself admits that his preference for "originalism" is purely a matter of opinion and that originalism and non-originalism of various types (including the "living" Constitution) are "two evils" of which originalism is the one "I prefer."[91] Confronted by the obvious problem with his preferred hermeneutic, however, Scalia admitted: "It's not always easy to figure out what the provision meant when it was adopted. I don't say it's perfect. I just say it's better than anything else."[92] But "originalism" is not, in fact, better than anything else. It is arguably even worse than the "living constitution" of the liberals, as it embroils conservatives in a fossil hunt for the petrified evidence of debatable 18th- century understandings, while the liberals confront head on the knotty issues of justice, morality and even theology inherent in such concepts as "life," "liberty," "property," "establishment of religion," "free

---

88. Antonin Scalia, "Common-Law Courts in a Civil-Law System: The Role of United States Federal Courts in Interpreting the Constitution and Laws," *The Tanner Lectures on Human Values* (March 8 and 9, 1995), 112.

89. *District of Columbia v. Heller*, 128 S.Ct. 2783, 2791 (2008).

90. Cf. Richard S. Kay, "Original Intention and Public Meaning in Constitutional Interpretation," 103 *Northwestern University Law Review* 703 (2009).

91. Antonin Scalia, "Originalism: the Lesser Evil," 57 *University of Cincinnati Law Review* 849, 862 (1989).

92. Quoted in David Gram, "Scalia talks up 'originalism' in UVM speech," *Associated Press*, October 9, 2004.

exercise of religion," "freedom of speech," "cruel and unusual punishment," "privileges," "immunities," and "due process of law."

The "conservative" idea that such concepts must mean only and forever what a modern-day Supreme Court justice surmises they meant to Protestants of the 18th century leads, ironically, to even more arbitrary moral outcomes than the "living constitution." For the "living constitution" at least allows for the possibility that someday the Court, departing from an eminently debatable "original" meaning or intent, might actually be able to correct objective moral or theological errors in an "original" understanding that *not even originalists* can agree upon. As we saw in the preceding chapter, this is what the NRA movement had hoped to do by way of a Constitutional amendment so that the document would "conform to the facts as they have actually been evolved," warning that "if this be not done, the Constitution will in time conform everything to itself." And here it is the liberals who sound like the voice of common sense when they cite Edmund Randolph, a Framer who sat on the Committee of Detail at the Philadelphia Convention, whose notes reflect that one of the "two essentials" observed in drafting the Constitution was "[t]o insert essential principles only; lest the operations of government should be clogged by rendering those provisions permanent and unalterable, which ought to be accommodated to times and events."[93]

That said, the "textualists" who argue that "no law respecting an establishment of religion" and "no religious test for any office" signify "support of religion in general" have failed to demonstrate convincingly how the religion clauses can be read that way. Nor have the "intentionalists" been persuasive in explaining how the search for the Founders' intention should ignore or selectively overlook the written intentions of the two Founders—Jefferson and Madison—who provided virtually the entire roadmap for America's journey into the previously unknown territory of "the sacred principle of religious liberty."

The debate between originalists and non-originalists aside, however, we must keep in mind that both conservative and liberal interpreters of the religion clauses are all agreed that *in no event does the Constitution permit America to constitute itself a Christian republic in any sense of the word*, as the NRA rightly observed of the Constitution's godlessness (while incoherently defending the separation of Church and State mandated by the First Amendment). The debate between the two schools is thus ultimately a non-debate. In consequence, nearly 130 years after the Supreme Court first mentioned it, Jefferson's "wall of separation" stands firm, for while complaining about the metaphor, not even the "conservative" wing of the Court proposes anything more than the most minimal permeation of the wall, leaving completely intact the strictest possible Church-State separation. The continual bickering between the two wings of the Court revolves only around the extent to which government can engage in trivial ceremonial "acknowledgments" of God and America's "religious heritage."

93. Quoted in John R. Vale, *The Constitutional Convention of 1787: A Comprehensive Encyclopedia of America's Founding* (ABC-CLIO: 2005), 107.

A perfect case in point is *Van Orden v. Perry*, in which a 5-to-4 majority hobbled its way to the conclusion that the display of the Ten Commandments on the grounds of the Texas State Capitol since 1961 was a tolerably "passive" and "historic" "acknowledgment" of "the role of religion in American life from at least 1789." The rationale for upholding the display, as expressed in Justice Rehnquist's plurality opinion (endorsed by four of the five justices in the majority), makes a mockery of the legend of the national government's "Christian foundations." Noting the "two faces" of the Court's Janus-like Establishment Clause jurisprudence, Rehnquist opines:

> This case, like all Establishment Clause challenges, presents us with the difficulty of respecting both faces. Our institutions presuppose a Supreme Being, yet these institutions must not press religious observances upon their citizens. One face looks to the past in acknowledgment of our Nation's heritage, while the other looks to the present in *demanding a separation between church and state*. Reconciling these two faces requires that we neither abdicate our responsibility *to maintain a division between church and state* nor evince a hostility to religion by disabling the government from *in some ways* recognizing our religious heritage. . . . The placement of the Ten Commandments monument on the Texas State Capitol grounds is a far more *passive use* of those texts than was the case in *Stone*, where the text confronted elementary school students every day. Indeed, Van Orden, the petitioner here, apparently walked by the monument for a number of years before bringing this lawsuit.[94]

That is, the Court's "conservative" wing (joined by a lone liberal, Justice Breyer) would permit "passive" displays of the Ten Commandments on public grounds precisely because such displays *have no significant religious influence* but are merely the functional equivalent of a display of antiquities in a museum. On the other hand, in a companion case decided the same day, *McCreary County v. ACLU*,[95] the Court's liberal wing upheld a lower court injunction banning the *recent* placement of copies of the Ten Commandments in county courthouses in Kentucky because that placement did not have longstanding "historical" significance but rather a "predominantly religious purpose."

Therefore, despite all the bickering, the conservative and liberal wings of the Supreme Court are in complete agreement that government may not convey the message that citizens should actually *follow* the Commandments. As Rehnquist is at pains to note in his opinion in *Van Orden*, such an impermissible message had resulted from posting the commandments in public school classrooms as the Court had earlier decided in *Stone v. Graham*. The two "ultra-conservatives" on the Court, Justices Scalia and Thomas, concurred with Rehnquist in *Van Orden*.

In his concurring opinion, however, Justice Scalia states that while Rehnquist's reasoning "accurately reflects our current Establishment Clause jurisprudence. . . ,"

---

94. *Van Orden v. Perry*, 545 U.S. 677 (2005) 683–83, 691.
95. 545 U.S. at 691.

the Court should adopt "an Establishment Clause jurisprudence that is in accord with our Nation's past and present practices," by which he means: "there is nothing unconstitutional in a State's favoring religion generally, honoring God through public prayer and acknowledgment, or, *in a non-proselytizing manner,* venerating the Ten Commandments."[96] Justice Thomas, in a separate concurring opinion, observes that Rehnquist "rightly recognizes that the [Ten Commandments] monument has 'religious significance' and "properly recognizes the role of religion in this Nation's history and the permissibility of government displays acknowledging that history."[97] Thomas would read the First Amendment to permit passive, museum-like "displays" of the heirlooms of America's "religious heritage." He adds, however, that the Court should "return to the views of the Framers and adopt coercion as the touchstone for our Establishment Clause inquiry," so that "Every acknowledgment of religion would not give rise to an Establishment Clause claim"[98] but only those which coerce nonbelievers. Thomas fails to note, however, that Madison and Jefferson alike regarded *any* form of governmental support for Christianity, even "non-preferential" recognition of all Christian denominations, to be not only coercive but "tyranny" and "religious slavery" *per se.* As the constitutional scholar Paul J. Weber suggests, Madison's "perfect separation" between government and religion would preclude government support of religion "even if that support be only financial, or only *honorary, laudatory or commendatory,* since these are discriminatory."[99] And Weber is writing *against* an absolutist reading of Madison's thought.

Hence even under Scalia's and Thomas's "ultra-conservative" reading of the First Amendment as applied to the States via the Fourteenth Amendment, the State governments are permitted far less than the remnants of Christian legal codes that were already under attack by the battering ram of the Constitution at the height of the NRA movement. The most "conservative" reading of the First Amendment today would allow the States and their political subdivisions nothing more than generic historical references to "the Supreme Being" invoked by the deistic Founders and Framers, some form of vague "favor" of "religion in general"—whatever that means—and a "veneration" of the Ten Commandments that, of course, must avoid any official declaration that the Decalogue binds the body politic as God's law. The NRA movement, with its call for an explicit recognition of the Social Kingship of Christ in an overwhelmingly Christian nation, would hardly have viewed this as an acceptable answer to the moral emergency the Constitution was helping to provoke even in the mid-1800s. Quite the contrary, in yet another echo of the Catholic teaching, its proceedings warned that "to sever the bond of connection between our nation and Christianity would be to consign us to inevitable national ruin."[100]

Today, however, even the Court's "conservative" wing would utterly reject any role for Christianity as a foundation of law or public policy. It is apparent that even

96. Ibid., 692.
97. Ibid.
98. Ibid., 697.
99. Paul J. Weber, "James Madison and Religious Equality: The Perfect Separation," loc. cit, 184–185.
100. *Proceedings* (1874), 2 (D. McAllister).

if they had their way, the Supreme Court's most conservative justices would not take us anywhere near the Christian commonwealth of the golden legend but rather to a place only a few steps removed from the First Amendment absolutism of their liberal colleagues. And yet we are expected to believe that the Establishment Clause does *not* mandate governmental hostility toward revealed religion! As they grapple with the liberals over the "meaning" of the First Amendment, the Supreme Court's conservative wing only confirms that the Founders meant to, and in fact did, end the alliance between civil authority and the Christian religion that had been the hallmark of Western civilization for fourteen centuries and still exists in those few Western nations (nearly all in Latin America) which have not completely embraced the cult of Liberty. Just as the NRA observed, "the Constitution . . . has powerfully inculcated the notion that politics has nothing to do with religion, and that the State, having no conscience itself, cannot demand a conscience in its servants . . . and a slow but steady decline of official integrity has been the result."[101]

Moreover, it should be obvious that the "conservatives" on the Court would join the liberals in striking down under the First Amendment any State statute or constitutional amendment that embodied the NRA's proposed language on the sovereignty of God and the Social Kingship of Christ. Yet, had such language been written into the federal Constitution by the Christian Founders of legend, no school of constitutional interpretation, not even the most liberal of non-originalists, could have found in the same document a right to abortion or private consensual sodomy, as the Supreme Court's liberal majority has infamously done.[102]

In fact, it is no coincidence that it is precisely in those Western nations whose constitutions still expressly invoke Christ or Catholic Christianity (e.g., Ireland,[103] Malta,[104] Bolivia,[105] Peru[106] and quite recently Hungary[107]) that the demand for such constitutional "rights" has been thwarted or rolled back. Granted, such nations are overwhelmingly Catholic. But what, besides a slavish attachment to the deistic Founders' notion of "religious liberty," prevented America's overwhelmingly

101. *Proceedings* (1872), 65 (T. P. Stephenson).

102. Cf. *Lawrence v. Texas*, 539 U.S. 558 (2003) (striking down Texas anti-sodomy statute as applied to "adult males who had engaged in consensual act of sodomy in privacy of home").

103. *The Preamble to the Constitution of Ireland*, adopted in 1937, reads as follows: "In the Name of the Most Holy Trinity, from Whom is all authority and to Whom, as our final end, *all actions both of men and States must be referred*, We the People of Éire, Humbly acknowledging all our obligations to our Divine Lord, Jesus Christ, Who sustained our fathers through centuries of trial. . . ."

104. Section 2 of the *Maltese Constitution* provides: "The religion of Malta is the Roman Catholic Apostolic Religion. . . . The authorities of the Roman Catholic Apostolic Church have the duty and the right to teach which principles are right and which are wrong. . . ."

105. Article 3 of the *Bolivian Constitution*, as amended in 2005, reads: "The State recognizes and supports the Catholic, Apostolic and Roman religion. . . ."

106. Article 50 of the *Peruvian Constitution* declares: "Within an independent and autonomous system, the government recognizes the Catholic Church as an important element in the historical, cultural, and moral formation of Peru and lends it its cooperation."

107. See draft text, adopted by the Hungarian President's signature on April 25, 2011, www.scribd.com/doc/52905269/Official-translation-of-new-Hungarian-constitution.

Christian majority from producing a Constitution that at least invokes God and Christ in a non-denominational fashion as a bulwark against legal innovations that attack the moral order? The Protestants of the NRA movement sought precisely such a Constitution in the late 1800s, and, as has been noted, NRA's President for a time was the retired Supreme Court justice, William Strong.

That is the difference between then and now: Then, it was still possible for even a Protestant member of the Supreme Court to advocate publicly that the Constitution was gravely defective on account of its failure to invoke "Almighty God as the source of all authority and power in civil government, the Lord Jesus Christ as the Ruler among the nations, his revealed will as the supreme law of the land. . . ." Now, the "conservative" *Catholic* majority of the same Court would regard such advocacy as lunatical and subversive of "American values." This bizarre state of affairs is not some recent perversion of the Framers' intention. Rather, it is just what the NRA predicted in 1874 when it warned that "what is left out [of the Constitution] may one day be formally declared un-American."[108]

Law Trumps Religion

But the situation is even worse than thus far suggested by the Supreme Court's First Amendment jurisprudence. The Court's own "conservatives" have made clear that the Constitution does not merely subordinate religion in the negative sense of making a "religiously neutral" government immune to its claims, which (just as the NRA warned) has been disastrous enough for the moral order in America. Beyond the disestablishment of religion, the Constitution *positively* subordinates religion by restraining religious acts whenever they come into direct conflict with a "neutral" exercise of governmental power, and this despite the First Amendment's Free Exercise Clause. Here, too, the NRA movement was prescient.

The process came to a historical head with the Supreme Court's decision in *Employment Division v. Smith*. In *Smith* none other than the "ultra-conservative" Justice Scalia, writing for the 6-to-3 majority, upheld denial of state unemployment benefits to two Native Americans who had been fired for the use of peyote for their religious rituals in violation of Oregon law, which prohibits possession of peyote as a controlled dangerous substance. The Court rejected the employees' argument that, in denying employment benefits under such circumstances, Oregon law infringed the free exercise of their Native American religion. While on its particular facts the decision appears reasonable, the Court's rationale makes it crystal clear that in the American polity, as in every Western polity today, religion is at the mercy of state power. Scalia's opinion contains this chilling observation: "We have never held that an individual's religious beliefs excuse him from compliance with an otherwise valid law prohibiting conduct that the State is free to regulate."[109] Even more

---

108. *Proceedings* (1874), 14.
109. *Employment Division v. Smith*, 494 U.S. 872, 878–79 (1990).

chillingly, Scalia quotes the liberal Justice Frankfurter for this proposition: "The mere possession of religious convictions which contradict the relevant concerns of a political society does not relieve the citizen from the discharge of political responsibilities."[110]

Scalia and the majority declined to apply the rationale of prior Supreme Court decisions that required a "compelling state interest" to justify laws substantially burdening the free exercise of religion. While the "compelling state interest" standard is hardly a bulwark of religious liberty—the State can always argue that its interests are "compelling"—Scalia's dismissal of the standard evokes the majesty of the Lockean "supreme Government" the Framers established: "To make an individual's obligation to obey such a law contingent upon the law's coincidence with his religious beliefs, except where the State's interest is 'compelling' . . . contradicts both *constitutional tradition* and common sense."[111]

Note well: Scalia, the Court's most "conservative" reader of the Constitution, says that *the Framers* made religious belief subject to general civil law. As Scalia concludes: "[T]he right of free exercise does not relieve an individual of the obligation to comply with a 'valid and neutral law of general applicability on the ground that the law proscribes (or prescribes) conduct that his religion prescribes (or proscribes).'"[112] Amazingly enough, Scalia's opinion in *Smith* quotes and relies upon the earlier mentioned decision in *Reynolds v. United States*—the very decision in which Jefferson's "wall of separation" metaphor, which Scalia and the other "conservative" Justices disparage, first appears in Supreme Court jurisprudence. Apparently missing the irony, Scalia quotes *Reynolds* for the proposition that the State cannot allow "the professed doctrines of religious belief [to be] superior to the law of the land, and in effect to permit every citizen to become a law unto himself."[113]

While the conduct at issue in *Smith* was the politically unpopular use of peyote, the principle Scalia enunciates as foundational to the American system extends to *any* form of religiously motivated conduct "the State is free to regulate" according to "the relevant concerns of a political society" and "the discharge of political responsibilities" by citizens. True, this principle does no harm where the general civil law at issue prohibits conduct that also violates the natural or divine law, such as suicidal snake handling or polygamy. In such cases, civil law morally *ought* to take precedence over the religious beliefs and practices of the individual. But, as the NRA movement was well aware, in our Lockean polity, founded on the social compact theory, "the relevant concerns of a political society" and "political responsibilities" are not subject to the limitations of any absolute theological standard—the Constitution, after all, does not even mention God—so that the objects of civil law can be, and often are, at odds with the natural and divine law. Consequently, the "ultraconservative" Scalia defends in principle vast governmental power to infringe the

110. Smith, 494 U.S. at 879.
111. Ibid., 885 (citations and internal quotations omitted).
112. Ibid., 879.
113. Ibid., 494.

very "religious liberty" the Constitution is supposed to enshrine, at least according to the golden legend.[114]

For example, State governments have already enacted "valid and neutral law[s] of general applicability" that legally penalize all of the following religiously motivated conduct: the refusal to comply with the orders of divorce courts which purport to dissolve sacramental marriages (recall the NRA's early condemnation of State divorce laws); the refusal to perform or recognize "gay marriages"; pro-life demonstrations that allegedly "interfere" with the business of abortion mills, or which trespass on judicially or statutorily created "bubble zones" where the pro-life speech of Catholics and other Christians has been prohibited;[115] the refusal of Catholic hospitals to dispense "emergency" contraception;[116] the refusal of adoption agencies to permit "gay adoption" or the refusal of local officials to certify "gay marriages";[117] and the refusal of Christian organizations to hire homosexuals,[118] to provide medical coverage for abortions and contraception,[119] or to provide health benefits for "same-sex couples." In one state, a wedding photographer has even been hauled before a human rights commission for refusing to photograph a "gay wedding,"[120] and in another a Methodist campground facility was stripped of its tax exemption for refusing to host a "gay marriage" ceremony at a pavilion on its property.[121]

In fact, in his dissenting opinion in *Romer v. Evans,* Justice Scalia himself declared: "homosexuals are as entitled to use the legal system for reinforcement of their moral sentiments as is the rest of society. But they are subject to being countered by lawful, democratic countermeasures as well."[122] *Romer* struck down as unconstitutional under the Fourteenth Amendment a voter-adopted amendment to the Colorado Constitution barring localities from passing laws granting special protected status to homosexuals as a class. Scalia's "conservative" protest against

114. Here the author is indebted to Kenneth Craycraft's work, which highlights the importance of the *Smith* decision and prompted my own further study of the Supreme Court's jurisprudence on this issue.

115. See, e.g., *Madsen v. Women's Health Ctr., Inc.,* 512 U.S. 753 (1994).

116. See, e.g., Wis. Stat. § 50.375 (2007).

117. See, e.g., "New York clerk faces lawsuit for refusing to sign same-sex 'marriage' license," http://www.freerepublic.com/focus/f-news/2786143/posts.

118. "Sexual orientation discrimination" in employment is banned in California, Colorado, Connecticut, Delaware, Hawaii, Illinois, Iowa, Maine, Maryland, Massachusetts, Minnesota, Nevada, New Hampshire, New Jersey, New Mexico, New York, Oregon, Rhode Island, Vermont, Washington, and Wisconsin. Religious exemptions typically do not apply to Christian organizations that are not actually engaged in a religious mission but rather provide services to the general public.

119. See, e.g., *Catholic Charities of Diocese of Albany v. Serio,* 7 N.Y. 3d 510, 522 (2006), where New York's highest court held, in keeping with the decision in *Smith,* that Catholic Charities of New York must provide employee health coverage for contraception under the "Women's Health and Wellness Act" because "the burden on plaintiffs' religious exercise is the incidental result of a 'neutral law of general applicability'. . . ."

120. John Jalsevac, "Christian Photographer Hauled before Commission for Refusing Same-Sex Job," January 30, 2008, www.lifesite.net/ldn/2008/jan/08013004.html.

121. Jalsevac, "U.S. Christian Camp Loses Tax-Exempt Status over Same-Sex Civil-Union Ceremony," September 17, 2007, www.lifesite.net/ldn/2007/sep/07091902. html.

122. *Romer v. Evans,* 517 U.S. 620, 646 (Scalia, J., dissenting).

this outcome was simply an appeal to the will of the majority—precisely the standard that would lead to America's moral decline and ultimate ruin, as the NRA had warned in its failed attempt to give the Constitution a foundation in Gospel morality.

One could multiply almost endlessly the possibilities for government suppression of religious practice or even belief that conflicts with "valid and neutral laws of general applicability" adopted by the majority as "lawful, democratic countermeasures." So long as the State can articulate some "relevant concern of a political society" to justify a law that is not specifically "aimed at the . . . restriction of religious beliefs," such as the supposed need for "reproductive health services," even the "ultra-conservatives" on the Supreme Court have left themselves no principled ground on which to oppose the consequent governmental oppression of Catholics and other Christians whose religion forbids compliance with such laws.

That is precisely the threat posed by a decision of the U.S. Department of Health and Human Services (HHS) in January 2012 that would have compelled Catholic Church-affiliated institutions to provide coverage for abortion-inducing pills, contraception and sterilization in health plans mandated under "Obamacare." Faced with the potential for nationwide Catholic civil disobedience led by the Catholic hierarchy—the thing the forces of Liberty fear the most—the Obama administration hastily announced an "accommodation" that achieved the same result with what a group of Catholic scholars denounced as a "cheap accounting trick": amending the dictate to require insurance companies to provide the contested coverage "free of charge" when exempt organizations refuse to pay for it.[123] This sleight-of-hand would inevitably result in the cost of the "free" coverage being passed on to the organizations in the overall premium they are forced to pay. The response from the United States Conference of Catholic Bishops (USCCB) was at first "curiously muted," advising that it saw "initial opportunities in preserving the principle of religious freedom," but a later statement declared that the policy "continues to involve needless government intrusion in the internal governance of religious institutions, and to threaten government coercion of religious people and groups to violate their most deeply held convictions. . . . The only complete solution to this religious liberty problem is for HHS to rescind the mandate of these objectionable services."[124]

The USCCB also called for passage of the federal "Respect for Rights of Conscience Act," whose preamble invokes Jefferson's statement to the New London Methodists in 1809 as "express[ing] a conviction on respect for conscience that is deeply embedded in the history and traditions of our Nation. . . ."[125] What the appeal to Jefferson was supposed to add to the Act's prospects for passage was far

---

123. "Statement by religious scholars on contraceptive coverage policy change," February 10, 2012, http://www.foxnews.com/interactive/politics/2012/02/10/statement-by-religious-scholars-on-contraceptive-coverage-policy-change/.

124. February 10, 2012, "Bishops Renew Call To Legislative Action On Religious Liberty," http://www.usccb.org/news/2012/12-026.cfm.

125. H.R. 1179, Patient Protection and Affordable Care Act, § 2(2).

from apparent. What was apparent, however, was that the Act had been cobbled together to provide a legislative patch for the gaping hole in the First Amendment regime of "religious liberty" so clearly exposed by the Supreme Court's "conservative" majority in *Smith*. The Obama administration's accounting gimmick, however, appeared sufficient to insure that the sleeping Catholic giant would remain in its Liberty-induced slumber, during which more than 50 million unborn children have been aborted since *Roe v. Wade* with little or no active resistance by the Catholic hierarchy.

The situation was not helped by the Court's attempt to cut back on *Smith* in a decision in an employment discrimination case, handed down the same month as the HHS dictate, in which the Court held that under the First Amendment there is a "ministerial exception" to employment discrimination laws respecting the hiring and firing of personnel actually engaged in "conveying the Church's message and carrying out its mission."[126] The decision in *Smith*, said the Court, "involved government regulation of only outward physical acts. The present case, in contrast, concerns government interference with an internal church decision that affects the faith and mission of the church itself." But compliance with "neutral laws of general application" usually involves "outward physical acts" by church-affiliated organizations and individual believers rather than an "internal church decision." Worse, the Court did not hold that the First Amendment rendered the federal judiciary powerless to intervene in religious discrimination claims involving ministers, but only that the "ministerial exception" is "*an affirmative defense to an otherwise cognizable claim, not* a jurisdictional bar."[127] Thus, a court would be required to determine case-by-case whether an employment position is sufficiently "ministerial" to be outside the reach of generally "neutral" anti-discrimination laws. It is not difficult to imagine the battles of expert opinion on religious matters that will now occupy the federal courts, which will decide who is a "minister" and who is not in close cases.

That this particular constitutional shoe has not dropped until recently does not change the fact that the text of the Constitution in no way precludes the result in *Smith*, but rather it has always pointed to the supremacy of "neutral" civil law over religion in all cases of conflict. In fact, Justice Scalia, a conservative "textualist," opines that the outcome in *Smith* is dictated by a reading of the Free Exercise Clause as "a textual matter."[128] And so it is, if one reads the text of the Amendment according to the Lockean principle, which happens to be the principle of the Framers, that religion is a strictly private matter ultimately subordinate to the public authority of Locke's "supreme government."

---

126. *Hosanna-Tabor Evangelical Lutheran Church & Sch. v. E.E.O.C.*, 132 S. Ct. 694, 708 (2012).
127. *Id.* at 714 & n. 4.
128. *Smith*, 494 U.S. at 878.

The Supreme Court's Nod to Locke

That this is precisely how the Supreme Court majority views the "original" meaning of the First Amendment was placed beyond all doubt by the post-*Smith* decision in *City of Boerne v. Flores,* in which the Court's "conservative" majority upheld denial of a building permit to the Archbishop of San Antonio for enlargement of a church that had been designated a historic landmark by the City.[129] *Flores* was decided after Congress, in response to the public outcry over the decision in *Smith,* passed the Religious Freedom Restoration Act (RFRA) of 1993, which reinstates the "compelling state interest" standard for any federal, state or local law that "substantially" burdens the free exercise of religion.[130] In *Flores,* the Court declared RFRA, which the Archbishop had invoked, was unconstitutional as applied to the States because Congress had exceeded its power to enforce the Fourteenth Amendment by requiring states and localities to show a "compelling state interest" for laws burdening religion. In his concurring opinion Justice Scalia—disagreeing, ironically enough, with the liberal Justice O'Connor—declares that the Founders, *following the philosophy of John Locke,* never had any intention of allowing the free exercise of religion to trump the maintenance of public peace through obedience to "general laws":

> [T]he affirmative protection of religion accorded by the early "free exercise" enactments [in the colonies and states] ... do[es] not support the dissent's view, since they contain "provisos" that significantly qualify the affirmative protection they grant.... Religious exercise shall be permitted *so long as it does not violate general laws governing conduct....* At the time these provisos were enacted, keeping "peace" and "order" seems to have meant, precisely, *obeying the laws....* This limitation upon the scope of religious exercise would have been in accord with *the background political philosophy of the age* (*associated most prominently with John Locke*), which regarded freedom as the right "to do only what was not lawfully prohibited"....[131]

Scalia further opined that George Washington's letter to the Quakers on abstention from military service merely expressed his "'wish and desire' that religion be accommodated, not his belief that existing constitutional provisions required accommodation...." As for Jefferson, he "did not in fact espouse the broad principle of affirmative accommodation [of religion] advocated by the dissent...."[132] Thus the Supreme Court justice widely considered the most conservative constitutional jurist in America today affirms that the First Amendment, which reflects the Lockean view of "religious liberty" as the "background political philosophy of the age," does not mean that anyone is exempt on religious grounds from "obeying the laws" promulgated by the "supreme Government" to which the people have

129. *City of Boerne v. Flores,* 521 U.S. 507 (1997).
130. 42 U.S.C. §2000bb, *et seq.*
131. *Flores,* 521 U.S. at 539–40.
132. *Id.* at 542.

"consented." Under the Constitution, religion is not only negatively subordinated to state power by its separation from government, but also positively subordinated wherever legislative enactments applicable to all happen to violate the religious convictions of particular individuals or churches.

And Scalia is right. To recall Locke's teaching on this point in the *Letter Concerning Toleration*, the "supreme Government" has the power to "alter the obligation of even some of the laws of God, and change the nature of vice and virtue" in order to address conduct deemed "destructive to human society," and God will respect that political judgment, "so much does he take care of the preservation of government." All the more will Locke's legal positivism prevail where, as in the Constitution, even Locke's remote deity has been removed from the scene. What was true all along, and what has been suggested throughout this examination of the modern Lockean social order first embodied in America, is confirmed by the leading voice for an interpretation of the Constitution according to its original "textual" meaning.[133]

In sum, the words of the First Amendment say what they say, and it was Madison's reading of those words "that was to be vindicated by history," as the federal judge and constitutional scholar John T. Noonan, Jr. has noted with approval.[134] The First Amendment's religion clauses are what they have always been, not what the keepers of golden legends wish they were today. And what they have always been, as even the Supreme Court's conservative majority demonstrates, is not a "neutral" accommodation of Christianity, nor an amiable "truce" between Christian denominations, nor a warrant for "non-preferential" government support of a meaningless "religion in general," but rather a patent negation of the Christian commonwealth or any form of state governed by the truths of revelation. Further, even the conservative wing of the Court has made it clear that the religion clauses provide no protection against any law of general application that reflects "the relevant concerns of a political society" and requires "the discharge of political responsibilities." The worst fears of the NRA movement have come to pass.

133. Nor has the First Amendment's "meaning" been altered in the least by the Supreme Court's recent decision in *Gonzales v. O Centro Espirita Beneficente Uniao do Vegetal*, 546 U.S. 418 (2006), wherein the Court unanimously held that while RFRA is unconstitutional as applied to the States and localities, it still binds the federal government to apply a "compelling state interest" test to federal laws and regulations. As the Court observed, the statutory "compelling state interest" test enacted by Congress is *not required by the First Amendment*: "[T]he approach later mandated by Congress under RFRA was not required as a matter of constitutional law under the Free Exercise Clause." In other words, Congress had to enact a special statute to provide protection for religious liberty *not to be found in the text of the Constitution itself*. But, as already suggested, even under RFRA the courts will readily find a "compelling state interest" to justify federal laws that impinge on religious beliefs, such as the Freedom of Access to Clinics Entrances Act (FACE) which criminalizes religiously motivated pro-life protests that "interfere with" or "intimidate" abortion "providers." In fact, the Supreme Court has refused to consider a challenge to FACE under RFRA, and the lower federal courts have uniformly held FACE constitutional. So, even under RFRA, the Lockean principle of the absolute supremacy of civil law over religion remains fully operational in the Constitution, the Free Exercise Clause notwithstanding.

134. John T. Noonan, Jr., *The Lustre of Our Country* (Berkeley: Univ. of California Press, 1998), 81; quoted in Craycraft, *American Myth of Religious Freedom*, 90.

The American Myth of Religious Freedom

What we see today—the thinly veiled assertion of state supremacy over all religious authority throughout the Western world—is exactly what Madison, Jefferson and the Framers accomplished in America as the first working model of Locke's principles. For the first time in Western history, the Constitution abolished the temporal and spiritual "dyarchy" and created in its place what Craycraft calls "a political monism, which (ironically) makes the state the *only* ultimate arbiter of religious legitimacy."[135] That is, the State declares that no religion has a claim upon it, and then it elevates its power above all religions.

Here Craycraft is following the indications of John Courtney Murray, who flatly contradicts his own defense of the First Amendment as pragmatic "good law" or "articles of peace" by arguing in a later chapter of the same book that modern democracies are based on a "monism of power" which involves "a rejection of the Gelasian thesis, 'Two there are,' which had been the dynamic of the Christian revolution."[136] Political modernity declares, on the contrary: "'*One* there is whereby the world is ruled'—the power of the people, expressing itself in the preference of a majority; and beyond or beside or above this power there is no other." Contemporary man, following the commandments first laid down by the Moses of the Enlightenment, "does not object to religion, provided that religion be regarded as a private matter which concerns only the conscience of the individual. In his more expansive moments he will not object even to organized religion—the 'churches'—provided they accept the status of voluntary associations for limited purposes which do not impinge upon the public order. But he will not tolerate any marring of his image of democratic society [as] . . . the One Society, with One Law, and One Sovereign, the politically equal people." The modern nation-state, Murray concludes, has "declared the Gelasian doctrine to be heretical and has outlawed it in the name of *modern orthodoxy*, which is a naturalist rationalism."[137]

It is none other than Murray, the supposed champion of "the American model," who identifies that very model as above all an interference with the perennial role of the Church as a socially constitutive agency. In the critique that undermines his own attempt at a Catholic defense of religious liberty in the modern sense, Murray observes that political modernity has "rejected *the freedom of the Church* . . . as the armature of man's spiritual freedom and as *a structural principle* of a free society."[138] The modern nation-state "has denied (or ignored, or forgotten, or neglected) the Christian revelation that man is sacredness, and that his primatial *res sacra*, his freedom, is sought and found ultimately *within the Church*."[139] Craycraft asks: "What else can Murray be talking about but the United States of America

---

135. Craycraft, *American Myth of Religious Freedom*, 115.
136. Murray, *We Hold These Truths*, 206.
137. Ibid., 210.
138. Ibid., 213–214.
139. Ibid., 215.

and its political and legal institutions?"[140] Murray confirms this in his own text, which observes that "*Madison's* 'republican principle' affords the Final Grounds for the Last Say on All Human Questions...."[141] Craycraft sees Murray's self-contradiction within the pages of the same book as a "dilemma." But the same dilemma confronts anyone who proposes to defend the Greco-Catholic Western tradition while praising America's radically Lockean departure from it. The NRA movement, like Thornwell's movement in the Confederate States, was trapped in the same dilemma when it advocated a union between the State and the Christian religion while rejecting any union between the State and the teaching Church.

Just as Locke would have it, then, the price for "religious liberty" in America and virtually every other Western polity today is an agreement on the part of believers that the authority of the State is supreme and unchallengeable by any religion or combination of religions. Nowhere was this demonstrated more dramatically than in the historic speech by John F. Kennedy to Southern Baptist leaders in 1960—an address that offers a striking parallel to Thomas Jefferson's letter to the Baptists of Danbury:

> I believe in an America *where the separation of church and state is absolute— where no Catholic prelate would tell the President (should he be a Catholic) how to act* ... where no public official either requests or accepts instructions on public policy from *the Pope ... or any other ecclesiastical source—where no religious body seeks to impose its will directly or indirectly* upon the general populace or the public acts of its officials.... I ask you tonight to follow in that tradition, to judge me on the basis of fourteen years in the Congress—on my declared stands *against an ambassador to the Vatican*, against *unconstitutional aid to parochial schools*.... I do not speak for my church on public matters—and *the church does not speak for me*.[142]

Only by giving assurances that his Catholicism would have no bearing on his exercise of political office, that his first loyalty was to America's civil government, not to the Vicar of Christ, and that (shades of Locke) he would oppose even diplomatic recognition of the Vatican, could John Kennedy hope to become the one and only Catholic President in the history of the United States. Kennedy, in short, had to promise to be the kind of Catholic of which John Locke would approve: one who bows before the majesty of the State, no matter what his Church teaches to the contrary.

Justice Scalia himself has expressed a complete acceptance of this Lockean view of the place of religion in the State. Speaking at the Gregorian University in Rome in 1996, he declared in perfect Lockean fashion that "[T]he responsibility of government is the here, not the hereafter.... I believe it is the job of the state to take care of the natural man, and it is up to religious individuals and associations to

140. Craycraft, *American Myth*, 119.
141. Murray, *We Hold These Truths*, 208.
142. "Address to Southern Baptist Leaders" (1960), U.S. State Department archive, accessed at http://infousa.state.gov/government/overview/66.html.

take care of the supernatural man."[143] Thus saith Locke, who, as we saw in Chapter 3, insisted that the role of the State is "confined to the care of the things of this World, which have nothing to do with the world to come,"[144] and that "care of souls . . . which neither does belong to the commonwealth nor can be subjected to it, is left entirely to every man's self."[145] Having neatly divided man into natural and supernatural selves precisely as required by Locke's new politics of the body, Scalia went on to say that in a democracy, which has nothing to do with man's supernatural self, the majority must have whatever it wishes, including the crowning "achievement" of Liberty, legalized abortion:

> If the people, for example, want abortion, the state should permit abortion in a democracy. . . . To say, "Ah, but it is contrary to the natural law," is simply to say that you set yourself above the democratic state and presume to decide what is good and bad in place of the majority of the people. I do not accept that as a proper function. . . .[146] And I am afraid that a lot of theologians waste a lot of their time becoming political scientists because of that notion that somehow the ends of Christianity will be achieved through the state. . . .[147]

It is fitting indeed that (as we saw in Chapter 3) it was none other than Locke who undermined belief in an immaterial human soul and anticipated the arguments in favor of abortion by calling into question the humanity of the fetus in his *Essay Concerning Human Understanding* (as did Hobbes in *De Corpore Politico*). Legalized abortion, which Scalia defends as a prerogative of the majority, is the ultimate illustration of the consequences of Locke's disjunction between man and his soul for political purposes. Abortion is an offense against divine and natural law that, according to the Christian teaching, destroys the moral integrity and threatens the eternal welfare of the souls of those who provide or obtain it, which would be a "private" matter according to Locke (and Scalia). Yet abortion also destroys the bodies of its victims and can cause either the death or long-term psychosomatic disturbance of the women who undergo the procedure. It is similarly impossible to segregate spiritual from somatic effects as to a host of other social evils traditionally prohibited under Christian legal codes, including the sale of pornography, prostitution, drug abuse, public lewdness, public drunkenness, public adultery, and so forth. It is impossible on account of the very thing Lockean politics tries to deny (with agreement from Scalia): the integral unity of body and soul, for which anyone who has read Dante's *Inferno* will achieve at least a literary appreciation.

Confronted with Liberty's culminating and absolutely inevitable debacle— legalized abortion in state-licensed "medical clinics"—Liberty's "conservative" defenders attribute it to an anomalous "judicial tyranny" representing yet another

---

143. Antonin Scalia, "Of Democracy, Morality and the Majority," transcript of Q&A following address at the Gregorian, May 2, 1996 in *Origins*, Vol. 26, No. 6 (June 27, 1996), 87.

144. *Letter*, 26, 28, 48.

145. *Letter*, 26, 27, 35, 48.

146. *Origins*, loc. cit., 87, 88.

147. Ibid., 87, 90.

dastardly subversion of the holy legacy of Jeffersonian democracy. But they conveniently overlook what Scalia frankly observes (and what the NRA movement prophetically deplored) as essential to that same legacy: the tyranny of the legislature that Locke describes as "*the supreme power* of the Commonwealth . . . sacred and unalterable in the hands where the Community have once placed it. . . ."[148] Even before *Roe v. Wade* was decided in 1973, legislatures in the majority of the States had already legalized abortion under limited circumstances, with New York permitting abortion on demand throughout the first 24 weeks of pregnancy.[149] If a popular majority, acting through Locke's supreme legislature, wishes to deny or demote the humanity of the fetus and thus legalize all or some abortions, there is no way to stop them on Lockean principles, and thus no way to stop them in America or anywhere else in the post-Christian West.

The idea that Christians enjoy "religious liberty" when they are bound by the proposition that the will of the majority trumps not only the will of Christ but even the natural law is, as Craycraft so rightly contends, "the American myth of religious freedom," which is part of a regime that inexorably "eradicates the insubordinate witness of orthodox faith."[150] That inexorable eradication is what the NRA movement had hoped to prevent by amending the Constitution to make it what it never was: the charter of a Christian nation. That serious Catholics have actually been persuaded that the very regime even the Protestants in the NRA movement decried as inimical to Christian social order is *favorable* to their religion is a testament to the power of the myth. But the reality, as Ralph C. Hancock writes, is that "the zealous Lockeanism of the American Revolution," which resulted in the "relegation of religion from the public to the private realm," reflects, not the vaunted "religious neutrality" of which we hear incessantly, but rather a "deep philosophical hostility in the first instance to revealed religion. . . ." and a veritable "anti-theology" of the State.[151]

Freedom of Worship?

Given the reality that Christianity and the Church have been wholly subordinated to state power under the Framers' regime of "religious freedom," conservative defenders of Liberty retreat to the last ditch, arguing that, nevertheless, believers still enjoy the freedom to practice "privately" the tenets of their respective denominations without state interference, thus benefiting from the Framers' judicious balancing of public and private interests to insure "public peace." The term "freedom of worship" is thus rather stealthily substituted for the full-blown "freedom of religion" the Framers supposedly secured. The argument does not survive even a moment's reflection.

148. *TT*, II.134.
149. See "Abortion in New York," *Time* magazine, September 7, 1970 ("Since New York State's liberalized abortion law became effective on July 1, some 16,000 women have obtained legal abortions").
150. Craycraft, *American Myth of Religious Freedom*, 25.
151. Hancock, "Religion and the Limits of Limited Government," loc. cit., 696.

First of all, we have already seen how under the First Amendment, as construed by the Supreme Court's "conservative" and *Catholic* majority, even purely "private" belief is subject to governmental restriction wherever it conflicts with "neutral laws of general application" enacted without reference to, and often in violation of, the tenets of traditional Christianity, such as state laws legalizing abortion and the purported termination of sacramental marriages, or prohibiting various forms of "discrimination" which Christians might be obliged in conscience to practice, or state and federal taxation for the government subsidy of abortion and contraception.

Beyond this restraint on the "private" practice of religion in particular cases, however, is a far deeper, broader and even more pernicious one that few have noticed: *the very disjunction between the "public" and "private" practice of religion is a thinly disguised but quite massive deprivation of religious freedom.* As William Cavanaugh has noted: "Christian denominations still thrive in the United States, but as optional, inward-looking affairs. They are not *publicly* true. . . ."[152] They are not *permitted* to be publicly true because the resulting truth claims on public authority would bring down the framework of the new kind of nation-state the Founders and Framers constructed according to a Lockean blueprint and which today's judicial "conservatives" dutifully help to maintain.

In a secular state such as ours, "private" believers are strictly forbidden to give any "public" expression to their faith that would challenge the State's monism of power. Hence even where they constitute an overwhelming majority of the electorate, "private" believers *are not free* to embody their beliefs in the laws or institutions of a political unit of any size—federal, state or local. For instance, according to the dictates of Liberty as implemented in America, where the First Amendment regime now governs the States (as the NRA rightly predicted long before the "incorporation" doctrine enunciated in *Gitlow*), it is legally impossible for a small town consisting entirely of Christians of various denominations to enact ordinances providing that the Ten Commandments shall govern community life, that local office holders must profess a belief in Christ, and that abortion, the sale of contraceptives and pornography, and other specified wrongs are prohibited within the town limits as contrary to the divine and natural law. Not even the otherwise almighty majority, not even a *unanimous* electorate, may act in any way that would violate Madison's "sacred principle of religious liberty," which paradoxically restricts the fundamental liberty, indeed the duty, of Christians to order their communities according to the law of the Gospel. A notable recent example of this radical restriction on the freedom of Christians in America is the philanthropist Thomas Monaghan's hasty retreat[153] from his plans to build a Catholic town in

---

152. Cavanaugh, *The Myth of Religious Violence*, 118.

153. *See* "Tom Monaghan's Pizza Pilgrimage," ePluribusMedia.org, 11 March 2006: "Civil libertarians are threatening to sue Domino's Pizza founder Tom Monaghan over his plans to build a new city in Florida . . . according to strict Roman Catholic principles. . . . If Monaghan gets his way, stores will not be able to sell pornography, pharmacies will be barred from selling condoms and other forms of birth control, and cable television companies will not be allowed to carry X-rated channels." Monaghan

Florida, which ended up being Catholic in name only. Madison and Jefferson, were they alive today, would have led the charge against Monaghan's proposed strictly Catholic town, just as they led the charge to disestablish even generic Christianity in Virginia.

As this study has demonstrated, Liberty has always been especially concerned with suppressing the action of the Catholic Church in social order because, as Locke rightly understood, the Church is the single greatest threat to the kind of polity Liberty demands: secular and pluralistic, with no "papist" alliance between government and revealed religion. We cannot forget how prominently the specter of "popery" figured in the Revolutionary propaganda that inspired the colonists to revolt against a king precisely on the suspicion that he was crypto-Catholic. The American constitutional scheme, like that of nearly all Western nations today, embodies the Lockean theologico-political principle that traditional Roman Catholicism is "the common enemy" of all right-thinking non-Catholic factions and, therefore, that Liberty must watch the Church like a hawk (or an American eagle) for the least sign that the "private opinions" of Catholics are threatening a breakthrough into the "public" sphere.

The principle that the operation of religious beliefs must be confined strictly to the realm of a private "freedom of worship" further limits religious freedom by "taming" even merely verbal religious opposition to error and vice at the level of public discourse. As Francis Fukuyama observes in his famous tribute (however cautionary) to the triumph of liberalism over the old order: "After a centuries-long confrontation with liberalism, religion was taught to be tolerant" and "was defanged by being made tolerant."[154] The toothless religion of so many contemporary Christians, including Catholics, arises from the operation of Locke's Law of Toleration in America and throughout the post-Christian West. The very existence of a Hobbelockean sovereign embodying and enforcing the Law of Toleration coerces religions to embody and enforce it as well.

As Fukuyama remarks in a passage that confirms our contention here, over time the instrumental elements of the so-called "peace treaty" among religions attain the status of supreme public virtues in themselves—above all, the "virtue" of toleration—which government imposes upon citizens *as duties transcending their "private" religious particularities* and thus impinging upon even "private" adherence to religion:

> *The liberal state growing out of the tradition of Hobbes and Locke engages in a protracted struggle with its own people.* It seeks to homogenize their variegated traditional cultures and to teach them to calculate instead their own long-term

---

abandoned his plans under threat of litigation: "I thought we owned the real estate, so we can lease to whoever we want . . . but there are laws and there were lawsuits out there" (Associated Press, July 23, 2007). In proper American fashion, the development company assured the public that "gays are welcome, too." Ibid.

154. Fukuyama, *The End of History*, 260, 271.

self-interest. In place of an organic moral community with its own language of "good and evil," one had to learn a new set of democratic values: to be a "participant," "rational," "secular," "mobile," "empathetic," and "tolerant." . . .

For democracy to work . . . citizens of democratic states *must forget the instrumental roots of their own values,* and develop a certain *irrational thymotic pride in their political system and way of life.* . . . Moreover, they must cease to see values like "tolerance" as merely a means to an end; *tolerance in democratic society becomes the defining virtue.*[155]

No less an authority than Sidney Mead, the great academic defender of the "American experiment" at the University of Chicago in the mid-20th century, explained the result of the process with evident satisfaction: "[T]he Republic's neutral civil authority *set limits on the absolutistic tendencies inherent in every religious sect,* preventing any one of them, or any combination of them, from gaining a monopoly on the definition of truth, and imposing its particular forms on the people. . . . Historically, *the way of the Republic has been the way the sects were constantly being pushed.* . . . The result is that today dogmatic insistence on the ultimate significance of any sect's particular tenets or observances seems to *have reached the vanishing point* except in citadels of impregnable isolation from the currents moving in the unfolding history of our world."[156] This study has been written from within one of those citadels of impregnable isolation: traditional Catholicism.

Nor is this outcome of merely recent emergence. It was already evident decades before the NRA movement deplored it, which is to say within the lifetime of the last of the generation of the Founders. As Gustave de Beaumont, the traveling companion of Alexis de Tocqueville, wrote to his mother: "nothing is commoner in the United States than this *indifference toward the nature of religions,* which doesn't however eliminate the fervor of each for the cult he has chosen." Beaumont wanted to know "how a lively and sincere faith can get on with a perfect toleration; how one can have equal respect for religions whose dogmas differ. . . ."[157] The answer, as our American experience demonstrates, is that they cannot. Over time, faith in the dogmas of traditional Christianity, especially as presented by Catholicism, could not coexist integrally in the same people who *also* have faith in the competing dogma of toleration. Hence Tocqueville himself wrote of his suspicion that even at the dawn of the American Republic there was "*a great depth of doubt and indifference*" hidden behind the outward piety of America's Protestant sects, and that "Faith is evidently inert." In the Protestant churches, he continued, "you will hear morality preached, of dogma not a word. Nothing which can at all shock the neighbor; nothing which can arouse the idea of dissent. . . . here, generally speaking, religion does not profoundly stir the souls." Rather, what Tocqueville saw among

155. Fukuyama, *The End of History,* 214–215.

156. Mead, "The Nation with the Soul of a Church," 281.

157. In Barbara Packer, "Signing Off: Religious Indifference in America," *There Before Us: Religion, Literature, and Culture from Emerson to Wendell Berry* (Grand Rapids, MI: William B. Eerdmans Publishing, 2006), 2.

American Protestants was a "pretended toleration which, in my opinion, is nothing other than good round indifference...."[158]

At that time (1831), Tocqueville was still able to say of Catholicism in America that "The Catholic faith is the immovable point from which each sect separates a little further, while nearing pure deism" and that Catholics were "taking advantage of the tolerance of their former adversaries, but [are] still at bottom as intolerant as they have ever been, as intolerant in a word as *people who believe*." But this was only because Catholics "forbid themselves all relations with the religious societies which surround them. I even suspect that their dogma on the liberty of conscience is about the same as [Catholics] in Europe; and I am not sure that they would not persecute if they found themselves the strongest."[159]

The insularity that protected the integrity of Catholicism in the midst of America's congenitally anti-Catholic *ethos* was made possible by the parish system, which managed to provide precisely the "citadels of impregnable isolation" to which Mead refers. But their fortress-like function would begin seriously to erode in about sixty years, when a newly emerging liberal wing in the American Catholic Church, led by Bishop John Ireland, began to sing Liberty's praises, prompting Rome itself finally to intervene against "the Americanist heresy." But that subject must await a later stage of this study. Suffice it to note for now that, as *The New York Times* observes with satisfaction, contemporary Catholics are voting for pro-abortion Democrats in vast numbers because they are "scattered across the American landscape, with the sun having long set on the empire of the parish, a source of boundary and social identity."[160] Even the Catholic population has merged fully into a body politic governed by the Law of Toleration; it no longer exhibits the intolerance of "people who believe."

On this score the sociologists have provided their usual empirical confirmation of the obvious. A recent study at Rice University revealed the non-surprise that "most Americans don't feel their religion is the only way to eternal life—*even if their faith tradition teaches otherwise*" and that sixty-eight percent of those surveyed agreed that "there is more than one true way to interpret the teachings *of their own religion*." Concerning Catholics, the study further observed that "More than most groups, Catholics break with their church, and not just on issues like abortion and homosexuality...."—a finding that prompted Archbishop Charles Chaput of Denver to lament that "The statistics show, more than anything else, that many who describe themselves as Catholics do not know or understand the teachings of their church." The sociologist who conducted the study concluded: "religion in America is, indeed, 3,000 miles wide and only three inches deep...."[161]

After more than two centuries under a political regime whose smothering "neutrality" obliterates all religious differences at the level of public life, at the level of

---

158. Tocqueville to L. de Kergolay, June 29, 1831, in George Wilson Pierson, *Tocqueville in America* (Baltimore: Johns Hopkins Univ. Press), 154.

159. Ibid., 155.

160. "Catholic Vote is Harbinger of Success," *New York Times*, February 9, 2008.

161. "Americans: My Faith Isn't the Only Way to Heaven," *Associated Press*, June 24, 2008.

"private" belief Americans have become "accustomed to a 'soft' Lockean Christianity characterized by peaceableness and love"[162]—a peaceableness and love that does not deny the right of the majority to "disagree" with the divine and natural law in such matters as "the right to choose" abortion, even if the soft Lockean Christian "privately" cannot "agree" with such "choices," which of course he will respect as prevailing law should he ascend to public office or the bench.

The resulting reduction of even "private" Christianity to a smiling toleration of what are objectively intolerable differences with others is viewed as a discovery of the true "essence" of religion uniting all Americans, or what Locke called "the chief Characteristical Mark of the True Church."[163] The liberal German Protestant theologian Paul Tillich presents this development as the point at which "religion breaks through its particularity, elevating it to spiritual freedom and with it to a vision of the spiritual presence in other expressions of the ultimate meaning of man's existence."[164] Somehow this "spiritual presence" never poses any impediment to the demand for divorce, abortion, pornography, "gay rights" or anything else the fickle majority may approve or tolerate as an outcome of the political process.

The Christian witness in opposition to error and vice has thus effectively ceased to exist in the same liberal State that boasts of its "freedom" for the "private" practice of religion. As Fukuyama observes: "Christianity in a certain sense had to abolish itself through a secularization of its goals before liberalism could emerge."[165] That is, the Framers' regime of "religious freedom" requires not just the subordination of Christianity by the State but also the triumph of Liberty over Christianity as a competing creed. Liberty has become the one religion on which all Americans can agree.

162. Morrisey, "Moral Foundations of the American Republic: An Introduction," *The Moral Foundations,* 14.

163. *Letter,* 23.

164. Paul Tillich, *Christianity and the Encounter of the World Religions* (NY: Columbia Univ. Press, 1963), 96–97, in Mead, "Nation with the Soul of a Church," 273.

165. Fukuyama, *The End of History,* 216.

21

The American
Confessional State

WHAT HAS BEEN SAID thus far should already have suggested that the secular state the Founders' created is not *purely* secular or *formally* atheistic, even if it excludes from its organic law any possibility of a commonwealth founded on the truths of divine revelation and is thus in practice the "godless, Christless blank" the NRA movement predicted. Quite the contrary, the birth of the American Republic represents the beginning of "a 'transfer of sacredness' from traditional Christianity to the United States itself"[1] in keeping with the general development of the sacred nation-state of political modernity. The sacredness of a nation-state that is no longer a Christian commonwealth necessarily gives rise to the civil religion first proposed by Hobbes and later advanced by thinkers of the "moderate" Enlightenment, including Rousseau, who coined the very term civil religion, as we saw in Chapter 4.

The American Civil Religion

After the dancing around Liberty Tree was over, the Spirit of Liberty left the Tree to be reincarnated in the new Republic. To recall the observation of Catherine Albanese noted in Chapter 5, the American Revolution "was in itself a religious experience, a hierophany collectively manifested and received, which provided the fundamental basis for American civil religion as we know it."[2] Perhaps the world's most renowned scholar on this subject, Robert N. Bellah, has observed that "[t]here is a sense in which the American Revolution and the American civil religion are the same thing. . . . I am pointing to that revolution in the minds of men that John Adams argued was the real revolution in America."[3] Recall in this connection John Adams's boast that the Revolution would mean not only freedom from the King but also "the illumination of the ignorant, and the emancipation of the slavish part of mankind all over the earth." In Chapter 4 we noted how Rousseau prescribed for his ideal state "a purely civil profession of faith, the articles of which it is up to the

---

1. Cavanaugh, *The Myth of Religious Violence*, 115.
2. Catherine L. Albanese, *Sons of the Fathers*, 6.
3. Robert N. Bellah, "The Revolution and the Civil Religion," in *Religion and the American Revolution*, ed. Jerald C. Brauer (Philadelphia: Fortress Press, 1976).

Sovereign to fix, not precisely as dogmas of Religion but as sentiments of sociability, without which it is impossible to be either a good Citizen or a loyal subject."[4] The American Republic represents the first embodiment of this type of civil religion, whose central dogma is Locke's Law of Toleration. In fact, "[t]he primary example of civil religion cited by scholars is that of the United States."[5]

The American civil religion is "a curious blend of Enlightenment and Christian themes and symbols,"[6] involving a "fusion of religion and secularism" that comes to us from Locke by way of "the thought of the heroes of the secular interpretation of the Founding, Thomas Jefferson and James Madison."[7] This fusion of religion and secularism subordinates not only Christianity, but even God Himself, to secular purposes that are paradoxically endowed with a religious force imposing itself on the body politic over and above all underlying religious differences among its individual members. The God of revelation, Jesus Christ, is the God the NRA movement pleaded for the national government to recognize in the Preamble at a time when the movement's members were convinced that "our national sins . . . have provoked the Divine displeasure." But this living and ever-present God, who intervenes directly in human affairs, punishes sin, chastises rebellious nations, judges and grants grace, is not part of what Albanese calls the "mythic worldview" from within which the drafters of the Constitution "were willing to consign the Almighty to oblivion."[8] Rather, the American civil religion invokes "a unitarian god that underwrites America's sense of purpose in the world."[9] The God in whom we trust, as our paper currency has declared since 1956, is not and never has been Christ, but rather the "Nature's God" of the Declaration of Independence, the Masonic "Glorious Being" of George Washington's presidential invocations, the unmentioned source of what the Constitution's Preamble calls "the Blessings of Liberty" that we nonetheless "secure to ourselves and our posterity" in Pelagian fashion by devising the appropriate political arrangements, including the state subordination of revealed religion.

This purely notional civil deity, however, has not failed to provide a commanding revelation of its own. Despite Madison's disclaimer of any divine inspiration for the Constitution, in the mythology of the Founding both the Constitution and the Declaration of Independence soon attained the status of God-breathed scriptures whose teaching (like the newly created government itself) overarches all religions, uniting and subduing them all under a set of divinely imposed super-dogmas given by the "Holy Author of our religion," to recall Jefferson's moniker for the Unitarian god who commanded the disestablishment of religion in Virginia. The Declaration and the Constitution, as Albanese writes, "quickly assumed [an] aura of sacrality" and the Constitution came to be seen not as a mere consensual arrangement

4. Cf. *The Social Contract*, IV.8.32.
5. Cavanaugh, *The Myth of Religious Violence*, 115.
6. Ibid.
7. Hancock, "Religion and the Limits of Limited Government," 698.
8. Albanese, *Sons of the Fathers*, 204.
9. Cavanaugh, op. cit., 116.

between parties to a legal document but rather "the greatest sacramental sign of the new republic...."[10] Thus did "[t]he fusion of religion and secularism" in the Founding acquire its analog to Holy Scripture in the two texts inspired primarily by Jefferson and Madison. And the teaching in these "scriptures," handed down to us by the first Apostles of Liberty, subordinates the teaching of the actual Scriptures just as effectively as the political structure the Framers erected subordinates Christianity.

The sermonizing of American politicians in the decades following the death of George Washington in 1799 provided a body of homiletics to go along with the sacred scriptures of the American civil religion. A well-known classic example is a peroration by former President John Quincy Adams during an address to commemorate the fiftieth anniversary of Washington's inauguration. After invoking the arrival of Moses and the children of Israel at the Promised Land just before Moses was withdrawn from the chosen people (as was Washington from the new chosen people of America), Adams depicts the Declaration and the Constitution as sacred texts that carry blessings or curses in accordance with the correspondence of the new covenant people to their teaching:

Fellow-citizens, the ark of *your* covenant is the Declaration of Independence. Your Mount Ebal [the mountain of curses], is the confederacy of separate state sovereignties, and your Mount Gerizim [the mountain of blessings] is the Constitution of the United States. In that scene of tremendous and awful solemnity, narrated in the Holy Scriptures, *there is not a curse pronounced against the people, upon Mount Ebal, not a blessing promised them upon Mount Gerizim, which your posterity may not suffer or enjoy, from your and their adherence to, or departure from, the principles of the Declaration of Independence, practically interwoven in the Constitution of the United States.*

Lay up these principles, then, in your hearts, and in your souls—bind them for signs upon your hands, that they may be as frontlets between your eyes[11]— teach them to your children, speaking of them when sitting in your houses, when walking by the way, when lying down and when rising up—write them upon the doorplates of your houses, and upon your gates—*cling to them as to the issues of life—adhere to them as to the cords of your eternal salvation.*

So may your children's children at the next return of this day of jubilee, after a full century of experience under your national Constitution, celebrate it again in the full enjoyment of all the blessings recognized by you in the commemoration of this day, and *of all the blessings promised to the children of Israel upon Mount Gerizim, as the reward of obedience to the law of God.*[12]

10. Albanese, *Sons of the Fathers*, 184, 202.

11. A direct quotation of Deuteronomy 18: "Therefore shall ye lay up these my words in your heart and in your soul; and ye shall bind them for a sign upon your hand, and they shall be for frontlets between your eyes."

12. John Quincy Adams, "Discourse to the New York Historical Society on the Fiftieth Anniversary of the Inauguration of George Washington," April 30, 1839 (paragraph breaks added).

On another occasion Adams posed the rhetorical question whether the "Declaration of Independence . . . gave to the world the first irrevocable pledge of the fulfillment of the prophecies, *announced directly from Heaven* at the birth of the saviour and predicted by the greatest of the Hebrew prophets six hundred years before?"[13] In the orations of Adams the fusion of the Founders' secular political aims and religion could not be more apparent. Even liberal Catholic "Americanists" would take up his themes a few decades later, arousing the fierce opposition of their "ultramontane" Catholic opponents.

In the same vein is this literal prayer to Father Washington by another great sermonizer of the American civil religion, Daniel Webster, speaking as Secretary of State in 1851:

> Great Father of your Country! we heed your words; we feel their force as if you now uttered them with lips of flesh and blood. Your example teaches us, your affectionate addresses teach us, your public life teaches us, your sense of the value of the blessings of the Union. Those blessings our fathers have tasted, and we have tasted, and still taste. Nor do we intend that those who come after us shall be denied the same high fruition. Our honor as well as our happiness is concerned. *We cannot, we dare not, we will not, betray our sacred trust.*
>
> We will not filch from posterity the treasure placed in our hands to be transmitted to other generations. The bow that gilds the clouds in the heavens, the pillars that uphold the firmament, may disappear and fall away in the hour appointed by the will of God; *but until that day comes, or so long as our lives may last, no ruthless hand shall undermine that bright arch of Union and Liberty* which spans the continent from Washington to California.[14]

The "bright arch of Union and Liberty" apparently did not extend to the slaves whose federal rendition and forcible return to their masters Webster had supported in voting for the Fugitive Slave Law of 1850 (a decision that had cost him his career in the Senate but did not prevent him from regaining his earlier position as Secretary of State).

Appropriately enough, some fourteen years after Webster's hymn to Washington, the interior of the dome in the rotunda of the Capitol Building was adorned by the aforementioned fresco entitled "The Apotheosis of Washington" (cf. Chapter 8). It was the work of the Italian artist Constantino Brumidi, who had been employed at the Vatican by Pope Gregory XVI—ironically, the same Pope who had denounced liberalism and religious indifferentism in his encyclical *Mirari Vos* (1831). We have already noted that Brumidi's fresco depicts "George Washington rising to the heavens in glory, flanked by female figures representing Liberty and Victory/Fame. . . ." As the government website explains: "The word 'apotheosis' in the title means liter-

---

13. John Quincy Adams, "Oration Delivered Before the Inhabitants of the Town of Newburyport . . . July 4, 1837," in *Albanese, Sons of the Fathers*, 192.

14. Speech on "The Addition to the Capitol," July 4, 1851, in *The Great Speeches and Orations of Daniel Webster* (Boston: Little, Brown & Co., 1879), 653 (paragraph breaks added).

ally *the raising of a person to the rank of a god*, or the glorification of a person as an ideal; George Washington was honored as a national icon in the nineteenth century."[15] The surrounding iconography depicts such celestial events as

Armed Freedom and the eagle defeating Tyranny and Kingly Power;

...Minerva teaching Benjamin Franklin, Robert Fulton, and Samuel F.B. Morse;

...Neptune holding his trident and Venus holding the transatlantic cable, which was being laid at the time the fresco was painted;

...Mercury handing a bag of money to Robert Morris, financier of the American Revolution;

...Vulcan at the anvil and forge, producing a cannon and a steam engine;

...Ceres seated on the McCormick Reaper, accompanied by America in a red liberty cap and Flora picking flowers.[16]

Of course, this is not the only artistic hymn of praise to Washington apotheosized. The astonishing Washington Monument, a 555-foot tall obelisk constructed between 1848 and 1884, contains "193 memorial stones presented by individuals, societies, cities, States, and nations of the world." All of humanity paid tribute to Washington as "the divinely appointed Moses who led his people out of the hands of tyranny."[17] Demonstrating both America's endemic anti-Catholicism and the religious character of the Monument, on January 16, 1854 a mob broke into a storage facility on the Mall to steal the "Pope Stone," a piece of marble the Pope (Pius IX) had sent for inclusion in the Monument as a gesture of good will. While an armed watchman stood by and did nothing, the "Pope Stone" was thrown into the Potomac to prevent the Monument's "defilement" after the protesters were unable to obtain the concession that it be placed next to another stone stating: "Americans were fully aware of the 'crafty, subtle, far seeing and far reaching power, which is ever grasping over the whole world, to sway with its iron scepter, with bloodstained hands, over the millions of its inhabitants.'"[18]

Saint Thomas and Saint Abraham are likewise immortalized in their respective quasi-religious shrines. The Jefferson Memorial, a mammoth affair modeled on the Pantheon in Rome, enshrines a 19-foot bronze statue of Jefferson that "was intended to represent the Age of Enlightenment and Jefferson as a philosopher and statesman." In activities befitting a religious shrine, "the Jefferson Memorial plays host to various ceremonies, including annual Memorial exercises [and] Easter

15. "The Apotheosis of Washington," www.aoc.gov/cc/art/rotunda/apotheosis/Overview.cfm.

16. Ibid.

17. Robert N. Bellah, "Civil Religion in America," *Dædalus, Journal of the American Academy of Arts and Sciences*, Fall 2005 (1967), 47.

18. Theodore Maynard, *The Catholic Church and the American Idea* (NY: Appleton-Century-Crofts, Inc., 1953), 71.

Sunrise Services. . . ."[19] The Lincoln Memorial is literally designated a temple by the federal government: "In this temple, as in the hearts of the people for whom he saved the Union, the memory of Abraham Lincoln is enshrined forever."[20] Within the temple, whose design was inspired by the Parthenon, "the Great Emancipator and preserver of the nation during the Civil War . . . sits immortalized in marble" on a throne-like chair surrounded by massive Doric columns. The Great Emancipator's "left hand is clenched in a manner depicting determination . . . to fight the war to its end in spite of the ongoing bloodshed."[21] But while a temple enshrines the assassinated President as a martyr for Liberty, there is no temple in the Capitol dedicated to the memory of the 620,000 souls slaughtered in the war Lincoln waged under the supposed heavenly warrant to preserve at any cost the union of New York with North Carolina or Maine with Mississippi.

Nor must we forget the saints and sacred shrines of the extinct Confederacy with its own saga of holy martyrdom for Liberty: the "Recumbent Statue" of Robert E. Lee in the "holy of holies" of the Lee Chapel, the "Mecca" of the twin gravesites of Lee and Jackson at Lexington, and the mammoth Jefferson Davis memorial erected in imitation of the Washington Monument. Only a lack of funds prevented completion of the construction of "a grand temple, designed by New York architect, Percy Griffith, as a memorial to the Confederate president." The project had to be abandoned after the laying of the cornerstone.[22] But Lee and Jackson, the sainted generals of the Lost Cause, have been raised to the national altars of Liberty along with their Northern counterparts, and today all of America recognizes their rightful place in the great canon of Liberty's progress, even if they are not saints of the first rank like Lincoln and Washington.

In addition to sacred scriptures, saints, and shrines, the American civil religion has its own religious relics. It was Jefferson himself who "advocated for 'reverence' of the Declaration of Independence and the 'holy purpose' of adhesion to it," and who expressed the hope that memorabilia surrounding the writing of the Declaration would be reverenced "*like the relics of saints . . .* to nourish our devotion to this *holy bond* of Union."[23] Among these relics was the writing desk on which Jefferson penned his draft of the Declaration. In a letter to his granddaughter, Ellen Randolph Coolidge, Jefferson informed her that "I happen still to possess the writing-box on which it was written," and that if her husband accepted it as a gift from him, he might live "to see it carried in the procession of our nation's birthday, as the relics of the saints are in those of the church."[24]

19. "Jefferson Memorial," www.nps.gov/nr/travel/wash/dc73.htm.

20. "Lincoln Memorial," www.nps.gov/linc/index.htm.

21. Ibid.

22. Donald E. Collins, *The Death and Resurrection of Jefferson Davis* (Lanham, MD: Rowman and Littlefield, 2005), 86.

23. In Cavanaugh, *The Myth of Religious Violence*, 115.

24. Jefferson to Ellen Randolph Coolidge, November 14, 1825, in *Family Letters*, 461–462, available online @ www.monticello.org/site/research-and-collections/fourth-july.

Drawing upon the analysis of Harvard sociologist W. Lloyd Warner, Bellah's famous essay "Civil Religion in America" even identifies a liturgical calendar of major feast days for the American civil religion:

> Memorial Day, which grew out of the Civil War, gave ritual expression to the themes [of] . . . a rededication to the martyred dead, to the spirit of sacrifice, and to the American vision. Just as Thanksgiving Day . . . serves to integrate the family into the civil religion, so Memorial Day has acted to integrate the local community into the national cult. Together with the less overtly religious Fourth of July and the more minor celebrations of Veterans Day and the birthdays of Washington and Lincoln, these two holidays provide *an annual ritual calendar for the civil religion.* The public school system serves as a particularly important context for *the cultic celebration of the civil rituals.*[25]

Memorial Day is the civil religion's analogue to All Souls' Day. In various public ceremonies the faithful departed are remembered, not for the repose of their souls (whose existence and eternal destiny are matters of "private" opinion), but for their blood sacrifice on behalf of the Republic. Warner describes the elaborate liturgical functions surrounding the event:

> The sacred symbolic behavior of Memorial Day, in which scores of the town's organizations are involved, is ordinarily divided into four periods. During the year separate rituals are held by many of the associations for their dead, and many of these activities are connected with later Memorial Day events. In the second phase, preparations are made during the last three or four weeks for the ceremony itself, and some of the associations perform public rituals. The third phase consists of scores of rituals held in all the cemeteries, churches, and halls of the associations. These rituals consist of speeches and highly ritualized behavior. They last for two days and are climaxed by the fourth and last phase, in which all the separate celebrants gather in the center of the business district on the afternoon of Memorial Day. The separate organizations, with their members in uniform or with fitting insignia, march through the town, visit the shrines and monuments of the hero dead, and, finally, enter the cemetery. Here dozens of ceremonies are held, most of them highly symbolic and formalized.[26]

Finally, the American civil religion has its own ultimate sacred symbol: the American Flag, which represents the incarnation of Liberty, just as the Crucifix represents the Incarnation of the Second Person of the Holy Trinity—an object so sacred that it must never be allowed to touch the ground. Cavanaugh cites a passage from Carlton Hayes's famed *Essays on Nationalism* that should give pause to any objective observer of that strange awe and reverence Americans are expected to display for a piece of cloth emblazoned with stars and stripes:

25. Robert N. Bellah, "Civil Religion in America," *Dædalus, Journal of the American Academy of Arts and Sciences,* Winter 1967, Vol. 96, No. 1, 11–12.

26. W. Lloyd Warner, *American Life* (Chicago: Univ. of Chicago Press, 1962), 8–9.

Nationalism's chief symbol of faith and central object of worship is the flag, and curious liturgical forms have been devised for "saluting" the flag, for "dipping" the flag, for "lowering" the flag, and for "hoisting" the flag. Men bare their heads when the flag passes by; and in praise of the flag poets write odes and children sing hymns. In America young people are ranged in serried rows and required to recite daily, with hierophantic voice and ritualistic gesture, the mystical formula: "I pledge allegiance to our [sic] flag and to the country [sic][27] for which it stands, one nation, indivisible, with liberty and justice for all."[28] Everywhere, in all solemn feasts and fasts of nationalism the flag is in evidence, and with it that other sacred thing, the national anthem.[29]

This veritable idolatry of a flag is not to be confused with love of one's country, for the Pledge of Allegiance is not to America as such, the land beneath our feet, but to the *flag* and to "the *Republic* for which it stands." What is enjoined upon one who recites the Pledge and salutes the flag, with hand over heart, is devotion to *the State*, to a particular form of government, rather than to the fatherland of traditional patriotic affections. Something quite distinct from the virtue of patriotism is at work here.

In fact, the very author of the Pledge, Francis Bellamy, was a "Christian socialist" and champion of "liberty, equality and fraternity" in the French mode, whose cousin, Edward Bellamy, was the author of the utopian novel *Looking Backward*, a huge best-seller which depicted America in the year 2000 as a socialist paradise. Bellamy wrote the Pledge in 1892, at a time when "immigrants were pouring into the country ... anti-Catholicism was strong [and] [r]eformers were fighting for universal public education, while heated debates were raging over the funding for parochial and public schooling."[30]

In other words, the Pledge was intended as a loyalty oath to impose doctrinal conformity on Catholics and other perceived threats to the civil religion. Bellamy's expressly stated aim was to use the public schools to inculcate a quasi-religious devotion to republican principles. "It is the same way," he wrote, "with the catechism, or the Lord's prayer."[31] Apropos this function of the Pledge, Teddy Roosevelt, then head of the Civil Service Commission, remarked: "The Common School and Flag stand together as the arch-typical of American civilization. The Common School is *the leading form in which the principles of equality and fraternity take shape*, while the Flag represents not only those principles of equality, fraternity

27. The official version of the Pledge has never used the phrase "the country for which it stands" but rather "the Republic for which it stands."

28. Hayes wrote before "under God" was inserted into the pledge in 1954.

29. Carlton Hayes, *Essays on Nationalism* (NY: Macmillan, 1926), 107, in Cavanaugh, *Myth of Religious Violence*, 117.

30. Dr. Shelly Lapkoff, "The Amazing History of the Pledge of Allegiance," historyofthepledge.com/history.html.

31. In Cecilia O'Leary, *To Die For: The Paradox of American Patriotism* (Princeton, NJ: Princeton Univ. Press, 1999), 178.

and liberty, but also the great pulsing nation with all its hopes, and all its past, and all its moral power."[32]

The Pledge—just as Bellamy wrote it, but with the addition of the words "under God" in 1954—is codified as federal law in the Federal Flag Code,[33] along with the proper rituals and rubrics for displaying and respecting the flag's sacred and untouchable status. The Code specifies how the flag is to be protected from any possibility of desecration by profane hands.[34] Although it contains no penalties for non-compliance, the Code prescribes reverence for the flag because it "represents a living country and *is itself a living thing*."[35] The living flag, the Flag Code admonishes, "should not be dipped to any person or thing," evidently because it is viewed as having a greater dignity than any person or thing.[36] When the flag passes by, all in its presence "should face the flag and stand at attention with their right hand over the heart, or if applicable, remove their headdress with their right hand and hold it at the left shoulder, the hand being over the heart. Citizens of other countries should stand at attention."[37] The Code even prescribes a proper dignified "funeral" for a tattered flag (preferably cremation).[38]

It is quite revealing that in America the same Christians who would never dream of any sort of public reverencing of a Crucifix, symbol of the very God in whom they profess to believe, nevertheless demand shows of humble public submission and even adoration before a banner that represents a mere earthly republic. In keeping with this religious reverence for the flag, the Supreme Court, in *Minersville School District v. Gobitis* (1940), upheld 8-to-1 a local school board's compulsory flag salute regulation and its expulsion of recusant Jehovah's Witnesses, despite their objection to what they considered state-enforced idolatry. In so doing, the Court provided the very rationale Justice Scalia would adduce nearly sixty years later in *Smith*: "The mere possession of religious convictions which contradict the relevant concerns of a political society does not relieve the citizen from the discharge of political responsibilities."[39]

Yet only three years after *Gobitis*, reversing itself 6-to-3 in *West Virginia Board of Education v. Barnette*, the Court implicitly recognized that state-mandated reverence for the flag does involve a matter of civil religion, observing that "no official,

32. In John W. Baer, *The Pledge of Allegiance: A Centennial History: 1892–1992* (Annapolis, MD: Free State Press, Inc., 2007), oldtimeislands.org/pledge/pdgech4.htm.

33. Cf. 4 U.S.C. §§(1)–(10).

34. The Flag Code provides that the Flag must never be: "displayed with the union (stars) down," "allowed to touch anything beneath it," "carried flat or horizontally," "used as wearing apparel, bedding, or drapery," "festooned, drawn back, nor up, in folds," "fastened, displayed, used, or stored in such a manner as to permit it to be easily torn, soiled, or damaged in any way," "used as a covering for a ceiling," or "have placed upon it, nor on any part of it, nor attached to it any mark, insignia, letter, word, figure, design, picture, or drawing of any nature." Cf. 4 U.S.C. (8), (a)–(i).

35. 4 U.S.C. §(8)(j).

36. 4 U.S.C. §(8).

37. 4 U.S.C. §(9).

38. 4 U.S.C. §(8)(k).

39. *Minersville Sch. Dist. v. Gobitis*, 310 U.S. 586, 594–95.

high or petty, can prescribe what shall be orthodox in politics, nationalism, religion, or other matters of opinion or force citizens to confess by word or act their faith therein."[40] The mandatory Pledge of Allegiance in effect at that time included the "Bellamy salute," which the Court described as "the 'stiff-arm' salute, the saluter to keep the right hand raised with palm turned up . . ." while facing the flag and pledging allegiance to the Republic.[41] As the Court noted, "[o]bjections to the salute as 'being too much like Hitler's' were raised by the Parent and Teachers Association, the Boy and Girl Scouts, the Red Cross, and the Federation of Women's Clubs."[42] The embarrassing resemblance to the Nazi salute (rendered palm-down) prompted Congress to amend the Flag Code to prescribe the current hand-over-heart gesture.[43]

The Jehovah's Witnesses involved in *Barnette* had been unable to avoid expulsion for "insubordination" even though they had proposed a substitute pledge in which they would declare: "I respect the flag of the United States and acknowledge it as a symbol of freedom and justice to all. I pledge allegiance and obedience to all the laws of the United States *that are consistent with God's law, as set forth in the Bible.*"[44] For reasons that should require no explanation at this point, mere respect for the flag as a symbol, but a refusal to salute it as a "living thing," and a promise to obey human law only if it comports with divine law, are heresies against the American civil religion. Nevertheless, the Supreme Court relieved the Witnesses of their excommunication from the public schools, upholding a state court injunction preventing enforcement of the mandatory pledge and Nazi-style salute.

Forty-six years later, however, in dissenting from the Court's 5-to-4 decision in *Texas v. Johnson*, which invalidated a Texas statute criminalizing flag-burning as "desecration of a venerated object," Justice Rehnquist protested: "The flag is not simply another 'idea' or 'point of view' competing for recognition in the marketplace of ideas. Millions and millions of Americans regard it with *an almost mystical reverence. . . .*"[45] Indeed they do. And it seems that no "loyal American" is permitted to suggest that there might be something odd and even idolatrous about this. Obstinate doubt or denial of the necessity of mystical reverence for the American Flag is heresy, and mistreatment of it is sacrilege and desecration.[46] Accordingly, in

40. *West Virginia State Board of Education v. Barnette*, 319 U.S. 624, 642 (1943).
41. *Id.* at 627.
42. *Id.* at 627–28.
43. Cf. 4 U.S.C.A. §4.
44. *Id.* at 627 & n.4.
45. *Texas v. Johnson*, 491 U.S. 397, 429 (1989)(Rehnquist, J., dissenting).
46. This author is personally familiar with an incident in which American Catholics on religious pilgrimage in France were accused of "desecrating" the American Flag their chapter carried in procession because they had stitched onto it an emblem of the Sacred Heart of Jesus to signify (as even the Protestant NRA movement recognized) His dominion over all nations. That an ancient Catholic symbol of God Incarnate was held to "desecrate" the symbol of an earthly government established by deistic revolutionaries in the 18th century reveals the extent to which America's civil religion is paramount to Christianity.

response to the decision in *Johnson*, Congress enacted the Flag Protection Act of 1989, imposing a federal prison term of up to one year on anyone who "knowingly mutilates, defaces, physically defiles, burns, *maintains on the floor or ground*, or tramples upon any flag of the United States."[47] By a bare majority of 5-to-4 the Supreme Court (following its rationale in *Johnson*), struck down the law in 1990, thus narrowly averting the federal criminal prosecution of heresy, sacrilege, and desecration respecting the flag.[48]

In sum, to borrow from Cavanaugh's summary of Hayes's sociological analysis, the American civil religion has all the elements of Christianity with none of its theological content: a Supreme Being, sacred scriptures, saints, martyrs, shrines, relics, liturgies and a liturgical calendar, feast days—including a Christmas (the Fourth of July) and a Feast of Corpus Christi (Flag Day)—a sacred defining symbol akin to the Crucifix (the Flag), and even an inquisition (the public schools as enforcers of patriotism and political correctness).[49] But there is also an underlying theology, and a Church to teach it.

An Anti-Theology of the State

According to the Lockean variant of "Christian liberalism," as Hancock calls it, Locke's ultimately illusory "limitation" of government to insuring the pursuit of self-interest without impediment by any governmentally recognized religious sanction is precisely what achieves the status of a religious principle in an "anti-theology" of the State. This anti-theology arose within a Calvinistic theological framework that takes the depravity of fallen man as an irremediable given—divine grace having nothing to do with political life—yet pronounces good the actions depraved man takes according to the "natural law" of self-preservation in the "state of nature" posited by both Hobbes and Locke. The anti-theology excludes Original Sin and thus the Greco-Catholic conception of justice as the activity of a morally integrated soul (delivered from Original Sin by grace) and happiness as the possession of virtue by such a soul. Hancock notes the "Lockean separation of body and soul" (evident also in Justice Scalia's remarks, as we have seen) and with it Locke's acceptance of "the Hobbesian premise that man can know nothing of happiness, but only 'of the conditions appropriate to the pursuit of what each man may call happiness.'"[50] From which it follows that "A Lockean political order is not based on any definite view of the whole, or any fixed understanding of the purpose of human life."[51]

If there is no universal understanding of a divinely established purpose of human

---

47. 18 U.S.C. §700(a)(1).

48. Cf. *United States v. Eichman*, 496 U.S. 310 (1990).

49. Cavanaugh, *The Myth of Religious Violence*, 117.

50. Hancock, "Religion and the Limits of Limited Government," 696, quoting Berns, *First Amendment*, 30.

51. Ibid.

life, yet there *is* a divinely authored "natural law" of self-preservation by all necessary means, then God "is pushed so far beyond the human world that divinity can provide no intelligible reference point above the common, material interests of humanity, but only *a spiritual sanction for the universalization of those interests.* Thus divinity is reduced to *beneficent power in service of humanity.*"[52] This divine servant of humanity is the deity presented by the sacred theology of the American civil religion, available to bless the waging of war—both civil and foreign—the conquest of territory, the launching of major programs, and all other national undertakings on a non-denominational basis, but never to countermand law or public policy adopted by government or by an electoral majority. The only God who could countermand what "We the People" have decided is the living Christ, but it was precisely He who had found no place in the Constitution, as the NRA had protested far too late to do anything about it.

Harold Bloom provoked widespread outrage but no serious refutation when he wrote in 1991 that what passes for religion in America "masks itself as Protestant Christianity but has ceased to be Christian.... I do not think the Christian God has been retained by us, though he is invoked endlessly by our leaders, and by our flag-waving President in particular, with especial fervor in the context of war. But this invoked force appears to be *American destiny, the God of our national faith.*"[53] The American Jesus of Lockean Christianity, marketed under a thousand different brands in a competitive "religious marketplace,"[54] has merged into one substance with the Unitarian god of the Founders. The "holy spirit" that proceeds from both the American Father and the American Son is the Spirit of Liberty, which inspired the Declaration and the Constitution "for the illumination of the ignorant, and the emancipation of the slavish part of mankind all over the earth."

What has arisen from the Founders' fusion of secularism and religion, therefore, is neither pure secularism nor atheism but rather what Mead terms "the cosmopolitan, universal theology of the Republic."[55] That is how Mead understands G.K. Chesterton's observation that "America is the only nation in the world that is founded on a creed. That creed is set forth with dogmatic and even *theological* lucidity in the Declaration of Independence...."

America as Teaching Church

America, Chesterton also said, is "a nation with the soul of Church."[56] Taking his cue from Chesterton, Mead explains—an explanation freely adopted here—that since under the American regime of religious "neutrality" no denomination "could plausibly claim to be, or to function as, 'the church' in the new nation, 'the *nation*

52. Hancock, 693.

53. Harold Bloom, *The American Religion*, 32.

54. Hatch, *Democratization of American Christianity*, 67.

55. Mead, "Nation with the Soul of a Church," 270.

56. G.K. Chesterton, "What I Saw in America," *The Collected Works of G.K. Chesterton* (San Francisco: Ignatius 1990), Vol. 21, 41–45.

came more and more so to function."[57] By assuming "a churchly function in becoming the community of righteousness," the American nation has emerged "as the primary agent of God's meaningful activity in history. . . ." Lincoln was not employing a mere trope in his declaration that "when the people rise in masses in behalf of the Union and the liberties of their country, truly may it be said, 'The gates of hell shall not prevail against them.'"[58]

Purporting to represent informed Catholic opinion, the late Richard John Neuhaus, a Lutheran minister who became a Catholic in 1990, said much the same thing as Mead concerning Chesterton's remark, offering the astonishing admission that "America is *the first creedal nation in human history. America did not just happen. It was professed into being. In that sense, America is the first universal nation,* for all who are convinced can join in professing its *creed. . . .*"[59] Contrary to what Neuhaus suggested, profession of the "creed" of the "first universal nation" has not been confined to those who are convinced of its truth. We have already seen in some detail that the American Revolution itself was an exercise in imposition of the "creed" by force wherever it met popular resistance. So was the Civil War, which was a bilateral Crusade: by the North, to recapture part of the Holy Land from infidels and return it to communion with the Holy See on the Potomac; and by the South, to establish by a Second American Revolution the "First Reformed America" of the Confederate States, wherein chattel slavery and the "conservative" hierarchical society it supported would have their rightful place in the true Protestant Promised Land of Liberty. As we will see in the second volume of this study, since the American Revolution virtually every Western nation, beginning with France, has adopted the "creed"—that is, Liberty—at the point of a gun. This would often occur with crucial assistance from "the first universal nation," happily reunited in a repaired Temple of Liberty in which division would never more occur. Recall Jefferson Davis's advice after the Civil War that "[t]he past is dead . . . before you lies the future—a future full of hope and golden promise; a future of expanding national glory, before which all the world shall stand amazed."

America is indeed a creedal nation; and Neuhaus acknowledged that this creed is a "'civil religion' that can too easily turn to idolatry," the prophylactic for which, inexplicably enough, he saw as an even firmer adherence to the "truths" enunciated by the Founders in their "curious mix of the Scottish Enlightenment and Calvinist Christianity" and their "Puritan-Lockean synthesis."[60] Neuhaus typifies the contemporary liberal Catholic who casts himself (*à la* Locke) as a prudent conservative, even as he presents the radical idea that there was a hitherto undiscovered universal validity, pressing even for Catholic acceptance, in the principles of a political regime devised by deistic Protestant thinkers who (*à la* Locke) despised

57. Mead, op. cit., quoting John E. Smylie, "National Ethos and the Church," *Theology Today*, XX (October 1963), 313–21.

58. Address of February 11, 1861, Lincoln archive, www.nps.gov/liho/indianapolis-_inaugural-journey.ht.

59. Richard John Neuhaus, *Doing Well and Doing Good* (NY: Doubleday, 1992), 4, 55.

60. Ibid.

Catholicism and the perennial philosophy integrated into Catholic teaching on the theologico-political question.

We will return to a consideration of Neuhaus's brand of liberalism in a second volume, which takes up the phenomenon of the "Americanist heresy" and the eventual papal condemnation of it in the context of the worldwide wave of revolutions following the revolution in France, the first inspired by the American example. Suffice it to say for now that Neuhaus himself suggests the conclusion toward which this chapter has been moving: that the "temple of Liberty" is the self-proclaimed successor to the Catholic Church, the Church of Churches and the Faith of Faiths, a religious world-society that "transcended and included 'all earlier distinctions, whether of Jew and Gentile, or of Greek and barbarian. . . .'"[61] The Republic "conceived in liberty and dedicated to the proposition that all men are created equal" embodies a new "universal vision . . . incarnated in a religiously pluralistic commonwealth." This new pluralistic commonwealth "is the bearer in history of the cosmopolitanism which, when and if incorporated in world institutions, may *compel* the nation-churches to live side-by-side in peace under law—*as our Republic compelled the heteronomous religious sects to do* until they discovered that the limitation of their conflicts to reason and persuasion was a viable path to union— that dialogue was a virtue."[62]

This new community of righteousness demands of its members not only toleration but also religious obedience to its new vision of a united humanity. According to Liberty's "theonomous cosmopolitanism," involving a fusion of the secular and the religious, the divine will itself has decreed that there shall be one fold and one shepherd—or else. The power of the State no longer serves the cause of the Gospel of Christ; it serves the cause of the gospel of Liberty. Hence, paradoxically but no less truly, "The deep meaning of the radical separation of politics and religion is their fusion."[63] The Founders and Framers executed perfectly the blueprint drawn up by Locke, who, "though widely credited with being the great philosopher of the separation of church and state" actually proposed "the most successful *uniting* of church and state in the history of modern political philosophy. Locke completely politicizes religion, and completely theologizes politics. But the new Lockean religion is a far cry from Christianity as it had ever been understood before. . . ."[64] And so is the Lockean fusion of secularism and religion that is the "cosmopolitan" deistic theology of the Founding.

Seen in this light, the motto "In God We Trust" on our currency, the congressional chaplains, the presidential proclamations of prayer and fasting, and so forth, are not, as Craycraft says, "anomalous to the intention of the First Amendment" as understood by Madison and Jefferson, but rather they are completely consistent with the supra-religious authority of Liberty as the demiurge, the active agent

61. Mead, "Nation with the Soul of a Church," 263.
62. Ibid,. 283.
63. Hancock, "Religion and Limited Government," 695.
64. Craycraft, *American Myth of Religious Liberty*, 40.

between the "Glorious Being" and man, first acknowledged in the rituals surrounding the Liberty Tree. For after all, the government we have is what "the Holy author of our religion" has willed, according to Jefferson, and what "the Christian Religion itself" requires, according to Madison. The cultural and ceremonial remnants of traditional religion tolerated in the national government, being devoid of any Christian doctrinal content challenging to the State, thus not only pose no threat to the reign of Liberty but actually facilitate it as instrumentalized religious props.

Martin E. Marty, the renowned professor emeritus of religious history at the University of Chicago, ties the existence of America's civil religion to Gustave de Beaumont's query about how the "personal" faith of the members of the various Protestant sects in America could "get on with such a perfect toleration." Marty argues that Beaumont's "tentative conclusion" that "their faiths were broad but not deep" obscures the deeper answer to the question, which "had to do with the character of the common faith."[65] That is, the common faith overrides all individual faiths (no matter how deep) wherever the two conflict.

One might wonder how a supposedly "Christian people" was induced to place this common faith above the dictates of Christianity as preached by their various denominations. Were the Protestant masses in Revolutionary America, their clergy included, duped into accepting Madison's and Jefferson's Locke-inspired theologico-political fusion? On the contrary, as Hancock rightly contends, the "Lockean subordination of Christianity to secular ends" is not some plot perpetrated by devious drafters "contrary to the intention of the great body of the people." Putting aside the rather underhanded manner in which the Constitution was substituted for the Articles of Confederation in the secret sessions at Philadelphia, the theologico-political aspect of the new national government (to be distinguished from its claims to authority over the States) was seen and accepted by the Protestant majority, both North and South, as representative of America's common faith: faith in majoritarian republicanism, the unfettered pursuit of happiness, the dogma of toleration, the sacred texts of the Declaration and the Constitution, and a distant generic deity who unfailingly blesses all these things, no matter what their outcome.[66] The NRA movement represents a significant although short-lived exception, but even fellow Protestants denounced its members as religious fanatics. Moreover, the NRA itself was hopelessly torn between its desire for a Christian republic and the contrary tenets of the American civil religion, especially dogmatic toleration of belief and unbelief indifferently and the separation of Church and State.

Hancock, therefore, misses the mark in his contention that the "Protestant Lockeanism of the first Americans" was not a contradiction in terms, that it did not arise from a "confusion of the brain" that left people unable to perceive any "incompatibility between the teachings of Jesus Christ and those of John Locke."[67]

---

65. Martin E. Marty, *Sons of the Fathers*, Foreword, xi.
66. Hancock, op. cit., 686.
67. Ibid.

The very fact that America's Protestant Lockeanism is an application of Locke's principles within a Calvinistic theological framework only demonstrates that it *is* a confusion; for Locke was nothing if not a confused thinker, and Protestantism in all its forms is a study in confusion and self-contradiction. Nowhere is the confusion inherent to Protestant Lockeanism more apparent than in the undoubtedly well-intentioned NRA movement, whose program literally amounted to proclaiming the existence of a Christian government that could not actually be Christian.

The same "confusion of the brain" is evident in the writings of Joseph Story, who, like NRA President William Strong, was a Supreme Court justice. Story's commentaries on the Constitution are considered a classic work on the subject, and yet we find Story arguing at one and the same time that government should "foster and encourage" Christianity "among all the citizens and subjects," but that the Founders were right to "exclude from the national government *all* power to act upon the subject of religion" and to refuse to require any religious test for office, so that "the Catholic and the Protestant, the Calvinist and the Armenian, the Jew and the Infidel, may sit down at the common table of the national councils. . . ."[68] Thus, Story, like the NRA, advocated a pro-Christian government that could not favor Christianity. The legal scholar Michael de Haven Newsom, in an essay on what he calls "The American Protestant Empire," catches the self-contradiction: "Having posited a Christian duty to encourage the religion, it is difficult to see how the national government would not be obliged to do so. Yet, because of the absence of a religious test for office . . . it is difficult to see how that Christian duty might be fulfilled."[69] It is not only difficult, but impossible.

What all of this means is simply that the vaunted "religious freedom" of Americans under the First Amendment does not exist. The regime established by the Founders allows only a relative free exercise of religion in the newly invented "private" sphere, while prohibiting the free exercise of religion and mandating adherence to the civil religion in the equally novel "public" sphere, especially when it comes to the Catholic Church. No one has exposed the nature of the fraud more deftly than Craycraft:

> But insofar as liberals claim that all religious beliefs are granted equal liberty under the American regime, they make a claim that is simply not true. Locke intended, and Madison understood, that the state's first concern is to protect its own peace and sovereignty, and therefore that *the definition of all liberties must be made by the state*, or at least approved by the state as not being in violation of the charter. But this state must necessarily deny the freedom of a church which presumes that *its* definitions ought to be the regnant ones. *The state makes a truth claim, and it cannot allow rivals. . . .* The reason there is no such thing as freedom of speech or religion is that *there is no such thing as the*

68. Joseph Story, Commentaries on the Constitution of the United States (Hilliard, Gray & Co., 1833), Vol. 3, §986, 992, quoted in Newsom, "The American Protestant Empire: a Historical Perspective," 40 *Washburn Law Journal* 187, 255 (2001).

69. Newsom., 255–56.

liberalism that claims to have invented them. In Fish's succinct phrase, "Liberalism doesn't exist."[70]

Here too Liberty has never delivered what it promised. Just as Liberty promised liberation from the "tyranny" of monarchy only to demand the subjugation of all to Locke's "one supreme government," so also has it promised "freedom of religion" while demanding the adherence of all to a supreme cult of civic tolerance under a strictly non-denominational God, who must never under any circumstances be identified with Christ and His claims on men and nations. The blessing this secular deity has bestowed in common on the members of all religions, or no religion, is the Republic, which every citizen, regardless of creed, has a duty to preserve intact as the sacred *traditio* received from the Founding Fathers.

As Father Washington declared in his first inaugural address: "The preservation of *the sacred fire of liberty* and the destiny of the republican model of government are justly considered as deeply, perhaps as finally staked, on the experiment entrusted to the hands of the American people." The preservation of that sacred fire requires the suppression of all religious convictions that might threaten the deposit of faith that has been handed down. As we see with John F. Kennedy's public renunciation of primary allegiance to the Catholic Church in order to be elected President, "the national magistrate, whatever his personal religious views, operates under the rubrics of the civil religion as long as he is in his official capacity. . . ."[71] The cult of Liberty, and it alone, enjoys perfect freedom and security in America and in every other Western nation where Liberty reigns today. The civil religion Rousseau envisioned was first established in the United States; the Republic whose constitution purportedly prohibits any establishment of religion in fact has one. In the divinely bestowed glory of its sacred secularity, America is a confessional state.

---

70. Craycraft, *The American Myth of Religious Freedom*, 100, 156.
71. Bellah, "Civil Religion in America," 46.

22

Mind-Forged Manacles

THE NEW SECULAR nation-state the Founders and Framers created is at least potentially capable of a Christian reform according to the same majority will it enshrines as the source of all sovereignty and authority. That such a reform has never materialized—the NRA movement, as we have seen, failed utterly—is not owing entirely to the political framework of the Republic. In its task of subordinating Christianity to state power and to the tenets of the civic religion that is its creed, Liberty has been aided by another phenomenon produced for the first time by "the American experiment": the tyranny of public opinion.

In his magisterial refutation of the myth of a "conservative" American Revolution, Gordon Wood observes that the Revolution "had created something like the general will, in which the course of the society was shaped by the mass of intellectual, moral and physical powers. . . . People now described society more and more as a 'mass' and for the first time began using this term in reference to 'almost innumerable wills' in a positive, non-pejorative sense. . . . The individual was weak and blind . . . but the mass of people was strong and wise."[1] Just as the Revolution led to the overthrow of any established Church, so also did it lead to the overthrow of established truths concerning religious and other matters. In post-Revolutionary America received wisdom was replaced by what Wood calls the "statistical collectivity" of the individual views of innumerable common people, which "added up to something far more significant than ever existed before. They became what Americans obsessively labeled 'public opinion.'"[2] As the organs of this new thing called public opinion—books, pamphlets, newspapers, posters, handbills—multiplied by the thousands, not only law, but truth itself came to be defined by the majority sentiment of the moment, unguided by any universally acknowledged moral or religious authority. As with the mass defection from mainline Protestant denominations already discussed, "[m]ost ordinary people were no longer willing to defer to the knowledge and judgments of those who were once their superiors"[3]—including the Founders themselves, as they were learning to their dismay.

The Federalists, Wood notes, were aghast at this development, protesting that

---

1. Wood, *Radicalism of the American Revolution*, 360 (internal quotation marks partly omitted), 360.
2. Ibid., 363.
3. Ibid., 362.

"people needed to know the criterion by which we may determine with certainty, *who are right and who are wrong*."[4] But where in what the Framers had built, beginning with a Constitution that makes no mention of God or His law, was there any place for such an immutable criterion of truth and error? For the Republicans—at least when it was convenient for them so to argue—the "criterion for determining who was right and who was wrong . . . was the opinion of the whole people."[5] Yet by 1821, after public opinion on the Missouri Compromise had failed to go his way, even Jefferson was complaining to John Adams that "The inquisition of public opinion overwhelms in practice the freedom asserted by the laws in theory."[6] If, by Jefferson's lights, this was true concerning a limited Congressional approval of slavery extension that he deemed disastrously inadequate to protect the purported property right in slaves, it was most certainly true of popular decisions in most states more than a century later to legalize the treatment of unborn children as even more disposable than the human chattels who worked on Jefferson's plantation.

The Law of Opinion

Here we are dealing with yet another Lockean paradox in the Temple of Liberty. Just as the Law of Toleration produces intolerance for absolute religious truth, so does Locke's Law of Opinion produce intolerance of any truth claim rejected by public opinion. To recall Locke's statement of his Law:

> Virtue and vice are names pretended, and supposed every where to stand for actions in their own nature right or wrong. . . .But yet, whatever is pretended . . . these names, virtue and vice, in the particular instances of their application through the several nations and societies of men in the world, are constantly attributed *only to such actions as, in each country and society, are in reputation or discredit.*[7]

In Chapter 3 we saw that under Locke's "law" right and wrong are commonly determined according to social approbation or disapproval in a given society, which in a democracy means the approbation or approval of public opinion. In the same section of the *Essay* Locke pays lip service to the law of God as the ultimate standard of right and wrong,[8] but since he denies that God's law is written on the heart or authoritatively expounded by any Church or other established authority, the way is open to morality by popular consensus. This, again, is in keeping with

---

4. Wood, *Radicalism*, 363.

5. Ibid., 365.

6. Jefferson to John Adams, January 22, 1821; in ed. Randolph, *Memoir, Correspondence, and Miscellanies*, Vol. IV, 338.

7. *ECHU*, II.28.10. Cf. Hobbes's variant of this "law," which he designated the fifth "Law of Nature": "COMPLAISANCE—that is to say, that every man strive to accommodate himself to the rest . . . the observers of this law may be called SOCIABLE . . . the contrary stubborn, insociable, forward, intractable. . . ."*Leviathan*, I.15.209.

8. Ibid., II.28.8.

Locke's method of providing in his writings "one trail for the skeptical and another for the pious, so that eventually the pious will have to follow the skeptics' trail if they wish to get anywhere."[9]

The outcome of the operation of the Law of Opinion in America is precisely as we predicted in our theoretical discussion of Locke in Chapter 3: "the paradoxical result of logical individualism and final democracy will be subjugation to the collective." That is, when public opinion is made the standard of right and wrong—with due "toleration," of course, for legally ineffectual "private" religious views to the contrary—the individual's contribution to the supposed "free exchange" of ideas in the public forum amounts to the same thing as his "consent" to be governed: submission to whatever the greater number decides. Or, as Tocqueville describes the paradox: "Not only is common opinion the *sole guide* that maintains for individual reason among democratic peoples; but it has an infinitely greater power among those peoples than any other. . . . *The same equality which makes him [each citizen] independent of each fellow citizen leaves him isolated and defenseless before the action of the greatest number.*"[10]

Writing only forty years after ratification of the First Amendment, Tocqueville already marvels at how the tyranny of public opinion in America has subjugated the individual mind in a way not seen even under the "absolute monarchs" of Europe. He offers his famous damning assessment: "I do not know of any country where, in general, less independence of mind and genuine freedom of discussion reign than in America."[11] What does Tocqueville mean by this affirmation, which will come as a rude shock to Americans who consider themselves the blessed beneficiaries of a "religious freedom" and "freedom of speech" that are unequalled anywhere in the world? In Europe, he explains, there was "no religious or political theory that cannot be preached freely in the constitutional states. . . . [and] does not penetrate the others; for there is no country in Europe so subject to one single power that he who speaks the truth does not find support capable of assuring him against the consequences of his independence."[12] This was so even as to those European states still ruled by Catholic monarchs or by the Pope himself (the papal states of Italy would not fall until 1859–60), for the holder of an unpopular opinion could find support, as the case might be, from the aristocracy against the people, or from the people against the monarch, or from the monarch against the people.

But "in the heart of a democracy organized as that of the United States," Tocqueville continues, "one encounters only a single power, a single element of force and success, and nothing outside it." That is, one encounters the popular face of the "monism of power" that is the essence of Liberty, the other face being the instrumentality of "representative" government. In America, Tocqueville observes, "the majority draws a formidable circle around thought. Inside those limits, the

---

9. Harvey C. Mansfield, "On the Political Character of Property in Locke," 29; cited in Pangle, *The Spirit of Modern Republicanism*, 164.

10. *Democracy in America*, II.I.2.

11. Ibid., I.II.7.

12. Ibid.

writer is free; but unhappiness awaits him if he dares to leave them." The writer who is so bold as to offend public opinion will not be subjected to an auto-da-fé or other physical restraint, but he will most certainly be "the butt of mortifications of all kinds and of persecutions every day." Tocqueville describes the sorry lot of anyone who—then, as now—sins against political correctness by publishing the wrong ideas:

> A political career is closed to him; he has offended the only power that has the capacity to open it up. Everything is refused him, even glory. Before publishing his opinions, he believed he had partisans; it seems to him that he no longer has any, now that he has uncovered himself to all; for those who blame him express themselves openly, *and those who think like him, not having his courage, move silently away.* He yields, he finally bends, under the effort of each day and returns to silence as if he felt remorse for having spoken the truth.[13]

The great irony here, Tocqueville noted, is that even under the worst of the absolute monarchs "despotism struck the body crudely, so as to reach the soul; and the soul, escaping from those blows, rose gloriously above it; but in democratic republics, tyranny does not proceed this way; it leaves the body and goes straight for the soul."[14] Public opinion says to its victims: "Go in peace, I leave you your life, but I leave it to you worse than death."[15] And once the sentence has been passed, "When you approach those like you, *they shall flee you as being impure*; and those who believe in your innocence, even they shall abandon you."[16]

The situation today is rather different, of course, from the one Tocqueville observed. Europe and Canada have raced ahead of America in following the logic of Liberty to its inevitable conclusion: the *formal* punishment of politically incorrect speech by civil and penal law. In America, for the moment, it is still possible to publish without legal penalty opinions that transgress the dogmas of Liberty and even argue for overturning them, as this study does. But the penalty exacted by public opinion is far more onerous today than in Tocqueville's time, given a network of mass media whose thundering, ubiquitous and instantaneous objurgation of political heresy Tocqueville could scarcely have imagined. Indeed, Tocqueville would have considered an apocalyptic fantasy the "formidable circle around thought" now prevailing. Politicians and other public figures who dare to question the right of homosexuals to marry each other and adopt children, for example, are cast beyond the pale of public life, and even the few "conservatives" who oppose "gay marriage" hasten to proclaim their full acceptance of the homosexual "lifestyle"—that is, sodomy—so long as it does not receive formal legal recognition as a marriage.[17] Such

13. Tocqueville, *Democracy in America*, I.II.7.
14. Ibid.
15. Ibid.
16. Ibid.
17. The defenders of Michelle Bachmann, a Congresswoman from Minnesota who is a vocal opponent of "gay marriage" and considered a leading "far Right" American conservative, hastened to proclaim to the *New York Times* that she and her husband "are absolutely not against the gays. They are

is the final outcome of the reduction of vice and virtue, via Locke's Law of Opinion, "to such actions as, in each country and society, are in reputation or discredit."

As it has been since the beginning of the history of Liberty, the guardians of public liberal orthodoxy are especially attentive to that most feared source of heresies: the Catholic Church. Craycraft mentions the telling example of the furor that followed publication of the late Cardinal O'Connor's article in *Catholic New York* warning that politicians who promote abortion are at risk of excommunication. In response the *New York Times* issued its own warning: "To force religious discipline on public officials risks destroying the fragile accommodations that Americans of all faiths and no faith have built with the bricks of the Constitution and the mortar of tolerance.... Stop leaning on Catholic public officials now working to heal, not divide, the rest of society."[18] That public opinion viewed O'Connor's simple statement of the duty of Catholic politicians to follow Catholic teaching as a threat to the very bricks and mortar of our Lockean regime is a startling reminder of how the reign of Liberty depends entirely upon restraining the freedom of the Church as a socially constitutive force.

Catholic politicians who defy the teaching of their own Church in order to support such evils as abortion take the same position as Burt Neuborne, a law professor who responded to Cardinal O'Connor's letter by remarking that "When you accept public office you're not a Catholic, you're not a Jew. You're an American."[19] (The reference to Jews is a distraction from the real message: a public official must not be *Catholic*, since only the Catholic Church opposes abortion without exception, whereas the vast majority of Jews, along with the vast majority of Americans, support at least some degree of legalized abortion.) That, in essence, is the position of Justice Scalia, whose judicial opposition to abortion is not based on any objective moral principle but solely on the Constitution's silence about the matter, so that, as he writes in his dissenting opinion in *Planned Parenthood v. Casey*: "The permissibility of abortion, and the limitations upon it, are to be resolved like most important questions in our democracy: by citizens trying to persuade one another and then voting."[20] Stripped of voting booths and other trappings, this reliance on "persuasion" to defend the good is the morality of the Roman Colosseum: thumbs up and the unborn live; thumbs down and they die. And such is the tyranny of public opinion.

just not for marriage." The *Times* noted gravely, however, that Mr. Bachmann was under suspicion of providing "reparative" or "gay-to-straight" therapy at two Christian counseling centers he operates, which would call into question the sincerity of his acceptance of homosexual conduct as legitimate. See Sheryl Gay Stolberg, "For Bachmann, Position on Gay Rights Reflects a Mix of Issues and Her Faith," *New York Times*, July 17, 2011.

18. *New York Times*, June 17, 1990, quoted in Craycraft, *American Myth of Religious Liberty*, 14.

19. *Washington Post*, June 16, 1990, quoted in Craycraft, loc. cit.

20. *Planned Parenthood of Southeastern Pennsylvania v. Casey*, 505 U.S. 833, 979 (1992) (dissenting in part).

Seminaries of Conformity

One cannot discuss the role of public opinion in subduing Christian opposition to the dogmas of Liberty without some mention of the system of secularized public education first established in America. We have noted Jefferson's plan for a system of "general education" by which people "would be qualified to understand their rights, to maintain them, and to exercise with intelligence their parts in self-government" and by which "every fibre would be eradicated of antient or future aristocracy; and a foundation laid for a government truly republican." Where education was concerned, "Jefferson was a complete secularist, never deviating in any significant degree," as is evident from his proposed bills for general public education in Virginia at the primary and secondary level, in which no provision of any kind was made for religious instruction.[21] Jefferson's contemporary critic, Edward Everett, who later became President of Harvard, protested that Jefferson's failure to provide for any department of divinity at the University of Virginia represented, amazingly enough, "probably *the first instance, in the world,* of a 'university' without such a provision."[22]

Jefferson, writes Leonard Levy, saw the public schools as essential to forming citizens who would "think republican thoughts" and "support the cause of liberty as he understood it."[23] Like the other Founders of the first rank, American *philosophes* of the Enlightenment, Jefferson had no use for the idea that had been a foundation stone of the Western tradition: that, as Plato's Athenian declares, the aim of education is to produce "the highest possible perfection of excellence in body *and soul.*"[24] As we saw in Chapter 1, this meant, for Plato, inculcating a "habit of mind . . . which must likewise be pursued by the man who would be like God. . . ."[25] Since the coming of Christ, this aim of education had naturally meant the study of God (theology) and the inculcation of Christian virtue. But for Locke, the aim of education is to direct a child's "natural Freedom," according to which "we . . . from our Cradles, *love Liberty.* . . ."[26] The way to control this love of Liberty is to inculcate in children a dread of shame—not from guilt over violations of God's law, which is not written on man's heart, but over *the disapproval of their fellow citizens,* which Locke admits is "*not the true Principle and Measure of Virtue,*" yet, according to him, "is that which comes nearest to it. . . ."[27] For Locke, then, the aim of education is, as Pangle observes, "to tame the original and naturally wild love of liberty by making it subordinate to and expressed by way of the concern for reputation" and a "*radical dependence on the opinion of others.* . . ."[28]

---

21. Levy, *Jefferson and Civil Liberties,* 9.

22. "University of Virginia," *North American Review* (1820), 10:113–37, 130; cited in Pangle, *The Spirit of Modern Republicanism,* 78.

23. Levy, 143.

24. *Laws,* 788c.

25. Ibid., 792d.

26. *Some Thoughts Concerning Education,* §§76, 148.

27. Ibid., §61.

28. Pangle, *The Spirit of Modern Republicanism,* 218. This author is indebted to Pangle's analysis, which is based in turn on Nathan Tarcov's seminal *Locke's Education for Liberty.*

Hence Lockean (and thus Jeffersonian) education is "education for Liberty," to use Nathan Tarcov's phrase; and education for Liberty means education in obedience to the Law of Opinion. And so would it be for public education in America, where the public schools would become virtual seminaries of social conformity according to the dogmas of Liberty: toleration, "inclusiveness," and respect for law as determined by an ever-shifting majority will. Thanks to crusaders like Horace Mann, within a generation of the death of James Madison free public education at the elementary school level was available in every state, and compulsory attendance laws were being enacted—first in Massachusetts and New York, and then in every state by 1918. By 1850, public schools for grades one through twelve had been established "in every place where there were enough pupils."[29]

Given the once militant faith of American Catholics, throughout the mid-19th century there was fierce Catholic opposition to compulsory common schooling in a wholly secular public school system that breathed America's endemic anti-Catholicism. Accordingly, at the Second Plenary Council of Baltimore held just after the Civil War (1866), the Catholic bishops of America declared that only a system of parochial schools could preserve the faith of Catholics living in a sea of religious indifferentism:

> The best, nay *the only remedy that remains*, in order to meet these very grave evils and inconveniences, seems to lie in this, that in every diocese schools— each close to the church—should be erected, in which the Catholic youth may be instructed in letters and the noble arts as well as in religion and sound morals. . . . In these schools, carried on under the eyes of the pastors, the dangers which we have just said inhere in the public schools will be avoided; the pupils will be kept free from that indifferentism which is now so rampant; they will learn to walk in the Catholic way, and to bear the yoke of the Lord from their youth.[30]

Naturally, the organs of American public opinion viewed this sort of thing as little short of seditious. An article in *The New York Times* from the summer of 1873, sensationally entitled "The War on the Public Schools," neatly encapsulates the conflict. Noting with alarm an initiative by Bishop Loughlin of Brooklyn to "compete with public schools and draw their pupils away" by establishing Catholic day schools "in every part of Brooklyn," the article includes an interview with a Father Maguire, pastor of Saint Paul's Roman Catholic Church, whose forthright statements were evidently printed in the hope of fanning the always smoldering flames of anti-Catholicism:

> Q.—You propose to ask the parents of Catholic children, and the children themselves, to leave the public schools and attend your school?
> A.—We propose to educate all the Catholic children who come in the tenets

---

29. Morison, *HAP*, 531.

30. Decreta, 430, 431, in Rev. J.A. Burns, *The Growth and Development of the Catholic School System in the United States* (NY: Benzinger Bros., 1912), 188.

of their faith. The public schools don't teach any religion; that is why I am opposed to them. *They make infidels; that's all.* ...[31]

The article includes the warning that while the Catholic initiative had "not been instrumental in materially reducing the attendance at the public schools ... new and more determined efforts are to be made to secure that object."[32] The battle had been joined not only in New York but also in other states, where Catholics fighting the indoctrination of their children in the public schools faced criminal penalties for refusing to participate in the system.

Catholic opposition to public schools finally achieved a victory with the Supreme Court's decision in *Pierce v. Society of the Sisters of the Holy Names of Jesus and Mary* (1925). In upholding a lower court injunction against enforcement of an Oregon law that would force Catholic parents to send their children to local public schools under penalty of fine or imprisonment, the Court issued its famous dictum: "The child is not the mere creature of the state; those who nurture him and direct his destiny have the right, coupled with the high duty, to recognize and prepare him for additional obligations."[33]

But while the guardians of Liberty were unable to achieve the "standardization" of children by legal compulsion, they eventually achieved it by cultural conquest. As we will see in the second volume of this study, by the 1890's Bishop John Ireland, leading the "Americanist" faction of the Catholic Church, would declare himself "a friend and advocate of the state school," support compulsory attendance laws with criminal sanctions, and call for the outright abolition of Catholic schools in favor of public schools wherein Catholic religious instruction would be reduced to an after-hours appendage to a secular curriculum. The outrage over Ireland's failed plan to end specifically Catholic education in America contributed mightily to his fall from grace in Rome and ended his dream of being made a cardinal, but it also signaled the fast-approaching assimilation of the great body of American Catholics into the milieu of Liberty. Today, the overwhelming majority of Catholic children attend public schools, and their cultural formation (even where Catholic schools exist) is generally indistinguishable from that of the population at large.

The "mind-forged manacles" of public opinion have proven perhaps even more effective than external legal compulsion in exacting Christian conformity to Liberty's requirements. Whereas, as Christopher Dawson writes, it is "the very function of the Christian to be moving against the world, and to be protesting against the majority of voices,"[34] by operation of the stifling Law of Opinion, subject in turn to the Law of Toleration, even the most "privately" orthodox Catholics have been trained to stay within the circle of acceptable public opinion—precisely as

31. "The War on the Public Schools," *The New York Times*, July 30, 1873.

32. Ibid.

33. 268 U.S. at 535.

34. *The Tablet*, CLXXXVI, No. 5943 (London), August 18, 1945; cited in Erik von Kuehnelt-Leddihn, *Liberty or Equality* (Front Royal, VA: Christendom Press, 1993), 123.

Locke had hoped they would in the society he envisioned, and which finally took shape in America and then throughout the Western world.

Today, as Erik von Kuehnelt-Leddihn has so aptly put it, "the omnipotent society rules through the public praise of labels and shibboleths," and "we see as a result all heresies, mischievous actions, immoral propositions making their conquests under an elaborate camouflage, in order not to challenge openly the forces of the social Behemoth which can be *far more potent than the state Leviathan.*"[35] The people are deceived or brow-beaten into quiescence by opinion-makers, and the manacled masses become an irresistible force for the destruction of all traditional religion and morality, even as the individual "private" observance of both is given an assiduous but completely meaningless "respect." One can only marvel at the work of Locke's amazingly effective tool in the construction of the first secular nation-state.

35. Kuehnelt-Leddihn, *Liberty or Equality,* 123.

23

The God That Failed

IN FOCUSING ON the first century of the American Republic as the first practical realization of a Lockean vision of Liberty, it is hardly necessary to demonstrate that the Founders and Framers devised their political creation with quill pens in one hand and Locke's writings in the other, although with Jefferson that was literally the case. To recall the caveat in Chapter 3, it is not the *origin* but the *function* of ideas that concerns us. The world we inhabit today—the world of Liberty—is surely a world that even Locke would view with horror. And yet it is the world that has emerged from the function of the ideas of the "moderate" Enlightenment he represented and which now passes for our "conservative" inheritance. That inheritance bears the name of the deity first enshrined in a temple on the Aventine Hill in 238 BC (cf. Chapter 5) and adored by the American revolutionaries as they danced around Liberty Tree. We turn now to a final assessment of the epic failure of this god and the consequences of that failure for a once Christian civilization.

Assessing Our "Conservative" Inheritance

The preceding pages have explored in a synthetic and narrative way the sociopolitical function of the ideas comprising our "conservative" inheritance in order to demonstrate their objectively radical outcome in the American experiment. It is now opportune to adumbrate an analytical breakdown of the specific elements of the American model resulting from the function of these ideas over time:

1. Government based upon the "consent" and "sovereign will of the people" as expressed through their representatives, rather than divine authority as the ultimate source and limit of all human authority.

2. The consequent emergence of "one Body Politick under one *Supreme Government*" according to Locke's *Second Treatise*—irrevocably consented to, but subject to the right to revolution/secession according to private judgment of grievances.

3. A legal positivism according to which the "one Supreme Government" can alter even the very concepts of virtue and vice, as foreseen in the *Second Treatise* and the *Essay Concerning Toleration*.

4. Religion reduced to the level of politically ineffectual private opinion according to the Law of Toleration enunciated in both the *Essay* and *Letter* concerning toleration.

5. The endless multiplication of religious sects as counseled by the *Essay Concerning Toleration*, insuring the inability of Christians to mount a united challenge to the power of the State.

6. As foreseen in the *Letter* and *Essay* on toleration, the *First Treatise* and the *Essay Concerning Human Understanding*, the softening of Christianity by its incorporation of the dogma of toleration under the Law of Toleration.

7. The consequent subordination of Christianity in particular and revealed religion in general to state power.

8. The corresponding emergence of a civil religion whose remote and depersonalized deity is invoked to bestow "the blessings of Liberty" and to approve of the wars and other undertakings of a post-Christian nation-state no longer governed by the truths of revelation or even the dictates of the natural law.

9. Unlimited freedom of speech and religion regarding "things indifferent" or "speculative opinions," except speech and religion deemed intolerant or politically incorrect (especially the social doctrines of Catholicism), as foreseen in the *Essay* and *Letter* on toleration.

10. At the same time, a paradoxical tyranny of public opinion that determines vice and virtue by the force of popular approbation or discredit under Locke's Law of Opinion.

11. An ever-expanding concept of "rights," including abortion, according to the Lockean principle of "self-ownership" enunciated in the *Two Treatises* and the *Essay Concerning Human Understanding*.

12. A paradoxical expansion of state power as the catalogue of Locke-inspired "rights" expands.

13. The dogma of the right to live in any way that one sees fit in keeping with Locke's concepts of "self-ownership," the "pursuit of happiness," and the non-aggression principle, without any legal limitation reflecting man's eternal welfare or the common good under its spiritual aspect.

14. A State united only by commerce, consumption, sports and entertainment, whose political life is dominated by pocketbook issues in keeping with a view of political society as having nothing to do with the soul but only the protection of property and "personal liberty."

15. A politics of the body replacing a politics of the soul, producing a people like those of pagan Rome in Saint Paul's time, who "sat down to eat and drink, and rose up to play."[1]

16. An academic formation in common schools that inculcates obedience to the Laws of Toleration and Opinion which maintain this status quo.

17. A relentless and catastrophic decline in both public and private morality, aided by laws and judicial decisions affirming that very decline as essential to the preservation of Liberty.

18. The consequent domination of all society by the secular State, whose monism of power fills up, even as it helps to expand, an ever-larger moral and spiritual vacuum.

It is manifest that these features of political modernity represent the realization of Hobbes's Leviathan, at which we have arrived along a path paved with the gold of Lockean liberalism. We are indeed Hobbes's "Generation of that great Leviathan . . . of that Mortal God, to which we owe under the Immortal God, our peace and defense."[2] Leviathan is the secular nation-state whose will as "Mortal God" is law no matter what the will of "the Immortal God," safely removed from human affairs, may enjoin to the contrary; and the peace it offers is a mere absence of public disturbance. The result is the destruction of anything resembling Christian social order and its replacement by a society in which everyone may do whatever he pleases so long as he allows the same "freedom" to others and raises no challenge to the Mortal God's absolute authority, which extends even to the determination of good and evil in the commonwealth. No one has assessed the final outcome more succinctly than Pierre Manent, the "chastened liberal"[3] whose profound insights have been cited repeatedly on these pages:

> Classical thought, which the tradition seeks to preserve, maintains that the human world, that is the city in the first place, should be founded on or, better, guided by what is proper to man, by what sets him apart from the animal, which should be always in the forefront. *Modern thought despairs that men will ever agree on what is proper to man, on human substance or ends*, and thus it wants to bracket the question of what is proper to man. It seeks to keep man in his efficacious indetermination so that, *by taking his bearings from what is not human but animal* and thus determined and necessary, he might construct a human world whose order is independent of human opinions, *where man can affirm himself without knowing himself*, where he can be free.[4]

---

1. 1 Cor. 10:7.
2. *Leviathan*, II.17.
3. Milbank, "The Gift of Ruling: Secularization and Political Authority," 222.
4. Manent, *City of Man*, 129.

We have arrived, as Manent recognizes, at a City of Man that no longer acknowledges the existence of a City of God—and this, remarkably enough, in the very midst of an endless profusion of "private" religiosity on which the secular State prides itself. A contented liberal, which we are all expected to be, is happily "an atheist under the true God, under the God in whom he believes."[5]

The Heart of Liberty

The rise of Liberty—our illusory "conservative" inheritance—has required nothing less than a resolute forgetfulness of what man is. And this self-imposed amnesia concerning man's nature is called freedom. Here again the United States Supreme Court has confirmed with approval a grim diagnosis of modernity. In defense of the right to abortion and the Court's refusal to overturn *Roe v. Wade*, Justice Kennedy declared as follows in *Planned Parenthood v. Casey*:

> At the heart of liberty is the right *to define one's own concept of existence, of meaning, of the universe, and of the mystery of human life.* Beliefs about these matters could not define the attributes of personhood were they formed under compulsion of the State.[6]

That a Catholic jurist who presumably believes "privately" in man's immortal soul and eternal destiny could utter a statement like this in all seriousness is a dramatic demonstration of how Liberty has radically converted the mind of Western man, leaving him defenseless against a final assault on the last faint remnants of the moral order of Christendom.

A defense of the *Casey* decision by Clifford R. Goldstein, editor of *Liberty* magazine, conceded that Kennedy's "notorious statement" regarding "the heart of liberty" sounds "more like a discourse on Spinozean metaphysics than on constitutional jurisprudence. . . ."[7] But it also sounds like a discourse inspired by the nominalist epistemology of the *Essay Concerning Human Understanding*, calling human nature itself into question in the context of Locke's doctrine of "the pursuit of happiness" according to each individual's conception of it, rather than the actual attainment of happiness ordered to the good for man, including God as *summum bonum*.

In fact, Kennedy's dictum, however melodramatic, is an assessment—no less telling than Manent's—of the final extremity of Lockean "conservatism," which has expanded like a supernova to become the entire universe of possible conservative outcomes of the political process, all of which are actually liberal outcomes. This is seen in a contemporary libertarian movement that advances the non-aggression principle, the radical "law of equal freedom," and a radically laissez-faire "market society" as a program to recover the "conservative" inheritance from our Locke-

---

5. Manent, *An Intellectual History of Liberalism*, 83

6. *Planned Parenthood v. Casey*, 505 U.S. 833, 852 (1992).

7. Clifford R. Goldstein, "Justice Kenney's Notorious Liberty Passage," *Liberty Online Magazine*, July–August 1997, www.libertymagazine.org/index. php?id=1585.

inspired Founding Fathers.[8] We are even told that the antebellum South, with its socioeconomic order based on chattel slavery, and its notions of nullification-at-will of unacceptable laws and secession-at-will from unacceptable governments, represents the "conservative" tradition of Liberty at its finest—a noble Lost Cause we should endeavor to recover (minus the embarrassment of slaves).

Recognizing the hypocrisy of "conservatives" who defend in principle the very "heart of liberty" they mocked when it made its throbbing appearance in *Casey*, Goldstein rose to Kennedy's defense against a fusillade of objections by so-called conservatives: "New Age jurisprudence" (Robert Bork); "open-ended validation of subjectivism that paves the way for drug abuse, assisted suicide, prostitution, and virtually anything else" (William Bennett); "'gaseously' written" (George Will); a "thing of almost infinite plasticity" (Michael Uhlman); and "a notorious mystery passage" (*First Things* magazine). Goldstein replied that "it's ironic that mostly political conservatives attack it, because at the heart of Justice Kennedy's at-the-heart statement is *the essential message of political conservatism*, and that is personal liberty." All the "conservative" objections were well founded, of course, but none of the objectors recognized that Kennedy's dictum had proceeded from the very conception of social order *the objectors themselves defend* in other contexts.

Goldstein catches the contradiction. He writes that while it might appear superficially that "all this metaphysical 'universe,' 'meaning,' and 'existence' stuff does sound like something uttered from a channeler or from Shirley McLaine . . . what Kennedy says does, in fact, encapsulate *basic Jeffersonian conservatism*. . . ." Had Kennedy proclaimed "the right to define one's own concept of existence, of meaning, of the universe, and of the mystery of human life" in the context of defending democratically enacted state laws *prohibiting* abortion, writes Goldstein, "this same quote would have been seen as sweeping summary of classical conservatism." Goldstein is right. Recall that none other than the "ultra-conservative" Justice Scalia, in his dissent from Kennedy's very opinion in *Casey*, declared that "The permissibility of abortion, and the limitations upon it, are to be resolved like most important questions in our democracy: by citizens trying to persuade one another and then voting."[9] Recall also that in his dissent in *Romer*, Scalia declared that "homosexuals are as entitled to use the legal system for reinforcement of their

---

8. It is precisely "the libertarian, purely free-market society" that the libertarian icon Murray Rothbard, panegyrist of the American Revolution, extols in his aforementioned *Ethics of Liberty*, which not only defends an absolute legal right to abortion but also calls for a total repeal of all "statist" measures of "prohibitionism" regarding conduct short of the outright physical invasion of another's person or property. Cf. *Ethics of Liberty*, 90, 97–112, 257–272. In his introduction to Rothbard's *The Betrayal of the American Right* (xi–xii), the prominent Catholic libertarian polemicist Thomas E. Woods, Jr. defends Rothbard as an authentic conservative of the Old Right versus the "statist" conservatives of the New Right. By the standard of post-Enlightenment liberalism as the logical development of Enlightenment principles, Rothbard is indeed a "conservative." By the standard of the Christologically-oriented Western tradition that the "Enlightenment" destroyed, the claim is simply absurd. Indeed, even the Enlightenment divines would find Rothbard's "ethics of liberty" appalling, though it proceeds from the very principles they advanced in order to conquer the tradition they despised.

9. *Casey*, 505 U.S. at 979.

moral sentiments as is the rest of society. But they are subject to being countered by lawful, democratic countermeasures as well."[10]

What passes for "conservatism" in America today freely concedes the right of abortion advocates and militant homosexuals to enshrine in law precisely their "own concept of existence, of meaning, of the universe, and of the mystery of human life," provided only that they do so via Locke's "supreme legislature," acting by a bare majority of representatives elected by a bare majority of the voters representing in most cases a distinct minority of the total population. As Justice Scalia flatly declares: "The States may, if they wish, permit abortion on demand. . . ."[11] Today's "conservative," following the "background political philosophy" of the Founding, would never think of allowing divine or even natural law to stand in the way of what the "supreme legislature" declares in keeping with Locke's dictate that while God's law "forbids vice . . . the law of man often makes the measure of it" and that for the "good of the commonwealth" human law may "limit and alter the obligation of even some of the laws of God, and *change the nature of vice and virtue*."[12]

The renowned Constitutional scholar Hadley Arkes rightly observed more than twenty years ago that in the judicial conflict over what the Constitution's morally freighted terms "mean" as applied to such matters as abortion, the liberals "profess that they are not legislating 'moral questions'" when in fact "[t]hey invoke the language of right and wrong . . . react to 'injustice' with moral outrage" and are "very much in the business of 'legislating morality,'" whereas the "conservatives," in reacting against the "judicial activism" of the liberals, have rejected any appeal to natural law or natural right and "in place of moral truths that hold their truth in all places" have appealed to "that which has been accepted, or rejected, by a majority." The result, Arkes concluded, is that "the cause of conservatism in politics *has been attached to 'positivism' in the law*, and that kind of marriage will be the undoing of political conservatism. For it will insure that . . . on matters of moral consequence conservative jurisprudence will have *nothing to say*."[13]

The liberals do not pretend, as the "conservatives" do, that the Constitution is a mere dry legal document and that there is no moral component to such constitutional terms as "life," "liberty," "property," "free exercise of religion," "freedom of speech," "cruel and unusual punishment," "privileges and immunities," "equal protection of the laws" and "due process of law." The liberals treat the Constitution as what it clearly is—a human rights charter with unavoidable moral and even theological implications—and they construe it in keeping with the liberal theological principles of the American civil religion. The "conservatives," on the other hand—citing the proto-liberal John Locke!—literally run from the field of battle, insisting that the battlefield does not exist.

This, then, is where Liberty has led our civilization along the path that began

---

10. *Romer v. Evans*, 517 U.S. 620, 646 (Scalia, J., dissenting).
11. *Casey*, 505 U.S. at 979.
12. *Essay on Toleration*, 145 (Cambridge ed.)
13. Hadley Arkes, *Beyond the Constitution* (Princeton, NJ: Princeton Univ. Press, 1990), 13, 15.

with the trial and execution of an inconvenient king and the forcible deposition of another by the privileged elites of 17ᵗʰ-century England: a liberalism that knows no bounds, opposed only by a conservatism reduced to legal positivism. And what both liberals and conservatives alike fail to recognize today is that it is precisely "the compulsion of the State" that Justice Kennedy decried in *Casey* by which Liberty has triumphed over the divine and natural law, the only real guarantors of human freedom. It is precisely the compulsion of the State that has replaced the perennial politics of the soul with Locke's politics of the body. From which it follows, just as Kennedy opines, that in the resulting sociopolitical order lives *in utero* can be treated as chattels at the whim of electoral majorities, or the whim of Supreme Court justices appointed by the "representatives" of electoral majorities. The same was true of the slaves, back when the Constitution that is the Magna Carta of Liberty declared in its unamended text that "We the People of the United States" had decided that slaves were chattels bereft of the rights of citizens.

What this means, of course, is just what the enlightened Founders, with their predominantly rationalist politics and deistic theology, set in motion: the definitive abolition of Christendom. The radicalism of the American Revolution, overturning the entire existing order of political society, has borne its increasingly bitter Lockean fruit in the constantly shifting sands of public opinion the Revolution itself created. It is poetically just that, as we saw in Chapter 9, so many of the Founders themselves lived long enough to be disgusted, appalled and even remorseful over the results of their own handiwork and its looming consequences for the world. We have never seen "the ultimate good of the world" a guilt-ridden John Adams hoped for in vain, but rather an accelerating civilizational debacle resulting precisely from "the present systems of paganism, deism and atheism" his friend Benjamin Rush decried and which the *philosophes* of the Enlightenment had promoted, as Adams admitted, to "undermine the Christian religion and the morals of the people as much in America as they have in Europe."

This study joins others written from the perspective of a growing post-modern disillusionment—especially but not only among Christians—with the results of the "political modernism" represented by the Founders and the "progressive 'grand tradition' as the key to the history of political thought." It is a disillusionment rationally compelled by "the unprecedented degradations of political life in our supposedly mature [20ᵗʰ] century: the banalization of civic and cultural existence in the 'bourgeois' democracies and . . . the chilling spectre of the emergence of Communism and Fascism in the very bosom of the 'ascendant' West."[14]

A Neo-Roman Sunset

Were he alive today, Adams undoubtedly would be unable to bear the spectacle of the once Christian West, "liberated" from the "tyranny of popes and kings," succumbing to a neo-pagan decadence that recalls the Roman Empire in the midst of

14. Pangle, *The Spirit of Modern Republicanism*, 9–10.

its fall. So strongly does the parallel suggest itself that the currently reigning Pope, exercising the very office Adams and all his enlightened brethren so despised, would declare it publicly in an address to the Roman Curia: "The sun was setting over an entire world. Frequent natural disasters further increased this sense of insecurity. There was no power in sight that could put a stop to this decline." Today as well, Benedict XVI continued, "moral consensus is collapsing, consensus without which juridical and political structures cannot function. Consequently, the forces mobilized for the defense of such structures seem doomed to failure.... *The very future of the world is at stake.*"[15]

After nearly fifty years of inexplicable optimism concerning "the modern world" inaugurated by the Second Vatican Council, the Pope, in view of the obvious, returns to the sober realism of his preconciliar predecessors, including the admonition by Pius XII in an encyclical on Catholic missions issued eleven years before the Council began:

> Venerable Brethren, you are well aware that almost the whole human race is today allowing itself to be driven into two opposing camps, for Christ or against Christ. The human race is involved today in a supreme crisis, which will issue in its salvation by Christ, or in its dire destruction.[16]

There is, of course, an unseen power that could avert final catastrophe: *Excita, Domine, potentiam tuam, et veni*—Arouse, Lord, Your Power and Come. So Pope Benedict began his address on that occasion, citing this and similar invocations in the Church's Advent liturgy that "were probably formulated as the Roman Empire was in decline." Like the Roman Empire, Benedict warned, democracy cannot survive without a "fundamental moral consensus.... Only if there is such a consensus on the essentials can constitutions and law function." But that consensus, "*derived from the Christian heritage*, is at risk wherever its place, the place of moral reasoning, is taken by purely instrumental rationality."

This is what the NRA movement recognized a century-and-a-half ago in the face of an unprecedented political regime that had positively excluded from its organic law not only Christ and the Gospel but even the barest mention of divinity. The national and state governments created after the Revolution were classic examples of "purely instrumental rationality," indeed the first of their kind in Western history. To recall Adams's sardonic boast, the men who created these new republican governments had not conducted "interviews with the gods" or been "in any degree under the influence of Heaven, more than those at work upon ships or houses," but rather had been guided "merely by the use of reason and the senses"—that is, reason separated from faith, and senses whose very authority had been called into question by the New Philosophy.

The Empire of Liberty that began in America is ending now, far more quickly than the Roman Empire, in the apostasy of peoples who once believed that the Gos-

---

15. Benedict XVI, *Christmas Greeting to the Roman Curia*, December 20, 2010.
16. Pius XII, *Evangelii Praecones* (On the Promotion of Catholic Missions), n. 70.

pel is the law of the land. Duly alarmed by the neo-barbarism of political modernity, but blind to the ultimate source of their fear, Christians in America fervently
invoke, not the Triune God in whom they believe, but the Holy Spirit of 1776 to save
them from the ravenous modern nation-state conceived in that very spirit. *Excita,
Libertas, potentiam tuam, et veni*—Arouse, Liberty, Your Power and Come. That is
the desperate petition of preponderantly Christian protest movements to a government that acknowledges no authority higher than itself and against which they dare
not invoke the name of Christ. Few there are like the survivor of a botched saline
abortion who rebuked the "supreme" authority of the United States Congress in the
name of Christ during her testimony before a House subcommittee:

> Where is the soul of America? Members of this committee, where is your
> heart? How can you deal with the issues of this Nation without examining her
> soul? A murderous spirit—and I say it again, a murderous spirit—will stop at
> nothing until it has devoured a nation. . . .
>
> Why do you think this whole room trembles when I mention the name
> Jesus Christ? It is because He is REAL! He is able to give grace for repentance
> that we need as Americans. We are proud and boastful and we kill without
> shame. . . .
>
> Good men have stood before us . . . they have stood up for righteousness,
> and today we are nothing but cowards in America. . . . We are under the judg-
> ment of God, whether or not we want to hear it. . . . I didn't die because I was
> supposed to be here today to say: Shame on America.[17]

But the grace of Christ and the judgment of God are deemed inoperative within
the framework of a regime that is constitutionally incapable of binding itself to the
Law of the Gospel, as the NRA movement warned far too late to avert the inevitable result. Not even Catholics in any considerable number have an awareness of
where they really stand in the midst of what they have been conditioned to believe
is an unparalleled regime of "religious freedom."

The political philosopher Eric Voegelin described political society as a "cosmion," or little world unto itself, within which symbols, ritual and myth create a
social reality that its members experience "as of their human essence."[18] For all his
Fifties optimism about the cosmion of the "American model" as a vehicle for recovery of the already lost Western tradition, it was he who admitted that the Enlightenment's "taboo on the instruments of critique"—meaning the "classic philosophy
and scholastic theology" that had supported a politics of the soul—led to the ruin
of "the decisive part of Western intellectual culture." The resulting destruction
"went so deep that Western society has never completely recovered from the blow,"
which is putting it mildly from our perspective more than half a century later.
The result of the Great Taboo is that "theoretical debate concerning issues which

17. Testimony of Gianna Jessen, *Hearing Before The Subcommittee On The Constitution Of The Committee On The Judiciary House Of Representatives*, Second Session, July 20, 2000 (paragraph breaks added).

18. Eric Voegelin, *The New Science of Politics* (Chicago: Univ. of Chicago Press, 1987), 27.

involve the truth of human existence is impossible in public" and public debate is reduced to "the game with loaded dice that it has become in contemporary progressive societies."[19] In the secularized cosmions that Liberty has created, including ours, the social reality that penetrates "our human essence" includes the dictate that participants in the political process must pretend that they are bodies without souls and avoid any mention of God, eternity or eternal consequences in the courts or halls of government.

Writing in the early 1950s in the midst of postwar confidence about the future of American democracy as a bulwark of the West, Voegelin perhaps was blinded to what anyone can see now. But today we know beyond doubt, as Alasdair MacIntyre has so famously observed, that "the barbarians are not waiting beyond our frontiers; they have already been governing us for quite some time. And it is our lack of consciousness of this that constitutes our predicament."[20] We are in this predicament because we have been induced to forget or to put aside what we really are and to practice the politics of the body instead of the politics of the soul.

Beyond the Diagnosis

What, then, is the alternative? Such is the supposedly unanswerable objection Liberty confidently poses in defense of itself, now that it has succeeded in expunging all recollection of the alternative from the historical memory of Western man.

The libertarians, reaching the last ditch of their defense of Liberty as a gift to humanity, now advocate the final liberal cure for the diseases of liberalism: total abolition of the State and its replacement by an "anarcho-capitalist" utopia. Many of them follow the vision of the late Murray Rothbard, the great guru of Liberty who never ceased to praise the Revolution that created the very state he never ceased to condemn. Such Rothbardian disciples as Hans-Hermann Hoppe (whose *Democracy: The God That Failed* was discussed in Chapter 1) now propose a fantasy world of "stateless societies" in which insurance companies and private arbitrators would provide "defense services" and "justice services" according to competing private legal codes.[21] Hoppe imagines that under this scheme "every single conflict and damage claim, regardless of where and by or against whom, would fall under

---

19. Voegelin, *The New Science of Politics*, 140–142.

20. MacIntyre, *After Virtue*, 263.

21. See, e.g., "The Private Production of Defense," http://mises.org/journals/scholar/Hoppe.pdf. Libertarian writer Roy Halliday explains this bizarre and patently unworkable substitute for a State: "In Hoppe's system, instead of having a uniform code of law imposed on everyone by the state, *competing insurance firms* would offer defense services tailored to customers who agree to specific rules of conduct, such as not to commit suicide and not to provoke attacks, and specific standards for such things as rules of evidence and assignment of awards and punishments. *Each citizen would be free to make a defense contract with a specialized insurance firm that enforces the legal code of his choice.* Muslims might choose to be judged by Islamic law, Catholics might choose Canon law, Jews might choose Mosaic law, and others could choose from a variety of secular legal codes. Cases involving parties who subscribe to the same legal code would be settled according to the laws of that code." Cf. royhalliday.home.mindspring.com/libelhtm.htm.

the *jurisdiction* of one or more specific insurance agencies. . . ."[22] While they propose to save the body of Lady Liberty by amputating her gangrenous limbs of government—which she has never been without for even a moment—the "anarcho-capitalists" merely advocate the modern state by another name, which, even if their utopian scheme were achievable, would only return through the medium of insurance premiums instead of ballots.

But what of those who look to a recovery of the abandoned Greco-Catholic tradition, adapted to modern circumstances, with its Christian moral order and characteristic decentralization of political power according to the principle of subsidiarity? Despite mounting disillusionment in America with what historian John Rao has called "the Grand Coalition of the Status Quo," there is still only verbal opposition to the conquering *Zeitgeist* in "the practically private publications of a handful of scholars,"[23] whose influence is all but nil. And we must agree with Manent the chastened liberal that even the most confirmed traditionalists among these voices of opposition are haunted by a loss of the "innocence and sincerity that alone would give meaning to the restoration of medieval Catholicism or the ancient city-state."[24] Manent quotes the proto-libertarian Benjamin Constant concerning the Catholic restorationists of post-revolutionary France, "who 'in declaring themselves champions of earlier centuries . . . are, in spite of themselves, men of our century,' who 'consequently, have neither the strength of their convictions nor the hope that ensures success.'"[25]

But it is Liberty itself that has deprived us of the hope that ensures success by convincing us that the overthrow of Christendom was inevitable and is now quite irreversible: There will be faction and violence if you abandon me, Liberty warns us, for only Liberty can control the chaos Liberty has unleashed. Our entire civilization has fallen prey to an ideological protection racket. Yet we are not protected, and in our fear of violence we pay tribute to violence. In only a few decades legalized abortion alone has claimed more victims for Liberty than all the wars in modern history combined; and the most "conservative" reaction to this holocaust in America is to insist that it be referred to the will of the majority for further (and seemingly endless) deliberation.

Our deliverance from this civilizational death spiral is far from inconceivable, however. Another triumph of the new orientation is that it has blinded us to the *political* significance of the spiritual reality that the great preponderance of the population of the Western world still consists of baptized Christians, with the Western popular majority (including Latin America) remaining at least nominally Catholic. If this inert majority were to be roused from its Liberty-induced coma by the leaders of a Church returned to militancy, the face of the earth could be renewed.

22. Hoppe, *Democracy: The God That Failed*, 252.
23. Voegelin, *The New Science of Politics*, 142.
24. Manent, *Intellectual History of Liberalism*, 91.
25. Ibid.

A demonstration of this potential for social *metanoia* has recently been seen in Nicaragua. In 2008, a century-old law permitting abortions in "hard" cases was overturned and a total ban on abortion reinstated under the parliamentary leadership of none other than Daniel Ortega, former socialist President of the country, following his reconciliation with the Church. An outraged Amnesty International spokesman denounced Nicaragua's "shocking and draconian law," demanding that "UN member states should take this opportunity to hold Nicaragua to account for a law that violates women's right to life, health and dignity."[26] The international press sounded instant alarms as typified by the lamentation in *The New York Times* that "Hopes among women's groups in Nicaragua . . . have been dashed" and that the law is "a throwback to the Middle Ages for women's rights. . . ."[27]

In the same year, one Catholic commentator noted the "seemingly miraculous transformation" of the Brazilian hierarchy, producing a "pro-life Pentecost" that has led the Brazilian bishops to adopt strategies that "are a lesson to the whole Catholic world," including the direct confrontation of "pro-choice politicians," the excommunication of doctors performing abortions, and a massive educational campaign depicting abortion procedures in graphic detail, with the result that "Brazilian lay Catholics are horrified by what they see, and are inspired to act against abortion." The bishops' goal is not only to "stop new anti-life legislation, but to eliminate all exceptions in Brazil's penal code regarding abortion."[28]

Nor are such encouraging developments limited to Latin America. In April of 2011, the predominantly Catholic nation of Hungary, its political clock reset to zero with the end of its status as a Soviet satellite, not only repudiated its Soviet-era Constitution of 1949, as amended in 1989, but adopted in its place *an explicitly Christian constitution* as the new Fundamental Law of Hungary, which went into effect on January 1, 2012.[29] The movement for the new constitution was not led by a Catholic, however, but by Hungary's Prime Minister, Viktor Orbán, the Protestant head of Hungary's Fidesz party—thus demonstrating the feasibility of a pan-Christian alliance for constitutional reform aimed at restoring some semblance of a Christian commonwealth along the lines the NRA movement failed to achieve in this country.

The new constitution—an actual example of the Christian commonwealth adapted to modern circumstances—begins with the invocation "O Lord, blessed be the Hungarian nation!" and proceeds to a formal "National Avowal of Faith" that declares in pertinent part:

26. "GOVERNMENTS URGED TO CONDEMN NICARAGUA ABORTION BAN," February 4, 2010, http://www.amnesty.org/en/news-and-updates/news/un-urged-condemn-nicaragua-abortion-ba–20100204.

27. James C. McKinley, Jr., "Nicaragua Eliminates Last Exception to Strict Anti-Abortion Law," *The New York Times*, November 20, 2006.

28. Matthew Hoffman, "The Pro-Life Pentecost in Brazil, and What it Means for the Rest of the World," March 20, 2008, LifeSiteNews.com.

29. Cf. English translation of adopted draft constitution, http://tasz.hu/files/tasz/imce/alternative_translation_of_the_draft_constituion.pdf.

We are proud that one thousand years ago *our king*, Saint Stephen, based the Hungarian State on solid foundations, and made our country a part of *Christian Europe.* . . .

We acknowledge the role Christianity has played in preserving our nation. . . .

Article Q of the Section entitled "Fundamentals" makes it clear that the National Avowal of Faith is no mere precatory preamble, but rather that "The provisions of the Fundamental Law shall be interpreted in accordance with . . . the Fundamental Law's National Avowal of Faith. . . ." The constitution prescribes a Coat of Arms topped by the Holy Crown of Saint Stephen I, canonized by Pope Gregory VII in 1038.

The National Avowal further declares that "after the moral defeats of the twentieth century, our need for spiritual and intellectual renewal is paramount." In keeping with that aim, Article II contains the "human life amendment" American pro-life advocates have sought in vain for decades:

Human dignity shall be inviolable. Everyone shall have the right to life and human dignity; *the life of the foetus shall be protected from the moment of conception.*

Delivering further defiant nays to the EU status quo, Article K (1) rejects "gay marriage," declaring that "Hungary shall protect the institution of marriage, understood to be *the conjugal union of a man and a woman* based on their independent consent; Hungary shall also protect the institution of the family, which it recognizes as *the basis for survival of the nation.*" And Article XV protects parental rights against state interference: "Parents shall have the right to choose the upbringing to be given to their children." During a later interview about the new constitution, Orbán was challenged about its provision respecting marriage. His reply declared forthrightly the constitutional principle that has never been more than mythical in America, where it is now considered unthinkable even by "conservatives" on what passes for the American Far Right: "But what we call marriage is exclusively for one man and one woman. *We are a Christian country.* That's a historical fact." And, even more provocatively: "Hungary is a Christian country. *Christianity is the tide.* Hungarians are individualistic and pro-freedom. But *freedom is not the property of the liberals.*"[30]

The developments in Hungary sent shockwaves throughout the Empire of Liberty. An editorial in *The New York Times* deplored "Hungary's Constitutional Revolution" which—horror of horrors—"accepts conservative Christian social doctrine as state policy. . . ."[31] While the editorialist conceded that "the Fidesz government

30. April 7, 2012, "An interview with Viktor Orban, prime minister of Hungary," http://www.Washingtopost.com/opinions/an-interview-with-viktor-orban-prime-minister-of-hungary/2012/04/06/gIQAaaMNoS_story.html.

31. Kim Lane Scheppele, "Hungary's Constitutional Revolution," *New York Times*, December 11, 2011.

has accomplished this constitutional revolution by legal means after a democratic election," only revolutions *against* conservative Christian social doctrine (violent or non-violent) are acceptable in the Empire. An alarmed report from the BBC fretted that the opposition parties "accuse the governing Fidesz party of imposing divisive right-wing ideology on the country," although the Constitution passed by an overwhelming vote of 262-to-44. Members of the EU parliament demanded an investigation into whether the constitution threatens to violate EU "values." Radio Netherlands fretted that "with references to God, Christianity, the Holy Crown of Hungary, the fatherland and traditional family values, critics have slammed the new constitution as discriminatory."[32] The Internet abounded with dire headlines.[33]

The developments in Latin America and Hungary demonstrate the falsity of an *eidos* of history (to borrow Voegelin's phrase) according to the Whig narrative of inevitable progress toward a democratic capitalism from which there is no turning back. The potential of even mass democracy and our "godless Constitution" (appropriately amended or construed) as vehicles for moral and spiritual regeneration lies no deeper than the next election or series of elections, if only political leaders would launch serious appeals to the dormant Christian consciences of scores of millions of voters. What will be needed is a national political figure with the courage to throw off the mind-forged manacles of public opinion, defy the threat of an Inquisition by the mass media, and simply declare that he will follow God rather than men and that his fellow Americans ought to do the same.

The campaign of former Senator Rick Santorum during the 2011–2012 Presidential election cycle provides a tantalizing hint of what could be. By his own admission, Santorum was a "nominal Catholic" before he underwent a profound religious conversion and married another nominal Catholic—the former lover of an abortionist—who had likewise rediscovered her faith. The Santorums abandoned their practice of contraception and had eight children, including a son who died shortly after birth and a daughter, afflicted by a grave genetic disorder, whom they could have aborted. On the Republican primary trail Santorum had the hardihood to criticize Barack Obama for his "phony theology" and to warn of the "dangers of

32. "Hungary Adopts Disputed New Constitution," www.rnw.nl/english/bulletin/hungary-adopts-disputed-new-constitution," April 18, 2011.

33. See, e.g., "Hungarian Constitution: 'Trojan Horse for Authoritarianism'" (EurActiv.com)("a more authoritarian political system ... threatens European values"); "New Hungarian Constitution Threatens European Values" (alde.eu)("serious threats ... to widely held European values: freedom, democracy, equality, non-discrimination...."); "Hungary's New and Dangerous Constitution"(atlanticsentinel.com)("this road leads to dictatorship"); "Hungary: New Constitution Enshrines Discrimination" (Human Rights Watch, hrw.org)("Hungary at odds with its obligation to uphold and respect human rights"); "EU Asked to intervene in 'worrying' Hungarian Constitution" (neueurope.com) ("offers the real prospect of banning both abortion and gay marriages, a concern shared by human rights groups"); "Berlin Blasts Hungary for New Constitution" (UPI) ("a gradual undermining of the country's democratic principles"); "Hungary's Proto-Authoritarian New Constitution"(compartive-constitutions.org ("breaks radically with its 1989 predecessor and the constitutional values it embodies"); "Germany Concerned About new Hungarian Constitution" (eubusiness.com)("hardly compatible with European values").

contraceptives." Taking aim at a foundational dogma of Liberty, he even described as "nauseating" John F. Kennedy's "call for strict separation of church and state" and his "idea that the church can have no influence or no involvement in the operation of the state," as expressed in the 1960 speech we noted in our discussion of the American civil religion in Chapter 21.[34] Santorum's criticism of Kennedy's public abjuration of Catholic loyalty while in office echoed a 2010 address by Archbishop Charles Chaput at Houston Baptist University, in which the Archbishop, with no less courage, said that Kennedy had "profoundly undermined the place not just of Catholics, but of all religious believers, in America's public life and political conversation. Today, half a century later, we're paying for the damage."[35] (The damage, of course, had been inflicted far earlier, as these pages have shown.)

Santorum is not presented here as another Thomas More, and we need not dwell on his own inconsistency under pressure or his foreign policy prescription for preemptive wars like the disastrous intervention in Iraq. The point is that it is possible even for a politician to challenge the grand coalition of the status quo; he need only open his mouth to speak, reminding people of who they are and what they owe to the God who made them and will judge the nations as Lord of History.

The problem, however, is that the grand coalition numbers many prominent Catholics among its inquisitors, all of them thoroughly converted to the civil religion. The Catholic "public intellectual" Gary Wills, for example, described by *The Washington Post* as "among many Catholics whose touchstone is the Second Vatican Council, which opened up Catholicism to the modern era," said this of Santorum's brave foray into political heresy: "Santorum is not a Catholic, but a papist."[36] Wills pronounced the anathema in perfect conformity with the Lockean magisterium by which America has been governed since the colonial radicals inveighed against the papist designs of George III. As *The New York Times* was at pains to mention, Wills spoke for the majority of America's reliably quiescent Catholics: "Many Catholics take issue with Mr. Santorum's approach to their faith. Mr. Santorum, polls show, has lost the Catholic vote in every primary contest so far, some by wide margins."[37] He lost the Catholic vote in the pivotal Ohio primary, which went 43% to 31% for Mitt Romney, a Mormon. This meant that it was Catholics who delivered the state's delegates to Romney, as white evangelicals voted for Santorum by 47% to 30% and Romney won the overall vote by a mere 1%.[38] For

34. Sheryl Gay Stolberg and Laurie Goodstein, "From 'Nominal Catholic' to Clarion of Faith," *The New York Times*, March 4, 2012, A1.

35. "Santorum not only conservative nauseated by JFK 1960 speech; view shared by many on right," *Associated Press*, *Washington Post*, February 28, 2012.

36. Ibid.

37. Stolberg and Goodstein, "From Nominal Catholic to Clarion of Faith," *The New York Times*, March 4, 2012, A1.

38. Dan Gilgoff, "Loudly Catholic Santorum Loses Ohio Catholics," March 7, 2012, CNN report, accessed http://religion.blogs.cnn.com/2012/03/07/loudly-catholic-santorum-loses-ohio-catholics/#s736045=&title=Family.

that matter, Catholics voted 54% to 45% for Obama in the 2008 Presidential election, thus ensuring his election.[39]

As if they represented some astounding *rara avis* no one would ever expect to encounter in America, the *Times* marveled that the Santorums "believe in a highly traditional Catholicism that adheres fully to what scholars call 'the teaching authority' of the pope and his bishops." This curious "teaching authority" is the very thing the progress of Liberty was supposed to have subjugated long ago, yet here was a Catholic politician in the year 2012 who seemed to think it might actually govern his public life in some way. "He has a strong sense of that," said George Weigel, another faithful Catholic adherent of the civil religion. In fact, said Weigel, Santorum is "the first national figure of some significance who's on that side of the Catholic conversation."[40] Weigel was right. That is how completely Liberty has tamed the Catholic masses. Under the Law of Toleration the generality of American Catholics have essentially been converted to the "soft Lockean Christianity" that Liberty requires for its subordination of revealed religion to the ever-increasing power of the secular state.

Santorum's plight demonstrates that there can be no prospect of an American *metanoia* unless political leadership is preceded by religious leadership in the Catholic Church. The commentator on the political turnabout led by the Catholic hierarchy of Brazil poses the pertinent question concerning the capacity of democracy to rebuild the collapsed moral order of the West: "What effect would such an approach have if all of the Catholic bishops of the world were to imitate the Brazilian bishops, and declare war on abortion, euthanasia, and other offenses against human life?" While the American population is only twenty-five percent Catholic, he queries: "If this 'sleeping giant' were to awaken, galvanized by clear preaching and educational campaigns that clearly reveal the crime of abortion, how could any political party stand against it?" How indeed? We have already seen that even the prospect of civil disobedience led by the Catholic hierarchy forced the Obama administration to backpedal on its "contraceptive mandate" in January 2012. Were the Catholic hierarchy to galvanize the laity and lead an unrelenting, massive civil rights movement akin to the civil rights movement of the 1960s, there can be little doubt that legalized abortion or any other targeted social evil would be eliminated rather quickly by the same democratic process that brought it about. The forces of Liberty know and fear this, even if the great dormant mass of Catholics is unaware of its latent capacity to effect social change.

Hence this critical study of the history of Liberty is not premised upon—nor does it reject, on the other hand—a restoration of monarchy as such. But where monarchy is concerned, not a few recognize what is evident from the history of the American Republic and our own experience of it: that Liberty has not abolished monarchy but only given it a new name, wedded to a post-Christian worldview

39. "How the Faithful Voted," The Pew Forum on Religion and Public Debate, November 10, 2008, accessed at http://www.pewforum.org/Politics-and-Elections/How-the-Faithful-Voted.aspx#1.

40. *The New York Times*, loc. cit.

with atomic weapons, vast armed forces, cruise missiles, and Predator drones at its disposal. Those who ridicule monarchical rule need to explain why the "imperial Presidency" does not represent, when all is said and done, Liberty's corrupt version of the oldest form of government in human history, from which America has never really escaped. Just as the anti-Federalists first perceived, the American federal system is a pyramid topped by an elective monarch wielding immense powers, including the power of life and death, with a congressional and judicial oligarchy in the middle and mass democracy at the bottom, driving the whole ensemble according to demagogic persuasion of a fickle electorate whose one unifying *desideratum* appears to be the Super Bowl.

Beyond the Constitution

Concerning the potential of our cosmion to reform itself by admitting into itself that which has hitherto been excluded, nothing but a lack of popular will prevents our Constitution from being amended or, more expediently, at least construed in accordance with the Christocentric sociopolitical tradition that Liberty has overthrown—just as the NRA movement hoped and a pan-Christian alliance in Hungary has actually achieved. In defense of his "originalism" against the claim that the Constitution ought to be construed objectively according to "fundamental values," Justice Scalia scoffed: "Are the 'fundamental values' that replace original meaning to be derived from the philosophy of Plato, or of Locke, or Mills, or Rawls, or perhaps from the latest Gallup poll?"[41] Here Scalia overlooks that in *Flores* he himself held that the Constitution's "original meaning" ought to be determined with reference precisely to *Locke's* thought as the "background philosophy" of the Framers' time and that, consequently, his own originalism is but a disguised search for fundamental values—the fundamental values of the Framers. But where does the Constitution state or even imply that its terms are to be construed until the end of time in accordance with the philosophy of the "moderate" Enlightenment? As for Scalia's scoffing reference to fundamental values proposed as replacements for his "original meaning," he conspicuously omits one source of which he is certainly acutely aware: the law of God as reflected in the natural law written on man's heart and promulgated to him in the Decalogue.

Hadley Arkes (who recently became a Catholic) rightly decries the attitude of America's judicial "conservatives," who view even application of the bare natural law as "a pretext for evading the discipline of the Constitution."[42] But, as he asks: "[W]hy would a constitution merit our faith if it were not committed in principle to justice rather than tyranny? Why *should* we summon our faith in the Constitution if there is no moral ground of conviction to support that faith?"[43] Indeed, to

41. Scalia, "Originalism: the Lesser Evil," 57 *University of Cincinnati Law Review* at 855.
42. Arkes, *Beyond the Constitution*, 14.
43. Ibid., 12.

return to the question first raised in Chapter 10, where we examined the Dred Scott case, how can judges even begin to ponder the issues of justice that come before them without recourse to an absolute moral standard for applying the Constitution's morally freighted terms to the questions presented? What Arkes rightly sees as essential to saving the Constitution from incoherence and malign application— "an independent ground of right and wrong...that does not depend on the vagaries of local cultures"[44]—can come only from the Decalogue and the Evangelical counsels. As between divine law and "original meaning"—which, after all, performs the function of a fundamental value—the proper standard to decide moral issues arising under the Constitution's morally freighted terminology is undeniable for Christians who are willing to defy the Great Taboo and be consistent with themselves.

The time has come for jurists who profess to be Christians to recognize that they are engaged in a final combat over morality, not merely dry legal terms that can be interpreted and applied as such. Christian jurists are called to oppose the relativistic moralizing of the liberals with the moral absolutes of divine law, the law whose basic moral precepts God has inscribed in His rational human creatures in keeping with their nature and ends. Judges who swear an oath to God that they will faithfully perform their duties under the Constitution and who, in the very chamber of the Supreme Court, sit beneath a frieze that includes images of Moses holding the tablets of the Ten Commandments, Charlemagne the Great and Louis IX, a canonized Catholic saint,[45] have no justification for behaving as if the very God to whom they have sworn their oath does not exist within the American juridical framework and that not even the natural law is of any account in the rendering of justice.

Surely, at a time when "the very future of the world is at stake" as Pope Benedict has rightly warned, Christian jurists who have taken an oath to God can summon up the hardihood to cite His law against liberal jurists who are clearly bent on defying it. And what, besides personal embarrassment, prevents a life-tenured judge from declaring the obvious truth that the Constitutional term "liberty" imposes the judicial duty to decide moral questions? To take abortion as the prime example, is there some principle higher than the Fifth Commandment that would forbid a judge to declare that the right to life secured by the Fifth *Amendment* extends to lives *in utero*, especially given that feticide is a crime in 37 States[46] and even federal law recognizes a "child in utero"[47] as a legal victim if injured or killed during

44. Arkes, *Beyond the Constitution*, 13.

45. Cf. Joan Biskupic, "Great Figures Gaze Upon the Court," *The Daily Republican,* March 11, 1998, dailyrepublican.com/sup_crt_frieze.html.

46. Christine Vestal, "States Expand Fetal Homicide Laws," Stateline.org, August 22, 2006 @ www.stateline.org/live/details/tory?contentId=135873.

47. See 18 U.S.C. 1841 (a) (1) ("Whoever engages in conduct that...causes the death of, or bodily injury (as defined in section 1365) to, a child, who is *in utero* at the time the conduct takes place, is guilty of a separate offense under this section"). See also, *Uniform Code of Military Justice,* Article 119a.

commission of specified violent crimes? (This is a dramatic sign of the utter moral incoherence of America's positivistic legal system: thanks to the "democratic process," the child *in utero* is treated in some jurisdictions as a life in being when a third party felon kills him, but not when his own mother kills him with the help of an abortionist, as permitted more or less by the law of every State.)

The objection that a judge's application of God's law to moral questions would constitute impermissible "judicial activism" is a dodge of moral duty supported only by an implicit "anti-theology of the State" (to recall Hancock's term) that is itself the result of judicial activism according to the requirements of Liberty. A judge, like a legislator or any other public official, is morally bound to act in accordance with the higher law when questions of positive law implicating morality are squarely presented to him under the Constitutional rubric of "liberty." And if we are going to look for the "original meaning" of *that* term, we ought to consult the Founder of the world rather than the founders of a particular civil society: "Ye shall know the truth, and the truth shall make you free."[48]

The answer to a liberal judicial positivism that violates God's law at every turn is not a "conservative" judicial positivism that punts moral questions back to the legislative Colosseum, where Christians (and everyone else who cares about preserving the moral order) are succumbing to the lions. No jurist should fear to follow a judicial philosophy reflecting what the American civil rights icon Martin Luther King—a Protestant minister—famously wrote from his Birmingham jail cell in the 1960s in a letter that reflects the entire Greco-Catholic tradition on the proper relation between God, Man and State:

> I would agree with St. Augustine that "an unjust law is no law at all". . . . A just law is a man made code that squares with the moral law or the law of God. An unjust law is a code that is out of harmony with the moral law. To put it in the terms of St. Thomas Aquinas: An unjust law is a human law that is not rooted in eternal law and natural law.[49]

It is time, in short, for judicial "conservatives," especially those who are Catholics, to recognize the truth we noted at the very beginning of this study: that "All human differences are ultimately religious ones."[50] And that is certainly true when it comes to differences over the question of freedom under the United States Constitution or any other document purporting to secure "human rights." The liberals certainly recognize this implicitly, which is why they are winning the culture war in America by rigorously enforcing their anti-theology.

48. John 8:32.
49. Martin Luther King, *Letter from a Birmingham Jail* (1963).
50. Quoted in Wilhelm Röpke, *A Humane Economy* (South Bend: Gateway Editions, 1958), 4, 75.

Changing History: A Thought Experiment[51]

It is not hard to imagine what would happen if Catholics in public life awoke from their Liberty-induced trance and remembered that the God who judges His creatures for failing to obey His law does not require a visitor's pass to enter the courtrooms and legislative chambers of the Western democratic republics. He is there already, and the same judges and legislators who routinely defy His will even piously invoke His name.

Suppose for example, that five of the six Catholic justices now sitting on the Supreme Court bench join in a majority opinion overruling *Roe v. Wade.* Let us suppose that this opinion holds that the Fifth Amendment protection against the deprivation of life and liberty without due process of law, applied to the States via the Fourteenth Amendment, extends to life in the womb. Suppose further that the opinion holds that the Fourteenth Amendment itself, which provides that no state shall "deprive any person of life, liberty, or property, without due process of law; nor deny to any person within its jurisdiction the equal protection of the laws" applies to persons *in utero.* Finally, let us suppose that the opinion ends with this astonishing declaration:

> The Constitution was not drafted and ratified in a moral or theological vacuum. The Framers lived in a society whose common law tradition still recognized the Law of God, and in particular the "divine positive law" of the Ten Commandments, as the ultimate source of human positive law. The classic commentaries of William Blackstone place this historical conclusion beyond serious dispute. The justices of this very Court take an oath to God, and we deliver our opinions while sitting beneath a frieze depicting Moses the Lawgiver holding the tablets containing the Commandments.
>
> We recall here Dr. Martin Luther King's historic declaration in his "Letter from a Birmingham Jail" in the midst of the civil rights movement of the 1960s: "One has not only a legal but a moral responsibility to obey just laws. Conversely, one has a moral responsibility to disobey unjust laws. I would agree with St. Augustine that 'an unjust law is no law at all.'" For too long, the legal distortions created throughout the fabric of this nation by our unprecedented decision in *Roe* have placed conscientious Americans in the same position as Dr. King, writing from his jail cell. Indeed, *Roe* has given rise to a new civil rights movement and concomitant social turmoil that show no signs of abating nearly forty years after *Roe* divided this nation in a way not seen since the abolition movement that followed the everlasting embarrassment of our decision in *Dred Scott v. Sandford,* 60 U.S. (19 How.) 393 (1857).
>
> But beyond a mere appeal to history, which provides the context for our textual interpretation, we hold today that the Constitution's morally freighted terms "person," "life," and "liberty" cannot be considered apart from the same

---

51. The material in this section is adapted from Chapter 20 of *The Church and the Libertarian* (Wyoming, MN: Remnant Press, 2010), by this author.

ultimate source of moral authority that Blackstone, our nation's common law tradition, and Dr. King had in view. As this Court observed in *Zorach v. Clausen*, 343 U.S. at 314, "We are a religious people whose institutions presuppose a Supreme Being." Men are creatures of that Supreme Being, accountable to Him for any human law that contravenes His law, which is written on the heart. Our unfortunate decision in *Roe* is such a human law. We overrule it today, not only in the name of history and tradition, but in the name of God.

That the issuance of such an opinion now seems absolutely inconceivable is in itself a demonstration of the depth and breadth of the dictatorship of Liberty. But what would happen if the Court so decided? The mass media would of course erupt in an unprecedented storm of outrage. There would be calls for impeachment proceedings to remove all five Catholic justices. But what would be the impeachable offense—that the five justices had violated their oaths to God by citing His law in their opinion? Who in the Senate would be foolhardy enough to lead a prosecution of five sitting Supreme Court justices based on their adherence to God's law, supported moreover by references to history, tradition and Saint Martin of Birmingham?

Consider the galvanizing effect the decision would have on a nation whose population is still overwhelmingly at least nominally Christian. Surely, in response to the liberal onslaught, conservative talk radio and TV would hail the justices as heroes, as would evangelical Christian leaders and even many members of the ordinarily craven United States Conference of Catholic Bishops. The Pope would hail the decision, emboldened by the courageous witness of the justices, and Catholics around the world would join the Pope. Certain orthodox Jewish leaders who have long allied themselves with Christians on moral and social issues would lend support to the justices as they come under attack by the media jackals and Congress. And what could the President do? Like Thomas Jefferson in his frustration over Justice Marshall's interference in his attempt to railroad Aaron Burr to the gallows (cf. Chapter 8), he would be reduced to ranting having no legal effect on the life tenure of the five justices. The justices would hold on to their seats and the "separation of powers" that was supposed to characterize the American Republic would receive a tremendous vindication.

In the States, pro-life initiatives in the courts and legislatures would gain powerful impetus. If not outright bans on abortion, state after state, freed from the dead hand of *Roe*, would be able to enact measures that drastically reduce the number of abortions. Christians would come out of hiding throughout the political process, now openly proclaiming that God's law ought indeed to govern positive law and judicial decisions, and what were we thinking before? The resulting rightward shift in national politics could produce a fundamental realignment in Congress and even another Catholic president, but this time one who would not be afraid to proclaim his faith while urging Americans to unite on the great moral issues of our time, using the bully pulpit of the presidency to preach national repentance and conversion of hearts while the liberals seethe with rage.

All of these things could well happen because five jurists had the courage to remind their nation that there is a God in heaven, that we must all die and face His

eternal judgment, and that both men and nations have a duty in this world to follow His law. In short, our imaginary Supreme Court scenario could be a defining
moment in the battle for the soul of the West, with the potential to change not only
the course of American history, but the history of the world. And what is to stop
this imaginary event from becoming a reality? Nothing, save fear of the powers that
be. When our leaders overcome that fear, the rescue of the West from the clutches
of Liberty can begin.

As the Protestant-led NRA movement recognized long ago, only when conservatives—both on and off the bench, in America and in every Western nation—begin
to invoke and defend the law of God, rather than the will of the people or the text
of a document standing alone, can there be any hope of regaining the vast moral
territory we have already lost and of avoiding a final defeat that can only mean the
destruction of what is left of the moral order and the overt persecution of believing
Christians throughout the Western world. Whoever among us still does not see this
is fiddling while the West burns.

The Hope of New Life

As Christopher Dawson observed of our situation, a recovery of our own tradition
has always been possible, even now: "However secularized our modern civilization
may have become, this sacred tradition remains like a river in the desert, and a genuine religious education can still use it to irrigate the thirsty lands and to change
the face of the world with the promise of new life."[52] The opinion-makers and secular statesmen who erupt in outrage at any sign of a recrudescent Christian moral
order evince an acute awareness of the immense spiritual power lying dormant
under the desert whose aridity they monitor assiduously for suspicious signs of
that new life. They sense how easily an awakened worldwide fraternity of the baptized, moved by a resurgent river of grace, could topple the imposing idol called
Liberty from its Sphinx-like dominance over the desert sands.

The burden of this study has been to demonstrate that if our civilization is to
survive, the idol must fall in the name of true freedom: the freedom that arises with
the social incarnation of the reality, heralded by the intuitions of Greek wisdom,
that we are the children of a loving God who bestows upon His rational creatures
both temporal blessings and eternal happiness if only men and societies will worship Him "in spirit and in truth,"[53] heeding the counsels of the Church He established with a mission to make disciples of all *nations*.[54] It is not even a Catholic but
a Protestant thinker who reminds us of the way back to what we have lost:

> Beginning with the flesh of Jesus and its presence in the church, theology alone
> can give due order to other social formations—family, market, and state. The
> goodness of God is discovered not in abstract speculation, but in a life ori-

52. Christopher Dawson, *Understanding Europe* (Garden City, NY: Doubleday, 1960), 255.
53. John 4:24.
54. Matthew 28:20.

ented toward God that creates particular practices that require the privileging of certain social institutions above others. *The goodness of God can be discovered only when the church is the social institution rendering intelligible our lives. . . .* For a Christian account of this good, *the church is the social formation that orders all others.* If the church is not the church, the state, the family, and the market will not know their own true nature.[55]

In his discussion of the West's "progress" from Christendom to the "cult of permission" and the "culture of death," the philosopher H. Tristram Engelhardt, Jr., writing from an Eastern Orthodox perspective, observes that "In the grip of Enlightenment dispositions regarding religion, few are inclined to recognize that the moral life once disengaged from a culture of worship loses its grasp on the moral premises that rightly direct our lives and foreclose the culture of death."[56] The Anglican scholar John Milbank has expressed this same conviction in a startling way: "Only a global liturgical polity can save us now from literal violence."[57] But it is precisely that global polity—Christendom—that Liberty has destroyed.

What Liberty has destroyed the Church has the power to rebuild, *mutatis mutandis,* by a concerted application of her now dormant yet potentially immense social force at the points where human history turns. In the end, this study stands for the proposition that Romano Amerio recognized in his masterwork on the consequences of the Church's mysterious self-subjection to the *Zeitgeist* in our time: "Faith in Providence thus proclaims the possibility that the world might rise and be healed by a metanoia which it cannot initiate but which it is capable of accepting once it is offered."[58] The offer must come first from the Church, as something intrinsic to her mission in the world, and then from leaders inspired and emboldened by her example, who will begin the task of restoring the sacred in the domain of the secular. That prospect is still nowhere in sight, however, for the offer and its acceptance remain impeded by a prevailing cynicism and resignation to an ever-worsening status quo, disguised as political prudence. Christianity having been locked up in the ghetto of private opinion with the agreement of Christians, who hold the key to their own prison, the secular state faces no challenge from a populace united by a public witness of the faith. Liberty's work is done, its reign secure.

We are citizens of the *Novus Ordo Seclorum* to which the American Revolution gave birth. Professed followers of Christ whose ancestors were united in "one Lord, one faith, one baptism"[59] and bowed their heads as one to the bells of the Angelus

55. D. Stephen Long, *The Goodness of God: Theology the Church and Social Order* (Grand Rapids: Brazos Press, 2001), 26, 28; in Thaddeus J. Kozinski, "The Good, the Right, and Theology," *Anamnesis,* www.Anamnesisjournal.com/issues/2-web-essays/13-the-good-the-right-and-theology.

56. H. Tristam Engelhardt, "Life & Death after Christendom: The Moralization of Religion & the Culture of Death," *Touchstone* (June, 2001), accessed April 18, 2011; www.touchstonemag.com/archives/article.php?id=14-05-018-f.

57. John Milbank, "The Gift of Ruling," 238.

58. Amerio, *Iota Unum,* 761.

59. Ephesians 4:5.

from Norway to Spain and the mission territories of the New World, including America, we assemble now in immense and nebulous political congregations composed only of social atoms, each with its own respectable but ineffectual opinion on matters religious. We exhibit excitation in the Lockean-Newtonian field of electoral politics, but fail again and again to maintain equilibrium, much less prevailing strength, against the opposing forces. We seem bewildered by this entirely predictable outcome in a closed system whose fundamental laws require us to manifest our discontent to supreme legislatures and high courts in dutiful submission to the sociopolitical banishment of Christ that is leading the system toward entropic self-annihilation—the heat death of our strange secular cosmion, walled off from any public connection to the living God in whom we all believe. We cannot affect the outcome because we have consented to move within that cosmion according to a social mode of Christianity that, as Louis Veuillot so vividly put it, is "sufficiently nothing to live in peace with the rest of the world."[60]

But the diagnosis is not inevitably terminal. A civilizational return to the sociopolitical recognition of man's true nature and destiny is as near as the God who has endowed us with infinitely more than "unalienable rights": a rational soul, an intellect governing our free wills, the law written on our hearts, reason perfected by the supernatural gift of faith, the capacity for regeneration in grace, the promise of life eternal. The divine dispensation Plato anticipated so many centuries ago in his quest for the good State that would foster the good man has always been ours for the asking. *Excita Domine potentiam tuam et veni ut salvos facias nos*—Stir up your power O Lord and come that you may save us. We need only call upon the Word Incarnate as one people and then watch the world begin to change again.

---

60. Louis Veuillot, *L'Illusion Libérale* (Palmé, 1866), 96 (English edition).

Bibliography

PUBLISHED PRIMARY SOURCES

Selected Primary Treatises

Saint Thomas Aquinas. *On Kingship.* Toronto: Pontifical Institute of Medieval Studies, 2000 [1949].

_____. *Summa Theologica.* New Advent online version, www.newadvent.org/summa/.

_____. *Summa Theologica* in five volumes. Westminster, MD: Christian Classics, 1981.

Aristotle. *The Complete Works of Aristotle*, Vol. II, Bollingen Series. Ed. Jonathan Barnes. Princeton: Princeton Univ. Press, 1984.

_____. *Nicomachean Ethics.* NY: Penguin Books, 2004.

_____. *The Politics.* NY: Penguin Books, 1992.

Augustine, Saint. *The Fathers of the Church: Saint Augustine, the City of God*, Books 1–7 and 17–22. Demetrius B. Zema, S.J. and Gerald G. Walsh, S.J., trans. Washington, DC: Catholic University of America Press, 1950.

Thomas Hobbes. *De corpore politico, or, The elements of law natural & politick.* Whitefish, MT: Kessinger Publishing, LLC, 2004.

_____. *Leviathan.* London: Penguin Books, 1985.

John Locke. *A Discourse of Miracles* in *The Reasonableness of Christianity.* Ed. I.T. Ramsey. Stanford, CA: Stanford Univ. Press, 1958.

_____. *An Essay Concerning Human Understanding.* London: Thomas Tegg, Cheapside (1841).

_____. *A Letter Concerning Toleration.* Ed. James H. Tully. Indianapolis, IN: Hackett Publishing, 1983.

_____. *Political Essays.* Ed. Mark Goldie. Cambridge: Cambridge Univ. Press, 1997.

_____. *The Reasonableness of Christianity.* Stanford, CA: Stanford Univ. Press, 1988.

_____. *Two Treatises of Government.* Cambridge: Cambridge Univ. Press, 2005.

_____. *Writings on Religion*, Ed. Victor Nuovo. Oxford: Oxford Univ. Press, 2002.

Baron de Montesquieu. *On the Spirit of the Laws.* Electronic Text Center: Univ. of Virginia Library, http://etext.virginia.edu/toc/modeng/public/MonLaws.html.

Plato. *Plato: the Collected Dialogues.* Bollingen Series LXXI. Princeton, NJ: Princeton Univ. Press, 1989.

Jean-Jacques Rousseau. *The Social Contract and Later Political Writings.* Ed. Victor Gourevitch. Cambridge: Cambridge Univ. Press, 2007.

Voltaire. *Treatise on Toleration and Other Writings.* Cambridge: Cambridge Univ. Press, 2000.

_____. *The Works of Voltaire*, Vol. XIX (Philosophical Letters) [1733] in *The Works of Voltaire, A Contemporary Version: A Critique and Biography.* John Morley, notes by Tobias Smollett, trans. William F. Fleming. NY: E.R. DuMont, 1901. Accessed at

oll.libertyfund.org/index.php?option=com_staticxt&staticfile=show.php%3Ftitle
=666&Itemid=27.

Selected Primary Documents

An Act for the Admission of West Virginia into the Union. Virgil Anson Lewis, *History of West Virginia.* Philadelphia: Hubbard Brothers, 1889.

Confederate States of America—Message to Congress, April 29, 1861 (Ratification of the Constitution) (Jefferson Davis). Yale Law School: Lillian Goldman Law Library. The Avalon Project, http://avalon.law.yale.edu/19th_century/csa_m042961.asp.

Constitution for the Confederate States of America (1861). Yale Law School: Lillian Goldman Law Library. The Avalon Project, http://avalon.law.yale.edu/19th_century/csa_csa.asp.

Constitution for the Provisional Government of the Confederate States of America (1861). Yale Law School: Lillian Goldman Law Library. The Avalon Project, http://avalon.law.yale.edu/19th_century/csa_csapro. asp.

Constitution of the Republic of Texas (1836). Univ. of Texas at Austin: Tarlton Law Library, Jamail Center for Legal Research. Electronic text: tarlton.law.utexas.edu/constitutions/text/1836cindex.html.

Constitution of the United States Of America. Official Transcript, http://www.archives.gov/exhibits/charters/constitution_transcript.html.

Constitution of Virginia. Virginia Legislative Information System, http://legis.state.va.us/laws/search/constitution.htm.

Emancipation Proclamation (1863) (Abraham Lincoln). Yale Law School: Lillian Goldman Law Library. The Avalon Project, http://avalon.law.yale.edu/19th_century/emancipa.asp.

Farewell Address (1796) (George Washington). Yale Law School: Lillian Goldman Law Library. The Avalon Project, http://avalon.law.yale.edu/18th_century/washing.asp

Georgia Declaration of Secession (1861). Yale Law School: Lillian Goldman Law Library. The Avalon Project, http://avalon.law.yale.edu/19th_centur/csa_geosec. asp.

Kentucky Resolution—Alien and Sedition Acts. Yale Law School: Lillian Goldman Law Library. The Avalon Project, http://avalon.law.yale.edu/18th_century/kenres.asp.

Message to the Senate and House Regarding South Carolina's Nullification Ordinance (1833) (Andrew Jackson). Yale Law School: Lillian Goldman Law Library. The Avalon Project, yale.edu/lawweb/avalon/presiden/messages/ajack001. htm.

Mississippi Declaration of Secession (1861). Yale Law School: Lillian Goldman Law Library. The Avalon Project, http://avalon.law.yale.edu /19th_century/csa_missec.asp.

Proclamation of January 1, 1795 (George Washington). Yale Law School: Lillian Goldman Law Library. The Avalon Project, http://avalon.law.yale.edu/18th_century/gwproc11.asp.

Proclamation on Whiskey Rebellion (1794) (George Washington). Yale Law School: Lillian Goldman Law Library. The Avalon Project, http://avalon.law.yale.edu/18th_century/gwproc03.asp.

Proclamation Regarding Nullification (South Carolina) (1832). Yale Law School: Lillian Goldman Law Library. The Avalon Project, yale.edu/lawweb/Avalon/presiden/proclamationsjack01htm.

Records of the Federal Convention of 1787. Ed. Max Farrand. New Haven, CT: The RFC, 1937.

Report on the Virginia Resolutions (1800) (James Madison). *The Founders' Constitution,* Chapter 8, Document 42, http://press-pubs.uchicago.edu/founders/documents/v1ch8s42.html.

South Carolina Ordinance of Nullification (1832). Yale Law School: Lillian Goldman Law Library. The Avalon Project, yale.edu/lawweb/avalon/states/sc/ordnull.htm.

Texas Declaration of Independence (1835). Texas State Library and Archives Commission. Electronic text: www.tsl.statetx.us/treasures/republic/declare-01.html.

Texas Declaration of Secession (1861). Yale Law School: Lillian Goldman Law Library. The Avalon Project, http://avalon.law.yale.edu/19th_century/csa_texsec.asp.

Virginia Declaration of Rights (1776). Virginia State Govt. archive: www.archives.gov/exhibits/charters/virginia_declaration_of_rights.html.

Virginia Resolution—Alien and Sedition Acts. Yale Law School: Lillian Goldman Law Library. The Avalon Project, http://avalon.law.yale.edu/18thcentury/virres.asp.

Virginia Statute for Religious Freedom (1786). University of Virginia Library. Electronic archive, religiousfreedom.lib.virginia.edu/sacred/vaact.html.

The War of the Rebellion, A Compilation of the Official Records of the Union and Confederate Armies ("Official Records"). Cornell University Library: "Making of America" electronic archive, http://ebooks.library.cornell.edu/m/moawar/waro.html.

Selected Primary Historical Writings and Addresses

Abigail Adams. *Letters of Mrs. Adams, the Wife of John Adams,* Vol. II. Ed. Charles F. Adams. Boston: Charles C. Tuttle and James Evans, 1841.

John Adams. *Proclamation of May 21, 1800.*

_____. *The Spur of Fame: Dialogues of John Adams and Benjamin Rush.* Eds., John A. Schutz and Douglass Adair. Liberty Fund: Indianapolis, 2001 [1966].

_____. *The Works of John Adams, Second President of the United States: with a Life of the Author.* Contrib., Charles Francis Adams. Boston: Little, Brown and Co., 1856, Vol. 10; accessed from oll.libertyfund.org/title/2127/193660/3103830 on 2011-02-08.

Edmund Burke. *Speech on Conciliation with the Colonies. The Founders' Constitution,* Volume 1, Chapter 1, Document 2. Univ. of Chicago Library, press-pubs.uchicago.edu/founders/document/v1ch1s2.html.

John C. Calhoun. *The Works of John C. Calhoun,* Vol. V. Ed. Richard K. Crallé. NY: D. Appleton and Company, 1855.

Mary Boykin Chesnut. *A Diary From Dixie.* NY: D. Appleton and Company, 1905. Kindle Edition.

_____. *Mary Chesnut's Civil War.* Ed. C. Vann Woodward. New Haven: Yale Univ. Press, 1981.

Henry Cleveland. *Alexander H. Stephens in Public and Private, with Letters and Speeches.* Philadelphia: National Publishing Company, 1866.

Jefferson Davis. *Jefferson Davis: the Essential Writings.* Ed. William J. Cooper. NY: Random House, 2004.

_____. *The Rise and Fall of the Confederate Government.* NY: D. Appleton & Co., 1881.

_____. *A Short History of the Confederate States of America.* NY: Belford Company

Publishers, 1890.

Frederick Douglass. *The Life and Times of Frederick Douglass*. Mineola, NY: Dover Publications, 2003 [1892].

_____. *My Bondage and My Freedom*. NY: Miller, Orton and Mulligan, 1855.

Ulysses S. Grant. *Personal Memoirs of Ulysses S. Grant*. NY: Cosimo, Inc., 2007 [1885].

Patrick Henry. *Address to the Virginia Ratifying Convention*, June 9, 1788, Univ. of Chicago Library, press-pubs.uchicago.edu/founders/documents/v1ch11s13.html.

Benjamin H. Hill. *Senator Benjamin H. Hill of Georgia: His Life, Speeches and Writings*. Atlanta: H.C. Hudgins & Co., 1891.

John Jay, James Madison, Alexander Hamilton. *The Federalist Papers*. New Rochelle, NY: Arlington House, 1966.

Thomas Jefferson. *The Anas*. In *The Writings of Thomas Jefferson*. University of Virginia Library. Electronic text: lib.virginia.edu/etcbin/toccer-new2?id=JefBv012.sgm& images=images.

_____. *First Inaugural Address*. *The Papers of Thomas Jefferson* at Princeton University. Accessed at www.princeton.edu/~tjpapers/inaugural/infinalhtml.

_____. *Jeffersonian Cyclopedia*. NY: Funk & Wagnalls Company, 1900.

_____. *Notes on the State of Virginia*. Ed. David Waldstreicher. NY: MacMillan, 2002.

_____. "Special Message on the Burr Conspiracy"(1807). Yale Law School: Lillian Goldman Law Library. The Avalon Project, yale.Edu/lawweb/Avalon/jeffburr.htm.

_____. *The Writings of Thomas Jefferson*. Ed. Paul Leicester Ford. NY: G.P. Putnam's Sons, 1898.

_____. *The Writings of Thomas Jefferson*, Vol. XI. Ed. H.A. Washington. Washington, DC: Thomas Jefferson Memorial Association, 1907.

John F. Kennedy. "Address to Southern Baptist Leaders" (1960). U.S. State Department archive, http://infousa.state.gov/government/overview/66.html.

Abraham Lincoln. *Abraham Lincoln: His Speeches and Writings*. Ed. Roy P. Basler. Cleveland, OH: World Publishing, 1946.

_____. *First Inaugural Address* (1861). Yale Law School: Lillian Goldman Law Library. The Avalon Project, http://avalon.law.yale.edu/19th_entury/lincoln1.asp.

James Madison. *Detached Memoranda* (c. 1817). *The Founders' Constitution*.

_____. *Memorial and Remonstrance* (1785). *The Founders' Constitution*.

_____. *Vices of the Political System of the United States* (1787). *The Founders' Constitution*, Vol. 1, Chap. 4, Doc. 11. Univ. of Chicago Library. Electronic Text: http:/press-pubsuchicago.edu/founders/document/v1ch4s11.html.

_____. *Virginia Remonstrance Against the Assumption of State Debts* (1790). In Lance Banning, *Liberty and Order: The First American Party Struggle* [2004]. Accessed at Online Library of Liberty, http://oll.libertyfund.org/?option=com_staticxt&static-file=show.php%3Ftitle=875&chapter=63862&layout=html&Itemid=27.

_____. *The Writings of James Madison*. Ed. G. Hunt. NY: 1900–1910. Digitized archival copy, accessed at archive.org/stream/writingsofjamesm01madi#page/n0/mode/2up.

Charles Marshall. *Lee's Aide-De-Camp*. Ed. Frederick Maurice. Lincoln, NE: Univ. of Nebraska Press, 2000.

National Reform Association. *Proceedings of the National Convention to Secure the Religious Amendment of the Constitution of the United States*. Philadelphia: As. B. Rodgers Co., 1872.

_____. *Proceedings of the National Reform Convention to Aid in Maintaining the Christian Features of the American Government and Securing a Religious Amendment to the Constitution of the United States*. Philadelphia: Christian Statesman Association, 1874.

Thomas Paine. *Common Sense, the Rights of Man and Other Essential Writings*. NY: Meridian Books, 1984.

Edmund Ruffin. *The Diary of Edmund Ruffin*, Vol. III. Ed. William Kauffman Scarborough. Baton Rouge: Louisiana State Univ. Press, 1972.

Alexander H. Stephens. *A Constitutional View of the Late War Between the States*, in two volumes. Philadelphia: National Publishing Co., 1870.

_____. *Recollections of Alexander H. Stephens: His Diary Kept When a Prisoner at Fort Warren, Boston Harbour, 1865; Giving Incidents and Reflections Of His Prison Life and Some Letters and Reminiscences*. NY: Doubleday, Page & Company, 1910.

Leo Francis Stock, ed. *United States Ministers to the Papal States: Instructions and Dispatches 1848–1868*. Washington, DC: Catholic Univ. Press, 1933.

Alexis de Tocqueville. *Democracy in America*. Eds. Mansfield and Winthrop. Chicago: Univ. of Chicago Press, 2000.

Albion W. Tourgée. *A Fool's Errand: A Novel of the South During Reconstruction*. NY: Cosimo Classics, 2005 [1879].

Augustine Verot, Bishop. *A Tract for the Times*. New Orleans: Catholic Propagator Office, 1861. Duke University Library Ebook and Texts Archive, http://www.archive.org/details/tractfortimesslao1vero.

George Washington. *The Writings of George Washington*, Vol. 5. Ed. John C. Fitzpatrick. Univ. of Virginia Library. Accessed at virginia.edu/Washington/fitzpatrick.

Sam R. Watkins. *Company Aytch*. NY: Touchstone, 2003 [1881].

Daniel Webster. Speech on "The Addition to the Capitol, July 4, 1851." In *The Great Speeches and Orations of Daniel Webster*. Boston: Little, Brown & Co., 1879.

SECONDARY SOURCES

Selected Articles and Addresses

P. Allard. "Slavery and Christianity." *The Catholic Encyclopedia*. NY: Robert Appleton Company, 1912.

David J. Alvarez. "The Papacy in the Diplomacy of the American Civil War." *The Catholic Historical Review*, Vol. 69, No. 2, Apr. 1983.

Paul Maria Baumgarten. "Johann Joseph Ignaz von Döllinger." *The Catholic Encyclopedia*, Vol. 5. NY: Robert Appleton Company, 1909. Accessed at <http://www.newadvent.org/cathen/05094a. htm>.

Robert N. Bellah. "Civil Religion in America." *Dædalus, Journal of the American Academy of Arts and Sciences*, Fall 2005 [1967].

_____. "The Revolution and the Civil Religion" in *Religion and the American Revolution*, ed. Jerald C. Brauer. Philadelphia: Fortress Press, 1976.

Sacvan Bercovitch. "How the Puritans Won the American Revolution." *The Massachusetts Review*, Vol. 17, No. 4, 1976.

Richard E. Beringer. *The Elements of Confederate Defeat.* Athens, GA: Univ. of Georgia Press, 1988.

Walter Berns. "Religion and the Founding Principle." In *The Moral Foundations of the American Republic.* Charlottesville, VA: Univ. of Virginia Press, 1986.

Daina Ramey Berry. "'We'm fus' rate bargain': Value, Labor and Price in a Georgia Slave Community." In *The Chattel Principle: Internal Slave Trades in the America*s. Ed. Walter Johnson. New Haven: Yale Univ. Press, 2002. Kindle Edition.

John Bigelow. "The Southern Confederacy and the Pope." *The North American Review,* Vol. 159, 1893.

Richard Maxwell Brown. "Violence and The American Revolution." In *Essays on the American Revolution.* Eds. Stephen G. Kurtz and James H. Hutson. Chapel Hill, NC: Univ. of North Carolina Press and NY: W. W. Norton & Co., Inc., 1973.

Orestes Brownson. "Introduction to Last Series." *Brownson's Quarterly Review,* January 1873. In *The Works of Orestes A. Brownson.* Detroit: H.F. Brownson, Vol. XX, 1887.

Paul Carrese. "Montesquieu's Complex Natural Right and Moderate Liberalism: The Roots of American Moderation." *Polity,* Vol. 36, No. 2, 2004.

William T. Cavanaugh. "Beyond Secular Parodies." *In Radical Orthodoxy: A New Theology.* Eds. John Milbank, Graham Ward, Catherine Pickstock. London: Routledge, 1998.

John Charvet. "Rousseau, the Problem of Sovereignty and the Limits of Political Obligation." In *Critical Essays on the Social Contract Theorists: Hobbes, Locke and Rousseau,* Ed. Christopher W. Morris. Lanham, MD: Rowman & Little, 1999.

G.K. Chesterton. "On Babies and Birth Control." In *The Well and the Shallows.* San Francisco: Ignatius Press, 2006.

_____. "What I Saw in America." *The Collected Works of G.K. Chesterton,* Vol. 21. San Francisco: Ignatius Press, 1990.

William Cohen. "Thomas Jefferson and the Problem of Slavery." *The Journal of American History,* Vol. 56, No. 3, Dec. 1969.

David P. Currie. "Through the Looking Glass: The Confederate Constitution in Congress, 1861–1865." *Virginia Law Review,* 90:1257, 2004.

Carl N. Degler. "Slavery in Brazil and the United States: An Essay in Comparative History." *The American Historical Review,* Vol. 75, No. 4, Apr. 1970.

Lawrence Dewan, O.P. "St. Thomas, John Finnis and the Political Good." *The Thomist* 64, 2000.

Frank L. Dewey. "Thomas Jefferson's Notes on Divorce." *The William and Mary Quarterly,* Third Series, Vol. 39, No. 1.

Thomas Di Lorenzo. "The Latest Defamation of Jefferson." www.lewrockwell.com/dilorenzo/dilorenzo100.html.

Ross Drake. "The Law that Ripped America in Two." *Smithsonian Magazine,* May 2004.

Jane Shaffer Elsmere. "The Trials of John Fries." *The Pennsylvania Magazine of History and Biography,* Vol. 103, No. 4, October 1979, 432–445.

H. Tristam Engelhardt. "Life & Death after Christendom: The Moralization of Reli-

gion & the Culture of Death." *Touchstone*, June 2001, touchstonemag.com/archives
/article.php?id=14-05-018-f.

William Fanning. "Pierre-Jean De Smet." In *The Catholic Encyclopedia*. NY: Robert
Appleton Company, 1908.

Patricia J. Ferreira. "Frederick Douglass in Ireland: the Dublin Edition of His Narrative." *New Hibernia Review*, Vol. 5, No. 1, Earrach/Spring 2001.

Paul Finkelman. "Scott v. Sandford: The Court's Most Dreadful Case and How It
Changed History." 82 *Chi.-Kent L. Rev.* 3 (2007).

Richard T. Ford. "Law's Territory (A History of Jurisdiction)." 97 *Mich. L. Rev.* 843
(1999).

Kevin M. Gannon. "Escaping 'Mr. Jefferson's Plan of Destruction': New England Federalists and the Idea of a Northern Confederacy. 1803–1804." *Journal of the Early
Republic*, Vol. 21, No. 3 (Autumn 2001).

Paul Leslie Garber. "James Henry Thornwell: Presbyterian Defender of the Old South."
Doctoral thesis, Duke University, 1939. Reprinted from *Union Seminary Review*, February 1943, accessed at http://www.archive.org/details/jameshenleythorn00 garb.

"Eugene Genovese: From Marxism to Christianity." Calvin College, January Series
Lecture, Part 5, 1-20-98. youtube.com/watch?v=xYYTSEodYy4&NR=1.

John Gerard. "Galileo Galilei." *The Catholic Encyclopedia*, 1909.

Alan Gibson. "Whatever Happened to the Economic Interpretation: Beard's Thesis
and the Legacy of Empirical Analysis." Paper delivered at annual meeting of Midwest Political Science Association, April 15, 2004.

Wayne Glausser. "Three Approaches to Locke and the Slave Trade." *Journal of the History of Ideas*, Vol. 51, No. 2, April–June 1990.

Charles A. Gliozzo. "The *Philosophes* and Religion: Intellectual Origins of the Dechristianization Movement in the French Revolution." *Church History*, Vol. 40, No. 3,
Sept. 1971.

Clifford R. Goldstein. "Justice Kenney's Notorious Liberty Passage." *Liberty Online
Magazine*, July–August 1997. libertymagazine.org/index.php?id=1585.

Steven K. Green. "Understanding the 'Christian Nation' Myth." 245 *Cardozo Law
Review* 250 (2010).

Hermann Gruber. "Masonry, Freemasonry." *The Catholic Encyclopedia*, Vol. 9. NY:
Robert Appleton Company, 1913.

Ralph C. Hancock. "Religion and the Limits of Limited Government." *The Review of
Politics*, Vol. 50, No. 4, Autumn, 1988.

David G.R. Heiser. "Bishop Lynch's Civil War Pamphlet on Slavery." *The Catholic Historical Review*, Vol. 84, No. 4, October 1998.

Dwight F. Henderson. "Treason, Sedition, and Fries' Rebellion." *The American Journal
of Legal History*, Vol. 14, No. 4., Oct. 1970.

Peter R. Henriques. "The Final Struggle between George Washington and the Grim
King: Washington's Attitude toward Death and an Afterlife." *The Virginia Magazine of History and Biography*, Vol. 107, No. 1, Winter 1999.

Mary Hershberger. "Anticipating Abolition: the Struggle Against Indian Removal in
the 1830s." *The Journal of American History*, Vol. 86, No. 1, June 1999.

Donald R. Hickey. "Federalist Defense Policy in the Age of Jefferson." *Military Affairs*, Vol. 45. No. 2, April 1981.

Charles F. Hobson. "The Negative on State Laws: James Madison, the Constitution and the Crisis of Republican Government." *William and Mary Quarterly*. Third Series, Vol. 36, No. 2, Apr. 1979.

Richard Hofstadter. "The Tariff Issue on the Eve of the Civil War." *The American Historical Review*, Vol. 44, No. 1, October 1938.

Wythe Holt. "The Whiskey Rebellion of 1794: A Democratic Working-Class Insurrection." Paper presented at The Georgia Workshop in Early American History and Culture, 2004.

Theodore Hornberger. "Samuel Johnson of Yale and King's College." *The New England Quarterly*, Vol. 8, No. 3, Sept., 1935.

Frederick E. Hoxie. "What Was Taney Thinking? American Indian Citizenship in the Era of Dred Scott." 82 *Chi.-Kent L. Rev.* 329, 335 (2007).

James Hutson. "James Madison and The Social Utility of Religion: Risks and Rewards." Library of Congress monograph, www.loc.gov/loc/madison/hutson-paper. html.

_____. "Thomas Jefferson's Letter to the Danbury Baptists: A Controversy Rejoined." *William and Mary Quarterly*, 3d Series, Vol. 56, No. 4, October 1999.

Gianna Jessen. Testimony at Hearing Before The Subcommittee On The Constitution Of The Committee On The Judiciary House Of Representatives, Second Session, July 20, 2000.

Samuel Johnson. "Taxation No Tyranny." In *The Works of Samuel Johnson*. Ed. Arthur Murphy. NY: Alexander V. Blake, 1837.

Sidney Kaplan. "The 'Domestic Insurrections' of the Declaration of Independence." *The Journal of Negro History*, Vol. 61, No. 3, July 1976.

Richard S. Kay. "Original Intention and Public Meaning in Constitutional Interpretation." 103 *Northwestern University Law Review* 703 (2009).

Thaddeus J. Kozinski. "The Good, the Right, and Theology." Anamnesis, www.Anamnesisjournal.com/issues/2-web-essays13-thegood-the-right-and-theology.

Isaac Kramnick. "The Great National Discussion: The Discourse of Politics in 1787." *William and Mary Quarterly*, 3d. Ser., Vol. 45, No. 1, Jan. 1988.

Jeffrey Langan. "Revolutionary Guilt." Paper delivered at Trialogos Conference: Tallinn, Estonia, 2007.

Howard R. Marraro. "The Four Versions of Jefferson's Letter to Mazzei." *William and Mary Quarterly*, 2d Ser., Vol. 22, No. 1, January 1942.

Martin E. Marty. "Sidney E. Mead: Historian of Religion in America." Accessed at http://www.harvardsquarelibrary.org/unitarians/mead.html.

Robert M.S. McDonald. "The Madisonian Legacy: A Jeffersonian Perspective." In *Madison and the Future of Limited Government*. Ed. John Samples. Washington, DC: Cato Institute, 2002.

Sidney E. Mead. "The Nation with the Soul of a Church." *Church History*, Vol. 36, No. 3, September 1967.

Harvey C. Mesesrve. "The Therapeutic Age." *Journal of Religion and Health*, Vol. 16, No. 2.

John Milbank. "The Gift of Ruling: Secularization and Political Authority." *New Blackfriars*, Vol. 85, Issue 996, March 2004.

Philip Milton. "John Locke and the Rye House Plot." *The Historical Journal*, 43, 3, 2000.

Michael de Haven Newsom. "The American Protestant Empire: a Historical Perspective." 40 *Washburn Law Journal* 187 (2001).

Steve O'Brien. "The Justice: Roger B. Taney." *The Latin Mass: The Journal of Catholic Culture and Tradition*, Winter 2011.

Peter S. Onuf. "Jefferson, Federalist." In *Essays in History.* Univ. of Virginia electronic archive, Vol. 35, 1993.

Samuel C. Pearson. Jr. "The Religion of John Locke." *The Journal of Religion*, Vol. 58, No. 3, July 1978.

Gary Potter. "Catholicism and the Old South: Part 2." catholicdiscussion.wordpress.com/2008/04/10/catholicism-and-the-old-south-by-gary-potterpt-2/.

Paul Rich and Lic. Guillermo De Los Reyes. "Towards A Revisionist View Of Poinsett: Problems In The Historiography Of Mexican Freemasonry." Published paper, www.h-net.org/~latam/essaysmason2.html.

Kirkpatrick Sale. "Getting Back to the Real Constitution?" www.counterpunch.org/sale10282010.html.

S. Gerald Sandler. "Lockean Ideas in Jefferson's Bill for Establishing Religious Freedom." *Journal of the History of Ideas*, 21, 1960.

Antonin Scalia. "Of Democracy, Morality and the Majority." Transcript of Q & A following address at the Gregorian, May 2, 1996. *Origins*, Vol. 26, No. 6, June 27, 1996.
_____. "Originalism: the Lesser Evil." 57 *University of Cincinnati Law Review* 849 (1989).

Calvin Schermerhorn. "The Everyday Life of Enslaved People in the Antebellum South." *OAH Magazine of History*, April 2009.

Arthur M. Schlesinger. "Liberty Tree: A Genealogy." *The New England Quarterly*, Vol. 25, No. 4, Dec. 1952.

George Shulman. "Hobbes, Puritans, and Promethean Politics." *Political Theory*, Vol. 16, No. 3, 1988.

Harry S. Stout and Christopher Grasso. "Civil War, Communications, and Religion: the Case of Richmond." In Randall M. Miller, Harry S. Stout, Charles Reagan Wilson. *American Religion and the Civil War.* NY: Oxford Univ. Press, 1998.

Richard Sutch. "The Breeding of Slaves for Sale and the Western Expansion of Slavery: 1850–1860." In Engerman and Genovese, eds *Race and Slavery in the Western Hemisphere: Quantitative Studies.* Princeton, NJ: Princeton Univ. Press, 1975.

William F. Swindler. "The Politics of 'Advice and Consent'." 56 *American Bar Association Journal* 540 (1979).

Allen Tate. "The Battle of Gettysburg: Why It Was Fought." Lecture at Lothrop Memorial Auditorium, Univ. of Minnesota, 4 February 1963, in *Allen Tate Papers*, Princeton University.

James Henley Thornwell. "Relation of the State to Christ." In *The Collected Writings of James Henley Thornwell*. Eds. John B. Adger and John L. Girardeau. NY: Robert Carter & Bros., 1873.

Herbert Thurston. "John Emerich Edward Dahlberg Acton. Baron Acton." *The Catholic Encyclopedia*, Vol. 1. NY: Robert Appleton Company, 1907. Accessed at <http://www.newadvent.org/cathen/01114a.htm>.

Benjamin Wachs. "Sociologist Philip Rieff haunts us from the grave." JWeekly. com, July 18, 2008, www.jweekly.com/article/full/35346/sociologist-philip-rieff-hau nts-us-from-the-grave/.

"The War on the Public Schools." *The New York Times*, July 30, 1873.

Paul J. Weber. "James Madison and Religious Equality: The Perfect Separation." *The Review of Politics*, Vol. 44, No. 2, April 1982.

Kenneth L. Woodward. "The Last Respectable Prejudice." *First Things*, October 2002.

Selected Books

George Rollie Adams. *General William S. Harney: Prince of Dragoons*. Lincoln, NE: Univ. of Nebraska Press, 2001.

John B. Adger and John L. Girardeau, eds *The Collected Writings of James Henley Thornwell*, Vol. III. NY: Robert Carter & Bros., 1873.

Catharine L. Albanese. *Sons of the Fathers: The Civil Religion of the American Revolution*. Philadelphia: Temple Univ. Press, 1976.

John K. Alexander. *Sam Adams. Revolutionary Politician*. Oxford: Roman & Littlefield, 2004.

Felicity Allen. *Jefferson Davis: Unconquerable Heart*. Columbia, MO: Univ. of Missouri Press, 1999.

Hadley Arkes. *Beyond the Constitution*. Princeton, NJ: Princeton Univ. Press, 1990.

John W. Baer. *The Pledge of Allegiance: A Centennial History: 1892–1992*. Annapolis, MD: Free State Press., Inc. (2007).

Bernard Bailyn. *The Ideological Origins of the American Revolution*. Cambridge, MA: Belknap Press of Harvard Univ. Press, 1992 [1967].

George Bancroft. *History Of The United States of America, from the Discovery of the American Continent*. Boston: Little, Brown and Company, 1875.

K. Jack Bauer. *The Mexican War, 1846–48*. Lincoln, NE: Univ. of Nebraska Press, 1992 [1974].

Charles A. Beard. *An Economic Interpretation of the Constitution of the United States*. NY: Dover Publications, 2004 [1913].

Carl L. Becker. *The Heavenly City of the Eighteenth-Century Philosophers*. New Haven: Yale Univ. Press, 2003 [1932].

Hilaire Belloc. *Economics for Helen*. Norfolk, VA: IHS Press, 2010 [1924], Kindle Edition.

Richard E. Beringer. *The Elements of Confederate Defeat.* Athens. GA: Univ. of Georgia Press, 1988.

Richard E. Beringer, Herman Hattway, Archer Jones, and William N. Still. Jr. *Why the South Lost the Civil War.* Athens, GA: Univ. of Georgia Press, 1986.

Ira Berlin. *Generations of Captivity: A History of African-American Slaves.* Cambridge, MA: Belknap Press of Harvard Univ. Press, 2004, Kindle Edition.

David Berlinski. *The Devil's Delusion.* NY: Crown Forum, 2008.

Walter Berns. *The First Amendment and the Future of American Democracy.* NY: Basic Books, 1976.

Iver Berstein. *The New York City Draft Riots: Their Significance for American Society and Politics in the Age of the Civil War.* Oxford: Oxford Univ. Press, 1990.

James H. Billington. *Fire in the Minds of Men.* NY: Basic Books, Inc., 1980.

Rev. Benjamin J. Blied, Ph. D. *Catholics and the Civil War.* Milwaukee: 1945.

Harold Bloom. *The American Religion: The Emergence of a Post-Christian Nation.* NY: Simon & Schuster, 1993.

Mark Mayo Boatner III. *The Civil War Dictionary.* NY: David McKay Co., Inc., 1959.

Paul F. Boller. *George Washington & Religion.* Dallas: Methodist Univ. Press, 1963.

Paul S. Boyer, Clifford E. Clark, Sandra Hawley, Joseph F. Kett, Andrew Rieser. *An Enduring Vision: A History of the American People.* Florence, KY: Wadsworth Publishing, 2009.

Mark L. Bradley. *This Astounding Close: the Road to Bennett Place.* Chapel Hill: Univ. of North Carolina Press, 2000.

Fawn McKay Brodie. *Thomas Jefferson: An Intimate Portrait.* NY: W.W. Norton & Company, 1974.

Everett Somerville Brown. *The Constitutional History of the Louisiana Purchase, 1803–1812.* Berkeley: Univ. of California Press, 1920.

Patrick J. Buchanan. *Churchill, Hitler and the Unnecessary War.* NY: Three Rivers Press, 2008.

Steven C. Bullock. *Revolutionary Brotherhood.* Chapel Hill: Univ. of North Carolina Press, 1996.

John W. Burgess. *Political Science and Comparative Constitutional Law: Vol. I. Sovereignty and Liberty.* Boston: Ginn & Co., 1893.

Rev. J.A. Burns. *The Growth and Development of the Catholic School System in the United States.* NY: Benzinger Bros., 1912.

J.H. Burns and Mark Goldie, eds *The Cambridge History of Political Thought: 1450–1700.* Cambridge: Cambridge Univ. Press. 2004 [1991].

William T. Cavanaugh. *The Myth of Religious Violence.* NY: Oxford Univ. Press, 2009.

G.K. Chesterton. *Saint Thomas Aquinas.* NY: Random House, 1974.

William Cobbett. *A History of the Protestant Reformation in England and Ireland.* NY: Benzinger Bros, 1896. Tan Books reprint.

Margaret L. Coit. *John C. Calhoun: An American Portrait.* Columbia, SC: Univ. of South Carolina Press, 1991 [1950].

Ambrose Coleman. *The Friars in the Philippines.* Boston: Marlier, Callanan & Co., 1899.

Donald E. Collins. *The Death and Resurrection of Jefferson Davis.* Lanham, MD: Rowman and Littlefield, 2005.

Jeffrey R. Collins. *The Allegiance of Thomas Hobbes*. Oxford: Oxford Univ. Press, 2005.

Frederick Copleston, S.J. *A History of Philosophy*. NY: Doubleday, 1985.

R.S. Cotterill. *The Southern Indians: The Story of the Civilized Tribes before Removal*. Norman, OK: Univ. of Oklahoma Press, 1954.

Don Juan Donoso Cortes. *Essay on Catholicism, Authority and Order*. NY: Joseph F. Wagner, 1925.

Joseph F. Costanzo, S.J. *Political and Legal Studies*. West Hanover, MA: The Christopher Publishing House, 1982.

Antonio Rafael de la Cova. *Cuban Confederate Colonel: The Life of Ambrosio José Gonzales*. Columbia, SC: Univ. of South Carolina Press, 2003.

Kenneth L. Craycraft, Jr. *The American Myth of Religious Freedom*. Dallas: Spence Publishing Co., 1999.

Hiram Martin Crittenden and Alfred Talbott Richardson, eds. *Life, Letters and Travels of Pierre-Jean De Smet*, Vol. IV. NY: Francis P. Harper, 1905.

H.W. Crocker, III. *The Politically Incorrect Guide to the Civil War*. Perseus Distribution-A: Kindle Edition, 2008.

Richard N. Current. *Lincoln and the First Shot*. Prospect Heights, IL: Waveland Press, Inc., 1990 [1963]. Reprint, Harper & Row edition.

Philip Davidson. *Propaganda and the American Revolution*. Chapel Hill, NC: Univ. of North Carolina Press, 1941.

Graham Davis. *Land!: Irish Pioneers in Mexican and Revolutionary Texas*. Texas A & M Univ. Press, 2003.

Varina Davis. *Jefferson Davis*, Vol. I. NY: Belford Company, 1890.

William C. Davis. *Jefferson Davis: the Man and His Hour*. LSU Press/Harper Collins, 1991.

W.W.H. Davis, A.M. *The Fries Rebellion, 1798–99*. Doylestown, PA: Doylestown Publishing, 1899.

Christopher Dawson. *Religion and the Rise of Western Culture*. NY: Image Books, 1991 [1950].

_____. *Understanding Europe*. NY: Sheed and Ward, 1952.

Matthew Q. Dawson. *Partisanship and the Birth of America's Second Party, 1796–1800*. Westport, CT: Greenwood Publishing, 2000.

Enrico Del Lago. *Agrarian Elites: American Slaveholders and Southern Italian Landowners, 1815–1861*. Baton Rouge: Louisiana State Univ. Press, 2005.

Donald D'Elia. *The Spirits of '76*. Front Royal, VA: Christendom Publications, 1983.

William R. Denslow and Harry S. Truman. *10,000 Famous Freemasons*. Missouri Lodge of Research, 1957.

John V. Denson. *A Century of War: Lincoln, Wilson and Roosevelt*. Auburn, AL: Von Mises Institute, 2006.

William Doyle. *The Oxford History of the French Revolution*. NY: Oxford Univ. Press, 1989.

Dinesh D'Souza. *Life After Death*. Washington, DC: Regnery Publishing, Inc., 2009.

Robert F. Durden. *The Gray and the Black: the Confederate Debate on Emancipation*. Baton Rouge: Louisiana State Univ. Press, 1972.

Clement Eaton. *A History of the Old South*, 3rd ed. Long Grove, IL: Waveland Press, 1975.

David J. Eicher. *The Longest Night: A Military History of the Civil War.* NY: Simon & Schuster, 2001.

John S.D. Eisenhower. *Zachary Taylor.* NY: Times Books, 2008.

Stanley Elkins. *Slavery: A Problem in American Institutional and Intellectual Life.* Chicago: Univ. of Chicago Press, 3d ed., 1976.

Cornelio Fabro. *God in Exile.* NY: Newman Press, 1968.

Drew Gilpin Faust. *The Creation of Confederate Nationalism: Identity and Ideology in the Civil War South.* NY: Vintage Books, Kindle Edition.

_____. *This Republic of Suffering.* Vintage: Kindle Edition, 2008.

Bernard Fay. *Revolution and Freemasonry.* Boston: Little, Brown and Company. 1935.

_____. *The Revolutionary Spirit in France and America.* NY: Cooper Square Publishers, 1966.

Michael Fellman. *The Making of Robert E. Lee.* NY: Random House, 2000.

David Ferguson. *Liberalism, Community and Christian Ethics.* Cambridge: Cambridge Univ. Press, 1998.

Edward Feser. *Locke.* Oxford: One World Publications, 2007.

Paul Finkelman, John F.A. Sanford. *Dred Scott: A Brief History with Documents.* Boston: St. Martin's Press, 1997.

Charles Bracelen Flood. *Lee: The Last Years.* NY: Houghton Mifflin, 1998.

Robert William Fogel. *Without Contract or Consent: the Rise and Fall of American Slavery.* NY: W. W. Norton & Co., 1989.

Shelby Foote. *The Civil War: A Narrative* in 3 Vols. NY: Vintage Books, 1986 [1958].

Gaines M. Foster. *Ghosts of the Confederacy: Defeat, the Lost Cause and the Emergence of the New South, 1860 to 1913.* NY: Oxford Univ. Press, 1987.

Dennis B. Fradin. *Sam Adams: the Father of American Independence.* NY: Clarion Books, 1998.

Douglas Southall Freeman. *R.E. Lee: A Biography.* NY: Scribner & Sons, 1914.

Francis Fukuyama. *The End of History and the Last Man.* NY: Free Press, 1992.

François Furet. *Revolutionary France: 1770–1880.* Oxford: Blackwell, 1988.

Hans-Georg Gadamer. *The Idea of the Good in Platonic-Aristotelian Philosophy.* New Haven: Yale Univ. Press, 1986.

Gary W. Gallagher. *The Confederate War: How Popular Will, Nationalism, and Military Strategy Could Not Stave Off Defeat.* Cambridge, MA: Harvard Univ. Press, 1997.

Peter Gay. *The Enlightenment: The Rise of Modern Paganism.* NY: W.W. Norton & Co., 1977.

_____. *The Enlightenment: The Science of Freedom.* NY: W.W. Norton & Co., 1969.

Eugene D. Genovese. *The Political Economy of Slavery.* Middletown, CT: Wesleyan Univ. Press, 2d ed., 1989.

_____. *Roll, Jordan, Roll: The World the Slaves Made.* NY: Vintage Books, Kindle Edition, 2011 [1976].

_____. *Slaveholders' Dilemma: Freedom and Progress in Southern Conservative Thought.* Columbia, SC: Univ. of South Carolina Press, 1994.

_____. *The Southern Tradition.* Cambridge, MA: Harvard Univ. Press, 1994.

Peter Gilmour. *Philosophers of the Enlightenment.* Edinburgh Univ. Press, 1990. U.S. edition, Totowa, NJ: Barnes and Noble, 1990.

Paul Glynn. *A Song for Nagasaki.* San Francisco: Ignatius Press, 1988.

Horace Greeley. *The American Conflict: A History of the Great Rebellion,* Vol. II. Hartford, CT: O.D. Case & Co., 1866.

Michael S. Green. *Politics and America in Crisis: the Coming of the Civil War.* Santa Barbara, CA: ABC-CLIO, LLC, 2010.

Steven Green. *The Second Disestablishment: Church and State in Nineteenth-Century America.* NY: Oxford Univ. Press, 2010, Kindle Edition.

L. F. Greene, ed. *The Writings of the Elder John Leland.* NY: G. W. Wood, 1845.

Herbert G. Gutman. *Slavery and the Numbers Game: A Critique of Time on the Cross.* Chicago: Univ. of Illinois Press, 2003 [1975].

James Haley. *Sam Houston.* Norman, OK: Univ. of Oklahoma Press, 2004.

Nathan O. Hatch. *The Democratization of American Christianity.* New Haven: Yale Univ. Press, 1989.

Chester G. Hearn. *When the Devil Came Down to Dixie: Ben Butler in New Orleans.* Baton Rouge: Louisiana State Univ. Press, 2000.

David S. and Jeanne T. Heidler, eds. *Encyclopedia of the American Civil War.* NY: W. S. Norton & Co., 2000.

James J. Hennessey. *American Catholics: A History of the Roman Catholic Community in the United States.* NY: Oxford Univ. Press, 1981, Kindle Edition.

Wallace Hettle. *Inventing Stonewall Jackson: A Civil War Hero in History and Memory.* Baton Rouge: Louisiana State Univ. Press, 2001, Kindle Edition.

Frederick May Holland. *Frederick Douglass, The Colored Orator.* NY: Haskell House Publishers. Ltd., 1969 [1891].

David L. Holmes. *The Faith of the Founding Fathers.* Oxford: Oxford Univ. Press, 2006.

Jerry Holmes, ed. *Thomas Jefferson: A Chronology of His Thoughts.* Lanham, MD: Rowman & Littlefield Publishers, Inc., 2002.

Michael F. Holt. *The Fate of Their Country: Politicians, Slavery Extension, and the Coming of the Civil War.* NY: Hill and Wang, 2004.

_____. *The Rise and Fall of the American Whig Party: Jacksonian Politics and the Onset of the Civil War.* NY: Oxford Univ. Press, 1999.

Hans-Hermann Hoppe. *Democracy: The God That Failed.* New Brunswick, NJ: Transaction Publishers, 2004.

Robert H. Horowitz, ed. *The Moral Foundations of the American Republic.* Charlottesville, VA: Univ. of Virginia Press, 2001.

Daniel Walker Howe. *What Hath God Wrought. Oxford History of the United States.* Oxford Univ. Press: 2007, Kindle Edition.

Jonathan I. Israel. *Locke, Spinoza and the Philosophical Debate Concerning Toleration in the Early Enlightenment.* Amsterdam: Royal Netherlands Academy of Arts and Sciences: 1999.

_____. *The Radical Enlightenment: Philosophy and the Making of Modernity.* Oxford: Oxford Univ. Press, 2001.

Margaret Jacob. *Living the Enlightenment.* NY: Oxford Univ. Press, 1991.

Werner Jaeger. *Paidea: The Ideals of Greek Culture,* Vol. I: *Archaic Greece—The Mind of Athens.* Oxford: Oxford Univ. Press. 1974 [1939].

_____. *Paidea*, Vol. II: *In Search of the Divine Center*. NY: Oxford: Univ. Press. 1971 [1943].

_____. *Paidea*, Vol. III: *The Conflict of Cultural Ideals in the Age of Plato*. Oxford: Oxford Univ. Press, 1971 [1944].

Philip Jenkins. *The New Anti-Catholicism*. Oxford: Oxford Univ. Press, 2003.

Clayton E. Jewett. *Slavery in the South: A State-by-State History*. Westport, CT: Greenwood Press, 2004.

Lawrence S. Kaplan. *Jefferson and France: An Essay on Politics and Political Ideas*. New Haven: Yale Univ. Press, 1967.

Sidney Kaplan. *The Black Presence in the Era of the American Revolution*. Amherst, MA: Univ. of Massachusetts Press, 1989.

Helmut Georg Koenigsberger. *Politicians and Virtuosi: Essays in Early Modern History*. NY: Continuum International Publishing Group, 1986.

Dimitri Kolgonov. *Lenin: A New Biography*. NY: Free Press/Simon and Schuster, 1994.

Lincoln Konkle. *Thornton Wilder and the Puritan Narrative Tradition*. Columbia, MO: Univ. of Missouri Press, 2006.

Isaac Kramnick, R. Laurence Moore. *The Godless Constitution: the Case Against Religious Correctness*. NY: W. W. Norton & Co., 1997.

Erik von Kuehnelt-Leddhin. *Leftism Revisited*. Washington, DC: Regnery Gateway, 1991.

_____. *Liberty or Equality: The Challenge of Our Time*. Front Royal, VA: Christendom Press. 1993 [1952].

Ward Hill Lamon. *The Life of Lincoln: From His Birth to His Inauguration as President*. Boston: James R. Osgood & Company, 1872.

Fr. E. Laveille, S. J. *The Apostle of the Rocky Mountains: The Life of Father De Smet, S.J.* NY: P. J. Kennedy & Sons, 1915. Tan Books edition, 2000.

Ross M. Lence, ed. *Union and Liberty: The Political Philosophy of John C. Calhoun*. Indianapolis: Liberty Fund, 1992.

John C. Lester, Daniel L. Wilson. *Ku Klux Klan: Its Origin, Growth, and Disbandment*. NY: Neal Publishing Company, 1905.

Mark R. Levin. *Ameritopia*. NY: Simon & Schuster, 2012, Kindle Edition.

Bruce Levine. *Confederate Emancipation: Southern Plans to Free and Arm Slaves during the Civil War*. NY: Oxford Univ. Press, 2005, Kindle Edition.

Leonard Levy. *Jefferson and Civil Liberties: the Darker Side*. NY: Quadrangle/New York Times Book Company, 1963.

Leon F. Litwack. *Been in the Storm So Long: The Aftermath of Slavery*. NY: Vintage Books, 2010, Kindle Edition.

D. Stephen Long. *The Goodness of God: Theology, the Church and Social Order*. Grand Rapids, MI: Brazos Press, 2001.

C.B. Macpherson. *The Political Theory of Possessive Individualism: From Hobbes to Locke*. Oxford: Oxford Univ. Press, 1962.

Pierre Manent. *An Intellectual History of Liberalism*. Princeton, NJ: Princeton Univ. Press, 1995.

_____. *The City of Man*. Princeton, NJ: Princeton Univ. Press, 1998.

Theodore Maynard. *The Catholic Church and the American Idea*. NY: Appleton-Century-Crofts, Inc., 1953.

David McCullough. *John Adams*. NY: Simon and Schuster, 2001.

Forrest McDonald. *We the People: the Economic Origins of the Constitution*. New Brunswick, NJ: Transaction Publishers-Rutgers University, 1991 [1958].

Andrew McLaughlin and Albert Bushnell Hart, eds. *Cyclopedia of American Government*, Vol. II. NY: D. Appleton & Co., 1914.

Edward McPherson. *The Political History of the United States of America during the Great Rebellion*. Washington: Philp & Solomons, 1865.

James M. McPherson, Gary W. Gallagher, Reid Mitchell, Joseph T. Glatthaar. *Why the Confederacy Lost*. NY: Oxford Univ. Press, 1992.

Myra McPherson. *Long Time Passing: Viet Nam and the Haunted Generation*. Bloomington: Indiana Univ. Press, 2001.

Sidney Mead. *The Lively Experiment: The Shaping of Christianity in America*. NY: Harper and Row, 1963.

William Meade. *Old Churches, Ministers and Families of Virginia*. Philadelphia: J.P. Lippincott & Co., 1899.

H.L. Mencken. *Prejudices: Third Series*. NY: Alfred A. Knopf, 1922.

John Milbank. *Theology and Social Theory: Beyond Secular Reason*. Oxford: Blackwell, 1993.

John C. Miller. *Sam Adams: Pioneer in Propaganda*. Stanford, CA: Stanford Univ. Press, 1964.

_____. *Triumph of Freedom, 1775–1783*. Boston: Little, Brown, 1948.

_____. *The Wolf by the Ears: Thomas Jefferson and Slavery*. Charlottesville, VA: Univ. of Virginia Press, 1991 [1980].

Robert Ryal Miller. *Shamrock and Sword*. Norman, OK: Univ. of Oklahoma Press, 1989.

Albert Burton Moore. *Conscription and Conflict in the Confederacy*. Columbia, SC: Univ. of South Carolina Press, 1996 [1924].

Frank Moore, ed. *The Rebellion Record*, Vol. III. NY: G.P. Putnam, 1862.

Samuel Eliot Morison. *The Oxford History of the American People*. NY: Oxford Univ. Press, 1965.

_____. *Sources and Documents Illustrating the American Revolution, 1764–1788*. Oxford, 1929.

Benjamin Franklin Morris. *Christian Life and Character of the Civil Institutions of the United States*. Philadelphia: George W. Childs, 1864.

John Watson Morton. *The Artillery of Nathan Bedford Forrest's Calvary: the "Wizard of the Saddle."* Nashville, TN: Publishing House of the M.E. Church, South, 1909.

John Courtney Murray, S.J. *We Hold These Truths*. Kansas City: Sheed and Ward, 1960.

Mark E. Neely, Jr. *Confederate Bastille: Jefferson Davis and Civil Liberties*. Milwaukee: Marquette Univ. Press, 1993.

Friedrich Nietzsche. *The Genealogy of Morals*. Mineola, NY: Dover Publications, 2003 [1913].

Alan T. Nolan. *Lee Considered*. Chapel Hill: Univ. of North Carolina Press, 1991.

Conor Cruise O'Brien. *The Long Affair: Thomas Jefferson and the French Revolution.* Chicago: Univ. of Chicago Press, 1996.

Stephen Jay Ochs. *A Black Patriot and a White Priest.* Baton Rouge: Louisiana State Univ. Press, 2000.

Cecilia O'Leary. *To Die For: The Paradox of American Patriotism.* Princeton, NJ: Princeton Univ. Press, 1999.

Kim Ian Parker. *The Biblical Politics of John Locke.* Waterloo, Ontario: Wilfrid Laurier Univ. Press, 2004.

Orlando Paterson. *Slavery and Social Death: A Comparative Study.* Cambridge, MA: Harvard Univ. Press, 1985.

Merrill D. Peterson, ed. *The Political Writings of Thomas Jefferson.* Chapel Hill: Univ. of North Carolina Press, 1993.

Jason Phillips. *Diehard Rebels.* Athens, GA: Univ. of Georgia Press, 2007.

George Wilson Pierson. *Tocqueville in America.* Baltimore, MD: Johns Hopkins Univ. Press, 1996.

Serhii Ploky. *Yalta: the Price of Peace.* NY: Viking, 2010.

Thomas Jefferson Randolph, ed. *Memoirs, Correspondence and Miscellanies from the Papers of Thomas Jefferson,* Vol III. Charlottesville, VA: F. Carr and Co., 1829.

James F. Rhodes. *History of the United States from the Compromise of 1850 to the McKinley-Bryan Campaign of 1896,* Vol. III. NY: Cosimo, Inc., 2009 [1895].

David A. J. Richards. *Toleration and Constitution.* NY: Oxford Univ. Press, 1986.

Philip Rieff. *The Triumph of the Therapeutic.* Wilmington, DE: ISI Books, 2005 [1966].

John Rist. *Real Ethics.* Cambridge: Cambridge Univ. Press, 2002.

James I. Robertson, Jr. *Soldiers Blue and Gray.* Columbia, SC: Univ. of South Carolina Press, 1998.

_____. *Stonewall Jackson: the Man, the Soldier, the Legend.* NY: MacMillan Publishing USA, 1997.

Cornwell B. Rogers. *The Spirit of Revolution in 1789.* Princeton, NJ: Princeton Univ. Press, 1949.

Wilhelm Röpke. *A Humane Economy.* South Bend: Gateway Editions, 1958.

_____. *The Social Crisis of Our Time.* New Brunswick, NJ: Transaction Publishers, 1991 [1942].

Murray Rothbard. *Conceived in Liberty,* Vol. IV, Auburn, AL: Von Mises Institute, 1999 (online edition).

_____. *Ethics of Liberty.* NY: New York Univ. Press, 2002.

_____. *For a New Liberty.* Auburn, AL: Von Mises Institute, 2002 (online edition).

Charles Royster. *The Destructive War: William Tecumseh Sherman, Stonewall Jackson, and the Americans.* NY: Vintage Books, Kindle Edition, 2011 (Knopf ed. 1991).

Anne Sarah Rubin. *A Shattered Nation: the Rise and Fall of the Confederacy, 1861–1868.* Chapel Hill, NC: Univ. of North Carolina Press, 2005.

R. J. Rummel. *Death by Government.* New Brunswick, NJ: Transaction Publishers, 2008.

John Salza. *Freemasonry Unmasked: An Insider Reveals the Secrets of the Lodge.* Huntington, IN: Our Sunday Visitor Publishing Division, 2006.

Philip Schaff. *The Principle of Protestantism as Related to the Present State of the Church.* Chambersburg, PA: Publication Office of the German Reformed Church, 1845.

Simon Schama. *Citizens.* NY: Alfred A. Knopf, 1989.

J.B. Schneewind. *The Invention of Autonomy.* Cambridge: Cambridge Univ. Press, 1997.

Thomas P. Slaughter. *The Whiskey Rebellion.* NY: Oxford Univ. Press, 1986.

Abbot Emerson Smith. *James Madison: Builder: A New Estimate of a Memorable Career.* NY: Wilson Erickson, 1937.

W.M. Spellman. *John Locke.* NY: St. Martin's Press, 1997.

Mark David Spence. *Dispossessing the Wilderness: Indian Removal and the Making of the National Parks.* Oxford: Oxford Univ. Press, 2000.

Cornelia Philips Spencer. *The Last Ninety Days of the War in North Carolina.* NY: Watchman Publishing Co., 1866.

Kenneth M. Stampp. *The Southern Road to Appomattox.* El Paso, TX: Univ. of Texas Press, 1969.

Peter F. Stevens. *The Rogue's March: John Riley and the St. Patrick's Battalion, 1846–48.* Washington, DC: Potomac Books, Inc., 2005 [1999].

Leo Strauss. *Natural Right and History.* Chicago: Univ. of Chicago Press, 1965.

Craig L. Symonds. *Stonewall of the West: Patrick Cleburne and the Civil War.* Lawrence, KS: Univ. of Kansas Press, 1997.

David P. Szatmary. *Shays' Rebellion: The Making of an Agrarian Insurrection.* Amherst, MA: Univ. of Massachusetts Press, 1980.

Michael Tadman. *Speculators and Slaves: Masters, Traders and Slaves in the Old South.* Madison, WI: Univ. of Wisconsin Press, 1996.

Frank Tannenbaum. *Slave and Citizen: the Negro in the Americas.* NY: Vintage Books/ Random House, 1946.

Nathan Tarcov. *Locke's Education for Liberty.* Chicago: Univ. of Chicago Press, 1984.

Alan Tate, et al. *I'll Take My Stand.* Baton Rouge: Louisiana State Univ. Press, 1994 [1930].

Augustine Thompson, O. P. *Cities of God: The Religion of the Italian Communes.* University Park: The Univ. of Pennsylvania Press, 2005.

Laurence H. Tribe. *Abortion: A Clash of Absolutes.* NY: W.W. Norton & Co., 1992.

George Tucker. *The Life of Thomas Jefferson.* Philadelphia: Carey, Lea and Blanchard, 1837.

Philip Thomas Tucker. *Irish Confederates: The Civil War's Forgotten Soldiers.* Abilene, TX: McWhitney Foundation Press, 2006.

Louis Veuillot. *The Liberal Illusion* [*L'Illusion Libérale*]. Kansas City, MO: Angelus Press, 1996 [1866].

Eric Voegelin. *The New Science of Politics.* Chicago: Univ. of Chicago Press, 1987 [1952].

Arthur Edward Waite. *A New Encyclopedia of Freemasonry.* NY: Wings Books, 1994 [1921].

Eric H. Walther. *The Fire-Eaters.* Baton Rouge: Louisiana State Univ. Press, 1993.

James Webb. *Born Fighting: How the Scots-Irish Shaped America.* NY: Broadway Books, 2004.

Mason Locke Weems. *A History of the Life and Death, Virtues and Exploits of General George Washington.* Philadelphia: J.P. Lipincott Co., 1918.

Mark A. Weitz. *More Damning than Slaughter: Desertion in the Confederate Army.* Lincoln, NE: Univ. of Nebraska Press, 2005.

Henry Alexander White. *Robert E. Lee and the Southern Confederacy: 1807–1870.* NY: G. P. Putnam's Sons, 1900.

David Williams. *Rich Man's War: Class, Caste and Confederate Defeat in the Chattahoochee Valley.* Athens, GA: Univ. of Georgia Press, 1998.

Brian Steel Wills. *The Confederacy's Greatest Cavalryman: Nathan Bedford Forrest.* Lawrence, KS: Univ. Press of Kansas, 1992.

Edmund Wilson. *Patriotic Gore: Studies in the Literature of the American Civil War.* NY: W. W. Norton & Company, 1994 [1962].

John Witte, Jr. *Religion and the American Constitutional Experiment: Essential Rights and Liberties.* Boulder, CO: Westview Press, 2000.

Gordon S. Wood. *The Radicalism of the American Revolution.* NY: Vintage Books, 1991.

Kenneth J. Zanca. *American Catholics and Slavery, 1789–1866. An Anthology of Primary Documents.* Lanham, MD: Univ. Press of America, 1994.

Howard Zinn. *A People's History of the United States.* NY: Harper Collins, 2005.

Hiller B. Zobel. *The Boston Massacre.* NY: W. W. Norton & Co., 1970.

Selected Church Sources

Benedict XVI. "Papal Address at Univ. of Regensbug." 12 September 2006.

John XXIII. *Veterum Sapientia*, 1962.

Pius XII. *Evangelii Praecones*, 1951.

Pius XI. *Quadragesimo Anno*, 1931.

_____. *Quas Primas*, 1925.

Pius X. *Vehementer Nos*, 1906.

Leo XIII. *Au Milieu des Sollicitudes*, 1892.

_____. *Diuturnum*, 1871.

_____. *Immortale Dei*, 1885.

_____. *In Plurimis*, 1888.

_____. *Libertas humana*, 1888.

Gregory XVI. *In Supremo Apostolatus*, 1839.

_____. *Mirari Vos*, 1832.

The Papal Encyclicals, in five volumes. Raleigh, NC: Pierian Press, 1981.

Catechism of the Catholic Church.

Index

as synthetic jurisdiction, 466–468
civil religion of, 594
American civil religion
as primary scholarly example of civil
religion, 594
description of, 594
elements summarized, 603
feast days of, 599
relics of, 598
American Revolution 16, 44, 46, 70,
120–123, 127–128, 130–132, 134–136, 138,
140–141, 144, 146, 154, 157, 159, 163, 165,
171–172, 184, 191, 239, 241, 245–246, 301,
329, 353, 358, 363, 437, 444, 481, 493, 593,
597, 610, 623, *passim*
and anti-theology of State, 587
and creation of public opinion, 610
and Freemasonry, 123
and Locke's doctrine of revolution,
77, 136
and Mexican War, 274
and mythical conservatism of, 168ff
and parallel with Civil War, 10, 166,
299ff, 304–305, 307, 363, 461
and parallel with the French Revolution, 167–168
and taxation without representation,
132
as conservation of slavery, 356
as early model of Lincoln's tyranny,
301
as Enlightenment fulfilled, 16
as Enlightenment in practice, 153
as inspiration for French Revolution,
527
as prepared by Enlightenment, 37
as religious experience, 593
as replicated in Texas Revolution, 264
conservative mythology of, 46ff
dictatorship of, 154–164
effect on religious unity, 544
invoked by Confederacy, 307, 359, 363
pretexts for, 130–133, 138–147
radicalism of, 16, 130–133, 625
replaces monarchy with expansive
new powers, 173–175
Americanist(s) 538, 552, 591, 606, 617
Americanist heresy 606

anarcho-capitalists, anarcho-capitalism 132, 628
as libertarian solution to abuses of
liberty, 628
Anderson's Constitutions 118–120
Anglican Church 138, 140, 518
disestablishment of in Virginia, 562
Annapolis Convention 176
anti-Catholicism 94, 491
and American Revolution, 138–140
and Know-Nothing movement, 227,
282–283, 293
and Mexican War, 272ff
and Pledge of Allegiance, 600
and "Pope stone" incident, 597
and public education, 616
as essential to Liberty, 47–48, 94ff
as "last respectable prejudice in
America," 94
anti-Federalists 188, 191–192, 194–195,
204, 254–255, 635
discern centralizing effect of Constitution, 504
predict Civil War, 207
prophesies of fulfilled, 187ff, 242
Antonielli, Giacomo, Cardinal 55
Aquinas, Thomas, Saint 2, 22, 38, 70, 75,
375, 637
and Aristotle, 38
Chesterton on, 22
completes synthesis of Hellenism and
Christianity, 21
on end of law, 91
on immorality of revolution, 74–75
on just war, 375
on political society as natural to man,
70
on unjust law, 637
philosophical realism of, 22
Aristotle 2, 16–18, 22–23, 49, 70, 91, 129
and Greco-Catholic synthesis,
defined, 16
as herald of Gospel, 21
as source of rational basis for Christian state, 23
attacked by Hobbes and Locke, 49–51
doctrine of substance adopted by
Church, 49

CPSIA information can be obtained
at www.ICGtesting.com
Printed in the USA
BVOW06s1349181116

468016BV00013B/18/P